KU-202-704

Contents

Contents

Contributors

Professor John Radford, joint editor of this book, is an Honorary Research Fellow at the University of East London (formerly North East London Polytechnic, and before that West Ham College of Technology). He was previously Dean of Science at the Polytechnic, and prior to that had built up there what became probably the largest Department of Psychology in the UK. He was largely responsible for the introduction of Psychology as a GCE subject, and for the founding of the Association for the Teaching of Psychology. His many other professional interests have included Chairmanship of the Psychology Board of the CNAA and numerous activities in the British Psychological Society, of which he is a Fellow. He took a BA General at Goldsmiths' College in 1955, and BA Honours in Psychology at Birkbeck College in 1961, where he obtained a PhD in 1965. He has published ten other books.

Ernest Govier, joint editor of this book, is Principal Lecturer in Psychology at the University of East London. He obtained BSc in Zoology from London University in 1968 and BSc in Psychology in 1972. He is a Chartered Psychologist and an Associate Fellow of the British Psychological Society.

Dr Andrew Burton is Senior Lecturer in Psychology at the University of East London. He has published two books on thinking and one concerned with aspects of neuropsychology. Recently he has worked on various projects concerned with hemisphere differences in cognitive function and the rehabilitation of brain-injured patients with language difficulties.

Brian Clifford is Professor of Psychology at the University of East London. He holds a DPE from Jordanhill College of Education (1967), a DipEd from London University (1969), a first-class BA Hons in Psychology from NELP (1974), an MSc in Artificial Intelligence from Brunel University (1986), and a doctorate from the University of London (1989). He is an Associate Fellow of the British Psychological Society, a Fellow of the

Cybernetic Society and a Chartered Psychologist. He has published two books, with three more to come, and over 80 papers in the field of applied memory research.

Jeremy Coyle is a former Principal Lecturer in Psychology at the University of East London. He is now a Director of two market research companies, Jeremy Coyle Associated Ltd and Networld Research Ltd. He obtained a BA Hons in English from Bristol University and BA Hons in Psychology from London University.

Philip Erwin is Senior Lecturer in Psychology at Manchester Metropolitan University. He obtained a BSc in Psychology in 1978, a doctorate in 1983, and a Diploma in Guidance and Counselling in Education in 1987.

Philip Evans is Principal Lecturer in Psychology at the University of Westminster. He read Moral Sciences and Natural Sciences at Emmanuel College, Cambridge, specializing in Psychology, and his PhD is from University College, Cardiff.

Harry Fisher was formerly Principal Lecturer in Psychology at the University of East London. He obtained BSc in Psychology in 1971 and is a member of the Mathematical Association and the British Psychological Society.

Mark Fox, BA, MSc, is Head of Assessment Services at SCOPE. He is the Associate Tutor for Professional Development for experienced Educational Psychologists at the University of East London. Previous to this Mark worked as a psychologist in the West Midlands and was in charge of Bromley School Psychological Service. He has a particular interest in pre-school children and the management and organization of School Psychological Services.

Clive Gabriel is Principal Lecturer in Psychology at the University of East London. He obtained BSc in Mathematics and Physics in 1965 and BSc in Psychology in 1970. He is a Chartered Psychologist, an Associate Fellow of the British Psychological Society and an Associate Member of the Market Research Society. He is chairman of Gabriel Ashworth Ltd, a marketing consultancy.

Judy Gahagan is a graduate of London University. She worked with Basil Bernstein on linguistic codes and language enrichment before teaching social psychology at the University of East London. She taught psycholinguistics and socio-linguistics on Masters courses at the Institute of Education, University of London, and later Applied Social Psychology at the City University. She has written a number of texts in Social Psychology. She is now working as a freelance writer and journalist and living most of the time in Italy.

Heather Govier is a freelance consultant in Educational Computing. She read Natural Sciences at Newnham College, Cambridge, specializing in Psychology. She graduated in 1970 and then moved to the Chelsea Centre for Science Education where she obtained an MPhil in the Psychology of Education.

Simon Green is a lecturer in Psychology at Birkbeck College, University of London. He has a BSc in Psychology from University College, Cardiff, and a PhD in Psychopharmacology from the University of London. He is a member of the British Psychological Society, the Brain Research Association, and the British Association for Psychopharmacology. Between 1983 and 1986 he was Chief Examiner in 'A' Level Psychology for the Associated Examining Board.

Len Holdstock abandoned a career in industrial administration when his interests turned towards psychology in the late 1950s. He obtained a PhD in Psychology in 1969 from Birkbeck College, London University. For most of the intervening period he has lectured in applied cognitive topics at the University of East London.

Clive Hollin was Research Assistant to Professor John Radford at North East London Polytechnic from 1975 to 1978; then Psychologist, later Senior Psychologist, in the Home Office 1978–82. He was awarded his PhD in 1980, moving to the post of Lecturer in Psychology at the University of Leicester in 1982. In 1989 he was appointed to his present post of Senior Lecturer in Psychology at the University of Birmingham. He is a member of the British Society of Criminology, the British Association for Behavioural Psychotherapy, the American Psychological Association, and Fellow of the British Psychological Society.

Carolyn Kagan is Principal Lecturer in Social Psychology at Manchester Metropolitan University. She also contributes to the North West Mental Handicap Development Team as an adviser to health and social services. After graduating from NELP in 1974 she did research for a DPhil in Oxford, before moving to Manchester and subsequently qualifying as a social worker. She has written two books on interpersonal skills for nurses and a wide range of other articles and reports. She belongs to a number of professional interest groups, including British Association of Counselling, British Society for Experimental and Clinical Hypnosis, British Association of Social Work, and the Social Policy Association.

Alan Labram, MSc, CPsychol, AFBPsS, is a Senior Educational Psychologist in the School Psychological Service, London Borough of Newham and Field Tutor to the MSc in Educational Psychology at the University of East London. He has a degree in Psychology from London University and a Master's degree in Educational Psychology from Edinburgh University. Current interests include the professional development of educational psychologists and the assessment and remediation of children's language difficulties.

Marian Pitts gained her first degree and PhD from University College, Cardiff. She has taught at North East London Polytechnic, the University of Tennessee and the University of Zimbabwe and is now principal lecturer in psychology at Staffordshire University and Honorary Research Fellow at the University of East London.

Allan Sigston is an educational psychologist. He obtained his first degree in Psychology at Birmingham in 1974 and a Master in Educational Psychology from University College London in 1978. He is currently working as an Associate Tutor on the MSc Professional Training in Educational Psychology at the Polytechnic of East London and doing professional development work in the London Borough of Waltham Forest.

David White is Professor at Staffordshire University. His research interests include the adjustments that men make as they become fathers, parent–child interactions, and health psychology. At present he is involved with projects in Britain and Zimbabwe concerning the primary prevention of AIDS.

Sheila Wolfendale has been a primary school and remedial teacher and educational psychologist. She has written extensively on learning difficulties, special educational needs and parental participation. Sheila Wolfendale currently runs the MSc Educational Psychology in the Psychology Department of the University of East London and was made a Professor during 1988.

Anne Woollett teaches developmental psychology in the Psychology Department, University of East London. Her research interests include the development of single children and twins within the family, and women's reproductive health, their attitudes and experiences towards infertility and miscarriage, motherhood and child rearing. At present she is studying Asian women in East London and is editing a book on motherhood.

Editorial foreword

The first edition of this book proved so difficult to produce that neither editor would have been able to envisage working on a second edition. Its existence, therefore, is yet another example of the triumph of hope over experience.

It is almost a decade since the first edition appeared and there have been substantial advances in many areas of psychology, a fact which provided the impetus for this revised edition.

In deciding on a strategy for the preparation of this book, we took the perhaps rather vain view that it should change through evolution rather than revolution; thus some chapters are largely unchanged, while others, for example, in the Social Psychology section, have been rewritten. New chapters on Language, Developmental Psychology, and Learning and Teaching have been included as has a chapter on how to prepare for examinations.

The overall structure of the book remains largely the same, so that anyone reading it from beginning to end will encounter a view of psychology which increases in its breadth, from the reductionist efforts of physiological psychologists to try to understand human behaviour; through the work of cognitive psychologists who concentrate on the individual's mental abilities and experiences; to the social psychologists, who try to understand human behaviour in its social context.

We have subdivided these sections between an opening section which deals with historical and methodological issues and a final section, in which, among other things, we try to show how the reader might apply some psychological principles to make learning about psychology a more efficient and perhaps more enjoyable process.

E.G.
J.K.R.

Preface to the second edition

Students, like policemen, keep getting younger, and anyone in the teaching business knows it gets harder to bridge, or even to appreciate, the widening gap. New degree students in the year in which this should appear will, at least, if coming straight from school, hardly recall the 1970s, when the first edition was written. My own student period of the 1950s and early 1960s will be historical. Yet it is interesting (to me at least) that I saw and heard such figures as Frederick Bartlett, Edwin Boring, Cyril Burt and Wolfgang Köhler, whose careers went back nearly to the beginnings of organized psychology – certainly they had known, as had my own professor, C. A. Mace, all the pioneers. Psychology still has a short history, in the well-worn phrase, although a long past.

This book begins with a sketch of the history because psychology, like its students, changes rapidly. It is notoriously prone to fashions. It is as much a mistake to think that nothing matters but the very latest experiments, as to live in the past. What appears to be relevant or 'with it' now, may or may not have lasting value; conversely sometimes the most abstruse research turns out to have practical use. Often the same basic issues remain under a change of language or of perspective. The language may be more accurate, the perspective wider, but not necessarily. The attempt to reach some balance of old and new is one of the feats of mental skill required of students of the subject of whatever age. Still more demanding is it to disentangle the more fundamental matters from the ephemeral.

This is particularly the case since psychology the discipline has yet to make very much progress with many most important aspects of behaviour – though at the same time the bounds are widening ever more rapidly. Psychology the subject, as it is exemplified in syllabuses and examinations, can (like any subject) only be a selection from the discipline. Our selection has been guided by the aims of first of all covering at least what is listed in the two existing GCE Advanced Level syllabuses; and then to provide a sufficiently full account to serve a first course in psychology as a major subject, such as may be found in the first year of a degree programme. Some students, we hope, may find enough to make the book of more lasting use. In practical terms, it is often helpful to refer back to a fairly introductory book when the range of specialized material threatens to become overwhelming. Psychology is, in our view, essentially a subject in which theory, investigation and practice are all closely linked. The orientation towards first courses, however, means that in this book there is rather more explicit emphasis on the first two and less on the third.

We have called this 'a textbook', which the dictionary defines as 'a manual of instruction; standard book in a branch of study'. The last phrase is more than we would claim. Rather, the book is, as was the first edition, an introduction given by a set of authors who (despite their editors' best efforts) have their own styles and their own ideas as to what is most important. Any student seeking an introductory book will be well advised to shop around; to compare material and opinion – an exercise in psychological method. This is not, as it has sometimes been called, 'the NELP textbook'. The Department of Psychology at North East London Polytechnic (before 1970 West Ham College of Technology, and from 1989 the Polytechnic of East London) has had many more members of staff than even the quite large number who have contributed here. However, all but one of the authors are or have been part of the Department and, we think, share its values. There has never been a 'party line', but what I wrote (with slight variations of wording) in the Preface to the first edition remains true.

Our shared view of psychology as a discipline (I wrote) holds that it is, or should be, objective, empirical, eclectic and humane. *Objective* means that one tries to distinguish what commands general agreement, because it can be demonstrated by reference to fact or logical argument, from what is the outcome only of opinion, tradition, heresay or prejudice, or indeed unreasoning belief of any form. It does not mean that psychology can, or should, avoid value judgements, indeed the preference for objectivity is itself such a judgement; it means being aware of values and of their sources and their implications. *Empirical* means that, whenever we can, we look for evidence. Generally, the preferred way of getting evidence is by experiment, for the reasons given in the first section of the book. But that is not the only useful way, and it is quite unscientific to reject any way of obtaining good evidence. In particular the experience of each individual is a valuable bonus for psychology which other disciplines, not concerned with human behaviour, cannot share. *Eclectic* means that we do not rule out in advance any source of information, though we do not accept every source uncritically. There have been scientists, including psychologists, who have felt that their methods or their theories were all that was necessary or even permissible. This is not only unscientific but self-defeating since such approaches become progressively isolated from reality. A really eclectic approach would mean that ideally a psychologist would be thoroughly familiar with many branches of learning beside a conventionally labelled 'psychology'. In a basic textbook most of these connections can at best be suggested. Finally, *humane* means concerned with, and about, human beings. Some approaches to psychology have seemed to neglect this; the more extreme behaviourism of the past, even perhaps some of the cognitive science of today. A self-styled 'humanistic' psychology has sometimes seemed to be interested in cornering what the others have neglected. We feel there is a wider, less dogmatic, British tradition – the tradition of Galton, Bartlett, Burt (yes, despite the sins of his old age), Broadbent and many others – which has always put human beings, with all their perplexing attributes, at the centre of its concern. We hope our book will be seen to be within that tradition.

There is a story that the late Norman Hartnell, dressmaker to the Queen, was once told that Her Majesty was 'not very with it'. He replied grandly: 'The Queen does not have to be with it. She is it!' Perhaps the same might be said of psychology.

John Radford
London 1990

Acknowledgements

Acknowledgement is due to the following for permission to use figures and tables in this volume.

Figures 6.1, 6.3, 6.6, 6.7, 6.8, 6.10, 6.11, 6.12, 6.13, 6.14, 7.2, 7.3, 7.4, 7.5, 7.6, 7.7, 7.9 and 7.11, from *Physiological Psychology* by Simon Green published by Routledge and Kegan Paul, 1987. Reproduced by permission. Fig. 11.3, from 'A Comparative and Analytical Study of Visual Depth Perception' by R. D. Walk and E. J. Gibson published in *Psychological Monograph* Vol. 75 No. 519. Copyright © 1961 by the American Psychological Association. Reprinted by permission. Figs. 11.4 and 11.7, from 'Plasticity in Sensory-Motor Systems' by Richard Held. Copyright © 1965 by Scientific American, Inc. All rights reserved. Fig. 11.5, from *Optics: An Introduction for Ophthalmologists* by K. Ogle published by the W. B. Saunders Company, Philadelphia, Pa., 1961. Fig. 11.8, from 'The Role of Frequency in Developing Perceptual Sets' by B. R. Bugelski and D. A. Alampay published in the *Canadian Journal of Psychology*, 15. Fig. 11.12, from 'Pictorial Depth Perception in Sub-cultural Groups in Africa' by W. Hudson published in *Journal of Social Psychology* Vol. 52, 1960, by Human Sciences Press, 72 Fifth Avenue, New York 10011, USA. Figure 15.1, from *Women, Men and Language* by Jennifer Coates published by Longman, 1986. Tables A.1, A.4, A.5 and A.10, from Tables 1, 13 and 18 of *The Biometrika Tables for Statisticians, Vol. 1*, edited by E. S. Pearson and H. O. Hartley (3rd edition 1966). Table 13.3 from 'Familial Studies of Intelligence: A Review' by T. J. Bouchard and M. McGue published in *Science*, Vol. 212, 1981. Table A.13, from 'A Distribution-free k-sample Test against Ordered Alternatives' by A. R. Jonckheere, *Biometrika Vol. 41*, pp. 133–45, 1954. Tables A.2 and A.3, from Tables III and IV of *Statistical Tables for Biological, Agricultural and Medical Research* by R.A. Fisher and F. Yates (6th edition 1974). Published by Longman Group Ltd., London (previously published by Oliver and Boyd, Edinburgh), and by permission of the authors and publishers. Tables A.8, A.9, A.12 and A.14 reprinted by permission from the *Journal of the American Statistical*

Association as follows: Table A.8, from Table 1 of 'Extended Tables of the Wilcoxon Matched Pair Signed Rank Statistic' by R. L. McCormack, 1965 Vol. 60 pp. 864–71; Table A.9, from 'Significance Testing of the Spearman Rank Correlation Coefficient' by J. H. Zarr, 1972 Vol. 67 pp. 578–80; Table A.12, from 'Use of Ranks in One-Criterion Variance Analysis' by W. H. Kruskal and W. A. Wallis, 1952 Vol. 47 pp. 584–621; Table A.14, from 'Ordered Hypotheses for Multiple Treatment: A Significance Test for Linear Rank' by E. B. Page, 1963 Vol. 58 pp. 216–30. Table A.7, from Table L of *Nonparametric and Shortcut Statistics* by Merle W. Tate and Richard C. Clelland. Danville, Illinois: The Interstate Printers and Publishers, Inc., 1957. Used by permission. Table A.11, from Table I of *Nonparametric and Shortcut Statistics* by Merle W. Tate and Richard C. Clelland. Danville, Illinois: The Interstate Printers and Publishers, Inc., 1957. Used by permission. Values at the left of the broken line were derived from Appendix 5A, 5B, 5C and 5D of M. G. Kendall's *Rank Correlation Methods* (4th edition 1970). Reproduced by permission of the publishers, Charles Griffin & Company Ltd. of London and High Wycombe. Other values were obtained by the method described by Kendall, *ibid.*, p. 84.

The authors and publisher are grateful to the Literary Executor of the late Sir Ronald A. Fisher, F.R.S., to Dr Frank Yates, F.R.S. and to Longman Group Ltd., London, for permission to reprint Tables III and IV from their book *Statistical Tables for Biological, Agricultural and Medical Research* (6th edition 1974).

Psychology as a science

This section describes some of the historical background to psychology and how it was developed, and, in doing so, gives an overview of psychology as a whole. Thus, many of the things said here are picked up and further discussed in later chapters. This section also includes chapters on the empirical methods which psychologists use in their investigations, together with the accompanying statistical procedures.

Scientific investigation, in its broadest sense, is fundamental to all modern psychology and investigations cannot be done or understood without at least a minimum grasp of techniques of design and analysis. The non-mathematical should not be put off: the computation involved is small. One of the most satisfying rewards of tackling psychology is to carry out an elegant, well-designed piece of research.

Chapter one

The development of psychology as a science

Clive Gabriel

Introduction

One of the major difficulties encountered when starting to study psychology is to find out what it is. It is tempting to take the easy way out by looking up the word 'psychology' in a dictionary and satisfying oneself with some neat definition, such as 'the science of behaviour and experience'. But this way will not provide you with any adequate picture of the subject, because 'psychology' has meant (and does mean) quite different things to people, depending on when they lived, where they worked, and, also, on

3

what sort of person they were. The aim of the first two chapters of this book is to present an adequate, if necessarily very brief and simplified, view of the nature of psychology, by discussing its development in the last hundred years or so. This chapter gives an account of the history of the subject until about 1950. The second chapter looks at more recent psychology. But first we need to clarify some ideas about 'science' and 'explanation'.

Before scientific psychology

The history of wondering, and pronouncing, on human behaviour and motivation is as old as history itself. That which took place before the 1870s (as well as some since) is now generally thought of as philosophy rather than psychology. One great step which marks the possibility of a clear division between philosophy and psychology was the founding by Wilhelm Wundt (1832–1920) of the first psychological laboratory in Leipzig, Germany, in 1879. Like so many 'firsts', this one is disputed, and it is sometimes claimed that the event first happened in Harvard University in the USA, the founder being William James (1842–1940); but whichever place, date, and person you accept, the 1870s were a uniquely important time for psychology.

The development of the early psychology laboratories was adumbrated particularly by the two-and-a-half preceding centuries of philosophical activity, during which the appeal to the authority of dogma for knowledge was replaced by an appeal to observation. The atmosphere for these brave ways of speculating about human mental activity was provided by contemporary discoveries from other areas of science. The most striking of these were Galileo's rejection of the belief that the Earth was at the centre of the universe and Harvey's discovery of the rudiments of the blood circulatory system. The one shattered the picture of man as being something quite exclusive in all creation, and the second reduced his body to something as mundane as a machine. Much later, Darwin removed the last obstacles to regarding humankind, not as a unique product of God's creation, but as a part of a continuous evolution of animal life.

The people who most prominently made clear the implications of this new picture of man for the study of what we now call psychology were the Frenchmen Descartes (1596–1650) and Comte (1798–1857) and the group which is often outrageously known as the 'English Empiricists', a large proportion of whom were Scottish and one of whom was Irish.

Descartes delineated the distinction between mind and body, supposing that the body needed no more than the rules of mechanics to understand it; it was, in his view, a machine. He further proposed that the interaction between body and mind took place in the brain (although, for the love of unity, he chose a rather improbable part of that organ).

The main difference between the philosophies of the British Empiricists and Descartes was in the latter's supposition that some ideas are present at birth, whereas the Empiricists believed that the development of mind happened by an accumulation of sensory experiences after birth.

By the mid-nineteenth century there was a strong current of philosophical thought which held that the organization of conscious experience was a fit subject for study; that sensation (stimulation impinging on sense organs) was a vitally important process in the gaining of ideas about the external world; and that the association of ideas or elements of experience was an important explanatory mechanism to show how simple ideas could combine to provide the complexity which is characteristic of human thinking. The next step seemed, to some thinkers of the time, to be to examine these ideas by experimentation. Thus, psychology, in something akin to its present-day meaning, came about.

Schools of psychology

Once psychology had established itself as an empirical study, that is, a study based on systematic observation rather than on reason alone, it developed and separated into different schools of thought, traces of which are still with us today. These schools differed in their subject matter, in what they thought psychology should be about, as well as in their methods of investigation. Each school has handed down some ideas and attitudes which are of value to contemporary psychologists; but some of the schools were much more diffuse in their formulations than others, resulting in their present-day influence being uneven in importance.

The idea of 'schools' is a convenient one which enables contemporary psychologists to look back and make sense of the welter of ideas and experiments which lie behind their own. From the point of view of members of the various schools, the organization of psychology may sometimes have seemed as clear as it can be made to look now but, most often, it must have seemed nothing of the sort: rather, a busy confusion with an occasional transient clear direction. But, as long as we are aware of this, we may usefully use the method to get a bird's-eye view of the past.

Structuralism

Wilhelm Wundt

Although Wundt founded his *Psychologisches Institut* in 1879, he was titled Professor of Philosophy in Leipzig from 1875 to 1920. His laboratory, with its many students, worked with a great solemnity of purpose on a range of problems, particularly those of physiological psychology, psychophysics, and reaction times, as well as on the analysis of experience, for which he is best remembered. He defined psychology as the science of consciousness and believed that its subject matter should be immediate experience rather than that experience which has been subject to conceptualization. For example, Wundt was not at all satisfied if a person told him that he saw a blue book. For Wundt, this was a far too high level of interpretation of the experience. The level he was trying to elicit was that expressed by 'blueness', 'rectangularity', 'depth', and so on. Two questions immediately occur: why should Wundt want to deal in such a low level of experience and how could he possibly obtain this seemingly unnatural type of information from people?

The chemistry analogy

Wundt wanted to build his new science of psychology along the lines of other sciences, hoping to achieve successes comparable to theirs. He dealt with the elements of experience in a way that was analogous to the way in which chemists discussed the elements of matter. Wundt believed that consciousness consisted of compounds which could be broken down into their constituent elements for our fuller understanding of them. Further, he considered that the elements of experience could be divided into two kinds, the ones 'out there' being 'sensations', and the others, within the person, being 'feelings'. He also used the word 'image' to describe elements of ideas, a concept closely related to sensation, but perhaps less vivid. Wundt systemized feelings and their compounds in various ways at various times, but none of his attempts convinced the scientific world for long. His best-known system of feelings was obtained by carefully examining his own mental processes whilst listening to clicks sounded in various rhythms and speeds and noting his feelings during and at the end of the sets of clicks. Wundt suggested from his procedure that feelings could vary along three independent dimensions: 'excitement–calm', 'pleasure–displeasure', and 'strain–relaxation'. However, these were just the dimensions of simple feelings or elements of conscious experience. Wundt believed that these elements of conscious experience were built into compounds and beyond these into complexes of experience; this idea became known as Structuralism. Yet in Wundt's scheme of things the attributes and characteristics of compounds could not necessarily be discovered by knowing the attributes and characteristics of their elements. This was, in Wundt's view, because the mind performs a 'creative synthesis' of elements when putting them together. This rather unsatisfactory way of linking elements and compounds was defended by Wundt with the chemical analogy: who, without knowing chemistry, would predict on 'seeing' the two gases hydrogen and oxygen that they could be synthesized into water?

Introspection

The method which Wundt and his students used to obtain their information about the elements of consciousness was that of introspection. This simply means that people were asked to examine and report on their own mental processes. Everyone has done this, and some people, you may have noticed, do little else, but Wundt's contribution was to bring order into the process. His idea was that introspection should be made to be replicable and lawful; that is, it should give similar results on different occasions, even when carried out by different people, and, further, differences in results should follow differences in instructions or problems in a systematic way. To become an 'observer', that is, one who introspects using Wundt's terms, involved a great amount of training. To see commonplace objects in the analysed way required by Wundt meant attaining what he called a state of 'strained attention' to the contents of consciousness.

The method of introspection, by itself, in the end proved inadequate as a way of gaining knowledge about mental processes. There were several reasons for this but the most basic was that when different laboratories gave different results there was no way of settling the issue. The most famous example of this happening was in a conflict between Wundt's laboratory and that of Oswald Külpe (1862–1915) in Würzburg.

Külpe, originally a student of Wundt, became professor at Würzburg in 1894 and, within a short time, had established a laboratory working along similar lines to that at Leipzig. However, whereas Wundt claimed that it was possible to study experimentally only the elements of conscious experience, Külpe saw no reason why higher mental processes should not be studied as well and picked on 'thinking' as a start. Külpe's studies repeatedly showed that problem-solving took place without the appearance of images in consciousness; that is, without the elements of conscious experience to be expected by Wundt's chemical analogy. It was like water resisting all efforts at reduction to hydrogen and oxygen. Wundt responded to this state of affairs by attacking the finer points of Külpe's introspective methods. Thus began a debate which exposed the weakness of the method of introspection when faced with conflict between two sets of researchers. It is a very fundamental weakness, depending ultimately on the impossibility of observing another person's mental processes in the way that any reasonable number of people may observe what goes on inside a retort in a chemical experiment.

Edward Titchener

Titchener (1867–1927) was born in England and became a disciple of Wundt in Leipzig. Later, he exported Wundt's methods and beliefs about the essential subject matter of psychology to the USA.

Titchener was every bit as awesome as Wundt, and he painstakingly, perhaps relentlessly, compiled a list of the distinct conscious elements of sensation which he published in *An Outline of Psychology* in 1896. The majority of the sensations were visual and most of the rest auditory. They came to a total of more than 44 000.

Although Titchener produced various reformulations of Structuralism during his life, he cannot be said to have introduced any new essence into psychology and, with his death, Structuralism also died. The analysis and presentation of the structure of the contents of consciousness no longer seemed to psychologists a useful way to proceed. There were two separate circumstances which made this the case: the inability and lack of promise of Structuralism's method of introspection to provide a cogent, generally agreed account of human mental life, and the existence of practicable alternative sorts of psychology.

Functionalism

Whereas it is easy to say what Structuralists believed – that it was essential for psychologists to study the structure of consciousness – it is not such a simple matter to say what Functionalists believed. As you might expect, they generally held that the function of consciousness was an important topic to study, but members of the school worked at a wide variety of topics.

The greatest single influence on functional psychology was Charles Darwin's work on the origin of the species. Functionalists were also influenced to work on a relative diversity of subject matter by rebellion against the dogmatic insistence of the contemporary Structuralists that psychology was essentially concerned with the structure of consciousness. In particular, they were influenced by the brilliant writing and inventive thinking of William James (1842–1910).

In one sense, structural psychology owed most in its underlying attitudes to philosophy, while functional psychology owed most to biology; and perhaps for this reason the attitudes underlying functional psychology are still with us, while no parallel situation exists with structural psychology.

Charles Darwin

The idea of evolution, that living organisms change and develop over time, is a very ancient one. Darwin's great contribution, in a series of publications from 1858 to 1877, was to provide the world with a carefully worked out account of the mechanisms of evolution. Darwin, however, failed to do the decent thing by stopping the account just before the arrival of man. This last fact, particularly, provided a great shock to very old habits of thinking, causing Victorian theologians to express anger and despair and psychologists to start work on a rich source of ideas.

Darwin's main thesis was that members of a species exhibit variability of characteristics and this means that some of them will be better suited than others to any given set of environmental conditions. By 'characteristic' is meant anything which may be attributed to the organism, for example, height or ferocity. Those members of the species who are best suited to the environment will be the ones who will reproduce most prolifically; indeed, under extreme conditions they will be the only ones to survive to maturity and be able to reproduce at all. These survivors of the struggle to reproduce will tend to transmit to the next generation that advantage, ability, or physical characteristic which enabled them to survive. This advantage will tend not merely to be transmitted, according to Darwin, but, because of the variability of characteristics, some of the new generation will have the advantage to a greater degree than others. If the environmental pressures remain similar over several generations, the process may be repeated until the advantage is so pronounced that a major change has taken place in the type of animal. Darwin proposed this mechanism of natural selection as one of the ways in which new species emerge.

The thesis caused uproar when first presented because of its implications for human origins; and, because of the enormous body of observation presented by Darwin in support of it, it could not easily be dismissed.

If the function of other abilities were to be discussed, why not the function of consciousness? Thus, Darwin raised the issue of the utility of consciousness. The importance of individual differences between members of species was also made clear by Darwin, and this lead was taken up by a group of statisticians and psychometricians who form a tradition of psychology in themselves.

Darwin's ideas also provided an immediate reason for supposing that observing animal behaviour would be of use in understanding human behaviour. Descartes had held the opposite view to Darwin, that studying animals was a pointless pursuit. His reason for this was his belief that animals were radically different from humans in having no soul. Darwin won; during nearly all of this century, a great deal of animal experimentation has taken place.

In *The Expression of the Emotions in Man and Animals* (1872), Darwin presented evidence and argued for the notion that emotional expressions are vestiges of actions and movements that, at one time in the evolutionary history of the species, had served some practical function. Again, by considering the use of emotional expression, Darwin focused on a field eagerly taken up by functional psychology and also provided modern psychology with its first look at man as an emotional being – unless you count Wundt's feelings of tension and relaxation to metronome clicks as emotions. Perhaps Wundt may have.

Finally, Darwin provided psychologists with an early example of the study of infant development. In 1877, he published *Biographical Sketch of an Infant* which comprised details of the development of his own son. Of Darwin's four main contributions to psychology, the importance of a functional approach (asking about the *uses* of mechanisms and characteristics) is the most pervasive. It will appear throughout this discussion of Functionalism and also as a declared or tacit assumption through the whole of this book. The other three main contributions, the importance of animal work, child psychology, and the study of individual differences, will be discussed at various points.

William James

William James' central place in the Functionalist school of psychology was not chosen by himself. The school was, in fact, labelled by Titchener in 1898. At that time, Titchener was attacking non-Structuralist psychology, and, for this purpose, he found it convenient to provide a name for the sort of psychology practised by James and his associates.

James was as different in personality from Wundt and Titchener as can be imagined. He had, in common with Freud, a wonderful literary gift combined with little or no interest in experimentation. James travelled much throughout his life and his attitudes were always very eclectic. He would have been incapable of declaring allegiance to any school or set of ideas; certainly none could have contained his divergence of thought. He was born into a wealthy and talented family and, for several years, threatened to become merely a wealthy dilettante. James looked at several posssible careers: painting, chemistry, biology, medicine and nearly became a full-time hypochondriac. He failed to qualify in any of these with the exception of medicine, in the efficacy of which he had little faith. From medicine, via emotional and physical crises, he went on to teach physiology, and a while later he taught a course on the relationship between physiology and psychology.

James remained principally a psychologist for a remarkably long time for him, but towards the end of his life he published in philosophy and in education. We are lucky that he dropped in on us: he brilliantly expressed a much-needed corrective to the all too pervasive Structuralism.

The influences on James included the overriding one of Darwin, often as transmitted by Galton, an important figure whose work will be discussed with the account of psychometry. James spent nearly twelve years writing a major account of psychology, *Principles of Psychology* (1890), which states his position on the whole range of psychological topics in which he was interested. The *Principles* presents a picture of people far more complete than that of the Structuralists. James pointed out that we act and feel and show emotion: not just think. Further, he tried to place all of our activities in a biological framework. Psychology was regarded at this time by James as the study of peoples' adaptation to the environment.

Consciousness

James believed that, to understand consciousness, one had to understand its function rather than its structure. This function, according to James, was to enable the organism to behave in ways most likely to lead to survival. Otherwise, he reasoned, how would it have been evolutionarily selected at all? James supposed that many repeated actions are first performed by the use of conscious thought but that, by practice, they became properly relegated to unthinking habit, thereby freeing consciousness for the acquisition of new actions and for functionally vital decision-making.

James believed the Structuralists to be mistaken in thinking that conscious experience was made up of analysable elements. He supposed that in their analyses they saw what they expected to see – a common enough occurrence! James saw consciousness as a unity and as something that flows; the 'stream of consciousness' is one of the most striking images he used to describe this view. He argued that the continuity of the stream of consciousness was not interfered with even by sleep: we pick up in the morning from where we left off at night, with no real break in our conscious experience of life.

James' view of consciousness is also one of a system of organic growth. Experience increases by a process of inclusion rather than one of association. As James pointed out we can never perceive the same event twice because on the second occasion the event is perceived by a person with different experience; Piaget was a more recent exponent of this view.

Habit

As can be gleaned from James' view of consciousness, unconscious habit also has a crucial part to play in his account of human life. He provided a theory of habit at two levels, physiological and social. His physiological explanation that habits are established by increased plasticity of pathways in the nervous system is plausible but, by now, very outdated. The account of the function of habit in running society also reflects an outlook of a 'place for everything and everything in its place', which is certainly weaker now than in James' day, but still the social function of habit is clear. While 'stream' was the image used for consciousness, 'flywheel' was that for habit. James saw habit as the great stabilizing force in society. It is the device by which the predictability of the behaviour of others can be kept within biologically efficient bounds.

Emotion

Unusually for James, in the area of emotion, he presented a clear, testable formulation. That is, he presented a point of view which suggested empirical ways in which it can be supported or refuted. He argued that if we see a frightening object and run, we feel afraid because we are running (due to the accompanying autonomic and skeletal changes), whereas common sense tells us that we are running because we feel afraid. This problem, concerning the order of the various components of emotion (experience, behaviour, and expression), is one which still concerns psychologists. As usual, common sense is inadequate and fails to deal with the complexities of the problem. James' theory of emotion is contemporary with a similar (although not identical) one presented by the Danish physiologist Lange. The two formulations have tended to be thought of together as the James–Lange theory.

The self

James attempted an analysis of the concept of self, proposing a hierarchy of 'selves' stretching from the 'spiritual me', to the 'bodily me', via a number of levels of 'social me'. The 'spiritual me' has, since James, tended to be left to theologians and mystics and the 'bodily me' to the medical profession. Social psychologists have, however, made much of the various types of 'social me', particularly during the last two decades, when accounts of real people have tended to re-enter psychology after a long period, during which only aspects of people were being considered by many (although not all) psychologists.

These topics do not exhaust the huge range covered by James. Before his arrival in psychology the subject was narrower and doctrinaire in its approach; he let fresh air into the subject and enabled a much broader view to be taken of the areas which psychology could encompass.

James' methods

James' contribution to methods by which we may gain knowledge about human life was not as far reaching as his widening of the subject area. James stayed with the Structuralists in regarding introspection as the psychologist's basic tool, he saw it as the exercise of a natural gift. This way of proceeding was, however, not the only one James recognized. Experimentation he accepted as valuable and was happy that others would use it. He himself, however, lacked the inclination and the patience.

James emphasized the desirability of comparative methods, that is, attempting to gain knowledge about the workings of one group by observing its similarities and differences with those of another; for example, human adults against animals or children.

Dewey and Angell

John Dewey (1859–1952) and James Angell (1867–1949) each published a paper which served to codify the achievements thus far of Functionalism as a school and to point out its advantages, not only over the, by then, ailing Structuralism, but also over atomism in general. Atomism is the doctrine that to understand the workings of a system it is best to break it down and understand the parts first.

Dewey (1896) continued the Functionalist argument that there was no point in regarding behaviour as an object of study unless it was in the context of understanding the organism's adaptation to the environment. Angell (1906) provided a very thorough exposition of the Functionalist position in which he represented its basic tenets.

The ends of Structuralism and Functionalism

Both schools were transformed: Structuralism into a matter of little more than historical interest; Functionalism into a belief in the importance of a biological substratum to experience and behaviour which was to underlie all future psychology.

Despite the huge difference between Structuralism and Functionalism there were many ways in which they were similar and every one of these similarities encountered a reaction. Both Structuralism and Functionalism allowed the importance of the unconscious part of mental life. The earlier schools agreed that introspection was a valuable method but Behaviourism was to attempt to dismiss it entirely, supposing only observable behaviour to be worthwhile data. Structuralism insisted upon and Functionalism partially tolerated the idea of atomism, that is, the idea of analysing phenomena in trying to understand them; Gestalt psychology was to reject this approach entirely, believing that, by disregarding the holistic aspects of mental life, one was disregarding its essence.

Structuralism and Functionalism were largely concerned with discovering statements concerning the similarities between people, but individual differences were studied by Galton (during the heyday of Structuralism and Functionalism) and later by a line of researchers who were particularly connected with the use of psychology in the selection and testing of people.

Both Structuralism and Functionalism accepted the existence of associations of greater and lesser complexity. They inherited the notion of association from philosophy. Three psychologists in particular, however, instead of accepting the association of ideas, events, and so on, chose to create associations and to study the circumstances under which this could be done. The rest of this chapter will discuss first these Associationists and then each of the reactions to the ideas shared by Structuralism and Functionalism.

Associationism

The three scientists in this part of the chapter hardly form a school, but they provide us with a convenient grouping to help understand the early work on the forming of associations.

Hermann Ebbinghaus

Hermann Ebbinghaus (1850–1909) originally trained in philosophy. Amongst other events in his early life he was involved in the Franco-Prussian war of 1870. Despite this, or perhaps because of it, 1876 found Ebbinghaus looking through the second-hand book stalls which then, as now, line the Seine in Paris. There he found a copy of Fechner's *Elemente der Psychophysik*, which event in the psychology of association is akin to the tale of the falling apple in Newtonian physics. Ebbinghaus, with an independence of spirit, engendered, no doubt, by many factors, but including a good private income, decided to ignore the edict of Wundt that higher mental processes were not amenable to psychological investigation and began to investigate learning by adapting Fechner's techniques.

Although the meaning of 'learning' in psychology will be made clear in later chapters it is important to realize now that 'learning' means those changes in humans or animals which are not attributable to maturation or disease. This definition, like so many others, causes more trouble than it clears up, but it will suffice to make it clear that 'learning' in psychology is not specifically connected with the concept of education or even of training.

By inventing a device called a 'nonsense syllable' Ebbinghaus was able to investigate the formation of associations between items which he supposed could not have been associated previously. Examples of nonsense syllables are ceg, zut, tis.

The result of his several years of utterly dedicated and very isolated endeavour was considerable understanding of the learning and forgetting of meaningless material. Ebbinghaus discovered that forgetting, the lack of availability of associations, happens quickly at first and then progressively more slowly and he quantified this and his other results.

While Ebbinghaus's work provided the firmest of foundations for its elaboration by other workers, psychologists now regard it as being of very limited interest because of its artificiality. Nearly all of the material that people learn is meaningful and this radically alters the way in which it is remembered and 'forgotten'.

The other two Associationists we shall discuss concerned themselves mainly with associations in animals.

Ivan Pavlov

Ivan Pavlov (1849–1936) was a dour man who did not like psychologists. He regarded psychological nomenclature as pretentious and useless. His own training was as a physiologist, to which study he stuck, investigating initally the innervation of the heart and digestive system and then brain function.

Pavlov discovered the rules governing the association between external stimuli, such as sights and sounds, and some types of glandular secretion. The experiments for which he is most famed amongst psychology students are those in which he taught dogs to salivate to the sound of a buzzer. Because he demonstrated that untaught dogs fail to do this he can be said to have formed an association between the sound of a buzzer and salivation. This process is now known as classical or Pavlovian conditioning. The description is not reserved only for the special case just mentioned but whenever a learned stimulus (for example, the buzzer) replaces a natural stimulus (for example, food).

Around this basic process, Pavlov worked to provide an enormous amount of information about the variables which, when manipulated, provide greater or lesser, stronger or weaker, learning. Pavlov was a great quantifier. He did not, for example, content himself with the observation that a dog salivated slightly or copiously but, rather, measured the rate and total amount of saliva secreted. The importance of quantification is a topic to which we shall return when summarizing the contribution of the Associationists.

Edward Thorndike

Edward Thorndike (1874–1949) took the principles known to circus trainers for generations and transmitted them into knowledge of great scientific value. Whereas Pavlov had investigated the associations between stimuli and glandular responses, Thorndike investigated the association between situations and voluntary muscular responses. To do this, he invented the 'puzzle box', which is a cage, out of which animals may learn to escape by some manipulation, such as pulling a wire loop. Thorndike motivated the animals to escape by enabling them thus to obtain food or to join their fellows. He used the time taken by an animal to escape as a measure of learning or, if it had previously learned, as a measure of remembering.

Thorndike explained his earlier work in two 'laws'. The first of these is the 'Law of Effect' which holds that the effects on itself of an action by an animal influences the likelihood of the animal repeating the action given the opportunity. This is an informal way of stating the law which, it is hoped, is clear. In Chapter 8 you will find its formal statement, together with an account of the conceptual difficulties to which such a seemingly simple idea can lead. Earlier in his career, Thorndike also supposed that associations were strengthened or weakened in ways independent of the outcome of the situation. This he called the Law of Exercise.

Although Thorndike's early work was with animals, he attempted to apply his learning principles to education, but this is not the part of his work for which he is now best known.

The contribution of the Associationists

At first sight, the contributions of Ebbinghaus, Pavlov, and Thorndike might appear disappointing in that, sometimes, their discoveries seem self-evident. But this is only true of the grossest account of their work. At this very gross level, they simply confirmed that humans and animals tend to associate certain events with certain behaviour. Their work is important, however, because they made, and led others to make, a very fine study of the conditions under which the formations of associations – learning – could be expected. This work was largely continued by a school of psychologists who have become known as Behaviourists: even Ebbinghaus's work was to be put under the heading of verbal behaviour.

The emphasis on quantification in psychology has been mentioned as something for which the Associationists should be given special credit. It is important that one realizes why working with quantities or scales is a matter of importance to psychology or, come to that, to science in general.

If we think we understand a system or part of a system we may check our understanding by predicting how it will behave. The more finely we can check the system the more we can confirm our understanding or realize that we did not understand it as well as we thought. Fineness of checking improves with our fineness of measurement. If, for example, we predict that it will rain over Southend Pier in 50 days' time, and it does so, we might or might not have discovered the key to the laws which govern the falling of rain. However, if we predict correctly that it will rain from 19.08 hours to 20.03 hours at that place on that day and at no other time we can be surer that we have understood the laws. To predict an event roughly is a less impressive demonstration of our comprehension of the rules governing it than to predict the event finely. We wish to be as impressive as possible in this way, and fine prediction involves finely quantified prediction.

The type of analysis of associations discussed here is dependent upon the notions of a stimulus, something which affects the organism, and a response, something the organism does because of the stimulus. Thus, the three scientists we have been dealing with needed to break down behaviour somewhat artificially. They adopted an atomistic attitude. The same type of attitude had been taken by Wundt concerning his chosen subject matter of the contents of consciousness. Atomism and a great concern with the problems of learning characterize an American-based school known as Behaviourism. A total rejection of trying to understand behaviour by breaking it down into small components characterizes a German-based school known as the Gestaltists. We need, now, to discuss these two schools.

Gestalt psychology

The German word 'Gestalt' is translated in several ways such as 'form', 'shape', 'configuration', or 'whole'. The word in psychology represents a school whose main tenet is that the subject matter of psychology should be treated holistically wherever possible. Favourite words of Associationists, 'stimulus' and 'response', were anathema to Gestalt psychologists.

The school's founder was Max Wertheimer (1880–1943) who was joined by Kurt Koffka (1876–1941) and Wolfgang Köhler (1887–1967). It began and flourished mainly in Berlin, but its three leading protagonists emigrated to the USA during the 1930s because of the threat posed to them by the Nazis. Thus Gestalt psychology was thoroughly introduced to the English-speaking world.

Max Wertheimer

Wertheimer began his campaign against atomism by doing experiments on apparent movement. Using a tachistoscope (a device for presenting visual stimuli for timed periods), Wertheimer illuminated two slits, one vertical the other at an angle, one after the other. He found that the subject's perception depended on the interval between turning off the light behind one slit and turning it on behind the other. If the interval was long (by visual perception experiment standards), say 300 msec (msec stands for millesecond which is one-thousandth of one second), then the subjects typically saw one slit go off and the other come on. If the interval was very short, say 30 msec, then the subjects saw first one slit on and then the other, but the fascinating case for Wertheimer was the intermediate interval of about 60 msec. At about this interval subjects reported seeing the slit of light move from one place to the other. This phenomenon, which has often been exploited in illuminated advertising hoardings, Wertheimer dignified with the name 'the phi-phenomenon'.

Wertheimer believed the phi-phenomenon was important to psychology because it provided a perception which defied analysis by Wundtian methods. You will remember that Wundt was not content with reports from his observers that they saw 'a book'; rather, he required an analysis of this percept into, for example, darkness, rectangularity, and so on. Wertheimer showed that his subjects, having observed the phi-phenomenon, could not analyse it into its elements in a Wundtian manner, even though those elements were there. This remained the situation however many times they cared to watch the phenomenon.

Thus, Wundt's atomistic type of analysis failed, nor could an Associationist approach of some other kind explain why two incidents in a particular relationship should look like something else. Wertheimer's solution to the problem was to point out that there was no problem if one accepted a Gestalt approach, that the phenomenon needs to be considered as a whole to provide a sensible unit with which to work. This principle is usually expressed in the phrase, 'the whole is greater than the sum of the parts'. In fact, the phrase has become such a cliché that it is tempting to suppose that it is devoid of meaning; but this is not true, it really does convey very clearly the main principle of Gestalt psychology. Later, Gestalt psychologists were to refer to atomistic, Associationistic psychology as 'bricks and mortar' psychology, the bricks being the atoms or elements and the mortar the associations between them. They believed that the important part of the matter was the wall. Further, in cases like the phi-phenomenon it was important (we are nearing the end of the analogy) to discuss walls because there were no bricks or mortar to be seen.

Wertheimer developed his early work on the phi-phenomenon until, in 1923, he published a set of principles of perceptual organization. In those he expressed the view that perceptual organization is spontaneous whenever an organism looks round its environment. We do not have to learn this organization because it is based on fundamental principles which can in turn be related to the organization of brain function.

The main principles of perceptual organization, according to Wertheimer, are proximity, similarity, closure and pragnanz. The first three can be made clear by diagrams:

```
        X   X       X   X
        X   X       X   X
```

Figure 1.1

The principle of proximity is illustrated by the fact that we most readily see the eight crosses as two squares made up of four crosses each. The elements of the diagram which are closest to each other are perceived as wholes.

The principle of similarity explains, according to Wertheimer, why we tend to see six rows rather than six columns in Figure 1.2.

Closure, as a principle, is demonstrated by the observation that we tend

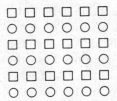

Figure 1.2

Figure 1.3

to perceive Figure 1.3 as three circles rather than two back to back semi-circles with a spare at each end. We tend to complete incomplete figures.

The principle of pragnanz is more difficult to illustrate, as you might have guessed from the fact that it remains in German. *Prägnanz* is simply the German for pregnant, or concise. It refers to the belief in a tendency for figures to be perceived as 'good' as possible. A figure attains goodness by being orderly, stable, simple, reduced to its simplest terms. One is not obeying the principle of pragnanz if one saw

Figure 1.4

as representing a state of affairs which could happily exist indefinitely.

Wertheimer supposed that all perception was organized according to these principles but he believed also that the experience of the perceiver would affect the perception.

Apart from his work on perception Wertheimer also carried out major work on the topic of 'thinking'.

Gestalt psychology and the brain

The Gestalt psychologists imagined brain processes underlying the organization of perception to be quite different from those imagined by the Associationists. Instead of a series of representations of outside events connected by associationist links, the Gestaltists supposed that isomorphism existed between the outside world and its representation in the cerebral cortex (that part of the brain where sensory input is primarily represented). 'Isomorphism' means literally 'same form'. The Gestaltists supposed that the brain was a map of the outside world. This means that if, for example, two objects are close to one another in space they will automatically be represented close to one another in the brain. This proximity, according to the Gestaltists, would cause an automatic interaction of the representations enabling them to be perceived as parts of a whole, the whole being the result of physiological inevitability, not the result of learning.

To understand more accurately the Gestaltists' notion of interaction by virtue of proximity, it is important to realize that they were influenced by the contemporary topicality of field theories in physics. These theories postulate (and, in the case of physics, clear evidence is available for this) that entities such as electric currents are not limited to their conducting wire but radiate a field all around them, strongly when close to the wire, and rapidly falling off but reaching zero only at infinity.

To use this kind of idea for the cortical representation of the outside world needs more direct physiological evidence, in fact the Gestaltists' notions received indirect support from the unlikely quarter of Karl Lashley (1890–1958), a Behaviourist.

Learning and problem-solving

The Gestaltists extended their principles of perception to provide accounts of learning and problem-solving. Learning was the central topic, not only for the Associationists, but also for the Behaviourists who were contemporary with them. Problem-solving was a topic which the Structuralists had considered previously.

During the First World War Köhler was interned on Tenerife. He took advantage of his confinement by studying the behaviour of apes who were given various problems to solve. The type of problem Köhler used was not totally unlike that used by Thorndike. The animal had to discover a technique in order to obtain food. By using apes, Köhler had rather splendid subjects in that he did not find it necessary to have the animals very hungry as Thorndike often did. To an ape, it appeared, a banana in the distance was a challenge.

Köhler's observations led him to conclude that the solution to problems are 'seen' in the literal rather than the metaphorical sense. Once the elements required for a solution are in reasonable proximity (e.g. a banana and a stick with which to drag it into the cage) then the solution may come, and, once it does, it comes quite suddenly as the Gestalt of elements forms. Thorndike's results with cats, however, needed explaining. Köhler held that they resorted to trial and error because Thorndike hid a vital element for the solution of the problem which is what prevented the sudden appearance of the solution.

Thus, for the Gestaltists, learning and problem-solving involved a holistic reorganization of the perception of the environment which is in strong contrast to the atomistic approach of the other schools. Wertheimer, in a late work, extended Gestalt ideas on learning and problem-solving to the case of human beings, but this work is perhaps of rather more pedagogical than psychological interest.

The great criticism of the Gestalt school's account of problem-solving, which does not seem to have been satisfactorily answered, is that their solution to problems often seems to be the same as ignoring them. This is a tempting way to run one's life but an ultimately unrewarding one. To criticize Thorndike for not presenting his animals with part of the solution seems strange when problems are problems just because some part of the solution is obscured.

The Gestaltists did, however, stimulate a great deal of work on the relative contributions of genetic endowment and learning to perception, which is described in Chapter 11.

Behaviourism

Behaviourism was as American in its main development as Gestalt psychology was German. The main tenet of the school, that psychology should be the study of behaviour, however, is attributable to the British psychologist William McDougall (1871–1938).

Whereas Gestalt psychology had, by modern times, shrunk greatly in its width of application, Behaviourism became an essential ingredient of mainstream psychology. By the 1950s the idea that psychology was, to a large extent, to be the science of behaviour, as distinct from that of consciousness, had become almost universally accepted and, thus, Behaviourism, as a widespread school, ceased to exist. This is parallel to the end of the Functionalists' clear existence as a school, once Functionalism had been widely accepted. Schools, in fact, seem to have been generated by a wish to protest against currently accepted ideas. If and when the ideas of a school becomes accepted, then loses its strong identity.

John Watson

John Watson (1878–1958) was the person who changed the emphasis of psychology from the study of conscious experience to the study of behaviour. That he was able to do this in a very short time speaks for the existence of two factors. The first of these was a readiness, particularly on the part of American and British psychologists, to accept change because of the difficulties into which introspection as a method had led Structuralism. The second factor was the ability of Watson as a polemicist as well as a scientist.

Watson began life as the sort of child most parents prefer not to have, eventually displaying socially delinquent behaviour. After his relatively short working life in academic psychology, during which he made his greatest achievements in the subject, he returned to 'delinquency' in the guise of divorce and re-marriage to a research assistant. For the United States of the 1920s this was delinquency indeed, and he was forced to resign his job at Johns Hopkins University. He spent the rest of his life making a great deal of money in the advertising industry and producing an occasional book on Behaviourism. As time progressed, Watson became increasingly concerned with the implications of learning theory for education and the organization of society. B. F. Skinner is another Behaviourist who, more recently, has turned his attention to the same kind of concern.

Watson's first published written account of Behaviourism came in an article in *The Psychological Review* of 1913 and in his book *Behaviour* (1914). He was clearly impatient with the in-fighting of the Structuralists particularly over the dispute between Wundt and the Würzburgers over the possibility of imageless thought. Watson felt that, if psychology was to progress, it would have to desert the method of introspection which, he pointed out, was turning psychology into a 'debating society'. For introspection Watson wished to substitute objective data.

Although Watson did not concern himself greatly with this point, it is worth considering the meaning of the term 'objective' because it is not always clear when a piece of evidence is to be regarded as objective. The problem becomes clear when one considers that all of the knowledge we have of the world is essentially private. We do not, in the last analysis, know if we see an object in the room; we simply know we have a sense-impression, a perception of the object. This knowledge is subjective. Even if the object is clear and plain to see, an armchair, for example, we only know of it subjectively; and if we are the only person who has ever been in the room or ever will go into the room, the statement, 'there is an armchair in the room', is a subjective one. In principle, the situation is not altered if a procession of observers peer into the room and note the existence of the armchair. But the situation is to some extent altered if the observers hold a meeting and agree that there is an armchair in the room. We are tempted, then, to say that the statement, 'there is an armchair in the room', is an objective statement. This idea of objectivity, as an agreement between observers, will have to do as its definition. Karl Popper thus defines objectivity as 'inter-subjectivity'.

One problem with introspection as practised by the Structuralists was that, given a dispute about what was in consciousness, there was no way in which more than one observer could check the situation. A further problem was that, to obtain the 'right' things in consciousness, one had to be trained properly and this reduced to being trained by the right people. This kind of psychological 'establishment' was not destined to appeal to Watson.

Watson, then, in the short term, substituted objective data for introspective data but it is essential to realize that, very soon, the Behaviourists were slipping in introspection, usually under the euphemism of 'verbal report'. But it had become complementary to and an aid to understanding the objective data rather than the main data itself. The new definition and methodology of psychology insisted upon by Watson opened the doors completely to animal psychology. Apart from the Cartesian objection to animals being used in psychology, that they had no souls and were thus fundamentally different from humans, the Structuralists had ignored animal psychology on the grounds that they possibly had no conscious experience but that, even if they had, they were distinctly inadequate at introspecting.

Like the Structuralists and unlike the Gestaltists, Watson was atomistic in his approach; he believed that, however complex a piece of behaviour appeared to be, it could be analysed into basic stimulus-response (S-R) units which he called 'reflexes'. In Watson's system these were of two types: those called by Pavlov unconditioned responses, for example salivation to the smell of food, which he supposed were instinctive, and those which he supposed were learned. A major task for psychology, according to Watson, was to identify those responses which were instinctive and those which were learned and to discover the laws governing learning (or habit formation as Behaviourists sometimes called learning). However, while others took this up, Watson, true to his concern with practicalities in life, dealt most of the time with stimuli and responses of a molar common sense size rather than a molecular, analytic size.

Watson's insistence on observing behavioural measures, rather than worrying about conscious states, led to some results of great interest, but also to what now seem to be almost absurdities. His account of learning depended largely on a basis of Pavlovian conditioning and he strongly opposed Thorndike's law of effect. An enormous amount of work has been done in learning theory since Watson's day, so that his own account of learning is now a matter for history rather than contemporary scientific interest.

Similarly, his account of memory is distorted by his determination to see human beings as S-R machines. The brain is simply a complex switch-room or telephone exchange, a passer on, not an originator or storer of messages. To avoid the plausible assumption that memories are stored and recalled in the brain, Watson put forward the implausible assumption that memories are largely after-effects in sensory organs. The lack of more than a 'telephone-exchange' brain in Watson's scheme presented him with particular difficulties in accounting for thinking, which he described as being simply implicit speech movements, a view which has received only circumstantial empirical support and which belongs to times past.

Whereas the difference between the common sense and the Jamesian view of emotion was in the order in which its components were supposed to occur, Watson predictably dismissed the component of emotional experience, restricting himself to the view that emotion consists of profound bodily changes particularly of the visceral and glandular systems. The viscera are the smooth muscled parts of the body such as the stomach and gut which, as you probably know if you have ever sat an examination, seem to be highly involved in emotion. In the case of emotion, Watson's assumptions led to some fascinating demonstrations of conditioned acquisition and loss of emotional responses which were a precursor of important later work, especially in clinical psychology. At first sight, Watson's simplified way of regarding human beings may seem pointless or just perverse, but it is important to realize that this enabled him to formulate clear predictions which were testable by experimentation. Furthermore, that experimentation was often able to decide between Watson's view and that of others. In this respect Watson was admirable; he was not frightened to stick his neck out.

Edward Tolman

Edward C. Tolman (1886–1961) accepted a Behaviouristic approach to psychology but one which was tempered by his interest in and knowledge of Gestalt psychology. The fact that the Gestalt school placed emphasis on perception and the organizing function of the brain led Tolman to change the S-R model of Watson to an S-O-R model, where 'O' means organism.

Tolman's major contribution was his theory of learning which was expounded in various publications covering 40 years, nearly up to the time of his death. The theory demonstrated his wish to re-introduce the person into psychology in so far as it used the notion of cognition. Cognition means knowing and Tolman suggested that even animals come to know a part of their environment. Further, these pieces of knowing coalesce to form an internalized map of the environment in the animal's brain: shades

of Gestalt psychology, indeed. Tolman's theory has received consider
empirical support, although it had some enormous difficulties, particularly
in the area of relating knowing to action, which demonstrate that it was far
from a completely satisfactory story.

Clark Hull

Clark Hull (1884–1952) was the person who most thoroughly developed
the Behaviourist account of learning. His theory went through three major
formulations and attempted to predict the behaviour of rats in mazes. It
was the last theory which attempted anything so ambitious. Hull's followers, notably K. W. Spence and N. Miller, tended to concentrate on
more limited problems within learning theory as the solving of any one of
these proved to be a formidable task.

Hull's theory of learning reflects his interest in mathematics as well as in
the physiological research of Pavlov. The theory can be likened to
Euclidean geometry. By starting with a set of axioms, Hull hoped by means
of deduction to produce predictions concerning behaviour. He then tested
the predictions experimentally, thereby supporting, or otherwise, his
axioms. In the cases where the predicted behaviour did not occur, attempts
were made to modify the axioms to put this right, while not at the same
time putting wrong deductions which had been confirmed in other experiments. The scheme of continuous guessing and checking was envisaged by
Hull early on as a corrective to what he regarded as the half-baked
formulations of other schools who did not, in his view, make the effort to
follow through their assumptions to their logical conclusion. So that you
may recognize it, it should be pointed out that the method of guessing and
checking is usually glorified by the title of 'hypothetico-deductive method'.
The guesses, the hypotheses, are not, however, usually as random as the
word 'guess' may imply, but are guided by previous experience and
knowledge which, when codified, is known as theory.

The difficulty which Hull and his co-workers met with in their grand
scheme was that it failed to converge to the point where the number of
explanatory devices was adequately smaller than the observations to be
explained. Hull's lasting contribution to psychology is the provision of a
variety of terms which have become part of its language and are most often
found nowadays in learning theory and its applications in clinical psychology.

B. F. Skinner

Burrhus Frederic Skinner (born 1904) has also largely concerned himself
with learning theory and like Hull has often used animals, although his

work has been extended by himself as well as others to account for and to attempt to modify human behaviour most notably in educational and clinical settings.

Skinner's attitude to research methods in psychology was originally inspired by Pavlov's view that if variables are adequately controlled, then the underlying order in the nature of things will become apparent. This view of research has contributed to Skinner's use and development of a characteristic approach to experiment which may be contrasted with that most often used by Hull and others. Skinner's method is to observe one animal or person rather than a group. Even if he does this several times it is not for the purpose of averaging the results, the typical Hullian procedure, but to check that the results obtained with one organism are not the result of some idiosyncrasy of that organism. Accounts of Skinner's work in various settings will be found in Chapter 8.

It is in Skinnerian work that an 'anti-organism', behaviourist, S-R rather than S-O-R, approach still survives as a useful complement to much modern psychology, which is concerned with the analysis and comprehension of the organism. This does not mean that users of Skinnerian techniques as a group have any particular beliefs about the organism. In fact, it is unlikely that many of them do think that consciousness is simply a more or less useless by-product of a basically S-R system. However, the simplified S-R scheme of things is found to be useful in various settings and excellent at predicting the behaviour of animals in some situations, which allows us to create further hypotheses about human behaviour. This is more than adequate justification for the approach which has come to be known as the 'experimental analysis of behaviour'.

Psychology of the unconscious mind

The modern consideration of the unconscious mind was developed largely by Sigmund Freud (1856–1939) beginning from about 1895. Thus, we go back to the time before Behaviourism and Gestalt psychology. The reason for leaving discussion of Freudian and related work to this late stage in the chapter is that it had little debate with the other schools, coming as it did from a different mix of antecedents and developing a different subject matter. Before considering any relationship of the psychology of the unconscious to other schools a word about terminology will be useful.

The system founded and developed by Freud was called by him and is still known as 'psychoanalysis'. Freud had many disciples at various stages of his career, two of whom founded major systems branching from his. That founded by Carl Gustav Jung (1870–1961) is known as 'analytical psychology' and that founded by Alfred Adler (1870–1937) is known as 'individual psychology'. These three systems, together with other related ones, form a school, having in common the belief that much human experience and behaviour springs from motives of which the individual is unconscious. Collectively, the various systems are most often known as 'psychoanalysis', which is all right as long as the context makes clear whether the term is referring to the specifically Freudian system or to the systems as a group.

Sigmund Freud

Freudian psychoanalysis is both an account of human mental life and behaviour and a therapeutic technique. This is a lot and it took someone of Freud's singularity of purpose and confidence about the rightness of his ideas to produce it all. He was, like Wundt, a tireless worker and an autocratic man. He rethought parts of his system as time went on, yet was extremely antagonistic to friends or colleagues who offered criticisms or even suggested modifications to his system.

Freud was a medical graduate who was initially influenced by the French hypnotist Charcot (1825–93). He used hypnosis with patients when he returned after a year in Paris to Vienna in 1886. However, he found his results only partially satisfactory. A medical colleague in Vienna, Joseph Breuer (1842–1925), also used hypnosis to deal with a case of hysteria (a psychiatric disorder), but the patient not only seemed to remember emotional experiences to which symptoms were attributed, but found that, after discussing these under hypnosis, the symptoms disappeared (usually temporarily, as it turned out). It was from Breuer's hint that Freud proceeded with working out psychoanalysis, soon dropping the part played by hypnotism.

The ideas of Freud are discussed in later chapters. Here it will have to suffice to describe his ideas very briefly so that the elements of particular interest and difficulty may be pointed out.

Freud invented a theory of personality based on the notion of 'fixation' at various developmental stages. These developmental stages Freud called 'psychosexual' stages, indicating the importance he wished to allot to sexuality in his system. Indeed the very life force, the prime motivator, in Freud's system is 'libido' which, at least in early versions of his system, is clearly sexual in nature. Freud also put forward an account of the forces which, in their dynamic (i.e. not static) equilibrium, constitute mental life. For this reason psychoanalysis (in general) is sometimes known as 'dynamic' psychology. The prime actors in this dynamic system are the id exerting instinctive, libidinous force, the supergo representing cultural, civilized forces and the ego which achieves some balance between the other two.

Freud's system in general has caused a great deal of controversy in psychology, but there are perhaps two points in particular to which people have often reacted strongly. The first of these is Freud's insistence that children enter a phase of sexual activity at about the age of four to five years, after which there follows a decline, the latency period, until puberty. The second point is his belief that much human motivation, especially that from the id, is unconscious. This means that humans may sometimes do things for reasons of which they are unaware and cannot normally become aware.

Psychoanalysis, as a therapeutic technique, includes free association to the elements of the patient's dreams and the interpretation of the patient's statements in terms of symbolic meanings. The process, in its classical form, is extremely lengthy, involving what Freud described as transference of libido to the psychoanalyst. In broad terms, the technique is conceived as a means of obtaining controlled regression back to the psychosexual stage at which the patient is supposed to have been fixated, that is, unable to progress through. While at this stage (in some emotional sense) the analyst attempts to right the previous wrongs so that the desired emotional maturity may be reached by the patient.

Freud came to his conclusions by seeing patients over many years and also by the process of self analysis. Freud's system is often criticized, indeed dismissed as mere fancy, on the grounds that his conclusions were obtained in a way open to the possibility that he simply recorded his own prejudices and views and that, by the undoubted charisma of his personality, he persuaded his colleagues to reach the same conclusions as himself. This criticism is neither of scientific nor pragmatic relevance for the following reasons: if one reduces Freud's beliefs to a set of statements, it is the job of scientists, in the case of dispute, to check these by replication, that is, by observing relevant cases, such as current patients, to see if they reach similar conclusions. To look at the reliability of the origin of the sources is to practise history, a practice only justified when the events are not still there to be observed. However, it is as useful to check Freudian hypotheses as to check Jamesian or Wundtian ones: they are not even entertained in their original form by those who would describe themselves as Freudians. Further, Freudian and neo-Freudian psychology is so vast in its aims that one should never fall into the trap of discussing the standing of Freudian hypotheses; always specify which ones. Several attempts have been made to test empirically Freudian-derived hypotheses in more or less modified forms, and the results, as one might expect, are mixed.

Carl Gustav Jung

Jung's analytical psychology differed from Freud's system, from which it stemmed, in several respects. The most radical of these were his account of the unconscious and the dismissal of libido as the central life-force.

Jung believed, obtaining his evidence in a similar way to Frued, that the unconscious was of two types, the personal and the collective. The personal unconscious is broadly similar to Freud's conceptualization, but the collective unconscious is an inherited unconscious knowledge of the essential experience of all mankind. The mechanisms of transmission of the collective unconscious have always been obscure. According to Jung, the collective unconscious expresses itself in an archetypal way, that is, its products represent concepts which are universal. One purpose of Jungian analysis is to recognize the archetypes behind dreams and fantasies. Jung believed that archetypes also occur in myths and fairy tales and are cross-cultural. Jung's attitudes to the notion of archetypes and their transmission showed a tendency to mysticism which pervades much of his work. The effect this tendency had on Freud, who was a convinced atheist, may be imagined. To go with his attitudes, Jung posited that the essential life force was essentially spiritual in nature, not sexual as it had been in Freud's system.

Jung was concerned with psychological 'types' and introduced into psychology the ideas of introversion and extraversion which were to become important in theories of personality (see Chapter 20). He is perhaps one of the most difficult psychologists to comprehend and it is certainly impossible to do anything like justice to what one is tempted to call his muse in such a short space as this. Like many original thinkers, his work can seem at times utterly profound but at others equally absurd. What is clear is that those parts of Jung's system which overlap in their coverage with that of Freud are probably even more difficult than Freud's to investigate empirically.

Alfred Adler

Adler produced an account of human behaviour and mental life which, for scrutiny, needs to be considered in terms of outcome rather than in terms of cogent structure as a system. This is not a criticism; there is no intrinsic merit in producing a grand scheme of things, and Adler certainly provided ideas and theoretical formulations even though these were often modified piecemeal.

Where Freud had libido and Jung a spiritual life force Adler has the extraordinarily down to earth will for power, a striving after superiority. He saw the essential part of human motivation as being conscious although he in no way denied the existence of unconscious motives. His emphasis was not, as with Freud and Jung, on the history of the patient's emotional life, but on its future. Largely as a result of this an Adlerian analysis is far shorter and less likely to become a way of life in itself than a Freudian or Jungian one.

None of these divergencies from the Freudian orthodoxy were destined to endear Adler to Freud, and Adler went his separate way in 1911.

The three systems

We have seen earlier the huge methodological difficulties encountered in trying to investigate psychology as a science of consciousness, but these difficulties become trivial when compared with those arising from trying to create a science of unconsciousness. Because of this, psychoanalysis has always stood apart from the other schools. It was born of medicine rather than biology or philosophy, and its subject matter has prevented it from really joining with and interacting with other schools. Psychoanalysis has been centrally concerned with clinical problems and, in its final assessment, whenever that will be, it will be important to consider it not only as a form of therapy but also as a description of human mental life and human behaviour.

Free will and determinism

The accounts of human life that we have been discussing vary in the degree to which they suppose that a person's actions are determined by some combination of their genetic inheritance with their immediate environment. Historically there have been two opposing views, the free will and the deterministic positions. The free will position holds that, in general, a person could do other than what they actually did; whereas determinism holds that every event is caused, human actions included, so that what happened was what had to happen. In fact these two poles describe the extremes, and between them there are many positions that have been adopted. While an analysis of these positions is of concern to philosophers, psychologists have tended to think out their theoretical position within psychology and then, perhaps, realize where they were within the free will–determinism debate, rather than begin with it.

Neither psychologists nor philosophers nowadays tend to have any truck with more extreme forms of determinism such as fatalism, which holds that the future is fixed. We are familiar with fatalism via Greek drama, and particularly in psychology via the Oedipus legend.

A more popular recent position is known as 'soft' determinism which accepts that our actions are caused but rejects the idea that this makes us less free because the causation is not a compulsion, thus soft determinists believe that free will and causation are compatible. This debate is important when considering reward and punishment. Soft determinists can defend these only as influences on action, moral considerations belong to the world of free will. The free will position has also always been favoured by most religions because, one imagines, it is difficult to have sin without it.

Psychometry

From the end of the last century throughout the whole period we have been considering, there have been psychologists who, usually with an eye to immediate application of their studies, have concerned themselves with the problems of mental measurement. They do not form a school in the sense that they actively worked together, hoping to solve the same problems; rather, they have usually been people who were faced with the need to solve a problem and who had the inventiveness to develop the solutions.

Galton, who has been mentioned already in the context of Functionalism, was the forerunner of modern psychometry. He supposed that intelligence was correlated with sensory ability (he had invented the first measure of correlation a little earlier in 1888). Thus, to measure intelligence, he set out to measure sensory ability. Not one to betray lack of enthusiasm for the task in hand, he arranged the collection some six years later of data from over 9000 people. James McKeen Cattell (1860–1944) had by then met Galton in London and published his paper *Mental Tests*, which gives an account of the uses to which such tests may be put as well as providing the term 'mental test'.

The progress of mental testing was threatened for a while by statistical objections to its validity but the situation was saved by the work of Charles Spearman (1863–1945) who worked under Galton in London. Spearman presented a two-factor theory of intelligence which held that any test result depended on tapping the general ability (g) of the subject as well as special ability (s). This theory was immediately challenged and has often been so since, but remains a usable underpinning for the theory of mental measurement.

Alfred Binet (1857–1911) was a French psychologist who faced the administrative problem in Paris of allocating some children of deficient intelligence to special schools. To solve this problem, he devised a series of graded tests each consisting of a group of different tasks, thus providing a broad tapping of the child's abilities. Unknown to Binet at the time, he had solved, in practical terms, what Spearman had solved theoretically. The result was a success and the Binet scale was translated into English. The need for testing conscripts in the First World War so that they could be successfully allocated to different tasks completed the acceptance of mental testing and since those days it has been a part of all our lives. Recently, however, the very basis and meaning of mental testing has again been called into question. Discussion of the problems will be found in Chapter 13.

Conclusion

This chapter has not attempted to present every contribution to psychology in the 75 years or so it covers. Some of the grosser omissions will be repaired in the next chapter. They involve work which makes more sense looked back upon rather than being sliced off at about mid-century.

It is customary to point out that schools in psychology were a developmental phase, akin to that seen in other sciences in their early days. They were weakened in about 1930 when their founders were dead and when there was dissension from within and psychologists realized that no school really did justice to the huge gamut of human experience and behaviour. The extent to which this is so is something we shall have to examine in the next chapter.

What is clear from our examination of the schools is the conflict between the poetic imagination and the influence of the machine. On the one hand, we have the Gestalt psychologists and the Psychoanalysts, who have a vision of humans which is born of the notions of completeness and uniqueness with full recognition of the place of awareness. On the other hand, we have the Associationists and Behaviourists with their vision of humans strongly influenced by the development of machines. Both may be useful models. The extent to which they have guided, and even made compatible, recent work is the essential if often tacit subject of the work we now need to examine.

Different approaches to the study of psychology

Clive Gabriel

Later psychology
Motivation
Instincts
Drive theories
Arousal theories of motivation
Hedonistic theories of motivation
Conclusion on motivation
Physiological psychology
Methods of physiological
  psychology
Physiological psychology and
  psychology
Social psychology
Content of social psychology

The methods of social psychology
Cognitive psychology
The methods of cognitive psychology
Cognitive psychology and a model
  of humans
Developmental psychology
The contents and methods of
  developmental psychology
Individual differences
Trait and type theories
The origins of individual differences
Science and explanation
Method in psychology
Ethics in science

Later psychology

A number of differences may be seen between later psychology and the psychology of the schools discussed in the last chapter. The emphasis on doctrine has lessened and that on empiricism and conceptual analysis has increased; it is rare nowadays to hear such confident prescriptions as to what psychology should be about or the level of analysis, holistic or atomistic, at which it should be conducted. This change has not come about because psychologists have all suddenly become especially tolerant people, but because it is now clear that what we have embarked upon in studying psychology is most probably a never ending task, rather than the few years to clear up the details, optimistically supposed by some of the earlier schoolmen. With the recognition of the complexities of the problem that we have set ourselves has come the acceptance that the routes to the answers cannot be clear and that the plural 'routes' is probably the realistic way of expressing the situation. Individual psychologists, being people, still, however, have their preferences for subject areas, as well as for methods, so that different areas of psychology are still recognizable.

One of the biggest changes that occurred in psychology during the last forty years or so was the growth of 'cognitive' psychology. Social psychology, developmental psychology, and applied psychology have all developed greatly since the era of the schools, and physiological psychology has revealed a great deal about the workings of the 'machine' which correlate with behaviour and conscious experience. It has also made some particularly exciting contributions to the area of motivation. Let us begin the account of later psychology with the problem of motivation.

Motivation

The problem of understanding why people do anything at all, and if they do something, why that and not something else, is basic to psychology. The problem may be broken down into the need to understand two components of motivation: driving force, and direction. Following is a sketch of the types of approaches to motivation which have been used to account for its problems.

Instincts

An early theorist who attempted to answer both parts of the question was William McDougall in his *Introduction to Social Psychology* (1908). As the title of his book implies, McDougall was concerned with the area of social psychology, but his aim was to find, for those involved in all types of work concerning societies (sociologists, economists, and so on), a firm psychological basis for their accounts of human behaviour. For McDougall, that firm basis was biological and based on the idea of 'instinct'. McDougall presented a list of twelve human instincts which grew to a list of eighteen by 1932. His idea was that all human motives could be derived from his list of basic instincts. McDougall was not really happy with the use of the word 'instinct' in this context, which is as well because neither was anyone else. He later used the term 'propensity' instead. Instincts, or propensities, in McDougall's sense, were said by him to be analysable into three components: a predisposition to notice particularly relevant stimuli in the environment; a tendency to feel an appropriate emotional impulse; and a predisposition to make appropriate movements.

In fact, McDougall's theory was very sophisticated, involving a concept of sentiments which were derived from instincts, the final behaviour not being supposed to be purely instinctual at all, but involving considerable learning. The reasons why the theory fell out of favour after a period of great success were threefold. First, behaviourism was emphasizing the importance of learning for behaviour. Secondly, the sociologists, economists, etc., for whom McDougall's theory was so obligingly prepared, made it clear that they did not want it: for them, 'society' was a concept they felt they could deal with without considering individual psychology. Thirdly, the concept of 'instinct' came under great suspicion for not explaining anything, but just stating the problem in a new way. For example, saying that one is eating because of an instinct to eat may sound acceptable, but then, why not say that one is roller-skating because of one's roller-skating instinct? This process could be continued indefinitely – renaming everything and explaining nothing.

The 1950s saw the return of the idea of instinct to psychology, but this time with clear circumspection. The term itself is usually replaced by 'species-specific behaviour', one of a set of concepts introduced by animal ethologists such as Lorenz, Tinbergen, and Hinde to describe the genetically-determined behaviours of various species. However, even these genetically-determined behaviours are more or less modified by learning, although some to a very small extent indeed. Species-specific behaviour has been described in sub-human species, but there is no reason to suppose that we do not exhibit it, although the very adaptability of humans speaks for the likelihood of a great proportion of learning in their behaviour.

Drive theories

Before the problems with McDougall's theories were clear, Freud had put forward his idea of libido as the energizing force behind behaviour. Other later theories, related to Freud's, supposed that the driving force was different in origin, and it was given different names; but the idea was essentially similar. In Freud's system, any particular type of behaviour could be supposed to be a transformation and canalization of libido, and Freud suggested mechanisms such as 'repression', by which these processes could occur. However, his and similar systems fail to say much more than that they suppose people behave because they live. There is no part of these systems which explains the vital point: why the general driving force takes the form of violin playing in one person, for example, and rock climbing in another.

A different theory of drive came from the learning theorist Clark Hull. Hull's system related hours of deprivation of a basic biological need, such as food, to variables, such as speed of running to reach food. Hull's system was extremely complex and he took note of many variables in the rat's behaviour other than drive. However, it is important to note two points: that Hull had no way of measuring drive – he inferred it from deprivation; and that he found his data best fitted the assumption that drives are not specific. This last assumption means that, generally, a thirsty and hungry rat will seek food more energetically than a rat which is only hungry. This last idea, that of generalized drive, has much in common with the idea of arousal which was to become important to the theory of motivation.

Arousal theories of motivation

The concept of arousal seemed to have a clear physiological basis in the activity of part of the brain-stem known as the ascending reticular activating system (ARAS). Indeed, for several years from the late 1940s it seemed that there existed a physiologically mediated continuum of general arousal or activation. Sadly, like so much in science, what seemed simple has proved to be complex. Nevertheless, arousal states of various types are still identifiable and the concept of arousal in one form or another has featured widely in motivation theory.

The arousal theory of motivation supposes, and evidence has supported this to some extent, that the organism will work to obtain intermediate levels of arousal, too little arousal leading to no behaviour or aimless behaviour, while too much arousal leads to panic or frantic agitation. This picture is adequate in so far as it explains why humans and animals will behave to avoid staring at blank walls for long periods of time on one hand, and do not sit by idly while the house is burning down on the other. There are also, however, all of the middle levels of arousal which cover most of life. To explain which response is made by humans at these levels of arousal, cognitive and social theories of motivation are usually called upon. For animals, hierarchies of preferences for different types of behaviour are often supposed to operate. In the human case, these further theories usually involve the notion of hedonism.

Hedonistic theories of motivation

Hedonism is the ethical doctrine that seeking pleasure is the purpose of life. As pleasure is a conscious experience which animals cannot report and maybe cannot have, the notion is modified in their case. This is done by treating as 'pleasurable' those stimuli which the animal will work to obtain.

In his formulation of the 'law of effect', Thorndike supposed that animals repeated actions when they were followed by 'satisfiers' and would avoid repeating them when followed by 'annoyers'. It was soon pointed out that this formulation led to a circular argument. Thorndike supposed food was a satisfier because animals would press levers for it and he supposed they pressed levers for it because it was a satisfier. However, there was no way of predicting, other than in this circular way, what would be a satisfier or what would be an annoyer. Meehl (1950) and Premack (1962) have solved this problem by demonstrating that satisfiers and annoyers have a general role by which they can be identified other than by the circular argument of Thorndike. Premack has presented a system of arranging behaviours in order, which enables one to predict the proportion of time an animal is likely to spend emitting any one behaviour. Further, he has shown that the proportions may be altered by depriving the animals of particular requirements.

Social psychologists have taken up the idea of hedonism in their accounts of motivation. A series of 'exchange theories' have been developed, the exchange referring to rewards and costs. These theories are also open to the criticism of circularity and again ways have been found to meet this criticism.

Conclusion on motivation

Because motivation is at the very core of psychology one cannot expect all, or even many, of the problems it presents to be neatly solved. Animal and human studies may still offer perspectives for each other, but it seems that the two areas are perhaps best considered separately, if only because of the greater use of secondary or learned motivation (the cognitive and social sort) in explanations of human behaviour. One difficulty with the psychological study of motivation is that the history of the subject has persuaded psychologists to look for answers by studying organisms in one environment, the laboratory. It has been apparent for some while now that the situation in which the behaviour takes place, especially in interaction with the organism's idiosyncrasies, plays a large part in the cause of behaviour exhibited.

Physiological psychology

Physiological psychology is concerned with discovering the physiological mechanisms whose action is concomitant with behaviour, experience and, indeed, all psychological phenomena. The relationship between physiological and psychological events is often complex, cause and effect by no means being always in one direction. Indeed, the relationship is often interactive, the physiological events and the psychological events serving to build up each other's intensities or damp them down. There are people who believe that, ultimately, all psychological events will be explicable in terms of physiological events, and this belief is known as reductionism. Whether or not reductionism is ultimately shown to be useful, it is not a view which need concern us now; pragmatically there is more than enough for us to discover in both physiological and psychological language.

The scope of physiological psychology is wide and covers a number of different subject areas. Research has developed rapidly in recent years on the mode of action of brain cells (neurones) and, most importantly, their junctions, which are known as synapses. These are important to psychology because of their role in learning and remembering.

At a gross level, physiological structures have been shown to mediate various psychological functions. Details of these systems and their functions will be found in the chapters on physiological psychology. Physiological psychology has also been important in the investigation of sleep cycles (sleep has been found to comprise a cyclical arrangement of different physiological and behavioural states), as well as in the wider investigation of the whole range of consciousness from coma, through sleep and wakefulness, to alert attention.

Methods of physiological psychology

Activity of the cerebral cortex, the outermost layer of the brain, is interpreted from records known as electroencephalograms, which term is mercifully usually abbreviated to EEG. This is the method beloved of illustrators of sensational articles about the horrors of mind-reading, thought control, and other Orwellian ideas. Electrodes are affixed to subjects' scalps, and these electrodes are sensitive to the very small electrical effects arising from the activity of the cortex. The signals from them are amplified and a continuous graph of the signals is automatically drawn. Readings from the graph may be correlated with sensory stimulation the subject receives or tasks he or she is asked to perform.

Measures may also be taken of the activity of the subjects' autonomic nervous system (ANS), which can be crudely defined as the nervous system controlling involuntary responses (Chapter 6 gives more detailed explanation). These measures are usually of heart rate, breathing depth and rate, galvanic skin responses (GSR), as well as readings of muscle tension. The galvanic skin response is a measure of conductivity between two points on the skin. Skin potential is also sometimes read. A further technique used by physiological psychologists is to implant an electrode at a specific point in the brain by means of surgery. The electrode may then be used either to stimulate that area of the brain with small electrical currents or else, by larger currents, to burn away a small area of surrounding tissue. This latter process is known as ablation. Stimulation and ablation are carried out mainly on animals, very rarely on humans, and then only for good clinical reasons.

Physiological psychology and psychology

As you will appreciate from this brief account of the activities of physiological psychologists, their work is not confined to one area of psychology (although it is more applicable to some areas than to others) but covers many areas in a symbiotic relationship with work which is behavioural or introspective.

Social psychology

Like physiological psychology, social psychology offers more than just its subject matter; it can be used as a viewpoint for all psychology.

The start of social psychology is usually taken as dating from the work of McDougall, who has already been mentioned in the context of motivation. His aim was to provide a firm biological basis for others who concerned themselves with the structure and function of society. It is important to note that social psychology is very concerned with the individual although it takes especial note of relationships with others. Social psychologists do not often talk of 'society' as a concept for study; this is the job of sociologists. Ironically, given McDougall's aspirations for a biological basis for social studies of various types, social psychology is often regarded by psychologists as being as far as one can get from physiological psychology, the two types of study involving very different techniques.

One of the earliest influential theoretical systems in social psychology was that of Kurt Lewin (1890–1947). Lewin was greatly influenced by Gestalt psychology; indeed, he is often regarded as a Gestalt psychologist. Like the other members of the school, he was impressed by and used the field theories then, as now, current in physics. However, he used the idea of a field to represent the person's interactions with various forces in their 'life-space', whereas the other workers had used the idea as the basis of a theory of brain function.

Lewin's idea of a person's life-space comprised a psychological map of their environment, that is, a map representing the physical world as mediated by their perceptions as well as the rest of their psychological world. Lewin's aim was to comprehend behaviour by supposing it to be the resultant of the vectors (lines representing forces in direction as well as magnitude) representing all forces in the life space. This model, therefore, incorporates the influence on behaviour of the environment as it is perceived by the individual. The idea of representing psychological 'forces' by vectors became influential in social psychology in the three decades following Lewin's death.

Content of social psychology

A considerable proportion of social psychology is concerned with the problem of social motivation in humans, that is, motivation which does not relate to basic biological needs without some intervening learning process; and in most human society that amounts to just about all behaviour. Attempts have been made to identify such motives, as well as to provide models for the resolution of situations where motives would be expected to oppose each other. Some of these social motives such as the postulated need for achievement (N Ach) are hypothetical constructs (complex ideas supported by evidence which is largely circumstantial), whose measurement is by questionnaire-type tests. These tests need to be subjected to procedures for ascertaining their reliability and validity. That is, we have to discover that the tests are measuring what we believe them to be measuring and are doing so reliably at different times.

Another major topic of investigation in social psychology is the study and measurement of attitudes and attitude change. An attitude is another hypothetical construct which is supposed to have a cognitive, an affective (pertaining to mood), and a behavioural component. The study of the influence of groups on their members' behaviour and beliefs, of non-verbal communication and interpersonal attraction comprise a few of the further topics which make up social psychology and which you will find discussed in later chapters. The study of how children become socialized, that is, learn the enormous amount of social skills and number of attitudes society requires them to have is sometimes placed under the heading of social and sometimes of developmental psychology.

Recently, many social psychologists have become concerned with the careful analysis and investigation of the terms they use, in the belief that we use these terms to construct reality.

The methods of social psychology

Social psychologists' data cover the gamut of possibilities: behavioural, introspective, and various other kinds of report, free or structured by questionnaire. The data have often been collected in laboratories but field work is also common.

For several years now social psychologists have been questioning the validity of their procedures. The problems they have encountered are of two types: those which are difficult to put right but clearly could be, given the will; and those which seem part of the very activity of social psychology. There has been concern about the heavy bias of samples of subjects used in social psychology experiments. Counts done on journal articles report that well over half the subjects used are students. Concern has also been expressed about the effects the experimenter has on the subjects by consciously or unconsciously communicating to them the requirements of the experiment. Another criticism is that social psychology is inadequate in predicting behaviour; that is, it fails to discover general laws governing social behaviour. The fact that students are so often used as subjects is a greater problem in social psychology experiments than in, say, physiological psychology experiments because the variables the social psychologist observes (social skills, for example) may be functions of socioeconomic class, intelligence, and so on. The trouble is that students are already biased in these ways: they are more intelligent than the general population and still tend to come more from middle-class families than from working-class families. One is, therefore, developing the social psychology of a small group which may lead to statements which are quite untrue for the rest of the population, who were not represented in the experiments. The problem exists for all types of psychology but has been emphasized by social psychologists, not without reason. In short, the problem is that students are more likely to be atypical of the general population on social psychological variables than they are on some other types of psychological variables. This problem is of very great practical importance. Its remedy may well be extremely costly in effort. It is not, however, a fundamental problem.

Rosenthal (1966) raised the problem of experimenter effects which, again, might occur in most psychology experiments but will be more powerful in an area of study which frequently requires responses involving value, rather than purely behavioural, responses. Various ways have been used to remedy this problem which have in common the use of 'blind procedures'; that is, none of those who come into contact with the subject know the experimental condition to which the subject is to be allocated. There are, however, other demand characteristics of experiments. It is often the case that subjects hypothesize what is expected of them and, depending on how nice or nasty they are, will tend to give the results they suppose are desired or the opposite results. Both niceness and nastiness are obstacles to undistorted results, and experiments need to be designed to minimize this effect. There are no general rules for this; the experimenter needs to exercise wit to reduce the problem.

The problem of the relative lack of predictive power in theories in social psychology is more fundamental but not at all hopeless. The underlying model behind much social psychological thinking is that people behave according to an economic calculus. Various actions are seen as having positive or negative utility, and an attempt is made to understand human behaviour as being the result of a reckoning of which choice of action will provide the best pay-off. The predictive power of this kind of theory is limited by the same matter which so lamentably limits that of economic forecasting: the problem is that the effects are so highly interactive. This means that any general statement such as 'people will like those similar to themselves' will be contradicted many times because so many factors will affect it and in real life these are not held constant. The same problem occurs in all science: the extent to which it can be dealt with depends on matters of complexity and measurement. We have to draw the distinction made by Karl Popper, while discussing physics, between prediction and prophecy. While it is often difficult to *predict* the outcome of a situation in social psychology, it is often possible, using theory, to provide a rationale for the outcome; that is, to show it fits the theory once one knows what the outcome is. Prediction is one of the severest criteria scientists demand before they are satisfied that an explanation of a phenomenon has been provided. However, a rationale is a type of explanation, if not one which is ultimately satisfying. We shall have to return to the topic of what constitutes a satisfactory explanation towards the end of this chapter.

Cognitive psychology

Associationists and behaviourists had concentrated on a stimulus-response (S-R) model of animals and man. Tolman (1932) had taken the step of modifying this scheme to an S-O-R- model, where 'O' standing for 'organism' indicated the view that the brain, indeed the central nervous system in general, was probably more than a busy telephone exchange. Cognitive psychology has attempted to analyse the structure and function of 'O'.

'Cognition' means knowing, and cognitive psychology has studied all of the abilities we use in knowing: perceiving, remembering, thinking, and so on. A very clear indication of how to proceed in cognitive psychology came from D. O. Hebb in *Organization of Behaviour*. Hebb suggested that, in order to understand the flow of information through the nervous system, one need not have a complete knowledge of the finest aspects of brain structure and function. Instead, one could race ahead of physiological knowledge by inventing a conceptual nervous system. While any account of the brain's working must ultimately be subject to the check of physiological credibility, the approach of the conceptual nervous system, building information flow models, has proved extremely constructive.

Early empirical work was begun by Colin Cherry, an engineer who concerned himself with what he called the 'cocktail party problem'. This is the problem of discovering how one may listen to the speech of one person while surrounded by many others speaking equally loudly in a crowded room. Why, if the person who is talking to one, is saying 'we had an awfully good time yesterday' and someone nearby is saying quite as loudly, 'the cow jumped over the moon', does one not hear some conflation of the two messages such as, 'the cow had an awfully good moon yesterday'? Cherry's method of answering this problem was to give various dichotic listening tasks to subjects. In these, different information was fed into each ear and the subject was asked to report what was heard, in other words to 'track' the message from one or other ear. The investigation of these and related problems was soon taken up, at first by Donald Broadbent, and then by a number of workers particularly in the UK and North America (for details see Chapter 10).

Eventually, models were developed, and these are still being modified, to account for the unknown facts about perception, selective attention, memory, and other aspects of the information processing system. The development of computers, which has occurred at the same time as the development of cognitive psychology, has provided inspiration for the building of some models and has also provided a useful analogy for higher level models designed to show the organization of other models.

Cognitive psychology, then, is not simply the science of behaviour, nor the science of conscious experience, but the science of information flow through people. Some of this flow may lead to behaviour and some of it may be conscious but neither is necessarily the case.

The methods of cognitive psychology

One method of psychologists in this field is to ask people what they saw, heard, or remembered after some sensory stimulation (and sometimes after a delay, during which they may be asked to perform some task or be subjected to other sensory stimulation). That is, subjects are asked to introspect. Watson's way out of the difficulty, when he had lambasted introspection as a methodological disaster, yet wanted to take notice of what his subjects said, was to say he was not using introspection at all; it was 'verbal response'. This need not be just casuistry; the distinction is in the attitude held by the psychologist. If a subject is asked to look into a tachistoscope (an instrument used for presenting visual stimuli) and say what he sees, the psychologist may get a response such as, 'it says ZRT'. If the psychologist assumes that the statement has meaning which is akin to that with which other subjects (and he himself) would endow the statement were they looking, he is using introspective method. If, however, the psychologist treats the statement as though it were a mere reflex in Watson's terms, something akin to conditioned salivation, then he has obtained a verbal response. It is hard to imagine why anyone would want a verbal response in this sense, unless they could not understand the language of the subject (an unpromising practice), or else were trying hard to defend a silly doctrine. It is clear that what cognitive psychologists ask subjects to do is to introspect.

A fundamental reason for objecting to introspection as far as behaviourists were concerned was that, in cases of dispute, the problem sometimes proved to be unresolvable, but there are practical differences between the practice of cognitive psychologists and that of structuralists. Wundt and his disciples were concerned with a type of report from subjects which did not occur spontaneously and which took careful training to obtain. They often succeeded in finding agreement between subjects at different places but hit trouble when they pursued more and more difficult tasks. Apart from straightforward instructions about where to look or listen, the subject in the type of experiment usually done in cognitive psychology is asked simply to report what he or she heard. During the last 40 years or so disputes have indeed arisen, caused by conflicting experimental results, but they have not led back to the mysteries of the training of subjects. Instructions given to subjects have often been found to alter results but instructions may be and have been compared and problems resolved.

While the methods of cognitive psychology have frequently included introspection, this has been a matter of convenience, not doctrine, as has been the case in the past. Other methods are indeed used, as may be seen from the chapters on memory, perception, and thinking. It is typical of the attitudes of post-school psychology that any other methods available will certainly be grabbed very quickly, as long as they help to solve the problems which concern cognitive psychologists.

Cognitive psychology and a model of humans

In the last chapter it was pointed out that some schools of psychology worked with a machine-like model of human beings, whereas others took a view which had more in common with the products of a poetic imagination. Clearly, the methods and model building activities of cognitive psychologists subscribe to the 'person as a machine' view; but a machine with a difference. It is seen as much more complex that that postulated by the associationists and behaviourists. Also, there is in general no claim by psychologists that their account of information processing is sufficient to explain all human behaviour and experience. Some believe this, with the corollary that the 'machine' needs to be complex enough to produce poetry; a sort of computer. Others believe that the production of poetry is not within the province of even the most complicated machine; they suppose that the machine is a mediator. While these conjectures are fascinating, it is not necessary to take one side or the other or even to indulge in them at all to practise cognitive psychology; the important thing is to understand the workings of the machine as accurately as possible.

Developmental psychology

In 1887, Darwin published an account of the diary he kept of the development of his own son. This is normally taken to be the start of modern developmental psychology. The first person to make the study a major part of their life's work was Granville Stanley Hall (1844–1924).

Hall was a remarkable person who investigated everything with superb enthusiasm. The fact that he was not one to do things by halves may be judged from the title of his magnum opus, *Adolescence: its Psychology, and its Relations to Physiology, Anthropology, Sociology, Sex, Crime, Religion, and Education* (1904). Hall was a strong proponent of evolutionary theory, especially that aspect which holds that ontogeny follows phylogeny; that is, that the development of the individual goes through stages representative of the development of the species. Hall left a wide, encyclopaedic basis for future study as well as a look into the future in his late study of geriatrics, until quite recently a lamentably neglected end of developmental psychology.

In general, developmental psychologists have been distinguished from others by the questions they have asked, rather than by their theoretical background, although there is one giant exception to this rule.

The contents and methods of developmental psychology

Developmental psychology rests on the notion that behaviour and experience at any stage of life is related to previous states. The early years, from conception to young adulthood, have received most attention from developmental psychologists and old age has the next share of attention. Middle life does not so often show such sudden changes of behaviour or experience, so that it has been comparatively neglected. This is like historians of ancient times mentioning only the great battles and other crises of society, thus giving an unnaturally exciting account of life to the unwarned reader.

Psychological theories of early life stress two types of unevenness in the flow of development: stages, and critical periods. Development is found to occur in more or less the same order (although at differing times) in all normal children. Thus crawling precedes walking while holding furniture precedes free walking. Further, these stages of locomotion will roughly correlate with development of speech and other achievements. Various workers, foremost amongst whom are Freud and Piaget, have used the concept of stages to delineate periods when particular abilities first appear, or during which characteristic behaviours are produced. Critical periods are periods during development in which it is supposed that a child is ready to take advantage of some particular set of experiences. Some critical periods seem more critical than others. The extent to which various successful adult functions depend on childhood experience is a topic discussed in later chapters.

Both the concepts of stages and of critical periods imply that development is neither simply a function of learning nor simply of maturation, that is, of the pure consequences of genes manifesting themselves at the appropriate times. Rather, development is, in general, the result of an interaction between heredity and environment. The meaning of 'interaction' is that any statement concerning the effect of learning on development must be qualified by describing the hereditary attributes of the person concerned, and, similarly, any statement about the effect of heredity on development must be qualified by describing the experiences encountered by the organism. At a common sense, qualitative level, the idea of interaction between heredity and environment is very clear; it is in attempts to quantify it that difficulties arise, indeed, the meaning of quantification in this area is a difficult concept. One way of dealing with this problem of quantification is to give scores to some piece of behaviour, aggressiveness, for example, and attempt to discover how much of the variance amongst scores is explained by heredity and how much by environment. Variance is a statistical term, it is simply a number which represents the dispersion of the scores; the smaller the variance the more the individual scores tend to crowd around their mean. Difficulty then arises in controlling both the learning available to the children as well as their heredity. These points will be taken up at various places in this book, but it is important that you realize now that any statement concerning the various contributions of heredity and environment to any human function is a statement in which there can be little confidence.

The main approaches to the development of childhood have been those by Freud, Piaget, and various learning theorists (Bandura, for example); these approaches have differed in both their content and their methods. All three have investigated various aspects of socialization, with Freud predictably concentrating on emotional development and Piaget on intellectual and moral development. Learning theorists have concentrated, to some extent, on mechanisms of imitation, which has led to a theoretical debate as to whether or not imitation may be understood in terms of the basic types of conditioning introduced in the last chapter. Whereas learning theorists have adapted conventional laboratory methods to the study of development, the methods of Freud and Piaget are idiosyncratic and their validity is often challenged. Freud's discussion of development stems from his psychoanalytic methods which, as has been mentioned in Chapter 1, leave much to be desired. Piaget's methods are semi-structured; that is, in his questioning of children, the aims and basic questions are standardized but, in recognition of the fact that children are not standardized, supplementary questions are sometimes added *ad lib*. These raise the methodological difficulty of distinguishing between asking and teaching.

The developmental psychology of senescence (old age) comprises distinguishing between normal and abnormal senescence and attempting to find successful management regimes for both. This is an area where psychology works with a range of other disciplines: psychiatry, neurology, and social work.

In all developmental work the need for more accurate observation has been felt. Children and the old are ready victims of anecdotal evidence, an awful combination of wishful thinking and sloppy observation, fit only for first wanderings in science. Developmental psychology is one area where theory has come almost too early and psychologists, aware of this, are successfully pushing the clock back, using techniques, such as time-sampling of behaviour, which have become readily available with the widespread use of aids such as video-tape recording.

Individual differences

One may consider people as being extraordinarily similar to one another or extraordinarily different from one another. Which viewpoint you take depends on how you compare them. A huge amount of psychology has arisen from studying the similarities between people; that which studies the differences comes under the heading of individual differences. Traditionally, this field has been divided into the main areas of personality and intelligence, with their attendant problems of measurement.

'Personality' is a term which, while easy enough to grasp roughly, is not easy to define, and it is even harder to make the definition operational. The problem is one of knowing where to stop studying the differences. While viewing everyone in the world as being more or less the same is clearly a gross oversimplification, viewing everyone as unique in every respect may be wonderful for the biographers but not for scientists who usually wish to see patterns in their subject matter.

Trait and type theories

Although these are commonly distinguished, they may be regarded as fundamentally similar, trait theories allowing more 'types' and being more flexible in the labelling of those they allow.

Trait theories, as typified by that of R.B. Cattell, are developed by obtaining, by various means, such as rating and behavioural observation, people's positions on various scales. Most of the scales used by Cattell (he began in 1946 with 171 of them) are bipolar, that is they have adjectives of opposite meanings at either end of the scale: examples are 'sociable-shy', 'wise-foolish'. Left like this, with a person rated on 171 variables, we might as well write a biography, indeed a biography may well be more digestible and give a clearer picture of the person than 171 numbers. Because of this, Cattell has, by various statistical means (cluster analysis and factor analysis), reduced the number of traits by taking advantage of correlations between them. The principles of these techniques are very simple, although in pre-computer days the arithmetic was very tedious. The idea of taking advantage of correlations can be readily understood by considering two of Cattell's original 171 traits. It is found that people's scores on the 'confident-submissive' scale are highly correlated with their scores on the 'conceited-modest' scale. This being so, we may reduce these two scales (together with several others) to one scale, say, 'dominance-submissiveness'. Thus, several of the 171 originals may be reduced to one 'source' trait. Cattell, in fact, ends up with no more than 16 source traits altogether with which to summarize his 171 original traits. It is worth noting immediately, however, that personality ratings alone have proved to be rather disappointing in the prediction of behaviour. Situational variables, especially when considered in interaction with personality, are far more predictive of behaviour than personality alone.

The best-known, contemporary type theory is that of H. J. Eysenck, who proposes that people may be scored on three continua: neuroticism, extraversion, and psychoticism. Thus, people are typified by these scores. Although developed quite independently, Eysenck's three dimensions may be likened to Cattell's by regarding them as the result of taking advantage still further of correlations which may be found between the source traits.

The origins of individual differences

The origins of individual differences is a topic which has received much attention in the past few years. Special attention has been paid to the particular problem of intelligence, especially because of the suggestion that scores on intelligence tests may be largely genetically determined, a suggestion that has caused social, political, and moral opinions to be expressed on all sides in answer to psychological and statistical problems. This overspilling of inappropriate, often affective reactions into a problem of cognition has slowed progress of our understanding of the issues involved.

As you will probably already have realized, the topic of the origins of individual differences is yet another place in which the heredity-environment issue is of major concern.

Science and explanation

The problem with defining 'psychology' is at least matched by that of defining 'science', indeed a whole area of study known as the 'philosophy of science' has grown up to consider this and related problems. Many philosophers from the Greeks to Bacon to various contemporaries have had a lot to say about the proper conduct of enquiry, but in the space allowed here we shall have to begin with one of the major twentieth-century philosophers of science, Sir Karl Popper.

Popper distinguished between two major problems which he wished to solve: the problem of demarcation, and the problem of induction.

The problem of demarcation is concerned with discovering the criteria that demarcate science from non-science. Growing up in Vienna early this century, Popper was particularly concerned with finding the rules which would justify his belief that Einstein's theories of relativity were scientific, while Adler's form of psychoanalysis and Marx's political theories were not. Popper concluded that to be scientific, a statement had to be potentially falsifiable. He pointed out that a crucial test of Einstein's general theory of relativity was provided by Sir Arthur Eddington's observation that light was subject to gravitational force. Popper held that had Eddington observed light going in straight lines, thereby falsifying Einstein's hypothesis, then Einstein's theory would have been dead at a stroke. Popper argued that psychoanalytical and Marxist theories were not of this nature: what evidence, he asks, would convince an Adlerian or a Marxist to abandon their beliefs? Popper's view of the attitudes of holders of 'non-scientific beliefs' can be illustrated as follows. If you agree with psychoanalysis, good; if you don't then that is because of your un-analysed repressions. If you agree with Marxist theory, good; if you don't then that is because of your class interests. Popper argued that these theories are too all encompassing in their explanatory power to allow proper tests of hypotheses generated from them and, therefore, by Popper's definition are not scientific.

The 'problem of induction' is the name given to the worry that scientific procedure does not rest on logic. The problem may be illustrated by the fact that one observation of the bending of light was enough to convince the Einsteinians that it was time to celebrate. After just a few such observations the matter was regarded as quite settled: light was subject to the laws of gravity. But this is arguing from the particular to the general, which is not logically defensible. The danger of supposing that if something happens a few, or any finite number of times, then it will happen generally is best illustrated by the well-known story of the scientific turkey who was delighted to note that every day a gentleman came in during the morning with copious amounts of delicious food. The turkey supposed that the man would come in every morning for the same purpose but, alas, a few days before Christmas he came in for quite a different purpose. This story does not imply that we should not dare to reach conclusions in science, but that scientific conclusions must always be tentative. Certainty and proof have no place in science.

Later philosophers of science have been much less convinced than Popper by the intimate connection between evidence and belief. Imre Lakatos, among others, has pointed out that scientists do not abandon theories once there is a disappointing experimental result, rather they explain the finding by pointing out special conditions which affected the readings concerned, or they simply list the finding as an anomaly and push on with their research, hoping things will become clearer later. Other philosophers have gone further and have defined science as 'what works', or hold that 'science' is the word with which we consecrate any activity which is approved of by governments and given research grants. Perhaps a reasonable working definition of a scientist is a person who attempts to make defensible statements following observations and submits these to the critical judgement of his or her peers.

There are several points to keep in mind whenever you are wondering whether or not to regard a statement as scientific.

Psychology as a science

1. None of the usual stereotypes will do, test tubes do not mean science any more than a cord jacket and pipe mean arts. Science can be practised by theologians in the ascription of documents to authors using stylistic analysis, and by archaeologists in the dating of materials. The person with the test tube may be behaving scientifically, or may be a bigoted dreamer intent on 'proving' his or her theory despite opposition and despite evidence.

2. Much philosophy of science, particularly earlier work, has been concerned with physics. But William Kneale made an excellent case for physics being the least typical of all sciences (defined as what is done in science departments); it is only physics which is concerned solely with principle, all other sciences are to some extent concerned with history – of rocks, of species, etc. So physics may be a poor exemplar of science in general and a particularly poor one for psychology.

3. The essence of science is not experiment, but rather observation. Geologists, for example, gain much of their knowledge from observation rather than experiment.

All scientific procedures aim to give as accurate a *description* as possible of the correlations between events; whether of the correlation between particular electric fields and the acceleration of electrons, or between particular methods of toilet training and later behavioural habits. Note that I have used the word 'description' as the aim of science rather than 'explanation'. Explanations are merely descriptions which satisfy the questioner and, for the while, make further questions seem unnecessary. The arbitrary nature of explanations can be seen by considering the child who asks why the trees are moving. 'Because the wind is blowing.' 'Why is the wind blowing?' 'Because of a severe depression centred on the Dover Straits.' 'Why is there a severe depression?' 'Because the earth revolves.' 'Why does the earth revolve?' 'Because ...' etc., *ad nauseam*.

We can, like the child, stop asking anywhere or nowhere.

Method in psychology

While far from complete, these two chapters have presented a picture of what psychology has been about. The existence of several tensions in psychology will, it is hoped, have become apparent during the discussion. These tensions often reduce to conflict between intuitive and methodical methods of gaining knowledge about mankind. This raises a basic and very interesting distinction between psychology and other sciences: other sciences study objects and events which are not the objects and events doing the studying. Because each of us has such immediate experience of being human, it is very tempting to indulge our intuition in trying to understand humans; but the pitfalls in this method make it unacceptable.

The major problem with proceeding by intuition is that people's intuitions are different, as are our own at different stages of our life. By depending on intuition, we thus consign ourselves to a modern 'Tower of Babel', everyone talking what to them is sense, and all the talk falling on non-comprehending ears. The claim science has to uniqueness is its ability to make statements which are regarded as true according to criteria which are there for all to see. This view of science does not mean that its practice is without assumptions or declared or tacit values, nor does it mean that science is in any way anti-intuitive. Intuition, in fact, has a worthy and recognized place in science as being one means by which hypotheses may be generated; but, once they are generated, we insist that they go through some system of checking, which may, or may not, seem intuitively reasonable, depending on who you are.

Intuition is not, however, the only way in which scientists obtain hypotheses for checking; a more formal way is by the use of theory. A theory is a general statement which serves two fundamental purposes: to enable us to remember various disparate experimental results and discussions, and to provide us with hypotheses for checking. These are known respectively as the mnemonic and heuristic functions of a theory. An example of a general statement serving as a theory in psychology is: 'the more predictable is reward during the training of an animal to make a response, the fewer trials it will take before the animal stops making the response once reward has ceased'. Because this is a general statement, it is not immediately testable. To test it, we need some initial conditions. For example, group of rats A has been rewarded for every fifth trial in training, group of rats B has been rewarded every nth trial, where the mean of n is five. With the theory and the initial conditions, we may immediately form the hypothesis that group of rats A will stop making the trained response after a fewer number of trials than will group of rats B.

If, on running the experiment and interpreting the results according to the appropriate methods, we find that our prediction is confirmed, then we may say that our theory is corroborated. Note well, 'corroborated' not 'proved'. 'Proof', in the way the word is commonly used, has no place in science: we have not demonstrated that our theory is true for goldfish, elephants, people, or even mice, just for some rats.

When we have tested a hypothesis, we may assume that our result would hold for all organisms which had an equiprobable chance of being in the sample tested. However, once a theory has been shown to hold for several species, we may use our knowledge of the relations between species to make a reasonable guess at which other species may also come under the domain of the theory. All of the remarks about species may also apply to types of people or any other convenient categorization. Those individuals, species, or groups for which a theory can be corroborated are called the domain of convenience of the theory.

The idea of a scientist as one who attempts to make defensible statements from observations leaves room for a wide variety of methods. Much of the psychology reported in this book comes from a preference for 'positivist' methods, that is those methods which are characteristic of the natural sciences: experiment, and sticking to the observable and the manipulable. However, people are not as predictably manipulable as electrons, and they report processes, such as thought, which are not directly observable by the experimenter, so there is growing interest in psychology in other types of specifically human scientific methods. Some of these methods have been long used in ethnography, the study of other cultures, as well as in other areas – some types of marketing research, for example.

Positivists examine their procedures and conclusions carefully in an attempt to make them as valid as possible, humanists do likewise, but whereas the methodological lynch pin of positivist validity is the experiment or other type of controlled observation, that of the humanists is the hermeneutic circle, a process of repeated interpretation and checking until the details of the events and their overall interpretation are fully consonant. The concept of validity is a complex one. Completing the hermeneutic circle is akin to the establishment of internal validity in the positivist model. Something like external validity is satisfied by various other humanistic model procedures such as the transferability of the findings to other similar events.

Attempts to explain events in terms of 'lower order' processes, for example, to explain conscious experience in terms of neurology, are known as reductionist explanations. These are sometimes favoured by positivists but are rejected by humanists who usually suppose that the understanding of an experience has to be in terms of the experiencer.

Ethics in science

Theologians and moral philosophers study the moral value of human conduct and try to deduce the principles and rules which ought to govern it. Because of the power of science-based techniques and devices to affect our lives, this study of ethics has, with the coming of science, been given whole new worlds to explore. Particular groups of scientists and most institutions which organize science have felt the need to devise a particular ethical code to govern the conduct of its members; the code is usually administered by an ethical committee. The motivation to draw up such a code has come from several sources:

- the personal feeling of some scientists that their work should not have negative consequences or involve damaging procedures;
- the belief that unless ethical control of their work is undertaken by the

scientific community then outsiders, representing pressure from society, will step in and control it for them in less sympathetic ways;
- the need of the individual scientist to have some protection from legal action or moral opprobrium should the research be felt to be unacceptable at a later date.

There is sometimes a tension between the desire of scientists to carry out some research and the desire of an ethical committee to stop it. Where one stands with respect to any particular issue will depend on one's own beliefs and feelings about right and wrong. One ingredient in a decision has to be the fact that the practice of science, like every other human activity, is not value free. To take an example from psychology, the very act of labelling some of the people who will help you carry out your work as 'subjects' reveals attitudes about human life and the way in which you believe it can be meaningfully and usefully investigated.

Chapters 1 and 2 are meant to have provided you with some historical and conceptual landmarks to enable you not to lose sight of the overall subject of psychology while studying the contents of the following chapters. The rest of the book consists of chapters on statistics for the purpose of hypothesis-testing and very much more detailed accounts of the large range of subject matter which comprises contemporary psychology.

Further reading

Brown, R., and Hernstein, R. J. (1975) *Psychology*. Methuen.
Doyal, Len, and Harris, Roger (1986) *Empiricism, Explanation and Rationality*. Routledge and Kegan Paul.
Eysenck, H. J., and Wilson, G. D., eds. (1976) *A Textbook of Human Psychology*. M. T. P. Lancaster.
Fancher, Raymond E. (1979) *Pioneers of Psychology*. Norton.
Hollis, Martin (1985) *Invitation to Philosophy*. Blackwell.
Kline, Paul (1988) *Psychology Exposed*. Routledge.
Lindsay, P. H., and Norman, D. A. (1977) *Human Information Processing*. Academic Press.
Maxwell, Nicholas (1984) *From Knowledge to Wisdom*. Blackwell.
O'Neil, W. M. (1982) *The Beginnings of Modern Psychology*. Harvester.
Phillips, D. C. (1987) *Philosophy, Science, and Social Enquiry*. Pergamon Press.
Stove, David (1982) *Popper and After*. Pergamon Press.
Wright, D. S. *et al* (1970) *Introducing Psychology*. Penguin.

Chapter three

Experimental and non-experimental methods

Jeremy Coyle and Brian Clifford

A psychologist may employ a variety of methods to study behaviour. He (for brevity we use the word 'he' here to stand equally for 'he' and 'she') might watch how children play together and note how they converse, how they co-operate or fight with each other, or how they withdraw to play alone. He might give a questionnaire to a representative sample of the voting population to discover their attitudes towards political issues. Alternatively, he could ask detailed questions of one person in order to establish why he chose a particular career. To such methods as these – observation, survey, interview – he can add the method of experiment.

An experiment can be thought of as a method for speeding up the rate at which observations can be made. Consider for a moment the position of an early astronomer. He would look at the various heavenly bodies, note the pattern of movement, make conjectures about how one governed the movement of another, and make predictions about future events based on the theories he had formulated about the mechanics of the universe. Events would confirm or deny the truth of his propositions. Some of his theories might have to wait a hundred years for the crucial testing event to occur.

If his calling had not made a patient man of him, he might long to intervene in the processes he observed. If he could move the sun a little closer to the earth, would that merely allow him to grow peaches in his garden, or would it scorch the moon, or disorientate the pole star, or bring the Trade Winds to the doors of St Paul's? Alas (for him, if not for us), he is powerless to intervene. He cannot manipulate things and see their effect. He cannot, in other words, experiment.

How does the psychologist stand in relation to our astronomer? In some respects, he, too, is restricted to observational techniques, as in the case mentioned above, for example, when he wishes simply to see how children play together. He can, however, manipulate this situation as well. He could introduce a stranger into the group, or change the number of boys or girls in the group and see what happened. This ability to intervene and change things in order to see the resultant effects gives him an enormous advantage over our astronomer, for he need no longer wait for nature to produce the conditions in which he can make his observations. He can construct the conditions himself. Forcing the pace in this way is the function of the experimental method.

Designing an experiment

How does he set about using the experimental method? He might start with a theory that is based on his own, or others', observations, or with a hunch that comes to him almost haphazardly. He might start with what seems to him to be a sound piece of common sense or the received opinion of the community. The source of the idea does not really matter, but the first thing to do with it is express it in a form that allows it to be tested. Let us suppose he has the notion that treating people kindly is a good thing. To test the truth of this proposition, he would need to know, for example, what was meant by 'kindly'. Does it mean justly, mercifully, indulgently, liberally – which, if any, of these? How could 'kindness' be applied? What is meant by a 'good thing'? Would people be more virtuous, more efficient, more contented if treated kindly? How would he measure this effect?

Formulating a hypothesis

In order experimentally to assess the idea, the psychologist has to formulate it in more precise and measurable terms. He will first look for *operational definitions* of 'kindness' and 'good thing'. Perhaps he will represent 'kindness' as rewards, or positive reinforcers, and look for their effect on the efficiency with which people perform certain tasks.

His original idea, of course, has lost its overtones and has been narrowed to the comparatively impoverished statement, 'positive reinforcement will increase efficiency'. This, unfortunately, is the sort of price that must be paid when we employ experimental methods. However, the compensating advantage is that we have a clearly defined, testable proposition which can lead us to reliable conclusions.

Let us consider this kind of statement more formally. When a psychologist states that 'positive reinforcement will increase efficiency', or says that 'noise will impair learning', he is putting forward a *hypothesis* that one thing has an effect on another. Putting this in technical terms, he is suggesting that the manipulation of an *independent variable* will produce a change in a *dependent variable*. In the two examples we have quoted, the independent variables are reinforcement and noise; the dependent variables that are influenced by these are, in the first case, efficiency, and in the second, learning.

Now that we have formulated an experimental hypothesis, a number of decisions need to be made before we are in a position to put it to the test. These include (a) how to represent and manipulate the independent variable, (b) how to represent and measure the dependent variable and (c) what type of experimental design to employ.

Manipulating the independent variable

The first of these is very much under the control of the experimenter. He is free to do virtually as he likes. Consider the second of the hypotheses quoted above ('noise will impair learning') and see what he might do with the independent variable, 'noise'. He might represent it in the form of pop music or of a tape recording of traffic in Piccadilly Circus and compare the efficiency with which people learned with that background noise with their learning in fairly quiet conditions. It is possible, however, that in a psychological laboratory he would use 'white noise' (a mixture of sounds at all frequencies within the audible range, so called by analogy with the visual spectrum where all colours, when blended, produce white). Let us suppose he adopts this course. He might then decide to compare the effects of white noise over a wide range of decibel values. This is quite posssible, but it involves techniques that are beyond the scope of this book. We are concerned here with comparisons between just two experimental treatments, e.g., 'noise' versus 'no noise'. (These experimental treatments, incidentally, are also known as *'experimental conditions'* or as *'levels of the independent variable'*.) Now our experimenter can finalize things. He decides that he wishes to compare the effect of a fairly loud background noise with that of the normal ambient noise one might be exposed to in a classroom. He accordingly determines that his two conditions shall be of 85 dB and of 60 dB.

Representing and measuring the dependent variable

His next concern is with the dependent variable. What material shall be learned? A passage of poetry? A set of complex instructions? A chapter from a textbook of psychology? A common recourse in psychology is to use lists of words or of nonsense syllables. These, at least, can easily be marked right or wrong. But there are still several ways in which the experimenter can obtain measures of this dependent variable. They include counting how many items a subject gets right or, alternatively, how many he gets wrong after one presentation of the list; noting the number of times the list of words has to be presented before a subject learns all the words perfectly; or taking the total time a subject requires to master the entire list. A decision must be made between these, and the experimenter may consider which will give his experiment the greater 'realism', as well as which is the most convenient or expedient to use.

Choosing a design

The decision about the type of design to employ is an important one. Many things need to be considered, such as the nature of the task the subjects have to do, the number of subjects available or the kinds of irrelevant variables that might intrude on the experiment and confuse or obscure the finding. The choice of design will also be important in determining the way in which the experimental data are to be analysed.

There are three basic designs available to us. They are:

1. Independent measures designs.
2. Related measures designs.
3. Matched subjects designs.

We need to examine each of these in detail.

Independent measures

This design involves taking all the people who are to be the subjects of an experiment and dividing them into two groups. If we return to our experiment on the effect of noise on learning, what would happen there is that one of these groups of people would learn the list of words under the 60 dB condition and the other would learn the list under the 85 dB condition. We would then want to compare the performance of the groups to see if they differed. There are obvious problems here. What would happen if the first (60 dB) group contained all the highly-motivated people or people with a higher average intelligence than the other group? If we looked at the scores and found those for the 85 dB condition to be lower, we could not conclude that this was due to the noise level, for it might equally be attributable to these differences in motivation or intelligence. Clearly, the groups must be as equal as possible. But in what respect? The answer must surely be in respect of all those abilities which could influence their performance on the learning task, for what we are trying to do is isolate the effect which is due to noise and noise alone. But, here, we have perhaps twenty people doing our experimental task, and they will differ with respect to practically any variable that we care to name as having a potential effect on their performance – age, sex, previous experience, educational background – as well as the two variables already referred to. We also know that introverts and extraverts are differentially affected by noise. How, then, can we create two groups that are equal? The best answer is to allocate the subjects at random to our two experimental conditions. This can be done very simply by writing the numbers 1 to 20 on pieces of paper and asking each person to draw a number. Those who select odd numbers form one group, while the other group contains those who select even numbers. Random number tables can also be used to create the groups. This random allocation of subjects to the two experimental conditions ensures that all the potentially interfering variables are divided quite unsystematically between the two groups.

It is important that this sorting process should be *random* as opposed to arbitrary. If, for example, the experimenter merely picked out what he thought was a 'random' group of ten, it is possible that he would alight initially on the people who were looking at him. They might well be the more highly-motivated or co-operative subjects and there could be a difference in the performance of the two groups which was primarily due to these variables. This would either enhance or obscure the differences due to noise and vitiate the experiment, for the experimenter would have confused – or, to use the technical terms, *confounded* – the effect of his independent variable (noise) with that of an irrelevant variable (motivation, or 'co-operativeness'), thereby making his data impossible to interpret.

It is obvious, however, that even if he randomly allocates his subjects to each of the two conditions he will not eliminate these irrelevant variables. They will always be present in his experiment, but if his sample is of reasonable enough size, the effects they create will be dispersed through the two conditions as 'random error' – as it is properly known – or, to use a more familiar term, 'noise'.

'Random error' or 'noise' is something which the experimenter cannot eliminate, he can only aim to minimize it and to prevent its sources from being confounded with the effects of his independent variable.

Let us see how this kind of design looks and when it might be used:

60 dB	85 dB
S_1	S_2
S_3	S_4
S_5	S_6
S_7	S_8
S_9	S_{10}

– where S stands for 'subject' and the numbers are those which each subject drew from the hat.

This design would be used, for example, in the following circumstances:

1. Where there is an adequate supply of subjects for the experiment to allow the randomization procedure to be effective (say, 20 to 30 in all).
2. When the stimulus material used in the experiment has to be the same for each level of the independent variable but cannot be exposed twice to the same subject.
3. When the experiment involves only one subject.

This last circumstance needs commenting on. We will quite often want to do an experiment on a single subject; sometimes we will be obliged to, simply because of the shortage of subjects. Suppose we wish to compare someone's visual and auditory reaction times. The statistical analysis we would have to perform would require that all these measures were independent of one another, that is to say, that the value of one reaction time is not influenced by the value of another. This, in principle, seems rather unlikely where a single subject is involved. There are two ways, however, of looking at this problem. One is to think of the subject as a source of a *population of potential reaction times*, from which an experimenter with a good experimental technique (e.g., using suitable time-intervals between collecting scores, adequately preparing the subject for the task, etc.) can obtain two samples of responses under the headings 'visual' and 'auditory'. If we are satisfied that this has been done, we might reasonably assume that the measures are independent. The second way to view this is to consider whether the reaction times we obtain can be organized in any way other than in two columns, with the headings 'visual' and 'auditory'. For example:

Visual	Auditory
RT_a	RT_q
RT_x	RT_i

Can one say that RT_a influences RT_q any more than it influences RT_x or RT_i? Does RT_x influence RT_i any more than it influences RT_q? Having collected these data, would it make any material difference if, within the columns, the scores were shuffled and written down in a different order? (To put this point in statistical terms, an independent measures design is one that assumes that scores are not paired across the two conditions, and that if we calculated a correlation coefficient for the two sets of scores, it would be as good as zero.) The essential point is that these scores do not come in pairs. Scores relate to other scores, perhaps, but in such an unsystematic, even chaotic way that they may as well be treated as independent measures.

Related measures

It is perhaps already clear by implication that this type of design assumes that the scores we obtain are *correlated*. Indeed, some writers use the term 'correlated measures' to describe this sort of design.

Let us see what it looks like.

	60 dB	85 dB
S_1	—	—
S_2	—	—
S_3	—	—
S_4	—	—

Here, we have our subjects working in each of our two noise conditions. An advantage of this type of design that can be seen immediately is that, for a given number of subjects, twice as many raw scores are obtained this way as in an independent measures design. It is not difficult to understand why the resulting pairs of scores are considered to be correlated. Suppose the task the subjects performed was one which required arithmetical skills, and we had three subjects of differing ability. They might produce scores that looked like this:

	60 dB	85 dB
S_1	10	8
S_2	6	4
S_3	3	1

By inspecting these scores, we can see not only that the 85 dB condition impairs performance, but also that our subjects have very different arithmetical abilities. S_1 performs best in both conditions, while S_3 performs worst. These scores very definitely come in pairs: they *correlate* perfectly. It would also be confusing if we shuffled the scores within each column, for, although that would not change the average score for each condition, it would obscure the identity of the score pairs and thereby cause us to lose the important 'second dimension' of this design.

Had we used an independent measures design in this particular example with, say, twenty subjects, all of different mathematical ability, the differences between our subjects, although divided at random between the two conditions, would still be, as it were, jostling within the columns, and the influence of our independent variable would have to compete against them in order to make its presence felt. In this related measures design, by having the second dimension of organization, we pin down this source of what otherwise would be random error and can thus see more clearly the differences that are due to subjects and those that are due to our main variable (noise).

Some precautions, however, need to be taken with this sort of design. If a subject is tested first under one condition and then under the second condition, he might well carry over the experience he has gained by performing under the first to benefit the second. Alternatively, he might find the tasks he is required to do boring or tiring. If so, he will perform worse in the second condition than in the first. This kind of effect is known as an *order effect*. If we were to compare his performance under the two conditions, we would not know whether the difference we observed was due to the independent variable or to some irrelevant variable, such as practice or fatigue.

Now, as we have said, it is essential in an experiment to isolate the effect of the independent variable alone and not have our observations distorted by the irrelevant variables that tug and fret at these efforts of ours to see just the one effect. In the case of the independent measures design, we endeavoured to neutralize the effect of irrelevant 'subject variables' by randomization. Here, although we have controlled those that are to do with subjects (e.g. intellectual ability), we find ourselves exposed to new ones that are to do with the order in which our subjects are exposed to the two conditions.

The solution to this new problem is known as *counterbalancing* – one subject is measured under Condition I first and Condition II second, another is measured under Condition II first and Condition I second. The 'order effects' such as 'practice' or 'fatigue' will consequently tend to cancel each other out. Of course, we would need to have half the subjects performing under one condition first and half of them performing under the other condition first. Naturally, the order for a particular subject must be randomly determined, and it is evident that, to counterbalance properly, an even number of subjects is required.

It should be emphasized that this, although the best available solution to the problem, is nevertheless not a perfect one. If, for example, a subject benefits more from performing first under Condition A, than under Condition B, the 'carry over' from A to B will be greater than that from B to A. In such a case, the order effect is said to be 'asymmetrical', and the counterbalancing procedure will be unsuccessful. The experimenter, therefore, must judge these effects to be symmetrical before he can confidently employ this technique.

Matched subjects designs

This type of design is really only a special case of a related measures design. It assumes that each subject in one condition is paired off, or 'matched' with another subject in the other condition. Let us take our original problem and suppose that we wish to see whether the ability in mathematical tests is influenced by noise. We might think we should 'pair off' clever subjects with other clever ones and dull ones with dull ones.

That way, differences in intellectual ability would be 'damped down'. If we represent 'cleverness' and 'dullness' in the form of scores in an intelligence test, we would have this kind of design:

60 dB	85 dB
S_{1A} (IQ 130) —	— S_{1B} (IQ 130)
S_{2A} (IQ 100) —	— S_{2B} (IQ 100)
S_{3A} (IQ 70) —	— S_{3B} (IQ 70)

We have matched our subjects by IQ score, and we might therefore expect to obtain correlated measures, with the 'clever' subjects producing the highest overall scores and the 'dull' subjects producing the lowest. The effect of noise would be seen 'overlying' this, as it did in our example.

But is it good enough in this experiment to match subjects only on IQ scores? Perhaps one of our 'dull' subjects is much more highly motivated than the subject we have paired him with. Perhaps one of our 'average' subjects hates mathematics. Perhaps one of our 'clever' subjects is off his form. Our 'matching' could be very unsuccessful. It is quite evident that, in principle, our 'pairs' should be matched on every variable that might influence their performance in this experiment. It would be impossible to list all the variables that might influence their performance; it would, in any case, probably be impossible to measure all these 'irrelevant variables' in such a way as to permit matching. And how many subjects might we need to produce even a dozen pairs of people matched perfectly, or even adequately, for IQ, motivation, attitude towards the experiment, and so forth? It is better, surely, to use an independent measures design, where all these variables are defined as 'noise' and committed to the neutralizing care of our randomization procedure. Better still, perhaps, to allow each subject his idiosyncrasies and let him, in a related measures design, bring them to each of our experimental conditions as (hopefully) a constant.

In practice, these designs are rare. They are mostly used in studies of twins, where the process of matching is more justifiable than in the case of other subjects. Even in these studies, however, the method is open to the sorts of criticism we have made.

Some further considerations

Situational variables

The designs considered above have one common purpose: they aim to reveal the effect of the independent variable in spite of the host of other variables that crowd the experimental scene and set up a confusing clamour. They use different techniques (e.g. randomization and counter-balancing) to deal with some of these irrelevant variables, but there are others that are not so much associated with particular designs as with the ordinary working conditions of a psychological experiment. They are known as *situational variables*. This term is used to refer to such things as the ambient noise in which an experiment is conducted: people conversing nearby, perhaps; the clatter of typewriters or the ringing of a telephone in an adjacent office; or traffic in the street outside. But in the experimental room itself there are others – differences between, say, two tachistoscopes which are used to present stimuli, or, more important, differences in the way in which the experimenter deals with his subjects.

This last problem can be a very acute one. There is a considerable literature, much of it attributable to Rosenthal, on 'experimenter effects', which demonstrates that effects which appear to be due to the independent variable are sometimes due to the experimenter's unwitting influence over his subjects' performance. Let us suppose that he expects his subjects to perform better under one condition. Whenever a subject does so, the experimenter might display almost imperceptible signs that reinforce the subject. He might hold his breath in anticipation, change his facial expression or shift his posture. Neither the experimenter nor the subject may be aware that these cues are being given and responded to, but they can have a marked, systematic effect on performance that is confounded with the effect of the independent variable and so makes the experimental findings impossible to interpret.

What can be done with such variables? We can endeavour to rid ourselves of them by conducting experiments in sound-proof rooms and using sophisticated computer-controlled apparatus. But this is a costly, tedious, and, possibly, unnecessary thing to attempt. What we normally do is try to avoid the grosser distracting influences on subjects by conducting experiments in places where a subject can concentrate reasonably on the task in hand, by using our apparatus sensibly and skilfully and by reducing the possibility of 'experimenter effects'. The latter can be accomplished, for example, by using standardized instructions and by keeping what might be called the 'social relationship' between experimenter and subject strictly controlled and minimal.

By these methods, the effect of many situational variables will be rendered unimportant. Some of them (e.g. variations in background noise) will tend to cancel each other out over the time-span of the experiment rather than obviously help or hinder the subjects' performance in any particular condition. There will, of course, be some occasions when an experimenter will want to examine very subtle behavioural effects which need elaborate (and costly) protection from the influence of situational variables if they are to be detected at all. In these cases, the experimenter has no choice but to take the necessary precautions. Such occasions will be comparatively rare, for there is a wide range of psychological phenomena robust enough to be studied experimentally without the fear that they will be 'drowned' by the effect of situational variables. It is also sensible to ask ourselves whether the search for very subtle differences is always worth the investment of time, energy and money. Is the difference we are looking for going to be of any consequence? William James once remarked that 'a difference that makes no difference is not a difference'. Any experimental psychologist might usefully ponder this.

Perhaps at this point we might draw together the main points that we have covered so far in this chapter so that they might be made to stand out more clearly.

First, an experiment involves the manipulation of an *independent variable*. It is the effect of that, and that alone, on a *dependent variable* that we wish to isolate. Other variables will tend to obscure this effect. Some of these are *subject variables* (e.g. motivational differences) and some are *situational variables* (e.g. background noise). We endeavour, by various means, to ensure that none of these works systematically to favour one of our experimental conditions and so become *confounded* with the effect of the independent variable.

In the case of an *independent measures design* we control irrelevant variables by randomly allocating subjects to each of our conditions. When a *related measures design* is employed, counterbalancing will eliminate *order-effects* provided that they are symmetrical. *Matched subjects designs* have limited utility because of the difficulties inherent in the matching process.

Control groups

We often use the word 'control' to refer to the process of managing the effects of irrelevant variables. This word is used in another, more restricted, sense in the phrases 'control group' or 'control condition'. A control group is used to give the experimenter a baseline against which he can compare the performance of another group. Let us suppose that he wants to see whether rewarding children with sweets will improve their performance in a weekly spelling test. He would take a group of children and divide them at random into two sub-groups. One sub-group would merely take the spelling test each week, with no special reward being given for success; the other might be promised, say, a bag of sweets if they spelt all the words correctly each week. Perhaps at the end of one term, the marks would be compared. The children who received no reward would be described as the 'control group'; those who were rewarded would be described as the 'experimental group'. The 'control condition' is the 'no reward' condition, the other is the 'experimental condition'.

This method of experimenting (in which either independent or related measures designs may be employed) assumes that the two groups differ only in respect of the variable we are interested in (in this case reward), and that otherwise they are equal both in composition and the way in which they are treated.

Correlational studies

The designs we have looked at already seem implicitly to have the purpose of looking at differences between two conditions. An experimenter, however, might well be interested in whether scores in two conditions or on two variables 'go together', or *correlate*. Does a child's performance in mathematics resemble his performance in English? Is his performance on a choice-reaction time task related to his intelligence? Such investigations are perfectly possible to conduct. There are two things to be noted about them, however. First, there is the interpretation of our findings. If we do discover that one variable 'goes with' another, we cannot conclude that they are causally related. In human beings, for example, height and weight tend to be correlated, but obviously height does not cause weight, nor vice versa. Nowadays, most of us are aware of the correlation between smoking and lung cancer, and equally aware that some people dispute whether the relationship is causal. It has been suggested, for example, that both smoking and cancer are the result of a possible genetic predisposition, which, therefore, must be regarded as the common causal factor. The distinction between correlation and causality is very clear when one considers what are known as 'spurious correlations', such as that which has been found between the increase in alcoholism and the increase in the salaries of Methodist ministers.

Generalizing from experimental findings

Over-generalization from experimental findings is, unfortunately, all too common. It must always be borne in mind that, if a difference is found between two experimental conditions, the difference is specific to the conditions that have been used. If, for example, a psychologist is interested in the effect of the delay on recall, he might ask one group of subjects to recall a list of words after a delay of ten seconds after presentation of the list, and another group of subjects to recall them after a delay of 30 seconds. He finds that his subjects remember fewer words after a 30-second delay than after one of only ten seconds. On the basis of this finding, he cannot conclude that all possible delay periods produce similar effects. Perhaps performance after a 60-second delay would not be materially worse than after a delay of 30 seconds. Equally, he cannot draw conclusions about the effect of a 20-second delay. It might well be the case that recall after 20 seconds is as good as after ten seconds or just as bad as after 30 seconds. To state the matter more formally, neither extrapolation nor interpolation is easily justified; each experiment gives us only a fragment of the total picture.

Another sort of generalization is sometimes discussed. It is pointed out that many psychological experiments are conducted on undergraduate students of psychology. Surely, it is argued, these subjects are an unrepresentative group; what is true for them may not be true for the general population.

Such an argument often mistakes the nature of psychological experiments. They are not surveys. If a profile of the population at large is required, a survey, not an experiment, is required. An experiment is primarily concerned with the effects of independent variables and usually treats the varying characteristics of the subjects who participate in it as random error, about which nothing can be said except that the smaller it is, the better. It follows, therefore, that using a fairly homogeneous group of subjects is an advantage rather than a liability for random error, in the form of individual differences, is thereby reduced.

It is with his independent variables, not with his subjects, that an experimental psychologist models the world and it is by his success in this that he must be judged. If his model does not reflect the 'real world', his conclusions will, to use Gerard Manley Hopkins' phrase, 'fable and miss'. However cleverly he controls extraneous variables, however pure his randomization procedures or elegant his counterbalancing techniques, his success ultimately depends on the importance of the independent variables that he manipulates and the way in which he represents them. Although it is often difficult to represent or manipulate many important psychological variables one must remember that methods other than experimentation exist. One must also be prepared to accept that knowledge accumulates in a slow, piecemeal fashion, in spite of the ingenuity with which it is sought.

Non-experimental research

As was said above, methods other than the true experiment exist in psychology because experimental psychology is only a part of scientific psychology, and there is no such thing as *the* scientific method. There is only a scientific approach: a way of thinking about and tackling a perceived problem. Thus, while to run a true experiment is to be scientific, to be scientific does not necessarily entail running a true experiment. This is just as well because there are many situations in life where a true experimental approach is neither applicable nor appropriate. If a phenomenon is unique, or rare (e.g. a particular head injury), or if it would be unethical to place people in certain situations (e.g. in pain), or the issue of interest has been-and-gone (e.g. suicide), then in these situations experimentation would not be possible.

Fortunately a large number of methods of investigation are available that can still allow investigations to proceed. This is so because, while the experiment is the most desirable way to investigate behaviour, allowing the least ambiguous conclusions to be drawn about the causes of an observed effect, there is a progressive diminution of control over the research situation that still results in serviceable research techniques. These research techniques are classed as non-experimental techniques and are serviceable because they can, at least, begin to give knowledge about, or insight into, behaviours of interest.

Non-experimental techniques have two main characteristics. The first is that no attempt is made to manipulate an independent variable. Rather we have an effect whose cause, or causes, we are seeking to discover. For example, do hot summers cause street riots? The second characteristic is that the data collection procedure must often compromise some degree of control in return for obtaining the data – this is the 'progressive diminution' referred to above. There are several varieties of non-experimental research, some of which were mentioned at the start of this chapter.

Correlational studies involve studying the relationship between variables, none of which may be the actual cause of the behaviour of interest: e.g. the relationship between years of schooling and salary level. While *all* research is correlational, in the sense that it seeks functional relationships between variables, what makes research correlational in the loose sense (i.e. the non-experimental sense) is the inability independently (deliberately) to manipulate the variables. One simply looks at the relationship between the two sets of existing data.

A second type of non-experimental methodology is *naturalistic observational research*, in which the researcher simply observes behaviour and perhaps categorizes it for later analysis. A variant on this method is the *artificial-naturalistic observation* method, where natural environments are artificially created to enhance observation.

A fourth category of non-experimental research is the *survey* method. Here people are asked to answer questions either in a face-to-face situation (interview) or by telephone, or in a written questionnaire which may be designed for self-completion or (usually if it is complex or lengthy) for completion by an interviewer. A fifth category is the *case study* which can be divided into several types, but especially archival research and case studies proper.

In what follows we will look in a little more depth at each of these last four types of non-experimental methodology.

Case studies

In *archival research*, public or private records are examined in order to test hypotheses about the cause of some behaviour of interest. This type of research involves the investigator in using data that he has had no part in collecting. The investigator simply examines or selects data for analysis that are held to be relevant to the investigation. Archival research is appropriate in many circumstances. For example, when data bearing upon the hypothesis of interest already exist, collecting new data would be wasteful. Secondly, ethical and logical considerations may make it impossible to conduct experiments relating the variables of interest, e.g. suicide or child sexual abuse.

A good example of archival research is the study by David Phillips (1977). He was interested in the question of whether some motor vehicle deaths were suicides rather than accidents. He hypothesized that if suicides were triggered by reports of other suicides, then motor vehicle fatalities should increase just after publicized suicides. He studied the police records of all motor vehicle deaths occurring in California during the week that followed the reporting of suicide on the front page of the State's two largest newspapers. Then he compared the fatalities with those in a control period in another year. He found a nine per cent increase in the number of fatalities in the week following the suicide report, with a maximum increase of 30 per cent on the third day after the stories appeared. By correlating the increase in fatalities following each story with the total circulation of all newspapers that covered the story, he showed (to his satisfaction at least) that there was a relationship between the publicity and number of motor vehicle fatalities.

Now, from considering the above study it should be clear that archival research has certain limitations. First, most archival data are collected for non-scientific purposes; thus they may not be in an appropriate form for scientific analysis.

Secondly, because archival research, by definition, is carried out after the event, ruling out alternative explanations for particular observed correlations may be difficult. Related to this point is the fact that a spurious hypothesis may be given unwarranted, purely fortuitous, support by analysing only a specific sub-set of the available data. A different hypothesis may have been supported if a different segment of the available record had been selected for examination.

Lastly, an archival researcher is at the mercy of any biases that occurred in the collection of the data. Police records, for example, are notoriously subject to bias. Many categories of crime are seldom reported to the police; police themselves may treat different types of crime differently in terms of fullness of reporting; and public interest and concern can gravely distort records from year to year as record keepers respond to these public influences.

Case study methodology is frequently opportunistic and *ad hoc*. Because case studies take many forms they cannot be neatly classified. However, a case study typically involves, first, a focus upon a single individual (i.e. an idiographic approach), second, the collection of multiple observations over time (i.e. the longitudinal approach), and third, an examination of the collected data for understanding, explanation, control, generalization or hypothesis building.

A good example of the opportunistic nature of case studies is Penfield's stimulation of the exposed brain of a patient undergoing surgery which resulted in speculation concerning the localization of highly specific and vivid memories in certain brain areas. Surgery of this kind, combined with a surgeon with the interests of Penfield, is a perfect example of how case studies can precipitate the search for new knowledge and can contribute to the organization and analysis of that knowledge.

Indeed, despite contravening nearly all the basic tenets of good science – numerous subjects (to increase the number of observations), randomly allocated to conditions, and manipulation of the independent variables – case studies have contributed greatly to scientific argument, if not actual advance. For example, Broca's studies contributed to knowledge of how language is organized in the brain, while Freud's development of psycho-analytic theory rests almost entirely upon case study material. And today, current neuropsychology is making great progress by studying single patients with unique presenting symptoms.

Here, however, we must draw a somewhat fine distinction between case studies as such, and single subject (N=1) research designs. There are two general types of single case methods: descriptive and experimental. In the descriptive type, the researcher concentrates on an exact description or report of the behaviour of a subject. In the experimental (N=1) method, there is also an effort to describe the behaviour as precisely as possible, but in addition the researcher manipulates some variable so as to determine its relationship with the behaviour being observed.

The case study method that we are currently discussing is of the former type: it is a purely descriptive procedure. However, some case studies come very close to containing the ingredients which would make them single subject experimental studies. This distinction can be made clear by looking at two studies – the first a pure case study, the second a case study that shifts into a single subject (N=1) experimental study.

In 1962, Lenneberg investigated a boy with congenital disability in the acquisition of motor speech skills. The medical and family histories of the boy were examined and physical examinations and psychological tests were given by Lenneberg. The boy's vocalizations were recorded for four years on a regular and frequent basis. The boy learned to understand English fully, yet could not speak it. This then is a pure case study because no intervention occurred – just careful recording of what behaviour was or was not present. The study did, however, serve to demonstrate that comprehension of a language does not require babbling in infancy or overt imitation of adult speech.

In 1973, Jones and Kamil, by chance, observed tool making and tool using in a bird species, the northern blue jay. The laboratory-reared jay, upon which the researchers were conducting unrelated experiments, was kept in a suspended cage that had newspaper beneath the cage floor. The cage floor was held in place by side struts. By chance, food pellets had collected on the ledge at the foot of the cage formed by the struts. Fortuitously, the jay one day was observed to tear a piece of paper from the pages of the newspaper under the floor and use the paper as a tool to rake the otherwise inaccessible food pellets close enough to eat. Based upon this observation and with knowledge that at certain times in its laboratory stay the bird had been deprived of food, Jones and Kamil hypothesized that tool using might be related to food deprivation levels. Thus, the hypothesis had come from the case study. To test the hypothesis, however, Jones and Kamil had to progress to a single subject (N=1) experimental design. They systematically varied the amount of food deprivation, the availability of paper, and the presence of food in the cage in order to observe the effect on tool making and using behaviour. As expected, they found that the incidence of such behaviour was a function of the manipulated variables. The case study part of this investigation also indicated imitation of tool making and using in other birds, which was then also experimentally tested.

From these examples of case studies it should be clear that such non-experimental methodologies can make important contributions to psychology, such as generating new hypotheses, aiding the understanding of rare phenomena, or demonstrating exceptions to otherwise well-established assumptions.

However, we have said earlier that such outcomes can only be provisional. This is because case studies have several important drawbacks. First, when used in clinical studies (and Bolgar (1965) has argued that case studies are 'the traditional approach of all clinical research') there is usually no adequate baseline measure of behaviour, and no follow up. This latter is important because improvements can occur without any treatment (the placebo effect), and these are often short lived. Second, because case studies are essentially idiographic, generalization is a problem. The so called 'existence proof' that case studies provide, testifies only to the presence of that condition in that particular individual. Third, and most important, it is impossible to determine which variables are responsible for change because control is impossible and thus confounding highly likely. Because we cannot attribute causality unambiguously, we cannot conclude much; the most we have with non-experimental case studies are interesting hypotheses, which, however, may prove to be very useful.

Surveys

In many ways surveys are the complete antithesis of case studies, in that they aim to collect data from a large number of people, usually in a non-face-to-face manner. They can be conducted in a number of ways – from the purely written answer to the written question contained in a mailed questionnaire, through the phone interview which is not face-to-face, but does allow flexibility of questioning, to the face-to-face interview. Whatever the type of survey, there are certain basic considerations that should be complied with.

The questionnaire or interview schedule should be as short as possible and care should be taken that early questions affect the responses to later questions as little as possible. The questions must not be ambiguous. Each item should address a single issue and do so in a clear manner. The following statement is ambiguous: 'School pupils should receive corporal punishment because this prepares them for the harsh realities of life'. This statement contains both an opinion about corporal punishment and a reason for it. A respondent may agree with the opinion but not with the reason, or vice versa. Questions must be written or asked in ways that do not bias the responses. Bias often enters when respondents could perceive one alternative as more socially acceptable than another – a phenomenon called 'social desirability'. This error should be avoided by wording questions so that each alternative appears equally socially desirable.

Attitudes can be measured by ticking boxes or circling numbers but it is better to measure the degree of agreement or disagreement rather than to require a simple yes or no response. This increases the sensitivity of the measuring instrument. Seven categories are the maximum that can be distinguished on most dimensions.

The response formats can range from the simple yes-no, through 5- to 7-point Likert-type scales, to multi-choice or open-ended formats. All types of response formats have their special purposes and advantages and disadvantages. For example, open-ended questions allow more insight into the respondents' thoughts on the question, but the fixed alternatives yield a much greater uniformity, and thus allow for easier analysis of the data.

All questionnaires or interview schedules should be piloted before being used in a study. This allows the investigator to see if the questions are clear and understandable to the respondent and whether the questions are asking what the investigators think they are asking (i.e. are the questions valid?).

A key consideration in survey methodology is to ensure that the data collected are representative of the population at large to which the results are to be extrapolated. This raises the issue of sampling. There are many ways of sampling currently employed in survey research; only a few will be discussed here.

Uncontrolled sampling

This involves questioning population sub-groups to which the researcher has access but no control over sampling (selecting), e.g. listeners to a local radio station. The results from an uncontrolled sample (phone-in poll) are worse than a rough estimate because they will be biased in the direction of the more vocal person who listens to that station.

Haphazard sampling

Sometimes the investigator has control over whom to sample but uses haphazard methods of obtaining people. For example, it may be decided, because of lack of time, to interview ten people in the street of whom five women, three teenagers and two elderly men are to be included. The haphazard sample is almost as worthless as the uncontrolled sample.

Probability sampling

The most satisfactory surveys obtain their respondents on a probability basis. That is, the researcher makes an effort to ensure that each person in the population of interest has an equal chance of being represented. The most straightforward technique is *simple random sampling*. Here a list of all the population of interest is drawn up and then a random sample is drawn from the list with the help of random number tables.

If a population with identifiable sub-groups that are likely to differ markedly in their responses is to be surveyed, validity can be improved by obtaining a *stratified random sample*. If 100 respondents are going to be used and it is known that the population of interest contains 45 per cent women and 55 per cent men, then the random selection should be 45 women and 55 men. Stratified random sampling ensures that the proportion of women and men matches the population of interest.

Random sampling, however, is not always possible or feasible. If this is the case then *cluster sampling* can be employed. Commercial polls, such as the Gallup Poll, employ this approach. If, for example, it was decided to discover the attitude of a school to 'school visits abroad' all the classes in the school, stratified by ages, could be listed and some proportion of the classes in each age category randomly selected as respondents.

It has been calculated that by employing only 1000 respondents selected by simple random sampling, or by cluster sampling, the characteristics of a population the size of the USA can be accurately assessed with a margin of error of only 3.2 per cent or four per cent respectively (Weisberg and Bowen, 1977).

These figures look (and are) very impressive but they can give the impression that surveys are easy techniques to employ. They are not. Let us look at one study to show just one of the pitfalls, albeit a major one. In 1973, *New Scientist* surveyed its readers on their attitudes to ESP (Evans, 1973). The results showed that 67 per cent of those responding considered ESP to be either 'an established fact' or 'a likely possibility'. This sounds like impressive evidence in favour of the scientific credibility of ESP until one discovers that the return rate on this questionnaire was only two per cent.

While there is no correct answer to the question of what constitutes an adequate, unbiased return rate, two per cent is certainly not acceptable. But what is? Several key survey studies have accepted return rates as low as 20–40 per cent. There are, however, ways of increasing this number that all survey investigations should employ to maximize the rate of return. First, inducements to respond usually bear fruit – prizes, gifts or rewards can be offered for completing and returning. Second, the attractiveness and clarity of the questionnaire can improve return rate. The length of the questionnaire is also important: there is always a temptation to build in as many relevant questions as possible since 'they are getting the questionnaire anyway'. Do not be tempted. There is a direct inverse correlation between length of questionnaire and return rate.

A well-worded accompanying letter, in which the respondent is made to feel important and involved, and which explains the reason for the questionnaire and the wider context of its application, can all increase returns. An SAE is also a necessary inclusion. We have already suggested that the ease of answering the questions is an important consideration. Here the investigator must trade off questions and question-formats that are maximally useful to him with formats that are maximally easy for the respondent. Most productive of improved return rates is the well-timed and well-worded follow-up letter or phone call.

That then is the survey; what are its advantages and disadvantages? As we have seen, one of its advantages is its low cost – a lot of data is obtained for minimal input in terms of hours invested. Questionnaire processing and analysis can be fairly easy if the questionnaire is well constructed. A mailed questionnaire also avoids biasing errors that can arise in face-to-face interviewing or experimentation, owing to the personal characteristics and variable skills of the interviewer. Surveys can afford anonymity to the respondent. This is important when the issues being addressed are concerned with sensitive areas of investigation. Surveys also allow considered responses on the part of the respondent and these can be more valid and reliable than spontaneous answers required in face-to-face interaction. Above all, the chief advantage of a survey questionnaire is that it allows wide geographic contact with large numbers of people.

However, the survey method also has its disadvantages. The questionnaire must be simple in order to allow unaided comprehension by the respondent. This methodology allows of no probing, clarification of ambiguity, or appraisal of non-verbal behaviour on the part of the respondent. That is, it is extremely rigid. There is no control over the actual filling in of the questionnaire, or who returns it. This leads to the most crippling disadvantage of the questionnaire – the possibility of a low response rate – which leaves the investigator with the difficulty of deciding how to estimate the effect of non-respondents on the results obtained and the overall generalizability of the research. The non-representativeness of the returned sample will undoubtedly introduce a bias into the study whose seriousness is impossible to assess. A last concern with survey techniques is that they rely solely upon verbal reports – and these may not be a good source of data (Nisbett and Wilson, 1977; cf Ericsson and Simon, 1980) and may not actually be in accordance with behaviour.

Observational studies

Observational research involves recording behaviour without attempting to influence it or change the environment within which it is occurring. While the most widely-known naturalistic observation studies have been done by anthropologists who carefully observe cultures other than their own, developmental psychologists observe children at play; social psychologists watch individuals interacting in various social situations; industrial psychologists watch people at work; educational psychologists observe children in the classroom, and comparative psychologists and ethologists study animals in the wild. Thus observational studies have loomed large in the development of all these areas of psychology.

Looking across all these studies it can be seen that the behaviour observed can be molar (large) or molecular (small); the observations may be structured or unstructured; and the observations may be made continuously or a sequence of observations may be collected either at fixed or random time intervals. In addition, observations may be made by an observer who is literally concealed from view, as in a 'hide' in ethological studies of animals, or high above street level as in the study by Collett and Marsh (1974) into male/female differences in avoidance behaviour on a busy pedestrian crossing. Frequently, observation of groups is done either by complete participant methodology, or by participant observation approaches. In the former, the observer is completely concealed within the group, the research objectives are not known to the group and the researcher becomes a fully-fledged member of the group. However, this complete participation approach has been severely criticized on ethical and methodological grounds and as a result participant observation is the more frequently employed technique. Here, the researcher's presence as a scientist is known to the group being studied and the participant observer tries to form close links with the group which subsequently serves both as informants and respondents.

Irrespective of the species or level of behavioural repertoire being observed, certain basic considerations must be dealt with in this methodology if the obtained data are to be scientifically meaningful. These considerations involve what to observe and when and how to observe. While it is now possible to make continuous records (via audio- and video-tape technology) a much better approach in observational studies is to use time sampling schedules. Time sampling is the selection of observational units at different points in time which has the advantage of assuring the researcher of representative samples of types of behaviour. However, this technique is inappropriate when the purpose is to observe events or behaviours that occur infrequently.

No matter how informal the observation is intended to be, the scientific validity of the resulting data can be enhanced by devising, beforehand, categories of behaviour that are explicit, exhaustive and mutually exclusive. This means that any one type of behaviour will be classified accurately only once – there will be no double or triple counting of the same behaviour. This structured observation results in data that are more reliable and more easily analysed. The categories can be developed into a checklist. An important consideration when observing behaviour is that interpretation should be kept separate from observation. For example, record that 'a child entered the room crying'. Do not record in the same place that this was 'probably due to frustration, loss of a toy, harsh words from teacher', etc.

Let us now look at two observational studies that begin to show the power of this methodology. Goodall (1963) spent several years living with a group of chimpanzees near Lake Tanganyika. She observed them using straws to get termites out of rotting trees, the first recorded observation of tool use by animals in their natural environment. She also observed cranes in their natural habitat (Van Lawick-Goodall, 1968), and again observed this species using tools; in this case, picking up rocks and hurling them at ostrich eggs to break their shells.

Fawl (1963) observed children for a complete day in their normal, natural surroundings. Among other things he found that the children averaged about 16 frustrating events a day. In previous *laboratory* studies frustration was seen to lead to aggression. In Fawl's study the child's usual response to naturally occurring frustrations was mild or no response at all. Thus, children usually did not exhibit aggression when frustrated in their normal environment.

These two studies serve to illustrate some of the useful functions that observational studies can perform. For example, they can be used as exploratory research which may be useful in formulating hypotheses for subsequent testing. They can be used to gain supplementary data to interpret or qualify findings obtained by other methods. Third, they can also be used as a primary method of data collection in descriptive studies. Importantly, the observational method must not be seen as divorced from the experimental method – it is a vital supplement to it.

The specific advantages of the observational method are, first, its directness. The observer sees directly the behaviour of interest, he does not have to rely on perhaps faulty introspective report. Second, it may be the only appropriate method: Gellert (1955) has indicated that children find it difficult to introspect and to maintain attention in long experiments. Third, it produces data on spontaneously occurring behaviour which are thus likely to be more natural and 'real' than those produced in a laboratory. Fourth, because it is spontaneous, the behaviour observed requires no deliberate active co-operation from the subject. Lastly, because it is naturalistic, this type of study can show the role of context on the behaviour being studied.

But there are also disadvantages to this type of research. First, by entering groups, observers, by definition, change the group, and more so with small groups than with large groups. Second, sampling of behaviour has the attendant problem of incomplete record and thus possible misinterpretation of the full behavioural repertoire. Third, observational studies are notoriously difficult to replicate because natural situations are fluid. One of the chief difficulties of observational methodology – which it shares with all other research techniques – is the unambiguous designation of causality: what is causing what. Because naturalistic conditions are complex, and the observer, as a deliberate strategy, is not manipulating any variables, it is extremely difficult to isolate a single variable or even a complex of variables that can be said to be causing the behaviour of interest. As we have seen with other non-experimental techniques, observational methods may provide little more than interesting conjectures or hypotheses. However, we have stressed above that this indictment of the methodology has force only if we see observational methodology as divorced from all other available techniques – and we have been concerned to stress that it is not. A last criticism of the natural observational approach is that it can be very wasteful in the sense that the behaviour of interest may occur only very infrequently. This problem has spawned another non-experimental technique to which we now turn: the artificial-naturalistic observation technique.

Artificial-naturalistic observation technique

This technique involves creating an artificial habitat or social situation and observing a sample of behaviour. An example of this approach would be the 'etho box', the rat cage or a zoo or, in social psychology, the famous Bull Dog and Red Devil summer camp situation.

The primary purposes of this approach are (a) to reproduce 'real life' conditions but under as controlled conditions as possible; (b) to ensure the behaviour of interest occurs as frequently as possible in order to obtain stable and reliable data. An example of an artificial-naturalistic study, which shaded into an experimental study, is one by Klopfer (1963). Klopfer placed sparrows in a room containing pine and oak foliage on a number of perches. The chipping sparrows preferred the pine perches and the white-throated sparrows showed no preference. The fact that Klopfer controlled or manipulated the type and number of perches actually renders this an experiment. However, it does serve to demonstrate a contrived naturalistic set-up.

Perhaps the most famous such set-up is the zoo. Here animals are present in situations similar to their natural environment. However, because of the reduction in size of the environment, the crowded conditions and the consequent limitations on the freedom of the creature, one must always be careful in generalizing observations to animals in their home environments. This, in fact, is one of the chief problems with artificial-naturalistic observation – the difficulty of extrapolation to the population of interest, because of the artificiality of the observing environment.

As with naturalistic observation studies, a chief difficulty is what and how to observe. Perhaps more than any other non-experimental technique this approach needs to be considered in conjunction with one or more of the other available approaches to research, because its virtue is its liability. By artificially creating a 'natural' environment, this approach runs the danger of eliciting behaviour which is typical of neither the spontaneous, context-dependent behaviour found in the wild, nor the planned, context-independent, deliberately engineered behaviour which occurs in the highly controlled laboratory.

This last research method thus serves to make the point that research methodology is as much art as science, and the art of compromise must be honed to a fine point if the best method is to be selected to produce the best results possible.

A decision framework

How then does a researcher go about selecting the appropriate methodology to answer his question? From the above it can be seen that there is no right answer: the circumstances, time, expense, and the nature of the question must all be considered in coming to a sensible decision.

However, there are a number of considerations that can render the decision more principled than it otherwise may be:

1. Data by themselves are of limited scientific value – the delineation of relationships is the chief end of investigation. This implies hypothesis formulation and is a necessary prerequisite for data collection. As a general rule, while non-experimental techniques are data-rich, they are relationship-poor.
2. Basic to meaningful study is the control of variance, i.e. maximizing induced variance, minimizing error variance, and controlling extraneous variance. On all three counts, non-experimental techniques do poorly.

3. Replication may be the only valid way of ensuring that a result is valid. The lack of standardization in non-experimental techniques, with their attendant loose protocols, renders replication difficult.
4. For a study to be of any worth it must have internal and external validity. Internal validity is the basic minimum without which an investigation is uninterpretable. It refers to how certain we can be that the dependent variable changes are due to the independent variables manipulated. External validity asks whether the results obtained can be generalized to other populations, times and situations. The problem is that features of a study which enhance one type of validity may detract from the other. Non-experimental techniques have problems with both types of validity, but especially internal validity.
5. Sources of error and the nature of control are important considerations in any study. Overlooking relevant variables, inadequately analysing and collecting data, inadequacy of sampling and investigator expectancies are as likely in non-experimental techniques as in the true experiment.
6. Bias is an ever-present problem. Studies must control it by avoiding it, distributing it, or by measuring and evaluating it. Non-experimental techniques do very poorly on all these requirements.
7. While causality may be a problematic goal of the scientific endeavour, a better alternative is still not available. All non-experimental techniques have problems in deducing unambiguously the presence of causation.

Further reading

Calfee, R. C. (1975) *Human Experimental Psychology*. Holt, Rinehart and Winston.
Cherulnik, P. D. (1983) *Behavioural Research*. Harper and Row.
Christensen, L. B. (1980) *Experimental Methodology*. Allyn and Bacon.

Chapter four

Statistics

Jeremy Coyle

The statistics used by psychologists are of two main kinds: those that describe data, and those that are analytical tools, capable of showing whether what we have observed is unusual enough to be taken seriously. The first of these are *descriptive*, the second *inferential* statistics.

Descriptive statistics belong to the tradition of 'statists' sums' which Mark Twain criticized in his much-quoted remark, 'there are lies, damned lies and statistics'. But descriptive statistics can only describe. They tell us what is the average national wage, what a horse's track record is, or how many families own freezers. The inferences we draw from them are our own. Mark Twain's criticism, therefore, applies not to statistics themselves, but to the familiar inclination of politicians to go mendaciously beyond the facts.

Describing data

The descriptive statistics we are concerned with here are of two kinds: measures of central tendency and measures of dispersion. Let us suppose

79

we wish to state how much money we normally carry on our person. We might say that, on average, it is five pounds. This piece of information is useful enough, but it would be desirable to know, in addition, whether the sum we carried varied much about this average. Do we always carry, say, between four and six pounds, or is this average based on very variable sums between a few pence and twenty pounds? Our friends who wanted to rely on us for the occasional loan of a couple of pounds would, in fact, be less interested in the average sum we carried (i.e. the measure of central tendency) than in knowing how much variability there was about this central value. For them, the measure of *dispersion* could be the critical one. Similarly, a teacher dealing with a class whose average IQ was 100, with all the members of that class varying between IQ 95 and IQ 105, would find it easier to 'pitch' his lessons at the right level than if he were confronted with a class of the same average IQ but with children in it whose IQs ranged from 70 to 130.

Let us now consider the various measures of central tendency and dispersion that we might use.

Measures of central tendency

All measures of central tendency are 'averages'. There are three of them: the *mean*, the *median*, and the *mode*.

The mean is the arithmetical average, the median is the 'middle' value, and the mode is the value that occurs most frequently.

Here are fifteen values:

$$3, 4, 5, 5, 5, 5, 6, 6, 8, 8, 10, 10, 10, 32, 33$$

To find the mean of these numbers, we add them all together and divide by fifteen. This gives us $150 \div 15 = 10$.

To find the median, we must first be sure that the scores are arranged in ascending or descending order and we then choose the middle one. In this case, it is the eighth one, which is 6.

For the mode, we find which value occurs most frequently. In this case, the most common value is 5.

These measures of central tendency, applied to the same set of numbers, yield three different values. Which one is the most apt? Which is the 'best' one to use? The answer depends partly on the nature of one's data, partly on what features of the data need to be brought out, and partly on the way in which measures of dispersion can be used to indicate how apt or representative our measure of central tendency happens to be. We will deal with this last point first.

Measures of dispersion

Measures of dispersion are also known as measures of 'spread', 'scatter' or 'variability'. They are used in such a way as to complement the measures of central tendency that we employ.

This time, we shall start with the mode. Its associated measure of dispersion is the *variation ratio*, which simply tells us what proportion of our observations are not 'modal'. Considering the numbers we had previously:

$$3, 4, 5, 5, 5, 5, 6, 6, 8, 8, 10, 10, 10, 32, 33$$

We saw that four of them were 'modal'. Eleven of them are not. The variation ratio for these data is found by determining what eleven is, as a proportion of 15. To do this, we divide 11 by 15:

$$11 \div 15 = .733$$

and state that .733 of our observations are *not* modal. By implication, of course, .266 *are* modal. (If you are not happy with proportions, you can transform them to percentages by multiplying them by 100, and saying, in this instance, that 73.3 per cent of the values we had are not accounted for by the mode.) We now have a measure that tells us how representative, or otherwise, the mode is. In this case, it does not seem to be very representative at all.

The median is complemented by measures of range. The *range* itself is simple to calculate. It is the difference between the highest and the lowest score. For the above data, the range is $33 - 3 = 30$ units.

The two measures together, therefore, tell us that the middle value is 6 and the range of values is 30. This indicates to us (as is, indeed, the case) that the values are mostly fairly low (in fact, half of them are below 6) and that there is a wide spread of values. This seems a fairly satisfactory description of the numbers we have. Suppose, however, that the last score were 100, instead of 33. 100 would look rather unusually high in relation to the others and the range of values now would be 97 (although the median would still be 6). Because of the sensitivity of the range to extreme, possibly freakish, scores, it is more common to eliminate the highest and lowest scores – to 'top and tail' the set – in order to avoid such misleading extreme scores. One way of doing this is to ignore the top 25 per cent and the bottom 25 per cent of scores and quote the range of the middle 50 per cent. This measure is known as the *interquartile range* (IQR).

Let us see what this does for our set of scores:

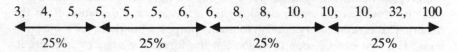

81

The interquartile range is found by subtracting the score that cuts off the top 25 per cent of all the values from the score that cuts off the bottom 25 per cent. Thus:

$$IQR = 10 - 5 = 5$$

We now say that the median is 6, and the middle 50 per cent of scores lie within a range of five about that central point. This seems a more satisfactory way to describe our set of values than by quoting the full range, for the 'freak' score of 100 is not permitted to distract our attention from where the bulk of the scores lie.

It is more common, however, to use the *semi-interquartile range* (SIQR) than the IQR. This is simply half the IQR and in this case it would be $5 \div 2 = 2.5$. (This value is to be understood as 'plus or minus 2.5'; that is, 2.5 units either side of the median.)

The last measure of dispersion complements the mean. It is the *standard deviation*. Although it is a less intuitively obvious measure than those we have seen so far, it is a very 'powerful' descriptive statistic which can cross the border, as it were, into the territory of inferential methods. It merits detailed treatment.

The standard deviation gives us an idea of how much, on average, the individual scores in our set differ from the mean of the set. To make things very simple, we will take only five scores and consider how we can obtain the standard deviation:

$$1, 2, 3, 4, 5.$$

First, the mean of these numbers is $\dfrac{1+2+3+4+5}{5} = 3$

The difference from the mean of each score is:

$$(1-3); \quad (2-3); \quad (3-3); \quad (4-3); \quad (5-3)$$

i.e. $\quad -2; \qquad -1; \qquad 0; \qquad +1; \qquad +2$

Now in order to *average* these differences, we must add them up and divide by the total number of differences. The problem is obvious. These values sum to zero; zero divided by five is zero. Our efforts to aggregate the differences will always come to nought unless we do something about their signs. The first thought is that we might ignore them:

$$2 + 1 + 0 + 1 + 2 = 6; 6 \div 5 = 1.2$$

We now state that the average distance of all values from the mean is 1.2 units – and 'plus or minus' is understood. What we have just done is calculated what is known as the *mean deviation* (i.e., the average deviation from the mean). This is satisfactory enough for many purposes but there are some problems. The first can be seen if we look at the formula we use to calculate it.

$$MD = \frac{\Sigma(|X = \bar{X}|)}{N} \qquad (1)$$

where: X = a given score
$\bar{X}$ = the mean of the scores
N = the total number of scores
Σ = the conventional summation sign (the Greek capital letter 'S') which simply instructs us to add up all the $X - \bar{X}$ differences that we have found

Note the two vertical lines that embrace $X - \bar{X}$. This is a modulus sign which tells us to treat all differences as positive – which is what we did.

A mathematician looking at this formula, however, might be less satisfied with it than we are, for the modulus sign effectively puts a block on algebraical manipulation. He would suggest, perhaps, that we remove the modulus sign, and get rid of the troublesome positive and negative values by *squaring* the differences. We would, of course, have to square the other side of the formula appropriately to preserve the equation; so we would have:

$$\text{Mean } squared \text{ deviation} = \frac{\Sigma(X - \bar{X})^2}{N} \qquad (2)$$

Treating our five numbers this way we obtain the following:

$$\frac{(-2)^2 + (-1)^2 + 0^2 + (+1)^2 + (+2)^2}{5} = \frac{10}{5} = 2$$

and we present our finding that the set of scores has a mean of 3 and a 'spread' (i.e. dispersion) of two squared units.

At this stage, we would surely protest to our mathematician that his desire to manipulate formulae had led him to commit a nonsense. What can 'two squared units of dispersion' possibly mean? His first rejoinder might be that we could easily take the square root of our calculated value and so return to the original units of measurement. Thus:

$$\sqrt{2} = 1.414^*$$

We might be inclined to accept this reply as merely a hollow little triumph of legerdemain and still resent the sacrifice of our commonsense measure, the mean deviation. Have we watched it having its parts squared and then square-rooted for no better reason than to please a mathematician?

* Those who are not very comfortable with mathematics might wonder why this answer is different from the original mean deviation. The reason is that our mathematician did not square the mean deviation itself. He squared the individual deviations and then averaged them. Squaring the mean deviation itself would have meant averaging the individual deviations first and then squaring them.

The answer, as you will suspect, is no. Let us first consider what our mathematician has done and then see why it makes such good sense.

When he took the sum of squared deviations (Formula 2) he was in fact calculating the *variance* of the scores. The variance, therefore, is the *mean (or average) squared deviation from the mean*. The symbol for variance is s^2 and the formula therefore would normally be written thus:

$$s^2 = \frac{\Sigma(X - \bar{X})^2}{N} \tag{3}$$

The standard deviation (s) is simply the *square root of the variance*. Its formula would therefore be:

$$s = \sqrt{\frac{\Sigma(X - \bar{X})^2}{N}} \tag{4}$$

Both of these formulae can be manipulated algebraically to produce:

$$s^2 = \frac{\Sigma(X^2) - \dfrac{(\Sigma X)^2}{N}}{N} \tag{5}$$

and

$$s = \sqrt{\frac{\Sigma(X^2) - \dfrac{(\Sigma X)^2}{N}}{N}} \tag{6}$$

These formulae are mathematically identical to formulae (3) and (4) and more convenient when using a calculating machine.

Now to consider why these measures of dispersion are superior to the mean deviation. First, note that the fundamental index is variance. (The standard deviation, by taking the square root of the variance, merely restores the original unit of measurement.) Variance is about squared deviations. This need not surprise us, for often squared units are the only apt units with which to describe the physical world. A glance at any textbook of physics will reveal formulae using all kinds of squared units to describe physical relationships. Acceleration, for example, is distance divided by time *squared*.

But why should this concern an index of dispersion? Solomon Diamond (*Information and Error*, 1963, N.Y., Basic Books) tells the story of 'the scatter-brained boy' who was surrounded by birds roosting on a heath. He shouted and clapped his hands to startle the birds into flight. In a few seconds they settled down and he noted how he had scattered them. He decided to repeat the experience, and shouted and clapped again equally loudly. Again the birds rose, dispersed and settled. He considered the sum of the distances of all the birds from their original roosting places. It seemed greater than after the first alarm, but not twice as great. Given that both alarms had been equally effective surely there should be twice as much scatter, or dispersion? Diamond points out that if the boy measured the *squared distances* of the birds from him and added them up, the second *sum of squares* would be twice the size of the first. The boy, in effect, was standing at a centre of a circle, measuring the distances of the birds around him. Those distances can be thought of as radii of the circle. To double the area of a circle, one doubles the square of its radius, for the area of a circle is given by πr^2. Diamond notes that 'the dispersion of scores of any kind is, in principle, not different from the scattering of birds on the heath'.

By using the variance (and the standard deviation), we thus capture an essential quality of dispersion that the mean deviation, for all its intuitive appeal, misses.

Choosing a descriptive statistic

We have now seen three measures of central tendency and their associated measures of dispersion. It is necessary to consider the circumstances in which they can be used appropriately. Let us suppose we stood at the entrance to the British Museum and noted the nationality of 70 visitors who entered during one half-hour period. Our observations were as follows:

British	American	European	Japanese	Arab
12	20	15	13	10

It seems evident that the most appropriate summary statistics to use here are the *mode* and the *variation ratio*. These will tell us that American is the most common nationality and that .714 (or 71.4 per cent) of the visitors are of other nationalities. We could not use the median, for who is 'the middle-ranking person'? How can one get a mean if that involves adding up all our observations and dividing by N? Such a procedure would be meaningless.

It is clear from this example that we are not at liberty to use just any of these statistics whenever we wish. One of the crucial things that governs their appropriate use is the level of measurement we have achieved.

Levels of measurement

Psychologists ordinarily use three levels of measurement: nominal, ordinal and interval scales. Ratio scales are less common.

The nominal scale

The nominal scale, the crudest of the three, involves classification, or sorting things into mutually exclusive categories. An ornithologist, for example, might record each observation he makes during the day and do so by species. Someone less familiar with all the different species of bird might sort the same observations into different, cruder categories (e.g. gulls/waders as opposed to kittiwakes; herring gulls/redshanks; bartailed godwits). Both these people, in statistical terms, are employing nominal scales although, clearly, the expert ornithologist has the more sensitive method of classification, that is, the more sensitive nominal scale.

It is useful to think of the nominal scale as being essentially about naming things. When someone says 'my name is Oliver Twist' he is, to put this statistically, establishing a category and entering the number of observations that belong in that category, i.e.

Category: Oliver Twist
No. of observations: 1

It can sometimes be slightly confusing when numbers are used nominally – that is, as classifiers, identifiers, or mere labels. The usual example given of this type of usage is that of numbers on footballers' shirts, which serve only to identify a player. Their numerical value is quite immaterial. The most skilful or expensive players, for example, are not necessarily given the highest numbers. In such cases, one must remember that the numbers in themselves are meaningless. They do not imply rank, nor can they be added, subtracted, multiplied, or divided in any informative way, for they are being used categorically, for purposes of discrimination only.

The ordinal scale

This represents a higher level of measurement than the nominal scale. It involves ranking. With this scale, we can say which is first, second, third, and so on in a sequence; which is biggest, smallest; highest, lowest; most beautiful, or ugliest. It involves comparison of one thing with another, or others. What it does not involve is the comparison of things with some objective yardstick. In the racing pages of newspapers you will find the previous record of horses presented as a list of finishing positions only, that is, as how they ran against other horses in particular races. We are not given their times for the course, which could be one possible objective yardstick.

When we use an ordinal scale to identify which is first, second, or third we must remember, therefore, that we do not imply that the difference between first and second is the same as the difference between the second and third. If we ranked Cinderella and her sisters according to their beauty, the difference between the first and second would be much greater than the difference between the second and third. The ordinal scale involves ranks and ranks only.

The interval and the ratio scale

Interval scale measurement has the great advantage over ordinal scale measurement that there are defined differences along the scale. We can say that the interval between one and two is exactly the same as the interval between 55 and 56. Scores that people obtain in tests are typical interval scale measures. There is no true zero point, however, for a score of zero, say, in a geography test does not mean that the person who obtains it knows nothing at all about geography. Such things as height, weight and volume, however, involve ratio scales which do have true zero points.

There is one important point to note about these levels of measurement. Consider any interval scale measurement: say an IQ of 100. As well as telling us what fixed unit of measurement is involved, this statement implicitly conveys the information that 100 *is less than*, say, 120 and that *is different from* any other number. In other words, interval scales contain the characteristics of both ordinal and nominal scales. The ordinal scale, of course, includes the features of the nominal scale. Thus, higher levels of measurement implicitly have all the qualities of the levels of measurement which are below them.

We can return now to the question of how to choose an appropriate descriptive statistic, and present the answer in a simple, tabular form:

Table 4.1

Level of measurement		Index of central tendency	Index of dispersion
(lower)	Nominal	The mode	The variation ratio
↓	Ordinal	The median	The semi-inter-quartile range
(higher)	Interval	The mean	The standard deviation

Note that any measure which can be used at a lower level of measurement can also be used at higher levels of measurement. The mode and the median, for example, could be used at the interval scale level, but the mean cannot be used at either of the lower levels of measurement. Traffic, so to speak, is one-way only – in the direction indicated by the arrow. This is because the characteristics of lower levels of measurement are present in the higher levels. For example, the mode can, as it were, attach itself to the 'nominal' features of an interval scale but the mean, depending as it does on arithmetical operations, cannot cope with scales that are too imprecise to make such operations permissible.

Frequency distributions

Whenever we have a set of values, or scores, and a count of how many times each occurs, we have a frequency distribution. The following data, showing the frequency of scores that occur within particular class-intervals, are from an aptitude test given to 53 apprentices:

Score:	31–35	36–40	41–45	46–50	51–55	56–60	61–65	66–70	71–75	76–80
Frequency:	2	1	5	8	11	10	9	4	2	1

We can represent these data graphically by plotting *frequency against value* and could produce either a frequency polygon or a histogram. Both of these graphs do essentially the same job. They show in a simple pictorial fashion how our scores are distributed, and we could use either method of representation. There are two subtle differences, however, between the two graphs which are worth noting in order to establish some concepts which will be of importance to us. First, by joining up the points plotted on the frequency polygon, we imply that scores exist between those which we have plotted. We could read off the implied, theoretical frequency, say, of the value 43.5. If this statement sounds sensible enough to you, reflect

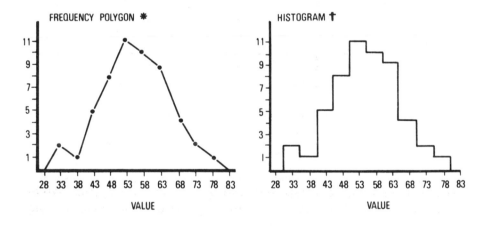

Figure 4.1

* The frequency polygon is conventionally constructed by joining the mid-points of class intervals with a straight line. Two extra points, for when the frequency is 0, are added at each end of the distribution in order to 'close' the Figure.
† The histogram is constructed by erecting rectangular columns the width of the class interval; the height is equal to the frequency.
    Note that in these graphs the class intervals are marked off in what are known as 'real limits' as opposed to the 'apparent limits' shown in the data above. It is more precise to do this. The implication is that theoretically possible scores can be accommodated, e.g. 35.4 would be included in the first class interval, while 35.7 would be included in the second.

for one moment that you are thereby implicitly acknowledging something which statisticians are perfectly comfortable with – namely *theoretical frequencies* (which could, of course, be fractional).

Now consider the histogram, and imagine it were constructed by filling in a square on graph paper for each frequency (i.e. column one would consist of two squares, column two of one square, and so on). What obviously follows is that the *sum of the frequencies* will be given by the total *area under the histogram*.

The idea of a normal distribution

One very important theoretical frequency distribution, in which the area under the delineating curve is constantly used, is the normal probability curve. It is bell-shaped and symmetrical – and looks like this:

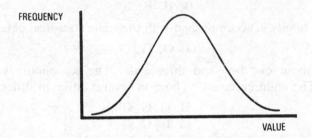

Figure 4.2

This is often known as a Gaussian distribution, after Gauss, the mathematician who first described its properties. We need to consider it in some detail.

The first thing we might note about it is that it seems to correspond with our intuitive understanding of the distribution of many variables. We have mentioned height already. If we write 'midgets' on the left hand side of the 'value' axis and 'giants' on the right hand side, we can see immediately that most of us feature somewhere between these extremes. A box of apples would have a similar distribution, with some apples being distinctly undersized, others being very large, but most of them being of 'middling' size. Indeed, it is the case that the normal distribution represents how a great number of variables are usually distributed. One can almost think of it, instead, as the 'usual distribution'. Because of its importance, we must understand some of its properties. One way to do this is consider another distribution, known as the binomial distribution, which resembles it quite closely.

The binomial distribution

Let us suppose that a couple wish to have four children. They wonder how many boys or girls they might end up with.
The possibilities are:

No. of boys: 4 3 2 1 0
No. of girls: 0 1 2 3 4

How probable is any of these outcomes? If we assume that the sex of a child is randomly determined, it is obvious that the couple is less likely to have four boys or four girls than a family of mixed sexes. The way we determine these probabilities is by listing the various possible combinations. An all-boy family is quite simple (statistically speaking). It can have only the following *sequence* of births:

B, B, B, B.

An all-girl family is accomplished with the same statistical ease:

G, G, G, G.

But how about one boy and three girls? The combinations are more complex. The children could be born in several different orders, namely:

B G G G
G B G G
G G B G
G G G B

The same would apply for one girl and three boys:

G B B B
B G B B
B B G B
B B B G

Two boys and two girls? You can list the six possible sequences for yourself. This process, however, yields the following:

Table 4.2

Sequence of boys and girls	No. of possible arrangements
Four boys and no girls	1
Three boys and one girl	4
Two boys and two girls	6
One boy and three girls	4
Four girls and no boys	1
Total	16

We can state the probabilities. There is a one in 16 chance of having four boys and no girls, a four in 16 chance of having three boys and one girl, and so on. The following Table shows these chances as percentages and as proportions.*

Table 4.3

	No. of possible arrangements	Percentage	Proportion
4 boys and no girls	1	6.25	.0625
3 boys and 1 girl	4	25.0	.25
2 boys and 2 girls	6	37.5	.375
1 boy and 3 girls	4	25.0	.25
4 girls and no boys	1	6.25	.0625
Total	16	100.00	1.0000

We can make a histogram for this distribution:

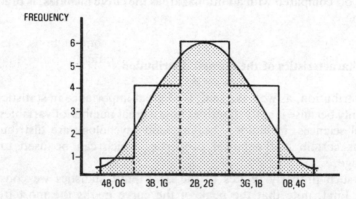

Figure 4.3

and, looking at the *area under the histogram*, we can obtain the *probability* of any of the combinations of children. Column 2, for example, contains four out of the 16 possibilities; it is one quarter, or 25 per cent of the total *area*. Now probabilities are usually expressed as *proportions*, so we would say that the probability of having three boys and one girl is .25.

Imagine, if you can, a couple who wished to have 24 children. We could make similar lists of possible combinations and draw a histogram of them.

---

* For the non-mathematical, percentages are based on 100, while proportions are based on 1. Proportions are fairly commonly used in statistics, which is why they have been introduced here.

The histogram would have many more steps to it. But it would, of course, always be 'stepped', no matter how many frequencies were plotted, for this distribution involves a *discrete* variable, that is, one that can assume only particular values – in this case, 'boy' or 'girl'. This particular distribution is known as the binomial distribution for it is derived from theoretical outcomes of the combination of two kinds of event. However, it does begin to resemble the normal probability curve which we have super-imposed on the histogram above. If we imagine that we had been dealing with a *continuous* variable, such as height, which can assume any value, including fractional ones, the 'steps' would disappear, and we should have a smooth curve whose shape is essentially the same as the bi-nomial distribution. Thus we can think of the normal distribution as a theoretical or idealized representation of certain very common frequency distributions for which N (the total number of scores or observations) is very large.

Note, however, that even when N is quite small, as in the above example, the 'fit' of the line to the histogram is quite good and the *area* it encloses, when you consider the pieces of the histogram that have been clipped off compared with additional areas the curve includes, is practically the same.

Some characteristics of the normal distribution

This distribution, as we have said, is of great importance in statistics. This is not only because it aptly describes how a great number of variables in the physical sciences, in biology, botany, and psychology are distributed; it also has certain mathematical properties which can be used to great advantage.

One such property relates to the descriptive statistics we considered earlier. First, note that the peak of the curve marks the most frequent value, the middle value, and the arithmetical average of all the values in the distribution; in other words, the mode, median, and mean coincide at the axis of symmetry. The next, and very important, fact about this curve concerns the standard deviation, which measures dispersion or the 'spread' of scores. It can be shown mathematically (although to do so would be beyond the scope of this chapter), that within one standard deviation either side of the mean, 68.26 per cent of all scores will be found, within two standard deviations either side of the mean, 95.44 per cent of all scores will be found and within three standard deviations either side of the mean, 99.74 per cent of all scores will be found. Let us consider an example. It is a fact that IQ scores are pretty well normally distributed. We will graph them as if they were.

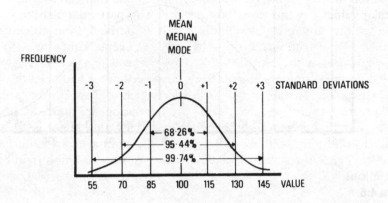

Figure 4.4

Average IQ, as we know, is 100. Furthermore, the standard deviation of test scores works out at 15 or 16 IQ points. Here, we have taken it to be 15, and marked off the values of *plus* one, two, and three standard deviations (115, 130, and 145) and *minus* one, two, and three standard deviations (85, 70, and 55) from the central point, or mean, of 100. (Remember that the standard deviation is to do with distance from the mean. The mean itself is obviously no distance at all from the mean, so it must have a standard deviation of zero.)

We can now state the following:

1. 68.26 per cent of the population have IQs between 85 and 115 (i.e. within − 1 and + 1 standard deviation from the mean).
2. 95.44 per cent of the population have IQs between 70 and 130.
3. 99.74 per cent of the population have IQs between 55 and 145.

Note that these statements are based on areas under the curve that are delimited by the different units of standard deviation.

Let us take the matter a little further. If we have a person whose IQ is 100, we know that 50 per cent of the population will have IQs as great or g eater. We also know that if we find a person with an IQ of 130, 2.28 per cent of the population will have IQs as great or greater. We can see how this is done by taking another look at the normal curve.

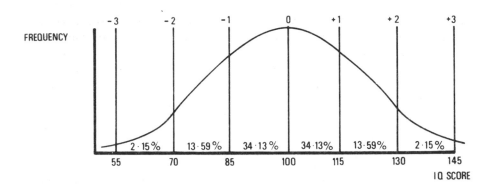

FREQUENCY

-3   -2   -1   0   +1   +2   +3

| 2·15% | 13·59% | 34·13% | 34·13% | 13·59% | 2·15% |

55   70   85   100   115   130   145

IQ SCORE

Figure 4.5

As can be seen, 2.15 per cent of the population lie between IQ 130 and IQ 145. Beyond 145, however, there is a further smaller fraction to be accounted for. We know that within plus and minus three standard deviations lie 99.74 per cent of all scores. Outside these limits, therefore, lie 0.26 per cent of cases; half of them (i.e. 0.13 per cent) being below 55 and half being above 145. We add .13 per cent to 2.15 per cent to obtain 2.28 per cent – the total percentage of the population having IQs of 130 and above.

It needs only a little reflection to realize that, when a variable is normally distributed, the mean and the standard deviation do more than merely describe it. For we know immediately how rare or common particular values of the variables are. We know, in other words, about their *probability* and this is why we pointed out earlier that the standard deviation goes beyond description into the realm of inference.

Inferential statistics

Inferential statistics are concerned with the probabilities associated with particular values of a statistic. They enable us to say, for example, whether a difference we observe between two measures of central tendency is a 'real' difference or not. The process by which we come to such decisions, however, is slightly unusual to those approaching statistics for the first time. What we must first do is establish some concepts that are basic to this process; but while we do so, it may help if one constantly bears in mind the origins of inferential statistics. These are to be found in the law courts of nineteenth-century France, to which mathematicians were summoned to give evidence on the fairness or otherwise of the various games of chance played in casinos. How often would a fair roulette wheel favour the house?

94

How often could a croupier draw the card he needed from a pack before he could be judged a crook? The critical thing to be resolved was the part played by chance. For, once the probabilities of particular events occurring purely under the influence of chance were known, comparisons could be made with what actually occurred, and the necessary conclusions could be drawn. The mathematicians provided the courts with theoretical distributions of outcomes when chance alone was assumed to be responsible for them.

(It is worth emphasizing at this point that the statistician's function is to calculate theoretical probabilities of one sort and another and to provide the instruments (i.e. the statistical testing procedures) that permit us to compare various features of our data with these theoretical distributions. The psychologist is responsible for collecting data, applying a suitable statistical test and drawing appropriate conclusions. This chapter is concerned only with these processes.)

Hypothesis testing

When we conduct an experiment, we look to see if an independent variable has an effect on a dependent variable. We might wish to see, for example, whether by varying the rate of presentation of stimuli, there is an associated change in the number of stimuli recalled. Accordingly, we prepare a list of 20 words and, in one case, present it at the rate of one word per second and, in the other, at the rate of two words per second. Recall is measured under each condition of presentation for each subject and our results look like this:

Table 4.4

	Condition I	Condition II
Rate of presentation:	1 per sec.	2 per sec.
Mean no. of words recalled:	8	6

and we ask ourselves is this a 'real' difference or not.

Whenever we do such an experiment, we should be aware that there are no fewer than three hypotheses which must be made quite explicit before we can either make full sense of what we are doing or perform any statistical analysis on our data.

The first thing is our *research hypothesis*. This is the 'larger scale' general hypothesis that 'rate of presentation of stimuli influences recall of those stimuli'.

The second is our *experimental hypothesis*. This is specific to what we propose to do. Here, it might state that 'words presented at the rate of one per second will show a different level of recall from words presented at the rate of two per second'. (This is the *operational statement* of our research hypothesis and it is important to recognize that evidence that confirms the experimental hypothesis does not automatically confirm the research hypothesis.)

The third is what is known as the *null hypothesis*. This lies at the very centre of statistical hypothesis testing.

The null hypothesis

The null hypothesis denies that any 'real' differences exist and holds that any observed differences are attributable solely to chance fluctuations in score levels. It plays devil's advocate to the experimenter and challenges him to prove that the differences he has obtained are due to the independent variable and could not reasonably be thought to be the product of chance variability.

Let us see how the experimenter contends with this. He has two samples of scores, whose means are 8 and 6. His experimental hypothesis states that they differ. More precisely, his experimental hypothesis states that *the populations from which these samples are drawn have different means.* Countering this, the null hypothesis states that *these samples are drawn from the same population.*

At issue is whether all possible scores in Condition 1 are qualitatively different from all possible scores in Condition 2. If we suppose that recall measures are normally distributed we can represent this conflict graphically:

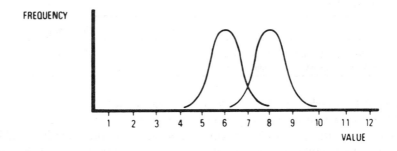

Figure 4.6

This is the experimental hypothesis: the two means, 8 and 6, belong to two quite different distributions.

The null hypothesis, however, claims that these two values belong to the same distribution. Thus:

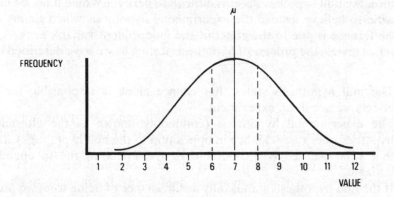

FREQUENCY

1 2 3 4 5 6 7 8 9 10 11 12

VALUE

Figure 4.7

How do we decide between these competing claims?

First, imagine that Figure 4.7 represents a plot of an indefinitely large number of scores, each of which is printed on a slip of paper and placed on a box. We then pick out 50 of them at random and calculate the mean of that sample. It turns out to be, let us say, 6.5. We replace the slips, shake the box to randomize the contents and draw another sample of 50. Its mean is 7.4. The difference between the two, therefore, is 0.9, which we record. We take another two samples similarly and compare their means; and so on until we amass a large number of such 'difference' scores. It is fairly obvious that big differences would be less common than small ones, and that, after doing this, we would be able to make some such statement as 'smaller differences of, say, up to 0.5, are common; but differences of, say, 2.5 or greater are extremely rare'.*

This is one way of approaching the problem of how we can decide between the experimental and the null hypothesis. The null hypothesis, remember, is claiming that any difference that is found is purely a product of chance. We now know, however, as a result of all our random pairings, that there is something quite lawful about the distribution of these chance differences. Small ones are common, but some differences are so large

---

* This statement would be based on our knowledge of the *distribution* of difference scores. The standard deviation of this distribution is known as the *standard error* of the difference. If you look at the formulae for related and independent *t*-tests in the next chapter you will see that their denominators have a form which closely resembles the formula for the standard deviation. In the case of the related *t*-test, the difference scores (in the numerator) are divided by the *standard error of the differences* to produce *t*, whereas in the independent *t*-test the difference between means (in the numerator) is divided by the *standard error of the means* to produce *t*.

that, by chance alone, they occur very rarely indeed. They are, in other words, very improbable if chance alone is responsible, and, as a consequence, the null hypothesis seems difficult to believe. Would it not be more sensible to believe instead the experimental hypothesis which claims that the difference is due to the effect of the independent variable?

Let us review the process of hypothesis testing as we have described it so far.

1. The null hypothesis states that chance alone is responsible for the effects we see in an experiment.
2. The experimental hypothesis (commonly known as the alternative hypothesis because it stands in opposition to the null hypothesis) states that what we see is attributable to the effect of the independent variable.
3. If the null hypothesis stands only a slim chance of being true, we prefer to believe its alternative, i.e. the experimental hypothesis.

Rejecting the null hypothesis

The last point, 3, above needs elaborating. Very simply, there is a fairly firm convention in psychology (and in most other sciences) that we refuse to believe the null hypothesis if it has only one, or less than one, chance in 20 of being true. This is usually expressed in percentage or proportional terms, i.e., 'a five per cent (or less) chance of being true'; or (more commonly) 'a probability of being true equal to or less than .05'. The short way of writing the latter is $p \leqslant .05$.

Thus, when we find a difference between two sets of scores that is so large that it could occur by chance alone only one in 20 times or less we reject the null hypothesis and accept the experimental hypothesis. In other words, we say that we are not prepared to believe the difference is a chance one; we prefer to believe it is a product of change in the independent variable; that it is, in fact, a *significant* difference.

The concept of significance

At this point, it is worth attempting to describe what 'significant' means. In statistics, something is significant if it is unlikely to be the product of chance alone. The probability of its being the product of chance alone, must, by convention, be .05 or less.

How do we know when a difference is significant? How do we know when $p \leqslant .05$? In general this provides no problem. We carry out a statistical test on our data and then consult tables which show what the probability is that our result could occur by chance alone. It would be quite beyond the scope of this chapter to deal with the origin and genesis of significance tables, but if you turn back to p. 90, you will see how one such table of probabilities can be constructed. Suffice it to say that a variety of tables exists to inform us of the probability of the null hypothesis being true under a variety of different circumstances. Statisticians create them; psychologists use them. Unless you are prepared to spend some considerable time on statistical theory, you would be better off concentrating your efforts on the task of becoming a competent *user* of statistical tests: You do not, in other words, have to understand the inside of a car engine in order to become a competent driver.

Type I and Type II errors

It may be clear already that, even if we declare that we have found a significant difference between two sets of scores, we have not eliminated the possibility that we are wrong in believing that the difference is attributable to the effect of our independent variable. The null hypothesis could still be true – in fact, we have stated that it has a one in 20 chance (or less) of being true. Overall, our conclusions will be more often right than wrong but there will certainly be occasions when we reject the null hypothesis when it is true. This is known as a *Type I error*, and it is obvious that the probability of committing this type of error is equivalent to the significance level that we choose. When we set our significance level at $p = .05$, we are settling for being wrong 5 per cent of the time. Sometimes, we will want to be especially careful before we are prepared to say that a difference is significant. We would not wish to market a drug, for example, whose efficacy was not assured. In these cases, we might set our significance level more stringently at .01 or .001, for the more stringent the significance level*, the less the risk of a Type I error.

But there is a price to be paid for defending ourselves so well against the chance of being wrong. We might fail to detect a difference that is really there. This is known as a *Type II error*.

The position is therefore as follows:

1. If our significance level is not stringent enough, we will commit a relatively large number of Type I errors, that is, we will be reporting that differences really exist when, in fact, they do not.
2. If our significance level is too stringent, we will commit a relatively large number of Type II errors; that is, we shall fail to report differences which actually are present.
3. Any scientist would rather err on the side of caution and risk a Type II error rather than a Type I error.
4. A decision must therefore be made about significance levels which,

* All pre-set significance levels are known as 'criteria of significance'. A criterion is denoted by the Greek letter α. Hence one reads in statistical texts such formal statements as 'Let $\alpha = .05$'.

while restricting the number of Type I errors, does not entail an unacceptable number of Type II errors.

5. The .05 level of significance is commonly judged to strike roughly the right balance between the risks of these two complementary types of error.

One- and two-tailed tests

Experimental hypotheses can be one-tailed or two-tailed. If you, the experimenter, have reason to predict that the values in one sample will be greater than those in the other, your hypothesis will be *one-tailed* and will have some such form as 'the mean of Sample A will be higher than the mean of Sample B'. If, however, your experimental hypothesis has the form, 'the means of Samples A and B will differ' and you are implicitly adding 'but I am not sure which sample will have the higher mean', your experimental hypothesis is said to be *two-tailed*.

The word 'tail' here refers to some theorectical distribution of a statistic. Suppose that the distribution concerned is the normal distribution. It has a central 'hump' and two 'tails' that trail off indefinitely. Now, we already know that if we want to reject the null hypothesis, we must have some value that is so unusual that we judge it unlikely to have been produced by chance alone. In the case of the normal distribution, where are these 'unusual' values to be found? Clearly the answer is that they are to be found in the 'tails', for the more common values cluster round the mean to produce the central 'hump'.

We also know that only values that can occur by chance 5 per cent, or less, of the time are extreme enough to be deemed 'significant', that is, extreme enough to allow us to reject the null hypothesis. The shaded areas of the

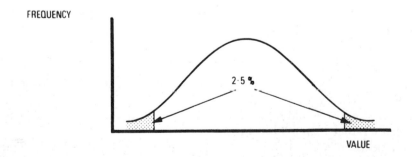

Figure 4.8

distribution show where the most extreme 5 per cent of scores are to be found; 2.5 per cent of them in one 'tail' and 2.5 per cent in the other.

A two-tailed experimental hypothesis is in effect saying 'the effect of the independent variable will be to produce a value which is extreme, but which could be located at either end of the distribution'. A one-tailed hypothesis is quite different. In effect, it says that 'the effect of the independent variable will be to produce an extreme value which is located at the end of the distribution that the experimenter specifies'. And if we now shade in the area occupied by the most extreme 5 per cent of values in only one end of the distribution, we have the following:

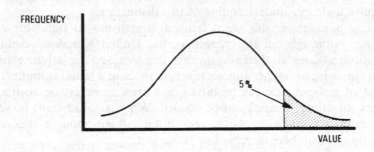

Figure 4.9

Whichever kind of hypothesis is involved, the *region of rejection* (as it is known) of the null hypothesis covers *5 per cent of the total distribution*. However, in the case of a one-tailed hypothesis, a less extreme value is needed to achieve significance. This is a benefit which comes from having a more specific hypothesis.

It is important to note that when you formulate a one-tailed hypothesis, the *region of acceptance* of the null hypothesis includes the other 'tail' of the distribution. What happens if, having predicted that values in Sample A will be larger than values in Sample B, the opposite turns out to be the case, and the size of the difference is so great that it would have proved significant if we had had the opposite hypothesis? The answer is that you have already defined such an event as one which does not permit the rejection of the null hypothesis. You have made your bed and must lie in it. The logic of hypothesis testing cannot be turned into caprice.

Types of statistical test

The tests we are primarily concerned with in this book are predominantly two-sample tests, although some multi-sample tests are included for those who might have the occasional need or desire to go beyond the limitations imposed by two-sample techniques. The specific function of each test is briefly described in the introduction to the tests presented in the following chapter. Here, we are concerned with some more general points which will help us to choose an appropriate test for our data.

Parametric and non-parametric tests

Although it is not difficult to distinguish between these two types of test, it seems worthwhile to define some basic concepts and terminology in order to acquire a clearer understanding of this distinction.

First, *a population*: this word is used in statistics to stand for all of anything. Although 'all the people in the United Kingdom' defines a population; so does 'all the foxes on Bromley common', or 'all the chimney pots in Ipswich', or 'all Mr Jones's reaction times to a visual stimulus'. The concept of a population can be broad or narrow, concrete or abstract. It can lack all utility; it can even be absurd. When a statistician, however, talks about a population, he is very often talking about a theoretical population of numbers or scores or some such.

A sample is a portion of a population. Usually it will be selected in such a way (e.g. randomly) as to be representative of the population from which it is drawn.

A parameter is a value referring to some characteristic of a population. Usually, such values will be denoted by Greek letters. For example, the mean of a population is denoted by μ (the Greek letter 'm', pronounced mu) while its standard deviation is denoted by σ (the Greek letter 's', pronounced sigma).

A statistic is a value referring to some characteristic of a sample. Usually, such values will be denoted by letters from the Roman alphabet. For example, the mean of a sample is usually denoted by $\bar{X}$ ('X bar') while its standard deviation is denoted by 's'.

Assumptions of a parametric test

As you might expect from the foregoing, parametric tests involve parameters. They, in fact, estimate population parameters and capitalize on the known properties of the normal curve. One such test is the *t*-test. There are two versions of it: one for independent samples and one for related samples. The following comments apply primarily to the independent *t*-test.

The theoretical distribution of t, from which significance tables are constructed, and against which we check the value of our test statistic, is derived on the assumption that the population distributions are normal and have equal variances.

Strictly speaking, if we are to use a t-test, our data should come from populations with these characteristics. However, it has been repeatedly demonstrated that even if these assumptions of normality and homogeneity of variance are violated it makes little difference. The t-test is therefore said to be robust in that it will tolerate quite marked departures from these assumptions.

To be more practical about these matters:

1. The normality assumption is not very important. If you can reasonably imagine that if you collected an indefinite number of scores, the majority would form a roughly central 'hump' in the middle of the distribution with the higher and lower scores tailing off at each end, that will be good enough.
2. Check the ranges of scores in each sample. If they are roughly the same, you can assume that their parent populations have similar variances. If they are markedly different, carry out an F test (see p. 133) which will tell you whether they differ significantly. Be particularly cautious about assuming homogeneity of variance if your sample sizes are unequal; for in such cases, your test could much more easily be invalid.
3. Remember that the independent t-test assumes that the data in both samples come from normally distributed populations with equal variances; you should check both samples for similarity with respect to these parameters. And this test is the one which can have unequal sample sizes. In the case of the related t-test you are not concerned with the parent populations of the two samples, but with a single set of difference scores. These should be from a (roughly) normally distributed population. No assumption about variances is involved. Furthermore, difference scores, even if derived from population distributions of quite different shapes, tend to be normally distributed. You can, therefore, afford to be much less diffident about using the related t-test than about using the t-test for independent samples.

It might be worth coming back to this part of the chapter when you have seen more of the tests we are talking about (see next chapter). In turn, we will revert to our treatment of the different types of test available to us.

Within the broad division into parametric and non-parametric tests, there are further subdivisions. There are tests of difference, and measures of correlation. There are also, if we go beyond the limits of two-sample methods, tests of trend.

Tests of difference

These are probably the most commonly used tests in psychological experiments. They may be tests of differences in central tendency, or differences in dispersion. We can, for example, test whether the *means* of two samples differ significantly (a *t*-test will do this for us) or whether two *variances* differ significantly. In order to choose an appropriate difference test, we must make the following decisions:

1. What sort of difference are we looking for?
2. What level of measurement have we for the dependent variable?
3. Are we dealing with an independent or related measured design?

That much will allow us to select a test; but, in addition, we must decide whether the test we use is to be one- or two-tailed. At the end of Chapter 5, we will present a 'decision-map' (not unlike that on p. 147 which covers descriptive measures) but we must first deal with other types of inferential techniques before it can be made complete.

Measures of correlation

Two variables are said to be correlated when the values on one of the variables allow us to predict the values on the other. Let us suppose I have a motor car that does exactly 30 miles to the gallon. If I tell you that I have ten gallons of petrol in my tank, you can instantly predict that I can travel three hundred miles. One variable, which we shall call Y, is the amount of petrol; the other, which we shall call X, is the number of miles I can travel. We can plot this relationship:

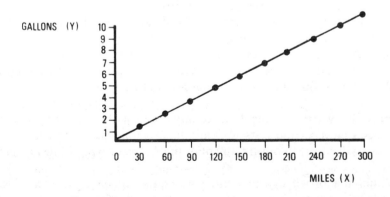

Figure 4.10

These two variables are *perfectly correlated*, that is to say, an accurate prediction is possible from one variable to the other. If, for example, I tell you that I have travelled 180 miles, you know that I have used exactly six gallons of petrol. X and Y are also *directly correlated*, which is to say that as mileage increases, consumption increases. The 'direction of movement' so to speak, on each variable, is the same.

Suppose, however, that I start with a tank full of petrol (ten gallons) and measure how much petrol I have left after 30, 60, 90 miles, and so on. As mileage increases, the quantity of petrol remaining in the tank decreases (see Figure 4.11).

The variables are still perfectly correlated, but the relationship is an *inverse* one, for 'the movement' on each variable is in *opposite directions*. A direct relationship as in Figure 4.10 yields a *positive correlation coefficient*: an inverse relationship, as in Figure 4.11, yields a *negative correlation coefficient*.

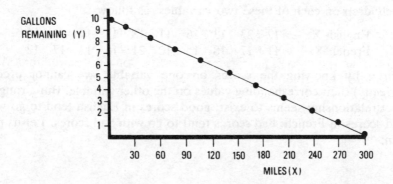

Figure 4.11

The values of a correlation coefficient can range from − 1 through zero to + 1. Perfect correlation gives a coefficient of unity (positive or negative); where no prediction is possible, the coefficient will be zero; but most of the time we have to deal with coefficients that are somewhere between these extremes.

If we plot the values of two variables that are imperfectly related, we get, instead of a straight line, a scattergram which will show a rough 'straight-line' relationship. When two variables do not correlate at all (i.e. when the coefficient is zero) no straight line relationship can be seen at all.

Thus:

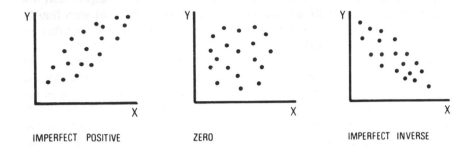

IMPERFECT POSITIVE   ZERO   IMPERFECT INVERSE

Figure 4.12

Suppose we wish to see whether children who do well in an English examination also do well in a French examination. We obtain the scores of ten children on each of these two variables, as follows:

English X:	12	23	13	15	11	18	17	14	16	15
French Y:	11	17	18	15	12	21	16	13	17	12

Clearly, by knowing the scores on one variable, we cannot predict (perfectly) their corresponding values on the other variable. But a roughly direct relationship seems to exist: good scores in English tend to go with good scores in French; bad scores tend to go with bad scores. Let us plot them:

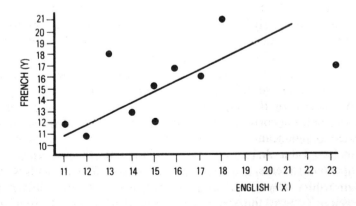

Figure 4.13

This approximates to the sort of direct relationship shown in Figure 4.12. In fact, for these data the correlation coefficient works out at + 0.58 (which is significant). What does this tell us? First, the positive sign tells us that the relationship is direct. Higher scores in English are associated with higher scores in French, and so on. Second, the value of 0.58 for the coefficient tells us that it is a less than perfect relationship. As a result, predicting French scores from the basis of the English scores will be imprecise. We can get an idea of how much imprecision there is by simply squaring the correlation coefficient, multiplying by 100, and reading the resulting value as a percentage. That percentage tells us how much 'guessing error' for Y scores is eliminated by knowing X scores. This is perhaps a little complicated. Go back to Figure 4.10. There, the coefficient would be $= + 1$. $1^2 = 1$; $1 \times 100 = 100$ (%). One hundred per cent of any guessing error for Y is eliminated by knowing X values. We can make a list of these *'guessing-error' elimination values* thus:

Value of correlation coefficient (whether + ve or − ve):	0	.1	.2	.3	.4	.5	.6	.7	.8	.9	1.0
'Guessing error' eliminated:	0%	1%	4%	9%	16%	25%	36%	49%	64%	81%	100%

As you see, until the coefficient is quite high, only a comparative small proportion of 'guessing error' is eliminated.

This concept is not to be confused with the *significance* of a correlation coefficient. That tells us whether such a coefficient could occur by chance only very infrequently. Imagine any four scores on each of two variables, X and Y. The X values are shuffled and set down; the Y values are shuffled and set down alongside the X values. What chance is there that the high scores will be 'paired off' on each variable, likewise the medium score and the low ones? Obviously, with only a few scores on each variable, the chances are quite good. If, however, we had a hundred scores on each variable the likelihood of obtaining consistent pairings is remote. The significance of a correlation coefficient is to do with this – namely the scope that chance alone has to produce systematically paired scores.

The implication of this is that when the number of scores on each variable is small, the correlation coefficient needs to be high before it can be regarded as significant, but as N increases, a smaller coefficient will be significant (see Table A.10, which clearly illustrates this point).

It is important to remember that the correlation coefficients presented in this book identify only the *linear* (i.e. straight-line) relationship between two variables. You can think of them as statistical techniques for drawing the best-fitting straight line through a scattergram. If our scattergram was as follows:

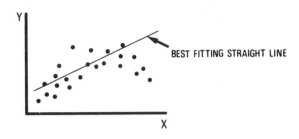

Figure 4.14

The best-fitting straight line does not fit very well because the relationship between the two variables is curvilinear. There are techniques for dealing with non-linear relationships but in this book we are restricted to identifying only the linear component.

Finally, note that, when a correlation coefficient is tested for significance, the null hypothesis usually states that the population coefficient is zero*, a one-tailed alternative hypothesis specifies the sign of the coefficient (i.e. the direction of the relationship), and a two-tailed alternative hypothesis does not.

Trend tests

The word 'trend', as used in statistics, has a more restricted meaning than it has in ordinary usage. It is used to describe a progressive increase, or decrease, in values across three or more levels of an independent variable. A trend test can therefore be thought of an an extension of a one-tailed test where more than two samples are involved. Like any other one-tailed test, trend tests require that the directional hypothesis is formed in advance of data collection. If, for example, you predict that scores will increase across three levels of an independent variable and it turns out that they actually decrease, you cannot switch your hypothesis to match the effect, for your data have fallen into what you had defined as the rejection of acceptance of the null hypothesis (see also the section on one- and two-tailed tests).

Degrees of freedom

You will find that statistical tests involve degrees of freedom. To use statistical tables, you often have to use the appropriate number of degrees

---

* Other null hypotheses can be formulated, but this is the most usual one. It is beyond the scope of this chapter to treat such variants of H_0.

of freedom in order to find the required critical value of a statistic. The concept is a difficult one to grasp in all its complexity, but it can be stated, in general, that the number of degrees of freedom associated with a statistical calculation reflects the number of observations or scores that are free to vary within certain restrictions. If we have a simple sum:

$$1 + 2 + 3 = 6.$$

How many values can be freely altered within the restriction that their total must be 6? The answer is any two of them, e.g.:

$$10 + 12 + x = 6.$$

We have changed the first two values, but the third, x, is now determined. It is not free to vary. It must be -16. This calculation, therefore, has two degrees of freedom associated with it.

There is only one degree of freedom associated with the choice of which leg you put into your trousers first. If you put your left leg in first, you are no longer free to vary which leg goes in second. The restriction within which you are operating here is, of course, that human beings, and trousers, have only two legs.

Now consider a more complicated example. Imagine we intend to shoe a horse. Theoretically, we could start on any hoof we liked – front, back, left or right. We could then choose any of the three remaining hooves; after that either of the remaining hooves; but the fourth hoof would be prescribed by our first three (free) choices. We can represent our choices in this way:

	Left	Right
Fore		
Hind		

Figure 4.15

(You can place a tick in any three boxes you wish, but when you have done so, you have no choice about which box to put your fourth tick into.)

So, as novice blacksmiths, we have three degrees of freedom associated with the order in which we shoe our horse's hooves. Before we embark on this venture, however, we decide to consult an experienced blacksmith. He tells us that we should not shoe a hind leg first, for there is a danger of being kicked if we do so. We must therefore start with a foreleg. Are we free to choose either of these? The blacksmith would tell us that we are not. Horses prefer to be approached from the side on which they are usually led – their left hand side – otherwise they can become nervous, and, again, we would be in danger of being kicked. In the interests of safety, therefore, we sacrifice one of our degrees of freedom by deciding to shoe the front left hoof first.

A blacksmith would now tell us that we should shoe the left hind hoof next, for it is easier to move the tools down the flank of the horse than to the other side of it. In the interests of convenience, therefore, we sacrifice another degree of freedom and shoe that hoof next.

Two hooves remain to be shod. We appear to have one degree of freedom, for we seem free to choose the right front *or* the right hind leg. The blacksmith would not give himself this freedom, however. To be on the safe side, he would start at the front. For him, therefore, the order of shoeing is wholly prescribed. By imposing the restrictions we have described he sacrifices *all* the degrees of freedom that appeared to us to exist.

Perhaps these things will give you the idea of degrees of freedom. Unfortunately to take the concept further we would have to enter the realms of theoretical statistics and that is well beyond our brief. From the practical point of view, however, it can be said that it is generally advisable to ensure that you have as many degrees of freedom as possible, for that increases your chances of detecting significant effects. Although – odd as it may seem – it is possible to have too many degrees of freedom, the problem occurs rarely in psychological experiments because of their small scale.

We come finally to the 'decision map' we discussed earlier in this chapter and which is to be found on p. 148. As you will see, the things that determine which is an appropriate test to use are:

1. the type of effect you are looking for (i.e. difference, correlation, trend),
2. the number of experimental treatments (samples),
3. whether your design involves independent or related measures,
4. the level of measurement (i.e. nominal, ordinal or interval).

Other considerations, such as whether you can assume normality and homogeneity of variance, will also determine the choice of test, but these organizing principles are fundamental and need to be well 'over-learned'.

Chapter five

Statistical procedures

Jeremy Coyle

Introduction

This chapter is primarily concerned with tests of significance. The descriptive measures it contains are the mean and the standard deviation (here presented for more complex data than were used for illustrative purposes in the preceding chapter). But as these are arguably the descriptive measures most useful to psychologists Chapter 4 should be consulted for further information about them.

The function and assumptions of each test are given in a brief introduction and the procedure for calculating each statistic is given step by step, with an accompanying worked example. With the exceptions of the mean, the standard deviation and χ^2, the data that are analysed are basically the same for all two-sample and multi-sample treatments. The reason for adopting this rather unorthodox way of doing things is to permit the user of this book to see for himself how different designs affect the way in which data are analysed and how tests differ in power.

The power of a statistical test

The 'power' of a test can be seen as its ability to detect the effect of the independent variable on the dependent variable. To put this another way, it is the probability of avoiding a Type II error. The power of a test is influenced by a number of things. One of them, obviously, is α, our criterion of significance; another is the size of sample (larger samples being better than smaller ones); yet another is the variance of the parent populations. We can, however, look at this in a simple way and say that the more the experimenter can, as it were, 'tell' the analysis, the more effectively it can operate on the data. For example, when you can 'tell' the analysis that the parent populations from which your data are drawn are normally distributed and have equal variances your data can be treated in a more sophisticated and effective fashion than if such information were not available. Similarly, if you 'tell' the test that two samples are related, you are giving it the information that the values in each sample tend to come in pairs; they are organized other than in just two columns, they are also organized by 'rows'. Again, if you 'tell' the analysis that the units of measurement are precisely defined (as inches or seconds, etc.), it has more to go on than if it merely assumes that the sample measures represent rank order only.

In general, therefore, what we might call an 'interval scale analysis' is more powerful than an 'ordinal scale analysis', which, in turn, is more powerful than a 'nominal scale analysis'. And, as we saw in the case of descriptive statistics, while statistics appropriate to lower levels of measurement may be used for data at a higher level of measurement, the reverse is not the case. In spite of this possibility, however, it must always be advisable to use the most powerful analysis, and the potential 'upward mobility' of statistics appropriate to lower levels of measurement should not be encouraged.

Note for the non-mathematical

It is perhaps worth reminding those who dislike mathematics that statistical formulae, although capable of algebraical manipulation, can be seen simply as a set of coded instructions which tell you how to calculate a statistic. You 'read the code' in the sequence specified in the old school-room mnemonic BOMDAS, standing for '*B*rackets, *O*f, *M*ultiplication, *D*ivision, *A*ddition, and *S*ubtraction'. First, work out what is in brackets; then do any multiplications, then divide, and so on. Here is an example:

$$x = \frac{a(b + c)^2}{n} + n - 15$$

where: a = 1
b = 2
c = 3
n = 5

Start inside the *brackets*: b + c = 2 + 3 = 5; still associated with the bracket is the instruction to square, so: 5^2 = 25
Now *multiply*: a(25) = 1 × 25 = 25
Now *divide*: $\dfrac{25}{n}$ = 25 ÷ 5 = 5
Now *add*: 5 + n = 5 + 5 = 10
Now *subtract*: 10 − 15 = − 5
And do not worry about having negative values as your answer. They are common enough. Remember, however, that

positive × positive = positive
positive × negative = negative
negative × negative = positive

Note that Σ ('sigma', the Greek capital letter S) is an instruction to add things up. It is a summation sign. Also, X stands for any given score, and it may have a subscript such as X_A, X_B, etc. These subscripts tell you which set of scores you are dealing with. Suppose we have two conditions under which we have collected test scores:

Table 5.1

Condition A	Condition B
1	5
2	6
3	7
$\Sigma(X_A)$ = (1 + 2 +3) = 6	$\Sigma(X_B)$ = (5 + 6 + 7) = 18

The mean from grouped data

The mean is an appropriate index of central tendency when data are measured at the interval scale level. Here we will calculate it for data which are grouped in class intervals.

Table 5.2 shows the IQ scores of a random sample of 150 twelve-year-old schoolchildren.

Formula

$$\bar{X} = \frac{\Sigma(fg)}{N}$$

where: f = the number of scores within a given class interval
g = the mid-point of a given class interval
N = the total number of scores

Table 5.2

IQ:	61–70	71–80	81–90	91–100
No. of children	5	13	21	44

IQ:	101–110	111–120	121–130	131–140
No. of children	39	20	7	1

Calculation

Step 1: Subtract the real lower limit of each class interval from its real upper limit and divide the result by two (e.g. for the first class interval):

$$70.5 - 60.5 = 10; \quad 10 \div 2 = 5$$

Step 2: Add this value to the real lower limit of each class interval and re-cast the table thus:

Table 5.3

IQ:	65.5	75.5	85.5	95.5	105.5	115.5	125.5	135.5
No. of children:	5	13	21	44	39	30	7	1

Step 3: Find the product of the mid-points of the class intervals and the frequencies; add these up and divide by N to obtain $\bar{X}$.

$$\bar{X} = \frac{(65.5 \times 5) + (75.5 \times 13) \ldots + (135.5 \times 1)}{N}$$

$$\bar{X} = \frac{14745}{150} = 98.30$$

The mean IQ score of these children is 98.30

The standard deviation

The standard deviation is an appropriate measure of dispersion when data are measured at the interval scale level. We will calculate it for the following random sample of ten IQ scores:

108, 92, 85, 121, 113, 76, 95, 103, 104, 94

Formula

$$s = \sqrt{\frac{\Sigma(X^2) - \frac{(\Sigma X)^2}{N}}{N - 1}} \qquad (6)$$

where: X = any given score
N = the total number of scores.

Calculation

Step 1: Square all the scores and add these squares. This gives $\Sigma(X^2)$
$(108^2 + 92^2 \ldots + 94^2) = 99825$

Step 2: Add up all the scores and square them. This gives $(\Sigma X)^2$
$(108 + 92 \ldots + 94)^2 = 991^2 = 982081$

Step 3: Divide $(\Sigma X)^2$ by the total number of scores and subtract the resulting value from $\Sigma(X^2)$.
$982081 \div 10 = 98208.1; \ 99825 - 98208.1 = 1616.9$

Step 4: Divide the outcome of Step 3 by N − 1
$1616.9 \div 9 = 179.655$

Step 5: Find the square root of the outcome of Step 4. This gives s.
$s = \sqrt{179.655} = 13.40$

The standard deviation of these scores is 13.40. If we assume IQ scores to be normally distributed, we can infer from this that 68.2 per cent of all scores lie within 13.4 IQ points either side of the mean. Here, the mean is 99.1, so between 85.7 and 112.5, 68.2 per cent of scores are to be found.

Note

1. Notice that, in the above formula, the denominator is N − 1. In general this is the more common formula, for it gives an estimate of the standard deviation of the *population*. The dispersion in a *sample* is found by dividing by N. The reason for this is that the standard deviation of a population is always likely to be larger than the standard deviation of a sample and we compensate for this by reducing the denominator by 1. This boosts the final value of s (see Diamond op. cit. for an explanation of this).

2. The percentage of scores in a population that fall within plus and minus one, two or three standard deviations from the mean is as follows:

Table 5.4

Type of distribution	Number of standard deviations from the population mean		
	± 1	± 2	± 3
Normal	68.2%	95.4%	99.7%
Symmetrical but unimodal	at least 57%	at least 89%	at least 95%
Any	−	at least 75%	at least 89%

The standard deviation from grouped data

This is a method of calculating the standard deviation when data are grouped in class intervals of equal size.

Formula

$$s = \sqrt{\frac{i^2}{N-1}\left\{\Sigma(fw^2) - \frac{(\Sigma fw)^2}{N}\right\}}$$

where: i = the real class interval size
f = the number of scores within a given class interval
w = the weight given to a class interval
N = the total number of scores

Calculation

This rather fearsome formula can easily be broken down into a step by step calculation. Thus:

Step 1: Estimate which class interval includes the mean of all the scores and give it a weight of zero. Give the class intervals *above* it positive weights, in ascending order, and the class intervals *below* it negative weights, in ascending order.

Step 2: Square all the weights.

Step 3: Multiply each frequency by the weight given in Step 1 and add up these values (remembering to take their signs into account). This gives Σfw.

Step 4: Multiply each frequency by the squared weight in Step 1 and add up these values. This gives $\Sigma(fw^2)$.

Step 5: Add up all the frequencies to obtain N.

Step 6: Square Σfw, found in Step 3; divide this by N and subtract the resulting value from $\Sigma(fw^2)$, found in Step 4.

Step 7: Find the real length of the class intervals by subtracting the real lower limit of any one of them from the real upper limit. This gives i.

Step 8: Square i and divide by $N-1$.

Step 9: Multiply the results of Step 6 by the result of Step 8 and find the square root. This gives the standard deviation.

To illustrate this method of obtaining a value for the standard deviation, we will use the same data as we used for the mean from grouped data.

Table 5.5

IQ:	61–70	71–80	81–90	91–100	101–110	111–120	121–130	131–140
Frequency(f):	5	13	21	44	39	20	7	1

Step 1: (w) -3 -2 -1 0 $+1$ $+2$ $+3$ $+4$

Step 2: (w^2) 9 4 1 0 1 4 9 16

Step 3: $\Sigma fw = (5 \times -3) + (13 \times -2) \ldots + (1 \times 4) = 42$

Step 4: $\Sigma(fw^2) = (5 \times 9) + (13 \times 4) \ldots + (1 \times 16) = 316$

Step 5: $N = 5 + 13 + 21 + 44 + 39 + 20 + 7 + 1 = 150$

Step 6: $(\Sigma fw)^2 = 42^2 = 1764$; $\dfrac{1764}{150} = 11.76$; $316 - 11.76 = 304.24$

Step 7: Taking the first class interval (61–70); its real lower limit is 60.5, and its real upper limit is 70.5.
Thus i = 70.5 − 60.5 = 10.

Step 8: $\dfrac{i^2}{N-1} = \dfrac{10^2}{149} = 0.671$

Step 9: s = 304.24 × 0.671 = 204.15; $\sqrt{204.15} = 14.29$

The standard deviation is 14.29.

Some general notes on the χ^2 test

χ^2 is used to test data which are in the form of frequencies. Essentially, it tells us whether the frequencies which we have differ significantly from the frequencies that we would be expected to have if the null hypothesis were true.

The case of one sample

Suppose we toss a coin 100 times and obtain a result of 54 heads and 46 tails. Are the frequencies we observe significantly different from those which we would expect on the basis of chance alone (i.e. 50 heads and 50 tails)? The χ^2 test will deal with this kind of question. Similarly, by observing the frequencies with which winners come from each of the six traps in a greyhound stadium we can check whether there is a significant discrepancy between what actually happens and our theoretical expectation that there will be an equal number of winners from each trap. In these two instances, we are talking about *a single set of frequencies*. There are two frequency counts involved in the first, and six in the second. Thus:

Heads　　Tails　　　　Trap No:　1　2　3　4　5　6

and

and the expected frequency for each 'box' can be obtained by adding up all the observed frequencies and dividing by the number of 'boxes', or categories. The χ^2 test, used this way, is known as a one-sample test because there is only a single dimension to the arrangement of categories; and this, the most common way of generating expected frequencies, gives us a *rectangular distribution* of expected frequencies.

The 2 × 2 case and the (r × k) case

χ^2 can also be calculated for a 2 × 2 contingency table. Suppose that 100 children are given the choice of studying either statistics or geography. We can cast the choices of both the boys and the girls into a 2 × 2 contingency table:

	Statistics	Geography
Boys	40	20
Girls	20	20

How do we now discover whether our observed frequencies differ from the frequencies expected under the null hypothesis? The important thing to note is the nature of expected frequencies. In the previous one-sample case, it made good sense to derive the expected frequencies by dividing the sum of frequencies by the number of categories. But, as far as the statistical test is concerned, what in fact we did there was allocate *equal proportions* of the total frequency count to each of the 'cells' or categories.

The same applies here, and the question that we are asking is whether the *proportion* of boys who choose each of the subjects is the same as the *proportion* of girls. The null hypothesis, of course, would state that the proportions are the same. How do we derive expected frequencies which have this proportional similarity? We take the *marginal totals* that are common to a particular cell, multiply them together and divide by N. Thus:

	Statistics	Geography		Marginal totals
Boys	40	20		60
		A|B		
		C|D		
Girls	20	20		40
Marginal totals:	60	40	**Grand Total (N) =**	100

Note that we have labelled the cells A, B, C and D for simplicity's sake. The expected frequencies would now be as follows:

	Statistics	**Geography**
Boys	36	24
Girls	24	16

A = 60 × 60 ÷ 100 = 36

B = 60 × 40 ÷ 100 = 24

C = 40 × 60 ÷ 100 = 24

D = 40 × 40 ÷ 100 = 16

This allows for the different number of boys and girls making up our 100 people (60 boys and 40 girls). And, by using these expected frequencies, we are setting up a null hypothesis which states that the proportional split of boys and girls between the two subjects is the same (i.e. 36 is to 24 as 24 is to 16; the proportions are .66 and .33 for both boys and girls). The method for calculating expected frequencies in the (r × k) case (i.e. where the contingency table is larger than (2 × 2)) is exactly the same.

There is, however, a general rule about expected frequencies that must be made clear:

Expected frequencies in at least 80 per cent of all cells in the contingency table must be 5, or more. In no case may an expected frequency be less than 1.

In the 2 × 2 case, no expected frequency can be less than 5. If this condition is not met, the Fisher Exact Probability test must be used instead (see Siegel, S., *Non Parametric Statistics*, 1956, McGraw-Hill).

If this condition is not met in the (r × k) case, adjacent cells may be collapsed together if it is sensible to do this.

Finally, whenever there is only one degree of freedom, Yates's Correction should be applied. This is known as a *correction for continuity* and involves subtracting 0.5 from the absolute value of each difference between an observed and an expected frequency. What this does is correct for the effect of forcing our observations into discrete categories. When, for example, we count the number of people who vote for and against a proposal, the division we observe is not truly a hard and fast one. Some who vote 'yes' will be only marginally in favour, while others will have no hesitation about doing so. Yates's Correction allows for this mathematically and has the effect of reducing the final value of χ^2, thereby compensating for the effect of an over-simplification of the 'true' state of affairs.

The χ^2 test (rectangular distribution)

This test tells us whether the frequencies we observe in a single set of categories differ significantly from those expected under the null hypothesis which states that all the frequencies should be the same. All observations are assumed to be independent.

Formula

$$\chi^2 = \frac{\Sigma(O - E)^2}{E} \qquad\qquad df = c - 1$$

where O = an observed frequency
E = an expected frequency
c = the number of categories

Suppose that we have counted the numbers of winners coming from each trap in a greyhound stadium during the course of a week's racing and we wish to test whether all the traps produce an equal number of winners. Our data are:

Table 5.6

Trap No:	1	2	3	4	5	6
No. of winners:	11	6	7	5	3	4

Calculation

Step 1: Add up all the frequencies and divide by the number of categories. This gives E, the expected frequency for each cell:
$11 + 6 + 7 + 5 + 3 + 4 = 36; \quad 36 \div 6 = 6$

Step 2: Take E from each observed frequency, square the resulting value and add up the squares. This gives $\Sigma(O - E)^2$
$(11 - 6)^2 + (6 - 6)^2 \ldots + (4 - 6)^2 = 40$

Step 3: Divide the result of Step 2 by E to obtain χ^2.
χ^2 is $40 \div 6 = 6.66$.

Step 4: Consult Table A.2 with c − 1 degrees of freedom to find the critical value of χ^2 for p = .05.
Table A.2 gives $\chi^2 = 11.07$ for 5 degrees of freedom.

Our calculated value is less than this and is therefore not significant. We cannot therefore reject H_o.

This means that although our observed frequencies may look different from the theoretically expected frequencies, the discrepancy is simply not large enough to be considered significant. (A practical implication of this, in this instance, is that perhaps we need more data in order to test the hypothesis adequately.)

The χ^2 test (2 × 2) case

This test tells us whether the proportional split of frequencies between different categories differs significantly from that which would be expected under the null hypothesis. All observations are assumed to be independent.

Formula*

$$\chi^2 = \frac{N \left\{ |AD - BC| - \dfrac{N}{2} \right\}^2}{(A + B)(C + D)(A + C)(B + D)} \qquad df = 1$$

where: A, B, C and D = cell frequencies in a 2×2 contingency table which has been labelled in this way:

$$\begin{array}{c|c} A & B \\ \hline C & D \end{array}$$

N = the sum of all four frequencies.

Suppose that of 50 people in a room, 28 were men, and 22 were women. Eighteen of the men and eight of the women were smokers. Is there a significant difference between these men and women with respect to smoking? We can draw up these data into a 2×2 contingency table:

	Smokers	**Non-smokers**	
Men	18	10	(28)
	A|B		
	C|D		
Women	8	14	(22)
	(26)	(24)	N = 50

Calculation

Step 1: Always check the expected frequencies first to ensure that the test will be valid. In any contingency table the best way to do this is to take the two *smallest* marginal totals common to a particular cell, multiply them together and divide by N. If this value is 5 or more, all is well. Here, the smallest marginal totals are 22 and 24:

$(22 \times 24) \div 50 = 10.56$ – We may proceed.

Step 2: Multiply together the frequencies in cells A and D; do the same for cells B and C, and take the smaller value from the larger. (The two vertical lines in the formula are a *modulus* sign which tells us to treat the difference between these two values as *positive*. Hence always take the smaller from the larger.)

$AD = (18 \times 14) = 252$; $BC = (10 \times 8) = 80$; $252 - 80 = 172$

---

* Note that this formula incorporates Yates's Correction (in the N/2 expression in the numerator).

Step 3: Divide N by 2, subtract this from the value found in Step 2, square the result and multiply it by N. This gives the numerator of the formula.
$50 \div 2 = 25$; $172 - 25 = 147$; $147^2 = 21609$;
$(21609 \times 50) = 1080450$

Step 4: Multiply together all four marginal totals and divide this into the value found in Step 3 to obtain χ^2.
$28 \times 22 \times 26 \times 24 = 384384$; $\chi^2 = 1080450 \div 384384 = 2.81$

Step 5: Consult Table A.2 with 1 degree of freedom to find the critical value of χ^2 for $p = .05$.
Table A.2 gives $\chi^2 = 3.84$ for one degree of freedom. Our calculated value is less than this and is therefore not significant. The proportional split of men and women into smokers and non-smokers is not significantly different.

The χ^2 test (r × k) case

This test tells us whether the proportional split of sets of frequencies across several categories differs significantly from that which would be expected under the null hypothesis. All observations are assumed to be independent.

Formula

$$\chi^2 = \Sigma \frac{(O - E)^2}{E} \qquad df = (r - 1)(k - 1)$$

where   O = an observed frequency
E = an expected frequency
r and k = the number of rows and the number of columns in the contingency table.

Suppose that 100 people from different social classes were asked how they kept their trousers up and we classified their replies as follows:

	Belt	Braces	Belt and braces	
Aristos	8	14	1	(23)
Bourgeois	17	12	10	(39)
Proles	14	4	20	(38)
	(39)	(30)	(31)	N = 100

Is there a significant association between social class and preferred method of trouser-suspension?

Calculation
Step 1: Find the expected frequencies for each cell by multiplying together the marginal totals common to it and dividing by N, the

sum of all the frequencies. (Check that at least 80 per cent of the cells have expected frequencies of 5 or more and that no cell has an expected frequency of less than 1.)

The expected frequency for the top left-hand cell, for example, is: $(23 \times 39) \div 100 = 8.97$ and the complete set of expected frequencies is as follows:

	Belt	Braces	Belt and braces
Aristos	8.97	6.90	7.13
Bourgeois	15.21	11.70	12.09
Proles	14.82	11.40	11.78

Step 2: Find the difference between each observed and expected frequency, square it and divide by that expected frequency. Add up all the resulting values to obtain χ^2.

$$(8 - 8.97)^2 = 0.9409; \quad 0.9409 \div 8.97 = 0.1048$$
$$(17 - 15.21)^2 = 3.2041; \quad 3.2041 \div 15.21 = 0.2106$$
$$(14 - 14.82)^2 = 0.6724; \quad 0.6724 \div 14.82 = 0.0453$$
$$(14 - 6.90)^2 = 50.4100; \quad 50.4100 \div 6.90 = 7.3057$$
$$(12 - 11.70)^2 = 0.0900; \quad 0.0900 \div 11.70 = 0.0076$$
$$(4 - 11.40)^2 = 54.7600; \quad 54.7600 \div 11.40 = 4.8035$$
$$(1 - 7.13)^2 = 37.5769; \quad 37.5769 \div 7.13 = 5.2702$$
$$(10 - 12.09)^2 = 4.3681; \quad 4.3681 \div 12.09 = 0.3612$$
$$(20 - 11.78)^2 = 67.5684; \quad 67.5684 \div 11.78 = 5.7358$$
$$\chi^2 = 23.8447$$

Step 3: Consult Table A.2 with $(r - 1)(k - 1)$ degrees of freedom to find the critical value of χ^2 for $p = .05$.

Table A.2 gives $\chi^2 = 9.49$ with 4 degrees of freedom. Our calculated value exceeds this and is therefore significant. (In fact the table value for $p = .01$ is 13.28, which is also exceeded. We may say therefore that this is significant beyond the .01 level.)

Interpreting such a finding can be quite difficult. By inspecting the tables of observed and expected frequencies, however, we can see that some large discrepancies make up the bulk of the overall effect. Remember, however, that this is strictly an 'overall' analysis. In many cases it is not so easy to see where the bulk of the effect comes from.

Model data for all subsequent analyses

The data below will be used in all subsequent analyses with the object of showing how tests differ in their power to reject the null hypothesis and how the analysis you use depends on the question you ask, on the design of your experiment and on the assumptions you make.

75	65	56	57
77	57	48	52
58	42	49	34
41	38	21	18
47	27	19	25
39	24	36	28
51	39	53	37
46	41	55	41
45	24	35	43
74	73	54	45

In each worked example that follows, these figures will be assumed to have come from hypothetical experiments which are described. If you compare the outcome of the various analyses, you will begin to appreciate what they each accomplish.

The Sign test

This test applies to two related samples when measurement is at the nominal scale level. It identifies the *kind* of difference that exists between pairs of observations (e.g. positive or negative) and determines whether there are more differences of one kind (or the other) than would be expected under the null hypothesis.

Dealing with our model data

Suppose that the data above are the results of an experiment on the Muller-Lyer illusion. Let us assume that ten subjects each produced scores under two conditions. Condition I used 'fins' and 'barbs' at an angle of 45° to the 'shaft'; Condition II employed an angle of 60°. The subjects used apparatus made up of a sleeve and an insert. To eliminate the bias resulting from either pushing in or pulling out the insert, the subjects used both methods of setting the apparatus under each condition. The order in which they did so was counterbalanced, and the scores are error expressed in millimetres. The experimenter hypothesizes that the values in Condition II will be lower (a one-tailed hypothesis).

Thus, our raw data would actually look like this:

Table 5.7

	Condition I (45°)		Condition II (60°)	
	Push	Pull	Push	Pull
S_1	75	65	56	57
S_2	77	57	48	52
etc.				

We now combine 'push' and 'pull' scores to produce a single combined score for each subject under each condition. Thus:

Table 5.8

	Condition I (45°)	Condition II (60°)	Sign
S_1	140	113	−
S_2	134	100	−
S_3	100	83	−
S_4	79	39	−
S_5	74	44	−
S_6	63	64	+
S_7	90	90	0
S_8	87	96	+
S_9	69	78	+
S_{10}	147	99	−

Calculation

Step 1: Mark the direction of difference between each pair of scores with a positive or negative sign, giving zero where no difference exists (see column headed 'sign' above). If you have a two-tailed hypothesis, go now to Step 3.

Step 2: If you have a one-tailed hypothesis, check that the majority of signs are in the predicted direction otherwise you must at this stage accept the null hypothesis. (In this case the majority of signs are in the predicted direction.)

Step 3: Count the number of times the less frequent sign occurs and call this value x.
Here $x = 3$.

Step 4: Count the number of pairs of scores that show a difference *other than zero* and call this value n.
Here n = 9.

Step 5: Consult Table A.6 with these values of x and n to obtain p. If p is less than .05, reject the null hypothesis. Here, for $x = 3$, n = 9, p = 0.254 (one-tailed), so we must accept H_o and conclude that there is no significant difference between the conditions.

Note

1. The sign test deals only with the direction of these differences. Because it is a nominal scale analysis, it is insensitive to the *size* of the differences. As far as the sign test is concerned, we might as well have written 'H' (for 'higher score') and 'L' (for 'lower score') and had data like this:

Table 5.9

	Condition I (45°)	Condition II (60°)
S_1	H	L
S_2	H	L
etc.		

In other words, if ever you have data like these (say ticks and crosses, 'yes' and 'no' responses) or any such simple dichotomies in a related measures design, the sign test is the test to use.

2. If you have more than 25 pairs of scores, use the following formula:

$$z = \frac{n - (2x + 1)}{\sqrt{n}}$$

To find z, get twice *x* and add 1; subtract this from n, the number of pairs of scores; divide the result by the square root of n and consult Table A.1 for the significance of z. Do not forget what is said in Step 2 above, however.

The Wilcoxon Rank Sum test

This test tells us whether the average of the ranks in one sample differs from the average of the ranks in another. It applies when we have two independent samples. The null hypothesis states that the two sets of ranks are, on average, the same.

Dealing with our model data

Let us suppose that the data on p. 124 are the results of an experiment conducted on 20 children to see if their performance in arithmetical tests was worse in the afternoon than in the morning (i.e. a one-tailed alternative hypothesis is involved). Each child drew from a hat a ticket with

Table 5.10

Condition I (am)		Condition II (pm)	
140	(2)	113	(4)
134	(3)	100	(5.5)
100	(5.5)	83	(12)
79	(13)	39	(20)
74	(15)	44	(19)
63	(18)	64	(17)
90	(9.5)	90	(9.5)
87	(11)	96	(8)
69	(16)	78	(14)
147	(1)	99	(7)
Sum of ranks:	94		116

a number on it between one and twenty. Those who chose odd numbers were tested in the mornings, those who chose the even numbers were tested in the afternoons. Each child was tested twice to help get a more representative index of his ability than a 'one-off' test would provide, and the two scores were combined to produce the information shown in Table 5.10.

Calculation

Step 1: Rank all the scores from highest to lowest regardless of which sample they are in. When ties occur, give average ranks. Add up the ranks in each sample. The smaller of these two values is T.
(Ranks are shown in brackets in Table 5.10, together with the two sums of ranks.) T = 94.

Step 2: If you have a two-tailed hypothesis, go now to Step 3. If you have a one-tailed hypothesis, check that the difference between the two rank sums is in the predicted direction, otherwise you must at this stage accept the null hypothesis.
(Here the higher rank sum is where it should be – the worse scores are in the pm condition.)

Step 3: Consult Table A.7 using n_1, the number of scores in the smaller sample and n_2, the number of scores in the larger sample to obtain the critical value of T for p = .05. Our sample sizes here are equal: both n_1 and n_2 = 10. Table A.7 gives T = 82 for p = .05 (one-tailed). Our calculated value of 94 exceeds this and is therefore not significant. The two sets of ranks do not differ significantly.

Note

1. Giving tied scores an average rank makes the test slightly more conservative, that is, it tends more towards a Type II error, or, if you prefer, leads us to err on the side of caution. Even if ties are numerous and extensive their effect is so small as to make it rarely worth the labour to correct for them.

2. Compare the outcome of this analysis with that which results from the Wilcoxon Signed Rank test and with the t tests.

3. When n_2 exceeds 20, use the following formula:

$$z = \frac{2T - n_1(N + 1)}{\sqrt{\dfrac{n_1 n_2(N + 1)}{3}}}$$

To obtain z, add one to the total number of scores (N), multiply this by n_1 and subtract the result from twice T. This gives the numerator of the formula. Multiply together the numer of scores in each sample; multiply that by N + 1; divide by 3. Take the square root of all this and divide into the numerator. Consult Table A.1 for the significance of z. Do not forget what is said in Step 2, however.

The Wilcoxon Signed Ranks test

This test applies to two related samples when the differences between score-pairs can be meaningfully ranked. The null hypothesis states that the ranked differences, when their signs are taken into account, will sum to zero. If we reject the null hypothesis, we can conclude that the values in the two samples differ significantly.

Dealing with our model data

Suppose that the experimental design and hypothesis were the same as for the sign test. We would have the same data, but on this occasion we can see how this test makes use not only of the *direction* of the differences but also of their *magnitude*. Thus:

Table 5.11

	Condition I (45°)	Condition II (60°)	d	Rank
S_1	140	113	−27	
S_2	134	100	−34	
S_3	100	83	−17	
S_4	79	39	−40	
S_5	74	44	−30	
S_6	63	64	+1	1
S_7	90	90	0	
S_8	87	96	+9	2.5
S_9	69	78	+9	2.5
S_{10}	147	99	−48	

Step 1: Find the difference between each pair of scores and note its direction with a positive or negative sign (see column headed 'd' above).

Step 2: Ignoring the signs for the time being, rank the differences giving the smallest difference Rank 1. Disregard any zero differences.

Step 3: Find the smaller sum of ranks which have the same sign. This gives T. If you have a one-tailed hypothesis and this value comes from differences whose sign does not conform to the direction of your hypothesis you must at this stage accept the null hypothesis. (Here, things are as we predicted, so we may continue.)
$T = 1 + 2.5 + 2.5 = 6.$

Step 4: Consult Table A.8 using n, the number of pairs of scores showing a non-zero difference, to obtain the critical value of T for p = .05. From Table A.8 for n = 9, T = 8 for p = .05 (one-tailed). Our calculated value is less than this and is therefore significant. We can conclude that the values in the two conditions differ significantly.

Note

1. When difference scores are the same, they should be given an average rank (see Siegel, S., *Non Parametric Statistics*, 1956, McGraw-Hill, for tie-correction technique, if you wish).

2. Compare the outcome of this analysis with that from the Sign test and the Wilcoxon Rank Sum test. This test is more sensitive than the Sign test, which failed to find a significant difference, because it takes the *magnitude* as well as the *direction* of differences into account. The Sign test is sensitive only to the latter. The difference between this test and the Wilcoxon Rank Sum test is to do with *Design*. Here we have 'told' the test that the scores are *paired*; in other words, that they *correlate*. The rank sum test did not 'know' this. As far as it was concerned, subject differences were mere 'noise' and had no such orderliness about them.

3. When there are more than 25 pairs of scores, use this formula:

$$z = \frac{n(n + 1) - 4T}{\sqrt{\dfrac{2n(n + 1)(2n + 1)}{3}}}$$

To obtain z, add 1 to n and multiply this by n. Subtract from this $4 \times T$. This gives the numerator. Find twice n and add 1; multiply this by $n(n + 1)$ and double the resulting value. Divide all this by 3, find the square root and divide this into the numerator to obtain z. Consult Table A.1 for the significance of z. Do not forget, however, what is said in Step 3.

The independent *t*-test

This tests whether the means of two independent samples differ significantly against the null hypothesis that the means are the same. As it is a *parametric* test, it requires interval scale measurement and depends for its validity on the assumption that the data are drawn from populations which are normal and which have equal variances. However, the test is robust enough to tolerate quite distinct violations of these assumptions.

Formula

$$t = \frac{\bar{X}_A - \bar{X}_B}{\sqrt{\dfrac{\left\{ \Sigma(X_A^2) - \dfrac{(\Sigma X_A)^2}{n_A} \right\} + \left\{ \Sigma(X_B^2) - \dfrac{(\Sigma X_B)^2}{n_B} \right\}}{N - 2} \times \dfrac{N}{n_A n_B}}}$$

$$df = N - 2$$

where $\bar{X}_A$ = the mean of Sample A

$\bar{X}_B$ = the mean of Sample B

n_A and n_B = the number of scores in Samples A and B
N = the total number of scores

Dealing with our model data

We can assume exactly the same design and a similar, one-tailed hypothesis as was described for the Wilcoxon Rank Sum test but here we would make the assumption that the parent populations from which our samples are drawn are normally distributed and have equal variances. Thus:

Table 5.12

Condition A (am)		Condition B (pm)	
	140		113
	134		100
	100		83
	79		39
	74		44
	63		64
	90		90
	87		96
	69		78
	147		99
ΣX_A =	983	ΣX_B =	806

Calculation

Step 1: Add up the scores in each sample and divide by the number of scores in each sample to find the two means, $\bar{X}_A$ and $\bar{X}_B$. Their difference gives the numerator of the formula. (If you have a one-tailed hypothesis, check that this difference is in the predicted direction, otherwise the null hypothesis must be accepted at this stage.)
$\Sigma X_A = 983$; $\bar{X}_A = 983 \div 10 = 98.3$;
$\Sigma X_B = 806$; $\bar{X}_B = 806 \div 10 = 80.6$;
$98.3 - 80.6 = 17.7$
(The difference is in the predicted direction.)

Step 2: Square all the scores in sample A and add up these squares. This gives $\Sigma(X_A^2)$. Do the same for Sample B to obtain $\Sigma(X_B^2)$.
$\Sigma(X_A^2) = 140^2 + 134^2 + 100^2 \ldots + 147^2 = 105281$
$\Sigma(X_B^2) = 113^2 + 100^2 + 83^2 \ldots + 99^2 = 70412$

Step 3: Square ΣX_A and divide by the number of scores in Sample A. Repeat this for the corresponding B values.
$$\frac{(\Sigma X_A)^2}{n_A} = \frac{983^2}{10} = 96628.9$$

$$\frac{(\Sigma X_B)^2}{n_B} = \frac{806^2}{10} = 64963.6$$

Step 4: Find $\left\{ \Sigma(X_A^2) - \dfrac{(\Sigma X_A)^2}{n_A} \right\}$ and $\left\{ \Sigma(X_B^2) - \dfrac{(\Sigma X_B)^2}{n_B} \right\}$

$105281 - 96628.9 = 8652.1; \quad 70412 - 64963.6 = 5448.4$

Step 5: Add together the two values found in Step 4 and divide the result by N $-$ 2.

$8652.1 + 5448.4 = 14100.5; \quad 14100.5 \div 18 = 783.361$

Step 6: Multiply n_A by n_B and divide this into N.

$10 \times 10 = 100; \quad 20 \div 100 = 0.2$

Step 7: Multiply the outcome of Step 5 by the outcome of Step 6 and find the square root of that value.

$783.361 \times 0.2 = 156.672; \quad \sqrt{156.672} = 12.516$

Step 8: Divide the numerator found in Step 1 by the outcome of Step 7 in order to obtain t.

$t = 17.7 \div 12.516 = 1.414$

Step 9: Consult Table A.3 with N $-$ 2 degree of freedom to obtain the critical value of t for p $= .05$.

From Table A.3 with 18 degrees of freedom, $t = 1.734$ for p $= .05$ (one-tailed). The calculated value of t is less than this and is therefore not significant. The means of the two conditions do not differ significantly.

Note
1. Compare the outcome of this analysis with the results of the sign test, the Wilcoxon rank sum test, the Wilcoxon signed ranks test and the related *t*-test.
2. *t* may have a negative sign. This merely reflects which mean is the larger and does not affect the way you use the significance table.

The related *t*-test

This tests whether the means of two related samples differ significantly, against the null hypothesis that they are the same. As it is a parametric test, it requires interval scale measurement and depends for its validity on the assumption that the differences between related scores are normally distributed. However, the test is robust enough to tolerate distinct violations of this assumption.

Formula

$$t = \dfrac{\Sigma d}{\sqrt{\dfrac{n\Sigma(d^2) - (\Sigma d)^2}{n - 1}}} \qquad df = n - 1$$

where d $=$ the difference between a pair of scores
n $=$ the number of pairs of scores

Dealing with our model data

We can assume exactly the same design and a similar, one-tailed hypothesis as was described for the sign test, but here we would make the assumption that our data were measured at the interval scale level and that the differences between score pairs were normally distributed. Thus:

Table 5.13

Condition I (45°)	Condition II (60°)	d
140	113	−27
134	100	−34
100	83	−17
79	39	−40
74	44	−30
63	64	+1
90	90	0
87	96	+9
69	78	+9
147	99	−48
		$\Sigma d = -177$

Calculation

Step 1: Find the differences between each pair of scores and add them together, taking their signs into account. This gives Σd. (If you have a one-tailed hypothesis, check that the sign of Σd is in line with it, otherwise the null hypothesis must be accepted at this stage.)

See column headed 'd' above. (Σd is negative, which reflects the fact that scores in Condition II are generally lower, which is as predicted.)

Step 2: Square all the differences and add up these squares. This gives $\Sigma(d)^2$, which must be multiplied by n.
$\Sigma(d^2) = (-27)^2 + (-34)^2 + (-17)^2 \ldots + (-48)^2 = 7141;$
$7141 \times 10 = 71410$

Step 3: Square Σd to obtain $(\Sigma d)^2$; subtract this from the outcome of Step 2.
$(\Sigma d)^2 = (-177)^2 = 31329; \quad 71410 - 31329 = 40081$

Step 4: Divide the outcome of Step 3 by n − 1 and find the square root of the resulting value.
$40081 \div 9 = 4453.444; \quad \sqrt{4453.444} = 66.734$

Step 5: Divide Σd (found in Step 1) by the outcome of Step 4 in order to obtain t.
$t = -77 \div 66.734 = -2.652$

Step 6: Consult Table A.3 with n − 1 degrees of freedom to obtain the critical value of t for p = .05.
From Table A.3 with 9 degrees of freedom, t = 1.833 for p = .05

(one-tailed). The calculated value of t exceeds this and is therefore significant. The means of the two conditions differ significantly.

Note
1. The sign of t may sometimes be negative, as in this case. This merely reflects the nature of the difference scores, and does not affect the way you use the significance table.
2. Compare the outcome of this test with the results of the sign test, the Wilcoxon rank sum test and the independent t-test. The outcome of this test is in fact that $p < .025$. This measures its power against its non-parametric counterparts, the sign test and the Wilcoxon signed ranks test. It also demonstrates how, in a related measures design, more information is, as it were, given to the analysis. Its parametric counterpart, the independent t-test, found no significant difference between the two conditions because it lacked this extra information.

The F test

This is the only test presented in this book which is concerned with differences in dispersion as opposed to differences in central tendency. It tests whether the variances of two samples differ significantly. It is a parametric test requiring interval scale measurement and it assumes that the data are from normally distributed populations. It is, however, robust and will tolerate distinct violations of this assumption. The null hypothesis would state that the variances are the same.

Formula

$$F = \frac{\sigma_A^2}{\sigma_B^2} \qquad df(n_A - 1) \text{ and } (n_B - 1)$$

where σ_A^2 and σ_B^2 = the variances of the two samples under comparison
n_A and n_B = the number of scores in Samples A and B

Dealing with our model data

Suppose we took the scores in the first two columns of our model data on p. 124 and asked if their variances differed significantly. Thus:

Table 5.14

Sample A	Sample B
75	65
77	57
58	42
41	38
47	27

Table 5.14 continued

Sample A	Sample B
39	24
51	39
46	41
45	24
74	73

Step 1: Calculate the variances of both samples using the method described on p. 115 but omitting Step 5.

$$\sigma_A^2 = 218.455; \quad \sigma_B^2 = 289.333$$

Step 2: In the case of a one-tailed hypothesis, divide the variance you predict to be larger by the variance you predict to be smaller to obtain F. In the case of a two-tailed hypothesis, divide the larger by the smaller variance to obtain F.

Here, we had no directional hypothesis. Therefore:

$$F = \frac{289.333}{218.455} = 1.324$$

Step 3: Consult Table A.4 with $(n_A - 1)$ and $(n_B - 1)$ degrees of freedom to obtain the critical value of F for $p = .05^*$.

From Table A.4 with 9 and 9 degrees of freedom, $F = 4.03$ for $p = .05$ (two-tailed). Our calculated value is less than this and therefore the difference is not significant. The two variances do not differ significantly.

Note. The fact that the difference between two variances is not significant is no proof at all that they are the same. The null hypothesis exists solely to be disproved in a probabilistic fashion and is by its very nature incapable of proof. This test, therefore, must not be used to give positive support to the assumption of homogeneity of variance.

Spearman's Rank-Order Correlation Coefficient

This is a non-parametric correlation coefficient which applies when measures on both variables are ranked. It gives an estimate of Pearson's product-moment correlation coefficient, which is its parametric counterpart. The null hypothesis against which the coefficient is (most commonly) tested is that the population coefficient is zero.

---

* In the case of a one-tailed test, the levels of significance shown in Table A.4 should be halved. Thus the 5 per cent significance level should be read as 2.5 per cent, and the 1 per cent as 0.5 per cent.

Formula

$$r_s = 1 - \frac{6\Sigma(d^2)}{n(n^2 - 1)}$$

where d = the difference between a pair of ranks
n = the number of pairs of ranks

Dealing with our model data

We will treat the combined scores of the first two and the second two columns, and suppose that they represent the scores on a test that we had devised to measure people's motivation. We pilot the test on ten people to whom it is administered twice – the second occasion being six months after the first – because we wish to see whether their scores are consistent. If they are, we can conclude that our new test is *reliable*, which is to say that it tends to produce similar results on each occasion that it is used. Thus:

Table 5.15

Initial Score		Score after 6 months		d	d^2
140	(2)	113	(1)	1	1
134	(3)	100	(2)	1	1
100	(4)	83	(6)	2	4
79	(7)	39	(10)	3	9
74	(8)	44	(9)	1	1
63	(10)	64	(8)	2	4
90	(5)	90	(5)	0	0
87	(6)	96	(4)	2	4
69	(9)	78	(7)	2	4
147	(1)	99	(3)	2	4
				$\Sigma(d^2)$ =	32

Calculation

Step 1: Rank the scores separately on each variable. (You may do so from highest to lowest or vice versa as long as you treat each variable in the same way.)

(Ranks are shown in brackets above, the highest scores on each variable having been given Rank 1.)

Step 2: Find the differences between all pairs of ranks, disregarding their signs; square them, and add them up. This gives $\Sigma(d^2)$ which must be multiplied by 6.

(See column headed d above, and column headed d^2 above.)
$\Sigma(d^2) = 32$; $32 \times 6 = 192$.

Step 3: Square n, the number of pairs of scores; subtract 1 and multiply the resulting value by n. $n^2 = 100$; $(100 - 1) \times 10 = 990$.

Step 4: Divide the outcome of Step 2 by the outcome of Step 3 and subtract the resulting value from 1 to obtain r_s.

$$192 \div 990 = 0.194; \quad r_s = 1 - 0.194 = 0.836$$

Step 5: Consult Table A.9 using n, the number of pairs of scores, to find the critical value of r_s for p = .05.

From Table A.9 for n = 10, r_s = .564 for p = .05 (one-tailed). Our calculated value exceeds this and is therefore significant. There is a significant positive correlation between the two sets of scores.

Note

1. r_s is significant beyond the .05 level – beyond even the .005 level.
2. We used a one-tailed test because our *implied* alternative hypothesis was that the scores would be positively related.
3. The fact that these scores correlate gives some account of why the 'difference' tests for related (i.e. correlated) samples detected significant differences between these two sets of values while the tests that assumed independence did not. (See the Wilcoxon Signed rank test and related *t*-test, and the Wilcoxon rank sum test and independent *t*-test. See also Pearson's product-moment correlation coefficient for these data.)

Pearson's Product-Moment Correlation Coefficient

This is a parametric correlation coefficient. It reflects the linear (i.e. 'straight line') relationship between two variables. It requires interval scale measurement and its significance can be tested if both variables are normally distributed and have equal variances. The null hypothesis against which the coefficient is (most commonly) tested is that the population coefficient is zero.

Formula

$$r = \frac{N\Sigma(XY) - (\Sigma X)(\Sigma Y)}{\sqrt{[N\Sigma(X^2) - (\Sigma X)^2][N\Sigma(Y^2) - (\Sigma Y)^2]}}$$

$$df = N - 2$$

where X and Y = scores on the X and Y variables

N = the number of pairs of scores

Dealing with our model data

We can adopt the same data as for Spearman's r_s (see p. 134) and also suppose that the same test of motivation is being assessed. On this occasion, however, we are making the assumption that the scores come from normally distributed populations with equal variances. (Incidentally, when the product-moment correlation coefficient is used for this purpose, it is known as a 'reliability coefficient'.)

Thus:

Table 5.16

Initial score (X)	X²	Score after 6 months (Y)	Y²
140	19600	113	12769
134	17956	100	10000
100	10000	83	6889
79	6241	39	1521
74	5476	44	1936
63	3969	64	4096
90	8100	90	8100
87	7569	96	9216
69	4761	78	6084
147	21609	99	9801
ΣX = 983	Σ(X²) = 105281	ΣY = 806	Σ(Y²) = 70412

Calculation

Step 1: Multiply together each pair of scores and add up these products. This gives $\Sigma(XY)$, which is then multiplied by N.
$$\Sigma(XY) = (140 \times 113) + (134 \times 100) \ldots + (147 \times 99) = 84276;$$
$$N\Sigma(XY) = 10 \times 84276 = 842760$$

Step 2: Add up the scores on each variable to obtain ΣX and ΣY and multiply together these two totals. This gives $(\Sigma X)(\Sigma Y)$.
(See above for these two totals. $(\Sigma X)(\Sigma Y) = 983 \times 806 = 792298$)

Step 3: Subtract the outcome of Step 2 from the outcome of Step 1. This gives the numerator of the formula. (If you have a one-tailed hypothesis, check that the sign of this value is in line with the prediction. If not, the null hypothesis must be accepted at this stage.)
$$842760 - 792298 = 50462$$
(We have predicted a positive relationship. The above value is positive, so we may continue.)

Step 4: Square each value of X and add up these squares. This gives $\Sigma(X^2)$, which must be multiplied by N. Repeat this for the Y scores, too.
(See columns headed X^2 and Y^2 above.)
$$N\Sigma(X^2) = 10 \times 105281 = 1052810$$
$$N\Sigma(Y^2) = 10 \times 70412 = 704120$$

Step 5: Square ΣX and subtract that from $N\Sigma(X^2)$; square ΣY and subtract that from $N\Sigma(Y^2)$
$$(\Sigma X)^2 = 983^2 = 966289; \quad 1052810 - 966289 = 86521$$
$$(\Sigma Y)^2 = 806^2 = 649636; \quad 704120 - 649636 = 54484$$

Step 6: Multiply together the two values found in Step 5 and find the square root of their product. This gives the denominator of the formula.

$$86521 \times 54484 = 4714010184; \sqrt{4714010184} = 68658.48$$

Step 7: Divide the numerator found in Step 3 by the denominator found in Step 6 to obtain r.

$$r = 50462 \div 68658.648 = 0.735$$

Step 8: Consult Table A.10 with $N - 2$ degrees of freedom to find the critical value of r for $p = .05$.

From Table A.10 with 8 degrees of freedom, $r = .632$ for $p = .05$ (one-tailed). Our calculated value exceeds this and is therefore significant. There is a significant positive correlation between the two sets of scores.

Note. The value for this coefficient is less than that for Spearman's r_s. To understand why this has occurred, look at the third and the eighth pair of scores. The Spearman coefficient sees the discrepancy between the *ranks* of these score pairs as 2 in each case; the Pearson coefficient is more sensitive and takes into consideration the fact that the 'real' discrepancies are not the same. In one case, the discrepancy is 27 and in the other 9. The Spearman coefficient, by taking into account only the rank position of each score, exaggerates the amount of agreement.

The Cochran test

This test applies when data in three or more related samples are measured at the nominal scale level. It can be thought of as the extension of the sign test in that it deals with dichotomous measures and tests the null hypothesis that the two sides of the dichotomy are similarly represented in each sample. Here, however, the dichotomy is expressed as '1' or '0', rather than as '+' or '−' as is conventional in the case of the sign test.

Formula

$$Q = \frac{(k-1)\{k\Sigma(T^2)-(\Sigma T)^2\}}{k\Sigma L - \Sigma(L^2)} \qquad df = k - 1$$

where T = the total for a given condition
L = the total for a given 'row'
k = the number of conditions

Dealing with our model data

Let us assume that all these scores were split at the median (44.5) to produce scores which were classified as 'high' or 'low', or 'pass' and 'fail'. Suppose ten candidates had each taken a four-paper examination: 'pass' is indicated by 1, 'fail' by 0. We now have a nominal scale and there are more than two related samples. The appropriate analysis is Cochran's Q, if we wish to find whether the papers are not of equal difficulty.

Table 5.17

	Paper I	Paper II	Paper III	Paper IV	L	L²
S_1	1	1	1	1	4	16
S_2	1	1	1	1	4	16
S_3	1	0	1	0	2	4
S_4	0	0	0	0	0	0
S_5	1	0	0	0	1	1
S_6	0	0	0	0	0	0
S_7	1	0	1	0	2	4
S_8	1	0	1	0	2	4
S_9	1	0	0	0	1	1
S_{10}	1	1	1	1	4	16
T:	8	3	6	3		

Calculation
Step 1: Add up all the 'ones' in each condition and find the sum of these totals. This gives ΣT, which is then squared.
(The column totals are shown above.)
$$T = 8 + 3 + 6 + 3 = 20; \quad (\Sigma T)^2 = 400$$
Step 2: Square each column total and sum these squares. This gives $\Sigma(T^2)$.
$$\Sigma(T^2) = 8^2 + 3^2 + 6^2 + 3^2 = 118$$
Step 3: Multiply $\Sigma(T^2)$ by k, the number of conditions, and from this subtract the outcome of Step 1.
$$118 \times 4 = 472; \quad 472 - 400 = 72$$
Step 4: Multiply the outcome of Step 3 by k − 1. This gives the numerator of the formula.
$$72 \times (4 - 1) = 216$$
Step 5: Add up all the 'ones' in each row and find the sum of these totals. This gives ΣL; which is then multiplied by k.
(The row totals are shown above.)
$$\Sigma L = (4 + 4 + 2 \ldots + 4) = 20; \quad 20 \times 4 = 80$$
Step 6: Square each row total and sum these squares. This gives $\Sigma(L^2)$
(See column headed L^2 above.)
$$\Sigma(L^2) = (16 + 16 + 4 \ldots + 16) = 62$$
Step 7: Subtract the outcome of Step 6 from the outcome of Step 5. This gives the denominator of the formula.
$$80 - 62 = 18$$
Step 8: Divide the outcome of Step 4 by the outcome of Step 7 to obtain Q.
$$Q = 216 \div 18 = 12.00$$

Step 9: Because Q approximates closely to χ^2, consult Table A.2 with $k - 1$ degrees of freedom to obtain the critical value of χ^2 for $p = .05$. From Table A.2 for 3 degrees of freedom, $\chi^2 = 7.82$ for $p = .05$.

Our calculated value exceeds this and is therefore significant. The performances on each paper differ significantly.

Note

This is an 'overall' analysis. It provides us with a general conclusion that subjects' performances on these papers are not the same. It does not, however, tell us which particular paper (or papers) differ from which other (or others).

The Kruskal Wallis test

This test applies to three or more samples of independent measures when data are at the ordinal scale level of measurement. It tests whether the sets of ranks differ significantly, against the null hypothesis that they are the same. This can be thought of as the extension of the Wilcoxon Rank Sum test to deal with cases involving more than two samples.

Formula

$$H = \frac{12\Sigma \left(\frac{R^2}{n} \right)}{N(N + 1)} - 3(N + 1) \qquad df = (k - 1)$$

where R = the sum of ranks in a given condition
n = the number of scores in a given condition
k = the number of conditions
N = the total number of scores

Dealing with our model data

Suppose that these scores were obtained by 40 children who had been allocated at random to do four tests (A, B, C, D) which were supposed to be graded in order of difficulty from A (easiest) to D (most difficult). When the tests were completed we simply ranked the performances of all the children (the highest score being given Rank 1) to produce the following:

Table 5.18

Test:	A	B	C	D
	2	5	9	7.5
	1	7.5	16	13
	6	22	15	32

24	28	38	40
17	34	39	35
26.5	36.5	30	33
14	26.5	12	29
18	24	10	24
19.5	36.5	31	21
3	4	11	19.5
R: 131	224	211	254

Calculation

Step 1: Rank all the measures from 1 to N, regardless of sample, giving tied scores an average rank. Then add up the ranks in each sample. This gives the values of R.

(Scores are already ranked above, and the sample totals (R) are shown.)

Step 2: Square each value of R and divide by the number of measures it is based on. Add up the resulting values and multiply this by 12. This gives the denominator of the formula:

$$12\sum \left(\frac{R^2}{n}\right) = 12\left\{\frac{131^2}{10} + \frac{224^2}{10} + \frac{211^2}{10} + \frac{254^2}{10}\right\}$$

$$= 12 \times 17637.4 = 211648.8$$

Step 3: Add 1 to the total number of scores and multiply this by N. This gives the denominator of the formula which must be divided into the numerator found in Step 2.

N + 1 = 41; 41 × 40 = 1640; 211648.8 ÷ 1640 = 129.054

Step 4: Multiply N + 1 by 3 and subtract this from the outcome of Step 3 to obtain H.

41 × 3 = 123; H = 129.054 − 123 = 6.054

Step 5: If the number of scores in the largest sample does not exceed 5, consult Table A.12 for the critical value of H for p = .05. Otherwise, treat H as if it were χ^2 and consult Table A.2 with k − 1 degrees of freedom.

From Table A.2 with 3 degrees of freedom $\chi^2 = 7.82$ for p = .05. Our calculated value is less than this and is therefore not significant. The four tests do not differ significantly in difficulty.

Note

1. This is an 'overall' analysis which simply tells us whether the difference between the average ranks of each condition are big enough to be considered significant. It does not tell us which particular condition, or conditions, differ from which other, or others. Compare the outcome of this analysis with the two-way analysis of variance by ranks and with Jonckheere's trend test.
2. See Note 1 on the Wilcoxon Rank Sum test.

Friedman's Two-way Analysis of Variance by Ranks

This test applies to three or more samples of related measures when data are at the ordinal scale level of measurement. It tests whether the average ranks for each sample differ significantly, against the null hypothesis which states that they are the same. This can be thought of as an extension of the Wilcoxon signed ranks test to deal with cases involving more than two samples.

Formula

$$X_r^2 = n(k - 1) \; \frac{12\Sigma(R - \bar{R})^2}{n^2 k(k^2 - 1)} \qquad df = (k - 1)$$

where R = the rank total for a given sample
$\bar{R}$ = the mean of the rank totals

which always equals $\dfrac{n(k + 1)}{2}$

k = the number of samples
n = the number of scores in each sample

Dealing with our model data

Suppose that the same four tests were being used as in the case of the Kruskal Wallis test, but instead of 40 subjects, only ten subjects were involved and they each did all four tests. The order in which they took the tests was randomized. We then ranked the scores of *each subject in turn* giving the highest scores Rank 1, to produce the following:

Table 5.19

Test:	A	B	C	D
S_1	1	2	4	3
S_2	1	2	4	3
S_3	1	3	2	4
S_4	1	2	3	4
S_5	1	2	4	3
S_6	1	4	2	3
S_7	2	3	1	4
S_8	2	3.5	1	3.5
S_9	1	3	3	2
S_{10}	1	2	3	4
R:	12	27.5	27	33.5

Calculation

Step 1: Rank the scores of each subject in turn, giving tied scores an average rank, then add up the ranks in each condition. This gives the values of R.

(Scores are already ranked above and the sample totals (R) are shown.)

Step 2: Multiply (k + 1) by n and divide this by 2 to obtain $\bar{R}$.
$$(4 + 1)10 = 50; \quad \bar{R} = 50 \div 2 = 25$$

Step 3: Find the difference between $\bar{R}$ and each value of R; square these differences, add them up and multiply this by 12. This gives the numerator of the formula.
$$12\Sigma(R - \bar{R})^2 = 12[(12 - 25)^2 + (27.5 - 25)^2 + (27 - 25)^2 + (33.5 - 25)^2]$$
$$= 12 \times 251.5 = 3018$$

Step 4: Square n and multiply this by k; square k and subtract 1; multiply these two values together. This gives the denominator of the formula.
$$n^2k = 10^2 \times 4 = 400; (k^2 - 1) = 4^2 - 1 = 15; \quad 400 \times 15 = 6000.$$

Step 5: Divide the outcome of Step 3 by the outcome of Step 4
$$3018 \div 6000 = 0.503$$

Step 6: Multiply n by (k - 1) and then multiply the outcome of Step 5 by this value to obtain χ_r^2.
$$10(4 - 1) = 30; \quad \chi_r^2 = 30 \times 0.503 = 15.09$$

Step 7: Treating χ_r^2 as χ^2, consult Table A.2 with k - 1 degrees of freedom for the critical value of χ^2 for p = .05.
From Table A.2 with 3 degrees of freedom, $\chi^2 = 7.82$ for p = .05. Our calculated value exceeds this and is therefore significant. The tests differ significantly in difficulty.

Note
1. This is an 'overall' analysis. It tells us whether the differences between conditions are large enough to be considered significant, but it does not tell us which particular condition, or conditions, differs significantly from which other, or others.
2. When k = 3 and n is less than 9 *or* when k = 4 and n is less than 5, X_r^2 does not approximate too closely to χ^2 and Table A.2 should not be used. In these cases, take the value that is found in Step 5, treat it as W, and use Table A.11 instead.
3. Compare the outcome of this test with that of the Kruskal Wallis test, which found no differences between the conditions. The reason for this is that, here, we 'told' the test that the scores were related, row by row. We found a similar effect working in the two-sample tests, where the Wilcoxon Signed Rank test revealed a difference that the Wilcoxon Rank Sum test failed to detect. (See the note appended to those two tests.)
4. Compare the outcome of this test also with that of Page's test for trend.

Jonckheere's Trend test

This test applies to three or more independent samples when data are at the ordinal scale level of measurement. It tells us whether scores show a progressive increase or decrease across the samples. It involves what can be thought of as an extended one-tailed hypothesis and, because of that, you must predict *in advance* the direction of the trend, otherwise the test is not valid.

Formula
When sample sizes are equal, no formula is involved. All that is required is a counting process which is described below. See the note below for dealing with unequal sample sizes.

Dealing with our model data

We shall assume exactly the same design as was described for the Kruskal Wallis test, but here we shall suppose that the experimenter was not hypothesizing merely an overall *difference* between the tests but had formulated the rather more specific hypothesis that scores would get *progressively lower* over the four tests. In this case, Jonckheere's test would be appropriate.

Table 5.20

Test:	A	B	C	D
	2	5	9	7.5
	1	7.5	16	13
	6	22	15	32
	24	28	38	40
	17	34	39	35
	26.5	36.5	30	33
	14	26.5	12	29
	18	24	10	24
	19.5	36.5	31	21
	3	4	11	19.5

(Your data may be in the form of ranks, as above, or remain as interval scale measures as our model data were. It is not necessary actually to rank them, for the counting process in effect does that for you. It is concerned only with whether one value is higher or lower than another.)

Calculation
The counting procedure is determined by our hypothesis. Consider the sample on the extreme left. Our hypothesis in effect states that samples to the *right* of it will on average have lower scores in them. What we do, therefore, is tally the number of scores that are in line with our hypothesis.

This process involves comparing each individual score with every score in the other samples. We start with the first score in Test A and count how many scores in Test B are lower than that. The answer is that *ten* of them are. We then tally the number of scores in Test C that are lower than this first score in Test A. Again the answer is *ten*. Moving to Test D and making the same comparison, the answer is *ten*. So far the count is 30.

We next consider the second score in Test A, and repeat the counting process. The third score is treated likewise and we continue until all the scores in Test A have been compared in this way with all the scores in the other tests. We then move to Test B, start with the first score there and go through the entire process again. Thence to Test C which is treated in the same way.

The sum of all the counts is P, and we consult Table A.13 with the appropriate values of k (the number of samples) and n (the number of scores per sample), to find whether it is significant.

For these data, the counts are as follows:

Table 5.21

											Total
Test A values	2	1	6	24	17	26.5	14	18	19.5	3	
No. of lower ranks in Test B.	10	10	8	5	7	4	7	7	7	10	75
No. of lower ranks in Test C.	10	10	10	4	4	4	6	4	4	10	66
No. of lower ranks in Test D.	10	10	10	5	8	5	8	8	7	10	81
Test B values	5	7.5	22	28	34	36.5	26.5	24	36.5	4	
No. of lower ranks in Test C.	10	10	4	4	2	2	4	4	2	10	52
No. of lower ranks in Test D.	10	9	6	5	2	1	5	5	1	10	54
Test C values	9	16	15	38	39	30	12	10	31	11	
No. of lower ranks in Test D.	9	8	8	1	1	4	9	9	4	9	62
									Grand total P =		390

From Table A.13 for k=4 and n=10 the critical value of P is 138 for p=.05. Our calculated value exceeds this and is therefore significant. There is a significant tendency to get progressively lower scores across the four tests.

Note

When sample sizes are unequal, the following formula must be used.

$$z = \frac{2P - \Sigma(n_i n_j) - 1}{\sqrt{\frac{1}{18}\{N^2(2N + 3) - 3\Sigma(n^2) - 2\Sigma(n^3)\}}}$$

where n = the number of scores in a given sample
n_i and n_j = the number of scores in any two samples under
comparison*
N = the total number of scores

Page's Trend test

This test applies to three or more related samples when data are at the ordinal scale level of measurement. It tells us whether scores show a progressive increase or decrease across the samples. It involves what can be thought of as an extended one-tailed hypothesis and, because of that, you must predict *in advance* the direction of the trend, otherwise the test is not valid.

Formula

$$L = \Sigma(wR)$$

where R = the rank total for a given sample or condition
w = weights assigned to the conditions according to the hypothesized direction of the trend.

Dealing with our model data

We shall assume exactly the same design as was described for the Friedman two-way analysis of variance by ranks, but here we shall suppose that the experimenter was hypothesizing not merely an overall *difference* between the tests, but had formulated a more specific hypothesis that scores would get *progressively lower* over the four tests. In this case, Page's test would be appropriate.

Table 5.22

Test	A	B	C	D
S_1	1	2	4	3
S_2	1	2	4	3
S_3	1	3	2	4
S_4	1	2	3	4
S_5	1	2	4	3
S_6	1	4	2	3
S_7	2	3	1	3
S_8	2	3.5	1	3.5
S_9	1	3.5	3.5	2
S_{10}	1	2	3	4
R:	12	27.5	27	33.5
weight (w):	1	2	3	4

* For example, if three samples were involved containing 5, 6 and 7 scores, $(n_i n_j) = (5 \times 6) + (5 \times 7) + (6 \times 7)$.

146

Calculation

Step 1: Rank the scores of each subject in turn, giving tied scores an average rank, then add up the ranks in each condition. This gives the values of R.

(Scores are already ranked above and the sample totals (R) are shown.)

Step 2: Assign a weight of one to the sample which is expected to contain the highest ranks, a weight of two to the sample expected to contain the next highest ranks, and so on until all samples have been weighted.

(Weights are shown above. Note that the highest ranks were expected for Test A, which has a weight of one. Do not confuse *ranks* and *numerical values*. Although 1 is the *highest* rank, *numerically* it is the lowest number.)

Step 3: Multiply each rank total by its assigned weight and add up all these values. This gives L.

$$L = (12 \times 1) + (27.5 \times 2) + (27 \times 3) + (33.5 \times 4) = 279$$

Step 4: Consult Table A.14 using the number of conditions (k) and the number of subjects (n) to find the critical value of L for p = .05. From Table A.14 for k = 4, and n = 10, L = 266 for p = .05. Our calculated value of L exceeds this and is therefore significant. There is a significant tendency for scores to get progressively lower across the four tests.

Statistical tests—decision map

	Tests of difference: 2 samples, Independent	Tests of difference: 2 samples, Related	Tests of difference: 3 + samples, Independent	Tests of difference: 3 + samples, Related	Tests of trend 3 + samples: Independent	Tests of trend 3 + samples: Related	Measures of correlation
NOMINAL	χ^2 (2 x 2) case	The Sign test	χ^2 (r x k) case	Cochran's Q			
ORDINAL	Wilcoxon's Rank Sum test	Wilcoxon's* Signed Ranks test	The Kruskal Wallis test	Friedman's test	Jonckheere's test	Page's test	Spearman's r_s†
INTERVAL	Independent *t*-test	Related *t*-test					Pearson's Product-Moment Correlation Coefficient (r)

* The requirement of this test is that the differences between the pairs of measures must be able to be meaningfully ranked. This means that the raw data must be virtually at the interval scale level.

† r_s is an index of agreement between *two* sets of ranks. If you have more than two sets of ranks and want to obtain an index of agreement between them, Kendall's coefficient of concordance (W) can be calculated. W can adopt any value between zero and one, but cannot be negative, as r_s can be. To calculate W, use the first five steps of the calculation for Friedman's χ_r^2. The value obtained at the end of the fifth step is W. χ_r^2 in fact is equal to $Wn(k - 1)$.

Figure 5.1 Statistical tests – decision map

Psychology as a natural science

This is, perhaps, not an ideal title for the section, since human beings are at all times part of nature. But, conventionally, 'natural science' refers to non-human species. Here we group the study of the behaviour of such species, and also investigations of the physiological basis of behaviour. Both these can be, and are, studies in their own right. But they have also various applications to human beings.

In the case of physiology, it may be suggested that, in principle, every sort of behaviour must have a physiological substrate. In only some cases has it been possible to demonstrate that this is so. Much more is known, for example, about the physiological conditions of emotion than about those for intelligence. Even if all physiological conditions were known, however, it would be a reductionist fallacy to suppose that we would then have a complete explanation of behaviour.

Animals, apart from their intrinsic interest, may provide a more convenient population for some experiments than humans. The white rat in particular has often been used as a sort of test-tube in which it was hoped to study some basic mechanism of learning. Or it may be – especially with the ethological studies – that the other species offers a sort of model of the human, useful for suggesting hypotheses that can then be tested.

Chapter six

Physiological studies I

Simon Green

Physiological psychology is concerned with the relations between the observable behaviour of organisms and their physiological make-up. Psychology itself uses observable behaviour as its subject matter, and there is no reason why every psychologist should concern himself with physiology; in fact, many psychologists reject any 'physiologizing' as the thin end of the wedge of reductionism. *Reductionism*, briefly, is the attempt to explain phenomena by reducing them to their component parts; e.g. in physics, the explanation of the behaviour of gases in terms of our knowledge of sub-atomic particles. But some are worried that the application of reductionism to psychology is leading to physiological explanations of behaviour which are somehow preferable to or more valid than psychological ones.

As physiological psychology is not yet sufficiently advanced to offer complete explanations of perception, memory, emotion, motivation, etc., in terms of brain mechanisms or hormonal levels, the argument is rather irrelevant. A more constructive approach would be to accept that observable behaviour is the product of, or mediated by, the physiology of the organism; it has physiological correlates, which may be studied and which represent an alternative level of explanation to the psychologist's observations and measurements. A complete description and explanation of behaviour would, therefore, involve both psychological and physiological investigations.

The physiological psychologist is interested above all in the nervous system. Although respiratory, circulatory, hormonal systems, etc., are also involved, the overall integration of stimuli and responses found in complex behaviour is achieved via the nervous system; and the specific structure to have attracted and held the imagination of physiological psychologists, neuropsychologists, brain scientists, and philosophers generally, is the brain. So most of this and the next chapter will be concerned with brain structure and function; but remember, the adjective is 'physiological', and a complete description of the physiological correlates of behaviour would have to go beyond the brain. It is this complete description that physiological psychology aims at.

Basic units

The body is composed of millions of cells, organized into tissues and then into organs. Each cell is specialized for some function – hormone secretion, oxygen transport, filtration of waste matter, etc. All have many functions in common – they respire, metabolize (i.e. carry out many complicated chemical processes to provide, in particular, for energy expenditure), absorb nutrients, etc. We have therefore to concentrate on what makes one cell different from another, rather than their common possession of basic structures such as a nucleus (containing the genetic material in the form of chromosomes, made up of DNA) and cytoplasm (the jelly-like fluid filling the cell).

The unit of nervous system organization is the *neuron*. Neurons are elongated (see Figure 6.1), with the cell body ('soma') extending into a relatively long branching *axon* on one side and into a number of relatively short *dendrites* on the other. Axons and dendrites are often referred to as 'neuronal processes'. The whole neuron is a single cell, with cytoplasm filling axons, soma, and dendrites.

Neurons come in a range of sizes and with an enormous variety of dendrites and axonal processes. The brain contains around 15 billion (15×10^9) of them, while the neuron connecting the spinal cord to the toes has an axon three to four feet long.

The specialization all neurons have in common concerns the cell membrane, the outer barrier of the neuron. This is semi-permeable,

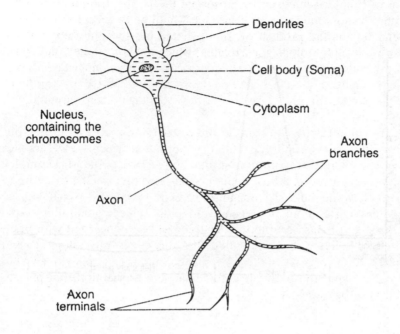

Figure 6.1 The neuron

allowing the passage of various electrically charged particles (ions) from inside to out and from outside to in. Usually there is a differential concentration of ions inside and out, leading to an electrical difference, or resting potential, of around −70 millivolts across the membrane from inside to out. The situation can be altered by stimuli of various sorts, especially small electric currents. Any stimulus which shifts the membrane towards electrical equilibrium (i.e. zero membrane potential) may provoke an *action potential* at that point on the membrane. As the potential across the membrane is decreased to a threshold of around −50 millivolts, there is an explosive increase in membrane permeability, enabling sodium and chloride ions to rush into the neuron and potassium ions to pass out; this rapid exchange shifts the membrane from −50 to around +40 millivolts in about a half a millisecond, and constitutes the action potential (see Figure 6.2). The electrical threshold is crucial, as action potentials are 'all-or-none' events.

After the action potential has peaked at +40 millivolts, the membrane rapidly returns to its resting state of a −70 millivolt potential. With a brief refractory period after the action potential during which the membrane is inactive, the whole sequence takes between two and four milliseconds, i.e. there must be an interval of at least two to four thousandths of a second before the membrane is able to produce another action potential.

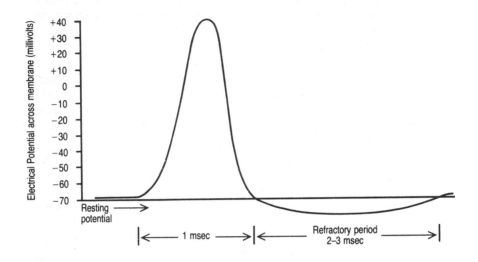

Figure 6.2 The action potential. Electrical changes across the neuronal cell membrane during an action potential

This gap becomes important when we consider what happens to the action potential. The structure of the neuronal membrane that enables action potentials to occur also enables them to travel along the neuron from the point at which they were first stimulated. Thus a wave of electrical activity (or 'depolarization', the explosive change in the membrane potential from −70 to +40 millivolts) passes along the neuronal membrane. If a thin wire recording electrode is placed on the membrane, it will record this wave as a blip of electrical activity; this is the nerve impulse. If action potentials are successively stimulated they will be recorded as sequences, or trains, of nerve impulses. Each part of the membrane travelled by an impulse will be inactive for two to four milliseconds. Thus the maximum rate of impulse transmission, or frequency, is between 250 and 500 per second. Each action potential is electrically identical to any other, and so the crucial properties of impulse conduction are the frequency and the patterning of trains of impulses over time.

Action potentials are usually initiated on the dendrites of the neuron and the nerve impulse is then 'propagated' (or 'transmitted') along the neuron in the direction dendrite → soma → terminals of all axon branches. Before considering the initiation of the action potential in more detail, there is one fundamental point to be made. Information in any nervous system is embodied, or *coded*, entirely by the frequency and patterning of nerve impulses. Sensory and motor systems, perception, memory, cognition and thought, emotion, personality, etc., are all represented by patterns of nerve impulses in appropriate parts of the nervous system.

This can be simply demonstrated. Using thin wire stimulating electrodes, a tiny electric current can be applied to single neurons or groups of neurons in the brain. As the brain itself has no sensory receptors, this procedure can be performed in human patients using only a local anaesthetic for the area of the head and skull through which a hole will be drilled to allow entry of the electrode into the brain. Such techniques are normally part of a screening programme before major brain surgery.

If the stimulating currents are within the naturally occurring limits for nervous system electrical activity, then the normal function of an area of the brain can be mimicked. As the patient is conscious, he or she can report any subjective experiences. It has been shown that visual experience (flashes of light), auditory sensation, 'automatic' vocalization, feelings of unease and euphoria and outbursts of aggression, recall of memories, movement of limbs and of individual muscle groups, increases and decreases in heart-rate and blood pressure, can all be produced by electrical stimulation of the appropriate part of the brain.

So we possess a brain of daunting complexity using a fundamentally simple electrical code for the information represented within it; i.e. if you want to be reductionist about it, our brains can be represented as machine-like. However, this machine has 15 billion working units each, as we shall see, having several thousand interconnections with other units, and produces human behaviour and experience; it is only machine-like if we upgrade our concept of what machines are and what they can do. Our most sophisticated machines – computers – are very fast information processors, and are much better at things such as mathematical computation than we are. However, no computer can as yet equal our higher cognitive abilities – visual perception, memory, learning, problem solving, etc. – or even our underestimated motor skills. The latest computers can perform *parallel* information processing, as opposed to coping with input *serially*, i.e. one after the other. This makes them a little more 'brain-like', but still leaves them at a primitive stage compared with the real thing.

The synapse

Neurons are not physically connected to one another. If they were, action potentials would simply travel haphazardly to all parts of the nervous system. Between an axon terminal and the next neuron is a gap, the *synapse* (see Figure 6.3). Only visible under the electron microscope, the synapses are measured in angstroms (an angstrom is one ten-billionth of a

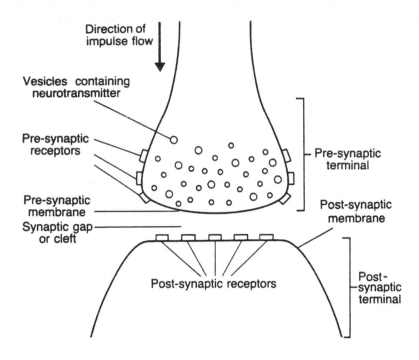

Figure 6.3 The synapse

metre), and present a barrier to the action potential: the action potential must be transmitted across the synapse to the post-synaptic membrane of the next neuron if it is not to be lost.

Transmission across the synapse is chemical. Quantities of the particular chemical (*synaptic neurotransmitter*) are stored within the pre-synaptic terminal in spherical storage packets called *vesicles*. When an action potential reaches the pre-synaptic region, it stimulates a number of vesicles to migrate to and merge with the actual neuronal cell membrane bordering the synapse, where they release their chemical contents into the synaptic cleft. The molecules of neurotransmitter diffuse across the synapse and combine with *receptors* located on the post-synaptic membrane. This combination is most simply seen as a 'lock-and-key' affair. The molecule of transmitter has a certain three-dimensional structure which is thought to match perfectly the structure of the receptor molecule.

This interaction between transmitter and receptor is short-lived, but while it lasts produces a change in the permeability of the post-synaptic membrane. This change is along the lines described for the initiation and propagation of the action potential, but the combination of a single molecule of neurotransmitter with a single receptor is insufficient fully to depolarize the post-synaptic membrane (i.e. it does not reach the electrical threshold for the generation of an action potential). Even the total amount of neurotransmitter released by a single action potential in the pre-synaptic terminal will be insufficient to initiate an action potential in the post-synaptic neuron, i.e. the nerve impulse will not cross the synapse, and the information it represents will be lost.

For synaptic transmission to occur, sufficient nerve impulses must arrive within a short space of time at the pre-synaptic terminal to stimulate the release of a sufficient quantity of neurotransmitter into the synapse; when combining simultaneously with many post-synaptic receptors, this quantity will be enough to depolarize the post-synaptic membrane to the level of the electrical threshold, and so initiate an action potential which will in turn be transmitted along the post-synaptic neuron. This additive effect of nerve impulses arriving consecutively at the pre-synaptic terminal is called *temporal summation*, i.e. summation over time. Alternatively, two or more axons may terminate close to the same patch of post-synaptic membrane; when impulses simultaneously arrive at these pre-synaptic axon terminals the combined release of neurotransmitter may be enough to trigger an action potential in the post-synaptic membrane. This additive effect, reflecting activity in two or more different axons, is called *spatial summation*.

In either case the frequency of nerve impulses in the pre-synaptic neurons is unlikely to be matched by the frequency in the post-synaptic neuron. There is one obvious function for this mechanism, but also a further complication. The obvious function is filtering out irrelevant information. If touch receptors on the skin are momentarily activated by dust particles in the air, nerve impulses travel along sensory neurons towards the central nervous system. If the activation is momentary, the concentration of impulses will be insufficient to carry across the first synapse in the chain leading to the brain and conscious awareness. Thus the information will be lost, or filtered out, a quite reasonable system for preventing the brain becoming overloaded with irrelevant information.

The complication is that synaptic connections are not one-to-one, or even of the same type. As a very rough estimate, any central nervous system neuron makes contact via synapses with thousands of other neurons. Thus a nerve impulse in one neuron is the summated product of thousands of inputs to that neuron, and an extra complication is that not all synapses are excitatory. In many synapses, the combination of neurotransmitter with post-synaptic receptor tends to *increase* the membrane's negative resting potential, i.e. moving it further away from the electrical threshold and making an action potential *less* likely. This *hyperpolarizing* effect is called an *inhibitory post-synaptic potential* (IPSP), in contrast with the depolarizing *excitatory post-synaptic potential* (EPSP) described previously. Neuronal activity reflects a sophisticated balance between hundreds of inhibitory and excitatory inputs.

Neurotransmitters

Chemical neurotransmission was first demonstrated by Loewi in 1921 (following 'creative' dreaming!) using the neural connections to the frog's heart (Loewi and Navratil, 1926). Over the next thirty years work concentrated upon the peripheral nervous system (as opposed to the central nervous system, the brain and spinal cord), particularly the synapses between the axons of motor neurons and skeletal muscles (the neuro-muscular junction), and it is still the case today that our synaptic models are based upon the peripheral nervous system or the accessible nervous systems of other animals.

Chemical neurotransmission at a central nervous system synapse was first demonstrated in the spinal cord (Eccles *et al*, 1954), and rapidly became accepted as a fundamental means of information transmission in the brain. By 1970 there were six established chemical neurotransmitters: *noradrenaline*, *dopamine*, and *serotonin* (all monoamines), *acetylcholine* (tertiary amine), *GABA* (gamma-amino butyric acid) and *glutamate* (both amino acids). It is a basic principle, now under attack but still not fully disproved, that a given neuron will secrete the same neurotransmitter at all its axon terminals (Dale's principle), and that neurons may therefore be characterized by their neurotransmitter. So the brain contains noradrenergic, dopaminergic, serotonergic, cholinergic, GABA-ergic, and glutamatergic neurons.

Added to this list by now are anywhere between 20 and 30 possible neurotransmitters discovered over the last two decades, whose precise role in brain function has not yet been identified. Some may be synaptic neurotransmitters in the classic sense, while others may be *neuromodulators*, influencing neurotransmission in subtle ways. Regardless of the ultimate outcome, brain chemistry has become the fastest-growing area of brain research, partly because the existence of a chemical bridge between neurons provides a valuable means of influencing brain function using externally applied chemicals and for modelling drug effects on behaviour, and partly through a combination of sophisticated biochemical and pharmacological techniques which have only become available in the last 15 years or so.

Synaptic receptors are specific to a given neurotransmitter. So, in line with the different transmitters there are dopamine, noradrenaline, acetylcholine, etc., receptors. As neurons receive many inputs via synapses, their dendritic and somatic membranes may possess many different types of receptor depending upon the types of input (Figure 6.3).

As a further complication, it has been discovered that beside post-synaptic receptors, there are also receptors on the pre-synaptic terminal itself; some of the neurotransmitter diffuses to these receptors (*autoreceptors*), where the effect is to inhibit neurotransmitter release from the pre-synaptic terminal, i.e. a negative feedback system: the more transmitter that is released the less likely it is to be released.

Neurotransmitter pathways

The study of the brain's neurotransmitters in relation to behaviour has expanded dramatically over the last twenty years. Early on it was discovered that at least some of these chemicals were distributed systematically in the brain, and this in turn has led to a particular method of conceptualizing brain-behaviour relationships.

In the brain, cell bodies of neurons tend to concentrate together in '*nuclei*' (singular '*nucleus*'). The axons of these neurons obviously have to travel from the nucleus, towards their eventual synaptic destinations on target neurons elsewhere in the brain. In some cases, a collection or bundle of axons from a given nucleus have the same target structure, which itself may be a nucleus or collection of nuclei. In such cases the axons travel together, making up a neural *pathway* or tract within the brain, and these pathways can be identified and named.

This neuro-anatomical approach has been going on since the nineteenth century, but has now been supplemented by chemical studies. It appears that a number of anatomically distinct pathways in the brain can also be defined in terms of the neurotransmitters they use, i.e. all neurons whose cell bodies make up a given nucleus and whose axons make up a pathway travelling from that nucleus to a target structure use the same neurotransmitter. Pathways organized in this way can then be labelled according to the neurotransmitter – noradrenergic, dopaminergic, cholinergic, etc. For each of the classical neurotransmitters mentioned earlier there exist two or three such pathways. As an example, Figure 6.4 outlines brain dopamine pathways.

The existence of such a systematic neuro-anatomical and chemical organization has led investigators to suggest that individual pathways will have specific roles in behaviour, and we will come across one or two of these hypotheses later on. It does mean that we can now associate categories of behaviour with *either* neuro-anatomical structures such as the hypothalamus or septum, *or* chemical pathways. As a cautionary note it should be emphasized that these 'long-axon' neurotransmitter pathways account for only around 20 per cent of all the synapses in the brain.

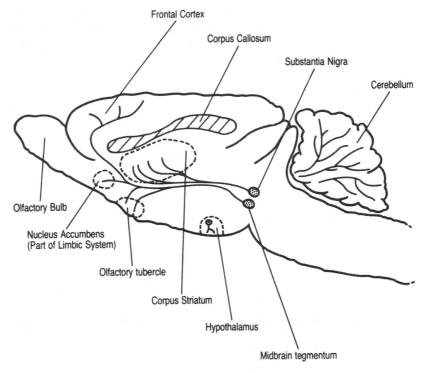

Figure 6.4 Dopamine pathways in the rat brain. The pathway from substantia nigra to striatum is involved in Parkinson's disease. The midbrain – limbic system – frontal cortex pathway may be involved in schizophrenia. The short pathway in the hypothalamus ('tubero-infundibular') controls the release of the hormone prolactin from the pituitary gland

Techniques for investigating brain function

The two principles of information transmission in the nervous system – electrical and chemical – provide two sets of investigatory techniques.

Electrical stimulation and recording

We have already mentioned the use of electrical stimulation to mimic the brain's natural activity. This necessarily involves localized stimulation using single wire electrodes, in some cases so small that individual neurons may be stimulated. For behavioural studies, stimulation usually involves larger electrodes activating many thousands if not millions of brain cells. At the top of the electrical stimulation ladder is electro-convulsive shock, in which large currents are passed through the brain to induce convulsive activity; this traumatic technique provides no insights into brain function, but is held by some to be a useful treatment for depressive disorders.

Electrodes may also be used to record the naturally occurring electrical activity of the brain. Recordings may be taken from single neurons (or single units), or from populations of thousands of neurons, while the evoked potential and EEG (electroencephalogram) recordings may involve billions of cells. *Evoked potentials*, as their name implies, are electrical changes evoked by, or 'locked' onto, a stimulus in the environment, e.g. a flash of light or a tone. They occur some milliseconds (thousandths of a second) after the stimulus, the precise latency (delay) depending upon the exact location of the recording electrode. Single unit recording can show evoked activity but, more usually, evoked potentials are taken from the cortex using recording electrodes placed directly on the skull, i.e. this can be a *non-invasive* technique. As the brain is constantly active, it is impossible to distinguish a single evoked potential from background electrical activity; repeated stimulus presentations are given, and a computer used to superimpose successive electrical recordings in the hope that the consistently produced evoked potential will emerge as the random background activity is averaged out. Measuring evoked potentials is thus a complicated procedure, and although it is useful in checking whether stimuli are being registered in various parts of the brain, the precise functional significance of evoked potentials and their relation to cognitive processing remains a matter of debate.

Building on the pioneering work of Caton and Galvani in the nineteenth century on the electrical activity of the brain, Berger introduced in the 1930s (Berger, 1929) the idea that the gross (i.e. large scale) electrical activity of the brain can reflect the subject's state of arousal, and he can be credited with introducing the EEG into neuro-physiology. The EEG is usually recorded from electrodes dotted over the skull surface, and reflects cortical activity. It represents the continuous activity of billions of neurons, and occurs in two major forms: it can be either *synchronized* or *desynchronized*. A synchronized EEG has, after appropriate computer-based analysis of the raw signals, a characteristic repeated wave-form, which may be identified by the number of waves per second (Herz). Greek letters are used to label waves of different frequencies. Thus the *alpha* waves dominating the EEG of the drowsy subject have a frequency of between eight and 12 per second (8–12 Herz), while the *delta* waves found in the deep sleep EEG have a frequency of around one per second. The desynchronized EEG, as its name implies, does not have a dominant and characteristic wave-form, but consists of irregular electrical activity. A fast desynchronized recording is typical of the waking, aroused state, and is also found in dreaming sleep (see later).

EEG patterns may also be recorded from large subcortical structures using invasive implanted electrodes, usually in animals. Particularly prominent has been the EEG recorded from the hippocampus, a large limbic system structure (see p. 176). This has a characteristic *theta* wave (4–7 Herz).

Chemical stimulation and recording

Since the earliest civilizations, *drugs*, often extracted from plants, have been used for their dramatic effects on perception, emotion and cognition. Today mescaline (from the dried cactus, peyote), psilocybin (from the so-called 'sacred mushroom' of Central America), opium and morphine (from the poppy), are still used for their hallucinogenic properties, while there is an enormous range of synthetic drugs used to alter behaviour and experience – anti-depressants, anti-anxiety drugs, anti-psychotic agents, pain-killers (analgesics), etc.

These compounds are known as *psychoactive* agents, as they influence psychological processes. A more general definition would be that drugs are chemical compounds with selective biological activity, i.e. that they produce specific effects on the cells which make up the body. Psychoactive agents have their actions on the cells of the nervous system, the neurons.

Most people would agree that agents used for the treatment of psychiatric conditions or 'abused' for their particular euphoric or hallucinogenic properties could be called 'drugs'. However, the definition is arbitrary, and subject to cultural factors. Cigarettes, alcohol, and coffee all contain chemical compounds (nicotine, alcohol, and caffeine) with selective biological activity involving brain neurons, and can affect psychological processes – attention, perception, vigilance, memory, emotion, personality. In addition they can all be associated with physiological and psychological dependence, and with a withdrawal syndrome if abstinence follows a long period of indulgence. Thus they qualify as 'drugs', and as 'drugs of abuse'. However, and despite the massive social and economic costs of smoking and drinking in particular, they are not usually referred to as 'drugs'. They have become part of the fabric of society.

Most classes of drugs used in psychiatry were introduced before much was known about the chemistry of the brain, on the basis of their clinical effectiveness. As information accumulated during the 1960s and 1970s on synaptic neurotransmission in the brain, it became increasingly possible to relate the behavioural effects of drugs to interactions with synaptic transmitters. Thus *'psychopharmacology'* or *'behavioural pharmacology'* evolved.

Over the last twenty years many drugs have been identified as having specific pharmacological effects at nervous system synapses. Given the complexity of synaptic neurotransmission, there are several ways in which it may be influenced, sometimes involving the injection of drugs through permanently implanted intra-cranial *cannulae* (tiny steel tubes inserted through the skull into the brain) onto specific sites within the brain. Among these ways are the following:

1. Drugs which are similar in structure to natural transmitters may act directly upon synaptic receptors, either to stimulate them (*agonists*) or to block them (*antagonists*).
2. Drugs may influence the release of the neurotransmitter from the pre-synaptic terminal. Amphetamine increases the release of dopamine and noradrenaline from their terminals, and is therefore an *indirectly-acting* agonist.
3. Drugs may interfere with the metabolic pathway of a given neurotransmitter, i.e. the way in which it is synthesized and broken down. Neurotransmitters are manufactured within neurons from raw materials transported in the bloodstream. Specific *enzymes* are essential for each stage of the process, and specific enzymes inactivate the neurotransmitter after its action at the post-synaptic receptor (otherwise post-synaptic stimulation would be continuous). In general we can say that interference at any point can have effects upon synaptic transmission. As examples, α-methyl-p-tyrosine inhibits (blocks) tyrosine hydroxylase, which is crucial to the manufacture of dopamine and noradrenaline. As a consequence, brain levels of these two neurotransmitters rapidly fall. (It is a general point that the total brain content of any transmitter will be released, broken down, and resynthesized within a matter of hours or days. Normal levels are sustained only by constant synthesis.)

   There is a group of anti-depressant drugs known as the monoamine oxidase inhibitors (MAOIs). Monoamine oxidase is an enzyme involved in the breakdown and removal of noradrenaline, dopamine, and serotonin from the synapse after they have combined with their respective receptors. Inhibition of this enzyme prevents the breakdown, and allows high levels of neurotransmitter to be maintained at and around the synapse, so producing high levels of synaptic transmission.
4. Drugs may have less specific actions. Anaesthetics seem in general to act upon the neuronal membrane, reducing its excitability, rather than upon the synapse.
5. Drugs may be used to produce specific chemical 'lesions', i.e. localized areas of damage after injection directly into the brain. These drugs are known as *neurotoxins*, and include 6-hydroxydopamine (6-OHDA) which is taken up by and destroys dopaminergic and noradrenergic nerve terminals.

For all the classical neurotransmitter systems, and for some of the newer candidates, we have comprehensive batteries of drugs to stimulate, block, increase levels of, or decrease levels of the neurotransmitter. We can also measure levels of brain neurotransmitters at post-mortem. In the living patient, our most direct insight into the brain's chemical working comes from analysis of *cerebro-spinal fluid* (CSF).

In the centre of the spinal cord lies the narrow spinal canal (see Figure 6.9). This continues up into the brain where it expands to form the ventricular system, consisting of fluid-filled chambers, the ventricles, which provide a means for the disposal of the waste products of brain metabolism. The CSF constantly circulates between brain and spinal cord, and a sample can be extracted via a hypodermic needle inserted between the lower vertebrae and into the spinal canal – the *lumbar puncture*. Analysis of CSF can reveal various aspects of the brain's metabolic activity. Presence of virus particles, for example, can confirm a diagnosis of meningitis (inflammation of the protective membranes covering the brain), while fragments of red blood corpuscles confirm that a cerebral haemorrhage has occurred. The CSF also contains the metabolic breakdown products of synaptic neurotransmitters, and some workers suggest a direct relationship between neurotransmitter activity in the brain and levels of metabolites in the CSF.

Lesions: physical destruction of brain tissue

The neurotoxin technique mentioned above is relatively recent. Until then, and still massively popular, a range of lesioning techniques dominated physiological psychology. Brain tissue has been damaged or removed by knife cuts, suction (especially the cerebral cortex in rats), injection of pure alcohol (the early frontal lobotomy of Moniz), focal (localized) cooling of specific sites, implantation of radio-active pellets, and most frequently, by electrolytic lesions. These latter involve thin wire electrodes implanted in the brain through which relatively high currents are passed. The heat generated by the current coagulates (electro-coagulation) the tissue in the immediate vicinity of the exposed tip of the electrode, effectively producing a small sphere of destruction.

A *lesion* usually refers to damage to a localized and small amount of brain tissue. An *ablation* – less common now as techniques and data focus upon smaller units of brain structure – refers more to the destruction or removal of whole brain regions, e.g. the cortex, hippocampus, etc. The very rare *lobotomy* refers to the physical destruction of a lobe of the cerebral hemisphere, while *leucotomy* refers to the cutting of pathways connecting various parts of the brain.

Recent developments in non-invasive procedures

An invasive procedure involves the penetration of the skull and brain for recording, lesioning, electrical and chemical stimulation, etc. It will, for practical and ethical reasons, often involve non-human animals.

Non-invasive procedures do not involve direct contact with brain tissue. Some, such as the electroencephalogram, have been used for many years. Others have only recently been introduced, and have led to a rapid increase in studies on the living brains of human subjects.

The *CAT scanner* (computed axial tomography) takes X-rays of the brain from many angles; a computer reconstructs these two-dimensional slices and then produces a three-dimensional overall view of the brain. Resolution (i.e. detail) is not yet high, so this technique is best for identifying large structures such as the ventricles, and for localizing large tumours and areas of haemorrhage, etc.

An even more recent technique is *nuclear magnetic resonance* (NMR) or, as it is increasingly known, *magnetic resonance imaging* (MRI). A powerful magnet is used to create a magnetic field around the head which aligns all the protons in the hydrogen atoms in neurons in the same orientation (it is apparently perfectly safe!). These are then bombarded with radio waves, and begin to resonate, producing radio waves of their own. These are recorded, computerized, and a three-dimensional picture of the brain emerges. The resolution and detail are on the whole better than with the CAT scanner.

Other techniques can be used to measure blood-flow to various brain regions (*cerebral angiography*), and techniques are becoming available to map out the distribution of neurotransmitter receptors in the living human subject. Doubtless progress will continue until we can measure detailed brain function during all aspects of behaviour. A fascinating illustrated review of these techniques can be found, surprisingly, in *National Geographic* magazine, January 1987.

The nervous system – organization and functions

Evolutionary considerations (see Figures 6.5 and 6.7)

Physiological psychology is primarily concerned with the advanced nervous system found in vertebrates – fish, amphibians, reptiles, birds, and mammals. This consists of a brain at the head of a spinal cord, with nerves distributed throughout the body. The vertebrate nervous system evolved from the *nerve-net* – a network of neurons and axons without any apparent organization, and able to handle only simple behavioural responses such as whole body contraction. This type of nervous system is found in primitive invertebrates such as the protozoan hydra, and is of interest to us only in that the elements – the neurons – function on exactly the same principles as those in our own brain, even down to the synaptic neurotransmitters involved.

A further stage in the evolution of the nervous system is reached with the insects and molluscs. Here we see some organization appearing. Neuronal cell bodies cluster together, and are surrounded by protective connective tissue to form *ganglia* (singular *ganglion*; in the brain, a protective coat is unnecessary, and such clusters are the *nuclei* referred to earlier). In addition the axons leaving the cell bodies in the ganglia to innervate (supply) the body tissues in part travel in bundles, again surrounded by a tough connective coat. Bundles of axons (occasionally dendrites) so bound together are called *nerves*; in higher vertebrates, the nerves travelling around the body will contain some hundreds of thousands of neuronal fibres.

In the ganglionic nervous system some regional organization is apparent, e.g. a head ganglion is usually identifiable. However, the internal structure of any one ganglion is comparable to that of any other, and the head ganglion of an insect is not directly comparable to the vertebrate brain (see Figure 6.5).

The evolutionary pressures leading to the development of a brain are discussed by Jerison (1973) in a stimulating book. He argues convincingly

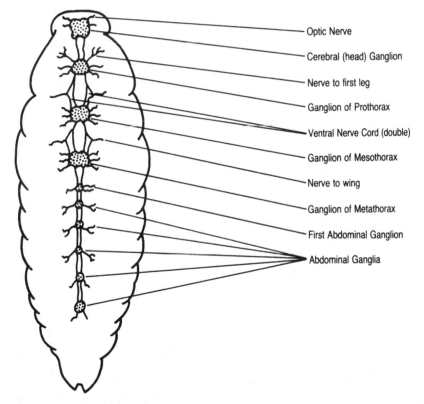

Optic Nerve

Cerebral (head) Ganglion

Nerve to first leg

Ganglion of Prothorax

Ventral Nerve Cord (double)

Ganglion of Mesothorax

Nerve to wing

Ganglion of Metathorax

First Abdominal Ganglion

Abdominal Ganglia

Figure 6.5 Dorsal view of the cockroach nervous system. Note the arrangement of ganglia throughout the body, connected by nerves. The cerebral ganglion is not equivalent to the vertebrate brain

that many of these pressures were sensory. It is still the case with present-day lower vertebrates that much of the nervous system is devoted to sensory and motor processes; analysing input from sensory receptors and producing motor responses (via control of skeletal muscles and internal response systems such as smooth muscle and glands). Even with mammals there is a high correlation between brain weight and body size – the larger the body, the greater the number of sensory receptors and response systems, and the larger the amount of neural tissue necessary to cope with them. Thus large animals have bigger brains than smaller animals.

As complex sensory systems such as eyes and ears (or their aquatic equivalent, the lateral line system, found in fish and amphibia and sensitive to changes in water pressure) evolved, and as these sophisticated receptors concentrated where they were most needed – the front or anterior end of the body which entered a new and possibly hostile environment first – the increase in neural tissue needed to process the vast increase in sensory input occurred close to the receptors, i.e. at the anterior end of the nervous system. Similarly, it can be argued (Jerison, 1973) that the significant increase in brain size in mammals as compared to reptiles occurred as a result of our 'mammal-like' reptilian ancestor occupying a nocturnal niche, where competition from the dominant but daylight-dependent large reptiles was minimal. Successful adaptation to a nocturnal habitat requires the development of sensitive olfactory (smell) and auditory systems to handle distant stimuli when vision is impossible; the neural tissue that evolved to cope with these senses contributed to the markedly larger brain, characteristic of mammals.

The brain has continued to evolve throughout the mammalian series. We (*Homo sapiens sapiens*) have a brain about three times as large as we would expect for a higher primate of our body size. However, there is nothing in its organization or in its detailed structure to distinguish it from other primates such as gibbons, chimpanzees, or monkeys; we have a large brain built on the primate pattern (Passingham, 1982; Walker, 1983).

Organization of the nervous system

The mammalian nervous system is, like the rest of the body, *bilaterally symmetrical*, i.e. if sliced through lengthways (the sagittal plane – see Figure 6.6), two identical mirror halves result. Vertebrates are also segmented organisms; although it is not immediately obvious, studies on the developing embryo show that we are fundamentally segmented in an analogous fashion to the earthworm, and in the adult one of the most obviously segmented systems is the nervous system. In the earthworm, the nervous system (Figure 6.7) is organized into a ventral nerve cord with paired nerves innervating (supplying) each segment. In vertebrates the nervous system consists of a brain at the head of a spinal cord, with paired

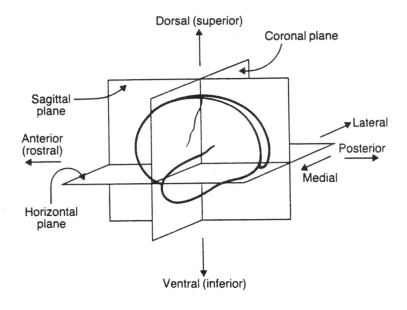

Figure 6.6   Planes of orientation in the brain

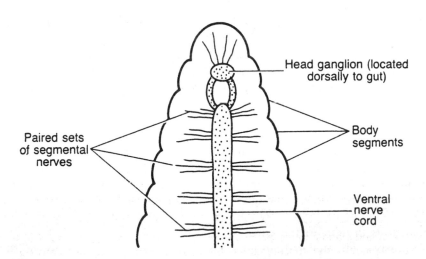

Figure 6.7   Outline of earthworm nervous system – anterior end of body. Compare segmental arrangement with vertebrate peripheral nervous system (Figure 6.8)

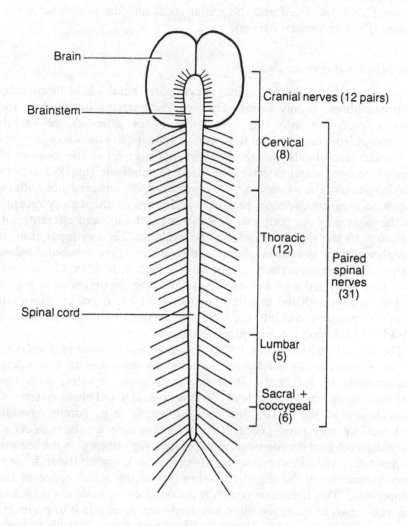

Brain

Brainstem

Spinal cord

Cranial nerves (12 pairs)

Cervical
(8)

Thoracic
(12)

Lumbar
(5)

Sacral +
coccygeal
(6)

Paired
spinal
nerves
(31)

Figure 6.8 Outline organization of vertebrate peripheral nervous system. Each spinal nerve contains thousands of neuronal fibres – motor axons of the autonomic nervous system, innervating the heart, smooth muscle of intestine and blood vessels, and glands; motor axons of the somatic nervous system travelling to skeletal muscle, and sensory fibres of the somatic nervous system carrying information from sensory receptors on the skin and in muscles and joints. The cranial nerves handle the sensory and motor functions of the head and anterior end of the body

spinal nerves leaving the cord to innervate the body. So an initial classification of the nervous system divides it into the *central nervous system* (CNS: the brain and the spinal cord) and the *peripheral nervous system* (PNS: the spinal nerves).

The peripheral nervous system

In primates, the 31 pairs of spinal nerves carry hundreds of thousands of neuronal fibres, mainly axons. They can be carrying information from sensory receptors into the CNS (*sensory* or *afferent*), or carrying commands from the CNS out to response systems, or effector organs, such as muscles and glands (*motor* or *efferent*) (Figure 6.8). The location and type of receptors and effectors are used to subdivide the PNS into two major systems. The *somatic nervous system* (SNS) includes those afferent pathways from touch, pain, pressure, and temperature sensory receptors on the surface of the body and in muscles and joints, and efferent motor pathways to the striped muscle of the skeleton. Sensory input from the complex sensory structures of the head (eyes, ears, the vestibular balance system of the inner ear) may also be seen as part of the SNS, whose overall role, in a simplified way, can be seen as allowing the organism to regulate its interactions with the external environment, i.e. it passes information from the outside world into the CNS and carries commands out from the CNS to skeletal muscle, providing movement.

The second division of the PNS, the *autonomic nervous system* (ANS), is, in a superficially analogous fashion, concerned with the internal environment of the body. It is a purely motor system, with fibres innervating the smooth muscle of the digestive tract and blood systems, the musculature of the heart, and various glands (e.g. adrenal medulla, pancreas, salivary glands, etc.). It is vital to *homeostasis*, the regulation of a constant internal invironment, as expressed, for instance, in the variation of heart-rate and blood-pressure in response to physical demands, in the smooth running of the digestive system, or in the maintenance of body temperature. This regulation is usually unconscious – you do not consciously ask your heart to speed up when you run – and to enable it to perform its functions the ANS has two branches. The fibres of the *sympathetic* branch tend to increase heart-rate and blood-flow to the skeletal muscles, open the respiratory passages, increase the release of adrenaline and noradrenaline from the adrenal gland, and in general prepare the animal for action: a state of peripheral or sympathetic arousal.

The fibres of the *parasympathetic* branch of the ANS innervate the same target organs as the sympathetic branch, but tend to have the opposite effects, i.e. slowing down heart-rate and blood-pressure, diverting blood to the digestive system, and in general calming things down and conserving energy. A dynamic balance is maintained between the two branches,

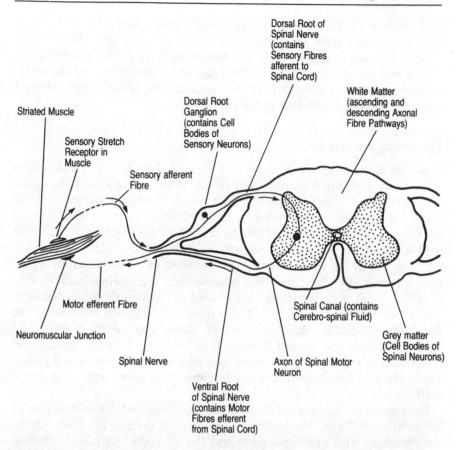

Dorsal Root of Spinal Nerve (contains Sensory Fibres afferent to Spinal Cord)

White Matter (ascending and descending Axonal Fibre Pathways)

Dorsal Root Ganglion (contains Cell Bodies of Sensory Neurons)

Striated Muscle

Sensory Stretch Receptor in Muscle

Sensory afferent Fibre

Motor efferent Fibre

Neuromuscular Junction

Spinal Nerve

Spinal Canal (contains Cerebro-spinal Fluid)

Grey matter (Cell Bodies of Spinal Neurons)

Axon of Spinal Motor Neuron

Ventral Root of Spinal Nerve (contains Motor Fibres efferent from Spinal Cord)

Figure 6.9 The spinal cord and the spinal reflex. The circuit from sensory receptor via afferent fibre to spinal cord, connecting with the spinal motor neuron travelling out via the spinal nerve to the striated muscle, is a local spinal circuit. Thus the knee-jerk reflex, for instance, can be produced in the patient otherwise paralysed by spinal cord damage. As the sensory pathways ascending to the brain are damaged, the patient would not feel the tap on the knee

shifting towards the one or the other in response to the body's demands, and moving back to equilibrium when the immediate demand has been coped with. We will deal with the ANS in relation to emotion and peripheral arousal later.

There is also a sensory system involved with the internal tissues. The *visceral afferent* network relays information from receptors in the smooth muscle of the gut and circulatory system to the CNS. Although not classified with the ANS, it can be seen as a less-developed sensory partner to the motor output of the ANS.

Apart from the somatic and autonomic nervous system fibres distributed via the spinal nerves, SNS and ANS fibres also make up the *cranial nerves* (see Figure 6.8). The twelve pairs of cranial nerves emerge from the brain stem rather than from the spinal cord, and supply the specialized senses (vision, hearing, balance, etc.) and musculature (e.g. those involved in speech and facial expression) of the head and anterior end of the body. Autonomic fibres, particularly in the vagus cranial nerve, supply visceral organs in the chest and abdominal cavities.

The central nervous system

The CNS is made up of the brain and the spinal cord. The spinal cord is continuous with the hindmost part of the brain, the *medulla*. In cross-section the cord is seen to consist of a central area of grey matter – the cell bodies of neurons – surrounded by areas of white matter – neural fibres coursing up and down the cord (Figure 6.9). A major function of the spinal cord is to connect the afferent and efferent fibres of the spinal nerves with the brain. Thus the white matter can be divided into various pathways, or tracts, named after the zones they interconnect: e.g. corticospinal (cortex to spinal cord), spinothalamic (spinal cord to thalamus), spinocerebellar (spinal cord to cerebellum), etc. These tracts carry specific information; of the three examples, the first conveys motor control of posture and fine movement, the second sensory input relating to pain, touch, and temperature, and the third sensory information from muscles and joints. There are also spinal-spinal tracts interconnecting zones within the spinal cord.

Damage to the spinal cord disrupts the ascending and descending flow of information. Clearly, the higher up the damage occurs, the more severe the outcome, with motor paralysis and loss of bodily sensation resulting from a complete high transection of the cord. However, even in cases of severe paraplegia (paralysis), some responses may still exist. As the cord is severely damaged, there is no voluntary muscular movement because the commands, formulated in the motor cortex of the brain, cannot reach the skeletal muscles via the spinal nerves; damage to neurons is usually permanent, although recent work on brain grafts and stimulation of axonal branching gives some hope of eventually repairing damaged pathways. But below the point of cord transection spinal nerves themselves are intact. Thus sensory information from, for example, stretch receptors in the knee joint is still transmitted into the spinal cord, and the final section of the pathway out from the cord via the spinal nerve to the muscles of the leg may still be functional. If the sensory input pathway has a direct connection to the motor outflow via spinal-spinal neurons, then a stimulus applied to the knee may still elicit the *knee jerk reflex*; obviously the subject is unaware of the stimulus, as the pathway ascending the spinal cord to the brain is broken. Even in intact subjects the knee jerk reflex is not subject to voluntary control, although they feel the stimulus. The difference is that

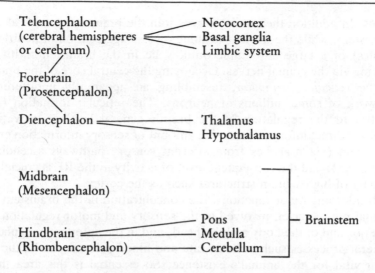

the intact subject can mimic the leg movement voluntarily, whereas the spinally damaged subject cannot (Figure 6.9).

Usually, autonomic regulation and, therefore, homeostasis in paraplegic patients is not badly affected – if it were, they would not survive. This is because a major component of the ANS leaves the CNS via the cranial nerves of the brainstem, within the skull, and is therefore unaffected by damage to the spine lower down.

The brain

The brain is the major concern of the physiological psychologist. In this section we give an overview of some of its major components and their role in behaviour, while the following chapter goes into more detail on selected topics.

The brain can be divided into some hundreds of separate structures, zones, nuclei (clusters of neuronal cell bodies), etc. Partly to simplify, and partly because data on the precise behavioural significance of many of them are lacking, the physiological psychologist usually deals with the major elements. A typical classification of the brain and its components is given opposite.

Hindbrain and midbrain

The *pons*, *medulla*, and *midbrain* make up the brainstem (which in some systems also includes the diencephalon). The medulla is a transition area between the spinal cord and the brain, and both pons and the midbrain also resemble the cord in containing large bundles of ascending and descending fibres. In addition the cranial nerves join the brain at intervals along the brainstem, while the nuclei (meaning a close aggregation of neuronal cell bodies) of a large autonomic outflow lie in the brainstem, with axons leaving via the cranial nerves. Occupying the central core of the brainstem is the *reticular formation*, resembling an apparently undifferentiated network of some millions of neurons. The reticular formation (RF) is central to the regulation of the brain's general level of activation. It receives direct information on the amount of sensory information entering the brain (via branches from afferent sensory pathways ascending the brainstem), and the consequent level of activity in the RF is crucial to the activity of higher brain structures such as the cortex.

Besides any other functions, the concentration in the brainstem of the cranial nerve nuclei, involved in the sensory and motor regulation of the anterior end of the body and the head, and in the autonomic regulation of visceral processes such as heart-rate and blood-pressure, make the brainstem vital for the animal's existence. So essential is this area that the concept of *brainstem death* is used by neurologists as an index of brain death. If various reflexes and responses indicative of brainstem function are absent, then the patient is defined as dead regardless of any residual spasmodic electrical activity higher up the brain. Experimental separation of the forebrain from the brainstem in animals has also been used to demonstrate the ability of the brainstem to regulate independently the body's vital functions within acceptable limits. In humans there is a rare condition called *anencephaly*, often associated with spina bifida, in which much of the forebrain fails to develop: the baby is severely impaired, but can still live as long as the brainstem regulatory centres are intact. So the brainstem can be seen as the site of 'essential' functions, even if many of them are not of interest to the psychologist.

The midbrain contains other structures of interest. The *superior* (above) and *inferior* (below) *colliculi* are concerned with eye movement control and with relaying auditory information onwards to the thalamus respectively. The *substantia nigra* is a large nucleus powerfully connected to the basal ganglia of the forebrain and concerned with motor functions. This would also be an appropriate time to emphasize that, in line with the vertebrate bilaterally symmetrical body, the brain is bilaterally symmetrical, and that any structure not actually in the midline therefore has a pair in the opposite (contralateral) half. So the colliculi and the substantia nigra are paired structures, along with virtually all the structures that go to make up the forebrain.

The *cerebellum* (Figure 6.10) is classified with the pons and medulla as the hindbrain, but has a distinctive appearance and structure that distinguishes it from the brainstem. After the neocortex, it is the largest brain structure in terms both of volume and the number of neurons. Indeed, some estimates (Blinkov and Glezer, 1968) give it as many

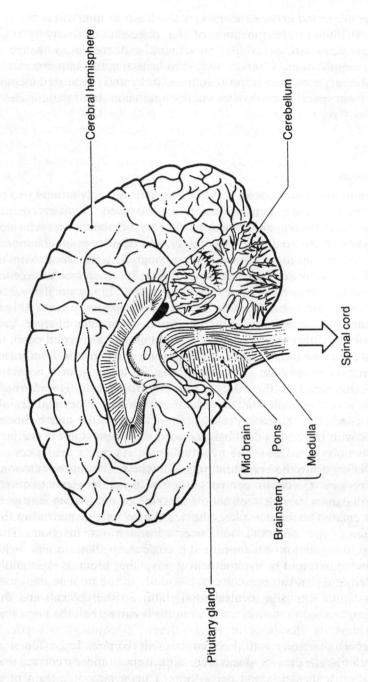

Figure 6.10 Midline (sagittal) section through the brain

Labels: Cerebral hemisphere, Cerebellum, Spinal cord, Medulla, Pons, Mid brain, Brainstem, Pituitary gland

neurons as are found in the neocortex, or even more, somewhere between 10 and 100 billion. The functions of the cerebellum principally relate to the co-ordination of bodily movement and the maintenance of (physical) equilibrium. Damage may produce tremor, impairments of skilled voluntary movements, unsteadiness, jerky unco-ordinated locomotion, and even speech disturbances via disrupted control of the muscles of larynx, pharynx, and lips.

Forebrain

Diencephalon

The *thalamus* and *hypothalamus*, although occupying only around two per cent of brain volume, between them are involved in many complex behavioural and physiological functions. The hypothalamus on each side is about the size of the tip of your little finger, and consists of some hundreds of thousands of neurons, i.e. a small number in comparison with the billions of neurons in cerebellum and neocortex. It is therefore an excellent example of the processing power of brain tissue. It lies on the ventral (lower) part of the brain, immediately above the *pituitary gland* (Figure 6.10) to which it is connected via the pituitary stalk or *infundibulum*. Via a combination of direct neural connections and chemicals carried down the infundibulum in the blood supply, the hypothalamus controls the secretion of the pituitary hormones. These hormones, including growth hormone, hormones to stimulate the adrenal and thyroid glands, *gonadotrophic* hormones which regulate the reproductive cycles in males and females via their control of hormone release from the gonads, and hormones concerned with the body's fluid balance such as vasopressin, are crucial to bodily function. In addition the hypothalamus, via direct neural connections travelling down the brainstem, regulates the activity of the autonomic nervous system. Given its control over the pituitary gland and ANS the hypothalamus can be seen as a higher-order controlling centre for functions related to homeostasis, the regulation of the body's internal environment. As we shall see later, through its involvement in physiological regulation, it is concerned in basic motivational drives such as hunger and thirst, and in the control of peripheral arousal, especially in states of emotion and stress.

The thalamus is a large structure lying above the hypothalamus. It is divided into around 17 distinct nuclei, but these can be classified into three major groups on the basis of their afferent (incoming) and efferent (outgoing) connections and their consequent role in brain functions. *Specific relay nuclei* project to and receive fibres from specific cortical areas concerned with sensation and perception. Thus a major function of the thalamus is to relay ascending sensory information on to the cortex, and it is notable that with the sole exception of olfaction (smell), all sensory

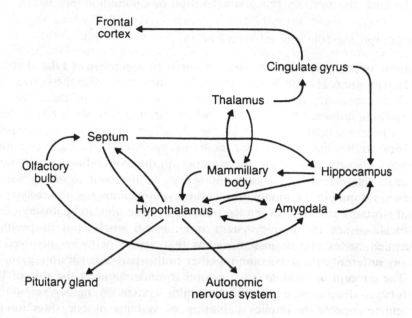

Figure 6.11 Some interconnections of the limbic system

systems project directly to the thalamus. This relaying is not a passive transfer across one synapse; a significant amount of sensory processing occurs in the thalamus, as we shall see in relation to the visual system.

Association nuclei project to and receive fibres from the association (i.e. non-sensory/motor) cortex. They do not receive inputs from the ascending sensory pathways, but are interconnected with other thalamic nuclei and receive some afferents from other subcortical structures. Their role in behaviour is as yet unclear, but is obviously related to the areas of association cortex they interconnect with; thus the dorso-medial nucleus may be involved in emotional and cognitive behaviours, such as memory, thought to be mediated by the cortex of the frontal lobe, with which it is reciprocally connected.

The *intralaminar* and *midline nuclei* of the thalamus are in evolutionary terms (phylogenetically) older than the rest. They receive inputs from brainstem regions, including the reticular formation, the cerebellum, and other subcortical structures. From the functional point of view, the most important projection system of these nuclei is a diffuse network of pathways innervating large areas of the cortex, i.e. a nonspecific system in comparison with the specific projections of the relay nuclei. The diffuse thalamo-cortical projection is thought to relay on to the cortex ascending impulses from the brainstem reticular formation, and therefore to mediate the cortical activation produced by reticular activation or stimulation (see later).

Telencephalon (the cerebral hemispheres)

Limbic system   The limbic system consists of a number of related structures (Figure 6.11). Each has substantial connections with the cortex and with diencephalic, midbrain, and hindbrain areas. They are therefore in a position to influence many types of behaviour, and their study has in some ways been the major concern of the physiological psychologist. Experimental studies have shown that the limbic system is involved in cognitive behaviours such as learning and memory, in the modulation of peripheral arousal as related to emotion and stress, in the control of aggressive behaviour, and in the modulation of the hypothalamus and all the systems that structure controls. Given the number of structures and pathways, it is difficult to see the limbic system as a unified whole, but its position between cortex and brainstem means that neural pathways involved in many different functions come together in this particular brain region.

The concept of *modulation* is crucial to understanding the role of the forebrain structures, especially the limbic system. A milder version of 'regulate', *modulate* implies a biasing of systems in one direction or another. Thus an amygdala lesion can produce placidity in monkeys, while septal lesions lead to a hyper-aggressive response. However, complete removal of the telecephalon does not prevent the production of integrated aggressive behaviour, i.e. the behaviour is organized at diencephalic and brainstem levels, but its appropriate display is modulated by higher brain centres.

Given their involvement in most aspects of behaviour, limbic system structures are referred to repeatedly in later sections. They illustrate one of the principles behind brain-behaviour relationships; although it is usual to consider one structure or one element of behaviour at a time, realistically no one structure is involved in only one behaviour, and no single behavioural component is the sole responsibility of any single structure. As an example, the *hippocampus* has been implicated in different aspects of memory, in behavioural inhibition, in emotional behaviour such as anxiety, and in feedback regulation of the hypothalamic-pituitary-gland system. Even though some of these hypotheses may be incorrect, there is no reason, given the processing power of a much smaller structure such as the hypothalamus, why the hippocampus should not be involved in many aspects of behaviour. Additionally, a cognitive process such as memorization is not a unitary process; there are sensory input pathways, brief sensory stores, short-term memory stores, long-term memory stores, and retrieval systems to enable recall and recognition. Obviously many brain structures will be involved in memory, and it is no surprise that a wide

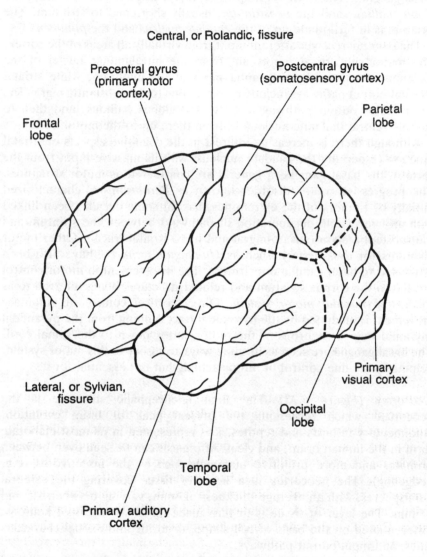

Figure 6.12 Side-view of brain, showing cortical infolding, lobes of the hemispheres, and primary sensory and motor areas

range of brainstem, limbic, and cortical manipulations have been shown to influence memorial processes.

Basal ganglia   These are a group of relatively large nuclei, including the *globus pallidus* and the *neostriatum*, usually shortened to striatum. The striatum is in turn made up of the *caudate nucleus* and the *putamen*.

The striatum receives afferent input from virtually all areas of the cortex. The major subcortical inputs are from the intralaminar nuclei of the thalamus and from the substantia nigra of the midbrain, while striatal efferent output pathways include a reverse one to the substantia nigra. The other major output pathway leads to the globus pallidus, and then to various ventral thalamic nuclei and from there on to the motor cortex.

Although there is increasing interest in the cognitive aspects of striatal function (especially the caudate nucleus, with its massive input from the cortex), the basal ganglia in general are considered as motor structures. The progressive motor disorder known as *Parkinsonism*, characterized initially by tremors of the extremities, has for some decades been linked with an irreversible degeneration of pathways between the striatum and the substantia nigra (striato-nigral and nigro-striatal tracts). Other motor disorders (or *dyskinesias*), such as *Huntington's chorea*, have also been attributed to basal ganglia impairment. The involvement in motor control has led to the corpus striatum and related structures being referred to as the *extrapyramidal motor system*. Direct cortical control of voluntary movement is mediated by the pyramidal tract running from the pyramidal (pyramid-shaped) neurons of the motor cortex down to the spinal cord. The basal ganglia are seen as in some ways accessory to this major system, helping in the fine control of motor activity but not essential for it.

Neocortex (Figure 6.12)   The final telencephalic structure is the neocortex, which represents the present peak of brain evolution. Rudimentary in birds and reptiles, it is represented in its most elaborate form in the human brain, and clear differences can be seen even between primates and more primitive mammals such as the insectivores (e.g. hedgehog). The neocortex is a layer of tissue covering the cerebral hemispheres, with an average thickness of 3mm, varying between 1.5 and 4.5mm. The layer of tissue is in turn made up of six layers of neurons, differentiated on the basis of cell shape, dendritic and axonal characteristics, and input/output pathways.

This six-layered arrangement seems fundamental to the neocortex, and therefore presents a logistical problem for brain evolution as the neocortex cannot increase its size by becoming thicker. It can only increase via an expansion of its surface area, and as it is attached to the cerebral hemispheres, this can happen only with an expansion of hemisphere surface area. However, this would imply an increase in brain volume, which has happened up to a point. Beyond that point, mechanical problems intervene: the brain is protected by the bony skull, which is supported by the skeleton and moved around by a sophisticated muscle system. As the skull enlarges, the support and movement demands become excessive. Therefore the brain has evolved an alternative method for increasing its surface area. The surface has *invaginated* ('infolded') upon itself, with deep clefts visible on the surface only as a patterning of lines (see Figure 6.12). This has the effect of increasing the surface area, and therefore neocortical area, without significant increases in brain volume. It also means that in the human brain only about a third of the two square metres of neocortex is visible on the surface, with the remainder buried in the clefts (*fissures* or *sulci*; singular *sulcus*). The visible surface neocortex between two fissures is known as a *gyrus* (plural *gyri*).

The patterning of fissuration on the mammalian brain is a crude index of evolutionary status; the most intensive infoldings are found in the higher primates and humans, while the surface of the rat brain is virtually smooth. Within a species the patterning is not consistent from one individual to the next, with only two major landmarks (the *central* or *Rolandic* fissure and the *lateral* or *Sylvian* fissure – see Figure 6.12) being readily identifiable.

The cerebral cortex contains around 15 billion (15×10^9) neurons, well over 90 per cent of all the neurons in the forebrain. Neuronal cell bodies appear grey under the light microscope, and the cortex is therefore accurately described as *grey matter*. A substantial part of the interior of the forebrain consists of axonal pathways interconnecting various structures, with nuclear masses such as the thalamus and limbic system distributed among them; the term *white matter* is given to these subcortical areas, taken from the microscopic appearance of densely packed axons.

The functions of the human cerebral cortex are in many ways the final frontier in physiological psychology, but although we tend to deal with structures in isolation, it is important to remember that the cortex is not independent of subcortical structures. It is not a layer mediating brand new functions superimposed on a phylogenetically older brain. The visual cortex is vital to the primate visual system, i.e. seeing. However, birds, reptiles, and fish, have perfectly efficient visual systems without the benefit of a visual cortex. Obviously the cortex enables more sophisticated cognitive functions to develop, but even with these the afferent pathways to the cortex and the efferent pathways transmitting the results of its deliberations can receive additional processing at subcortical way-stations.

Organization of the cerebral cortex   The cerebrum or telecephalon can be divided in various ways. First there is a left and a right cerebral hemisphere, and then each hemisphere can be divided into *lobes* (see Figure 6.12). These lobes are three-dimensional, consisting of the surface cortical layer and various subcortical pathways and structures. Thus the *temporal lobe* has buried within it the hippocampus and amygdala, while the basal ganglia lie more in the *frontal lobe*. The cortical surface of the hemispheres has, at various times throughout the last century, been subdivided in different ways. One of the more popular is the division by Brodmann (1909) into 47 distinct areas, differentiated by the precise type and arrangement of neurons within the six basic layers, i.e. not a functional but a neuroanatomical analysis.

A functional analysis of the cortex may be approached by dividing it into three types. *Primary sensory cortex* receives afferent inputs from the sensory relay nuclei of the thalamus, and is *modality*-specific, i.e. it deals only with one type of sensory input. So stimulation of the cells in the *primary visual cortex* of the occipital lobe evokes the sensation of light in awake subjects, and these same cells are activated by visual stimuli but not by sounds. Conversely stimulation of neurons in the *primary auditory cortex* of the temporal lobe (see Figure 6.12) evokes the sensation of sound, and they respond to auditory input but not to visual stimuli. Just behind the central fissure in the parietal lobe lies an area of cortex known from its location as the *post-central gyrus*. This is also a primary sensory region, responding to touch, pain, and pressure stimuli from the skin, muscles, and joints; from its association with the general body senses this region is known as *somaesthetic* or *somatosensory cortex*. Stimulation produces a sensation of numbness or tingling, and also reveals that the representation of the body on this area of the cortex is *topographic*, i.e. there is a point-for-point representation of the body surface in the somatosensory cortex. The representation is inverted, with feet and legs at the top and neck and face at the bottom. Parts more richly endowed with sensory receptors, such as the hands and face, take up proportionally more cortex.

These three major sensory zones are each surrounded by *secondary* cortical areas also dedicated to a given sensory modality (visual, auditory, somaesthetic), and in the cases of visual and auditory zones, by *tertiary* modality-specific areas. As we see later in relation to vision, primary, secondary, and tertiary sensory reception areas represent progressively more elaborate processing of sensory input, i.e. a transition between sensation and perception. While damage to primary reception cortex can produce complete loss of sensation (i.e. blindness, deafness, anaesthesia), damage to secondary and tertiary zones leads to higher-level loss, where physical sensation is retained but complex perceptual processes may be impaired.

Neurons in some other cortical areas also respond to sensory stimulation, but without discriminating between types, i.e. they are independent of the sensory modality, or *supramodal*. The best example of this type of cortex is the zone where parietal, occipital, and temporal lobes meet in the region of the *inferior parietal lobule*. These areas presumably integrate the products of sensory/perceptual processing from each of the modality-specific cortical zones, and would be crucial in the animal's 'world-view' and interactions with the environment.

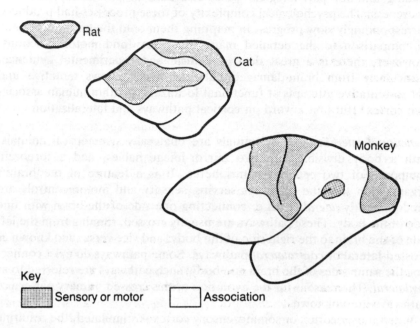

Figure 6.13 Comparative cortical functions across three mammalian brains

The *primary motor cortex* lies in the gyrus anterior to the central (Rolandic) fissure, the *pre-central gyrus* (see Figure 6.12). As with the post-central somatosensory cortex, representation is topographic, i.e. a point-for-point representation of the body on the cortical surface. Stimulation of the motor cortex results in isolated movements of individual muscles or muscle groups. Damage to this area produces paralysis, with a variable degree of recovery; the higher up the phylogenetic scale, the more severe and permanent the effects, with the cat being able to walk after ablation of the motor cortex, while primates, including humans, suffer permanent or semi-permanent paralysis.

Association cortex　In lower mammals most of the cortex is dedicated to the sensory and motor functions outlined above (Figure 6.13). Throughout mammalian evolution there is a trend towards an increase in the amount of non-sensory/motor cortex, and most of the cortical advantage seen in the human brain over primates lies in these zones. Assuming that the overall function of non-sensory/motor cortex is to mediate increasingly complicated interactions between sensory input and motor output (stimulus and response), it is given the generic name *association cortex*.

Most of the human cerebral cortex is association cortex. Within it lie controlling centres for higher cognitive functions such as speech and reading and for psychological constructs such as personality and self-awareness. The psychological complexity of these processes had produced correspondingly slow progress in mapping them onto the brain, especially in comparison to the detailed maps of sensory and motor functions. However, there is a great deal of clinical and experimental evidence, particularly from brain-damaged patients, which allows tentative and not-so-tentative attempts at functional localization within human association cortex. But first a word on cortical pathways and lateralization.

Functional lateralization   Mammals are bilaterally symmetrical animals, with a body divisible into two mirror-image halves, and a forebrain composed of two cerebral hemispheres. It is a feature of the brain's organization that the pathways serving sensory and motor controls are predominantly *lateralized*, i.e. connecting one side of the brain with one side of the body. These pathways are usually crossed, running from the left side of the brain to the right side of the body, and vice versa, and known as crossed-lateral or *contralateral* pathways. Some pathways do exist connecting the same sides of the brain and body; such pathways are referred to as *ipsilateral*. The reasons for the evolution of this crossed primary pattern of pathways are unknown.

When motor cortex or somatosensory cortex is stimulated, the resulting muscular activity or sensation occurs on the opposite side of the body. Damage to the motor cortex of the left hemisphere produces a *unilateral* (one-sided) right-sided motor paralysis, while damage to the somatosensory cortex of the right hemisphere would produce a left-sided anaesthesia. The auditory system is also predominantly lateralized, with signals entering the left ear being transmitted to the right hemisphere, while the right ear projects to the left hemisphere. However, functional ipsilateral auditory pathways do exist, and so unilateral damage to the temporal lobe primary auditory cortex leads to profound deafness in the contralateral ear and mild loss in the ipsilateral ear; complete deafness from cortical damage requires both auditory areas be affected, i.e. damage must be *bilateral* (both-sided). The visual system is the most complicated of our sensory systems, and is discussed in detail later. Briefly, the visual pathways leading from the retina of one eye to visual cortex are partially crossed. Half of the fibres are contralateral, and half ipsilateral. Thus the input to the visual cortex of one hemisphere consists of contralateral fibres from the eye on the opposite side of the body, and ipsilateral fibres from the eye on the same side, and severe damage restricted to one hemisphere produces a loss of half the visual field (field of view) in each eye (*hemianopia*).

Although ipsilateral, contralateral, and partially crossed pathways exist, the organization of sensory and motor systems is essentially symmetrical.

At the cortical level, left and right hemispheres are mirror images, and a description of sensory and motor representation applies equally well to both. However, this functional symmetry does not apply to association cortex, where we can find different effects of brain damage depending on the precise parts of the cerebral hemisphere involved and on the side to which the damage occurs. This functional asymmetry is discussed in detail later, and will be referred to in the following section.

Functions of association cortex   The cerebral hemispheres (telencephalon) are made up of neocortex and the subcortical structures of the basal ganglia and limbic system. They are divided into four *lobes*, the temporal, frontal, parietal and occipital (Figure 6.12). Each lobe therefore possesses a surface neocortical mantle plus subcortical structures and white matter. Damage to a lobe of the cerebral hemispheres via stroke, accident, trauma, etc., usually, therefore, involves tissue beyond the surface neocortex, and the behavioural effects of such damage may be difficult to localize precisely.

Although consisting mainly of visual sensory cortex, the tertiary visual areas of the *occipital lobe* can be regarded as association cortex where damage produces perceptual deficits which are independent of primary visual processes, such as sensitivity and acuity. These deficits are usually *agnosias* ('without knowledge'), a general term referring to perceptual loss. Thus damage to the left occipital lobe may produce *visual object agnosia*, an inability to recognize familiar objects or pictures, although they may be recognized by touch, i.e. it is a modality-specific impairment. Damage to the right occipital lobe tertiary zones may lead to *prosopagnosia*, an inability to recognize familiar faces, while damage to either side may produce *colour agnosia*, a failure to recognize colours even when discrimination is intact (i.e. a colour agnosic can tell that different colours are present), and *simultanagnosia*, an inability to handle more than one aspect of a stimulus at a time (e.g. given a picture of an elephant, the patient may list each feature and then realize what the whole thing is).

It is generally recognized that the *parietal lobe* is the most difficult to demarcate, especially in the postero-ventral areas where the occipital, temporal, and parietal lobes meet. The relevant parietal zones in this area include the *supramarginal* and *angular gyri* which represent zones for the integration of visual, auditory, and somatosensory information, i.e. they are supramodal, and damage to them has severe effects related to impairment in integrating sensory inputs.

Besides visual object agnosia and prospagnosia, these may include deficits in *cross-modal matching* (e.g. matching an object seen with the same object felt), *tactile agnosia* (inability to recognize objects through touch), and apraxia. Apraxia is an inability to perform purposive or skilled acts in the presence of intact sensory, motor, and intellectual functions.

Posterior parietal damage may produce *constructional apraxia*, where the patient cannot assemble the parts to make a whole, and left parietal damage *ideomotor apraxia*, where the patient cannot follow instructions but may perform the task spontaneously. Drawing ability is often severely impaired.

Another range of behavioural disabilities produced by parietal injury involves the subject's relationships with the surrounding space. The most extreme example is the *unilateral neglect* seen after parietal lesions; this, as its name implies, involves an apparent unawareness of the space to one side of the patient, opposite to the side of damage (i.e. a contralateral neglect), and is much more common after right-sided damage. The patient may draw only one side of a clock (with all the numbers crowded together), dress only one side of his body, and (if male) shave only one half of his face. Often they deny that any disability exists (*anosognosia*). Right–left confusion is also found, more commonly after left parietal injury, often associated with disorders of the body scheme such as *finger agnosia*, where patients seem unaware of their own fingers.

These symptoms of parietal lobe injury are not mutually exclusive, and neuropsychological diagnosis is often a case of probabilities and over-lapping categories. Many of the symptoms seem to involve the patients' ability to represent internally external space and their relationships with it, a function which involves integrating across sensory modalities and for which the parietal lobe is ideally placed.

The neocortex covering the *temporal lobe* contains primary, secondary and tertiary auditory projection areas, and damage to the second and tertiary areas produces high-level perceptual disturbances in hearing. Left-sided involvement produces problems in language comprehension, while right-sided damage may lead to *auditory agnosia* – a failure to recognize common non-verbal sounds.

Besides its major role in auditory processes, especially as related to the perception of speech, the temporal lobe also contains within it deeper-lying structures belonging to the limbic system. These structures, notably the hippocampus and the amygdala, are involved in cognitive and affective (emotional) functions. When they are damaged, either by accidental penetrating damage to the brain, subcortical trauma such as haemorrhage, tumour, or infection, or by surgical intervention in cases of temporal lobe epilepsy (see later), the consequences can be severe. Unilateral hippocampal damage can lead to memory impairment (specific to verbal material if left-sided, non-verbal if right-sided), while bilateral involvement produces severe *global anterograde amnesia*. Amygdala damage can, at least in non-human animals, lead to significant changes in emotional behaviour, particularly aggression.

The neocortical and subcortical components of the *frontal lobes* make up about a third of the cerebral hemisphere. The frontal lobes contain the largest amount of association cortex in the brain and consequently have been and remain a stimulating problem for the neuropsychologist. To distinguish them from frontal motor cortex, frontal association areas are usually referred to as *prefrontal cortex*.

Prefrontal cortex is directly connected to most other forebrain regions and structures. There are reciprocal connections with the sensory regions of parietal, occipital, and temporal cortex on the same side. Afferent ('to' the prefrontal cortex) pathways include a contribution from the non-specific thalamo-cortical radiation, connections with limbic system structures such as the amygdala, and ascending pathways from basal ganglia structures such as the substantia nigra. Efferent ('from' the prefrontal cortex) pathways link the prefrontal cortex with the thalamic nuclei, the caudate nucleus of the basal ganglia, amygdala, hypothalamus, and midbrain and brainstem regions.

This extensive and often two-way pattern of connections between prefrontal cortex and the rest of the brain implies that it will be involved in most aspects of behaviour, from perception through complex information processing to motor output. Despite this wide range of potential effects, damage to the frontal lobes has been observed, over the years, to produce behavioural changes consistent enough to be referred to as the *frontal lobe syndrome*.

Evidence comes traditionally from two major areas: injury through accident or disease (beginning with the classic case of Phineas Gage, a railway worker whose frontal lobes were effectively obliterated when, in 1848, a tamping iron was blown through them), and from the use of psychosurgical treatment for psychiatric disorders. The *frontal lobotomy*, or *prefrontal leucotomy*, is discussed later.

It was pointed out earlier that severe damage to the forebrain need not be fatal, and, in the case of prefrontal cortex, may produce significant but surprisingly mild changes in personality and behaviour. The frontal lobe syndrome has several components (reviewed in detail in Walsh, 1978). There is a loss of initiative and a diminution of abstract and creative thought. There is some loss of social inhibition, leading to irreverent and profane behaviour, coupled with a decrease in general anxiety and concern for the future. Although impulsivity is increased there is a profound loss of the ability to plan ahead, to organize behaviour across time and space to fulfil goals and intentions. In its place may be a tendency to perseverate in a given task, i.e. to fail to shift from an unsuccessful to a successful strategy, or to move on to the next component of a sequential problem. On a more general level the patient may vacillate between several action plans, never following one through to fruition.

Using recent techniques of PET scans and blood-flow studies, attempts have been made to localize functionally distinct zones within prefrontal cortex. Given its extensive connections, it is no surprise that Roland (1984)

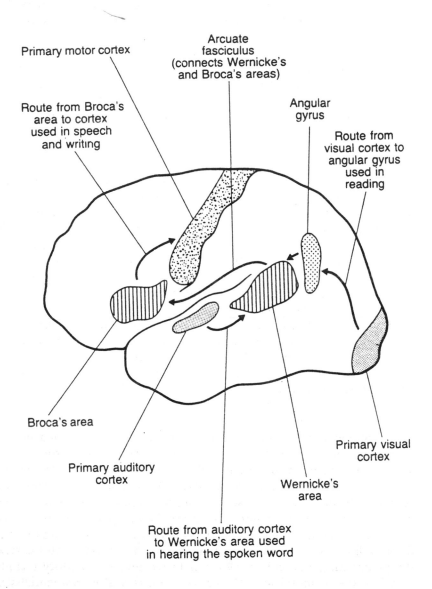

Figure 6.14 Components of the left hemisphere language system. Note how separation of the angular gyrus/visual cortex system from Wernicke's area prevents reading but leaves speech and writing intact, while damage to the arcuate fasciculus leaves language comprehension and production systems intact but desynchronized

should identify 17 such zones, although I, for one, find his general conclusion easier to grasp: 'in man one or more prefrontal areas participate in *any* structured treatment of information by the brain in the awake state' (my italics).

Language and the brain   We have mentioned previously how, in some cases, the behavioural effects of brain damage depend upon which side of the brain is affected. The clearest evidence for *hemisphere asymmetries of function*, or, to put it another way, functional lateralization in the brain, comes from the studies of language.

In the early years of the nineteenth century, several neurologists studied patients with unilateral brain damage and suggested a consistent association between left hemisphere damage and disorders of language (*aphasias* – involving speech production, speech perception, reading, and writing). Building on this work and using his own studies Paul Broca presented in the 1860s a hypothesis that an area in the posterior and ventral zone of the frontal lobe of the left hemisphere (now referred to as *Broca's area*) was the site of damage which led to speech problems. Carl Wernicke elaborated the model in the 1870s when he identified a region in the temporal lobe which, when damaged, again produced language difficulties: this area is now known as *Wernicke's area*.

The two syndromes were qualitatively distinct. Injury to Broca's area produced a severe impairment of expressive speech, while speech comprehension (e.g. following verbal commands) could be more or less intact. Damage to Wernicke's area produced a loss of speech comprehension, while speech production could be fluent, though confused, as patients could not monitor what they were saying.

Wernicke suggested that sound images of words and objects were stored in the temporal lobe, and transmitted to Broca's area which held the representations of speech movement. Loss of Wernicke's area preserved speech movements in the absence of speech comprehension (*Wernicke's, receptive*, or *fluent aphasia*), while loss of Broca's area preserved speech comprehension in the absence of fluent speech production (*Broca's, expressive, non-fluent*, or *motor aphasia*). The emphasis on Broca's area and speech production and on Wernicke's area and speech comprehension fits in well with the proximity of the former to the primary motor cortex of the precentral gyrus and of the latter to the primary auditory reception cortex in the temporal lobe (Figure 6.14). It should be emphasized that primary motor cortex is crucial to all motor activity including speech, and similarly auditory cortex is essential to the reception and analysis of all sounds, including speech. Damage to either will obviously affect speech production and comprehension, although specific deficits will usually be lost in the general patterns of motor paralysis and deafness respectively. Aphasias are, like other disruptions linked with the functions of association cortex, defined as occurring in the presence of intact sensory and motor processes.

Given the simple basic model of two major language centres in the left hemisphere, other forms of aphasia could be predicted, observed, and explained. Destruction of both Broca's and Wernicke's area results in a loss of both speech production and speech comprehension, termed *global aphasia*. Damage to the pathway connecting the two centres (the *arcuate fasciculus*) leaves both production and comprehension intact, but out of synchrony. Speech is fluent and spontaneous, while comprehension of speech and the written word is good, but the two are disconnected. This is seen best in the failure of the patient to repeat aloud a passage spoken to him; normally speech comes into the temporal lobe auditory reception area, is interpreted in and around Wernicke's area, and for repetition, passed immediately through the arcuate fasciculus to Broca's area where the motor output (speech) is prepared. Without the arcuate fasciculus, this cannot happen. The syndrome as a whole is termed *conduction aphasia*, and is one of a number of *disconnection syndromes*, so called as they appear to represent a separation of intact functions normally interconnected and co-ordinated (see Figure 6.14).

The other major area of language investigated has been reading. Disorders of reading are *dyslexias*, while total loss is *alexia*. Crucial to, for instance, reading aloud, is the conversion of the visual input to the internal linguistic code which is then conveyed to Broca's area where the motor response – reading aloud – is organized. Therefore damage to pathways connecting the occipital lobe visual reception areas to visual conversion centres in the *angular gyrus* of the parietal lobe can affect reading while leaving visual perception otherwise intact. As the angular gyrus is unaffected and still connected to Broca's area in the frontal lobe, writing is fluent. This can produce the bizarre syndrome of a patient who can write a page of coherent prose but cannot read it back, and is known as *pure alexia* or alexia without *agraphia* (loss of writing ability). We have two occipital lobes, and although the right hemisphere normally lacks language centres (for variations on the 'left hemisphere language' plan, see later), the right visual cortex is connected to the left hemisphere angular gyrus via fibres travelling across the brain in the corpus callosum. So, even in the presence of left visual cortex damage, reading can still be handled by eye movements which allow the words to be transmitted to the right visual cortex and then via the corpus callosum to the left hemisphere language centres. Pure alexia therefore normally requires two lesions to separate the angular gyrus from the visual cortex of both hemispheres – one in the occipital lobe, and one in that part of the corpus callosum carrying information from the right visual cortex to the left angular gyrus, known as the *splenium*.

As both these areas are supplied by the left posterior cerebral artery, haemorrhage or stroke involving this vessel could produce the necessary damage and a number of cases are known. Less common is brain damage that eliminates the angular gyrus – either directly, or by severing the pathways connecting it to other brain regions. The effects of such damage are severe. The angular gyrus appears to be crucial as a store of the internal representations of words that are essential for reading and for writing, and its loss results in a syndrome of alexia *with* agraphia – the inability to read and write.

This has been a simplified description of the role of Wernicke's and Broca's areas in aphasias and the role of the visual cortex and the angular gyrus in dyslexias and agraphias. The neuropsychology of language is a large and rapidly expanding field, and many of the old assumptions have been questioned.

The functional localization approach itself is probably an over-simplification. It appears, for instance, using the modern techniques outlined earlier, that damage to Broca's area is not essential for the syndrome of Broca's aphasia, but crucial is damage extending to both prefrontal cortex and to the basal ganglia. A more general problem is that these syndromes hardly ever occur in their 'pure' form; classification is a matter of which symptoms predominate in the clinical picture.

It may be that the various subprocesses involved in language are perfectly localized, but that brain damage invariably affects several functional areas and consequently produces mixed aphasias or dyslexias. Alternatively, given the processing power of even small units of neural tissue, it may be that no cognitive functions are perfectly localized, and that the gross division of impairments into exclusive categories is unjustified. This is the approach taken by Ojemann (1983), who, on the basis of experiments studying the effects of electrical stimulation of the brain on language functions, suggests that a division into an anterior speech production zone (Broca's) and a posterior speech comprehension zone (Wernicke's) is not supported by the evidence. Effects on production and comprehension were found equally in anterior and posterior cortical areas.

The neuropsychology of language is thus in a dynamic phase. What is undoubted is the contribution of the psychological analysis of brain-damaged patients to the cognitive modelling of normal language functions. This area is considered in detail in volumes such as that by Harris and Coltheart (1986).

Finally, it should be remembered that the commonest language disorder – development dyslexia in children – occurs in the absence of gross organic damage, and almost certainly represents a high-level problem in the organization of functions within and across hemispheres.

Chapter seven

Physiological studies II

Simon Green

Sensory systems

The world that we are aware of is a construction of our central nervous system. The building blocks are nerve impulses, travelling into the CNS along sensory pathways, produced by the various stimuli which surround us. Therefore, the only stimuli which we can be aware of are those which produce neural activity – action potentials or nerve impulses – in those sensory pathways.

The stimuli in the environment around us exist in various forms. Vision depends upon electro-magnetic radiation from the object, hearing relies upon mechanical pressure waves transmitted via the molecules in the air, touch is direct mechanical pressure on the skin, while taste and smell represent information coded as chemical structure. The crucial stage leading to our being able to sense and perceive these stimuli is the conversion of the various forms of energy into a neural code; i.e. whatever the stimulus, it is eventually coded as trains of nerve impulses travelling along sensory nerve fibres.

The conversion of stimulus energy into a neural code is known as *transduction*, and involves *sensory receptors*. These range in complexity from the highly specialized visual and auditory receptor cells found in the eye and ear, to the free nerve endings found in the skin which, even though barely modified from straightforward axons, are sensitive to painful stimuli and to heat and cold. Whatever their nature, the purpose of sensory receptors is to react to an appropriate stimulus by triggering action potentials in sensory afferent neurons.

With each of our senses, or *modalities*, we respond to (or are aware of) a range of stimuli; we see bright and dark objects, hear high-pitched and low-pitched sounds, taste sweet and sour foods. The range we respond to represents only a portion of the available range, and for every sensory modality we could find another species with a different battery of sensory receptors and which therefore responded to a different range of stimuli.

Our sensory systems may be readily divided into five traditional modalities – vision, hearing, touch, smell, taste – plus pain and *proprioception*, which concerns the awareness of bodily movement and position in space. They may be further classified into functional groups: e.g. *exteroceptive* senses, covering those modalities dealing with the outside world such as vision, hearing, touch, and smell; *proprioceptive* senses as above; and *interoceptive* senses, covering those sensory receptors handling information from internal structures, such as pressure receptors and glucose receptors in the walls of blood vessels. However, the most straightforward approach is to consider the various sensory modalities one by one. We shall outline the organization of sensory systems dealing with touch, taste, and smell, cover pain and hearing in more detail, and then discuss the visual system at length.

Touch

The sensation of touch comes in various forms, all involving stimulus contact with a variety of touch receptors in the skin. The sensations include light and heavy touch pressure, tickling and movements of a stimulus across the skin, cold and warmth, and pain. Categories overlap – a cold stimulus applied with heavy pressure can result in pain.

The receptors involved (*mechanoreceptors*, as they respond to mechanical or physical contact) number some hundreds in every square millimetre of skin surface although some regions are relatively well-endowed (e.g. the fingertips) and others relatively insensitive (e.g. the heel). There are several receptor *subtypes*. The most basic are the free nerve endings mentioned earlier, responding particularly to cold, warmth, and painful stimuli. Modified hair follicles respond to movement of hairs on the body surface, while *Meissner corpuscles* and *Pacinian corpuscles* are particularly sensitive to a stimulus moving across the skin and to a vibratory stimulus respectively. *Krause end-bulbs* and *Ruffini* endings are also found, although their specific functions are unclear. In fact the whole question of receptor specificity is unsettled, as there is some evidence that the whole range of touch sensations can be produced from areas of the body supplied only by nerve endings.

What is certain is that afferent sensory impulses from touch receptors on the body surface travel along sensory fibres in the spinal nerves to the spinal cord. After synapsing in the spinal cord grey matter, tactile information (i.e. not thermal or pain information) ascends the spinal cord, entering the hindbrain as a pathway which crosses sides and travels to the thalamus. After synapsing in the thalamus, this *somatosensory* pathway projects to the somatosensory cortex in the parietal lobe.

Throughout the somatosensory system, organization is *somatotopic*, i.e. point-for-point mapping of the bodily surface onto the somatosensory cortical surface.

Proprioception

This aspect of sensation covers body and limb movement and awareness of position in space. The relevant receptors include several of the touch mechanoreceptors already mentioned, located in and around limb joints. Awareness of limb movement (*kinaesthesia*) also involves receptors located on muscle fibres sensitive to muscle stretch. Proprioceptive sensory input enters the central nervous system along the somatosensory touch pathway, via the spinal cord, medial lemniscus, thalamus, and finally the post-central somatosensory cortex.

A vital contribution to proprioception is made by the *vestibular apparatus*, located in the inner ear. This organ is crucial to the sense of balance. In outline terms it consists of three *semicircular canals*. These structures are continuous with each other, but arranged in space so as to cover all possible orientations – the semicircular canals lie perpendicular to each other. The whole arrangement is fluid-filled, and the displacement of the fluid, produced by movement of the head in any direction, is picked up by specialized *hair cell* receptors and converted into afferent sensory impulses along the eighth cranial nerve. After a synapse in the brainstem, information travels to parts of the cerebellum, which are in turn connected to eye muscles and descending motor pathways to the spinal cord. The system controls body balance and the co-ordination of head and body movement.

Taste

The sensation of taste depends upon a molecular combination between the substance and a taste receptor. The receptors themselves are modified skin cells and occur in groups of around 50 on a taste bud. The taste buds are found clustered in small numbers in *papillae*, folds in the surface of the tongue.

Experiments on the subjective experience of taste suggest the existence of four primary taste qualities: bitter (e.g. quinine), sour (e.g. dilute acids), salt (e.g. sodium chloride), and sweet (e.g. glucose). However, although different taste buds may respond maximally to different primary tastes (e.g. bitter tastes are better sensed at the back of the tongue), it does not appear that there are four specific taste receptors corresponding to the four tastes. Rather, single receptors may respond more to one of them than others, but will still respond in some way to all. Activity in an afferent fibre will then represent a graded response across the population of taste receptors innervated by the fibre, and the final taste 'experience' will represent the pattern of activity across all sensory fibres. This would account for the fact that some tastes do not appear to represent one of the four primary qualities, or even a combination of them, and may, in fact, be literally indescribable.

Sensory fibres carrying information about taste travel via the cranial nerves to the medulla of the hindbrain, and thence to a relay in the thalamus and on to the cortex. The cortical representation of taste is in the post-central somatosensory cortex, just below and in front of the zone dealing with touch information from the tongue. The taste, or gustatory, pathway sends inputs to limbic and hypothalamic regions, which would be concerned with memory and emotional and motivational aspects of food taste.

Olfaction

The olfactory receptors lie in the *olfactory mucosa* at the back of the nasal air passages. These are effectively the endings of bipolar neurons (i.e. neurons with two long processes or axons), with the other long process extending centrally and making up the *olfactory nerve*.

Molecules representing the olfactory stimulus dissolve in the mucosal lining, bind to the receptor molecule and generate action potentials in similar fashion to the mechanism of taste sensation. The analogy is continued in the suggestion that seven primary olfactory qualities (smells) exist: ethereal (like ether), camphoraceous, musky, pungent, putrid, pepperminty, floral. However, evidence for highly specific receptors attuned to one or other category of smell is weak, and it appears that, as with taste, receptors will respond in some way to all smells. The smell finally perceived would then represent the pattern of activity across all olfactory sensory fibres.

Pain (nociception)

Pain pathways were outlined in the section on touch, but as this is an area in which major discoveries have occurred over the last decade, we shall present a little more detail of how pain pathways are thought to operate.

All pain receptors are free nerve endings, while painful stimuli can be mechanical, thermal, or chemical. Information representing 'pain' can travel via the spinal nerves to the spinal cord over one of two routes. The first uses axons covered with a fatty *myelin* sheath, while the other uses unmyelinated axons. The significance of the myelin sheath is that its presence enables nerve impulses to be transmitted much more rapidly along the axon; so the myelinated and unmyelinated pathways can be seen as representing 'fast pain' and 'slow pain' respectively. The actual conduction velocities are around 25 metres/second as against 0.5 metre/second, i.e. a transmission time difference of two seconds or more for stimuli travelling from hand or foot to the spinal cord, so explaining the experience of an initial sharp pain often followed by a duller and long-lasting pain from the same stimulus event, e.g. putting your big toe in a hot bath.

Pain fibres synapse in the spinal cord, probably releasing the recently discovered neurotransmitter *Substance P*. Information is then transmitted up to the brainstem and thalamus via spinal pathways. Many fibres synapse in the brainstem, other fibres pass directly to the thalamus, from where they are projected on to the somatosensory cortex.

The precise role of these various brain regions in pain perception is as yet unclear. Lesions and electrical stimulation of thalamic and midbrain sites have been shown to be effective in either producing the experience of pain or reducing it; indeed thalamic lesions are still sometimes used to reduce chronic pain in human patients. In addition, the potent *analgesic* ('pain-reducer') morphine is now known to act at specific receptors found particularly in midbrain regions. These *opiate* (named after the family of drugs from which morphine comes) receptors are stimulated, in the normally functioning brain, by the naturally occurring (*endogenous*) opiate *enkephalin*. It is assumed that enkephalin acts on opiate receptors to produce a powerful analgesic effect.

Substantial descending pathways exist between midbrain and hindbrain structures and the spinal cord which are almost certainly involved in

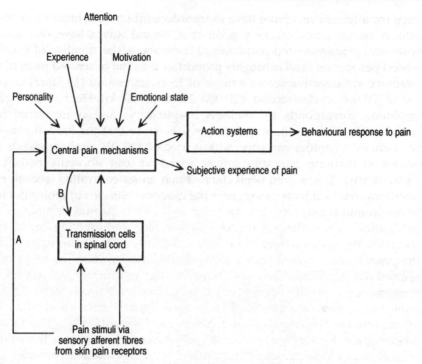

Figure 7.1 Pain pathways. Pain stimuli are transmitted via transmission neurons (T cells) in the spinal cord to the central pain mechanisms in midbrain and hindbrain. Besides this main pathway, these mechanisms also receive a faster input from pain stimuli (pathway A) which enables them to exert *feedback regulation* of the T cells (pathway B), making us more or less sensitive to pain stimuli. This feedback control is also influenced by a range of cognitive, emotional, and motivational inputs from higher brain centres. These factors can in addition affect our individual response to pain and our subjective experience

Source: Melzack and Wall, 1988

controlling our experience of pain. These descending pathways are probably involved in the cognitive and emotional modification of pain perception (Figure 7.1).

Hearing

The sensory receptors of the auditory system, buried deep in the inner ear, are mechanoreceptors. The stimuli, the sounds around us, exist as vibrations of molecules in the air which travel from the source to the ear as sound pressure waves, at around 1,000 feet/second. When the wave of molecular vibration arrives at the ear, it exerts a pattern of fluctuating pressure which corresponds to the original sound. It is this pressure pattern which the auditory receptors have to transduce into neural impulses in the auditory nerve. They are very good at it. Sound waves have two basic properties, *frequency* and *amplitude*. Frequency is the number of cycles (waves) per second, and is roughly proportional to the perceived pitch of a sound; we are sensitive across a range of 15 cycles/second (15 Herz) up to around 20,000 cycles/second (20,000 Herz or 20 kiloHerz – 20kHz). Amplitude corresponds to loudness or intensity, and is measured in *decibels* (dB). The loudness scale is logarithmic, so that the loudest sound the auditory receptors can cope with is around 120 dB, and represents a millionfold increase over the softest sound we can normally perceive (under 10 dB). It has even been claimed that under controlled laboratory conditions some subjects can register the random collisions of molecules in the air around them!

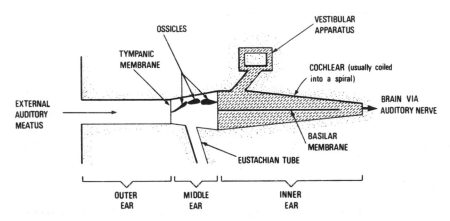

Figure 7.2 Diagrammatic representation of the human ear

The human ear is divided into outer, middle and inner sections (see Figure 7.2). The auditory canal acts as a resonator, collecting and guiding pressure waves to the *tympanic membrane*, or eardrum. Vibrations of the tympanic membrane are transmitted across the air-filled middle ear via the middle ear *ossicles*, three small bones (malleus, incus, stapes) which act as levers to increase the effective intensity of the tympanic membrane vibrations. The vibrations, representing the sound stimulus, eventually reach the oval window in the membrane separating middle ear from inner ear; movement of the oval window then produces correlated vibrations in the fluid-filled inner ear.

The inner ear includes the *vestibular apparatus*, and the *cochlea*, a spiralled structure containing the auditory sensory transduction apparatus. In between two compartments of the cochlea lies the *basilar membrane*, on which are around 25,000 *hair cell* receptors. Vibrations in the fluid-filled inner ear produce oscillations of the basilar membrane and associated movement of the hair cells. Movement of the hair cells leads to action potentials in the fibres of the auditory nerve to which they are directly connected, and so travelling sound waves in the auditory canal are finally transduced into neural signals.

Auditory pathways from each ear project to both hemispheres, providing extensive *bilateral* representation of auditory input in the central nervous system. Deafness after cortical damage requires a substantial bilateral destruction of tissue. However, despite this bilateral arrangement, it is accepted that the contralateral pathway is functionally dominant, with left ear input being preferentially processed by the right hemisphere and the right ear input by the left hemisphere. This is crucial for the rationale behind and the understanding of dichotic listening experiments, discussed later.

Vision

The visual system is the most complicated of our senses, as befits the sensory modality that we are most reliant on. A crude index of this complexity is the size of the optic nerves, each of which contains around one million nerve fibres, compared with the 30,000 or so in each of the auditory nerves.

Despite the daunting complexity, the visual pathways have been sufficiently studied, anatomically and functionally, to allow us to present a reasonably clear account of the early stages of visual perception.

Retina and optic pathways

The visual sensory receptors are contained in the multi-layered *retina* covering the rear two-thirds of the eye (the retina, incidentally, is derived during development from the same embryological cells as the nervous system, and can be seen as a true outgrowth of the brain rather than a separate peripheral tissue). Light energy from the environment, in the form of electromagnetic waves composed of photons, passes through the *cornea* and *pupil*, and is focused by the lens onto the retina. The retina is also unusual in that the receptor layer, containing the photosensitive elements, lies beneath the other cell layers making up the retina (see Figure 7.3); this means that the axons which eventually combine together to form the optic nerve travel across the retinal surface before passing

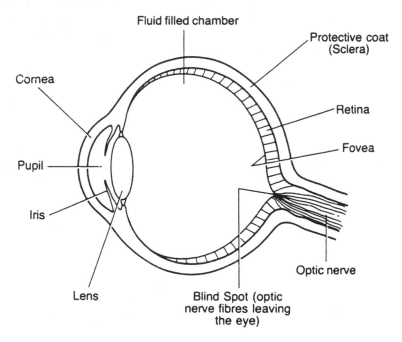

Fluid filled chamber

Protective coat
(Sclera)

Cornea

Retina

Fovea

Pupil

Iris

Optic nerve

Lens

Blind Spot (optic
nerve fibres leaving
the eye)

Figure 7.3 The eye

through the back of the eye at the retinal *blind spot* (so called as it cannot contain visual receptors and therefore cannot respond to light stimulation).

There are two types of visual receptor cells: *rods* and *cones*. Rods are specialized for vision in dim light, and cones for high acuity (resolution) and colour vision, which require more intense light. Although there are 120–130 million rods and only 5–10 million cones in the primate eye, the cones are concentrated in the *fovea*, that part of the retina which represents the centre of the visual field. As we move across the retina, relatively fewer cones and more rods are found with a consequent loss of acuity and colour vision. So, with eyes fixed straight ahead, we can see most clearly the centre of the visual field in front of us, with a progressive loss of detail towards the edges as the cones become less frequent. As we shall see, rods are inoperative in daylight.

Both types of visual receptor cell transduce light energy into action potentials in the same way. Rods and cones contain molecules made up of *retinal* (a form of Vitamin A) in combination with an *opsin*. Absorption of photons of light energy produces a change in the structure of retinal and a subsequent split in the retinal–opsin bond; the rupturing of this bond stimulates changes in the cell membrane of rods and cones, which eventually lead to the generation of action potentials.

Functional differences in the receptors are related to the different opsins found in them. The whole retinal–opsin molecule in rods is known as *rhodopsin*. To allow for vision in dim light, rhodopsin is higly sensitive to light, and in daylight it is permanently broken down into retinal and opsin, and therefore non-functional. When passing from bright into dim light, the period of adjustment we all experience represents the resynthesis of rhodopsin in the rods, upon which our night vision, such as it is, depends.

Each cone contains retinal in combination with one of three different cone opsins. The cone opsins make these receptors much less sensitive to light as such, but give them the ability to mediate high resolution of detail and colour in the visual world. In addition, the spectrum of colours we are able to perceive is based on the presence of three different opsins, i.e. the

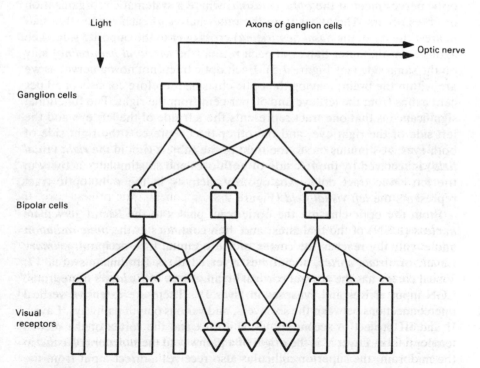

Figure 7.4 Cell layers of mammalian retina. (Note convergence of many receptors on to few ganglion cells, and overlap of connections.)

range of colours we are aware of is produced by different patterns of light stimulation across the three types of cone receptor.

Action potentials generated in the rods and cones are eventually reflected in nerve impulses travelling along optic nerve fibres. However, the relationship is not simple, as around 130 million receptors must converge onto one million optic nerve fibres. This convergence is mediated by specialized neurons in the other retinal layers (see Figure 7.4), and is not a simple channelling process. Rods and cones are directly connected to *bipolar cells*, which in turn connect with *ganglion cells*; the axons on ganglion cells constitute the *optic nerve*. Obviously many receptors contact the same bipolar cell, although a single receptor may interact with more than one bipolar cell. In addition, if the receptor → bipolar cell → ganglion cell is seen as a *vertical* pathway, there are important *lateral* interconnectiöns as well. *Horizontal* neurons form lateral connections in the receptor/ bipolar region, while *amacrine* cells perform the same function in the bipolar/ganglion cell zone. So substantial and sophisticated processing of visual input occurs within the retina itself.

Ganglion cell axons from all parts of the retina congregate and pass together as the optic nerve through the retina at the blind spot. The two optic nerves meet at the *optic chiasma*, where a systematic reorganization of fibres occurs. The axons from the inner halves of each retina (that half nearest the nose, the *nasal hemiretina*) cross over to the opposite side. The axons from the outer halves of each retina (the *temporal hemiretina*) stay on the same side (see Figure 7.5). Each optic tract (not now a nerve, as we are within the brain) leaving the optic chiasma therefore consists of 50 per cent axons from the left eye and 50 per cent from the right. The functional significance is that one tract represents the left side of the left eye and the left side of the right eye, and the other tract represents the right side of both eyes. A stimulus out to the right of the subject (i.e. in the *right visual field*) is received by the left side of both eyes and so stimulates activity in the left optic tract only. Analogously, activity in the right optic tract represents the *left visual field* (Figure 7.5).

From the optic chiasma the optic tract passes to the *lateral geniculate nucleus* (LGN) of the thalamus, and then continues as the *optic radiation* and eventually reaches the cortex of the occipital lobe-occipital, *primary visual*, or *striate cortex*, sometimes referred to as Brodmann's area 17. Visual cortex has the normal cortical arrangement of *six layers* of neurons. LGN input arrives and synapses in layer IV. There are extensive vertical interconnections between the six layers, and various output pathways. Layers II and III project to secondary visual cortex and the cortex of the medial temporal lobe. Layer V is the origin of a pathway to the *superior colliculus* in the midbrain; the superior colliculus also receives a direct input from the retinal ganglion cells, and uses the combined information to control the orientation and movement of head and eyes in relation to visual stimuli.

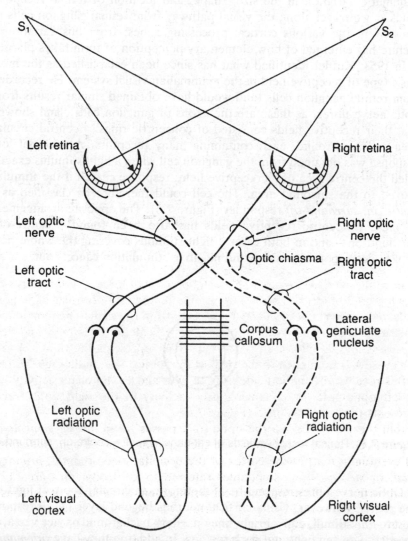

Figure 7.5 Optic pathways. With eyes fixated to the front, a stimulus (S_1) to the left of the subject is received by the right half-retina (hemi-retina) of each eye and transmitted initially to the visual cortex of the right hemisphere. Stimulus S_2 to the right of the subject is received by the left half-retina of each eye and transmitted to the left hemisphere

Retinal receptive fields and the cortical basis of visual form perception

The techniques used in analysing the neurophysiological basis of visual form perception revolve around the concept of *receptive field*. This refers to an area of the retina stimulation of which (by carefully controlled patches of light) produces a response in a given fibre or cell. There is a systematic variation in the size, shape, and location of retinal receptive fields as we travel along the visual pathway from retinal ganglion cells to neurons in the various cortical processing zones; from this variation a picture has emerged of how elementary perception of form takes place.

In 1953, Kuffler identified what has since been established as the most basic type of receptive field in the mammalian visual system. He recorded from retinal ganglion cells (and would have obtained similar results from optic nerve fibres, as these are the axons of ganglion cells), and showed that their receptive fields consisted of concentric rings: a central circular area and a surround, each containing many receptors. A maximal 'on' response was obtained from the ganglion cell when a light stimulus exactly filled the centre area of its receptive field; response ceased if the stimulus moved to the surround area. The cell could therefore be classified as a *centre-on, surround-off* responder (Figure 7.6). The opposite arrangement of these concentric receptive fields has also been found – centre-off, surround-on – and in both cases a light stimulus covering the whole field evokes no response; positive and negative stimulation cancels out.

Figure 7.6 Retinal receptive fields of cat ganglion cell – centre-on, surround-off

Optic nerve fibres respond best, therefore, to circular spots of light on the retina. However, visual cortical neurons beyond layer IV all respond best to *line* stimuli, e.g. a bright line on a dark background or vice versa, or an edge between light and dark regions. In addition they have *orientation selectivity*, in that the line stimulus has to be at a specific orientation (angle) on the retina; rotate the line a few degrees of arc and the firing rate of the neuron diminishes; at 90° to its characteristic orientation the neuron is virtually inactive.

Before considering the means by which the circular-spot responsive-receptive fields of LGN and layer IV neurons become the line-responsive receptive fields of other visual cortical cells, it would be appropriate to acknowledge the history of research in this area. Research into the mechanisms of visual perception is associated with the work of David Hubel and Torsten Wiesel. Beginning in the late 1950s and continuing up to the present day, they have establishd the structural and functional architecture of the visual cortex, pioneering the most painstaking and sophisticated experimental techniques; when only the results are presented, it is easy to overlook the problems of combining electrical recording from single cortical neurons with a retinal stimulus of suitable size and shape to activate it. In 1981 Hubel and Wiesel received, jointly with Roger Sperry, the Nobel prize for medicine.

Hubel and Wiesel (for a review of their work, see Hubel and Wiesel, 1979) identified several *functional* types of visual cortical neuron beyond layer IV. *Simple* cells respond to lines of a specific orientation on a specific part of the retina. *Complex* cells have receptive fields best stimulated by a line of specific orientation anywhere on the retina. The transition in receptive fields from concentric, to linear in one part of the retina, to linear anywhere on the retina, can be explained relatively simply. Suppose that a simple cortical cell receives its input from a group of layer IV neurons whose receptive fields are all of one kind (centre-on – surround-off), and which lie in an overlapping straight line on the retina (Figure 7.7). The most effective stimulus for that simple cell will then be *linear*, in a particular retinal location, and of a specific orientation and thickness, so that it covers the overlapping 'on' zones of the concentric receptive fields.

The next step in this converging flow of connections would be that several simple cells project onto a single complex cell. The simple cells would have in common a specific *orientation selectivity*, and although each is location-specific, together their receptive fields would cover the whole retina. So the optimal stimulus for the complex cell would be a line of appropriate orientation *anywhere* on the retina; in fact maximal activity is often produced by a line stimulus sweeping across the retina.

It seems that neurons in primary visual cortex perform a basic *feature detection* on incoming visual stimuli. Complex visual input is initially *broken down* into fundamental units, such as dots and lines, before converging operations at higher levels of the visual system reintegrate the results of basic analysis at lower levels. One might suppose that the logical destination for converging operations in the visual system is a set of neurons specialized to respond only to whole complex visual stimuli, i.e. the notorious 'Grandmother' cell is waiting to be discovered. However, it is a general view, and one held by Hubel and Wiesel, that although convergence probably continues into secondary and tertiary visual areas (i.e. several complex cells connect to a single 'hypercomplex' cell, which

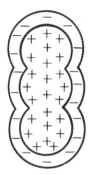 

Figure 7.7 Overlapping retinal fields produce receptive field of visual cortical cell. Most effective light stimulus = line-shape

will then respond to higher visual features such as angles, movement in a particular direction, etc.), primate visual perception does not depend upon a number of 'supercomplex' cortical neurons specialized to respond to 'whole' visual stimuli.

A microelectrode making a perpendicular penetration of the visual cortex (i.e. at right angles to the surface) passes through the six layers of neurons. There is an orderly arrangement of cells with those receiving the direct LGN input in layer IV, simple cells in layer III, and complex cells in layers II, III, and VI (the top layer, I, has few neurons, but mainly contains fibres travelling to and from the visual cortex). Simple and complex cells in layers II, III, V, and VI all have *linear* receptive fields of *specific orientations*, and Hubel and Wiesel were able to show that all the neurons encountered in a perpendicular penetration of the visual cortex (some hundred or so) had the *same* orientation, i.e. they can be considered an *orientation column* in which optimum orientation of the retinal receptive field is constant for all cells.

A similar penetration a millimetre away encounters a similar orientation column, but with the optimum orientation *shifted* round a few degrees, and it is clear that for the purposes of orientation selection, the visual cortex is architecturally subdivided into *vertical neuronal columns*. Hubel and Wiesel were then able to demonstrate the systematic organization of the orientation columns: a block of primary visual cortex one millimetre square and two millimetres deep (i.e. the cortical thickness) contains columns covering every possible stimulus orientation from vertical through 180° and back to vertical (Figure 7.8).

Such a block of tissue constitutes the elementary processing unit, or

Preferred line
orientation for each
column

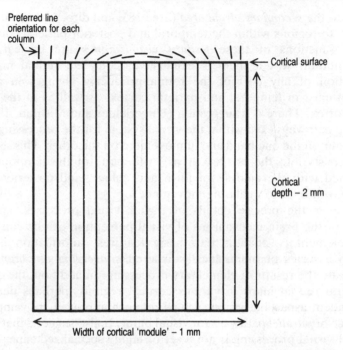

← Cortical surface

Cortical
depth – 2 mm

Width of cortical 'module' – 1 mm

Figure 7.8 Orientation columns, side-view. The visual cortex is organized into vertical neuronal *columns*. All neurons in a given column are selectively responsive to line stimuli on the retina with a specific orientation. The neighbouring column is similarly selective, but with the preferred orientation shifted by a few degrees. A block of cortex, 1mm by 1mm by 2mm deep, contains columns responding to all possible line orientations, and constitutes a functional 'module'. The visual cortex is made up of repeated versions of this basic processing unit.

module, of the visual cortex, whose overall functional organization is assumed to consist of repeated versions of this unit module. It may be that, as all cortical areas have similar columns of neurons, cortical function in general is organized on a *modular* basis. However, one major difficulty beyond the visual cortex is to identify the *'features'* which other sensory and associative areas are specialized to detect and operate upon. Feature detection in the visual cortex can be studied because simple visual stimuli are relatively easy to decompose into basic features such as orientation. Basic features or units of somatosensory sensation, language, thought, or personality, are difficult or even impossible to imagine.

Various efferent pathways leave the primary visual cortex. As mentioned earlier, connections from layer V neurons to the superior colliculus are involved in eye movement control, while layer VI cells send a projection back to the lateral geniculate nucleus; this is presumably involved in direct feedback modulation of visual input. The major pathways for the continued processing of visual information run from layers II and III to the *secondary visual area* (area 18), and directly or indirectly via area 18, to regions within the temporal and posterior parietal cortex. The precise functions of these *tertiary visual zones* are unclear. Visual representation within them is exhaustive; complete retinal maps (i.e. stimulation of any part of the retina producing changes in neuronal activity) exist in temporal and parietal cortex, as well as in the primary visual cortex. There is a suggestion (Ungerleider and Mishkin, 1982) that separate pathways exist within the visual system for the processing of form and colour on the one hand and of movement on the other. This separation then persists into the tertiary areas, with parts of the temporal cortex concerned with the analysis of form and colour, and posterior parietal cortex given over to analysing movement.

Whatever the precise details of higher visual processes, an overall picture of the brain mechanisms of visual perception can be constructed. After elementary analysis into basic features, information is passed through a series of hierarchically ordered *converging operations* which reintegrate the results of elementary processing. In addition, the existence of several retinal maps in various cortical regions, perhaps dealig with independent aspects of vision such as colour and movement, supports the existence of *parallel* pathways for visual input. It also suggests that the end-point of visual processing is not a set of highly specialized super-complex cells, but perhaps a pattern of neuronal activity across several cortical areas. The analogy used in Kandel and Schwartz (1985) is of the way a photograph can be seen as represented by the individual grains making up the picture.

Hemisphere asymmetries of function

The previous chapter discussed in outline the organization of the cerebral hemispheres, pointing out that while sensory and motor functions were evenly distributed across the ẅo hemispheres, those areas involved in the processing of language were usually found only in the left hemisphere. This discovery led to a general and continuing interest in *hemisphere asymmetries*, centring on two main questions. Is language always found in the left hemisphere, and are other high level cognitive abilities *lateralized* to one or other hemisphere?

The findings from surgery

Some of the most interesting and useful findings on hemisphere asymmetries in humans have derived from surgical intervention in cases of chronic epilepsy. Epilepsy is a result of a massive uncontrolled electric discharge in the brain, sometimes produced by a physical irritation (e.g. scar tissue after a brain operation) but sometimes of unknown origin. One form of epilepsy involves a *focus* in one specific area; the discharge begins here, and, as the brain consists of highly conductive material, may spread rapidly to other areas, eventually incorporating the whole forebrain. The symptoms include loss of consciousness during the attack and an amnesia for the seizure and the period leading up to it.

In the 1940s, an operation was devised, not to prevent the epileptic attack, but at least to prevent its spread from one side of the brain to the other in cases where the focus was unilateral (one-sided). This involved cutting the *corpus callosum*.

The corpus callosum connects the two hemispheres. It is a broad band of fibres connecting cortical areas on one side of the brain with cortical areas on the other. Although other bridges exist – particularly the *anterior commissure* – the corpus callosum is the means by which most impulses travel between the hemispheres. To accomplish its function, the callosum has in the order of 200 million fibres within it, as compared to the three million in the anterior commissure. If it is cut, effective communication between the hemispheres should cease (see Figure 7.5).

But is this communication important? The severing of the corpus callosum to alleviate severe epilepsy was performed partly because it did not appear to have any after-effects on normal behaviour. However, in the late 1940s and early 1950s, Sperry and his group looked at some of these patients again, using the rather sophisticated testing techniques of the experimental psychologist. They were able to show that *split-brain* patients (i.e. with corpus callosum transected; also referred to as a *commissurotomy* or brain bisection) do have severe behavioural problems which, however, they can adapt to in everyday life.

To demonstrate the functions of the separated hemispheres in the split-brain subject, Sperry had to devise special testing procedures, based on the anatomy of the visual pathways from the eye to the visual cortex. These were shown in Figure 7.5. Their arrangement, though complex, is systematic. Half of the fibres in each optic nerve cross over, or *decussate*, at the *optic chiasma* and eventually, after synapsing in the *lateral geniculate nucleus* of the thalamus, reach the visual cortex of the opposite hemisphere. The other half do not cross over, and eventually reach the visual cortex of the hemisphere on the same side. The system is *partially crossed*, involving *ipsilateral* ('same side') and *contralateral* ('opposite side') fibres.

Contralateral fibres connect with the visual receptor cells in that half of the *retina* nearest the nose (the *nasal hemiretina*), while ipsilateral fibres connect with the outer half of each retina (the *temporal hemiretina*; see Figure 7.5). Visual stimuli received on the receptor cells of the nasal hemiretina are transmitted to the visual cortex of the opposite hemisphere via the contralateral fibres, while stimuli received on the temporal hemiretina are transmitted via ipsilateral fibres to the visual cortex on the same side.

Usually head and eye movements make sure that our visual world is received on large retinal areas in both eyes, and is transmitted directly to both hemispheres. Even if a visual stimulus travels initially to the visual cortex of just one hemisphere, it is rapidly transmitted via the corpus callosum over to the visual cortex of the other hemisphere. However, in the split-brain subject, Sperry reasoned, a stimulus travelling initially to one hemisphere would *not* be transmitted to the other hemisphere as the corpus callosum has been cut; it would be confined to one side of the brain.

In addition he realized that if the subject looks straight ahead, a stimulus presented out to his right (the *right visual field*) would be received by the left half of each retina (see Figure 7.5), and transmitted to the left hemisphere visual cortex (via right eye contralateral fibres and left eye ipsilateral fibres). Similarly, stimuli presented out to the subject's left (the *left visual field*) would be transmitted to the right hemisphere.

So, using *lateralized* stimulus presentation Sperry could confine visual stimuli to one or other hemisphere of the split-brain subject. He presented his stimuli, such as words or pictures, on small cards, and using a *tachistoscope*, an instrument specialized for brief visual presentations (increasingly, researchers in this area now use microcomputers rather than tachistoscopes). The subject is instructed to look into the tachistoscope and to fixate a central point directly ahead. The card is flashed up for around 50 milliseconds, with the visual stimulus in the left or right visual field, i.e. to left or right of the fixation point. Sometimes the card has stimuli in both visual fields, for reasons which will become clear later.

When a stimulus – perhaps a word or a picture – is presented in the right visual field, it is transmitted to the left hemisphere. Most people (see later) have language centres (i.e. reading and speech) in the left hemisphere, and can therefore read out words and describe pictures using speech, and this is what happens in split-brain subjects. When stimuli are presented to the isolated *right* hemisphere in the bisected brain, there should be no mechanism for reading or speech, and so subjects cannot read out or describe the stimuli; in fact, they seems completely unaware of them.

Sperry wondered whether the absence of right hemisphere speech (a *response* system) might mask some ability at language comprehension, and to test this he decided to use the *contralateral* control of the left arm and hand by the right hemisphere. In the simplest demonstration, the left hand of the subject is placed behind a screen amongst an array of objects. A picture is flashed in the left visual field, is received by the *right* hemisphere, which can, even in the split-brain subject, instruct the left hand to select the object corresponding to the picture. More remarkably, the correct object can be selected even when the stimulus presented is the *name* of an object, i.e. the right hemisphere can *read* and *comprehend* simple nouns. Bizarrely, when the left hand emerges from behind the screen clutching the correct item, the subject cannot tell the experimenter what is going on –

speech is a *left hemisphere* function, and in this demonstration the left hemisphere has not seen the stimulus and has played no part in the response. Therefore it has no *awareness*, and cannot comment on or understand what the right hemisphere has been doing. Of course, if the word is presented to the left hemisphere, it can be read and the object selected, consciously, with the right hand. In the blindfolded split-brain subject, objects in the right hand can be described and named, while objects held in the left hand (connected to the right hemisphere) could not, and in fact could not be consciously registered at all.

Such studies (reviewed in Sperry, 1982; Sperry received the Nobel prize in 1981 for his work) showed a clear *disconnection syndrome*, with each hemisphere unaware of what the other one was doing; if two words or pictures are *simultaneously* presented to the two hemispheres, the split-brain subject cannot say whether they are the same or different, a task of some simplicity for the intact subject. In the disconnected brain, the hemispheres function independently. Of course, in normal life, this disconnection is not so apparent as the split-brain subject can move his eyes and head to ensure that stimuli are transmitted to both hemispheres.

Some findings, e.g. the language dominance of the left hemisphere, and the skill of the right hemisphere with pictures and faces, have been supported by research with normal subjects (see later), and Sperry's work in general has been instrumental in developing the whole research area of hemisphere differences. However, it must be emphasized that, even before their operation, split-brain subjects do not represent 'normal' brain organization. It is assumed that for most of them the epileptic condition was due to brain damage inflicted during prolonged labours (*perinatal brain damage*); oxygen starvation during difficult births causes convulsions in the infant brain which may be severe enough to produce physical damage. Years later (usually between the ages five and 15), the physical damage stimulates the epileptic attacks. It may also have provoked organizational changes in the newborn brain, which is extremely *plastic*, i.e. able to modify itself in response to damage. So the split-brain subject may have a reorganized brain which is then subjected to chronic and severe epileptic discharges, before the commissurotomy is performed. We cannot easily generalize from such subjects.

In addition there are, quite simply, not many of them. Only around 60 operations have ever been performed, and fewer than 20 split-brain subjects have been given extensive psychological testing, a very narrow data base for constructing models of brain function. In fact, as we shall see, our models rely predominantly on work with normal subjects.

However, an enduring contribution of split-brain research is to the study of consciousness and self-awareness. Our conscious life is largely verbal. We communicate using speech, we introspect using silent language, we reason and ruminate in words. Imagery has a part to play, but we are dominated by language, and therefore by the left hemisphere. If we think in words, then the thoughts reflect the left hemisphere at work. In the intact subject, thinking may represent an interaction between imagery, symbols, and the language used to manipulate them; the final expression of thought may well lie in its communication, i.e. the left hemisphere speech system.

In the split-brain subject the hemispheres are independent. The language-based self-awareness ('why did I do that?') can only describe left hemisphere functions; the right hemisphere is foreign territory. Intriguingly, in one or two of these subjects the right hemisphere as well as the left is capable of some expressive language (perhaps due to the early reorganization of the brain just mentioned). In one such patient (Ledoux *et al*, 1977) the left hand could assemble Scrabble letters to form answers to simple questions presented on cards to the right hemisphere ('who are you?'; 'what is your ambition?'). The answers were generally the same as those given by the left hemisphere, except that the left hemisphere wanted to be a draughtsman while the right hemisphere wanted to be a racing driver! These discrepancies suggested to the experimenters that the two hemispheres have separate and separable 'consciousnesses', but that, given their exposure to the same life experiences over many years, their processes and reactions are usually co-ordinated.

This is a fascinating field, and one in which the split-brain patient has a unique role. In the more routine areas of cognitive abilities and hemisphere function, we now rely much more on work with intact subjects.

Studies of other brain-damaged patients

Although the vast majority of contemporary investigations use normal subjects, a persistent minority of papers over the years have reported the consequences of accidental brain damage on hemisphere function. The causes of this brain damage include epilepsy, cerebro-vascular disorders, and traumatic brain injury.

Epilepsy was discussed earlier. Cerebro-vascular disorders include any interference with the blood supply to the brain, and include *strokes* (where the blood supply to a part of the brain is suddenly cut off by a thrombosis – a blood clot or air bubble plugging a narrow blood vessel) and *haemorrhages* (massive bleeding from blood vessels within the brain, usually caused by high blood pressure and/or congenital weaknesses in the cerebral circulation). Cerebral haemorrhage is always sudden and often fatal. Strokes may be equally sudden, but are far less likely to be fatal, depending upon the extent and location of the cerebral tissue normally supplied by the obstructed blood vessel. Brain neurons deprived of oxygen for more than ten minutes die, and strokes therefore produce *infarcts*, areas of dead and dying brain cells, and usually some behavioural impairment. Strokes are usually unilateral, and the side of the damage may be obvious from a subsequent temporary or permanent motor paralysis, i.e. left hemisphere stroke damage would result in a right-sided paralysis (or *hemiplegia*) of the body musculature. When there is no paralysis, interference with language functions may suggest left hemisphere damage in a right-handed patient, while the electroencephalogram and more modern neurological procedures such as CAT scans can localize brain damage in the living patient.

Similar procedures can be used to investigate the consequences of traumatic brain injury caused by car, industrial or domestic accidents, or by penetrating missile wounds. Patients with traumatic head injury usually form a more heterogeneous group than those suffering from cerebrovascular accidents, as particular cerebral arteries seem especially vulnerable to thrombosis and haemorrhage. However, there are fewer of the latter group, and most clinical work in the area involves epilepsy and head injury.

The patterns of abilities and behaviour of these patients should reflect the organization of the hemispheres for processing certain kinds of stimuli, and patients with *unilateral* (one-sided) brain damage would also be expected to show deficits on tasks considered to engage that hemisphere. The most obvious and important examples of this would be the language disturbances following left hemisphere damage described by Broca (1861) and Wernicke (1874), and referred to in the last chapter. Commonly in clinical neuropsychology, batteries of tests are used for assessing a range of cognitive abilities. Deficits, as compared with normals, may be shown on the 'verbal' subtests of, e.g. the Wechsler Adult Intelligence Scale (WAIS), and indicate left hemisphere pathology. Deficits on the 'performance' subtests may reflect right hemisphere pathology.

Another important test is the Wada test. This test involves injecting the anaesthetic sodium amytal into the carotid artery supplying one side of the brain. For the duration of the anaesthesia that hemisphere is non-functioning, and if it mediates language then language abilities are lost for that short period. Use of this test shows that 95–99 per cent of right-handers have language in the left hemisphere (Rasmussen and Milner, 1977). However, the Wada test usually involves speech production only, in line with the majority of clinical neurological studies, and does not imply that all aspects of language are equally lateralized. Remember that with the split-brain studies the isolated right hemisphere often revealed some rudimentary language ability, but rarely produced speech.

Studies of normal subjects

Studies of hemisphere involvement in various tasks show that types of stimuli elicit consistent hemisphere laterality effects. Brightness and colour discrimination, localization of *dots* within a matrix, line orientation, depth perception, pattern recognition, and faces, all produce an LVF (right hemisphere) advantage. Words, letters and digits all produce an RVF (left hemisphere) advantage, as does the localization of *letters* within a matrix. In auditory tasks, recognition of environmental sounds and various aspects of music such as duration, timbre and emotional tone may all produce an LEA (left ear advantage – right hemisphere). Spoken digits, words, nonsense syllables, backwards speech and normal speech produce an REA (right ear advantage – left hemisphere).

In general, the hemispheres may be characterized either by the stimuli that most effectively engage them (e.g. letters or faces), or by the mode of processing they employ. It is this latter approach that has been the most popular, and it has led to a series of overlapping *dichotomous* (two-way) descriptions of the two hemispheres. The simplest of these uses the two types of stimulus material which best distinguish the hemispheres – language and faces. Language is verbal, segmented, sequential, temporally ordered (i.e. distributed across time), and needs analysis into its components (words, letters) before it can be interpreted. Faces are constellations of visuo-spatial features, usually recognized via *parallel gestaltic* processes rather than via verbal mediation. Thus the original description sees the left hemisphere as verbal and the right hemisphere as non-verbal and visuo-spatial.

Since then, many dichotomies have been proposed. The following table presents some of them:

Table 7.1 Processing

Left hemisphere	Right hemisphere
Verbal	Visuo-spatial
Sequential	Simultaneous
Analytic	Synthetic, gestalt
Temporal	Spatial
Rational	Intuitive
Digital	Analogue
Intellectual	Emotional

Most can be reduced to the straightforward verbal/non-verbal distinction.

Using a whole range of experimental and clinical evidence, Bradshaw and Nettleton (1981) propose that the left hemisphere is specialized for the *analysis* and *production* of temporally ordered sequences of stimuli and motor activities. This explains its dominance of language comprehension and production, its fine-grained bilateral control of the oral musculature used in speech, and of the sequencing of skilled manipulative movements of limbs, hands and fingers (Kimura, 1977)

Faces seem to be the 'best' right hemisphere stimulus – so much so that it has been proposed that a specialist face-processor exists in the right parietal lobe (Carey and Diamond, 1977). Interestingly, the monkey also seems to possess neurons which are selectively responsive to faces (Perrett *et al*, 1982). Bradshaw and Nettleton suggest that the general specialization of the right hemisphere for faces and other visuo-spatial stimuli reflects an *holistic* strategy for processing stimuli. This they contrast with the *analytical* strategy of the left hemisphere. Hemisphere asymmetries in various tasks would then depend on what strategy is employed; so *analysing* music in detail would engage the left hemisphere, while *holistically* responding to the emotional tone would shift dominance to the right hemisphere.

Handedness and sex

The reasonably clear picture of functional asymmetries presented in the previous section works best when applied to male right-handed subjects with no family history of left-handedness. It becomes distorted when left-handedness (*sinistrality*: note that the Latin root for 'left-handed' and 'sinister' is the same) and/or sex is introduced as an additional variable.

Between 50 and 65 per cent of left-handed subjects have language in the left hemisphere, most of the remainder have language in the right hemisphere, while a proportion may have language bilaterally represented, i.e. in this latter case, showing more of a functional hemispheric symmetry than an asymmetry. The right-handed female subject shows, in general, the same pattern of asymmetries as the right-handed male, but to a lesser degree, i.e. there is evidence (McGlone, 1980) that the female brain is less lateralized than the male brain.

The clearest evidence for a less stable pattern of cerebral organziation in left-handers comes from the aphasic consequences of unilateral brain damage. Left-handers tend to have a slightly higher incidence of aphasia following right hemisphere lesions than do right-handers (13.7 per cent versus 6.7 per cent), and equivalent levels following left-sided damage (22 per cent versus 24 per cent: Hardyck and Petrinovich, 1977). Data on visio-spatial disturbances are comparable for the two groups.

The study of sex differences in cognitive processes and in cerebral laterality has a chequered history. Some authoritative reviews (e.g. Maccoby and Jacklin, 1975) conclude that males are superior on spatial tasks and that females excel on verbal tasks, differences that emerge in the years ten to 20 rather than before. These differences can then be related to hemisphere functional asymmetries, with the male brain being seen as more lateralized and the female brain as more symmetrical (e.g. Levy and Reid, 1978; McGlone, 1980; Inglis *et al*, 1982), usually in the direction of bilateral representation of language. Other, equally authoritative, reviews conclude that sex differences in cognitive abilities and/or lateralization are minimal and can effectively be ignored (Fairweather, 1982). Certainly, given the effort expended in the search for sex differences in cognition and brain organization, the results are not impressive either in amount or in consistency. Perhaps the most realistic conclusion is that performance on laterality tasks is a complex interaction between the specific task, sex of the subject, their handedness, and their family history of left-handedness (McKeever and Van Deventer, 1977).

Motivation

The psychologist is aiming to explain behaviour. The most fundamental question that can be asked is 'why behave at all?' Assuming that behaviour is not completely pointless implies that it has some purpose, or, in other words, is *motivated*.

The simplest example of the concept of motivation and its explanatory value is the hungry rat. We assume that depriving a rat of food for 24 hours induces a state we may call 'hunger' (a primary drive), reflecting a need for food to satisfy a *tissue deficiency*. To fulfil this need, the rat will learn to press a bar in a Skinner box to obtain pellets of food (primary reinforcer) and so eliminate 'hunger'. This sequence consists of energized and directed behaviour, i.e. a motivational sequence running from tissue deficiency to consummatory response and satisfaction.

The primary reinforcers for primary drives are obvious: food, water, the opposite sex. Stimuli consistently associated with the primary reinforcing stimuli may themselves become *secondary reinforcers*, capable of inducing and supporting secondary drives and learning based on secondary drive reduction. So maternal approval, consistently associated with primary nurturant reinforcers such as food and warmth, becomes a secondary reinforcer in its own right, and the child's behaviour may then reflect the secondary drive of seeking maternal approval. So, although originating in the reduction of primary drives, behaviour can become detached from its physiological sources. Although the explanatory power of this drive reduction approach can be impressive, we are now aware of many other factors involved in animal behaviour. Rats will learn to press bars for various non-nutritive and non-drive-reducing reinforcers such as saccharine and flashing lights, and their behaviour is now seen to be driven or guided by more than the reduction of simple physiological drives.

Hunger

The primary physiological drives are those behaviours aimed at maintaining *homeostasis*, i.e. sustaining a relatively constant internal environment. There are many measures of homeostasis, such as body weight, cellular and extracellular water content, and body temperature, and we deal only with a few of them within physiological psychology. Even for hunger and the regulation of food intake we concentrate on those foods which determine body weight, i.e. overall *caloric* intake in terms of *fats* and *carbohydrates*. Other dietary necessities such as *protein*, *vitamins*, *mineral salts*, and *trace elements*, are equally as important for bodily functioning, but details of their regulation are relatively unknown.

Apart from abnormal overeating or the dynamic phases of growth, body weight is regulated within fairly narrow limits in all animal species. One key aspect of this is that eating is usually *anticipatory* of future need, rather than a direct response to a central tissue deficiency. Animals normally take meals regularly, with water intake correlated with food intake, and neither is in response to extreme *deficit* signals; meal patterns are determined by external stimuli, cognitive processes such as habit, and by circadian rhythms. However, given the stability of body weight, actual food intake in the short term (i.e. meal size) and in the long term (over weeks, months, etc.) must be regulated, and it is the nature of this regulation that concerns us.

When rats or people eat, they do not eat for very long. Meal duration is reasonably consistent, and meal frequency also has a systematic pattern (Le Magnen, 1972). As we stop eating a meal long before the food can have been digested and fully absorbed into the body, factors other than body weight must be operating; we may therefore suggest a split between the control of *short-term satiety* (meal duration) and of *long-term satiety* (caloric intake over extended periods, regulating body weight).

In 1942 Hetherington and Ranson galvanized the study of feeding and hunger with their demonstration that lesions of the *ventro-medial hypo-thalamus* (VMH) produced a post-lesion *hyperphagia* (overeating), leading to a massive obesity in the long term. The hyperphagia was shown by a dramatic increase in meal duration and frequency, and led to the sugges-tion that the lesion removed a 'feeding cessation' or *satiety* centre. When, in 1951, Anand and Brobeck reported that lesions of the *lateral hypo-thalamus* produced a post-lesion *aphagia* (prolonged failure to eat), it appeared that this lesion destroyed a 'feeding-initiation' or *feeding* centre.

As the two major problems in this area were seen to be how feeding was begun and how it was ended, the discovery of feeding and satiety centres apparently solved the dilemma. Control was central rather than peripheral.

However, even though the ventro-medial hypothalamus may be a satiety centre, it still has to receive information from various mechanisms of 'satiety' telling it to inhibit feeding, and it has to have access to efferent, motor pathways to put that inhibition into effect. The identification of central satiety and feeding centres does not therefore eliminate peripheral mechanisms, and the last decade has seen a growth in interest in the central/peripheral interaction.

Let us now focus on peripheral mechanisms in feeding. The precise effect of food in the mouth is unclear, although taste sensation is clearly important – rats will overeat pleasant foods (they are particularly fond of chocolate biscuits), and *dietary* obesity can be produced fairly easily using certain operant schedules (Sclafani and Springer, 1976). In humans, too, increases in food intake can be produced by simply varying sensory aspects such as colour and shape (Rolls *et al*, 1982). Food in the stomach stretches the lining (gastric distension) and this is signalled directly to the hypo-thalamus. After the stomach food passes into the duodenum and on into the small intestine, and it is here that another short-term satiety signal comes into play. In 1972, Gibbs *et al* identified a hormone that they suggested had as a major action the suppression of feeding. This hormone, called *cholecystokinin*, or CCK for short, has now been shown to suppress feeding in rats deprived of food for up to 92 hours (Mueller and Hsiao, 1979), and also reduces food intake in obese humans (Pi-Sunyer *et al*, 1982). It is released from the upper intestine (i.e. duodenum and early portions of the small intestine) into the bloodstream in response to the presence of fatty acids in the intestine, although its detailed mode and site of action are unknown. There is some evidence that it acts directly on the vagal nerve, which carries afferent sensory information from the stomach and intestine to the brain (Lorenz and Goldman, 1982).

Things become much more complicated after the food has been ab-sorbed through the intestinal wall into the blood circulation through the liver. There are receptors for blood glucose (*glucoreceptors*) in both the peripheral liver circulation and in the ventro-medial hypothalamus. Activity in these receptors is proportional to the circulating levels of blood glucose, and in turn they affect activity in the neurons they are associated with. Peripheral glucoreceptors are served by branches of the vagus nerve, with glucoreceptor stimulation producing sensory impulses travelling to the central nervous system. Hypothalamic glucoreceptors are probably sited directly on hypothalamic neurons.

Levels of blood glucose respond rapidly enough to the ingestion and absorption of food for peripheral and central glucoreceptors to be given a role in the control of short-term satiety (Rezek *et al*, 1977), and make the list of such factors look something like this:

Control of eating and short-term satiety
Visual and olfactory stimuli associated with food
Presence of food in mouth
Presence of food in stomach (gastric distension)
Cholecystokinin (CCK) released from the upper intestine
Central and peripheral glucoreceptors

Other hormones, such as *insulin* released from the pancreas gland, also influence glucose metabolism, and will be briefly considered in relation to obesity and the VMH syndrome.

The ventro-medial hypothalamic syndrome

The VMH rat eats more palatable (tasty) food, by increasing the frequency and duration of meals. Such animals are over-influenced by the sensory aspects of food, eating abundantly of chocolate biscuits but refusing food contaminated with bitter-tasting quinine, food which the unlesioned hungry rat would eat. The VMH rat will not work so hard to obtain food, being easily put off by moderate operant schedules or by mild footshock; this suggests *lower* levels of motivation than deprived controls. VMH rats are also less active, more irritable, and less sexually active.

The post-lesion increase in weight of the rat is due almost entirely to increased deposition of fatty acids in the fat storage cells (*adipocytes*). If the behavioural hyperphagia (overeating) is eliminated by strict control of meal size, the VMH rat still becomes obese; if post-lesion weight gain is controlled to prevent obesity developing, the fat/non-fat ratio in the body still increases. These two observations suggest that the VMH rat suffers a profound metabolic disturbance, which shows itself in hyperphagia under appropriate circumstances. Apart from increased fat storage, other signs of this disturbance are increased blood levels of insulin (see later), increased glucose turnover (i.e. blood levels are roughly normal, but synthesis and breakdown are both increased), and high blood levels of lipids and cholesterol.

The number of fat storage cells (adipocytes) is determined by a combination of genetic factors and early nutritional experience; in later life the number is constant and only their fat content can change. VMH rats become obese even if hyperphagia is prevented and eating is normal, suggesting a profound shift in metabolism rather than a simple shift in body-weight set-point. Human obese subjects represent a heterogeneous (varied) collection of causative factors – genetic, nutritional, developmental, psychological (Leon and Roth, 1977). Family studies show the strong genetic influence on *basal metabolic rates*, i.e. how efficiently we burn up stored fats and carbohydrates for energy and heat production, a crucial factor in weight control (Bogardus *et al*, 1986). Socialization and habit formation are also important. So a simple equation between the VMH rat and the obese human is not justified.

However, there may be some physiological similarities. The VMH rat has chronically high blood levels of the hormone *insulin*, released from the *pancreas gland* near the duodenum. Insulin promotes the conversion of blood glucose to fats, stored in the adipocytes. So high levels of insulin produce low levels of blood glucose, and may therefore stimulate hunger and feeding behaviour. Interestingly, Powley and Opsahl (1974) reversed VMH obesity by cutting the *vagus nerve*, which normally stimulates the pancreas to release insulin; when the vagus is severed, blood insulin levels fall. In addition there is some evidence that obese subjects react to food intake with larger than normal insulin release (Johnson and Wildman, 1983), which may contribute to their increased appetite. In the VMH rat, and in some obese humans, there may therefore be a primary disturbance of insulin production.

The precise description and explanation of the VMH syndrome is still some way off. Carbohydrate and fat metabolism is physiologically so complex and so productive of chemical candidates for indexing energy consumption and body weight that the eventual model will represent a sophisticated fusion of physiology and psychology. It will have to incorporate hypothalamic mechanisms, fat storage, circulating glucose levels, hormone effects, and the peripheral regulatory systems described earlier in this section. So, even an apparently simple example of homeostatically-based motivation such as hunger, together with its most striking phenomenom – the VMH rat – still has many questions unanswered.

Non-homeostatic drives

Monkeys will do manipulative puzzles endlessly, with no obvious external reinforcement. Rats will learn to press bars in order to switch on a light in the chamber. Students do psychology courses. Most behaviour in animals and humans has no immediately obvious connection with homeostasis and drive reduction, but the following work has begun to shed light on this area.

In 1954 Olds and Milner were electrically stimulating various sites in the rat brain. They noticed that some animals repeatedly turned to that part of the cage where they had received stimulation. Olds and Milner assumed that they found the stimulation pleasurable. It turned out that these animals had, accidently as it happened, stimulating electrodes located in the *septum*. Olds and Milner followed this observation up by so arranging a Skinner box that rats could stimulate themselves by pressing the bar, and found that electrical stimulation of certain sites in the brain represented the most powerful reinforcement one could give an animal, preferable to food for the hungry or water for the thirsty. Bar-pressing for ESB (electrical self-stimulation of the brain) could be sustained for many hours at rates of 200–300 presses per hour, until fatigue intervened. The classic mapping work of Olds (Olds and Olds, 1965) showed that rewarding ESB could be produced from a range of sites within the brain, particularly from electrode placements along the median forebrain bundle, a large tract containing neuronal fibres ascending and descending from hindbrain to forebrain. The phenomenon is widespread, and has been demonstrated in rats, cats, monkeys and humans.

At first glance, ESB appears very different from natural rewards. It is extremely persistent, but extinguishes almost immediately if a bar-press is not rewarded with stimulation. After an inter-session interval, an animal may not spontaneously bar-press when replaced in the chamber; only after a few free 'priming' stimuli does it begin pressing. Performance deteriorates rapidly at long inter-stimulus intervals, and acquisition of partial reinforcement schedules is poor. These are characteristics not usually seen with natural reinforcers such as food and water. Moreover ESB does not *satiate*, and is therefore not based on any present or anticipated tissue deficiency. It appears to activate a higher-order reward network than that activated by natural reinforcers. External stimuli can elicit and guide behaviour, i.e. given that even feeding and drinking are also anticipatory and determined by habits and circadian rhythms, very little motivated behaviour is entirely 'driven' from inside the animal. The realization that behaviour can be elicited by external stimuli has given rise to the concept of *incentive motivation*, whereby stimuli can arouse and sustain behaviour independently of tissue deficiencies. It also means that in theory responses based on incentive motivation need not satiate – if incentive motivation is independent of tissue deficiencies, then it need not follow the 'normal' pattern of homeostatic drives.

Although speculative, this does provide a possible explanation for the effects of ESB, in particular its failure to satiate. It may be that the electrodes supporting ESB are directly activating the neural pathways involved in incentive motivation, arousing the animal but not satiating it.

ESB is a powerful and unusual phenomenon, and is still not entirely understood. Although artificially induced by the experimenter, its relationships with natural activities has helped and will continue to help in the explanation of the psychological and physiological bases of motivated behaviours.

Emotion and peripheral arousal systems

The physiological correlates of behaviour in the intact human may be studied in so far as they can be measured. We cannot intervenc in brain function using lesions or stimulation, but we can measure and record physiological variables which may reflect aspects of brain function.

The *psychophysiologist* works with intact humans, and measures various aspects of their physiology and neurophysiology (see, e.g. Martin and Venables, 1980). They record, as direct correlates of central nervous system activity, *electroencephalograms* (EEGs), and *evoked potentials* to stimuli such as lights and tones. As correlates of peripheral nervous system activity they can record *heart-rate*, the *skin conductance orienting response* (SCR; formerly the GSR, or *galvanic skin response*), *blood-pressure* and *blood-flow*, *skin temperature*, and other responses controlled by the autonomic nervous system. Blood or urine samples can be analysed for the presence of hormones such as *adrenaline*, *prolactin*, or *corticosteroids* (see later).

A key concept for the psychophysiologist is *arousal*, by which is usually meant peripheral arousal, i.e. the dominance of the autonomic nervous system by the sympathetic branch, leading to increases in sweating, heart-rate, blood-pressure, and higher blood levels of adrenaline and noradrenaline. Associated with this autonomic arousal is the activation of the *pituitary-adrenal axis*, whereby secretion of corticosteroids from the adrenal cortex is massively increased.

Whatever physiological responses are recorded may then be correlated with some change in behaviour. Does heart-rate fall during sustained attention? Do levels of corticosteroids vary during simple problem solving? Do schizophrenics have abnormal patterns of autonomic activity such as raised blood-pressure or increased sweating? The pattern that emerges is of a physiological response being the *dependent variable* (what is measured), and some aspect of behaviour or personality the *independent variable* (what is allowed to vary). This contrasts with physiological psychology, where the dependent variable is usually some aspect of observed behaviour, and the independent variable some controlled interference with a physiological system (usually the brain).

All of the physiological responses recorded by the psychophysiologist are ultimately controlled from the central nervous system, and in some cases act in turn upon the central nervous system. The nuclei controlling the autonomic nervous system lie in the brainstem (medulla, pons, midbrain), and electrical stimulation of these regions can produce changes in heart-rate, blood pressure, sweat-gland activity, etc. These centres are in turn modulated by higher brain structures such as the hypothalamus and limbic system. So even when we concentrate upon peripheral arousal, there are still central mechanisms in the background, regulating and modulating.

Peripheral arousal systems

The autonomic nervous system (ANS) was outlined in the last chapter. It is an *efferent* (motor) system conducting impulses from nuclei within the CNS out to target structures in the body. These include the heart, the smooth muscle of the digestive tract and blood vessels, and various glands such as the pancreas, sweat and salivary glands, and the adrenal medulla. The two branches of the ANS, sympathetic and parasympathetic, each connect with all target structures, and tend to have opposite effects.

The balance between the two branches is regulated by the brainstem ANS centres and is usually unconscious and automatic. We are *homeostatic* organisms, maintaining as far as possible a constant internal environment. This constancy involves a range of the body's characteristics, from temperature and the brain's oxygen supply to heart-rate and blood glucose levels. Such homeostatic regulation is the main function of the autonomic nervous system.

The provision of energy to meet the body's demands must fluctuate with need; sympathetic dominance or arousal involves energy expenditure (i.e. the sympathetic pattern is *catabolic*), while parasympathetic dominance is aimed at energy replenishment or conservation (i.e. the pattern is *anabolic*).

What all this implies, is that the system has evolved as a means of harnessing the body's metabolism to its physical needs. From this angle, the ANS has no *obvious* involvement in psychological phenomena; which is not to say that correlations between, for instance, various emotions and hormone levels do not exist, but that the *physiological demands* of the emotional state must be considered before valid conclusions can be drawn.

The psychophysiology of emotion lays great emphasis on the autonomically-controlled adrenal medulla. The adrenal gland lies just above the kidney, and is divided into two functionally independent

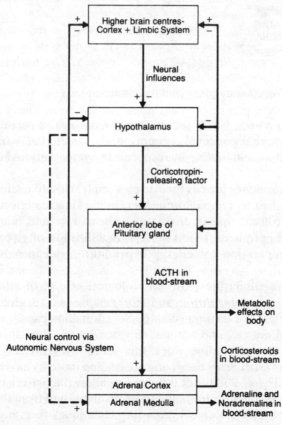

Figure 7.9 Hypothalamic-pituitary-adrenal system, and feedback control of ACTH secretion

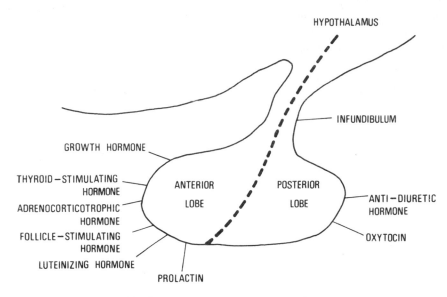

Figure 7.10   The pituitary gland and its hormones

components: a *cortex*, which secretes corticosteroids as part of the activation of the pituitary-adrenal system, and a *medulla*, which secretes *adrenaline* and *noradrenaline* in response to sympathetic ANS activation (Figure 7.9).

These two hormones are, as their names imply, closely related chemicals. Both are classified as *sympathomimetics*, mimicking the effects of general sympathetic arousal; that is, increases in heart-rate and blood pressure, constriction of peripheral blood vessels, mobilization of glycogen and fat reserves in preparation for energy expenditure, and increases in blood glucose levels.

Despite their similarities, the physiological effects of adrenaline and noradrenaline (or *epinephrine* and *norepinephrine*, to give them their American names) are distinguishable. Noradrenaline causes vasoconstriction in skeletal muscle, and adrenaline vasodilation. Both increase blood-pressure, but noradrenaline does this more by increasing peripheral resistance (via vasoconstriction), and adrenaline more by a direct action on heart muscle. These, and other differences, allow the pattern of peripheral arousal produced by noradrenaline to be distinguished from that produced by adrenaline by physiological recording techniques (see, e.g. Ax, 1953; Funkenstein, 1956).

Pituitary-adrenal system

The *pituitary gland* is suspended immediately below the hypothalamus by a short stalk, the *infundibulum* (Figure 7.10); it is not part of the brain, but intimately associated with it. The gland is made up of two lobes, the anterior (or *adenohypophysis*) and posterior (or *neurohypophysis*).

The two lobes are distinguished by the hormones they secrete into the bloodstream, and in the precise mechanisms whereby the release is effected. The posterior lobe releases *oxytocin* and *vasopressin* in response to neural impulses travelling down the axons of neurons whose cell bodies lie in the hypothalamus. The anterior lobe secretes a variety of hormones (see Table 7.2) in response to stimulation by chemicals manufactured in the hypothalamus, and travelling down to the adenohypophysis in the blood supply to the pituitary.

Table 7.2 Hormones released by the pituitary gland

Anterior lobe (Adenohypophysis)	
Growth hormone	(direct effects on metabolism to promote growth)
Thyroid-stimulating hormone	(stimulates thyroid gland to release thyroxin)
Adrenocorticotrophic hormone	(ACTH: stimulates adrenal cortex to release glucocorticoids and mineralocorticoids)
Follicle-stimulating hormone	(act together to promote testosterone release and sperm
Luteinizing hormone	cell growth in males, and oestrogen release and egg cell production and growth in females)
Prolactin	(promotes lactation, or milk production, by direct action on female mammary gland)
Posterior lobe (Neurohypophysis)	
Vasopressin	(anti-diuretic hormone: regulation of water loss via kidneys)
Oxytocin	(promotes milk release from breast, and uterine contractions during labour)

The pituitary gland has been referred to as the master gland of the body. Its hormones regulate, either directly or via an action on other glands, many aspects of the body's growth, metabolism, and reproductive behaviour (Table 7.2). Of particular interest to the psychologist is the adrenal cortex.

The adrenal cortex is controlled by the *adrenocorticotrophic hormone* (ACTH) released from the pituitary gland. The secretion of ACTH is in turn regulated by a chemical releasing factor (ACTH-RF) manufactured in the hypothalamus. ACTH passes into the bloodstream, travels to the adrenal cortex, and there stimulates the release of corticosteroids into the bloodstream (Figure 7.9).

There are many corticosteroids, broadly divided into two classes of mineralocorticoids and glucocorticoids. The former are involved in the balance of mineral salts and trace elements in the body, essential for normal physiological functioning of, e.g. the nervous system. The latter are concerned with the conversion of fat stores to glucose, and the suppressing of the body's protective immune response to infection or tissue damage; both these functions are part of the organism's preparation for energy expenditure and responsiveness to sudden stress – tissue repair can wait until danger has passed – and the release of glucocorticoids is a major component of the physiological stress response. Studies of the stress response usually involve measuring blood or urine levels of specific glucocorticoids such as *cortisone* and *corticosterone*.

The pituitary-adrenal system is extremely sensitive, with even mild but unexpected stimuli evoking an immediate release of ACTH and corticosteroids. If the stimulus is harmless, the system is damped down in an elegantly simple way; the release of ACTH from the pituitary is inhibited by levels of ACTH and corticosteroids circulating in the bloodstream, so that as soon as the pituitary-adrenal axis is activated it is tending to return to normal. It is a perfect *negative feedback system* (Figure 7.9).

The initial activation can be triggered by stimulus perception and evaluation by higher brain centres, which then excite the hypothalamus. If the stimulus is extremely threatening and/or arousing, these higher centres will override the negative feedback mechanism and sustain pituitary-adrenal activation at a high level; if the stimulus proves to be harmless, circulating levels of ACTH and corticosteroids are allowed to inhibit the pituitary and return the system to normal.

The peripheral arousal state associated with intense emotions involves ANS sympathetic activation and excitation of the pituitary-adrenal system. One reason for their close association is the presence in the hypothalamus of centres controlling both systems. Appropriate hypothalamic stimulation can activate the PAS, and it has been known for many years that hypothalamic mechanisms regulate the ANS (Gellhorn & Loufbourrow, 1963).

The psychophysiology of emotion

In 1884 William James invented this area. He proposed that, rather than an emotional feeling producing action, the action produces the emotional feeling. An object is perceived, and elicits a response, e.g. behavioural approach or avoidance, together with a range of peripheral changes in autonomic and endocrine (glandular) systems. The brain receives feedback from these physiological responses, and interprets the pattern in terms of an emotional feeling. So the pattern of extreme peripheral arousal associated with the sight of an aggressive predator is interpreted by the brain as 'fear'. This proposal conflicted with the more obvious view that the sight of the predator produces 'fear' which then leads to peripheral arousal and running away.

Around the same time the Danish physiologist Lange presented a similar hypothesis, and so the model of emotional feeling as depending upon feedback from bodily changes is known as the *James–Lange theory*.

The physiologist Walter Cannon (1929) was the next to pick up the argument, with a series of criticisms of the James–Lange model. He pointed out that animals still exhibit fear and rage responses after spinal transection (which eliminates sensory feedback from the body to the brain); that many non-emotional stressors such as high fever and anoxia (lack of oxygen) produce a peripheral arousal state apparently identical to the pattern supposed to produce 'rage'; that the sensory feedback system from the body (the *visceral afferent system*) is too primitive and too slow to code for a variety of rapidly occurring emotions; and finally that injections of adrenaline produce peripheral arousal, but do not lead to the experience of emotion.

Cannon proposed his alternative central model of action, in which the *thalamus* was responsible for emotional experience, and the *hypothalamus* for emotional expression and behaviour.

Despite Cannon's criticisms, it seems intuitively likely that peripheral arousal is correlated with some extreme emotional states such as fear and anger, and may interact with stimulus perception and evaluation in the production of the subjective emotional experience (it should be noted that James did restrict his ideas to the more 'primitive' emotions such as rage, love and fear). This hypothesis was given some encouragement by the work of Ax (1953). He used the known differences between the precise arousal patterns produced by the release of adrenaline and noradrenaline from the adrenal medulla to investigate possible correlations between emotions and peripheral arousal. Using a range of psychophysiological measures, Ax concluded that the state of fear was associated with adrenaline release from the adrenal medulla, and anger with noradrenaline release.

Funkenstein (1956) followed this up by correlating aspects of personality with adrenal medullary secretions. Subjects whose characteristic response to frustration was 'anger-out' showed the peripheral arousal pattern typical of noradrenaline, while those who demonstrated an 'anger-in' response had the arousal pattern typical of adrenaline.

Schachter and Singer (1962)

There are few definitive studies in psychology, few experiments whose methodological and theoretical framework have stood the test of critical analysis and replication. Those that have do so for a variety of reasons. They may actually be excellent studies, well designed, carried out, analysed, which produce significant and important results. Others, less impressive methodologically or in the pattern of results, survive to enter the folklore of psychology through their imaginative design and interpretation, and because their conclusions seem to make a lot of sense. Such a study is that of Schachter and Singer (1962).

Their starting point was the conflict between James's view that peripheral arousal produces emotion, and Cannon's criticism that the same peripheral arousal pattern was common to different emotions. In 1924 Maranon had failed to produce a true emotional state by injecting subjects with adrenaline – if James's ideas were valid, one would have predicted that induced peripheral arousal would produce some emotional experience.

Schachter and Singer point out that Maranon's subjects had a perfectly adequate explanation for their aroused state; they had been injected with adrenaline. They therefore hypothesized that subjects will always seek an appropriate explanation, or *cognitive label*, for subjectively perceived arousal, and if the explanation involves emotional stimuli, then an emotion will be experienced. So, if peripheral arousal is induced in subjects without their being given a suitable explanation, they will actively try to interpret their state in terms of the immediate cognitive environment; if this environment is systematically varied, then different subjective emotional states might result.

Using the pretence of investigating the effects of a vitamin supplement ('Suproxin') on vision, Schachter and Singer injected male subjects with either adrenaline or a non-active placebo. Adrenaline-injected subjects were either *informed* of the expected physiological consequences (increased heart-rate, tremor, palpitations, etc.), *misinformed*, or left *ignorant*. Their cognitive environment was varied in two ways. In the *euphoria* condition, a stooge (i.e. a confederate of the experimenter) acted in what might be classified as a manically happy way, playing with balls of paper and flying paper aeroplanes. In the *anger* condition, a stooge became progressively more angry and violent as he and the subject worked through an increasingly personal questionnaire (e.g. 'father's annual income?', 'do members of your family need psychiatric care?').

Schachter and Singer predicted that subjects experiencing a state of physiological arousal for which they had no explanation would interpret it in terms of their immediate cognitive environment; if the stooge was euphoric they would feel euphoric, and if the stooge was angry they would feel angry. Those subjects informed accurately as to the effects of the injection *do* have an appropriate explanation, and should therefore be unaffected by the stooge's behaviour. Subjects given the placebo should experience no peripheral arousal, and so should feel no need to interpret their state in terms of their cognitive environment (the actual arousing consequences of injections were checked using pulse-rate recordings).

Induced emotional state was assessed via behavioural observations by independent observers and subjective self-report. The predictions, in terms of degree of induced emotion, were that the adrenaline-misinformed and the adrenaline-ignorant groups would feel and act more emotionally than either the adrenaline-informed or placebo groups.

Schachter and Singer concluded that their results conformed to expectations. Subjects given no explanation for the arousing affects of their injection felt and acted more emotionally (euphorically or angrily) than informed subjects or placebo-injected subjects in the same experimental conditions. So 'emotional state' is determined not just by a state of peripheral arousal, but by an interaction between the state of arousal and the cognitive environment, and is therefore a combination of central and peripheral factors.

This is the conclusion referred to in subsequent reviews and descriptions of the psychophysiology of emotion. Recently, however, criticisms have been levelled at the Schachter and Singer study. Two attempts at partial replication failed to reproduce their findings (Marshall and Zimbardo, 1979; Maslach, 1979), and although neither of these studies is in turn free from criticism (Schachter and Singer, 1979), they do emphasize the need to read the original 1962 paper closely. Data analysis initially showed that of the four *dependent* variables (behavioural observation of expressed emotion, and subjective self-reports, for the two conditions of euphoria and anger), only the behaviour ratings in the anger condition produced a significant difference between the crucial groups, *adrenaline-ignorant* and *placebo*. Subsequent elimination of 'self-informed' subjects (those in the ignorant and misinformed groups who still attributed their physiological responses to the injection) from the analysis produced significant adrenaline-ignorant versus placebo differences for both euphoria and anger conditions, but again, only for the behavioural ratings and *not* for the self-report scores.

So the Schachter and Singer experiment does not unambiguously confirm that emotional states necessarily involve an interaction between non-specific peripheral arousal and appropriate cognitive evaluation, especially if 'emotion' is assessed using self-report. It does seem intuitively likely that perception of peripheral arousal plays a part in the origin and maintenance of emotional states, particularly the more intense ones of euphoria, anger, and fear. An arousal/cognition interaction would help resolve the James–Lange/Cannon dispute; peripheral arousal would be *necessary* (following James–Lange), but would not vary between emotional states (following Cannon). Distinctions between states would be ultimately cognitive. Such a picture is appealing, which may account for the rather uncritical acceptance of the whole of Schachter and Singer's theoretical position during the last three decades. But it does seem that the relations between emotion and arousal are not actually that straightforward, and this has also been demonstrated using other strategies.

Emotions have subjective and objective characteristics which may, with certain intensities of certain emotions, correlate with the presence of peripheral arousal. But peripheral arousal itself is not a *unitary* concept; heart-rate need not correlate with skin conductance activity, and adrenaline excitation is not identical to noradrenaline excitation. In fact the classical work in this area has largely failed to resolve the issue.

Using a novel approach, Ekman (Ekman *et al*, 1983) has studied the use we make of facial expression in conveying emotion. Using video techniques to analyse expression, he specified the precise pattern of contractions of the facial musculature which define any given emotion. The next step was to direct subjects in putting on a range of facial expressions to convey various emotions, i.e. precisely guiding the contraction of muscle groups into the appropriate pattern. Professional actors and scientists were used to minimize experimenter effects.

The emotional expression was held for ten seconds, during which physiological measures were taken, including heart-rate, finger skin temperature, skin resistance, and forearm muscle tension. When compared with pre-emotion baselines, changes in physiological measures significantly differentiated emotional expressions. 'Anger' was characterized by high heart-rate and skin temperature, and 'fear' and 'sadness' by high heart-rate and low skin temperature. 'Happiness', 'disgust', and 'surprise' were all associated with low heart-rate. Differences were less marked when subjects were asked to *relive* appropriate emotional experiences, an observation which will need to be analysed further. However, Ekman seems justified in concluding that what he calls *universal emotional signals* (facial expressions) do produce an *emotion-specific* autonomic activity. The precise mechanism is unclear, but the demonstration that *different* emotional expressions are associated with *different* patterns of peripheral arousal would appear to support the original ideas of James and Lange, and to go against the Schachter and Singer model.

As an alternative approach to the whole area, Frankenhaeuser and her group have over the last decade or so analysed the behavioural correlates of adrenaline and noradrenaline secretion in great detail, and their findings perhaps provide a more realistic picture of the psychophysiology of emotional states.

The adrenal medulla and behaviour

Adrenaline and noradrenaline are released from the adrenal medulla in response to activation of the sympathetic branch of the autonomic nervous system (Figure 7.9). Frankenhaeuser measures their release using urinary excretion rates, rather than measuring levels in the bloodstream which, although more direct, involves the additional stress of taking the blood sample.

A consistent and important finding is that adrenaline release is much more responsive, or *labile*, to psychologically-relevant stimuli; so much so that Frankenhaeuser's group work almost exclusively with adrenaline (noradrenaline release is increased significantly by *physical* stressors such as pain, cold, burns, and muscular activity).

The extensive work of Frankenhaeuser's group on the nature of the psychological stimuli most effective at producing an adrenaline response leads to some general conclusions. Overstimulation or understimulation both increase adrenaline levels, with the rise correlating with perceived discomfort. Emotion-arousing stimuli of any sort will produce an adrenaline response, with no distinctions between amusing, violent, or horrific films. Similarly effective are tasks which are either pleasant (playing bingo), unpleasant (unsolvable puzzles), or just tedious (simple but prolonged mental arithmetic). Although in some cases the adrenaline response appears to involve an element of emotional arousal, or at least emotionally-toned arousal, novel but emotional neutral stimuli are effective, as are conditions of uncertainty. The response to the latter may represent a physiological preparation for any eventuality, and in some of the situations a complex interaction between psychological stimuli and physical responses is clearly occurring. Doing IQ tests is an example where subjective involvement, emotional arousal (fear?), and intense physical activity (writing), combine to produce a massive release of adrenaline.

One of the more extraordinary findings reported by Frankenhaeuser is a sex difference in adreno-medullary reactivity. Females show little or no adrenaline response to a variety of stressors which are effective for males. These include cognitive tasks, and the taking of blood samples using a hypodermic syringe (Frankenhaeuser *et al*, 1976); females showed no rise in adrenaline levels from control relaxed conditions. There are instances where females do produce comparable reactivity, and these involve what Frankenhaeuser calls 'non-traditional' roles; adrenaline responses to achievement demands did *not* differentiate male and female engineers, bus drivers, or lawyers (Frankenhaeuser, 1983).

Females report similar levels of discomfort to males in these situations, so emotional reactivity cannot explain this finding. Frankenhaeuser feels that it is related to male/female differences in coping with achievement and other environmental demands, produced by early socialization and sex-role stereotyping.

The apparent stability of their adreno-medullary system may explain why females on average live longer than males (Frankenhaeuser *et al*, 1978). A key element in the damaging effects of stressful stimuli is the mobilization by adrenaline of the body's fat reserves, which results in high blood levels of free fatty acids. These would be expended in physical effort, if such was the appropriate response to the stressor. However, many *psychological* stressors activate the adreno-medullary system, but have no correlated physical response -- we sit in the car, tense, frustrated, and occasionally angry, but perfectly immobile. Fatty acids accumulate in the bloodstream, and contribute significantly to the furring up of the cardio-vascular system. Females, responding less dramatically to stressful situations, would accordingly suffer less physiological damage, even though they suffer equivalent levels of psychological stress.

Such a dramatic finding from one laboratory needs replication and extension before it can be fully accepted. If it were reliable, and assuming that the *emotional* ranges of males and females are roughly equivalent, it would *lessen* the likelihood that adreno-medullary activity determines or is even closely related to subjective emotion. The relative unresponsiveness of noradrenaline to psychological stimuli supports this conclusion, and casts doubt on the results of Ax and Funkenstein. The fact that most of the classical work quoted in this section has used as subjects *male* American college students might explain why the male/female difference has not been picked up before.

Adrenaline release produces peripheral arousal. Frankenhaeuser's work shows that it is not associated with particular emotional states, and over a century of work on emotion and peripheral arousal has failed to produce an acceptable model of their interaction. Peripheral arousal mechanisms evolved to provide for action – energy expenditure – in the face of environmental demands. Any attempt to link them to emotional states must start by assessing the *motivational* aspects of the emotion; does it lead to a particular behavioural response?

Sleep

The occurrence of sleep across the animal kingdom implies that it has a necessary function, but does not distinguish between physiological hypo-theses (e.g. tissue restoration), psychological hypotheses (e.g. processing of the previous day's experiences), or ecological hypotheses (e.g. safety from predation). The regularity of sleep patterns within the *circadian* (i.e. about a day's length, 24 hours) cycle needs explanation. Is sleep actively triggered by the brain in response to darkness or to some biological rhythm such as temperature; or perhaps by the daily build-up of some 'need for sleep' represented by, for instance, a drop in synaptic transmitter levels? Alternatively, sleep might be a passive process; the natural state, as it were, into which the brain falls unless incoming environmental stimulation is sufficient to arouse it.

No single chapter can deal with all the questions. We shall present some hypotheses relating to many of them, and then review the current status.

The states of sleep

Our definition of the various states of sleep relies heavily upon the *electroencephalogram*. Using EEG recordings, many levels of sleep may be identified. The waking EEG is characterized by *desynchronized* (i.e. no regular wave form) fast activity. *Slow-wave sleep* (SWS) consists of a *synchronized* EEG (i.e. a regular wave form with *amplitude* and *frequency*). As one passes from light SWS to deep SWS the amplitude and frequency of the waves in the EEG increase and decrease respectively, i.e. the waves become bigger and slower. In *rapid eye movement* sleep the EEG is desynchronized and fast, rather like waking activity, yet behaviourally the subject is deeply asleep, as intense stimuli are necessary to awaken him. So it is often referred to as *paradoxical* sleep, but, more usually as it is associated with *rapid eye movements*, as REM sleep. Originally it was thought that dreams occurred only in this phase, and it was consequently called *dreaming* sleep, but we know now that dreams can also occur in SWS.

Birds and mammals exhibit light and deep SWS and REM, oscillating between waking, SWS and REM. The pattern is highly consistent; animals fall from waking into light SWS, and then into deeper SWS. After some time in deep SWS, sleep lightens and they move back into light SWS. At this point a phase of REM is triggered, from which they move back into light SWS and the cycle repeats itself: light SWS → deep SWS → light SWS → REM → light SWS, and so on.

In humans the cycle duration (from the triggering of successive phases of REM) averages around 60 minutes, so a normal night's sleep may contain six or seven REM interludes. As our sleep lightens towards morning we spend more time in light SWS and so the REM phases (apparently dependent upon preceding light SWS) become more frequent. Thus the dreaming associated with REM becomes more common and memorable as we approach awakening.

The patterning of awake → SWS → REM represents a fundamental biological rhythm. Behavioural measures of the developing foetus in the uterus reveal rhythmic cycles of quiescence and activity. EEG measures of waking, SWS, and REM, in premature and full-term newborns, show that the periodicity (or cycle duration) at 36 weeks post-conception is similar to that in the eight-month-old infant (Stern *et al*, 1973). So, although the ratio of REM sleep to SWS alters during the first post-natal year, with the proportion of REM gradually declining from 70 to 90 per cent to around 20 to 25 per cent of total sleep time, the complex cyclical pattern of waking and sleeping seems to be *endogenous* (inbuilt into the nervous system) and therefore present from birth.

SWS and REM sleep are qualitatively distinct states. Both have physiological and glandular correlates alongside their EEG patterns, and these have stimulated various hypotheses as to the functions of sleep.

The functions of sleep

If sleep were necessary, total sleep deprivation should produce some physiological or psychological effects, analogous to the consequences of food deprivation. However, rather like prolonged hunger, the impetus to sleep increases with moderate deprivation without any dramatic break-down in body or behaviour. We can endure hunger for many days without permanent ill-effects, and we can endure sleeplessness for many days without permanent damage; impressively, performance on various cognitive tasks can be sustained at a high level even after several days of sleep deprivation.

This phenomenon has been used by some authors to demonstrate the absence of any psychological or physiological 'drive' to sleep (Meddis, 1979), and has led to explanations on a more ecological level. However, prolonged sleep deprivation can lead to psychotic breakdown, in the same way that prolonged hunger leads to malnutrition and death, and perhaps sleep resembles primary homeostatic drives more than seems immediately obvious.

An alternative hypothesis has been put forward by Oswald (1976; 1980). During the phases of SWS the brain is unaroused in terms of the EEG, but there is much peripheral activity. The pituitary gland secretes large amounts of growth hormone, which stimulates protein synthesis throughout the body, suggesting to Oswald that SWS is associated with general tissue restoration. During REM, the brain is very active, with EEG arousal and a 'waking' level of cortical blood flow; Oswald feels that this activity reflects recovery processes in the brain. So, whereas Horne (1978, 1979) sees SWS and REM in higher mammals as times of brain restoration, Oswald links SWS with the body and REM with recovery processes in the brain.

Sleep and biological rhythms

There are many rhythms in our biological and even in our psychological systems. They can be grouped, first into *circadian* rhythms, following a daily (24 hour) cycle and including body temperature (which varies by about three degrees over 24 hours, with the trough in the early morning), secretion of corticosteroids from the adrenal medulla, and the sleep/waking cycle. Secondly there are *infradian* rhythms, with a frequency of less than one cycle/day, including hibernation in squirrels and bears and the female menstrual cycle. Thirdly there are *ultradian* rhythms, with a frequency greater than one cycle/day, exemplified by the SWS/REM cyclical pattern during sleep.

Surprisingly, and although many of these rhythms can be influenced by environmental factors (*zeitgebers*), they follow the sleep/waking cycle in being largely endogenous. In higher mammals the *supra-chiasmatic nucleus* close to the hypothalamus is a critical pacemaker for many biological rhythms. If it is destroyed, many biological systems lose their cyclical nature, including body temperature and corticosteroid secretion. If the neurons making up the supra-chiasmatic nucleus are isolated from the rest of the brain, they maintain their own intrinsic rhythmical firing pattern.

There have been several studies of subjects isolated for many days in constant light or dark conditions (underground caves are very popular). Under these conditions the sleep/waking cycle settles to a steady rhythm, but the cycle length usually increases slightly to around 25 hours. The body temperature cycle also settles down, but becomes decoupled from the sleep/waking routine; interestingly, this makes it possible to demonstrate that subjects sleep much longer if they fall asleep at a high point in the temperature cycle rather than at the usual low point (Czeisler *et al*, 1980).

The desynchronization of the rhythms also implies that there must be at least two endogenous pacemakers in the brain, and that external stimuli (zeitgebers, such as light) can exert some influence – the sleep/waking cycle does extend when light/dark cues are unavailable. The effects of light are probably mediated by a pathway which runs from the retina to the supra-chiasmatic nucleus.

Jet travel across time zones and industrial shift-work are everyday examples which involve a decoupling of biological rhythms – you are biologically awake when external cues are telling you to sleep. The period of jet lag and the adjustment to new shift-work patterns can take several days, a time of biological discomfort as the sleep/wake cycle and other biological rhythms gradually resynchronize.

Brain chemistry, sleep, and the reticular formation

Approaches to the brain mechanisms of sleep represent an interesting developmental picture of physiological psychology. Up to the 1960s the area was dominated by EEG and neuroanatomical investigations focusing upon the reticular formation. Then Jouvet (1969; 1972) suggested that the various phases of sleep (SWS and REM) could be best understood in terms of neurotransmitters and chemical pathways.

A central question in the area was whether sleep was an active or passive process, i.e. was it actively generated by centres within the brain, or did it occur passively when sensory input fell below a threshold level, so representing, as it were, the 'natural' state of the brain when incoming stimuli were insufficient to arouse it?

When, in 1949, Moruzzi and Magoun first demonstrated the behavioural and EEG arousing effects of electrically stimulating the *reticular formation*, it seemed that an endogenous arousal generator had been identified. The brainstem reticular formation is a core of tissue running through the brainstem. It was originally thought to consist of a relatively homogeneous network (or *reticulum*) of short-axon neurons, whose single but essential function was to control, or modulate, the arousal state of the neocortex. This was achieved via ascending connections between the brainstem reticular formation and the neocortex, and hence the common term *ascending reticular activating system*.

The view that the reticular formation is a single homogeneous structure controlling cerebral arousal independently of sensory input is now seen as too simple. Around one hundred separate groupings of nuclei have been identified within it and, as we shall see, different groupings have different functions in relation to sleep and arousal. In addition it receives sensory input directly via branches from the sensory pathways ascending through the brainstem (sensory collaterals), and the patterns of activity within it are almost certainly responsive to the general level of sensory input.

In the 1960s attention shifted from neuroanatomy to the neurochemistry of sleep and arousal. Jouvet (1969; 1972) performed a series of drug and lesion studies to investigate the mechanisms underlying SWS and REM in the cat. His manipulations focused upon two major systems in the brainstem reticular formation, the *locus coeruleus* and the *raphé nuclei*. The locus coeruleus lies in the pons, while the eight or so nuclear formations comprising the raphé system spread from the medulla through the pons to the anterior midbrain. Using cats, he found initially that raphé lesions produced a selective loss of SWS, while damage to the locus coeruleus produced a selective loss of REM. Total destruction of the extensive raphé system led to an almost complete insomnia; anterior lesions were most effective at reducing SWS while posterior lesions were most effective against REM.

However, sleep can also be produced or decreased by electrical and chemical stimulation of sites in the forebrain, and so the full characterization of the role of the raphé system in sleep will probably emerge from a study of its interactions with these forebrain centres.

Early experiments (Jouvet, 1972) suggested that lesions of the locus coeruleus led to a selective loss of REM sleep. However, Ramm (1979), in a review of the vast literature on the brain mechanisms of REM, concluded that damage to the locus coeruleus had little or no effect on the production and duration of either REM or SWS.

A major problem with REM is that it is measured by using a number of different signs, each of which may involve a different brain mechanism. The paradox of REM is that although we talk about it as though it were a homogeneous phenomenon, we are still hard put to give it a clear and unambiguous definition. The various signs are given different degrees of importance by different workers, and given its multiple characteristics it seems likely that it will not have a single control centre such as the locus coeruleus.

The reticular formation and forebrain hypnogenic centres

So far we have concentrated upon the brainstem reticular formation in relation to arousal. However, we have known for many decades that electrical stimulation and lesions of forebrain structures can produce arousal or sleep in their own right, and we now know that these structures are of equal importance to the reticular formation in the control of sleep and waking.

Lesions of the *posterior hypothalamus* produce a sleep-like state (Nauta, 1946), more profound than that produced by lesions of the brainstem reticular formation. Stimulation of the *orbito-frontal cortex* also produces electrophysiological and behavioural sleep (Bremer, 1977). The induction of sleep by electrical stimulation suggests that sleep is an *active* process; there are centres whose normal function is to inhibit the waking patterns of brain and behaviour and to impose the various sleep patterns. There is still the problem of what controls these *hypnogenic* (sleep-inducing) centres, to which we turn in a moment.

Besides the orbito-frontal cortex there is a zone in the basal forebrain, just rostral (anterior) to the optic chiasma and usually referred to as the *preoptic area*, where stimulation produces sleep and lesions lead to severe insomnia (Lucas and Sterman, 1975). The orbito-frontal and preoptic hypnogenic centres are closely related, and Morgane *et al* (1977) have suggested the existence of a *frontal-preoptic-limbic cortical sleep system*, incorporating orbito-frontal, basal preoptic, and limbic mechanisms.

It is now clear that there exist in the brain centres or mechanisms responsible either for the production of arousal or for the production of sleep, and the next question is how do they interact? Bremer (1977) feels that ascending reticular activity both arouses the cortex and inhibits forebrain hypnogenic mechanisms; these mechanisms are *tonically* inhibited, in the sense that they are continually activated but the manifestation of this activity, i.e. sleep, is suppressed so long as reticular arousal is sustained. Once reticular arousal falls below a certain threshold, the forebrain hypnogenic centres are released from the tonic inhibition, exert their synchronizing influence on the brain, and produce sleep. As reticular arousal is partly dependent on general sensory input, sleep is both *active*, in the sense of being generated by specific sleep mechanisms in the brain, and *passive*, in the sense of being expressed only when general sensory input and reticular arousal fade away (Figure 7.11).

Hypnogenic centres are undoubtedly exposed to other controlling influences. The direct links between the reticular formation and the forebrain sleep centres would help explain how the endogenous rhythm can be overridden if sensory stimulation from the environment, arousing the reticular formation, were intense enough.

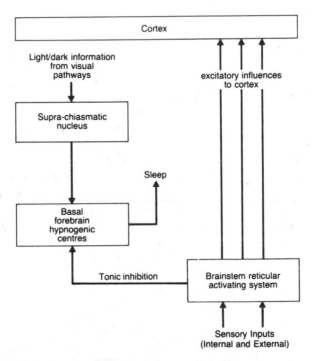

Figure 7.11 Reticular formation and forebrain hypnogenic centres. Reticular arousal is modulated by sensory inputs. When it falls below a threshold level, cortical excitability fades and tonic inhibition of hypnogenic centres is removed; they may then impose their natural function – sleep – on the brain, although they are still subject to control by endogenous oscillators in the supra-chiasmatic nucleus. (Other important centres, such as the thalamus and the midbrain waking centre, are omitted for the sake of simplicity.)

Further reading

Bloom, F. E., and Lazerson, A. (1988) *Brain, Mind, and Behaviour*. Freeman.
Green, S. (1987) *Physiological Psychology: An Introduction*. Routledge and Kegan Paul.

Chapter eight

Basic principles of learning

Philip Evans

Introduction

Elsewhere we have described naturalistic studies of animal behaviour (see Chapter 9). However, psychologists have also spent a good deal of this century performing laboratory experiments using animals with the express intention of formulating an analysis of how behaviour in general is shaped, organized and maintained. The role of evolution in adaptively shaping the behaviour of a particular species over the lifetimes of many individual members of that species was pertinent to the earlier chapter. The aim of the following chapter will be to see whether it has been possible to formulate general rules which govern the adaptation of an individual organism's behaviour to meet the pressures of its own unique environment. Adaptation, in this context, is synonymous with the term learning.

The search for general laws governing the learning process gains its momentum from the basic observation that simple and complex organisms alike seem to be capable of at least rudimentary learning, while in the most complex of all organisms – human beings – psychologists have tended to see most behaviour as learned. Roughly speaking, if we compare the balance of innately 'wired in' behaviour and learned behaviour, the balance shifts in favour of learning as we ascend from the lower to the higher animals. There are, however, other considerations. For example, we can, other things being equal, predict that an animal with a short lifespan, which reaches maturity very quickly, will not benefit from being genetically programmed to be a good learner; rather, it would be more helpful if it were endowed with a wide range of suitable innate responses ready for use very soon after birth. In an evolutionary context, then, we should see the capacity for learning itself as a piece of genetic programming, which, like anything else, will be tested, for a given species, by the pressures of natural selection. If the idea of being innately programmed to learn seems somewhat paradoxical, the reader has only to think about chess-playing computer programs. Here, the human creator is no longer content to supply a program with the ability to respond to specific moves, nor even to more general situations, but can build in a 'plasticity' which allows the program to alter itself as a result of its 'learning encounters' with its opponents.

But, given that at least rudimentary learning is seen across all species of animals, is it possible to give an account of its general operation, regardless of the particular species concerned? It might be helpful to draw an anology with someone wanting to investigate the workings of a particular part of a car; let us say the carburettor. S/he could take a particular model of car and study its carburettor and s/he would soon understand its function and method of operation. S/he might then move on to another model and discover that although the carburettor is of a different make, and indeed might look superficially very different, its method of operation and function are essentially the same. After some more experience with different types of carburettors it would be true to say that s/he knew something of the principles of carburation in cars. It is in this analogous sense that we want to see whether we can know about the principles of learning in organisms.

So, where do we begin? Pursuing our analogy a little further, our future carburation expert will hardly have begun with a study of the latest carburettor on the newest high performance model. Likewise, despite the interest it might have, we do not necessarily begin our investigation with human beings. As long as we are cautious about premature generalization of our findings we might begin with simpler 'model' species. For very good reasons, psychologists have chosen to carry out a lot of their laboratory experimentation using rats and pigeons. The first experiment, however, which we will consider utilized dogs.

An experiment by Pavlov

Ivan Petrovich Pavlov (1849–1936) was a celebrated Russian physiologist whose major interest, around the turn of the century, was the study of reflexes. In particular, he studied the salivation reflex in dogs. No one, least of all Pavlov himself, would have thought that his research would provide a foundation for the psychology of learning. After all, the reflex can be thought of as the purest example of innately 'wired-in' behaviour – a relatively simple response elicited by a relatively specific stimulus. However, during his work Pavlov became rather annoyed that the answers to his completely physiological questions were being hampered by the fact that, as the dogs became accustomed to the experimental situation, they would start to salivate and secrete stomach acids as soon as he himself walked into the room. These experimental nuisances he termed 'psychic secretions'. Pavlov, in studying them, soon came to see them as important in their own right.

The first question he asked himself was whether it was just the sight or smell of food that caused the salivation, or whether any stimulus, paired often enough with food, would have the same effect. To answer the question, he isolated just one seemingly neutral stimulus which on its own could not elicit salivation: he chose in fact a tone given by a tuning fork. He followed the tone, half a second later, by an insertion of food powder into the dogs' mouths. He repeated this pairing several times while recording the amount of salivation at every stage in the experiment. At the beginning salivation occurred only after a food delivery; but as the experiment proceeded, salivation commenced earlier and earlier until finally the secretion came before the food: that is to say, salivation was now elicited by a totally new stimulus – the previously neutral tone. This procedure is now termed 'classical conditioning'.

Classical conditioning

If a procedure is to have a wide degree of generality it has to be capable of being expressed in terms of nameable elements. What are those elements in classical conditioning? First, there is the unlearned reflex which one takes as a starting point. In the case of Pavlov's experiment we had a stimulus (food) and a response (salivation). Because, assuming the dog to be hungry, the relationship between these elements is automatic, or, to put it another way, unconditional, the food is known as the unconditioned stimulus (US) and the salivation is known as the unconditioned response (UR). The tone, or in more general terms the neutral element, is known as the conditioned stimulus (CS) and the novel response of salivation to the tone rather than the food is known as the conditioned response (CR). The whole procedure of Pavlov's experiment expressed in this general nomenclature is given diagrammatically in Figure 8.1. Various departures from that procedure are possible which will still result in conditioning, but the usual optimal interval between CS and US is short and of the order of 0.5 sec. Backward conditioning, where the whole order is changed and the CS follows the US, is a rare phenomenon, if, indeed, it occurs at all and is certainly beyond the scope of this introductory chapter.

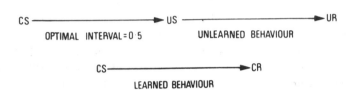

Figure 8.1 Diagrammatic representation of the standard classical conditioning procedure

Since the original experiments many more reflexes and many more species have been investigated, with the result that classical conditioning has become established as a learning phenomenon, capable of replication from one species to another. Where the same procedure gives the same results from one species to another with such reliability, one is perhaps justified in inferring a fundamental learning process shared by all organisms. Pavlov himself went further and believed that all learned behaviour, however complex, was, in principle, reducible to chains of conditioned reflexes. That belief is now, to say the least, debatable. However, we can outline one type of classical conditioning experiment which may give the reader some idea of the scope of the phenomenon in explaining behaviour.

The conditioning of emotional and physiological responses

When a person is anxious or afraid, certain bodily changes occur which can be measured using special instruments. One of these changes is in the electrical conductance of the skin. Because of the activity of tiny sweat glands, the skin becomes wetter and thus offers less electrical resistance. You may have noticed that when you become really anxious, the palms of your hands feel noticeably clammy; you do not, however, have to be that anxious in order that a sensitive device should measure a change in skin conductance. Indeed, the sensitivity of the response itself has led to its dubious use as a lie-detector in certain parts of the USA. But to return to the laboratory, if we can initiate a change in conductance (a so-called skin conductance response (SCR)), by a specific noxious stimulus, let us say a harmless but mildly painful electric shock, we have a ready-made unconditioned stimulus-response connection. Applying the Pavlovian procedure, it should be possible to pair an established neutral stimulus (CS) with the shock (US) and end up by eliciting an SCR (CR) to the CS alone. This indeed has proved eminently possible using human subjects. What, then, is the explanatory potential of this instance of classical conditioning?

The answer to this question comes from a consideration of the nature of the CS. In the laboratory, we might use a relatively meaningless stimulus such as a tone. However, conditioning also takes place outside the laboratory with an endless supply of possible CSs and noxious USs. Moreover, it takes place over a lifetime. If we say that the 'mental' correlate of our SCR is an emotion (let us say, anxiety) we are in a position to glimpse how conditioning theory may shed light on the acquisition of those bizarre and anxious behaviours seen in severe human neuroses. Moreover, classical conditioning could also explain the way each of us emotionally colours his own perception of the world. In a more general sense, a town, a house, a piece of furniture will have its own 'affective' meaning for us through particular emotional experiences.

A currently important area of research concerns the role of classical conditioning in 'psychosomatics' – how psychological events can influence disease processes. In particular Ader et al (1985) describe how immune-system responses can be conditioned. Such research strongly suggests some of the mechanisms which may be involved in the links which are increasingly being established between psychological events and episodes of infectious illness (e.g. Evans et al 1988).

We shall postpone further clinical speculations until we have said more about the nature of conditioning. Like the early researchers, we can best approach that task by asking ourselves a series of relevant questions, the answers to which will supply us with a variety of sub-topics.

Is conditioning permanent?

In order to investigate this question, let us return to Pavlov's laboratory and follow up those same dogs who have now learned to salivate to the sound of the CS tone. What happens, you may ask, if the experimenter carries on evoking the conditioned salivation response simply by presenting the tone (now on its own unaccompanied by food)? The answer is simple. The dog will eventually cease to salivate. This is a gradual process and is technically known as *extinction*. The first explanation that may come to mind is that the connection set up by the conditioning experience has to be 'reinforced' by the occasional re-presentation of the US (food), otherwise the connection simply breaks up and decays. Now, although the first part of that statement appears to be true (i.e. it seems that the connection has to be occasionally reinforced), the second part is untrue, and this can be demonstrated by the following procedure. Let us 'extinguish' the conditioned response in just the way we have described, and let us continue this procedure to the point where the dog no longer shows any salivation in the presence of the CS. If we now interrupt the trial either with a rest period, or, more briefly, by making a loud noise to distract the animal we shall find that the next presentation of the CS will produce the salivation response which we thought we had extinguished. Following a rest period this is known as *spontaneous recovery*. Pavlov discovered this effect and integrated it into his general theory. Basically, what he says is that the original conditioning is a form of active learning but so, also, is extinction. Far from the animal being passive in the extinction process, what it is learning to do is to inhibit the conditioned response. This view gains credibility if we look at Figure 8.2.

TIME

Figure 8.2

In Figure 8.2 we have deliberately omitted the parameters on the vertical axis, since they could be either a measure of the original conditioning or extinction. The point is that both follow the same pattern over time: acquisition and extinction curves have the same appearance. An unexpected stimulus, therefore, interrupts the inhibitory process, and the CR resurfaces, as it were. Hence Pavlov attributed the phenomenon to 'disinhibition'. Does this mean that conditioning, even if it goes underground, is really permanent? It would be foolhardly to take such a dogmatic view. Certainly, if we go on presenting unaccompanied CSs to the dog, it will, in time, reach a point of *zero extinction*, when no salivation can be elicited even after a rest or a distraction. And yet, even then, such a zero extinguished dog will be quicker to relearn the response than a completely naïve animal. So, it is not to be concluded that any link between the CS and the CR has decayed completely. Moreover, in the case of emotional conditioning, mentioned earlier, where anxiety or fear responses enter the picture, extinction is very difficult to achieve. This has led to some theorists such as Hans Eysenck to view certain traumatic conditioning as relatively irreversible. Conditioned anxiety can, as it were, be 'incubated'. The question, 'is conditioning permanent?' is therefore not a very fruitful one to ask; just as, in the related field of memory, it is often a sterile question to ask whether we ever completely forget anything, in the sense of its having decayed in storage.

What adaptive features does classical conditioning have?

If we had to learn a new response in every new situation, the flexibility of behaviour, conferred by learining, would soon be out-weighed, in so far as we would be spending all of our time in new learning and never, therefore, profiting from previous learning. It would make sense if some kind of transferability were built into the learning process. We know, of course, from our own experience that learned skills do transfer: an ordinary driving licence does not give me permission to drive a heavy articulated lorry; however, it is reasonable to suppose that I would be quicker at learning to drive the lorry than someone who had had no driving experience whatsover. In other words some of my skills can be transferred from one situation to another. Now, learning complex skills is far removed from the simple conditioned responses which we have been considering; and yet such conditioning also has transferability built into it, and this is seen in the phenomenon of *stimulus generalization*. Suppose we specify that the CS tone used in a Pavlovian-type experiment had a frequency of 500 Hz. After the CR has been fully established let us now see what happens if we test the dog with a different frequency CS tone, let us say 100 Hz above or below the training tone. We shall find that there is still a diminished but significant CR to the new stimulus. If we were to plot the magnitude of the CR stimuli above and below the training stimulus we would get *gradients of generalization* of the type seen in Figure 8.3.

Perhaps we should like to say that stimuli similar to the training stimulus have some natural capacity to evoke the CR. However, it might occur to the reader just how subjective the term 'similar' is. For instance, if we confine ourselves simply to a discussion of tone frequencies, where a physical dimension of similarity seems to be ready-made for us, we nevertheless encounter difficulty. Suppose our training stimulus was the note of middle C. Would a CR be greater in magnitude for the nearest F#

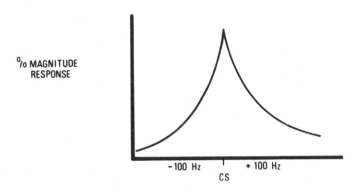

Figure 8.3

above middle C, or the more distant C octave above middle C? The answer (it even appears in rats) is that the more distant frequency is judged more similar and gives the greater response. Apart from the enchanting idea that we can talk of musical rats with a sense of octave, such a finding has other implications. These are most easily appreciated in a classic experiment by Razran using classical conditoning of human subjects.

He conditioned an electrodermal response, in the same way as we have mentioned already using mild electric shock as the US. However, rather than a tone as the CS, Razran used a visual stimulus consisting of the word 'sea'. When his subjects reliably gave an SCR to the presentation of the word, Razran tested their reaction to two words, both of which could be seen in some sense as similar. The first word was 'see' (defined as physically similiar since it is acoustically identical); the second word was 'wave' (in no way physically similar but semantically related). Razran's findings indicated that most response was obtained for the semantically similar word 'wave'. Semantic generalization can therefore be more important than physical generalization. The main problem then is the nature of 'similarity'; when this encompasses semantic similarity, we can envisage the generalization of the conditioned anxiety responses mentioned earlier to a wide variety of objects and situations, which make up totally idiosyncratic clusters of associated meaning for any individual. Perhaps this offers us some further insight into the acquisition of bizarre and neurotic anxieties in clinical patients; their diffuse anxiety may be idiosyncratically generalized anxiety responses.

What about unwanted generalization?

It is not always in the interest of an organism to show generalization of its learning. It could well be that a new stimulus, though perceived as similar to an old one, requires a very different response. Reverting to our driving skills example, imagine that you are well practised in the various habits associated with the driving of a manual gearbox car. Let us also suppose that you have the ingrained common, but perhaps not desirable habit of revving the engine at traffic lights. Further suppose that you now drive an automatic car. Unless you consciously prevent generalization of the habit, the consequence of revving up could turn out to be a little unfortunate.

So there has to be a check on generalization. Organisms must have a compensating capacity for learning discriminations, and this is just what we find even in the case of simple classical conditioning.

In a typical Pavlovian-type experiment, dogs were trained to salivate to the CS of a circle. At first, the animals showed typical generalization of the salivation response to circular-type figures, notably an ellipse. However, by presenting food powder (US) only in the presence of the circle and not in the presence of the ellipse, the generalization process was halted; the animals had learned a discrimination. Now comes the interesting question. The animal salivates to a full circle and not to a full ellipse, but what happens if we gradually start to introduce more and more ambiguous figures, ending up with a stimulus exactly half-way between a circle and an ellipse? The answer is that not only does the animal's discrimination break down, so does the animal! Emotional responses take over and the animal whimpers and howls as it is taken into the laboratory. Procedures of this kind have been deemed 'experimental neuroses', in the belief that they can shed light on the rudimentary mechanisms that may underline more complex human conflicts.

Can any neutral stimulus become a CS?

We might as well first raise the fundamental question of whether there can ever be such a thing as a truly neutral stimulus. To any organism, a perceived change in its environment (which is what a stimulus really amounts to) is important. Indeed, any novel stimulus evokes what is called an orientating response (OR). If we measure that response as we continue to present the stimulus over and over again, we find the response wanes to zero. The process is much akin to extinction, but because the OR to the stimulus did not require prior learning, the term *habituation* is used.

Now, the usual method of establishing the 'neutrality' of a potential CS, prior to conditioning, is to test it out by presenting it on its own before associating it with the US. If it in no way evokes part of the UR, then it is assumed neutral. If this procedure were not followed and the potential CS had already got some association with the UR, it would be very easy to think that one had established conditioning. However, such conditioning would be only apparent not real, and the term *pseudo-conditioning* has been coined for it.

Matters would be very simple if any stimulus (established as neutral in the sense given above) could be classically conditioned. But matters are not that simple.

It is readily apparent that certain CS–CR links are very easy to establish, while others are next to impossible. The terms *prepared* and *contra-prepared* have been coined by Seligman (1972) to describe (but not explain) such differences in conditionability. It is probable that organisms are biologically 'tuned' to properties of the environment which are important for survival. Potential dangers should then more easily come to elicit fear than neutral or potentially positive stimuli. Potentially rewarding stimuli by contrast should be more difficult to associate with fear. Conditioning studies with human subjects have shown, for example, that facial expressions involving positive emotion are less easily associated with painful events than negative emotional expressions (Ohman and Dimberg, 1984).

Instrumental conditioning

While the Russian researcher, Pavlov, was busy with his experimental dogs, an American psychologist, Thorndike, had been carrying out experiments with cats. Thorndike devised puzzle boxes: boxes from which the animal could escape if it could discover a certain trick, namely unhooking a catch. Thorndike noticed that the animals acquired the correct response in a gradual fashion and likened the process to trial-and-error learning whereby the correct response was gradually 'stamped in' as a result of being 'rewarded' by escaping. This he called the Law of Effect. Later on psychologists extended research to the laboratory white rat (an excellent learner) and to puzzles which enabled better observation and measurement of such learning – a simple T-maze, for example (see Figure 8.4).

Such apparatus enables the researcher to take more than one measurement of learning. He can look at the rate at which errors are eliminated and also look at the so-called 'latency' of the response – in other words the time involved in initiating a correct run of the maze. As research became even more systematic, psychologists such as Clark Hull began to investigate the effects of motivational factors in such learning. *Drive* was objectively defined in terms of the hours of food deprivation; *incentive* was defined in terms of the amount of food offered as a reward at the end of the maze. Hull and his colleagues hoped to build up a mighty edifice of behaviour theory in which the occurrence of any response was, in principle, predictable from a mathematical equation in which a finite

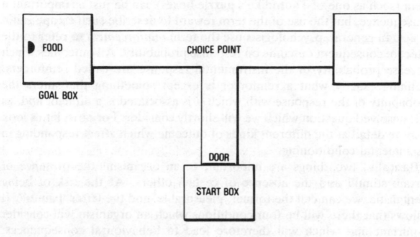

Figure 8.4

number of motivational and learning variables, such as drive and habit strength, interacted to give a final probability value for the particular response. Hull's school of research came to dominate the academic psychology taught throughout the middle period of this century; and yet, the promise of a complete behaviour theory was not fulfilled, despite the efforts of tens of thousands of hungry and hard-working white rats. Psychologists nowadays tend to shun the ideal of such an enterprise.

Despite the failure of the Hullian school, they and other animal experimenters have given us much information about how organisms in general do 'learn by reward'. Thorndike's 'stamping in' procedure is now generally talked about and investigated under the heading *instrumental conditioning*. The barest skeleton of the procedure is to follow a particular response with a 'reward', with the result that that particular response will increase in probability in that situation. The procedure is also called operant conditioning, particularly by the followers of B. F. Skinner (see later).

The concept of reinforcement

We have been content so far to talk about responses being learned by 'reward', but that is an oversimplification. In instrumental conditioning, we are really talking about a general learning ability, observable across species, which enables the organism to adapt its behaviour in the light of its environmental consequences for that organism. Consequences which are important for an animal, such as acquiring food when it is hungry, are quite easily spoken of as rewards. However, escaping from a noxious environment (such as one of Thorndike's puzzle boxes) can be just as important a consequence, but the use of the term reward to describe such escape is not so apt. In general, psychologists use the term *reinforcement* to refer to the effect of consequent outcome on response probability. All outcomes which increase probability of the instrumental response are called reinforcers. Defining exactly what a reinforcer is except something that alters the probability of the response with which it is associated is a difficult and, as yet, unsolved question which we will shortly consider. For now, let us look in more detail at the different kinds of outcome which affect responding in instrumental conditioning.

Basically, two things are important to an organism: the presence of certain stimuli and the absence of certain others. At the risk of being mentalistic, we can call the former 'pleasurable' and the latter 'painful'. It follows that there will be four conditions which an organism will consider important and which will therefore lead to behavioural consequences. These four conditions are summarized in Table 8.1:

Table 8.1

	Presentation	Removal
Pleasant stimuli	Positive reinforcement	Omission
Noxious stimuli	Punishment	Escape

It can be seen that the loose term 'reward' properly applies only to the positive reinforcement situation. The escape situation is similar in the sense that the associated response will become more probable, hence the term 'negative reinforcement' is sometimes substituted for escape. The other two situations have the opposite effect on response probability; a response followed by punishment (note: *not* negative reinforcement), other things being equal, will lead to a lowered probability of that response. Omission of a positive reinforcer will have the same effect as punishment, hence the term 'negative punishment' is sometimes substituted for omission.

What is learned in instrumental conditioning?

Thorndike and the early researchers mostly agreed that the nature of instrumental conditioning was the building up of habits or stimulus-response connections. Now, in an obvious sense this is indisputable. In all experiments, we come to see a functional probabilistic relationship build up between a stimulus and a response. However, the early researchers wanted to go further than this. They belonged to the Behaviourist school (see Chapter 1) and, therefore, sought to dismiss the importance of that which was not directly observable: cognition and consciousness. In so far as they were dealing with animals, it became an anathema to admit that anything of that kind went on inside the animal's head! Thus a direct mechanical link between stimulus and response was held, on faith, to be the actual nature of what was learned. It was as if the stimulus and response were wired up together by the blind operation of reinforcement. However, even in the early days there were 'cognitive' theorists such as Tolman who disputed the over-simplified Behaviourist view and indeed quickly caused modifications to simple Behaviourism as a result of their experiments.

Tolman showed that rats, once they had learned to run a maze, could, if circumstances demanded it, swim thought it. He also showed that rats in a cross-maze learned where to go rather than what to do, as demonstrated by their ability to proceed to the food regardless of their entry point to the maze. In essence, Tolman showed an animal's flexibility in its mode of response. He believed that the nature of learning was to perfect what he called 'maps in the head'. Rather than learning consisting of simple stimulus-response connections, Tolman believed that learning was about what stimulus goes with what other stimulus (S-S, i.e. stimulus-stimulus connections rather than S-R connections). The organism selects a response on the basis of this 'information'.

The debate between S-S and S-R theorists has now become largely historical. At a physiological level the attendant questions will not be answered for a considerable time and speculation is not profitable. At a behavioural level, everyone has agreed that, regardless of the physiological nature of learning, it is useful and possible to explore the systematic way in which events in an organism's environment and its responses develop into a functional relationship. Responses become measurably contingent upon events. The field of instrumental conditioning tends no longer to be about speculative S-R connections but about observable S-R contingencies (Rachlin, 1976; Davey and Cullen, 1988).

Is reinforcement a necessary condition of learning?

This question is closely allied to the previous one and is also largely historical. It can be seen that if Tolman is right that learning is essentially about the acquisition of information, one can draw a distinction between learning and performance. Reinforcement may not be necessary for learning; it may simply be the important variable which determines whether the animal translates covert learning into overt behaviour. Tolman and Honzig (1930) carried out a seminal experiment to try and demonstrate this. The experiment was to compare three groups of rats in a maze learning task. One group was given reinforcement (food) after each trial; the second group (control) was never given reinforcement; the third group was not given reinforcement until the eleventh trial. Tolman was able to show that the last group resembled the control group until trial eleven, showing little evidence, therefore, of learning. After trial eleven they very quickly caught up with the first group. The results are presented graphically in Figure 8.5.

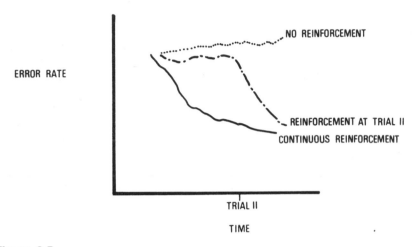

Figure 8.5

The experiment appeared to confirm Tolman's suspicion that 'latent' learning had taken place in the absence of reinforcement; when reinforcement was later introduced this 'latent' learning made itself apparent in the ease with which the Group 3 animals caught up with the Group 1 animals. Tolman's results could be countered by saying that there was some implicit reinforcement present in the earlier trials, e.g. being returned to the familiar home cage from the alien goal box. The trouble is that no one has been able to give a strict definition of reinforcement that covers all instances. We have, therefore, to make do with an operational definition, defining a reinforcer in terms of its effect on the probability of a preceding response. This, however, is essentially circular, and its circularity is particularly noticeable when we raise a question, such as 'is reinforcement necessary for learning?', where we need to have an outside criterion of what constitutes a reinforcer. Unless and until the concept becomes more refined any final answer to this question has to be shelved.

Is consciousness necessary for instrumental learning?

Many people enter and leave the area of conditioning with either an enthusiastic or a dispararging notion that it all boils down to what everyone knew already: the power of the stick and the carrot. Such a view needs so much qualification that it is in the end misleading. Nowadays, not many psychologists deny the importance of consciousness or awareness as something that often mediates between stimulus and response. We also know from our own experience that crude attempts to apply stick or carrot to human subjects very often give contrary results to those we would expect. A parent hitting a child for bad behaviour might not only fail to curb that behaviour but instead increase its likelihood. A political party holding out some obvious carrot to the electorate might be so mistrusted as to lose votes as a result. These examples demonstrate that, far from consciousness being necessary for instrumental conditioning, it may complicate it to the point of contrary findings. Conditioning is often most interesting as a phenomenon when reinforcement works gradually and blindly at shaping habitual patterns of behaviour which are not very often the focus of conscious control: a person's gait, his habitual mode of speaking, the attitudes he has come to hold (but has never consciously decided to hold). Certainly there seems to be evidence from a number of studies on 'verbal' conditioning that usage of certain words or types of words can be shaped by 'rewarding' them with approving utterances such as 'mm-hm' (Krasner, 1958). Although there are problems with measuring something like awareness, it does seem that these effects can be obtained without the subject being able to specify the contingency between the key words and the reinforcement. It goes without saying that much classical conditioning occurs without awareness. The whole area of interoceptive conditioning of visceral responses is an obvious case in point.

Classical and instrumental conditioning compared

We have described two rather different conditioning *procedures*. What we could, however, ask is whether these two different procedures reflect two fundamentally different learning *processes*, or whether, at root, there is just one process called conditioning. A quick look at the conditioning phenomena that we have mentioned might suggest that the differences may only be superficial. After all, both classical and instrumental responses undergo the same extinction process when either the US or reinforcer respectively is omitted. Moreover, the extinction curves in both instances follow the same pattern. The same similarity between the two kinds of conditioning procedure is seen when we examine the phenomenon of generalization. A rat which has learned (instrumentally) to press a bar for food when a tone sounds will show generalization of its behaviour in the event of similar tones being sounded.

Despite these similarities, a number of psychologists have put forward strong reasons for isolating two separate kinds of conditioning underlying the procedures. Perhaps most importantly, they have drawn a distinction between the type of response which is conditioned in each case. Classical conditioning deals with essentially involunatary emotional or glandular responses which are mediated by the autonomic nervous system; instrumental conditioning deals with essentially voluntary responses, which may be described as deliberate skeletal movements. This major division has been upheld by many notable psychologists including, in particular, B. F. Skinner. However, it was questioned in a series of experiments conducted by Neal Miller and colleagues. Miller managed to train rats to alter their 'involuntary' autonomic functioning in order to obtain a reward. Even before these well-controlled experiments, it had been shown that human subjects could also control supposed involuntary responses, such as heart-rate and blood-pressure, if they were provided with so-called bio-feedback. What Miller showed in his experiments was that this was not due to mediation by essentially voluntary responses, such as indulging in exciting fantasy, or making certain muscular movements. Miller's rats were totally paralysed and received reward in the from of direct stimulation of 'pleasure' areas in the brain. The only interpretation seemed to be that the rats were directly controlling autonomic responses.

However, Miller's experiments cannot be said to prove a one-process view of conditioning, since they leave open the possibility that the two kinds of procedure might still be more appropriate for different kinds of response, even if, in principle, involuntary responses can be instrumentally conditioned. Also, the experiments in this vein have since been plagued by serious problems of replication.

Schedules of reinforcement

We have scarcely yet mentioned one of the key figures in the development of learning principles, namely B. F. Skinner (b. 1904). And yet, it is to him and his colleagues that we owe most concerning our knowledge about the operation of reinforcement, particularly reinforcement *contingencies*. What do we mean by contingencies? Till now, our brief perusal of the field of instrumental conditioning has tended to assume a situation in which simple responses are stamped in by the operation of continuous rcinforcement after each correct response. Skinner's work takes us beyond this simple outline in two respects.

Skinner's work

First, he has been concerned with how more complicated responses can be shaped by reinforcing, at first, only gross approximations to the eventually desired response. In this way, quite extraordinary behaviour was engineered, the best known Skinnerian feat being ping-pong playing pigeons. Secondly, he has been interested in how conditioned behaviour can be maintained, not just by continuous reinforcement, but by *partial* (or *intermittent*) reinforcement. Such work is of great interest, since the behaviour of men and women in the real world is not usually followed by its due reward on every occasion. In other words, intermittent reinforcement of responding is nearer the real-life situation.

Before we outline some of Skinner's major findings, it is necessary to give a brief description of his typical laboratory method and apparatus. Skinner was the inventor of what has naturally enough become known as the 'Skinner-box'. This is essentially a chamber (see Figure 8.6), in which a small animal (usually a pigeon or white rat) is exposed to a highly-controlled environment. Reinforcement can be given automatically by a special mechanism linked to a bar, which the animal presses, or a key which is pecked. Skinner conceives of the organism continuously 'operating' on its environment. The behaviour can be studied in terms of small units called 'operant' responses. For this reason, Skinner uses the term *operant conditioning* instead of instrumental.

To return to the Skinner-box; obviously a naive rat cannot go straight up to a bar, press it, and receive a food reward. The behaviour is shaped; at first the rat will find out where the food-cup is located and a few carefully delivered pellets will keep the animal predominantly on the correct side of the box; later, the experimenter will demand more of the rat so that it must now at least be in contact with the bar; thus the final bar-pressing behaviour is shaped. Once a rat is fully trained in emitting the correct operant response, the Skinner-box comes into its own as a method of studying behaviour. One can introduce *discriminative stimuli* such as a green or red light which signals to the animal that reinforcement will or will not follow a bar press. Importantly, one does not have to follow a response with reinforcement on every occasion, and we now come on to a consideration of partial reinforcement.

One of the most important findings with regard to partial reinforcement of any kind is that the extinction process is lengthened. Let us examine what that, in fact, means. When a response is reinforced on every occasion (continuous reinforcement) the sequel in the extinction process of withdrawing reinforcement is a speedy diminution of responding. If, however, the organism's responding has been maintained by partial reinforcement, the extinction process is lengthened and, in some exceptional cases, can be avoided altogether. This is known as the partial reinforcement effect (PRE). Psychologists have put forward a number of theories to try to explain PRE, all of which possibly contain an element of truth. One common sense theory is that the animal has to learn to discriminate clearly between the acquisition/maintenance situation and the extinction situation

Figure 8.6 A pigeon in a Skinner-box

before it can change its behaviour (remember that extinction itself is a form of active learning not to respond). Now, in the instance of partial reinforcement the discrimination is not so easy since the organism has already learned not to expect reinforcement on each and every occasion; hence, the extinction process will take that much longer. Yet another theory bases PRE on inferred emotional responses which may be considered to be akin to conditioned frustration. These frustration responses can normally be thought of as motivating the inhibition of responding. However, in the partial reinforcement situation, such responses have been associated with the occasional presence of reinforcement; hence, the organism will tolerate much more frustration without a deterioration in performance. Although frustration responses are not directly observable, there is supportive evidence for this view in the common finding that the usual extinction process does lead to signs of emotionality in all organisms.

Specific types of schedule

Let us now be more exact about partial reinforcement. One can omit to reinforce an organism in many different ways. One could decide to reinforce every fifth, every tenth, or every fifteenth response; equally, one could, when the animal is responding properly, gradually make the

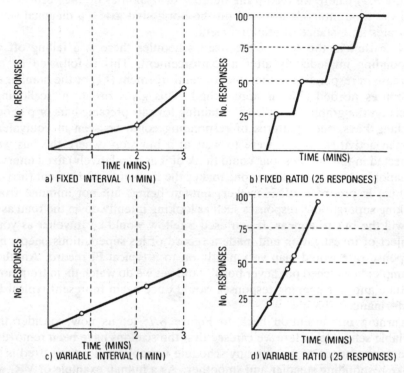

Figure 8.7 Cumulative records of different schedules (circles denote reinforcement)

reinforcement contingent upon the passage of time rather than the number of responses emitted; in other words the animal may be given a reward every minute, two minutes and so on. Ferster and Skinner (1957) discuss such schedules in great detail, but for our purposes we shall simply outline the two major types of schedule: they are *ratio* and *interval*, and they approximate to the examples given above. A ratio schedule requires the animal to make a fixed number of responses per reward; an interval schedule dictates that an animal will get a reward after a fixed time interval of responding regardless of how many responses it may make. Note the qualifying adjective 'fixed' – the schedules are known as fixed ratio (FR) and fixed interval (FI). However, it is equally possible to vary the ratio and vary the interval. Instead of reinforcement following every fifth response, for example, one could simply determine that on average the reinforcement will follow five responses. This is known as a variable ratio schedule (VR). Likewise, the reward which comes every five minutes on average would be an example of a variable interval schedule (VI).

These four major types of schedule give rise to typical patterns of responding which we can illustrate by the use of cumulative graphs (see Figure 8.7) where we record the number of responses on the vertical axis and the time intervals involved on the horizontal axis – a diagonal slash indicates an instance of reinforcement.

Note that in the case of the fixed schedules there is a falling off of responding immediately after a reinforcement. This is followed by an increase in responding as the time for reinforcement (FI) or the number of responses needed (FR) is approached. This gives rise to a 'scalloping' effect on the graph. Apart from obtaining for rats pressing bars or pigeons pecking keys, such patterns of responding could be seen in equivalent human activities. If you were to wait at a bus-stop, where the bus was expected in ten minutes, one could think of it as a (relatively) fixed interval situation; whatever responses one makes the time of reinforcement (arrival of bus) is preordained. However, human beings are not immune from making superstitious responses such as looking intently down the road as if to will the bus to appear. If you used a fellow would-be traveller as your subject of investigation and made a record of his superstitious peeps, his response rate would map very neatly on to a typical FI record. Another example: 'a watched pot never boils' – and yet we do watch them from time to time and our peeping responses would once again represent typical FI performance.

Turning our attention back to Figure 8.7, let us now consider the variable schedules. Here we can see that the scallops have been removed. The consequence of making any schedule variable rather than fixed is to make responding steadier and smoother. As a human example of VR, we can take the activity of playing a one-armed bandit. Here reinforcement is dependent on bar-pressing rather than time, but the number of bar-presses required for a reinforcement is variable. The kind of behaviour elicited in the gambler is obviously just what the machine's owner wants. A form of VR schedule is to be found lurking behind most gambling situations and partially explains the compulsive nature of the responding which it engenders: the fact that the investment of the responder is not usually equalled by his pay-off offers only a cognitive awareness which in some cases may be of little value in limiting compulsive responding.

Much contemporary operant research is concerned with more complicated scheduling of reinforcement, although this often involves 'packaging' of these basic schedules. Two broad types of schedules are of interest: concurrent schedules and consecutive schedules.

On concurrent schedules, an organism can choose between two schedules which are both available. For example, a pigeon may peck one of two keys, with different reward contingencies on each. Concurrent schedules have been much used in the study of choice behaviour (see below).

Consecutive scheduling involves 'chaining' one schedule to another. In the case of two schedules this may mean that they alternate. Signals may or may not be present which tell the subject which schedule is in operation. These sorts of schedule have been much used for studying predictability and preference for information (see below).

Choice and a quantitative law of effect

Thorndike's discovery of a so-called law of effect has been mentioned at an earlier point in this chapter. Many exciting developments in more recent operant research have focused on the quantifying of such a law. Herrnstein (1970), in particular, has been responsible for discovery and development in this area. On variable interval schedules it tends to be the case that the rate of responding (R) is an increasing negatively accelerated function of reinforcement frequency (r). This gives rise to the sort of hyperbolic curve illustrated in Figure 8.8. The exact form of the curve depends on two constants, namely the theoretical maximum response rate (R max) and the reinforcement frequency pertaining at half R max (Kh). The illustrated curve is then determined by an equation of the following form: $R = r \times R$ max $/ (r + Kh)$.

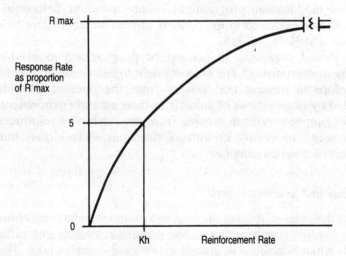

Figure 8.8

Even when we are considering a single response, we can view the situation as one in which an organism is choosing between responding and not responding. The predictive power of the equation is seen more clearly, however, when we consider an organism's behaviour when faced with two possible responses, in a concurrent paradigm, each associated with its own reinforcement frequency. How does a pigeon for example choose to allot its pecking responses between two keys when different variable interval schedules are linked to each? The answer in such cases is that the pigeon will 'match' its responding to the reinforcement 'pay-off' of the keys; if reinforcement is twice as frequent on one key it will peck that key twice as often. As long as certain procedural details are followed, e.g. scheduling a change-over delay, this matching law is robust across different species, including humans. Thus if 'a' and 'b' are the two schedules offered concurrently then Ra/Rb = ra/rb.

Matching is not seen in relation to all choice paradigms. Sometimes, for example, a pigeon will choose to respond on a single key which offers most reinforcement. Some have argued that the foundation of 'matching' is 'maximizing' the available pay-off. Thus matching is only in evidence precisely when it achieves maximization. These issues have been debated at great length by operant researchers (see, for example, Prelec, 1982). What is certainly true is that the matching law has been profitably applied to a range of interesting human behaviour, including vigilance (Baum, 1975), verbal behaviour (Conger and Killeen, 1974) and attention (Baron *et al*, 1988). Moreover, in so far as a quantitative law of effect instructs us to examine the reinforcement for alternative behaviours as crucially as target behaviours, it is not surprising that it has been used to plan behaviour modification programmes, where 'problem' behaviour can be seen as choice exercised in the context of possible alternative behaviours (Myerson and Hale, 1984).

Why should organisms in general be programmed to exhibit lawful matching or maximizing? The answer ought to lie in evolutionary fitness. It is therefore interesting that results from the operant laboratory are paralleled by observations of animals in their natural environments. Here their foraging behaviour in moving from one 'clump' of reinforcement to another seems to involve optimizing strategies which closely mirror the operation of a maximising law.

Behaviour and aversive events

Many of the rules governing the acquisition and maintenance of behaviour using rewarding consequences of the positive reinforcement variety have parallels when behaviour is shaped by aversive consequences. Thus, if an animal learns that it can escape a shock by pressing a lever, or jumping over a hurdle we would find that response will increase in frequency just like a positively reinforced response. For this reason *escape learning* is also referred to as negatively reinforced behaviour, and it appears to satisfy all the obvious canons of instrumental conditioning.

It is far more debatable to say that *punishment* procedures are so alike, since no particular response is being shaped. All that punishment may do is suppress a target response, and suppression and unlearning are not the same thing, as any parent should be able to testify. Child psychologists do not usually recommend using punishment as a standard way of shaping and controlling a child's behaviour. This is not only because child psychologists are kind people. There is a good deal of evidence to suggest that punishment techniques are, first, not particularly effective and, secondly, often have unwelcome consequences as side-effects. Let us examine some of these disadvantages of punishment procedures.

The disadvantages of punishment

In a laboratory we have almost complete control of an animal subject, so it is not surprising that a rat which receives a punishment for going down one alley rather than another will cease that particular response quite soon after the delivery of a few mildly painful electric shocks. Even in the laboratory we are not always likely to get such clear-cut results and paradoxical effects can result from such procedures. In normal life, the amount of control we have over other people is very properly limited and that applies to a parent and a child. Let us suppose that a parent punishes a child for aggression against other children, obviously in the hope that punishment will reduce the frequency of future aggressive encounters. This consequence, on its own, is, however, just one of many. Let us consider some other consequences:

1. The child learns to be selective about his aggressive encounters avoiding only those which are likely to come to the attention of his parents.
2. The child learns to avoid the presence of the aversive source of stimulation, i.e. the parent thus keeping punishment encounters to a minimum.
3. The child learns by example that his father can control him by what psychologists call 'power-assertive' techniques. Thus, as long as he also learns the first lesson that we outlined he should convince himself that, apart from the dangers of being caught, his own power-assertive ways of dealing with other children are just the thing.

None of the three outcomes above is desirable, nor were they intended. There is good evidence, however, to believe that they are very common outcomes. It is, for example, a well-established statistic that parents who use 'power-assertive' techniques of discipline tend to have distinctly more aggressive children on average.

There is another distinct disadvantage of punishment as a means of control. This derives directly from its vagueness in terms of goals. Punishment, at most, can only indicate what is undesirable or unwanted behaviour, it cannot indicate what is desirable or wanted. If a parent resorts to punishment as a way of bringing up a child, only offering criticisms, slaps, and shouting sessions, then it will not be surprising that the child will have little idea of what is expected of him. Add to this the established finding that power-assertive parents are also inconsistent in their demands of their children, and we have a very sorry picture and a very confused child.

There is yet another factor which needs to be mentioned, and that is that punishment, whether it be applied to a laboratory white rat or human kind, has attendant emotional consequences. Some years ago, Neal Miller carried out an experiment in which electric shock was given to a rat in a cage containing another rat. The shocked rat immediately attacked the other rat. Across species, aggression is a very common response to punishing consequences.

Avoidance and signals

We have so far looked at two procedures involving aversive events: escape and punishment. There is a third procedure which has been extensively researched by those involved in laboratory analysis of behaviour. It is called avoidance. Suppose we introduce in the normal escape procedure an additional stimulus which reliably predicts the arrival of the shock – for example it might be that a red light comes on a few seconds before the shock. We shall find that it is not long before the animal starts to make a response before the arrival of the actual shock. Rather than simply escaping the shock, it can now successfully avoid it altogether. This procedure is known as *signalled avoidance*.

Avoidance responses are often extremely durable once learned, and this led many early theorists to believe that it was classically conditioned emotional responses (CERs) roughly synonymous with 'fear' and elicited by the warning stimulus which actually motivated the instrumental avoidance response, which in turn was reinforced by fear diminution. This so-called two-factor theory involving classical and instrumental conditioning cannot so simply explain avoidance learning but there is equally no doubt that CERs can be involved (Mineka, 1979). Many would still hold such a conditioning model of phobic avoidance seen in clinical practice, albeit qualified by notions such as preparedness and generalization discussed earlier.

What is perhaps more interesting, given that such warning stimuli potentially elicit anxiety, is that they are often sought out. It is not perhaps surprising that signals which allow an organism to avoid successfully are sought out; it is less immediately evident why an organism prefers, for example, signalled inescapable shock to unsignalled inescapable shock. Yet, they certainly do. Rats will actually choose signalled shock despite its being more intense or more frequent than unsignalled. Why?

One possibility is that an organism likes to be informed. There are parallels here with the area of positive reinforcement schedules. Several investigators have demonstrated that rats and pigeons will show preference for component schedules where food delivery is signalled, even though no additional food is thereby earned. (For a review see Fantino and Logan, 1979.) However, such experiments have also demonstrated that such animals can be choosy about what sorts of information they show preference for. They will, for example, make an operant 'observing' response in order to know that food will be delivered on a certain schedule but not that food will be withheld (an extinction schedule). In a series of experiments Badia and his colleagues (Badia *et al*, 1979) showed the same sort of effect in regard to threatened shock. When a signal unreliably signals shock but its absence reliably predicts safety from shock, an animal will show preference for such information. When, however, the signal reliably signals shock but its absence does not guarantee safety it will not show preference. This has led to a theoretical view termed the 'Safety Signalling Hypothesis'. In so far as the hypothesis has received much general support, we may ask ourselves what lies behind it. As with the Matching Law discussed earlier, we may speculate that the answer may lie in evolutionary fitness. An animal in its natural habitat will often have two primary concerns: to feed well and to avoid falling victim to predators. It must therefore strike a balance in its time allocation between vigilant attention to 'warning stimuli' and feeding-related behaviour. An optimal strategy would be to concentrate on learning to recognize best those signals whose absence provide the surest guarantee of safety.

Humans are clearly more complex than animals in the business of preferring or not preferring information about dangers, or indeed reinforcement. However, there is a good deal of evidence that we, too, often prefer predictability to unpredictability. As is the case with other animals preference for information seems linked to utility that might follow in its wake. Predictability is sought in so far as it confers controllability. This has been confirmed in a number of experiments with human subjects (Averill *et al*, 1977; Evans *et al*, 1984). However, vigilance, involving looking out for warning stimuli, is only one of many 'coping strategies' available to human beings. In particular human beings are capable of cognitive coping strategies which enable them 'mentally' to avoid or reduce the intensity of a threat. There is also evidence that excessively vigilant coping is accompanied by heightened autonomic arousal, which may, in a chronic situation, be linked to stress and illness. Evans and Moran (1987) present evidence that persons scoring highly on Type A, thought to be a behaviour pattern associated with risk of coronary heart disease, are more prone to choosing vigilant coping and exhibiting higher cardiovascular arousal. Brady (1958) showed that 'executive' monkeys who exercised control over shocks developed more gastric ulcers than 'yoked' partners who had no control but received shocks as and when their executive failed to respond.

Brady's results are interesting because they are not predicted by a theory of learned helplessness advanced by Seligman (1975) which has been very influential over the last decade. For Seligman, initially at least, 'helplessness' – a lack of control – was seen as a disaster for organisms: a route to depression and indeed ulcers! Using mice as subjects but otherwise replicating Brady, Weiss (1977) found that the 'helpless' partners developed more ulcers than the 'executive' mice. Which pattern of results one gets, Brady's or Weiss's, seems to depend critically on the effortfulness of the control on offer, which points again to the importance of balancing the positive and negative aspects of predictability and controllability. Especially in the case of humans the answer depends on both the situation and the person. If we ask the simple question: will it hurt less if I can control it?, we find the answer is complex. That question and that answer provided Thompson (1981) with a nice title for her review paper, to which the interested reader can refer for further detail.

Conclusion

Some of the developments in modern learning theory which we have seen, particularly aspects of the Matching Law and Safety Signalling, emphasize a general way in which modern theory differs from classical behaviourism. No longer is the talk about stimulus-response connections. Instead theorists are more interested in specifying the broad but lawful correlations which can be plotted between behaviour and particular arrangements of discriminatory and reinforcing stimuli. Moreover, and to differing degrees, there is growing eclecticism in the language of debate. Cognitive and behavioural accounts of phenomena rub shoulders as never before, especially in the field of human behaviour (see Davey and Cullen, 1988). This will surely be an area of growth for the old 'learning theory' which so diligently has explored the behavioural potential of the white rat and pigeon.

Chapter nine

Animal behaviour

Philip Evans

Introduction

Even those whose primary interest is human psychology would admit that a study of their narrower domain is enriched by viewing human beings in a proper biological context: as a species which has evolved alongside others. Thus understanding something about the behaviour of other animals enhances the understanding of our own.

Traditionally two branches of scientific enquiry have been distinguished amongst those who have investigated the behaviour of infra-human species. They are 'ethology' and 'comparative psychology'. What first is an ethologist? The derivation of the term 'ethology' is Greek, but the meanings it has had over the centuries are various. Sometimes it has been used to describe a study of ethics and moral science; nowadays we use it to describe that branch of science which seeks to examine the behaviour of animals, predominantly in their natural environment.

Comparative psychology also deals with the behaviour of animals but the comparative psychologist has traditionally been interested in the manipulation and scientific control of behaviour under stringent laboratory conditions. The distinction between laboratory and field has not been a hard and fast one, but has certainly existed.

There is another distinction to be made between ethology and comparative psychology. Ethologists have in the main emphasized their role in understanding the function and evolutionary significance of *particular* behaviours for the *particular* species under investigation. Comparative psychologists, on the other hand, have more often used animals with the quite explicit intention of finding general laws about behaviour, with a clear view to generalizing across different species. Thus the species actually used in experimentation is of little importance except convenience: rats and pigeons have proven good 'conditioning' subjects; cats have been used in sleep research, a fact which has much to do with their propensity to sleep rather a lot.

This second distinction we have made is not cut and dried either. Psychologists who study learning principles through the use of laboratory animals are certainly the obvious heirs of those most closely identified in the past with the label of comparative psychology. However, the newer generation of such psychologists no longer blithely talks of 'general' learning principles, simply applicable across species. There is growing awareness that even when we look at development of behaviour over the course of an individual's life (so-called 'ontogeny') learning principles cannot be divorced from species-specific considerations, arising from the long evolution and development of that species (so-called 'phylogeny'). It is to the role of evolution in shaping behaviour that we now turn.

Evolution and behaviour

The term 'natural selection' is a familiar one for most people. It describes the mechanism by which traditional Darwinian evolution is said to work. It is often simplistically represented by the phrase: 'the survival of the fittest'. Thus all organisms compete for survival and those who live long enough and successfully produce offspring will contribute their genes to the 'gene-pool', which represents at any time the total genetic diversity within a defined group. A feature of classical Darwinian evolution is 'gradualism'. New species should evolve gradually through chance genetic mutation and slow competition of genes within gene-pools. Let us dwell a little on this matter.

There often appears to be some misunderstanding of the principle of natural selection. It is sometimes asked whether, as an explanatory mechanism, it is true or not. In an important sense its truth is not an empirical matter to be decided. That natural selection does occur is *a priori* true in the same way that 'two plus two equals four' is *a priori* true: essentially, '2 + 2' is another way of writing '4'. If someone disputes a mathematical proposition, we do not bother to argue, we send the person away to learn properly the meaning of our terms. So also the meaning of natural selection implies at least aspects of the concept of evolution. What can be more properly asked is this: does natural selection alone suffice to explain the observed pattern of evolution? Here the question does allow discussion. In particular the records we have of the past, in the shape of fossils, suggests to some that evolution may not always have been the gradual process entailed by the sole operation of classic Darwinian mechanisms. However, as we have implied, natural selection is always operating at the genetic level and it is the relevance of this to behaviour that we need to consider.

Most students are familiar with the idea of evolution appearing to act on the physical structure of a species: for example, selection pressures favouring emergence of the giraffe's long neck. Given that genetic factors do not influence only such 'morphological' features of an organism, but behavioural predispositions as well, we are poised now to consider some of the issues which have most radically been debated in the field of animal behaviour in recent years.

Altruism

Many earlier authors described aspects of animal behaviour within a species in terms of the evolutionary function it might have for the benefit and survival of the species as a whole. The implications of altruism and co-operation are not hard to glean. For example, worker bees will on occasion sacrifice themselves by leaving their sting and half-themselves inside an enemy attacking the hive. But isn't there a problem here? Surely such acts of self-sacrifice are a far cry from the ruthless, competitive self-interest entailed by a strict Darwinian view of natural selection, epitomized in Tennyson's ringing phrase 'nature red in tooth and claw'? It is individuals, not groups, which compete for survival. Indeed as Dawkins (1976, 1987) has been at pains to communicate, it is not even individuals, but genes which are in competition. The individual is merely the transitory bodily machine which acts as a vehicle for the destiny of genes from one generation to another. We therefore have to look twice at those apparent instances of co-operative and altruistic behaviours whose function seems to be for the good of the species as a whole. For example, Lorenz drew much attention to the fact that animals engaged in fights over territory or mates often refrain from doing fatal injury to each other. He went on to show how this might be for the good of the species. However, if we wish to be orthodox Darwinians, then we must account for such apparent gentlemanliness of conduct by showing how such behaviour satisfies the goals of the individual combatants, not the species to which they belong.

The arguments we shall use to reconcile the apparently opposing notions of self-interest and altruism will serve as an introduction to what has been called 'sociobiology': the aim of understanding social behaviour through an application of Darwinian principles. Argument is by appeal to plausible lines of reasoning rather than conventional proof, and sociobiological argument has stirred much controversy at times. What is undeniable is the impact of sociobiology since E. O. Wilson's (1975) seminal book of that title.

Let us return to our kamikaze bees. Clearly they are not helping with the propagation of their own genes by being programmed to commit acts of selfless suicide. That, however, is a little beside the point since worker bees are sterile. Their purpose is only to ensure the reproductive success of their queen, whose daughters they usually will be. Moreover each female worker has three-quarters of her genes in common with her sisters (an anomaly peculiar to the order of hymenoptera to which bees belong). Thus looking after sisters begins to make genetic sense and indeed would even do so if the individual worker were magically provided with offspring, having the usual 50 per cent of genes in common. Therefore the actual phenomenon of a sterile worker caste becomes more understandable.

The argument as put here is considerably over-simplified. There are other factors – male to female ratios, nature of breeding cycles – all of which need to be considered as part of a complex answer to the question of why worker bees have evolved as a sterile caste dedicated to the raising of younger sisters. But we have sufficiently made the point that we should look at things from the genes' point of view. What maximizes their fitness?

This leads us to consider something called 'inclusive fitness'. If we see traditional fitness as referring to the potential of an individual to propagate its own genes through offspring, the concept of 'inclusive fitness' invites us to widen the scope of things. Our own offspring will have half of our genes, but if we look at Table 9.1, we can see that other close relatives share considerable portions of our genetic makeup, too. Thus altruistic behaviour might well be expected to develop in groups where degrees of common kinship (relatedness) is high. The eminent biologist Haldane is reputed to have been asked whether he would lay down his life for his brother. He answered no, but affirmed that he would do so for three brothers, or even nine cousins. The witty reply perhaps best sums up the kernel of sociobiological argument in relation to altruism.

Much altruistic behaviour in a range of species can be seen in the context of inclusive fitness, even though our example drawn from the social insects is perhaps the most striking. Whenever we see altruistic behaviour which involves cost (C) to the individual, we usually find that the benefit (B) to the recipient is not indiscriminate but in direct proportion to the degrees of relatedness (R). More precisely a gene predisposing to an altruistic act would only be selected for if: $B/C > 1/R$.

As examples of altruistic behaviour we might mention alarm calling in squirrels and prairie dogs. In general it has been found that although alarm calling involves increased risk for the caller, it selectively helps 'kin'.

Altruism is not solely to be explained through the operation of inclusive fitness. There are examples of altruism between individual animals who are not kin. In some cases the altruism amounts to simple co-operation which mutually benefits both parties; joint hunting forays among male lions would be an example of such 'mutualism'. So long as one party cannot 'cheat' on the other there is nothing contradictory to a selfish gene stance in such examples of co-operation.

Table 9.1 Degree of relatedness of close relatives expressed in terms of proportion of shared genes

Relatedness = 0.5	Relatedness = 0.25	Relatedness = 0.125
Parents	Uncles and aunts	First cousins
Children	Nephews and nieces	Great-grandchildren
Siblings	Grandparents/children	

More difficult to account for are instances of so-called 'reciprocity' where A helps B today in the hope that B will help A tomorrow. This very human type of social co-operation has evolved in other animals, too, not least in other primates. Seyfarth and Chesney (1984) report a fascinating study, showing that, among vervet monkeys, one individual will attend to help-seeking calls of another unrelated monkey, but only if the monkey in need has recently earned credit by grooming the potential helper.

How can such reciprocity be selected for? If one starts with the assumption that selfishness is the general rule, then surely B should cheat on A? A, and individuals like A, would together with their aberrant genes soon be wiped out by the success of those who take advantage of any bizarre acts of altruism but who are not so silly as to endanger themselves by reciprocating. Non-altruistic, competitive strategies would seem to be inherently more stable ones, from the evolutionary point of view. Imagine that somehow a reciprocating population did develop; any mutant 'be-helped-but-don't-help' genes would be advantaged in this population, would spread and finally destroy any illusory stability.

Axelrod (1984) has shown, however, that co-operation can theoretically develop as a stable strategy if one assigns a reasonably large probability to the chance of two individuals re-meeting. Predictions of his model were tested in a simulated evolutionary game, and results showed that a reciprocating tit-for-tat strategy would under certain conditions resist invason by mutant genes. However, what is more speculative is how such co-operative stability would emerge in the first place. Possibilities of spread from originally kin-selected or random clusters of successful co-operativeness have been suggested.

We have devoted some space to discussion of altruism and co-operation. There is no topic which better illustrates the changes which have taken place in the science of animal behaviour in recent years. We now however turn to a perennial issue of importance: innate and learned factors in behaviour.

Innate versus learned behaviour

Lay people are often likely to attribute animal behaviour to instinct, by which they mean to imply that the behaviour in some way is built in to the animal concerned, the result of an innate capacity. Since instinct is also a term which has been used by investigators themselves, we begin by considering its meaning.

Nineteenth-century investigators had already noted fixed patterns of behaviour in various species of animals, and the word 'instinct' was used to explain why animals seemed blindly to engage in certain activities. Early psychologists, eager to make their discipline respectably biological, took up the concept. Psychologists, such as William James and McDougall, underpinned much of human behaviour with a plethora of separate instincts. We laugh because we have a 'laughing instinct', we weep under the influence of a 'weeping instinct', and so on. Nowadays, when we see that something can explain everything, we quite rightly suspect that it really explains nothing. So it was with the term instinct – it became overworked. When, a little later, psychologists began to discover the phenomenon of 'conditioning', the chaining of stimuli and responses by association, this seemed a much better way of broadly explaining man's extremely variegated behaviour. The adage was born that we are all 'products of our conditioning'. Innate factors in man's behaviour were banished from the mainstream of psychology, and only now are they making a powerful resurgence.

And yet, interest in innate patterns of behaviour did not die completely. There were scientists who continued to look at instinctive behaviour in animals generally, and though they tended not to make *homo sapiens* the object of their enquiry, they did, nevertheless, occasionally raise speculative questions about the viability of the 'infinitely conditionable' man of the experimental psychologist. These men, of course, were the ethologists. Notable amongst them have been two important figures: Niko Tinbergen and Konrad Lorenz. These two men laid the foundations of present-day ethology. Apart from amassing a large scientific literature of their findings, they also wrote extremely interesting popular accounts of certain parts of their work, e.g. *King Solomon's Ring* by Lorenz.

Fixed action patterns

Although it is natural to introduce the subject-matter of the ethologists by a mention of the term instinct, that particular word no longer occupies pride of place in many people's vocabulary. It seems immediately to beg too many questions about innateness. Rather, it is better to say that ethologists have found it easier to concentrate on apparently functionally important behaviour patterns which, nevertheless, can be easily identified and reidentified by different independent observers. It may, or may not, be appropriate to call such behaviours instinctive. Such rigid stereotyped behaviours have been called by Lorenz *fixed action patterns*. A multitude of examples could be given to illustrate the nature of fixed action patterns, but limitations of space enable us only to mention a few.

One of the classic examples which can be cited is the behaviour of the greylag goose. This bird builds its nest on the ground, and one of the constant problems that it faces is the tendency of an egg to roll out of the nest. The greylag goose then has to retrieve it. What interests us is just how it achieves the retrieval. The bird leans its head forward, puts its beak on the far side of the egg and gets the egg back into the nest using a scooping movement. The whole behaviour pattern is extremely stereotyped and admits of no variation. The bird could conceivably use its feet or its wing; the point is that it never does.

Another example which illustrates the amazing constancy of fixed action patterns comes from a study of courtship movements in the golden-eye drake. Observers recorded a particular part of the ritual known as the 'simple head throw'. Studying one particular individual, this movement was found to have an average time of 1.29 seconds. However, the variation from this average time could at most be measured only in hundredths of a second.

There is no doubt that there is a strong innate component in most fixed action patterns, and this is clearly seen when experimenters try to interfere with the naturally-occurring situations. For example, Lorenz and Tinbergen, having outined the egg retrieval behaviour of the greylag goose which we mentioned above, proceeded to present the bird with an egg of gigantic proportions. The bird nevertheless attempted to retrieve this egg using the same rigid method (see Figure 9.1).

Ethologists have tended to see fixed action patterns as the nearest thing to purely inherited behaviour. Often, it can be clearly shown that learning is not necessary in any way to the exhibition of such behaviours. Nor are such behaviours usually capable of serious modification, even when the circumstances may be altered either naturally or artificially. However, it is necessary to sound a note of caution here. It is, of course, possible to conceive of behaviour, even complex behaviour, being wired in to the nervous systems of species, which predispose the animal to perform fixed action patterns. But innateness should not be assumed in this way until the most rigorous investigations are done.

Certainly, rigidity of behaviour and stereotyped sequences of movement lead one to suspect the importance of innate factors; so also does the finding of a high degree of intra-specific similarity. However, such factors cannot in any way serve as criteria, since we see equally rigid and stereotyped movements in neurotic patients and experimental animals subjected to conflict. We would not want to say that these behaviour

Figure 9.1   Egg retrieval in the greylag goose (after Lorenz and Tinbergen)

patterns were innate – quite the contrary. We have a good idea of the kinds
of learning experience likely to produce them. The same argument applies
to intra-specific similarity; we know that cultures can be so powerful in
their influence as to lead to a very high degree of such intra-specific
similarity in man.

However, even when innateness appears to be a very probable
important factor, one should be careful. As an illustration, let us consider
the bladder-emptying reflex in the rat. A reflex is just about the simplest
fixed action pattern we can conceive of. Infant rats, in a particular
experiment not concerned with the bladder reflex at all, were removed
from their mother by Caesarian section. After the first day all the infant
rats were dead. It was discovered that they had died from rupturing of the
bladder. It was subsequently discovered that the reflex of bladder emptying
has to be triggered from the environment, in this case the action of the
mother in giving a slight kick to the offspring at birth. Once triggered, its
action is autonomous and needs no further prompting. Other examples
could be given of reflexes and fixed action patterns being at least partly
determined by environmental factors. Perhaps, therefore, we ought to
speak of inherited predispositions rather than inherited behaviour. In some
cases, the interaction of heredity and environment in the genesis of
behaviour patterns is much more complicated. In a moment we shall
discuss one example in full. First we should mention the powerful
experimental technique of the *isolation* experiment. Given that the simple
observation of stereotyped behaviour and rigidity cannot be sufficient to
assume a high degree of innateness, an obvious technique is to take young
animals at birth (neonates) and isolate them from their normal environment. If the behaviour in question still appears, this is good *prima facie*
evidence for innateness. Notice I have not said firm evidence, since the
reader should bear in mind that there is an equally important prenatal
environment in the womb, which the simple isolation experiment does not
control. Let us now look at the use of isolation and other techniques in just
one example, chosen because it illustrates a complex testing out of innate
and environmental factors.

Bird-song: inherited and learned components

Marler and Tamura (1964) and Konishi (1965) have given us a good account of the development of characteristic bird-song in the American white-crowned sparrow. This species is very widely dispersed along the Pacific coast of the United States and birds from different areas are known to have distinct 'dialects', superimposed on the standard bird-song of the species as a whole. If birds are reared in total isolation they do show as adults the characteristic song, even though they have in no way been exposed to the song of the adult during their development. Thus, clearly, the song itself is innately wired into the bird in some sense. The dialect, however, is not to be found in such experimental isolates and, therefore, involves learning experiences. Marler and Tamura found that the specific learning of the dialect takes place relatively early, indeed before the bird has ever sung a note. If birds are taken into isolation after three months, a recognizable accent is still present when the bird in isolation eventually begins to sing. Even more interesting, and something which we shall have more to say about later, the exposure to dialect seems to be required during a critical period. Isolates who are exposed to adult dialect song after four months are not affected by it, and the future song is the crude standard version.

Konishi continued the work of Marler and Tamura. By means of deafening the fledgeling birds (by surgical removal of the cochlea) he was able to show that birds need to hear their own song in order to produce even the inherited standard song. The mutilated birds were capable of producing only disconnected notes. Konishi also showed that deafening birds at any time before the birds had sung resulted in the same complete deficit. Only when the bird had actually produced a song, was it possible to deafen the bird and still leave the song unaffected.

How do we interpret these results to form a final picture of the interaction between inherited and environmental components? First, it appears, as we have said before, that what is inherited is not the song itself but the predisposition. We can call this a *template* of the song which is innately wired into the bird's nervous system. What the bird has to do is to use this template as a guide and ultimately match its own singing to it. We might say that the bird is *learning* to sing by copying a model; the model, however, happens to be internal and innate. Where, now, does the question of dialect fit in? It would appear that experiences in the environment, during a critical period, can modify the innately laid-down template, so that when the bird finally comes to using its template, that template has environmentally added accretions, i.e. dialect.

We have outlined the story of the white-crowned sparrow at length because it serves as a good example to establish how necessary it is in ethological investigations to be prepared for complex interactions between heredity and environment in the development of even those behaviours which the layman is likely to see as examples of good old instinct!

The role of external stimuli

So far, we have concentrated on the development of the fixed action patterns so often studied by the ethologist. We have done this in order to show the limitations of the old concept of instinct, and the improvement that is reaped by talking instead of innate and environmental components of behaviour. We now move on to look at the immediate environmental factors which determine the occurrence of fixed action patterns, regardless of how they have developed.

Sign-stimuli

One of the most widely-investigated species, with respect to the work of Tinbergen, has been the three-spined stickleback, a very common fresh-water fish. The fish does, in fact, spend much of the winter in estuaries, or even in the sea, but in the spring it migrates to rivers and streams. The male stickleback finds a suitable place for building a nest on the river-bed, and sets about finding a female to court and mate with. What is interesting to us is the different patterns of behaviour which are elicited by intruding male and female strangers. Male intruders are automatically attacked, females are courted. How does the stickleback know the difference? There are two distinctions which might be important: the male has a bright red underbelly whereas the female has not; secondly the abdomen of the female is swollen with the eggs she is carrying. What feature is important? Tinbergen first showed that it was indeed visual stimuli to which the fish responded. By putting a mirror in front of the male fish, he was able to demonstrate that the fish would attack its own reflection Having established this, he went on to build a number of 'model' sticklebacks, in which he varied the features that might be important in eliciting behaviour of attack. He showed that the shape of the fish was unimportant; only the red underbelly seemed to be the relevant feature (see Figure 9.2). The ethologists have called such highly selective stimuli in the control of behaviour *sign-stimuli*.

Let us consider one more example of sign-stimuli in operation. The chicks of the herring-gull obtain food quite reliably by pecking at the tip of the parent's bill. Regurgitated food is then given to the chick. The parent's bill is yellow with a red spot on the lower part. Once again Tinbergen was able to construct model bills in order to investigate just what were the important sign-stimuli in eliciting the vital pecking response of the chicks.

The features of the bill which were found to be important were (a) redness of the bill, and (b) the contrast of a spot against background. What

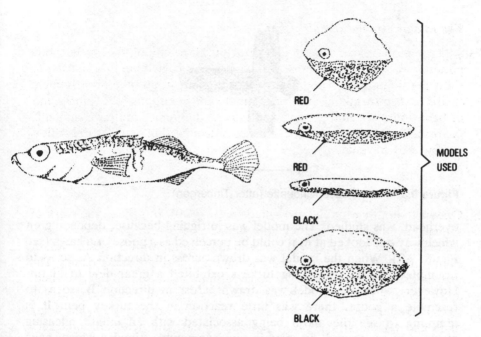

Figure 9.2 Models used to test for aggressive responses in the stickleback (after Tinbergen)

about the mechanisms which mediate between such sign-stimuli and response to them? Originally, Lorenz coined the term *innate releasing mechanism* (IRM) as an explanatory device. Unfortunately, this term has proven to be more of a hindrance than a help. For a start, we have seen already how cautious one has to be in applying the word 'innate' in any circumstances; its application can all too easily be questioned. Secondly, is it always true to say that the important property of the stimulus is that it releases the behaviour under study? We can conceive of many other functions for such a stimulus, such as an arousing or orientating function, or in some cases, indeed, an inhibiting one. Thirdly, the use of the singular term 'mechanism' implies just one single and, presumably, as far as the nervous system is concerned, central mechanism responsible for the behaviour. Once again, this is disputable. All in all the choice of the term IRM seems most unfortunate.

Let us look at some particular instances where the term IRM can be seen to go astray. In a well-known experiment by Lorenz and Tinbergen, the alarm response of young turkeys, confronted with a model hawk passing

Figure 9.3 Hawk-goose silhouette (after Tinbergen)

overhead, was studied. The model was intriguing because, depending on which way one looked at it, it could be perceived as a goose or a hawk (see Figure 9.3). When the model was drawn across in direction A, so as to resemble a hawk, the young turkeys exhibited a great deal of alarm. However, when the model was drawn across in direction B, so as to resemble a goose, there was little reaction in the turkey pen. It is tempting to see the alarm being associated with an innate releasing mechanism, triggered by certain environmental stimuli, which have achieved importance for very obvious reasons during the course of evolution. However, criticisms have also been made of the original experiments suggesting amongst other things that the young turkeys had had prior experience of geese flying over their pen. The fleeing response might, therefore, have been habituated to geese, but remained intact to hawk-shapes. The controversy over the innateness of this particular stimulus-response relationship continues, but it is clear that the term IRM cannot sensibly be used in 'explaining' such behaviour. Another critic of the early experiments was Schneirla, who argued that the actual resemblance to a hawk or a goose might be of little importance, and that what was important was the more primitive response of most organisms to an unexpected and sudden change in illumination, induced, in this case, more unexpectedly and more suddenly when the model comes in 'blunt end first', rather than tapering end first.

Let us now move on to the second objection to the term innate releasing mechanism. This, if you remember, centred on the term 'releasing'. Let us look at an example of behaviour where the term 'releasing' is clearly inappropriate. Young turkey chicks emit certain specific vocalizations which serve as discrete stimuli for the adult birds. But their function is not to elicit a response; it is, in this case, to inhibit one. Specifically, the sound of the young turkeys serves to prevent the adults from attacking and killing them.

Think back now to the egg-retrieving behaviour of the greylag goose that we mentioned earlier in this chapter. We mentioned that the egg did serve as a stimulus to elicit or release the retrieval, but retrieval is a complicated business, and it can be shown that the egg also serves to orientate the animal's response. Our examples, then, show us that stimuli do a lot more than just release behaviour; they can *inhibit*, as in the first case, or *orientate*, as in the second.

Our final objection to the term innate releasing mechanism was over the use of the singular form 'mechanism'. A single mechanism might indeed seem appropriate if we were talking always of just one single sign-stimulus controlling one single fixed pattern of behaviour. However, that is not always the case. While it is true that a herring-gull chick will peck most at a model which best resembles the parent's beak, we saw that pecking is recorded in other conditions, too, when the model is not maximally approximate to the real bill. This shows that the IRM, so-called, is only a kind of shorthand in the explanation of behaviour, and what we really require is a thorough knowledge of how the animal *processes* information (sorts out relevant from irrelevant detail) at all stages from the peripheral (the eye, the ear, the nose, etc.) right through to the central stage (i.e. the brain). First, let us look at an instance of fixed action pattern which depends solely on a peripheral mechanism. The example we choose comes from the mating behaviour of the silkmoth. The male moth reliably flies towards the female moth – not surprising really. However, when we look at what triggers this response we find that it is a certain odour given off by the female. Where do we find the mechanism which accounts for the selectivity of this response sequence? The answer is that we find it at the most peripheral level possible, i.e. the sense-organs of smell. Tiny *chemoreceptors* in the male send impulses through the central nervous system only when a particular odour is detected.

If we refer back to the pecking behaviour of the herring-gull chicks, we see that the stimulus which elicited the behaviour was not at all simple. It had at least two components. The contrast of the spot on the beak was the one component; the overall colour, red, was the other. Clearly more central analysis of the stimulus is required in this example.

So, our conclusion must be that the term 'innate releasing mechanism' is at best, and only in certain cases, a crudely descriptive one. True explanation can only come about by a thorough examination of the way in which a particular organism *filters* the relevant from the irrelevant aspects of the totality of environmental stimulation which impinges upon it.

Imprinting

In other chapters of this book you will find discussion of (a) behaviours which are learned, the implication being that within reason such behaviours could have been learned at any time, and (b) behaviours which, as it were, unfold at particular times and seem, for their essentials at least, not to require much in the way of specific learning opportunities, e.g. walking and talking. These latter behaviours are said to be examples of maturation processes. Imprinting combines some of the features of both types of development.

It was back in the last century that systematic observation first demonstrated that young chicks (two or three days old) had a tendency to follow any moving object. They would, in psychologists' parlance, *attach* themselves to one so-called mother figure. Incidentally, and as one might expect, this kind of attachment is most often seen in those species of birds which have the capacity to wander away from the nest very soon after hatching. The kinds of objects on which such a chick can become imprinted seem to be almost unlimited, varying enormously in size, shape, and colour. Experimenters have imprinted young birds on something as small as a matchbox or as large as an observational hide. Auditory stimuli can also play a part in the attachment process. Indeed, it has proved possible in some species to imprint the animal on a simple sound source. This, though, is rare.

One of the most noticeable facets of learned behaviour is that it improves with practice. Also, in so far as learned behaviour tends to be synonymous with environmentally-determined behaviour, it relies crucially on the ability of the organism to discriminate external stimuli. Both these factors can be shown to influence the acquisition of the *following responses*, which form the behavioural evidence for attachment.

Moreover, another well-known principle of learning theory is that a response which an animal learns to make in the presence of a stimulus will be elicited to a greater or lesser degree by any stimulus perceived as similar to the original stimulus. This is the principle of stimulus generalization. It can be shown that imprinted responses obey this particular law of learning.

Perhaps most surprising of all, there is some evidence (Solomon, 1980) that an imprinted response can be radically modified by reinforcement contingencies. Thus the well-known chicks' following response can be turned into its opposite – a non-approach response – if such behaviour produces the return of the mother figure. Imprinting, then, seems to occur in such a way as to obey most of the laws which apply to learned behaviour. So what makes it different? Where is its innate quality?

It seems that the unique feature of imprinting is that it must be innately laid down when the behaviour is first learned. This is the nature of the 'critical period'. In the case of the chicks' following response this critical period is typically between two and three days old. If one measures the accuracy with which a chick will discriminate and seek out a would-be attachment stimulus, then such a measure will 'peak' at the critical period (see Figure 9.4).

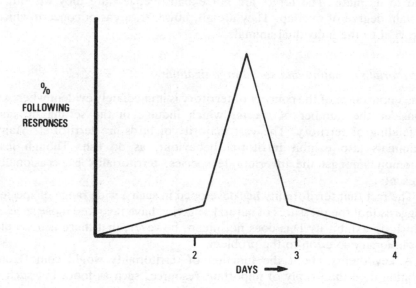

%
FOLLOWING
RESPONSES

2   3   4

DAYS ➞

Figure 9.4

On grosser measures, the chick may indeed show sensitivity to potential attachment stimuli at earlier or later periods, but when it comes to accuracy of learning the critical period is as narrow as depicted above. Scientists have speculated that the critical period develops as it does for the following reasons: before the onset of the critical period one may suppose that the perceptual and discriminatory potential of the chick leads to less accurate following behaviour; after the critical period fear becomes more fully developed and any new stimuli are likely to elicit avoidance behaviour. On this argument the critical period is the ideal compromise; it is the optimal point where discrimination is at its highest relative to fear.

Animal communication and social behaviour

Animals need to communicate and socially interact to different degrees and in different ways. In all cases, however, communication and social behaviour are to be seen in the light of each species' adaptation to its environment, its ecological niche, and the constant struggle at the individual level for evolutionary fitness. The fixed action patterns in response to well-defined situations, which we have already mentioned, are most in evidence when we address certain broad topics within the field of animal behaviour. In particular we can observe them frequently when we encounter an animal in relation to its territory, to rivals of its own species, and to its mate. The topics are not exhaustive, nor are they without a certain degree of overlap. They are all, however, areas of concern which are vital to the individual animal.

Territoriality, mating and social organization

The importance of the concept of territory is immediately evident when we consider the number of species which indulge in the setting up and defending of territory. The vast majority of birds are territorial. Many mammals also exhibit territorial behaviour, as do fish. Though less common amongst the invertebrate species, territoriality is occasionally present.

The fact that territoriality has developed in such a wide range of species suggests that the pressures of natural selection have favoured those species which do exhibit it. This does not mean, however, that there is a simple evolutionary solution to the problem.

A key theory about the function of territoriality would come from relating it to the supply of important resources such as food, but such a simple explanation cannot be the whole truth. Territories can vary enormously in terms of size, for example. Certain species such as the herring-gull have territories of limited extent within a colony and certainly do not obtain their food from the territory. Birds of prey, on the other hand, have very large territories (about one square mile) from which they obtain all their food. Apart from food supply, then, there must be other advantages accruing from the holding of territory. Such advantages could be freedom from disturbance by members of the same species, especially during mating periods. The general rule about territoriality is that although its exact nature differs enormously from one species to another, it is usually clearly relevant to the particular ecology of that species.

We begin with a consideration of those cases where the territory holder is for the most part a solitary animal, even though one could say that the group of territories constitutes a society of sorts. This is certainly the formula which applies in a number of bird species, amongst which the willow warbler is a good example. The male takes on a fairly large territory which will supply him with food; eventually he will share that territory with a mate and rear his young there. Although other territories are close by, such that all the ground in a vicinity is occupied, we can still say that each territory belongs to a solitary bird. The robin is also a highly territorial species in this sense, and will not lightly tolerate the presence of a rival of its own species. The other cardinal example of solitary territory holding is seen in that group of mammals known as the carnivores. Anyone who has kept a domestic cat will probably have observed its behaviour as it paces even one's own living room, rubbing up against furniture and indeed people in what appears to be an affectionate manner; the truth of the matter is rather different. Powerful scent glands are to be found on the cat's face which leave an olfactory message pertaining to its recent presence. Out of doors, various scents, and in particular urine traces, mark out the boundaries of his territory.

Here then are two examples of territories occupied by solitary animals. However, there are important differences even here: your own cat's territory is not his exclusive domain for a whole twenty-four hour period. The cat has to come to terms with the equally valid needs of all the other cats in the neighbourhood, and there is simply not enough space for all to have exclusive territory. The solution to the problem is as one might expect. The cats operate a time-sharing system. While the smell of urine is fresh, this acts as a signal to other cats which says 'keep clear'; as the smell gets stale the force of the signal is diminished and a neighbouring cat can claim that part of the territory as its own for another limited period. It will be seen that the system is very efficient; though a number of cats may be sharing the same geographical area the olfactory messages ensure that unwanted encounters are kept to a minimum.

Territoriality is intimately linked to a consideration of mating and parenting. In many birds, as we have seen, the male attracts a female or females to a territory. The better the territory, in terms of resources, the more mates he will obtain and the greater his reproductive success, always assuming he can defend the territory. On the other hand, females in a good territory will be paying a cost for it, if they prove to be a 'secondary' mate and have no male support with parenting. Monogamy in a poorer territory may be a better option.

Competing pressures towards monogamy and polygyny are also seen amongst mammalian species in regard to territory. Most female mammals are solitary, and therefore the size of territory a male can defend will automatically determine the extent to which he is polygynous. Usually the male will have little to do with raising offspring and his interest is solely in mating. However, it is noticeable that in the rare cases in which the male does involve himself in providing parental care (e.g. certain species of monkey and canid) monogamy is the rule and the male can thus be seen to be maximizing reproductive efficiency by offering such care.

In social animals the notion of territory often gives way to one of dominance or 'pecking order', where some individuals are higher in status than others. In vital matters such as access to food and mates, such individuals usually, but by no means always, have precedence. Neither territories nor dominance hierarchies are always rigid affairs however; e.g.

in primate groups especially, alliances can be struck up such that two inferior animals can dominate a superior.

In order to complete the transition from discussion of solitary territoriality to complete group living let us take somewhat arbitrarily three types of animal: the red deer, the wolf, and the primates.

In the case of the red deer the two sexes form separate herds and group-living is the rule during the summer, when the animals feed together. In autumn, however, the male herds disintegrate and with their antlers fully grown the males become very aggressive and put on elaborate displays for the benefit of the oestrus females. However, the mating season is quite short and the females soon return to their herd; likewise the males shed their antlers and regroup into their own herd.

Wolves have even more reason to live in groups, since they need to hunt in packs which means that a stable social organization is highly desirable. Some males are more dominant than others, but the group itself is at no time disrupted.

Of all animals, the primates are renowned for their highly developed social organization. The concept of territory becomes meaningless with respect to any individual animal. However, troops of monkeys can be said to have a territory. The troop may be as small as a single family in the case of the gibbon, for example. As a family they are territorial and make loud hooting noises if they detect other gibbons in the neighbourhood. Like the cat, however, the one group of gibbons does not, strictly speaking, own the territory. Auditory signals – like the olfactory signals of the cat – serve to minimize potentially threatening encounters. Other species of primate live in much larger groups than the gibbon. The gelada baboons live in colonies of up to 400; as one might expect there are sub-groups within such a large colony.

Within any grouping, there is usually a high degree of stability which is based on hierarchical considerations. High rank will, as we have seen, lead to preference when it comes to obtaining food and mates. Unlike hierarchies in other animals, however, primate groups are usually noted for their lack of aggressive encounters; threat postures by dominant males are not needed as much as one might expect, since subservience of the less dominant animals makes such postures redundant.

Rivalry and aggression

We have seen how some animals organize themselves in territories, but we have said nothing about exactly what happens when this territory is intruded upon by a rival. Usually the answer is simple – the intruder retreats under the threat of attack by the resident. However, the boundaries of territories are not as fixed as one might suppose. Manning (1973) compares a territory to an elastic disc, the centre of which is well defined as territory since any persistent intrusion will inevitably provoke an extremely aggressive response. As one moves out from the centre the response of the resident gradually becomes less pronounced, until a point is reached where the animal threatens only half-heartedly. In other words, there is not a fixed boundary on one side of which we see full-blown defence of territory, and on the other side of which we see no response at all. It is at these peripheral 'no-man's-lands' that threat displays are most in evidence. Threat displays are, essentially, therefore, a compromise when the tendencies to attack and to escape are about equal. Ethologists have made a special study of the idiosyncratic postures adopted by various species during peripheral boundary disputes.

Male cichlid fish face each other motionless with their gill covers fully raised, while in many birds and mammals the hair or feathers become erect. This common denominator suggests that the display itself is a more physical corollary to the autonomic activity associated with being in a conflict-ridden situation. Most boundary disputes do not go as far as actual physical aggression. Both animals involved keep up a mutual threatening until one of them retires. This is, of course, an over-simplified picture, and it would be wrong to conclude that for a given species there is a single identifiable threat display. We have said that the conflict – and, thus, the posture – results from the two tendencies of attack and retreat being equal, but they may be equal in different ways: both may be equal and low; both may be equal and high. It is likely that different threat postures are appropriate in the two cases. A nice illustration of the different postures associated with the interaction of increasing aggressiveness and increasing fear in the cat can be seen in Figure 9.5.

Similarly different results may follow the encounter. If both tendencies are high then the end of the threat situation is likely to be either attack or retreat, but, if both are low, other types of behaviour such as feeding or preening gestures may occur. Ethologists have called such interfering activities *displacement activities*, a term stemming from Lorenz's early 'psychohydraulic' model of instinctive energy which accumulates until finally it has to be released. One method of release is for it to be displaced into the sort of activities just mentioned.

This model has been sharply and widely criticized, not least because the working of such a model is very far removed from what we know about the functioning of the nervous system. A more credible view of displacement activity, is that it is a way of reducing anxiety attendant upon conflict. A bird, for example, during a long boundary dispute, may relieve its anxiety by executing a response immediately available in terms of the stimuli around it, such as pecking the ground. We may also mention one specific experiment. Raber (1948) found that turkey cocks showed displacement activity of a feeding or drinking variety during fights. However, the pattern of displacement depended critically on whether food or water was

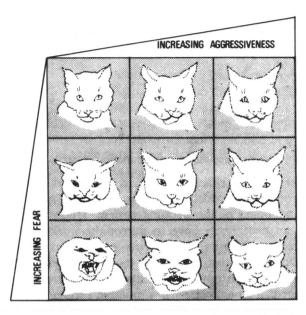

Figure 9.5 Changes in the facial expressions of the cat with their suggested motivational basis (after Manning, 1973)

available. This shows that displacement activity is under the control of the external environment, rather than being a result of hypothetical internal energy.

It is interesting to speculate why some threat displays develop into such highly ritualized and stereotyped form, given that they probably began as incidental displacement activity. Possibly ritualization and stereotypy serve to decrease disadvantageous and increase advantageous information. Thus it would be disadvantageous if the display revealed to a rival the exact balance of forces tending towards fight or flight, but it is advantageous to signal very umambiguously that a threat display is intended.

Similar lines of argument have been developed to account for the highly ritualized communications which are seen in courtship. It is to courtship we now turn.

Courtship

Courtship is a convenient term to describe those relatively fixed patterns of behaviour which occur as a preliminary to mating. It is fitting that this section follows on from a consideration of aggression, because we shall see that there is reason to believe that courtship and conflict behaviour are related. Certain species of spider illustrate the fact in a most alarming fashion. Here, the male must treat his mate with the utmost caution if he wants to avoid ending up as her dinner.

Because of territoriality mentioned earlier, many vertebrate males have strong conflicting motivations when faced with a potential mate; the female's behaviour must, therefore, serve to differentiate her as clearly as possible from that of an intruder. For this reason, many parallels can be seen between sexually motivated postures and *appeasement postures* (i.e. the typical postures adopted by a subservient animal when it gets in the way of a con-specific higher up in the peck order). In fact any behaviour which implies subservience is quite likely to be adopted as part of the courtship ritual. Thus, if we look at the great crested grebe we find that the courtship ritual involves an appeasement-type gesture which closely resembles the food-begging behaviour of the chicks. It seems then that the purpose of much courtship ritual is to bring about a reduction of aggressiveness necessary for mating to take place. Sometimes, it is the male who takes the initiative in de-escalating what could otherwise be an aggressive encounter by making movements resembling escape behaviour: we see such a pattern in the male chaffinch.

What we are saying, then, is that the courtship situation almost always involves a conflict between impulses towards sex, attack, and escape. We have already seen that, in the case of conflicting tendencies, displacement activities are almost invariably in evidence. Ethologists have been able to note many instances where such displacement activities have become ritualized and integrated into patterns of courtship behaviour. Tinbergen (1952) has termed these *derived activities*.

In certain cases, the derivation involves little change from the original unritualized behaviour. To return to the great crested grebe, one element in its courtship ritual involves presentation of nest building material; the derivation here is uncomplicated and clearly seen. In other species, however, the origin of derived activities has to be gleaned by looking at gradual changes which can be traced across related species. Morris (1959) has used this particular approach in investigating the courtship ritual of different species of grass finch. In the case of the spice finch, the male courts the female by using an extremely ritualized bow. From an examination of the less ritualized 'bows' of related species of finch, it seems that this particular ritual derives from the common displacement activity of beak-wiping.

It is quite often the case, then, that ritualized behaviour seems to evolve out of displacement activity. Presumably the behaviour begins under the motivation of conflict and later achieves an independence within general sexual motivation.

Courtship and identification

We may suspect that courtship rituals serve more than just one function: they certainly do seem to reduce conflict elements potentially present prior to mating. We may imagine, however, that another function may be important. An animal has to be able to identify an opposite sex member of its own species. Hybridization is almost always a 'bad thing' for a species; and yet we can often succeed in mating hybrids with the greatest of ease once we have introduced a male to a female. So, why does hybrid mating tend not to take place in the natural environment? The answer lies in the fact that species have developed clear courtship signals which lead an animal to its correct con-specific. In a number of lower species, for example, during the mating season the males get together and deliver *assembly calls* which serve to attract the females of their particular species. If we take two species of frog as our example, we can examine the function of these assembly calls in greater detail.

In certain areas, two quite related species of frog may share the same pond. In order to avoid hybridization it is clear that the assembly calls will have to be distinctly different so that discrimination leading to correct intra-specific mating can take place. This is, indeed, what we find. Interestingly, in other areas the two species are not found together, and one species will have a pond to itself. Ethologists have found that, in this case, assembly calls are quite similar. The rule, then, seems to be: related species inhabiting the same area will have different mating calls. Where there are exceptions there is usually a good reason; for example, two species of cricket living in exactly the same area have been found to have identical 'songs'. However, if we look more closely, we find that these two species have two different and non-overlapping mating seasons, so therefore there is no need for song differentiation.

A parallel to this line of argument can be seen in a comparison of alarm calls and mating calls in different species of birds. Analysis of the 'sound pictures' reveals a similarity of alarm call across different species, whereas mating calls are distinctly different.

We have already mentioned, in the context of rivalry and threat display, some possible reasons why ritualization of original displacememt activities might occur. In the case of courtship, speculations have also been made. Zahavi (1979), for example, has suggested that those who react to the signals are themselves selected to become more and more discriminating about courtship displays. Thus the more uniform and stereotyped the performances become, the more the good performer will stand out. The ritual hop of the zebra finch towards his hoped-for mate may provide the opportunity for her to assess his general agility against a clearly agreed standard.

Communication and sensory channels

So far we have looked at communication in relation to specific topics such as alarm calling, territory defence, and courtship. Let us now consider the general question of how animals communicate. Some signals are visual, some auditory, others are tactile or olfactory. Ecological restraints to a large extent determine the sensory channels used for communications. Thus visual signals are clearly of limited value to small nocturnal mammals, whereas scents and sounds have great potential. By contrast, visual signals may be of importance to animals living in open country, while auditory and olfactory communication might again be superior in habitats consisting of dense undergrowth or forest. Thus factors which favour efficient transmission of a signal will partially determine use of a particular channel.

That is not to say that subtler factors are not involved. Scents, for example, can vary in their volatility and so can be used in diverse ways. Territory marking by foxes is done by leaving long-lasting scent traces which can deter intruders during the several hours that the fox is patrolling different areas of territory. By contrast, the scent trails left by worker-ants build up rapidly, but, being volatile, decay quickly. This means that the trail exists only as long as the prey exists at the other end. When a new prey is discovered a new trail quickly replaces the old which efficiently fades away.

However, even the fastest decaying scent is a slow affair compared with the quick changes which can occur in visual, auditory or tactile signals. The rates at which signals can be changed, the range over which they will carry, their ability to go past obstacles, the ease (or, when considering predators, the difficulty) of locating their source, are all factors which will have relevance in the choice of sensory channel for a signal. Researchers have tried to show evolutionary adaptiveness by examining particular signals in relation to the sort of parameters just mentioned. Thus a particular bird-song may well be adapted in terms of frequency and other sound characteristics to optimize its reception according to the habitat of the bird (Krebs and Davies, 1987). Similarly monkeys may use high pitched screams during agonistic encounters within their group, but low-pitched 'long-range' vocalizations to warn off other groups. Krebs and Davies (1987) offer a more detailed discussion of these avenues of research.

The limits of animal communication

With one important exception, animals do not, unlike humans, communicate about things far removed in place or time. They communicate about immediate vital concerns to do with territory, mate, and predators. The only naturally occurring phenomenon which comes close to some of the more abstract characteristics of human language is the so-called 'language' of honey-bees, in which a complex dance conveys information about the direction, distance and quality of remote food. But even here, there is no flexibility. No bee has struck out for originality and adapted the dance to communicate about something else.

Are then the characteristics of human language unique to humans? Clearly spoken language itself is unique, but is it possible at least to teach other primates a system of communication with language characteristics?

Two decades of research involving attempts to teach sign or symbol languages to chimpanzees have not given us any conclusive evidence of a capacity for language among apes (Limber, 1977), although clearly much depends on how language is defined – and there is no universal agreement on that matter. What early chimp 'stars' such as Washoe (Gardner and Gardner, 1969) have demonstrated is the ability to string together signs in meaningful combinations, to use old signs in conjunction to come up with apt descriptions of novel objects or situations, and to accumulate a very reasonable vocabulary.

What has not been demonstrated is an ability to use (rather than just comprehend) a flexible but ordered grammar for generating anything more than the very simplest 'utterances'. Nor yet have we any compelling evidence of language transmission from ape to ape, or even linguistic exchange among apes, although such evidence may accumulate in the future. For the moment we shall end this section and the chapter on an agnostic note.

Information processing

Different aspects of what we are labelling information processing, for long periods, constituted virtually the whole of experimental psychology. Sensation and perception were the main preoccupation of Wundt and his immediate followers, 'thinking' that of Külpe, memory that of Ebbinghaus, while the Gestaltists concerned themselves with perception and problem-solving, and the behaviourists with learning. Added to this was the vast cognitive development system of Piaget and much of the work of the classical British psychologists, such as Bartlett. Further, there was the newer 'cognitive psychology' exemplified in the work of George Miller, Ulric Neisser, and others – to say nothing of the burgeoning research into language.

In many respects this section could have been called 'Cognitive psychology' but we have retained the heading of 'Information processing' because these chapters may be said to be written with the underlying assumption that people receive information about their environment, analyse it, and then manipulate it in thought and language.

Chapter ten

Basic perceptual processes

Heather Govier and Ernest Govier

An organism has access to information from its environment by way of sensitive tissues, which range from the simple photoreceptors in single-celled animals to sense organs as complex as the human eye. The basic physiology of such organs is discussed elsewhere; this chapter will be concerned with the cognitive processes involved in perception, that is to say, the way in which stimuli are interpreted by the organism.

Not all impinging stimulation is perceived. In experimental terms, perception always involves discrimination. We test whether or not an organism has perceived something by its ability to discriminate between the presence and absence of the stimulus or between two different stimuli. In the case of human beings, the discriminating response is usually a verbal one – the subject tells us whether he has seen or heard the stimulus. For animals, the response must be non-verbal – we know that a pigeon can discriminate between a red light and a green one by training it to peck at a key when a red light shows, but not to respond to a green light.

Two of the principal factors which affect the organism's perception of a stimulus are its past experience and its sensory thresholds. Many experiments have been performed which show that various experiences in an organism's development can contribute to later perception of the environment. This is true for experimental animals as well as man and will be fully discussed in Chapter 11.

Thresholds

The absolute threshold

Stimuli with intensities below a certain minimum value will not evoke any sensory experience. This minimum value is known as the absolute threshold and occurs for all sensory systems. However, the absolute threshold occurs at different stimulus intensities with different subjects and on different occasions with the same subject. It is not a constant value and must be measured afresh for each subject and on each occasion. One way of determining the absolute threshold, for example, of the visual system, is to seat the subject in a totally dark room, directing him to fix his gaze in a certain direction. The subject is then presented with a series of light flashes of varying intensities and must report whenever he sees a signal. When the data from such an experiment is analysed, it is found that there is no one intensity value *below* which the stimulus is never detected and *above* which it is always seen. Instead, there is a gradual gradient from intensities which the subject always reports seeing, through those which are sometimes detected and sometimes not, down to the lower intensities which are almost never perceived. An explanation of why this should be, uses the concept of 'neural noise'. At any one moment in time, some of the neurones in any sensitive system will be firing spontaneously. For example, in the visual system, recordings made in cats have shown residual neural activity in the retina and optic nerve, even when there is no light stimulation to the eye. When neural impulses are received by the brain, it must make a decision as to whether those impulses represent external stimuli or whether they are mere 'noise' or background activity. This decision process complicates the ascertainment of the absolute threshold because, with a given low intensity stimulus, the brain may sometimes 'decide' that a stimulus was present and on other occasions 'decide' that it was not. The intensity of stimulus which evokes a positive decision varies, depending on many factors in the internal and external environment of the subject.

If a graph is plotted of stimulus intensity against percentage of 'seen' responses, the following type of curve is obtained (see Figure 10.1). This curve is called a psychophysical function because it expresses a relationship between a psychological variable (the perception of the stimulus) and a physical variable (its intensity). The sloping part of the curve shows a region of stimulus intensities where detection occurs part of the time. In order to give a definite value to the absolute threshold, psychologists have agreed to define it as the intensity of stimulus which is perceived 50 per cent of the time.

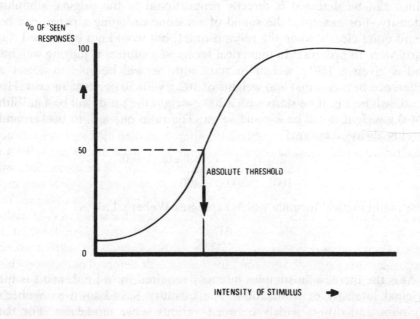

Figure 10.1

Difference thresholds

As well as being interested in the *minimum* intensity of stimulation which can be perceived, psychologists are also concerned with the *differences* in intensities between two stimuli required for them to be perceived as dissimilar. The minimum amount of intensity difference necessary before the subject can tell two stimuli apart is known as the difference threshold. As with the absolute threshold, the intervention of 'noise' and a decision process means that there is no one absolute value of the difference threshold. Again, it is defined as the magnitude of intensity difference between two stimuli, required for them to be perceived as different 50 per cent of the time. This value is alternatively known as the 'just noticeable difference' or j.n.d., a term invented by Gustav Fechner (1801–87) who was the first psychologist to study sensory thresholds empirically.

The difference threshold, like the absolute threshold, varies for different subjects and also for the same subject depending on motivation, physical condition, etc. However, the difference threshold also varies with the absolute stimulus intensity. This variation, unlike the personal and inter-personal ones, can be predicted according to a given law. This law is called Weber's law after Ernst Weber (1795–1878), who first discovered the relationship in 1846. He stated that the smallest difference in intensity which can be detected is directly proportional to the original stimulus intensity. For example, the sound of someone dropping a pencil can be heard quite clearly when the room is quiet, but would not be noticed if a party were in progress. In numerical terms, if a subject is judging weights and is given a 100 g weight to start with he will be able to detect a difference between that and weights of 102 g with 50 per cent success. His j.n.d. will be 2 g. If he starts with a 200 g weight the j.n.d. will be 4 g. With a 400 g weight it will be 8 g and so on. The ratio of j.n.d. to background level is always constant.

$$\frac{2}{100} = \frac{4}{200} = \frac{8}{400} \text{ etc. } = 0.02$$

The mathematical formula which expresses Weber's Law is

$$\frac{\Delta I}{I} = K$$

if ΔI is the increase in stimulus intensity required for a j.n.d. and I is the original intensity of stimulation. The quantity K is known as Weber's constant and differs widely between various sense modalities. For the change in pitch of a tone, $K = \frac{1}{333}$; in other words, we can detect a very small change in pitch. For the change in concentration in a saline solution, $K = \frac{1}{5}$; we are not very sensitive to change in saltiness. This is broadly true, although there is of course the complication of different units being used to measure intensities in different modalities.

Weber's Law holds fairly well over a wide range of background intensity but it does break down at the extremes, particularly at very low levels of stimulation. This is probably because at such levels the 'noise' in the system (i.e. the spontaneous residual firing of neurones in the absence of stimulus) becomes a significant factor.

Signal detection theory

In the last twenty years it has become apparent that the methods of determining a subject's threshold developed by the early psychologists presented the experimenter with some problems. For example, the experiments designed to find a subject's perceptual threshold used low energy stimuli; this means that on some proportion of trials the subject would be unsure about whether or not a stimulus had been presented. This of course provided fertile ground for the subject's guessing habits to affect the results. Furthermore the experimenter had no guarantee that his subject was not dissembling.

In order to deal with these problems experimenters introduced trials when no stimulus was presented. Originally, when this was done the experimenters tried to use the data collected from these 'catch trials' to account for the subject's guesses. However, if we deliberately set out to study the effect of the subject's guessing behaviour and to separate out this effect from his true perceptual sensitivity, then we may use the methods derived from so-called Signal Detection Theory. This is a mathematical model of stimulus detection, developed by communication engineers, from which it is possible to derive two supposedly independent measures of the subject's behaviour. First, ability to perceive stimuli correctly (d') and second, willingness to make a positive decision that a stimulus was presented (β). This latter measure, β, is the subject's criterion of caution, that is to say, the subject may decide to operate with a lax criterion in which case he will make more correct detections but he will also make more *false positive* errors, i.e. he will more often report the presence of a stimulus when no stimulus was in fact presented. Or he can operate with a stricter criterion, making fewer correct detections and fewer false positive errors. His criterion will be affected by many factors, his general motivation, his guessing habits, his expectations on each trial that a stimulus will be presented, his appraisal of what sort of accuracy is expected of him during the experiment, etc.

It is of course apparent that the subject's responses may be categorized as follows: correct detection, missed stimuli, false alarms and correct negatives, but we are only interested in the proportion of hits (correct detections) to the total number of stimulus presentations and the proportion of false alarms to those trials on which no stimulus was presented. If we run a subject nine times through our experiment, with the same signal strength while varying the proportion of trials on which a stimulus is really presented from say 10 per cent of the trials to 90 per cent, we should be able to study the effect of his altered expectations upon his criterion level, β. If we then plot the hit rate to false alarm rate for each presentation rate we will have a curve known as a Receiver Operating Characteristic curve which is an indication both of the subject's changing β and his sensitivity, d'.

A detailed discussion of the mathematics upon which calculation of d' and β are based is beyond the scope of this treatment, but one or two points should be mentioned. First, it is assumed that the subject has no threshold below which he will not detect the stimulus. Second, the model assumes that the subject's spontaneous neural activity fluctuates in a manner which is characteristic of the normal distribution and that when stimuli are presented the subject's neural activity is still characterized by the normal distribution but with a raised mean.

The first of the above assumptions seems odd as a 'trigger' or threshold is often built in to machines to make them more efficient, and the second assumption seems far too simple a description of the workings of the perceptual apparatus. It therefore seems likely that signal detection theory will be modified in the future to take account of these points. The reader who wishes to pursue the theory in greater detail may consult the treatment by J. P. Egan.

The general effects of stimulation

Stimuli above threshold level acting upon an organism may produce a response. The effects of stimulation fall broadly into two categories: the general effects, and the specific effects relating to object perception. We shall first discuss the general effects.

Sensory restriction

A number of experiments, started over thirty years ago, have indicated that efficient behaviour degenerates in human subjects who are deprived of all types of stimulation. In these experiments, college students have been paid to stay in isolation in sound-proofed cubicles, wearing goggles, and with their limbs tied up to prevent any tactile stimulation. Alternatively, they have been required to lie in baths of water at blood temperature, blindfolded, and using breathing apparatus. After a period of time under these conditions (which can vary from a few hours to a few days), subjects report great mental strain. They are unable to think clearly and logically, their minds wander, and they reach a state in which they are unsure whether they are awake or asleep. Some subjects have reported visual and auditory hallucinations. These effects may even continue for up to two days after the end of the stimulus deprivation. The interpretation of these results is complicated by the large variations in the experiences of individual subjects and also the discrepancies among the results obtained by different investigators. However, it is broadly true to say that subjects under such conditions of restricted sensory input function at less than their normal level of efficiency. This type of degeneration in efficiency is apparent in certain monotonous tasks such as radar scanning where the subject (or operative) is required to watch out for infrequent signals. Performance on this type of vigilance task can be improved by, among other things, the introduction of general stimulation such as background music for a visual task, or pictures to look at for an auditory task. In these cases the subject is not undergoing total *sensory deprivation* but his sensory input is so monotonous and unstructured that he could be said to be *perceptually deprived*. In experiments on perceptual deprivation subjects are, for example, required to wear diffusing goggles instead of blindfolds and, strangely, these subjects seem to show at least as much mental disturbance, if not more, than subjects in sensory deprivation experiments. It would appear that it is the lack of change in stimulation rather than the absolute reduction which leads to behaviour breakdown. Our brain seems to require a constantly changing sensory input for maximum efficiency.

This is not only true of the brain but also applies to the individual sensory systems. The ears, or the auditory centres of the brain, are very responsive to change in auditory stimulation but soon ignore persistent monotonous signals. For example, the ticking of a clock is easily ignored but if the clock for some reason stopped, the cessation of the ticking would be noticed. The eye reacts quickly to a moving stimulus but can be very unattentive to familiar objects which are still. This attention to changing stimuli has obvious survival value in a world where predator and prey are usually moving features.

Stabilized retinal images

As our sense organs normally respond largely to changes in the environment, it is interesting to see what happens when they are presented with an entirely stable perceptual field. This approach to the study of vision was first developed by R. W. Ditchburn in 1952.

When we survey a scene we make continuous eye and head movements which change the fix of our gaze. It is possible to prevent some of these movements by clamping the head and instructing the subject to fixate steadily on a small target. However, even under these conditions, the eye is constantly making small oscillating movements of which the subject is unaware and which he is unable to control. This tremor results in a constantly changing pattern of retinal stimulation even when the subject stares fixedly at one thing. It is impossible to stop these movements safely, but various devices have been produced which cause the image to move along with the eye. One such device is a tiny slide projector which is mounted on a contact lens. When the subject wears the lens the projector moves with the eye, causing the projection of the slide on a screen to move also. Wearing such a device, the subject is at first able to see the image projected onto the screen very clearly. However, within a few seconds the image begins to fade and may disappear entirely. More often, though, parts of the image disappear, and it has been noted that the disappearances are usually of an entire unit or block of the image rather than just random patches. For example, if a subject views a target like this in a stabilized vision

Figure 10.2

s/he is likely to see any of the following fragments of the image:

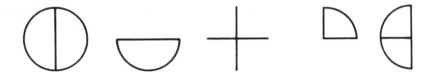

Figure 10.3

Frequently, the subject reports that as some parts of the image fade from view other parts come back so that s/he sees a changing pattern.

It is not clearly understood exactly what causes this phenomenon to occur. Some kind of neural inhibition or neural fatigue may be involved. This does not seem to occur at the retina, and the fact that meaningful elements of the stimulus disappear and reappear suggest that it may occur at quite a high level of neural processing, for example, the lateral geniculate body (see Chapter 6).

Sensory adaptation

Another of the general effects of stimulation is the way in which the sense organs are able to adapt to stimuli impinging upon them. If a stimulus persists, we become less sensitive to it, and, conversely, in the absence of stimulation, sensitivity increases. On first walking into a room, we can clearly smell both pleasant smells such as flowers or perfume, and unpleasant ones such as stale smoke. However, after we have been sitting in the room for some time we become less aware of the smell, even though there may be just as much smoke or even more than there was at first. Bath water may seem very hot when we have just stepped into it but it soon becomes comfortable as our senses adapt, even though the water temperature may remain the same. This phenomenon is perhaps most marked for the visual system. On first walking into bright sunlight it seems to hurt our eyes, but, as we adapt to the glare, we are able to see quite clearly. On returning to a dimly lit room, it is often impossible to see anything until our eyes have become adapted or accustomed to the lower light intensity.

One mechanism by which such adaptation occurs in the visual system is the contraction of the muscles in the iris which change the size of the pupil. However, this does not account for much of the adaptation. The main peripheral mechanism involved in dark adaptation seems to be biochemical changes which take place in the pigment cells (the rods and cones) in the retina. Exposure to bright light bleaches the photochemicals in the cells of the retina, making these cells less sensitive to light stimulation. When the bright light is removed these photochemicals regenerate, enabling the eye to respond to lower intensities of light. These changes in sensitivity are very dramatic. The eye at its most sensitive state, after a long period in total darkness, will respond to a stimulus $\frac{1}{100\,000}$ as intense as that required when the eye is at its least sensitive, after exposure to bright light.

Perceptual adaptation

Not all adaptation in sensory systems occurs at the peripheral level (in the sense organs themselves). Another series of experiments has shown that humans are capable of adapting to quite drastic changes in stimulation. Various psychologists, the first of whom was George Stratton (1897), have devised a variety of optical devices for distorting the visual world. The simplest of these are inverting lenses: pairs of spectacles which project an upside down image of the world to the wearer. When subjects first put on such spectacles they find it very difficult to do anything, and the world appears very bizarre. However, after some time things begin to look more normal, and after wearing the lenses for some days subjects find them- selves able to move around quite well. They have adapted to their distorted world. Moreover, subjects report confusion over their perceptions. They may be unable to say whether things still look upside down to them, although they do realize that there is something strange about what they see. On the removal of the lenses after they have been worn for several days, subjects report confusion and bewilderment which may last for several hours before their perceptual world returns to normal.

This type of adaptation is different from sensory adaptation, which is largely a physiological process, taking place mainly within the sense organ. Perceptual adaptation, on the other hand, must occur at a more central level of processing (i.e. in the brain itself rather than in the eye) and seems to involve an aspect of 'learning'. Interestingly enough, other animals do not seem able to adapt to this type of distortion of the visual field. Hens wearing distorting prisms show no improvement in their disturbed behaviour, even after three months. Monkeys show some sign of slight adaptation but nothing like as much as humans. Clearly, some quite complex processing must be involved in this type of adaptation. For a fuller discussion see Chapter 11.

The perception of objects

In the real world we are not much concerned with the general effects of stimulation such as those discussed above. Most of us never experience stabilized retinal images and few of us walk about wearing defusing goggles. We are concerned, however, with the perception of specific meaningful objects. Although our sense of taste and smell are stimulated by an elaborate pattern of chemicals, we do not perceive this pattern. We are aware, however, that we are having kippers for tea today! When listening to an orchestral concert only the trained ear is aware of individual notes or instruments; most of us hear only the music. This is even more true when we listen to speech; we are concerned with the meaning, not with the series of tones. Despite these examples, most of the work on object perception has been concerned with seen objects and, thus, much of the following discussion will be concerned with the human visual system.

Gestalt psychology

Any sensory experience is a product of a series of often quite discrete stimuli impinging on the organism. These individual stimuli are rarely perceived as such. The perception is of a pattern, not of its component parts. A television picture is composed of thousands of points of light but we are never aware of this. We see only the image shown on the screen. This type of phenomenon was the basis of a school of psychology known as Gestalt psychology. This grew up in Germany and Austria towards the end of the nineteenth century and the name Gestalt comes from a German word which means form or pattern. It was led by Max Wertheimer (1880–1943), Kurt Koffka (1886–1941) and Wolfgang Köhler (1887–1967). Proponents of the Gestalt school hold that components of a perceptual field are synthesized by the mind into a pattern or a Gestalt, i.e. that the whole perception is more than the sum of the individual parts and that the extra significance has been added inside the organism. There are four basic principles of Gestalt psychology: 'figure and ground'; 'segregation and differentiation'; 'closure'; and 'good Gestalt', or 'Prägnanz'.

The figure/ground principle relates to the problem of how the visual system is able to distinguish an object from its background. If all stimuli are simply arrays of coloured dots, how do we make out where one object ends and the next begins, i.e. how do we distinguish the figure from its background? This is not simply a matter of picking out identifiable objects, because figure-ground structuring in perception still occurs in the absence of these. Black and white patterns and certain wall-paper designs are perceived as figures upon grounds and in some cases figure and ground spontaneously reverse. A classic example is shown in Figure 10.4. This picture can be seen either as a white vase upon a dark background or two silhouetted faces looking at each other.

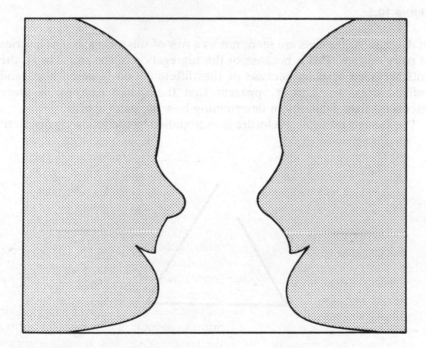

Figure 10.4

It is interesting to note that the ability to distinguish figure from ground is not learned. Studies of subjects who, blind from birth, have had their sight restored later in life show that they are able to distinguish figure from ground immediately, while other features of perception must be learned (see Chapter 11).

The second principle of Gestalt psychology, that of segregation and differentiation, is closely related to the first. The principles may be illustrated with dot patterns.

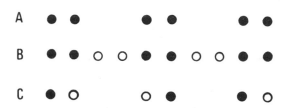

Figure 10.5

In diagram A, the dots are seen, not as a row of single dots, but as a series of pairs of dots. This is because of the segregation of the pairs. In B, the dots are seen as pairs because of the differentation between filled and unfilled dots. In C, it is apparent that the spatial nearness is more important than similarity in determining how the pairs appear.

The Gestalt principle of closure is exemplified by the following diagram:

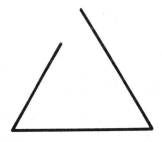

Figure 10.6

We perceive this as a triangle with a piece of one side missing. It has been found that subjects shown such shapes in a tachistoscope for brief intervals of time, report seeing the completed shape and are unaware of the break in the outline. They mentally 'close' the shape. The same happens when such shapes are used as stimuli in memory tasks. The subject, when asked to reproduce what s/he saw, will frequently draw a complete figure.

All these principles combine together to give the principle of 'good form' or 'Prägnanz'. The brain organizes a perception in such a way that the stimulus appears orderly, or a good figure. Take the following illustration:

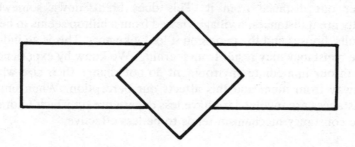

Figure 10.7

This figure is perceived as a square superimposed upon a rectangle. The rectangle is completed mentally according to the principle of closure. The square is the figure and the rectangle the ground. We do not see a ten-sided figure with two right-angled patterns inside it, as this would not be such a neat interpretation or 'good Gestalt'.

Object constancy

Not only are we able to distinguish a figure from its background, but we are also able to recognize a known object in a variety of different orientations. This ability is known as object constancy. The pattern of stimulation falling on the retina when we see our grandmother may vary wildly, depending on whether we see her from the front, back or side, whether she is sitting or standing and whether she is partly obscured by some object between us; none the less we still recognize her as grandmother. This must involve a high level of perceptual processing.

Location constancy

As our eyes move, or as we walk about, a constantly changing pattern of stimulation falls on our retina. We do not, however, see the world as constantly moving about. We know that the table is stable even though its image is moving. The ability to perceive objects as enduring and stationary is partly dependent upon the organs of balance in the middle ear.

Size constancy

Objects may be viewed at different distances. When they are so viewed, the image of the object falling on the retina will differ in size. The retinal image of a book held 10 inches away is twice the size of that when the book is held 20 inches away, yet the book does not appear smaller when it is further from us. We tend to see it as more or less invariant in size, whatever our distance from it. This does break down somewhat at unusually great distances, a village viewed from a hilltop seems to be made up of dolls' houses and the people in it look like ants. This is an indication that size constancy may result from learning. We know by experience that objects in our immediate environment do not change their size when we move away from them and this affects our perception. When unusually large distances are involved we have less experience on which to draw and thus the constancy mechanism tends to be less effective.

Colour and brightness constancy

Familiar objects appear to remain the same colour, despite variation in lighting conditions. Even coloured lights do not obscure our perception of the constancy of an object's colour, provided that there are sufficient contrasts and shadows. We perceive our writing paper as white, despite the fact that it may be covered by grey shadows or reflecting yellow light from a coloured street lamp. Colour constancy depends entirely on our having some knowledge of the perceived object and/or seeing it against a background of information about the intensity of illumination and the colour of surrounding objects. When these cues are removed colour constancy disappears entirely and we see the colour of objects.as true to the wavelength of the light reflected from them. For example, when a familiar object, such as a tomato, is viewed through a tube which obscures the outline and all background, its colour is no longer seen as invariant as the illumination of its changes.

Perception of depth

One of the problems in this field is how we manage to perceive a three-dimensional world when the image on the retina is necessarily a two-dimensional one. We believe that this is facilitated by recourse to certain 'cues' – aspects of the perception which give us information about distance and depth. These fall into two classes: binocular and monocular cues.

Binocular cues to depth

The image on the retina of the eye is two-dimensional, but the normal human observer has two eyes and thus two retinal images. These images are not identical. Because the eyes are separated in our head, the left eye receives an image which is slightly different from that received by the right eye. (This was first realized by Euclid in the third century BC.) If these two images are combined, a stereoscopic effect results. This effect can be clearly reproduced in a three-dimensional viewer or stereoscope. This device is similar to a pair of binoculars but instead of lenses each eye tube holds a two dimensional picture. By simultaneous presentation of two slightly differing pictures, one to each eye, a dramatic three-dimensional picture can be seen.

In normal vision, the slight difference between the two retinal images is termed retinal disparity and is easily demonstrable. Hold a pencil up in front of you at arm's length and, closing one eye, align the pencil with some distant object such as the window frame. Now open the closed eye and close the other. The pencil will appear to jump to one side as the second eye views it from a different angle. The image from one eye usually dominates the overall perception and in a right handed person the right eye is most commonly dominant. Eye-dominance can be determined in a similar way to the above. This time the pencil and window frame should be aligned with both eyes open. If you then close each eye in turn, the pencil will probably appear to shift more with one eye than with the other. If the greatest jump occurs when the right eye is closed then you are right eye dominant and vice versa.

Another depth cue which is dependent on the use of both eyes is convergence of the eyes. The nearer an object is, the more the eyes must turn inwards in order to focus on that object. Thus information from the orbital muscles which turn the eyes could be available as a further cue to depth.

Monocular cues to depth

It is clear that people who have lost an eye are nevertheless capable of judging depth as are two-eyed observers with one eye covered, and there must therefore be some alternative monocular cues available. The two binocular cues result from processes and structures which are inherent in the organism and are thus assumed to be independent of learning or experience. Such cues are called *primary cues* to depth perception, and there is one monocular primary cue which depends upon the accommodation of the eye. In order to focus objects at different distances from the eye, the lens must change its shape. These changes are brought about by the activity of the lens muscles. It is possible that information could be available from these muscles in much the same way as information from the orbital muscles. Of course, we are conscious of neither of these muscular changes as they are autonomic responses, but this does not preclude the possibility that the information may be being used at a subconscious level. However, this process only works over short distances. Anything further away than 25 feet is at optical infinity, in other words no further changes in lens shape occur after the object is further away than 25 feet. Therefore, there must be other cues available.

These final cues are called *secondary cues* and are assumed to be acquired through experience. They are not dependent on biological processes but are features of the visual field itself, and may be used by artists to create an illusion of depth in a flat picture. These cues are as follows:

1. *Overlap or superimposition.* If one object overlaps and appears to cut off the view of another then we presume the first object to be nearer.

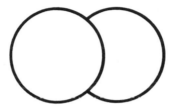

Figure 10.8

2. *Relative size.* In an array of similar objects smaller ones appear to be further away. This is especially true if the object is one which is known to have a constant size, e.g. a teacup.

Figure 10.9

306

3. *Height in the horizontal plane*. Objects which are placed higher up in a picture appear to be further away.

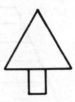

Figure 10.10

4. *Texture gradient*. The grain or texture appears to become finer as distance becomes greater.

Figure 10.11

5. *Linear perspective.* Parallel lines such as railway track appear to converge as they recede into the distance.

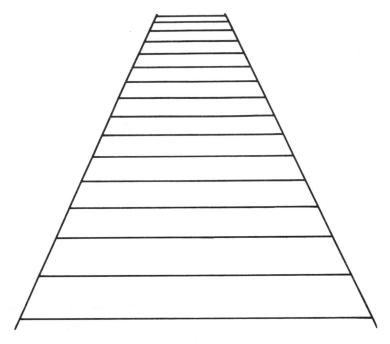

Figure 10.12

6. *Aerial perspective.* Objects at great distance appear to be slightly different in colour, e.g. the bluish tint of distant mountains.
7. *Relative brightness.* Brighter objects appear to be nearer if all other things are equal.
8. *Shadowing.* Three-dimensional objects present variations in light and shade. This can be used by an artist to create three-dimensional illusion.
9. *Motion parallax.* When the observer is moving, e.g. as a traveller in a train, the apparent movement of distant objects is slower than that of objects close by. Telegraph poles by the side of the track appear to flash by, while similar poles on a distant hillside move quite slowly.

Although the sensation of depth or distance produced by each one of these cues in isolation is not very strong, they can combine together to create a very compelling impression of depth.

To summarize, the cues to depth perception are as follows:

1. *Primary cues*
   Retinal disparity
   Convergence
   Accommodation

2. *Secondary cues*
   Overlap
   Relative size
   Height in the horizontal plane
   Texture gradient
   Linear perspective
   Aerial perspective
   Relative brightness
   Shadowing
   Motion parallax

Visual illusions

In the foregoing discussion of perception, various references have been made to situations in which our eyes seem to play tricks on us leading us to perceive something very different from reality. Such phenomena may be grouped together under the heading of visual illusions, and their study can tell us much about perceptual analysis.

Illusions of movement

Our perception of the movement of an object depends on changes in its position on the retinal image. However, as we move our heads around we produce a constantly-changing retinal image, and yet we do not perceive the world spinning around us. Despite the movement across the retina of their image, objects in the room appear to be stationary. Kinaesthetic feedback from the muscles and organs of balance is integrated with the changing retinal picture at a high level to inhibit the perception of movement. The disruption of this process results in dizziness when the world does appear to reel around. In the absence of this kinaesthetic feedback then, changes in position of objects in the retinal image are perceived as movement. It is thus possible to create the sensation of movement without any movement actually occurring. This creation of apparent motion is the principle by which moving films work. It was brought to the interest of psychologists by Max Wertheimer in 1912 and is commonly known as the *phi phenomenon*. A subject in a darkened room is seated in front of a line or sometimes a ring of lights. If these lights are flashed on and off in sequence, the subject perceives the illusion of a single light moving in a line or circle. This effect is sometimes used to create the illusion of movement in neon street signs.

The stroboscopic motion of cinema films is essentially similar to the phi phenomenon. The illusion of motion is created by presenting stationary stimuli one after the other.

When the eye perceives real relative motion the brain always tends to assume that the small objects are moving while large objects are stationary. If a subject is shown a stationary spot of light within a moving frame he will report that the spot is moving. This phenomenon is called *induced movement* and an everyday example of it is the apparent racing of the moon through the clouds in a windy sky. Similar illusions can be experienced when travelling by any kind of vehicle. In a train, it is often difficult to judge whether one's own carriage is moving or that of an adjacent train. Pilots and astronauts are so well aware of such confusion that they tend to trust their instrument panels rather than their eyes.

A third type of movement illusion is termed the *autokinetic effect*. If a small point of light is presented in a totally dark room, an observer will frequently report that the light is moving, although, in fact, it is not. This effect seems to be connected with eye movements, as, when such movements are minimized, the autokinetic effect is reduced. A theoretical explanation lies in the inability of the brain to 'decide' whether it is the movement of the eye itself or of the stimulus dot of light which is producing changes in the position of the retinal image. The brain has not enough data on which to base a decision and may come to the 'wrong' conclusion. This theory is supported by the fact that the introduction of any other features into the visual field will reduce and frequently abolish the autokinetic effect. It may be that a similar explanation could apply in the case of all the movement illusions discussed here. In each case the brain has not enough information on which to make an accurate decision and is, consequently, often mistaken. A similar theory will be put forward with regard to the geometric illusions described below.

Geometric illusions

The two most famous visual illusions are Muller–Lyer and the Ponzo illusions.

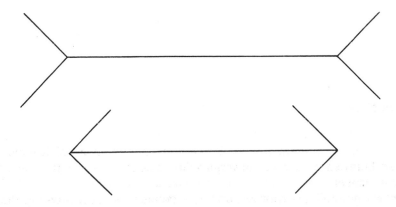

Figure 10.13

The Muller–Lyer illusion (Figure 10.13) is created by pairs of fins attached to the ends of straight lines of identical length. The line with the outgoing fins always appears longer. Not only is this true for most human observers but the illusion is also experienced by animals. We can ascertain this by training an animal to produce a response to the shorter of two lines. If such a trained animal is presented with the Muller–Lyer lines, it will respond to the one with the ingoing fins.

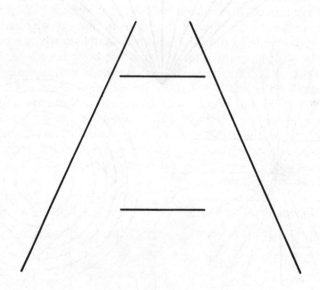

Figure 10.14

In the Ponzo illusion (Figure 10.14) two lines of identical length are placed between a pair of converging line segments. Here the top line appears longer.

Other illusions involve the distortion of lines by superimposing them upon certain backgrounds. In the drawings in Figure 10.15, straight lines appear to be curved and arches distorted.

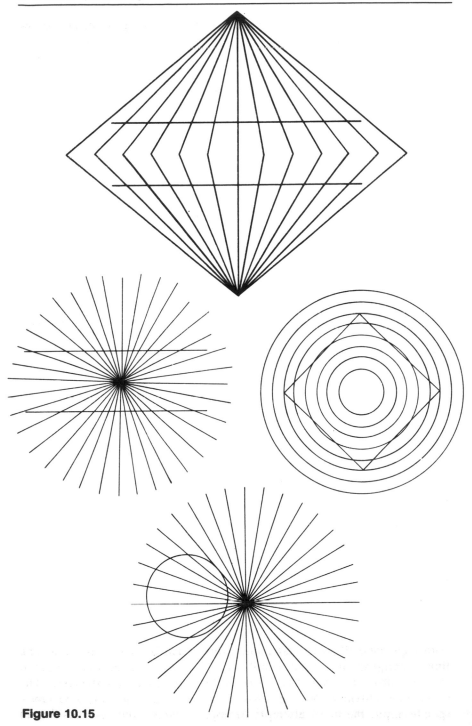

Figure 10.15

A third type of illusion involves a change in the apparent size of an object in changed surroundings:

Figure 10.16

The two centre circles are the same size but the one on the left appears to be larger. Similarly with the horizontal–vertical illusion below, the vertical line appears longer, although, in fact, the two lines are of equal length (Figure 10.17).

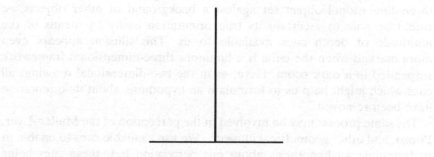

Figure 10.17

Towards an explanation

Although these illusions and many others have been known for a long time, their explanations are still controversial. One strongly-favoured theory relates illusions to the perception of visual constancies. The perceptual system is not a passive recipient of all stimulation. Given a specific input the brain attempts to apply meaning and searches for an hypothesis which is most consistent with all aspects of the stimulus. Sometimes this hypothesis changes from one moment to the next as in figure-ground illusions such as the one illustrated in Figure 10.4. Another well-known instance of this is the illusion of the Necker cube.

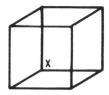

Figure 10.18

The above drawing is seen to represent a transparent cube the depth properties of which appear to change spontaneously. The corner x sometimes appears at the front of the figure and sometimes at the back.

The problem here seems to be lack of adequate information on which to base our hypothesis about what we are seeing. If the cube were a real three-dimensional object set against a background of other objects we would be able to ascertain its true orientation easily by means of the multitude of depth cues available to us. This illusion appears even more marked when the cube is a luminous three-dimensional framework suspended in a dark room. Here, as in the two-dimensional drawing, all cues which might help us to formulate an hypothesis about its orientation have been removed.

The same process may be involved in the perception of the Muller–Lyer, Ponzo, and other geometrical illusions. We use available cues to enable us to formulate an hypothesis about our perception but, these cues being misleading or inadequate, we are brought to the wrong conclusions.

In the case of these geometrical illusions, however, it is not so easy to determine why a mistake is being made. Clearly, there is no spontaneous reversal as with the Necker cube and thus a firm but mistaken hypothesis must have been made as to what comprises the stimulus. Several explanatory theories have been put forward. For example it has been suggested with regard to the Muller–Lyer illusion that the fins serve to draw the eyes past or within the lines. This, at best, is a rather vague description and can clearly be shown to be untrue. If the image of the arrows is stabilized on the retina the illusion is still apparent, although, clearly, no eye movement is possible.

Gregory's contribution

A more convincing approach is made by R. L. Gregory who, in his book
Eye and Brain, relates the perception of illusions to the various constancy
scaling devices discussed earlier in this chapter, in particular size constancy. A
book, or our hand appears to be the same size whether it is viewed from a
distance of 10 inches or 20 inches despite the fact that its retinal image will
be only half the size in the second instance that it was in the first. By the
reverse of this scaling process, a given size of retinal image will be
interpreted differently, depending on the estimated distance of the stimulus
producing that image. If we believe the object to be further away, we will
hypothesize that it must be larger for a given retinal image size. Both the
Muller–Lyer and the Ponzo diagrams contain features which could be
analysed as depth cues. In the Ponzo illusion, the outer pair of lines could
be considered to be cues to linear perspective. If this were the case, then
combination of that and the third monocular depth cue, i.e. height in the
horizontal plane should combine to give a strong illusion of depth. In this
three-dimensional percept the upper of the two inner lines is seen as
further away and, as it produces the same size of retinal image as the lower
one, the system will hypothesize that it must be larger.

A similar explanation can be put forward for the case of the Muller–Lyer
illusion. Here, the line with the ingoing fins provides linear perspective
cues which suggest that it might be the corner of an object which is pointing
towards us such as the corner of a building.

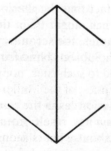 

Figure 10.19

The line with the outgoing fins looks more like the internal corner of a
room, where the corner is pointing away from us (see Figure 10.20).

The cues of linear perspective lead us to hypothesize that the vertical
line is nearer to us in Figure 10.19 than in Figure 10.20. Consequently,
the equal-sized retinal images of the vertical lines are interpreted as
representing different-sized objects, the more distant one appearing
larger.

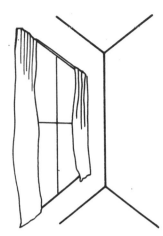

Figure 10.20

In support of this hypothesis is the fact that when the illusion figures are removed from their flat paper background and presented as luminous models suspended in a dark room, their three-dimensional interpretation is very striking. Gregory argues that it is only their superimposition on a flat paper background with its consequent conflicting cues (e.g. no texture gradient) that prevents us from seeing the Figures as three-dimensional objects.

Another piece of supporting evidence is the fact that the illusions only occur in organisms whose previous experience has taught them the basic depth cues. As was mentioned earlier in the chapter, the secondary depth cues are assumed to be learned from experience. Subjects blind from birth whose sight is restored in later life do not respond to such cues, nor do they experience the usual visual illusions.

It would appear, then, that the geometrical illusions as in the case of the Necker cube and reversible figure-ground drawings result from errors being made in the formation of an hypothesis about what is seen. These errors, yet again, result from incorrect interpretation of inadequate constancy cues.

However, Gregory's interpretation has been criticized and one most compelling illustration of where the theory falls short concerns a variation on the Muller–Lyer illusion (Figure 10.13).

In Figure 10.21 the two lines appear to be different lengths, as do the Muller–Lyer lines. However, in this variation there are clearly no linear perspective cues and it is very difficult to see how any 'misinterpretation of cues' hypothesis could account for the illusion.

We are left with an enigma.

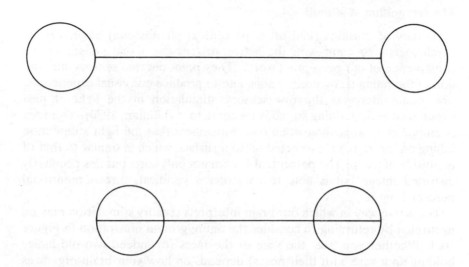

Figure 10.21

Figural after-effects

In the case of the visual illusions discussed so far the observer experiences the illusion when he first sees the stimulus involved. A further category of illusion is the figural after-effect, where the illusion is only experienced after viewing the stimulus for some time. If certain figures are viewed for a prolonged period with the eyes held as still as possible, distortions in vision may arise. For example, James Gibson noted in 1933 that if a curved line is viewed in this way and the gaze is then immediately transferred to a straight line, this line appears for a few seconds to be curved in the opposite direction.

Another famous after-effect is the waterfall illusion; if you stare at a waterfall for several seconds and then look at the adjacent bank it will appear to be moving in the opposite direction. A similar illusion is created by watching a parade for a long period: stationary objects viewed subsequently appear to move against the line of march. This effect can be produced experimentally by showing a subject a rotating spiral for several minutes and then instructing him to transfer his gaze to a stationary target. Subjects report that this appears to spin in the opposite direction to the spiral.

The explanation for these illusions probably lies in some inhibitory response within the nerves of the visual system. Inhibition theories have also been put forward as explanations of the geometric illusions, and it may be that, ultimately, all distortions of perception of this kind will be connected by a common theoretical explanation.

The recognition of stimuli

The study of illusions (and other perceptual phenomena) has led some psychologists to emphasize the active role of the visual system in the construction of our perceptual world. They point out that sensory stimulation of the retina is, by itself, inadequate to produce our visual experiences. The brain interprets the raw sensory stimulation in the light of past experience and, in doing so, adds meaning to it (Ullman, 1980). This idea is immediately appealing when one remembers that the light stimulation falling on the retina is projected on to a surface which is similar to that of the inside of a cup! The perceptual system not only sorts out this peculiarly distorted image but is able to construct a veridical, three-dimensional percept from it.

The active way in which our brain interprets sensory stimulation may be illustrated by returning to consider the figure/ground illustration in Figure 10.4. Whether you 'see' the vase or the faces (or indeed two old ladies holding up a vase with their noses) depends on how your brain organizes and interprets the data presented to it. The picture-stimulus does not alter at all, but your perception may.

Earlier in this chapter we introduced the principles of Gestalt psychology, which are, of course, merely *descriptions* of how some components of the perceptual field interact. The next question is *how* does this happen? What are the mechanisms of figure/ground discrimination, segregation, closure and the perception of 'the good figure'? In short, what are the mechanisms which enable us to recognize objects? This question, in common with so many others in psychology, has led to polarized theoretical positions, mainly because the two schools have tackled different aspects of the problem. One set of theorists argue that perception stems largely from a detailed analysis of the stimulus field, with the features and attributes of the stimuli being integrated to produce what is 'seen'. This is known as bottom-up processing and has much in common with the ideas of James J. Gibson, who developed his theory between 1950 and 1979. Gibson did not believe that our perceptions owe much to constructive interpretation by the brain, rather he emphasized the brain's ability to use information in the stimulus. Bruce and Green (1985) present a detailed, closely argued account of perception along these lines.

The other position, that our perceptions are mainly produced by processes which integrate existing knowledge into the perceptual system and thus add meaning to what is seen, is known as top-down processing. As we have seen, this position is often taken by psychologists studying illusions and ambiguous figures of one kind or another in order to explain the perceptual phenomena which occur under these conditions. We shall return to top-down or conceptually driven processing later.

Bottom-up processing

The nature of bottom-up or data-driven perceptual processing would seem to emerge from a consideration of the physiological structure of the perceptual cortex (see Chapter 1). The early work of Hubel and Wiesel (1962) indicated that the retinal image was analysed through the layers of the perceptual cortex in successively more complex ways until the output of the hypercomplex cells was integrated to form the perceptual representation of the stimulus. In other words, the constituent features of a stimulus were analysed first and then put together to form the perception of it. And, in fact, Marr (1982) has put forward a computer-based bottom-up model of stimulus recognition, in which he argues that perceptual analysis of a stimulus takes place in three major stages. The first stage produces a 'primal sketch' which is a representation of the pattern of light falling on the retina, based on information about the edges and textures of surfaces and objects. In the next stage, the '2 1/2D sketch', information about depth and orientation of surfaces from the observer's point of view only is derived. Finally, the '3D sketch' is produced which represents the object or objects in the stimulus field as independent of the observer's particular point of view by, for example, making use of the constancies of perception described earlier. Marr also showed that a computer programmed to apply the Gestalt laws of grouping to the data in his 'sketches' would correctly discriminate objects from background and some of the more obvious features of the objects. For example Marr's computer program could successfully separate the outline of a teddy bear. It could also discriminate the eyes and nose. However, Marr found that with more ambiguous stimuli the appropriate segmentation of the scene was possible only if additional higher level information was fed into the computer. For example, overlapping leaves could be discriminated only if the computer was programmed with the information that the stimuli were overlapping objects. This ties in with the notion, which has emerged from recent cognitive experiments, that the analysis of stimuli is not simply from the part to the whole; from the constituent features to the global stimulus.

There is now good evidence that global information about a stimulus is available to the brain before information about its detailed structure. This sounds an odd proposition but Navon (1977) devised experiments which illustrated the perceptual advantage which the overall or global properties of a stimulus may (under certain conditions) have over its detailed or local properties. Navon presented subjects with a stimulus whose overall structure was either consistent or conflicting with its detailed structure. Navon's examples were S and H, either composed of small Hs or small Ss.

```
H               H               S               S
H               H               S               S
H               H               S               S
H               H               S               S
HHHHHHHHHHHH                    SSSSSSSSSSS
H               H               S               S
H               H               S               S
H               H               S               S
H               H               S               S
```

The subject's task was to decide whether the name of the letter H or S had been spoken by a voice through a pair of headphones. Just before each auditory trial the subject was presented with one of the visual stimuli shown above. The first finding was that when the visual global letter was the same as the auditory letter, speed of auditory discrimination was faster than when the visual global letter was different from the auditory letter. The findings were approximately as follows:

Visual Stimulus		*Mean RT*
Auditory task +	no other task	550 milliseconds
Auditory task +	consonant global stimulus	560 milliseconds
Auditory task +	conflicting global stimuli	700 milliseconds
Auditory task +	neutral stimulus e.g. O or A	600 milliseconds

The interesting finding was that performance on the auditory discrimination task was completely unaffected by the detailed structure of the global letters. Moreover, most of the subjects did not notice that the large letters were composed of smaller letters. Even if the detailed structure of the visual stimuli was being analysed automatically, the results of that analysis were not able to affect the auditory discrimination task, whereas the global analysis was. The salience of the global nature of the stimulus is, of course, what the Gestaltists would have predicted.

Another experiment by Navon, using the same sort of stimuli, again provided evidence for the salience of global structure over local features. Subjects were asked to decide whether the global letter was an H or S and in another condition whether the local letters were H or S. The speed with which subjects identified the global letters was not affected by the nature of small letters but speed of identification of the local letters was much slower when they conflicted with the global letters.

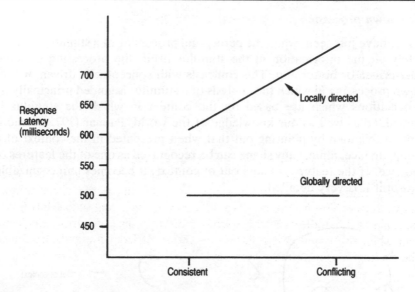

Figure 10.22 Stimulus relationship

This, on the face of it, constitutes good evidence that the first stage of the analysis of a stimulus (at least for a 'good' figure) may be global rather than local, but there is a problem with this view. It is now clear that global characteristics do not always interfere with processing of local features. As Kinchla and Wolf (1979) have shown, Navon's results were to some degree a function of the size of his stimuli; global stimuli which subtend 8° of visual angle or less are easiest to identify and Navon's effects are optimal when the global letters are about five times larger than the local letters. Kinchla and Wolf found that when the global letters were bigger than 8° of visual angle, the constituent letters were easier to respond to than the global ones. They therefore conclude that 'forms having an optimal size in the visual field are processed first'. This seems to mean that the results of the process of stimulus analysis are only available to affect other perceptual events and/or to be 'recognized' when that analysis has reached the level of a whole or 'good' figure. This tends to confirm that Gestalt assertion of the importance of 'goodness' of a stimulus. The Law of Prägnanz which asserts that the psychological organization of a percept will always be as 'good' as the perceptual conditions allow, does not precisely define the term 'good' but seems to include simplicity and symmetry. This 'law' or principle seems to suggest that the perceptual system attempts to find the 'essence' of a stimulus, an idea which has become ubiquitous in cognitive psychology and which Navon's work seems to support. We will return to this idea in the next chapter when we discuss the effects of cognitive disposition on perception and the formation of perceptual prototypes.

Top-down processing

As we have just seen, when the perceptual processing of a stimulus is based solely on the information in the stimulus itself, the processing is called data-driven or bottom-up. This contrasts with conceptually driven or top-down processing in which the analysis of a stimulus is guided principally by expectations which are based on the context in which the stimulus is embedded as well as our knowledge of the world. Palmar (1975) demonstrated this idea by pointing out that when presented in the context of a complete face, almost any shape can be recognized as one of the features of the face. If the feature is taken out of context, it becomes unrecognizable except if it is very detailed.

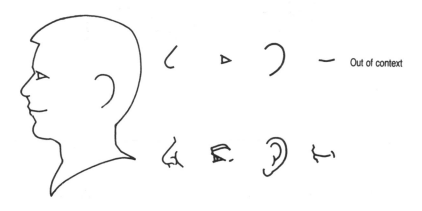

Out of context

Figure 10.23

There are many examples of how context determines perception, for example:

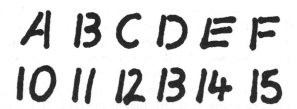

Figure 10.24

It is quite clear that the second character in the top line of Figure 10.24 is identical to the fourth character in the second line – but only when this is pointed out. Without such prompting one is seen as the letter B and the other as the number 13. Similarly the words in Figure 10.25 are clearly seen as The Cat:

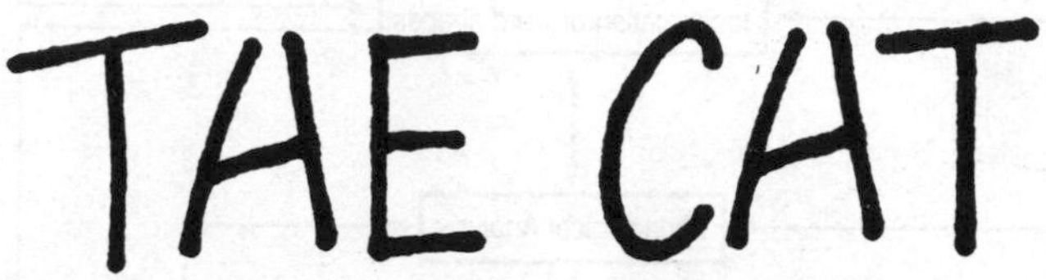

TAE CAT

Figure 10.25

But the two middle letters in each word are actually physically identical.

These are examples of context operating in an almost automatic fashion to determine perception, but in more ambiguous stimulus arrays the process of interpretation may be based on our knowledge of the world. For example, when we attempt to read poor handwriting, we may simply try to guess what a word might be on the basis of such of its physical attributes as we can discriminate, together with the meaning of the sentence of which it is a part. The sentence might be 'The footballer was sent off the pitch after committing a ————' when the last word is virtually illegible, but you may guess that the word is 'foul' because you know why footballers are usually sent off. This is a rather crudely obvious example of a conceptually driven search for the meaning of a degraded stimulus, but it suffices to illustrate the principle.

The diagram in Figure 10.26 illustrates how both bottom-up and top-down processes might combine to search for the meaning of a stimulus, in this case a poorly written word in a sentence:

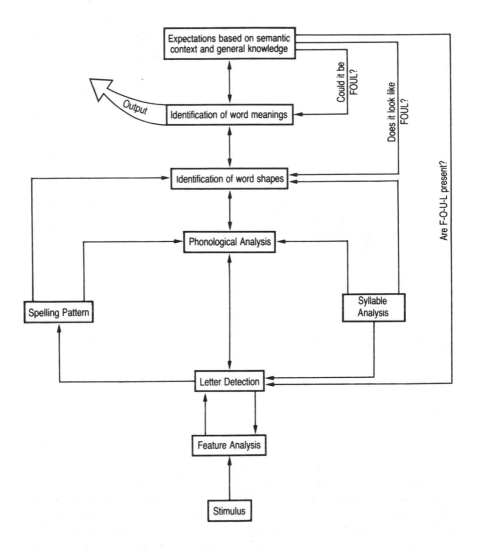

Figure 10.26 Top-down and bottom-up processing in word identification (adapted from Estes, 1975 and Wessells, 1982)

This model shows analysis of the spelling pattern (allowable vs non-legitimate letter sequences), and syllable analysis taking place in parallel. It also has phonological analysis (analysis of the sound of the word), as a higher level analysis than spelling pattern and syllable analysis. Moreover, the types/levels of analysis interact so that higher levels may contribute to the fine tuning of lower levels.

Parallel processing and stimulus recognition

A seminal experiment by Reicher (1969) illustrates the importance of recursive fine tuning in word recognition. He found that subjects were better able to identify a letter accurately when it was presented as part of a word than when it was presented either as part of an unpronounceable letter string, or by itself. This word superiority effect has been replicated many times in a variety of different ways (Baron, 1978; Solman, May, and Schwartz, 1981), and can thus be regarded as a robust effect. Reicher presented subjects with brief flashes of WORK or, for example, ORWK or just . . . K followed by a visual mask. The subjects were required to choose whether D or K had been presented in the first flash. They made fewer errors when primed with a word than when they were primed with a non-word or a single letter. Mezrick (1973) may have found the mechanism causing this effect; he found that the effect disappeared if subjects were told to say out loud each priming stimulus before choosing one of the two alternatives. The implication was that subjects automatically analyse the *words* phonologically and this helped in letter recognition but that, left to themselves, subjects did not analyse single letters in this way and further, that the results of phonological analysis were used to fine tune the lower level letter detection process.

Thus, there are two sorts of interaction between the different attribute analysers: the 'automatic' exchanges where their outputs 'affect' each other, both up and down the hierarchy of analysers and the deliberate use of semantic and general knowledge to make guesses about the nature of the stimuli.

The major problem with such a model is that it would appear to require far more time to operate than is observed in experimentation. An alternative conceptualization would be to have most of the analysis of a stimulus carried out by units operating simultaneously, i.e. in parallel (see figure 10.27).

There appears to be no theoretical reason why the stimulus attribute analysers should not operate in parallel using copies of a neural code of the stimulus. Thus, after an initial coding into a neural pattern, a word may be concurrently analysed at the level of syllables, spelling pattern, letter shape, phonemes and whole word shape. This may seem strange, but if it happened, it would help to explain the word superiority effect because a letter which is part of a word would be better analysed than a letter on its own, or one presented as part of a random letter string. There is no theoretical reason why semantic analysis should not take place simultaneously with the other modes of analysis; it does not necessarily require prior identification of the physical shape or of the phonological characteristics of the word. It is a pattern of neural activity caused by a stimulus which is analysed, not information about the acoustic shape of the word.

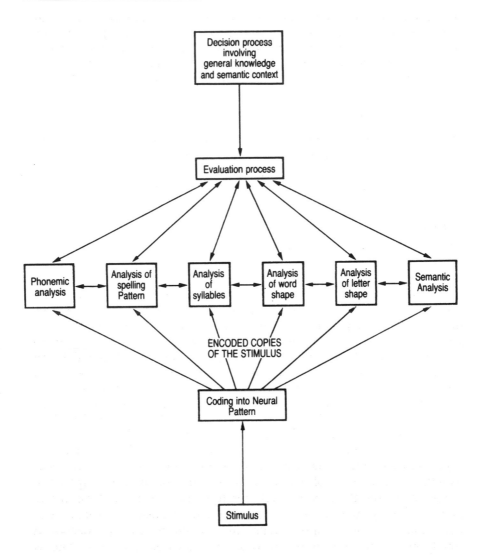

Figure 10.27 Parallel processing and stimulus recognition

The outputs from each type of analysis, phonemic, syllabic, word shape, etc., would be integrated and evaluated and the results of that evaluation would then be used to refine further the analysis until a decision could be made. Reicher's results would be explicable because a letter which is part of a word would undergo an analysis which would be refined by the results of the other analysers, whereas the analysis of a letter presented on its own or as part of a random letter string could not benefit from such a process. If both phonological and semantic analysis take place in parallel with all of the other stimulus attributes already mentioned, much of the data from other areas of psychology, such as subliminal perception, would become more readily understandable. The conceptualisation shown in Figure 10.27 serves merely to illustrate the broad principles of parallel processing but it poses many further questions concerning the details of how such a system could work.

The selective nature of perception

The final problem we shall deal with in this chapter is the issue of how we perceive or 'attend' to one object or task while ignoring others. This process is generally referred to as 'selective attention' by psychologists and is a much more complex feat than, at first sight, it seems.

The concept of attention

The study of attention is really the study of consciousness. As we shall see, psychologists have been loath to admit this since the rise of behaviourism in the 1920s, but it is, nevertheless, true.

The problem is, of course, that consciousness cannot be defined and some psychologists have taken the view that, if it cannot be defined, it cannot be investigated or even talked about in any meaningful way. Some have even gone so far as to hint that it might not exist or, if it does, it is of no importance. In order to sidestep the issue raised by the problem of defining consciousness, psychologists have taken to calling it 'attention', possibly in the hope that nobody will notice. As we shall see they have also taken a more sophisticated view of what constitutes a definition and modern experimental psychologists usually take care not to emphasize their subject's mental experiences when they report their experimental findings.

The stranglehold that an extreme form of behaviourism had on psychology was perfectly demonstrated in the area of attention. So great was its influence that nearly all references to attention or conscious experience disappeared from the experimental literature after the 1920s. Researchers saw very clearly the force of the argument that, as conscious experience is not available to public inspection, its nature cannot be reliably investigated simply by asking subjects to say what their own experience is. This is because equivalent experiences may be described differently or different experiences may be described as identical, without any means of checking the truth. Secondly, subjects might dissemble (a polite way of saying they might lie) or not be sure how to describe their experiences.

Some behaviourists went further; they argued that, as mental experience could not be investigated, it could not be proved to exist and that it was therefore of no significance to psychology. This view became important in the thinking and methods of those psychologists who sought to understand human psychology by studying the behaviour of rodents; the so called 'rat-psychologists', a rather unfortunate label perhaps.

It is, of course, a complete fallacy to suggest that because something cannot be proved to exist then it must be true that it does not exist – just because consciousness cannot be proved to exist does not mean that it does not! And, since it is the belief of each of us that, while a hot poker applied to our hand would not only burn our flesh and cause us to move our hand and utter a cry, but also result in our feeling a sensation which nobody else could perceive, we may as well assume that consciousness does exist and try to study it.

But, how should this be done?

Modern research into attention

The development of modern research into attention has been attributed by Neville Moray to three factors. First, 'operational' definitions of processes hitherto defined in terms of private experience were developed. This allowed for objectivity in research into attention. Secondly, the Second World War, catalyst of so much innovation, provided the conditions of urgency necessary to push forward experimentation into attentional phenomena. The rapid increase in the sophistication of communication systems provided human beings with situations in which they were presented with a great deal of information from multiple sources. This, of course, required answers to problems such as: how should the information be presented? How fast can a human operator switch his attention from one dial to another? Lastly, Moray highlighted the importance of the development of the tape-recorder, which has tremendously improved research into auditory attention.

The first important landmark in research into attention was the development by Colin Cherry of dichotic listening experiments in which the subjects had to 'shadow' or repeat aloud the verbal message that was presented to them through one ear while a different message was played to them through the other ear. The particular puzzle which originally inspired Colin Cherry and which he described as 'the cocktail party problem' was as follows. Imagine that you are at a noisy party surrounded by people enjoying their animated conversations: you are trying to listen to just one conversation and, by and large, you are succeeding. Now Cherry was interested in how we achieve this complex feat of perception. What factors affect our ability to select one conversation from the babble which surrounds us? This ability requires extremely complex analysing mechanisms, so complex in fact that no electronic device can, as yet, mimic our performance. The second question which Cherry posed for himself was, how much of the rejected conversations can we remember?

Let us look in some detail at what a dichotic listening test entails. Two different prose messages were recorded, both by the same speaker; one of the messages was presented to the subject's right ear and the other to the

left ear. The messages were presented via headphones
was to repeat one of the messages as he heard it; this '
shadowing. The point of requiring a subject to shado'
is to make sure that his attention is directed towar.
experimental equivalent of the cocktail party situation w.
listening to one conversation and ignoring others. Cherry was n
determine exactly how much of the unattended (non-shadowed) mess
the subjects could report. He found that they could always correctly
identify it as speech, but they could not identify any words or phrases or
even definitely identify the message as being English. A change of voice
from male to female could be detected and a 400 cps pure tone was always
reported. Reversed speech was thought to be normal by most subjects but
was thought to have 'something queer about it' by others. This all seems
quite straightforward really; the conclusion, of course, is that only the
physical properties of the unattended message are 'heard' by the listener
and the semantic content is completely lost.

The first theories

The filter theory

The earliest comprehensive theory of attention was proposed by Donald
Broadbent in 1958. The essential feature of Broadbent's theory was that
we are unable to analyse all the information which falls on our sensors. He
therefore proposed that somewhere in our brain is a mechanism or 'filter'
which limits the amount of information which has to be analysed to a very
high (semantic, in the case of spoken words) level. He therefore identifies
the higher levels of analysis as being where the bottleneck occurs (see
Figure 10.28).

Broadbent based this model on a great deal of research but a set of
experiments now referred to as the 'split span' experiments are regarded as
having been critical of Broadbent's thinking. In a typical split span
experiment subjects were presented with three pairs of digits, each pair
being presented simultaneously, one digit to each ear, at the rate of
one pair every half-second. After presentation, the subjects were
asked to recall the digits, which they did by recalling the three digits
presented to one ear followed by as many as they could recall from the
other ear.

From these results and those of Cherry, Broadbent concluded that,
when we select a message for high level analysis, we do so on the basis of
its physical properties (in the case of the split-span experiments the
information which is not selected is only retained for a very short period in
a short-term store, where it decays rapidly). If a message is allowed
through the filter, it enters the limited capacity channel where high level

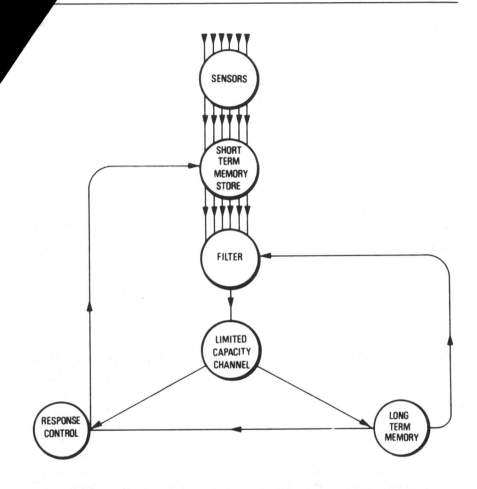

Figure 10.28 Broadbent's filter theory (after Broadbent, 1958)

analysis takes place with the aid of the long-term memory store. The results of this analysis may then produce a response.

In 1959, experimental evidence was published which conflicted with Broadbent's conclusions. In that year, Moray found that if the subject's own name was presented in the unattended message of a dichotic listening task, he would hear about one third of the presentations. These early results implied that Broadbent was wrong to suggest that filtering occurs before any analysis for meaning has taken place. Actually, this experiment by Moray parallels the anecdotal evidence of many people who claim to have heard their own name being mentioned in conversations to which they had not been paying attention. Very soon after this experiment by

Moray, Anne Treisman also found experimental evidence for high-level analysis of the unattended message.

Treisman's contribution

In a dichotic listening experiment carried out in 1960 Treisman asked subjects to shadow a message they heard through one ear while a different prose message was presented to the other (unattended) ear. Half-way through the task the messages were switched. At this moment the shadowers would repeat one or two words from what was now the 'wrong ear', before reverting to the correct ear. While this was happening the subjects were unaware of having temporarily switched ears. These results very strongly imply that the unattended message was analysed for meaning.

Treisman found, in an experiment carried out in 1964, that if a French translation of the attended message was presented as the unattended message in a dichotic listening task, then about 50 per cent of bilingual subjects realized that the two messages had the same meaning. Again, this argues very strongly for a high level of analysis of the unattended message.

On the basis of these, and many other, experiments, Treisman proposed her 'attenuation model'. This model is, in fact, similar to Broadbent's filter theory but Treisman's filter merely attenuates or weakens the signal strength of the rejected message. As applied to a dichotic listening task, both the attenuated rejected message and the attended message go deeper into the perceptual system for further analysis. Here, we find a major difference with Broadbent because Treisman is allowing for all inputs to be analysed at a high level. However, at this higher semantic level a second stage of selection takes place in which so called 'dictionary units' or word analysers are triggered if their signal strength is high enough. The triggering of a dictionary unit is perceived. Thus, as the thresholds of dictionary units are all different and variable, so biologically relevant and emotionally important words will fire their low-threshold dictionary units even when the signal strength of such a word has been attenuated

Thus Treisman's model allows a subject to hear his own name and a few other very special words even when they have been presented in the non-attended ear. The main problem with this model is that the first stage of filtering really appears to be redundant. If the thresholds in Stage II are variable, why not allow Occam's razor to cut off Stage I, and have the filter do its work after a high level of analysis of the input. Treisman admits that all inputs are analysed to a high level, so obviously, the bottleneck appears to be a function of consciousness not analysis.

Single filter, late selection

This brings us to the final theory of selective attention that we shall discuss. This theory was developed in 1963 by Anthony and Diana Deutsch. Its

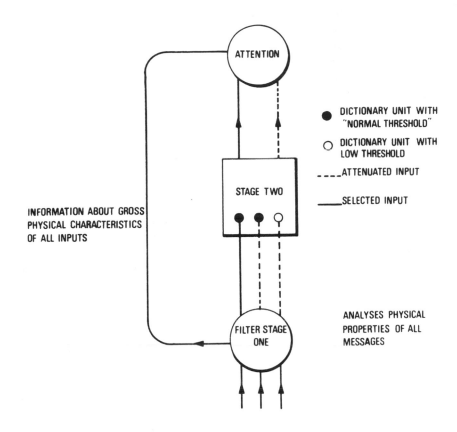

Figure 10.29 Treisman's attenuation model

main feature is that it allows for filtering or selection only after all inputs have been analysed to a high level, i.e. after each word (if the message is prose) has been recognized by the memory stem. From Figure 10.30, we can see that a message is analysed for its physical qualities and, on the basis of this, each word 'activates' its representation in the memory store. Simultaneously, the items most pertinent to the ongoing activity also excite their representations in the memory store. Those items which are excited by both mechanisms are allowed to pass into attention.

In summary, we may say that there are two major theories which have been offered in recent years as explanations of the phenomena so far discovered in the field of selective attention. Both theories allow a high level of analysis of the information processed by the sensors, although one theory (Treisman's) carries the implication that when two messages are physically different, i.e. presented dichotically or spoken in different

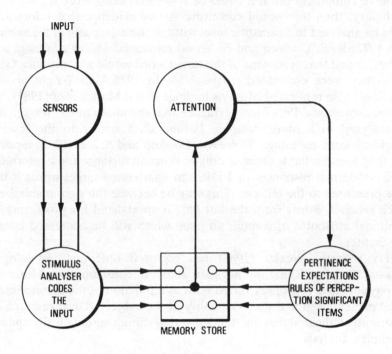

Figure 10.30 A single filter, late selection model

voices, then the unattended message will be attenuated, and it will not be analysed quite as efficiently as the attended message.

The fate of the unattended message

In 1969, Moray briefly mentioned in a publication that he had found that subjects would produce galvanic skin responses (minute increases in the electrical conductivity of their skin) to words which had been coupled with electric shock and then embedded in the unattended message of a dichotic listening task. The procedure he used was as follows: a subject was presented with a neutral word such as 'country' followed by an electric shock to his hand. After about fifteen trials Moray found that his subjects produced strong GSRs just to the presentation of the word country. He then presented 'country' to his twelve well-conditioned subjects, first in the unattended message and then in the attended message (AM). Three of his twelve subjects produced marked GSRs to the target word when it was presented in the unattended message (UM) even though they did not hear it. As Moray indicated, this experiment was carried out using very primitive equipment but if it could be replicated using more sophisticated machinery, then this would constitute strong evidence that information could be analysed to a semantic level without the awareness of the subject.

In 1972, R. S. Corteen and B. Wood replicated Moray's findings and, further, found that synonyms of the target word would also produce GSRs when they were embedded in the UM. In 1975 Von Wright and his colleagues also replicated Moray's findings as did Martin *et al* (1984), and in 1982 Govier and Pitts found evidence that the unattended message may be analysed in a more complex fashion than simply to the level of individual word meanings. However, Dawson and Schell (1982) reported that they found reliable changes only in skin conductance (now referred to as electrodermal responses or EDRs) to unattended target words if they were presented to the left ear. This may be because the right hemisphere, which receives words from the left ear, is specialized for processing the emotional attributes of stimuli, an issue which will be addressed later in this chapter.

Very recently Wexler (1988) has reported obtaining physiological responses to stimuli that did not gain access to consciousness. Moreover, the physiological responses varied both as a function of the hemisphere of initial presentation and the personality of the subject. Thus, research has persistently indicated that unattended verbal stimuli automatically undergo a complex analysis.

Divided attention studies

Since the mid 1960s, some researchers into attention have taken a somewhat different course. Instead of trying to unravel the processes involved when subjects are engaged in focused attention tasks, i.e. focusing attention on one source or category of stimuli, while ignoring others, as in a dichotic listening task, some psychologists have addressed the question of what happens when a subject is asked to engage in two tasks simultaneously.

We have all witnessed someone driving a car and talking; it seems to be very easy. But, if we analyse drivers' behaviour carefully, we find that they stop talking at points where they need greater 'concentration', e.g. at roundabouts. One interpretation of this is that the driver's information processing system cannot cope with the two tasks simultaneously, because both tasks are using the same parts of the system. This seems unlikely because driving and talking seem, on the face of it, to be very different tasks, but it may nevertheless be true.

As early as 1898, Welch showed that using the hand to grip something with as much force as possible would slow the subject's performance on a concurrent mental arithmetic task. It could be argued that if two such dissimilar tasks interfere with each other (in the sense that performance on one can only be improved at the expense of performance on the other) then *any* two tasks, however dissimilar, will interfere. But, as Michael Eysenck (1984) has pointed out, similarity between the tasks does matter. Using as his example an experiment performed by Segal and Fusella (1970) Eysenck argued that two tasks which have similar information processing characteristics will interfere more than two tasks which do not. In this experiment subjects were asked to use visual imagery while they were watching for visual signals on a screen. They were then asked to use auditory imagery while they watched for visual signals on a screen. The subjects made more errors in the former condition. But, when they were asked to listen for auditory signals while using auditory imagery, they made *more* errors than while using visual imagery.

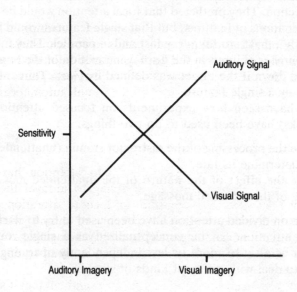

Figure 10.31

What, then, are we to make of all this? One interpretation is that because any two tasks interfere, they must be sharing some kind of general all-purpose processor which is involved in virtually all tasks. Moreover, because similar tasks interfere more than dissimilar ones, there must also be specific systems in our information processing architecture which are specialized to deal with different types of stimuli. Michael Eysenck (1984) has characterized these two kinds of processing thus:

1. The single multi-purpose processor has a very limited capacity, it is flexible and it operates in a serial fashion – that is to say, it deals with one stimulus at a time.
2. The specific processors seem to operate automatically and without any obvious capacity limitations, they are difficult to modify and operate in parallel.

The evidence that specific processors have the characteristics outlined above comes from an experiment performed by Treisman and Gelade (1980), in which subjects were required to search for a target item in a visual display, composed of between 1 and 30 items. The subjects either had to detect a stimulus on the basis of *one* of its characteristics, that is to say, they had to find an S or any blue letter, or they had to detect a stimulus on the basis of two of its characteristics, i.e. a green letter T. Treisman and Gelade called the former task 'feature' detection and the latter task 'object' detection. They predicted that focal attention would be required to detect combinations of features, but that single features would be analysed 'automatically', that is to say, very fast and in parallel. They indeed found that as the number of items in the display increased, the detection of target items slowed down if the target was defined by two features, but not if it was defined by a single feature.

Thus we have seen how experiments on focused attention (dichotic listening tasks) have been used to do two things:

– investigate the processing of the distractor stimuli (unattended message) to try to determine its fate.
– investigate the effect of the nature of the unattended message on the processing of the attended message.

Experiments on divided attention have been used to try to clarify the issue of whether attention can be conceptualized as a single multi-purpose processor or as a set of more or less independently operating processors specialized to deal with different kinds of stimuli.

Application of dichotic techniques

As we have seen, in the early 50s Donald Broadbent devised a dichotic task in which the subject was presented with three pairs of digits at 500 MS. intervals and was then required to recall as many words as possible. This has become known as the 'digit triad task' and has formed the basis of what is proving to be one of the most fertile methods of research in current psychology. In an important paper in 1967, Doreen Kimura presented a model of brain organization underlying audition in which the stimuli presented to each ear are transmitted first to the contralateral auditory cortices. That is to say, words presented to the left ear go first to the right hemisphere and words presented to the right ear go first to the left hemisphere. Kimura did admit the existence of auditory pathways between the left ear and left hemisphere and between the right ear and right hemisphere, but she pointed out that these 'ipsilateral pathways' were suppressed during simultaneous dichotic presentation. Furthermore, as the left hemisphere was thought to be specialized for verbal analysis, verbal stimuli presented to the left ear would be transmitted to the left hemisphere via the right hemisphere, with a consequent risk of some degradation in the process. The upshot of all this, according to Kimura, was that subjects ought to display a right ear edvantage (REA) when doing a dichotic digit triad task. This REA has been observed many times and is now known to be a very reliable phenomenon; moreover, a left ear advantage (LEA) has been obtained by many researchers when the stimulus material was non-verbal (either musical stimuli or emotionally toned stimuli). The interested reader may consult Sidtis (1981) for information on how to obtain large, reliable LEAs.

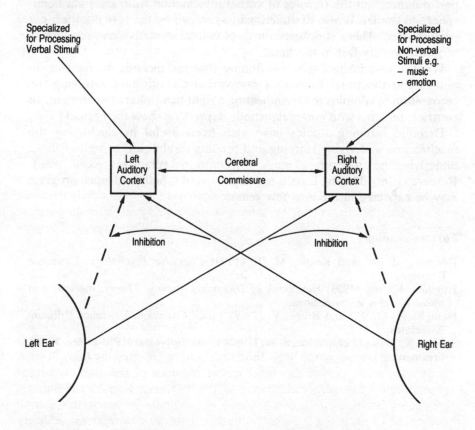

Figure 10.32 Kimura's model for dichotic listening performance

Perhaps the most exciting development in this area is the use of dichotic task of the kind described above to elucidate the brain dysfunctions underlying some psychoses and types of depression. There is now clear evidence that schizophrenics with paranoid delusions and/or auditory hallucinations show an unusually large REA in dichotic triad tasks involving words (Takahashi *et al*, 1987).

This, together with other research, indicates that paranoid/hallucinating schizophrenics may be suffering from a dysfunctional left hemisphere as well as dysfunctional transmission of information between the hemispheres (Nachshon, 1988).

The conclusion stems from the observation that the greater than normal REA shown by this sub-group of schizophrenics is due to the very poor left ear performance, not an improved right ear performance. In fact, the right ear performance is below that of normal control subjects. Thus, researchers have argued that, not only is the left hemisphere verbal processing sub-optimal, as shown by the poorer than normal right ear performance, but the transfer of verbal information from the right hemisphere to the left is also dysfunctional, as shown by the *very* poor left ear performance. These conclusions are, of course, tentative and research is progressing very fast in this area.

What is also intriguing is the finding that melancholic depressives do not exhibit the usual LEA in a non-verbal dichotic task involving the recognition of complex tones, indicating a right hemisphere impairment. In contrast, patients with non-melancholic depression show the normal LEA.

Dichotic listening studies have also been useful in elucidating the mechanisms underlying learning and reading disabilities, as well as those underlying the processing of music and emotional stimuli (Hugdahl, 1988). Research using dichotic tasks is moving forward rapidly and much progress may be expected in the next few years.

Further reading

Eysenck, M. W. and Keane, M. T. (1990) *Cognitive Psychology*. Lawrence Erlbaum.

Hugdahl, K., ed. (1988) *Handbook of Dichotic Listening: Theory, methods and research*. John Wiley & Sons.

Humphreys, G. W., and Bruce, V. (1989) *Visual Cognition*. Lawrence Erlbaum Associates.

Spoehr, K. T., and Lehmkuhle, S. W. (1982) *Visual Information Processing*. W. H. Freeman.

Chapter eleven

The development of perceptual processes

Heather Govier and Ernest Govier

One of the most long-standing controversies in the history of psychology has been concerned with the relative influences of innate factors and the environment on the development of perceptual processes. There have long been two opposing schools of thought: that of the empiricists; and that of the nativists.

The empirical position is that all knowledge comes through experience. This point of view was expressed in its most extreme form by John Locke (1632–1704), who held that the mind at birth is a *tabula rasa,* a complete blank, requiring experience to fill it with meaning and understanding. Thus, the newly born can derive no meaningful perception from the environment, such perception being built up as experiences multiply. A less extreme expression of the empirical view is attributable to Hermann Von Helmholtz (1821–94), who accepted that something was brought to perception by the physiological features of the organism. He held that it is by complex interaction between this physiological structure and the environment that the resulting perception is developed.

The nativists, on the other hand, believed that most fundamental perceptual processes are innate and independent of experience. Such a view was taken by many of the Gestalt psychologists and notably by Ewald Hering (1834–1918). For them, the infant comes into the world with a mind fully able to grasp all essential features of its perceptual field.

A third, and more recent, position finds some sort of middle ground between these two extreme philosophies and was expounded by Donald Hebb. He argued that studies of the structure of cell assemblies in the brain suggest an innate basis for visual perception (c.f. the nativists) but that these cell assemblies are built upon and influenced by the experiences of the organism, to form the perceptual processes of the adult (c.f. the empiricists).

Evidence on which to assess these divergent theories comes in modern psychology from a variety of different fields of study. Clearly, the examination of the physiological features of perceptual systems in both developing and adult organisms can shed some light on the issue. However, this aspect is fully discussed in Chapter 6 and will not be considered here. The study of visual illusions, too, is covered in Chapter 10. This chapter will be concerned with four basic sources of insight:

1. Studies of neonates both human and animal.
2. Studies of the adaptations made by subjects to distortions in their perceptual world.
3. Studies of the influence of various cognitive dispositions on perception.
4. Studies of the effects of cultural differences on perception.

Examination of these four types of research as set forward below represents a contemporary reassessment of the development of perceptual processes.

Studies of neonates

One way to assess the relative importance of nature and nurture in determining what we perceive is to compare the perceptual world of the adult with that of the newly born (or neonate). Any differences between the two must be due either to the influence of the environment or to maturational processes. Various controls enable us to disentangle these two influences, as we shall see below. Both human and animal neonates have been used in these studies, the most important of which have been carried out by five noted psychologists: Fantz, Gibson, Walk, Held, and Hein.

The work of Robert L. Fantz

Research by Robert L. Fantz and his colleagues has been concerned with the ability of the infant to perceive form, i.e. shape, pattern, size and solidity. The early work used newly hatched chicks as experimental subjects. Immediately after hatching, chicks begin to peck at small objects in their environment in order to find food. In these experiments the chicks were offered a variety of items to peck at and their pecking preferences were noted. All stimuli were encased in perspex to exclude the possibility of smell, touch, or taste influencing the choices. As the chicks were hatched in darkness and had no experience of real food, any discrimination must have been made exclusively on the basis of innate perceptual abilities.

The results of this experiment were quite conclusive. Chicks consistently preferred a sphere to a pyramid and a circle to a triangle, indicating an ability to perceive shape. That they could also perceive size was shown by selection of circles of $\frac{1}{8}$ inch diameter more frequently than circles of any other size, and, when tested for perception of three dimensionality, the chicks selected a sphere in preference to a flat disc. Clearly, the chick has innate ability to perceive the shape, size and solidity of possible food objects. Moreover, the preference for spheres of this particular size is highly adaptive, as this is approximately the size and shape of the food grains which constitute the chick's diet.

From studying chicks, Fantz turned to the study of human infants. But here he was presented with a major problem. Human babies are not self-sufficient organisms with the mobility and range of responses of chicks. They have, in fact, very little way of showing preferences between stimuli. Fantz, however, was able to use the only one available. He studied the eye movements of the young babies when presented with a choice of visual test objects. If the baby is seen to look consistently at one object more than another s/he must be able to perceive some difference between the two stimuli. This experiment is thus essentially similar to the one conducted with chicks and concerns itself with the question of whether the innate abilities seen in the chick persist higher up the evolutionary scale. Human infants are, clearly, less developed than newly hatched chickens with regard to motor abilities, so perhaps this is also true of their perceptual processes.

Fantz tested a group of human infants at weekly intervals from the age of one week until they were 15 weeks old. The stimuli used were four pairs of designs of varying complexity. One of these pairs consisted of two identical triangles, which were included to control for the possibility of differential response to some factor other than form. In the other three pairings, the infant was able to choose between the alternative figures shown in Figure 11.1.

Both in the case of the identical triangles and the cross and circle, the

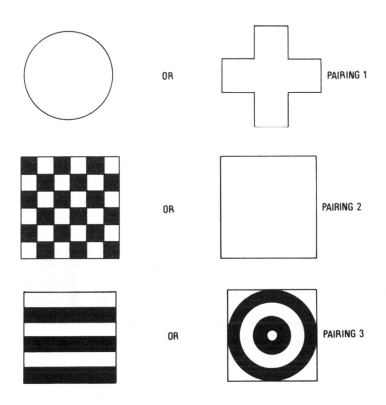

OR　　PAIRING 1

OR　　PAIRING 2

OR　　PAIRING 3

Figure 11.1

infants spent an equal amount of time looking at each figure in the pair. Moreover, with each of these pairs the infants quickly lost interest and either looked elsewhere or went to sleep. The more complex figures elicited far more interest, and, in both cases, the infants showed a preference by looking at one stimulus more than the other. Generally, the checkerboard was favoured in preference to the square, and the bull's-eye in preference to the stripes. Curiously, in younger babies (under two months) this preference lay in the other direction, i.e. the stripes were fixated more than the bull's-eye. The reason for this is unexplained. The important point, however, is that a preference is shown in the case of both complex pairs, indicating that the infant is able to discriminate between the two stimuli. This is true for all the ages tested. Human infants, then, are able to perceive form from the age of one week. Ethical considerations clearly exclude the possibility of keeping human infants in the dark, and it is thus conceivable that this level of perceptual skills is the result of influences occurring in the first week. However, similar findings have since been made for infants below the age of one week, strongly indicating that some degree of form perception is innate in humans.

In the case of the experiment with the chicks, it was suggested that their preferences were biologically adaptive in that they opted to peck at grain-like stimuli. An equivalent stimulus to the human infant is, perhaps, an adult face, as this will always accompany any attention to its needs. Accordingly, Fantz investigated infants' preferences among stimuli which approximated by varying degrees to an image of a human face.

In this experiment the stimuli were three flat objects the size and shape of an adult head. On one of these a stylized face was painted, on the second the same features were included but in a jumbled order, and on the third an area equal to that of the features was included at one end of the 'face'. All 'features' were black on a pink background.

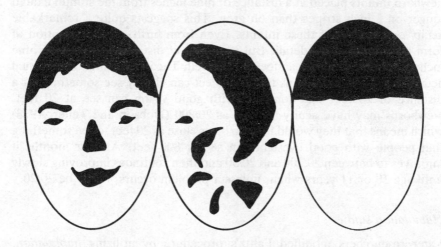

Figure 11.2

The three stimuli, paired in all possible combinations, were shown to the infants ranging from four days to six months old. In all cases the realistic face was preferred to the jumbled face and the third figure stimulated hardly any interest at all. In this study, although the degree of preference for the real over jumbled face was not large, it was consistent. However, in later studies Fantz failed to replicate this finding or found the effect only at certain ages. In fact, Fantz reported, in 1965, that this behaviour developed in infants sometime between four and 16 weeks, a finding later confirmed by Kagan, Henker, Hen-tov, Levine and Lewis (1966). A cautious conclusion from this line of research would be that there is an inborn predisposition to respond preferentially to more complex visual patterns and that, with the stimuli used in this experiment, the infant requires several weeks of visual experience before he prefers organized or 'meaningful' complex patterns to disorganized complex patterns.

Results using three-dimensional stimuli, however, were more clear cut. Infants over the age of two months consistently preferred to look at a three dimensional dummy of a head rather than at a white board of the same size and shape. Under the age of two months the flat object was preferred, perhaps because it was brighter than the solid model. These results suggest that, as the baby develops, changes occur either in the ability to perceive three-dimensionality or in the attention holding value of solidity.

In the next phase of his research, Fantz concerned himself with ascertaining the visual acuity of human infants. A similar procedure was used, but this time a plain grey stimulus was paired with a series of striped patterns which varied in the width of the stripes. Results here showed that newborn infants placed at a distance of nine inches from the stimuli fixated longer on ⅜ inch stripes than on grey. This suggests quite a remarkable acuity on the part of these infants. Even from birth, their perception of form has considerable detail. But it is only at distances of eight or nine inches that the newborn can focus quite well. The usual standard for visual acuity is 20/20 which means that a subject can clearly see something at a distance of 20 feet that someone with good vision can see at 20 feet. Newborns may have acuity as poor as 20/800 (Dobson and Teller, 1978) which means that they would have to be as close as 20 feet to see something that people with good eyesight can see at 800 feet. At four months it improves to between 20/200 and 20/50 and then continues improving slowly until age 10 or 11 years when, unless a problem occurs, it will be 20/20.

Habituation studies

Later researchers modified Fantz's procedure by utilizing *habituation*. They would present a baby with a single stimulus and watch the viewing behaviour. At first, the baby will look at the stimulus, but after a while it will cease to be of interest and s/he will not look at it. This *habituation* or boredom effect disappears if a new stimulus is presented, the baby will pay attention to it and look at it. Using this technique it has been possible to show that, even in the first days after birth, infants can discriminate, not only familiar from novel stimuli (Cohen and Salapatek, 1975), but also the difference between a square below a cross and a cross below a square (Antell and Caron, 1985). The technique has also been used to show that infants who are only 12 weeks old have normal colour vision (Bornstein *et al*, 1976).

Fantz's research was also the forerunner of the recent research into the 'looking behaviour' of infants which has shown that, in general terms, up to the age of eight weeks the infant's visual attention is directed at *where* objects are, i.e. s/he will locate an object and follow it with eye movements. Having found an object s/he scans edges and areas of contrast (Haith, 1980) so that up to six weeks infants even scan edges in faces (Haith *et al*, 1977). If the infant looks at features, it is the eyes or sometimes the mouth, if it is moving. Indeed, in the first few days after birth the newborn's perceptual apparatus and control of its mouth and tongue are so well co-ordinated that s/he can imitate mouth movements, like tongue protrusion and mouth opening (Meltzoff, 1985). At about eight weeks a baby's perceptual apparatus improves enough to enable it to move from simply finding objects to identifying them. At this point babies now look at facial features rather than edges and they can apparently recognize that 'small over big' has changed to 'big over small'. Using the habituation method, Caron and Caron (1981) have shown that babies between the ages of three and four months will respond to similar shapes arranged into new patterns, i.e. if the child habituates to a series of figures, such as to a small circle over a large circle and a small diamond over a large diamond, s/he will show renewed interest in a figure which reverses the pattern, i.e. a large triangle over a small triangle. Thus babies at this young age are already perceiving patterns of stimuli rather than just specific stimuli.

Finally, one can see how sophisticated a newborn's perceptual apparatus rapidly becomes, because at about 12 weeks babies can consistently discriminate the parent's face from other faces (Zucker, 1985) and by five or six months babies can usually perceive different emotional expressions, e.g. fear and happiness (Schwartz *et al*, 1985). This last ability is vitally important to enable the baby to learn how to behave in new situations. For example, given a new object in the environment, a baby of this age will check the mother's facial expression; if she shows fear, the baby will remain closer to her than if her face shows happiness (Zarbatany and Lamb, 1985).

The work of Eleanor J. Gibson and Richard Walk

Whereas Fantz studied the perception of *form* in developing animals, Gibson and Walk have investigated *depth* perception. Their work centres around a piece of apparatus which has become known as the 'visual cliff'. In the centre of this structure is a narrow plank on which the subject is placed. On either side of the plank there is a step down to a level floor area. To the right of the plank this step is very small, just a few inches, whereas to the left there is an apparent sharp drop of three or four feet. For the safety of the subject, a plate of glass covers this drop so that s/he cannot fall over. The experimental subject is able to choose between the two sides of the apparatus. A reluctance to move to the left (onto the glass over the cliff), as opposed to the right, would indicate that the subject is able to perceive the greater depth of the left hand cliff.

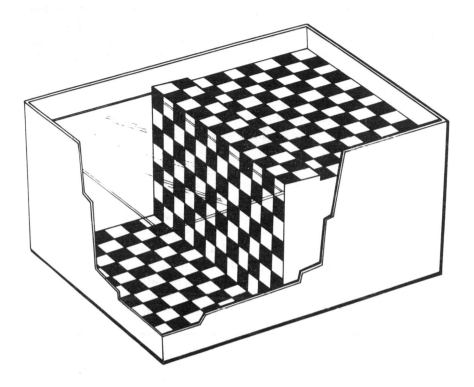

Figure 11.3

When human infants were used as experimental subjects they consistently refused to cross the glass on the deep side to reach their mothers but happily crawled across to them when they stood on the shallow side. This would seem to indicate that human infants are able to perceive depth and are aware of the dangers involved in a cliff. Of course, the children used in this experiment were all able to crawl and were therefore all at least six months old. This poses the question 'can younger children see depth?' This problem was tackled by Campos *et al* (1970) who used heart rate as an indication of depth perception on the visual cliff apparatus.

When children only 55 days old were placed on the shallow side their heart rate did not change, but when they were placed on the deep side there was a significant slowing down of the heart-rate. There is firm evidence that heart-rate deceleration is generally associated with curiosity rather than fear (Gibson and Spelke, 1983). Indeed, these babies actually cried less on the deep side than on the shallow side and showed behavioural signs of being 'interested' in what they could see.

It seems that 'fearful' responses to the deep side of the visual cliff appeared by nine months, at which age heart-rate acceleration was noted when babies were placed on the deep side (Schwartz *et al*, 1973; Richards and Rader, 1983). Bornstein (1984) has clearly shown that infants as young as eight weeks show avoidance responses to stimuli that are apparently

Visual acuity	Age	Perceptual ability
	Birth	
Poor visual acuity over 20 cms		Can perceive complex patterns (Fantz, 1961)
		Can discriminate objects from background but scans edges (Haith, 1980)
Dobson and Teller (1978) 20/800 vision		Will look at eyes or moving mouth (Haith *et al*, 1977; Meltzoff, 1985)
		Can discriminate new from familiar shapes (Salapatek, 1975)
		Can discriminate identical stimuli arranged in different ways (Antell and Caron, 1985)
		Begins to prefer to look at organized (meaningful?) patterns (Kagan *et al*, 1966)
	8 Weeks	
		Looks at features rather than edges of features in faces The relationship of stimuli in patterns becomes more salient (Caron and Caron, 1981) Can perceive depth (Schwartz *et al*, 1973; Bornstein, 1984)
	12 Weeks	
20/200 vision		Can 'recognize' parent's face (Zucker, 1985) Has normal colour vision (Bornstein *et al*, 1976)
	20–24 Weeks	
20/50 vision		Can perceive facial expressions associated with emotion (Schwartz *et al*, 1985)

Figure 11.4 Visual perception up to 24 weeks

looming towards their eyes, again indicating that depth perception operates at least as early as two months. In fact, infants as young as six days show evidence that they can perceive an object looming towards their eyes (Bower, Broughton and Moore, 1971).

However, the same apparatus has been used with a variety of animals and the results here are clearer and more easily interpreted. Chicks less than 24 hours old are able to perceive the visual cliff and never hop down on the deep side. The same is true of goat kids and lambs tested as soon as they can stand. Moreover, if placed on the glass over the 'deep' side these animals show marked fear despite repeated tactual experience of the solidity of the glass.

Rats, on the other hand, are less inclined to accept the evidence of their eyes over other senses. If they are able to feel the glass with their whiskers, rats will step down onto either side of the cliff but if the glass is lowered out of reach the cliff is avoided.

Kittens are not mobile until four weeks of age but, tested at this time, they are able to avoid the visual cliff. Similar findings were made for a variety of other animals, an exception being aquatic turtles which showed less avoidance of the deep side. Clearly visual depth is less biologically important to aquatic turtles and thus we are unable to say whether their depth discrimination is poorer than other animals or if they simply pay less attention to perceived visual depth, having no fear of a fall.

Gibson and Walk next investigated which of two visual cues was most important in determining depth perception. The two cues investigated were pattern density and motion parallax. In all the visual cliff experiments described so far the floor level was marked by a sheet of patterned material which was pasted directly under the glass on the shallow side and laid upon the floor some feet below the glass on the deep side. Thus the retinal images of the pattern elements and the spacings between them were smaller when viewing the deep side, giving greater pattern density than on the shallow side. This cue can be removed by using an enlarged pattern on the low side of the cliff such that the retinal image size of pattern elements on both sides is the same.

The second visual depth cue which could be used in assessing the visual cliff is motion parallax. When a subject moves its body or head, the apparent motion of the pattern elements is slower for the more distant elements than for the nearer ones. This is similar to the effect seen from a railway carriage, where nearby objects seem to flash by while distant ones move much more slowly. In the case of the visual cliff this can be removed by pasting patterns directly below the glass on both sides of the cliff with the 'deep' side pattern elements reduced in size to maintain pattern density differences.

In the first condition, with pattern density equalized, chicks and rats still prefer the 'shallow' side. Clearly, both species can discriminate depth using motion parallax alone. In the second condition, with motion parallax cues removed, day-old chicks showed no preference while rats preferred the side with the larger pattern, i.e. the 'nearer' surface. However, the rats used in this experiment were somewhat older than the chicks and it is possible that they had learned to respond to pattern density. This suggestion is supported by experiments with dark-reared rats which, like the chicks, stepped down equally on both sides when motion parallax cues were removed but not when they were present. It would appear, then, that in these animals motion parallax is the innate cue for depth perception while responses to pattern density are learned later.

Experiments involving dark-rearing

Before we can declare that an animal has innate ability, we must be certain that there are no opportunities for learning between birth and testing. In the experiment described above the rats appeared to show an innate response to pattern density. However, when rats which had been kept in the dark from birth were tested there was no such response.

Rearing animals from birth in darkness would seem to provide an answer to the problems encountered with those species in which infants at birth are very limited in their range of responses. Kittens, as has already been pointed out, are not mobile until four weeks old and therefore cannot be tested on the visual cliff or any similar task before this age. During these four weeks the normally-reared kitten receives much visual stimulation, giving opportunities for perceptual learning to occur. Thus, their avoidance of the 'deep' side of the visual cliff may be seen as a result of learning rather than innate factors. This suggestion is supported by the fact that dark-reared kittens will step or rather fall down equally on either side of the visual cliff apparatus. Apparently, in kittens, the ability to perceive depth is not innate as it is in rats and chicks.

By rearing animals in the dark, we remove all possible opportunities for visual learning. Thus, we should also be able to draw some conclusions about the relative influences of learning and maturation using this technique.

Fantz found that monkeys reared in the dark showed no improvement in performance on perceptually guided tasks with increasing age, unlike normally-reared monkeys. Deprived of opportunities for learning, the animals make no progress. This would seem to suggest that improvements with age in the normally-reared animals are due to learning rather than maturation. However, the dark-reared animals do not simply fail to improve, they, in fact, show distinct deterioration as they get older. Older animals take longer to learn perceptual skills after removal from the darkness than do younger ones. This poorer performance of the older animals was originally thought to indicate that there is a critical age for the development of visual perception. Deprived of stimulation during this period the animal later learns perceptual skills only after extensive experience and training. Again maturational influences seem to be compounded with learning.

There is, however, an alternative explanation for the poorer performance of the older, deprived animals which confounds the issue still further. Perhaps rearing animals in the dark actually leads to a physical deterioration in the perceptual system. Such an explanation is supported by evidence from a variety of sources. Chicks which have been reared in the dark from hatching to 10 weeks of age are unable to recognize and peck at grains, although normal chicks are able to do this immediately on hatching. Clearly, there has been loss of ability in the dark-reared group. Development of cataracts on the eyes of some of the groups suggests that physical deterioration of the eyes may be involved. Such deterioration has been clearly seen in the dark-reared monkeys and cats, where post mortem examinations of the eyes have found retinal damage. The damage occurs at many levels of the perceptual system; in chimpanzees, dark-rearing for between six months to $2\frac{1}{2}$ years results in the absence of retinal ganglion cells (Chow et al, 1957). In cats even periods of deprivation as short as $3\frac{1}{2}$ months result in deterioration of the retina and optic tract (Weiskrantz, 1958) and dark-rearing has also been found to result in biochemical abnormalities of the retina (Riesen, 1966).

Light deprivation may also have severe effects on more central levels of the perceptual system; it may significantly reduce the activities of cells in the lateral geniculate nucleus. Moreover, monocular deprivation also leads to abnormal development of the visual cortex; Hubel (1979) surgically closed either the right or left eye of two-week-old monkeys and showed that the development of the ocular dominance columns (groups of cells which respond to stimulation of either the right or left eye) was disrupted. The columns associated with the closed eye were reduced while those associated with the open eye were larger than normal. There was evidence of a critical period between three and six weeks after birth during which exposure to patterned stimulation seemed necessary for normal development.

Physical retinal damage is reduced if animals are reared, not in total darkness, but in diffuse light. In such experiments, the animals are fitted with diffusing goggles which allow a homogenous field of light to impinge upon the retina, but there is no patterned stimulation. Although physical damage to the retina is not found in animals so reared, their performance on perceptual tasks is still poorer than that of normally-reared controls. The ability to differentiate the brightness, size and colours of stimuli appeared to be intact, but they could not seem to perceive movement very well or distinguish between geometrical shapes. However, they did begin to learn visual skills when exposed to a normal visual environment although the speed at which they acquired competence seems to depend on both the species of animal and the period of visual restriction.

Some researchers, notably Colin Blakemore, have raised kittens in visually restricted environments in which the animals were exposed only to specific visual patterns. For example, the kitten might be raised in a chamber where all it can see are *either* vertical *or* horizontal stripes. Blakemore (1973) found that a kitten raised in the 'vertical' environment seemed to be blind to horizontal lines and vice versa for a kitten raised in a horizontal environment. Furthermore, these kittens had developed cells in the visual cortex which responded only to line stimulation appropriate to environments in which they were reared. Leventhal and Hirsch (1975) have further refined this sort of study and found that exposure to diagonal lines allows the development of cortical units which respond to both horizontal and vertical lines, but exposure only to horizontal and vertical lines prevents the appearance of units which respond to diagonals. This seems to indicate the horizontal and vertical detectors are basic units requiring less specific visual input for their development but that diagonal detectors require more specific stimulation in order that they may develop. As Movshon and Van Sluyters (1981) have pointed out, the main structural plan of the visual cortex seems to be innately drawn and the environment 'validates' the plan and actively contributes to the development of some parts of it.

Studies of humans

The few cases of humans who have had their sight given to them after being blind from birth have provided less insight into the process of perceptual learning than might be imagined. The largest body of evidence was provided by Von Senden (1932) who described 65 cases of people who had had surgery to remove cataracts. In general, they were, at first, unable to name or distinguish between simple objects or shapes but with long periods of experience of sight, some eventually developed useful vision; generally these were the more intelligent, active and better educated patients. However, some gave up the attempt to use their sight and reverted to a life of 'blindness'; this was often associated with severe depression. As we have seen from studies of visually deprived animals, the situation is a complex one and a great deal of detailed information must be collected before conclusions may be drawn. On the face of it, such a case was that described by Gregory and Wallace in 1963. They reported that 'S.B.', who had been blind since he was six months old, had his sight restored at the age of 52 with a corneal graft operation; within a few days he could walk about the hospital without having to use his sense of touch, he could read a clock accurately, and he would rise at dawn to watch the world go by outside his hospital window. He could name many of the animals in London Zoo correctly because he had stroked pet animals and had others described to him as he grew up. In fact, he seemed to be able to name most things by sight if he was familiar with them by touch, especially if he could discern a particularly characteristic feature. His perception of distance was accurate only if he already knew the size of objects by touch. He could immediately recognize upper case letters which he had learned by touch (indicating good cross-modal transfer of information), but it took him a long time to learn lower case letters even to the point of reading simple words.

In one episode S.B. was shown a lathe, a tool he had heard about and wanted to use. On simply looking at the lathe he could not identify any parts or 'understand' it at all, but when he was allowed to touch it he closed his eyes, ran his hands over it and then stood back, opened his eyes and said, 'Now that I've felt it, I can see it'. What this may mean is, of course, open to interpretation, but it is reminiscent of the experience of looking at an ambiguous figure, e.g. Figure 11.9, and not being able to 'see' the man or the rat without prompting.

Sadly, S.B. became severely depressed, possibly because of the realization of missed opportunities throughout his life and he began to sit in the darkness in the evenings rather than turn on the light! He gradually gave up an active life and died three years after his sight was restored.

It is very difficult to draw conclusions about the development of vision in normal subjects from such cases as S.B.'s. He had developed touch skills which may have interfered with the development of his visual sense. The emotional disturbances caused by suddenly being given sight may cloud attempts to understand exactly what such patients can see. For example, S.B. became terrified of crossing the road when he could see the traffic, whereas before he was confident. Moreover, the severe depression which is common in many cases, may be an important factor when attempting to determine the nature of the new visual sense.

Most importantly, nothing is known of the possible physical deterioration of the visual system in such patients while they were blind, a state of affairs which severely limits the value of these findings. The study of light-restricted animals has highlighted this factor.

Finally, as Richard Gregory has pointed out, 'adults with restored vision are not living fossils of infants'.

The work of Richard Held and Alan Hein

We have seen that dark-reared kittens seem effectively blind with regard to the visual cliff on first exposure. Held and Hein have further investigated the perceptual abilities of neonate kittens. Their hypothesis is that, in the case of those animals in which perceptual abilities are not innate, such as kittens, the acquisition of these skills depends not only on exposure to visual stimulation but also on motor activities. They argue that it is only by moving about in a visually rich environment that normal sensory–motor co-ordination can develop. Passive exposure to such an environment is not adequate to produce normal behaviour. They tested this hypothesis using a piece of apparatus which has become known as the kitten carousel (see Figure 11.5).

Two kittens are placed in the apparatus together. One kitten is housed in a basket, from which only the head protrudes. There is room inside the basket for limb movement but the kitten's legs cannot touch the floor of the apparatus. The second kitten is allowed to move about freely within the confines of a drum. It is attached to a harness connected to the basket containing the first kitten in such a way that its movements are transmitted and thus both kittens receive the same visual stimulation while inside the drum. The walls of the drum and centre post are covered with a repeated, striped pattern.

In the classic experiment, the pairs of kittens were reared in darkness until strong enough to be able to move the basket containing a kitten (eight to 12 weeks of age). They were then placed in the carousel, with the same kitten in the basket on each occasion, for three hours each day,

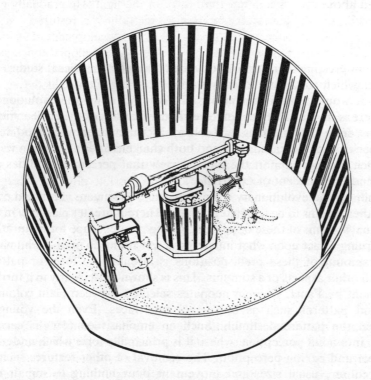

Figure 11.5 (From 'Plasticity in Sensory-Motor Systems' by Richard Held. Copyright © 1965 by Scientific American, Inc. All rights reserved.)

spending the rest of the time in darkness. After 30 hours in the apparatus the active kitten showed normal sensory motor co-ordination. It avoided the deep side of the visual cliff, blinked when an object approached its eyes, etc. The passive kitten, however, showed no such responses although it soon learned to do so after being allowed to run about in a lighted environment.

Kittens, then, must learn sensory–motor skills of this nature. They are not innate. Moreover, in order to require such skills it is necessary for the animals to move around under the power of their own muscles in a lit environment where they can see the results of their movements. However, we must draw a distinction between perception, on the one hand, and sensory–motor co-ordination, on the other. The experiments of Held and Hein do not prove that the passive kitten cannot perceive the increased depth on the one side of the visual cliff or the objects moved towards their eyes. It may simply be that the kitten has not learned the correct response for such situations. This is a confounding factor in the case of most of the experiments with developing animals. This experiment is also open to many of the difficulties of interpretation of dark-rearing procedures discussed above.

Conclusions

Several interesting conclusions can be drawn from these studies of neonates which contribute to nativist-empiricist argument.

First, it would appear that in organisms lower down the evolutionary scale there is innate ability to perceive salient features of the environment. Chickens, soon after hatching, are able to discriminate between food items and other environmental stimuli, and both chickens and rats avoid a visual cliff. Such findings support the nativist view that perceptual abilities are innate and independent of experience.

Further up the evolutionary scale, however, in humans, apes and even kittens there seems to be less that is innate. There is greater plasticity in the perceptual systems of these organisms, giving greater scope for maturation and learning to act upon what innate predispositions do exist. In humans, the paramount of these predispositions is attention to form or pattern above all other aspects of a stimulus. This is shown most clearly in a further experiment by Fantz, wherein neonates selected between plain coloured discs and patterns such as bull's-eyes and faces. Even the youngest preferred the patterned stimuli. Such an emphasis on form is carried through into adult perception, where it is principally form which underlies all object and person perception. The removal of other features such as depth, colour, usual size, and movement does nothing to impair our recognition, as the success of black-and-white photography proves. For humans, then, the position taken by Donald Hebb seems to be the most accurate. There is some innate bias for visual perception, but it is only by complex interaction between this and the maturation and environment of the individual, that the adult perceptual capabilities are developed. Such a system underlies the great adaptability of higher organisms.

Adaptation to perceptual distortion

Johann Kepler (1571–1630) was the first person to argue that the image of an object falling on the retina is inverted by the lens of the eye. His theoretical analysis was subsequently confirmed by Scheiner (1575–1650), who cut away the opaque outer layers at the back of the eyeball, making the image on the retina visible. From this time on, philosophers and natural historians speculated on how this inverted image comes to be perceived as upright. Perhaps Lotze (1852) made the most sensible contribution to this argument when he pointed out that the orientation of the image on the retina is irrelevant as every other geometical property of the image is distorted on the retina, which, after all, is a most peculiar shape on which to project an image. One of the implications of this view, especially in the light of empiristic arguments, is that, given the opportunity for perceptual–motor experience, the perceiver could perceptually and behaviourally adapt, even were the image to be artificially reinverted. Further, it would be intriguing to find out what would happen to subjects' perception if they were exposed to grossly transformed visual input for long periods. Would they adapt to their new visual world by altering their motor responses to it, or would they adapt by sorting out their new perceptual problem so that the world once again looked 'normal'? In any event, if they adapt at all to this new world this has implications for our understanding of the role of experience in the development of perception.

Stratton's experiments with inverting lenses

With the background outlined above, George Stratton (1896) devised an experiment which has become one of the most widely cited investigations in the history of psychology, which is rather odd because, as we shall see, his results are controversial even to this day. His apparatus was a tube containing a lens system which produced an inverted image which was then re-inverted by the lens of the eye to produce an upright image on the retina. This apparatus was worn over his right eye, the left being blindfolded. Stratton used himself as the subject because he found it difficult to persuade others to wear his apparatus for days or weeks.

The main part of his investigation lasted for eight days, during which he wore the lens system for a total of 87 hours. While he was not wearing the apparatus, both his eyes were blindfolded. During the time that he wore the apparatus, Stratton just went about his usual routine; he did not engage in any controlled perceptual motor tasks.

Stratton reported that, at first, he experienced a great deal of visuo-motor disruption, so much so, that at times he shut his eyes to avoid considering the visual data with which he was presented. As the first day wore on, he became better able to accept the scenes around him as they were presented. But he was still aware that the part of his environment not in his immediate vision was in a different orientation. By the fourth day, Stratton reported that he was starting to imagine the unseen parts of his environment as also being inverted and by the eighth day everything appeared harmonious by which he seems to mean that he had begun to feel himself to be upside-down and to feel normal in this state.

The feeling one sifts from Stratton's reports is that his visual sense of up and down was not affected by his experiences, even though he had learned to adapt his behaviour. This feeling is supported by Stratton's report of his experiences as the apparatus was removed. He immediately recognized the visual orientation as the pre-experimental one, but, even so, he found it surprisingly bewildering, though definitely not upside-down. This absence of an up-down after-effect is strong evidence that perceptual adaptation did not take place to the inversion effect of his apparatus. However, he did experience an after-effect which caused the scene before his eyes to swing and sweep as he moved his eyes thus indicating that location constancy had been disrupted by adaptation to a different set of rules.

More experiments with inverting lenses

In 1930 P. H. Ewert tried to repeat Stratton's experiment but, as is so often the case with an attempted replication, Ewert began by altering the apparatus; he used a binocular optical system. His subjects wore the inverting goggles for between 175 and 195 hours. Ewert's aim was to determine finally whether, during such an experiment, there was any perceptual adaptation, rather than just an improvement in the subject's ability to cope with his transformed vision. To this end, he devised two tests which he administered on each day of the experiment. In the first test, the subject was presented with coloured blocks placed in a line extending from his observation point. The subject was asked to name the colours of the nearest and farthest blocks. The results were quite clear; up and down and right and left judgements were always inverted with no evidence of up/down adaptation even after the 14th day of the experiment. Ewert also tested for motor adaptation and found considerable improvements, for example, in touch localization.

A further series of experiments by Frederick Snyder and Nicholas Pronko (1952) and J. Peterson and J. K. Peterson (1938) which focused mainly on the question of motor adaptation contributed to the findings that these newly learned visuo-motor adaptations are extremely resistant to forgetting, to the extent that, two years after their experiment, performance wearing inverting goggles was not significantly poorer than at the end of the 30 day experimental period.

The final set of experiments that we shall discuss in the context of inverting lenses were performed by Ivo Kohler (1964). For all three experiments Kohler used an optical device which utilized a mirror; its effect was to invert the image on its vertical axis without reversing left and right. He carried out three experiments, but we shall be concerned only with the third, which lasted for ten days. Kohler concluded on the basis of this third experiment that upright vision could be achieved if the subjects were encouraged to move about and touch objects in their environment. The familiarity of objects was also found to be important: the more familiar the object, the greater the probability that it would be seen upright. Kohler also reported that, on removal of the inverting apparatus, subjects sometimes saw objects as upside down, but this happened only for the first few minutes.

Thus, Ewert's findings appear to be contradicted by those of Kohler. Perhaps we may explain their differences in terms of the different experimental apparatus and procedures. Kohler's apparatus only inverted the image, it did not reverse left and right; Ewert's apparatus not only inverted the image but also reversed right and left, as well as producing depth inversion. Although Ewert's experiments lasted for up to 195 hours his subjects were not encouraged to practise a wide variety of perceptual motor tasks; in fact, most of their time was spent being assessed in the laboratory. This is in contrast with the experience of Kohler's subjects, who were encouraged to move around and pick up objects. Lastly, we must note that in the experiments discussed here a total of nine subjects were used – a very small number when we consider the problem of individual differences which must limit extrapolation.

The prism experiments

In 1928 experiments along the lines of Stratton's transformed stimulation studies were begun by James J. Gibson. This researcher used prisms set in goggles as well as other devices, but for the moment we shall confine ourselves to a discussion of the effects of wearing prisms. One of the effects produced by a prism is to distort vertical lines by making them appear curved. A prism with its base to the left will make a straight vertical line appear curved with its centre pulled to the left (Figure 11.6).

Furthermore, this curvature of lines is only part of a more comprehensive property of prisms by which variations in the angle, curvature, and distance of observed objects may be produced. This comes about because the angle at which a light ray is caused to deviate varies as the angle that it makes with the front face of the prism changes, such that rays entering at an oblique angle are made to deviate more than rays entering at right angles. Thus, if the eyes move behind the prism or the head and goggles move while the eyes remain fixed on an object, very complex 'variable' distortions will arise. Prisms also produce colour fringes which appear along the borders of light-coloured objects. This is because light rays of shorter wavelengths are bent more than long ones. Finally, prisms produce colour displacement effects, wherby adjacent areas of different colours are separated leaving a dark area between the colours.

Gibson's subjects were the first to discover adaptation to line curvature and colour fringes produced by prisms. The subjects adapted to these constant distortions in the relatively short duration of Gibson's experiment, but adaptation to the more complex variable distortions produced by prisms was not noted until Kohler reported such adaptations in his subjects. The so-called variable distortions take the form of concertina effects, such that, wearing prisms with bases pointing to the right, a subject who turns his head to the left but his eyes to the right sees an image which contracts horizontally. If he turns his head to the right and his eyes to the left the

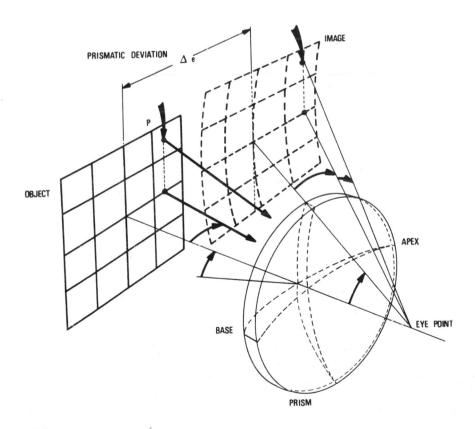

Figure 11.6

image expands horizontally. Kohler's subjects suffered severe after-effects when they removed their goggles at the end of the experimental periods, which resulted in contraction or expansion of the image depending on the position of the head and eyes. These after-effects disappeared after two or three days.

The colour stereo effect

Several devices apart from the prism arrangement described above were used in Kohler's series of experiments, but we shall discuss only one further type of prism device here. Kohler found that if his subjects wore goggles with the base of each prism pointing outwards (away from the nose) this produced a variety of distortions; the most interesting from our point of view is known as the colour stereo effect. The two prisms refract colours at different angles according to their wavelengths, but in opposite

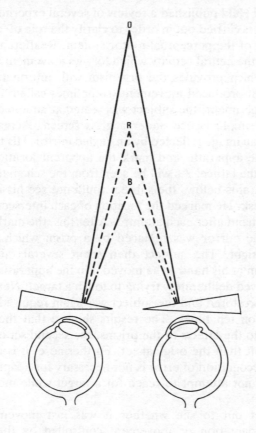

Figure 11.7

directions. As the bases face outward the blue end of the spectrum is bent outward more than other colours. This means that the eyes must converge more to focus blue images than red images, making blue appear closer than red, with other colours appearing to lie between them.

One of Kohler's subjects, wearing these goggles, described an incident in which he saw a woman wearing a red blouse walking along a street. She appeared to have no upper body with the red blouse following a few feet behind her moving its empty sleeves in time with the movements of the arms!

Now, the most important finding about the colour stereo effect is that even after wearing the prisms for 52 days Kohler's subjects did not report the slightest adaptation to this distortion. So far, this finding remains without any completely satisfactory explanation.

The role of active movement in adaptation

In 1965, Richard Held published a review of several experiments which he and his co-workers carried out in order to clarify the role of 'reafference' in the organization of the perceptual-motor system. Reafference is the term used to describe the neural activity which follows movement initiated by an organism and which provides the organism with information about the results of this self-produced movement (sometimes called 'feedback').

In the first experiment, the subject was seated at an apparatus in which he could see a simple lattice under a glass screen. Actually, what the subject saw was an image reflected by an angled mirror. His task was to put his hand into the apparatus and mark the apparent location of the four intersections of the lattice. As will be seen from the schematic representation of the apparatus below, the subject could not see his hand while he carried out his task. He marked the location of each intersection ten times, withdrawing his hand after each attempt. After this, the marking sheet was removed and the mirror was replaced by a prism which displayed the images to the right. The subject then spent several minutes looking through the prism at his hand as he moved it in the apparatus. None of the movement involved deliberately trying to touch a target. Next, the original conditions were restored and the subject was again required to mark each lattice intersection ten times. The results showed that the subjects had begun to adapt to the effects of the prisms, the second set of marks being further to the left than the original set. Furthermore, it is apparent from this study that recognition of error is not necessary for adaptation to occur (the subject did not attempt to reach for a target while moving his hand under the prism).

Held then set out to see whether it was just movement that was necessary for adaptation or movement controlled by the subject. He repeated the procedure outlined above, except that, during the time the

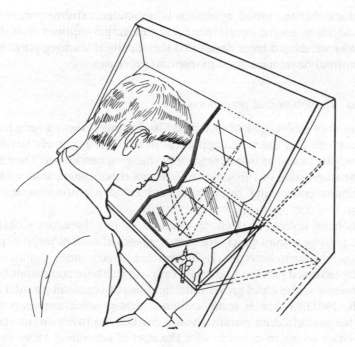

Figure 11.8

subject was looking through the prism, he had his arm strapped to a board which was pivoted at the elbow. Subjects looked through the prism under three conditions:

1. No movement of the arm.
2. Passive movement: he kept his arm limp and it was moved from side to side by the experimenter.
3. Active movement, in which he moved his arm from side to side himself.

The results showed that approximately half an hour of active movement, i.e. Condition 3, was all that was required to produce complete compensation for the displacement caused by the prism, whereas passive movement, Condition 2, produced no adaptation. Thus, Held concluded that as the same visual feedback was available to the subjects in the active and passive condition the differences in adaptation must have been due to the element of self-initiation of movement in Condition 3. For a comparison with Held's work using animals see the kitten carousel experiment in the first part of this chapter. Held went on to argue that it is important that movement is self-produced because an organism will be able to gain information about the movement of objects relative to its own anatomy only if it has information about its commands to its own muscles.

The studies of adaptation to distorted visual input reviewed here lead us to conclude that the visual apparatus is, in adults, extremely flexible and able to adjust to severe interference and changing conditions. It is difficult to see why we should have developed this facility if learning plays no part in the normal development of perceptual processes.

Stimulus orientation and perception

The studies of adaptation of distorted visual input reviewed here have led us to conclude that the visual apparatus of adults is extremely flexible and able to adjust to severe interference and changing conditions. Therefore, it might be interesting at this point to contrast these conclusions with some observations concerning orientation and the recognition of stimuli in children.

It has been noticed that young children (about three years old) often confuse pairs of stimuli which are mirror images of each other, e.g. p and q or b and d. Such 'lateral' confusions are much more common than vertically reversed pairs, e.g. p and b or q and d. These confusions become less common as the child grows older and usually cease at about 11 years (Serpell, 1971). There is some evidence that practice improves performance because children usually show a marked improvement at about six years, which seems to coincide with the start of schooling. More evidence that practice is important comes from a study by Clark and Whitehurst (1974) who showed that even children of three and four could learn to discriminate the left–right reversed letters with training.

Children who experience severe problems in learning to read, but who do not have any other more general cognitive dysfunction, for example, low IQ, mental retardation or an obviously uncorrected visual disturbance which might explain their reading disability, are often referred to as having a condition called dyslexia. A common characteristic of children with dyslexia is an inability to distinguish left–right reversed letters (Sidman and Kirk, 1974). Indeed, Casey (1986) has shown that five-year-old children who have especial difficulty discriminating between mirror image shapes, often experience difficulties learning to read as they get older.

The fact that children sometimes seem unable to distinguish between stimuli which are presented in different orientations may be associated with an interesting phenomenon to do with the recognition of the human face. If six-year-old children are presented with photographs of familiar faces, they are better able to identify them when they are presented upside down than adults can (Carey and Diamond, 1977). This seems at odds with the conclusions of the adaptation studies in that, in this context, the perceptual system seems to become less flexible in adults whereas the adaptation studies indicated that adult perception remained flexible. Perhaps the contradiction is more apparent than real. Adaptation studies involve prolonged training; subjects are not simply tested with strange stimuli. One might speculate that adults have learned to deal with faces in one particular orientation, but they would be quite capable of learning to deal with them upside down. Young children have not yet undergone the training process which will limit their performance with stimuli presented in unexpected orientations.

Personal factors affecting perception

Here, we shall consider the proposition that our perception is dependent, not only upon the structure of the environment and objects in it, but also upon certain dispositions and processes within the perceiver.

Organizing processes in perception

Expectation and perception

It is quite easy to demonstrate the effect of expectation on perception. An early experiment performed by Bruner and Minturn (1955) showed that if subjects were expecting to see a number and were presented with very brief flashes of 13 and then asked to draw *exactly* what they had seen, they drew the number 13, but if they were expecting a letter they drew a B. Bruner and Minturn concluded that when there was ambiguity in the stimulus array, resolution was brought about on the basis of the context in which the stimulus was set.

Bugelski and Alampay (1961) have shown that a similar expectation effect can be induced without verbal instructions. They presented half their

Figure 11.9 From 'The Role of Frequency in Developing Perceptual Sets' by B.R. Bugelski and D.A. Alampay, published in the *Canadian Journal of Psychology*, 15

subjects with a series of pictures of animals, after which they presented all their subjects with an ambiguous 'rat-man' figure (Figure 11.9) for identification. The pre-trained subjects generally saw a rat, while subjects who had not been given pre-training, usually saw a man.

An experiment which appears to illustrate the same sort of process was performed by Leeper (1935). He found that if he presented a subject with a figure which portrayed a young woman (B), followed by an ambiguous figure (A), then the subject reported that (A) was a picture of a young woman. The parallel effect was produced by prior presentation of (C) in which case (A) was seen as an old woman.

But, this powerful predisposing effect is probably not simply due to expectation, because if you present a subject with a sequence of C–B–C–B–C–B–C–B, he expects C (the old woman), but if you now present A, he usually reports seeing B (the young woman). So it seems that expectation is not always the dominant organizing factor in the perception of ambiguous (ill-defined) stimuli.

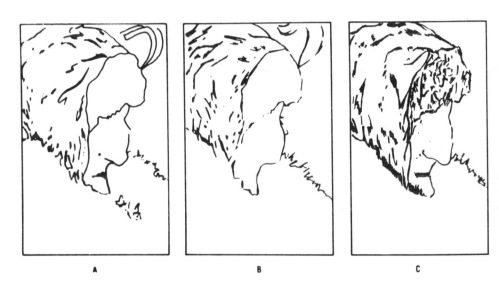

A B C

Figure 11.10

Prototype formation

A set of experiments on the perception of ill-defined stimuli have provided some insight into how the perceptual system can extract information from stimuli, in a surprisingly sophisticated way, which then influences the perception of subsequent stimuli. Posner and Keele (1968) used three random nine-dot 'prototypes'.

Four distortions of each prototype were prepared by moving each dot a certain distance from its position in the prototype according to a rule which meant that the average position of each dot in the distortion was the same as the prototype.

The subjects were then trained to categorize each of the 16 distortions into the four piles appropriate to the prototypes. Each category was given a name. When subjects had mastered this task they were required to sort another set of cards into the four categories; this set of cards contained a mixture of 'old' and 'new' distortions and the prototypes themselves. The 'old' distortions produced a 20 per cent error rate and the 'new' distortions produced a 50 per cent error rate; chance alone would have produced a 75 per cent error rate. Prototypes produced a 32 per cent error rate, indicating that the subjects had learned about them without having studied them directly. In a later study Posner (1969) found that if he asked subjects which of a selection of dot patterns they had been presented with in phase I of the experiment and which were 'new', they were more likely to classify the prototype as previously seen rather than new. But, this effect was not observed for previously unseen (new) distortions. This implies that the prototypes have a qualitatively different psychological significance compared with ordinary distortions.

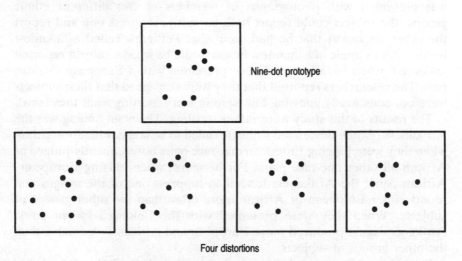

Nine-dot prototype

Four distortions

Figure 11.11 Illustrative example (adapted from Posner and Keele, 1968)

This sort of experiment, and there have been many variations since Posner's original work, demonstrates how powerful the brain is as a *classifier* of information, in this case visual information. This ability to classify, to see similarities between stimuli, is, of course, one of the most important factors underlying our ability to make sense of the world. But, when it is not tempered by more subtle, higher order cognitive processes, it may often result in a tendency to stereotype and indulge our hostile attitudes to those people or things which fall into categories of which we do not approve.

Perceptual categorization and attitudes

The interaction between our attitudes and our powerful tendency to categorize was investigated by Thomas Pettigrew, Gordon Allport, and Eric Barnett (1958). They, rather ingeniously, used binocular resolution to investigate how members of the five main ethnic groups in South Africa perceived one another. These researchers used 122 subjects drawn from Afrikaner, English, Coloured, Indian and African populations of Durban. Each subject was presented with pairs of head and shoulder photographs of members of four ethnic groups, African, Coloured, Indian, and European in all combinations plus intra-group pairs. These pairs of photographs were presented stereoscopically for an exposure duration of about two seconds. Immediately after exposure, each subject was required to name the race he thought he had seen. The responses fell into several different categories. When both eyes were presented with photographs of members of the same race, the subject could be either right or wrong in his judgement. When he was presented with photographs of members of two different ethnic groups, the subject could report both correctly, suppress one and report the other, or report that he had seen what Pettigrew called a 'manifest fusion'. An example of a manifest fusion would be when a subject reported 'coloured' when in fact he had been presented with a European–African pair. The researchers reported that they were convinced that their subjects were not consciously guessing but were in fact reporting what they 'saw'.

The results of this study were rather startling. The main finding was the Afrikaners (Dutch-descended whites) tended to be comparatively accurate when they were judging European one-race pairs but frequently judged as African all other one-race pairs. Furthermore, when judging European–African pairs, the Afrikaners tended to suppress one of the images and report either European or African more often than the other groups of subjects. When they were presented with the Coloured–Indian pairs, Afrikaners again produced more European and African judgements than the other groups of subjects.

Pettigrew, Allport, and Barnett interpreted these findings as being consistent with previous research which has shown that judgements made by highly emotionally-involved subjects tend to be extreme, i.e. that people with strong beliefs tend to see issues in 'black and white' (in this case both literally and metaphorically). The argument here seems to be that questions of race are of paramount importance in the life of Afrikaners and this tends to polarize their judgements in racial issues, and, furthermore, this mechanism can influence perception.

Some points to bear in mind, however, are that this study uses highly artificial stimulus arrays, briefly presented, and that, even if the subject reports his perceptions rather than his guesses, this does not mean that his real-life perceptions are in any way similar. Secondly, this study has now been replicated but we are left with the central issue. Do Afrikaners really 'see' exactly what the other races see but differ from them in their willingness to attach labels to these perceptions, or are they actually less likely to 'see' a fusion? At the moment we cannot be certain.

Personality and perception

Individuals differ from one another in many obvious ways. We all know people who are sociable, energetic and happy, others are loners, yet others are characterized by their meticulousness or their generosity. It would be of great interest to know whether people whose personalities differ so markedly also perceive the world differently. Witkin and Berry (1975) argued that virtually all of our mental life is affected by underlying processes which give our mentation coherence and direction. This mental coherence, Witkin called 'cognitive style', and our cognitive style determines how we deal with the world in a psychological sense.

Witkin identified two types of cognitive style using the 'rod and frame test'. In this test the subject sits in a darkened room and can only see a vertical rod inside a frame. The frame is rotated and the subject has to adjust the rod so that it is vertical. Obviously, the subjects may be influenced in their judgements by the position of the frame as well as relying on their own sense of balance and other bodily cues affecting their sense of the vertical. Those subjects who perform the task accurately are known as field-independent and those who are influenced by the frame are called field-dependent. Field-independent people are said to be less socially conforming, more inner-directed, more analytic and active in their interactions. Field-dependent people are said to be conforming, eager to make a good impression, sensitive to their social surroundings and less self-reliant. Interestingly, the same sorts of categorizations can be made of people's performance on the embedded figures test (see Figure 11.12); subjects who have difficulty finding the target figure would be field-dependent, while those who find the target figure easily would be field-independent.

These researchers have sorted people into two categories on the basis of a perceptual test and then looked for personality factors which might be associated with (and possibly causally related to) the perceptual typology. Another method is to start with personality categories and look for differences in perception. The most frequently researched personality factors are extraversion and introversion (see Chapter 20 for a description of these personality dimensions). The most common finding is that introverts are far better at tasks requiring sustained attention. After approximately 30 minutes of sitting watching for a blip on a screen or listening for a click through headphones, extraverts begin to perform very poorly, compared with introverts. Research carried out by Stelmack *et al*, (1977) using electrical recording techniques has shown that the primary sensory cortex of introverts is more sensitive to auditory stimuli than that of extraverts. Using more straightforward techniques the same general principle (that introverts are more perceptually sensitive) has been confirmed for vision (Siddle *et al*, 1969) and touch (Coles *et al*, 1971).

Using the idea of cognitive style one might predict that the person most likely accidentally to knock into you and upset his cup of tea all over you in a crowded room would be a field-independent extravert!

Motivation and perception

The idea that our perception may be coloured by our likes and dislikes, our emotional state and personal values, is widely held to be true by the general public. In this section we shall review some evidence that this is, to some extent, true.

Value effects on perception

Perceptual overestimation (accentuation) of the size of objects due to their value has been noted in many experiments. The results of the overwhelming majority of these studies confirm the following general conclusion: we tend to perceive valued objects as larger than they really are but only if the value of the objects has been associated with their size, e.g. increasing coin size is related to increasing value of those coins (with some exceptions, this is true for the coins of many countries of the Western world).

A typical early experiment was designed by Jerome Bruner and Goodman and reported in 1947. In this experiment 30 ten-year-old children were used as subjects, ten poor children, ten rich children and ten children drawn at random from the population of Boston (a control group). Each child sat in front of a screen, on which was a spot of light. A knob under the screen controlled the size of the spot. All the subjects had to estimate (by manipulating the size of the spot of light) the size of penny, nickel, dime, quarter, and a half dollar in that order and then in reverse order.

Control subjects had to judge the size of grey cardboard discs which were the same size as the coins used. The results of these trials were expressed as percentage deviations of the size of the spot of light from the true size of the coins being judged.

The main finding of this experiment was that all children significantly overestimated the size of the coins by an amount which increased with the value of the coin, not its true size. Thus, even though a dime (10 cents) is smaller than a penny (1 cent) its percentage overestimation was greater. The one exception to this was the half dollar which Bruner and Goodman suggest may have been too valuable then for a ten-year-old child to be able to form any real feeling of its worth. These findings, then, seem to substantiate the hypothesis that attitudes may have an organizing effect on perception.

Those studies which have produced findings which are apparently contradictory to those of Bruner and Goodman have one thing in common: the 'value' of the stimuli used has nothing to do with their size. For example, concentration camp survivors do not reliably overestimate the size of discs bearing a swastika. Clearly, whether a swastika is large or small or on an object that is large or small is of no relevance to its importance. Thus, size is not associated with the importance of swastikas in any special way.

Perceptual defence and sensitization

Much of the interest among psychologists investigating the effects of motivation on perception has been focused on the phenomena known as perceptual defence and perceptual sensitization. Leo Postman, Jerome Bruner, and Elliot McGinnies utilized the concepts of perceptual defence and sensitization in 1948 when they put forward the hypothesis that personal value systems were determinants of perception. This led to a series of experiments which indicated that subjects had lowered visual recognition thresholds for words which had highly valued or pleasant associations and higher thresholds for words which had unpleasant or taboo associations. In their main experiment Postman, Bruner and McGinnies used 25 subjects, all of whom had completed Allport-Vernon personal value questionnaires. Each subject was then shown 36 words, one at a time, in a tachistoscope. The words represented the six scales of the personal value profiles (theoretical, economic, aesthetic, social, political, and religious); thus the theoretical value scale words were: *theory, analysis, logical, science, research,* and *verify* while the social value scale words were: *sociable, kindly, loving, devoted, helpful,* and *friendly.* Now, if a subject has a low social and high theoretical value profile, his thresholds for words like *logical* and *analysis* should be lowered because of 'perceptual sensitization' and raised for *sociable* and *loving* because of 'perceptual defence'. The results of the experiment seemed to confirm the existence of the mechanisms of sensitization and defence, and, further, early experiments, notably by Elliot McGinnies, concentrated on replicating the perceptual defence effect. Again this was done by tachistoscopic presentation of words, but, this time, half of the words were chosen as emotionally neutral, e.g. apple, broom, glass and the other half as emotionally arousing taboo words, e.g. whore, penis, belly (our sense of what is a taboo word has obviously changed since 1949!). The subjects' recognition thresholds were determined by exposing the words at 0.01 seconds then at 0.02 seconds, etc. until it was correctly reported. McGinnies found that his subjects displayed significantly higher recognition thresholds for the emotionally-toned words than they did for the neutral words. This, of course, was interpreted by him as clear evidence for perceptual defence; however, there are alternative interpretations.

Howes and Solomon (1950) made two main points:

1. The difference in threshold between neutral and emotional words is due to the greater familiarity with the written form of neutral words because they occur with much higher frequency in generally available literature than 'taboo' words.
2. It is not that subjects fail to recognize the emotional words as quickly as neutral words; it is merely that they feel loath to report their perceptions until they are absolutely sure about what they have seen.

This perceptual defence versus response bias controversy has continued more or less to the present day, with perhaps the best attempt to settle it being an elegantly designed experiment by Worthington (1969), in which he utilized brightness scaling at the threshold of awareness. Worthington used 160 subjects, who were required to judge which of two faint spots of light presented successively on a screen was brighter. In fact they were objectively identical. Embedded in each spot of light was a very faint subliminal word. Nine different words were used which had previously been rated for emotionality by an independent group of judges. Worthington found that when one of the spots of light had a word rated high on emotionality embedded in it, it was rated as dimmer than a spot of light with an emotionally neutral word embedded in it even though the subjects were completely unaware of the verbal stimuli.

This experiment very neatly provides us with firm evidence that the perceptual defence effect is not due to a reluctance on the part of the subject either to say out loud or even admit that he is aware of any taboo words. In fact, in the Worthington experiment, the subjects had no idea that any words were being presented to them at all. If this experiment is successfully replicated we will probably be justified in regarding the perceptual defence effect as a manifestation of a sensory regulation mechanism. However, we must now introduce a note of caution in our interpretation of the 'perceptual defence' effect. It seems most odd that we should have evolved a mechanism which would allow our unconscious minds to censor emotionally arousing stimuli, especially as this effect seems to occur only with stimuli which are very faint either because they have been presented very fast or at a very low intensity. Indeed, one would have imagined that the selection pressures on our evolutionary ancestors would have been in the direction of making us as sharply aware as possible of faint but threatening stimuli. As perceptual defence seems to be a fact of life, how are we to deal with the evolutionary arguments outlined above?

A possible explanation might rest on the evolution of consciousness itself. This new development would require the parallel development of a mechanism which would control the input into consciousness, which is a limited capacity system. Once a mechanism which controls entry into consciousness is arrived at, it becomes easy to see that the organization of the system which may produce the most efficient selection under most conditions, may, under the special conditions of a perceptual defence experiment, result in what appears to be an anomaly. In any event, there would seem to be absolutely no necessity to imagine that the 'perceptual defence' effect results from an attempt by our unconscious psyche to protect us from rude words. The reader who wishes to pursue this highly controversial topic further can do no better than read the excellent treatment by Norman Dixon in his book *Preconscious Processing*.

Sex differences in perception

So far this chapter has concentrated on visual perception but some interesting differences have been noted between the perceptual abilities of male and females in the areas of taste and olfaction (smell). It seems to be the case that females have a more sensitive olfactory sense than males (Money, 1965) and that this difference is produced by the action of the hormone, oestrogen. Evidence for this emerges from the fact that the acuity of a woman's sense of smell varies during her menstrual cycle, becoming most acute in the middle of the cycle when oestrogen levels are highest. In fact, doses of oestrogen can be shown to improve the sense of smell in women whose levels are too low.

Females also perform better than males on tests of auditory acuity, especially at higher frequences (McGuinness, 1972) and they also seem to be more sensitive to painful stimuli than men; again this is an effect which seems to vary in the menstrual cycle (Tedford *et al*, 1977).

If we look at visual perception we find that about 5 per cent of males in white populations of northern European extraction suffer from a type of partial colour blindness called green weakness or deuteranomaly. The condition is caused by a gene on the X chromosome and leads to a ratio of 20:1 affected males to females. Affected individuals see the colour red as reddish brown, bright green seems to be tan and olive greens are indistinguishable from brown. Another partial colour blindness condition called red weakness or protanomaly affects about 1 per cent of males and, again, it is caused by a gene on the X chromosome. The vision of females seems to be poorest just before and during menstruation; administration of the hormone progesterone may return vision to normal in females whose vision is disrupted most severely. Females do, however, appear to dark-adapt in poor light conditions quicker than males (McGuinness, 1976). Thus, in many respects, females seem to be more sensitive to their environment, a conclusion which supports the finding that they are more field-dependent than males. Thus, it is not surprising that males appear to be better able to distinguish a target shape from its surrounding context. This can be demonstrated using what is usually called an 'embedded figures test', an example of which is shown in Figure 11.12 below.

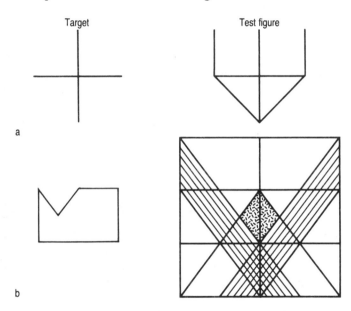

Figure 11.12 Embedded figures test

The subject's task is simply to identify the 'target' in the complex figure and typically males do this faster than females. It has also been reported that males who are insensitive to androgen have reduced spatial ability, while females with unusually high androgen levels have increased spatial competence (Peterson, 1976). Finally, Yen (1975) has pointed to evidence which suggests that spatial ability may be influenced by a sex-linked gene; certainly it has been reported that females with Turner's Syndrome (a disorder in which one of the two X chromosomes is missing) may have a problem with some kinds of spatial perception (Mange and Mange, 1980).

Cultural influences on perception

Visual illusions

The principal thrust of work in this area has been concerned with visual illusions and constancies. This work originated with W. H. R. Rivers who worked with the natives of the Torres Straits as long ago as 1901. He concluded on the basis of his findings that the reactions of his subjects to the visual illusions with which he presented them were largely determined by their own particular environment. A later, and much more extensive, investigation was carried out by Marshall Segall, Donald T. Campbell, and M. J. Herskovits who published their results in 1963. This study took six years to complete during which 1,878 subjects were studied from locations in Africa, the Philippines, South Africa and America. These researchers found that non-European subjects were less susceptible to the Muller–Lyer illusions but that some groups of non-Europeans were susceptible to the two horizontal-vertical illusions in the study. (For information on these illusions see Chapter 10.)

Segall, Campbell, and Herskovits hypothesized that the greater susceptibility of the Europeans to the Muller–Lyer illusions was due to the relatively widespread occurrence of rectangularity in their environment which results in a bias to interpret angles drawn on a two-dimensional surface as representative of rectangular, three-dimensional objects. The relatively less 'carpentered', non-European environment would not encourage the development of such a perceptual bias; hence the Muller–Lyer illusion tends to 'fail' with individuals developing in these conditions.

Now, this explanation must be treated with caution for the following reasons. First, the mechanisms underlying the perception of geometrical, visual illusions are still under debate. Thus it is by no means certain that the experience of rectangularity is especially important. Secondly there may be other cognitive or biological differences between the Europeans and the non-Europeans which account for the experimental findings. Certainly, there is some evidence that biological characteristics, such as the pigmentation of ocular structures, for example the iris, may affect the perception of visual illusions. Thus, blue-eyed subjects are more susceptible to the Muller–Lyer illusion whereas brown-eyed individuals are less susceptible. This, of course, could easily confound research into cultural differences in perception if brown-eyed peoples are compared with populations with large proportions of blue-eyed members (Coren and Porac, 1978).

However, biological differences apart, there is growing evidence that it is familiarity with the artistic and graphical conventions used in the test materials that are the most important factors in perceptual differences between cultures. Evidence for this stems from a study by A. C. Mundy-Castle and G. K. Nelson (1962) who studied an illiterate community of white forest workers in South Africa. In spite of the 'rectangularity' of their environment they were unable to give appropriate three-dimensional responses to two-dimensional symbols on a standard test. Neither were their responses to the Muller–Lyer illusion significantly different from a sample of non-Europeans; but they were significantly different from those of ordinary white adults.

Similarly, the finding of Segal *et al* that some groups of non-Europeans were more susceptible to the horizontal–vertical illusion cannot be attributed simply to the openness of the terrain on which these groups lived because Jahoda (1966), working with Ghanaian subjects, found no support for the hypothesis that groups living in open country would be more susceptible to the horizontal–vertical illusion than groups living in dense tropical forest. Moreover, Gregor and McPherson (1965) found no significant differences between two groups of Australian aborigines on the Muller–Lyer and horizontal–vertical illusions, in spite of the fact that one group lived in relatively urbanized life in a 'carpentered' environment while the other group lived primitively in the open.

So we have evidence that there do appear to be differences between ethnic groups in how they respond to some illusions. However, we also have some evidence that these differences do not seem to be caused by the different physical environments of the groups (Jahoda, 1966; Gregor and McPherson, 1965), but that perhaps familiarity with the test materials, drawings and pictorial representation in general, may be an important factor (Mundy-Castle and Nelson, 1962).

The perception of line drawings

Further evidence highlighting the importance of this last factor comes from an intriguing study reported in 1966 by A. C. Munday-Castle. He set out to investigate how Ghanaian children responded to depth cues in pictorial material. He used 122 children aged between five and ten years, who were shown the pictures in Figure 11.13 and asked a series of questions about them.

From the children's answers it became clear that they frequently misinterpreted details in the pictures, but their mistakes were not haphazard. They frequently correctly recognized the class to which the object belonged but seemed to guess which member of that class was represented, using their own experience as a guie, e.g. the deer was called a goat, sheep, cow, dog, ass, horse, or camel. More interestingly, it was clear that, with the more abstract representations, the children did not even get the class right, their mistakes being often the result of failing to respond to cues of three-dimensionality; e.g. in Card 3, the road was often mistaken for an object such as a mill or tree which the children said would prevent the man and the deer seeing each other. Similarly, the horizon line was almost always described as a ruler, stick or piece of string.

The second problem highlighted by this study was that of cultural effects on responses, by which we mean the rather striking finding that about 35 per cent of the children answered the questions in a peculiar, imaginative way. For example, one child said (Card 1) that the man could not see the 'goat' because his attention was focused on the lion (elephant), which he

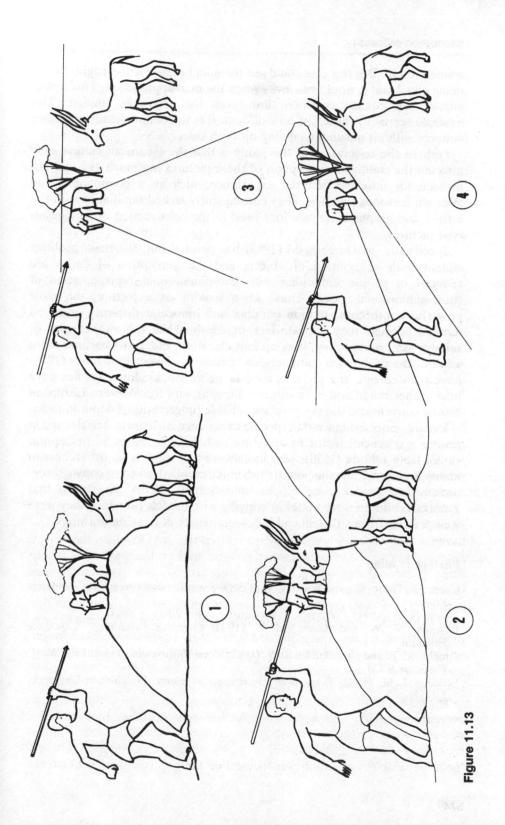

Figure 11.13

wanted to kill. But the goat could see the man because it was frightened of being killed and it would run away when the man approached. This sort of answer was equally common throughout the age-range studied. This example serves to show just how difficult it is to communicate with other cultures without misunderstanding on both sides.

Perhaps the conclusion of this study is that the Ghanaian culture only affected the children's perception of these pictures inasmuch as it did not provide for informal pictorial experience, such as is commonplace in Western European homes. They consequently lacked familiarity with the artistic and graphical conventions used in the construction of European-type pictures.

Specifically, as Deregowski (1980) has pointed out, the main problem is that both recognition of objects and the perception of depth are reduced in people unfamiliar with two-dimensional representation of three-dimensional space. Thus, when looking at a picture, the most powerful depth cues, motion parallax and binocular disparity, must be ignored because they indicate lack of depth, while the weaker cues of relative size, perspective, overlap and elevation, etc. must become more salient. The problem is compounded because, as Hagen and Jones (1978) have pointed out, the pictures used in many cross-cultural studies have been rather crude and even subjects familiar with the Western European artistic conventions did not produce reliable judgements of depth in them.

Finally, more evidence that specific experience with the materials used in testing is a crucial factor in assessing cultural differences in perception comes from Jahoda (1979), who has shown that there is no differences in ability between Ghanaian and British children when asked to copy a three-dimensional model using blocks, and Serpell (1979) has shown that Zambian children were better at copying wire models (at which they were well practised), but British children were better at copying drawings.

Further reading

Coren, S., Porac, C., and Ward, L. M. (1989) *Sensation and Perception*. Academic Press.

Dixon, N. F. (1981) *Preconscious Processing*. John Wiley & Sons.

Eysenck, M. W. and Keane, M. T. (1990) *Cognitive Psychology*. Lawrence Erlbaum.

Spochr, K. T. and Lehmkuhle, S. W. (1982) *Visual Information Processing*. W. H. Freeman & Co.

Wilding, J. M. (1982) *Perception: From sense to object*. Hutchinson University Library.

Chapter twelve

Memory

Brian Clifford

Introduction

Memory is one of man's essential survival systems; without a memory we would not exist for more than a few hours. In everyday life many different types of demands are placed upon us. Broadly speaking, we use our memories in the short term when we receive a telephone number from the operator, or when we try to remember directions which have just been given to us. We also use our memories in the short term when we try to remember how much the cashier demanded, how much we gave her, and whether the change we received was correct. These two senses of short-term memory (as a passive storage system and as a working or processing 'space') differ somewhat, but in both cases short-term storage is regarded as an essential requirement for efficient transaction with our environment. We use long-term memory when we are sitting our A levels, when we try to understand what the teacher is really saying, or again when we dial, almost unconsciously, our familiar home telephone number. Now, these two memory systems are obviously not unrelated because that which is now classifiable as an old memory was, at one time, new input and, as such, employed short-term storage. But, while not unconnected, many psychologists feel that they can be separated, and ought to be so, in order to understand better the total system we call memory. It is this question – to separate or not – that has troubled psychology acutely since the 1960s but more generally from the beginning of the science of behaviour.

The distinction between STS and LTS

William James (1890) was one of the first psychologists to make the distinction between primary memory as one type of memory that endures for a very brief period of time, and secondary memory, 'the knowledge of a former state of mind after it has already once dropped from consciousness'. Meumann (1913) made the same type of distinction. Now, while these historically very old views were based on introspective evidence, more recently the same distinction between short-term store (STS) and long-term store (LTS) has been suggested by laboratory studies and by investigation of patients in a clinical setting. More specifically, the evidence for such a separation comes from physiological studies, from amnesic patients, and from a number of experimental manipulations based on testing retention over different periods of time.

Physiological studies

The physiological basis of an STS–LTS dichotomy has been most strongly argued by Donald Hebb (1949). Hebb distinguished between reverberating activity (the active trace) and structural change (the structural trace). These two traces were equated with short-term and long-term storage respectively. He speculated that incoming stimulation sets up reverberatory activity in the receptor and effector cells which are involved in the sensation. With repeated stimulation and reverberation, a structural change occurs, possibly of a neuro-anatomical or neuro-chemical nature. During the early part of this process, interference or disruption can be caused by further incoming information. That is, the active trace is very fragile; the structural trace is not. This theory has an important affinity with consolidation theory ('give me a minute to let it sink in'), which suggests that perseveration (continuation in time) of neural activity is necessary for the consolidation of the trace. Interference is more likely the shorter the length of time perseveration has gone on.

There is some experimental support for the Hebbian theory. Duncan (1949) applied electric shock to the brains of rats at various times after they had learned a maze and observed its effect on retention of this new learning. If perseveration is necessary for learning, but is interfered with, deficits in retention ought to be observed. This is what Duncan found: the shorter the delay between learning and shocking, the poorer the retention of the learned behaviour. If the administration of shock was sufficiently delayed, no impairment of learning occurred.

Clinical evidence

Studies of amnesic patients give strong support for the belief that memory has at least two components. Patients suffering from Wernicke-Korsakoff's syndrome, an alcohol-related illness, exhibit gross long-term storage defects but little impairment of short-term storage. For example, they cannot remember what day, month, or year it is but they can repeat back perfectly a series of digits or letters which they have just been given. This normal STS capacity but impaired LTS has also been well documented in amnesic patients other than alcoholics (e.g. Baddeley, 1982).

The converse has also been shown. Patients exhibiting neurological deficits have been examined (e.g. Shallice and Warrington, 1970; Basso *et al*, 1982) who have intact, good LTS in the sense of memory for everyday events but grossly impaired ability immediately to repeat back even two digits.

Thus, the evidence of good memories for long past experiences but poor memories for what has just gone, together with the converse, is strong evidence for the belief that we must distinguish between at least two types of memory.

Laboratory evidence

The third line of evidence for the distinction between STS and LTS comes from the psychology laboratory proper, and especially free recall studies. In free recall, the subjects are presented with a list of items which they then must try to recall – but in any order they choose. When this technique is employed, one of the most reproducible effects in psychology occurs (at least after the first one or two trials); it is known as the serial position curve (SPC) effect. The SPC is characterized by good recall of the first few items presented by the experimenter (the primacy effect) and good recall of the last few items presented (the recency effect). The middle items are usually poorly recalled.

The relevance of the SPC is that the two end peaks of the curve (primacy and recency) are held to represent output from LTS and STS respectively. Now, if it could be shown that one peak could be altered while the other remained intact, this would be very good evidence for a distinction between two separate and separable memory systems. This can be achieved. It has been found that the nature of the words presented for

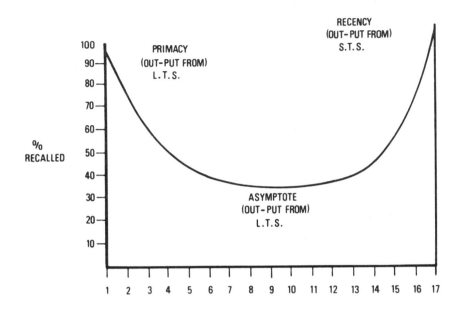

Figure 12.1 Hypothetical serial position curve (SPC) showing primacy and recency peaks and their source

recall does not affect recency but does affect primacy. For example, word frequency has no effect on recency, but common words (high frequency of usage) are better retained in LTS than are low frequency words. The imagibility of words, i.e. the ease with which we can form 'pictures' of the thing referred to, has been found to have little effect on recency but large effects on primacy. Again, lists containing either acoustically similar words (e.g. fail, sail, hail) or semantically similar words (e.g. huge, great, large) have little effect on recency but a large effect on primacy. The repeated presentation of a word in a list has no effect on recency but does affect primacy. In contrast to all the above, delaying recall after presentation of a list has no effect on primacy but does massively depress recency.

These above findings are taken to be powerful experimental evidence for an STS–LTS dichotomy. From everyday life, from physiology, from amnesic patients, and from the experimental psychologist's laboratory much the same story emerges: it seems necessary to distinguish between two distinct memory systems – STS and LTS. The next question to ask is in what ways do they differ.

The characteristics of STS and LTS

The characteristics of the two main memory stores have been shown to differ along a number of dimensions. These dimensions are:

1. Entry of information: how the to-be-remembered items get into the different memory systems.
2. Maintenance of information: how a person can go about storing or consolidating material to retain it best.
3. Format of information: the form of the material held in memory.
4. Capacity: the amount that can be held in the various systems.
5. Information loss: the causes of forgetting.
6. Trace duration: how long we remember information for.
7. Retrieval: how we recall information when we need it.

These different characteristics are shown in Table 12.1.

Table 12.1 Characteristics of the short-term store (STS) and the long-term store (LTS)

Features of memory	Levels of memory	
	STS	LTS
1. Entry of information	Requires attention	Rehearsal Semantic processing
2. Coding (i.e. the transferring of a stimulus into a format that can be retained by the cognitive system)	Phonemic Articulatory Visual Possibly semantic	Semantic Phonemic Visual
3. Storage format	Phonemic Articulatory Visual Images	Lexicons Grammars Knowledge of the world Propositions
4. Capacity	Small (2.5–7 items)	No known limit
5. Maintenance of memories	Continued attention Rehearsal	Repetition Organization
6. Memory duration	Up to 30 seconds (if not rehearsed)	Minutes to years
7. Forgetting	Displacement Possibly decay Possibly interference	Loss of accessibility Possibly interference Possibly repression Possibly systematic distortion of the memory trace
8. Retrieval	Automatic	Search and decision process Possibly direct access

Qualifications

Now while, in broad terms, these different characteristics of STS and LTS hold true, it is the case that some contradictory evidence exists. The accumulation of such conflicting findings underlies the attack on the dichotomous view of memory, i.e. that memory comprises two major parts: short-term and long-term memories.

Entry of information

While it is generally true that attention is required to enter items into STS, it is not always the case. From the selective attention literature, a study by Donald McKay in 1973 is interesting. He showed that, if one group of subjects was presented with an ambiguous sentence in one ear, to which they were to attend (the attended channel), such as 'the boys were throwing stones at the bank', and into the other ear, which they were not required to attend to (the unattended channel) they were presented with the word 'river', their recall of the attended message differed from that of a group given the same ambiguous message on the attended ear, but the word 'savings' on the unattended channel. That is, the subjects given the word 'river' on the unattended ear behaved as if they had been presented with a sentence to recall about throwing stones into a river. The subjects who had received the word 'savings', however, behaved as if they had been presented with a sentence about throwing stones at a building. Remember, both groups had been given exactly the same message to attend to and thus recall. Of equal importance was the fact that both groups were unaware of the unattended channel word as shown by the fact that they could not recall the unattended-ear word. Thus, although no attention had been allocated to these words, nonetheless they had entered STS and had served to disambiguate a potentially ambiguous sentence. Additionally, in order to create these different interpretations of exactly the same sentence, these two words must have been processed at a semantic level; that is, the *meaning* of the words must have been appreciated by the subjects, not just the *sounds* of the words.

Format of information

Another area where evidence is not as clear cut as Table 12.1 would suggest is in the format of information. One of the thorniest problems in current memory research is the form of storage of information in STS. Is it acoustic (the sound of the word), articulatory (the speech pattern of the word), visual (the visual pattern of the word) or semantic (the meaning of the word)? The earliest studies suggesting that STS was acoustic were by Richard Conrad in 1962 and 1964, who presented a series of letters which subjects had to remember for later recall. Where errors occurred in recall, they were similar to the correct letter's sound, e.g. 't' was wrongly recalled as 'b' 'p' or 'd'. This acoustic confusion suggested that items are coded or processed on an acoustic basis. From this initial experiment many researchers then went on to argue that the coding of items in STS was acoustic. However, at most all that could legitimately be deduced was that acoustic coding was one possibility. Because letters were used, it would seem reasonable to argue that semantic (meaning) coding would not (a) be very easy or (b) be very beneficial, and therefore would not be used. If one were to use semantic material, and semantic coding was known to be beneficial, or necessary, then the story may be rather different. This was shown to be the case by Harvey Shulman who, in 1970, demonstrated that semantic coding did occur in STS, if it was possible, due to the material, and if it was beneficial or necessary, due to the task demands.

Shulman visually presented lists of ten words and then tested for recognition memory by means of a visually presented probe word which could either be a homonym of a presented word (ball-bawl, pray-prey, board-bored), a synonym of a presented word (talk-speak, leap-jump, angry-mad) or identical to a presented word (board-board, speak-speak, pray-pray). The subjects had to say whether the probe word had been present in the list of ten words. The error rates were very similar for both the homonym and the synonym probes, thus strongly suggesting that semantic coding was going on in STS because to make an error on 'talk' and 'speak' requires that the similarity of meaning of the two words has been rendered available. That is, the two words were being matched at a semantic level. Thus experimental evidence now strongly suggests that semantic coding occurs in STS, while logic, and everyday observation of communication, would also support this contention.

Capacity

The last qualification to Table 12.1 which we will discuss here (but there are others) is that of capacity. It would generally be conceded that STS capacity is small. But the real question is how small is small? The number of items which a person can repeat back word and order perfect is said to represent his/her memory span. This memory span is, in turn, held to reflect the limited capacity of the STS. Typically, a person can only repeat back five to nine items, depending on whether the items are digits, letters, or words. However, if input words are in the form of a connected sentence then, at least for oldish children and young adults, the memory span expands to twenty words. George Miller has pointed out that it is not the number of items as such that defines the limitation but the number of 'chunks' or meaningful units. A digit, letter, word, or sentence can be seen as one chunk, but the number of items within a chunk can and does differ. This is an extremely interesting aspect of memory which we will pick up again under organization.

While most psychologists working in the area of memory have accepted the possibility of a dichotomy, qualifications like those above have led some to argue that a unitary memory system may be a better way of conceptualizing the known facts (e.g. Craik and Lockhart, 1972). However, before we look at this view we will retain the distinction between STS and LTS for its heuristic usefulness in a discussion of how we forget.

Theories of forgetting

Psychologists have been much exercised in elucidating the process of memory failure. All memories do not fade at the same rate, or in the same way, but we do seem to forget over both long and short periods of time. Why should this be? There are a number of possible explanations or theories, such as the passive decay theory, systematic distortion of the memory trace, interference theory, displacement theory, motivated forgetting and retrieval failure. Over and above these psychological accounts of memory failure, physical trauma, drug abuse, and senility, where actual brain cells or systems are destroyed, are other causes of memory loss. However, only the psychological accounts will be discussed here.

Passive decay theory

This theory suggests that memories fade over time, unless maintained by rehearsal or repetition. Now, while time itself cannot be an explanation it is argued that, as time goes on, so metabolic processes occur which degrade the memory trace which was set up during the initial learning and remembering. Weathering in physical geography would be an appropriate analogy for this theory.

Systematic distortion of the memory trace

The early proponents of this theory of memory failure argued that memories were not so much lost as distorted. They also held that errors of distortion increased over time. Wulf (1922) found that when subjects were asked to reproduce a line drawing which they had been presented with some time earlier, their drawing showed certain characteristic distortions compared with the original. If the presented shape looked like some familiar object the recalled shapes looked even more like the familiar object. Secondly, it was found that the reproduced figures became more symmetrical, and, thirdly, any irregularity in the original stimulus became accentuated in the reproduced figure. It was also found that the longer the time between seeing and reproducing the figure, the greater was the distortion. After the initial flush of success for the Gestalt psychologists, who could explain this in terms of 'goodness', problems began to appear in 1945. Hebb and Foord demonstrated that distortions were no greater after long delays, provided you tested different subjects at the different time intervals, and not the same subjects repeatedly. There is now a fair amount of evidence that large distortions are due to repeated reproductions by the same subject. Over and above the time factor, it has also become clear that systematic distortion occurs, not only during storage, but also at input and at retrieval.

These distortions testify to the active striving of humans for coherence; and this coherence stems from the person's pre-existing schemas – packets of information stored in memory representing general knowledge about objects, situations, events or actions. Note, while strictly speaking the plural of the Greek word 'schema' is 'schemata', conventionally the anglicized version 'schemas' is used, as it is here. We will be discussing schemas more fully when we look at Bartlett's work a little later (p. 403).

Motivated forgetting

A complete account of remembering and forgetting cannot ignore what the person is trying to do – both when he remembers and when he forgets. Repression, a Freudian term (see Chapter 16), suggests that some memories become inaccessible because of the way they relate to our personal feelings. Memories can be 'forgotten' because they are unacceptably associated with guilt and anxiety. Clinical evidence testifies to the reality of motivated forgetting. The amnesic syndrome, often brought about because of physical trauma or pathology, can also be produced by great emotional shock. In these cases forgetting is highly selective and focused. The memories forgotten are those referring to self – name, family, home address, personal biography. However, it is somewhat doubtful whether motivated forgetting ever occurs in normal, everyday life, or whether it has ever really been shown in the laboratory. Paul Kline (1972) argues persuasively for its reality in the laboratory, and reviews evidence which shows that if you inform some subjects that they have failed a test which they have just taken, then their recall of these test items is much poorer than subjects given no such feedback. The line of reasoning is that if you provide 'failure' feedback the subject becomes anxious and hence represses the emotional stimuli and this leads to poor recall. The problem, as Michael Eysenck (1975) indicates, is that exactly the same failure to recall occurs if you give 'success' feedback! Thus, an arousal hypothesis may be a better explanation of everyday forgetting of this type than Freudian repression.

Interference theory of forgetting

This account of forgetting does not use times as an explanation, but rather stresses that it is what we do between initial memorization and eventual recalling that is crucial. Within this interference account of memory failure there is interference caused by prior learning on later learning (pro-active interference, or PI) and the interference caused by later learning on earlier learning (retro-active interference, or RI). A very basic concept in interference theory is similarity: the more that two things (people, words, situations) resemble each other the greater the potential for interference. Thus, basically put, interference theory explains forgetting by the fact that we constantly learn or do new things which have a greater or lesser degree of similarity to things we have learned or done, or will learn to do, and, thus, we are likely to confuse this old and new learning. From this emerges a real problem for interference theory: do we ever actually forget anything, or do we merely 'hide' it by new or old memories? That is, does new learning cause unlearning of old knowledge, or does it merely compete with it? Although most old, and still a few new, introductory texts on memory devote a large number of pages to interference theories of forgetting it is now being realized that the theory is very paradigm-specific, by which I mean that it seems to hold only for very circumscribed laboratory situations. Thus interference theory, once regarded as 'one of the most successful and established theories in psychology' (Kintsch, 1970), is on the wane. Leo Postman himself, the great exponent of the theory, has said that the concepts of PI and RI have 'failed to generate a model of the forgetting process which can be shown to have general validity'.

Retrieval failure

The basis for this theory of forgetting is the belief that memories are seldom lost, they merely become inaccessible. There is a popular belief that nothing is ever forgotten – we just fail to retrieve the memory when required because of insufficient cues or reminders. Now while hypnosis has been cited as a technique for supporting this belief it is generally agreed that this strong assertion is untestable. If we cannot recall something is this because we have not yet been given the 'best' cue, or does it mean that despite being given most or all cues possible, the memory cannot be recalled, thus we have forgotten it? However, academic psychology makes the distinction between accessibility and availability (Tulving and Pearlstone, 1966). That is, just because we cannot recall a desired piece of information does not mean that we do not know it. Quite often, in fact, we know that we know it. This is the famous 'tip of the tongue' phenomenon. Accessibility to stored information is governed by retrieval cues, or retrieval routes. These retrieval cues can either be encoded along with the to-be-recalled material or they can be provided later as prods or pointers which govern where we will search in memory. Endel Tulving and Donald Thomson have developed this theory most thoroughly; from a cue-dependent forgetting theory, to an encoding specificity principle. While the encoding specificity principle lacks falsifiability, and is, therefore, of little value, the 'hypothesis' form is useful and informative. Tulving has produced a great deal of evidence for this hypothesis, but perhaps the clearest evidence for it comes from a fairly old study by Abernethy (1940) who presented material to be learned to two groups of subjects. One group both learned and recalled in the same room while the other group learned and recalled in different rooms. The recall of the former group was much higher, suggesting that the closer we can reinstate the environment of learning at the time of recall, the better will be that recall. Note how your memories of a holiday come flooding back if you once return there.

Displacement

The last theory of forgetting we will consider is that of displacement. If memories are finite storage banks (see above) then it would seem somewhat obvious that there is a possibility that if you enter yet another piece of information you will 'push out' a previously stored memory. While this theory has been applied to long-term storage the evidence is purely anecdotal: the absent-minded professor, or the professor who refused to learn his students' names because for every name learned he lost the Latin name of a flower. The application of displacement theory to STS seems much sounder because here we know that STS is a limited capacity system, unlike LTS, which may be unlimited in capacity, the only limitation being one of retrieval.

Each of these theories explains some cases of forgetting but no one theory explains all forgetting. Further, no one theory even fully explains forgetting from either STS or LTS, but some are better or more general than others.

Forgetting from STS

Decay theory, interference theory, and displacement theory have been the chief contenders as explanations of STS forgetting. Two chief techniques can be cited as sources of resolution, the Brown–Peterson technique and the serial probe recall technique of Waugh and Norman. The Brown–Peterson technique involves presenting subjects with a number of trials, each trial comprising the presentation of three items, then asking the subjects to perform a task which prevents rehearsal of these three to-be-remembered items and finally asking for recall of the three items. The important manipulation is the length of time the subjects perform the interpolated rehearsal-prevention task. Brown argued that in the absence of rehearsal, memorized items should decay over time. This was shown. Forgetting of the three items was complete after as little as 18–30 seconds. While this was good evidence for the decay theory (coupled with rehearsal

– see below) there remained one possibility in terms of interference theory: if it could be shown that there was little forgetting on the first trial, but progressively more on the second, third and fourth trials, then pro-active interference could be occurring. Geoffrey Keppel and Benton Underwood (1962) argued that they showed precisely this. In their study using the Brown–Peterson technique no forgetting was shown on the first trial. However, Alan Baddeley and Donald Scott (1971) collected evidence from a number of their own studies and indicated that, providing certain precautions in terms of design were taken, forgetting did occur on the first trial. Thus, it seems that decay rather than interference was the better explanation of STS forgetting.

More recently, there has been a general acceptance that, in fact, displacement may be an even better explanation. The reference experiment is the serial probe technique of Nancy Waugh and Donald Norman (1965), who presented their subjects with series of digits at different speeds, and, when the list presentation was over, re-presented one of those digits and asked the subjects to recall the digit which followed that re-presented item in the original list. The different rates of presentation determined the time of items in STS and, thus, would indicate the relevance of decay theory, while the probe recall determined the number of items which intervened between a to-be-recalled item and its actual recall, thus allowing investigation of displacement theory. In general, displacement was supported: the greater the number of intervening items, the poorer the recall of the probed digit. There is, however, some evidence for decay theory because slower rates of presentation did produce slightly poorer recall.

The general conclusion which follows from the above is that interference theory has little to recommend it, decay theory has some validity, but that the best explanation of why memory for new information is so elusive resides in a displacement account.

What about these frustrating situations when we cannot remember that which we know we know? This is the problem of LTS forgetting, to which we now turn our attention.

Forgetting from LTS

Several of the theoretical explanations of STS forgetting reappear in accounts of LTS failure. These are trace decay and interference, and to those are added retrieval failure, systematic distortion of the memory trace, and motivated forgetting.

While systematic distortion of the memory trace and motivated forgetting will not be discussed here for the reasons outlined about, it must be borne in mind that, undoubtedly, some forgetting from LTS is due to those factors.

The choice between decay, interference, and retrieval failure is nicely made in an experiment by Endel Tulving (1968), who presented a list of words and then asked the subjects to recall all they could remember. He then took away their answer sheets, and without re-presenting the list, asked them to recall again. This was repeated a third time. The important finding was that the same words were not recalled on each of the three trials. One would have difficulty explaining these results in terms of interference because one would have to argue that that which had been unlearned on trial 1 was present on trial 2 or 3. Decay theory would be an unsatisfactory explanation of why items not recalled on either trial 1 or trial 2 could be recalled on trial 3 because more time would have elapsed between presentation and the third recall. The above results are easily explained by assuming that different retrieval cues or schemes are employed on different recall trials. Thus the possibility exists that perhaps much less is forgotten than we believe, and what is fallible is the selection or the provision of the appropriate cues. As with the STS explanation the story is much more complex than this, but for our purposes the generally accepted position is that in normal everyday life we fail to recall that which we know we know because we are unable to set up correct or appropriate retrieval cues.

Special issues

Rehearsal

If there are in fact two memory systems, an STS and an LTS, then we must ask how information gets from one to the other. The traditional answer has been 'rehearsal'. However, the term rehearsal has recently come under attack either as not being necessary or as being too global a concept. Richard Atkinson and Richard Shiffrin (1968) suggest that rehearsal has two functions: maintaining items in STS, and transferring these items to LTS. There are also two associated assumptions which go with this dual function: that time in STS and the number of repetitions are vital for transfer of information to LTS. The longer the stay in STS, or the greater the number of rehearsals, the better the chance of remembering at a later date.

Recent research, however, suggests that neither time in STS nor number of rehearsals predict storage in long-term memory. Fergus Craik and Michael Watkins (1973) asked subjects to remember only critical words (defined as words beginning with a certain letter) in lists which were presented either rapidly or slowly. The placing of critical words relative to non-critical words determined the amount of time an item spent in STS, and potentially the number of rehearsals given to an item. Retention over the long term was unrelated to either duration in STS or number of implicit or explicit rehearsals. This led Craik and Watkins to differentiate between maintenance rehearsal and elaborative rehearsal. The former is sufficient to retain items in the short term, but the latter is necessary for retention over a long term. Maintenance rehearsal can be conceptualized as repetition of the item in its presented form, elaborative rehearsal involves the elaboration of the input item, this often involving a semantic recoding or an associative linking of the words with pre-existing knowledge.

It is possible that if elaborative processing is adequately employed, storage can be achieved without any 'rehearsal' (in the sense of repetition) whatever. That this is possible is indicated by studies on incidental learning where subjects are not led to expect a recall test and therefore are not predisposed to rehearse. James Jenkins (1974) has performed many experiments where separate groups are asked either to 'estimate the number of letters in the words which I will present to you', or 'give a rhyming word to each of the words I will present to you', or thirdly, 'give me an association to each of the words I will present you with'. These are the cover tasks which hide the fact that memory is actually being studied, but they also involve processing the words in different ways. It is found that 'associative' processing produces very good recall. Thus, in the absence of rehearsal, as it was originally conceived, long-term retention can be good.

Thus it is not the amount of rehearsal but rather the type of rehearsal or processing which is crucial. The more meaningful the processing of information the better the eventual retention. What could this 'more meaningful processing' entail? This question, which we shall now address, has raised very serious doubts about the dichotomous nature of memory and has suggested that a 'levels of processing' account may be a better conception of the human memory system.

A 'levels of processing' approach to memory

Together with the criticisms of the 'boxology' approach which we made in terms of capacity, storage format, and attention, the theoretical shift from structure to function or process has led to the conclusion that, rather than looking at memory as a series of holding stages, it may be better to see memory as the by-product of what we actively do with information as it comes to us. Depending upon what we do, the type of memory we have will differ. If we simply wish to retain information momentarily in order to deal efficiently with our environment – such as dialling a person's telephone number – then we will merely process these numbers in a maintenahce way, or in what Fergus Craik and Robert Lockhart (1972) called a type 1 way (we may simply repeat them over and over again). We have no need to store it permanently, therefore we do not expend much 'cognitive effort' on it, and, as a result, the memory we have is not at all durable. If, however, for what ever reason, we wish to make sure that we learn something which we will not forget then we expend a greater amount of cognitive effort on the material. This 'cognitive effort' is best characterized as an attempt to relate new information to old, previously learned, information. This view of memory has been most forcibly argued by Frank Restle (1974) who conceptualized memory in terms of a 'degree of organization' principle. The better we can organize new material, i.e. relate it to existing knowledge, the better it will be retained.

This is altogether a more realistic way of viewing memory because it does not treat memory as a system separate and separable from our thinking, perception and knowledge systems. This is especially the case where the material we are trying to remember is new in the sense that words are not. When we are asked to 'remember' a list of words we are not really learning them, because they are in memory already; we are simply being asked to remember that a specific word has been presented. When we read stories or hear sentences, however, they have not been previously stored and could not have been because they are infinite in number. Thus the explanations of memory for digits, letters, and words may not suffice as explanations of memory for novel, complex material. It is precisely in this latter case that a level of processing or a degree of organization approach is most exciting in its potential. Thus, memory comprises several levels, but they are not different memory stores with information being transferred unidirectionally from one to the other. When we are asked to remember, we encode into existing cognitive structure, the depth of processing being determined by what we are attempting to do.

Now, while the levels of processing account of memory is not without its detractors (e.g. Eysenck, 1978, 1984; Baddeley, 1978) it has proved to be a fruitful framework for investigating memory phenomena. The theory has generalizability and it has been shown that if you make judgements about faces which are 'deep' (e.g. that face is kind) rather than judgements that are superficial (e.g. that is a female face) then memory for these faces is better in the former case (e.g. Bower and Karlin, 1974). Likewise, deeper processing of textual material and of filmic or TV material leads to better recall than when people process these media superficially.

Of late, the 'depth of processing' account of memory has been revised to include the idea of 'elaboration' and 'distinctiveness' (e.g. Ellis and Hunt, 1983). These two concepts help to explain what 'depth of processing' could entail. If we devote a lot of attention to incoming information we are likely to be elaborating upon it, that is, working out what the new information relates to, what it could be related to, how it is similar to or different from other material in memory, etc.; we elaborate or 'add to' the incoming information. Now, by virtue of adding to this new information we actually make that information more distinctive. The greater the information we have about an object the more distinctive that object becomes. For example, if we are told, in a party game, that 'I am thinking about a large, grey African animal' we are unclear whether it is an elephant or a rhinoceros. One further bit of information will serve to make the object distinct: 'long nose' or 'horn'. It is in this sense that the three concepts of depth, elaboration and distinctiveness hang together and are felt to go a long way towards telling us how to remember important material and how to prevent its loss.

However, just when it was felt that the issue of whether to study memory processes or memory structures had been settled, in favour of a focus on process, a whole new research effort awoke – focusing upon memory structures. This recent research involves the concept of working memory.

Working memory

Baddeley and Hitch (1974) began with the question: if memory does comprise two basic systems, an STS and an LTS, what function does the STS serve? While the Atkinson and Shiffrin model (1968) gave a reasonable account of the *laboratory* data (see above) it had difficulty with evidence provided by STM-deficient patients. If STS was essential to transfer information to LTS then such patients should have a major long-term memory problem. Evidence indicates that they did not. This is odd. A number of possibilities thus present themselves: either STS is not important in the human information processing system; or STS is important, but it is a more complex structure than a mere 'holding' stage in the human information processing system. The idea that STS was more than a holding store was in fact suggested by Atkinson and Shiffrin (1971) when they argued that not only was information held in STS for a limited period, but also that, while there, the information had 'control processes', such as attention and rehearsal, applied to it. However, the modern view of STS is even more complex than that. The idea that Baddeley developed was that of a short-term working memory system. This working memory system is not identical to the old-style STS, conceptualized as a unitary storage system, but is seen rather as a multi-component structure, comprising a central executive or 'attentional control system' (Baddeley, 1988) supplemented by two principal slave systems, the articulatory loop and the visuo-spatial scratch pad, and possibly a third, the primary acoustic store.

The central executive is the heart of the working memory model, although it is the most poorly researched, being, according to Eysenck (1984), the last area of ignorance. The central executive is assumed to integrate information from the slave systems and from LTS, and to play a critical role in planning and controlling behaviour. According to Baddeley and Hitch (1974) the central executive can be employed for storage or processing, in a trade-off type relationship. The central executive seems to be involved in degenerative diseases such as Alzheimer's disease, and undoubtedly in many many more cognitive processes, which involve integrating information from different sources and carrying out plans and intentions.

The articulatory loop is a limited capacity phonological store: i.e. information is represented as it would be if spoken, and the 'memory' includes the muscle movements necessary to produce these sounds. This memory trace decays within 1–2 seconds, unless it is refreshed by a rehearsal process involving subvocal speech. It can also convert visually presented items into an articulatory form – the letter 'a' into the sound of the letter 'a'. A malfunctioning articulatory loop can cause problems in language comprehension and in learning new foreign languages. The articulatory loop may also play a vital role in learning to read (e.g. Jorm, 1983).

The visuo-spatial scratch pad deals with visually presented material and also spatial reasoning. The various imagery mnemonics, useful in cramming for exams, may depend upon the operation of the visuo-spatial scratch pad component of working memory which has been referred to as the 'inner eye'. Images may be characterized as more or less shadowy refabrications of ordinary perceptions and a person may experience images in one or several of his ordinary sense modalities. Mental imagery has been considered important in memorization since the time of the Greeks, who perfected methods of using imagery as an aid to memory.

The early associationists held that part of the meaning of a word lay in the image which the word evokes. The word comes to evoke an image through its repeated occurrence contiguous with the object which it symbolizes. In time, the word comes to evoke an image, just as the object produces its percept. Thus, it could be argued that if the 'recallability' of a word in part depends upon the richness of its association network, then words with images as associations obviously have a greater probability of being recalled than words which do not, assuming that both types of words have verbal associations.

There are several types of mnemonics (rules of learning that improve recall) but the function of all of them is to provide a means by which new material can be very quickly integrated into an existing memory structure. The user of the mnemonic simply has to form a conscious association between the to-be-remembered material (we shall stick to words) and an item which already firmly exists in his memory. A very simple visual mnemonic, e.g. the method of loci, or the method of places (Yates, 1966; Wollen, Weber and Lowry, 1972), would involve the subject in imagining a familiar house during presentation of, say, a word list; he would try to image each word written on the wall of a room in this house. In fact, the more bizarre and eccentric the image association, the greater is the probability that it will be effective: the word could thus be magnified in large letters of a brilliant colour on an unusual part of the room. In order to recall the word list, our mnemonist simply takes an imaginary stroll through the house looking into each room to 'see' which words are there. If the process of association-formation has been successful he will be able to recall the words which have been associated with each room.

One of the easiest mnemonics useful for remembering short word lists requires that the mnemonist calls to mind the numbers 1 to 10 and then remembers the first word that comes to mind which rhymes with that number, for example, 1 – gun, 2 – shoe, 3 – tree, 4 – door, and so on. Suppose that the to-be-remembered word list consists of ten words, the first two being chair and lion; the mnemonist has to imagine (visualize) an association between, for example, gun and the first to-be-remembered word which here is 'chair', then shoe and the second word 'lion', and so on. Again, the more bizarre the association, the better.

The primary acoustic store (which Eysenck, 1986, calls the inner ear) is accessed by auditory input directly – we cannot help but hear someone talking to us. Visual input can also enter this sub-system by being converted to phonological form (i.e. being processed by the articulatory loop). According to Hitch (1980) this input system is crucially concerned with retaining recently heard speech.

The upshot of this new line of memory research is to favour very markedly the argument that the best way to proceed is to conceptualize memory not as a unitary system or function, but rather as an alliance of interacting systems serving different functions and operating in different ways. Only time will tell whether this approach, or an approach focusing upon processes or strategies will result in a better understanding of memory and how to go about improving it in children and adults in diverse situations.

Organization

We have argued above that good memory depends upon the subject actively organizing the to-be-remembered material. John Meyer (1973) has stated that to remember is to have organized. Now, while this is not necessarily the whole story, there is more than a grain of truth in it. The evidence that people actually do strive to organize material for later recall, and that this organization has beneficial effects, became obvious as a result of what appeared to be a very trivial change in research methodology. The change was from a stress on serial recall to a stress on free recall. In serial recall, the subject must correctly recall the items and recall them in the same order as they were presented, while, in free recall, correct item recall is demanded, but the subject can recall the items in any order he chooses. This simple change unlocked the door on a whole unexplored area of human memory. By allowing free recall of the items, psychologists could begin to see just how subjects were going about memory tasks.

Now as we have already seen, psychologists are fond of postulating dichotomies to explain their data, and the explanation of the efficacy of organization is no exception, being polarized into storage and retrieval accounts. The first account states that organization has its beneficial effect at storage because it serves to reduce the amount of material to be remembered by hierarchically grouping the material, or chunking it. For example, the words cat, dog, parrot, and tortoise could all be grouped under the heading 'pets'. The opposing view is that organization has its effect at retrieval due to the fact that organized items have greater uniqueness and hence an increased number of retrieval routes or 'tags' associated with them. However, the assumption we will work on is that organization has a beneficial effect because it aids both storage and retrieval. It is likely that whenever a subject detects the possibility of an organizational scheme he processes the input words into this scheme and retains both the retrieval (organizational) scheme and the individual items. You will remember from our section on rehearsal that, providing an item is processed adequately (deeply), no rehearsal in the sense of repetition is necessary. Fitting the word into an overall organizational scheme may be sufficient processing to ensure recall. At retrieval the subject probably evokes his organizational scheme and then decides if internally-generated words are sufficiently familiar to constitute a response.

It has become clear from a vast amount of research that subjects can organize material either because the material has intrinsic organizational properties (e.g. all the list words refer to either cars, animals or colours), or subjects organize material in terms of some personal idiosyncratic principle. The first type of organization can be referred to as experimenter-imposed organization (EO). The second type of organization is referred to as subject-based organization (SO). Categorical organization refers to the fact that the input words can be grouped into a greater or lesser number of semantic categories, as, in our example above, cars, animals, and colours. Here the work of Bousfield is seminal, and this technique is still employed today, with various gradations of refinement. He began by sampling a number of semantic categories for exemplars (e.g. category: animal; exemplars: horse, lion, etc.) and then randomly mixing these exemplars into a sixty-item list and presenting them to subjects for memorization. This procedure ensured that all the animal exemplars did not come one after the other in the input list. The important question was whether this random input would be recalled in a principled, non-random way. If recall did exhibit category-clustering of exemplars, then good evidence would exist that subjects actively processed and organized the list for later recall. Principled free recall was exhibited, and has been confirmed by numerous other researchers.

Further evidence for categorical organization comes from the study by Pollio and Foote (1971) who studied temporal aspects of recall. These researchers showed that items within categories were recalled rapidly, but long delays occurred between categories (e.g. lion-tiger-panther – pansy-rose-violet). Segal (1969) supported categorical organization by showing that if category labels ('animals') were presented randomly among list of exemplars (tiger, desk, animal, pansy, lion) the category label preceded the category exemplars at recall. Lastly, a 'some or none' effect has been shown by Cohen (1966) where, with categorizable lists, either several exemplars from a category are recalled, or none at all.

Limitations

So predictable has this categorical organization effect become that more recent research has taken for granted that it will happen and has begun to look for other characteristics of organization, such as its limits and mechanisms. Current research seems to suggest that, while categorical organization does exist, it is limited both in the number of categories that can be efficiently handled (about six) and in the number of words in each category. These inherent limitations have been shown most clearly by Tulving and Pearlstone (1966), who varied both the number of categories and the number of exemplars per category by presenting lists of 12, 24, and 48 words containing categories of one, two, or four exemplars in each. Half the subjects were simply asked to recall the words, while the other half of the subjects were given category names (cues) at recall and were asked to recall the presented exemplars. The cued recall subjects recalled more words (exemplars) than the non-cued subjects, but this was due to recalling from more categories, not from recalling more exemplars from any one category. That is, the cued and non-cued subjects did not differ in the number of exemplars recalled from any one category. This shows clearly that there seems to be a limit to the number of words recallable from each category. The second limitation of organization (the number of categories that can be handled) was shown by providing the category labels to the non-cued subjects after they had indicated that they could remember no more words. If more words were then recalled, this would be good evidence for a limitation in terms of the number of categories that could be remembered. Such additional word recall was exhibited. (Note also that this is an example of the availability–accessibility distinction talked of above.)

While category-clustering serves the function of showing that subjects can utilize organizational schemes inherent in the material, it fails to show just how 'active' the subject really is in memory situations. A more powerful demonstration of organization would be achieved if the material to be recalled did not have any (obvious) organizational schemes such as categories contained within it, but principled recall was still observed. This is precisely what subject organization (SO) achieves. This paradigm also avoids the inherent danger of EO in that the latter builds on the assumption that, because the list has intrinsic organizational properties, these properties should be used and therefore be the criterion by which one deduces organization on the part of the subject. The problem with this is that if the experimenter's assumption does not match the subject's actual organizational method then the subject will be assumed not to have shown organization, whereas in fact all that can be said is that the subject did not use the experimenter's organizational scheme. Subject-generated organization has been demonstrated in a number of ways such as looking for repeated output-grouping despite different input orders over a number of lists, but especially by what is called part-list or transfer learning. Tulving (1966) argued that subjective organization involves schemes for memorizing the whole list, i.e., subjects are not merely concerned to organize one or two items into a memorable unit, but rather they are concerned to maximize recall by generating an overall organizational scheme which includes all the to-be-remembered items. If this is the case, then if items a, b, c, d, e, and f form a list and then the subject is later asked to learn a list comprising a, b, c, d, e, f, g, h, i, and j, the possibility exists that the organizational schemes for the first and second lists may conflict, resulting in the odd findings that learning part of a list inhibits the learning of the whole list compared with subjects who have no chance to learn the first part of the list. Tulving (1966) showed this counter-intuitive finding. He used two groups, with one group (Group 1) learning 18 words which would later be incorporated into a 36 word list, while the other group (Group 2) also learned 18 words but these words were not to be incorporated into the later 36 word list. The interesting question was whether Group 1 or Group 2 would learn the 36 words faster. From trial two onwards the subjects who had initially learned 18 irrelevant words learned the 36 word list faster! Tulving interpreted these results as indicating that Group 1 had initially developed an overall organization scheme for the 18 words, which, when these 18 words were incorporated into a 36 word list, was inappropriate, while Group 2 simply evolved a new organizational scheme for new material. This part-whole transfer effect has also been shown to work in reverse (whole-part).

The process of organization

Research has thus gone beyond simply demonstrating the fact of organization. We now know quite a bit about the process. For example, it seems that organization has its effect both at storage and retrieval (e.g. Mandler, 1972); that the efficiency of organization is limited both by the amount of information we can contain within an organized unit and the number of such organizational units we can effectively utilize; and, lastly, it has become obvious that the number of ways a person can organize any set of information is very large.

But perhaps the most exciting work in the last few years is that concerned with the question of how students organize connected discourse or texts for retention. This literature is very complex but rather clear principles are emerging. These principles basically follow those found in word-list research and are based on hierarchical grouping of content. In any text, the ideas expressed are of differential importance. If one has ever tried to write a précis, this point will be conceded. It seems that, in remembering connected discourse, the relative importance of the idea units clearly predict recall, i.e. the more important or central the idea, the more likely it is to be recalled. It seems that texts can be represented as hierarchical in nature, that is, within the logical structure underpinning the actual text, conceptual units can be isolated, and be shown to interlink in hierarchical form, such that from the central or core idea other ideas lead off in an ever spreading network. The function of a central idea is clearly shown by John Bransford and Marcia Johnson (1973) who presented a difficult-to-comprehend passage to one group of subjects and also gave them the title ('Washing Clothes') before they read the passage. Another group of subjects were given the passage, and then the title after they had read it, while the last group received only the passage and no title at any time. The argument advanced was that the title is the central idea. Recall of words in the passage was then requested and the 'title plus passage' group was found to surpass by far both the 'passage plus title' and 'passage only' groups. The finding that the 'passage plus title' did not differ significantly from the 'passage only' strongly suggests that either the organizational scheme must be present at input, or, at least, that it must be capable of generation during the ongoing input. Giving a retrieval or organizational plan (title) after encoding has gone on does not aid memory.

Throughout this discussion of organization we have been concerned to stress organizational schemes in terms of hierarchies which have the properties of low storage requirement and high inference components. From our argument that memory is a by-product of integrating incoming information with existing knowledge, a fairly clear prediction would then be that our existing knowledge has this hierarchical structure. To see whether, in fact, it does is the focus of the next part of this chapter.

Semantic memory

That part of long-term memory which is concerned with our stored knowledge of facts, laws, and principles is referred to as semantic memory. This should be distinguished from our long-term memories of personal events and episodes which have happened to us in our lives. This latter memory has been referred to as episodic memory (Tulving, 1972). While these two memories are undoubtedly intimately connected they can be conceptually distinguished, and here we shall deal only with semantic memory.

All the knowledge that underlies human cognitive ability is stored in semantic memory. From this premise certain things follow:

1. Semantic memory will be involved in problem-solving and logical deduction, in question answering and fact retrieval, and in the development and utilization of language.
2. The amount of information stored in memory is staggering.
3. Semantic memory must therefore be organized, not haphazard.

It was precisely with these assumptions in mind that one of the earliest and best evolved theories of semantic memory was developed. In 1969 Allan Collins and Ross Quillian published their 'cognitive economy model' of human semantic memory, which was developed from a computer simulation model of language processing.

Collins and Quillian argued that knowledge was stored in the form of a hierarchical network of concept nodes, each concept being linked with a number of other nodes in a superset–subset relationship. Their most often quoted hierarchy (see Figure 12.2) should help render the basic structure of their model clear.

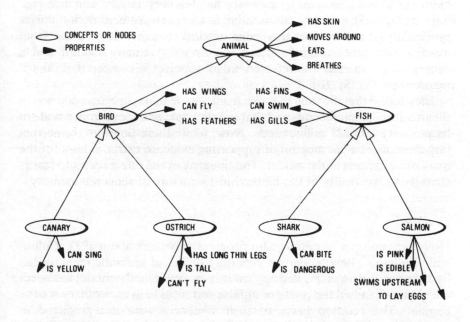

Figure 12.2 A hypothetical memory structure for animal, bird and canary (after Collins and Quillian, 1972)

As can be seen, properties are stored non-redundantly, i.e. that which is true of animals, birds and canaries (e.g. breathing) is stored only at the animal node, and is therefore applied to canary by implication (inference), due to the latter's membership in that animal hierarchy. Thus, Collins and Quillian's model is characterized by a low storage requirement but a high inference component. Now, it is all very well generating a computer program which will handle language, but the important question to ask is whether it in any way represents human memory. To test whether, in fact, the simulation model adequately modelled the human system Collins and Quillian used a true–false reaction time (RT) technique whereby subjects were presented with a sentence such as 'a canary is a bird' and the time taken by the subject to answer true (yes) or false (no) was measured. On the bases of their model Collins and Quillian predicted that it would take time to move from one node to the other. Secondly, they suggested that where one step depended on the completion of another (prior) step the times would be additive. Thirdly, they postulated that the average time for any step would be independent of which particular level of hierarchy was involved. In order to verify or falsify these predictions Collins and Quillian need both property (P) and superset (S) sentences. These two basic types of sentence could each have three levels. For example, 'a canary is yellow' would be called a P_0 sentence (being a property sentence with no hierarchical links involved); 'a canary has feathers' is a P_1 sentence (see Figure 12.2) and 'a canary can breathe' is a P_2 sentence because it involves properties but also involves traversing two links to arrive at 'breathes' from 'canary'. Sentences such as 'a canary is a canary', 'a canary is a bird' and 'a canary is an animal' are referred to as superset sentences 0, 1 and 2 respectively (S_0, S_1, S_2).

They found that the time to move from a node to its superset node was in the order of 75 milliseconds and that the time taken to move from a node to its property was 225 milliseconds. Now, while these times are somewhat task-dependent a fair amount of supporting evidence exists, at least for the qualitative aspects of the model. The linearity of the effect seems to testify strongly to the reality of the hierarchical structure of semantic memory.

Critique

However, since its inception, and progressively since about 1972, Collins and Quillian's (1969) cognitive economy model of semantic memory has had certain criticisms levelled against it. For example, the model has never adequately handled the problem of false instances such as 'a canary is a fire engine'. The reaction times to such sentences were not predicted or predictable, and despite having looked at five possible explanations Collins and Quillian (1972) had to conclude that no satisfactory or adequate answer was at hand. Obviously an adequate account of human functioning will have to explain both positive and negative instances of knowledge verification.

Over and above this major failing, other problems have arisen, such as the possibility that people do store information repeatedly, and that because of this, some information is more available than others because of the individual's past learning. A second attack is based on the belief that Collins and Quillian's data (RTs) may be an artifact of category size. For example, there are more animals than birds and thus verification of an instance of animal should take longer than verification of an instance of bird. That is, the greater the number of instances the slower RT will be. A third possible explanation of the Collins and Quillian findings could be in terms of imagery (Jorgansen and Kintsch, 1973). They suggest that the higher up the hierarchy one goes, the less concrete or imagible is the instance or concept. It is very difficult to image an animal – without imaging a specific animal. It is, however, easy to image a canary. The last attack on Collins and Quillian which we shall discuss is the argument that the RT data of the cognitive economy model could just as easily be explained by similarity, or what is called 'feature overlap'. Concepts which are more distant in a conceptual hierarcy have fewer features in common (e.g. mammal and collie) than concepts which are close together (e.g. dog and collie). It has been proposed that subjects prime a positive response when two concepts are similar and would thus predict the Collins and Quillian RT findings, without having to postulate that knowledge is stored hierarchically. In fact similarity ratings of concepts are better predictors of judgement times than distances in a conceptual hierarchy.

These various attacks on Collins and Quillian's interpretation of their RT data has led to a suggestion that knowledge is not, in fact, stored hierarchically but, rather, in some other format. The nature of this alternative organization is not at all clearly specified and, in fact, when it is given 'flesh' there seems little to differentiate it from the Collins and Quillian model (though this is far from being a consensual statement).

Currently, a form of network model of semantic memory still holds sway. In 1975 Collins and Loftus presented an augmented version of Collins and Quillian's cognitive economy model, in which it is still argued that our concepts are linked with each other, but now the network of concepts is much less strictly hierarchical. Now some links are more important than others (due to past learning, for example), and one hierarchy can link directly into another, different, hierarchy. Thus an animal-bird-robin hierarchy will link directly to a colour network via the link between 'robin' and 'red breast'. In addition, this rejuvenated network model has a visuo-spatial (imagery) dimension so that we can now activate 'dog' either by hearing the word 'dog' or by seeing a picture of a dog.

This model is itself not without its critics; some say it is so much of a hybrid that it cannot be falsified. This is based upon its complexity. And

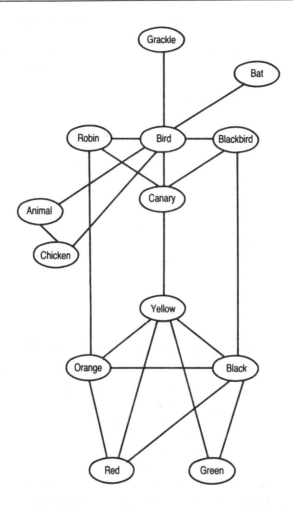

Figure 12.3 The structure of semantic memory as seen in the Spreading Activation Model (after Collins and Loftus, 1975). Note, the different lengths of 'connections' between concepts: the symmetry of Collins and Quillian's (1969) model has gone, and the structure is now more heterarchical than hierarchical

yet its complexity is almost certainly far short of the truth. Much, much more complex models will be needed if we are truly to explain the complexity of the human brain.

The concept of semantic memory is a fairly new field of enquiry and errors in theory and methodology are therefore to be expected. The polarization of theories should not serve to frustrate the student of memory but rather should serve to indicate the fruitfulness of the field and its importance. The overriding concern is that logical models should not carry the day simply because of elegance, power and parsimony; the overall need is for a psychological model of knowledge structure and the way it develops and is utilized. Semantic memory research has a very long way to go, but it has made its first faltering steps, and we must now be concerned with its growth to maturity. However, this maturity may never be realized because interest has shifted, at least for the present moment.

Schemas, scripts, and frames

Throughout this chapter constant reference has been made to the fact that memory can be improved if new input material is related to old, existing knowledge. Yet 'semantic memory models' seemed to be missing something. They seemed to be investigating highly artificial, limited knowledge. Knowledge that wasn't really the stuff of everyday life.

A key feature of current memory research is an attempt to explore and investigate 'the stuff of everyday life'. A central concept in this investigation is that of schema. While schema theory originated with Kant, and was used by the neurophysiologist, Head, it became prevalent in the writings of Piaget and of Bartlett in 1932. While these two researchers used the term in slightly different ways both were agreed that schemas were 'distillates of past experience'. Bartlett examined the way in which a person's memory for stories could be affected by his own attitudes, beliefs, motivation, and general cognitive style. Typically, subjects were presented with a short story and, after various intervals, they were required to reproduce it. Bartlett found his subjects very often appeared to modify the story in such a way as to make it more consistent with their own frames of reference. The most frequently quoted example of this aspect of Bartlett's work is one of his stories which tells of two Indians who are canoeing on a river when they meet a war party and are invited to join it. One of the Indians joins the raiding party but is wounded in the ensuing fight. He is brought back home and dies at dawn the following morning. The story also includes a reference to ghosts, which can either be viewed as central to the whole story or as figments of the imagination of the dying Indian. The English subjects of this experiment seemed to interpret the story in such a way as to make the ghosts unimportant and they were generally omitted from the later reproductions. This and other very common alterations made to the story during recall led Bartlett to formulate several generalizations; some subjects indulged in a lot of elaboration and invention especially after long delays before recall; there was much rationalization so that details were made to fit in with a subject's pre-formed interests and tendencies. Two other common results were noted: if one subject was asked to recall the story frequently then the form and items of remembered detail very quickly became stereotyped and did not change much with repeated recall; however, in the case of infrequent reproduction, omission of detail, simplification of events and structure, and transformation of items into more familiar detail went on so long as unaided recall was possible. Finally, the most common finding was that accuracy of recall in a literal sense was rare.

Bartlett emphasized the idea that remembering is not just the reactivation of memories which have been stored and which have remained unchanged during storage. Instead, Bartlett describes the act of remembering as being a process of reconstruction based on 'schemata'. He thus emphasized the active nature of memory, and only recently has cognitive psychology rediscovered that the production of memory involves the subjects' expectations or inferential reasoning.

So, at present, the evidence appears to indicate that we interpret meaningful material in terms of existing knowledge, attitudes, beliefs, and expectations and that this interpretation is accurately remembered and is very resistant to change.

When we have experienced something once or twice we retain the skeleton of what was common to these various particular experiences and actual details may be forgotten. Thus schemas can be regarded as 'ideational scaffolding' upon, and in terms of which, new material can be 'hung' or interpreted and given meaning. Van Dijk (1981) defines schemas as high-level complex knowledge structures. The important point to grasp is that schemas are active knowledge structures. Current schema research has been concerned to refine and explain more fully their nature and function. What has this research uncovered?

Schemas have four main characteristics. First, schemas have variables or slots which have to be filled for completeness of understanding. These slots are filled by either *instantiation* (e.g. if the information is provided directly by the speaker, the text or the film) or by *default* (by inference) if it is not presented directly. Thus if we are told that the golfer 'sliced his shot' we know (by inference) that he used a golf club. Second, schemas exhibit embedding, i.e. components of schemas may themselves be schemas, e.g. faces and eyes; letters and words. This notion of embedding implies the possibility of nesting of schemas. Thus, person-schemas which include trait, attitudes and actions can be nested within goal-orientated schemas such as power, happiness, wealth. Think of how Macbeth fits into goal-driven behaviour patterns (schemas). Third, schemas can differ in their level of abstractness. Some are very concrete (getting ready for school) while some are quite vague (getting a 'good' job). Fourth, schemas represent general knowledge of the world rather than definitions of objects or events. This gives the notion of schema greater flexibility. This means that the components, attributes and relations of a schema are not always necessary, certain or universal – rather they are possible, probable and likely. To use Rosch's (1978) term, attributes of schemas vary in typicality with respect to a schema. Paying for school meals in the 'school dinners' schema is typical but not strictly necessary.

So far we have concentrated upon the static structure of schemas, but they are far from being inert. Rather our previous knowledge actively engages currently attended-to material and critically determines whether and how we will learn new knowledge. Schema-based knowledge does this in a number of ways:

1. The schema provides the background knowledge or context that is needed for guiding *interpretation* of specific input; without this context nothing is interpretable.
2. A second function of schemas is to provide background knowledge that is relevant to generating *inferences*.
3. A third function of schemas is to generate *expectations*. Once a schema is generated the content of that schema provides the knowledge needed for the comprehender to expect and predict future events and states.
4. Another function of schemas is to guide the comprehender's *attention*. It does this in two ways:
   (a) by directing attention to the place or location in an informational display where parts of the schema are expected to occur. For example, if you track eye movements in scanning a face these eye movements are highly predictable – they follow the face schema of eyes, mouth, and nose. An embarrassing example of schemas directing attention is the great difficulty people have in *not* looking at a missing body part when introduced to someone with an arm, leg, finger or ear missing;
   (b) by directing attention to parts of an information display which deviates from the context of the schema – devotees of video games will appreciate this point! Basically it means that we are attracted to and by the unusual.
5. A fifth function of active schemas is constant *correcting and adjusting* schema-relevant action via feedback. While performing goal orientated behaviour individuals execute actions in order to achieve consequences that satisfy goals.

Of late schema theory has been very successful in explaining a great deal of everyday memory, and not a little of what goes on in schools. So successful has the application of the concept been that some investigators are concerned that the concept is so general as to be unfalsifiable. This has led to the evolution of more specific concepts such as frames (Minsky, 1975, 1978) and scripts (Schank and Abelson, 1977). In an attempt to specialize the rather amorphous concept of schema, frames have been argued to be more circumscribed than schema and to be predominantly concerned with object- and situation-specific knowledge. Likewise, scripts are concerned with the specific knowledge we have about specific actions and events, like visiting a dentist or going to a disco. While each of these concepts contribute something unique to the explanation of memory we lose little by regarding them merely as smaller-scaled schemas.

Conclusion

This chapter has been concerned to indicate both enduring issues in the study of memory, such as rehearsal, organization, why we forget, why we remember, but also issues that are far from settled, such as whether memory is unitary or duplex or multi-structured. In addition, 'big issues' about strategy and the best way to approach understanding of how memory works have been addressed, for example, whether a process-orientated or a structure-orientated approach will have the greater pay-off. Throughout the chapter however it is hoped that the examples chosen and the topics discussed indicate that memory research is progressively addressing the issue of ecological validity: does the research say anything about real-life memory? It will have been noticed that certain issues are no longer addressed, not because the issue is finally settled, but rather because it is felt that the question it was addressing is no longer relevant, or that the right question was being raised at the wrong level. Semantic memory's usurpation by schema theory is a case in point. Here questions concerned with what we do in real life dictated the agenda of issues to be discussed. It is hoped that a glimpse of the current memory agenda has been given by this chapter.

Further reading

Baddeley, A. D. (1976) *The Psychology of Memory*. Harper and Row.
Baddeley, A. D. (1986) *Working Memory*. Oxford University Press.
Cohen, G., Eysenck, M. W., and Le Voi, M. (1986) *Memory: A cognitive approach*. Open University Press.
Gregg, V. (1975) *Human Memory*. Methuen.
Gregg, V. (1986) *Introduction to Human Memory*. Routledge and Kegan Paul.
Wright, D., Taylor, A., Davies, D., Slukin, W., Lee, S., and Reason, J. (1970) *Introducing Psychology: An experimental approach*. Penguin.

Chapter thirteen

Intelligence

John Radford and Clive Hollin

The measurement of intelligence

One of the most basic problems faced by psychologists is that, so it seems, no two people are exactly alike. Even identical twins (see below) are not identical in every respect; and each has his or her own individual thoughts and feelings, however similar they may often be to those of their twin. This problem is not one shared by many other sciences, or at least is less serious elsewhere. Physicists, for example, seek to understand the forces underlying *all* matter. Dynamics is concerned with *general* laws of movement, not primarily with particular moving objects. Even biologists deal mainly with classes and sub-classes rather than with individual members of a species.

Some psychologists (for example, Gordon Allport, 1897–1967) argue that it is uniqueness that we must study; it is precisely individuality that makes us human. Partly for this reason, some psychologists (for example,

H. J. Eysenck, b. 1916) maintain that the central concern of psychology is the study of individual differences.

The differences between people have fascinated scholars, scientists, and writers for centuries. From at least the time of Hippocrates (c. 460 BC) there have been attempts to devise some kind of orderly classification. Systematic attempts to measure the differences, to establish their distribution, range, and limits, have however been made only in the last two hundred years. For various reasons, the greatest amount of effort, at least until quite recently, has gone into the study of intellectual abilities; and in particular, into the investigation of what has come to be labelled intelligence.

Definitions of intelligence

Psychologists are sometimes criticized for trying to study intelligence when they cannot agree on what it is. This criticism is due to a misunderstanding of the purpose of scientific definitions. These are perhaps best thought of as labels or direction-signs. They are useful if they are generally understood and agreed upon. The sign 'exit' is useful, without having to define precisely the nature of exits or say whether the doors are hinged, sliding, or revolving. The sign, 'way out' would do just as well. (Signs can be misleading. There is the story of the showman who, in order to hurry the crowd along, labelled the way out 'This way to the egress'.)

It is only fair to admit that psychologists themselves have, especially in the early years, contributed to the confusion, partly by their disagreements, and partly by apparently thinking that definitions are not so much merely convenient labels as declarations of territorial rights. It will be useful to try to see what psychologists have intended to convey in using the term 'intelligence'.

As Burt (1955) points out, the concept of intelligence came into vogue largely due to an upsurge of interest in the writings of Herbert Spencer (1820–1903) and Francis Galton (1822–1911) who were among the first to use the term 'intelligence' more or less in its modern sense. For different reasons, they both believed in the existence of a general ability superordinate to and distinct from special abilities; an ability which was the basis for intellectual achievements of all kinds. This notion received support from the hierarchical view of the nervous system expounded by the leading neurologists of the period John Hughlings Jackson (1834–1911) and Charles Sherrington (1857–1952). Cyril Burt himself accepted the theory of a general cognitive capacity probably dependent upon the number, complexity of connections, and organization of the nerve cells in the cerebral cortex. The concept of 'intelligence' gradually became widely accepted, and attempts to define it proliferated. There have been three main sorts of definition: *intuitive* definitions have relied on experience and judgement;

logical definitions try to tease out the implications of the way the word is actually used; while the *empirical* approach generally starts from accepted usage and from what has been scientifically established, derives hypotheses from this, seeks evidence to test the hypotheses, and tries to construct a theoretical model to accommodate the results. Here are some examples:

Intuitive 'The ability to carry on abstract thinking' (Terman); 'The capacity to acquire capacity' (Woodrow); 'The power of good responses from the point of view of truth or fact' (Thorndike).

Vernon (1960) classified definitions of this type as biological, psychological, or operational. Freeman (1962) divided them into those emphasizing (a) power of adapting to the environment; (b) capacity for learning; (c) capacity for abstract thinking.

Definitions of this type may be useful starting points, but cannot really be accepted as conclusive.

Logical Probably the most important analysis is that of Gilbert Ryle (*The Concept of Mind*, 1949). He argued that 'intelligence' is not to be considered as an entity inside the organism, causing it to act in a certain way; nor is it an attribute such as 'tall' or 'British'; rather it is a dispositional concept describing certain sorts of behaviour. However, there is no list of behaviours which can be always so described: rather, any sort of activity can, in principle, be carried on intelligently or unintelligently – playing cards, washing dishes, or resolving mathematical equations. To say that someone is intelligent means that he or she characteristically acts in intelligent ways in the things that they do. The intelligent individual acts in ways logically related to the desired end result; is ready to deal with new circumstances if they arise; and is able to innovate. Howe (1988) has recently revived some of these arguments.

Miles (1957) described intelligence as not only a 'disposition word' but also as 'polymorphous' and 'open'. Polymorphous means that, as with a word like 'games' or 'farming', two examples may have no individual characteristics in common. Open means that the list of possible characteristics of intelligent behaviour is endless.

Empirical This approach originates with the work of Francis Galton and was continued by a line of British psychologists, Karl Pearson (1857–1936), Charles Spearman (1863–1945), and Cyril Burt (1883–1971), who were closely associated with University College, London. All favoured the concept of one general quality of 'intelligence', common to a wide range of activities, though they had somewhat different ideas about the nature of this quality. The idea became famous with Spearman's 'two-factor' theory (1904). He suggested that a number of psychological capacities existed, each involving both a general intellectual factor and another factor specific to that capacity. The first he labelled 'g' or general

409

intelligence; and he considered that it consisted essentially in the ability to see relationships.

A parallel line of thought developed in the United States, where stress was laid rather on the analysis of intellectual abilities into a number of separate factors. Thurstone (1938) felt that the evidence justified the naming of seven 'primary mental abilities'. Guilford (1967) developed this further and defined no fewer than 120 factors which constitute 'intelligence'. To an extent, this difference depends less on basic theoretical issues than on preferences for what are considered the most economical practical ways of interpreting the results of factor analyses (see below).

Sternberg and Berg (1986) compared definitions of intelligence favoured in 1986 as compared with 1921. They found a surprisingly high similarity in definitions over the 65 years, although there was a prominence given to 'metacognition' in the more recent definitions not found in earlier times. (Metacognition is knowledge about and control of cognition; perhaps best viewed as 'thinking about thinking'.)

In spite of the cautions of Ryle and others, there is still a temptation to think that because there is a word 'intelligence', there must be a thing that corresponds to it. In fact the word as generally used is only a convenient grouping of certain ways of behaving. Other people may, and other cultures certainly do, group behaviours differently from ourselves.

Reliability and validity

Given that it is possible to identify, from whatever standpoint, some important intellectual ability or capacity, it is clearly useful to be able to measure it. From the start, the measurement of psychological characteristics – termed psychometrics – has had both a theoretical and a practical purpose. Galton's purpose was to identify those qualities that made for great achievement in both individuals and the race, and then find means of increasing them. Alfred Binet (1857–1911), who produced in 1905 the first intelligence test of modern type, did so to solve the practical educational problems of identifying those children in the schools of Paris who needed special education. The need to classify army recruits when the United States entered the First World War in 1915, many not speaking English well, led to the production of group tests, and to testing on a massive scale: one and three-quarter million by 1919. (For the use of intelligence tests in education today, see Chapter 25.)

To be of use, any measuring instrument must be *reliable* and *valid*. *Reliability* is often interpreted as consistency; but, as Cronbach (1960) points out, the term often covers two rather different aspects. He distinguishes between the internal consistency of a test, the extent to which the different parts or items agree with each other; and stability, the degree to which the test produces consistent results when used for successive groups of subjects.

The best-known way of establishing internal consistency is the split-half method. The items of the test are divided into two groups; they are then all scored for each of a set of subjects; finally the two sets of scores are correlated. An improvement on this is provided by the Kuder–Richardson method, which gives not just the correlation coefficient for one arbitrary division of the items, but the average coefficient that would result from splitting the items in every possible way. To establish stability, the test–retest method is generally used. The test is given to the same group of subjects on two occasions, with an interval between in which it is hoped that the subjects will have forgotten their exact first responses but will not have altered substantially in their performance.

It should be clear that reliability is a relative, not an absolute, matter. It depends upon assumptions (such as the stability of subjects) and upon decisions about the selection of groups of subjects and conditions of administration.

Validity refers to the question of whether we know what a test is measuring. It is sometimes said that a test is valid if it measures what it is supposed to measure. This is slightly misleading since, because of the theoretical uncertainties of psychological concepts such as intelligence, we do not always know what a test ought to be measuring. Some cases of invalidity are relatively obvious; for example, if a test involved a lot of writing, we might be measuring handwriting skill rather than intelligence. There are several ways of improving validity, or perhaps better several varieties of validity. These are summarized in a report of the American Psychological Association (1954). The most relevant to intelligence are concurrent validity and predictive validity.

Concurrent validity and *predictive validity* refer to the comparison of scores on the test with scores obtained from some other source. This could be another test, or performance on a task or series of tasks, or judgements of trained observers. The difference between concurrent and predictive validity is that in the first case the two sets of scores are taken at or about the same time; in the second, they are separated by an interval, possibly of several years. Clearly both have an element of circularity: for example, if a test is validated on children against the judgements of their teachers, those judgements are almost certain to be affected by what the teachers know of their children's performance on similar tests.

Construct validity hopes to avoid this. The idea is that a test should be derived from some theory which has testable consequences. This is rather obviously desirable, but also obviously difficult, due to the lack of any generally accepted theory. In principle, construct validity, if established, would ensure that the test measured 'real' intelligence. It is, at best, an unsolved conceptual puzzle whether such a term as 'real intelligence' has any meaning.

For completeness we should mention face validity, which means, approximately, whether a test looks valid. This makes good sense for tests of, say, history knowledge, in which the questions should be about items on the syllabus. However, for psychological tests it is generally less useful.

Standardization

Standardization is a concept analogous to calibration. It is the process of ensuring that the measuring instrument accurately corresponds to the appropriate criteria. Thermometers, for example, can be checked against standards of heat such as the boiling point of water. It was realized by Galton that there are no such objective absolutes for most psychological characteristics. New tests of intelligence can only be checked against other measures of 'intelligence', which may be tests, or achievements, or the judgements of other people, and so on.

In standardizing a test we are seeking to establish a scale of measurement (see Chapter 5). Such scales can be more or less informative, and the advance in the development of a test consists in moving from a nominal scale (i.e. classifying) to an ordinal scale (i.e. ranking), to an interval scale (in which items are an equal distance apart). There are also ratio scales which start from an absolute zero, but very few psychological measures are of this kind. Intelligence tests are normally of the interval type.

The process of standardizing involves the administration of numbers of possible test items to large groups of people, who represent the 'standard' population. Some items will prove to be valid and reliable and will be retained; others will not and will be rejected. The process is much more complex than this suggests, for judgements must be made about the actual construction of items, their balance in the test as a whole, avoidance of response bias, etc. The last of these, to give one example, can be readily demonstrated. Ask a group of subjects to imagine they are answering a questionnaire, no matter on what, in which the answer to each item is yes or no. Then ask them to write down their replies to the first three items. On the first item, there will almost invariably be a large majority of yeses.

It must also be noted that no population chosen for standardizing a test can possibly be fully representative of the human race as a whole. The most that is normally practical is a sample representative of one group in one country; and even this is a very long and expensive task. This must be remembered when the test is used, as tests often are, to assess individuals from other groups. The results from tests used in such circumstances may not be useless, but they do involve a further set of judgements and assumptions.

The result of the standardization process is a set of norms for the completed test which takes the form of a distribution of scores given by the standard population. It is generally assumed that psychological variables, and intelligence in particular, will tend to be normally distributed. The

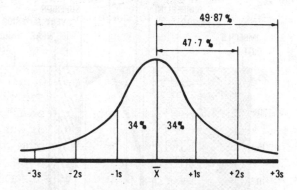

Figure 13.1 The normal distribution. X̄ indicates the mean, or arithmetic average. s indicates a standard deviation. This is a measure of the spread of the data, such that 68% fall within one standard deviation above and one below the mean. These two figures can be used to summarize the results. Thus, if the heights of men were measured, they might be summarized (in inches) as M = 67±3. This would mean that the arithmetic average was 5′ 7″; 68% of men were between 5′ 4″ and 5′ 10″; 95% between 5′ 1″ and 6′ 1″; and so on (after Radford and Kirby)

concept of a normal distribution is derived from statistical probability theory and was initially developed by Gauss (1809).

The assumption relating 'normality' to psychology was first made by Galton, who argued that, as intellectual abilities must have a physical basis, they should follow the normal distribution as other physical traits (such as height) had been shown to do by Quetelet (1835).

In reality, it is found that natural phenomena *tend* to fit the normal (or Gaussian) curve which is a mathematical abstraction. An example of such an approximation is given in Figure 13.2 (although contemporary psychologists would be unwilling to use labels such as 'imbecile' and 'superior').

One particular difficulty with many psychological phenomena is that they cannot be observed directly, like height, but must be inferred from behaviour. The investigator has to decide what is to count as intelligent in order to measure it; and one criterion for the choice is that the items will yield a normal distribution.

Another important aspect of the normal distribution is that it underlies factor analysis, one assumption of which is that the data do in fact conform to this pattern.

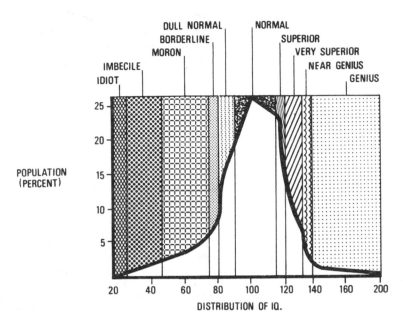

Figure 13.2 Interpretation of intelligence quotients on the Stanford-Binet (after Merrill)

The use of factor analysis in research on intelligence

What is factor analysis?

Factor analysis derives from the concept of correlation (see Chapter 4), the extent to which two variables go together. In studying the structure of human abilities, it is usual to administer a number of tests to a large number of subjects and obtain a score for each test. All these scores can then be intercorrelated, yielding a correlation matrix. An example is shown in Table 13.1.

Table 13.1 Correlation matrix for nine aptitude tests (from Guilford, 1967)

Tests	2	3	4	5	6	7	8	9
1	.38	.55	.06	−.04	.05	.07	.05	.09
2		.36	.40	.28	.40	.11	.15	.13
3			.10	.01	.18	.13	.12	.10
4				.32	.60	.04	.06	.13
5					.35	.08	.13	.11
6						.01	.06	.07
8							.45	.32
								.32

The three outlined clusters of correlations, because of their sizeable correlation coefficients, indicate that these are groups of tests with something in common not shared by the other tests. Factor analysis is a mathematical technique which enables us to make specific this kind of interpretation. The final result of a factor analysis is usually a measure of how much variation in performance on all the tests may be accounted for by one common factor, and of the extent to which additional factors are necessary. It is possible to 'extract' statistically the effect of the factor common to all the variables (the general factor) and still find correlation patterns suggestive of further common influences. The process is repeated until all the remaining correlations are statistically non-significant.

Thus if we factor analyse the correlations of Table 13.1, we first compute the correlation of each test with a few factors. Such correlations between test scores and factors are known as 'factor loadings'; if a test correlates 0.02 on Factor I, 0.16 on Factor II, and 0.83 on Factor III, it is said to be most heavily loaded on Factor III. The correlation matrix of Table 13.1 yields the factor matrix of Table 13.2.

The outline factor loadings show tests which are most highly correlated with each of the factors. The clusters are the same as those in Table 13.1, but, due to the analysis, have a greater accuracy. Test 2, since it is loaded equally on Factors II and III, cannot be a 'factor pure' test.

The factors which have been identified must now be interpreted. This is done by inspecting the contents of the tests which are most heavily weighted on each factor. They may be given a plausible name (such as 'general intelligence') or one made up for the purpose, or just numbered. Thus, while the factor analysis itself is a mathematical process, the interpretation and naming of the factors is a strictly psychological undertaking.

Table 13.2 Factor matrix for nine aptitude tests and three factors (from Guilford, 1967)

Tests	Factors		
	I	II	III
1	.75	−.01	.08
2	.44	.48	.16
3	.72	.07	.15
4	.08	.76	.08
5	−.01	.49	−.01
6	.16	.73	.02
7	−.03	.04	.64
8	.02	.05	.66
9	−.01	.10	.47

Criticisms and comments

While factor analysis is an important and useful mathematical tool which may be gainfully employed by psychologists, it has definite limitations, among which are these:

1. As already indicated, the statistically-produced factors do not emerge conveniently labelled 'general intelligence', 'spatial ability', etc. The interpretation of a statistical factor as a psychological dimension requires careful justification.
2. The method itself can give answers only to the questions it is set about the data presented. The method gives no indication as to what material should be analysed at the start. It cannot give information about abilities for which there is no valid test.
3. The final result of the analysis is not a description of the composition of intelligence, or any other psychological quality. It simply provides a number of mathematically equivalent statements. To fasten upon any of these and form a theory from it involves further assumptions, either mathematical or psychological.
4. There exist alternative methods of factor analysis which yield slightly differing results. There is also some debate about the precision with which the factors are determined. The issues are complex and, as yet, unsettled. As a result of the differing analyses the theoretical interpretation of the test results may differ.

The nature of intelligence

Factorial approach

The use of the statistical technique of factor analysis gave rise to a number of ways of describing the nature of intelligence. These factorial, or psychometric, theories were concerned to identify the components of intelligence, the distinct abilities which form what we call intelligence. A number of theories based on a factorial approach have been presented since the turn of the century.

Spearman and general intelligence, 'g'

Charles Spearman (1863–1945) is generally recognized as both the inventor and first user of factor analysis. He concluded that individual differences in test performance could be accounted for by one general factor, common to all the tests, and a series of specific factors, each peculiar to one task. The general factor he labelled 'g' or general intelligence. This was the origin of the 'two-factor' theory of intelligence, which led to the extremely influential hierarchical model developed by later British workers. Spearman believed he could identify the essential nature of intelligence. This was, in brief, the ability to see relationships: a concept which has been embodied in very many subsequent test items, often of the form 'a is to b as c is to ?'.

Sir Cyril Burt and the hierarchical system

Cyril Burt (1883–1971) was the first British educational psychologist (1912) and remained an influential figure to the end of his life. It now seems certain that in later life, from about 1950, he fabricated data on twin studies to support his views on intelligence. While the falsified empirical support is valueless, the views themselves are still of interest.

One of Burt's major theoretical contributions was the extension of the two-factor notion to a hierarchical model, consistent with Sherrington's work on the organization of the nervous system. As Burt put it: the measurement of any individual for any one of a set of traits may be regarded as a function of four kinds of component: namely, those characteristic of (1) all the traits, (2) some of the traits, (3) the particular trait in question whenever it is measured, (4) the particular trait in question as measured on a particular occasion.

The first of these Burt identified as intelligence or 'innate general cognitive ability'. At the next level, a number of studies show that the most important distinction is between verbal and non-verbal abilities. Figure 13.3 shows how such a hierarchical model might be conceived.

To some extent it is a matter of choice whether one prefers this sort of

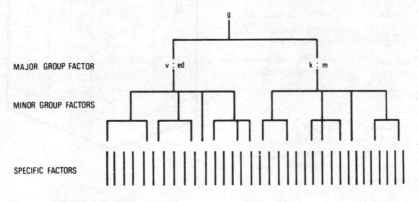

g = GENERAL INTELLIGENCE
v : ed = VERBAL - EDUCATIONAL ABILITY
k : m = SPATIAL - MECHANICAL ABILITY

Figure 13.3 Suggested arrangement of the hierarchical arrangement of intellectual abilities. It should be noted that this is a suggestion. No studies have firmly established that this is a correct model in every detail (after Vernon)

arrangement, or what has been called the more 'democratic' one of several independent factors. L. L. Thurstone (1938), for example, identified seven 'primary mental abilities': spatial ability, perceptual speed, numerical ability, verbal meaning, memory, verbal fluency, and inductive reasoning.

J. P. Guilford and the structure of intellect

The most extreme version of a multi-factor theory so far developed is that of Guilford (1967, 1982). He argued that we must consider three dimensions in analysing intellectual capacities. These are (a) the basic psychological functions involved, e.g. memory, or *operations*; (b) the type of material being processed, e.g. semantic or symbolic, or *products*; and (c) the form that the information takes in the course of being processed, e.g. units or classes, or *contents*. According to Guilford, the number of possible operations is five, of products six, and of contents four. This gives a total of intellectual abilities of $5 \times 6 \times 4 = 120$. This is expressed diagrammatically in Figure 13.4.

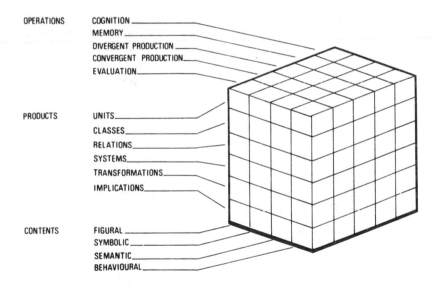

Figure 13.4 Guilford's scheme of ability factors (after Guilford)

Following this theoretical analysis Guilford has carried out extensive investigations to test the reality of the theory, and see how far it describes real-life behaviour, such as solving problems. It appears that there is good evidence for some of the factors or abilities, and less strong evidence for others. Guilford and his co-workers seem a little like astronomers searching for new stars which they know ought to be there but which have not yet been established. It also seems that for practical purposes of predicting what a given person will be able to do in certain circumstances, say at school or university, Guilford's complex of abilities is less useful than the simpler models or indeed just one measure of 'general intelligence'.

R. B. Cattell and crystallized and fluid intelligence

Cattell (1963) proposed a theory of intelligence which presupposes that the general factor found in tests is in actual fact a function of two conceptually distinct, but correlated, factors. These he named crystallized and fluid intelligence. Crystallized intelligence applies where what is required are habits of skilled judgement which have become set through learning and experience. Such skills are of less use in new situations, requiring new or adapted responses. Here fluid intelligence is appropriate. Although Cattell suggests ways of separating these two experimentally, it is not clear whether they are in fact two abilities or merely two modes of working.

Cattell has also argued that intellectual factors cannot really be isolated from personality factors. The establishment of measurable traits of personality is more difficult even than for intelligence, but Cattell has shown correlations between some of these, such as motivation, and others such as achievement, which in turn is related to intellectual abilities.

Information-processing approach

These accounts are all closely linked to the techniques of factor analysis. Some more recent approaches take rather different starting points. Information-processing or cognitive approaches are concerned with an understanding of the mental processes which contribute to intelligence. For example, some studies have examined the speed of information-processing, others have been concerned with strategies and accuracy of solving complex problems. The American psychologist Robert J. Sternberg has formulated an influential information-processing theory of intelligence.

Sternberg's componential model

The starting point for Sternberg's model is the assumption that when faced with a task, say an item on an intelligence test, the individual possesses a set of mental abilities or processes – which Sternberg terms *components* – that work in an organized way to produce the final response to the test item. Sternberg (1984) suggested three mechanisms of 'intelligent functioning'. *Metacomponents* refer to the higher-order processes such as deciding upon the nature of the problem and selecting the best way to advance towards a solution. *Performance components* are those mental processes which actually carry out the selected problem-solving strategy. *Knowledge-acquisition components* are the processes involved in learning new material. Further components have been included: *retention-components* include the processes involved in retrieving information from memory; *transfer components* include those processes employed in generalizing information from one situation to another.

While much of Sternberg's experimental work is concerned with identifying the critical components in solving problems of the type found in intelligence tests, he is also concerned that theories of intelligence should be relevant to the real world. Thus, Sternberg (1985a) argues that a fully comprehensive theory of intelligence should involve a much wider range of components and processes than are found in the rather restricted world of IQ testing. This broader 'practical' or 'social' intelligence might need to attend to issues such as the ability to learn from experience; the ability to think in abstract terms; the ability to adapt and survive in a changing environment; the ability to motivate oneself to complete the tasks life sets. Conventional tests of intelligence tell us something about the first two, but very little about the latter two. This, of course, sets the problem of the usefulness of IQ tests as they are formulated at present. As Sternberg points out of IQ tests: 'Although such tasks are not unheard of in the everyday world, they are not typical of the kinds of things people normally do in their lives'. The question then becomes one of whether performance in real life can be reduced to components as seen in somewhat artificial laboratory tests. Similar arguments for a much broader view of intelligence are made by Frederiksen (1986) and Raaheim (1984).

Gardner's theory of multiple intelligence

Gardner (1983) proposed a fresh way of considering intelligence, an approach which has similarities to factorial and information-processing views, yet contains a number of new ideas. In common with factorial theories, Gardner proposes a number of distinct abilities. These are: 1. linguistic; 2. logical-mathematical; 3. spatial; 4. musical; 5. bodily-kinesthetic; 6. personal.

Unlike factorial theorists such as Spearman and Burt, Gardner suggests that these six abilities are not part of a general intelligence, but rather *are* intelligences themselves. Thus Gardner argues that these six intelligences are independent of each other, each functioning in its own individual manner, according to its own rules, in its own system.

The first three intelligences are commonplace, as measured in standard IQ tests. The latter three are seldom seen as even part of intelligence, so their elevation by Gardner to the status of an independent intelligence, rather than part of a general intelligence, is a radical departure from convention. Musical intelligence, Gardner argues, consists of the ability to perceive pitch and rhythm and is the basis of musical ability. Bodily-kinesthetic intelligence concerns control over one's body, such as found in gymnasts and mime-artists; and control over instruments, such as in cricketers and engineers who are able to use objects – bats, balls, tools, etc. – with extreme finesse. Personal intelligence can be divided into *intra*-personal and *inter*personal components. The former is concerned with self-perception and self-monitoring one's own thoughts and emotions, and the ability to use this information to guide one's actions. The latter, inter-personal intelligence, is sensitivity to other people, including the ability to discriminate accurately the moods, intentions, and behaviours of others, and to use this information to behave appropriately.

If Gardner's theory departs from factorial theory, the same is also true with regard to cognitive theories. In keeping with mainstream cognitive opinion, Gardner is concerned to discuss the way in which the intelligences function both in terms of the cognitive operations involved and the role of physiological processes. Where Gardner departs from the mainstream, as with factorial theories, is in his suggestion that the intelligences operate as modular systems, without needing a 'central control' to co-ordinate and guide operations. The implication of this view is that while the intelli-gences may interact, one might have high levels of one and low levels of another. Localized brain damage might impair one intelligence, leaving the others intact. Occasionally, severely retarded individuals are very good at one particular, if limited, ability, such as drawing or playing an instrument.

Gardner also suggests that while heredity and learning will influence the level of each intelligence, the effects of the culture cannot be ignored. This may determine which intelligences are valued most and the use to which abilities are put. The broader conceptualization of intelligence advanced by Gardner may help to explain why, for example, academically able individuals sometimes struggle to achieve; and, alternatively, why it is not always the 'brightest' pupils and students who advance furthest in their chosen field.

As Sternberg has pointed out, and as illustrated by Gardner's theory, the factorial and information-processing theories are not incompatible. The former attempts to identify the clusters of intellectual abilities which exist; the latter seeks to explore the working of the abilities themselves.

H. J. Eysenck and biological intelligence

Eysenck (1986) argues that approaches to intelligence can be classified into biological, psychometric, and social. Or rather, that there are three meanings of 'intelligence'. Sternberg, for example, is concerned, according to Eysenck, with social intelligence. Sternberg defines intelligence as 'mental activity directed towards purposive adaptation to, and selection and shaping of, real-world environments relevant to one's life' (Sternberg, 1985a). But this sort of definition, Eysenck holds, is far too loose and general for scientific study. The psychometric approach of Spearman, Thurstone, Cattell and others has been much more useful but still gives rise to difficulties. What is needed is a biological approach, in other words an attempt to discover what physical characteristics underlie intelligent behaviour. This was originally Galton's approach. He thought, for example, that more intelligent people would have a faster-working nervous system, which could be measured by, say, reaction times. He was not able to demonstrate this, but Eysenck now presents evidence that it is indeed so; he reports correlations of more than 0.60 between short RT tasks and standard intelligence tests. Even higher correlations, up to 0.80, have been found using another physiological measure, evoked potentials. Eysenck argues that speed of information processing is a fundamental property of biological intelligence; so that this approach will enable us at last to have a truly 'scientific' theory of intelligence.

The origins of intelligence

Much of the debate over the origins of intelligence has centred on the issue as to whether it is a product of the environment or inherited. Practically every possible position has been proposed and attacked, and the issue has at times been utterly confused by misunderstandings, ignorance, and political arguments. While psychologists must be aware of such factors, and of the social and moral effects of their work, they must also distinguish the various scientific issues, and acknowledge their importance.

While the term 'hereditary' usually implies resemblances between parents and offspring, there are also systematic lacks of resemblances which give information as to the workings of heredity. We must distinguish between the phenotype and the genotype: that is, the characteristics which an individual manifests, and the genetic characteristics which an individual inherits but may or may not exhibit. The hereditary units that an individual receives from his or her parents are carried by chromosomes which are structures found within every cell of the body. A chromosome is composed of many individual determinants of heredity called genes. These are large molecules of deoxyribonucleic acid or DNA. Genes occur in pairs, one of each pair coming from the sperm (male) chromosomes, and the other from the ovum (female) chromosomes. There are 46 chromosomes per body cell and approximately 1,000 genes per chromosome; hence, it is extremely unlikely that, by chance, any two human beings would have the same heredity. Exceptions to this occur in multiple births. Only twins are sufficiently frequent to give study populations which yield reliable psychological results. However, of the two types of twin-pair, only *monozygotic*

(MZ) twins share the same heredity. In the case of *dizygotic (DZ) twins*, two separate ova are fertilized at the same time (by two sperms): the resulting twins are genetically no more alike than any pair of siblings (brothers and sisters).

It is best to regard as 'nature' only the genetic constitution of the individual, a particular combination of genes determined at the moment of fertilization. All other influences from that point on should be regarded as 'nurture' or environment. Thus both prenatal and postnatal conditions are 'environmental'. Now it is known that a given environmental factor can interact differently with different specific genetic material. For example, a rise in temperature affects the number of eye facets in the fruit fly *Drosophila*; yet identical changes in temperature have different effects upon flies having different gene constitutions. Further, every individual member of a species has a slightly different environment; even identical twins are born one after the other. It is a fundamental characteristic of living things, which becomes more important the more complex the organism is, that they interact only with some aspects of the environment. Animals, and above all humans, select from their environment.

Thus, apart from having a unique genetic constitution, each member of the species has a unique environment; and each developed individual is the product of the interaction between the two. This interaction effect led D. O. Hebb (1949) to postulate two types of intelligence, which he named Intelligence A and Intelligence B. These correspond to genotype and phenotype: A is an innate potential, the capacity of the brain for development; B is the ability of the developed brain. While neither can be directly observed, Hebb claimed that B is '... a much more direct inference from behaviour than Intelligence A, the innate potential'.

There would probably be general agreement that it is meaningless to regard any psychological characteristic as the result of either heredity or environment alone. However, it is possible to investigate empirically the relative contributions of each set of influences. Anastasi (1958) lists five main methods: selective breeding; normative development studies; structural factors in behavioural development; the effects of prior experience upon behaviour; and studies of family resemblances, of which twin studies are a special case. As far as intelligence is concerned, it is the last method that has received the greatest attention.

Studies of family resemblances

Evidence for the inheritance of intelligence comes from the numerous findings that the closer the family, that is the genetic relationship, the higher the degree of similarity on a range of psychological characteristics, and certainly on intelligence. Bouchard and McGue (1981) collated all the published reports that conformed to strict methodological criteria, of which there were 111, and summarized them as shown in Figure 13.5.

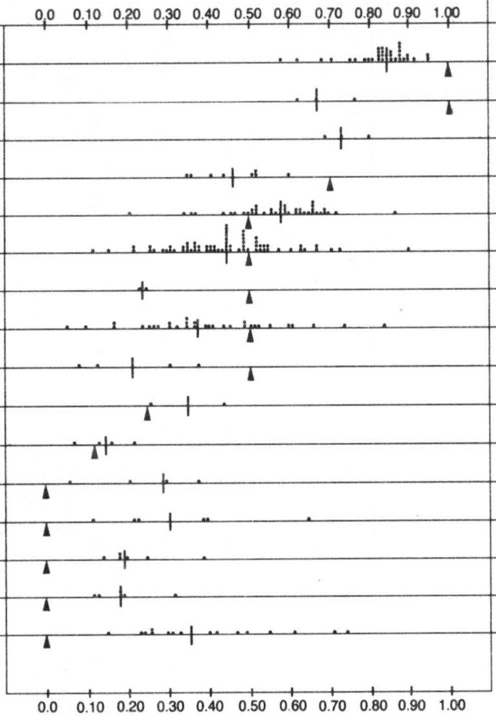

	0.0 0.10 0.20 0.30 0.40 0.50 0.60 0.70 0.80 0.90 1.00	No. of correl- ations	No. of pairings	Median correl- ation	Weight- ed aver age	χ² (d.f.)	χ² ÷ d.f.
Monozygotic twins reared together		34	4,672	.85	.86	81.29 (33)	2.46
Monozygotic twins reared apart		3	65	.67	.72	0.92 (2)	0.46
Midparent-midoffspring reared together		3	410	.73	.72	2.66 (2)	1.33
Midparent-offspring reared together		8	992	.475	.50	8.11 (7)	1.16
Dizygotic twins reared together		41	5,546	.58	.60	94.5 (40)	2.36
Siblings reared together		69	26,473	.45	.47	403.6 (64)	6.31
Siblings reared apart		2	203	.24	.24	.02 (1)	.02
Single parent-offspring reared together		32	8,433	.385	.42	211.0 (31)	6.81
Single parent-offspring reared apart		4	814	.22	.22	9.61 (3)	3.20
Half-siblings		2	200	.35	.31	1.55 (1)	1.55
Cousins		4	1,176	.145	.15	1.02 (2)	0.51
Non-biological sibling pairs (adopted/natural pairings)		5	345	.29	.29	1.93 (4)	0.48
Non-biological sibling pairs (adopted-adopted pairings)		6	369	.31	.34	10.5 (5)	2.10
Adopting midparent-offspring		6	758	.19	.24	6.8 (5)	1.36
Adopting parent-offspring		6	1,397	.18	.19	6.64 (5)	1.33
Assortative mating		16	3,817	.365	.33	96.1 (15)	6.41

| 0.0 0.10 0.20 0.30 0.40 0.50 0.60 0.70 0.80 0.90 1.00 |

Figure 13.5 Familial correlation for IQ. The vertical bar in each distribution indicates the median correlation; the arrow, the correlation predicted by a simple polygenic model. (From Bouchard and McGue, Familial studies of intelligence: a review. *Science*, 1981, 212, 1055—8.)

These results show clearly that correlations rise with increasing closeness of relationship. They also show, of course, that correlations rise with similarity of environment. Even unrelated persons reared together show correlations of up to 0.4.

It was Galton who suggested the study of twins in particular to disentangle the effects of heredity and environment. As he pointed out, the advantage is that at least one side of the equation is under control, since monozygotic twins have theoretically identical genetic constitutions. For example, in the Louisville Twin Study (Wilson, 1979), 374 pairs of twins were followed longitudinally from three months to six years of age. The monozygotic twins correlated about 0.8 for intelligence, compared with about 0.45 for both dizygotic twins and ordinary siblings. These were all cases of children who were reared together. Further, as they got older, the monozygotes tended to become more alike, the dizygotes less so. Further reports of this group (Wilson, 1986) give similar results.

A number of criticisms can be made of twin studies. There are technical statistical arguments, which however would probably not affect the results very dramatically. There are also objections to the use of twin studies as such. Vandenberg (1966) distinguishes four main arguments. First, there is no way of controlling the genetic variability between groups of twins. One sample of twins may include inherited tendencies towards certain sorts of behaviour which are not typical of twins in general. A related point that Vandenberg might have made is that twins themselves are not necessarily typical of the general population; there is known to be a 'twinning factor', such that certain families tend to produce DZ twins (Herman, 1984). Second, when MZ and DZ twins are compared, it is generally assumed that the environment is held constant, but this is not necessarily so; MZ twins may create for themselves more similar environments. However, Vandenberg (1984), in a further discussion, concludes that characteristics of twins do not in fact cause greater similarity but are the result of prior similarity. Third, the twin method deals only with variance within families, which is part of the total variance; no account is taken of variance between families. Lastly, many early studies suffered from errors in identifying identical twins, which is a much more technical matter than might appear. This does not really constitute a problem now, but evidence has been found that even so-called 'identical' twins are not necessarily identical, due to the allocation of genetic material that occurs at the splitting of the fertilized egg.

These are all important points, but it is unlikely that they affect the general results very greatly. On the whole, errors in one direction will be balanced by those in the opposite direction.

It is less easy to see just what we can conclude. It seems clear that both genetic and environmental factors must be involved; and it is also self-evident that, within any population selected at random, there is a wide variation in intellectual capacity. The argument turns on attributing values to sources of variation within populations. It should be noted that it is not possible even in principle to say, in the case of any individual, how much of his or her intelligence (or any other trait) is inherited or otherwise, since it is impossible to partition the variance in a sample of one. Further, even when the variance can be partitioned, it is not justifiable to conclude that there are fixed environmental or hereditary components of intelligence; intelligence is not a product like a car with engine made in one plant and bodywork in another.

Thus it is rather misleading to speak of intelligence being x per cent inherited, as for example did Burt (1966). Using a statistical method of partitioning the variance he concluded that intelligence is 80 per cent inherited and 20 per cent environmental. In fact, all that can be inherited is a potential, and we do not yet know how this reacts with environmental factors to produce behaviour that can be labelled 'intelligent'. Some of the complexity is shown in studies of race and environment.

Race, culture, and class

Race

In everyday use the word 'race' most often refers to some discriminable group to which the speaker can identify him or herself as belonging or not belonging. Just what constitutes a separate race of human beings is often not clearly defined. The so-called 'Aryan race' which Hitler's National Socialists sought to preserve was defined by a confused collection of cultural, physical, and supposed historical factors and was, in fact, nonsense.

The clearest, although still quite complex, way to consider race is biologically. In particular, it seems best to start with the definition that a race is a reproductive community sharing a common gene pool. This definition applies to the human population as a whole: thus, different 'races' are sub-groups and all the sub-groups overlap to a greater or lesser extent. For example. Eysenck (1971) reports that estimates suggest an admixture of about 25.30 per cent white genes in present-day Negroes in the USA. The overlapping is caused partly by the common origin of groups which have subsequently separated, and partly by interbreeding. And overall, the common genetic inheritance of the human species far outweighs the differences between sub-groups.

Early attempts to distinguish races depended upon obviously observable characteristics. For example Blumenbach (1775) proposed a classification based on skin colour. This is both invalid and unreliable. Modern methods make use of advances in serological genetics, which permits accurate identification of specific genes from the chemical reactions of the components of human blood. As the number of blood genes identified increases, so it becomes necessary to increase the number of recognized races. Morphological, that is bodily, characteristics can also be used, and Dobzhansky (1962) has proposed a system involving as many as 34 different characteristics. Some studies (e.g. Pollitzer, 1958) use both morphological and serological methods in attempting to classify subjects according to race.

Taking the definition of a common gene pool, it is widely accepted (e.g. Garn, 1961) that three types of genetic populations can be distinguished. These can be termed geographical, local, and micro-geographical or minor races. The largest unit is a population confined within a broad geographical area, such as Australian, European, Asiatic. Another example is the native population of the Americas, the Amerindians, who share, among other characteristics, a low incidence of the genes for Type B blood. The separate American peoples within the Amerindian group, such as Navahos or Guarani, are examples of 'local' races. Other examples from elsewhere are Basques, Gypsies, Bantu: such groups are often separated from others by physical and/or social barriers. The smallest groups it is generally useful to distinguish are, as Gottesman (1963) calls them, 'significant pockets of variation'. He reports, for example, distinct micro-races, differing by blood-group genes, in Wales.

Thus, it is certainly possible to distinguish between races on purely biological grounds, without considering cultural factors. As has been pointed out, the races so distinguished do overlap considerably; and where the lines are drawn depends upon decisions as to the degree of difference that is important. The questions that arise for psychologists concern the possibility of behavioural differences between the races that are distinguished. There is evidence for differences in, for example, sensory-motor and perceptual abilities; but here we are concerned with intellectual abilities. As it happens, it is this question that has aroused the greatest controversy. The most hotly-debated issue has concerned the Negro populaton of the United States, and it is on this that the greatest amount of research has been done. This issue illustrates some of the general problems.

Shuey (1966) comprehensively reviewed some hundreds of studies comparing intelligence test scores of white and Negro children. She found that these studies, with very small variance, showed that groups of white children had a mean IQ some fifteen points, or one standard deviation, higher than Negro groups. It has also been generally found that, among Negroes, females tend to score higher than males. Jensen (1969) gives an average of three or four IQ points difference. These findings are shown in Figure 13.6.

A wealth of criticism has been directed at these and similar investigations. It has been suggested, for example, that groups of Negroes and whites are not comparable for various demographic reasons. Shuey (1966),

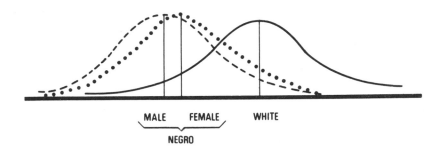

MALE   FEMALE   WHITE

NEGRO

Figure 13.6 Diagrammatic distribution of intelligence quotients of whites, and Negro males and females (from Eysenck)

however, quotes a study in which two groups were matched on age, education, occupation of parents, geographical areas of childhood home, army rank, number of years in the service, marital status, urban or rural background, personality, and attitudes to test-taking. A difference of nearly one standard deviation still emerged. Again, it is suggested that Negroes are at a disadvantage when the tester is white. Shuey gives the results of nineteen studies in which Negro children were tested by Negroes. There was no difference as compared with similar investigations using white testers.

In general, it appears that the difference is a consistent one, and not due to accident or error. It is more difficult to say what can be concluded from this. Shuey argued that there must be a strong genetic component to intelligence; and Jensen (1969) and Eysenck (1971) agree. Shuey found, for example, that the differences were greater on abstract tests items, which are seen as relatively environment free as compared to verbal items. Further, genetically hybrid groups of subjects score closer to the white than do the purer Negro groups. It also appears that southern Negroes are inferior to northern on IQ; and that those who migrate to the North gain in IQ. It could well be, of course, that these groups are also genetically different. Indeed this is possibly an example of different genetic constitutions interacting differently with different environments.

Jensen (1969) has further argued that Negro and white children should be given different styles of education, fitted to their different modes of intellectual functioning. This is far more contentious, since we do not know what sorts of education are best suited to different ways of thinking, even if these were established.

It must also be remembered that the difference is only an average one: even on the standard tests, very many individual Negroes score above the white average.

However, perhaps the crux of the argument is that as has already been explained, any test of intelligence is only a selection from the extremely wide range of intellectual skills that human beings can display. This sample is, in general, correlated with success in the society in which the test was constructed. We cannot infer from test scores anything about superiority in general; nor can we conclude that groups who score below the average of the standardizing population are necessarily less competent generally. This is because competence is defined by the environment, not by tests. As Cole and Bruner (1971) put it: 'The problem is to identify the range of capacities readily manifested in different groups and then to enquire whether the range is adequate to the individual's needs in various cultural settings'.

Although the greatest amount of attention has been paid to the Negro–white issue, there is some evidence from other groups. For example, Lesser *et al* (1965) compared six- and seven-year-old children of Chinese, Jewish, Negro, and Puerto Rican communities in New York City, in respect of their verbal reasoning, numerical, and spatial abilities. Distinctively different patterns appeared, which were quite consistent across social classes within the communities. The Jewish group, for example, excelled at verbal ability, the Chinese at spatial (the full results are given by Butcher, 1968).

In an important series of studies Vernon (1965) compared West Indian, Canadian, American Indian, Eskimo, and Scottish children. A complex pattern emerges. It is clear that groups from a poor cultural and socio-economic background, with little education and unstable home life, do less well on tests, particularly in practical-spatial and some abstract non-verbal abilities. The main lesson from this is the difficulty of disentangling test performances from actual attainments, either educational or practical, and sorting out the complicated interaction of causes.

Another example of this is the rise, over a period of 50 years (1932–82), in average national intelligence in several countries, in particular Britain, Japan, and the USA, reported by Lynn and Hampson (1986). It was thought at one time that because there is a negative association between intelligence and family size, the less intelligent must have a higher rate of reproduction, so that this must lead to a decline in average intelligence. Lynn and Hampson summarize studies showing, on the contrary, average rises per decade of 1.71 IQ points in Britain; 7.70 in Japan; and 3.0 in the USA. The Japanese rate however is slowing down. Lynn and Hampson suggest the main reasons are improvements in health and nutrition, and greater stimulation from TV, games, books, and from parents with more leisure and smaller families. There may be some genetic factors such as different patterns of marriage in these three countries. But we do not know how varying genetic endowments interact with different, and changing, environments.

Culture

In the investigations just mentioned the groups are distinguished by both racial and cultural factors. The latter are even harder to define exactly. Broadly, 'culture' refers to the humanly-created environment in which each individual lives. Culture does not include the physical environment, but it does include the uses to which the environment is put. Similarly, culture does not include genetically determined characteristics, such as skin colour, but it does include the behaviour that may be occasioned by members of a group sharing a particular colour. Cultural groups, even more than racial ones, overlap and intermingle. There are now probably no groups remaining anywhere in the world which are not in some measure affected by western culture.

Nevertheless, it is possible to distinguish culturally different groups on the basis of observed differences in basic human practices such as child-rearing, marriage, tool-making, food-getting, religion, and so forth.

There is evidence that between such groups there are also more strictly psychological differences. For example Gregory (1966) reports that Zulus are less susceptible to the Muller–Lyer illusion (see Chapter 10) than are Europeans. This is a relatively trivial, but at least measurable, effect due, Gregory argues, to the 'uncarpentered' environment in which Zulus traditionally live.

The question of intellectual differences is much more complex. Some of the reasons have already been discussed, but there are further problems. It must be first noted that when any test of intelligence is given to members of a group, what is being measured is only a sample of Hebb's Intelligence B. Vernon (1969) called this sample 'Intelligence C'. Any cross-cultural comparisons made, are made between Intelligence C samples, which may or may not be valid and reliable.

Further, it must be stressed again that any test of intelligence derives its validity, ultimately, from comparisons with other assessments of behaviour, which are themselves cultural matters. No attempt has, so far, been made to establish psychometric tests which would be universally valid. Indeed it may be impossible to do so, since human behaviour and culture never stand still but are continuously evolving. It is true that there are some theories of intelligence, such as those of Spearman, Piaget, and Eysenck, which might claim such validity but their claims have not been systematically tested. There is some evidence that cross-cultural comparisons can be made using Piaget's stages of cognitive development, but even here it is difficult to be sure just what a particular result means. For example Laurendeau and Pinard (1962) reported a large scale experiment which showed that measures of Piaget's stages could be established in a different population from Piaget's; in this case, children in Montreal.

However, it is quite a complex and even subjective matter to assess Piagetian stages (see Chapter 16).

Thirdly, the very activity of assessing intellectual functions is one which is strange to many cultural groups. Irvine (1966) points out that the learning task involved in jut becoming familiar with and understanding the concept of multiple-choice items is quite formidable for most Africans. He lists six sources of unwanted variance in test scores. Irvine was particularly concerned with African groups, but the problems are more general.

1. The content of the test itself.
2. The form and style of the test.
3. The transfer which takes place between practice items and actual test items, especially when the material is unfamiliar.
4. The particular educational or cultural bias of the test items.
5. The motivational influence of strange (other culture) testers who are likely to be European.
6. Error variance.

It may be pointed out that the only way to equate cultures absolutely would be to make them identical, in which case the possibility of cross-cultural comparisons would cease to exist.

Nevertheless, even given all the difficulties, and the inadequacies of measuring instruments, it is possible to establish some of the factors that definitely do affect the level of test scores in a given population, remembering that it is Vernon's Intelligence C that is in question. Vernon (1965) lists eight such factors.

1. Physiological and nutritional deficit.
2. Perceptual deprivation in pre-school years.
3. Repression of independence and constructive play.
4. Family insecurity.
5. Female dominance (this may favour verbal as compared to spatial abilities).
6. Defective education.
7. Linguistic handicaps.
8. Adult roles and adolescent aspirations (in minority cultures children may be affected by a gradual realization of their depressed status, lack of opportunities, etc.).

Although these are all clearly-identified factors, it must still be remembered that they constitute handicaps only in relation to some standard. It is relatively easy to say what is the standard of nutrition required for normal development, but much harder for a psychological variable such as male or female dominance, which in any case varies widely even within a culture. It is very likely that individual children are differently affected by even the 'same' amount of dominance, for example.

Despite all these problems, it is possible to explore more and more systematically the modes of thinking characteristic of different cultures. Several of the leaders in this work are or have been based at Harvard University, such as psychologist Jerome Bruner, and anthropologists, such as Michael Cole.

Cole, Gay, Glick, and Sharp reported a series of studies of the Kpelle people of Liberia in *The Cultural Context of Learning and Thinking* (1971). As well as general observations of cultural practices, they used various experimental techniques to examine such abilities as logical reasoning and conceptual thinking. Among their major conclusions was that the differences in thought processes between different cultural groups lie not so much in the processes themselves, as in the situations to which they are applied. The Kpelle subjects, for example, were quite able to reason logically, but were more accustomed to do so in social situations. Abstract problems (such as most intelligence tests include) were new to them.

Cole *et al* think it significant that the Kpelle equivalent for 'clever' was not applied to such activities as rice farming or car repairing but to skill in social relationships. A farmer might be thought lazy or hard working, but not 'clever'. Similarly, they found subjects could, for example, clearly explain how children should be raised, but not the principles of good house-building (even though they could, in practical terms, do both).

Similar studies, for example by Irvine (1969) and Wober (1972) and Super (1983), show that different cultures group abilities in varying ways. Super concluded that the Kipsigis' (of Kenya) notion of 'intelligence' is 'a highly verbal cognitive quickness ... a skill particularly valuable for politicians, teachers, market traders and social mediators ... the ability quickly to comprehend complex matters, and to use that comprehension in verbal interaction and the management of interpersonal relations'.

Despite such variations, Berry (1984) and others think it will eventually be possible to establish 'universals' of cognitive competence, in the same way that we recognize biological, linguistic and cultural universals which are common to all human groups.

Class

The human environment is both social and physical, and here we can mention only some of the many aspects that may be important.

Like the previous two ways of distinguishing groups (race and culture) social class is not easy to define. Perhaps the simplest criterion is an economic one, since it is an objective fact that some families have higher incomes than others. This, however, gives us a division which does not exactly match what most people mean by 'social class'. It might be argued, for example, that (say) a school teacher in a country town, a university graduate, is more likely to correspond with what most people mean by 'middle class' than a 'working class' factory worker who may have a higher income. In considering studies of class, therefore, it is desirable to know what criteria are being used; income, occupation, education, style of life, or others.

One of the largest and most famous studies relevant here, however, did not start from a definition of social class. This began in September 1921 when L. M. Terman and his co-workers selected from the state schools in California the 1,500 most gifted children aged 3–12: approximately the top 1 per cent on standard intelligence tests. A great deal of other information was also gathered about these children, and the group has been re-examined at intervals over the subsequent years.

About a third of the group came from the homes of professional people, and a half from those in the higher ranks of business. Fewer than 7 per cent came from families of semi-skilled or unskilled workers. A second very conclusive finding was that the more intelligent individuals, in general, excelled in almost every other respect: they were, rather naturally, more advanced in school work; but they were also taller, fitter, better adjusted socially, and more likely to be leaders in group activities. As the group made its way through life, these advantages were, on the whole, maintained. The large majority retained or improved their social status, many becoming distinguished in particular fields.

It will be obvious that this work does not show why high IQ scores are linked to social class; and it is most likely that parents in the middle and upper classes not only transmit through heredity some of their own ability, but also provide more intellectually stimulating home environments for their children.

The complex way in which the different variables interact has been shown in many other studies. For example Teasdale and Owen (1986) studied a sample of 241 18–26-year-old young men in Denmark who had been adopted. They took measures of social class, intelligence, and educational attainment. The highest correlation was between educational level and the social class of the adoptive fathers (0.36); the correlation with social class of the biological fathers was only 0.17. Intelligence correlated with social class about 0.2 in both cases. All these correlations are low, although significant.

More generally in studies of fostered or adopted children there is usually a higher correlation between the intelligence of the children and that of their biological than their adoptive parents, indicating a genetic contribution (Loehlin, 1980). On the other hand fostering homes tend to be 'better' than the natural homes, which includes some class factors, and there is evidence that placing children in such homes does raise intelligence scores; for example the classic study of Skeels (1966), in which a mean IQ of 64 of deprived orphanage children at nineteen months rose, after adoption, to 96 at six years.

'Better' environments undoubtedly involve very numerous factors, from food and clothing to intellectual stimulation; and the factors interact in ways that are exceedingly hard to disentangle. One example of this, in which there has been much recent interest, is the possible effects of lead in the atmosphere. Lead in high doses is certainly toxic and can have severe effects on the central nervous system. In the modern environment some lead is likely to be absorbed from the air, particularly from car exhaust fumes. Many studies have suggested that this is associated with lower intelligence test scores in children. Marlowe (1985), reviewing the literature, concludes that the issue 'no longer needs or deserved prolonged debate. Protective social action on lead would benefit the future of all children.' David (1984) summarizes evidence that lead can be harmful even at considerably lower levels than those previously used as a definition for lead poisoning. He also points out one of the main problems in establishing such effects, namely that of biological variability: in other words not all children may react alike. A given dosage might be harmful to some children yet not show up very strongly in overall statistics.

Such conclusions might well seem enough to cause legislators to insist on lead-free petrol, as is indeed the case in many countries. From a scientific point of view, however, it is not so simple. Smith (1985), reviewing the same research, discusses such methodological issues as sample selection, outcome indicators, and the fact that exposure to lead is related to socioeconomic level. Socially disadvantaged children are more likely to have higher levels of lead; and she concludes that when these factors are controlled it appears that it is the social disadvantages, rather than the lead itself, which produce any deficit in measured intelligence. Harvey (1984) agrees. Winneke and Kraemer (1984) report studies of children in 22 German cities. They found lead-related deficits of visual-motor integration and of reaction performance but not of general intelligence; and all the lead effects were very small compared with those of social background.

Such research cannot justify any complacency about possibly harmful man-made changes in the environment, but it does show something of the complexities still to be unravelled. Svancara (1984), reviewing American and European studies, concludes that to understand and interpret human development, information on historical, physical, biological, psycho-physiological, socioeconomic, cultural and other changes must be considered; and we are yet far from being able to say how all these various factors interact. This certainly applies to intelligence.

Further reading

Butcher, H. J. (1968) *Human Intelligence: Its nature and assessment*. Methuen.

Gardner, H. (1983) *Frames of Mind: The theory of multiple intelligences*. Paladin.

Kirby, R., and Radford, J. (1976) *Individual Differences*. Methuen.

Sternberg, R. J. (1985) *Beyond IQ: A triarchic theory of human intelligence*. Cambridge University Press.

Storfer, M. D. (1990) *Intelligence and Giftedness: The contributions of heredity and early environment*. Jossey-Bass.

Tyler, L. E. (1963) *Tests and Measurement*. Prentice-Hall.

Vernon, P. E. (1979) *Intelligence: Heredity and environment*. Freeman.

Chapter fourteen

Thinking

Andrew Burton and John Radford

Definitions and basic concepts

The task of understanding the process of thinking is one of the most important challenges for psychology since, in some form, thinking would seem to be an ingredient of all but the simplest of human activities. Such generality produces problems of definition, however, since a very wide range of mental activities could reasonably be given as examples of thinking, e.g. planning, reasoning, imagining, making decisions and judgements, and so on. One possibility is that there are different types of thought process which operate under different circumstances and are more or less independent of one another. Another possibility is that there are common threads or core features which all, or at least the majority of, the various different forms possess.

To begin with, thinking seems to involve more than simply reproducing our existing knowledge. Being a good thinker is not the same as having a good memory. Though it may well involve the use of stored information, thought is not merely a process of memory since it involves processes of *interpretation* and *inference* by which one goes, in some sense, beyond the knowledge. In fact, the Gestalt psychologists distinguished reproductive thinking, the process of reiterating a previously successful response to a problem, from productive thinking, where insight into a new rule or principle has occurred.

A second feature of thinking is that it is often a *goal directed* activity. We tend to associate the use of thinking with situations where no response is readily available, i.e. where we are faced with a problem and need to attain various goals in order to solve it.

Third, thinking appears to be an activity which occurs in *stages* and is *controlled* by strategies or plans selected according to the perceived goals.

These criteria are very broad and may often be difficult to apply in practice. For example, much thinking would seem to involve both reproductive and productive elements, the goals of thinking may be only vaguely defined and thinking can (occasionally!) occur so quickly it may be quite impossible to distinguish different stages. It is not possible, therefore, to use the criteria to draw a neat dividing line between the territory belonging to thinking and to other cognitive processes. This, of course, is very much in keeping with the current climate of opinion in cognitive psychology in which all cognitive processes are seen as based upon a highly interactive system of information processing components.

The study of thinking

Thought processes have been studied from very many different theoretical points of view, and one reason for the difficulty of integrating all the various results is that investigators have been asking quite different sorts of questions. Often they have used different methods. Here are some of the main orientations.

Behaviourist

In its early, rather dogmatic version, the behaviourist approach assumed that thinking, since it goes on inside the head and thus cannot be observed, was not something that could be studied at all. J. B. Watson did allow the study of the supposed very small movements of the mouth and larynx which he believed went on when someone was said to be thinking, and which, he argued, actually were thinking. This was the 'motor theory', now probably only of historical interest.

Later behaviourists also tried to bring thinking within the fold by considering it as something that can be observed, but in a more sophisticated way. Bourne, Ekstrand and Dominowski (1971), for example, rejected the definition of thinking as an internal process controlling behaviour. Rather, the phrase 'she is thinking' describes a person doing something. To specify what this is, four aspects must be considered: knowledge, skill, intention and performance. Each of these can be observed and measured, and thus studied objectively. It will be seen that even now when the main fashion in psychology has moved from behaviourist to cognitive, much of the experimental work still follows this plan.

Psychometric

The measurement of intellectual abilities might seem to be closely linked to thinking. In practice, however, they have often been carried on quite separately and for different purposes. Some of the theories described in Chapter 13, in particular those of Gardner, Guilford, and Sternberg, try to encompass a wider range of the factors involved in thinking in different situations than did the older concept of one main sort of intelligence – 'g'.

Psychoanalytic

Freud theorized that thinking originates in the fact that human infants cannot, by themselves, immediately get what they need to survive, such as food and warmth. The need is accompanied by a memory or image of what is wanted; but some way is required to distinguish between the image and the reality, and then to control movements and expression (ultimately, language) in order to obtain what is wanted. Freud also distinguished between two modes of thinking, the primary and secondary processes. The latter include the (fairly) rational, conscious thought we are usually aware of; the former follow other, non-logical principles and are generally unconscious. Freud was far from the first to point out that we are not aware of all our thought processes. His revolutionary innovation was to see that thought processes that are not conscious and rational must develop first, both in the species and in the individual. Conscious, rational thought emerges later in favourable circumstances; and it can easily be disrupted by the primary processes. On the other hand these processes seem to play a useful role in more creative or artistic aspects of thinking.

Gestalt

The Gestalt psychologists, reacting against the analytic approach of Wundt, argued that the mind works with wholes (or 'gestalts'), not units; we hear a tune, not a succession of notes. They were primarily interested in perceptual processes, but the principle can be extended to thinking, particularly to problem solving. This would involve seeing a total situation and then mentally restructuring it so that it is seen in a new way, a process they termed 'insight'. An example is Kohler's famous ape, Sultan, 'seeing' that two poles could be put together to make a longer one – long enough to reach a banana. Apart from the difficulty in specifying just what is to count as insight, one main criticism is that problem solving seems to depend much more on practice and learning than the Gestalt psychologists suggested.

Piagetian

Piaget's theories are described in Chapter 16. They have not been universally supported but, rather as with Freud, many of the underlying concepts have been widely influential. Among these are, that thought develops through interaction between the organism and the environment; that there are qualitative differences between processes at different ages; that development involves a sequence of stages; and that internal representation of the world is not exact, but rather a kind of model.

Vygotsky and the troika

Lev Semenovitch Vygotsky (1896–1934) was an exact contemporary of Piaget who, like him, came to psychology from a different area. Piaget trained as a biologist, Vygotsky began in literature and the theatre. In contrast to Piaget's very long productive career, Vygotsky did only ten years of psychological work before his premature death. But he inspired other Russian psychologists, by many of whom he was regarded as a unique genius. His two outstanding followers are A. R. Luria (1902–79) and A. N. Leontyev (1904–79). The three are sometimes known as the 'troika', which is or was a carriage unusual in that a centre horse trotted between shafts while two outside horses galloped – and perhaps not quite such a good image given the furious pace of Vygotsky's work and ideas.

These developed in the revolutionary fervour of post-1917 Russia, and were part of the attempt to create a new society and new sciences consistent with Marxist doctrine. Vygotsky sought to develop a Marxist psychology, and at the same time devise ways of dealing with practical problems such as those of education. Three themes form the core of his theoretical approach (Wertsch, 1985b): reliance on a genetic or developmental method; the claim that higher mental functions have their origin in social processes; and the claim that they can be understood only by analysis of the tools and signs that mediate them, specifically language. As so often happens, revolutionary ferment was followed by a period of repression and stagnation. Stalin ordained that all psychology was to be based on Pavlov; and only from about 1960 have Vygotsky's ideas re-emerged in what has become known as the cultural history school. Luria worked on (among other things) the emergence of consciousness and higher mental processes – thinking – through language, that is effectively through culture and education; Leontyev developed a theory of the evolution of the mind in stages: sensory, perceptual and intellectual, which are the results of biological evolution, and then a further stage of human consciousness which depends on cultural historical evolution (Madsen, 1988).

Instrumental conceptualism

This phrase is not now much seen but refers to the work of J. S. Bruner and others, which likewise has influenced the general direction in which the study of thinking, indeed psychology as a whole, has developed. *A Study of Thinking* by Bruner, Goodnow and Austin (1956) was one of the first to introduce what would now be called a cognitive view of problem solving in terms of strategies rather than trial and error. Later Bruner formulated a theory of different modes of thinking that develop successively in children – enactive, iconic, symbolic. This derives partly from Piaget, but puts much more emphasis on the role of the environment, particularly the cultural environment, in cognitive growth, showing the influence of Russian ideas.

Computer simulation and artificial intelligence

The aim of computer simulation studies is to use the rapid processing of information that they provide in order to test out some idea as to how behaviour might work. Such an idea is often called a model. There is some disagreement as to whether, given a model that seems to replicate the behaviour, we then have an explanation of that behaviour. In principle any sort of behaviour can be simulated, but there has been particular interest in cognitive processes; perhaps partly because it has been felt that there is a similarity between them and computers, but largely because of the enormous growth in use of computers to process vast quantities of information, to solve problems, and to control other systems. Many aspects of these have come to be called, generally, artificial intelligence.

Phenomenological

The word 'phenomenology' has had various uses in philosophy. Perhaps most generally, it refers to the study of things as they appear to be, rather than of some supposed reality lying behind the appearance. Edmund Husserl (1859–1938) tried to give accurate descriptions of phenomena as they present themselves in consciousness: or rather of the essences of phenomena, devoid of all the usual presuppositions and prejudices of the mind. Part of Husserl's doctrine was that consciousness is intentional. This recurs in the work of Maurice Merleau-Ponty, whose theory of cognition stresses the way in which what we know of the world is, so to say, created in the act of knowing it. In recognizing an object, we do not note a set of items and then put them together; rather the object emerges from the general perceptual field, and only afterwards can we identify the particular stimuli that make it up. This process centres on the body and its movements, since it is through these that we relate to the world; or rather, perhaps, they constitute the relationship. The body is part of the 'I' that knows and perceives, just as we do not say 'my body is hungry' but 'I am hungry'. These complex ideas, which are only hinted at here, have perhaps not directly inspired a great deal of experimentation, but have contributed to important changes in psychology; for example, the general revival of interest in conscious experience, and some of the so-called 'humanistic' ideas.

Introspection and consciousness

Experimental psychology began as the study of consciousness, using the method of systematic introspection. The experimenter tried to observe and record his own sensations and feelings as objectively as possible. A typical situation would be reporting on the beats of a metronome, which seem to form rhythms even though one knows they are perfectly regular. It is the sensation which the introspective psychologist studied, not the sound itself. The difficulty with this, as Wundt realized and Kulpe demonstrated experimentally, is that many mental processes, including much of what we call thinking, cannot be got at in this way.

This led to the method being abandoned in favour of the observation of behaviour. More recently consciousness has been readmitted as part of psychology, and introspection as a method. Usually, however, it is not the systematic procedure of Wundt, but simply a record of a subject's thoughts as he carries out some task, such as solving a problem. Many experimenters, for example P. C. Wason, have found that what subjects say does not necessarily match what they do: the right solution can be accompanied by the wrong reason, or even vice versa. This is not particularly surprising, since most major theorists since Freud have held that information is processed in more than one way. One of the objects of Ulric Neisser's influential book of 1967, *Cognitive Psychology,* was to tie together several such theories with the concept of multiple and sequential modes of information processing.

Cognitive psychology

From being a label for some aspects of behaviour, contrasted with affective (feeling) and conative (motivational), the term 'cognitive' has come to mean a general approach to psychology, one which in the last 20 years has been the prevailing fashion. Some Departments of Psychology in the United States have hastened to rename themselves 'Departments of

Cognitive Science'. As far as the study of thinking is concerned this has perhaps had two main effects. One is to re-emphasize such aspects as consciousness, imagery, and language. The other, almost paradoxically, is that the label 'thinking' has tended to disappear (for example it is no longer a section head in the *Psychological Abstracts* which summarize published research). In this book we have taken the opposite tack by reinstating it – in the first edition we used the term 'information'.

Current research on thinking

Recent research on thinking, while partly deriving from the various perspectives we have just described, has become more closely integrated with other aspects of psychology. As a result, different questions have been posed producing a variety of new research trends. One theme that continues to run through these is that of problem solving, and we shall make use of this to provide a framework for our account of the various current concepts and points of growth. Let us start with a simple anagram problem:

MAITANXONEI

When you have tried this, think about the tactics you used. Was your strategy completely haphazard? Almost certainly not: your knowledge of the rules of English spelling would suggest that there is little point in trying to identify the word by placing 'NX' or various other combinations at the beginning. Although there may have been an element of trial and error, it is more likely that the use of different strategies based on this knowledge played an important part in the process of solution. The use of strategies allows us to make *inferences* from the data of the problem. Since the making of inferences is often seen as a key characteristic of thinking, the first and one of the most important topics for investigation in thinking, therefore, is the nature of the strategies we use in solving problems and the factors which affect the inferences we draw as a result of using them.

A second point about the anagram problem is that it produces *individual differences*. People take different amounts of time in finding the word and set about the task in different ways. The second important theme in current research is therefore concerned with the cognitive basis of individual differences in thinking and whether they can be systematically related to various components of the information processing system.

A third point about anagram solving is that, as crossword puzzle solvers know, performance improves with practice – we can 'learn' through experience how to solve this sort of problem more efficiently. A third topic in recent research therefore concerns the possibility of extending this idea to more complex forms of thinking. Is thinking a skill and can we *train people to think more effectively*?

The final strand in current research concerns *developmental aspects* of thinking. If given to children of different ages, one would expect to find age related differences in performance on the anagram problem. Any complete account of thinking therefore needs to include a developmental perspective. What changes in thinking occur with age and what is their cognitive basis?

Reasoning

Research on reasoning is concerned with the strategies used by people to make inferences when solving logical problems. 'Logical' is a term which is used in different ways. In popular speech it is often used to describe behaviour which is sensible or appropriate in particular circumstances ('He did the logical thing'). According to the strict definition, however, logical thought is thinking which makes use of specific rules in order to reach conclusions which are valid. The particular rules used depend on the nature of the system of logic which is applied. Valid conclusions are not necessarily true or sensible. For example, it might be argued that all drugs are bad for you and therefore that since tea is a drug, drinking tea is bad for you. This conclusion is perfectly valid, given the *premises* stated, but most people would regard it as empirically unsound.

Historically, logical thought has often been raised on a pedestal and portrayed as one of the highest forms of thinking to which humans can aspire. The reasons for this include the belief that logical thought allowed the fullest expression of the faculty of reason with which humans but not animals were endowed; and also that one could feel more secure about knowledge acquired through pure reasoning since it was uncontaminated by the intervention of sensory information which might be unreliable. It is possible to detect elements of these ideas in some of the earlier work on reasoning carried out by psychologists. In more recent research, however, the idea that logic might provide a standard for evaluating the effectiveness of human thinking has more or less been abandoned and studies of reasoning are seen as of interest primarily because of the light they can throw on the processes of inference people use.

Many textbooks concerned with logic have catalogued the mournful miscellany of errors of reasoning to which we are prone. Several of the early experimental studies appear to reinforce this negative picture. For example, in their often quoted study of 'atmosphere effects', Woodworth and Sells (1935) asked subjects to evaluate various syllogisms, i.e. arguments of the form:

	All As are Bs
	All Cs are Bs
Therefore	All As are Cs

They found subjects generally performed rather badly, often apparently failing to analyse the logical structure of the problem and accepting invalid conclusions because they based their judgements largely on irrelevant 'nonlogical' factors such as the 'atmosphere' of acceptance created by the use of the word 'all'. Morgan and Morton (1944) also studied syllogisms, using various different kinds of task content. The aim was to examine whether subjects were able to keep the process of logical evaluation separate from their own personal opinions about the content. The results showed that subjects often apparently accepted conclusions which were not valid but which they happened to think were true.

In 1968 Wason published the results of an experiment which used a reasoning problem (known as the 'Selection Task') which came to dominate research on reasoning for many years after. Many variations of the task have been carried out but typically subjects are presented with four cards such as are shown below:

B　　　　**N**　　　　**3**　　　　**7**

Subjects are informed that each card has a letter on one side and a number on the reverse. They are then given a sentence which states a simple rule about the cards: 'If there is a "B" on one side of the card, there is a "3" on the other'. The subject's task is then to select the card, or cards, which would have to be turned over to find out if this statement is true or false. Faced with this task, most subjects give 'B' and '3' as their choices, reasoning that anything other than a '3' on the back of the 'B' will falsify the statement and that if the statement is true, then there ought to be a 'B' on the back of the '3'. Yet the logically correct choices are 'B' and '7' since these are the only cards which, when turned over, *could* falsify the statement. Subjects seem ready to accept this for 'B' but not for '7' yet a 'B' on the reverse of the card showing '7' would demonstrate the statement to be false. The choice of the card showing '3' is not strictly correct since nothing on its reverse could falsify the statement though a 'B' would corroborate it. The majority of subjects eventually agree (usually somewhat reluctantly!) to accept the correct choices.

These findings proved to be very robust and were readily reproduced by Wason and his colleagues using a variety of task materials and formats. The general interpretation favoured, especially in the earlier investigations, was that the results revealed a genuine lack of insight into an important type of logical relationship. Subjects were said to choose cards which could verify rather than falsify the rule. In fact Wason and Johnson-Laird (1970) proposed an 'insight' model of performance in which subjects progress through various stages of insight and gradually 'learn' the correct responses. Such a view would seem to have important implications for concepts of human rationality and perhaps also to throw into question the model of formal operational thinking described in Piaget's theory (see Chapter 16).

Not surprisingly, however, this interpretation has not gone unchallenged. A common objection is to argue that people are 'logical' but that such tasks are artificial and unfamiliar and are not valid measures of true ability. Since most subjects do not receive training in formal logic, the results are therefore no more surprising than if they had been asked to carry out some other unfamiliar task such as juggling oranges. This is a powerful argument and one which cannot be overlooked. It should be noted, however, that in Wason's studies, subjects rarely seem to respond randomly; their choices, though incorrect, are remarkably consistent, suggesting they may have a common basis. One possible explanation for the consistency is that the subjects' choice of cards is determined by an interpretation of the task or problem which is different from the one intended by the experimenter. Subjects may therefore reason perfectly correctly but apply their reasoning to a different version of the rule being tested. The idea that erroneous conclusions might be due to the use of alternative interpretations of the premises of a problem rather than to faulty reasoning was most forcibly argued by Henle (see e.g. Henle, 1962) who observed that many cases of apparently illogical thought may be due to subjects ignoring or mis-interpreting important information. Often this may be because they hold some strong personal opinion about the content of the problem which makes it difficult for them, as she puts it, 'to accept the logical task'.

To apply Henle's explanation to the performance of subjects on the selection task would mean finding an interpretation of the task for which 'B' and '3' are the correct choices. One interpretation of the task which subjects might use (suggested by verbal reports quoted by Wason himself) is that the aim is to choose cards which will prove the rule to be true. This might lead to a choice of cards 'B' and '3' which could prove the rule true. Apart from its circularity, however, this argument does not seem entirely convincing since presumably 'B' could also falsify the statement. Interestingly, Wason (1969) also found that even telling subjects to choose cards which would prove the rule false had very little effect on their performance. Henle's main point, however, is an important one: when people make errors in reasoning tasks, one cannot be certain that they are the result of the use of an incorrect *process* of reasoning unless one also knows what interpretation of the task is being used. A major problem in testing this, however, is the difficulty of obtaining a satisfactory measure of the subject's interpretation which is separate from the conclusions drawn. Unless this can be done, it is difficult to see how the proposal can be properly investigated.

The importance of content in reasoning

Suppose you are a medical researcher involved in examining the relation-ship between the disease AIDS and the HIV test. What sorts of people

445

would it be necessary to investigate in order to test the validity of the hypothesis *if you have AIDS then you are HIV+*? People with AIDS? Those without? People who are HIV+? Those who are not? The logical structure (if . . . then) of this task is equivalent to the original selection task but when used within a more concrete problem, it seems much more straightforward: you need to test patients with AIDS to see if they are HIV+ and those who are *not* HIV+ to see if any of them are AIDS sufferers. People who are HIV+ but who do *not* have AIDS are not critical to the hypothesis since they may be HIV+ for some other reason. Several experimental studies have demonstrated the effect of 'concreteness' very clearly. Wason and Shapiro (1971), for example, presented subjects with the statement 'If I go to Manchester I travel by train' together with four cards showing, respectively, *Manchester, Leeds, train, car*. On the reverse of modes of transport cards there were names of destinations and on the reverse of destinations were modes of transport. As in the original 'abstract' form of the selection task, subjects were required to say which cards should be turned over to find out whether the statement was true or false. Performance was found to be far superior compared with the more abstract form, the majority of subjects correctly selecting *Manchester* and *car*.

Reasoning without logic?

The above findings suggest it may be useful to distinguish between logical *competence* and *performance*. Just as Chomsky suggested for language (see Chapter 15), the performance of people in logical tasks often seems to fall short of their true competence, especially where the tasks involved are rather abstract or unusual. Why should the content of the task be so important? If we understand a rule, why are we not always able to apply it? To say that it is because of the 'unfamiliarity' of the task begs the question of *why* unfamiliar tasks should be less capable of drawing out the underlying competence. One possible answer is to be found in the work of Johnson-Laird (see e.g. 1982) who has suggested that logical problems are not necessarily solved using some form of 'mental logic'. Instead, Johnson-Laird proposes a theory of 'mental models' to explain the performance of subjects in reasoning tasks. In his studies, subjects were asked to decide what conclusions could be drawn from various types of syllogistic argument; for example:

All the beekeepers are artists
None of the chemists are beekeepers

Johnson-Laird's suggestion is that such problems are solved by constructing mental representations of the premises which integrate the various elements, e.g. perhaps by conjuring up a mental image of a collection of artists, some of whom are also beekeepers wearing protective headgear; pictured separately is a group of chemists in white coats. In deciding whether a particular conclusion may be drawn, it is compared with the mental model: if the model does not explicitly disallow the conclusion it is accepted as valid. In the present example, for instance, the conclusion 'none of the chemists are artists' would be accepted. In fact, Johnson-Laird found that about 60 per cent of subjects regarded this conclusion as valid even though it is not. The problem lies in the failure to consider alternative mental representations of the premisses, e.g. models in which some (or even all) of the chemists, although not beekeepers, are also artists. When all possible interpretations are considered it can be seen that only one conclusion – 'some of the artists are not chemists' – is valid but in Johnson-Laird's study, no subject actually made this response. Johnson-Laird argues, however, that this is not because of a failure of subjects to understand or apply some abstract logical rule but because they have neglected to consider the relevant mental model of the premisses. This is hardly surprising since the construction and interpretation of mental models places a considerable demand on 'working memory'. In line with this, Johnson-Laird found that the greater the number of different representations which can be constructed for a problem, the poorer the performance. Abstract logical tasks may be more difficult to handle because it is more difficult for subjects to build and modify the relevant mental representations of the task components.

Though it has been developed mainly through the study of syllogistic reasoning, the mental models approach represents an important shift in research and theory in that reasoning is assumed to be achieved by the use of strategies for representing information rather than by the application of logical rules. Various other recent lines of research reinforce this change in emphasis from logical to cognitive and various other 'non-logical' (not to be confused with 'illogical') factors. Evans (1984) for example has advanced a two-stage theory of reasoning. In the first, *heuristic* stage, items of what are considered to be 'relevant' task information are selected from the problem as presented; in the second, *analytic* stage, various processes operate on the information selected in order to draw conclusions. Various 'non-logical' factors play a part in both stages. Evans and Lynch (1973), for example, showed that subjects tend to choose 'B' and '3' in the Selection Task simply because those are the symbols mentioned in the statement to be tested. This seems to increase the perceived 'salience' of those cards and biases subjects towards choosing them, irrespective of their true relevance. The process, which they term 'matching bias', is not consciously controlled. Similarly, the particular wording used in such tasks may trigger associations with more natural uses of the same words. For example, conditional sentences (if ... then) are commonly used to refer to causal relationships or temporal sequences ('if he travels by car he always feels sick'). These everyday connotations can then influence the selection of what is considered relevant. As a result, some items which are relevant may be incorrectly classed as irrelevant. 'Concrete' logical problems may be easier to solve partly because they facilitate the selection of task relevant information perhaps by stimulating the retrieval of memories of similar problems or by helping people to construct a scenario in which potentially relevant information is more salient, e.g. Manchester railway station standing full of empty trains while hordes of students arrive by the carload.

In this section we have concentrated on studies of deductive reasoning. Space does not allow any discussion of research on a variety of other similar tasks such as those involving inductive reasoning and statistical judgement which also require subjects to make inferences. In general, however, these areas of research do not suggest conclusions which differ substantially from those drawn so far. When any form of inferential task is presented there is no simple mechanical computation of the logical 'truth values' of the different elements of the problem. A range of factors seems to influence the process of reasoning. Many of these may be best described as non-logical rather than illogical in the sense that they do not reflect the operation of faulty logical rules. In addition, some are the result of an inappropriate transfer of the strategies used in more practical everyday problem solving. The research also demonstrates the need to re-examine the old question of whether people are or are not rational. Sometimes they are, sometimes they are not. This is precisely what would be expected if, as some have suggested, the process of thinking is a form of skilled activity since the quality of performance will vary according to the circumstances. In some reasoning tasks it will be easier for people to make inferences which are, according to the external yardstick of logic, valid. The question of whether these inferences are based upon the use of some system of mental logic, however, is currently the subject of much debate. It is certainly no longer considered useful simply to examine how well thinking measures up to some hypothetical logical, or other, standard. As Evans (1984) argues, psychology should attempt to understand the nature of inferential behaviour rather than to pronounce it rational or irrational. Not all, however, have fully accepted Johnson-Laird's radical account of how we might reason without logic.

Although commonly and justifiably criticized for its artificiality, research on reasoning has been successful in underlining the great variety of processes and factors that seem to be involved in reasoning both in practical and more formal abstract tasks and in some respects at least has enabled us to put forward more detailed accounts than were offered in earlier times.

Artificial intelligence

The arrival of the first digital computer around 40 years ago provided psychologists with a new model for human thinking based on the idea of the mind as an information processing device. The main analogy is between the processes of thought and the manipulation of information by means of a computer program (i.e. the software) rather than between the human brain and the physical machinery of a computer (i.e. the hardware). It is useful to distinguish artificial intelligence (AI) from computer simulation. Although there is some overlap, in the latter the aim is to test a theory of human performance by expressing it in terms of a working computer program. The purpose of AI is to use a computer to carry out particular tasks such as diagnosing a fault in a machine or recognizing voices which are normally carried out by people. The manner in which these goals are achieved may or may not mirror the mode of performance in humans.

One of the main contributions of AI is that it can quickly reveal ambiguity or deficiencies such as lack of clarity or explicitness in a theory. A good example of this is to be found in the work of Marr (1982) whose computer-based research on pattern recognition demonstrated the inadequacies of earlier feature extraction theories. Such work would probably count as an example of what Gardner (1985) calls 'weak AI' – the computer simply provides a way of testing how people might carry out a certain activity. The success of projects such as The General Problem Solver (see e.g. Newell and Simon, 1972), a large program capable of playing chess and solving a range of mental puzzles, and flexible programs for understanding natural language such as SHRDLU (Winograd, 1972) has led to stronger claims. The ability to program a computer to solve such problems using the same strategies thought to be used by humans suggests that computers can be said to behave intelligently. Perhaps all intelligent behaviour, no matter how complex, is reducible to the manipulation of various mathematical and logical symbols and therefore is capable of being realized within some form of computer program.

In general, AI has been successful in encouraging cognitive psychologists to think about how complex forms of human behaviour might be achieved. Computers have also been taught how to learn and to use *heuristics*, i.e. ways of selecting potential forms of solution with the highest chances of success rather than simply to consider all possibilities in a 'brute force' fashion. Opponents of AI especially in its 'strong' form, however, point to the relatively limited achievements of many AI programs which often turn out to be restricted to a much narrower range of problems than would be expected of a device showing genuine intelligence. Another objection is that programming a computer to give the same output as a human is not the same as simulating the processes used in producing the output. Successful chess playing programs, for example, still work mostly by a 'brute force' examination of all the possible available moves even though this is clearly not the method used by human players. Some of the most vociferous critics also argue that the use of machines to simulate human behaviour will always be limited in several crucial respects. In the case of Searle (1980) this amounts to a rejection of the whole basis of cognitive psychology since he argues that to explain intelligent behaviour only two sorts of concepts are required: those relating to subjective mental states such as beliefs, wishes, desires and intentions and those concerned with the neurophysiological events by which the brain realizes these states. There is no third 'intermediate' level at which knowledge is represented by symbols and manipulated using rules. Other criticisms are that human beings have a 'fringe consciousness', are tolerant of ambiguity and are motivated to perform tasks in more complex ways. They also get bored and tired. Such objections are not fundamentally damaging to the AI enterprise, however, since there seems no *a priori* reason why a computer program should not be given these characteristics. A more searching criticism is that there are fundamental differences between biological and mechanical systems especially in the sense that there are some things which humans know by virtue of having a body. Thus, although many devices are capable of acquiring knowledge in diverse ways, no organism that does not have a human body can know things in the same way (Weizenbaum, 1987). Ultimately, however, the issue is not to decide whether a computer is analogous to a human being in every respect but to explore the extent to which it is a useful tool for investigating cognitive processes and provides a satisfactory model for complex human performance.

Expert systems

As Cohen (1983) has noted, the current limitations on AI are partly technological and partly theoretical. The forthcoming so called 'fifth generation' computers are widely expected to bring about significant advances in AI especially in research into *expert systems*. An expert system is a form of intelligent computer program designed to assist with a specific activity such as medical diagnosis or fault finding in a piece of machinery. Most consist of a knowledge base which incorporates expert knowledge, often expressed as rules, about the particular field and a device for applying the rules to particular inputs (e.g. a set of symptoms) and suggesting a hypothesis. One of the current limitations is that as the size of the knowledge base increases, the problems of organizing the information and retrieving it also begins to increase. Processing speed is also limited by the machine's hardware in which only one operation at a time can be carried out, creating a bottleneck. Fifth generation computing devices will make use of a completely different form of computer architecture which allows extensive simultaneous processing of different instructions in parallel. This will enable the computer to support very large knowledge bases, to retrieve information and carry out instructions very quickly and will perhaps also allow the user to interact with the computer using natural language. The resulting programs will undoubtedly encompass a much greater span of knowledge and be potentially more versatile. This will probably make some types of expert system more expert but progress with others seems likely to depend on first reaching a fuller understanding of the form of knowledge possessed by experts.

Individual differences

In terms of cognitive processes, what is the difference between people of high, average and low ability? Until recently the subject of individual differences in thinking suffered prodigious neglect at the hands of cognitive psychologists. Traditionally seen as the domain of *psychometrics* (see Chapter 13) there have been only isolated attempts to study variations in types, strategies and styles of thinking. In recent years, however, there have been signs of increased interest. The most outstanding example of this is probably Sternberg's information processing theory of intelligence (see Chapter 13).

Speed of processing

Empirical research on individual differences has also been growing. One source of individual variation is simply speed of responding, a principle enshrined in many aptitude tests. This is not to say that speed alone is sufficient – we can all think of people who rush into things and make a complete mess of them. In a processing system such as the human mind, however, where resources are limited, faster processing could produce qualitative as well as quantitative differences in performance since information held in working memory may decay to a point where it can no longer be retrieved if processing is too slow. Indeed, some studies have found a modest correlation between measures such as reaction times and intelligence test performance (see e.g. Mackintosh, 1986). This might suggest that individual differences in intelligence are simply a function of an individual's overall efficiency of information processing. The strength of the relationship between speed of processing and intelligence, however, also depends on the level of intelligence of the individual. The highest correlations are found with people of lower intelligence. At the higher ability end, the relationship is very slight (Lally and Nettelbeck, 1977). Gross measures of processing speed such as reaction times, therefore, seem to reflect large *between* group differences in intelligence but are unlikely to be sensitive enough to variations in ability *within* a more selected range to be a useful index of individual differences.

Measures of speed within particular types or stages of processing may be more useful. Many researchers have emphasized the benefits of an information processing approach for understanding individual differences. This involves the identification of the different components of processing required by a particular task or set of tasks. Once identified, the contribution of the separate components can then be examined. Sternberg (see e.g. Sternberg and Gardner, 1983) discusses the use of this approach applied to individual differences in tasks requiring analogical reasoning (e.g. mouth ... taste: eye ...?). Each of the different stages of processing envisaged was found to contribute a separate amount to the overall solution time. A further finding of particular interest was that although subjects of high reasoning ability were faster overall, they were actually slower at the 'encoding' stage of such problems. Sternberg suggests this may be because more skilled reasoners appreciate that time spent encoding information accurately at the beginning can speed up subsequent stages of processing. Hunt (see e.g. 1980) suggested that an important source of variation in verbal ability might be the speed with which very elementary verbal processing operations are carried out. In reading, for example, visually presented symbols may need to be 'decoded' into their name forms. Hunt devised a special task to measure the time needed to carry out this verbal decoding and correlated the scores with various measures of verbal intelligence. The task was found to discriminate well between groups of individuals differing widely in verbal intelligence, e.g. college students, poor readers and children with learning difficulties. Within a more selected population such as, for example, college students, the overall correlation is significant but quite modest – close to what Hunt refers to as the '0.3 barrier' which he claims such tests rarely break through.

Research on individual differences in speed of processing has therefore produced mixed findings. Global measures of processing time are certainly correlated to some degree with measures of general intelligence but are not sufficiently sensitive to provide a simple alternative index. Research on the speed with which an individual is able to carry out particular processing operations have been more useful in pinpointing specific sources of individual differences. Speed alone, however, seems to provide only a partial explanation of cognitive differences between individuals.

Strategies

Differences in knowledge are another potentially important source of individual differences. Those who are more able may simply know more. (In fact, this could be why they are able to process information more quickly.) In this context, 'knowledge' can be construed very broadly and includes specific items of information (e.g. knowing what a prime number is) as well as various forms of procedural knowledge (e.g. knowing how to do a 't' test). Of greater importance, according to, e.g. Sternberg, however, are various forms of more general 'strategic' knowledge which he refers to as 'metacomponents'. Metacomponents are higher order executive skills of problem solving concerned with, for example, problem identification and goal setting, planning and selecting strategies and monitoring their effectiveness. Sternberg argues these are a major source of individual differences in thinking in that many people may possess the specific skills required to solve a problem but lack the skills of overall strategic control necessary to co-ordinate them. Strategies of processing are clearly difficult to measure since, setting aside introspective reports, they have to be inferred mainly from differences in the frequency or types of errors or from large differences in processing time. Various studies, however, have revealed some interesting strategy-based differences between groups differing in general intellectual ability (see e.g. Sternberg, 1985a, b). For example, when faced with simple verbal and arithmetical puzzles, gifted children seem to be better at selecting relevant from non-relevant task information compared with children of average ability. In addition, higher ability children are more likely to be able spontaneously to transfer their knowledge to problems not previously encountered. This is particularly noticeable when children with severe learning difficulties are investigated. As the 'distance' increases between existing knowledge and new tasks to which that knowledge needs to be applied, the more difficulties those of lower intelligence seem to experience (Campione *et al*, 1985).

Training in thinking?

Mental activities seem to improve with practice just as physical skills do. Experiments on problem solving also show that prior exposure to specially selected problems can facilitate solutions to others which differ in content but have a similar structure (Gick and Holyoak, 1980). This leads to the possibility that various forms of thinking may be improved through training, an idea which may be traced back as far as Plato. In recent years a number of specially designed training programmes have been devised which are intended to develop various thinking skills such as creativity (e.g. De Bono, 1976; Gordon, 1961) and powers of analytical reasoning (Whimbey and Lochhead, 1980). The programmes vary considerably in their aims, content and structure, some being intended for children (e.g. Feuerstein *et al*, 1980), some for adults and others or for those with severe learning disorders. Although several of them have been used extensively for many years with large numbers of subjects, the majority have not been subjected to rigorous scientific scrutiny in the sense that we cannot be sure that if improvements do occur, they are genuinely due to the specific content of the programme. There is also some uncertainty about whether the skills acquired are limited to the materials used in the programmes or whether subjects would generalize them to novel tasks. (For a recent review, see e.g. Baron and Sternberg, 1987.)

Answers to these sorts of questions may be more easily obtained from less ambitious smaller scale investigations. In a series of studies, Fong *et al* (1986) examined whether various forms of training in statistics would generalize to how people reason about imaginary everyday 'statistical' problems. The focus of training was the law of large numbers: a random sample is more representative of the distribution from which it is drawn, the larger the sample. The results showed that the frequency and quality of statistical arguments used in answering a series of test problems were greater in a group of subjects who had received prior training, even in problems where the relevance of the law of large numbers was not so obvious. Subjects who had received training were also successful in identifying 'decoy' problems to which the law was not applicable. The study suggests that there may indeed be generalization of specific forms of training to problems drawn from outside the immediate area of training. Transfer of knowledge cannot be taken for granted, however, and it should be noted that the problems under investigation were relatively simple.

Some cultural/developmental aspects

Thinking can be considered as involving complex skills, but there are different approaches to the ways in which such skills might develop. Several of these are described elsewhere in this book; for example learning theory, and more recently cognitive theory. Another view is the Piagetian one. As a biologist by training Piaget was interested in how the living organism takes what it needs from the environment and incorporates it, thereby itself growing and changing – the processes of assimilation and accommodation. It is also possible, on the other hand, to start from the environment rather than the organism. It is fairly clear that without a human social and cultural environment, a human baby could hardly develop normally, even if it survived physically. There are some such cases, one of the earliest and most famous being the unfortunate Victor, the 'wild boy of Aveyron' (died 1828). Devotedly taught by his tutor, J. M. G. Itard, Victor painfully acquired only the rudiments of human behaviour (Lane, 1977). One difficulty with all such cases is not knowing what they were like to start with; in some cases they may have been abandoned because they seemed to be deficient in some way. Nevertheless more recent cases of deprivation such as 'Genie' (Curtiss, 1988) seem to bear out what must be logically true: without access to human behaviour and in particular human speech, a child could not develop these for itself.

L. S. Vygotsky was born in the same year as Piaget, but in contrast to him began his career in the study of literature and the theatre, and only worked on psychological problems for the last ten years of his short life. His central interest was the relationship of thought and language, in which he saw the key to understanding the nature of human consciousness. In *Thought and Language* (1934, English version 1962) Vygotsky outlined a theory and a programme of investigation to show how thought develops through the internalization of action and particularly of external speech. Language and thought, according to Vygotsky, have different origins, as can be seen in both animals and children. Thinking, he seems to argue, originates in the need to restructure a situation; language originates in expressive utterances and in the need to communicate. Vygotsky considered that language for the child had two functions: one, that of monitoring and directing internal thought; the other, that of communicating with other people. It is the inability to separate these that results in what Piaget labelled 'egocentric' speech. The latter, however, gradually separates out into inner speech and external speech. These are quite different modes or 'planes' as Vygotsky calls them, with different syntax. Inner speech appears relatively disconnected and incomplete. It deals in 'sense' rather than 'meaning'. By 'sense' Vygotsky meant the whole complex of psychological events aroused by a word. 'Meaning' is a restricted part of sense; what a word stands for, like a dictionary definition. Language and thought can be considered as two partly overlapping circles: the area of overlap is 'verbal thought'. Both thought and language can exist independently. An example of thought without language, according to Vygotsky, is tool using, and of the opposite, repeating a poem learned by heart.

Vygotsky's ideas were officially suppressed by the Communist Party in Russia (the book was banned for 20 years from 1936), but were kept alive by those he inspired, particularly A. S. Luria and A. N. Leontyev, and more recently have had a much wider influence. Vygotsky had two main aims in his psychological work: to formulate psychological theory along Marxist lines, and to develop effective ways of dealing with practical problems, especially those of illiteracy and remedial education (Wertsch, 1985b). (It may seem odd, in view of the first aim, that his ideas were suppressed, but illogic is a feature of totalitarian regimes.) Three aspects of Marxist theory were particularly important in shaping Vygotsky's ideas, according to Wertsch (1985a). There was first the method, involving the identification and analysis of some complete living unit as a model or microcosm of the whole. An example from Marx is the concept of 'value'; for Vygotsky, it was word meaning. This is a unit because it retains the essential properties of thought and language, and cannot be further divided, for example into the sound and what the sound stands for, without losing them. Second was the belief in activity as a basic concept in psychological theory; and third was the view that individual psychological functioning has social origins.

This is consistent with a Marxist view that the only way to bring about psychological change is by altering social conditions. If peasants are to be rescued from what Marx had termed 'rural idiocy' and led along the road to socialism, their whole way of life must be altered. Such ideology lies behind Stalin's policy of collectivization, with its resulting deaths of many millions, and the recent Romanian policy of destroying villages and small towns. Seeking rather to understand the process than to judge it, an interesting example of research is the work of Luria in Uzbekistan, Central Asia, published in English in 1976 though done many years before. He was able to compare groups with three degrees of involvement in the new society that was coming into being: non-literate peasant farmers in traditional villages; young people in collective farms, with some literacy; and women attending teacher training schools. Luria examined among other things verbal reasoning based on syllogisms, such as: precious metals do not rust, gold is a precious metal, does gold rust or not? He found that often, when a problem involved premises or inferences which non-literate subjects did not themselves know to be true, they often refused to accept them and argued that they could only judge on what they themselves had seen or knew from reliable people to be true. For example:

'In the Far North, where there is snow, all bears are white. Novaya Zemlya is in the Far North and there is always snow there. What colour are the bears there?'

'We always speak only of what we see; we don't talk about what we haven't seen.'

'But what do my words imply?' (repeats problem)

'Well, it's like this. Our tsar isn't yours and yours isn't like ours. Your words can only be answered by someone who was there, and if a person wasn't there he can't say anything on the basis of your words.'

'... But on the basis of my words – in the North, where there is always snow, the bears are white, can you gather what kind of bears there are in Novaya Zemlya?'

'If a man was sixty or eighty and had seen a white bear and had told about it, he could be believed, but I've never seen one and hence I can't say. That's my last word. Those who saw can tell, and those who didn't see can't say anything.'

(Another, younger, respondent) 'From your words it seems that the bears are white.'

'Well, which of you is right?'

'What the cock knows how to do he does. What I know, I say, and nothing beyond that!'

Whether this is rural idiocy, or peasant cunning in the face of a nosy stranger, it is probably too late to say.

There have been many other studies of thinking in different cultures; some are mentioned in the chapter on Intelligence. Curran (1988) points out that competence must be distinguished from performance. She quotes Irvine (1978) as saying that among the Wolof people of Nigeria it is unusual to ask people over the age of seven questions to which one already knows the answer (as all our psychological tests do): it may be taken as aggressive or a trick. Again, it is often found that thinking is related to situations in which there is a need for it, and in which there has been practice. Blurton-Jones and Konner (1976) describe the extensive knowledge of animal behaviour possessed by the !Kung-San hunter-gatherers of the northern Kalahari desert of Botswana (incidentally yet another native people currently – 1989 – being driven from their homeland). They clearly distinguished in their knowledge between evidence and hearsay, and were highly expert trackers, which involves both making inferences and testing hypotheses. Terezinha Carraher found that street-trading children in Recife, Brazil, were better at the sums they did in the course of selling than the same sums in school; and they used different methods (Carraher, Carraher and Schliemann, 1985). At the same time the street arithmetic is more limited than formal mathematics, which can serve as what Bruner has called an 'amplifier of thought processes'.

The distinction between formal and practical thinking goes back to Aristotle, as Sylvia Scribner (1984) points out; one typical of philosophers, and superior, the other of artisans and those whose social function is to get things done. Scribner studied practical thinking in a milk processing plant. Following Bartlett, she regarded skilled practical thinking as goal-directed and varying adaptively with the changing properties of the problem; contrasting with formal academic thinking in which a single method is used to solve all problems of a given type. As is typical of skills, in the milk plant expertise was a function of experience, eventually becoming 'visual', that is, automatic.

As mentioned, Vygotsky and his followers were particularly interested in the role of language in thought. This issue arose also in the work of Edward Sapir (1927) and Benjamin Lee Whorf (1957). The Sapir–Whorf, or Whorfian, hypothesis, is essentially that language influences the way we think and even the way we perceive the world. It is well known that languages differ in their vocabularies and grammatical forms even for the same class of object or event. A famous example is that of the colour spectrum given by Brown (1965) (see Figure 14.1).

Such an example does not prove that those using the language see the spectrum differently. Glucksberg (1988) points out that the spectrum is a continuum which can be divided arbitrarily, but at the same time colour perception and conceptualization are cognitive universals determined by

English

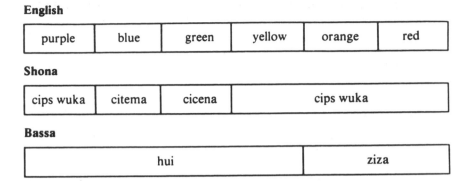

purple	blue	green	yellow	orange	red

Shona

cips wuka	citema	cicena	cips wuka

Bassa

hui	ziza

Figure 14.1 The colour spectrum in three languages (after Brown)

the properties of the human visual system. He quotes evidence that there are four psychologically primary hues, red, yellow, green and blue (plus black and white). Subjects can describe any sample from the visible spectrum using these, but cannot do so with less. Nor does it follow that a particular thought cannot be expressed in a language. It has been said that if this were so, Whorf could not have written articles dealing with the Zuni or Hopi languages, entirely in English.

An example of more recent research is by Terry Kit-Fong Au (1983), who re-examined an experiment by Bloom (1981) comparing English and Chinese speakers. In English, what are called 'counterfactuals' use the subjunctive: 'If X were to happen, Y would follow' (implying that X has not happened). Chinese lacks this construction, and also the distinction between tenses, and thus has to use two forms, one where the negative is generally known ('If I am the US President, then I do so-and-so') and one where it is not ('Mrs Wong not know English. If Mrs Wong know English, she do so-and-so'). Bloom constructed a story embodying such counter-factuals, in English and Chinese versions, and gave it to native speakers of each language, who were then asked whether the implied negatives were the case. 98 per cent of English speakers replied correctly and only 7 per cent of Chinese. Bloom concluded that the language affected the reasoning. Au argued that the result was in fact due to the unidiomatic nature of Bloom's Chinese version; using a more idiomatic version, he found Chinese speakers had no difficulty. He also found that American high school students did less well than Chinese subjects in Hong Kong.

It is perhaps most likely from a common sense point of view that thought and particular languages continuously interact within a total cultural context. English has a vocabulary some three times greater than any other language, growing as more and more people use it for more varied purposes, making different selections from and additions to it. Inasmuch as this gives the possibility of a greater range of expression, it would seem to provide a more versatile instrument of thought.

Further reading

Gardner, H. (1986) *The Mind's New Science: A history of the cognitive revolution.* Basic Books.

Gilhooly, K. J. (1988) *Thinking: Directed, undirected and creative,* 2nd edn. Academic Press.

Kail, R., and Pellegrino, J. W. (1985) *Human Intelligence: Perspectives and prospects.* W. H. Freeman.

Chapter fifteen

Language

Part I The psychology of language
Marian Pitts

Part II The acquisition and development of language
Harry Fisher

Part I The psychology of language

Language is one form of communication. Its use is not restricted to communication – it is extensively used for thinking and conceptualization. There are other, non-verbal, forms of communication – facial expression, eye contact, posture, even dress can all communicate and convey information. This chapter, however, is mainly concerned with language as verbal communication.

There are three main questions which arise in respect of language:

> how do we produce it?
> how do we understand it?
> how do we acquire it?

The first part of this chapter will deal with the language of adults. It will consider the processes by which speech is produced and those by which it is understood. Speech production and comprehension have been the subject of much experimental investigation which is characterized by competing theories or explanations which often try to link production with comprehension. Often this experimentation has taken place in the laboratory using very simple language as its starting point. More recently, there has been increasing interest in the social influences on the speech we use. We will look at the study of conversation in natural settings and at the sociological variables which influence the speech we use and choose to use.

Speech production

Psychologists have not progressed very far in explaining how we move from abstract ideas to a stream of continuous speech which expresses clearly our wants or opinions. This is mainly because the articulate speaker in full flood presents speech which is rapid and coherent and difficult to slow down or analyse. Psycholinguists have therefore tended to concentrate on what happens when this articulate fluent stream of speech is disrupted in some way or another. Much of the evidence for explanations of how we speak is derived from pauses, slips of the tongue, speech errors of other types, and the speech produced by people after brain injury of some kind.

Pauses and spontaneous speech

Spontaneous speech, unlike written text, contains many mistakes, false starts, hesitations and silences. Brief silences can broadly be divided into filled and unfilled pauses. Filled pauses are those filled with ahs, ums, etc. Radio editors edit these out from recorded interviews: it's called de-umming. Unfilled pauses are brief silences, brief being a minimum of 200 milliseconds of silence. Goldman-Eisler (1968) was one of the first people to study these pauses. She estimated that anything from 4 per cent to 54 per cent of time in discussion is silence, with around 35 per cent being the average – hence one third of our speaking time is occupied in this way. She designed an experiment to study the function of pausing; she collected a series of strip cartoons and subjects were asked both to describe the events in the strip and to interpret them. She had subjects repeat this task twice for the same cartoon, thus getting a measure of the effect of spontaneity. She found that speakers spent twice as much time pausing during the interpretation phase of the task as during the description of the cartoon, and that there was a significant decline in pausing between the first time the task was tackled and the second time. She suggested that pausing is related to planning an utterance. It's thinking time in other words. Butterworth

(1975) also considers that the planning of the next bit is what occupies pauses and also finds about 32 per cent of speaking time is occupied in this way. He suggests the planning is for the choice of lexical item, especially 'informational' or complex or unusual lexical items. This argument is unfortunately open to the criticism that it is circular. Pausing occurs – why? – cognitive processing is occurring – where? – at the start of sentences – how do you know? – because we pause there ... etc.

Slips of the tongue

An historian, nervous before his first lecture which was on the History of the Welsh-Speaking Peoples, decided a drink might steady his nerves. It did, but unfortunately also resulted in his tongue not doing what his brain had intended. He introduced his topic as a history of the 'welsh-peeping speakles'. This sort of error is often known as a 'spoonerism' after the Reverend Spooner of Oxford who was (in)famous for his mistakes.

Victoria Fromkin (1973, 1980) has carried out serious study of these errors to see what they might tell us about the way we plan and produce speech. She has found that slips of the tongue can be of several types. One type is a whole word exchange – this is when two complete words are transposed: one milk of pint please, put the bench on the cat. In nearly all these cases, these word exchanges occur within a clause and only very rarely do they occur across clauses; this is evidence, she suggests, that speech planning takes place clause by clause.

Exchanges involving only parts of words – single morphemes or phonemes are also fairly common; Spooner's errors are examples of these. Again, this is taken as evidence that our planning of speech involves selection of appropriate phonemes and then addition of necessary morphemes, such as pluralization, before the product is uttered.

Freud had a rather different explanation for speech errors. He suggested that slips of the tongue occur when an unconscious message or desire is competing with the one the speaker intends to deliver: so an error can indicate ambivalence about the message being delivered overtly. Simonini (1956) offers an example to illustrate this: Are you a man or a mouse – come on squeak (speak) up! An explanation of speech errors in psychodynamic terms has not been widely accepted by psycholinguists, but Ellis and Beattie cite experiments by Baars (1980) and Motley (1980) which offer some support for Freud. Subjects are required to say aloud pairs of words or non-words as quickly as possible. Some of the non-words are designed to allow the occurrence of slips of the tongue which may reveal unintended interests. The experiments were run on male subjects by either a male experimenter or an attractive female experimenter 'provocatively attired'. With the second experimenter, subjects produced more speech errors of the type associated with target stimuli which were 'goxy firl' and 'bine foddy' than other neutral non-words. An explanation in terms of general increased nervousness with the second experimenter is countered by the fact that other non-target stimuli did not produce an increased number of errors.

The 'tip of the tongue' phenomenon

We have all had the experience of searching for a particular, usually uncommon word, which is temporarily unavailable to us. We experience the word as on 'the tip of the tongue' (TOT). Brown and McNeill (1966) carried out a famous experiment to investigate TOTs. They required subjects to report a word after listening to its dictionary definition. Subjects who experienced TOT were questioned about the sought-after word. Frequently, they could reject wrong suggestions for it, say something about its length and number of syllables; often they could correctly suggest what it might begin or end with – the whole word though remained resolutely unavailable. Browman (1978) studied a large number of TOTs and found the first phoneme was correctly reported in 51 per cent of cases and the last phoneme in 35 per cent. These findings shed some light on how words might be stored in our mental lexicon (internal dictionary); in this respect it must be very similar to an ordinary dictionary: words are ordered alphabetically and we locate them by looking up the beginning few letters.

Clinical disorders of speech and language

Useful information about normal speech production may be available from studying people who have suffered a loss of this ability. The most common type of language difficulty among adults is aphasia (more accurately known as dysphasia – disordered language). These difficulties are often the result of a 'stroke', or cardiovascular accident (CVA). This occurs when the blood supply to the brain is temporarily disrupted. The main feature of the differing types of problems associated with strokes and head injuries is a difficulty in word finding, similar to TOT just described. The person may have problems in finding 'content' words such as nouns and verbs. Or they may have plenty of nouns but very little left in the way of the small 'function' words which mark out syntactic relations in sentences. Other patients suffering from what is known as 'jargon aphasia' will produce a jumble of words often unrelated to the questions they are trying to answer and frequently containing made-up words known as 'neologisms'. These differing problems seem to be related to the areas of the brain which have become impaired. Researchers such as Coltheart and others have studied individual cases of language problems following a stroke and tried to see what can be learned about normal language production and processing from them. Ellis, Miller and Sin (1983) studied a jargon aphasic patient and concluded that neologisms were associated more often with infrequent words; and hence the process of retrieval is similar to that experienced during TOT. Many patients who have difficulties in retrieving words can nevertheless produce some well-rehearsed speech such as nursery rhymes or familiar greeting with no apparent difficulties: it is likely that this sort of speech (automatic speech) may be mediated in some sense by the right hemisphere. Saffran *et al* (1980) and Coltheart *et al* (1980) have studied patients who cannot read with a view to explaining the role of the right hemisphere in normal reading. Should it be confirmed that the right hemisphere has some role to play in normal language processing than there would be clear indications that therapy following a stroke might utilize these areas. There remains the question though to what extent we can be confident that examining 'failures' in a system can tell us about that system when it is functioning normally.

This debate about how easily we can extrapolate from disfluency to fluent speech dominates the area of speech production. We still can say very little with certainty about the natural and successful act of mature speaking.

Speech comprehension

The basic task of speech comprehension is to unravel the meaning or idea from the physical characteristics of what is being said. This applies both to listening and reading, although the research has tended to examine these two modes of comprehension separately. We shall examine the comprehension of spoken language here. First, we have the task of recognizing and identifying the words being uttered.

The cohort model

Marslen-Wilson and fellow workers have suggested a simple but intriguing explanation of word recognition. They argue that at the onset of a particular target word, all possible words are mobilized and made available for processing. For example, with the word 'treatments', as the first part (phoneme) – 'tre' – of the word is accessed, all words *not* beginning with that phoneme are 'stood down' and left unconsidered. The next phoneme will allow another large batch of possible contenders to be discounted – 'treat' – and so on. By the end of the target the only candidate left available should match the target – 'treatments'. This sounds like a lengthy and cumbersome process but in fact Marslen-Wilson has demonstrated that it can be remarkably fast and efficient.

The model leads to a number of predictions which have been tested in simple and elegant experiments. Some words have combinations of letters and sounds which occur rarely in English and hence will allow for the discounting of contenders well before the end of the word has been reached. Such a word is 'trespass' where the combination 'tresp' is unique in English and can only lead to 'trespass' or its associated words – 'trespassing', etc. For other words it is necessary to proceed to the very end before alternatives can be discounted – 'trea ...' would be an example where there are a number of possible root endings – treacle, treadle, treasure, treatment, etc. One would predict that in a task where subjects have to press a button as soon as they hear a target word then they should be faster in 'trespass' type words than in equivalent non-unique words. This has been found to be the case (Marslen-Wilson, 1980).

Not only information contained within the words is subject to these considerations. Information from the syntactic (grammatical) structure of the sentence should allow syntactically inappropriate options also to be discounted. Thus the structure of the sentence will allow verbs to be discounted from filling a 'noun' slot – 'Pass me the ...' will cue for a concrete noun, for example. The nature of the information being conveyed by the sentence (semantic context) should also reduce the possibilities for choice enormously. Unfortunately these more general considerations are less easily transformed into neat experimental paradigms.

The spreading activation model

Aitchison and others advocate a rather different model of speech processing (McClelland and Elman, 1986). She points out that the cohort model makes no real allowance for provisional identifications – this is when we hazard a guess or make assumptions about what is coming next. The cohort model also relies upon the first part of the word being heard distinctly – this is essential for the original cohort to be mobilized. We know, though, that people can identify words when the first part is blurred or missing, 'Please shut the ... ate', for example. How can the cohort model account for this? Aitchison suggests the need for a model which allows a continual update and revision of initial uncertain guesses as to the nature of the target heard. She considers a model which would begin the process of word recognition by alerting or activating certain likely candidates as the context sets the scene for the target and the initial part of it is heard; as more information comes into the system those items which match the new information will become even more active while others will fade. Finally, there should be only one (or perhaps a very small bunch) of items which are active. Should any of these fail to meet the requirements of the context, then it is possible to backtrack and reactivate other similar items. The main difference between these two types of model is that the cohort assumes readiness as the initial state, from which items are 'stood down'; while spreading activation theories begin with a state of quiescence from which certain items are 'called up'.

It begins to seem a bit like volunteering either by stepping forward from a line or by being the only one *not* to step back!

Syntactic processing

This probably begins as soon as the first units of the sentences are received. It is likely that we normally make informed guesses or assumptions about the structure of what we are about to hear and assume a basic structure of the form: noun phrase, verb and then another noun phrase – 'the angry dog bit the frightened man'. More complex sentences are broken down into 'sentoids' which conform to this basic pattern. Bever (1970) suggests that in these sentoids the first noun phrase is regarded as the actor, the verb is the action and the second noun phrase is the object, as in the example just given. So sentoids are assumed usually to take the form actor-action-object. This form is very common in English – at least 80 per cent of these statements take this simple, active, affirmative declarative (SAAD) pattern. A number of experiments (Slobin, 1966; Mehler and Carey, 1967) seem to confirm that this structure is the easiest to recognize and understand.

An alternative view is a gap-filling process. According to this view, a hearer will hold certain phrases in memory until they can have a syntactic structure reliably assigned to them. This model predicts that a sentence of the type: 'the witch who despised sorcerers frightened little children' should be easier to process/understand than a very similar sentence such as 'the witch whom sorcerers despised frightened little children'. This sentence would require 'whom' to be held and transposed to occur after 'despised'. Wanner and Maratsos (1978) did indeed find that sentences of the second type caused extra problems of understanding, but the reasons for these difficulties remain a matter of some debate.

Sentences which are *not* of the SAAD type have been studied by Wason (1965) and Clark and Chase (1972). They found that 'the car is not blue' is more difficult (takes longer) to comprehend than 'the car is blue'. This finding remains consistent across a wide range of sentences and procedures. One reason may be the relative infrequency of occurrence in natural language of this type of negation. When we use negatives in natural speech it is often to point out or refer to the exception to a rule or expectation. 'I'm not going out tonight' implies that I usually do. 'The Dean is not a man' implies that he usually is. When negative sentences performing this function are used experimentally, they are significantly easier to comprehend than negative sentences not implying exceptionality.

Semantic processing

Communication generally takes place within a context where certain conventions are observed. These conventions can aid in sentence comprehension as they can form the basis of what is expected to be heard. Grice (1975) suggests four conventions which can aid comprehension in conversation – the normal form of language use. These are:

> quantity – be informative, but not overly so
> quality – be truthful
> relation – be relevant to the preceding context
> manner – be clear

Hearers assume that the speaker is in general trying to be informative, truthful, relevant and clear unless there are cues to indicate otherwise (facial expression, game playing context, etc.). Failure to follow these rules can result in misunderstandings or heated exchanges.

Discourse comprehension

We rarely speak in single, isolated sentences and in recent years psycholinguists have become more interested in how we understand and remember longer passages of speech or writing; this is called discourse comprehension. When reading or listening to discourse we try to make sense of it by anticipating its direction or drift. Much research on the strategies for this anticipation has been guided by the work of Clark and Haviland. They suggest that people make use of strategies. One such strategy is known as the given/new strategy. This strategy requires that first we identify which parts of a sentence are 'given' or familiar and which contain information that is novel or new. We then need to find the antecedent to match the given information and attach the new information to that point.

If we encounter a sentence which gives information for which there is no obvious antecedent, then we should have difficulty in comprehending it.

Clark and others have used the comprehension time method to study this process. Subjects are required to press a button when they have read and understood a sentence. It is possible by this measure to compare 'simple' and more difficult sentences. An example of the use of the given/new strategy can be seen from this pair of sentences:

> A. She put the jelly in the fridge.
> B. The jelly was still warm.

In understanding and responding to sentence B we identify the jelly as given information relating to its antecedent in sentence A. We mark 'it was still warm' as the new information and relocate it with the jelly's whereabouts in the fridge.

A rather more complicated process involves a 'bridging inference'.

> A. Anne entered a lot of races last year.
> B. This year she won again.

Here an inference is required concerning Anne's success in last year's races in order to comprehend sentence B accurately.

Haviland and Clark (1974) have shown that discourse requiring bridging inferences takes longer to comprehend than the simple discourse presented earlier.

If we cannot find antecedents in previous sentences for our given information by employing such strategies as bridging then we may have to employ more complex strategies – the understanding of indirect statements and figurative language necessitates more complex manoeuvres.

A. It's time Fred retired.
B. You can't teach an old dog new tricks.

This pair of sentences is readily understood as relating to the same topic and yet by the sort of strategies we have considered so far, it should be extremely difficult to follow.

Psycholinguists are finding such areas as the comprehension of metaphor to be a useful testing ground for theories of discourse comprehension.

Conversation

Conversation is a cornerstone of the social world; it is also a complex cognitive process involving the planning, generation and timing of spontaneous speech.

In some senses the biggest problem we may face in a conversation is going from silence to speech and from speech to silence, i.e. getting started and ending.

When we meet someone we can employ a variety of speech rituals to begin conversation. Some of these rituals are 'pseudoapologies' such as 'excuse me but', 'sorry to bother you', etc., or we may indulge in more formal introductions such as, 'Hello I'm Fred', 'Hello I'm a visitor here'.

When we are dealing with someone we know, these early rituals are unnecessary; instead we may use such devices as exclamatory remarks which invite some sort of reaction from the listener: 'Well, I never', 'Good heavens', etc. All these represent devices to begin; a refusal to reply to such invitations is often taken as a sign of aggression to be met with a direct question, 'what's the matter with you today?'

Keenan and Schiffelin (1976) remind us that the speaker must first secure the attention of the listener, either by verbal or non-verbal techniques, that the speaker must articulate clearly and provide sufficient information for the listener to be able to identify people and objects referred to in the conversation, and that the speaker must provide sufficient information for the listener to reconstruct the semantic relations existing between the referents in the discourse.

Another major element of conversational interaction is turn-taking. This is the smooth transition from one speaker to another; it usually occurs with little overlap or gap between speakers. Psychologists have tried to find out which cues are used to alert a potential speaker to the end of a turn so that he can move in to take a turn, and the transition can take place smoothly.

Sacks, Schegloff and Jefferson (1974) describe certain linguistic warnings that the end of a turn is nigh – if we say 'and finally . . .' then we are duty bound to relinquish the floor. A direct question to someone also indicates a new turn is about to be taken.

Duncan and Fiske (1977) show that specific signals are sent out by the finishing speaker; these are changes in intonation such as a drop in pitch or loudness, certain stereotyped phrases and the use of non-verbal signals such as gesture and gaze. These latter are probably of less importance as telephone conversations seem no less smooth in their transitions than face to face conversations.

Beattie (1983) analysed turn exchanges in conversation and did find that most included at least one terminating cue of the sort we have just considered, but some turns were successfully taken without any of these cues, so clearly we do not know the whole story yet.

Interruptions

A basic violation of this convention of smooth turn taking occurs when a speaker is interrupted. Many studies have looked at the variables associated with interrupting. Rim (1977) for example found both personality and intelligence to be important in predicting rate of interrupting: less intelligent people interrupted more often than more intelligent people; those who scored high on neuroticism or extraversion interrupted more frequently than less neurotic or introverted speakers.

Zimmerman and West (1970) carried out a well known study of mixed sex conversations. They found that 98 per cent of interruptions were made by men on women. Men did not interrupt other men very often and women never interrupted men. Esposito (1979) found similar differences amongst four-year-old girls and boys.

Beattie (1983), however, studying mixed sex tutorial groups at a British university did not find these sex differences and it seems likely that the factors underlying this effect are more complex than originally supposed. Beattie did though find some interesting differences between the rate of interruptions during political interviews. He compared interviews with James Callaghan and Margaret Thatcher in 1979 – at the time the former was Prime Minister and the latter still Leader of the Opposition. He found that Margaret Thatcher was interrupted far more frequently than James Callaghan. Beattie suggests that this difference of about 20 per cent in attempted interruptions had less to do with the sex of the two politicians than with their differing speech styles. He demonstrates that Mrs Thatcher often gives syntactic and prosodic indications that she is about to come to the end of a turn when she is really still in mid-stream. She frequently drops the pitch of her voice and stares at the interviewer in mid-flow when these are two of Duncan's turn terminating indicators described earlier. Note though that these attempted interruptions of Mrs Thatcher rarely succeed: long periods of simultaneous speech usually result in Mrs Thatcher still holding the floor and the conversation! Bull and Mayer (1988) studied recent interviews of Mrs Thatcher and Neil Kinnock. They report that both politicians were interrupted equally often, but that Mrs Thatcher commented upon such attempts 'may I just finish . . .', sometimes even when no attempt at interruption had been made. Clearly the study of such interviews can tell us a lot more about the mechanisms which govern turn-taking.

Saying goodbye

Sometimes we can give notice of the end of a conversation very explicitly – 'well, it's been nice talking to you . . .' – but more often a period of disengagement is required when there is some negotiation between the two participants as to when precisely the conversation will end. These negotiation skills are not always easily acquired and we have all had experience of trying unsuccessfully to end a conversation. The most effective technique would seem to be to put physical distance between yourself and the speaker; this cannot operate of course with telephone conversations which are an interesting case to study for ending techniques – one can always resort to the excuse of having been cut off!

Children's conversations

It is only very recently that attention has been directed towards conversations among pre-school children. Nevertheless, findings from three- and four-year-olds can tell us a lot about how the conversational skills we have been considering are developed. Attention-getting to begin a conversation among children is often achieved by non-linguistic means such as tugging the clothes of the potential listener, or by shouting. Children learn only gradually the conversational rule that if you are spoken to you should reply. Dore (1977) found that only 27 per cent of questions addressed to three-year-olds received a reply, and even among seven-year-olds statements sometimes went unacknowledged. Garvey and Berninger (1981) studied turn-taking in pre-school children and found a gradual decrease in the length of the gaps between turns as children got older; interruptions were fairly frequent but overlaps between children's speech were relatively rare. By the age of three or four children have usually already acquired many of the rudimentary skills required for conversation management.

Social influences on language

Sociolinguistics is about the importance of language to people, from small groups to whole nations. It is concerned with language variety and the implications of such variation. People differ in how they speak both from one another and across situations, adapting their language to suit the context or occasion. Some countries, such as Greece and Haiti, have two language varieties – usually referred to as high and low varieties which have separate functions. The high variety is appropriate for formal, legal or educational situations, while the low variety is more relaxed and informal – used between friends or within the family. Although English does not have such a clear split between language varieties, we all vary our choice of words, our pronunciation and our grammar when moving from one situation to another.

Several classic studies have examined the relationship between linguistic variation and other variables, in particular, social class. William Labov studied New Yorkers and Peter Trudgill studied people living in Norwich. They came to very similar conclusions from these different settings; people varied in their language use according to their social class and the situation in which they were speaking. Typically, the pattern to emerge from their results was like this:

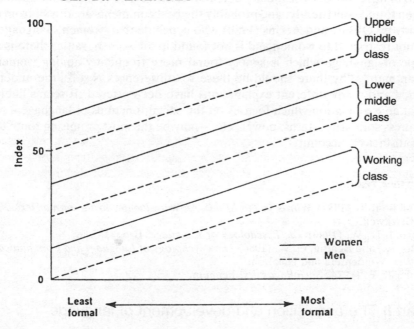

Figure 15.1 A diagrammatic representation of stratification according to social class and sex (after Coates, 1986)

People use the standard or prestige form of English more as the situation becomes more formal, and the middle classes use the standard form more than the working classes in all situations. Examples of standard English forms are 'walking' (where the 'ng' sound is pronounced) and 'hammer' where the 'h' is sounded, as opposed to 'walkin' and 'ammer' as the non-prestige forms. The reasons for this systematic language variation are complex: studies of attitudes towards forms of English by Howard Giles have shown that standard forms are regarded as superior in many ways, although there is no sound linguistic basis for this view. It would seem to be the type of speech which is encouraged and aimed for when we are in a position to think ahead about our choice of style.

In addition to class differences, there are also sex differences found in language use. One major difference is that in most speech settings women use more of the standard or prestige forms of speech than men; this has been reported from studies conducted in Norwich, Glasgow, West Wirral, Edinburgh and many other areas of Britain and the United States. Other studies of speech have examined whether certain characteristics of language choice and intonation patterns vary between men's and women's speech. Women are said to use adjectives more frequently, to emphasize their speech more, to employ tag questions – 'this is interesting, isn't it?' – and to have a richer vocabulary of colour terms. None of these features has been found consistently, and probably the best comments are drawn from a study by O'Barr and Atkins (1980) who conclude that 'women's language' is not restricted to women and is not found in all women, rather there is a type of language which is simply found more frequently among women than men. Why there should be these sex differences is still little understood and many different explanations have been offered. It seems likely that an explanation which focuses on the social functions of language – to express solidarity, status, power, etc. – may be the most promising route to a satisfactory account.

Further reading

Aitchison, J. (1987) *Words in the Mind: An introduction to the mental lexicon.* Blackwell.
Carroll, D. W. (1986) *The Psychology of Language.* Brooks Cole.
Ellis, A., and Beattie, G. W. (1986) *The Psychology of Language and Communication.* Weidenfeld and Nicolson.
Trudgill, P. (1974) *Sociolinguistics.* Penguin.

Part II The acquisition and development of language

The second part of this chapter considers how children acquire language and how it develops. Some requirements of an adequate theory of acquisition are dealt with along with five very different approaches.

Selected details of the developmental sequence are considered, from communication by means of smiles and gestures to multi-word utterances. The role of individual differences is discussed as well as the impact of other aspects of cognition on language development.

Theories of language acquisition

Common sense suggests that children acquire language by imitation and from parental teaching. Child speech is clearly modelled on parental (or caretaker) sounds, and the early picture book naming routine, among others, provides opportunities for parental teaching. These processes account for only part of what is acquired; some of the child's early utterances include items which are clearly not imitations – neologisms like 'timbo' which could be words but happen not to be, and, later, past tenses like 'gived' for gave and 'taked' for took are unlikely to have been heard from adults. Further, it would be most unusual at any age to find a child whose utterances consisted of unmodified imitation. Thus while imitation is clearly involved its role is at best only partial. The notion of imitation is, of course, limited in that it applies to descriptive rather than to explanatory accounts. Also, as will be seen later, the study of links between maternal influence (in naturalistic settings) and language development has produced equivocal findings.

What then needs to be explained? Specifically, how each child learns his own language; but this involves more general issues. Much is already known about the acquisition and development of language which any plausible theory must account for. Pinker (1979) in the journal *Cognition* divides this evidence into six areas. The issues raised might be formulated as questions as follows.

1. What is it about language which makes it learnable?
'Learnable' is used in the special sense that the infant acquires it merely from exposure to it, and virtually without explicit instruction. (Walking is learnable in this sense by infants, but not the moves in chess.)

2. How is it that a child can acquire any language as its native language? Skinner (1957) proposed that each child acquired it by means of operant conditioning. Since each language has its own grammar, Chomsky holds that each child behaves as if it had innate knowledge of a universal grammar which treats each language as a special case. It has also been seen as consistent with the notion of a general problem solving capacity which has language as a special domain. (See also the sections on Skinner and Chomsky.)

3. How does the child learn so much about language in so short a time? By the age of three most children use well-formed sentences, draw

on a vocabulary of 1,000 words or more and are well on their way to communicative competence. Critics have questioned the notion of 'so much'. Is there anything to compare it with? Miller (1965) makes the comparison with the time it would take to learn all possible sentences separately. He claims that only with a generative (creative, rule governed) system is it possible to acquire 'so much'.

4. How is what a child learns about language related to environmental input?
This will include both the linguistic environment, e.g. the speech of others, as well as the non-linguistic environment in which this speech is set.

5. How are the several stages of the developmental sequence linked together?

6. What are the links between the development of language and other aspects of cognitive development?
This includes the development of perceptual discriminations, attention and memory.

These questions are wide ranging and it is hardly surprising that there is no theoretical approach which adequately covers any of these areas, let alone all of them. The last five of these questions will form the focus of the remainder of this chapter. The first question represents a relatively recent way of investigating language acquisition, called Learnability Theory. This is a linguistics enterprise which seeks to determine the characteristics of a system which is 'learnable' (in the sense described above) by induction from a set of sentences, with the kind of limited feedback that psychological studies have shown to pertain (Gleitman and Wanner, 1982; Chapter 10).

A number of major proposals have been made which address various aspects of the questions discussed. Five (of many) such proposals will be considered briefly in the next section. The particular choices were dictated partly in the interest of diversity and partly in terms of the influence exerted in accounting for aspects of acquisition and development.

Five approaches

B. F. Skinner (b. 1904)

As a learning theorist, Skinner sees no need to differentiate between language and other behaviour. Speech and language are held to be acquired by operant conditioning. The emphasis is upon learning through experience, according to the principles proposed by learning theorists. The innate prerequisites for the acquisition of behavioural responses are few: the capacity to form stimulus-reponse associations, and to discriminate between and to generalize among stimuli. This capacity is not confined, of course, to humans.

According to this view, the random or imitative sounds uttered by infants become, through selective reinforcement afforded by parental attention and praise, increasingly like adult sounds. The verbal responses are shaped by the parents, who, as time goes on, tend to withhold rewards until the standard sound is matched by the child's own, or until the word used matches the situation. Thus a parent might say 'what's this' holding up a biscuit, but delaying handing it over until the infant has produced the appropriate verbal response (which may, of course, be anything between 'b' and 'biscuit' according to expectation).

The case that Skinner proposes for language acquisition is, thus, a simple extension of his views about behaviour in general. The acquisition of language, or to use Skinnerian terminology, verbal behaviour, comes about according to the same laws of reinforcement by which animal behaviour is shaped.

In this way, Skinner deals with both of the central questions posed. 'What' a child acquires when he acquires language is a set of verbal responses; 'how' he acquires them is by the process of operant conditioning.

The strict Skinnerian view has been criticized on the grounds that the child is seen as being only passively involved in language acquisition. The opponents of this sort of approach point to the way in which children behave creatively with language. That is, not only do children understand sentences which they have never heard before, but they also utter both words and sentences which are novel. Thus, words like 'sheeps', 'goed' and 'oftenly' are unlikely to be products of imitation alone. The thrust of these criticisms is not that the proposals are implausible, but that they fail to fit the facts of language acquisition.

The quantity of empirical evidence bearing directly on the Skinnerian view of acquisition is small; some work assessing the influence of various types of model for imitation will be discussed later.

Noam Chomsky (b. 1928)

Noam Chomsky, in a thorough review of Skinner's book, *Verbal Behaviour* (1957), presented a number of arguments aimed at demonstrating the inadequacy of a learning-theory approach to acquisition. He contended that it is untrue that children learn language only through the meticulous care of adults who shape their verbal repertoire, and that '. . . a grammar is no more learned than, say, the ability to walk is learned'. Since the late 1950s Chomsky has advocated a view diametrically opposed to that of Skinner. For, while Skinner emphasizes the influence of 'nurture', on acquisition, Chomsky sees 'nature' as playing the dominant role. He holds that the structure of language, that is, the sound system (phonology), the rules for forming words by combining sounds (morphology), and the rules for combining words (syntax), is, to a considerable degree, specified biologically. That is, just as it is a part of 'human' nature to walk upright, so it is also natural to speak and understand language. Experience serves not so much to teach, as to activate this innate capacity for language.

An infant, whatever the nationality of his parents, or his country of birth, if placcd in a foreign language community where he had contact only with the new language, would acquire that language in much the same way as a native infant. While the Behaviourist sees in this something about the universality of the way in which caretakers shape the language of children, it can also be interpreted as indicating the presence of universal structural elements in language. Chomsky holds that implicit knowledge of these linguistic universals must be part of the innate equipment of each child. The acquisition of language takes place as the development of this endowment. Two sorts of universals are distinguished: 'formal', and 'substantive'. Formal universals are those relating to the overall structural properties of language, whereas substantive universals are linguistic elements found in all languages – for example, certain kinds of sounds are common to all languages, as are such categories as noun and verb.

Chomsky's theory has stimulated an enormous volume of research both on acquisition and adult usage. (It is important to note that Chomsky, a linguist, has conducted no psychological experiments himself. Nevertheless, many psychologists have undertaken work stemming from his proposals.) While some of the work (on linguistic universals, for example) has produced findings consistent with Chomsky's predictions, at least in broad outline, other work has begged the question as to whether the similarities in acquisition across languages are to be accounted for in terms of innate and universal linguistic information, or in terms of common innate cognitive capacities underlying the capacity for language.

Chomsky has, further, argued that the child acquires the grammar of his language, not so much by learning it, as by using the speech he hears to choose among possible grammars stored in what he has termed the child's language acquisition device (LAD). It is held that this is the more remarkable because of the 'meagre and degenerate' sample of speech usually available for this purpose. The speech used in the home is rarely formal, and frequently consists of the abbreviated and half-finished sentences used among intimates. It is questionable, however, as to whether the grammar needs to be obtained from speech only. For the child hears this speech in a social context, and it seems possible that he uses this as a means of deciding what the sound means.

Chomsky's work has provided an elaborate and cogent statement of the nativist position. It was not intended to suggest that mechanisms like imitation and reinforcement were inappropriate explanations, but rather to demonstrate that learning-theory approaches by themselves were inadequate. There is a measure of agreement among psychologists here, but research carried out since 1960 has produced only limited support for Chomsky's account.

Eric Lenneberg (1921–75)

Eric Lenneberg, in his book, *Biological Foundations of Language* (1967), drew on a wide range of studies, anatomical, physiological, neurological, genetic and pathological to support the thesis that biological endowments make language uniquely possible for man. These include some which suggest that verbal behaviour is linked with a considerable number of anatomical and physiological characteristics of the human physique; for example, the lateralization of the speech function in the left cerebral hemisphere of the brain, special co-ordination centres in the brain for speech, and special respiratory tolerance for prolonged speech activities. Lenneberg drew attention to the difference in development potential between the human and chimpanzee brain. The human brain at birth is about 24 per cent of its adult weight while the chimp brain is some 60 per cent. He further held that there was no evidence to suggest that any non-human form had the capacity to acquire even primitive stages of language development. In the late 1960s and early 1970s, a number of chimps were trained in language-like behaviour. To what extent Lenneberg's claim needs to be modified in the light of such studies, if at all, is not clear. It is possible that several chimp studies, now in progress, may provide further light. While animals do not acquire human language, however much they are exposed to it, in humans, acquisition of language goes on in spite of dramatic handicaps for some children. Children of parents who have no spoken language, or who are themselves deaf, for example, acquire language without any great delay. Lenneberg also points to linguistic features common to all languages as consistent with the notion of human language as species specific. He further cites the regularity of the developmental sequence of acquisition: babbling at about six months, the first 'word' at about twelve months, the two-word 'sentence' by about two years and competence in communication which is complete in a basic sense by five years of age.

That this sort of pattern is to be found across widely different languages and cultures is attested by the work of Slobin and his colleagues. Pathological case histories also indicate that beyond the age of puberty, when language function has been lateralized in the left hemisphere (for the great majority), the capacity for further language acquisition decreases dramatically. This, then, is some of the material brought to bear on the thesis of the uniqueness of language to man. Lenneberg held that human language is a species specific cognitive capacity, a view shared by Noam Chomsky.

In spite of the clear demonstration of the involvement of physical maturation in the acquisition of language, it is impossible to specify in neuro-physiological terms the relationship between them.

Jean Piaget (b. 1896)

Piaget cannot accept either the Behaviourist or the Chomskyan view of language acquisition, and, while his own approach entails the notion of a strong maturational influence, he proposes that language development grows out of the changing cognitive processes of the child, which in turn reflects the changing nature of the interactions between the child and his environment. This view sees the period before the onset of language as one in which the child comes to know his world in such a way as to enable him to make sense of at least some of the vocal sounds that he hears. Interaction with the environment will be largely in terms of caretakers, food, the consequences of an increasing ability to move about, and such like; and it is not surprising that his early words are dominated by those referring to salient aspects of his world. This is a plausible account of the onset of speech, but one which is difficult, in practice, to test. Clearly, infants do understand much about their world before they begin to speak. It may even be that this understanding is an essential ingredient for language. The important question, however, is whether, by itself, the understanding is sufficient to account for language acquisition. Helen Sinclair-de-Zwart (1969), one of the team of Genevan researchers, has provided data which offer some support for the supposition that cognitive changes precede rather than follow language changes.

It will be seen in the next chapter that this theme is central to Piaget's view of development. What evidence is there to support this point of view? It was noted earlier that the bulk of the work performed by Piagetian psychologists is based on a clinical approach, in which children are required to perform tests and answer questions in situations ingeniously contrived to investigate changing cognitive strategies.

Four- and five-year-old children appear to believe that the amount of a liquid changes with the shape of a container. Thus water from a standard beaker poured into a narrower vessel elicits a response indicating that the amount of liquid is now considered to be greater. Most children of four years of age will respond in this way while most children of six years and more will be able to compensate for the decrease in the width of the container, and maintain that the quantity of liquid is identical (has been conserved) across the two situations. This task, conservation of volume (one of a range of Piagetian conservation tasks), was used to divide the children into three groups: total absence of conservation, intermediate stage, and conservation present.

The children's verbal capacities were explored, using both production tasks (where the children's use of language is examined) and comprehension tasks (their understanding of words used by others). The following linguistic features were examined:

1. Use of comparatives (larger, smaller) as opposed to absolute terminology (big, small).
2. Use of differentiated terms like 'short' and 'thin' as distinct from an overall application of 'little'.
3. The type of sentence used to co-ordinate the two dimensions, e.g. 'This is tall but it's thin'.

The comprehension task 'find a pencil which is longer but thinner' was performed correctly by practically all the children; but, while the three groups did not differ in this task, there were striking differences between the extreme groups on the description tasks. Of those children who 'conserved', the large majority used comparatives; those who did not, used absolute terminology almost exclusively. Those with conservation all used different terms for different dimensions; of those without, three-quarters used a single term, e.g. 'small' for both 'short' and 'thin'. Those with conservation were more skilful in combining descriptions: 'this pencil is longer but thinner, and the other is short but thick'. The group without conservation mostly described only one dimension, or used four separate sentences.

A further series of experiments attempted to teach the group without conservation the verbal skills which distinguished the other group. Having completed this verbal training the children were again assessed to see whether this had made a difference to their ability in the conservation task. In the event, it had not for 90 per cent of the children, whose ability to conserve remained unchanged. It had, indeed, proved difficult to teach the non-conservers some of the verbal skills. It was relatively easy for them to learn to use differentiated terms like 'short' and 'thin', harder for them to use 'plus' and 'minus' ('*plus*' and '*moins*') to produce comparatives, and still more difficult for them to learn combined descriptions. While the verbal training did bring about an awareness of the relation between the height of the liquid and the width of the stem, it did not bring about the ability to 'conserve' for volume.

This provides some support for the Piagetian view of the relation between language and intellectual operations, that language is not a sufficient condition for bringing about intellectual changes; and that, indeed, it is changes in intellectual operations which initiate changes in language.

M. A. K. Halliday (b. 1925)

Halliday is critical of an approach to language (like Chomsky's) which refers almost exclusively to structure, to the neglect of function. When a child acquires language he acquires both. What constitutes a 'proper balance' between the two is problematic; Halliday's account of acquisition has as clear an emphasis on function as Chomsky's has on structure. He draws attention to the communicative function of cries, smiles, gestures and eye-contact, long before the appearance of words. Halliday described six such functions observed in the development of his own son, between 9 and 18 months of age. These all reflect aspects of social interaction and include the satisfaction of his various needs, self expression, and the manipulation of those around him. They are later supplemented by a seventh function, later because it requires language, by means of which the child attempts to inform a listener of something novel in the environment. For Halliday, meaning originates in social interaction, and acquiring language is 'learning to mean' (the title of his book on this aspect of his work), and at the same time 'learning his culture'. From those seven functions emerges the adult language conceived within the same functional framework. A significant problem with this approach is that of translating the theory into terms which will permit of wider empirical enquiry.

The five approaches considered here are based on very different sources of information. Two, at least, draw on little more than common observation. Skinner's account is based mainly on an elaboration of his operant conditioning principles, drawing on earlier studies for support. Chomsky's account, similarly, does not rest on any special observation of young children, but is based on his linguistic work on the structure of language. Lenneberg does draw on his own empirical studies of both children and adults, albeit principally within a clinical context. Only Piaget and Halliday base their findings on observations of children in the process of acquiring language. It is to a consideration of methodology that we now turn.

Research methods

It is difficult, though not impossible, to experiment on the language of children in the first two years of life. Thus the method most often used is observation. This may be done without any intervention although it is usually systematic. Observations may be made regularly at fixed times and places or under specified conditions, such as when the child is playing with certain toys.

The development of children's language has often been recorded in diary form. Charles Darwin kept a diary of his own son's development. Such diaries provide records which are remarkably consistent about a number of different aspects, for example, the way in which children's early understanding of word meanings tends, at first, to be overextended. The word 'cow' might be used for a cow or a pig or a horse, and the word 'moon' for a range of articles which have the property of circularity. But diary data have limitations: they are necessarily selective and normally only record what does occur, when frequently what fails to occur is also important.

More recently, tape and video apparatus have made it possible to re-examine the original observations with a consequent increase in accuracy. They also allow repeated inspection by a number of observers and the possibility of assessment in terms of inter-observer reliability. The raw data are then transcribed into written form prior to analysis. Studies of this kind are thus inherently very time consuming, and in order to complete research projects within a reasonable period it is usually found necessary to restrict the number of subjects, typically to two or three and rarely more than ten. This inevitably limits the generality of the findings.

One of the most useful features of the video recording is that it records virtually 'everything'. This makes possible a range of related exploratory investigations; any or all of such factors as the child's gestures, his direction of gaze, the presence of toys, maternal comments and so on, may throw light on the child's own speech and understanding.

Data from an observational study normally represent only 'what occurred with what', restricting analysis to some measure of association. One might wish to investigate, for example, the effect of some maternal behaviour on the child's speech. Correlation analysis alone provides limited help, being unable to specify the direction of influence. This may be from mother to child or the reverse, or, while the data are being collected, sometimes one and sometimes the other. In the absence of corroborative evidence correlational indices need to be interpreted with caution.

From communication to language

The child's first word is often an eagerly awaited event, yet it is doubtful whether it is recognizable, except in retrospect, perhaps. The title of this section was used by Bruner (1975) to describe events leading up to the transition through the borderland that contains the first word. This section traces the changes which occur as the child passes from the prelinguistic stage through the one and two word stages.

Precursors of language

First words rarely appear before the child is 10–12 months old, but language-like capacities are in evidence long before that. It has been shown that infants only a few weeks old can distinguish the mother's voice from that of someone else as well as make fine discriminations between similar sounds. The infant's own voice, active from birth, soon moderates from seemingly uncontrolled crying to include murmurings and soft cooings, particularly during feeding, and at about six months, repetitions of single sounds, like 'ma-ma-ma-ma' which can give the impression of playing or practising with sounds. All this time the infant is becoming more active socially, particularly following the advent of the smile at about six weeks. Soon, much of this activity takes on the appearance of intentional communication. Thus, important features of language, if only in rudimentary form, appear to be in evidence from an early age. What follows is a consideration of some further possible precursors of language made available by more systematic methods.

Several studies have used video recording to examine the simultaneous movements and actions of mother and child. Colwyn Trevarthen (1974) has published such a study under the title 'Conversations with a two-month-old'. Among the interesting proposals to emerge from this work is that from a few weeks old infants behave differently towards objects as compared with people. With objects they show signs of visual exploration, tracking and trying to grasp. Communication-like behaviours, however, were reserved for people. These included co-ordination of activity between mother and child like the turn-taking of normal conversation. It also included what the author called pre-speech, a soundless moving of the lips and tongue by the infant. Associated with this from time to time were gestures like those of adults involved in animated conversation.

Bruner has also described the development of communication skills within the pre-linguistic period. One such is the establishment of a common focus of attention by mother and child. In the first instance the mother's following of the child's gaze means that she knows what he is attending to and is the better able to interpret his needs and actions. It was also found that as early as four months, in some cases, infants also follow the gaze of another. Thus a system of joint selective attention develops which provides a basis for communication, and a procedure for the establishment of common reference. Serving something of the same purpose is pointing. By eight months, possibly earlier, the outstretched arm which reaches towards an object loses the grasping feature it had, replacing it by a directional gesture. By about one year the infant no longer grasps at the picture on a page but touches it, finally, with just the index finger. Such routines provide support for rudimentary naming.

Bruner further describes the infant's development of a strategy for enlisting help in joint activity as a major feature in the establishment of a wide basis for acts of communication. The infant is well equipped with unmistakable vocal patterns which are used to draw attention to his distress. Bruner calls this the 'demand mode'. Once the infant comes to expect attention to such calls the urgency of the distress call is reduced to an initial call interspersed with pauses, possibly anticipating attention; this is the 'request mode'. Should this fail the infant reverts to the demand mode. Next in order is the 'exchange mode' in which the infant calls or gestures for some object, which by 8–10 months he not only receives but also gives back, often with appropriate vocalization such as 'ta' in either or both directions. This sequence of socializing functions passes into the 'reciprocal mode' in which the child is capable of enlisting help for performing a task, like putting various shapes into a toy letter box, which needs two people, not only to perform the task but to co-ordinate the effort. The infant seeks guidance by means of repeated eye contact with the helper. This procedure is built not just on the ability to vocalize, but also on the ability to interact to some purpose by means of vocal and non-vocal signals. This is a pattern for an act of communication.

Piaget saw the emergence of the first words in terms of the approach of the end of the sensorimotor period (see Chapter 16). Whereas the infant's representation of the outside world has to this point been in terms of actions, words confer upon him a new mode, a symbolic one. Aspects of the world around can be represented by symbols, in this case, by words. The transition to verbal communication, when it does come, is not sudden. Nonverbal communication, what Halliday has called protolanguage, exists for some time side-by-side with 'babble' type words and 'proper' words, words which label objects in the environment; gradually these label words begin to dominate and the babble words to disappear.

Beyond this transition it has been customary to describe next a one-word stage followed by a two-word stage. It is important that these should not be taken as referring to well defined and homogeneous periods, but rather as indicating the dominant type of data met with in two consecutive periods. Development proceeds throughout, sometimes barely perceptible, but at others incredibly fast.

Single-word utterances

One example of variability which occurs within what has been called the one-word stage can be seen in some of the work of Martyn Barrett (1986). He draws attention to the way in which children may rapidly change the way they use words. For example, the first appearance of his son Adam's uses of the word 'duck' (pronounced 'dut') when the baby was one year and two days old (1:0:2) was in the context of hitting one of his three toy ducks off the edge of the bath. For some days it occurred only on such occasions, and was context bound in this sense. Then he said the word while playing with the duck in a different situation and in response to the question 'What's that?' (1:0:15); then on seeing a yellow toy duck (1:0:17), and real ducks (1:1:6). The use of 'duck' was on the way to becoming decontextualized. At (1:5:18) he used it while looking at real swans, and at real geese, and at (1:6:7) while looking at a picture of a quail. This insight into one boy's use of the word 'duck' covers a period of over six months, from a much underextended use to a vastly overextended use. As other words enter the child's vocabulary, correctly employed – words like 'goose' and 'swan' which draw contrasts between their referents and the duck – 'duck' moves towards the standard use by the elimination of alternatives like these.

It may be inferred that such changes in use are related to changes in the meaning of the word for the child, and the step-by-step approach to standard usage has been seen as a potential source of insight into the relation between vocabulary and conceptual development. Eve Clark (1973), for example, drawing on both diary data and experimental findings has provided support for her semantic features hypothesis. This held that word meanings were based on semantic features (or components), some related to perceptual or other cognitive features, like atoms of meaning. Thus an underextended use of a word would be the outcome of too few semantic features, overextension with too many, and changing of meaning with gaining or losing features. One of a number of objections to this approach was that while it was highly suited to an object clearly belonging to one category or another on the basis of its features, it was not so useful in dealing with the gradual changes which may take place within a category. Robins and sparrows might be regarded as prototype birds with chickens less so, and ostriches much less so. Binary (yes or no) features are unable to convey the gradual variation.

The holophrase

What do these early single-word utterances mean, and what does the child mean by them? Probably different things at different times. Single-word utterances have frequently been interpreted by both parents and psychologists as having the force of complete sentences (or holophrases). Support may be drawn from the way in which children use the same utterance in different contexts and with different intonation. For example, a child might point to her brother's sock and say his name, and anyone present might add, 'Yes, it's Tom's sock'. On another occasion she may tearfully utter his name to a parent, having recently been teased by him. The 'rich' interpretation which draws on the context as well as the utterance may suggest possession in the first case, and the role of agent (in the child's distress), in the second, suggesting sentences like, 'This is Tom's sock' and 'Tom made me cry', though only 'Tom' was uttered. In neither case does it appear appropriate to construe the utterance as having a simple labelling function.

In 1970 David McNeill argued that holophrastic speech was consistent with the notion that even very young children had a working knowledge (Chomsky's tacit, i.e. untaught, knowledge) of basic grammatical relations, that, 'the facts of language acquisition could not be as they are unless the concept of a sentence is available to children at the start of their learning'. In addition to the sort of evidence considered above he drew attention to the use of label words in the absence of their referents. He instanced a child pointing to the place on the refrigerator where bananas were usually kept, uttering 'nana'. Again, interpretation of the utterance as a label seems less plausible than that of some kind of statement or question.

Plausible as the holophrase or sentence-word is, its dependence on 'rich' interpretation admits of speculation. Even if some links between banana and refrigerator are implicit in the child's pointing, are these links necessarily in sentence form?

Complex messages

In 1976 Greenfield and Smith provided a significant alternative to the holophrase position. They proposed that children use the single uttered word to create complex messages rather than sentences. The difference between this and the holophrase position is that the nonverbal context is taken as it is to provide the remainder of the message, rather than transformed into sentence material. The complex message thus consists of the combination of the single word with such nonverbal elements as gesture, intonation and the objects and action involved in the situation.

These proposals arose from their observational study of the one word utterances of two boys, Nicky and Matthew. They propose that their findings show that the function of the single word changed over the period of the investigation. At first it simply accompanied some action performed by the child, but added no information to the message. One example of this is when the child waves and says 'bye-bye'. The message of the wave is not added to by the spoken word. In the fourth and final stage the spoken word plays a vital role in the message, and is aimed to bring about a change in an entire event, as when 'again' is used to bring about the repetition of part of an ongoing event. Between these two Greenfield and Smith describe two further roles played by the uttered word.

They further claimed that the single-word utterances were used in such a way as to emphasize that aspect of the message which maximizes the communicative value of the utterance. They found that the four functions just mentioned were acquired in the same order by both boys. In a more fine-grained analysis of twelve roles, summarized by the four considered, the correlation between acquisition orders for the two boys was very high.

An outstanding weakness of the study is, of course, that it involved only two boys, imposing severe limitations on the generality of the findings. Subsequent work in this vein has provided some support and has again drawn attention to the skilful way in which children insert single words into action contexts to communicate so efficiently, in spite of linguistic immaturity, that hearers experience the utterances as if they were complete messages. Greenfield and Smith claim that 'a semantic approach which derives grammar from relations among perceived aspects of the real world opens the way to a theoretical treatment of one word speech as continuous with later grammatical development'.

McShane (1980) sounds a cautionary note. He proposes that for early single-word utterances where naming is involved, children may not be aware that they are naming objects. It is as if the child learns a word, that is learns to make a sound that is somehow appropriate in a given context, but only later, perhaps weeks after, divines that this sound is the name of something specific in the context.

Later, often suddenly, at some time during the months which precede the child's second birthday there normally occurs what has been variously described as the 'vocabulary explosion', the 'designation hypothesis' and the 'naming insight'. It is as if the child has become aware that everything has a name. He continually demands of his caretakers the names of common items, and has great delight in using them. His vocabulary increases very rapidly and he begins to use words in combination, as in 'see sock', 'mummy push', 'that knee', 'big boot', 'two sock', 'a celery'. Some of them, like the last two in this list, are clearly not copies of adult speech.

Multi-word utterances and the acquisition of syntax

While two-word utterances take over from single words it should not be supposed that utterances are exclusively of two words in the period following the second birthday. There are considerable differences among individuals. Some quite normal children have barely begun at this age, but by the time two-word utterances are established in the repertoire of a child, his speech is likely to include one-word utterances and perhaps the occasional three-word sequence. Nevertheless two-word utterances are dominant and their arrival offers further insights into the language acquisition problem. As soon as two words are used in sequence the question of order arises, providing an opportunity for the investigation of the beginnings of syntax. Work in this area was widespread in the sixties. One early suggestion was that children learn the grammatical order of words by a process of contextual generalization, a generalization resulting from learning which position certain words usually occupy. The learning was based on the child's observation of the adult model. Braine (1963), who proposed this, was able to find only limited experimental support for the hypothesis. He provided an alternative approach to the question of the acquisition of syntax by listing all the two-word utterances of three two-year-olds, Andrew, Gregory and Steven, over a given period. His hypothesis predicted that the order of the words in the two-word strings would be consistent with the normal adult order. On examination of the information collected this was frequently not the case. Neither were the words combined randomly, and Braine set out to describe what appeared to be a primitive but systematic syntax by which the two-word strings might be obtained. There was no suggestion, of course, that the three boys consciously used these ordering rules, but rather that the rules provided an accurate description of their linguistic behaviour.

He identified two groups of words in their utterances, one involving a small number of words which occurred frequently (which he called pivot words), and a much larger group which occurred less frequently (which he called open words). The pivot class included such words as 'allgone', 'my', 'it' and 'get', while the open class had words such as 'ball', 'baby', 'book', 'daddy', and 'push'. Most frequent among the output of these three boys were strings like 'allgone shoe' (a pivot followed by an open word), and 'push it' (open plus pivot). Pivot words rarely appeared alone but open words did. Thus while 'ball', 'daddy' and 'push' might be found as one-word utterances, 'get' and 'my' rarely, if ever, did. From such findings Braine proposed a detailed syntax capable of accounting for both the one- and two-word utterances of the three boys. The notion of writing grammars in this way was hailed with some enthusiasm because it offered an additional way of investigating language development; by writing grammars for individuals or groups at different times direct comparisons might be made to follow specific changes in language over time. This promise was not fulfilled for a number of reasons. As data from other studies became available it was clear that the syntax for Braine's subjects was not equally appropriate for other children. For example, while in his study pivotal constructions accounted for 75 per cent of all utterances, in another the corresponding figure was only 17 per cent. Some children, it was found, do use pivots like 'more' and 'no' on their own. A further problem was the occurrence of combinations which contained no pivot, e.g. 'Kitty ball', 'Daddy car', contrary to Braine's expectations.

Bloom (1970) also found such combinations. One of these has become famous, i.e. 'Mommy sock'; it was found in two different contexts and Bloom proposed to account for this and similar combinations in semantic rather than syntactic terms. In one context 'Mommy sock' was said while having a sock put on by the mother; in the other the child said it while pointing to a sock which belonged to the mother. In context these identical utterances might be seen as having different meanings, the first, a comment on what was going on and the second a statement of possession. (Pivot grammar does not allow such a distinction to be made.) Several investigators have preferred to interpret two-word utterances in semantic rather than syntactic terms, arguing that the expression of meaning represents a (if not the) central purpose of language. The regularities of the two-word utterances have accordingly been seen in terms of such semantic units as agent, object, possession, location, etc. where agent stands for someone who does something, object for an entity which has something done to it, for example. In favour of this semantic approach it has been argued that it provides a grammar which is less abstract than pivot grammar, that the child's real world would seem to be much more likely to be occupied by agents, objects and the like than by open and closed classes of word. There is much evidence to suggest that children from different parts of the world are saying much the same sort of thing at the two-word stage. Roger Brown (1973) proposed that all the meanings expressed could be accounted for in terms of eight relations and three operations, the relations including agent–object (mummy sock) and the operations, recurrence (more milk), non-existence (allgone milk) and nomination (this [is a] cup). Drawing on a wide range of material, Brown showed that this basic list accounted for some 70 per cent of his two-word data, although in some recent work this figure is smaller.

Both syntactic and semantic approaches have provided insights into the problems involved in accounting for the linguistic output of the early two-year-old. Neither has proved entirely adequate. Among the difficulties encountered have been those associated with the changing nature of the output as language develops, and the wide differences between individuals. Together they may cover some of the variability which has limited the generalization of findings.

Our account of language development so far has been mainly in terms of linguistic elements: words, syntax and semantics. It is clear that other factors influence its course and that our account would be deficient without a consideration of them. Important among them are the linguistic environment – the people in the child's life and the ways in which they talk to him and the personality of the child which makes his developmental story unique. We consider these in the next two sections.

Motherese

Interest in the influence of the immediate linguistic environment, normally an environment in which the mother plays a major role, arose in the context of Chomsky's contention that while exposure to language was necessary for development, its influence was limited. It was the child's innate linguistic endowment which directed and powered the development. The child was exposed to what Chomsky described as a degenerate sample of language, the normal domestic noises and unsystematic speech of intimates. The many who reacted against this pointed to the care normally taken by those concerned with the infant, and in particular the mother, to modify their normal speech in ways intended to enhance communication with the infant. A range of research projects provided support that this was so. The special register adopted includes speaking more slowly, using exaggerated intonation, and utterances which are short and simple. This became known as motherese. The next step was to determine whether motherese was associated with language acquisition and development. Videotaped records of mothers in natural play situations with a child have shown some, but surprisingly few, links between maternal behaviour and infant progress. An unexpected finding, for example, was the absence of a link between length of maternal utterance and length of child utterance. Some stable links have been found; one example is that between the mother's use of 'yes/no' questions and the child's use of such auxiliary verbs as 'did' and 'can'. This has been seen as a consequence of the close association of the two in use, and the prominence of the auxiliary at the beginnings of the questions, 'Did you wash your hands?' 'Yes/No'. 'Can you find it?' But clear findings of this kind are few.

One study did show that more advanced speech was addressed to linguistically more advanced children, providing some support for the notion of mothers who are 'fine tuned' to the child's linguistic needs. However, the fine-tuning (or omniscient mother) hypothesis is at variance with the finding that most parents appear to be ignorant of their child's special linguistic needs. Shatz (1983) also proposed and tested the 'executive child' hypothesis, which proposes that it is the child who tunes in to the linguistic environment, taking from it that which is appropriate at each stage. This hypothesis has done little better than the other. Both appear to be involved but in highly specific contexts.

One of the most influential assessments of the motherese hypothesis has been presented by Gleitman, Newport and Gleitman in the *Journal of Child Language* (1984). The title of an earlier paper by these authors provides something of a summary of their findings in this area. It is: '"Mother, I'd rather do it myself": some effects and non-effects of maternal speech style'.

Some recent work has suggested that substantial influences on the development of language may be linked with interactions between the linguistic and non-linguistic environment. Harris *et al* (1986) have shown that in their study of the maternal speech of two groups of children, one showing a normal rate of development, the other slower than normal, clear differences were apparent between the two groups in respect of the opportunities they were afforded for making the link between these two environments. Mothers of the children in the slower group made fewer references to objects at the centre of the child's attention, and more references to objects other than those to which he was attending. They further changed the topic of conversation without providing an appropriate non-verbal context. Here the study of utterances in context has yielded rich supporting evidence for the distinction between the roles of the two groups of mothers.

The role of individual differences

Two recurrent themes in the literature considered have been the limitation of studies using small numbers, and the failure to give an account of the child's role in language development. Several of the sets of findings considered have shown only limited validity outside the original subjects. Bruner, Halliday and others have depicted the child as a willing and eager partner in communication from an early age. It would indeed be surprising if such differences as arise among children – even in motivational terms alone – should not play a part in their personal development of language.

In a review of work carried out in this area, Nelson in 1981 drew attention to the inadequacy of the typical research paradigm of the previous decade, where, she argues, consistent with a Chomskyan expectation of a near universal sequence, it was appropriate to study small numbers of children in order to identify significant features of development; examination of the role of individual differences was irrelevant to such an enterprise.

She draws attention to some of her early work to investigate the role of individual differences, and to the need for alternative paradigms to take account of these in a climate where the number of known factors involved in language development had increased considerably, to include, for example, both social and cognitive factors. Bloom in 1970 and Nelson in 1973 had reported differences in the vocabularies of their subjects. Nelson, examining the first fifty words of each of her eighteen subjects, identified two groups in terms of the types of words they had acquired. Both groups had a preponderance of labels. For ten of them this amounted to about 75 per cent, as compared with about 53 per cent for the others. The latter, however, had more social patterns, like, 'stop it', 'I want it', than the former. The former she called 'referentials', the latter 'expressives'. The earlier work of Bloom had produced a similar contrast between nominals (dominance of labels) and pronominals (pronouns, principally personal pronouns). Some subsequent work saw this contrast in functional terms as between analytic (reflecting an interest in naming elements) and holistic (concerned with the expression of broader, complete statements). While these contrasts are not drawn in the same way, they represent some measure of overall agreement about this manifestation of individual differences. The work subsequent to Nelson's review and up to 1986 provided further support, and demonstrated ways in which these differences had been seen to arise. This was principally in terms of maternal influences – expressive mothers tended to have expressive children – particularly where the rapport between mother and child was optimal in the sort of terms discussed earlier in the work of Margaret Harris and of others, where mothers' comments were aimed at whatever was of central interest to the child, and were appropriate and well timed.

These, then, are the differences which emerge. But what of their psychological significance? Do they represent a conflict with earlier findings or are they complementary? Are they related to recognizable past or present states of the child? Do they have stable long-term consequences? Would the data yield different findings if different word categories, say child centred rather than adult centred, were used? At present there are no clear answers to any of these questions.

Language development and cognition

Research beyond the two-word stage

Development beyond the 'vocabulary explosion' proceeds quickly and, because of the child's ever-widening competence, on an increasing variety of fronts. Beyond the two-word stage, not only does the increased number of words provide additional problems, but the child's increasing conversational skills offer new insights into language development in terms of comprehension skills. The earlier research is described more accurately as the study of 'learning to talk' than 'language development'; language embraces comprehension as well as production. Most of the research done beyond this early stage is carried out within restricted domains, but with aims to shed light on, for example, the acquisition of the passive, or on the influence of particular factors on progress in communicative competence, but also to contribute to wider and more general issues. It is with one such problem that we are concerned in this section. Pinker, whose requirements for an adequate theory of language development were considered earlier, stated it thus, 'the mechanisms described by the theory should not be wildly inconsistent with what is known about the cognitive faculties of the child . . .'.

Language and cognition

It is convenient to think of language as one form of cognition, one way of knowing the world around us. Others include attention, memory and our perceptual and conceptual abilities. Pinker's proposal poses the problem of describing the links between them, perhaps here in particular, the link between language and conceptual activity, though this may necessarily involve other aspects of cognition. Two very different positions will be considered here, one associated with Piaget and the other with Chomsky. Piaget held that it is cognition which affects language and not the reverse. Chomsky holds that language progresses according to its own development rules; it is not wholly dependent on cognition. Several workers have adopted positions similar to that of Piaget, including Macnamara (1972) and Cromer (1974), who framed his Cognition Hypothesis thus: 'we are able to use the linguistic structures that we do largely because through our cognitive abilities we are enabled to do so ...'. Chomsky maintains his view of innate linguistic mechanisms guided by tacit knowledge of a transformational generative grammar with support from the views of his Massachusetts Institute of Technology colleagues who see language comprehension, among other functions, as a domain specific module in a complex cognitive architecture.

Only a minute fraction of the evidence available can be mentioned here; the interested reader is referred to Cromer's chapter, 'The Cognition Hypothesis' in the Penguin *New Perspectives in Child Development* (1974). In support of the Piagetian position, Sinclair (1969) draws attention to the onset of language. The arrival of the first word fits the observed time for the ending of the sensori-motor stage, and it is argued that the timelag allows necessary cognitive development to take place. It may indeed be necessary, but it cannot be argued that it is sufficient. Sinclair also offered experimental evidence that language enrichment cannot be used to bring about the cognitive process of conservation (see the earlier section on Piaget). Among others who have taken up this position is Eve Clark, who sought to account for semantic development in terms of semantic features she called 'atoms of meaning'. Semantic development happened by including additional features to established words. These linguistic features she linked with cognitive universal features proposed by Bierwisch (1970). Clark produced a wealth of empirical support for this view.

In support of Chomsky's position are a series of studies in which changes in language take place apparently without any correlated cognitive change. Negation, for example, typically takes place in three phases, non-existence, as in 'no more'; rejection, as in 'don't'; and denial, as in 'that not lollipop'. While the sequence is constant, no corresponding cognitive motives were observed. Much the same was found in the case of the acquisition of personal pronouns. It is of interest in this context to refer to the 'Mommy sock' study of Bloom referred to earlier. The rich interpretation of the two contexts is consistent with two different cognitions; the appropriate language, in one case to indicate possession, in the other to describe an action, however, were not available. It has also been observed that appropriate language does not always match the cognitions because of the linguistic difficulties involved. For example, by six or seven years of age the average English-speaking child is competent in the use of plurals. Such is the linguistic complexity of this system in Egyptian Arabic that children are usually well into their teens before it is mastered.

In the light of such evidence Cromer proposed a weak form of his Cognition Hypothesis: 'we are able to understand and productively to use particular linguistic structures only when our cognitive abilities enable us to do so. Our cognitive abilities at different stages of development make certain meanings available for expression. But in addition we must also possess certain specifically linguistic capabilities in order to come to express these meanings in language ... Though language development depends on cognition, language has its own specific resources.' This approaches a reconciliation of the Piagetian and Chomskyan positions. There are those who regard these proposals as at best conditional on unsubstantiated assumptions (see, for example, Atkinson in his *Explanations in the Study of Child Language Development*, 1982), but many have seen them as persuasive, and as a substantial contribution towards an account of language development.

Further reading

Aitchison, J. (1983) *The Articulate Mammal,* 2nd edn. Hutchinson.
Ellis, A., and Beattie, G. (1986) *The Psychology of Language and Communication.* Weidenfeld and Nicolson.
Harris, M., and Coltheart, M. (1986) *Language Processing in Children and Adults.* Routledge and Kegan Paul.

Development of the individual

This section constitutes, so to speak, the other half of 'individual' psychology, balancing Section three. A notion which goes back at least to Thomas Hobbes (1588–1679) is that a complete account of behaviour must include three levels of phenomena: physiological, individual and social. Psychology, as a distinct discipline, has perhaps spent most time and energy on the middle level, which is peculiarly its own. At the other two levels, specialists are closely allied to other disciplines: physiological psychologists to physiology; social psychologists to sociology and anthropology.

Chapters in this section present an account of how the milieu in which we grow up may affect our psychological development. The Personality chapter gives a description of how psychologists have tried to reduce the dazzling complexity of human behaviour by trying to categorize people. The final chapter sets out the attempts which have been made to understand abnormal behaviour and psychological states.

Chapter sixteen

Three accounts of human development

Harry Fisher

In many ways, age-related changes in the behaviour of children are similar, in spite of variations in cultural backgrounds. One aim of an account of development must be to supply a theoretical framework which will accommodate these similarities and provide a basis for the prediction of others. One of the accounts to be considered is made in terms of processes held to be involved in all behaviour-change. This is the learning-theory account which takes the view that 'development is just learning'. The other two accounts are framed in terms of pervasive aspects of human behaviour, Piaget's being concerned with intellectual, and Freud's with personality development. These three accounts provide an introduction to some of the basic issues involved in contemporary research and to the vocabulary of developmental psychology.

Learning-theory and development

Learning is the process by which more or less permanent changes in behaviour come about, through experience or practice. Behaviour-changes related to temporary states of the organism, like illness, fatigue, drugs, and injury, are not in this category; neither are changes which take place due to maturation. As has been seen in the case of language acquisition, it is not always possible to decide which factor, if either, dominates, since it seems likely that both are at work most of the time and that each may influence the other. It is characteristic of maturational processes that there is a regularity about the developmental milestones. The development of mobility in the infant normally progresses from sitting to crawling and thence to kneeling, standing and walking. Many hold that, in this sequence of changes, maturation is dominant.

Learning-theory is the name given to the body of knowledge based primarily on studies in which an external stimulus becomes associated with an overt response, in most cases, by procedures known as conditioning. Three approaches to learning will be considered here. Two use conditioning procedures as the means of establishing new associations, while the third involves changes in behaviour brought about by observation. The general aim of learning-theory is to provide the basis for an explanatory account of as wide a range of behaviour change as possible, animal as well as human, in terms of a small number of principles for establishing new stimulus-response bonds. The validity of these principles has been widely demonstrated in animal experiments. A considerable volume of research in the developmental context has investigated the extent to which these same principles may apply to human behaviour, and much recent research has been concerned with conditioning and learning in early infancy.

Classical conditioning

Not all behaviour is learned. Some, like sneezing, salivating and eye-blinking, appears to be elicited automatically by appropriate stimuli. This is known as reflex behaviour. Classical conditioning is the name given to the process whereby an association is formed between a previously neutral stimulus and the reflex behaviour. The best known example, possibly, is that in which Pavlov, the Russian physiologist-turned-psychologist, succeeded in inducing a dog to salivate to a previously neutral stimulus like the ticking of a metronome. Thus the reflex response of salivation, usually reserved for digestive purposes, became conditional on (or conditioned to) the ticking of the metronome. This was brought about by allowing the metronome to tick for a few seconds, stopping it and at the same time presenting the dog with some dry food. After a dozen or so trials the dog salivated at the sound of the metronome, and the *conditioned reflex* had been established. (Further details of Pavlov's experiments are to be found in Chapter 8.) It was for this that Pavlov became famous, and he believed that his method provided a means of gaining fundamental insight into the learning process.

The American behaviourist, J. B. Watson, was of the same mind. He believed that there were three distinguishable emotions, love, anger and fear, each initially evoked by a limited set of stimuli. He argued that these responses were innate, since, for example, loss of body support, or a sudden increase in noise, invariably produced distress in young infants. He demonstrated how fear could be learned, by conditioning this response to noise to other, previously neutral, stimuli. In particular, he set out to condition a fear of furry creatures in a nine-month-old infant. Albert, as the infant was called, had no such fear at the outset of the procedure. In the initial session, as the child reached out to stroke a tame white rat, a loud gong was struck behind him. Naturally the child was startled. By the end of the seventh such weekly session, the child began to exhibit fear and avoidance in the presence of the rat without the sounding of the gong. In particular, this was seen as the way in which irrational fears could be acquired in childhood. In general, it was interpreted as showing that it was possible, in principle, to imagine the establishment of all sorts of stimulus-response bonds in this way. Conditioned reflexes were, thus, seen as providing a sound, explanatory basis for a wide range of behaviour-change. Indeed, there were those who held that all learning could be explained in terms of chains of conditioned reflexes.

It was observed that Albert had also become afraid in the presence of other objects which were white and furry – a rabbit, a dog and a white-bearded man. The fear had generalized. Generalization provided a further explanatory concept for accounting for the extension of the response to similar stimuli. Discrimination was seen as a complementary notion, conditioned responses being elicited only by specific stimuli. The concept of higher-order conditioning – whereby a further neutral stimulus becomes conditioned to a previously conditioned neutral stimulus – was seen as a possible way of accounting for complex human behaviour.

It is possible to see this sort of behaviour-change in infants. They suck innately at a nipple, but not at the sight of a feeding bottle. Yet, after several months of bottle feeding, infants frequently make sucking movements when they see the bottle. A considerable amount of recent research has demonstrated the wide range of the neonate's susceptibility to conditioning. It has, at least in principle, indicated that this means of learning may be extensively involved. It has been suggested that both conscience and language, for example, may be areas in which classical conditioning operates.

Operant conditioning

This mode of learning is associated with the name of B. F. Skinner, the American behaviourist. Sometimes also called *instrumental conditioning*, it involves the learning of associations between the responses of the organism and events in the environment. It differs from classical conditioning in that it is the response which initiates the process of learning. In the animal experiments in which it has been demonstrated, as soon as the animal makes a response, usually a movement, of the sort required by the experimenter, a 'reward', usually a food pellet, is delivered to it. This is repeated the next time a suitable response is made, so that the animal comes to associate the response with the arrival of the food pellet. In this way the behaviour of animals has been shaped, and they have been taught a range of behaviours not usually associated with them. Skinner has, for example, conditioned pigeons to play a version of ping-pong by this means. In this case pecking at the ball constitutes the operant (or instrumental) response while the consequent food serves as reinforcement, and the associations learned are between the emitted response and the reinforcement (rather than between a stimulus and a response as in classical conditioning).

Reinforcement

This is needed to maintain as well as to shape new responses, and has been extensively investigated under laboratory conditions. In some experiments, reinforcement has been given every time the required response was made (continuous reinforcement), in others not every time (partial reinforcement). In this last category, a rat may receive reinforcement on, say, every tenth trial (fixed ratio) or every ten seconds (fixed interval). Other schedules of partial reinforcement used are variable ratio and variable interval.

In general, continuous reinforcement produces the quickest learning, while partial reinforcement produces the strongest, that is, the learning which will persist for longest in the absence of the reinforcers. The persistent gambler seems to provide a fair example of this sort of behaviour. His reinforcement (winnings) come only occasionally but, in view of his persistence, sufficiently often to maintain the operant responses of picking the 'winner'.

In common with a host of other psychological concepts reinforcement, while useful, is difficult to define. What is particularly difficult to decide is what makes a reinforcer reinforcing. It is easy to see why a hungry rat is reinforced by a food pellet, but, once the concept is used in the context of human behaviour, the matter becomes more difficult because of the vast range of environmental events – food, sympathy, information, attention, absence of attention, and so on – which function as reinforcers. To avoid this difficulty, an operational definition of reinforcement is given. Thus, any stimulus-event which, following a particular response, increases the probability of the repetition of the response is regarded as a reinforcer. While it is unsatisfactory to be unable to be more specific about the nature of reinforcement, perhaps it is not altogether surprising in the light of the range of complexity of possible learning situations.

Reward and punishment

Prior to Skinner's work on operant conditioning, one of America's early psychologists, E. L. Thorndike, proposed that animals learn responses, the consequences of which they find 'rewarding', and drop those found 'punishing'. That is, it was the effect of making the response which determined whether learning would take place or not. This was Thorndike's Law of Effect, a law which has an immediate intuitive appeal.

It supposes that 'punishment' will have an effect opposite to that of reward (or reinforcement), that is, instead of increasing, it will decrease the probability of repetition. Thorndike's own experiments obliged him to abandon the punishment half of the law. Subsequent animal experiments have confirmed these findings.

Since punishment is practised both by society and by parents as a means of changing the behaviour of deviants, it is important to try to assess the relevance of the experiments. One possible reaction is to refuse to accept the relevance of laboratory-based experiments in contrived and restricted contexts as valid for wider, real-life situations. If, however, the principles are accepted as valid, it seems that punishment, as a strategy for removing unwanted behaviour, has only limited potential. Further experiments have suggested that unwanted behaviour can be removed more efficiently by experimental extinction. This is a procedure whereby an animal continues to respond but no reinforcement is given. Under such a regime, the frequency of responding gradually weakens until it disappears. In human terms, the suggestion is that raids on the biscuit tin can be more efficiently discouraged by leaving it empty than by smacking or admonishing the raider.

Sufficiently severe punishment will, of course, suppress the undesired response but will not deal with the motivational origins. Indeed, it is argued that such punishment with children may produce undesirable emotional consequences in the wake of the frustrated aim and the fear of future punishment.

Punishment may be effective if the suppression of the undesired response is seen in a context where alternative responses exist which may be rewarded. Thus milder punishments, the criticisms of a trainer or teacher, low essay grades and the like, usually serve these ends. Sporadic punishment of the same offence may only serve as a reinforcer. Some of the persistently undesirable behaviour of children in classrooms has been seen in this light. In the interest of keeping the lesson moving, a teacher may well ignore minor offences for most of the time. The times when he stops to rebuke offenders may produce such a diversion as will reinforce the behaviour. Operant methods have been systematically used in some schools with acute behaviour problems. The basis of the system is the rewarding of desirable behaviour (by praise or the awarding of privileges) and the ignoring of undesirable behaviour as far as possible. When it is not possible, offenders are moved to a 'time out' room. This approach has been used at widely differing levels from English primary schools to down-town ghetto schools in New York. The reports published claim a measure of success.

Language acquisition

Reference has already been made (Chapter 15) to Skinner's account of language acquisition in terms of operant conditioning and of Chomsky's objections to it. It is sufficient here to restate that it was not Chomsky's intention to suggest that operant conditioning was not involved, but rather that such an explanatory device was inadequate to account for all aspects of language acquisition.

Operant conditioning in infancy

As with classical conditioning, recent research has shown that infant behaviour can be modified by operant procedures within the first days of independent life. There are, of course, limits to the variety of response in the neonate's repertoire, but sucking, headturning, and later, vocalization and smiling, for example, have all been brought under the control of operant procedures. Learning by operant conditioning is thus a potentially powerful source of influence on behavioural development from a very early stage.

Classical and operant conditioning – limitations

The learning theorists believed that the central issues involved in giving an account of human behaviour were those which had to do with learning. Classical and operant conditioning were regarded as fundamental principles of behaviour, capable of providing an objective insight into all learning in animals, children, and adults. Subsequent work questioned the validity of assuming so comprehensive a role for conditioning. In particular, the validity of transferring findings from laboratory experiments on animals to real-life situations with humans has been questioned. As has been amply demonstrated, human learning is influenced by language, and to that extent is qualitatively different from animal learning. Furthermore, classical and instrumental conditioning appear to describe acquisition of associations by an organism which is largely passive and virtually at the mercy of the environment. Viewed in this way, accounts based on conditioning appear appropriate only to limited areas of human and animal learning.

Learning by observation

In contrast to the early conditioning experiments, based mainly on animals, learning by observation has been studied using mainly nursery school children. That children learn in this way is no new discovery but it was not until the early 1960s that systematic studies were undertaken. The experimental design involved, first, showing a group of children a real-life episode, or a film, in which a model (usually adult) behaved in a given context in some extraordinary way. The children were later observed individually in a similar context, to assess the extent to which this behaviour was imitated. It was important that the piece of behaviour filmed should be extraordinary and not a usual part of the child's repertoire, so that the criterion for its imitation could be clear. The behaviour of these children was compared with that of a control group who did not see the film.

A considerable number of experiments have studied the learning of aggressive behaviour. In a typical episode the model would be seen making an attack on an inflatable (Bobo) doll of a size usually a little larger than the watching children. The unusual feature of the attack was that it might involve, say, lifting and throwing the doll, or attacking it with a wooden hammer. The findings indicate that, compared with a control group, those children who saw the episode behaved in a much more aggressive way with the doll, much of the aggression following that of the model. This was the same whether the experimental group saw a real episode or a film, or whether the model was child or adult. Using this basic design Bandura and Walters and a number of colleagues have investigated the sorts of factors that influence the likelihood of imitation of observed behaviour.

In a further experiment where the model exhibited aggressive behaviour, one group saw the model rewarded (with sweets and lemonade) for his behaviour; another saw the model 'punished' (in terms of a severe scolding for his brutality), while the control group observed neither the rewarding nor the punishment. Subsequent individual observation showed that the levels of imitation differed among the three groups. The 'model-punished' group showed much less aggression than the other two. Thus, the 'model-punished' group might be seen as sharing the punishment of the model, and the differences between the groups seen in terms of the *vicarious punishment* as against *vicarious reinforcement*. When children taking part in this study were individually asked to imitate the behaviour of the model and were directly rewarded for doing so, there were no differences. Children from all three groups were equally aggressive. The vicarious punishment was associated, therefore, with the lower performance of aggression in the previous phase of the study. It appeared that the acquisition of the aggressive behaviour was not different from that for children in the other groups.

It is of considerable importance to notice that the aggressive behaviour acquired came about by mere exposure. The children were not instructed to attend to and try to imitate what they saw: just seeing it was sufficient. Furthermore, Bandura has shown that absence or weakness of performance cannot be construed as absence of acquisition.

What is true for aggressive responses has also been demonstrated for a range of others. Thus, children have been shown to learn to solve problems, and to make moral judgements, among other tasks, by observing others. Learning complex tasks would be extremely difficult if conditioning were the only means. Thus, learning to drive a car, to play golf, or to play a piano can be done more efficiently by the intervention of a teacher who can demonstrate what is required.

Further studies have investigated a range of model-variables involved in the performance of observed behaviour. For example, models whom the subjects perceive as similar to themselves elicit greater imitation than those perceived to be dissimilar: a child is more likely to imitate another than to imitate a cartoon character. Similarly, the perceived warmth, power and attractiveness of the model have been shown to increase performance. However, it has been shown that acquisition is no less likely with models seen as cold or lacking in power or unattractive.

The studies of learning by observation have raised a number of problems as well as providing a wealth of information about the way in which learning may take place outside the laboratory. Of the problems, the notion of imitation is an important one, for it provides no clue as to how the learning takes place, merely an index that it does. Imitation of others is so common that some have seen it as a human instinct. In a study where children were directly rewarded for imitating one aspect of a model's behaviour, it was found that other aspects were also being imitated. Many children imitate their parents in this way, reproducing attitudes of stance and gait, verbal mannerisms and tone of voice, as well as similar opinions. This more general imitation of the characteristics of another has been called identification. It has been seen as an important process in personality development by Freud and others, and this concept will be further considered later. Recent research with infants has suggested that learning by observation is possible within the first three months, and is therefore a potentially powerful means of adaptation.

There is some overlap between the concepts of conditioning and learning by observation. Both, as has been seen, draw on the notion of reinforcement. But they appear to relate to different sorts of tasks. Observational learning relates to the combining of a number of established acts, for example, learning to co-ordinate arms, feet, head and breathing in learning to swim. The shaping of behaviour, on the other hand, appears to be specially suitable for the establishment of behaviour patterns which are, in total, new. There is, thus, a sense in which these two sorts of learning can be seen as complementary.

While two approaches to learning have been considered here, one in terms of conditioning, classical and operant, and the other in terms of observation and imitation, other forms have been described. Gagne, a learning theorist, has proposed a hierarchically organized system of eight different types of learning which he describes as signal learning, stimulus-response learning, chains (of stimulus-response connections), verbal associations, multiple discrimination, concept learning, principle learning, and problem-solving.

Evaluation

As an account of development, the approach in terms of conditioning is general rather than specific. It was the aim of early behaviourist researchers to identify principles underlying the learning process, and to demonstrate their relevance to behaviour-change in general, including, of course, developmental changes. The principles identified stem mainly from animal experiments, but there have been, from the earliest days of the behaviourist enterprise, experiments demonstrating the effects of conditioning procedures on children, albeit in no great volume and in widely differing contexts. More recently, studies with infants have underlined the potential importance of conditioning from an early age. In many cases, however, experiments have involved highly specific stimuli within strictly controlled environments unlikely to correspond closely to real-life conditions. A cautious conclusion, therefore, is that such experiments demonstrate that conditioning processes may be involved in development. Other experiments, like the conditioning of fear of things white and furry in Watson's subject, Albert (see p. 499), demonstrate the principles in action in a more realistic setting. Particular experiments, however, permit only limited generalizations. The generality of the involvement of conditioning in development must, thus, be regarded as inferred, rather than demonstrated.

It seems likely that, whatever the importance of the role of conditioning, other factors are involved. The notion of maturation is not denied by behaviourists so much as held to be of limited explanatory value. Thus this approach makes no appeal to changing biological factors to account for significant changes in behaviour.

In the case of learning by observation, systematic empirical work, using a range of modelling and imitation techniques on children of different age groups, provides a coherent demonstration of its role in development.

The single feature of child development which poses perhaps the most serious question for the learning-theory approach is that class of responses which may be regarded as 'novel' in the sense that it seems unlikely to have come about as a result of deliberate teaching or the imitation of a model. Child language at certain stages contains examples of such innovations – new words or near-lawful errors like 'gonned' or 'wented' for went, 'Weetabik' as a singular for an apparent plural Weetabix – which suggest a rule-governed behaviour distinguishable from repetition. This same sort of innovation is to be seen also in early locomotor behaviour, where individual children develop highly original means of moving from place to place.

Thus, while there seems little doubt that both conditioning and imitation are involved, neither, alone, would appear capable of providing the basis for an adequate account of development.

Piaget's account of development

The paradox

The work of Piaget presents something of a paradox. There is a clear contrast between the technical shortcomings of much of his work and the richness of the insights which he has contributed to psychology, in particular to the psychology of cognitive development. Flavell, who has written an eminently readable summary of his work to 1963 (*The Developmental Psychology of Jean Piaget*), lists some of the complaints levelled against his work: it is difficult to understand in translation and in the original French; there are frequently large gaps between theory and the related empirical work; and there is a 'persistent disinclination' to use theory to generate testable hypotheses. But this is only a beginning. 'He simply did not conduct his research in such a way as to make a very convincing case for even the major configurations of his stated results' (Flavell, 1963). He is also accused of a general want of reporting accuracy, communicative inadequacy, careless sampling, subjects chosen only by age and availability, using procedures which varied from subject to subject, providing results in terms of subject protocols rich in detail but without statistical analysis, not even means and standard deviations, interpretation of data in a manner described as unparsimonious, and of appearing 'to force unwilling data into preset theoretical moulds'. This is but a sample of what Flavell describes as Piaget's 'bad habits'. Yet in spite of such shortcomings, many of which are obvious even to the beginner in psychology, Piaget's contribution has been massive in the sense of having drawn attention to a wide range of stable and systematic aspects of cognitive development in considerable detail.

Genetic epistemology and child psychology

Piaget was trained as a zoologist, but regarded his central interest as genetic epistemology. Epistemology is the study of knowledge, how we come to understand the world around us. Piaget's genetic epistemology thus focuses attention on the origins of knowledge as they may be manifest in children. This illuminates certain aspects of his work which must be considered as underdeveloped had child psychology been for him an end in itself; issues were retained and researched only in so far as they had a contribution to make to genetic epistemology.

Piaget's account of cognitive development owes much to biological notions. Each organism has its own characteristic organization. This determines its unique and invariant way of functioning, and thus the way in which it interacts with its environment. A living plant, for example, is so organized that it invariably takes nutrition from its soil environment in solution, given an adequate water supply. The plant's growth and development is a joint function of its way of extracting nutrition and the properties of its environment. Should these properties be less than adequate, or the extraction process be impaired, the plant's development will be abnormal. Piaget's account of cognitive development is seen in terms of this inter-actionist model, and draws freely on biological terminology. In the early 1970s Piaget likened cognitive development to biological epigenesis. This is a theory in which biological development is seen as a gradual modification of organization and the production of new structures, as opposed to the mere growth in size of a complete, preformed miniature organism. This approach to development raises fundamental questions about the nature of the qualitatively different stages required by this notion, and about the processes by means of which one stage passes into the next. Similar questions thus also arise in the case of cognitive development.

Methodology

It is always important to examine theoretical propositions in the light of the methods used to collect the data to which they look for support. Nowhere is this more important than in the case of Piaget's account of cognitive development, for his methods are singular and controversial. His work in psychology dates from 1921. He died in 1980 and had published his findings over the intervening period. Practically all of his early work and most of the subsequent work was dominated by a single-minded application of the 'clinical method' to the task of providing an account of cognitive development. Essentially this was an interview between the experimenter and a child. (With preverbal children it might take the form of a game-like interaction between them.) This might be described as an S R S R ... approach, for a stimulus (frequently a question) was employed to elicit a verbal response from the child; this response in turn was used by the experimenter to generate a further stimulus, eliciting a further verbal response from the child, and so on, the experimenter using the procedure to investigate some aspect of the child's intellectual functioning,. While the general theme would be constant across different children, the stimuli (apart from the first, perhaps) were usually not the same, being generated in terms of the child's responses. Having considered responses from a number of children Piaget would publish his conclusions with individual protocols, such as the following, in support. (Piaget was investigating the notion of 'same number' in a five-year-old (Hug) by placing counters in correspondence with a model row.) Hug (5;0), for a collection of 15 counters, said:

'I don't know how many there are. I don't know how to do it' (to find the same number).

'Try.' (He collected a few counters and then spaced them out so that they resembled the model.)

'Are they the same?'

'Yes'.

'How many are there (model)?'

'I don't know.'

'Then how do you know they are the same?'

'I looked twice' (model and copy). 'It's right.'

The topic of such conversations might concern remote events, like dreams, or immediate events, like the escaping of air from a punctured ball, or they might concern aspects of the solution of a task being carried out by the subject.

With the youngest children the verbal component would be inappropriate and other indicators used. In this case the supporting protocol would consist of a description of what took place with supporting detail of the subject (name and age), and materials.

Piaget was well aware of the advantages and limitations of the clinical method, and familiar with the controversy surrounding its use in psychiatry. High on the list of advantages must be the flexibility of its operation in the hands of a skilled experimenter, and its consequent potentiality to reveal unique and individual findings. The latter provide clear constraints on overgeneralization. Such effects might be lost in a statistical average. But the method's dependence on the skill and integrity of the experimenter, with its vulnerability to the effects of unwitting bias (in choosing hypotheses, in questioning, in 'leading' throughout the interview) represents serious problems. Happy to use statistics in his earlier zoological work, Piaget rejected its application where subjects had received the different treatments inherent in the clinical method.

For Piaget the clinical method represented what he saw as optimum in terms of his aims. Its inevitable hazards had to be lived with. Some, at least, of (what Flavell calls) Piaget's 'bad habits' arose from the calculated risks he was prepared to take. The method persists in the work of his colleagues. Others have felt it necessary to repeat some aspects of his work using rigorous experimental procedures. It says much for the quality of the insights revealed by the clinical method that such replications have provided 'a fair degree of confirmation' (Halford, 1972).

Cognitive development

It was upon evidence drawn from studies based almost exclusively on the clinical method that Piaget proposed an account of cognitive development in terms of adaptation and organization among other 'functional invariants'.

Intellectual development

For survival, each organism must be able to adapt to its environment. Adaptation includes the possibility of structural changes. By analogy, intellectual development is seen as adaptation involving psychological structural changes. Piaget held that we inherit a specific mode of doing business with the environment and that it is this which makes intellectual development possible. This mode is seen as remaining constant throughout life (in Piagetian terminology, it is a functional invariant), and changes in structure are due to its operation. Two conceptually distinct processes are seen to be operative in adaptation: assimilation and accommodation. A biological example of these aspects of adaptation can be seen in the case of intake of food by an organism. Assimilation involves the modification of what is taken in to fit existing structures.

Accommodation, a process whereby the organism modifies existing structures to meet the demands of the changed environment, may be seen in the physical changes which may be necessary to incorporate the food as well as the biochemical changes which take place as a result of the intake of food. Intellectual development is seen in analogous terms. The existing cognitive structures operate on the environment in the assimilation of new information, which, in turn, is accommodated by, and produces changes in, existing structures. These two aspects of adaptation will be seen as serving complementary functions. In the same way, Piaget pairs the term 'organization' with adaptation to indicate the progressive nature of intellectual functioning. Each time a child solves some new problem in his interaction with the environment, his intellectual development moves one step nearer to maturity. Confronted by the same problem, a procedure is now available for its solution. The attainment of this new level of adaptation is called equilibration.

Piaget described the structure of the intellect in terms of schemas and operations. Schema is used to denote the internal representation of a well-defined sequence of physical or mental actions. Neonates are held to possess a number of innate schemas, relating to such actions as sucking, grasping, looking, and crying. As development proceeds, these schemata will be further elaborated, and links formed among them.

The term 'schema' thus covers the most elementary sort of cognitive structure. Operations are more complex structures, usually acquired in middle childhood, and form the basis of the most complex forms of mental functioning. An operation in the sense used by Piaget has been described as 'an internalized action' or 'an action which takes place in imagination'. As with the term 'schema', Piaget nowhere sets down an exhaustive definition. A distinctive property of an operation is that it is reversible, that is, a child who is able to think 'operationally' is able to imagine not only a particular action, but also that action which will undo the first. Thus, subtraction may be used to reverse addition. A different sort of example of reversibility is to be found in the knowledge that pouring back all the individual glasses of water into the water jug will result in the same quantity of water as was present before the glasses were filled. Operational thinking is essential to intellectual activity; without it Piaget held that the child is unable to recognize that in the above example, the quantity of water is invariant, in spite of the transformation which takes place when the glasses are filled from the jug. Piaget held that it is because the four-year-old is unable to think in terms of inverse operations that he is unable to perform accurately on conservation tasks. That is, he is unable to appreciate that, when the liquid from a tall slim glass is poured into a wider glass, the amount of water is the same. The different liquid levels appear to persuade him against conservation. This is but one example of conservation. Others, mentioned later, include conservation of number and of mass. It was central to Piaget's aim to give an account of the development of intellectual structures from the simplest beginning, the innate schemas, to operational thinking.

Stages of intellectual development

Piaget has identified a series of stages and substages in cognitive development, the order of which he regards as fixed since each presupposes the level of adaptation reached in the previous stage. The stages themselves are thus structurally distinct, and the four main stages are named in accordance with the dominant cognitive structure, as follows: sensori-motor (birth to about two years), pre-operational (two to seven years), concrete operations (seven to 11 years), and formal operations (upwards of 11 years). While most people reach the stage of concrete operations there are some who do not reach the final stage.

The child in the *sensori-motor period* knows his world dominantly in terms of perceptions and actions. When other means of knowing, memory and language, become available, this stage is at an end. The neonate has a few ready-made independent shemas, which gradually become co-ordinated into more complex schemas. Piaget describes how this comes about in terms of six sub-stages, beginning with actions described as reflex exercises, which develop through the gradual organization of action-perception schemas. Early in this stage a small object is something to be grasped, sucked, and looked at. Later it will be shaken, but if it drops it will quickly be forgotten. Most parents have observed babies drop things out of their cots and prams. At first they pay no further concern to the object, but later it becomes a good game to drop it and 'insist' on its return. Thus what seemed earlier to be 'out of sight, out of mind', is no longer so; the child appears to be able to think of an object which is not present. Piaget calls this the concept of object permanence. It suggests the establishment of a capacity to represent actions and objects internally. At about 12–18 months children begin to use words and this provides a further means of representing aspects of the environment. Action-perception schemas are no longer the child's sole means of knowing the world.

While this first period is dominated by interactions involving a present environment, the final stage (formal operations) is characterized by a mode of thinking which can be completely dissociated from the environment. Between them are two stages representing the relative facility with which internal representations are handled. In the first, pre-operational, they are handled imperfectly, being tied to a single, egocentric, viewpoint. In the second, released from this restriction, the individual is no longer constrained by his own viewpoint, but is able, by using reversible operations, to see other possibilities. When this is the case the stage of concrete operations has been reached.

The pre-operational period can thus be differentiated from the previous stage by an increasing use of internal representation of the environment. The child can remember, imagine, and pretend. It is differentiated from the operational stage by the limitations of egocentricity. At this stage, a child's judgements are dominated by his own unique viewpoint. Such a child is unable, for example, to select from a series of photographs of a model landscape one that represents a viewpoint different from the one he sees it from. Similarly, a boy who asserts that he has a brother will deny that his brother also has a brother. At this stage, the child fails to realize the invariance of matter against perceptual change. He also fails to conserve for number. If two rows of pennies are placed in one to one correspondence, a child at this stage will agree that each row has the same number. Yet, if in one of the rows of pennies some are placed closer together, he will now judge there to be fewer in this row than the other. He is apparently unable to perform the reverse operation of spreading them out again in his mind's eye.

The period of concrete operation is characterized by the acquisition of reversible operations, demonstrated in terms of success in conservation tasks. This process, however, takes time. In the early part of the period, conservation mistakes are still possible. For example, suppose a child is presented with two balls of clay of the same weight and size. If one of them is subsequently rolled into a sausage shape, the child at the pre-operational stage will say that mass, weight, and volume have all changed. A child in the early concrete operations stage is clear that the mass remains constant, but holds that weight and volume are changed. Later still he appreciates the conservation of both mass and weight – but not volume, until somewhere around 11 years of age. This period concerns operations, because the child needs to be set problems relating to concrete objects rather than abstractions in order to understand logical relationships. For example, the child who is mid-way in the period and competent at seriation tasks, where he is required to arrange in order blocks of different size, may well find difficulty when presented with a similar abstract task (e.g. John is taller than Jack, Jack is smaller than George, who is smallest?).

The period of formal operations is characterized by the ability to solve problems in the absence of the concrete objects and situations to which the problem relates. Thus, a child at this stage is able to manipulate propositions like those above to obtain the correct answer. He is further able to regard the several possibilities of a given problem as hypotheses to be tested, and to locate salient variables, and examine their effects in isolation and in all possible combinations.

An experiment used to investigate formal operational thinking is one described by Piaget and Inhelder on the oscillation of a simple pendulum. The subject is set to determine what governs the time taken to complete one swing of a pendulum, in this case a weight suspended by a string. Possible variables involved are the length of the string, the size of the weight, the length of the swing and the strength of the initial push. It is, in fact, the first of these which is the relevant variable. The subject's task is, therefore, to isolate its effect from that of the others. The pre-operational child tends to believe that it is the strength of his initial push which matters, but he is incapable of separating the effects of the several factors. The child at this stage of concrete operations can vary each fact or factor systematically and observe the relation between the length of the string and the time of the pendulum's swing, but he, too, is incapable of isolating the effect of this variable. This isolation is, typically, only achieved by the child in the period of formal operations, or perhaps the stage of 'scientific thinking'.

Evaluation

Any evaluation of Piaget's work must take account of the massive contribution he made to the field of cognitive development, which includes not only the insights which stemmed from the work in which he was personally involved, but also from the vast amount of research his work has generated. It would be difficult to overestimate the influence Piaget and his school at Geneva have had in this field of inquiry. Yet 'More than most, Piaget's system is susceptible to a malignant kind of premature foreclosure' (Flavell, 1963). Doubtless there are many who base such a reaction on the extent of his departure from the normal scientific canons, while others reject his theoretical position. Here some of the main problems and assets are considered briefly to provide the reader with insight into the issues involved in making one's mind up about Piaget.

Departure from normal scientific canons and the use of the clinical interview constitute an important group of problems. Since many of the issues they raise have been discussed earlier, nothing more will be said here.

A second problem area is that which concerns the interpretation of Piaget's data, much of which are based on verbal responses. Since language skills improve with age, there are no sure grounds for supposing that changes in the content of the responses are due to cognitive changes. They may simply reflect an unrelated increase in verbal fluency. The empirical evidence does not help, for while sometimes cognitive development does appear to be related to language development, at others it does not. This issue is considered in more detail in the final section of the chapter on language.

Flavell (1963) argues that the structural complexity of Piaget's account of the intellectual life of middle childhood is excessive. Of the concrete operational stage he writes, 'It is our judgement that Piaget's bent towards mathematics and logic, ... and towards symmetry and order, has led him to see more coherence and structure in the child's intellectual actions than are really there'. This is a claim that Piaget's theory is too strong in at least two ways: that it over interprets the data, and predicts greater uniformity than is found. Flavell has described a less complex model which he sees as more realistic yet within Piaget's overall approach.

The problematic notion of 'stage' or 'period' or 'level' has been seen by many as a source of unresolved conceptual problems. The problems are practical as well as theoretical. A major theoretical problem has been that of how to define a concept which will describe different levels of intra-age cognitive homogeneities, or similarities, when some nine distinct meanings for 'level' can be distinguished; and when the cognitive activities are influenced by so wide a range of personal and environmental factors that it becomes problematic as to how the 'homogeneities' might be identified in practice. Since they are to be seen in structural terms, they should facilitate strong predictions. Instead they specify only the kinds of knowledge required for a range of behaviours. This leaves the concept of 'stage' as fuzzy at best. Flavell nevertheless sees it as serving the useful function of labelling significant uniformities in the developmental sequence.

Piaget's system covers cognitive development as far as the adolescent signs of formal operational thinking. It has been argued that this can hardly be exhaustive; several suggestions have been made for the inclusion of a distinctive mode of thinking beyond the formal stage. Bruner (1959) proposed a distinction between the intelligence of Piaget's subjects, and Piaget's own intelligence used to conceptualize their intellectual operations. Arlin (1975) has conceptualized post-formal thought as a mode of problem finding, distinguishing it from the problem-solving quality of formal thought. Post-formal thought is considered further in Chapter 18.

These are just some of the problems to which Piaget's system gives rise. Any one of them might be taken as grounds for rejecting at least a significant part of the work. Thus Brown and Desforges (1979) state, 'In our view Piaget offers no adequate explanation of cognitive development.' Flavell approached the task of evaluation holding that in the interests of scientific progress it is important to consider not only the problems, but to 'direct most of one's energies into milking the system for all that is, or might be, positive or useful in it'. He views the problems of the Piagetian system in the light of the 'significant assets, accomplishments and contributions' it contains. Among these he cites the assimilation–accommodation model as providing a unifying principle to describe cognition from birth to maturity, and requiring an organism which is active in its own development; also the way in which Piaget has provided support for the notion that each present state of knowledge has its antecedents. Nothing appears from nowhere.

Some measure of the soundness of the Piagetian system can be inferred, Flavell argues, from its capacity to contribute to related disciplines. Among those he mentions arc philosophy, psychometrics and education. His central concern with the origins of knowledge is relevant to substantial issues, and the multitude of face-valid measures of intellectual performance used in his studies furnish both types and tokens of a wide range of psychometric instruments. *The Language and Thought of the Child* (1926) and *The Child's Conception of Number* (1952) are but two of many early publications which have a clear interest for those involved in education. Almost from the first there has been a strong interest in applying Piagetian findings to teaching techniques. In both the USA and the UK this interest is as strong as ever.

Flavell also proposes that Piaget's distinctive developmental–descriptive approach constitutes a positive contribution. It demonstrates simply that children improve in the performance of a number of tasks as they grow older. Its critics are those who see the proper business of psychology as investigating cause–effect relationships, and regard age (by itself) as an independent variable of doubtful value. Here one sees the constraints of Piaget's epistemological aims on the research he carried out. Those looking for cause–effect relationships raised the issue of the role of individual differences. For Piaget this was of secondary interest; his research objective was the fact and form of development in the average normal child. The developmental–descriptive approach was well suited to this end

Enough has probably been said to show that making one's mind up about Piaget is a complex task. Piaget was not the ideal spokesman for his own work, and evaluations are beset by the differences between Piaget's own aims and what other workers believe they ought to have been. Halford (1972) has offered a summary evaluation as follows: '... the majority of both empirical investigators and theoreticians have been more willing to embrace Piagetian phenomena than the Piagetian conceptual system. ... The phenomena themselves are striking, easy to demonstrate. ... The system is immensely complex and subtle, very poorly expounded, and riddled with gaps and inconsistencies, apparent or real.'

Further reservations

Prominent among those who have admired the work of Piaget, though with considerable reservations, have been Peter Bryant at Oxford, and a number of colleagues who have attempted to make good Piaget's occasional omission of considering explanations other than his own. Piaget used his '... skill and ingenuity as an experimenter' (Bryant, 1982) to explore some of the remarkable mistakes made by the developing child, frequently to infer the absence of some cognitive skill, e.g. failure to conserve, or failure to decentre (i.e. to see a situation from different viewpoints). Some of their findings indicate that young children may well have the abilities excluded by Piaget, and that the errors may arise from sources other than the shortcomings of their logic.

An example of this comes from the study of transitive inference by Bryant and Trabasso (1971). Transitive inference tasks are of the form, given A>B and B>C to make some inference about the relative sizes of A and C. Piaget (1952) noted that most children in his group of four to six-year-olds failed to respond correctly to 'Is A>C?'. (The actual propositions were more concretely given as 'Ann is taller than Belle', etc.) He saw this as an inability to integrate the two propositions, i.e. as an absence of appropriate logical operations. Bryant and Trabasso showed that poor performance may also be due to forgetting. They did this by teaching the inequality relationships between adjacent pairs of the series A>B>C>D>E (A, B, etc. were sticks different in length and colour) and then testing them on the relationship between B and D which had not been seen together. Children as young as four were successful if they remembered both B C and C D. In general, those children who were successful were also those who remembered both premises, while those who did not do well were mainly those who forgot one or both.

Piaget considered the conservation to be a test of invariance. One who understands conservation knows that the transformation, spacing out the coins, or pouring the water into containers of different diameters, or rolling the ball of plasticine into a long sausage does not alter the number of coins or the volume of water, etc. Does failure in this task demonstrate a failure to understand the principle of invariance? Does success demonstrate understanding it? Bryant (1982), in the review, *Piagetian Issues and Experiments*, draws attention to an alternative account. Where there is failure on this task it is suggested that the child might be induced (albeit unintentionally) to report a change simply because the experimenter has manipulated the apparatus of the experiment, spreading out the coins, for example. Though the change does not alter the number of coins, it does alter something. An experiment of Donaldson and McGarrigle (1974) supports this notion. A 'naughty teddy bear' is introduced to make the manipulation of the apparatus appear accidental. The change takes place during a scuffle. There is no show of deliberation about it, though the change clearly takes place. In this case many more of the four to six-year-olds reported no change in the crucial attribute than in the traditional form of the task.

Thus, failure in this task need not imply a want of understanding of invariance. Neither is it the case that success guarantees understanding. A child may respond correctly having not grasped the nature of the perceptual change, or having not inferred its superficial implications. Such are the issues to which Bryant and others have drawn attention. Their impact has been to stress the controversial nature of many of Piaget's proposals. It is not his findings; these are frequently replicated. It is the interpretations placed on them which raise questions and cast doubt on the theoretical structure.

Freud's account of development

The development of personality

An important key to the understanding of Freud's account of development is the context in which it was made. Freud was a clinician, interested in patients who were 'mentally ill' and in one way or another maladjusted. His interest in the origins of the abnormalities suggested the prior history of the individual and, in particular, childhood as likely sources. His account of development thus grew out of the details he gained from what his patients told him about themselves and has, therefore, an implicit goal, the attainment of emotional maturity. Freud's central concern is the development of personality and the contingencies which mould it. In particular, Freud saw these as being in large measure related to the way in which the natural urges (in Freudian terminology, instinctual energy) were regulated by the individual and the world around him.

The biological energy model

The notion of biological energy, of inborn instinctive forces, is central to Freud's concept of human personality. It is in this sense that this theory of personality is referred to as 'dynamic'. That human life is regulated by physical energy is incontrovertible. Freud was not concerned with physical but psychological energy. He distinguished three sources or channels for the instinctive drives, one concerned with self-reproduction (sexuality – sometimes called the libido), one with self-preservation (which includes drives like hunger and pain) and one with dominance – aggression. Plausible as this notion of psychological energy is (often compelling in the clinical situation) it has remained untestable. It was further assumed that the amount of energy for a given individual was fixed, and that energy could be invested in or tied to (Freud called this cathexis) thought, action, objects, and people, but that cathexis in respect of one object depleted the total supply of energy.

Personality structure

In broad, structural terms, development starts with the id, viewed as the storehouse for instinctual energy. The neonate is regarded as all *id*, which demands instant cathexis. Frustration cannot be tolerated. As the infant becomes increasingly aware of his environment the second structure, the *ego*, develops. This is the executive part of the personality which mediates between the demands of the id and constraints of reality. The *superego* emerges between about four and six years of age and, continuing the analogy, represents something like a combination of the judiciary and the legislature, adding to the combination constraints in terms of ideals, conscience, and the demands of society. The ego is not always capable of wise mediation among the conflicting demands. The outcome of un-resolved conflict is anxiety. Freud saw the ego as continually engaged in the reduction of anxiety by realistic means. Failure is marked by ego-defence mechanisms, symptoms of which are held to be seen in aggression, depression, phobias, rituals, and obsessions. Repression is held to be the most powerful of these defences, as, by it, the ego is seen as removing the source of anxiety from consciousness to the unconscious. It is in repressed sources of anxiety that Freud saw the most significant roots of mental pathology.

Stages of psychosexual development

Dominant among the urges for satisfaction is the libido. Freud described development in terms of the body zones primarily associated with libidinal satisfaction at successive stages. Libidinal satisfaction assumes a more explicit sexual form as the child grows. Its earliest form, in the first year of life, is concerned dominantly with the mouth. Satisfaction, warmth and comfort are gained by sucking, licking and tasting. Freud called this the *oral* stage. In the second year of life it is the anal region which is the most cathected, and the child shows much interest in defecation and urination and the associated activities. This *anal* stage is succeeded at about four years of age by the *phallic* stage, when the source of libidinal pleasure is the genital region. It is during this stage that the Oedipal (Oedipus, in Greek mythology, killed his father and married his mother) conflict is said to confront the child, who at this time Freud saw as desiring direct sexual relations with the opposite sex parent, but experiencing anxiety in the face of the discovery of his desires by the same-sex parent. The boy is said to fear castration at the hands of his father, and the girl punishment from the mother to add to her believed castration. Resolution of the conflict for both boy and girl is to identify with the like-sexed parent, identification involving not only the showing of affection for, but also the adoption of the ideals of the like-sexed parents. The illicit incestuous desires are repressed and the resolution of the Oedipal conflict is marked by the birth of the superego, based on the identification made, and the societal norms mediated by the parent.

The period which follows is, in contrast, one of relative calm and stability. This, the *latency* period, sees no major personality development, but is a time of considerable social and intellectual development. It continues until the onset of the adolescence. A new stage, *the genital*, marks the beginning of a period of renewed sexual interests and the establishment of a coherent set of sexual attitudes.

Freud saw each of the stages as entailing a unique set of problems to be solved in the interests of the future personality. The prevention of cathexis or its over-indulgence could result in *fixation*. Freud used this term to carry the notion of biological energy so firmly engaged at a less mature level, that it is not available for more mature functioning. Fixation at the oral stage was associated with later gluttony, alcoholism, optimism or pessimism, and at the anal stage with adult obstinacy and meanness. Fixation at the phallic stage is held responsible for the great majority of adult neuroses by psychoanalytically orientated clinicians.

Evaluation

Freud's account of development, like Piaget's, concerns a major dimension of human functioning. For Piaget, the development of the child was seen in intellectual terms, for Freud it is in personality–emotional terms. In contrast with Piaget's developing child, whose intellectual development is built upon his interaction with the world around him, Freud's child is passive and a product of inner forces and outer restrictions.

The overwhelming appeal of his account must rest partly in its plausibility and partly in the potential it offers as an account for a wide range of human activity and experience. Estimates of the originality of the notions he handled have varied, but it is indisputable that his presentation of these notions stimulated a great deal of research inside psychology as well as much interest and speculation outside it.

Much of the experimentation which has gone on has failed to produce any considerable body of support. Three main areas of general criticism may be identified, relating to source of data, methods, and explanations. The source of Freud's data was his patients, who were exclusively adult and abnormal in some way. Freud observed no children directly. This would seem to detract from a developmental account, for it can, at best, be only partial. Further doubt has been expressed as to the validity of making generalizations from an abnormal population.

As with Piaget, the limitations of the clinical method have been raised. With Freud, the case is more extreme since the evidence collected concerns events, some of which were long gone and subject to selection, interpretation and fallible recollections

While it is not difficult to find evidence consistent with Freud's view of development, it has not been possible to establish it as clearly preferable to others. His approach to scientific discovery was based on observation and nduction. Theory emerged as a result of his extensive clinical experience. The nature of the theory put forward puts much of it beyond experimental test, because of the difficulty of drawing falsifiable hypotheses from it; those hypotheses which have been derived (by others) from the theory and tested have produced equivocal findings. Even among psychoanalytically-inclined clinicians there have been significant objections to Freud's theory, as will be seen in the next part of this chapter.

Freud's work has, notwithstanding these alleged weaknesses, been effective in the founding of a vigorous tradition of interest in child development from the psychoanalytic viewpoint.

Post-Freudian alternatives

Those who have folowed Freud can be divided into (a) those who developed the work along strictly Freudian lines, and (b) those who challenged basic assumptions in Freud's theory. Among the former were Anna Freud, daughter of Sigmund, who holds that factors such as parents' attitudes towards their children play as important a part as instinctual factors, and Melanie Klein, who claims that forerunners of the superego are evident during the first two years and that the aggressive drives play a more important part than sexual ones. Both have worked extensively with young children, and have developed methods of analysis suitable for children as young as two years.

Among the latter, Horney, Sullivan and Fromm have challenged most of Freud's assumptions. Though differing among themselves, they agree that:

1. Rather than biological factors, it is the social and cultural ones which are basic to our understanding of human personality.
2. Features of Freudian theory, like the Oedipus complex and the formation of the superego, are cultural rather than universal traits.
3. Interpersonal relationships are important contributors to the development of personality.
4. Personality determines sexual behaviour, rather than being determined by it.

It is characteristic of these post-Freudians that they concern themselves principally with the ego and the social context with which it deals. Erik Erikson has proposed an alternative account of personality development to that of Freud. He lists eight *psychological stages*, each of which is held to be critical for the development of certain fundamental aspects of personality. As Freud emphasized the influence of psychosexual crises, so Erikson emphasizes psychosocial crises. The similarity between the two will be seen in Table 16.1, which summarizes Erikson's proposals.

Table 16.1

Psychosocial stages	*Personality dimensions*
1. Oral-sensory (first year)	Basic trust v mistrust
2. Muscular-anal (2–3)	Autonomy v shame and doubt
. Locomotor-genital (3–5)	Imitation v guilt
4. Latency (5–12)	Industry v inferiority
5. Puberty and adolescence	Identity v role confusion
6. Young adulthood	Intimacy v isolation
7. Adulthood	Generativity v stagnation
8. Maturity	Ego integrity v despair

It will be seen that Erikson's analysis of personality development embraces the full life span from birth to maturity.

Comparison: which theory of development?

There are considerable differences among the three accounts outlined. These include differences in generality; the learning-theory account differs from the others in that it is a general while they are special theories. It also differs from the two others in respect of attainable goals; for, while Piaget's child is approaching intellectual and Freud's child emotional maturity, it prescribes no such goal or direction for development. Furthermore, both Freud and Piaget draw on biological changes to account for development but the learning theorists do not. A further difference concerns the part played by the child: Piaget's child develops only in terms of his transactions with the world around him, but the other two accord the child a passive role, where development is dominated by either environmental stimulation on the one hand, or the conflict between instinctual forces and the demands of an external reality on the other.

It is perhaps understandable to want to ask which account is right? Or at least, which is to be preferred? To be in a position to give an answer implies the existence of criteria for being 'right' or 'preferable'. Features of the theories like testability, the range of empirical data accommodated, and the extent to which elaboration is possible, give some guide to the second question but not the first. As has been seen, the different approaches have their own internal strengths and weaknesses and it is probably at this level that evaluations can most easily proceed. For the three accounts are undoubtedly different because of their different view-points, and differences of this sort are not necessarily to be seen in terms of contradictions. Each account has something to contribute to an understanding of development; where marked differences occur, these serve to underline the complexity of the task involved in the construction of a single integrated account.

Further reading

Baldwin, A. L.(1967) *Theories of Child Development*. Wiley.
Donaldson, M.(1978) *Children's Minds*. Fontana.
Erikson, E. H.(1963) *Childhood and Society*. Norton.
McGurk, H.(1975) *Growing and Changing: A primer of developmental psychology*. Methuen.
Meadows, S.(1986) *Understanding Child Development*. Hutchinson.
Mussen, P. H., Conger, J. J., and Kagan, J.(1974) *Child Development and Personality*, fourth edn. Harper and Row.
Smith, P. K., and Cowie, H. (1988) *Understanding Children's Development*. Blackwell.

Chapter seventeen

Development in the early school years

Harry Fisher

Developmental psychology

This chapter and the next will be concerned with some aspects of developmental psychology. Development has been described as 'those processes which are biologically programmed or inherent in the person, and those ways in which the person is irreversibly transformed by interaction with the environment' (Neugarten, 1973). The task of the developmental psychologist is to provide in objective terms a description of these changes, and where possible, to offer an explanatory account in terms of variables linked with them. In an earlier chapter the pioneer work of Freud on personality development, and Piaget on cognitive development was considered, both resting on detailed developmental descriptions and both accounted for in terms of separate theoretical frameworks which have been found acceptable in varying degrees. This work reflects the emphasis placed at that time on development in childhood as compared with later development. Both descriptions are consistent with the notion that their respective developments were complete by adolescence, i.e. with the completion of Freud's genital stage, and Piaget's stage of formal operations. In contrast, the work of Erik Erikson, also considered earlier, sees psychosocial development as continuous throughout life.

Life span development

Much of the current work in developmental psychology is set within a life span context. Baltes (1980) has been influential in exploiting this approach to describe development in terms of three major influence systems which interact to produce very different patterns of development. The first of these influence systems is described as 'normative age graded', and covers those influences which are largely age related; beginning at school age five, and speaking a first 'word' between 12 and 18 months are examples. The second system, described as 'normative history graded', refers to influences associated with a particular generation, like the Irish potato famine or the First World War. The third group subsumes those life events which are non-normative, that is, they are neither age- nor history-related but are specific to a given individual. This would include a disabling accident, for example, or inheriting a fortune. Each of the three systems may be primarily biological in character (e.g. the disabling accident), or primarily environmental (the fortune), or some compound of the two. This approach thus provides a systematic framework for the description of developmental patterns throughout life.

A different approach to the problem of providing a systematic coverage of the range of factors which influence development was proposed by Bronfenbrenner (1979) in terms of an ecological model of development. This reflects an increasing recognition of the importance of situational influences on development, so that studies of development become studies of development-in-context. He conceptualized situational influences in terms of sets of different generality, so that the more general include less general influences, for example, local government influences would be regarded as more general, i.e. less direct, than home influences in the development of the child. The most general system is the macrosystem. It includes the exosystem which, in turn, embraces a mesosystem; this includes several microsystems. The macrosystem refers to constraints on change in terms of the social conventions and ideologies adopted by a particular subculture, for example, the number of hours a man is expected to work to earn a living wage. The exosystem is less remote than this and has to do with contexts which also affect the individual only indirectly. For example, conditions of work which affect the parents directly may, by affecting home conditions, influence the child. The mesosystem relates to contexts in which the individual is directly involved; these contexts are known as microsystems, examples of which are the home, and the school. Thus the situational constraints on the child's development may be seen as compounded from this series of nested systems, so that, for example, what the child experiences within the home may be traced to the influence of social institutions . Much of both past and current development is carried out at the level of a single microsystem; Bronfenbrenner's ecological model is intended to provide a foundation for a fuller account of the link between changes in the environment and development.

What is to be considered in this chapter are some of the important psychological changes which take place between six and 11 years of age, opening approximately with the advent of formal schooling and closing as puberty becomes established. Such changes include: learning to get along with age mates; beginning to develop appropriate masculine and feminine roles; developing a conscience, a sense of morality and a scale of values; and developing attitudes towards social groups and institutions (Havighurst, 1972).

As has been noted above, the accounts given of these changes are dominantly in terms of single microsystems. The home, the school and the peer group are importantly involved in all of these changes, and as formal schooling begins, the balance among them changes. Up to this point the child has seen the world about him largely in terms of views pertaining within the home. Now, spending a large part of each weekday in school, others begin to influence that view – teachers, administrators and, possibly most influential, the peer group. It is the dawning of this influence which provides much of the impetus for and character of the development within this age range. Comparisons among members of the peer group take place throughout life and provide an enduring source of changes of beliefs, attitudes and conduct. This influence begins here, in the early school years, supplementing changes brought about within the home. Some of the ways in which the peer group affects such changes will be considered before examining specific areas of development.

Peer group influence

The influence of the peer group on its members reflects its function as an information exchange within a potentially vast population which draws on a range of devices. Whiting and Whiting (1975) showed that the ways in which the peer group influences the individual are different from those used by the family. They made comparative anthropological studies of peer and family relations in six farming groups (located in India, Japan, Mexico, the Philippines, Kenya and the USA). They found that in spite of wide social differences among them, peer group interactions were characterized by both pro-social behaviour and aggressiveness. In contrast, parent–child interactions were intimate, dependent and nurturant. These behaviours were only rarely observed in the 'other' group. The authors proposed that these findings provide support for the notion of universal differences between adult–child and peer interactions across cultures. Peer group influence operates over a wide range of variables including preferences, 'No one wears those things any more', moral values, 'It's not fair', and beliefs, 'Everyone knows that X is better than Y', among others, and it is at this time that children are becoming increasingly conforming as they move away from an earlier egocentrism. The way in which groups evolve and come to exert influence has been demonstrated by a number of studies carried out by Sherif and his colleagues (1951, 1961) in the context of a summer camp for boys. In one of these, known as the Robbers' Cave experiment, two groups of boys were involved, 11 in each group. All the boys were strangers to each other at the start, and in order to study within-group changes the groups were kept separate for the first few days. In the second phase the two groups were brought together in a conflict situation, which involved win–lose contests with planned frustration manipulated to increase tension between the groups. The third phase involved the reduction of inter-group conflict by, for example, introducing a common enemy, or a task which demanded co-operation. The study provided insight into the social changes which took place both within and between groups. It was noted that consistently:

1. Norms emerge in all groups, whether or not they are aware of the other group;
2. Each group produces a hierarchical authority structure;
3. Extreme roles, like leaders and more adherents, appear early;
4. Norms and rules strengthen in the light of the knowledge of the existence of the other group.

To the extent that such small scale experimental studies can be generalized to 'real-life' situations within the larger and more amorphous peer group, they provide useful indications of the ways in which group influence is exerted on its members.

Peer group modelling

The group also influences its members through individuals who on some grounds – their friendliness, good looks, perceived competence, the power they exert, among others – induce others to imitate them, although they may not intend to do so. Research in this area has been mainly in terms of behavioural acts (in some of the early work this phenomenon was referred to as 'behaviour contagion') because these are so readily observable, though it seems not unlikely that it might extend to attitudes and beliefs.

Close relations between peers are maintained in terms of mutual reinforcement of this kind, so that those who are most reinforced are likely to
be those who are generous reinforcers themselves. Bronfenbrenner (1970)
has drawn attention to the different ways in which such relations are used
in different cultures. In Russia where community needs are more highly
valued than individual needs, conformity to group norms is encouraged in
the schools by setting the peer group to support the teacher by giving them
duties to perform. In the USA where individuality is highly valued the
expression of anti-adult views is frequently regarded as a healthy sign. The
passage through early childhood sees the gradual extension of peer group
influence as intellects and personalities develop.

Friendships

Early childhood is a time when children form their first close friendships.
Here the bond is not just imitation, though that may be involved, but the
discovery, for the first time, of someone with whom they can share easily
things they have in common, hobbies, school-talk and all manner of
interests. Age and sex are important determinants of 'best friends';
geographical proximity of homes and schooling are others. As to whether
friends are drawn together because of similar personalities, one investigator (Davitz, 1955) collected data which suggested that, rather, they
perceive each other as similar because they are friends. Friendships are
more or less stable relationships within the peer group, and offer further
insight into peer group influence – that of a group united by age and
divided by sex, with family-based views of the world which now, at times,
clearly differ from it, disseminating information in terms of its social
structure.

These, then, are some of the ways in which the peer group is involved in
development. This is, of course, but one of many sources of influence, and
something of the complexity of the interactions among these and others
will be seen in what follows in specific areas of development characteristic
of the early school years.

Play

What is play?

Play is, of course, a characteristic and pervasive feature of the behaviour of
healthy children; this alone provides a rationale for the interest of
psychologists in it. A definition of play, however, is hard to come by. The
difficulty is that we use the single word 'play' to describe a number of very
different kinds of activity. It is, for instance, used of the activity of an
infant who repeatedly drops a toy and looks for it to be returned, or of two

people involved in a game of chess, or of a child pretending to drive a noisy motor cycle. Some psychologists, notably behaviourists, have, understandably, rejected the notion of play as vague and scientifically useless; they hold that the different manifestations of play should be investigated separately. Others have sought to provide a more integrated account of play. Wittgenstein, a linguistic philosopher, and others, have argued that terms like 'play' represent a range of concepts which have features – or family resemblances – in common, each concept having some, but not all, of these features. Psychologists who have taken this view have attempted to describe separate features and the relations among them. As will be seen in the work to be considered there is some overlap between the two approaches.

Play: two views

Prosser (1985) has provided a child's view of play by considering quotations taken from answers given by his seven-year-old granddaughter to the question 'What do you mean by play?' He chose the following answers:

> 'Doing something you don't need to.'
> 'It makes me happy.'
> 'You want to feel grown up.'
> 'Not real; you want to feel like somebody else.'
> 'You've got nothing else to do.'

The first two of these and the last offer insight into the motivational aspect of play; the activity itself appears less important than the pleasure it affords the child. The other two hint at the possible functional significance of those types of play which involve role playing and make-believe play. Both have a cognitive component, role playing representing knowledge of relationships among different social groups, and make-believe play requiring an ability to consider hypothetical relationships. The child's answers reveal some of the features of play by suggesting contrasts between play on the one hand and work, reality, boredom and constraint on the other. Similar insights have been obtained from more formal studies.

A different approach to the problem of what play 'is' is to distinguish between different types of play. An early classification of this sort was proposed by Parten (1932). She distinguished six types of play from her observations of nursery school children at free play, calling them unoccupied, solitary, onlooker, parallel, associative and co-operative. In unoccupied play the child may just stand and look around, or perform apparently random and goalless movements, while in solitary play the child is absorbed in what he is doing, for the time being in no need of outside assistance and unconcerned with whatever else is going on. Onlooker play is distinguished by the child's interest in the play of others, without joining in. In parallel play several children may be carrying out similar activities at the same time, without interacting with one another. The last two, in contrast, involve some interaction between participants in some related activity; associative play, however, involves little organization beyond, perhaps, the sharing of equipment whereas co-operative play involves social activity within a group with a sense of social cohesion, engaged in an organized activity, such as a team game.

There is some sense of temporal sequence in these six types of activity, running from early (unoccupied) to late (co-operative), though it seems likely that they may persist in some form well beyond the nursery and pre-school years, and coexist rather than form a fixed sequence. Spectator sport, for example, has affinities with onlooker play, and solitary play with all those activities, including hobbies of all sorts, which are best enjoyed by one alone. Co-operative play may be represented later not only by team games but also by all manner of social activities, where the sophistication of the 'play' changes in keeping with cognitive development and knowledge of the world.

Freud: play and catharsis

Freud saw play in terms of feelings and emotions. He describes its purpose as cathartic. This view of play is to be found in the writings of Aristotle; catharsis was probably originally a medical term meaning to purge or cleanse. On this view, then, children play to relieve pent up emotions. The psychoanalytic theory of play is a particular case of the cathartic view in which Freud demonstrates the way in which the more specific of his constructs fit within the notion of catharsis. The cleansing is seen as brought about by play which serves to reduce unpleasant excitation associated with pent up emotions. An example of this is play which repeats the details of unpleasant circumstances of which the child has been the victim, as when the child feeds make-believe medicine to a doll again and again. Freud argued that this reduces excitation by putting the child into an active rather than a passive role, and that the repetition further strengthens the child's feeling of being in control in the sort of situation in which, earlier, he was not. Much play can be seen in terms of the Freudian defence mechanisms to achieve the same end. Projection, for example, may be seen in the way in which children compensate for loneliness by the use of imaginary companions. Similarly, catharsis might be brought about by displacement, as when a child wilfully damages a sibling's property instead of taking it out on the individual. Such devices are seen as leading to the feeling of mastery of the situation by the child. They have been widely used as a basis for play therapy.

This view of play is developmental in that it describes play in terms of problems characteristic of Freud's stages of psychosexual development.

For example, role play representing identification with the same sex parent would be appropriate during the phallic stage, but play in this stage which was oral in character, e.g. repeated biting, would not. Such comparisons, of course, afford a basis for diagnosis. These stages were based on information obtained from Freud's adult patients about their childhood experiences. The subjective and retrospective nature of this information, drawn from an abnormal population, has been seen as placing severe limitations on the generality of Freud's model as a whole, and thus of his account of play.

Erikson: playing it out

Mention has been made in Chapter 16 of Erikson's eight stage life span theory of development. The accounts of play given by Erikson and Freud have much in common. The clinical context of their work makes the case study of central importance as a source of information. Both view play as a means of externalizing emotional problems. When adults are faced with such problems they may 'talk it out'. The limited language skills of young children preclude this, but they are able, according to this approach, to 'play it out'. 'Talking it out' becomes increasingly important as language develops. Thus, it is argued, observation and interpretation of play offer insight not only into the child's emotional problems, but also into development in more general terms. Like Freud, Erikson uses psychoanalytic constructs (id, ego and superego, levels of consciousness and defence mechanisms, for example) to interpret his observations. In addition Erikson draws on what is known of the social and cultural environment to interpret the play of the individual. It is this, together with his emphasis on the development of the ego, which distinguishes it from orthodox psychoanalysis; in his own words, 'A human being ... is at all times an organism, an ego and a member of society and is involved in all three processes of organization' (*Childhood and Society*, 1965, p. 31). 'Play is a function of the ego, an attempt to synchronize the bodily and the social processes with self' (p. 204). Erikson, like Freud, sees development in terms of a genetically determined sequence, thus providing a universal component. Erikson, however, holds that the individual is 'organism, ego and a member of society from birth', as distinct from Freud's view as all id to begin with, only gradually becoming socialized with the development of the ego and superego. A further difference between them is the scope of the development described. For Freud, this closes with the genital period (12–18 years of age). Erikson, however, sees development in life span terms, detailing three distinct stages beyond Freud's genital stage, the play of the child being just the precursor of adult activities which may be seen as play – the creative problem-solving of the adult, for example. From the earliest days play affords the ego a means of self-expression which may be evaluated by the child against the ever present social norms, leading to mastery in the form of self-help, and serving to resolve the crises defined by the eight psychosocial stages.

Erikson's account of play shares with Freud's criticisms relating to the limitations of the clinical approach and the validity of psychoanalytic constructs. On a number of counts his account has proved preferable to that of Freud. These include the following:

1. The breadth of information on which it is based. Whereas Freud's child data were obtained only from what his adult patients remembered of their own childhood experiences, Erikson's were based on case studies of children, as well as adult studies in a variety of social settings.
2. The additional emphasis on present (social) determinants of behaviour to that originating in the past, e.g. fixations and repressions.
3. The notion of continuity in the development of play in life span terms.

Piaget: play as adaptation

Piaget conceived of play in terms of the interplay between the adaptive processes assimilation and accommodation considered in Chapter 16. Where the two are in equilibrium there is adaptation, that is, the individual makes a response to the environment which is appropriate. For example early grasping is accomplished by enclosing an object between the four fingers and the palm of the hand. This method sometimes fails when the object is very small; appropriate handling of these has to wait upon the development of the opposition of thumb and forefinger. This accommodation makes it posssible for the infant to manipulate objects of various sizes. Thus here the activity of holding represents a balance between assimilation and accommodation. The balance, however, is a temporary affair, the process of equilibration moves on as the infant gains in strength and dexterity. Disequilibrium means that one or other of the two processes dominates; for the infant assimilation is frequently the more evident as the child appears to enjoy repeating mastered activities. It was this, 'pure assimilation', which Piaget regarded as play. Repeating an activity in order to understand it was regarded as investigation or exploration rather than as play, since it is adapted to external reality. Play, in contrast, is adapted to the child's internal reality.

This view of play is consistent with what is to be observed of its onset, developmental sequence and decline. Without assimilation and accommodation play is not possible; this may be the case in the brief period when the neonate's contact with the environment is dominantly passive. With the onset of the sensory motor period a sequence of activities of increasing complexity emerges which involves both processes. An early activity of this kind is the grasping reflex already referred to; the infant will repeat the action with evident dedication. Piaget referred to this as 'practice play'.

With the advent of object permanence, and the child's ability to use language, the nature of play changes to make use of these representational abilities. This is 'symbolic play'. It includes make-believe play, where a knotted scarf can stand for a baby, or a block of wood for a car. It also includes role play by means of which a child may manipulate his internal world, taking on roles which are active and dominant to replace real-world roles which are passive and limited. Story telling also develops and the child appears to enjoy the repetitions with little or no modification.

'It's not fair' is a claim heard increasingly as children of school age find themselves in competition with others. Such claims are associated with Piaget's operational period which leaves behind the limitations of egocentricity. Games and social relationships now involve rules which must be fair to everyone. This represents an underlying ability to deal with several aspects of a situation at once, and to rules which are reciprocally binding on all participants in a game. Play in the periods of both concrete and formal operations is described as 'games and rules'. In some games, draughts for instance, the rules are embodied in specified moves, analogous to concrete operations; in others, like American football, the actual movements are much more abstractly related to the rules. Assimilation now functions in terms of adherence to the rules. What satisfied the player or the spectator is not merely that specified goals have been achieved, but that they have been achieved according to the rules.

Piaget also saw the gradual decline of play in terms of the interplay between assimilation and accommodation. New experiences are a constant feature of early childhood, ensuring a preponderance of assimilation well into middle childhood. Beyond this the number and rate at which surprises demand the assimilation process is likely to decline in favour of accommodation and the elaboration of established schemata.

Evaluation of Piaget's account of play must be seen in the context of his methods, considered in Chapter 16. Little, if any, of the work on which the above conclusions are based rest on the accepted canons of hypothesis testing. Yet among Piagetians and others these canons are seen as useful but limiting, and incapable of providing the sensitivity of the clinical interview or the richness of the data it provides; they would want to regard the clinical approach as no less scientific than the other. There is no clear sense, therefore, in which it can be claimed that Piaget's data confirm the predictions of his theory, since theorizing and the collection of data appear to have a variable relationship. The theory sometimes predicts the observations and sometimes grows out of them. What can be said is that Piaget's account of play is coherent within the outlines of his broad and complex theory of cognitive development.

Piaget's account of play, like Freud's, extends only as far as the limit of this general framework. Beyond adolescence both are silent about play. Unlike Freud, there is little about the involvement of emotion in play.

Piaget's early description of cognitive development was given in terms of a fixed and invariant series of steps, the completion of each being required before passing on to the next. There is considerable cross cultural support for the constancy of the sequence, but some evidence which suggests that development may not be stagelike, and the different stages may coexist and development proceed in time as an upward spiral. Each time round the spiral each aspect of development may be dealt with at a higher level suggesting that the original account of cognitive development may have overemphasized the discontinuity.

The three accounts of play considered above are different because they emerge from studies of different problems. Freud links play with emotional development, Piaget links it with intellectual development and Erikson links it with factors in the social and cultural environment. Although these separate links are proposed there are clear areas of overlap; Freud and Piaget have accounts which do not progress beyond adolescence, Piaget and Erikson both emphasize the influence of social factors, Erikson and Freud both use psychoanalytic constructs, and all show a preference for stage-wise development. For such reasons the three accounts of play coexist rather than compete, each serving the system within which it is conceived. Together they provide some insight into the complex role which play has in development. Other approaches, using methods different from the clinical approach which unites these three, have added to what is known about play; for example, ethological studies have expanded the detail of the various activities which can count as play, and experimental approaches have provided insight into factors (e.g. imitation) which influence the acquisition of certain types of play (Bandura, 1977; Hutt, 1966).

Moral development

The study of moral development involves the identification and description of processes by which individuals come to internalize and adopt the norms of right and wrong of their society. The processes may be conceived in terms of cognitive, behavioural and affective aspects of morality. For convenience these are usually studied separately though it seems likely that there are links among them. Probably the most coherent developmental account is to be found in the work of Lawrence Kohlberg into the cognitive aspect; it represents the development and extension of the work of Piaget in the same area, which investigated the ways in which children of different ages viewed rules and made judgements about hypothetical situations involving moral conflict. The investigation of the behavioural aspect of morality has provided insight as to what individuals do in a moral conflict as distinct from what they say. Studies have been carried out, for instance, of the child's ability to resist temptation, providing indications of the capacity for implementing internalized rules. The effective aspect of morality in children has been concerned with the emotional reaction to transgression of rules, where guilt reactions were used to infer the reality of the rules for individuals. Each of these three aspects will be considered in turn.

Piaget: morals and marbles

Piaget used the method of clinical interrogation to gain insight into the development of the child's moral judgements. In one extensive study he questioned children of different ages about the rules governing a popular local game of marbles, to follow the ways in which these changed over time with different individuals. In another he presented them with short 'moral' stories, which they were asked to evaluate. The stories came in pairs. One, for example, would describe an individual who, through a clumsy, if well intentioned act, occasioned extensive damage, while the other described a similar individual who, engaged in deliberate mischief, brought about little damage. The subject was asked to judge which of the two was worse, and why. Younger children chose the one who did most damage, while older children chose the intentional villain. Piaget used this kind of data to construct a description of the developmental sequence of moral judgements. He proposed two clear stages, an earlier, heteronomous and a later, autonomous, stage, the age of seven to eight years providing a rough boundary between them. Heteronomous implies 'subject to another's law', autonomous, 'subject to one's own law'. Thus for the younger children moral sanctions are external and vested in parents and other adults. Older children regulate their own conduct, having established principles of their own in line with social norms – but occasionally in defiance of them. Piaget saw these two stages as a reflection of two defects of cognitive functioning, namely moral realism and egocentricity. Because of the first the child does not distinguish subjective from objective phenomena, viewing adult rules as fixed and inevitable; the second means that the child views rules from his point of view alone, entailing an inability to regard moral rules as relative to persons and situations. The later autonomous stage sees the child disabused of both limitations. Children in the two stages thus differ in their view of rules, their view of right and wrong, and consequently their view of justice. In the earlier stage, rules are regarded as absolute and unchangeable; in the later stage, rules are regarded as means of regulating social intercourse, to be changed if all concerned consent. Right and wrong to the immature child are judged by the letter of the 'absolute' rules. It is only in the autonomous stage that intentionality is used in evaluating right and wrong. Justice, for the younger children, is concerned with the punishment of misdeeds, again according to the letter of the law. Only in autonomous children is punishment seen as a means of demonstrating corporate displeasure for antisocial acts. Piaget described the change from one stage to the next as a change from a morality of authority to a morality of co-operation.

Evaluation

This pioneering work of Piaget raises a large number of issues, three of which will be considered here. The first concerns the heteronomous–autonomous distinction. Subsequent research using similar methods has provided substantial support for both the distinction and the sequence. This includes a large body of cross cultural studies as well as extended longitudinal studies; overall it is suggestive of a universal distinction and sequence. The benefit of hindsight suggests that Piaget's proposals may be somewhat coarse-grained, for while he proposes two types of moral reasoning Kohlberg (1976) proposes six. (See, however, the detail in the next section.)

A second issue is that of the clarity of the account of the developmental change from one type to the other. Piaget identifies several groups of factors, social, emotional and cognitive, which are likely to influence development, such as the social development of the child as a result of the increasing negotiations with the peer group on a reciprocity basis, the changing nature of the relationship between parents and the child, in the light of peer group influence, and the changing nature of cognitive functioning (particularly the decline of egocentric thinking). All of these are highly plausible sources of change. There is, however, little in Piaget concerning their relative importance or the ways in which they interact to bring about the transition.

The third issue concerns the link between Piaget's description of moral reasoning and his sequence of stages of cognitive development. It has been questioned whether the stage of formal operations adequately reflects what is found in mature moral reasoning, particularly the frequent emotional content. There is also evidence to suggest that significant changes can be brought about by experience, and that it should be possible, therefore, to distinguish, in a principled way, between the naïve, albeit 'formal', intelligent judgements of the adolescent and those of a mature adult who has, say, a long professional experience in making judicial rulings. This is also a criticism of Piaget's definition of the formal stage. This will be considered in more detail in the next chapter.

Kohlberg: moral judgements

The work of Lawrence Kohlberg (1976) rests on and extends that of Piaget and offers insight into some of the problems considered above. Like Piaget he sees moral development in terms of an invariant series of stages and uses answers to questions about moral dilemmas as his data. In one of these, for example, Heinz steals from a chemist a drug which would save his wife's life. He is too poor to buy it at the exorbitant price the chemist is asking. The subject is then asked a series of questions: should Heinz have done that? Was it wrong or right? Why? Was the chemist right to charge a greatly inflated price? Using the answers to such questions for a range of dilemmas Kohlberg proposed three levels of moral judgement: pre-conventional, which embraced most children under nine and some delinquent adolescents; conventional, accounting for most individuals from their teens onward, and post-conventional, representing a morality of self-chosen principles which only a small fraction of adolescents and adults attain, and then not usually until the twenties. Kohlberg divides each of these levels into two stages as shown in the table below; this provides a much abbreviated summary of his proposals.

Table 17.1 Moral judgement: Kohlberg's six stages

Level 1 Pre-conventional

Stage 1 Heteronomous Morality. Wrong is what is punished. Right is what remains. Obedience is required for its own sake.

Stage 2 Instrumental Purpose and Exchange. Right is what brings rewards. Right is also what is fair.

Level 2 Conventional

Stage 3 Conformity with Mutual Interpersonal Expectations. Right is living up to what friends expect of you. Being good means having good motives and keeping trusting and respectful relations.

Stage 4 Social System and Conscience. Right is keeping society's laws except in extreme cases where they conflict with other social duties.

Level 3 Post-conventional

Stage 5 Social Contract and Individual Rights. Right is acting in such a way as to be sensitive to other people's (different) commitments to the social contract. Some absolutes, e.g. life and liberty, to be maintained regardless of majority views.

Stage 6 Universal Ethical Principles. What is right is determined by principles of conscience, e.g. the sanctity of human life, justice, equality.
(Theoretical) The principles are not explicitly dictated by society-only specific enactments of them. The principles of conscience may conflict with aspects of the social contract.

Thus, answers consistent with stage 1 might include 'He should steal the drug' (or 'He should not steal the drug'), while stage 6 might include 'He has to act in terms of the principles of preserving and respecting life' (or 'He ought to act not only according to his feelings towards his wife, but also in the light of all the lives involved').

Evaluation

There are substantial similarities between the approaches of Piaget and Kohlberg, the latter supporting and extending the former. Both propose a fixed sequence of stages, seeing the progression from one stage to the next as powered by the interaction of the genetically unfolding cognitive development with experience and knowledge of the world. Both also stress the importance of the social influence of the peer group in these changes. They also share certain criticisms, e.g. that the stages are not discrete, but overlap. Bronfenbrenner and Gabarino (1976) have drawn on anthropological studies to suggest that while these stages are identifiable in western cultures they are by no means universal. Related are criticisms that the moral dilemmas are (a) not typical, that is, not the sort of problem situation usually encountered by young people; (b) situationally restricted, in that they require a rational approach, without the emotional context – and occasional irrationality – which mark the real-life dilemma, and (c) inadequate, in terms of inter-judge reliability. It is the case also that both Piaget and Kohlberg failed to distinguish between conventions (like driving on the left of the road) and moral rules (e.g. against stealing). Whereas conventions can be changed if everyone concerned agrees, moral rules cannot. Weston and Turiel (1980) showed that four to six-year-olds, within the heteronomous period, could distinguish between them. These are some of the issues which wait on further empirical investigation and need to be considered in the light of other work in the area. The original work, Kohlberg (1976), was based on a 20-year longitudinal study of 50 boys aged between ten and 16 years, seen at three-year intervals. The stages he proposed have been observed not only in his own work, but also in that of others using cross-sectional as well as longitudinal methods. Recently, Kohlberg and his colleagues have revised some aspects of the theory (Colby *et al*, 1983). Among the effects of the use of a new and more reliable scoring system has been the provision of further support for the original sequence as far as stage 4; stage 5 was found to occur only rarely and stage 6 not at all. This stage is thus now regarded as theoretical, that is as a distinction which can be made, but for which there is no valid evidence.

Moral behaviour

A different viewpoint on moral development has been established from the point of view of moral behaviour, or moral action; of interest is what people do as distinct from what they think. This involves a variety of approaches, a sample of which will be considered here.

Experiments have been performed which suggest the involvement of classical as well as operant conditioning in moral development. Parke

(1974), for example, showed that it was possible to inhibit three-year-olds' touching of a toy by telling them that it might break (conditioned anxiety response). Telling them that it belonged to another child had very little effect on the three-year-olds but had a clear effect on the five-year-olds. This was used to draw the distinction between the classically conditioned effect on the younger children and the cognitively based approach effective in establishing moral controls with the older children.

Social learning theory sees moral development as learned behaviour; this learning differs from conditioning in that the subject is seen as learning by observation, imitating what he observes apparently because of some desirable feature/s of a model who might be a parent, relative, teacher or other admired person. Introduced by Albert Bandura in the early 1960s, this approach is essentially experimental; its predictions are for individual differences in development as opposed to a common stage-based sequence, development being contingent on continued imitation. Studies of altruism, pro-social behaviour including helping those in distress and generally showing a selfless concern for the welfare of others have been made from this viewpoint. Martin Hoffman (1975), who has contributed substantially to this research, has shown that altruism increases in incidence and variety as the child gets older. Children may engage in altruism as early as the second year, though often this is as a result of prompting and rewards. A marked increase in altruism, both in incidence and variety, is associated with the influence of the peer group in the middle and late years of childhood, for most, but not all children. A critical factor underlying altruism is empathy, the ability to share the feelings of another; quite young children sometimes appear to be involved in empathic crying, and a mobile child will often approach and touch a crying child. Empathy is informed by being able to see things from different points of view. It has been shown that the disciplinary style of the parents plays an important role in the development of altruistic behaviour; their own altruistic example and their assignment of responsibility and maturity demands are practices which have been demonstrated as promoting altruism (Radke-Yarrow *et al*, 1975). The Social Learning Theory approach has also been used to give an account of the acquisition of antisocial behaviour (in contrast to the pro-social altruistic behaviour); this will be found in the section dealing with the influence of television.

Cheating

An early study of moral behaviour was concerned with children's behaviour when faced with a choice between two alternatives, one of which is seen to be morally wrong. The *Character Education Inquiry* published in 1932 by Hartshorne and May addressed this question. Twelve thousand children were put into situations where they could cheat, lie or steal – at

537

home, in the classroom, in athletics and in party games. They were mistakenly under the impression that their actions were private. The data were used to provide an answer to the question as to whether honesty is a general trait or whether it is situation specific. The findings were surprising. The correlation between bad behaviour in one setting and bad behaviour in another was low, averaging about 0.34. Even when the settings were similar, in school tests, for example, children behaved inconsistently. It was concluded that in terms of the tests performed, honesty was largely situation specific rather than a general personality trait. A subsequent re-analysis of the data modified the latter part of this conclusion by showing that there was a significant, if small, tendency for children who were honest on one test to be so on others. Subsequent studies of different measures of honesty have tended to confirm that they are positively correlated. Thus whether a person resists the temptation to cheat, lie, or steal is clearly influenced by his personality, as well as by the situation, Hill (1980) drew similar conclusions. He found, for example, that students cheat more when they know that the results will be displayed, and also when there is no adult invigilation of examinations. Like Hartshorne and May he found that cheating did not appear uniformly, but was specific to the situation. Similar findings appear also to apply to altruism.

It seems likely that early experience within the family plays an important role in moral development. The direct evidence allows very few generalizations apart from that concerning the pervasive influence of the mother. Perhaps the most direct evidence of the influence of child rearing practices comes from a comparison of family conditions between delinquents and matched non-delinquents. The non-delinquent typically comes from a home where the bonds of affection between child and parent are strong, where moral demands on the child are firm and explicit, and where misdemeanours are punished consistently and with some emphasis on reasoning and explanation. Punishment is rarely physical. The delinquent, by contrast, usually comes from a home where bonds of affection are weak, and where punishment is frequently based on physical or verbal assault; punishment is both inconsistently applied and variable in severity. But since there are also 'good' children who come from 'bad' homes and 'bad' children who come from 'good' homes this is clearly not the whole story.

The school and the peer group: role development

That these two agents of socialization play a major role in development is evident from the time over which they operate, if on no other grounds. School in the UK occupies at least 11 years. Access to playgroups, nursery school, and sixth form college can increase this to 15 years; similar figures apply in the USA. It is also evident that major changes take place during this time – physical, cognitive, social and emotional – in which each of these two agents has a part to play. The peer group influence is part of the influence of the school but distinct from it; much peer influence takes place entirely outside the school. While the direct influence of the school may extend to as much as 15 years, that of the peer group continues throughout life, constant comparisons being made among age cohorts. The onset of the influence of school and peer group is for practical purposes almost simultaneous; together they communicate what society deems appropriate. This includes the provision of a view of the world outside the home, and opportunities for each individual to find a place in it. The home has already provided a range of experience preparing the child for the world outside, including some of the ground rules for social interaction and the implications of such roles as mother, father, son, daughter, brother and sister. The school and peer group now offer an increasingly wider sampling of the world outside the home, and a wider range of roles, which now arise in the context of a numerically greater 'family' in the peer group, a wider sample against which the individual may evaluate and modify his own role.

Gender role development

'One man in his time plays many parts.' In what follows this quotation from Shakespeare seven such parts or roles are listed: infant, schoolboy, lover, soldier, justice of the peace, old man, and second childishness, some clearly obligatory and some not. They are but seven of a vast range of parts that an individual learns to play. This section is concerned with the development of sex roles and gender roles. A distinction between them may be made in the following way. Sex role has been used to refer to roles played by boys or roles played by girls, on the assumption that there is a sharp 'boys will be boys and girls will be girls' distinction between them and that the remainder, when these are withdrawn from the total population, will be small and abnormal. Gender role has been used to describe a wider variety of conduct and attitudes not constrained by the male/female dichotomy and taking into account that girls may exhibit what have been taken as masculine traits and boys, feminine traits. Both notions are of use in describing the phenomena of role development.

The development of such roles is a feature of middle and late childhood. Studies of playmate preferences and attitudes indicate that by three years of age children prefer playmates of their own sex (Maccoby and Jacklin, 1974), and from five to 11 discriminate in favour of their own and against the other sex. Informal groups of peers which form during middle childhood are mostly single sex; at least part of their activity appears to be concerned with emphasizing group differences, contributing to the polarization and serving the interests of the development of sex roles in both groups. Information about their knowledge of their sexuality has been obtained by asking young children directly about themselves or indirectly about dolls having clearly represented genitalia, 'Are you/Is this a boy or a girl?' By the time they are seven years old most children know the right answer. Their knowledge appears to involve the realization that each child is either a boy or a girl, that sexual identity is stable over time, and that it is also stable across different conditions, of, say, dress and hairstyle. Among the youngest of the subjects of Kohlberg (1966), whose ages ranged from two to five years, a number were aware of their identity – boy or girl but entertained the possibility that this might change if they were to dress differently, or if their hair were longer or shorter. Several studies have shown that most three-year-olds could accurately identify the sex of dolls on the basis of dress, but were much less accurate using genitalia. By six most children know that sexual identity is stable over time. One year later it is also seen as consistent in spite of changes of clothes and length of hair (Marcus and Overton, 1978). Thus by middle childhood these notions are established and provide an adequate basis for the establishment of sexual stereotypes.

Sexual stereotypes

These are generalizations about supposed characteristics of male and female behaviour which are widely held. One form taken is in terms of dichotomies such as 'women are emotional, men are unemotional; women are intuitive, men are logical'. Or, in comparative form, 'girls are more sociable than boys, are more suggestible than boys', etc. Whatever form they take they frequently represent widely accepted beliefs which are resistant to change. It is in the implied link that such stereotypes as 'he is aggressive because he is a man' present a challenge to psychology. They beg two main questions: the extent to which supporting evidence can be found, and the grounds on which many persist in the absence of such evidence. These raise two further questions: where sex related differences are found, what kinds of account are appropriate and to what extent is it possible to choose among them? In their massive work, *The Psychology of Sex Differences*, Maccoby and Jacklin (1974) showed that both in psychology proper and in 'folk' psychology there was little or no support for some proposed male/female differences. There was, for example, no support for the notions that girls are more sociable or more suggestible than boys. On the other hand the literature provided extensive support for the stereotype which sees boys as more aggressive than girls. This was practically independent of age and type of aggression. Across different cultural settings it was found that from the time that social play begins, boys are involved in different forms of aggression, physical, make-believe, and verbal, more frequently than girls, and that this difference is stable at least as far as adolescence. They also found considerable support for the superior mathematical ability of boys from about 12 years or so onwards, as well as for the superior verbal ability of girls from about 11 years.

These three are among the best attested stereotypes and invite explanation. Whether there is something common to aggression, mathematical, and verbal ability remains to be seen, but the question points up the problem of deciding on the nature of explanation to be sought. While a parsimonious account might be sought to embrace all three, and such others as there are, it would seem simpler to approach each of them singly at first, particularly as different types of account might be appropriate.

Why do sex role stereotypes persist?

In some cases they persist because they provide an adequate description of things as they are, agreeing broadly with the findings of empirical studies. The greater aggressiveness of boys is a good example. Not all boys are aggressive or more aggressive than girls, but most of them are. Others persist because they embody some half truth or some aspect of the truth which may apply in restricted domains, and yet others because they are conventionally acceptable. There is also considerable evidence that traditional sex roles are maintained by the considerable use made of them by the media. Surveys of popular children's TV programmes and books consistently depict males as aggressive and rewarded for action while females are seen as passive and deferential.

Androgyny

Stereotyped accounts of sex role development emerged from a tradition in which masculinity and femininity were regarded as opposite, and describable only in terms of attributes which were themselves opposites. Indeed such attributes were used as indicators of psychological health (Bem, 1975). A man was regarded as healthy to the extent that he presented a good number of masculine attributes. He was not supposed to exhibit gentleness or affection, for example, as these were feminine attributes. It was not until the middle of the 1970s that a plausible alternative to the binary division of attributes was proposed. This held that the whole range of attributes should apply to women and men. The same person might be described as having both masculine and feminine attributes. ('Androgyny' comes from 'andro', male, and 'gyne', female.) Bem and others have examined the validity of this notion by dividing their subjects into the categories masculine, feminine, androgynous, and undifferentiated on the basis of their responses on the Bem Sex Role Inventory. This is a questionnaire based on 20 items each of traditionally masculine attributes (assertive, independent ...), feminine attributes (gentle, understanding ...), and neutral attributes (likeable, friendly ...). Subjects were classified as masculine if they had high masculine and low feminine scores, feminine if they had low masculine and high feminine scores, androgynous if they were high on both, and undifferentiated if they were low on both. In a series of experiments designed to elicit responses in 'masculine' or 'feminine' situations, it was found, as predicted, that masculine typed subjects scored significantly higher than feminine typed subjects in masculine situations. The reverse was true in feminine situations. Androgynous subjects were high in both. Such findings, among a range of others, provide support for this alternative approach to describing the development of the 'sex' role in a more flexible way, drawing on traditional male and female features, and in addition distinguishing between androgynous and undifferentiated roles.

The pioneering work in this field has been largely in the hands of Bem (1975) and Spence and Helmreich (1978). The latter developed a Personality Attributes Questionnaire (PAQ) which, like the BSRI, provides a measure of androgyny. There is also a child PAQ which has produced further support by demonstrating a link between androgynous children and androgynous parenting.

One by-product of this movement has been the stimulation of interest in the influence of the father in development. The earliest literature gives the mother pride of place in child rearing, with little or no reference to the father. Differential involvement of fathers has been clearly demonstrated; for example, it has been shown that androgynous fathers participate more in child rearing activities than masculine fathers.

The notion of androgyny has not replaced traditional views of sex role development. Erikson, for example, holds that psychological differences between males and females arise from anatomical differences (his 'anatomy is destiny' doctrine); with others he has maintained that it is these which dominate sex role development, initiating early differences in childhood and continuing as the basis of an important social process throughout life.

The social influence of television

Albert Bandura and his colleagues showed that changes in a range of children's behaviour do not require the repeated pairing of response and reinforcement associated with animal studies, but may be effected by observation. What was to become the foundation of Social Learning Theory was based on the findings of experiments like the following. A child watches through a one-way screen as an adult model punches and generally ill-treats an inflatable child-sized (Bobo) doll. As a control, a different child observes the same adult model walk into the room and simply ignore the doll. In the next stage of the experiment the two children are separately observed as they wait for a short while in the room with the Bobo doll.

Typically, if there is any contact between child and doll it is the first child which is involved and the behaviour aggressive, following the same pattern as the aggression observed. These findings were repeated using much larger sample sizes. The findings are hardly surprising. Perhaps the occurrence of the response after only a single exposure may be mildly so, but the findings were stable over a range of studies. The implications of one trial learning by observation were far reaching, and have been largely realized by subsequent research.

Elaboration of this basic design offered insight into the influence of a range independent variables. Take the models, for example. The level of imitation was usually higher when the model was adult rather than a child, and with a friendly rather than unfriendly adult. It was possible also to investigate whether such effects were stable over time (they frequently were); also to study the effect of punishment or reward for the model on imitation level – the latter normally evoked more imitation . . . and so on. Common sense, maybe, but a rich area of enquiry. Of course it begs important questions, for example, does this have anything to do with real life? Are there corresponding findings for pro-social behaviour? Can it be established that television can act in the same way to modify behaviour? Can attitudes and beliefs be shown to be vulnerable to manipulation in this way – social or buying attitudes, for example? These questions, and others, will be considered in what follows.

Research methods

The rapid spread of television in the 1950s was matched by the interest shown in its influence. Early studies were concerned with the influence of television as such, more recent studies with the investigation of the impact of specific content. Of considerable importance among these have been those concerned with the influence of television violence upon the community. Three main types of enquiry have been employed: laboratory studies, field studies – real life studies to the extent that the data are collected outside the laboratory and in 'natural' context – and experimental field studies which combine the characteristics of the other two. Each approach has its limitations; laboratory studies frequently have only limited direct relevance to real life (or limited ecological validity), while naturalistic observations often lead to correlational analyses which cannot reveal the direction of influence (whether X is aggressive because he watches violence on TV, or whether he watches TV violence because he enjoys aggression). Many of the effects studied in this area have been shown to be stable across all three types of enquiry.

Television violence: findings

These have attracted wide interest and several extensive surveys have appeared from academic sources (e.g. Stein and Friedrich, 1975) and other public bodies, including government-sponsored reports in the UK and USA; a report from the American National Institute of Mental Health was published in 1982. On the basis of published findings many investigators and reviewers are prepared to see the strong relation between watching TV violence and aggressive behaviour in causal terms; this includes film and even cartoon violence. An idea of the stability of the link between these variables can be gained from the findings of Huesmann (1983). This was a correlational study run over ten years. It was found that reliable predictions of [peer group ratings of] aggression at 18 could be made from the viewing habits of the same subjects at eight.

Aggression: individual differences

The findings indicate that a number of factors are associated with individual differences; these include sex, habitual levels of aggression, and age.

Women watch TV violence less than men and are less aggressive. They are, however, equally susceptible to it. Research in this area has been mainly on males, and Stein and Friedrich (1975) suggest that the extent of female reaction to TV violence may have been underestimated because male/female comparisons on female appropriate aggressive behaviours have usually not been made.

One of the conclusions drawn in the USA Surgeon General's report of 1972 was that those who were most likely to be affected by television violence were children whose level of aggression was already high. It was argued in some quarters that if this were so the public objection to TV violence was misplaced. The report shows, however, that while there is a strong tendency towards aggression in such children the effect is by no means confined to them.

The clearest developmental trends include an age-linked preference for more violent programmes, and a corresponding reduction in anxiety on exposure to screened violence. These are also linked with other developmental trends, notably with the increasing influence of the peer group and the declining influence of the parents. In middle childhood TV violence can lead to aggression towards people as well as objects. It is most likely when the target is a member of the peer group and least likely for a known adult. The likelihood of aggression is also related to the anxiety-arousing properties of the situation (Stein and Friedrich, 1975); in turn these implicate the influence of personality variables, for children who show signs of anxiety in the presence of violence are less likely to react aggressively (Biblow, 1973).

The differential susceptibility to anxiety offers some account of the considerable differences found in the middle childhood literature on aggression. Against a background of wide ranges in both cognitive and emotional sophistication, reaction to TV violence is influenced by both peer groups and parental norms. Those children who have absorbed society's disapproval of violence may be expected to be inhibited to some extent in their own use of aggression. For some, repeated exposure brings about habituation, anxiety arousal declines and the inhibition decreases, reinforced by the conduct of appropriate models. This provides some outline of a possible Social Learning Theory account of the effects of exposure to screened violence.

An alternative account in terms of catharsis has been proposed, according to which observation of screened violence should provide a vicarious outlet for aggressive impulses. Thus aggression should decrease with exposure (Feshbach and Singer, 1971). While this may be the case for some children it would appear to be contrary to the findings considered above.

Television and pro-social behaviour

It would seem at least possible that those processes which underlie the establishment of antisocial behaviour in the form of aggression should also be involved in the establishment of pro-social behaviour. There is considerable evidence that this is so, such behaviours as helping, sharing and co-operation, among others, having been effected by imitation of peer and adult models. Such findings have frequently emerged from laboratory studies which raise the same problems of generalization to the natural effects of television met earlier. Now many studies have been carried out using television programmes popular in the USA such as 'Sesame Street' and 'Mr Roger's Neighbourhood'. The latter has a primary focus on social and emotional development, and Friedrich and Stein (1973) report that pre-school children learned a range of pro-social behaviours – helping, trying to understand another's feelings, among others – from seeing four episodes of this series. 'Sesame Street', originally concerned with mainly cognitive skills, also introduced social and emotional aspects. These programmes were directed at slightly older children; they too produced appropriate imitative behaviours in target behaviours, including helping, sharing, self-regulation (learning to wait), and imaginative play.

As with aggression, this imitation was moderated by the perceived status of the model, or what happened to him. Thus the extent to which pro-social television succeeded was influenced by such factors as reward and punishment to the model, the nurturance (warmth, friendliness) of his manner, or the similarity of the television characters to the watching child.

Television and social influence

The preceding discussion provides evidence of some of the ways in which changes of behaviour may be linked with television viewing, and some limited support for the notion that 'all television is educational television'. Overall, however, its potential is constrained in virtue of its interests in entertainment and advertisement. Stein and Friedrich propose that 'Television is a source of information about the world, its social relationships and its social structures. But it is not a mirror of society; it is a prism which selects and focuses attention on the values of the dominant culture.' Gerbner (1972) concluded that these values were vested, in the USA, in the young, the middle aged, the beautiful, and those of high status. Surveys of prime time television reveal that ethnic minority groups are stereotyped as ridiculous, foreigners are more frequently cast as villains, and frequent viewers present more traditional sex role stereotypes than less frequent viewers.

Thus those who gain social information in large measure from television obtain a digest which does less than justice to the rich variability which exists, but such views will frequently be modified by real-world experience and from comment from media outside television. Many have seen children as specially vulnerable to possible distortions of social knowledge because of their intellectual immaturity, and have drawn attention to the responsibility of producers who present interpreted views of the world to their audiences.

The teacher and the school

The teacher and the school are intended to play important roles in the development of the child, primarily in educational terms. In this section the role of the teacher as role model and prophet, and the influence of early schooling on socially disadvantaged children, will be considered.

The teacher as a model

'Geography was my best subject, I liked the teacher.' Individuals discussing their education frequently make this link between being good at something and a person who helped and directed their early efforts in the enterprise. The middle school pupil who likes his teacher will often spontaneously imitate practically anything that comes to hand – the teacher's gestures, favourite phrases, habits of dress, even hair styling – however inappropriate this may be. Sometimes this broadbased inclination to imitate includes the teacher's area of expertise; the admiration covers the methods and goals, and the teacher serves as a model which may be valued beyond the immediate school context. The opposite case exists, of course, where a pupil may abhor everything the teacher is or stands for. The link between pupil and teacher is probably a complex one, reflecting the pupil's needs and interests and the teacher's personality and expertise. One possible way of identifying a 'good teacher' is in terms of the numbers of pupils who imitate and subsequently succeed in his subject. This is much as the cognitive Social Learning Theory considered earlier would predict in relating imitation to the perceived status of the model. A variable which might be seen as likely to encourage imitation is teaching style, since this may be taken as a form of nurturance. Particularly in examination subjects, those teachers seen as effective are likely to inspire imitation, particularly in respect of skills taught. Bennett (1976), in an examination of the effects of different teaching styles, found that under a formal teaching regime pupil attainment was greater (in reading and mathematical skills) than those in an informal regime. The latter did no better than the former in imaginative writing, and anxious children felt insecure in the informal regime. Those in the informal regime would be disinclined to imitate the teacher's ways, not only because it is inconsistent with the autonomy encouraged in this approach, but because of its perceived ineffectiveness in this context. (Thus, at least, the advocate of the traditional approach would argue.) Bennett also reports the presence of interactions among teaching style, pupil personality, and pupil behaviour which impose constraints on the interpretation of the findings.

The teacher as prophet

A persuasive volume of experimentation suggests that the teacher has a more subtle effect on development in terms of his expectations of his pupils' progress. Expectations represent a more or less informed guess that X, say, will be a high flier, that Y will not stand the pace or that Z will constitute a constant source of disruption to others. These expectations appear to become, in some cases, self-fulfilling prophecies. Empirical tests of the Pygmalion Effect, as it has been called, have sought to establish (a) that different pupil treatment is associated with different expectations, and (b) that the treatments result in appropriately different pupil performance.

It has been shown that, for pupils having low expectations, teachers will expose them to less material than those with high expectations, and that they typically spend more time with the latter (Firestone and Brody, 1975; Rowe, 1974). In the Oak Hill study, Rosenthal and Jackson (1968) found that different treatments were associated with appropriately different subsequent performances. All pupils in this study were tested initially on verbal and reasoning abilities. The teachers were led to believe that this test was intended to detect those pupils who were about to go through an intellectual growth spurt. In confidence they were informed of the names of those expected to show this spurt, but in fact these had been chosen at random, one in five of the population being taken. Eight months later the tests were repeated with the entire population. The randomly allocated 'spurt' group were found to have made significantly greater gains than the remainder.

This was a controversial finding and the considerable publicity it received evoked extreme reactions, those who accepted the findings seeing in them implications for education (e.g. training teachers to display high expectations), while the remainder were highly critical of the study and the conclusions drawn. In a recent review Brophy (1983) drew attention to the fact that the Oak School study had not been replicated, although several attempts had been made. He pointed out that public discussion had drawn teachers' attention to expectation phenomena and had made them less likely to act on information given to them about their pupils, thus sensitizing subsequent experimentation. He is, however, prepared to accept the positive results of the study with six- and seven-year-olds as strong support for the Pygmalion hypothesis in view of corroborative studies from a number of other sources. Rosenthal (1976) analysed 300 studies of expectation effects in different settings, including classroom and laboratory studies, and found 37 per cent of reported results significantly (at the five per cent level) in favour of the hypothesis. Most non-significant differences were in the predicted direction. Differences in the wrong direction were below chance level. Brophy concludes, 'These data imply that teacher expectations do not always or automatically function as self-fulfilling prophecies, but that they can and do have such effects'.

Given this, how can such effects be mediated; how can teacher expectation be linked with pupil performance? A number of different answers have been suggested. The following is a paraphrase of the model suggested by Brophy (1983):

1. Teachers form differential expectations of pupil performance in early contacts with the pupil.
2. Led by these, teachers behave differently towards different pupils.
3. This communicates the expectations to the pupil concerned.
4. Assuming the consistency of teacher behaviour over time, it sems likely that student self-concept, achievement motivation, among other variables, will be affected, i.e. enhanced or otherwise.
5. Such effects are likely to complement and reinforce the teacher expectations, the pupil being more inclined to conform to them than he otherwise might.
6. Ultimately this will be reflected appropriately in pupil performance, 'indicating that teacher expectations can function as self-fulfilling prophecies'.

A recent review of mediation of interpersonal expectancy effects (Harris and Rosenthal, 1985) discusses alternative views of this effect.

School and the disadvantaged child

What effect, if any, has disadvantage on the development of the child? If it has a deleterious effect can special schooling help? Such questions were attracting the attention of psychologists in the 1950s and have been the centre of active research since. Disadvantage here refers to social disadvantage such as poverty, broken homes, parental unemployment, homelessness, and frequent changes in location of accommodation, as distinct from physical disadvantage for which special schooling has long been available in some form. These questions have been posed in two contexts, the effect of early disadvantage and the effect of ongoing disadvantage.

For some time it was taken for granted that adverse early experience was invariably associated with subsequent deleterious effects, especially in terms of emotional and social adjustment. Bowlby (1951) showed that there was a relation between early mothering experiences and later adjustment. Among his maladjusted juvenile patients a substantial proportion had been deprived of satisfactory mothering in early childhood. It was argued that the normal bonds between mother and child had not been established, and that this was at the root of the maladjustment. Subsequent studies showed, however, that this link was not inevitable. Among children who had suffered similar unsatisfactory early rearing experiences were those who had no such later problems, and it was concluded that children were differentially vulnerable, or differentially resilient to such experience (Clarke and Clarke, 1960).

A recent case of extreme disadvantage may serve to illuminate some of the issues raised. 'Genie', a 14-year-old girl when found in 1970 in California, had suffered exceptionally harsh conditions from about 20 months. She was virtually isolated from normal human customs and had lived her days alone and harnessed to a potty chair. At night she was caged in a bed which had a wire mesh top, and restrained in a kind of strait-jacket. If she made any noise the father beat her and barked at her. Her mother, dominated by this psychotic individual, provided little if any comfort for the child. When found Genie was severely undernourished, malformed and unsocialized. She could not stand and was unable to speak (Curtiss, 1977). Under the care of the Children's Hospital in Los Angeles she made a remarkable, if only partial, recovery. She gradually came to accept social norms, though there were exceptions. She also made progress in communication, but this too was partial. Within a year Genie was making single word utterances, and later, two and three word sentences, simulating the normal infant progress but more slowly. Some aspects of normal language development did not appear, e.g. the vocabulary explosion, and the normal use of questions among others.

Very few children suffer such severe and prolonged deprivation; Genie's resilience is self-evident but her vulnerability is emphasized by the restricted nature of the recovery she made. Thus while there is no inevitable link between early deprivation and later maladjustment, it remains a possibility that an important fraction of children are vulnerable to such accidents. In the early 1960s it was felt that in both the UK and the USA there was evidence that less extreme disadvantage and deprivation than Genie suffered was hindering the development, and especially the educational development, of large numbers of children; in consequence a number of compensatory education, or intervention, schemes were set up.

Compensatory education

Of a number of different forms of intervention those to be considered are primarily cognitive in nature. Their description draws heavily on distinctions made by Clarke and Clarke (1986).

Pre-school intervention studies

Pre-school education, in nursery school and play groups, has a long history in both the UK and the USA. It has been seen as an advantage enjoyed mainly by the rich, so that children of poorer families entered their first year of school at a disadvantage which could jeopardize their future development and career prospects. It was, at least in part, to try to break the poverty/poor education cycle that pre-school intervention was introduced. In the USA Project Head Start was introduced in 1965. It was designed to provide children from low income families with an enriched environment which would offset the effect of this disadvantage. The enrichment, which was variously defined and implemented, ran for one year. Subsequent tests of these children showed that some, but by no means all, had benefited. Head Start was far from being an unqualified success, and it became clear that those programmes which succeeded were among those most carefuly planned. It was also concluded that a single year was not always adequate. Clear evidence of the success of some early intervention comes from the Perry Pre-School Project (Schweinhart and Weikart, 1980). This was a carefully controlled study, with comprehensive pre- and post-testing of the experimental and the control group children, carried out over a 20-year period during which contact was kept with a high proportion of those involved. On a range of indices, including the number of years spent in compensatory education, completion of high school and post-high school education, and finding employment, the experimental children have a more favourable outcome than the controls. While this shows what is possible from pre-school intervention, the details of the study make it obvious that generalization is strictly limited. The subjects were of low ability and came from a poor black neighbourhood; expectations were typically low. The project maintained a high staff–student ratio (one adult to six children) and included one home visit each week. Such stringent design features must severely limit generalization.

Nevertheless initiatives in the UK, following Urban Aid and the Educational Priority Area projects (Halsey, 1972), have produced further support for the effectiveness of pre-school intervention. One approach has been to assess what normal pre-school groups achieve in practice. Osborn and Milbank (1985) report on a study of over 9000 children, a sub-sample of all the children born in England, Ireland and Wales during a specified week in 1970, for whom details of pre-school attendance, if any, was known. Follow-up at five and 10 years of age showed advantage for those who had attended pre-school groups as compared with those who had not. Since there was no pre-test the relative standing of the groups at the outset was not known; thus it could not be assumed that different outcomes were related to pre-school attendance. It is known, however, that playgroups are dominantly attended by the children of the well-to-do, while nursery education is attended by children of lower income families; children of low income families frequently have no pre-school attendance at all. Osborn and Milbank (1985) resorted to statistical manipulation of variables like type of neighbourhood, number of children in family, mother's employment status, 12 variables in all, so as to make the comparisons more meaningful. Again a clear advantage was found for those who had had pre-school experience. Some caution is necessary as to the final interpretation of the findings, since, as has been seen, the pre-school attendance variable is confounded with a range of social variables.

Intervention during the school years

Project Follow Through was initiated in the USA in 1967 when it was found that the gains which may have accrued from pre-school intervention soon began to diminish. It had become evident from Head Start that different kinds of enrichment were needed in different communities, and this was made a feature of Project Follow Through. It was found that the intervention was associated with positive effects on social and intellectual development in ways which discriminated in favour of the 'experimental' group, but, as in Head Start, that some types of intervention are more successful than others.

A different approach to compensatory education has involved the setting up of nurture groups within the school to offset the effects of adverse circumstances in children's home lives. The study was set in an inner city area of London where the incidence of such factors as unemployment, overcrowding and poverty is high, and the associated stress capable of interfering with the young child's adjustment to the demands of the infants' school. Boxall (1976), who pioneered this work, intended that the groups should serve to develop the children's trust in adults. Many, she held, lacked this trust. The teachers involved in running the groups aimed, therefore, to maintain a warm and generally nurturant atmosphere, treating the children as if they were their own. Allowance was made by treating them as younger than they actually were, and tantrums were tolerated up to a point. Physical contact was encouraged and parents urged to be involved.

All who took part were convinced that the project had made a positive contribution to the children's adjustment to adults and to the school, but no formal assessment was made. Indeed it is difficult to see how this can be possible in a project which draws so heavily on such imponderables as sympathy, affection and intuition.

Another British study (Tizard *et al*, 1982), following the Perry study, investigated the effects of two types of intervention, one based on parental coaching and the other on extra reading practice at school. All the children involved came from working-class backgrounds, and the two intervention conditions were compared against appropriate control groups. After two years there were significant gains for the children in the home intervention condition but not in the extra teaching condition. One year later it was clear that the advantage for the home intervention group had persisted. Teachers of reading have made good use of this finding. Where remedial intervention is required, the investment in parental teaching, appropriately guided and monitored by class teachers, is now a standard technique.

Overall, then, the work on compensatory education has produced some encouraging findings. Martin Woodhead (1985) has concluded, 'From research now available there are strong positive indications about the long-term benefits to be derived from well-planned pre-school provision.' It would appear from the discussion above that the same sort of conclusions might also be drawn for later intervention. However, not all workers in this field share this optimistic view. Baratz and Baratz (1970) are among those who have seen the equivocal findings of Head Start as grounds for abandoning early childhood intervention. Among the issues raised between those adopting these opposing reactions is that of specifying the nature of the disadvantage being compensated for. Some take the view that this is in the nature of a specific 'deficit', cognitive, social and emotional; others conceive of it in terms of a 'difference', which might be cultural and/or motivational in origin. Intervention in the absence of agreement on this matter may not only render the research meaningless, but also begs the question of the propriety of the research, it is argued. Only in those cases where the nature of the disadvantage is specified, as in the Tizard *et al* study referred to above, is intervention justified. The debate continues.

Further reading

Branthwaite, A., and Rogers, D. (1985) *Children Growing Up*. Open University Press.

Howe, M. J. A. (1984) *A Teacher's Guide to the Psychology of Learning*. Blackwell.

Kaye, K. (1984) *The Mental and Social Life of Babies*. Methuen.

Chapter eighteen

Development in adolescence and adulthood

Harry Fisher

This chapter takes up some further issues of development, treating the notion of development as useful throughout the life span. In particular it is concerned with development in adolescence and beyond. While interest in development beyond adolescence is comparatively recent much has already been achieved in some areas. Adult cognitive development is one such area, and recent findings are considered.

Puberty

During the period of puberty the body of the child is transformed into that of a young adult. The complex of processes involved takes, on average, three to three-and-a-half years for girls, and anywhere from two to four years for boys. The onset of puberty for girls is earlier than it is for boys by about one year. At the close of this phase of development the body is capable of mature sexual functioning. Under the influence of the pituitary hormones, the sex glands increase their production of sex hormones, and the growth of mature sperm in the male and ova in the female begin. At the same time, related endocrine activity stimulates the growth of bone and muscle and initiates a marked and rapid increase in height (the growth spurt). The complex of changes includes those relating to the size, shape, and proportion of the body, as well as its functioning, among a host of others. These include development of pubic hair, of other secondary hair and the eruption of second molars (the wisdom teeth) for both sexes, the enlargement of the breasts and pelvic breadth, and the onset of menstruation for girls. Boys develop a change of voice, enlargement of genitals, the appearance of beard, and seminal emissions. It seems reasonable to suppose that some of these changes may precipitate problems, physiological, social, and psychological, to which the individual needs to adapt.

Adolescence

'Adolescence' derives from a Latin verb which means 'to grow' or 'to grow to maturity'. It is used to refer to that period which marks the transition from childhood to maturity, but, while the onset is associated with the several physical changes appearing at puberty, a criterion for its completion is problematical. While some use the mature sexual function as the mark of adulthood, others use an arbitrary age criterion such as that relating to possession of voting rights, or certain legal responsibilities. A behavioural criterion begs the question as to what constitutes mature or adult behaviour. Adolescent behaviour has been described as 'negative'. In more detail it has been seen as including such features as a need for isolation, a disinclination to work, antagonism to family, friends, and society, indulgence in 'martyr' type fantasy, heightened sensitivity, irritability, obstinacy, and frequent revolts. It is unusual to find correspondingly positive descriptions of adolescent behaviour, although they are undoubtedly present. The traditional picture of adolescence is that of a period of 'storm and stress' contrasting sharply with the behaviour and experience both of the child and the adult. In giving an account of the psychology of adolescence, the developmental psychologist is faced with a number of questions. These include the following: to what extent are descriptions of adolescence in the above terms accurate and typical of youth across both social and cultural divisions? To what extent are any psychological changes attributable to physiological changes? What is the importance of cultural context?

Physical maturation rates: variability

While puberty normally follows the sequence set out in Table 18.1, variations are to be found which reflect a number of influencing factors. There are, for example, considerable differences in age for the onset of puberty; using the onset of menstruation (menarche) as the criterion gives an age range from nine to 17 years (see Table 18.1). This makes for difficulties in interpreting the psychological impact of this change, for example, in the primary school-girl of nine and the working girl of 17.

The variability of physical maturation is related to both environmental and genetic factors. Tanner (1973) has shown from records in Scandinavia, the USA and western Europe that the average for the menarche declined from about 16.5 years in the 1860s to about 13.5 in the 1960s. Over the same hundred years there was also a steady increase in average height among adolescents. These trends, which now appear to have levelled out, appear to be related to the improvement of general health and nutrition levels; possibly also to a general decline in family size.

Tanner (1972) also produced evidence which points to genetic involvement in the variability of physical maturation. He found that identical twin girls differ in the age of menarche by less than three months on average. The corresponding differences for fraternal sisters and two unrelated girls are 13 and 19 months respectively.

Table 18.1 Sequence and approximate timing of sexual changes during puberty

Girls	Age (years)	Boys
Budding of nipples.	9–10	
Appearance of pubic hair. Budding of breasts	10–11	Growth of penis and testes.
Growth of external and internal genitals.	11–12	Prostate gland becomes active in producing semen.
Breasts fill out.	12–13	Appearance of pubic hair.
Menstruation, range 9–17. Hair under armpits.	13–14	Growth of penis and testes.
Earliest normal pregnancies.	14–15	Voice change; hair under armpits; down on upper lip.
Voice deepens.	15–16	Mature sperm, range 11–17.
Skeletal growth stops.	16–17	Face and body hair.
	21	Skeletal growth stops.

Source: After Katchadourian, 1977

The problems of early and late maturing

Considerable differences occur in both the age of onset and the rate of progress of puberty. In general, early maturers develop more rapidly than late maturers, and this tends to produce, among adolescents of the same chronological age, large differences in maturity. Thus, at 15 years of age an early maturer might appear as a fully grown adult, while a late maturing contemporary is still very much a child in appearance. Data from standard personality inventories suggest that there are strong links between physical and psychological maturity. A number of studies indicate that early maturity for boys is a social asset. They were rated high on such variables as self-assurance and socially appropriate behaviour, where late maturers were rated low. These latter were also rated low in physical attraction and poise. Thus, late development for a boy can be something of a handicap. A study carried out on men in their early thirties, who had previously been studied as adolescents, showed that psychological differences between early and late maturers had persisted to a marked degree. Late maturers were still more dependent than those maturing early. Early maturity in girls may not confer the advantage it does for boys. Faust (1960) found that very early maturing girls were ill at ease on account of their greater height.

In another study high valued personality traits were attributed to those (12-year-old) girls who made up the majority and whose development was prepubertal. One year later, the early maturing girls scored more, and in the following years attracted the sort of preference accorded to early maturing boys. Late maturing girls have also been shown to have problems of social adjustment which persist beyond the attainment of biological maturity, but less so than late maturing boys. Some studies in this area (e.g. Harper and Collins, 1972) failed to find consistent effects associated with early and late developing girls, perhaps representing less clear cultural preferences in the case of girls, for such features as height and figure. While early and late maturation have to do with biological factors, the problems with which they are associated are in large measure socially mediated. In a study of the status of early and late developers it was found that, for Italian boys living in Italy, there was little preference for early as compared with late developers; but for Italian as for American boys living in the USA, late developers were at a disadvantage. This was interpreted in terms of an American preference for the features of early maturity – height and 'manliness' – as against an Italian preference for dependent behaviour in adolescence.

Effects of early and late maturation have also been found on school attainment. Early maturing adolescents scored higher than late maturers on standard tests (Douglas and Ross, 1964). These findings come from a British longitudinal study of 5000 children, all born in a particular week in March 1956. The conclusions to be drawn, however, are not clear, for performance is also related to family size and social class. Larger families are associated with later puberty and with poorer school performance, and the early–late advantage is much greater in lower social class groups. School performance thus does not depend simply on early or late maturation, but also on a number of interacting factors. A smaller Swedish study, Westlin-Lindgren (1982), provides some support. Here also it was found that early maturers had higher performance levels; this study also produced a much greater performance difference linked with social class differences. Again, the interpretation of these main effects needs to be made against a complex of interacting factors.

Biological–psychological links

Freudian and post-Freudian psychologists, as well as anthropologists, have sought to provide accounts of development in terms of unfolding sexuality.

Blos (1962), for example, saw adolescence as a second individuation process, the first having been that encountered by the child in attempting to control the unacceptable urges of psychosexual development. Following the latent period the adolescent is seen as involved in a second outburst of these problems. Thus personality development is seen in terms of sexual development. This approach is now much less influential than it was, being seen as emphasizing sexual to the neglect of other (e.g. social) factors.

A different approach is to be found in the social recognition of the dawning of sexual maturity in initiation ceremonies carried out in many traditional societies on both males and females. These ceremonies are centred on sexual development and the rites confer mature status. It is plausible that such enactments are associated with psychological changes. To what extent such changes have common components, whether they play a significant role in adolescence or leave only a temporary trace, is not known; the work in this field has been carried out mainly by anthropologists who had other, non-psychological problems to solve. Of course, the initiate is expected to meet the requirements of the newly mature, but these may be more social than psychological. The rites may – by accident or design – serve other purposes in the life of the society, reinforcing the authority of those who carry out the rites, for example, or the fostering of male solidarity (in male-dominated societies), or simply signalling the break between mother and child.

Adolescence and the quest for ego-identity

The development of a sense of identity has been seen as an important task of adolescence. To obtain some answer to the question 'Who am I?' might indeed be seen as a task which continues, to some extent, throughout life, but there are a number of plausible reasons for considering it of particular relevance during adolescence. These are to be found in the rate and extent of the changes which accompany adolescence in an industrialized society. After a period of childhood which is characterized by gradual changes and a consistency of role, the adolescent becomes quickly immersed in a complex of biological, social, and intellectual changes which provide grounds for self-consideration not met before. The evidence considered earlier indicates something of the way in which the changes of puberty draw reactions from society and from the individual concerned. There are numerous related problems to which the adolescent must adapt. To take but two, the problems associated with growth and the general increase in muscle which has been seen as producing the 'clumsy' adolescent; and the now more insistent sexual urges. These latter may give rise to conflict in view of social constraints. Indeed the 'storm and stress' attributed to adolescence by some of the early investigators, was seen as stemming from such conflict. The adolescent also becomes subject to new patterns of social pressure. Following a period where dependence – for physical, social and emotional sustenance – has been vested in the parents, who also initiated and regulated independent behaviour, the adolescent is confronted with expectations of a more radical sort. These concern his ability to cope with vocational matters and the attendant crises of choice and readjustment. There are additional pressures to conform to peer group expectations, again frequently representing a radical break with the conduct of the preceding period of childhood. Piaget contends that it is as a result of the interaction between biological changes and social pressures that 'adolescent thinking', that is, formal operational thinking, is born. It is this which confers the capacity to think about his own thought, about what is possible as distinct from what now pertains, and about the future. This widening of the conceptual horizons thus suffuses adolescent thinking, providing the possibility of new solutions to old problems, so frequently a theme among adolescent activists, and labelled idealism. Since there are those for whom formal operational thinking is never realized to any considerable extent, this period must also provide in cohesive adolescent school communities the greatest possible contrasts in intellectual functioning, and a correspondingly extreme range of approaches to the quest for identity, a source of further confusion for those involved in it.

It is Erikson who has characterized the extreme possible outcomes of adolescence in terms of 'identity versus role confusion'. His account of the search for identity sees it as a quest to establish a new sense of continuity, the former having been broken by the complex of changes entailed by puberty. The adolescent's task is seen as an attempt to integrate previous identifications, the former 'self' and the present social opportunities and constraints, in order to attain a sense of continuity for himself and for those with whom he has to do. In order to achieve this, adolescents will sometimes temporarily over-identify with popular figures, almost to the point where their own identity is obscured. Where the quest for identity is frustrated, role confusion results, and delinquency and psychopathology may follow. This view of adolescence has found some measure of acceptance, particularly within the United States. As with Freud's views, it is descriptive and based on clinical observations.

It is clear that a sense of identity will be influenced by a number of factors. There are a number of studies which show the importance of child–parent relationships to this end. A warm, interactive relationship between the adolescent and both parents facilitates the establishment of a strong sense of identity. The same-sex parent provides a model for personal and social standards, while the opposite-sex parent provides a source of critical approval of this model. Adolescents with such parents typically have fewer conflicts, and a greater capacity for coping with those which do arise, than those without. They also, typically, have clearly defined and favourable perceptions of themselves. Studies of the family regime have revealed that the 'democratic family' (one in which the child enjoys, as part of a warm relationship with parents, the freedom to disagree with them, involvement in family decisions, and a fair measure of autonomy) produces self-reliant adolescents. The 'authoritarian family', in which the parents institute plans without reference to the adolescent members of the family, and administer (mainly physical) punishment in accordance with rules adopted, again without reference to the children, tends to produce adolescents who, while they are compliant, incline to be deceptive and lacking in self-esteem. The search for ego-identity is thus facilitated by the existence in the home of adequate models of autonomy and co-operation, and an active involvement in the democratic family regime.

Kohlberg's studies of moral development, described earlier, support the general thrust of Piaget's views of the effects of the dawning of formal operational thinking. It further serves to contrast the moral views of childhood with those of adolescence, and to draw attention to the great sensitivity of the adolescent to moral issues. The morality of middle childhood is described as conventional, in that it reflects the expectations of the individual's immediate social context. By contrast, adolescent morality is capable of reaching a level which is characterized by the application of autonomous principles which have a validity apart from such authority contexts.

The sudden engulfment of the adolescent in so wide and radical a set of changes provides possible grounds for the 'negativity' of adolescents described earlier, as well as the storm and stress which has traditionally been associated with adolescence. Common experience suggests that to describe all adolescents as 'negative', and invariably involved in stress during this period of development, would be to overgeneralize. An adequate account of adolescence must accommodate the facts that wide differences exist in these respects, and that while some, perhaps many, are 'negative' and 'storm-tossed', others apparently by-pass calmly from a pleasant childhood to agreeable young adulthood, even within the constraints of the social competitiveness which exists in an industrial society.

Twenty statements and four states

A number of methods have been used to obtain information about the nature of, and changes in, ego-identity in adolescence. One of these requires individuals to supply 20 short answers to the question, 'Who am I?' The resulting statements supply a range of biographical details. Administered at intervals to the same individual these provide details of the changes observed; administered to a sequence of age groups, with adequate numbers in each, they offer insight into general changes over time. Montemayor and Eisen (1977) used this approach, taking statements from groups of subjects aged ten, 12, 14, 16 and 18, with about 50 subjects per group. Younger subjects typically produced statements of the kind, 'I am Tom; I live in Cedars Road; I like swimming . . . etc', while older subjects produced more abstract statements, of the sort, 'I am an individual; I am a human being; I hate prejudice . . . etc'. These statements were categorized as referring to possessions, to physical self, occupational and to ideological matters, etc., a total of nine categories in all. Significant age differences were found in all categories, though there were different patterns of change over time among them. There were, however, no marked changes at 14 and 16 years which might be taken to signal an adolescent crisis. In general the pattern of change was gradual and consistent with a view of adolescence as a phase of busy but normally non-disruptive development.

A second approach is based on Erikson's own work. 'The danger of this stage [adolescence] is role confusion. Where this is based on a strong previous doubt as to one's sexual identity, delinquent and outright psychotic episodes are not uncommon' (Erikson, 1965, p. 253). This quotation provides a reminder that Erikson's notion of an adolescent identity crisis is shaped by Freudian doctrine and the clinical method. His modification of the doctrine to provide a psychosocial as opposed to a psychosexual view was a change which attracted wide approval, reflecting the view that the influence of the latter had been exaggerated.

'The adolescent mind is essentially a mind of the moratorium, a psychosocial stage between childhood and adulthood . . .' (Erikson, 1965, p. 254). Erikson acknowledged that the quest for ego-identity – 'knowing who one is' – is one which continues to some extent throughout life, but that the magnitude and rapidity of the biological and social changes which take place in adolescence make this a period when identity-related turmoil is specially to be expected. One way in which this might arise is in the context of a moratorium – here a period during which all manner of facets of identity might be tried out (for one's own or others' approval) without any permanent commitment. This might involve aspects of physical appearance or habit (e.g. changes in hairstyle and handwriting), changes in interest (why not try pot-holing?), ambitions and religious affiliations, among others, all undertaken in the knowledge that they may or may not last. Some work which has shed light on Erikson's notion of an adolescent identity crisis has been that of James Marcia (1966, 1980) which differentiated among four different states in identity formation. To Erikson's notion of a moratorium state he added states of 'identity diffusion', 'identity foreclosure' and 'identity achievement'. In the diffusion state the individual is unclear about his identity, aims and alliances. An individual who has made premature decisions in order to avoid the anxieties of unresolved crises is said to be in the 'foreclosure' state, while one who has emerged from such crises with firm decisions about self-definition, commitments and goals is in the 'achievement' state. The four states were strictly defined in terms of the types of answers given during a standard interview, which was designed to explore identity status in specific areas, notably political beliefs, occupational views, religious beliefs and attitudes to sexual behaviour. Thus an individual in the diffusion state in respect of religious beliefs would be likely to produce answers indicating no clear ideas of the issues involved, while someone in the achievement state would be expected to produce answers consistent with a firm grasp of such issues. While the four stages are not sequential, diffusion is taken as the least mature and achievement as the most mature. A number of studies have been carried out on the age distribution of these four states. Identity achievement was not frequently found in 11 to 13-year-olds, as might be expected, but the proportion did increase as adolescence proceeded; diffusion and foreclosure states were most frequent at all levels in the cross-sectional study of 11 to 17-year-olds carried out by Archer (1982). An earlier study using males from 12 to 24 years showed that almost half of them had not attained achievement status by 24. The findings from these two studies, and from others, suggest that the quest for achievement status may continue well beyond adolescence.

Waterman (1974), reporting a longitudinal study on 94 university students, thus providing an account of changes in the same individuals over time, showed that more of them achieved identity status in their final year than did three years earlier (39 as compared with 12), but that at this age (20–21 years) about 56 per cent were still in the diffusion and foreclosure states. Munro and Adams (1977) found that achievement status had a significantly higher incidence in working males than in a sample of college males of the same age. The authors saw it as possible to regard college life as an 'extended moratorium period'; this raises the problem of the relationships among the four states, since it seems possible that in certain social climates the moratorium state may be more highly valued than the achievement state ('better to travel hopefully than to arrive').

While the data considerd provide general support for the notion of a movement among the four states towards identity achievement, they also show that this is frequently not accomplished within what is normally regarded as adolescence; further, as in other studies, there is no clear sign of a single, well defined crisis. The changes observed have appeared more as a range of problems to be solved than the emotional crisis described by Erikson. This suggests an alternative view of adolescent development as concerned with the attempted solution of a number of problems of adjustment, some common to all, but others individual and situation specific. There is other evidence which fits this picture better than the single crisis model. O'Connell (1976) found in a study of married women with school-aged children that most reported increasingly strong experiences of identity change accompanying such events as marriage, the birth of a first child, and the occasion of children going to school. It seems possible that career progress may bring about similar changes in self-image. The notion of a succession of problems of adjustment to be solved is germane to Coleman's (1980) focal theory of adolescence to be considered presently.

The generation gap

G. Stanley Hall (1904) saw adolescence as a time of storm and stress, a recapitulation of the troubled development of the human race. This suggests a universal or near universal experience of a troubled adolescence. As has been seen, there is now little or no substantial support for the recapitulation theory. Alternative accounts have been sought in terms of the physical, intellectual and social changes with which adolescence abounds. During the 1960s the so-called 'generation gap' was identified as a source of unrest in adolescent experience. The metaphorical gap was that between parent and child viewpoints, a gap which is deepened by the influence of the peer group on the adolescent. The differences between the antagonists embrace conduct, morals, ambitions and companions, among others. The parents' viewpoint is often presented as conservative and intended to protect the adolescent against the consequences of his inexperience; the adolescent frequently sees it as an attempt to impose standards no longer relevant and aimed at the inhibition of freedom. Literature and common experience attest that the phenomena of the generation gap predate the 1960s. What is at issue is whether the proposed gap is the source of serious altercations between parents and children, whether adolescents experience inner turmoil because of it, and to what proportions of the adolescent population these apply.

The findings from a range of studies suggest that:

1. The generation gap is indeed real, but brings about serious consequences in only a minority of cases (about 10 per cent or less).
2. The experience of inner turmoil affects some 20 per cent, at most, of the adolescent population, some more seriously than others.
3. Studies of parent–peer differences may, in producing positive findings, have obscured the extent of the considerable common ground between them, and have inadvertently exaggerated the size of the 'gap' and its psychological importance.

Among others in the 1960s and early 1970s, Floyd and South (1972) presented evidence of a change in adolescence from parent- to peer-orientation. At 11, parent orientation was dominant, but by 17 peer orientation had taken pride of place. While this distinction was clear, it soon became apparent that a complete account of parent–child relations would require evidence of the extent of the agreement between parents and peers. On the attitudes they tested Orloff and Weinstock (1975) found some 80 per cent agreement between them. Thus the difference figures alone provide an over-simplication of the matter. Further examination revealed that peers and parents influence different domains; peers to a large extent influenced clothes, hairstyle and leisure activities and related things, while parents were concerned with long-range issues, like schooling and careers, in a way in which peers were not. Parental influence is known to be affected by the style of parenting adopted, autocratic and permissive parents being much less likely to have a persuasive influence than democratic parents.

In the light of such evidence the case for a simple account of the generation gap is significantly reduced. This is not to deny that differences do arise between parents and their children on account, partly, at least, of age-related differences in viewpoint; it is rather that the incidence of such differences has been exaggerated. In the Isle of Wight study, to be described shortly, disputes between parents and children were graded as 'any altercation' or 'criticism' or 'rejection', the last named being the most serious. Rejections of fathers by daughters (nine per cent) had the highest incidence; rejection of mothers by sons (three per cent) and by daughters (two per cent) were much less frequent. The figure for 'any altercation' given by boys was 42 per cent and by girls 30 per cent; these figures differ from those obtained from parental interviews which were 18 per cent and 19 per cent respectively. Similar figures were obtained from a survey of more than 11,000 16-year-olds (Fogelman, 1976). This showed that 86 per cent got on well with the mother, and 80 per cent with the father. The agreement between these two major studies indicates that only a minority reported experiencing the kind of conflict associated with the generation gap. Certainly nothing like a universal phenomenon is suggested.

The Isle of Wight study (Rutter *et al*, 1976) collected data from the entire population of 2,303 14 to 15-year-olds on the island off the coast of Hampshire; they, and their parents and teachers completed questionnaires. Further information was collected from two subsets, one, a random sample of the total population, and the other a group whose earlier questionnaire indicated a possibility of deviant behaviour. Those in the two subsets completed further questionnaires and each was interviewed individually by a psychiatrist. It was from this data that the above detail of the role of the generation gap was obtained.

A second aim of this study was to investigate the experience of inner turmoil, as part of adolescent storm and stress. Partly this has been conceived as complementary to the 'external' problems of the generation gap, and partly as independent of it, the turmoil representing the adolescent's attempt to come to terms with his changing world. This produces problems concerned not only with parents, but also with life at large and the philosophical and practical issues it raises. On the basis of the questionnaire and interview data it appears that many adolescents experienced some degree of inner turmoil; the incidence of severe depression was, however, small. Comparison with other age groups indicates a slightly increased incidence of inner turmoil in adolescence, and the authors conclude that 'Adolescent turmoil is a fact, not a fiction, but its psychiatric importance has probably been overestimated in the past'. The Isle of Wight study provides a useful perspective on prominent aspects of adolescent troubles in general, and on the influence of the generation gap in particular. It underlines the reality of both external and internal representation of these troubles for a minority, and indicates that earlier views of the storm and stress of adolescence may have been overdrawn.

Coming of Age in Samoa

A different view of adolescence, one in which storm and stress play little, if any, part, has been described in the anthropologist Margaret Mead's (1928) book, the title of which heads this section. In it she put forward a case for an experience of adolescence as 'the age of maximum ease'.

Her study of the coming of age of Samoan girls, and the experiences of young people of the Arapesh of New Guinea, strongly suggested the involvement of cultural pressures as the origin of adolescent stress in industrialized society. For, in both of these 'primitive' societies, where such pressures are largely unknown, the course of adolescence described by Mead is one which much resembles the gradual and continuous development associated with our middle childhood, where dependence and independence coexist, the change from the former towards the latter progressing gradually, without marked discontinuities.

In the case of adolescence among Samoan girls, Mead recorded that the only differences between adolescent girls and their prepubescent sisters were the obvious bodily changes. There were certainly no differences in respect of revolt against authority, emotional distress or displays of idealism. She also reported negligible differences between late- and early-maturing girls. Comparing these phenomena with those for American adolescent girls she concluded that it is the differences in social environment which offer an explanation. The detailed differences cited may be divided roughly into two groups. The first concerns the characteristic way of life of the Samoan people (in the late 1920s). This was casual in the extreme, the distresses and disagreeable episodes of life being susceptible of speedy solution by mutual agreement. Thus, adolescents, growing up in a society where harassment was virtually unknown, were themselves subject to no extraordinary pressures. The second relates to the extreme simplicity of Samoan life, in respect of the limited number of choices available for each individual. For while the children of an industrialized society are faced with an array of groups differing in religion, standards of morality, and politics, the Samoan child is confronted by no such range of choices, but lives and grows with social constraints which are simple, minimal, and clear. It is the effect of the wide range of alternatives, and the pressure to choose among them, which Mead saw as the discontinuity, making for unrest among the adolescents of 'civilized' societies.

Much the same sort of evidence was cited in the case of both boy and girl adolescents of the Arapesh. The choice of a wife for a boy in childhood means that the two may use both homes for a considerable time before the formal marriage, and in this way one of a number of possible discontinuities at adolescence is dealt with.

This dominantly social and cultural view of adolescence was supported by distinguished anthropologists, including Ruth Benedict and Franz Boas, and has enjoyed a long period of influence, but with less than total approval. A recent work by Derek Freeman (1983) sets out some significant problems associated with the Samoan work. He points to Mead's relative inexperience (at 23) and to the limited time (six weeks) she spent learning Samoan. He questions the extent of the rapport she was able to establish, since she lived with a white family rather than among the Samoans, and hence the reliability of the information elicited from her informants. Since this frequently had to do with their sexual practices it would have been easy to mislead her, intentionally or otherwise. Only half of the 50 females she interviewed were post-pubertal, thus restricting the sample size. These and other criticisms are discussed in Freeman's *Margaret Mead and Samoa: the making and unmaking of an anthropological myth* (1983). They are linked with objections that anthropological studies both earlier and later than Mead's present an account of life in Samoa which differs in a number of respects from hers; for example, family bonds are strong – not invariably diffuse; sexual promiscuity was, and is, discouraged; and co-operation did not pre-empt fierce competition. But Freeman's own data have been called in question. In the nature of things the number of those able to testify as to pre-1920s Samoan customs is limited and memories possibly modified by recent missionary and military incursions. The more recent work also begs the question of the validity of some of his own work, carried out over 20 years ago. In spite of this many have accepted that Freeman's strictures properly call Mead's evidence in question; for them, whether Mead's work provides support for the notion of an adolescent experience which is virtually free from crisis must remain an open question.

As has been seen, factors influencing potential crises have been linked with changes in role and status. It can be argued that societies which make such changes easy, by making the child and adult roles parts of a continuum, may produce an adolescence which is relatively free from crises. Benedict (1934), for example, has described how some transitions were made easy for Cheyenne Indian boys by accepting their hunting catches as part of a father and son contribution to the common feast. This suggests a continuity which could help in the transition to adult status. Such phenomena would afford general support for Mead's point of view, but as yet the volume of evidence is not substantial.

Theories of adolescence

Coleman (1980) proposed that existing accounts of adolescence might be divided into two, psychoanalytic and sociological. Both assume that adolescence is a time of crisis, but while the psychoanalytic sees this as internal, and concerned with imbalance among id, ego and superego, the sociological approach locates the crisis as external and related to factors which regulate the demands of society – what adolescents ought to be and do. There are varieties of each, of course. Among those discussed above are the distinct psychoanalytic views of Freud, Blos and Erikson, as well as those of Anna Freud and Laing, which have not been considered. That this twofold division is less than watertight can be seen in Erikson's emphasis on the influence of sociological as well as psycho-dynamic variables. The two are methodologically distinct, the psychoanalytical approach using the clinical interview and the sociological using survey techniques.

Coleman's own work provides the basis for an alternative account which does not require a crisis. He examined 800 boys and girls of 11, 13, 15 and 17 years of age in a number of problem areas including parental relationships and self-image. These, and others, he found to become central at different periods of adolescence, for some individuals early, for others late, and that solving the associated problems was achieved in most cases one at a time, rather than reaching crisis level by being overwhelmed by several all at once. For different individuals specific problems would appear at different times, producing idiosyncratic developmental patterns. Coleman called his account a Focal Theory because of the way in which adaptation proceeds by focusing now on one, and then another problem. This was the dominant pattern for his subjects; problem areas were tackled in turn rather than *en masse*. The methodology employed by Coleman was such that highly stable developmental sequences were a possible outcome. No such pattern emerged. Individuals solved, or part-solved, or shelved problems which, for highly idiosyncratic reasons, had become prominent. They were, albeit, the same sort of social, emotional and cognitive problems which adolescents meet and which were considered earlier, but the order in which they occurred and the manner in which they were approached were individual. This no-crisis view of adolescence is consistent with empirical evidence considered earlier.

Development in the post-adolescent years

This is a long period extending from the late teens to the seventies and beyond, and for the purpose of presenting a life-span account of development it has been divided in a number of different ways. One of these, due to Havighurst (1952), describes some of the main developmental tasks encountered in early adulthood (18–30 years). They include selecting a mate, learning to live with a marriage partner, starting a family, rearing children, managing a home, and getting started in an occupation. In his scheme of things these tasks must be mastered in order to pass to the next phase.

This is middle adulthood (30–55 years), which has its own tasks, including achieving adult civic and social responsibility, assisting teenage children to become responsible adults, development of adult leisure time activities and accepting the physiological changes of middle life.

What Havighurst calls late adulthood (55 years and over) others have referred to as growing old. Its developmental tasks include adjustment to decreased physical strength and health, adjustment to retirement and to the death of a spouse and meeting social and civic obligations.

The psychology of ageing has been extensively researched in recent years and a large number of issues have been raised. In this section only a small sample of these can be considered. These will be taken mainly from the late adulthood years because of their intrinsic interest, but inevitably this will involve what is happening in the years preceding. The issues considered will concern biological ageing, since this is basic; social ageing, because it resists tidy solutions; and cognitive ageing because this has been one of the most widely researched areas of all. It will be argued that to give an account of each of these as part of a process of global and unrelieved decline is an oversimplification and inconsistent with evidence which indicates systematic adjustment to maintain the status quo until late in life.

Adjustment to biological ageing

The manifestation of the ageing process is a complex of age-related changes in behaviour and experience. For convenience the three aspects listed above will be considered separately, and this will include comment on the ways in which the individual adjusts to these changes. The changes themselves are rarely sudden. When assessed in retrospect they are frequently, but not exclusively, seen in terms of decline. The young adult still runs for the bus, and pursues ambitions and social recognition, where late adulthood does so rarely, if at all.

Bee and Mitchel (1980), in their book, *The Developing Person*, describe the biochemical, physical and sensory changes in such terms as smaller, slower, weaker, lesser and fewer. In old age, for example, height tends to decrease due to spinal changes and the tendency to stoop; loss of calcium means that bones become more brittle, and break more easily. Such fractures are slower to heal, as are skin wounds. Scratches which have disappeared from a young child within 24 hours are to be seen days later in the elderly. Nerve impulses are slower, too, and are reflected in slower response times. Muscles are reduced in mass and become weaker.

There are noticeable declines in sensory functioning, vision is impaired by the thickening of the cornea, and hearing, particularly of higher frequencies, restricted because of wear and tear on the small bones of the middle ear. The loss of elasticity of the eardrums also contributes to this. Hormonal function also declines. In women the reduced level of oestrogen plays the major role in bringing about the menopause, the ability to reproduce being completely lost during the early fifties. There is a decrease in body hair and in the number of natural teeth as well as taste buds; both taste and smell are impaired. Some functions remain virtually unchanged, for example homeostasis, the maintenance of the internal environment of the body.

Since ageing is universal and predictable, adjustment to it is similar across peoples, although there are some cultural differences. A vast array of remedies and devices, from pills and spectacles to sheltered accommodation and plastic hip joints, are brought to bear on maintaining an acceptable quality of life in Western societies. The healthy elderly learn to live within their biological limits, though what these limits are varies from person to person. In most Westernized societies there is an age set for retirement from work, but there are a number of places where compulsory retirement is unknown. In a small number of these the normal milestones of biological ageing appear to have been altered, and many of the inhabitants of high mountain communities live to ages well above 100, though some of the figures have been challenged.

This raises the question of the extent to which biological ageing can be extended, and what factors may influence this. In settlements like Vilcamba in the Andes mountains of Ecuador, both men and women work out of doors until they are over 80, and the elderly are accorded a high social status. Can such factors as a rarefied atmosphere, a sense of usefulness and outdoor manual work influence biological ageing? Are there other factors?

Adjustment to social ageing

Late adulthood is a period of declining social activity. The number and frequency of social contacts decrease for a number of reasons typical of this period. They include failing health, restricted mobility, reduced income and the depletion of the number of friends by death. Other major life events which have a social impact are retirement and the death of a spouse. The first effectively removes many daily contacts, established over the years, while the second entails a major loss of companionship as well as the emotional trauma and the, at least temporary, decreased wish to seek out the spouse's friends.

Whether it is possible to account in some principled way for the adjustment made by the individual to such varied social changes is problematic. Some attempts have been made. Cumming and Henry (1961), for example, saw social decline in terms of a reciprocal activity whereby the individual withdraws from society and society from the individual. This disengagement theory is seen as describing an inevitable progression, and one in which the individual and society acquiesce. For the individual, emotional involvement with others is gradually replaced by self-concern.

This is an account of ageing based on survey data, but it would seem likely to exclude a sizeable fraction, particularly those whose personalities make withdrawal repugnant. Havighurst (1968) has proposed an activity theory which not only rejects the notion of reciprocal disengagement, but sees optimal ageing as linked with the maintenance of such activities as will ensure possession of satisfying roles.

Neither of these theories of the course of social adjustment has been widely accepted. Nor has a plausible social exchange theory, in which society and the individual are involved in exchanges, e.g. a leisure role for an earning role, at retirement. This has something of both disengagement and activity theories, the exchange allowing for both decline and individual choice of activity, thereby accommodating those who choose some combination of the two. Neugarten (1972), among others, has stressed the importance of personality in the final choice of late adult lifestyle. What provides individual satisfaction in this area is widely variable; it creates problems for the search for a systematic description.

Adjustment to cognitive ageing

It is not unusual to hear older people complaining about their own failing memories, and how easy it is to remember things from the distant past as compared with their fleeting memories of things in the immediate past. But age-related cognitive changes are much more widespread, and, as with biological and social changes, it would be easy to see the evidence in terms of a widespread decline. There is a wealth of recent research evidence, of which Salthouse (1986) has provided a detailed review. He identifies five major age trends, '. . . processes for which there is unequivocal evidence of age difference'. The differences represent a performance decline in many cases. The five major trends are as follows:

1. Reasoning and decision making. For reasoning, data were drawn from such tasks as Raven's Progressive Matrices, and series completion tasks.
2. Memory. This covered a full range of tasks and techniques including memory span, cued and free recall and recognition of a range of types of information.

3. Spatial skills. Here tasks included object assembly, picture completion and block design, subtests of the Wechsler Adult Intelligence Scale.
4. Perceptual motor and cognitive speed. The tasks used exploited a range of cognitive skills: perceptual, memory and language tasks performed under time pressure.
5. Sensory factors. Tasks used here investigated the detection and discrimination of sensory information.

An additional trend was noted; age differences in favour of younger subjects were obtained as a function of task difficulty; the more difficult the task, the greater the difference. Salthouse concludes, 'Taken together, the five categories of specific processes and the general tendency of age differences to be proportional to overall task complexity present an imposing, and rather depressing, picture of the effects of ageing.'

However, to interpret these findings without further enquiry would, as Salthouse points out, invite oversimplification. There are, for example, cognitive data which show no appreciable change over time, and others which show a positive change. In addition there are design problems associated with experimentation in this area. These will be considered presently. In order to illustrate some of these difficulties some recent experimental work will be considered; the studies chosen are among the most careful and rigorous in the area.

Language comprehension in old age

Under this single heading Gillian Cohen (1979) reported three experiments investigating the comprehension of spoken language. Comparisons were made between two groups of subjects, one young, of average age in the mid-twenties, the other old, with a mean in the late sixties. Each group was further divided into high and low education levels. In the first experiment subjects listened to a short message and were asked, immediately afterwards, two questions. One required verbatim information, that is, explicit statements presented in the message, while the other required an inference to be drawn from the facts presented. (They did this for 16 such messages in all.) It was found that all four groups (generated from the young, old and high, low education divisions) were better at answering verbatim questions than inferential questions. In the old versus young comparison for the high education group no deficit was found for the verbatim questions, but inference questions produced a large difference in favour of the young group. The absence of a significant effect on the verbatim questions was taken as suggesting that the greater difficulty found in making inferences was not due to memory loss. Taken together with the finding of a large inference deficit in the old group when the message was presented faster, it was suggested that it is the several steps of the reasoning process which are vulnerable to time pressure.

In the second experiment subjects were tested on their ability to detect anomalies. This was intended to investigate further the suggestion that the age deficit has more to do with the reasoning processes than with recall. They listened to short spoken messages, and were then asked to judge whether each contained a mistake or an unlikely statement. (In a typical example, an early part of the message informed the listener that X had no bread, while later in the same message X was described as making sandwiches.) Detection of anomalies requires the combination of separate pieces of given information, or combination of this with knowledge of the world. It was found that the old group did significantly worse at this task than the young, as predicted.

The third experiment investigated age differences in story recall. This requires the retention of facts together with their organization within the story. In such a task the memory is overloaded; one possible strategy to maximize recall is to concentrate on gist rather than on detail. Since gist requires both, that is the detail itself and the inferred organizational properties, it seemed likely that this was a task that older people would find more difficult. This is what was found. The old group recalled much less than the young group. The story was coded for its organizational properties in terms of summary propositions, and it was clear that the younger group had made better use of these in recall than the older group.

In a subsequent paper, Cohen (1981) reports two further experiments. These investigated the difference between problem solving in written and spoken form. The first involved short questions involving logical puzzles, and the second were based on questions on material from an explicit or implicit text. In both cases the written form was easier. For older subjects the differences were large and significant, for the young, small and non-significant. Both experiments provide support for the view that, when inferences are required, the elderly are disadvantaged if at the same time they are required to take in new material – even when this is read, and thus available for re-reading.

An accurate account?

These two experiments provide a small sample of the detailed experimentation, and by extension, the rich empirical corpus which underlies our knowledge of age-related changes in cognition. Yet Salthouse (1982), among others, has expressed doubt as to whether this provides an accurate account of cognitive ageing. The problem is not only to provide a just account of the relevant data, but also that of specifying what findings are relevant. One possible strategy is to allow the dominant finding of overall decline to rule. Adjustment to cognitive ageing then becomes a matter of following the advice of the authors of particular papers. Cohen (1979), for example, recommends that when addressing old people, messages are kept short and explicit. This, however, would be an over simple use of the data. The data themselves are problematic in that they are neither integrated nor systematic; they have been described as 'a scrapbook-type collection of findings ...' (Rybash *et al*, 1986). In spite of the large body of research, they yield no integrated theory of either memory or comprehension, for example. There are, furthermore, findings, frequently in respect of language abilities, which do not fit the pattern of overall decline which dominates the survey data; some show no change, others actually improve with age.

The experiments themselves also raise problems of interpretation: the extent to which the experimental task represents some real-life function must inevitably pose a problem in the case of tightly controlled laboratory contexts, e.g. even in such carefully chosen tasks, making inferences, detecting anomalies, remembering stories, as those used in the Cohen (1979) study above. Further, cross-sectional studies of ageing require a younger control group, and it must be that sometimes the two groups differ on dimensions other than age, dimensions which have to do with the individual characteristics, educational, motivational, etc. of the two cohorts. Salthouse (1982) has considered the ecological validity problem from a different point of view. He asks why the age differences so evident in the laboratory are not equally evident in real life. He offers the following explanations: individual differences are large, so large that variations within one age group may be indistinguishable from those between two groups; the laboratory task may be a trivial aspect of behaviour not important in normal functioning; the tasks are not demanding, so that virtually everyone can do them; the tasks are overlearned, that is, so frequently performed that they present difficulty to no one.

Alternative approaches

It is not surprising in face of such problems that alternative approaches should have emerged. Age-related changes in cognition have been of interest to workers in widely different but related fields, for example, information processing, cognitive science, genetic-epistemology and psychometrics. Drawing on findings from these fields, Rybash, Hoyer and Roodin (1986) claim, '... we paint a different portrait of adult cognition than the irreversible decrement model developed from affectively neutral and ecologically irrelevant laboratory studies ...'. Their portrait, the Encapsulation model, draws data from this wider field and depicts not only the insistent decline, but also the emotional overtones of cognition which are involved in the approach to everyday problems, and the effects which expert knowledge and wisdom have on tasks which show improvement with age.

The genetic epistemological approach has its basis in Piagetian psychology, but Rybash *et al* reject the suggestion that the formal operations stage can provide an adequate basis for an account of adult cognition by itself. The formal stage is based on the application of logic: it enables its users to manipulate premises in order to identify valid conclusions, valid, that is, within the constraints imposed by the system of operations. Real life problems are only rarely of this type; they may have several alternative solutions, or none at all. Real life questions frequently arise in open systems of this type, rather than in closed systems. Further, formal operations deal in categories of reasoning which cannot embrace the experience of the user; and it may be argued that they impose an emphasis on probability and abstraction at the expense of the actualities of real life.

This is not to be taken as a total rejection of the formal stage; it has a part to play in closed system problems. Something more is required to provide the basis of an account of adult cognition. Rybash *et al* identify several functions which arise in adult development, e.g. new styles for reasoning, new ways of organizing knowledge and new ways of processing such variables. The work of Arlin (1975) provides an example of new types of reasoning. Looking for a fifth stage in Piagetian theory she proposed problem-finding as distinct from problem-solving which she associated with Piaget's formal stage. She examined both of these in a group of young adult artists. They performed equally on measures of formal reasoning, but those identified as creative and original scored higher on measures of problem finding. The two groups were also distinguished in the way they viewed their work; problem-solvers were inclined to think of a work as fixed and unalterable once it was finished, while the problem-finders viewed their work as capable of further development.

Perry (1968), in a longitudinal study, observed changes in the type of thinking which characterized his students. As freshmen they approached their intellectual and ethical problems as having set solutions which it was the responsibility of authority figures to teach them. In time this was replaced by a realization of the inherent subjectivity of all experience, and they were temporarily upset by the implications of the relativity of knowledge and value systems. After various intervals they came to terms with this and became committed to some particular way of approaching problems in terms of relativistic thinking. Arlin (1984) proposed that it was such thinking which induced the flexible viewpoint taken by the highly creative artists considered above.

Relativistic thinking and problem-finding are just two of a number of forms held to differ significantly from formal thinking, and which develop in the post-formal period. Dialectic thinking is another such form (dialectics is that branch of logic which deals with the rules and modes of reasoning). Studied first by Sinnot and Guttman, it has been more recently championed by Basseches (1980), who studied the views of freshmen, seniors and faculty members (representing increasing maturity) on the function and process of education. He found that the use of dialectic thinking increased with maturity. Using the same grading of subjects on a task which supplied pairs of arguments (one dialectic, the other not) on various topics, he found increasing preference for and understanding of the dialectical arguments with increasing maturity.

There is thus evidence that beyond adolescence, reasoning is not confined to formal modes, but broadens to encompass other approaches more appropriate to the solution of real life problems. The roots of these approaches beg explanation.

Cognition and decline

So also do findings which do not show decline with age. There is no shortage of such data. Salthouse (1982), for example, cites the vocabulary, information and similarities subtests of the WAIS as showing no decline. Birren (1955) found no age decline in verbal fluency, indeed there was a suggestion of increase. In a range of tasks of crystallized intelligence (involving verbal skills and others related to formal education), Nesselroade, Schaie and Baltes (1972) found performance to remain constant, or improve even into the eighties, confirming findings of Horn (1970, 1982). Botwinick (1978) found, in contrast, that performance on fluid intelligence tasks (reflecting the ability to solve novel problems) increases at first, then declines consistently from middle age, although longitudinal studies have failed to find this decline. Labouvie-Vief (1980) and others in this field hold that neither crystallized nor fluid intelligence shows an appreciable decrement until after seventy.

Cognition, affect and self

Rybash *et al* (1986) hold that an adequate account of adult cognitive development requires reference to related social contexts. They cite recent work which shows that adult comprehension becomes increasingly socially orientated with age (Kramer, 1983). They further argue that self-knowledge also contributes to this process, and that in real-life evaluations cognition is linked with emotion. The work of Lazarus (1966, 1981) and colleagues on adaptation indicates that the primary appraisal of a situation is cognitive and subjective; the subjective component influences the emotional response made; events are only stressful if they are interpreted as such. Secondary appraisal is also cognitive in character, prompting a review of possible consequences and personal resources. Thus adaptation to real-world situations grows out of a train of evaluations intermixed with affective experiences, uniquely determined for each individual.

Cognition and organization

An adequate account of the development of post-formal thinking involves explaining the synthesis of what is already known with continuing new inputs. It is plausible to suppose that this takes place in terms of increasing organization of knowledge in categories or domains. General support for this notion is based on structure of intellect models, but the final details of the synthesis (e.g. the number and structure of domains) would appear to be determined by the individual in the light of his experience and interests. The broad features of particular domain specific models follow established theories; Piaget took an interactionist view, while Chomsky, and Fodor (1983) take a strong nativist view, suggesting that humans have a number of 'genetically hard wired, autonomous cognitive subsystems' (modules) through which they come to understand reality (this is linked with Fodor's modular theory of mind, to be mentioned later). Several models take the Piagetian view as a starting point. Berzonski (1978), for example, lists six domains, figural-, semantic-, behavioural-, and symbolic-content, and aesthetic-, and personal-knowledge as his model of the formal operations stage. Each domain will develop in line with personal preference. One problem with this proposal is that such different domains as figural-content and personal-knowledge should stem from Piaget's all-embracing logical-mathematical principles. Among those who reject the Piagetian basis is Gardner (1983), who lists seven domains, or codes of human intelligence, linguistic, spatial, musical, logical-mathematical, bodily kinaesthetic, intra-personal, and interpersonal (see Chapter 13). This approach is linked with the modular model of Fodor (1983) which conceives of the mind as organized into relatively independent units (modules) which process the input in parallel. The modules are domain specific, that is, deal with specific aspects of the input, and it is this property which makes Gardner's model a distinct alternative. It should be noted that modules, as conceived by Fodor, are strictly concerned with input processing, while domains give meaning to the input. Both models offer an account of the domain specific nature of the development of post-formal thinking, one based on the Piagetian tradition and the other on the notion of a modular mind. Both represent the synthesis of extensive literatures, but as yet provide only preliminary conclusions. Many details remain, for example, there is recent evidence that development of thinking and knowledge is influenced by being organized within domains (Kiel, 1981, 1986), i.e. that organization is functional as well as structural.

Adult cognition – the encapsulation model

Rybash *et al* (1986) propose that 'by examining how adults cope with real-life problems we paint a different portrait of adult cognition'. One reason why this portrait is different is that it sets out to portray a much broader conception of adult cognition. A second reason is that a much greater range of empirical work is brought to bear, some of which has been briefly considered in the immediately preceding sections. The additional detail is a mixed blessing, for while a synthesis of findings from different fields provides strong internal support, the sheer volume and diversity of it militates against identifying substantial synthesis. Only an outline of their 'portrait' – the Encapsulation theory – is possible here and the interested reader is referred to their work.

They see adult cognition in terms of three inter-related dimensions, namely processing, knowing and thinking. Processing refers to the functions of various psychological resources to accept and utilize information. Detail has emerged from work in the psychometric and information processing fields. As people get older processing becomes much less efficient. Knowing covers the growth, representation and organization of knowledge systems. From work in the fields of artificial intelligence and cognitive science it appears that with increasing age and experience, the organization of knowledge systems becomes increasingly complex and takes on the stature of expertise or wisdom and is integrated within appropriate domains, or categories of knowledge. Information concerning developmental changes in thinking from the genetic-epistemological school has drawn attention to the appearance of qualitatively different styles. These allow an approach to be made to the solution of real world problems, which are frequently open and sometimes ill-defined. The term 'thinking' here accommodates both problem-solving and problem-finding.

The integration of the features of the three dimensions rests on the proposal that throughout adult development, processes as well as information become increasingly encapsulated within particular domains, so that not only does the knowledge representation increase in complexity, but so also do the processes for its management. The authors claim 'The continued encapsulation . . . represents an adaptive and necessary function in the development of expert knowledge and post-formal thinking'. It provides an account of some of the findings considered earlier. Acquisition of new material, which becomes less efficient with age, may be seen as due to the absence of appropriate contextual material encapsulated within established domains. Some indirect trade-off is possible wihin such a system where ageing may also serve to furnish expert systems as the result of encapsulated knowledge and processes. Such systems offer an account of task performance which shows no change with age, or even improvement, in terms of the availability of domain specific support, where the existence of expert systems would predict good performance. As has been seen there are authorities who claim that much of human cognition is of this kind.

It will be apparent, even from this brief description, that the Encapsulation model is at once more ambitious and more vulnerable to criticism than one more narrowly based. Its intended comprehensiveness must be set against its frequent vagueness in respect of operational definitions, which include such diverse elements as self-system, affect, domains of expertise and commitment among others. There is the further difficulty of meeting the demands of an encapsulation model which needs to describe both the growth of domain-specific knowledge as a universal process, as well as factors to account for the development of expertise in different cultures. While considerable integration of theoretical and empirical findings has already been made, gaps remain, e.g. the means used to identify how component processes build domains of expertise remain to be explored. Among the achievements of the Encapsulation model is the way in which it has accommodated an account of the ways in which real-world problems can be approached with an account of self-adapting aspects of cognition which function to stem its own decline.

Further reading

Coleman, J. C. (1980) *The Nature of Adolescence*. Methuen.

Hayslip, B. jnr., and Panek, P. E. (1989) *Adult Development and Ageing*. Harper and Row.

Clarke, A. M. and Clarke, A. D. (1986) 'Thirty years of child psychology'. *Journal of Child Psychology and Psychiatry*, 27, 6, 719–60.

Chapter nineteen

Young children and their families

Anne Woollett and David White

With few exceptions young children grow up in families and so much of what they learn about themselves, about other people and about the outside world they learn from their family. They spend a great deal of time in the home with their family and even when they are away from home they are often still with one or more family members. This then is the most influential factor in shaping young children's lives and in providing support for children while they explore new situations and learn about new people. However, no two families are identical and so each family provides a different context for its children's development. The composition of families varies, some are headed by two parents others by only one, some have resident grandparents others do not, some have one child others have more children. Each family member has a different influence on the child. Children learn different things from their mothers, fathers, siblings, etc. Because of differences in composition and differences in the behaviour of family members each family encourages its children to develop somewhat different characteristics and skills.

In this chapter we examine the characteristics and competence of young children, how these develop and change over time. We consider the response of family members to these characteristics and their implication for the sorts of relationships that children develop with their families, including the earliest attachment relations. Children's relationships with mothers, fathers, brothers and sisters are compared, focusing on the varying environmental contexts they provide for development. The influence of the family on children's development also depends on the cultural context, on family size and composition and on changes within the family, including family breakup and divorce.

Early behaviour: infants' repertoire and family reactions

Physical development

When they are first born, infants are not well developed physically compared with the young of other species, but during the first two years they gain control of their limbs. By six months infants can sit up, they can stand with support by nine and then begin to move about on their own, crawling or walking, with running and jumping developing later. From about four months, infants begin to show fine control of their hands; by about nine months they use precise pincer movements to pick up small objects. Because their physical development is slow, babies are dependent on the people around them to feed them and care for them and to approach them to talk or play with them. Later, when they can move about and talk, infants initiate interactions more.

Infants' perceptual and behavioural competence

Babies are competent in a number of ways from birth; they can suck, cry, smile, look around, turn their heads, vocalize and respond to sounds and they have an enormous capacity for learning and taking in information. Their competence develops rapidly during the early months forming the building blocks from which later competence and interactions emerge.

Sucking is a reflex action, available from birth. Infants suck to take in milk and stop when they are full or uncomfortable. They can control the strength, the frequency and duration of their sucks in response to changes in their environments (Rovee-Collier and Lipsitt, 1982). At first sucking is associated with feeding but later other things, like fingers, dummies and toys are taken to the mouth. Sucking such things pacifies a crying child and provides a way of finding out about objects (Dunn, 1977). (See Piaget and sensori-motor thinking.)

From the moment they are born infants cry. They use different types of cry when they are hungry, in pain, angry or tired. Exposure to babies helps people to distinguish these cries; the greater the exposure the greater the skill. Thus, midwives with a lot of experience of babies can identify the different cries of unfamiliar babies. Women with less experience (such as the average mother) identify the cries of their own baby but not the cries of unfamiliar babies whereas the average father does not have sufficient exposure to babies to identify even his own baby's cries (Wasz-Hockert et al, 1968).

Crying signals an infant's distress and is one of the first communication systems they use. To begin with, babies have no intention of communicating, they cry because they are uncomfortable. However, their cries signal something to other people, who respond by picking them up, comforting or feeding them. As a result, the expectation develops that future cries will be responded to in similar ways and the cry becomes part of the baby's communication system which can then be used deliberately.

At birth, smiles appear to be simple reflexes, triggered by stroking the lips. Over the next four to five weeks smiles appear spontaneously, as a response to internal sensations denoting that the baby is comfortable. At this stage smiles do not occur in response to any external events. Between three and eight weeks, true social smiling develops. Babies smile in response to a wide range of external social events, but the combination of faces and high pitched voices is one of the most reliable ways of eliciting smiling during the first six months. At this age smiles also vary according to circumstances. When babies smile at their mothers' face, their smiles come fairly quickly and last a long time compared with smiles to a female stranger. During play different smiles are used. These come quickly, are of short duration but of great intensity. These different smiles convey different messages about infants' emotional states. They can be signs of enjoyment, of affection and sometimes an invitation to interact. Smiles are powerful, highly rewarding signals to caretakers who often work hard to encourage them (Turner, 1980).

From the early weeks the infant's visual system is quite sophisticated and infants can register and process information. Young babies can also look around, fixate on objects and visually explore their environments. They look most at objects which move and are patterned and from an early age they focus on people, especially when those people speak. By six months babies use gaze to control the stimulation from their mothers, looking at them to maintain their mothers' attention or looking away to terminate interactions (Stern, 1977).

Babies have a good sense of hearing; they blink and startle to loud noises minutes after they are born, they soon locate sounds by turning their heads in the appropriate direction and they discriminate between sounds of different loudness, duration and pitch (Eisenberg, 1976). Infants are sensitive to human voices and are rapidly able to distinguish between their mothers' voices and those of other females. Babies begin to babble or vocalize in the first three to four months, using an extensive range of sounds and intonations long before they begin to talk. These vocalizations allow babies to communicate to others a variety of things about their moods and their needs. Vocalizations also serve to establish and maintain contact with others.

Play in infancy

Play refers to activities which children take pleasure in performing. The activities infants find pleasurable change with age. In the first few months repetitive actions, their own as well as other people's, seem to give most pleasure. They enjoy repeating sounds and body movements. They also enjoy watching others, looking at their gestures and facial expressions, including smiles, and listening to their vocalizations. Repetition is important in game playing, too. Babies favour games, such as peekaboo and pat-a-cake, which involve repetitive actions (Garvey, 1977).

As well as being pleasurable, play facilitates development in a number of ways. Play with objects helps develop manipulative skills and co-ordination and provides an opportunity to learn about objects. As babies get older they become more curious about objects and their play involves finding out about objects and the relationships between them. A nine-month-old spends a long time studying objects, comparing them with one another, seeing how they fit inside one another and so on (Garvey, 1977).

Play with people is the basis for the development of children's communication skills; it provides a framework in which they learn to trust caretakers and learn about other people. Through games, children learn a number of important features of social interactions, especially turn-taking and communication skills which are a necessary precursor of language (Bruner, 1978).

The development of behaviour patterns

The range and function of infants' behaviour patterns are quite extensive, giving the clear impression that even young infants make sense of their worlds and communicate a considerable amount of information to those around them. These patterns develop and change. Some cease to be so important. Crying, for instance, may be replaced in many situations by vocalizations, gestures and later by language. Some behaviour patterns become more differentiated so that the infants' state or needs are less ambiguous. Others generalize to other situations, extending the range of ideas and needs that children can discover and communicate. Behaviours are also integrated or combined into patterns or schemas (see sensori-motor development). For instance, infants combine looking at an object with pointing or vocalizing about it. Or they follow up one behaviour with another, so that having gained someone's attention through vocalizing, they may smile, gesture or make more sounds. Combining behaviour patterns in these ways adds substantially to the information conveyed.

Infants' behaviour patterns serve a number of functions. They indicate the infant's needs, interests and emotional states. They also bring close caretakers who can supply those needs. By being treated as if they are trying to communicate, infants are taught the rules of social interaction and communication and become increasingly adept at these skills. They also learn that what they do is of interest to others (both positively, as they babble and smile, and negatively, as they cry or cannot be consoled) and that they can demand and hold the attention of people in their environment (Turner, 1980).

Individual differences in infancy

The extent to which infants use these different behaviour patterns varies. Some infants consistently cry more than others, and when they cry some are more easily consoled than others. Some infants have sleeping and waking patterns that are more easily predicted than others. Infants can be very active, always moving their arms and legs, while others are more still and content to stay in one place. The things which attract and hold infants' attention also vary. Some infants are most attracted by people, others by things which move and others take more notice of noises. Some infants like to spend time watching or exploring an object whereas others pass quickly from object to object (Stratton, 1982).

Parents' reactions are also determined by their expectations about their babies and how they interpret their babies' behaviour. A major source of expectations is associated with a baby's gender. When parents first see their newborns, the main information they have is whether the baby is a boy or a girl. This knowledge creates a series of expectations so that parents, and especially fathers, see and behave differently towards their sons and daughters, even when the babies are very similar. They see boys as strong and handsome and girls as pretty and dainty and they hold and talk to sons more than to daughters (Rubin, Provenzano and Luria, 1974; Woollett, White and Lyon, 1982). When a three-month-old child was introduced as a girl, 'she' was thought to be fearful and anxious but when the same child was introduced as a boy, 'he' was seen as inquisitive and adventurous (Condry and Condry, 1976).

Infants vary in temperament, that is in their characteristic ways of responding. From about two weeks, parents describe their infants as differing on dimensions including things such as mood, sociability, adaptability and persistence (Thomas and Chess, 1977). Thus some babies are described as easy, friendly, happy and adaptable and others as touchy, fussy, withdrawn and inflexible. Although infant characteristics can change, they are often fairly stable. Ratings of boys' sociability, for instance, is fairly steady from infancy to adolescence. Their sociability in adolescence could be predicted fairly well from their sociability in infancy. Girls' sociability is less stable in the early years; their sociability in adolescence could be predicted from age six or seven but not from infancy.

Children's characteristics, including their size, attractiveness and temperament, affect the ways parents respond to them. Parents of difficult or irritable infants may find it harder to feel positive about their infants and be responsive to their infants' signals (Huntington, Simeonsson, Bailey and Comfort, 1987) and hence to form and maintain strong attachments. When mothers are less responsive, their infants, in turn, form less secure attachments to mothers (Goldberg, 1981).

When babies' behaviour is highly predictable, parents learn rapidly when is the best time for feeding, sleeping and playing and they can accommodate their babies' preferences. In contrast when babies are less predictable, it may take parents longer to feel confident about knowing how to deal with their babies' needs. Babies also come to recognize the consistency and predictability in their families' behaviour. During feeding, for instance, mothers tend to talk to their babies when they are not actively engaged in sucking. If this happens consistently, babies orient to the mother and attend to her face between bursts of sucking. As they interact with one another, infants become more predictable to their families and, in their turn, families become predictable to infants so their behaviour becomes more integrated. Children acquire a better sense that they can control their environment and parents come to believe that they are competent parents (Turner, 1980).

In the first two years there are large changes in the infants' behavioural repertoire, learning and information processing capacities and in their communication and social interactions. The individual characteristics of infants and their developing competence has an impact on those with whom they interact and with whom they form attachments.

Attachment

Infants are more confident and secure when familiar people are present; they are more curious and more willing to explore. Their confidence is increased by their knowledge from past experience that if they are frightened there are familiar people around to protect and comfort them.

Infants' confidence and trust are signs that they are relating to some people as individuals and that they are becoming socially and emotionally dependent upon them. These relationships are known as attachment relationships or more simply as attachments.

A theory of attachment

One of the most influential theories of attachment is the ethological theory of Bowlby (1969). The central assumption is that the attachment process has adaptive significance and helps ensure the survival of infants and their development as competent human beings. Bowlby describes four behavioural systems which operate in an adaptive manner: attachment, affiliation, wariness and exploration. Infants need to find out about their world, the physical world and the world of people, but this world is potentially dangerous and needs to be approached with caution. Consequently when infants encounter new situations, their initial reaction is to be wary and to seek the support of known and trusted figures. To this end the attachment system is activated. It consists of behaviours which promote proximity with attachment figures, including approaching, clinging and crying to bring them close. These behaviours are adaptive as attachment figures protect infants from threat. It would, however, be maladaptive if infants did not learn about their world, and so, if nothing untoward happens, their wariness habituates and the attachment system is replaced by exploration of the social or physical world. While infants explore, they monitor the position of their attachment figures, so they always know where their secure base is. In a similar way, when children meet new people, they treat them warily at first. If nothing happens to upset them, wariness is replaced by affiliation and they begin to make overtures to the unknown person, looking, smiling and vocalizing, from a safe distance at first.

Bowlby also points to the considerable variations in the children's early attachment relations. In some families infants are treated more consistently and positively and are encouraged to explore. In others their treatment is less consistent and their opportunities for exploration are restricted and consequently they are less confident or secure in their attachment relations and less trusting of people. These early attachments provide a foundation on which later relationships and the ability to handle stress are built.

Measuring security of attachments

The security of attachment relations have been explored in the laboratory by putting infants into what is known as the 'strange situation' which activates the attachment and wariness systems. Children are placed in unfamiliar surroundings and their reactions observed in seven episodes. Each episode, lasting three minutes, is marked by the departure or return of attachment figures or a stranger. Infants' reactions to the departures and returns of attachment figures and strangers are classified using a system described by Ainsworth *et al* (1978). This divides infants into those who are securely attached (the majority) and those who are insecurely attached. Securely attached infants typically explore the unfamiliar surroundings until a stranger enters when they draw closer to the attachment figure. On the departure of the attachment figure they protest and actively search for the departed figure. On their return they seek to interact with the attachment figure. Insecurely attached infants show one of two rather distinct patterns leading them to be described in Ainsworth's study as 'ambivalently attached' or 'avoidantly attached'. The ambivalent infants explore little in the presence of familiar figures, are distressed when they are absent but then show little interest in maintaining contact with the familiar figure on their return, often seeking contact and then angrily rejecting it when it is offered. In contrast avoidant infants show little interest in interacting with familiar figures and no distress when those figures depart. The reactions of children to the 'strange situation' reflect their temperament as well as their security of attachments (Belsky and Rovine, 1987).

The behaviour of infants in the 'strange situation' is predictive of their behaviour in other settings and at other points in time. Infants who are securely attached to their mothers explore more and with greater confidence than insecurely attached infants when at home with their mothers (Ainsworth *et al*, 1978). With familiar child minders and with unfamiliar adults, securely attached children are confident and accepting, avoidant children show social withdrawal whereas ambivalent children show unhappiness and uncertainty in their responses (Main and Weston, 1981). Peer relations, too, are linked to the quality of early attachments. Preschool children who are securely attached at one year are more willing to share and are better at initiating and maintaining interactions with both familiar and unfamiliar peers than are the insecurely attached. They are viewed by nursery teachers as being higher on self-esteem and empathy. Moreover, they are less aggressive and whine and complain less. Not surprisingly, they are more popular with peers and have more friends (Sroufe, 1983). With their profile of continuing poor social relationships, insecurely attached children might be expected to show signs of maladjustment and behaviour problems. Such a relationship between insecure attachment at one year and later problems exists for boys but not for girls (Lewis *et al*, 1984).

Problem solving skills also appear to be influenced by early attachment relations. Securely attached infants explore their environments and as they get older develop intellectual curiosity. Later, at ages two and five years, they show enjoyment when presented with a problem, they get involved in the problem and persevere with it until a solution is found. Insecurely attached infants show little exploration and later have poor problem-solving skills (Arend, Grove and Sroufe, 1979).

The links between early attachment relations and later skills may be, in part at least, a result of a continuing level of caretaker sensitivity across the pre-school years. Parents who are sensitive to their infants may facilitate the development of secure attachments in infancy and later good peer relations and intellectual performance. This idea is supported by evidence that when caretakers are under stress, their level of sensitivity declines and their infants' attachments become less secure (Vaughn *et al*, 1979).

Family influences: mothers, fathers and siblings

Children grow up in families which provide consistent and reasonably permanent relationships. In families children first learn social and cognitive skills; they learn about themselves and others, how to relate to and care for people, how to cope with their first disappointments and losses and how to influence their environments. Families are continually changing; new children are born, children grow older and leave home, children and parents get sick, become unemployed or take new jobs and parents get divorced and remarry. Families vary in their size and composition, in their expectations of parents' and children's behaviour and in the personalities and coping strategies of their members. In this section we look at the nature and functions of family relations and the influence they have on children's development.

Mothers

Although other family members, friends, neighbours and childminders are important in children's lives, mothers still take the major responsibility for childcare and spend most time with their children. Because they spend so much time together, mothers and children get to know one another well, their likes and dislikes, moods and interests and they can predict one another's reactions. Mother–child relationships are emotionally charged; mothers love, protect and care for their children but they also restrict their activities, curbing their expression of emotions and making them fit into adult routines.

Parenting styles

Mothers vary in their styles of childcare. The emotional relationship between mothers and children may be more or less accepting, responsive and child-centred, with some mothers showing more warmth and involvement in their children and their activities than others. Some mothers are more controlling and restrictive, wanting their children to do what they are told compared with others who are more permissive and allow their children a greater say in what they do. There is more open communication in some families than others. In some families children as well as parents discuss family activities, giving their reasons for their views and influencing the final outcome. In other families parents make all the decisions and these may not be explained to the children. Mothers also differ in the extent to which they demand mature, independent or socially acceptable behaviour. Some children are expected more than others to dress themselves, look after themselves, play independently and do well at school. Baumrind (1973) has suggested that parents' behaviour can be grouped into one of three distinct patterns or clusters which she calls authoritarian, permissive and authoritative. The three parental patterns have different implications for children's social, emotional and intellectual development, what she calls 'instrumental competence'.

Parents whose parental style she calls *authoritarian* tend to demand high standards of behaviour and performance from their children, requiring them to obey and live up to standards set by the parents. They may insist, for example, that children play quietly together and may be very strict in enforcing their rules, becoming very angry if their children make a noise. Their demands are not discussed with the children, nor are they explained. They are not told, for instance, that they must be quiet because their mother is ill or that they will be taken to the park later to run around freely. Authoritarian parents do not encourage initiative or independence nor do they listen to their children's viewpoint or take notice of their ideas and preferences. They express little warmth; there are few hugs and cuddles or verbal expressions of affection. Children brought up in authoritarian families do not demonstrate a high level of instrumental competence. They tend not to take social initiatives, they lack achievement motivation, are low in self-esteem, lack confidence around peers and are sometimes aggressive and hostile to other children. They seem to have little sense of being able to control their environment and develop few strategies for doing so. These characteristics persist into adolescence, especially for boys.

Permissive parents have a very different approach to childcare. They are more child centred, accepting and tolerant of their children's impulses, and so are unlikely to respond negatively and become angry if their children behave in inappropriate or socially unacceptable ways. The children of permissive parents are much less likely to be punished for noisy or destructive play. Permissive parents make few demands for mature behaviour or performance, allowing children to regulate their own activities and make their own decisions. They discuss and explain their actions and the basis of their rules, involving children in their discussions, but they are much less insistent that those rules or decisions are kept to. So, for example, children may be involved in the decision about acquiring a dog and may commit themselves to taking it for a daily walk. However, if after a few weeks the children tire of the daily walk, permissive parents may not demand that they stick to the agreed rules. Permissive parents are moderately warm and express affection towards their children but are unlikely to express their anger, impatience or annoyance. Their parents' easy discipline and acceptance of their behaviour means that children are not presented with clear expectations for mature behaviour and given little feedback. They have less opportunity, for example, to learn that if they break other people's toys or do not respect their feelings, others get angry and upset and may not want to share their toys in future. Children of permissive parents, like the children of authoritarian parents, tend to be low in instrumental competence and perform less well on tasks of social and cognitive skill. They are aimless and impulsive with little self-reliance and self-control.

It is interesting that children raised in these two different parenting styles, authoritarian and permissive, perform poorly on measures of instrumental competence. Baumrind (1973) suggests that while their techniques of childcare may differ, both kinds of parents tend to shield their children from stress. Authoritarian parents do this by restricting their children's activities, with the result that children rarely encounter stressful events and have little opportunity to learn how to deal with them. In contrast, while permissive parents do encourage new activities, their permissiveness means that their children rarely have to cope with the consequences of their actions.

The third parental style which Baumrind discusses is *authoritative*. Authoritative parents give their children considerable freedom but they have clear limits. They assume they have more skill and knowledge than their children and so are willing to restrict them when they think that is for the best. So, for example, although children may be encouraged to move around freely in the back garden, they may demand that they stay close and do as they are told in a busy street. They expect a fairly high degree of mature and independent behaviour, whether by feeding themselves, looking after younger children, concentrating on a task or by expressing themselves clearly. Authoritative parents are prepared to explain their behaviour and their rules and to listen to and consider their children's opinions and contribution. They express both positive and negative emotions, displeasure at bad behaviour as well as affection and pleasure at things their children do well (Baumrind, 1973). The children of authoritative parents tend to show greater instrumental competence. A parental mixture of moderate discipline, sensitivity to children's needs and demands for mature behaviour seem to provide a context in which children develop self-esteem, independence, resourcefulness, achievement motivation and good relations with peers and adults. These positive outcomes were still apparent in adolescence, especially for boys.

Other workers report somewhat similar results. Parents' use of reasoning, consistent discipline and the expression of warmth are positively related to children's self-esteem, internalized control, prosocial attitudes and intellectual achievement (Maccoby and Martin, 1983).

Cause and correlation studies look at the ways in which parents' behaviour is associated with children's social and cognitive competence. However, we need to be cautious about assuming that parents' behaviour *causes* their children's characteristics. Parents' behaviour may be a response to their children's behaviour, rather than its cause. Parents who are punitive, for instance, may have children who are more aggressive because they learn how to be aggressive from their parents. But it could also be that when faced with aggressive children, parents tend to become more punitive, setting up a model for further aggression. To know which explanation is most useful, we would need to consider how parents behave to their other children or to study families longitudinally, to observe which happens first, parental punitiveness or children's aggression.

Mother–child interaction

Mothers' and children's behaviour is often observed to study directly the ways in which warmth, control or maturity demands are translated into behaviour. These studies demonstrate that mothers' behaviour to their infants differs from that to adults. With their infants, mothers use exaggerated facial and vocal expressions which are built up slowly and maintained for long periods with much prolonged mutual gazing. There is a great deal of vocalizing together or 'chorusing' especially as interactions become lively and excited, and a great deal of looking and vocalizing together with mother looming in close, all features uncommon in adults' interactions with one another (Schaffer and Crook, 1978; Stern, 1977). To children who are beginning to talk, mothers use short, simple sentences, repetitive and highly intelligible language which is usually about what children are saying or doing and hence what they are attending to. These features of mothers' behaviour ensure that the model they present of social and language skills is easily perceived and contains little ambiguity, maximizing their children's opportunity to learn.

Mothers' behaviour acknowledges the limited, but fast developing, competence of their infants. They are sensitive to their children's age, level of competence, interests, moods and temperament. Mothers' sensitivity and the variations in their styles of responding are associated with the development of children's instrumental competence. In the first year, children benefit most from visual and social stimulation and the opportunity to interact with mothers (Wachs and Gruen, 1982). Mothers provide a considerable amount of stimulation, repeating and expanding their children's behaviour and also showing them how the behaviours they are using can be combined, extended and made more dependent on other people's responses. For instance, mothers demonstrate that pointing can be used more effectively if it is combined with looking, to ensure that people are looking at what is being pointed to, or with vocalization, to focus attention on what is of greatest relevance to the child (Schaffer and Crook, 1978). This stimulation is highly dependent on what infants do and how they respond to mothers' behaviour. From an early age infants influence their interactions with mothers; for example they increase the amount of stimulation from mothers by looking at them, smiling, vocalizing or even by stopping their feeding (Stern, 1977).

In their children's second and third years, mothers' verbal stimulation, their responsiveness to their children's verbal and social signals and their encouragement of children's exploration fosters development (Wachs and Gruen, 1982). In its repetitiveness and its grammatical simplicity, mothers' language (called motherese) provides their children with information about how language is segmented, about grammatical and semantic rules, about appropriate topics of conversation and ways to address people. As children become more skilled, mothers use longer and more complex utterances, their language is less bossy and takes a more conversational tone and they allow children to regulate the topic of conversation more (Bates *et al*, 1982). The focus of their conversation also changes; with 18-month-olds, mothers mainly supply words for the pictures in books, at two and a half they ask children questions about the pictures and with three-year-olds they put the pictures into the wider context of other similar objects (Wheeler, 1983).

Mothers are also sensitive to the expression of emotions by their children, including love and excitement at reunion, fears, temper tantrums and food fads. By their acceptance of children's emotional expressions mothers provide an example of how children can understand and respond to the feelings of others (Dunn, 1986; Dunn, 1988; Newson and Newson, 1968).

From three years of age onwards children whose mothers are consistently responsive to their social signals and language perform well on a wide range of social and cognitive tasks, including intelligence tests, spatial and other-perspective taking and social sensitivity, language development and the use and understanding of social and moral rules (Bates *et al*, 1982; Belsky *et al*, 1984; Maccoby and Martin, 1983; Wachs and Gruen, 1982). Mothers' responsiveness to their children's interests and moods may ensure that the models they provide are appropriate and of interest to their children who are thus motivated to learn and to use the skills they see modelled. When mothers are sensitive in these ways children are more likely to be securely attached (see earlier section on attachment). Children who are poorly attached, who are fearful and anxious, may find it difficult to explore, to respond to initiatives and use people and events to further their understanding. In turn fearful or passive behaviour may elicit less stimulating, interested or sensitive behaviour from mothers.

Mothers are not always sensitive and responsive. At times they get annoyed, express disapproval and demand mature behaviour or compliance with their rules (Dunn, 1988; Tizard and Hughes, 1984). Their expression of negative as well as positive emotions gives children feedback about the consequences of their behaviour and information about the world children occupy. Tizard and Hughes point to the learning potential of arguments and disputes between mothers and their four-year-olds. Such arguments can centre on a wide variety of topics and provide the child with information about the activities of family members, the characteristics of babies, the nature of baby care and development, domestic matters such as shopping and managing budgets, the physical world such as why bicycles break when big children ride on them, relationships and the social world such as what are men's and women's jobs and how to persuade people to do things for you, like mending a broken bicycle. Through disputes and exposure to their mothers' negative and positive emotions children may begin to build up concepts of themselves which are complex and multi-dimensional, incorporating positive and negative aspects.

From this analysis it is clear that the constituents of good mothering are various and ever changing. They involve providing children with appropriate models of behaviour and general rules, sensitivity to children's needs, moods and increasing competence, the ability to modify what they do and say to match changes in their children's behaviour and encouraging their children, through stimulation and emotional support, to demonstrate increasingly mature and cognitively sophisticated skills.

Fathers

The features of father–child relations which are important for children's development are similar to those discussed in previous sections for mother–child relations. In many respects mothers and fathers behave similarly to their children (Lamb, Pleck and Levin, 1985). They both employ a distinctive register, known as motherese, when speaking to young children, with a great deal of repetition and expansion of children's utterances (Golinkoff and Ames, 1979). Like mothers, fathers stress turn-taking in their games and interactions with their children. For both parents their parental style (whether authoritarian, permissive or authoritative) influences children's behaviour in the same way (Santrock *et al*, 1982). They both serve as attachment figures. More securely attached children, whether the attachment is to mother or father, show greater interest in unfamiliar adults than those who are less securely attached, although less than children who are firmly attached to both parents (Main and Weston, 1981). Both parents encourage children to play with 'sex appropriate' toys, although fathers enforce this more rigidly than mothers (Langlois and Downs, 1980). They provide stimulation which is developmentally appropriate, so that as children get older they maintain interactions for longer periods with more exchanges in each interactive sequence (Vandell, 1979).

Despite all these similarities there are some differences and it is generally the differences between mothers' and fathers' behaviour which are emphasized. These differences can be seen clearly in parents' play. For most fathers playing with their children is an important activity which occupies much of their time with their children. Fathers spend less time at home than mothers and hence overall they play less with children, but when they are at home their play is very concentrated as they engage in few other childcare activities (Clarke-Stewart, 1978). Fathers' play tends to be idiosyncratic; one father plays quite differently from another and fathers often play very differently on different occasions, making them unpredictable and not easy to follow. In general, their play tends to be very physical, with much rough and tumble, throwing into the air and bouncing around. It tends to happen in bursts and often in short sequences as fathers combine play with other activities such as watching television or reading the newspaper. Fathers' physical style of play seems to encourage children to explore their environments and try out new activities and this is thought to be associated with greater independence and intellectual development especially for boys (Huston, 1983).

In contrast mothers are at home with their children more and so play with them at length and at times throughout the day. Their play tends to be more repetitive than fathers' and they tend to persist longer with play sequences, so children can predict more readily what is going to happen and can fit into the game. Mothers constrain rather than encourage their children's boisterousness, encouraging quiet and concentrated activity. Mothers tend to play similar games to one another, often with a strong educational component and using verbal stimulation. They may, like fathers, provide support for their children's cognitive development, but their support takes different forms; while fathers foster development through curiosity and activity mothers do so through concentrated verbal exchanges (Clarke-Stewart, 1978; MacDonald and Parke, 1984).

There is a suggestion that the more playful fathers are the more influence they have on their children's social, emotional and intellectual development. Lamb finds that Swedish fathers spend less time playing with their children than do American (and British) fathers. Even when Swedish fathers spend a great deal of time with their children they have a smaller impact on their children's development than do mothers (Lamb et al, 1982). Playful American fathers have more influence on their children's development (although again their influence is not generally as large as that of mothers). Lamb believes that through their playfulness fathers become important and interesting to their children, so that they attend to their fathers, value their opinions and follow their example. Thus fathers have an influence on their children because their playfulness makes them more salient to the children.

Individual differences in parental involvement

The general picture of mothers' and fathers' behaviour presented here conceals many individual differences. Parents' behaviour may vary from day to day, as a function of factors such as tiredness or other demands on their time. But there are other variations which are apparent early in their children's lives. Some fathers are more involved with their children than others and some mothers are more sensitive and talk more to their children than others. These variations result from many factors including parents' personalities and general interaction strategies, from their responsiveness to others, their confidence in their parenting role, whether or not they are depressed, their general attitudes to childcare and the characteristics of the children themselves. The quality of the relationship between mothers and fathers also has a strong bearing on the involvement of both parents and especially the warmth and involvement of fathers with children (Belsky *et al*, 1984; Heinicke, 1984), as does their level of job satisfaction (Grossman, Pollack and Golding, 1988).

Mothers' and fathers' behaviour is also, to some extent, influenced by their working roles outside the home. Fathers who are major caretakers, in so-called 'role reversal' families, are more sensitive to their infants and spend more time imitating them, especially their vocalizations, than do fathers who are not the major caretakers. On the other hand, they are also like traditional fathers in that they encourage children's play and adventure seeking more than mothers (Field, 1978; Lamb *et al*, 1982). Fathers who are away from home a great deal spend less time around their children than fathers who are not, but regardless of the amount of time spent with the children, they tend to engage in similar activities and kinds of play (McHale and Huston, 1984). When mothers work outside the home, they play intensely with their children when they are at home, with the result that fathers and children in such families have less opportunity to play together (Crouter, Perry-Jenkins, Huston and McHale, 1987; Pederson *et al*, 1982).

Children's characteristics, including their gender, influence how their parents behave towards them, both as infants and as they get older. Fathers and, to a somewhat less extent, mothers encourage independence in boys more than in girls; boys are allowed to go to and from school unsupervised, to play outside the home more and to leave the house without revealing where they are going at an earlier age than girls (Huston, 1983). Children's sex also influences the academic and career aspirations of parents, especially of fathers. Another child characteristic which affects parents' behaviour is competence and disability; fathers spend less time playing with and helping their handicapped children the more severe the handicap (Cooke and Lawson, 1984).

Brothers and sisters (siblings)

Most children are brought up with others; fewer than one in five children are only children. Sibling relations begin with the birth of a second child; the family is enlarged, first born children have to share their parents' attention and parents have to consider the needs and interests of two children (Dunn and Kendrick, 1982). Younger children always have an older brother or sister to watch, look after them and later to play with, and from the start they share their parents' attention so that for them the impact of a new baby may be less than for first born children.

Children often become more demanding and more difficult when siblings are born but also more independent, wanting to feed and dress themselves and playing on their own more. Mothers often attend to their needs less quickly or less sensitively than before, there are more confrontations and disputes and mothers are more controlling. The new baby replaces the child as the main focus of family activity and discussion as mothers and children do things together for the baby. Children fetch things and watch the baby. The baby's characteristics, competence and lack of competence, likes and dislikes are talked about and comparisons are often made with the older child. The new sibling increases the number and the variety of interactions and discussions, providing children with the opportunity and the motivation to consider the perspective of another person (Dunn and Kendrick, 1982).

The two worlds of childhood

Children live with parents and siblings, sharing the same space, holidays and celebrations, friends, neighbours and family pets and as a result, they have similar backgrounds, histories, concerns and interests. Like those with parents, sibling relationships tend to be highly charged emotionally and long lasting, providing companionship and emotional support often well into adult life (Ciricelli, 1982).

At the same time, sibling relations differ from those with parents and children and parents have different expectations of each other. Parents protect, look after, control and teach their children and are committed to understanding their children's viewpoint. Children learn, co-operate, help and obey their parents and are dependent on them. Sibling relations, in contrast, tend to be more reciprocal with greater mutuality, sharing, initiating and terminating interactions. Siblings engage in different activities together, with more jokes, games, vulgarity and imitation than with parents. Siblings are more alike, in that their skills and power are comparatively limited, and they are less able and less committed than parents to understanding and respecting one another's perspectives. Relations with parents and with siblings represent 'two worlds of childhood' (Hartup, 1983), distinct and different worlds, but ones which are connected because children's social interactions with and secure attachments to parents prepare them for participation in sibling and peer relations.

Interactions between young children and their siblings

From before their first birthday, children watch their older siblings and there is a great deal of talking and intense play, with older children acting as initiators, companions and models. Infants respond to their older siblings' interest and become attached to them, missing them when they are absent and being less upset in the 'strange situation' when older siblings are present (Stewart, 1983). Play between young siblings is often aggressive and excited, involving mutual attention and imitation, bouncing and making noises together, often accompanied by laughter. At first older children tend to initiate games and aggressive play but younger children initiate more and become more aggressive as they get older (Abramovitch *et al*, 1982).

Siblings display, very openly, a wide range of intense feelings; they love and hate one another, tease one another and quarrel, are inseparable and affectionate and play happily and co-operatively. Sibling relations vary considerably; some are consistently more positive and harmonious than others, some siblings co-operate well and others quarrel constantly. Same sex siblings tend to get on better and play more together than different sex siblings. Older siblings and those with a large age gap are often closer. The quality of early relations between siblings and children's relations with their mothers also have an impact. Jealousy and arguments between siblings, for instance, may result from parents' greater attention to or involvement with one of their children. This may be an issue particularly when one child is sick or handicapped and needs more parental care and attention.

Perspective taking

Sibling interactions and relations provide a distinct cognitive and emotional context for development, encouraging shared understanding, trust and affection and at the same time jealousy and quarrels. Children are concerned when their siblings are distressed; they recognize their feelings and show practical, if limited, knowledge of how to comfort them. They tease and provoke one another, snatching toys or comforters which are precious to their siblings and taunting them with objects or situations which scare them. Sibling relations may provide one of the first contexts in which children demonstrate their ability to understand the feelings, intentions and needs of people other than themselves. Perspective taking with peers or adults who are less similar or with whom children's relations are less intense is not observed until somewhat later (Dunn, 1988; Dunn and Kendrick, 1982).

Perspective taking is often encouraged in pretend play. Siblings make and 'drink' cups of tea, go shopping, play mothers and fathers and pretend to be firemen, teachers and characters from television programmes. They co-operate as partners in fantasy, developing new elements. At first older siblings take the more active part, setting up and organizing games, but younger children are increasingly involved, acting out different roles, negotiating rules and handling arguments and disputes (Hartup, 1983).

Indirect influences on child development

We have suggested a number of ways in which mothers, fathers and siblings may influence children's development directly through their relationships with them, their pressures and support for mature behaviour and the models and emotional context they provide. Psychologists have concentrated on one-to-one interactions between children and their mothers, fathers and siblings, but within families, relationships and the influences they have on development are more complex. Interactions between children, their parents and siblings take place within a framework of other interactions. Mothers' discussions with their young children, for example, may be interspersed with discussions with fathers, telephone conversations with grandmothers, chats with neighbours over the garden fence or arguments with older children. Indeed, the amount of language mothers address directly to a child may be small compared with the amount of language children hear their mothers addressing to other people. What is going on around children, the general emotional atmosphere of the home and how friendly or involved family members feel towards one another are all factors which may influence their interactions with one another, and hence indirectly influence children and their development. The sources of indirect influences on children and the ways in which they operate are often varied, complex and not easy to observe or measure (Bronfenbrenner, 1986). Some indirect influences and their implications for development are discussed.

The presence of a third party

When mothers, fathers and siblings are alone with children they behave differently than they do when there is someone else present. Fathers, for example, talk more to their children when they are alone than when mothers are present and so the verbal stimulation children receive from fathers varies according to the amount of time they spend alone with them (Golinkoff and Ames, 1979).

Mothers' behaviour is also affected by the presence of others. Mothers of pre-school children interact less when fathers are present in the house, even if they are not in the room (Clarke-Stewart, 1978). And their language to younger children is altered by the presence of older siblings. Mothers speak less to their two-year-olds and they are less responsive when older children are present. When their older siblings are present, young children speak less, but they are exposed to language which is more complex, has a greater conversational feel and is about a greater variety of topics (Woollett, 1986).

In their turn mothers' presence also alters the interactions of siblings. They interact less, are more aggressive and less sociable when mothers are present (Corter et al, 1983). Mothers are aware of these effects and consider that their children get on better when they are not present. In many cases, however, family members are not aware of such indirect effects.

Setting an example

When family members are together with young children, they set one another examples of how to behave, and of expectations and demands of children. Thus, for example, parents come to adopt more similar holding positions as their children get older. At first parents often adopt dissimilar positions, with mothers tending to hold babies closer to their bodies than fathers and fathers preferring a face to face position. Over the first six months, however, the positions they adopt become more similar (White, Woollett and Lyon, 1982).

The games parents play, their expectations and demands of their children also converge as they observe what their children can do and what they enjoy when they interact with others. It has been suggested that fathers' major influence on their daughters' intellectual development may be indirect, through the expectations they articulate to mothers. Mothers then incorporate fathers' expectations which find expression in mothers' interactions with their daughters. In reconstituted families the expectations of a new parent may bring about changes in children's behaviour. The increased maturity demands made of children by a new stepfather may then be built into the mother's expectations and demands (Santrock et al, 1982).

General atmosphere

Each person contributes to the general family atmosphere and helps mould the social, emotional and cognitive environment in which children develop. Children are influenced by the emotional security, stimulation and sensitivity of those with whom they interact. If the atmosphere is happy and harmonious, children are more secure, attend to family members and they in turn are more responsive than is the case in families where there is tension and discordant relations. The atmosphere within the family may be affected by people's perceptions of their ability to fulfil their family roles. Unemployment or depression may create stress for parents which undermines their perceptions of themselves as good or competent parents. This in turn may make them less responsive to their children and their behaviour. A positive change in family circumstances, for instance when mothers return to work outside the home, may change not just the mother's mood but may have an impact on the whole family, making the adults happier, more relaxed and more responsive (Lamb, 1982).

Interactions within the family

Each family member influences the behaviour of others. A new baby in the family has a direct effect, through the sibling relations created, but the baby's presence also influences, indirectly, children's relationships with their mothers. In the same way, fathers' presence provides an opportunity for one-to-one interactions between father and child. However, fathers influence mothers' relations with the child. The quality of marital relations may be a major factor affecting how each parent feels about their role and their ability to interact with their children. When fathers are supportive, mothers have more positive attitudes towards mothering, they are more satisfied with their role and feel that they are more competent. This, in turn, makes them respond more sensitively to their children. And mothers may influence fathers' behaviour. When mothers want their partners to be involved in childcare and feel that they are competent, fathers are more involved and have a greater influence on their children's development (Lamb, Pleck and Levin, 1985).

Family members may influence one another, too, by their effect on each other's self-esteem. Thus if a mother feels that her relationship with one of her children is poor or that the child is out of control, she may feel that she is an inadequate and incompetent mother. This may have an indirect effect on her other children if her handling of them changes, becoming more controlling, more punitive or less responsive. The behaviour of the first child has an indirect effect on the experience of another by altering the mother's self-esteem, her coping strategies or parenting style.

When the relationship between parents deteriorates they become preoccupied with their own concerns and are less available and less responsive and sensitive to their children. In addition, each parent provides less support for their partner's relationship with the children. Children may, therefore, receive less attention and less sensitive handling from their parents at a time when they feel less secure because of their parents' quarrels. Their parents' lack of responsiveness may make them behave untypically, in ways which meet with insensitive rather than sensitive handling and negative rather than positive responses from their parents (Vaughn et al, 1979).

Family interactions: an overview

From this discussion of the behaviour of mothers, fathers and siblings and their roles in development, it is clear that children's relationships are multi-faceted. Their behaviour with different family members has much in common and the skills of communication and interaction learned in one context transfer to others. But there are differences. These include differences in responsiveness, in social, cognitive and linguistic skills, in commitment to understanding the child and taking their perspective and in encouraging curiosity and sex-role behaviour. At first mothers and fathers are the most important figures in children's lives but as they grow older children's outside contacts increase and with them the variety of models, supports and interactions.

Children grow up in networks of social relationships, and, in addition, much of what they learn is about their social world. They learn about people, about how they are likely to behave, how their behaviour may vary according to their mood, personality and the presence of other people. They learn about themselves, the kind of people they are, how others respond to them, what it means to be a girl or a boy, black or white, handicapped or sick in this society. Children's families are the world in which they first grow up and develop but also the world they learn about.

Two kinds of experience and their influence on children's development have been considered. These are direct one-to-one relations between children and family members and the indirect effects of a relationship between two people on a third. In addition, children themselves have a powerful part to play in their social worlds. Their personality and charac-teristics influence the reactions and the behaviour of those around them. Children are not just the passive recipients of socializing experiences. One characteristic which may influence their social experiences and their development is the child's sex. This is discussed in the next section.

Parents and sex role identity

Parents care for, look after and play with their boys and girls in many similar ways, but their children's gender is an important determinant of their behaviour. Parents dress their boys and girls differently and buy them different toys (Maccoby and Jacklin, 1974). At birth, even before they have any experience of their babies, parents see girls as more delicate, softer and boys as stronger, more co-ordinated and more alert, even though girls tend to be more resilient and less vulnerable to disease, malnutrition and a number of hereditary anomalies (Rubin, Provenzano and Luria, 1974). From an early age fathers engage in boisterous play more with their sons and cuddle daughters more and later they have more contact with sons (Hensall and McGuire, 1986; Lewis, 1986; McGuire,

1982). Fathers are less involved with their children's care and know them less so may be more likely to resort to stereotypical patterns of interaction. Mothers tend not to differentiate boys and girls in the early months; the differences in their behaviour emerge only later. This may be a result of their greater knowledge and responsiveness so that their behaviour to boys and girls differs only as their children's behaviour becomes more stereotyped in the second year.

Parents are more protective of their daughters, encouraging their dependency and keeping them close to the family (Lewis and Weintraub, 1974). Girls are more closely chaperoned and they are encouraged to bring *one* friend home to play. Mothers explain things more to girls, there is more discussion of intimate topics such as menstruation and sexual abuse and they are encouraged to take a person- rather than a thing-oriented approach (Newson and Newson, 1986). Girls are more exposed to adult models and more susceptible to parental, and especially maternal, influence. As a result they become more nurturant, develop superior verbal skills and their identity and self-esteem are more closely linked to their identification with their mothers (Maccoby and Jacklin, 1974). The birth of a sibling may have a greater impact for girls, as the close relationship between mother and daughter is disrupted by the new family member (Dunn, 1984).

Boys are encouraged to explore, to achieve, to be independent and competitive. They are allowed to play out more than girls, to go farther away from home, are supervised less and, not surprisingly perhaps, have more traffic accidents (Lewis and Weintraub, 1974; Newson and Newson, 1986). They play more aggressively, being both aggressors and victims of aggression more than girls. Boys are rarely allowed to deviate from typical 'masculine' behaviour; while tomboy behaviour is an acceptable option for young girls, deviation from appropriate behaviour for boys is 'sissy' and discouraged. Boys are more likely to have problems in school, with reading and speech difficulties and more emotional problems. After age ten they begin to do better than girls in visual spatial tasks and later in mathematical abilities (Maccoby and Jacklin, 1974).

There are considerable variations in mothers' and fathers' behaviour to their boys and girls, with some parents behaving in more stereotypical ways than others. These variations relate to parents' personalities and sex role orientation. Warm and nurturant parents are generally associated with more stereotypical sex role behaviour in their children. Fathers' absence, their coldness and being uninvolved may disrupt the learning of 'masculine' behaviour in boys and result in lower achievement and less successful heterosexual relationships in girls. Fathers appear to influence their daughters indirectly, by their attitudes and support for mothers' behaviour, as much as directly through their interactions with their daughters (Huston, 1983).

Parents are responsive to the activities in which their children engage and the extent to which they conform to sex role patterns. What constitutes appropriate sex role behaviour changes as children grow up. Girls, for instance, are often expected to be delicate and pretty as babies, subdued and compliant as children and domestic and responsive as adolescents. As children's and parents' expectations change over time, their interactions and the reactions of each are continually modified.

Families in flux: variations in family form and functioning

Much of the analysis of families assumes that families consist of two parents and a small number of children. Families, in fact, vary widely and psychologists are increasingly aware of the need to study different family forms and consider their implications for relationships between family members and the impact these may have on children's development.

Historical changes

Families are smaller than they were in the past; most families have two or three children. Families of four or more children are now unusual as are only children (Butler and Golding, 1986). With smaller families, parents have more opportunity to be involved and show greater concern for their children's psychological welfare. There have been changes in attitudes to childcare and to fathers' roles. Fathers express more interest in childcare and some are more involved in looking after their children than was the case in the past (Woollett, White and Lyon, 1982). At the same time more children are growing up in families where there is no father. As a result of greater acceptance of illegitimacy, single mothers are more likely to bring up their children and less likely to have them adopted (Butler and Golding, 1986). Better health together with unemployment and early retirement may mean that some grandparents are now involved in childcare (Tinsley and Parke, 1984).

Divorce and remarriage rates have increased in the last fifteen years and more children experience family breakdown. By age five, 10 per cent of a sample of children born in 1970 were not living with both parents (Butler and Golding, 1986). Marital breakdown and divorce bring about major social, emotional and financial changes for families and children. Parents are often bound up with the divorce and its impact on themselves, their self-esteem and the changes it brings in their lives. As a consequence they tend to have less energy for their children and may be less responsive to their children's needs and emotional problems. Remarriage is also more common and a considerable number of children now live in 'reconstituted' families with parent, step-parent and step-brothers and sisters. Remarriage may bring a new stability, but one which requires adjustments to a new step-parent and sometimes step-brothers and sisters. The effects of divorce on children varies according to their age and sex, with very young and adolescent boys having most adjustment problems (Kurdek, 1981).

Changes within families

Families change over time. The birth of a first child brings about major readjustments for parents in their relationship with one another, friends and family as they establish a relationship with the child and adjust to new routines and concerns (Belsky *et al*, 1984). The birth of a second child may change some of those relationships; some fathers, for instance, develop closer relationships with older children (Dunn, 1984). As children grow up, go to school, make friends outside the family, become more independent and eventually leave home, the amount and the kind of care they need and their relationships with parents alter (Newson and Newson, 1968; Newson and Newson, 1976).

Relationships and interactions within the family also vary with changes in parents' employment outside the home. Mothers tend to stop working when the first baby is born and take major responsibility for childcare. They return to work later as children get older; one half of mothers have returned to some kind of work by the time their children are five (Butler and Golding, 1986). Fathers generally expect their involvement to consist largely of providing financially. However, higher rates of unemployment and mothers' employment outside the home may alter parents' expectations and increase fathers' activity. Children growing up in such families have available more varied role models and attitudes to sex roles available (Hoffman, 1984).

Cultural variations

Social, cultural or ethnic differences are another major source of variation among families. There have been a number of studies which have explored cross-cultural differences in child care and development but studies within this culture have been largely confined to examining social class differences (for example, Newson and Newson, 1968). For accounts of parenting by mothers from different ethnic groups we need to look at novels or oral history studies.

Some families have more children than others and live in close networks of relatives, and especially female relatives. In large families children receive less one-to-one contact with mothers but they have a variety of relatives and siblings to care for them on a regular basis and who are potential attachment figures. In such networks children may be rarely left alone. In spite of these differences attachments are formed in similar ways and infants express their attachments similarly across the range of cultures studied (Ainsworth, 1967).

Family size interacts with other variables which have an impact on family functioning and children's development, making it difficult to separate the effects of particular variables. These include social class, single parenthood, poverty and mothers working outside the home. In the study of children born in 1970, Butler and Golding (1986) report that West Indian children are more likely than average to be in families labelled social class IV or V, to be living with one parent, to have more brothers and sisters and mothers are more likely to work outside the home. Asian children are also more likely to be labelled as social class IV and V and to come from larger families, but they tend to be living with both parents and mothers are less iikely to be working outside the home. The meaning and experience of different variables also has to be considered, for instance the value placed on children in general and on large families in different ethnic groups.

English is not the first, or indeed the main, language spoken in some families and some children grow up speaking two or more languages, one at school, one at home and perhaps even a third in the playground. Studies rarely consider the acquisition of two or more languages and the insights bilingual mothers and children may offer on the general process of language acquisition. When mothers and fathers do not speak English fluently they may be less aware of and less susceptible to fashions in childcare attitudes and changes in practices articulated in the media and contribute less to formulating those attitudes. Attitudes and expectations which have changed include views about mothers' and fathers' roles, parent–child relations, discipline and conformity to parental wishes.

In all cultures, childcare is predominantly the responsibility of women. Men are more involved in some families than others, depending on mothers' and fathers' expectations of their involvement. Other factors may also play a part in some ethnic groups. One such factor *may* be mothers' fluency in English; fathers may be more likely to take their children shopping or discuss children's schooling with teachers if mothers speak little English.

Familics differ in their expectations of children's bchaviour and thc extent to which gender, age or position in family define appropriate behaviour. In some families there may be greater expectations that children help with tasks in the work place, the home and with other children. There may also be clearer definitions of what are tasks for boys and tasks for girls in some families than others (Sharpe, 1978).

Debates around parenting and childcare practices assume that parents expect their relationships with their children to be fairly easy going and friendly with parents considering and making allowances for children's lack of skills and their unwillingness to delay having their needs met (Newson and Newson, 1976). Baumrind's work on parenting styles suggests that there is not necessarily a consensus; not all parents place a high value on independence, self-motivation and assertiveness and different ethnic groups may have different concepts of a 'good' or 'mature' child.

Instability in the family

Most children grow up able to talk, communicate and interact with others in reasonably adequate ways, suggesting that while differences between families are considerable, the impact of variations in parental behaviour or family interaction patterns should not be over estimated. There may be many ways of bringing up children who are mature, well adjusted, happy, positive about themselves and able to relate to others.

Some variations in family composition and functioning, however, are associated with problems of development, adjustment and coping for young children. Separation from mothers and disruptions of attachment bonds and family interaction patterns are associated with difficulties, especially if the separation is prolonged, the children have little previous experience of separation and when children are ill (Rutter, 1981). Often the effects of such separations are short term, so although children may be distressed and their behaviour disruptive for a time, they soon settle down. The difficulties some children experience at the birth of a sibling may result initially in the disruption of family interaction patterns with an improvement as new patterns are established (Dunn, 1984). In other circumstances the effects of instability and altered family patterns are more disruptive with longer-term effects. Family breakup and divorce often result in a wide range of problems, including problems with intellectual development and academic performance and difficulties in relations with teachers and peers (Fine, 1987; Furstenburg and Seltzer, 1986; Hetherington et al, 1982; Wallerstein and Kelly, 1980).

Most of the studies which examine the effects of family change and instability on development compare children with and without particular experiences and use retrospective designs, tracing back the histories of children with difficulties to identify common factors. These studies point to possible links between life events and their impact for children. A more powerful technique is to study children prospectively noting life events and circumstances and children's reactions as they occur. Such studies are not often undertaken because they are expensive and because of the long wait for data. Werner and Smith (1982) carried out a twenty-year longitudinal study of children growing up on an Hawaian island. The children were assessed at intervals to gain information about their temperament, rate of development, IQ, school performance and relationships with parents and others. Information was collected from mothers about obstetric history, family circumstances, caretaking procedures, childrearing practices, problems experienced by the child and experiences the child found stressful. School, social work and medical records were also examined. The histories and characteristics of children who developed psychiatric or educational problems or who turned to crime were examined and compared with children without problems. The events most closely associated with later problems were late birth order (first borns had fewer problems); prolonged separation from the mother in the first year; parental discord in the first two years; repeated childhood illness; father absent from home a good deal; family breakup; a mentally ill parent; a handicapped brother or sister and death of a sibling or parent.

These factors have in common that they introduce unpredictable and unwelcome change into children's lives and they interfere with the formation and maintenance of close attachment relations. When parents are mentally ill they may behave in unpredictable ways, be unresponsive to children's needs and the stimulation they provide may be unrelated to their child's behaviour. When parents have many children or a child who is handicapped they may not be able to deal effectively with the demands on their time and energy and hence be less attentive and less responsive to their child. The lack of responsiveness may hinder attachment, social and cognitive development. Prolonged separation from the mother, especially when associated with environmental change and the loss of familiar sights, objects and people, causes children distress and may interfere with the establishment of attachment relations and increase their needs for parents' attention (Wallerstein and Kelly, 1980).

Individual differences in resilience and stress resistance

There are large individual differences in the reaction of children to instability in family life. Some children seem more resilient and cope well, whereas others have enormous problems. A variety of factors seem to be associated with greater resilience, making children less vulnerable or providing them with some 'buffering' or protection when things go wrong.

Certain child characteristics or personality factors are associated with greater resilience. These include temperament, high self-esteem, high IQ, and being born a girl. Werner and Smith (1982) in their longitudinal study demonstrate that individuals who as babies are sociable, active in visual exploration of their environment and have good early co-ordination are less likely to respond to later adversity with rebellion at school, delinquency or psychiatric illness. When parents are under pressure, whether as a result of housing conditions, family finance or marital problems, they are more likely to be irritated by their children and to treat them insensitively. However, if a child is easy going and makes fewer demands of parents, she or he may experience fewer problems in relationships with parents and be less affected by deteriorating family circumstances.

Individuals whose self-esteem is high and who are intelligent are less likely to develop behaviour problems, even in the face of extreme adversity

(Rutter, 1978; Werner and Smith, 1982). In addition, even when they do succumb, they recover more quickly (Garmezy, 1984). These children are more able to think of a range of solutions and to have developed good coping strategies with the result that their self-esteem is high and they feel confident about their ability to cope.

A close relationship with someone who is sensitive may help buffer children against adverse life events. Thus children who have good relationships with their mothers are better able to cope with the adverse effects of a deterioration in their parents' relationship, their fathers' absence or the death of a close friend. For school-aged children resilience is increased if they attend a school that provides a structured and caring environment and a clearly defined and consistently enforced sets of rules. These seem to offer stability and coupled with a supportive attitude from teachers and pupils ensure that children are better able to resist the effects of adverse life events (Dunn, 1986; Hetherington *et al*, 1982; Rutter, 1978).

Also important in determining how children react are the number of adverse events with which they have to cope. Most individuals can cope with one adverse event at a time, but when they come together their impact is much more disruptive (Rutter, 1978). The long-term effects of adverse experiences depend on the nature of subsequent events. For instance, complications during delivery can lead to brain damage which may influence children's later cognitive competence and sociability. Whether or not there are long-term effects depends on the stability of the family in the early years; children are able to recover from obstetric complications when there are no additional adverse experiences (Werner and Smith, 1982).

Children whose parents divorce are exposed to multiple losses and adversities. To the loss of a parent may be added a change in the family home and hence in friends and neighbours who could provide stability and support. The family's standard of living often drops, sometimes substantially; one-parent families are among the poorest in Britain. Children show less disturbance after divorce if their lifestyles are less affected and the loss of a parent is not compounded by other social and economic losses (Kurdek, 1981).

Instability in children's lives may be associated with problems of various sorts, especially when there are multiple stresses and disruptions. Instability resulting in the loss of or weakening of attachment relations is most disruptive but a close and continuous relationship probably protects children best.

Summary

In this chapter we have seen that the development of young children is influenced by their experiences in their families. This influence persists and affects the way children approach new situations and how they are influenced by those new situations. One example of this was seen in the section on attachment. Security of early attachments is influenced by parents' sensitivity in their treatment of their children. In its turn security of attachment affects children's later confidence in exploring new situations and new social relationships. Early experiences within family settings shape the way children perceive themselves and their world, it shapes their confidence and level of self-esteem.

Families consist of a number of members who influence one another both directly and indirectly. To a large extent family members have similar values and interests and similar aspirations for the developing child. Consequently, different family members often act in a complementary manner, encouraging similar attributes and skills. Sometimes they do this via slightly different routes. Thus fathers encourage intellectual development by encouraging their child to be independent and curious. Mothers encourage similar development by their verbal stimulation and use of educational games. Nevertheless each family member provides the child with somewhat different experiences and so to some extent encourages the development of different qualities.

With the passage of time families change. Families can change in a number of ways, including the birth of another child, the death of a family member or by family breakup and divorce. Such change calls for adjustments and there is frequently some disruption to normal functioning. For instance, following the divorce of their parents children often become more aggressive, whiney, inattentive and socially withdrawn. However, most children are sufficiently resilient to overcome such adversity and to develop normally and the adverse effects are fairly short lived. As well as being a potential source of stress, families also have the potential to increase the resilience of developing children and make them better able to cope with adversity.

Chapter twenty

Personality

Marian Pitts

Introduction

It has been claimed that there are as many definitions of personality as there are personality theorists. Each definition reflects the approach of the theorist who suggests it. A widely accepted definition of personality is that offered by Gordon Allport. He describes personality as 'the dynamic organization within the individual of those psychophysical systems that determine his characteristic behaviour and thought' (Allport, 1961). Personality theorists study not only particular aspects of a person, they also try to study the whole person. Consequently, the study of personality can overlap with many other areas of psychology such as perception and memory.

There are a number of major controversies in the study of personality and we will examine these first and then consider some of the major schools of personality theory. Finally, we will consider the ways in which personality can be assessed.

A primary consideration is whether or not one can determine a *general disposition* to behave in one particular way rather than another. The behaviourist movement in psychology did not accept the idea of a general disposition of behaviour. Behaviour was regarded as a number of stimulus-response sequences and general patterns of responses occurring across situations were not considered. Other psychologists place great emphasis on a general, usually in-born, predisposition to behave in certain ways. These theorists may not take sufficient account of the ways in which a specific situation may influence a person's behaviour and reactions to that situation. A more useful approach to personality probably lies somewhere between these two extreme points of view. A person may, in general, have a tendency to be sociable and outgoing, but her/his behaviour in any given situation will be determined not only by that predisposition but by the way in which s/he perceives the specific situation.

A second major difference between personality theories is the degree to which they emphasize each person's individuality. Some personality theorists, such as Gordon Allport, place great emphasis on the uniqueness of the individual's personality. The approach is known as the *idiographic* approach. Idiographic theorists try to study an individual for a long period of time and believe that comparisons between people are of limited value only. In contrast, other personality theorists such as Cattell and Eysenck try to establish the major dimensions of personality on which people may differ, but which are present to some degree in everyone. This is known as the *nomothetic* approach to personality. Once again, the resolution of this disagreement may be a compromise. We can look for the similarities between people and yet also consider the individual's own adjustment and expression of predispositions. It is worthwhile to bear in mind while reading this chapter that these initial orientations of the personality theorists will lead them to emphasize some concepts at the cost of others.

Some theorists discussed in this chapter make use of the concept of *traits* as a means of investigating personality. Cattell could be called a trait theorist. Traits may be defined as covariant sets of behavioural acts. They are organizing principles which can be deduced from human behaviour. Examples of traits would be sociability and impulsiveness. These are recurrent and stable aspects of an individual's personality. Other theorists place more emphasis on the concept of *type*. For example, the traits of shyness, subjectivity and rigidity are included in Eysenck's dimension of introversion. Some typologists, however (for example Kretschmer or Sheldon), have supposed that every individual can be so placed in one of a limited number of categories, or types, having certain specified characteristics.

Finally, the issue of *consistency* should be considered. To what extent is it possible to describe a person as punctual, conscientious or aggressive? One element implied by such a description is that on a variety of occasions, or in a number of different situations, a person will display the particular trait ascribed to him or her. A major dispute in personality research centres around this point. Mischel (1968) argued that behaviour is influenced more by the situation a person is in than by that person's disposition. He pointed out that someone might well behave similarly in similar situations but that if the situation changes drastically, a person's behaviour may well change also. He cites an early study – Hartshorne and May (1928) – which found only a low correlation (0.3) between different tests of honesty in primary school children. Other studies such as Dudycha (1936) also report very low correlations for other traits such as punctuality, when measured in a variety of different situations. Mischel points out that there can be a danger of *reification* of traits. That is, to assume that there is some tangible thing called honesty which can be present or absent in an individual and that this can *cause* a person to behave honestly.

Partly as a result of Mischel's criticisms of trait theories, alternative approaches have gained sway. The most extreme could be called a situationalist approach. This suggests that behaviour is very largely governed by the situation in which it occurs. Put someone in a situation where heroism is called for and s/he will be heroic. This view would seem to be as limited as the one Mischel criticizes and a more subtle approach has developed known, inevitably, as the 'person × situation' or the interactionalist view. As you might guess, this view says that behaviour is the outcome both of situational variables and person variables, in consideration and in interaction with each other. An example of the sort of research prompted by this approach is found in Moos (1969). He studied people in a variety of settings within a psychiatric hospital and measured several different behaviours – smoking, drinking, etc. He found 'person' factors accounted for some of the variation, 'situation' factors also accounted for some of the variation and that the interaction between person and situation factors accounted for the most variance in behaviour. It is tempting to ask what else is left after person and situation have been accounted for.

Trait theorists have tried to answer some of the telling criticisms made by Mischel. Eysenck and Eysenck (1980) have pointed out that a trait such as extraversion is reliably related to a number of different biological and behavioural variables, and that statistically one could achieve higher correlations simply by increasing sample size and taking multiple measures of the trait.

The debate continues with neither side showing signs of modifying position in the light of criticism; perhaps that is one of the reasons that these 'grand' theories of personality have lost some of their sway in recent years. Increasingly there is a trend towards 'narrow' band theories which simply take one aspect of personality and try to see its effect on behaviour and experience.

We shall now examine several personality theories and try to evaluate them. What do we require of a good personality theory? In general, we expect a good theory of personality to offer an explanation or account of why people should behave as they do and, to some degree, enable us to predict how they will behave in the future. A good personality theory should describe, explain and predict a person's behaviour in terms which are meaningful to us.

The first school of personality we shall examine is the psychoanalytic school.

Psychoanalytic theories

Sigmund Freud (1856–1939)

Sigmund Freud was born in 1856 and died in London in 1939. For most of his life he lived in Vienna and it was there that he devised what is probably the most influential theory of personality ever produced. Freud studied medicine and became interested in the physiology of the nervous system: on a visit to Paris he was introduced to the use of hypnosis for the treatment of hysteria. Freud used this technique for some time with his patients but, gradually, he came to the conclusion that it was unnecessary to hypnotize the patient, and he moved on to use the technique of free association. In this method, the patient is asked to relax on a couch and then simply describe what comes into the mind, no matter how absurd or irrelevant it may seem. Freud found this method useful in helping him to understand the causes of his patients' problems. This technique formed the basis of all Freud's observations and led him to suggest the theory of personality we shall now consider.

For Freud, all behaviour has a cause: no form of behaviour, however bizarre, arises without a reason and it was the search for these reasons which occupied most of Freud's theorizing. Freud also believed that the reasons for behaviour are not always immediately apparent to an individual. He suggested that unconscious processes exert a powerful influence over a person's behaviour. The free association technique might reveal some of these influences. Freud emphasized the importance of the early years of life. He argued that the experience of these years moulded the psyche and determined the personality which would develop in later life. The technique of free association tapped experiences which were associated with these early years. For a discussion of Freud's theory of the development of personality, see Chapter 16.

Freud also analysed his patients' accounts of their dreams. He described the interpreting of dreams as the 'royal road to understanding the unconscious'. He argued that we are able to give free expression in our dreams to emotions and ideas that we censor from our waking thoughts.

He found many symbols in dreams which he interpreted as sexual in origin. The principle of causality also underlies Freud's interest in the mistakes people make in their everyday lives. Again, he argued that these apparently random events have causes and are expressions of unconsious processes. Thus, even accidental errors of speech were considered by Freud to be worthy of examination and explanation since they offered insight into the unconscious. See Chapter 15 for further discussion of speech errors.

Freud describes the personality as made up of three systems: the id, the ego and the superego. Each system has its own functions and course of development, but in the mature personality the interrelations between them are strong. The *id* is the driving power behind a personality: it is the psychic energy of the person. The id is a combination of sexual and aggressive needs: by sexual needs Freud meant more than simply a sexual act; he included the seeking of pleasure and the gratification of bodily needs.

The *ego* develops in order to control the energy of the id and its effect on the relation of a person to the world. We need to modify our basic drives towards immediate gratification when they are in conflict with societal needs and it is the ego that enables us to do this. It operates by what Freud called the reality principle: via this the ego manages to curb the impulses of the id in order that immediate gratification be put off for a more fulfilling, longer-term gratification.

The third element in Freud's theory of personality is the *superego*. This develops as the child learns, through its parents, the values and ideals of society. The child incorporates these values and gradually adopts the moral and ethical code of the parents. The superego is sometimes represented as the conscience: Freud referred to it as the primitive, unconscious conscience. It can be seen that the forces of the superego and the id may be in opposition: the role of the superego is to curb those primitive responses represented by the id if they are in conflict with societal norms. It is the role of the ego to act as a balance for these two opposing forces and this implies that, for Freud, people are continually in a state of conflict and their behaviour is determined, in part, by how these internal battles are faring. If the id is dominant anxiety may develop in the person, and this may be coped with in a variety of different ways. Perhaps the best known of these ways is by means of *defence mechanisms*; many defence mechanisms have been suggested and we shall discuss only one or two here. Anna Freud (Freud's daughter) describes some of the major defence mechanisms as *repression*, *projection*, and *regression*. All these mechanisms are said to work at the unconscious level: the person is not aware, for example, that he is repressing something.

Freud emphasized the importance of repression. It is the repression of energy which can result in motivated forgetting. But what is repressed is not lost; it is stored in the unconscious and can be regained into conscious-ness at a later time. Freud argued that if a person becomes anxious about something s/he may seek to deny its existence, thus reducing anxiety. This can, however, lead to a disruption of normal behaviour since the person is no longer aware of the reasons for her/his actions. Thus we may have apparently unreasonable fears which are based on an experience which we have repressed or 'forgotten'. While repression is held to be a feature of the ego, it may also develop as a consequence of a strong superego.

With projection people cope with anxiety, not by denying its cause but by unconsciously attributing the feelings to someone else. If they feel hostile to someone they cope by arguing that the person is hostile towards them. This can be effective in relieving anxiety and can also provide an excuse for repressing their true feelings. They can rationalize and legitimize the expression of their hostility. Ultimately, however, this is not a very effective way to reduce anxiety since the person who receives the projec-tion may well resent the hostility expressed and become hostile in return.

Freud believed that regression is the process by which an individual seems to revert to former ways of behaving and gratifying needs. For example, a person who feels threatened may chew her/his nails without being aware of it. Regression is a mechanism sometimes seen in a child who has recently had a new baby brother or sister. The child may have been fairly independent until the birth of the sibling, but will suddenly become much more clinging and reliant on parents. Thus, by means of the defence mechanisms described above (and it is suggested that there are others), the ego manages to control the inevitable conflict between the demands of the superego and those of the id.

To summarize these ideas, it is possible to think of Freud's three major components of personality in the following way. The id is the biological basis of personality; it provides the driving force behind a persons's behaviour. The ego is the psychological component of personality and it develops measures to cope with the demands of the id and the superego. The superego is the (unconscious) moral component of a personality; it develops from the pressures an individual faces from living in a society. Because the wishes of society are often in conflict with the desires of the indiviudal, the ego is equipped to cope with the reconciliation of these two opposing forces.

Evaluation:

Probably no other theory in psychology has created such controversy, not only among psychologists, but also in the general population. It is difficult for us to imagine the outrage the theory originally caused. Freud's emphasis on people's sexuality and its origins in childhood was out of keeping with the general views of the time, and ideas that we now find acceptable were thoroughly shocking to Freud's early readers.

It is a demanding task to evaluate a theory of personality which seeks to be so broad and to encompass all human behaviour. If there are so many different processes at work within a person, how can we say at any given time which are directing behaviour? One of the major difficulties is that it is hard to find methods suitable to test Freud's theory. Freud regarded his careful collecting of data from his patients and his emphasis on the principle of causality as the basis of a scientific approach to personality. Nevertheless, it is important to be aware that much of his evidence comes from single case studies and, when the theorist is also the therapist, as was the case with Freud, it is not possible to be confident that bias has been removed.

Let us consider certain features of Freud's theory and examine the evidence for them.

Freud described repression as 'the cornerstone on which the whole of psychoanalysis rests'. There have been many attempts to demonstrate experimentally that repression will occur after information threatening to the ego has been encountered. An example of this work is an experiment by Zeller (1950). Zeller gave subjects a set of nonsense syllables to learn: he then sorted his subjects into two groups, such that both groups were of equal ability on the syllable learning task. Both groups were then required to perform a psychomotor task. The control group of subjects was allowed to succeed at this task, but the experimental group was forced to fail. In this way, Zeller argued that ego threat had been introduced into the experimental group. Zeller suggested that the ego threat would be generalized from the psychomotor task to the learned syllables. On a further testing of recall of the syllables the experimental group performed less well than the control group. Zeller argued that the former had repressed the syllables. Both groups then performed a second time on the psychomotor task but, this time, both groups were allowed to succeed. Hence, for the experimental group the ego threat was lifted and, as Freud would predict, on a subsequent test of the learning of the nonsense syllables both groups performed equally well. This experiment and others like it were thought to provide strong support for Freud's explanation of repression.

Holmes has criticized these experiments. He suggests that it is not repression that causes the experimental group to perform poorly after failure in the psychomotor task. Rather, Holmes claims, response competition, or interference, is the basis of these results. Subjects who have performed poorly on the psychomotor task are likely to be concerned and this will reflect on their performance, causing interference in their ability to recall the syllables. In order to test this suggestion, Holmes and Schallow (1969) designed a similar experiment to that of Zeller. Three groups of subjects learned a list of high frequency nouns. Each group was then shown a series of Rorschach ink-blots (this test is discussed in greater detail on

p. 635). The groups were given the nouns from the learning task and were asked to choose which were appropriate to describe the ink-blots. Group 1 (the ego threat group) was told that its choices of nouns indicated some degree of pathology. Group 2 (the control group) was told it was simply helping to test a scoring system and the experimenter was not interested in their individual responses. Group 3 (the interference group) was told that the ink-blots test investigated perception and it was shown random film sequences between presentation of the ink-blots to cause interference. All these groups were then retested on their recall of the high frequency nouns. They were then debriefed (that is, the true purpose of the experiment was explained to them) and they were tested again for their recall of the nouns. Figure 20.1 shows the results for these three groups. It is clear that there is little difference between the interference group and the ego-threat group. Both differ from the control group. Holmes and Schallow argue that interference can account for the results of both groups 1 and 3. Furthermore, if ego threat were operating in group 1 then one would expect it to be reflected in the repression of those words which had been associated with the 'pathological' responses to the ink-blots. The patterns of recall for the nouns did not differ for this group from the pattern for the interference group. Thus it would appear that the concept of interference is sufficient to explain all the results that have been taken to provide evidence for Freud's theory of repression. This does not of itself, of course, refute the theory, which in any case is concerned with emotional development in childhood, not with laboratory situations.

Eysenck has also criticized the experimental work which is cited to support Freud. He discusses an experiment by Daston (1956) which examines the relation between paranoia and homosexuality. Freud suggests that paranoids have repressed homosexual tendencies. Daston found that paranoids recognized words relating to homosexuality which were presented tachistoscopically more readily than did normal subjects. This experiment has been cited as evidence to support Freud, but Eysenck argues that, if the homosexual tendencies of paranoids are repressed, then perceptual defence should operate and these words should be recognized less easily by paranoids than by normal people.

This study, and many others, are reviewed by Kline (1983) who argues that there is a wealth of evidence from both experimental and cross-cultural studies which could be taken to support Freud. Eysenck has reviewed the same evidence and cannot find any specific support for Freud's theory. He describes the theory as follows: 'what's new in these theories is not true, and what's true is not new'. This debate is likely to continue, so let us look elsewhere to evaluate Freud further.

A good way to evaluate Freud's theory is to look at its applications. Much of Freud's theory developed from his observations of his patients in Vienna. The techniques he used, such as that of free association, have

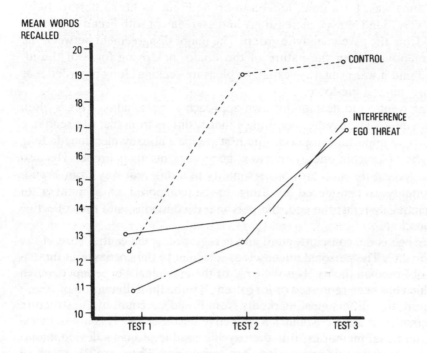

Figure 20.1 Mean number of words recalled on: Test 1, before experimental manipulation; Test 2, after experimental manipulation; Test 3, after debriefing (Holmes, 1974)

formed the basis of many of the therapies used today; the relationship between therapist and client is still central to all forms of psychotherapy. Many of us make use of concepts emphasized by Freud (for example, the concept of unconscious motivation), and his influence has spread beyond psychology to literature and anthropology. Indeed he is probably now held in higher regard in those disciplines than in psychology itself.

The neo-Freudians

During his lifetime Freud attracted followers to his way of thought. Many of them came to reject certain aspects of his theory and developed theories of their own. All of them, however show a clear debt to Freud in their writings. Two of his most famous followers are Carl Jung and Alfred Adler.

Carl Jung (1875–1961)

Carl Jung was, for a time, looked upon by Freud as his successor. Jung, however, found himself increasingly in disagreement with Freud and broke away from the psychoanalytic group. The major disagreement between the two men was about the nature of the libido, or driving force of the id. Freud said it was primarily sexual, or pleasure-seeking. Jung regarded it as a more general life-force.

Jung went on to develop his own approach to personality. This is often known as analytic psychology. Jung's theory differs from that of Freud in a number of important respects. The first we have already mentioned: Jung thought of psychic energy in more general terms than Freud. He also characterized the structure of personality in a different way from Freud. Personality is considered by Jung to be composed of a number of interacting systems: the ego, the personal unconscious, and the collective unconscious.

The ego is the conscious mind and is regarded as the central core of the personality. The personal unconscious is similar to the unconscious dimension of Freudian theory. It is the total of the individual's experience, much of which has been repressed or forgotten. It is the third dimension of Jung's structure that differs most markedly from Freud's account of the structure of personality. Jung postulates a collective unconscious. This holds ancestral and racial memories; it is the psychic residue of man's development. Within the collective unconscious are archetypes. These are the result of experiences which have become embedded in the human mind. Evidence for the existence of archetypes can be found in myths and folk-lore. Some examples of archetypes would be God, the wise old man, death and rebirth. Jung uses the evidence of these recurrent themes in the mythologies of a number of different cultures to argue for the existence of archetypes. He claims that they are also recurrent in free association and in the phantasies of psychotics. The validity of this can be questioned. Many experiences are common to all cultures and so it should not surprise us to find these common experiences reflected in our dreams and our literature. We do not need to postulate a collective unconscious in order to account for them. Carl Jung is also known for his use of the terms introversion and extraversion. These concepts will be discussed in the part of this chapter concerned with H. J. Eysenck.

Jung also popularized the technique of word association. In this technique, a person is presented with a word and asked to respond with the first word he thinks of. For example, the experimenter might say 'black' and the subject would probably respond 'white'. Jung suggested that hestitations before responding, or bizarre associations, might be indicators of complexes within the individual. This assertion is very difficult to test, but it seems, intuitively, to have a certain validity.

618

We have discussed the difficulty of evaluating Freud's theory; how much more is this the case with Jung! Very few workers have elected to investigate the validity of his suggestions about the structure of personality. He is widely admired and regarded by some as a great thinker but his influence on mainstream psychology has been slight. Nevertheless, we can find in Jung's writings a more optimistic view of man and his future than is found in Freud, and this is certainly a characteristic of later approaches to personality, such as those of Maslow and Rogers.

Alfred Adler (1870–1937)

Adler broke with Freud in 1911. He, like Jung, disagreed with Freud's description of the libido and its sexual nature. He argued that people are motivated primarily by social drives. He postulated that we should examine psychological maladjustment in terms of a person's relation to society. Adler introduced a concept which has passed into our general vocabulary – 'the inferiority complex'. Adler believed that a person is born with a striving for superiority and perfection that causes him or her to move constantly towards new goals. With the achievement of any goal, one sets oneself a higher one. Feelings of inferiority arise from a sense of imperfection in the tasks attempted. The courses people take to achieve their goals are individual: hence each person has a unique lifestyle. Adler's theory of personality places a greater emphasis on the social factors which affect personality; he places less emphasis on the unconscious processes that are central to the theories of Freud and Jung.

Evaluation:

Because Adler stresses the individuality of any person's struggle against inferiority, it is extremely difficult to arrive at clear predictions from his theory. Possibly the only certain prediction is that every individual will be different and that doesn't get us very far.

However, Adler has made some predictions about the effect of birth order on the patterns of behaviour which will typify each child in the family. First borns are secure and happy until they have to cope with the changes that come with the birth of a second child. Until then, they have been the centre of attention, and anxiety could arise when the child no longer feels the sole recipient of parental love. This child may have problems in later life: Adler suggests s/he could become delinquent or neurotic. The second child will be ambitious. S/he will constantly strive to outdo the elder sibling; s/he will be orientated towards the world and will strive for recognition there rather than within the family where attention is shared with the elder sibling. The youngest child (of three) will be the 'baby' of the family. In later life, s/he will be a sociable person but will not strive for success in the way the second child might; s/he may also have difficulties adjusting to the world beyond the family.

The evidence that has been collected to support these ideas is meagre. Goodenough and Leahy (1927) asked teachers to rate children on a number of traits such as aggression, introversion, submission, etc. For the fourteen traits they used, they found that the average percentage of unfavourable ratings that children received was as follows: for oldest children, 22.5 per cent of the ratings were unfavourable, for middle children, 20.6 per cent and for the youngest children, 16.5 per cent. These differences are very small; the difference between oldest and youngest is only 6 per cent and it is difficult to establish the basis for deciding that traits were unfavourable.

Other factors than birth are likely to be very important in determining personality: the sex of each child and the gaps in ages between the children must also be very influential. The evidence for Adler is very insubstantial and it would be unwise to place too much credence in his views.

We have reviewed three of the major theories of the psychoanalytic school of personality. All three are imaginative and thought-provoking, but only Freud's has played a major part in the empirical investigation of personality.

The theories we shall examine next are *type theories* based on observations of body size and shape.

Constitutional theories

Since the time of the ancient Greeks, there have been those who believed that a person's personality can be deduced from their physique; we tend to think that fat people are jolly and that muscular men are aggressive. Advertisements urge us to change our physique; if we develop our bodies the change will be reflected in the way people respond to us. What truth is there in the belief that there is a relation between personality and physique?

Ernst Kretschmer (1918–1964)

Kretschmer was one of the first psychologists to examine scientifically the relationship between physique and personality. As is often the case in this area of psychology, he based his observations on patients in clinical institutions. He compared those patients who had been diagnosed as schizophrenic with those diagnosed as manic depressives. He found major differences between them in terms of their average body size. Schizophrenics, typically, were tall and rather thin; he called this type asthenic (weak). Manic depressives were, in general, short and plump (so much for our notion that these people are always jolly!). He called this body type pyknic (thick). Kretschmer also examined people not in clinical institutions and described their average body size as athletic.

These are interesting findings, but there is doubt about their validity. Schizophrenia typically develops in late adolescence, thus Kretschmer's sample of schizophrenics was of mainly young people. Manic depression, on the other hand, is often a disease of middle age. It might be argued that Kretschmer was classifying the body changes that occur through a life-time: middle aged people are generally stouter than young ones. This would have biased his results and produced evidence which tells us very little about personality.

William Sheldon (1901-1985)

Sheldon's work began where Kretschmer's ended. His concern was to try to map the relationships that might exist between physique and temperament. Sheldon believed that biological factors were extremely important as determinants of human behaviour. He sought to identify these factors to provide a firm basis on which to build a study of human behaviour. He hypothesized a biological structure (the morphogenotype) which underlies physical characteristics. He suggested that this morphogenotype influenced not only the observable physical characteristics of a person but also, indirectly, that person's personality.

His studies began in this way: Sheldon took photographs of 4,000 college men and sorted them into types of physique. He identified three major dimensions of physique which he called endomorphy, mesomorphy and ectomorphy. The type of physique which he called endomorph was round and soft (rather like Kretschmer's pyknic type). Mesomorphs were muscular and broad-shouldered (athletic in Kretschmer's typology), and ectomorphs were narrow-shouldered and skinny (asthenic). These are descriptions of body types at the extremes of the dimensions. A person can be described in terms of how he or she resembles each of these three types of physique. Using a seven-point scale, one might score: two for endomorphological characteristics, six for mesomorphological characteristics and one for ecto-morphological characteristics (2, 6, 1). These ratings result in a description of a person's physique. Sheldon calls this the person's somatotype.

Having characterized and classified a person's physique Sheldon turned to temperament and attempted a similarly ambitious task. He scoured the literature on personality and drew up a list of the trait names that he found there: there were 650 in all. He reduced this list to 50 by considering the overlap between them. Sheldon and his fellow workers then selected a group of 33 men and carefully observed them for a period of a year. They rated each of the men on each of the 50 traits. By the use of factor analysis Sheldon reduced these 50 factors to three major clusters. He called them viscerotonia, somatotonia and cerebrotonia.

A person who scores highly on those traits describing viscerotonia is a lover of comfort, someone who needs approval for his or her actions and who can relax easily. Sheldon describes this person as 'bold as a rabbit'. A person who could be classified as extreme in somatotonia is noisy and aggressive, always on the move, Sheldon says s/he is 'fearless as a mastiff'. The third type, the extreme cerebrotonic, is tense and hesitant, rather a social isolate and not fond of action. Sheldon says that in the face of a problem s/he 'closes up like a clam and seeks a hole to crawl into'.

After this analysis, Sheldon was able to consider the relationship between his typology of physique and that of temperament. In 1942 Sheldon reported the results of a five-year study he had made of 200 men. He rated them for temperament as a result of interviews and observations and he typed their body build according to the dimensions described above. He then looked at the degree of association between his two sets of figures: those for physique and those for temperament. He found a highly encouraging set of relationships. Endomorphy correlated highly with viscerotonia, mesomorphy with somatotonia, and ectomorphy with cerebrotonia. These correlations were all of the order of + .80: a degree of correlation which is rarely found in psychology.

Evaluation:

The extent of Sheldon's work is impressive, but in this lies one of its major flaws. Sheldon himself scored his subjects both for physique and temperament. He firmly believed there was a strong relationship between the two and had clear ideas of what this relationship might be. Indeed, he thought he was measuring the same factor at two different levels: that physique was directly related to temperament. This in itself must make his findings rather suspect. Rosenthal and others have shown how an experimenter can unwittingly bias their findings in the direction they expect. We are not suggesting that Sheldon deliberately rated his subjects in ways which would confirm his theory but, in psychology, we place greater credence on work carried out by independent observers who do not have clear preconceptions of what the findings might show.

Sheldon maintained that to require total ignorance on the part of the investigator would make it impossible to obtain meaningful results and there is much to be said for this point of view. Furthermore, even if independent judges rated the subjects for temperament we would not remove completely the problems of bias. As we mentioned earlier, most of us have stereotypes of the fat, jolly person and, because of these stereotypes, it is difficult to guarantee that a rater will not be influenced by them.

Bearing in mind these criticisms of Sheldon's work, there are some experiments which lend support to his theory. In a major study of delinquents, Glueck and Glueck showed that delinquent boys differ from non-delinquent boys in body-type. The delinquents tended to be mesomorphic rather than endomorphic or ectomorphic. This is not an unlikely finding. It is probable that a good muscular physique is likely to suit the life-style of a delinquent. An individual who has a certain physique may be rewarded for certain behaviours and punished for others. Mesomorphs may be successful if they are aggressive and dominant, whereas ectomorphs may often fail to gain success through aggression and so learn other techniques of gaining their own way. The relationship that Sheldon found is therefore a plausible one, but one cannot argue that the differences in physique are directly the cause of differences in personality – except in the general way just indicated, where social expectations and differential success and failure rates may mediate the relationship.

Sheldon's typology is not a strong theory: he was concerned to type people on the basis of careful observation, and the predictions that can be derived are not numerous.

Factor-analytic theories

Raymond Cattell (b. 1905)

Let us now turn to two psychologists who have also tried to use statistical analysis to aid the development of a personality theory. The first of these is Cattell. Cattell sees the aim of personality research as enabling us to predict what a person will do in a given situation. His investigations of personality make use of the factor-analytic technique described in Chapter 13. Cattell began by examining the names used to describe traits or characteristics of personality. He used a list of 18,000 trait names and reduced this enormous number to 160. Looking at the clustering he found by factor analysis, he reduced this number again to about 16 factors which he considered to be the major ones which underlie personality. These factors he called source traits. He claims that these source traits manifest themselves in clusters of surface traits. These are relatively unstable, and Cattell maintains that many psychologists have been misled by observation of these surface traits; he claims that only by factor analysis can we uncover the source traits which are stable and which form the basis of our personality. Figure 20.2 shows a list of these major source traits. Cattell prefers not to label them with names because he thinks this is misleading; he simply gives each a letter.

Further factor analysis of these source traits has revealed second order factors; that is, some traits are themselves correlated and can be subsumed under a more general second order category. The two most important second order traits are those called exvia-invia and anxiety. Cattell considers that these, while interesting, are not as useful for prediction of behaviour as the source traits and it is at the level of source traits that he claims useful predictions of behaviour responses can be made. Cattell emphasizes that personality traits are only some of several factors which can influence behaviour. A person's state of mind, at any given time, can

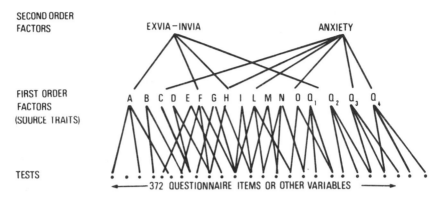

Figure 20.2 Diagram to illustrate Cattell's level of factors

also affect behaviour. For example, I may, in general, be a sociable person, but on a particular evening I may choose not to go out with friends.

Hans Jurgen Eysenck (b. 1916)

Hans Jurgen Eysenck published his first account of his model of personality in 1947. Since then, he has expanded and modified his theory several times. The basis of his theory, however, remains the same. Eysenck claims that personality can be represented on two dimensions which are uncorrelated with each other. He isolated these dimensions, labelled extraversion and neuroticism, by factor analysis. In 1952 he isolated a third dimension which he calls psychoticism.

Eysenck places his work in a historical context by pointing out the similarities between the dimensions he has found and those described by Galen and others through the centuries. Galen described four main types of personality: choleric, melancholic, sanguine and phlegmatic; and these four types have recurred at regular intervals in personality descriptions. Kretschmer, for example, made use of a typology very similar to that described above. Eysenck's attempt to type personality was not, therefore, new but it has a number of novel features. He has tried to make his theory of personality scientific: hc has used psychometrics and experimental techniques and has generated hypotheses which can be tested. The theory is new in attempting to establish dimensions on which individuals can be measured, rather than intuitively inferring a number of groups, into one of which every individual is supposed to fall.

Eysenck has also tried to make his theory a total one in that he has worked to give it validity at different levels of analysis. At the lowest level of analysis, there are specific responses or acts of behaviour; on a higher level, there are habitual responses, i.e. acts which recur under similar conditions. On a yet higher level are found traits. These are theoretical constructs which are based on correlations that have been observed at the level of habitual responses: these traits are characteristics such as rigidity and persistence. Finally, Eysenck claims there is the level of the type: this is a second order factor; for example, extraversion. In this way, knowledge of the type of a person should enable us to predict not only the general characteristics of that person, but also how they may respond in specific situations.

The foundation of Eysenck's theory of personality is a reliance on the biological basis of his dimensions. A person's location on the extraversion–introversion scale is held to be a function of the balance between the excitatory and the inhibitory processes within the cortex; while the degree of neuroticism possessed is presumed to be a function of the relative lability or excitability of the nervous system. This part of Eysenck's theory is a development of basic ideas about the relationship between physiology and behaviour postulated by Pavlov, and another Russian worker, Teplov.

Pavlov noticed that certain of his dogs were more difficult to condition than others and he suggested this was because they were more cortically inhibited. He also noticed that certain patients called hysterics were also difficult to condition, and extinguished conditioned responses quickly. Hysterics tend to be neurotic extraverts, while dystemics tend to be neurotic introverts. Eysenck verified these observations. Thus, on the neurological level certain predictions can be made and experimentally tested. Some of these predictions will be, for example, that:

1. Extraverts condition less easily than introverts (demonstrated by Franks).
2. Extraverts would show greater figural after-effects (demonstrated by Eysenck).
3. Introverts would be more difficult to sedate (shown by Shagass).
4. Drivers prone to accidents would be high on extraversion and neuroticism (shown by Shaw and Sichel).

Evidence from these sorts of experimental studies has been used by Eysenck to argue that his theory of cortical inhibition has been supported. But the link he claims between the neurological and behavioural levels is not at all clear. Other workers, for example Claridge, have suggested that the findings could be explained more simply in terms of basic differences between people in their levels of arousal.

The level of traits of behaviour is most simply measured by a questionnaire devised by Eysenck. This questionnaire will be discussed in the part of this chapter on personality assessment. Eysenck claims that his theory is useful, not only at the biological and individual levels, but also at the social level. He suggests that beliefs and attitudes can be linked to his two major dimensions. He suggests a dimension which he calls 'tough-mindedness' (someone who is practical and materialistic). This is a projection onto the field of attitudes of the characteristics of the extravert. 'Tender-mindedness' (someone who is thoughtful and idealistic) is a projection of the characteristics of an introvert. This dimension of tough/tendermindedness has been isolated, again by factor analysis, and is considered to be orthogonal to the dimension of radicalism/conservatism. According to Eysenck, someone who is a communist in beliefs is likely to be tough-minded and radical; a person who is fascist is likely to be tough-minded and conservative; while a person who is pacifist may be tender-minded and radical. Persons who have strong religious and moral beliefs tend to fall in the quadrant of tender-minded and conservative.

Evaluation:

Eysenck has extended his theory into a number of areas. He has, for example, attempted to explain criminality in terms of inadequate socialization as a result of poor conditioning. Thus, according to Eysenck's theory, criminals should be high on the extraversion and neuroticism dimensions. In fact, it has been suggested that there are two sorts of criminal: the introverted sort who condition quickly to their undesirable environments, and the extraverted sort who do not condition at all and so do not learn to obey the rules of society. The evidence for these assertions is confused. Some workers have found support for Eysenck's suggestions, but many have not.

Even the basic prediction that extraverts condition less easily than introverts has been shown to be far more complex than was originally thought. Conditioning seems to be determined, at least partially, by the intensity of the unconditioned stimulus and the sort of reinforcement schedule employed. In particular, Gray and others have argued that highly extraverted and highly neurotic individuals should be difficult to condition by a passive avoidance schedule (Gray calls this fear-conditioning), and that this is the basis of the differences found in conditioning, rather than more general differences in conditioning by all types of schedule.

There are other problems with Eysenck's theory. He has been accused of concentrating too much on extraversion and has not expanded, to any degree, the supposed biological basis of neuroticism; he has used the terms excitation and inhibition of cortical activity very loosely. Recently, these concepts have been linked with the concept of a strong or a weak nervous system (briefly, the ease with which the person can be aroused). Evidence seems to confirm that introverts have a weak nervous system and extraverts have a strong one as measured by the electroencephalogram (EEG).

A further problem for Eysenck is that the unitary nature of extraversion has been questioned. It is known that questions concerning extraversion on the Eysenck Personality Inventory (EPI) tap two factors – sociability and impulsivity. Eysenck claims that the dimension of extraversion is neverthe-less unitary, but Carrigan suggests that the two factors should be con-sidered independently. She proposes that the sociability factor may result in a well-adjusted type of person, while the impulsivity factor may result in a maladjusted type.

Problems of factor analysis

Factor-analytic approaches to personality are a welcome alternative to the abstract theorizing which has characterized many of the approaches we have described in the chapter so far. Use of this technique makes it more likely that we can derive experimental hypotheses about the theory and, by putting these to the test, we can evaluate the theory and consider possible modifications.

There are, however, many problems associated with the technique. A worker in this field has to decide whether to employ orthogonal or oblique systems of factor analysis. Analysis by orthogonal methods requires that the factors extracted are uncorrelated, or at right angles to each other. Oblique analysis allows factors which are partially correlated with each other to emerge. Cattell uses the latter method and derives several major traits. Eysenck prefers the former and, hence, arrives at his two major factors. The orthogonal method has the benefit of economy on its side; but this method can produce factors which are too gross to enable us to make any specific predictions, although Eysenck's theory has probably given rise to more testable hypotheses than any other. The oblique method can give rise to a further set of correlations between the factors that emerge. Cattell reports second order factors which, to some extent, represent the relation-ships between his original first order factors.

Methods of factor analysis can be used to test observations made by people working in the clinical setting. If the two, very diverse, methods – clinical judgement and factor analysis – agree about the major dimensions of personality, then we can be a little more confident about them. But, as we mentioned earlier, Cattell claims there is an important difference between source traits and surface traits, and it seems likely that there might be disagreement about which of these two kinds of traits the clinician is examining.

Another major difficulty with the use of factor analysis is the contention that one gets out only what has been put into it. This means that analysts have to have a theoretical basis to determine the measures they choose to consider. This is perfectly in order as long as one is aware of this: factor analysis is merely a tool for use in personality research; it cannot produce a new theory of personality 'out of the blue'.

Finally, there is the problem of labelling and identifying the factors which emerge. Cattell was unwilling to do this; certainly, once we have called Factor A, say, neuroticism, we have perhaps given it a concrete reality which does not make it readily apparent that, far from being a single, unified characteristic, it is a cluster of factors.

Nevertheless, bearing these observations in mind, it does not seem unreasonable to welcome an approach to personality theory which attempts to cut through the largely subjective element at present contained in many major theories. Certainly, factor-analytic theories such as Eysenck's have encouraged more empirical research than almost any other type of theory – and this can only be to the general good of the area.

Self theories and self-actualization

Gordon Allport (1897–1967)

Gordon Allport often argued against the main trends in personality theory. While most of the theorists have been looking for common characteristics between individuals and attempting to classify these into broad bands, Allport has maintained the idiographic viewpoint that each individual is unique and unlike any other; so far as that is literally possible. His approach relies heavily on case study as the basis for investigating and reporting personality findings.

It is often useful for an area of investigation to have its critics: personality theorists are fortunate to have had one of the good sense of Allport. Allport emphasized the self and the essential unity of an individual's personality. His approach may be useful in describing an individual's known behaviour, but it is of little use as a predictor of future behaviour in a variety of situations. One can make few generalizations, even about one individual, which will hold in all future cases. We need to be able to generalize in order to explain, and it could be argued that without this faculty, personality has no place in a science of psychology.

Carl Rogers (b. 1902)

Carl Rogers shares Allport's views about the importance of studying the individual. Rogers is primarily a therapist and, from his work with his clients, he has developed an orientation to personality which concentrates on the self. As we have seen from the descriptions of the psychoanalytic school, it is not unusual for personality theorists to begin their investigations from a clinical setting.

Carl Rogers and his followers have a view of people which differs in many ways from the other major theorists we have considered. Rogers sees people as rational and whole beings who have the greatest knowledge about their own feelings and reactions. Thus, Rogers differs from the psychoanalytic theorists who stress the degree to which a person's personality is unconscious and hidden. Rogers stresses self-knowledge as the basis of personality.

Unlike the factor-analytic theorists, Rogers emphasizes the uniqueness of the individual: his consideration is not 'in what ways are these people the same?' but 'what makes each of them different?' The major concept of Rogerian theory is the self. The self is the core of the individual. Some of the major properties of the self are that it develops from interactions with the world, that it aims for consistency, and that it can change as a result of interactions. Rogers also claims that there is a basic need for positive regard which can overshadow all other needs; there develops out of this a need for self-regard. Rogers suggests that an individual may have problems, such as neurotic disorders, if there arises a discrepancy between the experiences of others responding to her or him, and the self-concept. For example, a man may think of himself as a generous person, but he may find others responding as though he were mean. He will have to modify his self-concept or cope with what may be a distortion in the perception of others' responses.

Evaluation:

Many psychologists have welcomed Rogers' attempts to consider the totality of the individual and his positive regard for clients in therapy. Certainly it is a useful antidote to the general view that one can treat aspects of an individual without concern for a person in her or his own right.

However, as a theory of personality, the Rogerian approach has certain drawbacks. It may well be a naïve approach that uses as its basis the self-report. Can we be sure that we know ourselves as clearly as Rogers would claim? Rogers does not explain fully how the personality develops and it is again difficult to make specific predictions from this theory. Rogerian theory has had its major impact in psychotherapy. The client-centred therapeutic approach moves away from the ideas of the therapist as expert and places the emphasis on the client. Rogers has made extensive use of tape-recordings of his therapy sessions, and this has allowed others to check claims made by the therapist of success in changing the viewpoint of the client. We cannot evaluate the logic of Freud's deductions from his therapeutic sessions; we can at least make some beginning with Rogers.

Self-actualization

The term 'self-actualization' has been variously used and it is not always clear that different writers have meant the same thing by it. One source of the concept is Jung's theory of 'individuation' – approximately, the realization of oneself as a person. Another source is a theory of motivation proposed by Henry Murray, which supposes that human needs are arranged in a hierarchical system. Some, such as those for food and shelter, are more basic, and must be satisfied before those that are higher can receive attention. A. H. Maslow developed these ideas and argued that the highest need is for 'self-actualization', which involves the development of an individual's potential for those characteristics which make us most human: love and affection, aesthetic experiences, altruism. He considered that this implied a new alternative to the two main traditional approaches to psychology, behaviourism and psychoanalysis.

This has given rise to a very large number of related theories and programmes designed to increase self-awareness and self-development. At the present time any objective assessment of the value and efficacy of these is lacking.

George Kelly (b. 1905)

Cook (1984) tells us that when George Kelly first read Freud he described his reaction as 'incredulity that anyone could write such nonsense, much less publish it'. He said that psychoanalytic theory was 'only a few short steps removed from primitive notions of demoniacal possession and exorcism' (1955). The personality theory that Kelly himself advocated could not be more different from Freud's. He stresses rationality, conscious problem solving and decision making. He emphasizes the control people have over their lives; he advocates 'constructive alternativism' – 'even the most obvious occurrences of everyday life might appear utterly transformed if we were constructive enough to construe them differently'. Everyone is an amateur scientist – constructing and testing theories of the world and how it operates. There is no place for unconscious forces, nor for biology or emotions in Kelly's account. The purely rational being is described and contrasted with Freud's shambling beast. Kelly's theory acted as a forerunner to a more cognitive approach to personality which has become increasingly important in recent years.

Narrow band theories

Increasingly there is a trend towards 'narrow band' theories which simply take one aspect of personality and try to see its effects on behaviour and experience. Many aspects have been studied but perhaps one of the more interesting is what is known as the Type A Behaviour Pattern (TABP). Strictly speaking this is not a measure of personality: it is a set of characteristic behaviours and responses to situations which have been implicated in the development of coronary heart disease. Type A behaviours tend to include several of the following characteristics: competitiveness, restlessness, a strong sense of time urgency and a sense of pressing commitments or responsibilities. When faced with a problem which has resisted resolution a Type A person will redouble his efforts. It can be thought of as the White Rabbit's response – 'I'm late, I'm late, for a very important date. No time to say hello, goodbye, I'm late, I'm late, I'm late'. Several studies have found a relationship between these behaviours; in particular, the reactions to stress and pressures and the development of coronary heart disease.

Friedman and Rosenman (1974) reported on a study which has come to be known as the Western Collaborative Study. A large number of healthy men between the ages of 39 and 59 in San Francisco were examined. They were interviewed and on that basis were described as Type A or not (Type B). They found that after eight years a number had developed symptoms of coronary heart disease. More than twice as many men who had originally been described as Type A had developed coronary heart disease as those who were considered to lack Type A characteristics. Since then this finding has been substantiated several times, although there are disputes about which particular aspects of the Type A Behaviour Pattern might be especially implicated in the development of coronary heart disease and how best to measure Type A.

Studies have also focused on the role of personality in the development of other diseases. Early research by Le Shan (1959) and others described a 'cancer-prone' personality. Several characteristics were identified as being associated with the development of cancer: there was a tendency to keep in emotions – not to express them openly. This was especially the case with anger and resentment. There was also a supposed inability to form and maintain deep personal relationships. More recent prospective studies have tended to support some of these findings. Thomas and Duszynski (1974) studied 1000 medical students for nearly 15 years. They found that those who developed cancers reported less family closeness than those who did not. The explanation for these findings is via the role of stress. People with weak social support networks are likely to experience greater stress; stress lowers the immune system and that, in turn, can aid the development of cancers.

These studies, while useful when speculating on the development of particular aspects of personality and behaviour or what might change them, do not provide an all-encompassing description of a person. It may be that this rather less ambitious approach to personality may nevertheless yield more substantial and practical results than the grand theories of the past.

Personality assessment

So far in this chapter we have looked at several different approaches to personality. As you will have learned from the other chapters in this book, psychologists endeavour not only to describe behaviour, but also to

631

measure it. We want to know not just that John is aggressive, but by how much he is more aggressive than his fellows. We come now to the variety of attempts that have been made to measure personality. There are two assumptions behind these attempts: that a person's personality, once formed, can be constant across situations and time; but also, paradoxically, that it can change as a result of experience. There are at least three major ways in which we can measure personality: by questioning people directly about their feelings and behaviour, by making inferences as a result of their responses to material and by directing, observing, and measuring their behaviour.

Self report

Interviews

We conduct interviews for many different reasons but the purpose of most of them is that we are trying to understand and assess a person. Interviews form the basis of many types of therapy; by listening to and questioning people the therapist hopes to gain insight into their motivations and personality; Freud and Rogers both began with the patients' verbal report and made their inferences from it. This is largely a subjective method: it can pinpoint areas of a person's psyche which it might be fruitful to explore. However, there is a danger that interviewers may read into a person's report what they expect to find there.

Attempts have been made to make the interview less subjective and more open to public scrutiny and evaluation. Rogers tape-records many of his therapy sessions, so that the basis of his conclusions can be examined by others. Another frequently used method is a content analysis of the verbal report. The core of this method is that one constructs categories and counts the amount of verbal behaviour which falls into each. One might look, for example, for the expression of defence mechanisms or of conflict in a person's report. Changes in the structure of the content analysis over a number of sessions can be used to check against a therapist's reports on the progress of the individual. The therapist may report that the person is feeling less hostile as the therapy sessions progress; the expression of hostility, as measured by the content analysis, should also decrease. If this is the case then there would seem to be some basis for the therapist's claim.

Even a relatively structured interview is subject to bias. People may report their feelings in a way that they think the therapist will approve. There is also no guarantee that a reduction in the expression of hositility within the interview is an indication of a general reduction of hostility in a person moving from situation to situation. Aspects of non-verbal behaviour evidenced during an interview can be clues to personality.

Type A People are known to speak more rapidly, to pause less frequently and to interrupt more often than Type Bs.

A major way in which psychologists have tried to measure personality is by the use of paper and pencil tests. These have the advantage that, while relying still on the person's report, they are quicker to administer than an interview and they are less open to accusation of bias. It is possible to administer the same test to a person at different times and check whether the responses are similar on all occasions. To re-run an interview is more difficult.

Questionnaires

The most widely used of all questionnaires is probably the Minnesota Multiphasic Personality Inventory (abbreviated to MMPI). This test was devised in 1942 to discriminate between different types of patients in a psychiatric unit; it is now widely used in a variety of settings. The test has 550 questions, to which a person is asked to respond 'true', 'false', or 'cannot say'. These questions fall into nine clinical scales which are shown in Table 20.1.

Table 20.1 Clinical scales of the MMPI

Psychiatric disorder	Manifestation
1. Hypochondriasis (Hs)	Concerned about physical functions
2. Depression (D)	Depressed, dejected
3. Hysteria (Hy)	Unrealistic, insecure
4. Psychopathic deviate (Pd)	Irresponsible, egocentric
5. Masculinity-femininity (Mf)	Degree of gender identification
6. Paranoia (Pa)	Aggressive, sensitive to criticism
7. Psychasthenia (Pt)	Insecure, apprehensive
8. Schizophrenia (Sc)	Withdrawn, oversensitive
9. Hypomania (Hm)	Impulsivity, excessive activity

A problem with these scales is that they are based on traditional diagnostic categories which have, to some extent, been abandoned in recent years. The scales are not independent of each other in the way one would require for orthogonal factor analysis, and this may also be a problem. Nevertheless, the devising of the MMPI was a step forward in the objective testing of personality.

Other widely used paper and pencil tests of personality are those devised by Cattell and Eysenck. Cattell's 16PF Questionnaire is a direct test of his 16 factors (source traits) of personality that have been described above. The Eysenck Personality Questionnaire (EPQ) is an attempt to measure the three major factors which he claims underlie personality – neuroticism, extraversion and psychoticism. This is a comparatively short questionnaire.

People are asked to respond 'Yes', or 'No' to questions such as 'Do you like to go to parties?' 'Are you impulsive?' From responses to the questionnaire people can be scored for neuroticism, extraversion and psychoticism. Eysenck has paid particular attention to the reliability and validity of his questionnaire and it is widely used, especially in experimental settings.

A major problem with personality questionnaires is that subjects may try to 'fake good'; that is, they may try to fill in the questionnaire in such a way as to give the most favourable impression of themselves. Some questionnaires, such as the EPQ, try to overcome this problem by introducing into the questionnaire certain questions which will show this response bias if it is operating; but this works only to a limited extent.

In spite of these drawbacks, the questionnaire method of assessing personality seems to be one of the most successful and appropriate. It is increasingly used and is often supported by other techniques in order to gain as accurate a picture as possible of an individual's personality.

Other types of self report

A rather less limiting test of personality than the questionnaire has been developed by Stephenson. It is called the Q-sort technique. A person is presented with a large number of statements of the sort 'I am an anxious person'. He is asked to sort these into a number of piles according to how well he thinks each statement reflects his self-concept. The examiner can then build up a picture of the individual. Alternatively, the person may be asked to sort the statements in such a way that they reflect how they would like to be. Thus, the examiner can compare how a person sees himself with his ideal-self. This technique makes use of Rogers's approach to personality which sees the self as a central construct. A therapist could see from this technique whether therapy was leading to a closer relationship between a person's self-concept and their ideal-self.

You will remember that the EPQ had a sub-scale incorporated into it to counteract the possibility of a person 'faking good'. The Q-sort has no such scale; the examiner is forced to assume that the responder is not influenced in the sorting by what s/he thinks is desirable. The examiner also has to place complete reliance on what the people know of themselves.

Another test which faces similar problems to those encountered by Stephenson's Q-sort is Kelly's Role Construct Repertory Grid. This test has been constructed from Kelly's Personal Construct Theory. Kelly sees people as being in many ways like scientists. They develop constructs which enable them to predict and interact with the world. The Repertory Grid test is designed to elicit these constructs. A person is given a list of a number of roles, for example, teacher, employer, friend. S/he is asked to list people who fulfil these roles. The names of these people are then presented in threes to the person who is asked to indicate how two of the three are similar and the third one different. For example, s/he may say that two of them are generous while the third is mean. Gradually a matrix can be built up by this process and examination of this matrix may indicate which dimensions are important to that person.

This technique is designed to inquire into the way a person sees the world. The test is useful as a preliminary investigation of personality, but it has only very limited predictive power and suffers from one of the problems we have mentioned before, that of interpretation; it offers very few clues as to why people see the world as they do.

Projective techniques

Side by side with the attempts just described to standardize and to make objective the assessment of personality there is another approach. Some psychologists see a questionnaire as too limiting: they do not seek to impose their organization of personality on others. They have tended to use much less restrictive methods of assessment.

Word association tests

These tests have a long history in psychology. The psychologist presents a word and asks the subject to respond with the first word thought of. It is hoped that an analysis of the sorts of responses and response times given to this task will lend insight into the primary concerns and desires of the person being tested.

Ambiguous stimuli tests

There are other, more refined tests which share the rationale just described. In these tests, the emphasis is on finding stimuli that are ambiguous and that have few clues to the subject of how to respond. It is hoped that in this ambiguous setting subjects will reveal their concerns. The most famous test of this type is the Rorschach ink-blots test. This was devised in 1921 by a Swiss psychiatrist, Hermann Rorschach. He chose ten ink-blots from a large number which he generated. People are asked to tell the examiner what they see in each ink-blot. When they have responded in this way to all ten ink-blots the examiner then questions the subject about the interpretations to try to elucidate what determined the responses. Originally the ink-blot test was used as an aid to diagnosis in psychotherapy. The usual responses to the ink-blots were established and unusual responses were examined for clues to the person's state of mind. The Rorschach test assumes that much of the response is determined by unconscious processes; that people will project their feelings into the ink-blot. Therefore it is supposed that this technique will give valuable insights which would not be found by direct interviewing or by a standard paper and pencil test.

Another frequently used projective test is the Thematic Apperception test (TAT) which was developed by Morgan and Murray in 1935. This test comprises 30 pictures which are highly ambiguous; the subject is asked to tell a story around each picture. Again, there is no correct or incorrect answer to this test and so the subjects have very few clues to guide the stories that they make up. The examiner can record the time taken to begin to tell the story, s/he can also look for themes which recur within the stories. Major themes that are frequently studied by this test are, for example, to what degree the stories told indicate a motivation for achievement, a desire for affiliation, or a fear of failure.

The TAT, like the Rorschach test, suffers from problems of validity and accuracy of interpretation. The examiner may have expectations about the sort of themes which could be contained in the stories and this may bias the interpretations. Many studies have shown that training examiners to recognize indicators of themes has not led to great agreement between them in interpreting the stories.

It is clear, then, that the advantages of projective techniques – their flexibility and the provision for freedom of expression – lead directly to several major disadvantages. The tests are difficult to score, and the scores themselves need careful interpretation. Precisely what does the frequent appearance of a theme in the stories tell us about a person's personality? Projective techniques can be useful, then, but their drawbacks have led many workers to search for other methods of personality assessment.

Direct observation

If we wish to know how people behave why do we not simply observe them? Occasionally, we do, but the observation can never be total; personal privacy does not permit that. Instead, we can sample some part of a person's behaviour. During a period of time we can count how much of a particular sort of behaviour is occurring, for example, how many times a child behaves aggressively in the playground. This can be very useful: the psychologist could use conditioning schedules to try to reduce the amount of aggression the child displays; direct observation scores could indicate how successful the schedule has been. However, this does not really explain the behaviour that is measured. The psychologist is still at the stage of observation and description. We can, however, use how a person behaves in a specific situation as an indicator of the personality and this is discussed below.

Behaviour tests

There are numerous laboratory situations which are used to distinguish between different types of personality. Some of them will be discussed here to give a flavour of the sort of work that is done.

The rod and frame test

Subjects in a laboratory are asked to adjust a rod which is in a tilted frame. The apparatus is in a darkened room and so subjects have no clues to what is the true horizontal or vertical. This test is designed to measure field dependency. This concept was suggested by Witkin in the 1940s. Field dependency is the degree to which people are influenced by the situation which surrounds them. In the laboratory it could be clues about the perceptual field, in the social setting it might be the attitudes of the people they are interacting with. Thus performance on the rod and frame test may give valuable insight into a person's more general behaviour patterns.

The embedded figures test

This task is also designed to measure field dependency. A person is shown a figure and then asked to find it in a larger and more complicated design. Again, it is possible to tell from performance on this task whether s/he is greatly or only slightly influenced by the surroundings.

These tests are very useful: they are objective, and it is possible to check their reliability by retesting the subjects and the findings suggest that these characteristics of field dependency endure for a long time in a person's life.

The lemon drop test

Eysenck and his followers used a large number of experimental tests to discriminate between extraverts and introverts. Some of these have already been mentioned in the discussion of his theory. A test not previously discussed is the lemon drop test. Introverts have a greater state of cortical arousal than extraverts; they react more strongly to sensory stimulation. If a standard number of drops of lemon juice are placed on subjects' tongues they will tend to salivate much more if introvert than if extravert.

Figural after-effects

It can also be predicted from Eysenck's theory of personality that highly extraverted people will develop figural after-effects more rapidly and more strongly than will introverts. This has been found to be the case, and so the test will successfully discriminate between the two personality types.

We have seen here that experimental tests can successfully be used to measure personality. These sorts of investigations enable psychologists to record results in an objective and unambiguous manner, and the conclusions drawn from the tests can be re-examined to determine their generality. It seems probable that future work in the area of personality research will make greater use of these techniques.

Conclusions

This has been a very brief overview of some of the major aspects of personality theory and personality assessment. Historically personality has been a major area of psychology; ideas and approaches which have developed in personality are now used more generally, practical applications of theory can be found in the areas of clinical and occupational psychology. Nevertheless there is sometimes a feeling of frustration and lack of direction when studying personality. Theories come and go and today's 'hot' topic can rapidly become yesterday's fad. Meehl (1978) generates 20 reasons for the slow progress of what he calls 'soft' psychology; Kline (1983) complains that research funding for personality is now difficult to find. But the problems which personality theorists confront still remain. Psychologists will continue to search for answers to these questions, it remains to be seen whether current directions in personality theory will usefully guide this search.

Further reading

Cook, M. (1984) *Levels of Personality*. Holt, Reinhart and Winston.
Kline, P. (1983) *Personality: Measurement and theory*. Batsford.
Hampson, S. E. (1983) *The Construction of Personality*. Methuen.
Perrin, L. A. (1984) *Personality*. Wiley.

Chapter twenty-one

Abnormal psychology

Philip Evans

Who's who?

You are at a social gathering of some sort and somebody approaches you with the usual question: 'And what do you do?' You reply (if you are, as yet, inexperienced in matters of convenient untruths): 'Well, actually, I'm a psychologist.' Immediately you will be assumed an expert in all things concerned with bizarre behaviour, funny experiences, and, of course, nervous breakdowns. In short, you are taken to be an expert in *abnormal psychology*. The reason why this specialization within psychology should become synonymous with psychology as a whole on the part of a majority of the lay public is not hard to glean. For a start, there are many superficially similar words in existence: psychologist, psychiatrist, psycho-analyst, psychotherapist, and so on. Little wonder that this creates some confusion.

It would be true to say that the last three persons mentioned are always in some way concerned with the 'abnormal'; so are *certain* psychologists; those who have made it their academic interest for teaching and research; and more narrowly those *clinical* psychologists, who have taken a specific post-graduate training to enable them to work professionally in the applied field, dealing amongst others with the 'mentally ill' – a concept which we shall have to explore the meaning of a little later. First the reader should carefully examine the definitions below, which will clarify the 'job specifications' of those confusing people whose professional titles share the same five initial letters.

Psychiatrist: A qualified medical practitioner who has subsequently undergone training in what is termed 'psychological medicine'. The psychiatrist may undertake a diagnostic and therapeutic role, or may refer patients to a clinical psychologist or psychotherapist. In any event, the psychiatrist usually fulfils the global role of being medically responsible for a 'patient'.

Clinical psychologist: A qualified psychologist who has subsequently specialized and undergone professional training in the discipline of clinical psychology which involves the diagnosis and psychological treatment of mentally ill patients. The other therapeutic role does not include the prescribing of physical treatments, unlike the psychiatrist. As psychological treatments have become more diverse and, arguably, more powerful, so the therapeutic role of the clinical psychologist has grown. It is usual to find the clinical psychologist 'eclectic' in approach to therapy, with perhaps a bias towards the use of behavioural therapy. This is in contrast to the psychoanalyst.

Psychoanalyst: Strictly speaking, a therapist who more or less rigidly follows the method of psychological treatment devised by Sigmund Freud during the first thirty or so years of this century. The term is sometimes expanded to include practitioners of allied methods of therapy: analytic psychologists – followers of Carl Jung; individual psychologists – followers of Alfred Adler; and a host of post-Freudian and neo-Freudian schools of therapists. Most but not all psychoanalysts are also medically trained and are also psychiatrists. Because of the time-intensive nature of this kind of treatment – and, some would say, because of its limited applicability and difficulties in defining and assessing efficacy – it tends to be practised privately.

Psychotherapist: An umbrella term to describe anyone who undertakes the psychological treatment of patients, or 'clients' – a sometimes preferred term, which does not have medical overtones.

Who's ill?

We have now dealt sufficiently with the overlapping array of authority figures – the professionals. In search of their diverse talents come the so-called mentally ill. What are we to make of such a label?

Throughout history, and across societies, there have always been people who have been singled out by the rest of the community as odd, because of their behaviour. The term 'abnormal psychology' therefore, in its strictest sense, presents us with no problems. If a piece of behaviour is odd or abnormal in the statistical sense it can be justifiably studied under the rubric of abnormal psychology whether the behaviour in question be an incoherent and apparently meaningless flow of verbiage from a hitherto normally-speaking adult or a coherent and meaningful flow of musical compositions from a four-year-old child prodigy. Abnormal, in essence, should be a neutral non-evaluative adjective in terms of its application. It is equally clear that the adjectival phrase 'mentally ill' is not. Quite clearly there is the implication that something is 'wrong' with the mentally ill. The trouble is that the term 'illness', borrowed from the field of medicine to describe physical suffering and physical damage, or something capable of producing suffering or damage, loses a lot of its exactitude when prefixed by 'mental'. Treating physical and mental illness in this kind of parallel fashion would not be so bad if the resulting confusions did not often raise serious moral questions. Let us examine some of these.

A physically ill person is usually in a position to admit he is suffering and in need of treatment. Moreover, the doctor can usually point to something which can be identified as a cause. (This can be an over-simplification but we cannot explore every avenue of argument.) People who are often, and perhaps conveniently, labelled mentally ill by a society do not always subscribe to the view that they are suffering from an illness; still less would they agree that they are in need of treatment; still less can any doctor point to a simple cause. The moral issues are easily highlighted by example. In the Soviet Union perfectly sane (by Western criteria) dissidents have (until very recently at least) been labelled mentally ill and delivered into the hands of Soviet psychiatrists. Closer to home, it has, until quite recently, been common practice to commit homosexual men and women for treatment as mentally ill, despite the lack of any evidence to show any abnormality other than a different, but by no means rare, sexual orientation. The truly abnormal willingness of some homosexuals to undergo such procedures is, of course, amply explained by their living at odds with a traditionally 'homophobic' society.

The examples I have used are, of course, the easy ones, much used by other writers (see Szasz, 1970) who are antipathetic to the term mental illness.

Is the remaining area of psychiatry meaningfully covered by the term mental illness? Let us take a very common and less controversial mental illness: depression. However much one is concerned with definitions and exact use of terms and their moral implications, it is sobering occasionally to conjure up pictures of real people. Anyone who has worked in psychiatric establishments will have seen the real suffering, anguish, and despair of the truly depressed patient. Moreover, s/he will have felt a primary duty to help this patient, and the question whether the patient is really ill will not readily intrude on the performance of that perceived duty. However, it is possible to ask oneself afterwards what aid it has been to have called that condition an illness. Moreover, one can also perhaps see the dangers in labelling psychological mood-states in terms of illness. People who may be sad, very sad, for good reason become, with the wave of a verbal wand, victims of depression. People who are justifiably anxious in their day-to-day lives become sufferers from neurosis. And the trouble with such conceptual transformations is that they can be positively harmful in directing attention away from genuine causes of suffering requiring social and, perhaps, ultimately, political attention towards a vague and ghostly inner cause, which may be a mere convenient fiction. This really is the source of disagreement between those who advocate a so-called medical model (many psychiatrists, for obvious reasons) and those who do not (an increasing number of clinical psychologists whose training has emphasized the importance of social learning in the development of normal and abnormal behaviour). However, it is important to turn the above argument round and admit the possibility that in certain cases it may be equally frustrating to divert attention away from possible causes of a physical nature. To make an extreme point, one would not appreciate a mis-diagnosis where a psychological confusional state, caused in reality by the consumption of toxic substances, has been interpreted in the light of a disturbed childhood. Equally, it is a plausible hypothesis to see certain forms of very severe and irrational depression as being caused by a biological predisposition to toxicate one's own brain periodically.

What, then, do we conclude from this argument? The term 'illness' cannot be said to be either rightly or wrongly applied in this area in any general sense. Undoubtedly, as our knowledge progresses certain 'conditions' or 'disorders' will be able unambiguously to be called illnesses; equally, others will not. The term 'mental illness' is, therefore, not a particularly helpful all-round term. Do we, then, for the present, do away with all the well-known labels of psychiatry – schizophrenia, neurosis – along with their less well-known subdivisions and types? I think not. It is wrong to confuse the question of illness labels with the question of classification. Classification can, and should, be a neutral term, just as it is for the psychologist interested in classifying 'normal' personality types, response strategies, or whatever. Every science must go beyond the individual case in order to find some order before further work can be done. One could draw a parallel with botany and the pioneering work of Linnaeus, whose contribution was primarily a classificatory one. If we forget about illness as such, and simply ask ourselves how we can understand and help people with manifest psychological problems, it is surely helpful if we can discover some order in such problems. One does not have to be one hundred per cent committed to the medical model in order to appreciate that words like 'symptom' and 'syndrome', traditionally medical words, can have a sort of classificatory value even when we are not sure about the 'illness status' of the condition we are describing.

The classification of 'disorders'

Organic syndromes and the psychoses

Let us then look at a traditional type of classification in the field of psychiatric disorders. We could begin, closest to the field of medicine in general, with those disorders which, despite their observed pathology in terms of intellectual and emotional functioning, are clearly related to physical factors: mental retardation, and organic brain syndromes. The latter can encompass a wide variety of conditions: bizarre behaviour resulting from specific traumatic injuries to parts of the brain, damage to the brain as a result of acute or chronic poisoning (e.g. alcoholic), and last, but not least, chronic deterioration of mental functioning as a result of arteriosclerosis and other problems affecting the brain of the aged which accounts for many of the so-called *senile dementias*. In addition, there is a host of rarer specific syndromes leading to mental and physical deterioration, e.g. Huntington's chorea which is genetically transmitted. Some of these disorders are qualified by the adjective *psychotic*, which is really only a kind of shorthand way of saying that the disorder is characterized by very severe impairment of mental functioning, impairment of language, perception, and memory processes, as well as emotional dysfunction. We shall continue to use the term 'psychotic' (and later 'neurotic') because they still have very general currency but it is worth pointing out that they no longer figure in the most recent classification scheme devised by American psychiatrists.

Non-organic psychoses

Not all psychotic behaviour can be so readily attributed to physical factors, and this brings us to our next category of psychiatric disorder: psychoses not directly attributable to physical causes. By far the biggest subcategory here is *schizophrenia*. The schizophrenic is the layman's traditional idea of a madman, the lunatic: this is the patient who thinks he is God, or Christ, Napoleon, or a computer, and he can weave a more or less coherent *modus vivendi* around such a *delusion* – he has, in other words, a delusional system. We shall look at schizophrenia in a little more detail after our survey of psychiatric disorders in general and we shall find that not all schizophrenics have such a florid delusional system. At present it suffices to point out that the schizophrenic does not suffer from a split personality, as is so often assumed – a disintegrated personality is nearer the mark.

The other major psychosis within this category has been variously termed: manic-depressive psychosis or psychotic affective disorder. As those names suggest, the disorder is characterized by very severe mood swings, which periodically affect the patient for no apparent reason. The clearest cases involve a cycle from abnormally elevated mood (*mania*) proceeding down through normality to a deep depression, where the patient lies in bed, for perhaps weeks at a time, completely unresponsive to other people or to his own needs. However, not all cases are so simple, and the cycle may, for example, miss out mania entirely and consist simply of periodic bouts of severe and inexplicable depression.

It will have struck the reader that, although at present these disorders are not clearly related to organic causes and are, hence, not categorized as such, they nevertheless do not seem readily explicable in terms of learning or psychological experiences – they seem too bizarre and unrelated to life events. For this reason, many are of the opinion that the eventual causes (and remedies) will come from traditional medical and biologically-slanted research. The psychologist's present role in therapy has more to do with management than cure (though in the case of schizophrenia there has been a vocal minority opinion, represented for example in the writings of R. D. Laing, that schizophrenia can be seen as a psychological adjustment to an existence felt to be truly terrifying and self-destroying. This view is still most easily assimilated by the reader through the pages of Laing's early book *The Divided Self*).

Neurotic disorders

The psychologist's major theoretical contribution comes in our understanding of the next traditional category of disorders known as the neuroses. Unlike psychotic patients, neurotic ones are not grossly out of touch with reality. By and large, they live their lives much as everyone else but with an awful, handicapping sense of anxiety which sometimes becomes too much, so that the patient is forced temporarily to opt out and seek help – the only meaning that can really be given to the confusing term, nervous breakdown. Some neurotics have more specific symptoms, unlike the general anxiety neurotic just described. For example, phobic patients are even more like normal people, except that they have some object or situation which, when encountered, fills them with absolute terror. They may be so incapacitated by having to avoid the source of their phobia that they are forced to seek treatment. Yet another, and rarer, form of neurosis involves the patient in a compulsion to engage in senseless rituals, such as washing one's hands a hundred times a day, counting every advertisement hoarding on the way to work and so on. Such behaviour may strike the reader as so odd as to justify the term psychotic. However, unlike the psychotic type of patient, the obsessional neurotic has complete insight into his behaviour – he is the first to admit that it is crazy. Since anxiety enters the picture in some way in all neuroses, and since the conditioning of anxiety responses is something the trained psychologist can claim to know something about, it is not surprising, as I have just said, that psychology has increased our understanding of the nature and treatment of these disorders.

There is, however, one particular neurotic disorder, where it is sometimes claimed that anxiety (or at least conscious anxiety) does not enter the picture. The patients are so-called *conversion hysterics*, much treated in the early years by Freud. The patient develops a physical symptom such as a paralysed arm (or even blindness) and yet, there is no physical damage to account for the symptom and, indeed, before Freud's time, these patients were officially classified as malingerers. Freud's own view was that the symptom had symbolic meaning and could be traced back to some forgotten source of trauma. Anxiety becomes too intense to be felt consciously and is repressed, eventually finding indirect expression in some meaningful physical symptom. Other than complaints about the symptom, the patient seems totally carefree, showing what the text-books refer to as *la belle indifférence*. It is, however, questionable whether more than a few patients really exhibit such happy indifference. A learning theory of conversion symptoms would probably simply point to the possibility of their being learnt because of some reinforcement value (after all, many internal responses, felt previously to be involuntary, are now known to be susceptible to shaping by reinforcement – see Chapter 8). However, Freud writes very eloquently and the reader could do no better than consult Freud's original writings – perhaps the intriguing case of Fräulein Anna O. – to consider the possibility that a symptom may be learnt because it has meaning for the individual at an unconscious level.

Usually categorized alongside the neuroses is depression. Sometimes one speaks of *reactive* depression to contrast this with the psychotic depressions already mentioned. Reactive implies that the depression can be linked to life events, even though it may since have developed its own momentum leaving the patient depressed in the absence of good reason. Depression which does not seem to relate to any circumstances, such as psychotic depression, is referred to as endogenous, suggesting an inner cause.

Psychosomatic disorders

Related to anxiety and stress, but usually categorized separately, are the psychosomatic or psychophysiological disorders. Unlike hysterical conversion symptoms, these disorders are real physical disorders with manifest pathology: an ulcer, a skin rash, an attack of asthma are all physical and sometimes very dangerous symptoms. The term psychosomatic merely emphasizes that psychological factors, such as exposure to stress, are heavily implicated in the onset of such symptoms. Of course, since most illnesses can be said to be multi-determined (being in the presence of a flu virus is not sufficient to catch flu) we now talk of nearly all illnesses having a psychosomatic component.

When someone makes a move, of which we don't approve ...

To end our survey of types of disorder we move on to a rather dust-bin type of class, sometimes not very aptly called personality disorders or character disorders. This is also the area where ethical considerations, which we noted earlier, occur. Soviet dissidents and homosexuals would have been placed here; so would any person who is an embarrassment to his society rather than himself – Jews in Nazi Germany were taken to be hopeless cases of flawed characters and there were professors of psychiatry who argued the case in favour of the Third Reich. That said, there are undoubted examples of the need to have some sort of category for a psychopathic murderer (psychopathy: a deeply anti-social personality, incapable of feeling guilt, shows no evidence of learning pro-social behaviour through exposure to society's normal sanctions, and, on these and other criteria, can usually be differentiated from the ordinary criminal) or for someone who actively seeks sexual intercourse with six-year-old children (paedophile), or someone who is quietly killing himself with injections of heroin or slugs of whisky or meths (addict).

We need no longer, I think, dwell on the immense difficulties of making hard and fast rules about who to commit to care under the auspices of this label: marijuana users but not tobacco users? the cocaine sniffer but not the obese? The psychologist has, probably sensibly, devoted more of his time to studying obesity and smoking behaviour than 'character' disorders.

If this were a text devoted exclusively to abnormal psychology it would be time now to begin chapters in detail on all the separate disorders which have been outlined. In these limited pages, that is not possible. Therefore, the best approach is perhaps to consider just one or two topics in further detail, giving the reader some introduction to the methods that psychologists and allied workers use in both the investigation and treatment of various symptoms. The reader who wishes to go beyond a simple introduction can consult one of the many textbooks given over exclusively to abnormal psychology, e.g. *Abnormal Psychology – An experimental-clinical approach* by Davison and Neale (1990).

More about schizophrenia, and something about research

Schizophrenia is a good topic with which to begin; and it is so for several reasons. First, it is by far the most common severe mental disorder affecting adults. The majority of the in-patients of a psychiatric hospital are likely to be diagnosed as schizophrenic. Hence research into finding the aetiology (essentially, the main causative factors) of schizophrenia and, it is hoped, a remedy is a formidable enterprise. Secondly, the problems that arise in attempting to do research are legion and also highlight methodological difficulties which can be generalized to other areas within the field of abnormal psychology.

Problems are first encountered when we try to give a strict definition of schizophrenia. A typical attempt at a definition would have to point out that schizophrenia is a *generic* name for a group of disorders characterized by a disintegration of emotional stability and judgement involving contact with, and appreciation of, reality. This in turn produces considerable impairment of personal relationships and intellectual functions.

Now, in the case of a florid schizophrenia we may be presented with a picture of someone very clearly 'out of contact with reality' and so on, since he is suffering, perhaps, from delusions of the kind we have already mentioned earlier in the chapter, and perhaps also, he may appear to be hearing and answering to non-existent voices (auditory hallucinations). But what if the patient shows no such florid symptoms but just seems to have withdrawn into a world of his own, showing no interest in anything outside himself? He may show a few eccentric mannerisms, but that is all. How do we diagnose this case? The answer is unfortunately that some psychiatrists would say that this was still a case of schizophrenia, while others would not. The symptom of withdrawal in the presence of a few eccentricities is far more likely to be diagnosed schizophrenia in the United States than in Britain, although attempts are increasingly being made to 'bridge' such gaps in diagnostic arguments.

Traditionally, psychiatrists have felt able to distinguish sub-categories of schizophrenia each with certain distinguishing features. In 'catatonic' schizophrenia, for example, an individual will typically alternate between periods of wild manic excitement and complete immobility, maintaining perhaps some bizarre posture for a long period of time. These symptoms are less common than they used to be, since early drug treatment seems particularly successful in preventing at least the motor aspects of catatonic reactions. More common is 'paranoid' schizophrenia in which delusions and sometimes hallucinations centre on persecutory and grandiose themes. The patient may believe that he is really an important figure, who has been cheated out of recognition by a conspiracy, and who is therefore in danger from those who seek to keep him silent. He may over-hear voices whispering about him or believe that messages are being beamed through the television set or that his house is bugged by the CIA. A final category of schizophrenia is termed 'hebephrenic' and is characterized by the most disorganized behaviour. Here delusions and hallucinations tend to have less coherence, behaviour is often silly and child-like, emotional expressions may be totally at variance with context; the patient may exhibit apparently meaningless rituals, invent new private words ('neologisms') and altogether appear to be in an incoherent world of their own.

Such pen portraits may help the reader to form some more concrete picture of what is implied by the use of the label 'schizophrenia'; they have not, however, done much over the many years to bring that reliability of 'diagnosis' which should be the first requirement of those who, in this field, would wish to pursue a medical model.

Unreliabiltiy of diagnosis has, of course, disastrous implications for carrying out thorough research. Let us illustrate this by the following example. Suppose a researcher is interested in showing that schizophrenia has a substantial genetic component and that heredity is largely responsible for the transmission of the 'disease'. A powerful technique of investigation is to look at identical and non-identical twins and establish concordance rates for them. If, for example, you had ten pairs of identical twins where one twin was schizophrenic, you would go on to investigate the status of the other twin, and you may find that in seven out of ten cases the other twin was also schizophrenic, thus giving a 70 per cent concordance rate. Now, suppose you have done this for a sample of identical and non-identical twins and you now have two figures for concordance. If the figure for identical twins is substantially higher than that for non-identical twins which we will assume is, in turn, higher than for ordinary siblings, then we have presumptive evidence of a genetic factor; and if the absolute figure is itself high then we have evidence of a substantial genetic factor. Needless to say, such research has been carried out by many researchers in many countries. One of the earlier North American studies obtained monozygotic (identical twin) concordance rates of between 69 and 86 per cent – very high compared with dizygotic (non-identical twin) rates of only 10 to 15 per cent. This, of course, appears to be presumptive evidence for a strong and significant genetic factor in schizophrenia. However, later Scandinavian research (admittedly on smaller samples) puts concordance rates for both kinds of twins below six per cent! Gottesman and Shields (1972) come somewhere in between, confirming the American work in terms of a big difference between identical and non-identical twin studies, but putting the concordance rate for monozygotic pairs somewhat lower, at around 40 per cent. There can be no question that inadequately agreed criteria for diagnosis is the single most important factor accounting for such discrepancies.

Rosenhan (1973) created a storm in psychological and psychiatric circles by publishing an article in *Science* magazine entitled 'On being sane in an insane place'. The import of the article was, quite simply, to shock people into considering the vagaries of diagnosis in schizophrenia. He sent members of his research team into psychiatric hospitals and instructed them to fabricate just one symptom: that they heard voices. Any other questions about their current psychological state or their family history were to be answered honestly. After being diagnosed as schizophrenic and admitted to hospital the pseudo-patients had instructions to drop the faked symptom and behave totally normally. Rosenhan describes how this was all to no avail and that even quite normal activity on the part of the pseudo-patient (taking notes about what was happening) was reported by the nursing staff as evidence of abnormality. Only certain fellow-inmates gave evidence of having certain suspicions. Rosenhan's study has since been exposed to some criticism, but it had its intended effect of raising severe doubts about the use of schizophrenia as a diagnostic label.

Despite diagnostic difficulties research carries on, as indeed it should; and most researchers try to make sure that at least the sample of schizophrenics they use is reasonably homogeneous, i.e. similar in type to one another so that any conclusions reached may, hopefully, be generalized to similar types in the population. But further difficulties can then arise. Let us take another line of research to serve as an example in this respect.

There has been much speculation that schizophrenia and its attendant psychological symptoms are primarily the result of the faulty operation of certain brain chemicals, with perhaps the propensity for such faulty operation being genetically programmed. Thus, a search has been under way for many years to isolate offending substances and a long list of candidates have gone in and out of fashion; adrenalin, and related compounds, taraxein, and currently, dopamine. Many years ago now, some researchers thought they had solved the enigma of schizophrenia by discovering a simple, but apparently inexplicable, deficiency in iodine compounds; it remained inexplicable and fascinating just as long as it took to discover further that the hospital salt was bought cheaply and lacked the usual iodine nutrients. Control for diet in such studies now goes without saying. However, the difficulty of determining whether any finding is truly causative rather than a result of anything to do with background and life-style, including diet, can be a formidable difficulty.

Psychologists have tried to tell us more about the schizophrenic by studying his cognitive behaviour. Has the schizophrenic got some sort of specific memory deficit? Does he have difficulty storing, coding, or retrieving information? Does he have difficulty filtering irrelevant input from relevant, and, if he does, is this because he is perhaps chronically under-aroused or over-aroused? Models are constructed, and the psychologist goes about testing the models by giving batteries of cognitive tasks to do. Now, although much useful work has been done in this area, interpretation is often difficult because schizophrenics are usually receiving very powerful medication in the form of drugs known as the major tranquillizers, notably chlorpromazine, and the effects of these drugs is confounded with the schizophrenia under investigation. Attempts to get round this difficulty present other problems: for example, the simple solution of taking patients off their drugs a week or so before the research, as well as raising ethical questions if the drug seems to be controlling the schizophrenia fairly well, may be useless if the schizophrenic is thereby made incapable of concentrating on the relevant task.

So is there any reasonable methodology which is problem-free? The answer is certainly no, but that is, arguably, what research is all about, and, in all the above areas of research, good work has been done and is being done, simply because the researcher is aware of the type of problems we have outlined. Perhaps we should end this discussion of schizophrenia by outlining what might seem to be a common sense research project. You may say that, since we have no complete evidence that the causes of schizophrenia are biologically based, and because the very existence of some identical twins who are discordant shows that any genetic factor must have to interact with the environment to determine schizophrenia, we should therefore look very carefully at the past histories and present environments of all the schizophrenics we can lay our hands on. Why not simply gather all the information we can, and perhaps we may come up with the vital missing ingredient?

The answer is that this has been done by many people across many years. A lot of the resulting work has also run into the last of the methodological problems that I want to mention. Such work has for the most part been retrospective: such information as has been got has been acquired after the person in question has been diagnosed as schizophrenic. Now, the trouble with retrospective information is that it is notoriously unreliable, especially if it is 'family history' sort of information got from relatives and friends of the patient, who are quite understandably influenced in their response by the current situation of the patient. Not only that; the researcher himself may want to discover certain patterns in the background of the schizophrenic and thus unconsciously bias his research. It would be much better all round if the information could be acquired and documented before the person became schizophrenic, but the problem here is one of numbers: how many people do you have to collect masses of information from over many years before you get enough records of people who later become schizophrenic? This kind of longitudinal research – following up your subjects over a period of time – is extremely expensive and time-consuming. However, Scandinavian researchers, led by Mednick, have engaged in just such an enterprise but have got round the problem of prohibitive numbers by adopting a so-called 'high-risk group' methodology. Mednick and his colleagues chose to study limited samples of children over many years and included the key sample of children with schizophrenic mothers, who were deemed, therefore, to be high-risk for schizophrenia. The high-risk group has since divided itself into those showing signs of disturbance and those not, and Mednick *et al* (1981) have reported on a number of variables which differentiate them: parental separation, birth complications, early onset of schizophrenia in the mother, autonomic responsivity. Interestingly, the predictor variables seem different for boys and girls.

We have deliberately approached this outline of schizophrenia with the aim, not of giving a potted portrait of schizophrenics, but of showing what kinds of questions have been raised by those interested in finding out more about its nature and origin; in particular, we have tried to show the pervasive difficulties that the genuine researcher will always encounter. For the reader to appreciate those difficulties is of very general value.

More about neurosis, and something about behavioural therapy

If psychologists have been able to offer little in the way of a cure for schizophrenia as yet, they have managed to make therapeutic inroads with respect to certain disorders. Before the 1960s the psychological therapies given to neurotic patients tended all to be based, sometimes strictly, sometimes not so strictly, on the psychoanalytic method developed by Sigmund Freud. Unfortunately there was (and still is) no hard evidence to show that the method achieved more than chance success rates: neurotic patients do improve with time, even in the absence of formal therapy. What appears to be the case is that such therapy does help certain individuals but might actually make others worse by encouraging the patient to talk forever about himself, his past, his complexes, anxieties, guilt-feelings, and dreams, and never get round to doing anything about changing himself. With its emphasis on neurosis being caused by an interplay of blind unconscious forces, the Freudian model does not naturally give the patient a feeling of responsibility or control. Hence, the improved and what may be termed 'recovery-retarded' patients cancel each other out, leaving a chance level of performance for the therapy as a whole.

In 1958, a psychiatrist called Joseph Wolpe published a book entitled *Psychotherapy by Reciprocal Inhibition*, which can be seen as the beginning of the behaviour therapy movement. Wolpe had previously been using psychoanalytic-type methods and had become disenchanted by them and, searching for something new, started reading articles and books from the field of academic psychology, in particular the field of learning theory (see chapter 8). It occurred to Wolpe that, since everyone, including Freudians, tended to agree that people became neurotic largely as a result of experience, that was tantamount to saying that neurotic behaviour is learned; and, if it is learned, it should be governed by the same laws of learning which were being espoused by learning theorists in their psychological laboratories; moreover, psychologists had also studied 'un-learning' or extinction processes, and surely they should, if applied to neurotic behaviour, approach the status of therapy.

Now, the learning theorists had traditionally dealt in stimuli and responses, and Wolpe's first job was to try to conceptualize neurotic behaviour in similar terms. The easiest neurotic disorders to begin with were phobias, where it is possible to see the feared object or situation as a stimulus and the fear as a response. The principle of reciprocal inhibition in the learning theory of Clark Hull stated that if two incompatible responses to a stimulus are put in competition, the stronger will come to dominate and gradually extinguish the weaker by the process of inhibition. Earlier in the century, Watson and Rayner had reported the famous case of 'Little Albert' who was made phobic of furry objects by pairing the presentation of a white rat with a loud noise; Albert's supposed phobia was then extinguished by feeding him chocolate in closer and closer proximity to the rat. The pleasant response of eating chocolate could be seen as vying with the fear and since this response competition took place at first some distance from the phobic object the pleasant responses won the battle. The next battle, taking place a metre or so nearer the rat, was made easier and so on till the phobia was completely extinguished.

Now, Wolpe realized two things: first, he could not readily feed chocolate to his adult patients and, secondly, not all objects of phobic response can be positioned so many metres away from a patient in a consulting room. In terms of learning theory, he had to find alternative, reciprocally inhibiting, responses and, in certain cases, alternative, stimulus substitutes. He solved the first problem by suggesting three responses which could be said to be antagonistic to anxiety: assertiveness, sexual interest, and self-governed relaxation. With respect to ordinary phobias, as opposed to social and sexual anxieties, it is the third type of response which has become important: patients can be given training in progressive muscular relaxation or, alternatively, a sort of self-induced, semi-hypnotic state, which would limit the capacity to feel afraid. Wolpe solved his second problem by suggesting that the mere imagination of the phobic object should conjure up enough anxiety to enter into the deconditioning process and that such deconditioning would generalize to the real-life situation. Thus, by imagining oneself closer and closer to one's source of fear but always remaining relaxed and never moving ahead too fast, Wolpe envisaged the successful extinction of a phobia. He was right. This method of *systematic desensitization* has had tremendous success in the eradication of many phobias, particularly relatively clear-cut and simple phobias, and it is still one of the most widely-practised behavioural therapy techniques. That said, it is still a matter of much debate as to why the technique works, and Wolpe's original rationale in terms of reciprocal inhibition is not the only one nor the most plausible.

This is instanced by the success of another behavioural technique which is so much the opposite of desensitization at first appearance that it would seem to contradict the rationale of the earlier treatment. It is called 'flooding' – the patient is literally flooded with as much anxiety as possible in the presence or imagined presence of his phobic object. Under the supervision of the therapist he is encouraged to tolerate as much anxiety as he can until the anxiety is forced to dissipate itself by the very passage of time. The fear that such a procedure may make the patient worse is very much contradicted by experience and, indeed, sometimes the phobia is cleared up in remarkably fewer sessions than required by desensitization. The fact that both methods of treatment have creditable track records suggests an at least partly shared rationale: both treatments deliberately confront patients with the source of their fears and both treatments, at different paces, could be said to be teaching a certain tolerance of anxiety which may effectively prevent the patient from allowing fear to feed on fear to the point of panic-responding. In a simple fashion, both treatments refuse to reward the patient for escaping from the source of his fears; equally simply, learning theory states that a systematically unrewarded response will be supplanted in an organism's repertoire of behaviour.

Although not all neurotics have phobias, it is still true that phobic features are present in a number of cases of general anxiety neurosis, and, thus, the treatments described have some ilace in therapy. Moreover, it is possible for the therapist to identify inner sources of anxiety – thoughts and preoccupations – which he may wish to desensitize. In this way these treatments can be seen as general techniques for anxiety relief.

The behaviourally-orientated therapist adopts, in the case of neurotic patients in general, an attitude which can best be described as 'problem solving'. He tries to see the patient as being under the control (in a learning theory sense) of his present environment, rather than being the victim of his past lingering on in the form of inner and unconscious determinants of his present behaviour. The difference is one of emphasis. In stressing the present situation, the therapist can try to discover real contingencies between the way the patient feels and acts and the shifting background of his immediate environment, including the way other people behave towards the patient himself. By focusing on particular sources of anxiety, the therapist may be in a position to encourage the patient to experiment with new and alternative responses which, in turn, will shape a new environment which will, in its turn, shape the patient's existing modes of feeling and acting. The same sort of strategy is often used to treat depressed patients, who may be seen as having lost control over sources of 'reinforcement' in the environment as a result of a severe upheaval, such as a loss of a loved one. The traditional emphasis on past history, beloved of psychoanalysis, is not totally ignored by the eclectic behaviour therapist; he is, however, usually, and correctly, quick to point out that current factors maintaining abnormal behaviour are possibly more important than past factors precipitating such behaviour.

This is especially seen in the direct application of operant conditioning methods to encourage mentally disturbed or handicapped patients on a ward to 'emit' more self-reliant and pro-social behaviour. A 'token-economy' may be established where tokens (exchangeable for rewards) are used to reinforce daily behaviour in regard to such things as dressing, washing, eating and general social intercourse. The results can be clearly beneficial when such programmes are run well, but close attention needs to be paid to implementation and shaping staff behaviour as much as patients'.

Other treatment methods

Overview

Behaviour therapy techniques have traditionally been developed and utilized by psychologists, whereas biologically orientated psychiatrists have tended to favour physical methods of treatment, and psychodynamically orientated psychiatrists have favoured variants of psychoanalytic therapy. Other more recent developments in the area of cognitive psychology have led to the formulation of cognitive therapies, although in practice behavioural and cognitive aspects often overlap in any treatment package devised for a particular client. Finally there exist some 'independent' schools of therapy which have enough meritorious or distinguishing features for them to have achieved some general impact beyond a narrow clique of practitioners. We present here no more than a brief guide to treatment methods.

Physical treatment

The major method used by psychiatrists to treat their patients is the use of drugs (chemotherapy). Phenothiazine compounds are used in vast quantities to treat schizophrenia. There is no doubt that they often reduce the most florid manifestations of the disorder and have led to a revolution in its management but they do have undesirable side-effects and do not in any way constitute a cure, in the conventional medical sense. Severe affective ('mood') disorders are also routinely treated by chemotherapy. Manic conditions are often spectacularly controlled by a simple inorganic compound: lithium carbonate. Tricyclic drugs, which affect levels of brain amines such as noradrenalin, are successful in relieving severe cases of depression. Finally, much used (and, some would say, much abused) have been the minor tranquillizers, or benzodiazepines, for the management of anxiety and neurotic disorders. Criticism of their abuse has centred on two aspects: their capacity to induce addiction when prescribed for frequent and lengthy use, and secondly their being used as a crutch when the active learning of relaxation and coping techniques may in fact be fostered by psychological or behavioural therapy methods.

The use of electroconvulsive therapy (ECT) has over many years proven efficacious in the relief of otherwise intractable depression. Under anaesthesia, and following injection of a muscle relaxant, a current is delivered to one or both sides of the patient's forehead, thus inducing a controlled convulsion. Although the safety and efficacy of the treatment is established, we are still unclear about how the method works. Many psychiatrists would advocate the use of physical and psychological methods in depressive disorders, on the grounds that sometimes the physical treatment can break a vicious circle of depression and withdrawal, allowing the patient to become more responsive to psychological intervention which can then address the social and personal dimension which may be implicated in the depressive episode.

A physical method of treatment which is very rarely used involves surgical removal of brain tissue – so-called 'psychosurgery'. Apart from the ethical issues involving informed consent, there are other difficulties with such intervention: its effects are irreversible and they are often more unpredictable than one would like. A refined form of leucotomy is still occasionally used to relieve obsessional or compulsive symptoms which combine intolerable severity with proven intractability to any other method of treatment.

Cognitive therapy

Although this is a convenient title to introduce certain developments in the field of therapy it is also misleading to think of cognitive therapy as distinct from behavioural methods of treatment, of the sort already discussed. Behaviour therapy was introduced on the back of experimental psychology as it existed up to the beginning of the 1960s. In the last three decades experimental academic psychology has become cognitivized, and it is therefore inevitable that this has been reflected in the cognitivization of behaviour therapy. This began with cognitive reformulations of classic behaviour therapies such as desensitization (Wilkins, 1971) and has continued in theories such as that of self-efficacy (Bandura, 1977) which stress the importance of cognitive processes in mediating therapeutic change even when behavioural procedures are used.

Direct attempts to modify and, particularly, to restructure cognitions have sprung from cognitive theories of disorder. Ellis (1984) describes the essentials of his 'rational-emotive therapy' which sees much 'pathological' anxiety as stemming from irrational beliefs (often concerning a need to be always competent and loved by all). Beck (1967) pioneered the cognitive view of depression, seeing the affective processes as resulting from faulty cognitive operations. Abramson *et al* (1978) have further suggested that faulty attributions and the perception of helplessness may be important in some depressions. Cognitive restructuring therapies attempt to focus on and change the underlying beliefs and perceptions which are said to maintain the disorder. There is some evidence that cognitive interventions are effective in the treatment of depression (Wilson *et al*, 1983) even though cognitive theories of depression have yet to be properly formulated and evaluated (see Power and Champion, 1987). The essence of cognitive therapies is to make the client first of all aware of the belief system he has. This can be done by the therapist directly, or by methods of role-play where, for example, the client may switch roles with the therapist and by arguing rationally against himself, can bring irrational beliefs into sharper focus.

Other psychotherapies

Freudian and neo-Freudian methods have dominated much psychotherapy with an emphasis on gaining insight into disorders through access to the unconscious. This in turn is gained by free association (saying everything that comes into one's head without censorship), recording and relating dreams, and the development of transference such that unconscious projections are made on to the figure of the therapist which, when appropriately interpreted, shed light on early important relationships with parental figures. Not all psychotherapists have been convinced that insight is the primary route to 'cure'. Carl Rogers in developing his client-centred therapy believed that the qualities of the therapist – particularly empathy, warmth, and genuineness – allowed each client to embark on natural and inevitable processes of self-repair and self-growth. Rogers and his followers have been more generally influential in promoting empirical research to support what are too often vague and unsubstantiated assertions in the area of psychotherapy. Rogers' belief that the therapeutic relationship fosters the emergence of 'real self' has echoes in many other therapist/writers, not least existential psychoanalysts, such as Fairbairn, Guntrip, and Laing.

To take our discussion further into every avenue of therapy would involve us in drawing up a very long list indeed of individual methods which may or may not emphasize group involvement, may or may not describe themselves as humanistic, existential, or analytic, and so on. They all have their advocates and their adherents; no doubt many have much to recommend them. But no scientific statement can be made concerning their relative efficacy (as if they were antibiotics!) and since they tend to operate for the most part in the market-place what perhaps is needed is a good comprehensive consumer guide.

Psychology as a social science

It is sometimes said – indeed it is sometimes the subject of an examination question – that all psychology is social psychology. This is really one of those rather frustrating 'it all depends on what you mean' remarks. It is true that (as far as we can guess) very little normal development would take place if a child were reared in complete isolation. (The nearest examples are the 'feral' children: but there is never any certainty that they were normal to start with.) On the other hand, it is not true that you cannot study any important aspects of behaviour without taking all the social factors into account simultaneously. All the preceding sections demonstrate that.

Conversely, there are many aspects of behaviour which are more or less defined by their social context. It is meaningless to speak of racial prejudice without the existence of at least two races, or of group dynamics without a group. Just as with physiological psychology, there is a fairly distinct group of social psychologists who have developed particular techniques for dealing with these sorts of behaviour. And there is, once again, the question of deciding on an appropriate level of explanation.

Chapter twenty-two

Understanding other people; understanding self

Judy Gahagan

Professional psychologists and ordinary people alike are concerned with understanding people – their motives, that is the reason for their actions, and their psychological qualities, that is their personalities. The differences between the professionals and everyone else lie in the purposes to which the knowledge will be put, and the systematicity and objectivity of the search for that knowledge. The former aim to construct scientific laws and the latter simply guidelines for their everyday transactions with others. The former must make explicit the data on which their theories are constructed and test them under the rules of scientific method. The latter work with fluctuating and partially conscious intuitions which may seldom be put to any rigorous test. Of course this division is overstated. Many lay people, writers, interviewers, teachers, for example, may have to make more explicit and generalized judgements about motives and personality, than is common for everyday purposes. Likewise the professional psychologist may use everyday hunches and observations which unconsciously inform the direction of scientific research. In this chapter we are going to look at the convergence of professional and lay psychology – that is, the professional psychologist's study of the lay person as psychologist – the study of person perception, how the ordinary lay person sets about understanding other people.

Traditionally person perception has been split into separate areas of study, although in the real world it is rare that psychological processes are really separable. But scientific methodology demands their fragmentation.

The two areas are attribution theory, the study of how ordinary people infer causes and motives for the behaviour of others; and impression formation, the way in which, from limited data, we build up impressions of another's personality. Note here that the study of these processes is not concerned with their accuracy or correctness, but rather with the way people set about making inferences from available information.

Attribution theory

Attribution theory is concerned with the way ordinary lay people (assuming these are a homogeneous group) infer the causes of behaviour in others. Finding the reasons for the behaviour of others is an important step in forming an impression of their personalities. For example, if we see someone acting meanly, our interpretation of this depends on the reasons available for his behaviour. If we learn that other people have consistently exploited him, this throws a very different light on his behaviour compared with that where we can find no external reason at all. The latter case may lead to the judgement that the mean actions stem from a mean character and this will shape all our future interactions with that person, and our judgements of his other qualities.

This example brings us immediately to the first and fundamental stage of the attribution process, that of inferring external or internal causes of behaviour. Internal causes can be physical factors, like health, energy level or hormonal changes. Or they can be psychological, like habits, attitudes, abilities or lack of them, and general personalty traits. External factors can be classified as physical, social or 'pure chance': economic conditions, climate, temptations, barriers and the like on the one hand, and the demands of social situations and roles, pressure from other people, widely held norms of conduct and so forth, on the other. However, a further dimension, important for judgement, is the perceived stability of the cause. Mood, for example, usually fluctuates, but talent does not. Similarly, extreme poverty is constant in its influence, whereas the demands of a particular situation, like the conventions of a funeral or a wedding, are transitory. The following represents a useful two-dimensional classification:

	Internal	External
Unstable	mood, tiredness, mistaken ideas	luck, weather, opportunity, situation
Stable	talent, personality, attitude	climate, social class, laws/customs

Figure 22.1 (after Weiner, 1974)

This classification represents the most basic decisions we have to make when understanding the reason for another person's actions. For the most part factors internal to the person, especially if they are stable factors, give us a better basis for guessing what the person is generally like and for predicting his behaviour in the future. It is not therefore surprising that we show a preference for attributing behaviour to internal stable causes, for it provides, at least, the illusion of a stable and predictable world. Fritz Heider, the first person to study systematically the attribution process, called this preference 'the fundamental attribution error' (Heider, 1958). It is charmingly illustrated in an experiment by Ross, Amabile and Steinmetz (1977). They invited their student subjects to participate in a quiz game, and then randomly assigned them to the role of either questioner or contestant. The questioners were asked to think up absolutely any question, however obscure, so long as they knew the answer, to ask the contestants. Afterwards, questioners, contestants and onlookers were asked to rate the knowledgeability of the participants. Results showed that the questioners were rated as more knowledgeable, even though it was obvious to all that the situation was clearly devised to give the questioner a total advantage and indeed the roles could, having been randomly allocated, be reversed. A similar process is at work when we attribute the achievements (and similarly failures) of public figures to their unique qualities, entirely discounting chance and opportunity.

The lay psychologist

During the 1960s and 1970s there was a strong current of thought which viewed the lay psychologist as operating like the professional scientist in the search for the causes of behaviour. Harold Kelley, in particular, provided a model of the process which had a strong influence on subsequent research (Kelley, 1967, 1973); it was called the 'co-variation principle'. Like any scientist, he claimed, the lay person looks for patterns of co-variation in searching for causes, in this case for co-varying patterns between actions and the situations in which they occur. Three types of co-variation are important: consistency, that is the degree to which a behaviour is stable over time; distinctiveness, the degree to which the behaviour happens only in response to this situation and no other; and consensus, the degree to which most people behave, or would behave like the actor in question. Information from these three sources is used to decide whether the behaviour stems from within the actor or the situation. An example will show the simplicity of Kelley's argument. We see a man shouting at a dog. Is this more to do with the man (internal cause), or is it more to do with the dog (external cause)? The *consistency* factor makes us ask whether he always does this or whether this is a unique instance. If the latter, we will guess that it's something to do with the dog's behaviour at that moment (external); if the former, then something in the man is responsible (internal). The *distinctiveness* factor leads us to ask if he only shouts at this dog or at all dogs. If only at this one we judge it to be caused by this dog (external); if at all dogs then it is something in him (internal). Finally we ask about *consensus*. Do other people shout at the dog too, or not? If consensus is high and others behave similarly we judge the cause to be the dog rather than the man.

This model makes some very specific predictions about the attributions people will make if given information about these three factors, thus permitting a simple experimental technique for testing them. You simply provide subjects with a description of a piece of behaviour and the circumstances in which it occurs, and vary the information about consistency, distinctiveness and consensus. Subjects are then asked to indicate how far the behaviour was caused by something in the person or something in the situation. A number of studies have lent some support to Kelley's predictions. However, a number of them have suggested that consensus information has weaker effects on the attribution process than the other two factors. Read (1983) found that consensus information reliably affected subjects' attributions only in the absence of any other information at all, and led them to assume external causes. We shall come back to the significance of consensus information a little later.

A critique of Kelley's concept

Kelley's model generated a great deal of research, but it illustrates some fundamental problems both with theory and method in attribution research. One is – and Kelley recognized it and elaborated his model – that it is extremely rare for people to have these three (or any other) sources of information in complete form, and to be asked to make a definitive judgement. Normally we have to hazard guesses about the three factors. That is, the experimental variables are not good samples of the way such variables appear under natural conditions, and this limits the ecological validity, that is, the extent to which it matches up to real life, of the experiment. Kelley of course realized that typically our information is far from complete, and he proposed that we carry with us causal schemata about the probability and weighting of the three different kinds of information and made a number of suggestions as to their nature. But a much more serious defect is that the model seems to suggest that we use such analyses for all attributional judgements. Yet it must be obvious that a lot of the time we do not. Behaviour which is strongly normative, like laughing at parties or being sober at funerals, or police holding up the traffic, do not require causal analysis for there is sufficient reason available, and in such situations it is unlikely that we go through a complicated Kelley analysis.

So one very important question the attribution theorist has to ask, and which has received rather scant attention, is this: under what circumstances does the lay psychologist behave like a professional psychologist and draw inferences about the causes of behaviour, and under what circumstances does he simply take for granted some ready-made explanation? He probably does at first when no simple, ready-made explanation is available, or when a very precise objective (for example, in legal assessment of responsibility, or making an assessment of someone for a job) is at stake. In support of this Lalljee *et al* (1982) found that explanations of unexpected behaviour were more complex than for expected behaviour. If the situation was familiar and the behaviour unexpected, the explanation was in terms of the person (internal). If the situation was unfamiliar and the behaviour was unfamiliar the explanation was in terms of situation (external).

Lalljee (1981) also observed that people often hold others accountable for the situations which they get into. The degree to which they do so certainly depends on their implicit theory of motivation. For example people who believe in *unconscious* motives in such phenomena as accident proneness, for example, are likely to believe that situations are 'created' and don't 'just happen'. This thinking, of course, undermines the whole distinction between internal and external causes of behaviour on which much attribution research is based. What *is* clear is that for attribution theory to advance these two areas of research-schemata about what is usual or unusual behaviour, and implicit theories of motivation, will have to be more widely investigated.

Lalljee points out, too, that even a simple variable like consistency changes its meanings according to the behaviour in question. For example, getting divorced four times in five years seems a lot more frequent than jogging four times in five years. Lalljee suggests plausibly that people don't wait for information about behaviour and surrounding circumstances and then infer inductively backwards to causes. Rather they carry around a large fund of plausible hypotheses about reasons for actions and choose one when the appropriate situation crops up, according to specific cues available. We should remember at this point, too, that different cultures have particular 'ready-made' explanations for conduct. For example we are unlikely to use such explanations as 'witchcraft' or 'possession', but there are many cultures in which these would be commonly invoked as causes of behaviour.

One difference between the lay psychologist and the professional psychologist is that the former is very rarely a disinterested observer of other humans. For everyday purposes the lay person is strongly influenced in judgements by motives outside the disinterested pursuit of knowledge. And other motives lead to biases in the attribution process. For example right-wing politicians are much more inclined to attribute responsibility for misfortune and poverty to the person than to social conditions. Judges in chauvinistic, patriarchal societies are inclined to attribute the responsibility for rape to the female victim. Research has established that we are more likely to hold a person responsible if his behaviour has serious consequences (regardless of how intentional this was) than if the consequences are trivial. The effect is dramatically enhanced if these consequences affect us personally. Jones and Davis (1965) called this tendency 'hedonic relevance'. In one ingenious experiment Jones and de Charms (1957) set up small groups of subjects and gave them problems to solve with prizes attached for good performance. Unknown to them, in each group an experimental stooge had been planted who behaved so incompetently that the group's performance was undermined. Although these stooges behaved identically, in some groups the failure prevented only the stooge from getting a prize and in others it prevented all group members from getting a prize. Afterwards group members rated each other on dimensions of competence (an internal attribution). Where the stooge's incompetence had affected everyone's outcomes he was judged as markedly more incompetent.

Explaining failure

The role of motives in distorting the attribution process is clearly visible in what are called 'self-serving biases'. This refers to the explanations people give for their own successes and failures, and as the saying goes, 'success has many fathers but failure is an orphan'. There is an understandable tendency for people to attribute their successes to internal factors, like ability and effort and character, and their failures to situation, like task difficulty, bad luck, unfairness of others and so forth. A typical experiment involves putting subjects through some task, giving them (erroneous) feedback about their success or failure, and then asking them to give reasons for the quality of their performance. Using such techniques Zuckerman (1979) found subjects overwhelmingly blamed failure on the situation and success on ability and effort. This has been found in attributions regarding others with whom one is closely identified. For example Winkler and Taylor (1979) found that fans attributed the successes of their own teams to the high standard of play, and failure to bad luck and 'poor breaks'. This self-serving bias has been found in cultures as distant as Nigeria and China. Sustaining high self-esteem, regardless of the truth, seems to have some important value for mental health!

Finding reasons for one's own behaviour and finding them for the behaviour of others shows certain characteristic differences. There is a strong tendency to give external, situational reasons for one's own behaviour, and as in the 'fundamental attribution error', to give internal, dispositional reasons for the behaviour of others (Jones and Nisbett, 1972). One reason for this finding may be that for an outside observer the actor is the focus of attention, the situation is background. The actor himself, however, is far more aware of situational demands and the way his behaviour changes to suit them, hence he attributes more weight to external causes. Salience certainly is a factor in the attributional process, for we tend to attribute more responsiblity to someone in a group who is distinctive in some way, for example, being the only woman in the group, or being the only person of a particular race (Taylor and Fiske, 1978).

In summary, the attribution process is fundamental in forming impressions of others because, for the most part, the only data we have is their behaviour and the circumstances in which it occurs. Finding causes is an important stage in sifting the informative from the trivial and building up a picture which allows us to build up expectations about the person in future. Having decided that an action was caused by meanness or generosity, we then have one little building block for constructing a more complex picture. And thus we pass on to that other area of research in person perception: forming impressions of personality.

Forming impressions of personality

The causes of another's behaviour, in so far as the extent to which we believe them to be internal and stable, provide us with information about the person's disposition or personality. Such attributions are not, however, the only available source of data. We form impressions from many sources – physical appearance, occupation, other people's accounts, hunches whose basis we can't specify. The resulting impression is thus often nebulous and changeable. Once again the professional psychologist has to extract and 'freeze' some common processes whereby we form impressions of others.

Impressions are based on quite minimal cues for, in the words of Jerome Bruner, 'we go beyond the information given'. This means that we infer from what we know (or think we know) the presence of other qualities for which there is no direct evidence. For example, from the wearing of a suit and careful reading of the financial pages of the newspaper, we may infer punctuality, orderliness and lack of imagination, though there is no rational basis for this inference. Underlying this process is what psychologists call our 'implicit theory of personality'. Once again we are concerned with co-variation – the way in which phenomena appear, or fail to appear, together. In this case, our theories of how attributes co-vary.

Thus our impressions of others are constructed partly from our observations of them and partly from our theories about the co-variation of traits. In short, like the professional, the lay psychologist works with a mixture of theory and data. It is a kind of trade-off. The more we think we know already about a person, the less attentive we are likely to be to *actual* data from them, particularly data that are contrary to our theory. If we 'know' that a bank clerk is orderly and unimaginative we don't bother to notice the small signs that he is otherwise. One of the biases of the lay psychologist is that of searching for evidence that confirms, rather than scientifically searching for the case that disconfirms.

Implicit personality theory

The research literature on impression formation has a longer history than that of attribution theory, and has covered a wider field of enquiry. The earliest research was concerned with implicit personality theory. The difficulty with a lot of this research was that it involved judgements about the co-variation of traits independently of any particular target person. For example, Bruner and Tagiuri (1954) simply gave subjects various trait words and asked them to calculate the likelihood that any trait would be present or absent with another trait, for example, how likely was it that intelligence and independence would go together? Another, extremely influential study by Asch (1946) involved presenting subjects with short lists of words describing personality in which one term would be varied. For example, one group of subjects received the list with 'warm' as one of the traits, and the other group had 'cold'. They then had to imagine and describe other aspects of the imaginary person and to indicate from a further list of adjectives which other traits would be present. Asch was interested in discovering whether some personality traits are perceived to have a determining effect on the global impression. He found, in this case, that the warm/cold items did make a crucial difference to the overall impression of that person. Repeating the experiment with the cue words 'polite/blunt' showed little effect. Later studies explained this in terms of the whole constellation of terms presented in the stimulus list and the words presented for measuring the impression. For example, knowing whether someone is warm or cold does not help us to predict whether they will be sportive or reflective. But it does, apparently, help us to predict whether they will be spontaneous or sociable. Asch was suggesting something further – that the presence of certain traits, like warm or cold, changes the actual nature and meaning of other traits. For example, 'warm intelligence' is different from 'cold intelligence'.

It is not clear whether such research is simply concerned with word meanings or really touches on implicit theories of personality which are activated when we are trying to judge a person. It tells us little about the way in which data are spontaneously organized when confronted with an actual person. Later research benefited from the introduction of statistical techniques which allowed the analysis of large amounts of spontaneously generated real descriptions over a period of time. This technique of multi-dimensional scaling was applied, for example, to the study of the implicit personality theory of the American writer Theodore Dreiser. By examining the descriptions of persons in his novels the researchers found the regular co-variation of certain traits – for example, free with unconventional, and successful with conventional (Rosenberg and Jones, 1972).

Another technique, addressed to the same issue, was developed by George Kelly (1955) and called the 'repertory grid technique'. This involved a subject writing down a list of people who played particular roles in his life – friend, boss, admired person or whatever. Each one would be placed together with two others and the subject asked to state in which way the one was similar and different from the other two. This produced a list of terms used by the subject and from this point it was possible to explore further the dimensions of the terms (their opposite poles), the ways in which they were associated with each other, their importance and centrality. For example, a subject could be asked which other traits would change if one particular one was changed. This clinical method is a way of examining in depth one subject's implicit personality theory. Together with multi-dimensional scaling it would be possible to combine data from many subjects to uncover shared 'implicit personality theories'.

Stereotyping

Collective belief about traits shared by a category of person is called a stereotype. It is a shared implicit personality theory applied to a social or physical category; for example, that attractive people are also happy and successful, that fat people are lazy and placid, that bank clerks are orderly and dull, that Jews are devious and avaricious. Given the importance of such beliefs in sustaining prejudice or justifying political practice (for although stereotypes do not have to be negative, when they are their effects are dangerous), it is not surprising that stereotyping has occupied a lot of space in the social psychological literature. The simplest way of uncovering stereotypes is to provide subjects with a list of social categories, for example, ethnic groups, and a list of trait words, and ask them to assign the traits which most typify a particular group. This is exactly what Katz and Braly (1933) did in an important study. Their criterion for the existence of a stereotype was the concordance across subjects. That is if, for example, 75 per cent of subjects allocated the traits obedient, hardworking and proud to Japanese this would be taken as evidence for the existence of a stereotype. The Katz and Braly study showed very high degrees of agreement between subjects, that is, the existence of marked stereotypes among their subjects. It was possible to compare the different ethnic groups in terms of favourability. At that time, for example, the Turks had the worst stereotype and white Americans the best. Studies repeating Katz and Braly's technique over a period of a quarter of a century have been able to chart interesting changes in the strength and content of stereotypes over time which could be related to events in the world. For example, by 1969 Karlins, Coffman and Walters had found overall a considerable fading of stereotypes and changes in favourability – for example Negroes and Turks had improved markedly in subjects' eyes and Americans and Germans had lost their position a little.

The problem with this technique, as in other areas of person perception, is that it forces judgements and provides too much information at once, thus missing important elements in the real phenomenon, and undermining the ecological validity of the findings. Stereotyping, after all, involves a number of distinct stages: allocating someone to a social or ethnic category in the first place; making judgements about the characteristics held by that category; and inferring, therefore, that the individual must share those characteristics. Much research has only been concerned with the second of these processes. The other thing is that the technique is subject to the artifacts of social desirability. As stereotypes, especially about racial categories, become less acceptable, subjects are less likely to give prejudiced responses even if secretly they are prejudiced. A better technique involves the provision of unobtrusive information about a social category. A good example is a study by Razran (1950). The subjects were shown pictures of girls on a screen and asked to rate them for various psychological qualities. Some time later they were presented with the same pictures, but this time the girls were identified with names which sounded Irish, Jewish or Italian. The changes in rating as a result of additional information was the measure of ethnic stereotyping. In this case it was found, for example, that Jewish-sounding girls were rated higher on intelligence and ambition, but lower on niceness.

The maintenance of stereotypes

The voluminous research on stereotyping has revealed a fund of interesting information; physically attractive people are happier, more successful, more competent and better adjusted than unattractive people (Berscheid and Walster, 1974); that poor people are less competent than the wealthy (Darley and Gross, 1983); that Americans are materialist, Germans industrious, Italians passionate and black Americans musical. Such theories may contain some kernel of truth but, as they stand, they are virtually untestable. Stereotypes are strongly influenced both by historical events (for example the Turkish occupation of many countries and their massacre of the Armenians may have furnished some fuel for their earlier unpopularity), and they are reinforced by popular media whose producers also share the stereotype.

However, behind stereotypes, as behind all implicit personality theory, lie certain habits of cognition. One of these is the tendency to see co-variation where it doesn't exist. For example, in one study (Weiss and Brown, 1977) subjects were asked to keep a daily record of their predominant mood, over a two month period. They were also asked to keep records of other events that might influence their mood, like weather, amount of sleep, general health, day of the week, sexual activity and so forth. At the end of this period they were asked to indicate how important these latter factors were in determining mood. The researchers had, of course, statistical records of the real co-variation and reported mood. From their records it was clear that most co-variation was between day of the week and mood, but the subjects reported amount of sleep as being the main co-variant. This was probably due to an implicit theory many people hold that adequate sleep and mood are related.

This tendency is even more marked with events which are very rare. For example, in the past, people would relate an eclipse of the moon, an infrequent event, with the outbreak of a rare illness, another infrequent event. The fact that two rare events occur together leads people to think that there is some real connection in nature. This is not irrational because where events have a low probability of occurring at all, and an even lower probability of occurring together, it means we have little opportunity either to establish or to disconfirm whether an apparent association is more than chance. In terms of the present argument, red hair and wild temper are neither particularly common. The occurrence of the two together can be sufficient to launch a stereotype.

The persistence of stereotypes and implicit theories of personality are also sustained by selective attention and inattention to data from others: by selective coding of events and by selective recall of events. In one study (Duncan, 1976) subjects were shown a video of a discussion between two men which became heated. At one point one man gives the other a rough shove. Subjects had been set the task of categorizing all the behaviours they viewed on the screen, including, of course, the shove. The sequence was identical for all groups, but the race of the actors was not. Either they saw two whites, two blacks, or a black and a white with either the white or the black doing the shoving. The results showed clearly that the shove was coded as aggressive when coming from a black man, especially if his partner was white. When it came from a white man, it was categorized as fooling around.

Then, as lay observers we are very inclined to show distortions in memory to fit our implicit theories or to fit our current 'knowledge'. The following study is a good example. Subjects were given short biographies of a woman. A week later they were given additonal information, in one group to the effect that later in life the woman had embarked on a homosexual relationship, in the other group a heterosexual relationship. Some time later they were asked to recall the original biography. There was clear evidence of distorted recall along the lines suggested by the later information. For example, the first account had included information about the woman dating boys while a teenager. Those told about the lesbian episode omitted this element in their recall (Snyder and Uranowitz, 1978). In real life we see this process strongly at work when we account for some present situation in terms of the past. For example, if someone has a mental breakdown, previously innocuous behaviours will now be seen as early 'symptoms'. The sociologist Erving Goffman drew attention to this process in the case conferences of doctors and relatives when a patient is admitted to mental hospital; he called it 'the betrayal funnel'.

Accuracy and person perception

At the beginning of this chapter, it was stressed that the study of person perception is not concerned with the validity or truth of the lay person's perceptions of others' motives and characters, but with the processes of inference involved. This is because there are severe technical and theoretical difficulties about establishing the accuracy of the lay person's observations. For one thing it is difficult to establish a criterion of 'what a person is *really* like'. We could use standardized personality tests, except that these in themselves are subject to a variety of errors and provide a superficial picture of personality. With the attribution process, we have to accept that causes may not be determinable, they may be, and probably are, a complex mixture of factors. One might imagine that the target persons themselves could give the 'real truth about what they are really like and why they acted as they did'. However, people may be just as unaware of their own motives and of how they appear to others, as others are to them. It is not surprising that little effort has gone into examining the question of accuracy.

Another point is that the attributions people make about causes of behaviour depend on the kinds of question asked. The question 'Why did Harry marry Jean?' may really mean 'Why Jean?' 'Why marry and not live with?' 'Why marry or live with anyone?' The meaning depends on the context in which the question is asked. Similarly, in forming impressions of personality much depends on the purposes to which the judgement will be put. A job interviewer has a narrower range of interest than a potential partner, and the person interested in dynamic psychology another domain of interest altogether.

Finally we must remember that, in life, our beliefs about other people infiltrate our dealings with them, and may result in a self-fulfilling prohpecy, that is a belief which by its expression is made to come true. There is voluminous research in psychology which shows the power of self-fulfilling prophecies. Studies which show how teachers' beliefs about children's abilities actually result in changes in those abilities (Meichenbaum *et al*, 1969). In one study (Snyder *et al*, 1977) male subjects were asked to speak for a few moments to an unknown female on the phone, allegedly for the psychologist to study the acquaintance process. Half of the men were told that the unseen woman was attractive, the others that she was unattractive. Observers could hear either just the woman or just the man, but they knew nothing about the prior attractiveness manipulation. Both observers and the men had to rate the woman on a number of dimensions. In the attractiveness condition she was rated by both observers and by the men as more confident, animated, enjoying the conversation more, liking the partner more. The 'unattractive' women were rated as more 'altruistic, kind and modest'. If beliefs can have such a clear impact on the target under these highly restricted conditions, then we must suppose that the role of self-fulfilling prophecy in the real world is extremely powerful. It undermines hope of being able to demonstrate the accuracy of people's beliefs about one another, and demonstrates the limitations of trying to separate psychological processes, like perception and interaction, from one another.

Understanding self

At the heart of all these judgements, beliefs and impressions sits a ghost. That ghost is something we call 'self'. Psychologists have had an uneasy relationship with it. A science which has based its methods on the idea that the human psyche can be transformed into the same kind of matter as that studied in the physical sciences, whose qualities are determined by factors which can be revealed by deterministic approaches, is seriously threatened by such a ghost. For one thing it raises the possibility of free will. All the mechanisms of attention and memory, of alterations in consciousness, of self-control and personal change may in the end lie in the hands of a self which eludes psychologists.

Nevertheless, in spite of this fraught relationship, the study of self has been rich and diverse, and in the last twenty years or so, ingenious. It has opened up the dimensions of self-experience which can be studied. By way of introduction let us look briefly at them.

The experience of self

Our experiences of self can be classified in a number of ways. There is the bodily self; in normal consciousness we have a sense of boundary between sensations in our own bodies and the outside world. We know our toothache is *our* toothache and not someone else's, and we feel the difference between toothache and, say, jealousy or resentment; there is the psychic self, which, similarly, we feel to be located within our own heads – our thoughts and feelings and intentions are ours. Indeed it is a symptom of mental breakdown when people begin to argue that their thoughts are being produced by other people or by radio waves or Martians (oddly enough deterministic psychology takes the view that our experience and behaviour *is* controlled by factors external to the self); then both as bodies and psyches we have a sense of that which is visible to the world and that which resides inside us, hidden. We have some vague conception of how we look to other people, and an equally vague notion of how we look to ourselves alone. Most people get a shock when they see themselves suddenly in a mirror. Similarly we have some idea of the *person* we are to others – and indeed we may be as many persons as there are others. And we have a variety of conceptions of that private person that others do not see – and this may be equally fluctuating. The most important distinction of all is that between self as subject and self as object. The subjective self is experienced as an agent of action. That is the experience of free will (even though this may be illusory): I feel as though I choose to eat bacon for breakfast and not jelly or caviar. I feel as if I am the agent which makes me get up, shut the door, pick up a magazine. Indeed, sometimes I have the experience of having to force myself to do things, like diet or stop smoking. This is the subjective or agent self. The objective self is experienced as something which can be seen, responded to and judged by others. It is literally the experience of self-consciousness, which if too acute can be unpleasant and disruptive. Since this distinction is so important, we might as well start with some research which has examined it.

Wicklund (1975) argued that objective and subjective self-awareness are fluctuating states, and that we cannot be in both states at once. Imagine that you are playing tennis. You get into position to serve. All your consciousness is concentrated in the sequence of muscular movements – your consciousness *is* the action. Suddenly, out of the corner of your eye, you see someone watching – someone you'd like to impress favourably. Immediately you become aware of yourself in their eyes – that is, you become self-conscious; in Wicklund's terms, you become objectively self-aware. Wicklund and his colleagues argued that objective self-awareness has important consequences both for performance and for self-esteem. In a number of experiments, he and his colleagues manipulated objective self-awareness by introducing mirrors, tape-recordings or audiences and examined the subjects' performances on a task under these conditions. Usually it was impaired. His argument about self-esteem is an interesting one. Basically he argued thus: that normally objective self-awareness leads to lowered self-esteem. This is because our aspirations about ourselves nearly always outstrip the reality. A success makes us feel temporarily elevated, but soon we have our sights on some higher criterion or achievement, behind which the real self continues to lag. Objective self-awareness heightens the discrepancy. Only occasionally, at some moment of success and triumph (for these moments fade very quickly), is objective self-awareness a pleasant experience and one which enhances performance.

Wicklund also suggested that the origins of objective self-awareness (OSA) emerge from the infant's experience of negative reactions to his behaviour from his caretakers, a subject which we'll return to shortly. It seems that self-consciousness is acquired, for young children, before the age of about three, show little sign of it. It also appears to be a form of consciousness limited almost exclusively to humans. There is only rudimentary evidence for consciousness of self in the closest species of apes.

Subjective self-awareness is manifested in that sense of control which people variously experience regarding their own actions and fates. Indeed the very fact of talking about exercising self-control testifies to its existence in many domains of life. In fact there is much evidence that a sense of control, not only over one's behaviour but one's outcomes, is important for well-being (at least in our society). For example, Schultz (1976) studied the reaction of elderly people living in a residential institution to changes in the arrangements for their volunteer visitors. One group could make their own arrangements with their visitors (high control), and the others had no influence over the visits. There were marked effects on the health and morale of the latter group (it must be pointed out that the practice of using subjects on a non-voluntary basis for testing procedures which affect them adversely is entirely unethical!). Extensive work with animals, too, has shown characteristic patterns of deterioration when they lose the possibility of controlling stimuli (Seligman, 1975). This deterioration resembles the apathy of people suffering from depression. Loss of a sense of efficacy leads to passivity.

Locus of control

People certainly vary in the degree to which they *do* feel in charge of their lives. This has been revealed in extensive research by Rotter (1966). He devised a scale called the Internal–External Locus of Control Scale. It requires people to choose from pairs of statements the one which most reflects their belief. For example:

Getting a good job depends mainly on being in the right place at the right time.

Becoming a success is a matter of hard work, luck has nothing to do with it.

The assumption is that these beliefs reflect people's sense of their own capacity as agents. Research validating the scale has shown that people high on an Internal Locus of Control are more active in attempting to manipulate their environment. And typically they are of higher social status. This indicates that one's sense of control is a product of the environment in which one lives, and the lower ones's social status the less control one genuinely has over events.

But the self which we are most conscious of, most of the time, is indeed the objective self of Wicklund's objective self-awareness. It is the self which is visible to other people and which we bring to social situations. Here, too, there is evidence that individuals vary in the degree to which they are conscious of the impressions they make on others. Snyder (1974) devised a scale to measure what he called 'self-monitoring', that is the tendency to be aware of oneself and to modify one's behaviour in social situations to make a good impression. The scale included items to do with the extent to which one is able to act a part, to vary one's behaviour in different situations, and to hide inner states in order to fit in. Ajzen (1982) found that people who were low self-monitors revealed much more openly signs of fatigue and boredom. He also found that they revealed much more consistency of behaviour from situation to situation, the high self-monitorer being able to act and present a self in public.

Self-schemata

What is this self or character which we take with us onto the social stage? Just as we have an 'implicit theory' of what another person is like, so we have 'theories' about what we are ourselves. Many psychologists have suggested that we develop a fairly stable 'self-schemata', which is just as resistant to change as our fixed ideas and stereotypes about other people. One study of self-schemata was that carried out by Markus (1977). Her evidence for a developed schemata was extremity of self-ratings on dimensions such as 'independence', 'sociability' and the like. She argued that those attributes which we feel we have to a high degree are those which are the most important and enduring aspects of the schemata. She found in a subsequent study that people failed to process information which was incongruent with their schemata. The problem with this work is that it does not allow the possibility of people having a picture of themselves as moderates, for such people would be classified as having a poorly articulated self-schemata.

This and another study suggest that our self-schemata is a precious possession which will be vigorously defended against attempts to undermine it. Swann and Read (1981) measured various aspects of the self-schemata of subjects, including a measure of self-esteem. They were then put into groups for some bogus purpose and told the others in the group would either like them or dislike them, and that they would be rating each other afterwards. They were allowed to read these evaluations and the investigator simply observed how long they spent reading the ratings. They found that the most time was devoted by those with high self-esteem reading evaluations of others who gave them positive ratings, and, most interestingly, *an equal amount of time was spent by those with low self-esteem reading negative evaluations*. In a later stage of the study subjects were allowed to spend a few minutes talking to a person who had rated them. The conversations were observed and rated for evidence of subjects *eliciting* congruent behaviour from other people. All this work illustrates the social nature of the self, and reflects the tradition in sociology of seeing the self as an essentially social product. The work on the *self-fulfilling prophecy* described earlier in this chapter provides further evidence that the behaviour of others is important in the development of self-schemata. Once this is established, however, we probably interact rather selectively, avoiding those whose perceptions of us are incongruent with our own views of ourselves.

Self-esteem

The most important aspect of self-schemata is self-esteem. People vary greatly on how they value themselves, and this evalutation can be measured. The study of self-esteem has a long history, reflecting, no doubt, its extreme importance for people's behaviour and well-being. It has been considered variously to be the gap between one's *ideal* self and one's *actual* self, and the gap between one's ideal self and 'reality'. Rosenberg (1965) developed a scale which consisted of such items as:

> I certainly feel useless at times.
> On the whole I am satisfied with myself.

In validating the scale he found that people who scored low on self-esteem received independent ratings from others as being more miserable and easily discouraged. They also were less active and sociable and thought that others rated them negatively too. Thus self-evaluation has an impact on behaviour, which is likely to be self-reinforcing. On the whole we regard high self-esteem as normal and low self-esteem as maladaptive. This does not mean that high self-esteem is necessarily based on a more accurate perception of self. As with the perception of others it is difficult to establish a criterion for assessing accuracy. In one study the investigators simply compared the judgements of social competence which members of a small group gave themselves and each other. Some of the subjects had previously been classified as suffering from depression (low self-esteem is the most important component of depression). The depressed subjects rated themselves more negatively than the non-depressed subjects did. However, their ratings of themselves were much closer to the ratings given by the others than were the ratings of the non-depressed group, who continually overestimated themselves in this respect. The question remains whether it is more adaptive to recognize the truth or to maintain a high level of self-esteem!

In the humanistic psychology movement, self-esteem is considered an essential ingredient of an optimally functioning person. Carl Rogers, a leading writer and therapist, spoke, not so much about *esteem* as about *positive self-regard and acceptance*. He was concerned with the widespread phenomenon of people who simply could not and would not accept aspects of themselves, and the way in which this rejection led to distortions in the self-concept and a split between the self-for-others and a hidden real self. He argued that the origin of this lay in the fact that small children are extremely dependent on their parents, and on their parents' approval, and indeed, a basic human need is love and acceptance by other people. However, parents have to 'bring their children up', that is to say, they have to disapprove and punish certain aspects of behaviour. It often happens that during this process, the aspects of self which these disapproved behaviours represent not only become suppressed (which is a necessary condition of living in society) but pushed out of consciousness altogether, that is, repressed. This produces the incongruence mentioned above, and blocks the essential growth of a person to being completely themselves, and realizing all their potential, which Rogers, Maslow and others called *self-actualization* (Rogers, 1961).

Self-knowledge

Do we have more knowledge about ourselves than we do of others? Common sense suggests that people have privileged access to information about themselves, which they cannot have of others. Psychological research suggests that the matter is very much more complex. Even judgements of one's own emotional states are dependent on external cues. Research by Schachter and Singer (1964) showed how the manipulation of physiological arousal normally associated with emotional states was labelled as anger or euphoria as a consequence of (a) what the subjects were told by the experimenters, and (b) the situation they found themselves in. They suggested that inner cues to emotional states are often diffuse and ambiguous, and we rely on information outside ourselves to clarify exactly what we are feeling. Bem (1967) argued similarly about our judgements of our own attitudes. Over many areas of life, he suggested, we do not have strong views. We infer our attitudes from our observations of our own behaviour. In effect we say, according to Bem, 'I must like watching soap-operas, because I am always doing it'. It has been found (Deci and Ryan, 1980) that people who are *paid* to do something like it less than when they are unpaid, or simply initiate it themselves. In the former case they attribute their behaviour to the payment, in the absence of payment (or any other form of inducement) they conclude that they must *like* the activity.

The study by Weiss and Brown, quoted earlier in the chapter, showed how little subjects may be aware of the real influences on their behaviour. If we consider the issue of self-serving biases in attributing causes for success and failure, and if we consider the selective nature of attention and memory for information not in accordance with a theory we hold, it seems unlikely that we 'know ourselves' any better than we know other people. Indeed, given the protectiveness towards our self-schemata and self-esteem, the chances are that as relatively dispassionate observers, we are more likely to be acute in our judgements of others than of ourselves.

The search for general laws in the psychology of person perception and of self-concept is extremely fraught. In this chapter we have touched little on the problem of individual differences. The lay psychologist who is being studied by the professional is as elusive as the proverbial 'man in the street'. Clearly non-psychologists vary enormously in the sophistication and analysis which they bring to bear on their understanding of others. Virtually no allowance has been made for this source of variation in the research. Similarly, people vary greatly in the attention they pay to self and in the sophistication with which they try to analyse their own feelings, motives and natures. Furthermore it must be remembered that we live in an acutely individualistic society where self is important. It is hard to imagine other cultures where self is engulfed by one's social role, or where people hardly conceive of themselves as separated from those around them. This means that all our research findings in this area are unlikely to achieve the status of general laws of behaviour, but to be relevant only in our own social context. As in other areas of psychology, we have to consider what has been outlined here as culturally and historically relative.

Further reading

Fiske, S. T., and Taylor, S. E. (1984) *Social Cognition*. Addison-Wesley.

Goffman, E. (1971) *The Presentation of Self in Everyday Life*. Penguin.

Mischel, T., ed. (1977) *The Self: Psychological and philosophical issues*. Rowman and Littlefield.

Nisbett, R., and Ross, L. (1980) *Human Inference: Strategies and shortcomings of social judgement*. Prentice-Hall.

Oatley, K. (1985) *Selves in Relation*. Methuen.

Rogers, C. (1961) *On Becoming a Person*. Houghton Mifflin.

Chapter twenty-three

The effect of others on our behaviour

Carolyn Kagan

Most people live with and meet many other people in the course of their lives. Do we have any understanding of how people affect each other? This broad question underlies the study of social influence, and it illustrates many of the obstacles that socal psychologists, attempting to use empirical (often experimental) methods to explore social behaviour, come up against. We find, for instance, examples of how cultural values and possible political pressures have shaped the ways in which findings have been presented, interpreted and used; we see, too, how pressing social concerns have suggested fields of study, and how common themes emerge despite wide differences in method and context.

Most people reading this book will have taken an examination at some time. As a general rule we sit in an exam room along with many other people, also taking the same exam, and with other people – invigilators – watching us. Do we do well under these conditions? Why might this be? Why do we stop when invigilators tell us to? Once people start asking for extra paper, why do people who do not need any, also ask for some? If a fire alarm were to go off during the exam, would we know who would take charge? Why do some people lead others effectively, while others do not? What would make people help a colleague who fainted as the exam finished, when everyone wanted to rush away? Under what conditions might people start a brawl as they leave the exam room? All these questions have been studied, albeit not in the context of taking an exam! They involve issues of social facilitation; obedience, compliance and conformity; leadership; helping behaviour; and aggression, and we will consider each of these.

Does the mere presence of other people affect our behaviour?

Social psychologists have demonstrated that the mere presence of other people does, indeed, affect our behaviour. In a much cited study, Triplett, as long ago as 1897, noted that cyclists (he was himself a keen cyclist) doing time trials, obtained much better times when other riders were either in direct competition with them or were riding with them, than when they were alone. This effect has become known as 'social facilitation'.

Social facilitation and social impairment

Triplett, and many researchers since then, suggested that the presence of others has an energizing effect, and this leads to improved performance. Very many studies have been carried out on the social facilitation effect and, not surprisingly, it is not as simple as it once seemed. The studies have shown that other people – whether present as either an active or passive audience, or as co-actors also engaged on the task in hand – facilitate or improve performance on simple or well-learned tasks. If the tasks are new or complex, the presence of others leads to impaired performance. Thus a 'social impairment' effect has also been observed. How can these inconsistencies be explained?

Arousal and drive-reduction

Robert Zajonc (1965) offered an explanation that emphasized the role of physiological arousal. The presence of others, he suggested, causes people to become aroused or anxious. This arousal energizes performance, and in the case of simple and well-learned tasks this means that performance is enhanced or facilitated. For new and complex tasks, though, it is well-learned or dominant responses that are energized, and these interfere with the tasks in hand, leading to disrupted or impaired performance. The energizing of dominant and well-learned responses serves to reduce the arousal, and Zajonc's hypothesis is sometimes referred to as the 'drive-reduction hypothesis'. However, Zajonc's explanation says little about why the presence of others should produce arousal. Several suggestions have been made to account for this.

One suggestion is that in the presence of other people, we are concerned that we are being evaluated by them, and experience what is known as 'evaluation apprehension'. This is plausible, but it does not account for the finding that incidental audiences – other people just in the same place at the same time, with no reason to evaluate us – also give rise to a social facilitation effect. But some writers, notably Erving Goffman, would question whether we are ever free from the expectation that other people might evaluate us in some way.

An alternative explanation is that of 'distraction-conflict', the suggestion is that in the presence of others, people have to decide whether to pay attention to the task or to the other people. In other words, the presence of other people distracts them. Baron, Moore and Saunders (1978) suggest that distractional conflict leads to the arousal and heightened motivation to do better. They do not say why this should be, although they provide evidence that non-social forms of distraction (such as flashing lights or noise) produce the same kind of arousal during the performance of a task.

Furthermore, subjects in the experiments themselves do report experiencing distraction. These arguments indicate that the social facilitation effect may simply be an example of the arousing properties of any external stimuli, and not a specifically social phenomenon. They also point to the importance of asking subjects what they think of the explanation being devised to account for their behaviour and experience. Social psychologists are increasingly aware of the wealth of information to be got from subjects themselves about their social behaviour, and there is growing interest in attempts to engage subjects in parts of the research process. Whenever we have two (or more) different explanations for the same observation, we can do one of three things. We can choose one explanation in preference to the others, or we can assert that the same effect could be produced for different reasons and leave it at that. Alternatively, we can try to find yet another explanation that incorporates features of all the original ones. Such a compromise is to be found in the theory of objective self-awareness, put forward by Shelly Duval and Robert Wicklund (Wicklund, 1975).

Objective self-awareness

The theory of objective self-awareness combines evaluation apprehension and distraction conflict. The idea behind the theory is that our attention is focused either inwards on ourselves, or outwards on the environment. When we attend to ourselves we are in a state of objective self-awareness (OSA) and when we attend to the environment we are in a state of subjective self-awareness (SSA). We can change very quickly from SSA to OSA as a result of being exposed to what are called self-focusing stimuli. These stimuli can be anything we notice that makes us think of seeing ourselves as others see us. For example, mirrors, cameras, polished windows, and, importantly for this discussion, other people all help us see ourselves as others see us, in other words, as objects. When we are in a state of OSA, Duval and Wicklund suggest that this will eventually result in our thinking badly of ourselves. We focus on our shortcomings and this leads us to experience negative feelings about ourselves in the form of anxiety.

We have seen, then, that the presence of other people facilitates performance of simple and well-learned tasks, but impairs performance of new and complex tasks. Neither the explanation in terms of arousal, evaluation apprehension nor distraction conflict is sufficient in itself to account for the experimental findings, although the theory of objective self-awareness may be useful in so far as it combines elements of all the other explanations.

Social loafing

The work on social facilitation would seem to support popular notions that working in a group is more productive than working alone. However, several researchers have found the opposite to be the case. Where a group of people are engaged in working together on a task, the individual efforts of members of the group seem to decrease. We do not try as hard when there are other people helping us as when we are alone. Experiments on 'social loafing', as it is colloquially called, have shown, for example, that when other people join in (or are thought to join in), people stop clapping or cheering so loudly, pulling as hard in a tug-of-war, or putting as much effort into evaluating poems as they do alone. But if we believe our personal lack of effort will be noticed and that others will know we have been 'loafing', or if we believe we have a unique contribution to make to the activity, loafing is less likely to take place.

Social impact theory

The most widely accepted explanation of social loafing is offered by social impact theory, developed by Bibb Latané and his colleagues (Latané and Nida, 1980). According to social impact theory, any outside pressure directed towards a group is divided among the group members. Thus the greater the number of people in a group, the less the impact of such a force on each group member. Conversely, the greater the number of outside forces or pressure on one person, the greater the effect they will have. 'Impact', then, is taken to be the sum of the social forces impinging upon a person from the presence of others. Latané suggests three variables that will increase the salience of other people, and thus their impact. The first of these is strength or power. This includes such things as status, role, and age. To give a talk to a group of five people, when one of these people is your teacher, is more stressful than if they are all colleagues. The second is the number of people. The more people present, the greater their impact. It is more stressful to talk to 50 people than to three. The third is immediacy, which refers to the closeness of the other people in time and space. The impact of others is greater if they are actually present than if they are, for example, watching through closed circuit television. Latané suggests that as strength, immediacy and number of others present increase, so does their impact, but that each increment in impact is less than the previous one. The increase in size of a group, for example, from two to three people has a greater impact than the increase in size from 14 to 15 people.

Figure 23.1 summarizes social impact theory, and it should be clear that social impact theory can account for both social facilitation and social loafing effects.

Both social facilitation and social loafing are effects produced by the presence of other people when they make no direct attempts to influence people.

Crowd behaviour

People are often surprised to find that they have been involved in shouting obscenities, committing acts of vandalism or indulging in supposedly wild and impulsive behaviour, as part of a crowd. Early writers on crowd

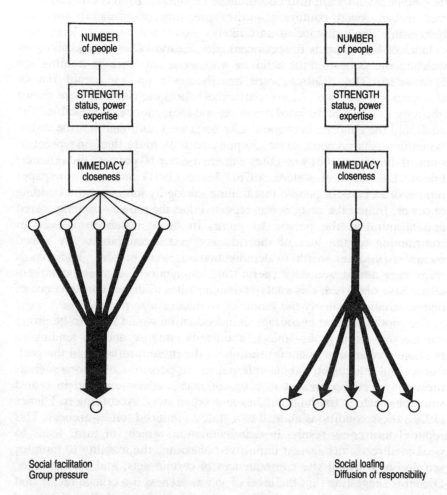

Figure 23.1 Social impact theory

behaviour referred to the 'madness' of crowds and wrote of how large groups took on an 'identity' of their own, irrespective of the people involved. Many social psychologists, nowadays, particularly in the USA, evoke the concept of 'deindividuation' to account for such behaviour.

Deindividuation is a condition in which people are said to feel anonymous and to lose awareness of their own distinguishing characteristics. As a result, they cease the usual monitoring of their own social behaviour and act with less restraint. Furthermore, they reputedly lack a concern about what others will think and have less fear of punishment for antisocial acts. Unfortunately people often perpetrate antisocial acts when deindividuated. However, not all deindividuated acts are aggressive and helping behaviours are also encouraged. Deindividuation is one condition that makes social contagion – the spreading of (usually) antisocial behaviours 'like a disease' – more likely.

In a well-known study of social contagion, Edward Diener and colleagues watched the behaviour of children who were out 'trick-or-treating' on Hallowe'en. The children were heavily made up and could remain anonymous if need be. At one particular house, the children were shown into a room which had a bowl of sweets and some money on the table. The adult told the children they could take one sweet, and then left the room. When the children were alone, 20 per cent took more than one sweet or some of the money, but when they were in a group 60 per cent did (Diener, Fraser, Beaman and Kelem, 1976). Mann (1981) analysed newspaper reports of 21 cases of people threatening suicide by jumping off a building or tower. In half the cases it was reported that the crowd watching jeered and encouraged the person to jump. In those instances, conditions contributing to the loss of individuality and accountability by crowd members (in other words to deindividuation) were present. The crowds were large and it was dark (permitting anonymity). As many commentators have observed, this analysis demonstrates a further consequence of deindividuation, namely the tendency to dehumanize people.

The conditions that encourage deindividuation would seem to be group membership (and group unity), anonymity, intense activity leading to physiological arousal, a concentration on the present rather than the past/future, and a focus on events external to the person. Conditions such as these may well be present at religious mass conversions and in crowd situations such as football matches and urban riots. According to Diener (1979), these conditions all lead to a state of reduced self-awareness. This reduced awareness results in deindividuation, which, in turn, leads to weakened restraints against impulsive behaviour, the inability to monitor self and to consider the consequences of certain acts, and so on. Thus, Diener is suggesting that the level of self-awareness is a crucial factor that mediates between the predisposing conditions for and the effects of deindividuation. An alternative type of explanation, which tends to be favoured by European psychologists, is a social cognitive one, which emphasizes the way in which individuals follow norms (rules or standards) that have developed within the group.

How do groups influence their members?

Groups have tremendous influence over their members irrespective of particular strategies that people in the group adopt, and different types of influence arise. Not all influence leads to changes in attitudes and behaviour, and it may be useful to distinguish between some of the terms used for different types of influence. *Conformity* refers to a change in either behaviour or beliefs as a result of real or imagined group pressure, when no direct request has been made. *Compliance*, on the other hand, describes the situation where people go along with a direct request, thereby changing their behaviour, but not necessarily their attitudes. Neither conformity nor compliance need necessarily result in private acceptance. *Obedience* may involve either conformity or compliance, as it is the following of directions of an authority. For there to be an authority, there must also be a subordinate, so obedience is closely linked to role.

Conformity

Most attempts to distinguish a group from a collection of people make some reference to the extent to which people identify as members of the group and share some expectations that they should recognize and stick to the rules or standards set by the group. The more strongly members identify with the goals and purposes of a group, the more likely they will be to conform to the norms of the group. If all the members identify strongly with the group, it will be a cohesive group, and one that is better able to influence its members.

Group identification

Perhaps the best-known study of group identity is the field experiment known as the Robbers' Cave study, conducted by Muzafer Sherif and colleagues (Sherif, Harvey, White, Hood and Sherif, 1961). They worked with 11- and 12-year-old boys attending a summer camp in the USA and as part of the camp activities they divided the boys into two groups, the Red Devils and the Bulldogs. The groups were given activities to do so that members began identifying with their own group. The more they did things together in their groups, the more cohesive the groups became. The two groups were then given tasks to do in competition with each other and very soon inter-group hostility grew. Boys from each group started to dislike and fight with members from the opposite group. They also tried hard to be more successful in the various activities. All the boys belonging to each group were found to identify strongly with their own group, and to value the ways in which their group behaved. They all conformed to their own group's standards or norms. Sherif *et al* suggest that categorizing the boys differently and creating conflict between the groups led to strong in-group identification (from which out-group hostility developed).

Henri Tajfel and his colleagues in Bristol set out to discover the *minimal* requirements of group membership that would produce conformity to some group norms. Tajfel found that schoolboys who were randomly allocated to different groups showed preference for members of their group as opposed to members of the other group. It was not necessary to give them tasks of any sort, either competitive or co-operative. This led Tajfel to suggest that categorization into groups is an important determinant of group identity, which itself will lead to conforming behaviour. (Both Sherif and Tajfel developed complex accounts of how group identity leads to prejudiced and hostile behaviour.)

In these studies, the boys either knew each other before the experiment (Tajfel) or got to know each other during the study (Sherif). Studies have also shown that even in newly formed groups, norms very quickly develop. They then act as a source of influence on people to conform (or at least comply) with other members' views.

Classic conformity experiments

Ambiguity

Another famous experiment was conducted by Muzafer Sherif in 1935 (see Sherif, 1936). Sherif sat people in a dark room and asked them to observe a small spot of light, which, although stationary, appeared to move. (This is known as the autokinetic effect and it occurs automatically.) When asked how far the light had moved, subjects sitting alone quickly developed a stable frame of reference and made all their judgements of movement within a small range. There were considerable differences in range between subjects. When asked to make their judgements with other people (i.e. in a group) subjects' judgements converged with the range of judgements offered by others. It seemed as if a group norm was developing. They conformed about 80 per cent of the time when the judgements of the range of distance were manipulated by the experimenter. (Typically the experimenter would use confederates, who had been given specific movement ranges to report, as the other group members.) In this experiment, the subjects had little reliable information of their own on which to base their judgements. The situation was ambiguous, so it seems sensible that they would take into account what other people said (although, interestingly, subjects usually claimed not to have been influenced by the other group members). When subjects had the illusion explained to them and they knew the light did not move, they no longer conformed to other people's judgements. This suggests that people accept the influence of others in an attempt to assess the reality of a situation; if they know the reality, they are not susceptible to the influence.

Group pressure

Conformity effects are not, however, eliminated by the ability to assess a situation accurately, as demonstrated by Solomon Asch in 1956. Subjects were asked to judge which of 3 lines on a board appeared to be the same length as a single line on another board. The task was very easy and 90 per cent of people could make the right choice. In the experiment, one target subject was unknowingly placed with a group of 5–6 confederates. Each person was to state their choice out loud with the target subject speaking last. The first few times that sets of lines were presented, everyone made the right choice. Then the first member made a wrong choice, the second member agreed with this decision and so on. By the time the target subject had to speak, all the others had made incorrect choices. What would this subject do? Over a series of experiments, Asch found that 15 per cent of subjects conformed on three-quarters or more of the actual trials, although no subject conformed to the incorrect choices on every one of their 12 trials. There is no suggestion here that subjects believed they were wrong and others were right. They simply showed conforming behaviour. The conformity effect only appeared if there was total agreement amongst confederates in giving the wrong decision. If confederates disagreed with each other, target subjects stuck with their own original decisions. In Asch's experiment there was less conformity than in Sherif's but it was, nevertheless, present. It is unlikely that subjects looked to other group members for information in Asch's experiment as the situation was unambiguous. They knew they were right. So why conform? It is generally thought that they conformed because they did not wish to appear different: they wanted to be approved of and liked by other group members, so they succumbed to group pressure. They knew that what they said was wrong, but they said it anyway. Subjects probably thought that 'going along with the group' was the best thing to do in the circumstances.

As we have seen, not all subjects did conform in Asch's experiments. Other experiments similar to Asch's have suggested that individual differences make it more likely that people will conform. Subjects who are led to believe that other group members are better at the task than they are themselves will be more likely to conform, whereas those that believe that other members are worse than they are, will not. It seems then that subjects' evaluation of their own ideas in comparison with others' affects their susceptibility to influence. Linked closely to this is the finding that subjects who have a low opinion of themselves generally (i.e. have low self-esteem) are more susceptible to influence. Many studies indicate that women are more susceptible to influence than men. However, if the task is changed to one that women are interested in, they show *less* susceptibility to influence than men!

Implications of the conformity experiments

A great deal has been said (partly as a result of Asch's experiments) about the irresistible forces of group pressure, the ways majorities will inevitably influence minorities and how people will conform mindlessly to the dominant status quo. As with much of the extrapolation from experimental studies in the laboratory to the social world, most of these assertions are unjustified. Nevertheless, the experiments themselves did receive widespread publicity. Social psychologists are now faced with an interesting question. If people become aware of social psychological findings, does their behaviour change? There is a growing conviction amongst social psychologists that the nature of socal psychological phenomena does indeed change over time, and that the assimilation of social psychological findings, as just described, contributes to these changes. Attempts to replicate Asch's experiments in the late 1970s and early 1980s have on the whole failed, and this might be one reason why. Other reasons will, of course, be the effects of other kinds of more general social changes, such as greater 'permissiveness' in some sectors of society.

It is useful to distinguish between *informational influence* (as in Sherif's study) and *normative influence* (as in Asch's study). Informational influence is the influence to accept information from another person as evidence about our own reality. The process is rational and we may or may not be happy about acknowledging the role of other people's views. Normative influence is the influence to conform with other people's positive expectations. This is not such a rational process: it works by reinforcing our own positive feelings which come from being accepted and approved of by others. Normative influence will be increased with strong group identity and group cohesion.

Anti-conformity and deviance

We suggested that people do not always conform to majority influence, so in what circumstances will people resist? Evidence from many different kinds of experimental and field studies indicates that a determined, consistent minority can influence other group members. Furthermore, the more members have conformed in the past, the more their deviance is tolerated by the group. People earn what are known as 'idiosyncrasy credits' as they conform to group norms. The more they accumulate the more the group will tolerate deviance in the future. If, however, people adamantly refuse to conform to group norms, in laboratory studies at least the group will isolate them after attempting to bring them back in line. This process underlies the labelling theory of deviance. If people are labelled deviant, others will behave towards them in ways that make it difficult for them to conform and they continue in their deviance. Such deviance is not usually, however, anti-normative. Generally people that do not conform to one set of norms (i.e. are deviant) do conform to another set. In other words, deviance is, itself, bound to norms. Let us take, for example, a 'rebellious teenager'. She or he may reject the family norms and behave in seemingly quite deviant ways. Parents may find this perplexing until they see that many other young people behave in the same (deviant) ways. They are all conforming to a different set of norms.

Even in well-controlled laboratory experiments (and certainly in the social world) not everyone will conform. Some people do just the opposite. Researchers investigating people's willingness to comply with their medical or psychiatric treatment have developed the concept of reactance. Reactance is, essentially, a type of obstinacy that some people show when others try to get them to do things. It is thought that reactance is one way in which we try to assert some control over situations in which we see ourselves as relatively powerless. The result of reactance is a refusal to comply with what is being requested. By understanding reactance, we may be able to understand why some people fail or even refuse to co-operate in therapy, to take medication regularly, or to go into hospital when summoned for an operation.

Overconformity

It is also possible to overconform to a particular set of norms. People who do this tend to lose their sense of individuality and cease to monitor their own behaviour. This helps create the conditions for deindividuation, discussed earlier, and one way to become deindividuated is to over-conform.

The conformity debate is part of a much wider debate about people's ability to exercise free will and to express their own uniqueness. While most people do claim a certain amount of freedom, they also reveal what is known as the 'superior conformity of the self'. Many experimental studies have pointed to the tendency we have to overestimate the extent to which our own behaviour is normative, as compared with other people's. We do this while still celebrating our uniqueness. If we did not conform and could not rely on the conformity of others, we would not be able to make predictions about how the social world operates. We could not rely on other people to avoid colliding with us in the street, to pay for their goods in a shop, to greet old friends, and so on. Up to a point, conformity underpins the social order.

What are the different ways we influence each other?

John French and Bertram Raven suggested that social power could be divided into six types. They defined social power as the potential influence of some influencing agent over some other person. The bases of social power are coercion, reward, reference, expertise, information and legitimacy.

Coercive power is our ability to punish other people if they do not comply. The threat of punishment may be effective in the short term, producing changes in overt behaviour but not in beliefs. It is an inefficient form of power because the people who are being coerced must be watched to see if they do what is required or not and thus whether the punishment must be given.

Reward power is our ability to reinforce compliant behaviour. Reward power is similarly inefficient. It, too, may produce short-term changes in behaviour and people must be watched to see if they deserve a reward. When the rewards stop, compliant behaviour will also stop.

Referential power is more subtle and more efficient. This is the power we have if we are liked or respected, simply because we are liked or respected. The power lies in the extent to which people identify with us, as the source of power. Incidentally, we may not be aware of our referential power over people. Referential power can produce long-term changes in behaviour, but they will only last as long as the initial attraction lasts. It is unlikely that the influence will lead to private acceptance, although it may do if people internalize changes, and begin to identify with us.

Expert power and the power of information, however, can lead to change in opinion as well as in behaviour. While people believe in our expertise they will be influenced by us; but as soon as our expertise is questioned, so our influence will dwindle. Similarly, so long as people accept the information that we give them as true, we will be influential. Expert power is transmitted through social relationships, but the power of information is not socially dependent: information is power, independent of who gives it.

Legitimate power is, arguably, the strongest, most efficient form of power. If people accept that we have the right to control them and accept the rules that say we have this right they will comply with almost any requests we make of them.

These forms of power are not independent of each other and at any time people may be subjected to more than one type of power. What power can be exerted by, for example, works supervisors who are liked a lot, know a great deal about the work in hand, are able to allocate overtime and who work in highly structured, hierarchical organizations? They would be able to influence employees through referent, coercive, reward, expert/ information and legitimate power.

Do we always do as we are told?

A particular role relationship that has attracted a lot of interest is the authority relationship. Social roles are the positions in a social system that people hold. Role expectations, to a large extent, define how different roles are played (this idea is similar to the labelling theory of deviance mentioned earlier). In an authority relationship, the authority figures (people occupying the authority role) will *expect* subordinates (people occupying the subordinate roles) to do as they are told. Similarly, subordinates will expect to do as they are told because they accept the legitimate power of the authority (in the sense discussed above). There are many instances, daily, when people excuse their behaviour with the plea 'I was only doing what I was told', and those studying obedience attempt to make sense of this excuse. In Nazi Germany, many of those involved in inhuman brutality claimed they were following orders and they, themselves, were not vicious, cruel people. In an attempt, initially, to demonstrate that people from the United States of America would not commit cruel and inhuman acts simply because they were told to, Stanley Milgram conducted what are, perhaps, the best-known of all social psychological experiments.

The obedience experiments

Milgram wanted to duplicate the kind of situation in which one person orders another person to commit an atrocity. He advertised in a local newspaper for men to participate in a memory and learning experiment at Yale University. When subjects arrived they were introduced to another subject (really an actor who was Milgram's confederate) by an experimenter wearing a white coat, carrying a clipboard and appearing competent and stern with a firm tone of voice. Subjects were told that the experiment was to investigate the effects of punishment on learning. One subject was to be teacher and the other (always the stooge) to be learner. The teacher was to help the learner by giving him electric shocks every time he made a mistake. By prearrangement, the learner made many! The teacher helped strap the learner into a chair and watched the experimenter fasten an electrode to his arm. The wires from this led to an electric shock generator next door. Unknown to the teacher, the generator was not switched on and no shocks were actually given. The teacher was then seated in front of the shock generator. This had 30 levers, clearly labelled from 15 to 450 volts at 15 volt intervals. Groups of levers were labelled 'mild', 'very strong', 'very intense', 'XXX danger, severe shock'. The teacher was told to give the learner an electric shock each time he made a mistake, starting at the lowest level and increasing the shock by 15 volts on each mistake. To illustrate what a shock was like, the teacher was given a 45 volt shock which stung considerably. By arrangement, on receiving a 75 volt shock, the learner began to grunt and moan; at 150 volts he demanded to be let out of the experiment; at 180 volts he cried out that he could no longer stand the pain; at 300 volts he refused to provide any more answers. At this point, the experimenter told the teacher to treat no answer as a mistake and to continue with the shock programme. If at any point the teacher said he did not want to continue, the experimenter replied with a sequence of prearranged comments, using as many as necessary before the teacher continued. These were:

'Please go on.'
'The experiment requires that you continue.'
'It is absolutely necessary that you continue.'
'You have no other choice, you *must* go on.'

If at any point the subject refused to obey after the fourth instruction, the experiment was terminated.

The dependent measure in this experiment was the number of shocks a subject was willing to give before giving up. Milgram had asked some Yale psychiatrists and other mental health workers to predict the behaviour of people in this experiment. They thought that most people would stop at 150 volts, when the learner first demanded to be let loose; that fewer than 5 per cent would go as high as 350 volts; and that 0.001 per cent would go all the way to the top. Of 40 subjects in the experiment, 26 went all the way to the top; 5 stopped at 375 volts; 4 stopped at 315 volts; and 5 at 300 volts. Subjects did not give increasing electric shocks calmly and in fact many of those who did go all the way were often quite distressed – nevertheless, they continued when instructed to.

None of the subjects suspected that the learner was not really being shocked and when told this and introduced to a live, healthy learner at the end of the experiment, they showed considerable relief.

Explanations of the obedience experiments

Milgram suggested that because the experiment was conducted in a highly prestigious, scientific establishment and appeared to be a legitimate research study, subjects may have abdicated responsibility for their behaviour, investing the competent experimenter with this responsibility. To test this Milgram repeated the experiment in the nearby city centre, in a marginally respectable office. The experiment was promoted as a piece of research for industry, conducted by a private firm. All reference to Yale University was dropped. Once more, to his surprise, Milgram obtained similar results. Other explanations for the findings were offered. Subjects were indeed encouraged to obey. It could have been that the gradual escalation of the punishments gave subjects no clear breaking point from which to move from obedience to disobedience. Thus, any attempt to monitor and regulate their own behaviour would have been difficult. In addition, they received encouragement rather than discouragement doing what, in normal circumstances, would have been prohibited, and this led to increasingly serious violations. This seems to suggest that, given the chance, people will behave in ways that are normally prohibited.

Subsequent experiments showed that the closer the teachers were to the learners, the more readily they disobeyed; if the experimenter was not physically present but left recorded instructions subjects more readily disobeyed; if orders were given and subjects could set their own level of shock, very low levels were chosen; if subjects were told they, themselves, were responsible for the outcomes, rather than the experimenter, there was less obedience; the presence of other people who disobeyed orders reduced obedience; and if the experimenter appeared incompetent, obedience was reduced. So it seems that we can identify some of the conditions that will increase the likelihood that ordinary people will obey destructive orders. These include diminished responsibility, lack of opportunity to monitor own behaviour, physical distance from the targets of destructive behaviour, surveillance by authority, receiving orders from authority, isolation from others that refuse orders and the perceived legitimacy of the authority issuing the orders. Milgram's experiments were replicated in Australia, Jordan and West Germany, which makes it difficult for people outside the USA to claim 'it couldn't happen here'. What these experiments show is that authority roles are, indeed, powerful.

Implications of the obedience experiments

Milgram's experiments have had far reaching effects. Not only are they probably the most widely publicized social psychological experiments, but they have been quite severely criticized by other social psychologists for being unethical. Critics ask whether telling subjects at the end of the experiment (debriefing them) that they had not really hurt the learner is sufficient, and question whether there were not long-term, psychologically damaging consequences to the subjects. Although Milgram claims that there were no lasting effects to his subjects, it is unlikely that any ethics committee in a research establishment would permit such a study today. This illustrates rather well how past social psychological investigations can shape future investigations. It is unlikely, too, given the widespread awareness of Milgram's experiments, that subjects would behave in similar ways in such experiments nowadays – another example of the way assimilation of social psychological findings can change the very nature of the processes under scrutiny.

Simulated prison study

Some people have suggested that Milgram's experiments could be role-played and subjects asked to behave 'as if' the experiment was real. Others have devised complex extended role-plays manipulating different aspects of obedience and role. One such study was conducted by Philip Zimbardo and his colleagues at Stanford University. They sought to demonstrate that people's behaviour in highly structured situations with clear role expectations (e.g. a prison) is typical, and more a function of their role rather than their personality.

Zimbardo advertised in local newspapers for 24 normal, college-age men to take part in an experiment lasting 14 days. They were told (truthfully) the general purpose of the experiment and offered $1500 to take part. When 24 men had been carefully assessed to ensure they had no psychiatric history or symptoms, they were recruited and divided into two groups of prisoners and guards at the toss of a coin (compare Tajfel's experiment). The guards were given a general briefing about the dangers of being a prison guard, but were not told how to act: it was up to them to establish the prison rules. They were equipped with role-props, such as sticks, uniforms and mirrored polarized glasses. The experiment began with the prisoners being picked up at home, unexpectedly, by 'policemen' and taken to a police station where they were finger-printed and 'booked'. They were then taken, blindfolded, to Zimbardo's mock jail, which was in the basement of the Psychology Department of Stanford University. There, they were stripped, searched, deloused and given prison clothing with numbers on it. They were shown to the 'cells' where they were to spend the next fortnight. However, the experiment had to be stopped after six days because of the alarming changes in behaviour of both prisoners and guards. After an early rebellion was 'quelled' by the guards, the prisoners became passive, lethargic and depressed and some began to show signs of severe disturbance (one man had to be 'released' after 36 hours as he displayed uncontrollable fits of crying and screaming). The guards, at the same time, became increasingly brutal and sadistic, harassing prisoners in senseless and dehumanizing ways. They appeared to enjoy their acts of cruelty. Prisoners seemingly lost their sense of personal identity and social responsibility, even letting a fellow prisoner spend the night in a small cupboard, rather than give up their blankets (an option given them by the guards). Zimbardo suggested that this study demonstrated the power of role and group membership on people's behaviour. What is clear is that the conditions for deindividuation were ripe. Prisoners were allocated a number rather than a name, and were given baggy, nondescript uniforms. Guards, too, wore uniforms and were able to 'hide' behind their polarized glasses. Zimbardo suggested that the deindividuation of both prisoners and guards was an important influence on their behaviour.

Implications of the prison study

Critics have suggested that the results may have been due to the fact that subjects knew they were taking part in an experiment on prison roles and so they behaved in a typical way. It was also suggested that the 'dehumanizing' props given to the guards encouraged extreme behaviours. Interestingly though an attempt to replicate the experiment in Australia in more humane conditions (no uniforms, plenty of open 'exercise' area, etc.) had similarly to be stopped long before the end of the proposed time for similar reasons (Lovibond, Adams and Adams, 1979).

Zimbardo's study also raised an outcry about the ethical issues involved, although Zimbardo, like Milgram, claimed there were no adverse consequences for his subjects. On the contrary, he noted later that many of his subjects had gone on to do voluntary work in prisons or had become advocates of penal reform. This may, however, be an indication of just how much psychological distress participants had suffered.

Both Milgram and Zimbardo used men in their original studies. Replications of Milgram's experiments, using women, indicate they would act in the same way, but there have been no replications of the prison study using women.

Who are the most effective leaders?

Leadership is a specific type of social influence: it is the process of influencing group members towards achieving group goals. As an area of study, leadership is interesting on two counts.

First, the research reflects a wide range of methods. Field and laboratory experiments as well as correlational studies abound, and while challenges to the ecological validity of the laboratory studies and the objectivity of field studies have been made, they all lead to similar conclusions.

Second, it is an area of study where ideological and political influences on the 'objectivity' of researchers is apparent.

Characteristics of leaders: trait approach

In the 1950s there was a profusion of attempts to identify the characteristics of leaders. These studies were based on the premise that leaders are born, not made, in other words, some people will inherently make good leaders because they possess a 'leadership personality' and others will make bad leaders. People cannot, then, learn to lead – nor can they be trained. Instead, the task is to find people with certain traits and put them in leadership roles. Randle (1956) gave psychological tests to, and interviewed, 1427 executives from 27 companies in the USA. Thirty traits were identified which differentiated between good, mediocre and bad leaders. Good leaders were found, for example, to possess more drive, intelligence and motivation than poor leaders. However, other studies have identified different characteristics of good leaders. In general, there is no agreement between studies, but rather a lot of overlapping results. Furthermore, and importantly for correlational studies such as these, the relationship between different traits and quality of leadership is not strong and no characteristics seem to predict leadership in all situations. A further problem is the difficulty of deciding whether certain traits produce good leaders or being a leader leads to the adoption of certain traits.

Leadership style: behaviour approach

Another approach is to examine behaviour rather than personality. The Ohio State Studies, as they are known, were carried out in the 1950s. The behaviour of supervisors in different work settings was analysed. A list of 1800 specific behavioural incidents was compiled and this in turn was reduced to a list of 150 different behaviours, on which a questionnaire (the Leader Behavior Description Questionnaire or LBDQ) was based. From numerous studies using the LBDQ, two basic kinds of behaviour have been identified, namely those concerned with *consideration* and those concerned with *initiating structure*. Behaviours typical of consideration make employees feel like valuable people whose feelings of well-being are important. Initiating structure behaviours focus on getting the job done. Many subsequent studies indicate that supervisors who show high levels of *consideration* behaviours elicit fewer grievances and less turnover amongst their employees, whereas the opposite is true for supervisors engaged in *initiating structure* behaviours. Interestingly, though, if a supervisor shows consideration behaviours as well as those initiating structure, they counter-act the latter's negative effects. In other words, we can, as leaders, push group members hard as long as we show consideration at the same time.

A particularly influential field study of leadership styles has been that by Lewin, Lippitt and White (1939). (Kurt Lewin is the founder of the 'Human Relations School' which has been a dominant force in industrial psychology for the past 30 years or more.) They set out to compare the levels of aggressive behaviour and productivity in after school hobby groups of ten-year-old schoolboys, working under democratic and auto-cratic leadership. The democratic leader involved the boys in all the decisions about how they were to work, whereas the autocratic leader issued instructions. Each group was to have had democratic and autocratic leadership in turn. One group reacted so (unpredictably) aggressively to democratic leadership that the researchers claimed the leader had not really behaved democratically. After the study had begun they therefore incorporated a third category of leadership style – laissez-faire leadership. Here the leader took little or no part in the decision making process, and made no attempt to structure the activities. (It was not until 1960 that Lippitt and White admitted to this procedure. In 1939 the experiment was reported as *designed* around three leadership styles, autocratic, democratic and laissez-faire.) The authors reported a high level of aggression under all conditions for one group and the remaining three showing more aggression under democratic than autocratic leadership, with productivity being highest under autocratic leadership. Yet, despite these findings, Lewin, Lippitt and White concluded that democratic leadership was more efficient and produced less frustration, less aggression, or both. This study, complete with its conclusion of the superiority of democratic leadership, has been widely and uncritically presented in textbooks and journals and has been particularly influential in industrial psychology circles where the prevailing view has favoured democratic leadership. How can this be? There are many different ways that the issues raised by this study can be explained. It can at least be suggested that both in 1939, and again in the 1950s and 1960s, when the democratic, 'free' USA was threatened by Hitler and by Stalinist Russia respectively, there was strong pressure to produce results in a certain direction. The role of ideology, transmitted through the personal and cultural values of the researchers, on experimental findings, is not confined to research on human subjects. Bertrand Russell wrote:

> One may say broadly that all the animals that have been carefully observed have behaved so as to confirm the philosophy in which the observer believed before his observations began. Nay, more, they have all displayed the national characteristics of the observer. Animals studied by Americans rush about frantically, with an incredible display of hustle and pep, and at last achieve the desired result by chance. Animals observed by Germans sit still and think, and at last evolve the solution out of their inner consciousness.
>
> Russell (1927) pp. 32–3

Russell obviously had in mind the experiments of Thorndike and Kohler in particular. Lewin's study provides a good example of how 'experimenter expectations' can reflect cultural values. The distortion of the design of the experiment shows the pressure researchers were (and possibly still are) under to conduct 'objective and scientifically sound experiments'. Field experiments are notoriously difficult to control, which is why many researchers take refuge in the laboratory and this is where the emergence and functions of leadership roles have been studied.

Functions of leadership roles: interactional approach

Robert Bales and his associates were interested in the emergence of leaders in groups which have no designated leaders. He devised the 'Leaderless Discussion Group' (LDG) paradigm which formed the framework for very many experiments. Groups of strangers (2–6 people) were invited to meet for 40 minutes once a week for four weeks to discuss a topic for which they received a five page brief beforehand. There was no problem and no solution to be found from the discussion, which was to be held for its own ends. The group discussion was taped and observed through a one-way screen, where a number of observers coded the interactions between people into several categories. A simplified version of the categories used by Bales is shown in Table 23.1

Using this information, as well as asking participants, after each session, who they liked best, who had the best ideas and who stood out as the best leader, Bales could study the emergence of leaders over time. Bales found that two quite distinct but complementary leadership roles emerged. Initially, in different groups, those people with the best ideas, and who

697

Table 23.1 Simplified categories used in Bales's interaction process analysis

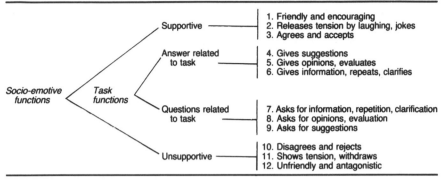

gave a lot of task-related answers were considered to be the leaders; they were also liked. In subsequent sessions they became less liked and those people who gave a lot of supportive comments emerged as being the best liked. While Bales acknowledged the artificiality of his experimental groups, which revealed, at best, the very earliest developmental stages of groups, he argued that two quite distinct leadership roles emerged, reflecting the needs of the group. The first fulfilled task-related functions (the *task* leader) and the second fulfilled interpersonal functions (the *socio-emotive* leader). Bales concluded that differentiation of leadership functions was necessary to the survival of a group and that the bifurcation (splitting into two) of the leadership role helped fulfil this function. It is worth mentioning at this point that this dual leadership role is very similar to the different kinds of leadership behaviour identified from the behavioural perspective discussed above. The differences between *consideration* and *initiating structure* behaviours are very similar to the differences between *task* and *socio-emotive* leaders. Quite different kinds of studies indicate, then, that different people display different styles of leadership and that groups need both kinds. There is considerable controversy, still, as to whether two people are necessary to fulfil the different leadership functions and whether they can both be met by the same person. While laboratory studies may be criticized for telling us little about how real groups work, there is surprisng similarity as we have seen between these laboratory and naturalistic studies.

Legitimacy of leadership power

One important factor that characterizes most real life groups, in contrast with laboratory groups, is the legitimate power that leaders have. In work groups, for instance, there is usually an institutional or organizational basis for legitimating who leads, and why. In informal groups, legitimacy is the result of members choosing their own leaders on the basis of their expertise or some other relevant criterion. Some studies have suggested that in those real life groups where the leader has little legitimacy, the bifurcation of *task* and *socio-emotive* leadership occurs. Otherwise, both functions have, generally, to be fulfilled by the same person if the leader is to be effective.

There is a danger that, by identifying our concern with leadership, we fail to take account of those that are led, or of the different circumstances in which leaders are operating. It is quite possible, for example, for the performance of group members to determine leader/supervisor style rather than vice versa.

Leadership effectiveness: systems approach

Fiedler (see, for example, 1978) proposed that the effectiveness of task-oriented and person-oriented leadership styles depends on the favour-ability of the situation for the leader. The favourability of the situation is defined according to three variables, which combine to reflect the ease with which leaders can influence group members. These variables are:

1. Group atmosphere or leader–member relations: if group members get on with each other well, are loyal towards and show confidence in their leader, the situation is favourable.
2. Task structure: the more clearly structured the task the more favourable the situation.
3. Position power: the more legitimate power the leader has, the more favourable the situation.

Leadership style was obtained by asking the leaders of small work groups to describe and evaluate their least 'preferred co-worker' (LPC) from previous work settings. Fiedler assumed a high LPC score (positive rating) reflected a friendly, accepting, person-oriented leader, whereas a low LPC score (negative rating) reflected a distant, demanding task-oriented leader. Fiedler examined many different real life groups and analysed them in terms of leadership styles and favourability of the situation. He found that effectiveness in achieving group goals depended on both leadership style and the situation. His findings were complex, but broadly they suggest that low LPC leaders (task-oriented) were more successful in those situations that were either very favourable or very unfavourable, whereas high LPC leaders (person-oriented) were effective in those situations of moderate favourability. The different combination of variables of situational favour-ability and effective leadership style are shown in Table 23.2.

Fiedler's model has been criticized on several fronts. The assumptions underlying the LPC score as a measure of leadership style have been challenged, as have some of the statistics he used to demonstrate the relationship between leadership style and situational favourability. Nevertheless, the model does manage to relate leadership functions and

Table 23.2 Leadership effectiveness and favourability of the situation

Favourability of the situation			
Group atmosphere	Task structure	Position power	Most effective leadership style
Good	High	Strong	Task oriented
Good	High	Weak	Task oriented
Good	Low	Strong	Task oriented
Good	Low	Weak	Person oriented
Poor	High	Strong	Person oriented
Poor	Low	Strong	Person oriented
Poor	Low	Weak	Task oriented

roles to personal styles and situational factors. Crucially, it conceptualizes leadership as a process of mutual influence between leaders and followers and thus does not fall into the trap of exploring the leadership role in isolation. It is able to account for why one particular leadership style will not be effective in all situations and it points to the possibility of training leaders to respond flexibly in different situations. The essential question is not whether both task and socio-emotive functions can be fulfilled by one person, but how the functions required of leaders change as situations change and how leaders themselves can be helped to respond flexibly to changing group circumstances. The question of whether leaders are born or made, that began this discussion, is now irrelevant. Leadership is conceptualized as neither a process nor a role, but rather as part of a dynamic system of mutual influence.

When will we help each other?

Interest in altruism and helping (more recently known as prosocial behaviour) was fuelled by concern over some widely publicized emergencies where people did *not* help others. The incident that is most frequently cited as the catalyst to helping research is the murder of Kitty Genovese in New York in 1964. The incident is well documented. Kitty was fatally stabbed in three different attacks by the same assailant in the early hours of the morning. Thirty-eight people living nearby witnessed the attacks but no one went to her aid. After quite a time, one person, anonymously, called the police after seeking the advice of two friends.

In 1985 a small girl, Leonie Keating, was heard and seen wandering around a caravan site in Great Yarmouth, England, in her nightdress, calling for her mother in the middle of the night. No one went to her. Leonie was later found sexually assaulted and dead in a ditch some way away. Why did no one help her? Similar instances appear in the newspapers daily. Onlookers, neighbours and bystanders seem reluctant to help others, even if they are obviously dependent and distressed.

Rather than study the types of people who will/will not intervene to help, several studies have tried to tease out the different circumstances in which people will or will not help others in distress. These include simulation of emergencies, requests for assistance, and analyses of real life catastrophes. Before discussing the issues raised by these studies, we will consider the development of some of the social norms (or standards) that underlie helping behaviour.

The development of helping behaviour

A fundamental moral principle of many major religions, including Christianity, Islam, Hinduism, Buddhism, and Judaism, is that we should help others in need, even when there are no obvious rewards for doing so. This principle is thought to be the cornerstone of civilized human society. Although there may be examples of this extreme form of helping among humans, by and large, helping behaviour can be thought of in terms of rewards (where the helper stands to gain or lose by helping) and the acceptance of certain social norms. It has been suggested that four norms are particularly relevant. The first is the *norm of social responsibility* – advantaged people *should* help those more needy than themselves. This norm is likely to have the greatest impact if the people to be helped are obviously dependent, and if the costs to the helper are low. Related to this is the *norm of social justice* – it is only necessary to help people who do not deserve their suffering. If people are seen to be responsible for their suffering they are less likely to be helped. The third norm is the *norm of reciprocity* – if we help, we are likely to be helped when the needs arise; alternatively, we help because we were helped ourselves in the past. This norm is likely to have greatest impact where helpers can see how they have been or could be helped themselves; they can see 'what's in it for them'. A fourth norm is the *norm of justified self-interest* – we will only help in so far as we can retain what others like us have. Thus, if the costs of helping lead helpers to be in a worse position than others whom they consider to be like them, they will not help. The very process of comparing ourselves with others leads us to experience a particular act as either costly or rewarding. Three broad frameworks in which we can understand helping and not helping have been developed.

Approaches to the study of helping and prosocial behaviour

Social learning

The first is a social learning framework. Social learning theorists suggest that we learn to help through a variety of channels, the most widely discussed being observation. Children need to observe others helping in order to learn to help. In helping situations, such as giving donations to charity, offering to give blood, and so on, seeing others helping incites greater helping behaviour. From this perspective, Robert Cialdini and colleagues propose three stages in the development of helping behaviours in children. The first stage is one of pre-socialization. Children are reluctant to help because they feel they may have to sacrifice something. In the second stage, children become aware of the norms that incorporate some notion of reward (for example, people that help will be rewarded, in some way, for helping). At this stage, they help others in order to get rewards for themelves. Lastly, they enter a stage of internalization. Helping, itself, becomes rewarding and makes people feel good, and can therefore occur in the absence of other extrinsic rewards. Social learning theory accounts suggest that people's motivations to help change as they get older. It also suggests that features of the situation, both antecedent (before the act) and consequent (following the act), will determine the extent to which people will help. One idea within social learning theory that has received relatively little attention in the context of helping, is Albert Bandura's concept of 'self-efficacy' or the belief that we can be efficacious in a given situation. Anecdotal accounts of 'I didn't think I'd be much use' and the like are common, but few studies have looked at the belief itself as a determinant of helping.

Empathy

A rather different framework is one that incorporates physiological arousal with a rewards–cost analysis. This seeks to explain what happens to us in an emergency and what might determine whether or not we will help in such circumstances. Jane Piliavin and her colleagues present the argument in this way:

Our witness of another person's distress, directly or indirectly leads to physiological arousal. The greater our arousal, the more likely we are to help. Following Stanley Schachter's (1964) theory about the labelling of emotional states, she suggests that we then label this arousal as a particular feeling or emotion. If the label is personal distress, we will help in order to relieve the distress and thus the arousal. If we see the distressed person as similar to ourselves, we may label the arousal as empathy. In other words, we experience the other person's distress as our own. Our major concern is, then, to alleviate the distress and to help. However, before helping, we will evaluate the situation in terms of the costs of helping versus the costs of not helping.

Social cognition

The third approach is cognitive and pays little attention to our affective (emotional) state (Latané and Darley, 1970). First, we have to notice something that has happened and we then need to interpret the situation as one where help is needed. After taking cues from the environment, we must then assume personal responsibility to help and lastly must choose and be able to offer some specific form of assistance. At any point in the process we can decide not to help. Furthermore, the presence of other people can stop us helping at any point. Let us turn now to some of the investigations that throw some light on the complexities of helping behaviour.

Experimental studies of helping and prosocial behaviour

Simulations of emergencies

Many different kinds of emergencies have been simulated. In one study (Latané and Rodin, 1969), strangers (one target subject and several stooges) were shown to a waiting room by a woman. The woman went behind a curtain and carried on using a filing cabinet. While they were waiting in the room, reading, from the room they had passed came a scream and a crash. Subjects waiting alone invariably went to investigate. If, however, a subject was with a group of stooges, all of whom seemed unconcerned at the commotion, s/he seldom went to help. It seems from this and a variety of other similar studies that if other people are present, helping is less likely. One explanation for this is diffusion of responsibility. When we have to take personal responsibility (when we are alone, for instance) we are more likely to help. The impact of other people may, however, be nothing to do with diffusion of responsibility. It could be that people judge the reactions of others as a basis for deciding how urgent a situation is and whether or not to help. Indeed, it does seem, from the experimental evidence, that the ambiguity of the situation is important in determining people's readiness to intervene. People seem to try to work out what is happening by taking cues from other people or from the situation. (There are similarities here with the work on conformity discussed earlier in the chapter. There, too, other people's reactions were important sources of information in ambiguous situations.) Other findings from this type of experiment indicate that people help more when they know *how* to help; they help less when they perceive others present to be more competent to help; and they help more if the 'victim' is thought to be similar to themselves. We can see, from these experiments, elements of all three explanations for helping behaviour.

Requests for assistance

Another type of study that has been widely used is the investigation of responses to requests for assistance. Typically, a confederate of the experimenter will make a request of members of the public in different situations and accompanied by various excuses. One study involved people simply being asked to give someone a small amount of money. Thirty-four per cent of people gave the money on being asked, with no reason given; 64 per cent gave money if the excuse was to pay for a phone call; and 72 per cent gave money if they were told the person's wallet had been stolen. The greater the legitimacy of the request, the more likely people seem to give assistance. However, any excuse is better than no excuse. Generally the findings indicate that if people observe others assisting they, themselves, are more likely to. The lower the material costs (for example, time involved) and the less the personal costs, the more response. It is interesting to consider, then, why justifying a request should make a difference, and an explanation for this may be found in the earlier discussion of norms. The norms of responsibility and of justice indicate that we feel more pressure to help other people if they make legitimate requests for our help. Richard Eiser suggests that this notion of deserved-ness is an important one. His argument centres around the idea of justified self-interest, alluded to earlier. Experiments indicate that if people are thought to deserve their suffering, help is likely to be withheld. However, if we, as just and fair people, see the suffering of others as undeserved, we have to consider offering assistance with the possibility of forgoing some of the benefits we, ourselves, have earned. To help us decide whether to act or not, we look to other 'just and fair' people like ourselves for definitions of how to act justly in this situation. We are then able to 'do our bit' and to give, while retaining as much as others, similar to ourselves, have. If we do not make this comparison, Eiser suggests, we will always be able to see others worse off than ourselves and there will then be no limit to what we will give. This comparison process depends very much on how we define our relationships with others and is a crucial factor in helping us guess the relative costs and rewards of helping. Even if an act is costly, it may be seen as justified.

Social comparison has been shown to play a part, too, in professional helping relationships. There is evidence to suggest that the extent to which clients or users of, for example, medical and social services are liked and perceived to be similar to those giving the service affects the quality of the service. The more similar and more liked the users are, the better the service they receive. Aspects of the situation and the thoughts and beliefs of the potential helpers (that is, their social cognitions) have both been shown to affect the readiness with which people will help or give assistance to others.

Person-situation debate

There has been a debate since the mid-1970s about the relative contribu-tion of aspects of the situation and aspects of the person to social behaviour. This is called the person-situation debate. Generally the findings of many different kinds of study suggest that it is neither to the situation nor to the person that we should look for our answers, but rather to the interaction between them. The work concerned with altruism and helping is one sphere where greater emphasis has been placed on situational factors than person factors. Some research, however, has indicated that there are some individual differences that affect the readiness of people to help.

Those people who are in a positive frame of mind are more likely to help. It has been noticed that sunny days lead to good moods and a greater preparedness to help! People who have recently experienced a success, too, are more likely to be generous with their time and assistance. Guilt seems to motivate people to help others, and there is evidence to show that those who have committed a transgression will be more likely to help because, it is suggested, such activities help to relieve their own negative feelings, an explanation related to the arousal hypothesis discussed above.

Deindividuation (see earlier discussion) has also been shown to encourage helping behaviours, which may explain why so many people who help others remain anonymous. Perhaps if they were sure of being identified they would not have helped in the first place, a notion that apparently goes against a reward–cost analysis. Intuitively it would seem that rewards would be greater if the helping act were acknowledged. However, the embarrassment and publicity resulting from such an acknowledgement may well contribute to the costs of helping and outweigh the benefits.

Thus several individual differences have been recognized. All in all, though, it would seem that social cognitions are the most important set of variables for understanding helping and not helping. The ways in which we sum up a situation, the victims' deservedness, our own abilities and responsibility to help, and the potential costs and rewards of helping will affect whether or not we help. In other words, the ways we construe situations will determine whether or not we will help, as we try to make sense of the situation and our own action or inaction. So, the claims that Kitty Genovese's neighbours thought the incident was a lovers' quarrel or the beliefs that parents have the sole right to protect and discipline their children as an excuse for non-intervention in child abuse cases, illustrate rather poignantly the role of such cognitions. We can see, too, from these examples how cultural values can be conveyed into social psychological study, not this time via the experiments but by the (potential or actual) subjects.

What makes us aggressive?

Aggression and violence refer to behaviours that reflect deliberate attempts to cause harm or to injure other people. We can distinguish between instrumental aggression which is displayed in order to receive

705

some kind of benefit or reward and hostile aggression, the display of which has as its primary objective the injury of someone else. It is hostile aggression that we will be discussing here. Before we go on to explore some of the person and situation factors that increase the likelihood of aggression, let us look at some of the theories that have been put forward to account for aggression.

Accounts of aggression

Biological theories

Biological theories assume that human aggression is essentially the same as aggression in animals and can be explained by, for example, androgen levels, instincts, and competition for resources for survival, especially food and sexual partners. While some sociobiologists emphasize biological explanations of certain aggressive phenomena, such as male rather than female aggression, fighting and vindictiveness spurred by sexual jealousy, social conflict in times of high unemployment (scarcity of resources, etc.) most social psychologists point to the important moderating influences of culture, socialization and thought. Nevertheless, some suggestions about the control of violence stem directly from biological theories, as we shall see later in the discussion.

Frustration–aggression hypothesis

Leonard Berkowitz (1969) refined Neil Miller's (1941) frustration–aggression hypothesis. In its original version, the frustration–aggression hypothesis suggested that aggression was the direct result of frustration, itself defined as the 'blocking of goal-directed activity'. Berkowitz developed the links between frustration and aggression as follows. First, he expanded the definition of frustration to include relative deprivation. Relative deprivation is the subjective experience of disappointment or a failure of expectations. So what to someone may not be frustrating to another person may be experienced as such. Second, he suggested that frustration led to physiological arousal which had to be labelled as anger if it is to lead to aggression. Finally, Berkowitz argued that this anger resulted in aggression *only* if there was a suitable or appropriate target in the environment: 'free floating' aggression did not occur. The process is shown in Figure 23.2.

The process in Figure 23.2 should be familiar. It is similar to the drive-reduction theories of social facilitation (Zajonc) and helping behaviours (Piliavin). There is considerable experimental support for the frustration-aggression hypothesis in one form or another, and we will explore some of this later on. However, there are also situations where there is no clear antecedent frustration. Arguably, Milgram's experiments considered earlier in the chapter involved aggressive behaviour. The perceived

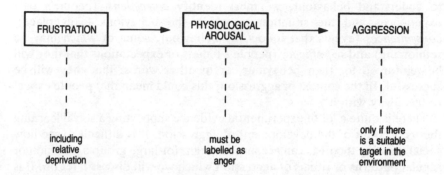

FRUSTRATION	⟶	PHYSIOLOGICAL AROUSAL	⟶	AGGRESSION
including relative deprivation		must be labelled as anger		only if there is a suitable target in the environment

Figure 23.2 Frustration–aggression hypothesis and social aggression

legitimacy of the form of aggression in that situation was seen to be important if subjects were to administer severe electric shocks willingly. Henri Tajfel (1978) suggests that the perception of legitimate aggression and legitimate targets of that aggression are useful concepts for under-standing aggression that occurs independent of frustration. Furthermore, he suggests that it is useful for drawing the links between individual motivational states (that is frustration/anger) and people's behaviour in hostile inter-group settings.

Social learning theory

Social learning theory accounts of aggression may also throw some light on aggressive behaviour with seemingly no antecedent frustration. Even within the frustration-aggression hypothesis Berkowitz's idea of 'appropriateness' was introduced in an attempt to explain why aggression occurs in response to frustration in some instances and not in others. But how do we know what is appropriate in a particular situation? It is likely that we learn it through socialization and this inevitably suggests processes of social learning. Our different learning histories may predict our dif-ferent responses to frustration. Social learning theory suggests that through the process of reinforcement, including observation, imitation and identi-fication with appropriate 'models' children learn acceptable and unaccept-able behaviours. In other words, they become socialized into their own communities or sub-cultures. Important socializing agents at different points in children's lives are family, school, peers and the media. Children with aggressive parents or friends, who watch aggressive television pro-grammes, would, according to social learning theory, be more likely to become aggressive adults. Social learning theorists would suggest that a careful analysis of the total situation is the only way fully to understand any particular act of aggression. Perhaps the most prominent social learning theorist, Albert Bandura (1977a), suggests the following analysis. In order to understand behaviour, we must identify *antecedents* (people's past experiences and the situation in which the behaviour takes place), *consequences* (events that follow the behaviour, some of which may be reinforcing) and *self-efficacy* (people's beliefs or expectations that they will be reinforced for their behaviour, or in other words, that they will be successful. In the context of aggression, this could mean that people expect to 'get away with it').

There is quite a lot of experimental evidence supporting a social learning theory account of the development of aggression. It is difficult to see how social learning theorists can account, though, for large group aggression or regular patterns or rituals of aggression which we will discuss later on. It is difficult, too, always to see what the nature of reinforcement in hostile aggression is. One view is that aggression offers the opportunity for people to wield power, which, itself, can be an important part of their social identity.

Social power

A social power analysis would suggest that people administer or threaten harm to others as a means of gaining compliance or of carrying out retribution. This would be the exercise of coercive power. All around us there are instances of how aggression linked to coercive power is legitimated. Parents are permitted to punish their children for disobedience. Until 1986 teachers in many state schools in England and Wales were also permitted to use physical aggression in the form of corporal punishment to deal with insubordination in children. Such aggression may be seen as attempts by relatively weak people to (re)gain control and have their authority acknowledged. This, in turn, contributes to enhancing their self-esteem. This excuse has often been offered for parents abusing their children ('just going a little too far') or men being violent towards women ('they needed to be shown who's boss'). Social workers, police and courts, in their attitudes to dealing with these acts of aggression, often legitimate the use of violence in the domestic contexts either by failing to intervene ('it's just a domestic dispute') or to charge perpetrators or by handing out light sentences. This has led many feminist commentators to decry what seems to be the institutionalized acceptance of aggression and violence as a tool of exercising social power.

Social factors influencing aggression

A series of influential studies in the social learning tradition by Albert Bandura and his colleagues (Bandura, 1973) have pointed to the role that imitation of significant others can play in the development and display of aggression. Their basic experiment was to allow nursery school children to witness someone else (the model) hitting a large inflatable doll (the 'bobo' doll). The children were then shown into a room that contained many toys, including a bobo doll. Compared with children who had not seen the aggressive model, these children were consistently more aggressive, copying the model they had just seen. What would make the children copy the behaviour they had just seen? By varying different aspects of the basic experiment, Bandura suggested that if the models were important (for example, adults) or significant (for example, children's mothers) the children would be more likely to copy them. Furthermore, if the model was seen to be rewarded, aggression increased. If the doll was identical, the children would be more likely to copy the behaviour than if it was only similar. Also, if the doll moved dramatically, the children continued to aggress, whereas if it hardly moved, they soon stopped. This indicates that to continue, an aggressive act must be reinforced. This may explain why, in real life, some children copy the aggression they see on television and others do not – only the first group get reinforced in some way for the aggression they show. They may, for example, get approval from their friends or attention from adults for their behaviour. While the bobo doll is only a doll, there is some evidence to suggest that similar imitation occurs in real life. Children will copy aggressive acts they have seen on films if exposed to identical situations afterwards. The environmental 'triggers' (that is, identical targets for aggression as seen on film) are important, as we shall see when we explore some environmental influences on aggression. In Bandura's experiments, children could have been forgiven for believing that it was all right to be violent towards the doll – or why was this adult (the experimenter) showing them the violent scene in the first place? In real life there are prohibitions and sanctions against aggressive acts as well as reinforcers (praise, approval, esteem) for them from some sources. Bandura's work suggests that these reinforcers will be more effective if they are given by people who are admired or respected.

Mass media influences

The mass media (broadcasting, newspapers, television, films, books, and videos) are important sources of models for children and adults alike. Occasionally we hear of dramatic and violent acts being committed exactly as the perpetrator had seen them on television or at the cinema. In nearly all these instances, environmental circumstances leading up to the violence were similar to those on the scenes on the screen. The role of television in inciting aggression in children has been the focus of a lot of attention in the USA where it was estimated by one of the major television companies that a child will watch 2,336 violent acts every year. Several studies have measured the amount of aggression children show towards each other after watching either aggressive, neutral or prosocial cartoon programmes. They find that those children who were aggressive before watching the aggressive cartoons became significantly more aggressive after viewing them, whereas children who were aggressive before watching the prosocial film, helped more subsequently. From more long-term, correlational studies in USA, Finland, and Poland, evidence has emerged to indicate that the more violent television primary school children watch, the more aggressive their behaviour towards classmates. Similarly, the amount of violence 8-year-olds watch on television has been shown to predict the amount of aggression the same children show at age 18 years. However, as with all correlational studies, the direction of causality is unclear. Do aggressive children seek out violent television to watch or does violent television make them aggressive, or both? In an attempt to tease out some of the issues and to understand why the relationship between aggressive children and violent television seems to hold for boys but not for girls, researchers looked for explanations in the social context in which children watch television. First they found that children did not always watch television alone. If they watched in the company of adults who commented on and criticized the use of violence they were less likely to be aggressive. Second, boys were rewarded more frequently for their displays of aggression than girls, reflecting differential socializing patterns for boys and girls (in the USA anyway). Third, evidence has accumulated to suggest that the more aggressive children were, the more parents were likely to use physical punishments towards them – but once more the direction of causality is not clear. The single best predictor of children's aggression, however, seemed to be their social popularity. The more unpopular they were amongst their peers, the more aggressive, but again there are problems of causality. This raises the possible role of frustration in moderating the effects of media violence, or of self-esteem and identity and the need to exercise social power. One thing is clear, there is no straightforward relationship between violence on television and aggressive behaviour. The potential effects of television violence can, however, be moderated by aspects of the situation in which the programmes are viewed.

Presence of other people

The presence of other people at the scene of a potentially violent episode can lead to violence. We do not know why this is. We do know that the presence of others leads to arousal (see earlier discussion on social facilitation), so if there are cues in the situation that lead to people labelling this arousal as anger, and if there are legitimate targets for aggression, it is likely that it will result. Other people may goad potentially aggressive people, effectively encouraging them and thereby reinforcing their aggression when it occurs. If they continue to encourage, aggression will increase. It could be, though, that with other people present people try to create a favourable impression and in situations where aggression is presumed to be valued (for example, among football supporters) aggressive displays will be more likely. In this case not only are the aggressors receiving social reinforcers (approval) they are also gaining self-esteem and possibly exercising social power.

Environmental/situational factors influencing aggression

Eliciting stimuli

Berkowitz and Frodi (1977) suggest that if there are cues in the environment that have previously been associated with aggression, evidence suggests aggression will be more likely to occur. Even the mention of someone's name, previously associated with anger and aggression, may involve further aggression. Young people who have had prior aggressive confrontations with the police, for example, may more readily aggress in police presence in the future. The process can, of course, work in reverse. Police officers who have had previous aggressive encounters with certain members of the public may more readily be aggressive towards the same people in the future. Closely linked to environmental triggers to aggression is what has become known as the 'weapons effect'. In a potentially volatile situation, the sight of an object that is clearly and unambiguously associated with violence (for example, a gun) may incite greater aggression. The sight of the weapon, it is argued, makes frustrated people more angry and thus more likely to be violent (Turner, Layton and Simons, 1975). Examples of this effect can be seen in some accounts of the inner city disturbances in England during the early 1980s (see, for example, the Scarman (1981) and Hytner *et al* (1981) reports).

Stressors

Many different environmental stressors have been identified, including noise, smells and heat. As they increase, aggression increases. Why is this? As we experience more stress, we become bad tempered and increasingly frustrated which leads, in accordance with the frustration–aggression hypothesis, to increased aggression. However, an interesting feature relating to environmental stressors and aggression is that as they increase, far from people becoming more and more aggressive, after some time they become less aggressive. This can be explained with reference to the general arousal curve which predicts that arousal of any sort only facilitates behaviour up to an optimum point, after which it debilitates performance. (This issue is similar, again, to that discussed earlier in relation to social facilitation.) A slightly different account of the effects of environmental stressors relates to our attempts to regain control over our environments. As we feel stressed we try to exercise control; if thwarted in our attempts to do this we try harder and sometimes more aggressively; if still unable to regain control we give up and lethargy, rather than aggression, sets in.

Thus the greater and more prolonged the stressors the more likely that lethargy will result. It has been suggested, largely anecdotally but with some attempts to demonstrate it statistically, that civil disturbances (riots) more often take place during long, hot summers.

Disinhibitors

Some people have suggested that aggression will occur in those situations that remove inhibitions and control of behaviour. Alcohol is frequently a factor in violent crimes and evidence from experimental studies does, indeed, suggest that people more readily aggress towards others if they have had even a small dose of alcohol. It is generally thought that alcohol suppresses those mechanisms in the central nervous system that normally inhibit aggressive behaviour. However, the effect is not a straightforward biological effect. The disinhibiting effects of alcohol depend in large part on the thoughts and expectations of the people doing the drinking and the way they interpret the situation they are in.

Other features of the situation that seem to have disinhibiting effects are those that lead to deindividuation. People in crowds, who are able to feel anonymous and as a result cease to fear punishment or retribution, are more likely to commit aggressive acts. In the policing of the miners' disputes in Britain in 1984–85, the police on occasion wore their uniforms without even the numbers on their epaulets which they usually wore. Thus they were virtually indistinguishable from each other, and could easily have become deindividuated.

We have already seen that in Zimbardo's prison study, participants were more likely to act aggressively and inhumanely when deindividuated. Zimbardo (1970) conducted a laboratory study in which women were clothed in bulky nondescript coats and hoods. In this state they gave stronger electric shocks to other people than did women who were not so anonymously attired (that is, were still individuated). People in a deindividuated state seem to exercise less than the usual amount of self-control and this disinhibition may lead to increased aggression. There is some contention whether or not anonymity, the wearing of uniforms or being in a crowd does, in fact, lead to deindividuated behaviour, or whether in such circumstances norms of behaviour are set up to which people adhere. From our earlier discussions of social influence in groups, it is likely that the more cohesive a group of people, the more likely it is that norms or standards of behaviour will be set up. This brings us to discussion of the role of ritual in aggression.

Ritual and aggression

Erving Goffman is widely known for his work on interaction rituals. He suggests that a great deal of everyday behaviour follows regular patterns;

people understand and follow rules of conduct and these enable them to interact predictably with each other. Similar analyses have been applied to apparently mindless aggressive situations. Peter Marsh (1978) did some detailed analyses of so-called football-aggro, the fighting between rival groups of football fans. He found, contrary to popular conceptions and the mass media coverage of football violence, that people rarely got hurt. Instead, what emerged, was a complex picture of ritualized, symbolic aggression. The groups of fans would appear, dressed in their team's regalia, and assemble behind the grandstands. They then proceeded to display hostile postures and shout insults at each other. One or two lads from each side would edge threateningly towards each other and then retreat. After this display, each side would proclaim their victory, relating to reporters and anyone else who wished to hear, the stories of injury, blood, broken teeth and so on. Re-describing the acts in this way made them into socially significant acts. The performance was turned into a ritual, which gave esteem to all those partaking of it. Over a period of four years, Marsh got sufficient information from football fans about what was and was not 'permitted' in a fight between rival fans to be able to identify some of the rules that underlay their behaviour. Sometimes, of course, people do get hurt. Although the way the media reports crowd behaviour at matches it would seem that clashes always result in injury, Marsh suggests that they usually do not. There is, it seems, order (rules and norms) in violent chaos.

Social cognition and aggression

We have already mentioned some of the cognitions that influence the likelihood and force of an aggressive act.

Cues in the environment have to be interpreted and their links with aggression acknowledged before they can exert an influence on aggression. Some of this interpretation may be very quick and people may not realize what it was that triggered their violence until some time afterwards. Nevertheless, the attribution of meaning to environmental cues is crucial if they are to elicit aggression.

When people are frustrated, they seek to explain their frustration. If they find a good reason for their frustrations, it is unlikely to lead to aggression. If, however, they perceive their frustration to be caused by inhibitory or illegitimate means, they are likely to get angry, and this may result in aggression. Similarly if they dislike a frustrating agent, or interpret the source of their frustrations as intended attack, they are also likely to resort to violence.

The way in which people define a situation may induce their aggression, possibly through the mediation of arousal. So, for instance, if people evacuate a building on hearing a fire alarm and are confronted with banks of fire-fighters as they leave the building, they may be unlikely to feel or behave aggressively. If, however, instead of fire-fighters they meet armed soldiers they redefine the situation and their reactions may be very different. In both situations, they are aroused, but one situation may lead them to label their arousal as safety, whereas the other may be labelled as confrontation. When people share the interpretation of events, as in this instance, frustration, arousal, and aggression become group phenomena. We will now look, briefly, at group aggression in more detail.

Group aggression

Henri Tajfel and his colleagues have conducted many studies on inter-group conflict. We have seen in earlier parts of the chapter that categorization alone helps group members identify with their group and Sherif's Robbers' Cave study suggested that if groups engage in competition with each other they are more likely to feel hostile towards each other.

Tajfel (1978) suggests that individual arousal states will be translated into group aggression under three conditions. There must be, as we have said, a social sharing of the interpretation of events. In addition, there must be a common popular 'theory' about their social causation. Lastly there must be a wide consensus about appropriate action. As Tajfel points out, groups do not randomly 'see and destroy' (although this may happen at times), instead they 'search and destroy'. The group's aggression is selective: this selectivity is governed by a social consensus (for example, about who should be attacked) and generally this consensus points only to certain targets of aggression. Group violence is nearly always selective and shows a degree of structure and direction over time. Tajfel suggests that central to an understanding of inter-group hostility is the concept of social identity. We are committed to a group only in so far as it gives us positive social identity. Hostility towards outgroups may enhance our sense of identity or belonging to the group. At different times and in different circumstances we may reassess the extent to which the groups to which we belong give us a sense of identity, and this appraisal is based on many different factors. Suffice it to say here that social identity is a changing phenomenon, but is, according to Tajfel, one that must be understood if we are really to get to grips with inter-group hostility.

The reduction and control of violence

Recommendations for the reduction and control of violence reflect the different theoretical explanations of aggression discussed at the beginning of this section.

Biological perspectives would suggest two ways of controlling violence. The first is via surgical or chemical means. Various attempts to remove parts of the brain or to castrate aggressive men, or to alter their hormonal profile, have met with limited success. The second is to channel aggression into socially acceptable outlets. This idea derives from instinct-theories of aggression. Many people believe that competitive sport, or shouting loudly, for example, channel or release aggressive tendencies through strenuous physical exercise. However, evidence suggests that physical exercise increases arousal and thus may increase, not decrease, aggressive potential.

Several suggestions for controlling aggression derive from *frustration-aggression and social learning perspectives*. If incompatible responses (such as relaxation) are rewarded, aggression should decrease. If labels other than anger for the state of arousal are available (for example, humour), aggression should not follow arousal. Exposure to successful non-aggressive models should place limitations on learning aggressive behaviour and, in the short-term only, punishing aggressive acts should stop them. If cues to aggression are removed aggression should not be triggered, and lastly if a delay of the aggressive act can be brought about this should allow for the aggression to subside which makes aggressive acts less likely.

Social power perspectives suggest that if we are taught non-aggressive social skills we may be able to assert our authority without resorting to aggression and develop more appropriate and non-violent ways of resolving conflict; ways should be found for us to get self-esteem without being dehumanized. Linked to this is the recommendation that we should all work towards developing norms that do not excuse or justify the use of threats or punishments in any circumstances. One solution to interpersonal conflict is the use of mediators. Increasingly family mediators are used in divorce and separation cases and neighbourhood mediators in disputes between neighbours. In both cases these are attempts to avoid violence and law suits. If ways can be found, too, of enabling people to remain individuated they are perhaps less likely to engage in violence. Linked to this, in the context of inter-group hostility, is the implication that if groups were able to give their members sufficient social identity without displaying hostility to other groups, violence may reduce.

Social cognitive perspectives would all imply that the sense we make of the situations we are in affects our propensity to aggression. We will be less likely to be angry if we can find reasons to explain our feelings of arousal as legitimate, or to assume non-aggressive intentions to other people and to stimuli in the environment.

Further reading

Brigham, J. C. (1986) *Social Psychology*. Little, Brown.
Brown, R. (1986) *Social Psychology*, 2nd edn. Free Press.
Brown, R. (1988) *Group Processes: Dynamics within and between groups*. Blackwell.
Hewstone, M., Stroebe, W., Codol, J.-P., and Stephenson, G. (1988) *Introduction to Social Psychology*. Blackwell.
Marsh, P. (1978) *Aggro: The illusion of violence*. Dent.

Attitudes

Philip Erwin

Introduction

The term 'attitude' derives from the Latin *aptus*, the same root as aptitude. It denotes a posture or fitness. A little over a century ago the term attitude was used to refer only to physical posture. We've all seen classical paintings of models that were no doubt told to adopt a reclining attitude. Current use of the term attitude is more commonly in terms of a psychological construct. In modern usage a laid-back attitude would be a psychological rather than physical state!

The concept of attitude has been described as 'probably the most distinctive and indispensable concept in American social psychology. No term appears more frequently in the experimental and theoretical literature' (Allport, 1954). Some early authors even went so far as to define social psychology as the scientific study of attitudes (Thomas and Znaniecki, 1918). Most modern social psychologists prefer to see their discipline as somewhat broader.

As you might expect from the above paragraph, there is a vast literature on the nature, functions and measurement of attitudes. In this chapter I will give a brief history and overview of the nature and function of attitudes, the attitude–behaviour debate, attitude change and persuasion, methods of measuring attitudes, and prejudice. The significance of attitudes in the 'real world' will be especially clear in the sections on persuasion and prejudice.

Nature of attitudes

DeFleur and Westie (1963) distinguished two major ways of conceptualizing attitudes, in terms of *response probabilities* or as *latent processes*. Response probability theorists (e.g. Bem, 1967) view attitudes as consistency in behaviour or self-descriptions. Do you usually eat brown bread? If so, we can regard this consistency in your behaviour as representing your attitude to brown bread. Most theorists prefer to go one step beyond the immediately observable and postulate some mediating process or structure.

If an attitude is a latent process this may be accounted for in behavioural or cognitive terms – lever and template models respectively (Campbell, 1963). Template models see attitudes as our window on the world. Their frame determines and limits what we can see and how we interpret it. From this perspective attitudes are seen as playing a part in the definition given to stimuli. The classical triadic model of attitude, which is examined later in this chapter, falls into this category. Lever models take a contrary perspective and see attitudes as being elicited by specific stimuli. From this perspective attitudes are dormant until activated, they do not actively structure the way an individual perceives his world. This approach is represented by Doob's (1947) behavioural model and Fishbein and Ajzen's (1975) influential theory of reasoned action.

These very different ideas about the nature of attitudes needless to say have produced some very different definitions of the concept and so it is now appropriate to consider these definitions in detail.

Definitions

A great many definitions of attitude are possible, as might be expected for such an important and central social psychological concept. Allport (1935) considered over a hundred different definitions of attitude, examination of considerably fewer should serve our purpose adequately. First, the classic triadic model:

> 'A learned predisposition to *think*, *feel* and *behave* toward a person (or object) in a particular way' (Allport, 1954).

The triadic model of attitudes has an ancient and venerable history (dating back at least as far as the Greek philosopher Plato, *c*400BC) and dominated the attitude literature from the late 1950s; even now it remains possibly the most influential model of attitudes. Several important points about this definition are worth noting.

First, attitudes are learned. They are social entities, the product of socialization and experience rather than heredity or constitution. This does not, of course, deny that personal characteristics and constitution have an effect on attitudes; it simply means that these effects are indirect, via differences created in an individual's life experiences.

Second, this definition, in common with most definitions, sees attitudes as predispositions to respond in a given way; it recognizes the existence of some pre-existing latent process and goes beyond the simple observed consistency of behaviour. A predisposition also implies that attitudes are relatively permanent and enduring entities.

Third, as considered by psychologists, attitudes are always about or directed towards some actual or abstract object. In the appropriate jargon, they possess a referent. A school teacher may well tell a pupil that he has a slovenly attitude but this is not a correct psychological use of the term as no referent is evident.

Fourth, and finally, this definition is specifically of a triadic model. It links together affect, cognition, and behaviour. Here we see the major point on which the triadic model differs from lever models. Lever models emphasize the central importance of affect, the emotional or evaluative component of attitudes.

Spurred on by many studies finding apparent inconsistencies between attitudes and behaviour, many authors have tried to redefine attitudes as unidimensional constructs. This approach was evident in the definitions of early researchers into attitude scaling and from the 1970s onwards appears to be gaining popularity and more general acceptance. Definitions of attitude based on this approach are given below:

> 'Affect for or against a psychological object' (Thurstone, 1931).

> 'An implicit drive producing response' (Doob, 1947).

'A person's evaluation of any psychological object' (Ajzen and Fishbein, 1980).

Thurstone (1931) saw attitudes as falling on a simple positive–negative continuum and as being closely related to behaviour. This view was soon to be threatened by apparent inconsistencies in the attitude–behaviour link (see the section on this topic, below) and this led other early authors to develop models to try to explain how a single attitude could produce a variety of behavioural responses.

Doob's (1947) theory, in postulating some internal mediating response, allowed the flexibility to explain how a single attitude could produce a variety of behavioural responses. The cost, however, was the removal of attitudes from direct linkage with behaviour. To restore this position Allport argued that the unidimensional concept of attitude was over-simplified and proposed the more complex triadic concept in his now famous definition of attitude.

Unfortunately the attitude–behaviour debate makes it clear that a rigid triadic concept is difficult to sustain. Since the 1970s, unidimensional models (especially that of Fishbein and Ajzen) have gained in credence and popularity as a tenable alternative which may genuinely be allowing the ability to predict behaviour from attitudes.

To follow this ongoing debate, the triadic model of attitudes will now be outlined, its status in view of the attitude–behaviour debate will be examined, and Fishbein and Ajzen's theory of reasoned action will be considered as an alternative.

The triadic model of attitudes

As noted above, this model of attitudes has a long and illustrious history; it sees attitudes as having three components:

1. Affect.
2. Behaviour.
3. Cognition.

The implication of the triadic model is that these three components form a system and are interdependent. A change in one component of the system should produce changes in the other components in order to maintain consistency.

Evidence exists that the cognitive and affective components of attitudes are indeed closely related. A classic study by Rosenberg (1960) used post-hypnotic suggestion to change subjects' affect (feelings) towards Negroes. Subsequent measures of the subjects' cognitions showed a corresponding change in direction. This study had a number of flaws. For example, from a total group of only 22 subjects those that were 'good' hypnotic subjects were allocated to the experimental group and the others constituted a control group. It is quite conceivable that subjects that are easily hypnotized are not representative in the dynamics of their attitude system. Despite reservations about the methodology of Rosenberg's study it has generally received support from subsequent research.

The same consistency has not been achieved in attempts to demonstrate a relationship between behaviour and the cognitive–affective components.

The attitude–behaviour debate

A central concern of attitude theory for a number of years has been the relationship of attitudes (as cognition and affect) to behaviour. This is especially important for the triadic model which sees behaviour as an integral component of attitudes.

Research has cast doubt on there being a strong attitude–behaviour relationship. The famous study of LaPiere (1934) is often cited to support this position. Beginning in 1930 and continuing for two years, LaPiere toured the United States with a Chinese couple and visited 251 hotels, motels, 'auto-camps' and restaurants. Despite this being a time of supposedly high prejudice against orientals they were turned away on only one occasion, 'from a rather inferior auto-camp'. Six months later these various establishments were written to and asked if they would accept Chinese customers. Over 90 per cent of returned questionnaires indicated that Chinese customers would not be served. Clearly this was at variance with what had actually happened.

There are a number of methodological problems with this study (e.g. who completed the questionnaire – was it the same person serving in the restaurant or on reception in the hotel? Did it matter that the Chinese couple were well dressed and had expensive luggage? Is refusal more difficult face-to-face?) but it nevertheless illustrates the apparently capricious nature of the attitude–behaviour link.

Other research has provided, at best, only equivocal support for such an attitude–behaviour relationship. Wicker's (1969) review of over thirty studies testing the relationship between attitudes and behaviour concluded that the relationship was weak, rarely above 0.3 and often near zero. This review has been much criticized (e.g. many of the studies it uses are weak methodologically and there is no inter-study comparability in terms of measuring instruments or definitions). Hanson (1980) in a similar review made the distinction between highly controlled laboratory studies and field studies where other competing influences might also be exerting an effect. Hanson found that the majority of laboratory studies supported an attitude–behaviour link (18 out of 26), while most field studies did not (16 out of 20). It appears that in the real world competing attitudes and other influences may prevent an attitude achieving behavioural expression.

Fishbein and Ajzen (1975) have tried to resolve the problem of the apparent inconsistency between attitudes and behaviour by proposing a theory which explicitly splits the classical, triadic model of attitudes and views attitudes and behaviour as separate though related phenomena. This theory will now be examined.

Fishbein's theory of reasoned action

This theory is in accord with commonsense and is presented in a form which makes its assumptions explicit, and its predictions testable and falsifiable. Through a series of mathematical equations an individual's attitude can be dissected and the components which give the attitude its significance established.

The theory of reasoned action sees intended behaviour as the result of only two main factors: attitude towards an act and subjective norms. Normative beliefs are what other important, relevant people expect one to do. The relative influence of attitudes and norms may vary in different instances. Other factors, such as situational, demographic, and personality influences, are seen as being mediated by these two components.

Attitude towards an act and subjective norms can each be analysed into their component parts, which may be assessed in various ways, e.g. by the paper and pencil responses of subjects. The components of attitude are consequently very easy and straightforward to assess. The overall attitude is obtained by simply slotting appropriate items of information into the general attitude equations.

Before proceeding further I should emphasize three points. First, the focus of concern of this theory is attitude toward an act, *not* toward an object. An example will clarify. To find out why a person is studying psychology we should look at the person's attitude toward studying psychology rather than the person's attitude to psychology itself. The reason for this distinction is quite simple. As is evident from the attitude–behaviour debate, a given attitude toward an object only predicts the overall pattern of behaviour, other factors may intervene before a behavioural intention is realized. Because external influences are taken into account, behavioural intention is a better and more consistent measure than behaviour itself.

Second, it is extremely important that all variables be treated at the same level of specificity as the behaviour they are attempting to predict. It is quite possible for a racially prejudiced person to exclaim truthfully that 'some of my best friends are black'. A general attitude or prejudice does not necessarily predict behaviour toward specific individuals in specific situations.

Third, subjects are often asked to rate a set of attitudinal beliefs obtained from another group of subjects. This has been criticized and does appear to reduce the ability of attitudes to predict behavioural intentions and immediate behaviour. It does not appear to affect the ability to predict behaviour in the longer term (Rutter and Bunce, 1989). It is probably preferable for subjects to supply their own list of beliefs and rate these.

Functions of attitudes

An alternative way of conceptualizing attitudes is not to attempt to determine their structure but rather to see their form and existence in terms of the functions they serve for the individual. The most famous functional approach to attitudes, that of Katz (1960), outlines four basic functions of attitudes, though note that these are not mutually exclusive; an attitude may be serving several functions simultaneously. The four functions of attitudes outlined by Katz are:

1. Instrumental.
2. Ego defence.
3. Value-expressive.
4. Knowledge.

An attitude may be held because it serves an instrumental or utilitarian function, it entails reward values; it has served and is expected to serve in the future to maximize rewards and minimize punishments for the individual. Note, however, an interesting aspect of this function: behaviour theory tells us that partial or intermittent reinforcement would be expected to produce attitudes more resistant to change than would continuous reinforcement. This has significant implications. When watching news programmes on television one often sees demonstrations and counter-demonstrations and these can become quite violent confrontations. The demonstrators might do well to ponder the results of their actions. If their intention is to change the attitudes of the opposition it is likely to fail. This is hardly surprising and would be expected for several reasons which we will touch on in due course. What is perhaps less immediately obvious, however, is that this confrontation and aggression may actually strengthen the attitude of the opposition at least in part because of the mechanism of partial reinforcement (this scenario would also produce effects on attitude change because of group dynamics but that topic is discussed elsewhere in this book).

The ego-defence function sees attitudes as a mechanism to bolster the self-concept and self-esteem. This is often seen as the basis for racial prejudice. Attitudes may help someone feeling insecure and threatened to feel superior. There is, of course, a price to pay for this secure bliss – a distorted view of the world. Prejudice, which often serves this function, really does seem to tell us more about the perceiver than the perceived.

The value-expressive function allows individuals to express their individuality, values, and group membership. For example, the attitude of punk rockers to styles of clothing and dress, and hence the way they do dress, may serve to indicate group membership and loyalty.

The knowledge function is based on the idea that we are motivated to understand and control our world. This is a cognitive aspect of attitudes and is closely linked with social cognition and the concept of cognitive schemata. Fiske and Taylor (1984) define a schema as 'a cognitive structure that represents organized knowledge about a given concept or type of stimulus'. The negative behaviour of a disliked person or group can be made understandable by categorizing it as being due to their inferred dispositions and traits. A specific form of schema is the stereotype, which is often the cognitive basis of prejudice. A stereotype is simply a schema consisting of 'a set of characteristics that is assumed to fit a category of people' (Schneider *et al*, 1979).

Attitude change and persuasion

Historically these have been approached from two angles. Carl Hovland and his associates began their research at Yale University at the time of the Second World War and, perhaps not surprisingly in view of the urgent need to understand what makes propaganda effective, adopted a very pragmatic approach to attempting to establish factors important in attitude change and persuasion. Many subsequent researchers adopted a more theoretical approach. In early research the dominant theoretical approach was cognitive dissonance theory (Festinger, 1957); of this and subsequent theories more in due course.

In this section I will start with an analysis of persuasion based on the approach and work of the Hovland–Yale group and then continue with an examination of various theoretical approaches, focusing on cognitive dissonance theory, self-perception theory, and the recent and increasingly influential elaboration-likelihood model of Petty and Cacioppo (1981).

The Hovland–Yale approach

Over two thousand years ago the philosopher Aristotle (*c*300BC) noted that apparent persuasion may be due to characteristics of the person attempting the persuasion, the quality of the message itself or the characteristics of the audience which may make them more or less easy to persuade. In this age of many and diverse media, the medium of presentation of a persuasive message should also be taken into account. As we shall see, all of these factors may indeed be influential, though they need not necessarily achieve their effects in the same way.

McGuire (1969) distinguished a sequential series of processes necessary for persuasion and attitude change:

1. Attention.
2. Comprehension.
3. Yielding.
4. Retention.
5. Acting as a result.

The Hovland–Yale school saw attention and comprehension as important for the actual learning of the message, but one needs also to consider various influences on motivation to explain whether a recipient actually accepts or rejects the learned message. And, even if the message is learned and is accepted, one needs to be able to note a change in behaviour in order for a change in attitude to be recognized. This raises the issues of social norms, the motivation to behave in certain ways, and the relationship of attitudes to behaviour ... but we won't go back to these debates.

The implication of the five stages in persuasion noted by McGuire is that when persuasion is unsuccessful it may be because of a failure at any one of the stages. From the perspective of McGuire's (1969) model, source, message, and audience factors may be seen as primarily exerting their influence on persuasion through their effects on the above stages. Their effect on one or more of the above stages may be to enhance or retard the process of persuasion. For example, perhaps a more intelligent audience is more attentive? It is also conceivable that such an audience may comprehend a message better and so see any flaws in the argument. Effects can be on many levels and not necessarily in the same direction at different stages. The example of intelligence will be examined further when the effects of audience characteristics on persuasion are reviewed.

Message source

The source of a persuasive message may be a person, group or institution. Possibly the first philosopher-psychologist to recognize the importance of source factors in persuasion was Aristotle who argued that 'good men' are believed more in general and especially so on issues where the facts are uncertain.

Identifying a source gives additional information to that contained in the message. Social approval and liking is rewarding and similar communicators or those of high status may be trusted to give us an insight into the 'correct' and appropriate attitudes to hold.

Two main lines of research on source effects in persuasion have developed, these are effects due to the attractiveness and likeability of the source, and effects due to source credibility. It is important to distinguish between these factors as they may produce their effects in different ways. Research appears to indicate that expertise may affect how a recipient thinks about a message while attractiveness may have a more direct impact (Mills and Harvey, 1972).

Credibility

If you read about some impending technological or medical advance would you be more likely to believe that it will happen soon if you read it in a scientific journal or a tabloid newspaper? A classic study by Hovland and Weiss (1951) showed substantial differences in attitude change depending on just such differences in source credibility.

Apparently irrelevant factors may affect the status and perceived credibility of a communicator (e.g. race or sex). Status effects may have important real-world implications. Film and TV stars are frequently made use of in advertising endorsements. The testimony of experts may significantly influence the interpretation of evidence and outcome of trials for serious crimes such as rape (Brekke and Borgida, 1988).

Credibility is, of course, in the eye of the beholder, and in some situations different people may well make different attributions. An important consideration may be the amount of interest the recipient has in an issue and the perceived intentions of the communicator. Himmelfarb and Eagly (1974) note that laboratory studies are typically on unimportant issues and use high credibility sources – this may explain many of the reported significant effects. Where an issue is highly relevant or threatening, or an individual has prior knowledge, source effects are much less. Hass (1981) has suggested that in these circumstances high credibility sources may actually increase the thought and attention given to the details of a message.

The perceived intentions of the communicator may also affect the trust we have in him and his credibility. Trust is increased if a communicator argues against his own self-interest or has nothing to gain (and may even lose out) because of his advocacy. A criminal advocating longer prison sentences for persistent law breakers is likely to be more persuasive than a policeman or lawyer advocating the same position (Walster *et al*, 1966). This attributional effect may also explain the power of 'hidden camera' advertisements, where ordinary shoppers extol the virtues of some product that the manufacturer would like us to believe we can't live without.

Attractiveness

Attractiveness is yet another significant factor in persuasion. Research has examined both physical appearance and likeability.

Attractive sources usually produce greater persuasion, though Chaiken (1979) suggests that at least part of the reason for the greater persuasiveness of attractive individuals lies in their other correlating characteristics such as better communication skills and higher self-esteem.

Subjects are also more persuaded by communicators perceived as similar and liked. A communicator's expression of initial similarity to his audience on some issue may encourage such liking and an attribution of credibility. Weiss (1957) calls the advocating of this already accepted position 'beating the dead horse'. Though a good persuasive argument is still needed, there is less resistance and criticism of a subsequent message.

The sleeper effect

A curious finding of some early research on source effects in persuasion was the occurrence of a delayed action 'sleeper effect': differences in the acceptance of a persuasive message due to course credibility seemed to disappear with the passage of time. A highly credible source may produce a lot of immediate attitude change but this effect may decline with time; for a low credibility source the opposite might occur, attitude change may increase as the quality of the message is recognized and the character-istics of its source are discounted. Perhaps this provides some justification for the cooling-off period now required for insurance sold door-to-door. With the passage of time the extraneous effects of a good salesman may be discounted and the product will stand or fall on its own merits as the potential client has a chance to dissociate information from sales pitch.

Early reviews suggested that the evidence for the sleeper effect was over-stated. Gillig and Greenwald (1974) cast doubt on the genuine existence of the phenomenon. More recent research and reviews (e.g. Gruder *et al*, 1978; Pratkanis *et al*, 1988) indicate that the sleeper effect may in fact occur but only under very specific circumstances.

An attributional explanation

Some theorists have stressed attributional explanations for many of the source effects that have been noted (e.g. credibility as represented by expertise and trustworthiness). They may be effective by bypassing the comprehension side of persuasion (Wood and Eagly, 1981).

The attribution approach has been criticized as having limited applic-ability because people will often not have sufficient information on which to base an attribution (Cialdini *et al*, 1981) – though people often do seem to manage with only minimal information in the real world. An alternative cognitive model, Petty and Cacioppo's (1981) elaboration-likelihood model, is discussed in detail later in this chapter.

Message characteristics

Message characteristics are perhaps the most immediately obvious factors influencing the persuasiveness of a communication. A large number of characteristics have been researched and the more significant and systematic influences will now be examined.

One- vs two-sided messages

One might predict that a message providing both sides of an argument would be seen as more honest and hence produce greater persuasion. Hovland *et al* (1949) did indeed find subjects with knowledge about a critical issue or negative initial attitudes were more persuaded by two-sided messages.

Most advertisements are one-sided, this is probably most effective for established, popular products with brand loyalty and few competitors. If the audience is well informed about the product and its alternatives, it is not widely preferred, or counter-advertising is likely, then two-sided arguments may be most effective and produce an 'inoculation effect' which may increase resistance to counter-persuasion. Next time you watch television advertisements, reflect on the strategy they are adopting – if nothing else, you'll find it makes them more interesting.

Implicit vs explicit conclusions

A message with implicit conclusions may be more effective (increase retention and yielding) providing one can be sure that the person is able, motivated and has time to draw his own conclusions (McGuire, 1968). Self-persuasion is very powerful. If people are not given time to draw conclusions, or the recipient is less motivated or intelligent, then explicit conclusions may be more effective.

Confidence

The confidence which a communicator has in his own argument can be an important factor determining how his message is received. Using a simulated jury technique, Maslow *et al* (1971) varied the last speech for the defence. Though over-confidence can be off-putting, overall, persuasion increased as the confidence of the message increased – whether this confidence was expressed verbally or nonverbally.

Fear

A large amount of the research on message effects has looked at the impact of fear arousal. This approach to persuasion may be considerably more effective than simply emphasizing the positive consequences of accepting a persuasive message (Robberson and Rogers, 1988). The persuasive power of fear in communications is a highly relevant topic in these days when vast amounts of money are being spent on advertising concerned with drug abuse and AIDS.

Attitude change which reduces fear should be rewarding because of the reduction of an aversive state; fear should also be effective because it will increase attention and reduce the ability to make complex choices (i.e. dominant responses tend to occur and so the subject is less able to produce counter-arguments).

Leventhal (1970) suggests that for fear to be effective in promoting attitude change it is necessary for the recipients of a fear appeal to perceive the threat as severe and with a realistic possibility of affecting them.

Responses to a perceived threat may be to deny it or to be persuaded about its significance and take appropriate avoiding action. Taking appropriate action rather than denying the threat may occur if realistic coping behaviour is possible, otherwise the denial of the threat may be perceived as the only alternative for the recipient; under these conditions attitude change may actually be in the opposite direction to that sought.

Some examples from recent health care research and campaigns may highlight the points made in the above paragraphs. First, the point that a threat must be perceived as severe and realistic. Wober (1988) found that a British televised AIDS information campaign did increase knowledge about the disease but that this militated against behaviour change! The authors suggested that this may be due to strengthening viewers' beliefs about being at low risk from AIDS. Clift and Stears (1988) provided some evidence to support this interpretation. British undergraduates exposed to an AIDS information campaign showed reduced concern over social and physical contact with AIDS patients. These studies show that fear was not a consequence of these AIDS campaigns when viewers could perceive themselves as being in low risk groups.

Second, people with the same attitude may show different coping behaviours. A study by Brown and Fritz (1988) showed that knowledge about AIDS and attitude towards AIDS patients and homosexuals was only minimally related to tolerance and coping behaviour. But what of individuals who do perceive themselves at high risk and with only a limited range of realistic coping behaviours available to them? Injecting drug abusers are such a group, and they have shown an increase in realistic coping behaviours (though this is still a minority of users), such as decreasing the sharing of needles or sharing more selectively (Hopkins, 1988).

Audience characteristics

The characteristics of the recipient of a persuasive communication may substantially affect the impact of the communication. These characteristics may be of two major types, interpersonal or intrapersonal. Interpersonal factors would include the person's social network and other external influences. Intrapersonal factors would include aspects of personality, attitudes and so on. Each of these factors will be examined in turn.

Interpersonal factors

The social context of a communication, and the functions it serves for the individual, may be an important determinant of its persuasive impact. An individual does not exist in a vacuum, he will be influenced by his culture, friends, acquaintances, and the members of various social groups to which he belongs. To treat any persuasive communication solely as information and in isolation from these other sources of influences is a very limited perspective with little explanatory power.

Intrapersonal factors

Many aspects of personality and individual differences have been investigated, e.g. authoritarianism, cognitive complexity, intelligence, anxiety, and self-esteem. There are many apparently contradictory results in this literature. The effects of intelligence and initial attitudes will be examined as important and representative issues in this area.

Intelligence For a number of individual characteristics, often apparently contradictory results can be explained quite parsimoniously in terms of McGuire's (1968) theory. Intelligence is a good example of this.

Though most studies show intelligence and ease of persuasion to be inversely related, some studies do show a direct linear relationship. McGuire's model would explain these contradictions by arguing that as intelligence increases so this increases reception (attention, comprehension, retention), especially of complex messages. Hence an apparent increase in persuasion. But acceptance also requires yielding and this decreases as intelligence increases, especially for simple messages. Taken together the combined effect may be to produce a relationship between these individual differences and persuasion which follows an inverted-U shape: persuasion increasing with intelligence up to a certain level and then declining as intelligence level increases further. This explanation for the apparently contradictory results of research examining the relationship between persuasion and intelligence has been directly tested and supported (Eagly and Warren, 1976).

Initial attitude The social judgement theory of Sherif and Hovland (1961) suggests that if a persuasive communication is sufficiently close to existing attitudes then it will be assimilated, but if it falls outside this 'latitude of acceptance', into the 'latitude of rejection', then the message will be contrasted, appear more extreme, and could actually produce a change in the opposite direction. A number of studies have confirmed this assimilation–contrast phenomenon in social judgement (e.g. Manis *et al*, 1988); but what determines the size of these zones of acceptance and rejection? We are certainly more open to persuasion on some issues than others.

The size of the latitudes of acceptance and rejection is affected by two closely related factors, ego involvement and extremity of initial position. Attitudes which are very significant and personal are often also extreme;

prejudicial attitudes are a good example of this. Trying to change such attitudes, which have a large latitude of rejection and a small latitude of acceptance, is, to say the least, difficult. If it were not our society would probably have far fewer problems due to prejudices of various sorts.

Inoculation effects

McGuire (1968) suggested that exposure to a brief communication which the recipient can refute can serve to immunize him against the full persuasion attempt. The implication of this is that a two-sided message can be more effective because of the trust it inspires *or* it could actually inoculate subjects against future similar attempts at persuasion.

The potential utility of inoculation as a means of promoting health and welfare is significant, as is shown in a study by Telch *et al* (1982): many teenagers smoke because it's seen as 'cool' or 'tough'. Telch found that 7th grade children (about 13 years old) given practice at refuting and counter-arguing against social and peer pressures to smoke were inoculated against pressures to adopt the habit. This strategy was very successful. Follow-ups at nine, 21 and 33 months showed subjects were 50 per cent less likely to smoke than non-inoculated subjects. Inoculation works because subjects become motivated to defend their beliefs and gain practice in defending beliefs which, until previously attacked, they may have accepted without realizing that they were open to question.

Propaganda often misses a valuable technique when it seeks simply to strengthen existing opinions rather than confronting alternatives and so providing inoculation.

Accidental inoculation could also have potentially serious negative consequences. A number of examples spring readily to mind, but one will suffice. Despite well-founded intentions, if not handled well the new GCSE in Civic Responsibility may have this unfortunate side effect; it seems debatable whether it will raise consciousness and make participants more caring or whether it will provide at least some participants with the inoculation to resist future pressures toward this prosocial position.

Audience availability

Despite techniques of persuasion, people tend to avoid explicit attempts to persuade them. We tend to expose ourselves to opinions and perspectives that we support, whether this be in the mass media or in personal contacts. Even the information that we do receive is subject to selection and interpreted. This is known as selective exposure and selective attention. People predict that they won't be persuaded by advertisements and forewarning does reduce persuasion, especially if the recipient's attitude differs from that of the message.

In a study of a televised American presidential campaign debate between Nixon and Kennedy, Sigel (1964) found that viewers had greater attention, better memory, and selective distortion of the message support- ing their own views. They noticed more of the good points in their own candidate's performance and the poor aspects of the opposing candidate. On this basis, sometimes an indirect approach may be best; such an approach could minimize people avoiding the communication and at the same time, because of distraction, could also prevent the possibility of inoculation effects and counter arguments.

Attitudes as a system

Successful persuasion takes into account underlying attitudes, values, and needs as well as the attitude of interest. As we have already seen, attitudes may be based on fact, social, or ego defence motives. An attitude serving a knowledge function may be changed by contrary information. This is unlikely to be the case with attitudes serving an ego defence function.

Medium of communication

Would an identical persuasive message presented in written form, on the radio, or on the television have the same persuasive impact? Common- sense alone tells us that differences may well be likely. To determine the impact that the medium of communication may have on persuasion it is necessary to examine the characteristics of the different channels.

Characteristics of channels

Persuasive communications are most effective when they are specifically designed to suit their channel of presentation. As such there is no 'best' channel. Even within a medium there may be substantial differences in the quality and complexity of a message and these may have a marked impact on the effectiveness of persuasion. The best channel in a specific instance will depend on a number of factors such as the target audience, interest value, personal relevance, ease of comprehension of the message, and the characteristics of the source. A medium may highlight source, message or audience characteristics.

Likeability of communicator may be more important in video or audio than in written messages (Chaiken and Eagly, 1983). In the audio-visual media there are many more cues to attend to (e.g. nonverbal behaviour), some of which may actually distract from the message. Because of their transient nature they also tend to deal in simple, easily and rapidly grasped messages; complex messages may be perceived as frustrating and unplea- sant. The audio-visual media do seem relatively potent sources of influence and yielding is often greater than for print (Chaiken and Eagly, 1976). For easily comprehended messages this medium may be the most effective.

Complex messages may be best in the relatively permanent form of print, which readers can consume at their own pace. This characteristic probably explains why arguments in print are received more critically than those on the audio-visual media (Maier and Thurber, 1968).

Social context of the mass media

Despite the undoubted significance of the mass media in persuasion one must not lose sight of their impact in absolute terms. Immediately an advertisement is shown on the television we do not all rush out to buy the product. In comparison with more powerful and flexible personal appeals, the mass media may come a very poor second (Jacoby, 1976).

Personal communications and mass media messages are not separate and it appears that mass media attempts at persuasion may be most influential when they integrate with the individual's social experience. A number of theories and models have been proposed to explain the means by which mass media messages may be socially disseminated. One of the most influential of these is Lazarsfeld *et al*'s (1944) two-step flow theory of media influence.

Lazarsfeld *et al* (1944) examined the effects of an American presidential campaign on voters' behaviours. He found that such a campaign had little direct influence except to reinforce existing attitudes. However, he also noted that individuals voted in groups and that within these groups there were opinion leaders, individuals more informed about various issues. These individuals were more attentive and better able to evaluate communications about these issues (there may be different leaders for different topics). Thus the leader may be influenced by various communications and the group may be influenced by the leader who is known, trusted, and attended to. A two-step process demonstrating the significance of mass media attempts at persuasion and their relationship to their social context.

Theories of attitude change

The 1950s and 1960s were times of great activity in psychology and many theories were proposed at that time which were to remain influential for decades and prompt a vast amount of research and secondary theorizing. At this time one of the most active areas in psychology was the study of attitudes and many of the theories proposed concerned the nature of attitude formation and change. Petty and Cacioppo (1981) outline at least twenty theories of attitude change and persuasion. Needless to say, we cannot examine all these theories and so this discussion will focus on what has been by far the most influential theory of attitude change, Leon Festinger's (1957) Cognitive Dissonance Theory. This theory will be outlined and evaluated, major and more recent alternatives will be considered, and an integrating perspective will be discussed.

Cognitive dissonance theory

Festinger's (1957) theory is founded on the basic assumption of all of a vast host of cognitive consistency theories, that there exists within the individual a striving to be consistent. This notion has already been touched on in relation to the triadic model of attitudes.

Dissonance theory has promoted a great deal of research, has a broad range of applications and can predict and explain many counter-intuitive findings, such as rewards associated with a task making it intrinsically less attractive. This has been recognized as having significant implications and raising important social questions. Should children be rewarded for schoolwork, for example? From this view it is most definitely one of the most successful of its generation of attitude change theories.

Festinger theorized that dissonance occurred and was experienced by a person when that person held two cognitions which implied the opposite of each other. This was considered to be an aversive state. The more important the dissonant attitudes and the larger the number of dissonant attitudes the more aversive the experience is supposed to be.

Because of the aversive nature of dissonance, people are motivated to reduce it, to restore consonance. This can be achieved by changing attitudes or behaviour. As attitudes are usually easier to change than behaviour this is often the observed effect of dissonance. An example may clarify this phenomenon. If you can only afford to buy one record but like two equally well what will ultimately be the result when you choose which one to purchase? Cognitive dissonance theory would argue that you should feel dissonance because of the difficulty of your decision. Did you make the right decision? You may possibly reduce this feeling of tension by finding justifications for your choice, or by altering your relative evaluation of the competing items. You may even avoid the dissonance by avoiding making the decision at all.

The original formulation of cognitive dissonance theory was extended by Brehm and Cohen (1962) to emphasize the role of commitment and volition. The effect of this was to draw attention to dissonance as a post-decisional conflict. The notion of perceived freedom of choice and commitment to a decision can apparently explain the occurrence of incentive rather than dissonance effects under certain conditions. If we feel that we had little say in a decision or choice among alternatives we may come to prefer that which rewards us most or costs us least.

A further major modification to the original formulation of dissonance theory was proposed by Aronson (1969) who suggested that dissonance is greatest when the self-concept is threatened. If you think about this for a while you will see that this is a very sensible idea. If someone regards themselves as a failure then when they make what may be potentially or actually a bad decision it is likely to fit in very well with their self-concept. No dissonance there! Similarly if a decision is on an issue which the individual perceives as unimportant then the possibilities for dissonance are minimal. This factor may be a very significant moderator of dissonance effects.

Severe criticisms have been levelled against dissonance theory (e.g. Chapanis and Chapanis, 1964; Greenwald, 1975). First, the theory can be vague and almost untestable. It is difficult to measure or quantify the actual degree of dissonance that an individual experiences and the fact that dissonance can be reduced in several ways sometimes makes it difficult to predict its consequences. Second, many of the classic dissonance studies can be subjected to severe methodological criticisms. Finally, a number of alternative explanations of apparent dissonance effects are often possible. Bem's influential self-perception theory is discussed below; a number of other alternatives have also been proposed.

As pointed out at the beginning of this discussion, cognitive dissonance theory has been a successful theory in terms of a number of criteria, but the above criticisms must be borne in mind when making a final evaluation of the theory.

Self-perception theory

A number of alternatives to dissonance theory do exist: one of the earliest and most influential is Daryl Bem's (1965, 1972) behavioural approach. Bem argues that people's attitudes and emotions are at least in part the product of observations of their own behaviour (not dissimilar to the James–Lange theory of emotions). For Bem attitudes are inferred from behaviour rather than being the cause of behaviour. Just as an observer might infer our attitudes from the way we behave so might we ourselves determine our attitude in this way. From the perspective of this theory a change in attitude is simply an updating of the individual's attitude on his perception of his current behaviour and its causes.

From this self-perception perspective Bem has replicated dissonance studies and found support for his theory – at least to his own satisfaction.

Many criticisms have been raised against Bem's controversial theory (e.g. Greenwald, 1975). Like dissonance theory it has a number of ambiguities. Also, many studies appear to indicate that attitudes which are important to the individual do tend to produce concordant behaviour; it seems mainly for relatively unimportant attitudes that the reverse situation might apply (Kahle, 1984).

Cognitive elaboration

It has been argued by Petty and Cacioppo (1981) that in general large differences in comprehension are required in order to produce changes in attitude. Most studies don't have such large differences and recall and retention of a persuasive message may have less of an effect on attitudes and behaviour than suggested by McGuire. Factors such as knowledge and interest may make differences in the cognitive processing of a message more significant. The current dominance of the information processing perspective in psychology is reflected in the cognitive response approach to attitude change. This will now be examined in more detail.

Cognitive effort and ability A main tenet of the cognitive response approach is that an individual's motivation to process a message will affect information processing. This is apparent, for example, in the number of message relevant thoughts, counter-arguments, and (possibly) disagreements that are listed by subjects when exposed to a persuasive communication. Note that this does not imply any differences in attending, comprehending or learning a persuasive message.

Where an individual is concerned about an issue there will be a motivation to pay close attention to the content and quality of a persuasive message, i.e. to exert greater cognitive effort in order to retain perceived freedom in an area regarded as important. The theory of psychological reactance (Brehm, 1966; Brehm and Brehm, 1981) argues that attempts to influence directly may backfire by threatening the individual's perceived freedom of choice and hence elicit a defensive reaction in the opposite direction to that desired.

Some support for this notion was provided by Petty and Cacioppo (1977) who showed that subjects forewarned and presented with information counter to important beliefs and attitudes tried to invent counter-arguments immediately in order to protect their perceived autonomy. Distractions could, of course, prevent this counter-arguing (Festinger and Maccoby, 1964). Many advertisements have a great many distractions and an unkinder person than I would relate this advertising strategy to the above observations.

Where the persuasive issue is of little personal relevance or importance the perceived loss of freedom is minimal and has little or no effect on counter-arguing or attitudes.

Central and peripheral routes Petty and Cacioppo (1981) propose an *elaboration-likelihood model* of persuasion and argue that persuasion may be via two routes, a central route or a peripheral route.

The central route to persuasion involves the active processing of the message itself. Petty and Cacioppo argue that this route is likely when an individual is motivated to think about the attitude issue, as when the issue has personal relevance. As such conditions produce greater cognitive effort and elaboration, the quality of the arguments in the message is of paramount importance. Factors inhibiting message relevant thought (e.g. distraction) will reduce message effects via the central route.

Persuasion via the peripheral route occurs when cognitive elaboration of the message is minimal and non-message factors account for obtained attitude change. For example, source characteristics such as credibility may have their effect via the peripheral route and so mainly occur when a subject's motivation or ability to process the message content is low.

Types of attitude change

So far this discussion has looked at some very different approaches to attitude change phenomena. Kelman (1958) outlines a perspective which may provide some integration of these various views. Kelman argues that persuasion may take several forms, different theories may in fact be trying mainly to explain different types of persuasion. Compliance with a powerful, feared communicator may be behavioural conformity rather than necessarily involving a change of attitude. In similar fashion, attitude change could be based on identification, liking or attraction to the source of a message. Of course, if the source ceased to be feared or to be attractive and liked then the basis for attitudes based on compliance or identification may also cease to exist. These forms of persuasion are relatively superficial. Note that much of the Hovland–Yale research was on factors affecting compliance and identification.

True persuasion may be the product of internalization. This would be the acceptance of information from an expert or knowledgeable source. This form of attitude change may be relatively permanent and resistant to attempts at counter influence as it may involve accommodating existing attitudes to the new information. Much of the more theoretically guided work, e.g. by Fishbein and his associates, would fall into this category.

A point worthy of note is that the distinctions made above would fit in quite neatly with Petty and Cacioppo's (1981) theory. Compliance and identification may be seen as peripheral routes to persuasion while internalization would be viewed as persuasion via a central route.

Measuring attitudes

As we have seen, attitudes have been defined in many different ways, and what one chooses to measure and how one chooses to go about measuring it may well be determined by one's theoretical orientation. Attitudes are hypothetical constructs, they cannot be directly observed and their existence is inferred from a person's behaviour. This behaviour can of course take many forms. It may be a person's real life actions, their verbal statements, or their filling in of attitude scales. The fact that the measurement of an attitude ultimately depends on behaviour emphasizes the importance of the attitude–behaviour debate which was discussed previously.

What to measure

Behaviour can be used to reveal attitudes in a number of ways. In terms of increasing formality and structure, the major approaches have been direct observation of behaviour, projective methods, and formal attitude scales. There are also a huge number of miscellaneous techniques which have appeared in the literature and which seem to show the amazing creativity of some researchers.

Observing behaviour

If attitudes are simply behavioural consistencies then observing behaviour is the most obvious way of measuring them. However, a number of problems make this task a little less easy than it might first appear. First, attitudes may be situation specific, very complex to observe and difficult to delineate. This implies that multiple observations are necessary – which may prove expensive in terms of both time and money. Even if one has the time, money and inclination to measure attitudes through observing behaviour, there is still the second issue of validity of the data collected. Are the observations unbiased? This issue could be addressed by having more than one observer and comparing their observations; this would reveal any subjectivity. The difficulty of recording behaviour could also be reduced by the observers using a set of categories in which to classify the behaviour. If we were watching who someone sits next to on a bus we might use categories such as age, sex, race, seat position, etc. Finally, and most problematic, it is sometimes very difficult to observe people unobtrusively. A study examining what people talk about in various places in a city could well produce the embarrassing finding that in all locations the central interest is being stared at by strangers! So, a useful technique for gathering attitude data, but very difficult to do well.

Attitude scaling

Attitude scales provide a fairly quick and simple method of assessing attitudes. They also provide quantitative data which facilitate comparisons, can be used in research, and in statistical analysis.

Measurement assumptions

Implicit in the process of measuring attitudes is the notion that they fall on a continuum and it is assumed that the scale of measurement is linear, that a higher score indicates a stronger attitude. Methods of scale construction aim to ensure unidimensionality, that all items are measuring the same thing, which means that either attitudes are accepted as unidimensional or else only part of a more complex attitude is being measured and the consistency of other components is assumed. Yet again we encounter consistency explanations of attitude and the ramifications of the attitude–behaviour debate.

The goal of determining strength and direction of attitude is a common aim of formal scaling methods. Attitude scales also aim for reliability (that responses are consistent), and validity (that the scale measures what it purports to measure). These last two factors are discussed in more detail below.

Reliability and validity

After item analysis of a pre-test the final version of a test is usually given to a representative group of subjects to provide data for calculating reliability and validity coefficients. These are important indicators of the quality of a test.

The reliability of a test is quite easy to assess, it is simply the consistency of a respondent's answers to test items. Validity is much more difficult to assess. If we ignore the rather dubious criterion of face validity (i.e. that the scale simply looks as if it is measuring the construct of interest), we are left with trying to find associations with some specified criterion measure (e.g. future behaviour or responses to other similar scales) and the gradual accumulation of confirmatory evidence.

Thurstone scales

The first attitude scale was developed by Thurstone (1928) who proudly announced in the title of his paper that 'Attitudes can be measured'. This method of attitude scaling has been termed 'the method of equal appearing intervals'.

A Thurstone scale usually consists of a series of 20 or 30 statements which have values, established in the course of scale construction, ranging from 1 to 11. The maximum number of items is limited by possible fatigue effects, though with too few items reliability and accuracy are reduced.

The values of these items are usually equally spaced over the whole of the 11-point range (e.g. at intervals at 0.5). Note that the values associated with items (which are given in brackets in the example) do not actually appear on the scale. Respondents simply tick those items with which they agree. Their attitude is the median (middle) score of all those that they ticked. An example of items from a hypothetical Thurstone scale is given in Table 24.1 below.

Table 24.1 Example of items from a hypothetical Thurstone scale

1. Modern civilization could not exist without nuclear power (11)
2. Nuclear power is a necessary evil (5)
3. The use of nuclear power should be discontinued immediately (1)

The method of constructing a Thurstone scale is fairly straightforward, if somewhat laborious. Initially a large pool of attitude statements is collected. These try to sample the broad range of positive and negative responses that are possible on the topic concerned. These items are then reviewed for possible ambiguity, appropriate language, relevance and so on. This scale is then given to a number of 'objective judges' to rate on an 11-point scale. Those items rated consistently are retained, the median of the judges' ratings is calculated and from these a number of items at approximately equal steps along the 11-point scale are selected for the final version of the scale.

Advantages: The Thurstone scale was the first formal method of attitude scaling to be developed and as such it is a well-known and established method. Its main advantage is that it provides a good indication of where a person falls on a particular attitude dimension, it also permits norms to be calculated so that the individual can be compared with other individuals or groups.

Disadvantages: This technique uses 'unbiased judges' in its pretest. Is it possible to find such perfect, objective individuals? Even if one can find unbiased individuals, is it better to have judges rather than individuals reporting their own attitudes? Taking subjects' attitude scores as the median of the values attached to the items with which they agreed also means that Thurstone scales tend to reduce the extremity of attitudes revealed.

Likert scales

Rensis Likert's (1932) method of summated ratings is possibly the most popular method of attitude scaling. The hypothetical Thurstone scale in Table 24.1 is reproduced in Likert scale format in Table 24.2, below. Respondents simply tick or circle their level of agreement with each item. The scales are usually marked on a five or seven point scale, say from strongly disagree (1) to strongly agree (7). Because some items are positive and some negative, to keep the scoring consistent it is inverted for negative items (i.e. for negative items strongly agree is scored 1 and strongly disagree is scored 7). A respondent's attitude is simply the sum of his/her scores on each of the individual items.

Table 24.2 Example of items from a hypothetical Likert scale

1. *Modern civilization could not exist without nuclear power*

strongly agree	agree	slightly agree	uncertain	slightly disagree	disagree	strongly disagree

2. *Nuclear power is a necessary evil*

strongly disagree	agree	slightly disagree	uncertain	slightly agree	disagree	strongly agree

3. *The use of nuclear power should be discontinued immediately*

strongly agree	agree	slightly agree	uncertain	slightly disagree	disagree	strongly disagree

Likert scales are fairly straightforward to construct, the procedure is not dissimilar to that of Thurstone scaling.

As with Thurstone scaling, the first step is to collect a large number of attitude statements. For the pre-test a number of subjects are asked to rate their agreement with each statement on a seven point scale (strongly disagree / disagree / slightly disagree / undecided / slighty agree / agree / strongly agree). The subjects should be representative of the group for which the scale is intended for use. Note that unlike Thurstone scaling, subjects are asked to rate their own agreement/disagreement with the items, rather than trying to act as 'judges'.

Responses to each statement are scored from one to seven and preliminary attitude scores are obtained for each subject by summing across all the subject's statement scores. For 40 statements this would give a score between 40 and 280. The higher the score the more favourable the attitude.

Once a set of rated statements has been obtained, those which are the best discriminators of the attitude being measured are retained for the final version of the scale. In an ideal world we would correlate each statement with some external criterion, perhaps in the case of nuclear power we might take membership of CND or Greenpeace as a criterion. Usually a good, objective criterion is not available, but there is a way around this. The internal consistency of responses to items can be used to indicate predictive value.

The more positive a person's attitude the more likely he should be to endorse favourable statements and the less likely he should be to endorse unfavourable statements. In effect what we do is correlate the scores on each item with each subject's pre-test score. To be absolutely correct, though it usually makes only a minimal difference, we should actually correlate the item score with the sum of the scores on the remaining items. This item analysis used to be rather hard work as it involves calculating a correlation coefficient for each statement, and there may be several hundred statements in the pre-test. Fortunately we now have computers. Those items with the best correlations are retained for the final version of the scale.

Advantages: It is usually argued that Likert scales are quicker to construct than equivalent Thurstone scales, though this claim has been disputed. The respondents in the pre-test are subjects indicating their own responses, they are not attempting to be unbiased judges and so this removes concern over whether such a role play is feasible. Despite simplifications in method of scale construction the Likert scale is generally found to have equivalent reliability and validity to that of Thurstone scales; the two forms of scale usually correlate highly (Edwards, 1957).

Disadvantages: The main disadvantage of Likert scales in comparison to Thurstone scales is their lower level of accuracy. The precise origins of a given score are ambiguous on a Likert scale. Two items producing a total score of eight could achieve this by each being rated four or by one item being rated seven and the other one. So what would a score of eight mean? Although a higher score indicates a more positive attitude there is no indication of the magnitude of differences. A score of four is higher and more positive than a score of two but it is not necessarily twice as positive.

Often the trade-off of labour involved in scale construction for slightly less accuracy is appropriate but this sort of decision must be made on an informed basis and with the aim and intended use of the scale being borne in mind.

The semantic differential

This technique was originally developed by Osgood, Suci, and Tannenbaum (1957) in their study of the meaning of concepts. The concept (i.e. the attitude object) is rated on a series of usually evaluative bipolar adjectives. A typical format is presented in Table 24.3, below. Note that the format of the scale is quite flexible. The points on the scale may be left unlabelled or they may be given a verbal or numerical label; similarly the scale may contain fewer or more than seven points.

Table 24.3 Example of a hypothetical semantic differential scale

Wise:	_____:	_____:	_____:	_____:	_____:	_____:	_____: Foolish
Good:	_____:	_____:	_____:	_____:	_____:	_____:	_____: Bad
Dirty:	_____:	_____:	_____:	_____:	_____:	_____:	_____: Clean

The adjectives used in a particular study are crucial if results are to be meaningful. Adjectives may come from several sources, the most obvious being a pilot survey or interview.

A variety of ways exist to score semantic differential scales. On evaluative scales responses could be transformed into numbers such that one stood for very negative and seven for very positive. The sum of ratings on these scales would then represent the positivity of the attitude toward the object. A very sophisticated approach might use factor analysis and compare subjects via their factor scores.

Advantages: It is a relatively simple and fast technique. It doesn't force respondents into making global judgements and is direct. It correlates well with the Thurstone and Likert methods previously discussed.

Disadvantages: This directness of the technique can be advantageous but it can also have drawbacks as it may provoke a negative reaction from some subjects and, like most self-rating scales, is open to faking. The adjectives also may not be relevant or meaningful to the respondent and may even be interpreted differently by different people. Adjectives with negative–positive poles are often randomized for which pole appears at which end of the rating scale, but this does not prevent response biases due to the influence of the scales preceding the one currently being marked. Most of these problems are not insurmountable and this remains a very useful technique.

Indirect methods

As we have seen in the above sections, direct scaling of attitudes is now very sophisticated. Despite this there are still some unanswered questions. For example, are we normally aware of and do we have insight into our attitudes? To what extent do formal scales actually produce or at least structure the way we experience and report the attitude they purport to measure? Formal scales are also more susceptible to faking.

Whichever method one uses to measure attitude, it is useful if findings can be confirmed by another method; this evidence confirms that the attitude being measured is not simply a product of the method of assessment.

Social psychologists seem to be very inventive when it comes to devising methods of measuring attitudes and a huge variety of topics could be included in this section. I will focus on the bogus pipeline technique and projective tests but a few other methods will be briefly touched on to show the variety of approaches.

The bogus pipeline method

One way of attempting to avoid social desirability effects in measuring attitudes has been to try to use physiological responses as a measure of attitude. Westie and DeFleur (1959) recorded galvanic skin response (changes in the electrical conductivity of the skin), vascular constriction of the finger, and characteristics of the heartbeat while subjects viewed pictures of Caucasians and Negroes. The assumption was that level of physiological arousal is directly related to feeling about the attitude object. Although this assumption may seem very reasonable at first sight, it is by no means universally accepted by psychologists and certainly doesn't give the direction of the response (i.e. whether it is positive or negative).

In a series of experiments in the 1960s and early 1970s Hess and his associates conducted a series of experiments showing that subjects' pupils dilated in the presence of pleasant stimuli (photographs of attractive members of the opposite sex, for example) and constricted in response to unpleasant stimuli. This observation caused great interest at the time as it seemed to provide an unobtrusive means of measuring direction *and* strength of attitude. In fact, eastern jade traders have known this effect for many years and in the bargaining over this precious stone it has no doubt had great influence. However, like a great many psychological effects it is important to understand the limits of the phenomenon. Hess's results are important but they do have limitations. For example, later studies found that the pupils of females also dilated in response to pictures of men with constricted pupils. Presumably the constricted pupils communicated a negative attitude or threat and the response of dilating pupils could be interpreted as appeasement. Overall, research points to pupilar dilation and a number of other similar techniques such as gaze duration as better indicators of intensity of feeling rather than direction.

The bogus pipeline technique of Jones and Sigall (1971) may be seen as a development of the physiological techniques discussed above. It seems more of an attempt to rescue traditional attitude scaling than to represent a totally new or different approach. The basic idea is that many scales (e.g. assessing prejudice) may produce defensive reactions. Most people prefer not to be thought of as prejudiced or bigoted. But if an individual thinks he might be found out ... maybe it is better to be thought a bigot than to be thought a lying bigot! Working on this principle, if one could manage to convince a subject that he was to be attached to what is basically a very sophisticated lie detector (i.e. that will detect his initial response, before he is actually required to make an overt behavioural response) this could well improve the response to your attitude test. Of course no such sophisticated machine exists, but all one really needs is a bank of impressive looking machinery with a few flashing lights; as long as the subject thinks that the machine can have insights to his real attitude that is all that is required.

In bogus pipeline studies, to convince the subjects that the machinary works a few pre-tests are usually carried out. Subjects typically complete a short questionnaire and try to see if they can deceive the machine. These questions are usually fairly innocuous so the subject doesn't produce defensive responses. Of course, the subjects' answers to the pre-test are leaked so that the machine can then appear to produce the appropriate insights. In the Sigall and Page (1971) study this was achieved by leaving the scale near to a slightly open door so that it could be read from the corridor. What an interesting picture this paints of social psychological research in action!

Advantages: Many interesting pieces of research have been conducted using the bogus pipeline paradigm. Though the procedure is more involved than administering a questionnaire, it may be very useful for sensitive topics.

Disadvantages: The bogus pipeline has been subject to a number of hotly debated criticisms. For example, it may be subject to demand character-istics, to cueing the subject into giving specific responses (Cherry *et al*, 1976). A number of the technique's supporters dispute this criticism (e.g. Gaes *et al*, 1978; Arkin and Lake, 1983).

The bogus pipeline is also only likely to be useful with relatively uninformed subjects. If the technique became very widely known or subjects were sufficiently knowledgeable about the possibility of such an instrument then its effect could be negated.

Overall, although the utility of the bogus pipeline is still controversial, it would seem to be worthy of a place in the range of techniques used to assess attitudes.

Projective techniques

Many of the alternatives to attitude scaling are often much more subtle and may require a good deal of specialist training to be used effectively. Projective approaches include interpreting inkblots or ambiguous photographs, completing unfinished sentences or stories, and judging or guessing answers to supposed questions of fact. All these approaches present subjects with ambiguous or partially structured material and then infer attitudes from the responses or interpretations of the subjects.

Advantages: These techniques permit greater freedom of response on the part of subjects and so may be giving a truer picture of a person's attitudes. They also can be relatively unobtrusive; subjects are often unaware of what is being assessed and so may produce fewer defensive responses (though this may raise some interesting ethical issues).

Disadvantages: Responses need not necessarily be a projection of feelings and attitudes on the part of the subject, he may simply be stating a cultural stereotype or describing the situation as he knows and has experienced it. For example, interpreting a photograph with black and white people in as having blacks in a menial role need not reflect prejudice, it may simply reflect the social arrangement as the subject has experienced it.

Projective approaches also suffer considerable methodological problems. Their test–retest reliability is poor, the qualitative nature of the data collected makes comparison across respondents difficult, and interpretations may vary considerably between different people administering the test.

Conclusions

The different ways of measuring attitudes that have been outlined above clearly show that there is no perfect method of measuring attitudes. Each approach has its advantages and limitations. From this perspective it is understandable that many social psychologists advocate a multi-method approach to measuring attitudes. If several flawed techniques each none the less indicate the same attitude one can be at least a little more confident that the finding is not an artifact of technique. Despite the widespread agreement that the above statement would obtain from most social psychologists, it is unfortunate that most studies do not adopt such an approach and measurement often reflects other demands (such as time, cost, etc.) and is based on a simple self-report attitude scale. This state of affairs is serious for the body of psychological knowledge that is being established; it is even more serious if this body of knowledge is to be applied or if it exerts an influence on social policy.

Prejudice

In this chapter we have examined attitudes and at several points the topic of prejudice has been touched on. This is not surprising or simply due to my selection of studies to discuss; much research was driven by the desire to understand prejudice and discover ways in which it could be reduced. This was very much an idea in keeping with many early definitions of psychology which saw it as concerned with the 'prediction and control' of behaviour. Though from a very different perspective, contemporary research, e.g. on measurement problems, shows that the study of prejudice may still be significant for general theory and research on attitudes.

Nature of prejudice

Prejudice is a specific type of attitude and, as might be expected, based on the earlier problems of defining attitudes, it is open to a variety of definitions. It can be seen as an overall evaluation based on the beliefs an individual holds about some other group and its members. It can equally well be defined in terms of the triadic model of attitudes, as a predisposition to think, feel and act in a given way to some other group and its members. Both definitions do have a core of agreement, a recognition of the role of affect. This is perhaps especially significant in that prejudicial attitudes do often appear to be very strong and personal and particularly resistant to change. Perhaps the most famous definition of prejudice is that of Allport (1954):

> 'An antipathy based upon a faulty and inflexible generalization. It may be felt or expressed. It may be directed toward a group as a whole, or toward an individual because he is a member of that group.'

This definition makes a number of important points. First, it emphasizes that prejudice does have a cognitive/belief component but that this is faulty and inflexible because it is over-generalized to apply to all members of the out-group. This cognitive basis of prejudice is a stereotype. Its resistance to change may be due to prejudicial attitudes often primarily serving an ego-defence function. Any threat to such an attitude may be a threat to the individual's whole self-concept, self-worth, and ability to understand his world. Prejudice is both incorrect and irrational.

As has been indicated above, the cognitive bases of prejudice are stereotypes. These may take two main forms. Individuals will have their own preconceptions of the characteristics of various groups, but these will

745

also contain a substantial component absorbed from the individual's culture and sub-culture.

The cultural stereotypes on which prejudice is based appear to be relatively persistent. Katz and Braly (1933) asked students at Princeton University to indicate the applicability of a list of 84 character traits (e.g. intelligent, musical, lazy, happy-go-lucky) to a number of racial groups (e.g., American, Negro, Italian). Personally, I wonder why they had Negro and American as separate groups – there are American Negroes. There was generally strong agreement among subjects about the characteristics of the various racial and ethnic groups. Follow-up studies in 1951, 1969, and 1982 confirmed that although stereotypes were weakening a core image remained (e.g. the intelligent, ambitious, shrewd Jew) and subjects still showed agreement about cultural stereotypes.

Second, Allport's definition states that prejudice is an antipathy that may be felt or expressed. Note that this means that it is possible to hold prejudicial attitudes toward some out-group without ever showing discriminatory behaviour. The contrary is also true. A person may discriminate against an out-group without being prejudiced against them, perhaps to please and be similar to friends. Discrimination is simply behaviour, and as the attitude–behaviour debate informed us, behaviour may or may not reflect attitudes. A point particularly worth noting about this definition is that it labels prejudice as negative, an antipathy. Many authors would argue that over-generalized positive attitudes would still constitute prejudice – and recent years have certainly seen instances of positive discrimination, a term I find rather confusing as to discriminate in any way implies that groups are treated differently; to discriminate positively toward one group implies that one must be negative, or at least less positive toward some other group.

Third, and finally, Allport's definition emphasizes that prejudice is based on group membership. Any *identifiable* group may be the target of prejudice. This makes prejudice a much broader phenomenon than might be initially imagined. Prejudice may be on the basis sex, race, religion, physical appearance, names, clothing or any of a whole host of other characteristics, and we can all be victims and perpetrators. Of course some prejudices may be more significant or vehement, but the only crucial factor determining if a characteristic can form the basis of prejudice seems to be that we must be able to distinguish membership of some real or imagined group.

Origins of prejudice

Many explanations have been offered to account for prejudice. These have been rendered on many levels, from historical, sociological, and psychological perspectives – and of course there may be a grain of truth in all of these, they are not mutually exclusive. Some of the proposed explanations constitute good accounts of the possible origins of prejudice, others are good at explaining how prejudice may be maintained, and yet others help us explain why individuals may differ in their levels of prejudice.

The historical perspective sees current prejudices as originating in historical inequities. So, for example, prejudice against blacks in the USA can be seen as a vestige from the days of slavery.

A sociologist might prefer to place more emphasis on prejudice as a product of the social and cultural structure of society. Barriers to social mobility, population density, urbanization, industrialization, communication, and competition for employment might all contribute to prejudice.

From a sociological perspective prejudice may be a justification for the economic exploitation of a minority group. It may also justify their being used as a scapegoat in explaining society's economic ills. In times of economic recession increases in prejudice in those feeling most threatened is a well-documented occurrence.

Psychologists have presented a number of perspectives on prejudice. One approach may emphasize the knowledge function of attitudes. Prejudice may enable an individual to make sense of his world. Stereotypes simplify the world and make it more predictable and potentially rewarding.

Prejudice, like all attitudes, is learned and this has been an obvious focus of attention for many psychologists. In children as young as about four years old racial attitudes can be seen emerging and changing as the child develops and learns the norms and stereotypes of his family and culture (Davey, 1983).

Personality and psychodynamic theorists have explained prejudice as a characteristic of the individual rather than simply of learning. Prejudice may essentially function as an ego defence mechanism, an individual may project his own shortcomings onto another group and blame them for his failures.

Adorno *et al* (1950) in attempting to explain the anti-semitism of Nazi Germany argued that early socialization may lead to distinctive personality types. So, for example, severe, rigid child rearing practices may in turn produce a rigid, 'authoritarian personality'. The child's frustration during child-rearing could not be directed to the all-powerful parents and so must be displaced. This way of coping with hostility by displacing it, and a rigid view of the world combine to produce a personality set ripe for prejudice. Although a number of criticisms have been levelled against Adorno's research into the authoritarian personality, a number of subsequent studies have confirmed the relationship between this characteristic of personality and prejudice.

Related to both learning approaches and psychodynamic approaches to prejudice is a scapegoat theory based on the frustration–aggression hypothesis of Dollard *et al* (1939). This theory, at its most basic, argued that aggression was the product of frustration. Prejudice is similarly hostile and could likewise be viewed as the consequence of frustration, as the blocking of some goal-directed behaviour. There is indeed some evidence that if prejudiced people are set frustrating tasks or punished then their ambient level of prejudice increases.

Reducing prejudice

We have already devoted considerable attention to examining attitude change and persuasion, so presumably all we need to do is to apply these principles to prejudice. Alas, such presumptions might be premature for, as our general consideration of the nature of attitudes has shown, they may serve significant functions for the individual and we are not dealing with people in isolation from their historical, cultural, and social context. These factors combined seem to suggest, and this is probably in accord with your commonsense conclusion, that changing prejudicial attitudes is far from easy.

Theorists have suggested that through inter-group contact stereotypes may be broken down. Many studies have shown that this does seem to work (e.g. Barnard and Benn, 1988), though this assumes positive, friendly, perhaps mutually dependent contact. Competitive contact, as is perhaps often the situation in our society, can actually aggravate prejudice. Similarly, social structures may be such that prejudice may be broken down but only within limited confines, perhaps in the workplace. Certainly legislation can go some way toward avoiding discriminatory behaviour, and one might hope that attitude would ultimately come into line with behaviour, but changing attitude is no easy or short-term matter. Changing attitudes also requires changes in society.

Further reading

Ajzen, I., and Fishbein, M. (1980) *Understanding Attitudes and Predicting Social Behavior*. Prentice-Hall.
Kahle, L. R. (1984) *Attitudes and Social Adaptation*. Pergamon.
Petty, R. E., and Cacioppo, J. T. (1981) *Attitudes and Persuasion: Classic and contemporary approaches*. William Brown Company.
Thomas, K., ed. (1971) *Attitudes and Behaviour: Selected readings*. Penguin.
Zimbardo, P., Ebbesen, E. B., and Maslach, C. (1977) *Influencing Attitudes and Changing Behavior*, 2nd edn. Addison-Wesley.

Psychology and education

One could argue that good education is the bulwark of civilized society. In this section we provide a brief insight into how some intellectual and physical skills may best be taught, together with specific advice on how to tackle, what is to some people, the anxiety-ridden task of studying for examinations.

Chapter twenty-five

Learning and teaching

Part I Teachers and children
Mark Fox, Alan Labram, Allan Sigston and Sheila Wolfendale

Part II Skill acquisition
Len Holdstock

Part I Teachers and children

Promoting children's learning

Assessing the contribution of psychology within education

The relationship between psychology and education has remained an unresolved and sometimes vexed issue. The relative influence of psychology upon teaching and learning processes is not easily assessable given a multiplicity of variables impinging upon schooling, and the place of psychology within teacher training courses is ambiguous. For decades now a psychology element in teacher education has been thought to be an essential requisite, though there has not traditionally been a consensus regarding the most relevant brands of psychology, the psychological orthodoxies which ought to be taught, and the range and depth of knowledge required by the tutors who lecture to teachers in training. The dangers of diluting psychology and trivializing hard-won psychological insights into learning derived from research has latterly exercised psychologists in higher education, particularly those involved in teacher training (Francis, 1985).

Articles in the *British Journal of Educational Psychology* over many years attest to a considerable amount of research into the application of psychological theories and constructs to educational processes. It is also evident, at face value, that a number of key subject and knowledge areas within psychology, such as learning theories, individual differences, developmental and social psychology and so on have significant bearing upon active teaching and learning. Indeed second year psychology undergraduates when asked between 1985 and 1987 to cite those parts of their psychology degree they felt to be applicable to education had no difficulty in generating lists and articulating their relevance.

The view of these contemporary students is then in line with the writings of Morris (1958), and Peel (1956) who outlines 'a role of educational psychology' and who therefore is on record in perceiving a discipline that has come to be called 'educational psychology' which is a marrying of psychological theory and its application to educational practice. It is important to acknowledge that Peel stressed the scientific rigour that should inform and guide all research and its applications. Writing in the same year Coladarci (1956) asserted that 'the teacher, then, must be an active, continuous inquirer into the validity of his own procedures' (p. 490) and saw the teacher's role as one of hypothesis-tester into the effectiveness of his teaching and children's learning.

As far as the application of psychology to education is concerned, then, the 'psychologically-informed' teacher is perceived to be in a key position and the route to the provision of such teachers is acknowledged to be through appropriate teacher training. The application of psychology to education through research activity as referred to above is another major area. A 'subject-count' of articles in the *British Journal of Educational Psychology* in the period 1984–88 confirms an enduring research preoccupation with core aspects of teaching and learning (Kyriacou, 1985), cognitive processing competence (Underwood and Underwood, 1987), children's perceptions (Little, 1985), reading (Crispin *et al*, 1984; Hannon, 1987).

Acknowledgement of the important contribution of research into educational processes is reflected in the long-standing existence of the National Foundation for Educational Research, which carries out research and development on a sponsored contractual basis. Major research programmes of the last few years, which are heavily influenced by psychological constructs and methodologies, include investigations into mathematics learning, evaluation of particular programmes such as the government-instigated TVEI (Technical, Vocational Educational Initiative), appraisal of initiatives to integrate children with special educational needs into mainstream schools. Yet another example of effectively applying psychology to education is the now widespread use of behavioural approaches to learning, teaching, classroom and behaviour management. Earlier work on behaviour modification has led to a proliferation of proven techniques applicable in a range of classroom and out of school settings, such as in the home (Vargas, 1977; Fontana, 1984).

A third major manifestation of the inter-relationship between psychology and education is the provision over the past 60–70 years of educational psychologists who are currently employed by local education authorities. Prerequisite qualifications of these applied psychologists includes a degree in psychology, teaching qualifications, teaching experience, and a postgraduate professional training at higher degree level. The terms of reference for educational psychologists (EPs) are wide-ranging, though there are core responsibilities, which include assessment of intervention with children's learning, behaviour, emotional difficulties, involvement in the educational placement of children with designated special needs and handicapping conditions, in-service training and support work with teachers, parents and others concerned with children.

Competencies and skills

These activities presuppose a whole range of competencies in relevant areas of applied psychology including a clear rationale for working with and on behalf of children, which can, for example, encompass problem-solving strategies, matched with working concepts of individual differences. In a recent policy document on the work of EPs, the Association of Educational Psychologists delineates four headings within which are grouped professional activities and requisite skills. These are: communication; gathering information; effecting change; evaluation. The following short selected extracts from the document may serve to convey the perceived match between a prior grounding in psychology, teaching experience and the specific ways in which psychology is offered by EPs to other practitioners:

'The hypothesis-testing method of working employed by EPs . . . has as

753

an essential component the gathering of relevant, accurate and comprehensive information from a wide variety of sources ... the central knowledge base is in essence the whole field of the psychology and development of children and young people ...'

'Skills and knowledge include ... development of rigorous experimental designs aimed at monitoring and evaluating projects involving individuals, groups, institutions and whole systems ... the design of recording and record-keeping techniques ... the design of questionnaire and interview procedures ... the use and interpretation of measures of change in ability, skill-development and educational performance.' (A.E.P., 1986)

Norwich (1983) critically probes the specific and unique nature of the EPs' contribution, pointing out that 'child psychologists ... derive their identity from the involvement in the understanding and explanation of children's psychological processes ... this would include research into and development of psychological methods used in providing for children's needs' (p. 116). He wants it generally acknowledged and acted upon that applied psychology in the areas of child development and education, like any discipline, has limits to its relevance, applicability and remit.

While it is valid to be cautionary about the parameters of any discipline, it is equally tenable to emphasize how educational psychology, whether academic in origin or applied within schools and other settings, continues to be concerned with the perennial preoccupations of teachers, namely,

- how best to promote individual and group learning,
- how to create effective learning environments,
- how to teach effectively.

A substantial body of literature, mainly American, now exists in learning and educational psychology (Gagné, 1985; Ausubel *et al*, 1978) which is both empirical and discursive and which exemplifies the inextricable relationship of psychology to education. Some of these eminent writers are optimistic about the contribution that psychology can make to children's learning. Bloom conceptualizes 'alterable variables' in education and children's learning (1979). In his model there are a number of variables that are neither stable nor static and which can be manipulated positively to effect measureable change in children's learning rate and output. His polarization demonstrates the difference between a static view of children's innate ability versus a 'no-ceiling to intelligence' view; emphasizes the underused power of teachers as a means of actively promoting learning; de-emphasizes the negative effects of an allegedly depriving home, but promotes the 'home environmental process' variables, including the 'curriculum and teaching style' that exists in each home.

In the following sections we go on to explore a small, selected number of key aspects of teaching, learning, curriculum areas, the important subject of reading, concepts of special need and exceptionality, with a view to illustrating the relationship between education and psychological research and practice.

The influence of schools upon children's development and learning has received intermittent attention over the years and is currently under scrutiny because of the radical, far-reaching implications of the 1988 Education Reform Act, the National Curriculum and stages of assessment of educational progress, as is mentioned later in the chapter.

The influence of schools as institutions

The importance of schools as objects of study has long been recognized within psychology and sociology. Schools are a formative factor in children's and young people's development both in terms of intellectual learning and in assisting the socialization of the child into society.

In an obvious sense schools ought to be highly influential in these processes for if we consider how the waking hours of five- to 16-year-olds are spent they are likely to be in school almost as long as in their own homes, with teachers for as much time as they are in the company of their parents and spending more time with same age peers than with their brothers and sisters. Yet up to the early 1970s social scientists commonly suggested that schools accounted for little of the variability between individuals, and by implication reflected rather than influenced the major divisions in society.

Bernstein (1970) ventured the view that middle class biases so permeated education that 'education cannot compensate for society'. On a different tack Jensen (1969) argued that the inheritance of cognitive abilities all but overwhelmed environmental factors in determining academic outcomes. A further group of theorists argued similarly in respect of family factors.

Subsequently the shift of both research activity and evidence has moved towards schools' ability to maximize the achievement of beneficial goals for their pupils; and as changing schools seems much more realizable than radically restructuring society, interest has been attracted to the topic from all political viewpoints.

A number of studies carried out in the Inner London Education Authority shed some light on the issues. Michael Power and colleagues showed large differences in the rates of recorded delinquency between a group of schools that remained stable over time and appeared not to result from differences in intake or areas in which pupils lived (Power, Benn and Morris, 1972).

Rutter, Maughan, Mortimer and Ouston (1979) examined a wide range of educational outcomes including attendance, conduct and academic performance. After making statistical allowances for the effects of differences in socio-economic background and cognitive abilities in the intakes, some schools seemed to come out consistently better showing positive correlations between these disparate measures so that, for instance, pupils in a school with good attendance tended to show better conduct as well.

A similar study of primary schools provides further evidence of the influence of school membership although cognitive and non-cognitive effects seem to be more independent of one another than in the secondary school. Indeed the authors go as far as to say that '. . . the results confirm that in determining pupils' progress during the junior years (taking account of initial attainment), school membership is far more influential than background factors, sex and age' (Mortimer, Sammons, Stoll, Ecob and Lewis, 1988).

The research referred to is drawn from a wide range of studies that indicate differential effects of schools on such dimensions as 'disruptive' behaviour, examination passes and rates of children identified as having special educational needs. The consistency of these findings and specific studies like Mortimer *et al (op cit)* tend to suggest that these effects are not marginal differences detected by sensitive statistical techniques but are at least on a par with other less alterable variables related to children's intellect and background. Reynolds (1987) offers a concrete example that easily translates to the sphere of job opportunities '. . . that individual schools have effects on academic development, amounting to one and a half "O" or CSE passes'.

Mechanisms accounting for differences between schools

Some researchers have pointed out wide variations in the proportions of time schools schedule for learning and that pupils spend in curriculum related activities (academic engaged time) or even more pertinently, doing work that is challenging and likely to engender new learning (academic learning time). As might be expected the more academic engaged/learning time the more curricular progress and the less 'difficult' behaviour is exhibited. Psychologists investigating pedagogy have identified a number of teacher behaviours and classroom factors that correlate with higher levels of task engagement (e.g. Brophy, 1986).

A considerable amount of evidence has amassed regarding the efficacy of parental involvement in the educational process, particularly in facilitating early reading skills (Topping and Wolfendale, 1985).

From a more social psychological perspective research into the interactions within schools has proved illuminating. Hargreaves (1967) showed that pupils placed in the low stream of a secondary school developed a subculture deviating from the rest of the school through differential treatment and the adoption of 'deviant' self-concepts.

In a later study Hargreaves, Hestor and Mellor (1975) have described how teachers develop stable stereotypes of pupils that may ultimately lead the pupil to behave in ways that more closely fit the stereotype.

One productive line of reasoning developed from Rutter *et al (op cit)* has been the notion that schools have a pervasive ethos. A school with a positive ethos values each member of the school community. This could be communicated in many ways such as emphasizing pupils' successes, frequent displays of pupils' work, consistency and fairness in applying rules and so forth.

Developing more effective schools

One method of changing what happens in schools has been prescription from outside, an obvious example being the instigation of the National Curriculum in the United Kingdom; however, there is little this approach can offer to address the differences between schools and the consequent inequalities of opportunities that may arise for their pupils.

Among practitioners there has been a progressive recognition that organizations amount to more than the sum of their parts. Like other organizations, schools tend to maintain current practices among their members and as a result they are fairly resistant to simplistic interventions like staff training in isolation.

A useful perspective has been derived from 'systems' theory (e.g. Maher and Illback, 1982). Briefly a school's development can be facilitated through looking at cohesive parts of the organization, analysing these sub-systems, designing changes, then implementing and evaluating them. Ideally this should be a cyclical process more akin to growth than prospecting for a definitive solution. Emphasis is placed on the resulting new structures, procedures and content arising from the deliberations but also, crucially, on the process by which decisions are made and implemented such that all parties share the endeavour and have ownership of the outcomes. There are some examples of schemes that have formalized this type of approach to make it more widely accessible, like the *Guidelines for Review: Internal Development in Schools* (McMahon, Bolam, Abbott and Holly, 1984). Although such initiatives need to belong to schools it is often useful for schools to have an external consultant. This role and the more general application of psychology to issues of organizational development represent a major but, at the time of writing, largely unrealized contribution from psychologists working in the field of education, such as applied educational psychologists described earlier in the chapter.

Teachers' handling strategies

While it is true to say that teachers are constantly concerned with what their pupils learn it is also true that teachers are often faced with behaviour which is difficult or disruptive such that learning of any kind is problematic. School rules and sanctions will often be sufficient for troublesome behaviour to be curbed but in those instances where these fail or are inappropriate teachers have the task of devising alternatives or of facing the prospect of the child being excluded or suspended from school. Some of the most successful strategies in changing behaviour are based on behavioural techniques. Writers such as Westmacott and Cameron (1981) have stressed the importance of defining offending behaviour in precise terms and avoiding labels which pass for descriptions. Examining behaviour in the context in which it occurs is vital. This includes listing the antecedents to the behaviour, the consequences to the behaviour and the effects of the consequences. Fundamental to this approach is the idea that where behaviour is followed by a consequent event which is pleasurable, the behaviour is more likely to be repeated. Such reinforcements, as they are called, differ from person to person but do not have to be extraordinary. Within schools reinforcements for desired behaviour such as teacher praise and visual feedback of progress in the form of charts can be effective. Often, undesirable behaviour has been learned through a schedule of reinforcement making it very difficult to eliminate. Teaching acceptable behaviour which is incompatible with the offending behaviour and which is rewarded is a more effective method of producing behavioural change than punishing.

Reading

Although most children do not start their formal education until they enter school at the age of five years, they bring with them a range of skills and expertise upon which their future education can be built. In no sector of the curriculum is this more important than in the acquisition of reading skills. Even without prior formal instruction in reading, children will already have acquired to a greater or lesser degree many of the fundamental perceptual and attitudinal prerequisites to reading. They will have developed the perceptual skills necessary to perceive letters on a page, see groups of letters as separate from others and yet as every infant teacher knows, they will differ widely in the extent to which they can 'read'. Researchers have attempted to discover why this is. Is it due to intelligence, memory, cultural background, reading ability of parents or perhaps some physiological determinant?

Among those children who do not read well at an early age a common feature appears to be the opportunity to observe and take part in reading activities which are enjoyable, satisfying and, most importantly, the presence of a sympathetic and model peer or adult to share these (Clark, 1976). While it is not uncommon for parents to read to their children, many have undervalued such activities and so attempts have been made to validate these and where extra help is required to give them some structure. Starting in the mid-1970s the development of parental involvement in children's reading has really taken off in the 1980s, with the emergence of paired reading as a researched valid and successful technique (Topping and Wolfendale, 1985, *op cit*). Essentially the technique consists of training parents and children to read together material of the child's choosing with a clear correction and support procedure and with the option of the child enabled to read alone. The technique, although apparently simple, does require parent and child to undergo some prior training since it is all too easy for parents to misunderstand the aims of the session. These are not primarily to jump on every error, to practise word-building, to discourage guessing or to improve spelling but are rather to promote reading through understanding the functions of print, to gain familiarity with written (as opposed to spoken) language by providing a meaningful, enjoyable and frequent experience.

Within schools, however, teachers still face the task of identifying those children with reading difficulties and developing for them an appropriate classroom approach. Many teachers have turned to tests of reading ability in order to identify such children. Tests such as the Burt Word Reading Test (1921) and the Schonell (1942) are administered individually and require the child to read correctly, isolated and unrelated words of increasing difficulty. These are then totalled to provide a reading age which can be compared with the child's chronological age to determine the extent of any disability. Such tests can be used only with children who have already acquired a sufficiently large sight vocabulary for a sample to be taken. They have been criticized as having very little resemblance to real reading as the words have been taken out of context and so provide no measure as to whether or not the child understands what he is reading. The term 'barking at print' has been used to describe children who successfully read aloud without understanding. Such tests are not designed to provide guidelines on how children who are failing to read should be helped. The idea of a child having a 'reading age' has also been criticized as having little meaning. A reading age of eight years might mean that if you averaged the ages of children reading at this level it would be eight or that most eight-year-olds read at this level. Nevertheless this approach has led to a much used single word approach to reading using 'flash-cards'. Words are written in large print on a piece of card and the teacher typically will sit at the front of the class showing each card in turn so that the children can read it aloud.

Other tests have attempted to break down reading into component parts to enable these to be assessed. The Neale Analysis of Reading Ability (Neale, 1966) requires the child to read aloud a series of graded paragraphs. It not only gives a measure of accuracy but also comprehension and rate. It provides a scheme of analysis and diagnostic features that go some way in providing pointers for teachers. However, the child has to be a fairly fluent reader already in order to complete the test.

Approaches by teachers to remediating children's reading have been varied but a long-standing one has been that of phonics. Essentially, children are taught the sounds of individual phonemes. They are then trained to break down words into phonemes, to read or sound these and then to reconstruct the word. Although the approach has a certain face validity and has had some success, it has been criticized (e.g. Smith, 1978). He argues that in the English language as with many others the same group of letters can sound differently according to context, e.g. 'broom' and 'brook'. Furthermore, even whole words can sound differently according to context, e.g. 'row'.

A different way of evaluating children's individual strengths and weaknesses on attainment tasks goes under the general term of 'Curriculum Based Assessment' (e.g. Ainscow and Tweddle, 1979). This approach is not based on the use of standardized tests giving norm related scores but rather aims to break down tasks into component skills. Each child's performance on a set of skill based tests leads to an individual programme of teaching. When the child has mastered those skills to the level of a pre-set criterion further assessment leads to new targets. One example of this is the procedure of direct instruction. Typically this is characterized by a set of published material which is highly structured. A set of placement tests is designed to ensure that an individual child is started at the most appropriate part of the programme. These are followed by quick-fire lessons requiring verbal responses from the child and followed up by practice and generalization exercises.

Precision Teaching is another approach which provides rapid feedback to the teacher. Individual behavioural objectives in reading are set for each child and the child's performance both in terms of accuracy and speed can be checked by a set of daily exercises (Solity and Bull, 1987).

Assessment and exceptionality

Children progress at different rates through the curriculum and educationists have always considered it of central importance to assess children's progress in order to understand the effects of education. If education does not move the child through the curriculum then education has had no effect.

There are a number of reasons why children are assessed in schools. Macintosh and Hale (1976) have made a useful summary of these reasons:

1. Diagnosis – of pupils' strengths and weaknesses.
2. Evaluation – of the effectiveness of teaching.
3. Guidance – of suitable subject choices or career.

4. Prediction – of pupils' potential and ability.
5. Selection – to place pupils in a particular school.
6. Grading – to assign pupils to a particular group.

Norm referenced and criterion referenced assessment

An initial distinction needs to be made between norm referenced and criterion referenced assessment. The purpose of norm referenced assessment is to compare children with each other and particularly with the sample of children on whom the assessment was originally standardized.

Criterion referenced assessments, on the other hand, are designed to discover an individual child's performance in a particular area. A criterion referenced assessment is not designed to compare performances between different children. An example will illustrate how the two different types of assessment give different but equally valid information.

Athletes in the Olympics have to succeed on both criterion and norm assessments if they are to win a gold medal. The criterion referenced assessment is the qualifying time needed to make it to the games. For each event there is a set criterion which athletes have to better to gain entry to the event. There is no restriction to the number of athletes who can achieve the criterion.

To win a gold, however, you have a norm referenced assessment, a comparison with your peers – you have to be first. The time, the criterion referenced assessment, is no longer important. However, as Rowntree (1977) has pointed out assessment in practice tends to involve both norm and criterion referencing. Thus the criteria for a place at the Olympics change over time as the norm for the event changes.

A second distinction needs to be made between intellectual assessment and curriculum based assessment.

Intellectual assessment

The first psychological attempt to assess children's progress in school was made in France. At the turn of the century the French government was concerned about children who were failing in school and Binet, a psychologist, was employed to assess which children were unable to learn. He devised with his colleagues the Binet–Simon Intelligence test (later revised as the Stanford Binet). Though Binet did not claim that his test was measuring genetically determined intelligence this was the start of what is now known as intelligence testing. Binet saw his test as a means of describing how well children learnt at school in relation to their peers. It was therefore for him norm referenced and at least partly curriculum based.

However, Binet's assessment quickly took on additional and different

761

characteristics when imported to the USA and Britain. Blum (1978) and Cronbach (1970) have described in detail the social forces that changed Binet's original conception of intelligence testing for assessing which children required a simplified curriculum to one designed to prove the genetically determined basis of intellectual assessment. Intelligence testing is based on the belief that a child's progress through the curriculum rests on intelligence which can be psychometrically determined.

The practice of assessing intelligence has developed significantly over the years with a great many tests developed since Binet. The most commonly used by psychologists are the WISC (Wechsler Intelligence Scale for Children) and the BAS (British Abilities Scale). The popularity of intelligence testing is largely due to the belief that knowing a child's intelligence will help the teacher predict the child's future achievement. Adults who know a child's IQ will usually restrict their perception of the child both if the child has a low IQ score, 'You can't expect much from Mary – she won't pass the exam' or a high IQ score, 'You can do better than a B+ grade – *you* should be able to get an A'.

In both cases the adult is making assumptions about the future performance of the child in the light of an intelligence test. The research, however, would not support the belief that you can predict a child's success in the adult world by IQ. For example a child's future income and occupational status is more dependent on the number of years' schooling than it is on an IQ score (Bowles and Gintis, 1972 and 1973).

Curriculum based assessment

A different method of assessing children's progress in school is known as curriculum based assessment which was referred to earlier. Its fundamental postulate is that children's progress in school should be directly assessed by measuring their progress on the curriculum. Such assessments can be either criterion or norm referenced. In the past it has been largely norm referenced where the pupils' results in examinations were compared with their peers. The criterion for success was not defined. This is what examination systems such as O and A level attempted to do. The difficulties with this form of assessment is the fact that the child's knowledge is assessed on one day in normally one form – essay type questions. Curriculum Based Assessment has moved this to a criterion referenced assessment procedure. Objectives are designed to clarify exactly what is being taught.

By focusing on clear objectives the class teacher can monitor a child's progress. If the child has difficulties in a particular area of the curriculum the objectives in this area can be broken down into smaller steps and the child can receive additional teaching in this area. This can usually be done within the confines of the classroom by the child's regular teacher.

The 1988 Education Reform Act ought to facilitate the use of curriculum based assessment as a way of monitoring the effects of education. All children between 5 and 16 in maintained schools follow a National Curriculum. Though each school decides how the curriculum is going to be organized this has to be done within a framework of the statutory programme of study, attainment targets and assessment arrangements. All children will be assessed at 7, 11, 14 and 16. It is proposed that assessment for the National Curriculum should be curriculum based and criterion referenced, with these monitoring procedures.

Special educational needs

In every school there are children who, for a number of reasons, have difficulty progressing through the curriculum. These children who require additional provision or specialized teaching are said to have special educational needs. 'Special educational need' is a term introduced by the 1981 Education Act which requires children who are having such difficulties to be assessed by a multidisciplinary team of professionals, including educational psychologists (see above). If it is found that they require specialized provision then this has to be provided. Some children with special needs go to special schools so that they can have the specialist teaching and equipment that they require. Many however stay in the normal school as most educationalists believe that children with special needs should be integrated with their peers. Warnock (1978) estimated that up to 20 per cent of children will at some time or another during their school career have special educational needs.

It is important to remember that these days a child with special educational needs is defined by performance on the curriculum not by speculating about some intellectual deficit. Children are no longer described as intellectually subnormal. Many children with special needs have sensory difficulties, visual or hearing impairment and that is why they require extra specialized provision. Others have physical difficulties. There are other children who do have learning difficulties with part (or all) of the curriculum. They may for example have difficulties with reading (see above), or writing, learning mathematics or a foreign language. Psychologists know enough about how children learn to realize that it is simplistic to say that these children fail to learn because they have limited intelligence.

So the term special educational needs does cover a wide range of children with learning, behaviour, sensory difficulties. A rather contentious category is that of the 'gifted' child, for some educationalists, teachers and parents of highly able children take the view that such children who learn very quickly, absorb new skills at a fast rate, and outpace their classroom peers should also be seen as having special educational needs.

To meet *their* needs the curriculum would have to be adjusted, extra teaching and stimulation provided. But 'gifted' was omitted from the 1981 Education Act which defined special educational needs and it is left to individual local education authorities and schools as to how they cater for children of 'exceptional ability' (Leyden, 1985).

Children's progress on the curriculum needs to be carefully assessed. This monitoring provides feedback to teachers on the effects of their teaching and allows them to modify and alter the instructional strategies that they are using in the classroom. However, as Ingenkamp (1977) has warned assessment has to be used for the right reasons, that is 'the only assessment which is educationally justifiable is that which promotes the individual learning process'.

Further reading

Blum, J. (1978) *Pseudoscience and Mental Ability. Monthly Review.*
Desforges, C. (1988) 'Psychology and the management of classrooms'. In N. Jones, and J. Sayer, eds., *Management and the Psychology of Schooling.* Falmer Press.
Galloway, David, and Goodwin, Carole (1987) *The Education of Disturbing Children.* Longman.
Smith, F. (1978) *Reading.* Cambridge University Press.

Part II Skill acquisition

The nature of skill

The meaning of skill in psychology

In psychology, 'skill' means any acquired ability which has been developed by some process of learning at least to the point where it is of some practical use to the individual. Most writers would want to go beyond this and to require that, for a skill, the learning should continue until the ability is automatic. Only then does it become 'accurate, effortless and smooth'.

Skills may be acquired in three ways. The individual may attend a course of formal instruction at an institution of learning, perhaps a technical college, a company which has an apprenticeship scheme, or perhaps be trained as a pilot at a flying school. A second way is to teach oneself, by trial and error, as with boiling an egg, or perhaps with the aid of a manual, as with driving a car, or operating a cine-camera. Another possibility is that the individual is a pioneer in some process or activity and that only self-instruction is available. This second method rarely produces the best results, and tends in time to give way to formal schemes of training, where the course designers understand, either implicitly or explicitly, the psychology of skill acquisition. The third method is through social processes by the interaction and association with one's elders and peers. This method is informal, and although fundamental, is also very limited. It is probably adequate for basic motor skills such as walking, but is very limited for learning a language; there is usually an ethnic limit on pronunciation, accent and vocabulary, and many basic conventions and attitudes are transmitted in this way. The third method can lead to severe deprivation and may be difficult to put right later. We do not include in skills vital biological functions like breathing or digestion; they are outside the domain of psychology.

All the following are called skills in psychology:

- walking,
- speech,
- reading to oneself,
- using a mallet and chisel,
- riding a bicycle,
- driving a car,
- typing.

But we would not call the following skills in the psychological sense; we shall see why a bit later:

- managing a company,
- being the captain of an aircraft,
- cabinet making.

Hierarchical organization of skills

Let us look at the skill of driving a car. We find it composed of component lower order skills, such as steering and braking. These components could be taught separately until proficiency is reached and then be combined into the higher order skill. But by the time a person goes to a driving school the component skills probably already exist, or partially exist. The higher order skill of driving is built up by organizing the lower order skills of steering and putting one's foot down to an appropriate stimulus. Driving a car, in the sense of conducting it from one point to another, is probably taught by the school as a whole, rather than part by part. It is further probable that at some time in one's early life the skill of steering an object has been built up from even lower order skills such as reaching and grasping. Thus, any skill can be thought of as a hierarchical structure. The instructor has to discover how far the individual has already built up the hierarchy and then build upwards from that point. We must not suppose, however, that all skills are established by only building upwards. Existing skills which are close to the new skill required may be adapted by what is called 'transfer'. The organization of the hierarchy is much the same, but the new skill is applied to perhaps a different machine or set of circumstances. Learning to ride a motorcycle may thus shorten the training period in learning to drive a car, or a graduate in history may be encouraged to believe that, because he has the skill of making decisions on the available evidence, he will be able to manage a company with abbreviated training and experience. More technically, much of pilot training is undertaken on simulators of greater or lesser reality; the validity of the training has to be proved by how good the transfer is to the real thing.

Sets of skills

We have to distinguish hierarchies of skills from 'sets of skills', and this is why we cannot call being captain of an aircraft a skill, nor can we call cabinet making a skill. An aircraft captain must acquire an appropriate *set* of skills, consisting perhaps of:

- being able to fly the aircraft routinely,
- being able to file a flight plan and navigate,
- being able to cope with both likely and unlikely emergencies,
- being able to inspect the aircraft for safety before flight,
- being able to command the crew,
- being able to communicate with air traffic control,
- and other abilities.

Thus, the curriculum of a flying school is quite long. There is another important point. From time to time, in accordance with commercial practices and the advance of technology, the functions of any occupation change; this is especially true wherever computers are involved. Humans tend to do what they are good at, leaving computers to do what they are good at. Fortunately for humans, in the occupational sense, human and computer abilities are largely complementary. Computers take over many of the lower order perceptual-motor skills, leaving humans to develop and use higher order skills such as recognizing patterns, using judgement (weighing up pros and cons) and dealing with novel problems. The task of the pilot of one of the latest passenger aircraft, the Airbus A320, is very different from that of, say, a post-war Avro York, hastily redesigned from a wartime bomber.

Similarly cabinet making cannot be called a skill, since it may be done in a variety of ways. A very high-class cabinet maker may interview customers, design the furniture, make parts himself and supervise workmen who do some of the work. He will require the set of skills appropriate to that whole task. Another way of making cabinets uses extensive division of labour. Every individual involved may perform only one of these tasks, or even, with mass production, only part of a task, perhaps repetitively. Still more recent in cabinet making is the application of computers. Cabinets can be made by computer numerical control (CNC). All the old skills which might be called 'the trained hand and the trained eye' may now have gone. The skilled people close to manufacture may now be toolmakers and computer programmers. In general, as society and technology change, the skills required change quite fundamentally, and this has led to a great deal of strife in the past, even to Luddism and the destruction of machines by people who once had highly paid skills.

Occupational uses of the term 'skill'

It requires only a short step now to see that the occupational use of the term 'skill' or 'skilled' is very different from the psychological one. We have seen that psychologically we cannot call the captaincy of an aircraft a 'skill'. But the employment market does. Really what is meant is that the captain has a set of skills appropriate to the job or task. The job or task is the external demand on the individual, what he is paid for doing. The set of skills are the trained mental and physical resources the captain has to achieve the task.

The job or task (the terms tend to be used with confusing interchange-ability) typically use only some of the skills the individual possesses. Some may have been used in former employments but are now redundant; others (recreational skills, domestic skills and general skills) will have been created outside any formal process of training. The employment market also uses the term 'unskilled' meaning a labourer or clerk without formal training. But many informal skills are important such as walking or speech. Only newly born infants do not possess skills.

Novice and expert behaviour compared

Meaning of 'novice' and 'expert'

For our purposes, a 'novice' is a person who does not possess a particular skill, nor any related skill. He may well have other skills which are quite different, and may be quite intelligent. But the novice is a person who has just embarked on a task which is strange, with the intention to perform well. He may be beginning an elementary course in some subject.

'Expert' means a person who has made much progress in acquiring a skill, and perhaps is near completion of the course and will obtain a certificate of proficiency.

Table 25.1 summarizes the main differences in behaviour. Much of this is very familiar, since all of us remember trying to acquire skills at some time or other. At the beginning we were at a complete loss, and needed some encouragement to continue. At the end we found we could do what we previously thought impossible, and can offer no explanation as to how we

Table 25.1 Main characteristics of novice and expert performance

	Novice	*Expert*
Speed	Slow, poorly synchronized	Task paced; fast if necessary
Errors	Many, almost any kind	Few; tend to be organized 'chunks'
Observable quality	Clumsy, jerky, exaggerated or excessive	Smooth, integrated
Feedback and attention	Every movement monitored	Occasional monitoring of large chunks
Introspective information	Performance helped by subject verbalizing	Behaviour automatic. Attempt to verbalize disrupts performance
Cognitive demands	Only one task possible at a time	Able to do some other (non-competing) tasks
Fatigue	Rapid fatigue. Short daily sessions	Minimal fatigue. Brief rest every two hours; five-day week for lifetime

were able to do it. We can just perform the task adequately, or even very well. Among the familiar differences between novice and expert or skilled behaviour are differences in speed, the number and type of errors made, the observable quality to an onlooker, and how rapidly fatigue occurs. Speed not only means working faster but getting the timing right so that it fits in with task requirements, e.g. in cricket hitting the ball with the bat when it has reached the right place. Errors are not only fewer but different in character, an important point we shall return to a bit later. Quality is different too: the expert does not need to pay continual but only intermittent attention to relevant details of the task. Speed and smoothness are now so fast that to see them for purposes of analysis requires a slow motion camera. Such an analysis is necessary to discover what a skilled walker or runner does, or in industry slow motion photography is necessary in 'time and motion studies'. In this way, skills can be transmitted from those who have them to novices.

The dramatic differences between novice and expert behaviour are so great that many people have wanted to say that the difference is qualitative rather than quantitative. Certainly we can point to features in skilled behaviour that are not there without the skill.

Chunking of output

We have already hinted that acquiring skill is a matter of building up organized structures, and such structures are observable in skilled behaviour. When we begin to type, for example, unless we learn touch typing, we have to use the 'hunt and peck' method, which has become even commoner now that so many people who haven't the available time to learn touch typing must communicate with the computer via a QWERTY keyboard. Once the paper is properly inserted, and perhaps we have written down exactly what we want to type on a separate piece of paper, the correct key has first to be located and struck; the result has to be checked by looking at the paper, and this has to be done for every character in the message. Even if we stay with the 'hunt and peck' method, gradually we will be able to avoid all the checking which had to be done, and be able to locate keys as word or even sentence sequences. This is reminiscent of what seems to happen in short-term memory (see Chapter 12). It is as easy to remember the sequence BBC or USSR as it is to remember a single digit, and as easy to remember 'little Jack Horner sat in a corner', because these structured sequences have been built into long-term memory, and can easily be transferred as a 'chunk' to short-term memory. Errors also tend to occur in 'chunks', especially when there is a novel ingredient in a well-practised task. Suppose we decide to visit a friend's house on the way home. It is very easy to forget to do so, or even to visit the wrong friend if the latter is more often visited. The more attention has been distracted during the journey home, the greater the probability of making the error (Norman, 1981; Rasmussen *et al*, 1987; Reason, 1987). The word 'chunk' has been used here, since it describes observable behaviour, but many writers believe the clues provided about the nature of organized internal structure are so strong that they are called 'schemata', a term first used in psychology by Bartlett (1932).

Doing two things at once

Can we do two things at once? The answer is that life would be very much more difficult if we could not, but there are some conditions to be fulfilled. Note that we are talking about psychological behaviour, that which we need to do to perform a task, and not about the vital functions such as breathing and standing up without losing one's balance. The most important point is that we can do two things at once if they are both skills. It is possible to listen to the radio and drive a car or, for a skilled typist, to do simple copy typing and talk to a friend. But these examples readily show the second limit; neither task must make much 'cognitive demand'. That is to say, neither must impose difficult decisions upon us such as dealing with a difficult road junction. If we want to negotiate the junction without an accident, then we have to stop talking. Suppose we have a radiophone. Although the advice is to stop driving anyway when using the radiophone, if the conversation requires difficult decisions then we must stop the car to think about the right answers. Some tasks are so demanding in terms of 'mental workload', as this is alternatively called, that the only skills we can perform simultaneously are simple manipulative skills such as pressing the right key on a keyboard or putting a piece of paper in an appropriate place. Where the task requires more than one skill, as in the case of an air traffic controller, such as working out the best courses, speeds and heights for the aircraft in the sector as one skill and giving instructions to pilots as a second skill, these must be done at separate times rather than simultaneously. A common complaint from air traffic controllers is that the number of aircraft to direct is so great that there is not enough planning time.

There is a third condition for being able to perform two tasks simultaneously; that they do not require the same physical or motor resources. We can talk as well as drive a car when neither requires too much mental workload: the car needs eyes and limbs for control, whereas talking needs ears and mouth. There is no competition for the input and output channels. If we needed to know the speed of the car, however, we would have to stop looking where we are going in order to look down at the speedometer; the time is much reduced for a 'head-up display' (Smyth *et al*, 1987). For further information on perception, see Govier and Govier, Chapter 10.

The determinants of skill training

Which of the following help in training a skill?

– Motivation,
– Verbal instruction,
– The trainee's present attainment,
– Practice,
– Guidance,
– Feedback (or knowledge of results),
– Training devices,
– Beautifully engineered simulators,
– Good instructors.

The answer is that every one of these factors can be important, or even vital. But, equally, every one of them can be ineffective or even reduce learning unless they are properly administered according to an understanding of the psychology of training. Most important of all is that each is incorporated in proper sequence in a Programme of Training (Gagné, 1962; Caro, 1973). It is just as important to stop giving any of these factors when the trainee is ready for the next stage of the training programme as to give them at all. It is imperative to understand this principle; without it attempting to train anybody at anything is baffling.

We find in this principle exactly the same as for the manufacture of any product. If we were to ask the question: which is the most important tool in cabinet-making, a chisel, a screwdriver, a power drill, a plane or sandpaper, we would know from our common sense that the answer would be each of these in its proper sequence, and when each has done its job, we go to the next stage. Indiscriminate use of a chisel would only lead to damaged wood, not a beautiful piece of furniture. Surprisingly, this common-sense point has often been absent in the attempt to create human skills.

Designing a training programme

Designing a training programme consists of the following stages:

1. Task description

The job the expert has to do must be described. The description must be what the expert will be able to do on completion of the training programme, and must be in physical (i.e. not at this stage in psychological) terms, e.g. safely convey a new Airbus A320 from the factory to Paris, or sell 10,000 sets of *Encyclopaedia Britannica* to reluctant housewives.

2. Task analysis

Any task or job may be composed of a number of dissimilar parts. Suppose, for example, we had a job description for a police officer. He would have to know relevant parts of the law, including the details of police procedure and what constituted a crime, the road traffic laws, how to give evidence in court. He would have to be able to cope with any emergency, to give first aid, to deal with minor fires or to call help or to deal with a civil disturbance. He must also be able to give directions on how to get from A to B. If the officer, when fully trained, is unable to do any of these the human consequences could be very serious. The course of training will therefore consist of a number of subjects taught concurrently, in different periods each day or week.

3. Psychological translation

The job or task is the physical demand placed upon the person. Training is the development of the resources with which the person will meet the demand. From this translation a formal set of skills can be listed and described, and it is these with which the trainee leaves the course, often with a certificate of competence or licence to practise.

4. Selection

The training institution must then decide on its human raw material, invite and test candidates who possess enough lower order skills onto which it can build the required hierarchy. Selection may be strict, but sometimes the training institution, perhaps one of the armed forces, will allow some candidates in below par and give them remedial training first. Often candidates will not have done well enough at school in terms of literacy and numeracy. The selection will depend on how well the training institution is at doing its job, i.e. how well the instructors understand the psychology of training. It will also depend on the equipment, but no equipment, no matter how well engineered, can make up for poor instruction. This point comes out particularly strongly in the design and use of simulators. Also important are the career alternatives available to the applicants. Not so many boys now want to be locomotive drivers; on the other hand, girls are now socially qualified to do so.

5. Sequences of training

For every skill identified, the course will be made up of a sequence of experiences, such as classroom instruction, exercises and testing. There is a fairly definite order about this sequence, as will be seen in the next section. As soon as the applicant is shown to be ready for the next stage, from the results of appropriate tests, he must be transferred to the next stage, or he will regress or be severely damaged in terms of acquiring the skill.

Administering a training programme

Motivation is, of course, important, and in childhood learning may be shaped by appropriate small rewards. When we are considering motivation at a flying school, however, the motivation must come from the trainee's own achievements, i.e. from the acquisition of the skill itself. We do not find police colleges dispensing Smarties after every correct performance on a test. In overall terms the trainee must not become anxious about whether or not the course can be satisfactorily completed. Especially at the beginning, the trainee must not feel lost, confused or unwanted. Something positive has to be done, along the lines of a host making a guest welcome.

There is often a period and programme of induction in which the rationale of the course and how the institution will provide what is required are explained. Since the trainee will emerge with obvious and marketable skills, that is as an expert, there may well be a credibility gap in the mind of the trainee. It is the nature of any skill that what at first cannot be done at all can later be done in an easy and accomplished manner. One way to do this is to begin with a parade of affluent and accomplished 'old boys' who are able to recount how dreadful they were when they started. The allocation of each trainee to a personal tutor or counsellor is also valuable.

Indoctrination

For many occupations, it is necessary for the trainee to get an early appreciation of how he stands with regard to society, since every employed person serves society in some way or another, and in turn, receives reward. Each occupation will have its own ethos, its own taboos, honours and medals. At any time of assessment, it will be these that are counted to determine success or failure. In order to perform any skilled task for the community, the expert will be granted fairly definite privileges necessary to perform the occupation, but these must not be abused, and in exchange, each occupation must offer something which is beyond the call of the ordinary duties of life. There must always be some dedication; some guarantee that the expert will not give up on the customer, patient or client when the going gets sticky.

For a civilian aircraft pilot, the main duty must always be to secure the safety of the flight and not embark on journeys which are hazardous. A military pilot, on the other hand, must 'press on regardless' without much concern for his personal survival, and even be prepared to sacrifice the crew if the mission requires it. For those engaged in the medical profession, the primary concern is for the health and life of the patient, as is made clear by the Oath of Hippocrates. Journalists, being one of society's checks on abuse by the powerful, require special privileges, but these must not be abused into prying into the private lives of 'celebrities'. A jobbing plumber is able to wander freely through private homes, giving an opportunity to be inquisitive or dishonest. It is this dedication which supplies the intrinsic motivation through the course. The old saying is that one volunteer is worth ten pressed men. Censure from one's peers is the severest form of trial; few people want to be loners; we are talking about social pressures and we may as well harness nature in the training of skilled behaviour.

Techniques of training

Training and information

The good instructor controls the acquisition process by an appropriate flow of information to the trainee (Annett, 1969). There are two broad categories of information. That which is given before the trainee makes any attempt to perform a task or any part of a task, is called 'guidance', and tells the trainee what he has to do and how to do it. It can be given at any time before the trainee's response, right up to the moment of performance. The other broad category is called 'feedback', or knowledge of results, and tells the trainee how well he has performed the response or required behaviour. It may be given at any time after the response, right from the moment the response has started. The effect of the feedback is assessed on the trainee's next attempt (sometimes called 'one-shot'), or on a larger or much larger sample of responses (long-term effect). In general, the 'one-shot' improvement need not be correlated with the long-term effect (Hammerton, 1977).

Guidance

Verbal guidance

Every training course makes much use of verbal guidance, unless the trainees are infants or animals. This is true for any adult course, even when the skill to be acquired is largely perceptual–motor rather than mostly cognitive. If one learns golf at a golfing school, the initial instruction is verbal. Even when the instructor is physically demonstrating the skill himself, he will verbally draw the attention of the trainee to various points about his stance, the placing of the ball, and the swing of the club. If one is even less than a novice and completely innocent, all the relevant objects must be learned by name, not just so that they can be referred to, but also so that the trainee finds them easy to think about. The golf trainee must understand the terms club, tee, flag and pin as well as ball, swing, stance and uplift. Of course, these terms must only be introduced as appropriate. Later, there will be more complex terms, perhaps to do with the strategy of playing the game. Often such instruction is best given on a one-to-one basis, but with good instructors much will have to be successfully done in classrooms. One-to-one instruction is best kept for individual problems in learning, while in class the instructor should deal with general difficulties. Frequently the trainee will be given diagrams or perhaps slow motion video; there is a skill even in taking notes; and there will be assessment.

Physical guidance

In this the instructor actually leads the body and limbs of the trainee through the correct motion. Again, it is frequently done with golf or other sports, but it could also be done in drama school, teaching musical instruments, or in a dual seat trainer aircraft where the trainee might hold his hands on the controls while the instructor moves them properly.

Low rate of error

Vitally important, especially at the earliest stages of skill acquisition, is that the trainee does not acquire bad habits. These are difficult to remedy, or, in extreme cases, the trainee may be flawed for ever. This is a reason, of course, for a good institution to take over individuals early for imparting the most basic skills, especially those involved with literacy and numeracy. In practical terms, it means that the trainee's individual error rate must be kept very low and requires individual assessment and instruction.

Prompting and cuing

Alternative names for guidance are 'prompting' and 'cuing'. The term 'guidance' tends to be used for perceptual-motor skills, 'prompting' for verbal tasks (for example, trainees learning to sort letters into the right pigeon holes for the Post Office), and 'cuing' for the correct detection of simple stimuli (for example, a radar operator learning to discriminate a target from noise). In each case, the trainee is either told verbally exactly what to look for or given an easily detectable example.

Feedback

Feedback is the information the trainee is given after the performance. It has a variety of forms; it may tell the trainee simply whether his performance is good enough (e.g. 'hit' or 'miss'); or it may tell the trainee the kind of error he has made (e.g. 'too hard and too low'); it may give the magnitude of the error; or may give advice on how to improve performance. It may be given trial by trial, or only after the completion of a block; quite subtle variations have strong effects on the trainee's progress.

Extrinsic feedback

Extrinsic means that the feedback will not be there in the expert performance. It is temporary, and serves only as a scaffolding until the trainee has learned to acquire feedback information for himself. For these reasons extrinsic feedback belongs only to early parts of a course, otherwise it becomes an indispensable prop, which would mean that the trainee cannot perform the expert task without it. A simple example would be asking a trainee to draw a line exactly 40mm long without a ruler. If it is within the limits set by the instructor the feedback may be simply the word 'good', or the actual error may be measured. Another example would be after the trainee takes a swing with the golf club the instructor says 'you didn't keep your eye on the ball'.

There is a second reason extrinsic feedback should be used only in early parts of the course. It is then that only simple actions will be required of the trainee. Later, these simple or lower order skills will be built into more complex higher order skills, and it is difficult to target the feedback onto exactly what is wrong, or to tell by this means what the correction should be. At the stage in learning a language where the subject is learning the translation of a word into its foreign equivalent, the feedback 'wrong' may be helpful. At the stage where he is composing sentences, simply to say 'wrong' would almost certainly do more harm than good.

Intrinsic feedback

Intrinsic feedback is that which will be available to the trainee in the expert performance of the task. It may, for example, be given by instruments which the trainee has learned to interpret, such as the artificial horizon in flying an aircraft, or there may be a warning buzzer if the monitoring computer detects that the pilot has initiated a dangerous manoeuvre.

Intrinsic feedback has to be found and used by the trainee or expert himself. This means not only sensing it but also diagnosing its importance and deciding exactly what to do as a consequence. Thus intrinsic feedback is not only complex in perceptual-motor terms, but also in cognitive terms. It needs to be thought about. Intrinsic feedback may be *augmented* in several ways. A book written for a child to read may have big and bold letters, and a new word may be presented in several different ways and contexts. In pilot training, a mock-up training device may be used with larger than normal instruments, but that would not be possible in the expert version of the task. There may be computer generated information stating what the error is and suggestions as to what to do. With modern complex equipment, such information may be available on demand at the expert stage also.

Proprioceptive feedback

The basis of much skilled activity, whether it is motor activity like throwing darts, something a bit more cognitive like changing gear in a car or speaking, is the skilled use of muscles. Training builds up the abilities of the proprioceptive sense to acquire and enable use to be made of information about the position of the limbs, and to compare such information with where the limbs ought to be. We include, besides position information, much other information such as hardness and texture of objects, their temperature and probably acceleration and velocity. That is why touch typing takes so long to learn before expert performance is possible; but it frees the visual sense to take care of higher order task requirements such as the format of what is being typed and the meaning of the words. The 'hunt and peck' typist has to alternate his vision between keyboard and paper, and may only be able to give partial attention to the words themselves. QWERTY keywords are used with computers as well as typewriters, and much work is being done on avoiding the difficulty of finding the right keys; examples are: allowing the operator to touch the correct word printed on the screen, or to use a 'mouse' which the operator moves about the table controlling the movement of an arrow which points to any one of several alternatives on the screen (Legge and Barber, 1976; Stammers and Patrick, 1975).

Stages in skill acquisition

Training as a progressive sequence

Earlier we asked the question: which of several training sequences is the most effective? We soon discovered that question to be too naive. Depending on what skill has to be trained, each of them will usually be a valuable item in a proper sequence. If given out of that order that technique can be ineffective, or even damaging.

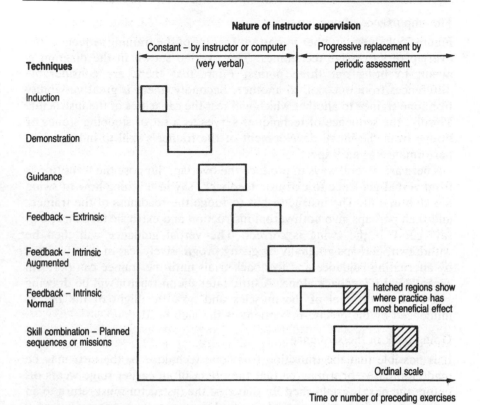

Figure 25.1 Sequencing of techniques in instruction – note overlap of successive techniques

The general sequence

Figure 25.1 shows the general sequences of techniques used in training a skill. It must be stressed that this will be substantially adapted or modified to meet any specific case, just as the sequence of planing, jointing, sandpapering and polishing is modified when producing a cabinet to meet one purpose or design rather than another.

The general objective is to get to the intrinsic feedback stage as soon as possible, i.e. without lingering in any stage if the trainee has been brought to readiness for the next. Expressed alternatively, the objective is to make the trainee independent of the instructor; the great danger is to create dependence on him or on the controlling information he has to offer.

As it stands, the diagram tends to represent the creation of a skill in some sport such as golf, or perhaps the adult learning of a second language, where the first language is available to give early instruction. For learning to drive a car, the sequence needs substantial modification; there would be much less extrinsic feedback and much more verbal instruction.

The importance of overlap

Figure 25.1 shows another important feature of the training sequence, the overlap of successive techniques. The overlap shown in the diagram is meant to bring out three points. First, that there are considerable differences from one skill to another. Secondly, there is great variability from one trainee to another which will test the capacities of the instructor. Thirdly, the sequence of techniques serves as a set of stepping stones or bridge from the initial development of the trainee's skill to independent performancc as an 'cxpcrt'.

There are several ways to produce the overlap. Suppose the transition is from verbal guidance to extrinsic feedback, say in teaching how to swing the club in golf. The instructor has to judge the readiness of the trainee, and then perhaps give both verbal instruction and extrinsic feedback, e.g. say 'good' if the swing is correct. The verbal guidance will then be withdrawn, perhaps gradually by giving progressively less of it or perhaps by alternating guidance and feedback trials until the trainee can perform acceptably by feedback alone. A little later the instructor will be drawing attention to the feel of the muscles and how the flight of the ball is influenced by the precise movement of the club head.

Going back in the sequence

It is possible that the transition from one technique to the next may be made too early, or it may be that the effect of an earlier stage wears off before the next is established. In that case the instructor must return to an earlier stage. It is even possible to find errors in the performance of a highly skilled person; it frequently happens when the expert has been self taught or badly taught. If this happens the defective skill must be identified; there may be some wrong movement by a batsman in cricket, or a pilot may be making judgements based on his senses when he should be using the information from instruments. That part of the total skill must then be retrained by going back to the beginning of the sequence and following through until the expert stage has been reached in the skill. After that, the partial skill has to be recombined with the old satisfactory parts of the skill, either using the working environment, or simulating it as closely as possible. Otherwise, one skill will be conditioned to the training environment, and the older defective skill conditioned to the working environment. There is, unfortunately, always the danger of regression, which emphasizes the importance of keeping the error rate low during the whole training process.

Practice

The old adage that 'practice makes perfect' is thus shown to be no more than a half-truth, and a rather dangerous half-truth at that. Extended practice on any exercise should not be given until the trainee can find the relevant information for him and this does not occur until the intrinsic feedback stage.

The power law of practice

In a very wide range of tasks whether perceptual-motor or cognitive, once the trainee is performing the task correctly, performance tends to improve according to what is known as the 'power law of practice'. Figure 25.2 shows a plot of time taken to perform the task over the number of trials taken, or, if the individual is performing regularly, length of time.

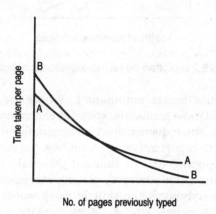

Figure 25.2 Performance of two typists. A uses the 'hunt and peck' method. B is training to be a touch typist

When practice has become effective, there is a comparatively rapid improvement at first, but the rate of improvement slows down. By making a suitable mathematical transformation, taking the logarithm of both time taken to perform the task and the number of prior performances, the curve becomes a straight line (Figure 25.3).

Not too much should be read into the fact that this is a straight line. No theory properly accounts for it, and it should be thought of rather as a useful summary of progressive improvement. It is notable that improvement can go on for a very long time, often years. Crossman (1957) found evidence of improvement in the hand rolling of cigars after up to seven years of practice.

Automatic behaviour

It is also possible that the most important feature of a skill – automatic behaviour – comes only after extended practice (we might almost change

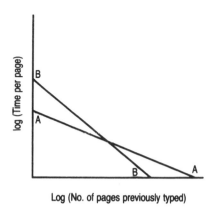

Log (No. of pages previously typed)

Figure 25.3   Figure 25.2 replotted by taking logarithms of both time and practice

the adage to 'practice makes automatic'). Where the skill requires an integration of several movements, the speed of execution makes control by feedback impossible, the sequence must be automatically planned, and the individual is unable to report anything about how the skill is achieved. The skill can only be demonstrated by doing it. Musical examples are much quoted in the literature (for example, playing arpeggios and chords), but more familiar to everybody is the skill in using words. The subject has learned to speak phonemes (the most elementary sounds of speech), combine these into words and words into sentences. Much processing activity must go on in the brain for this to happen, but whatever happens cannot be reported by the subject. The individual phonemes are each modified so that there is a smooth transition from one syllable to the next and often no interval will be left between one word and another. A corresponding skill must be built up in the brain of the listener. What happens is not at present understood, and no attempt to simulate these properties of speech on the computer has been successful, except in the most trivial cases (Boden, 1987).

A worked example

Learning to play golf

Let us work out an example of the principles of the sequencing of techniques fairly fully – with learning to play golf. The account is fictional, but although not very faithful to the game of golf, it is meant to be very faithful to the psychological principles.

Two of my friends are very keen on golf, and persuaded me to take up the game. 'Don't make the mistakes we made, though; you must take the game very seriously to enjoy it properly; so get yourself proper tuition.'

One day I went to the clubhouse with them, and they introduced me to the secretary. At first we sat in the bar, talking very generally about the greatness of the game. Then my two friends went off to play a round, leaving me with the secretary. The clubhouse was very impressive, and he took me to the trophy room, with oak panelled walls and deep carpeting. Everything was highly polished. Around the walls were glass cabinets containing all manner of cups and plates which the members had won. There were photographs, some very new and others very old, and I thought I had seen some of the names before. Away from the walls were free-standing glass cases, containing much used golf clubs and mounted golf balls. The secretary explained these at great length. I remember one of the balls had been struck by the Aga Khan many decades ago and another had scored 'a hole in one'.

'Well, to business,' said the secretary, leading me to his office. I filled in a membership form and paid an annual subscription. With beautiful timing, Georgina came in – she was to be my instructor for putting. I noted down several appointments with Georgina over the next few days.

All this is induction, *and however little it is usually dealt with theoretically by psychology, any course of training would be much lost without it.*

I turned up for my first appointment, and Georgina took me to the club shop. At first I was to buy only a few articles, apart from a number of balls, since I was expected to lose many. We then went out onto the eighth green. 'We'll start with this one,' explained Georgina, 'it's the easiest, as smooth as a billiard table and dead level.'

We approached the eighth hole. Georgina placed one of my golf balls on the ground. 'Now, I would like you to watch how I do it,' she said. 'I want you to pay particular attention to exactly where and how I place my feet, exactly how I hold the putter with both hands, and my stance – that is, how I shape my body to play the best stroke.' Georgina stood exactly as I have seen them stand on the television. She gently tapped the ball, and it went into the hole in a beautiful straight line. This is demonstration.

Georgina smiled. 'Now you try,' she said encouragingly. 'Remember the three things: where and how you place your feet, your stance, and your grip on the club.' Georgina spent some minutes moving the various parts of my body into the right positions, and when she was satisfied I felt very oddly contorted. 'Now, we will make the putt,' she said. 'Only a gentle tap, draw the putter away about six inches, you will be able to keep your eyes on the ball and putter. Now, in your own time, bring the putter into gentle contact with the ball.' I moved the ball about one foot, only one quarter of the journey towards the hole. This is guidance.

To my surprise she said: 'Not too bad. Now watch me again. Feet, stance, grip. Square the face of the putter to the ball. Only a gentle tap needed.'

Unerringly, to my great admiration, again the ball went into the hole. I then tried again, and did a bit better. Sometimes Georgina demonstrated again, but most times she would fuss about my feet, stance, grip. Eyes on the ball, square face. This is alternation between demonstration and guidance.

After a few more lessons, Georgina was demonstrating very little and only occasionally helping me with my body positioning. What she was saying more and more often was 'good' when I had got something right, or telling me how I had done it wrong. As I improved, we moved further and further away from the hole, and then to a more difficult hole which had 'left hand borrow'. This is extrinsic feedback.

My putting was improving, and I was very pleased. I took all the putting lessons Georgina had time for, and said 'Oh, well, I won't spoil the ship for a ha'p'orth of tar' when my bank statement came in. One day, Georgina said: 'You've done very well; but now I want you to be much more independent. So far, I have been your brains and eyes. Now you must develop your own golfing brain and eye. But especially you must get the feeling of it. Your body, your hands, your feet, all your body muscles will tell you what is right and wrong.' Georgina got me to pay attention to all these feelings and would watch me with progressively less and less comment. At first my performance declined, but then I seemed to get it, I can't really say how. If I looked at Georgina, her face would usually be dead pan, and I knew this meant, 'it is your golfing brain and body we are developing'. Occasionally, I would notice a cloud drift across Georgina's face; but more and more often an encouraging twinkle in the eye. Then she let me do some putting without any supervision, with only the occasional lesson. This is intrinsic feedback.

Oh, I forgot to say, that in parallel with my putting lessons, I had been taking lessons in driving (golf driving, of course). That's where you get quite muscular and give the ball an enormous biff off the tee, and get the ball up the fairway towards the green.

I had taken the advice of my friends and had not tried to teach myself, even with the aid of some golfing books and videos I had bought; I would not be tempted by them until much later. So I had yet to play a game of golf, and before I was allowed to do so, a tentative date was made for me to go before the handicapping committee of the club. One morning at 10 o'clock sharp, I stood before the bench, rather like court proceedings. The committee and I discussed my progress, considered the written reports from my two instructors, and after some whispered discussion, the chairman of the committee said, very deliberately: 'the committee feel that you are ready to play a real game of golf, in which you can do both driving and putting. Initially, you will have a handicap of 30, but we feel you will be able to improve to about 15 after much further tuition. We wish you the very best of golfing luck, and hope you will have a long and happy association with the club. You are now a full member, and are authorized to wear the tie and blazer in public.' We all shook hands, and went off to the 19th hole.

Next day, I played my first real game of golf, using both a driver and a putter as the lie of the land required. I lost to the other player, but slightly beat my handicap. This is skill combination. From now on, I could practise, practise, practise, and get that handicap down towards my target of 15.

Although the example is in golfing terms, a very similar scenario could be made up for any other skill, for example, learning to fly a light aircraft, or something verbal-cognitive like learning a second language. All the elements, or techniques, will be there with different emphases.

If I had attempted to acquire the skill by self instruction or poor instruction, it is very likely that some remedial treatment would be necessary. The good instructor would then try to identify what was wrong, and I might be taken back to the beginning of the sequence – to demonstration. But somehow my bad habits would have to be eliminated, which is mostly a matter of luck and dedication.

Attention and skill

Complementary concepts

The concepts of attention and skill are complementary. Human behaviour, as we saw briefly in the early part of this chapter, only makes much sense when we understand the nature of the task on which the individual is engaged. Attention is the means by which behaviour is continuously directed towards the task, in perception of relevant information, in the choice of action which is appropriate given that information, and in the skilled performance of the task where that skill is available. Although no analogy may be pressed too far, attention works in a somewhat similar fashion to the chief executive in a company or other purposeful institution. They are both aware of the organization's current purposes or goals, and are aided by guidelines such as attitudes, values or company policies. Attention, or the chief executive, is the controller of the organism, responsible for achieving the goals or acquiring or allocating the resources as opportunities allow. For the human organism skills, or for the company, skilled workers, are allocated to tasks or sub-tasks, and are either closely or perhaps only occasionally supervised. While the skills are at work, the attention (or chief executive) is freed to use its processing abilities on meeting the problems of the individual or company which need to be thought about, or about which decisions or judgements have to be made. Checks on the progress of the skill are made intermittently, and new directions are then given. The more novel the task, the more redirection; the more familiar, the longer the skill can go on without such direction.

Where one or more skills are possessed, and these measure up to the current task demands, provided they do not compete in terms of input channels (senses), cognitive resources (mental workload) or output channels (muscles), attention acts as the general controller, thinking ahead to new allocations of resources needed as the task changes.

A new perspective on 'novice' behaviour

What happens, however, when the skills do not exist, or have not been brought to the expert quality of performance? We then have all the attributes of novice behaviour shown in Table 25.1.

But we can take a different view of this, showing matters in a very different light. When the skill has not reached the expert stage or does not exist, we then have the whole of attention or the chief executive doing the job himself as best he can making the best use of what he remembers of similar tasks performed satisfactorily in the past, or by trial and error, trying to create a new ability which works satisfactorily. A new principle of performing the task may emerge, or more likely the experience will lead to the creation of an ad hoc rule known as 'heuristic' (Simon, 1957). A 'heuristic' is a 'rule-of-thumb', at present incapable of being deduced from more general principles, but which works well enough for practical use.

Given the creation of the heuristic, it will be applied on future performances of the same task, in terms of the company analogy, at the 'middle-management' stage, but if used with sufficient frequency, will ultimately be performed as a skill, that is, smoothly and automatically, provided it lies within a narrow range of the much repeated experiences.

Still taking this different perspective, we find in the chief executive performance a very powerful human ability, the ability the captain of an aircraft has to use if he meets with an emergency or any new problem which was not foreseen or reduced to routine. A most important point about this problem solving ability is that, up to the present time, nobody has been able to programme the equivalent onto a computer, which is why no machine or process can as yet be made entirely automatic. Captains of aircraft are still needed to fly with the aircraft to deal with such emergencies; human intervention is still necessary to cope with problems at nuclear power stations, and when emergencies do occur, the human faculty which we have called 'attention' will have to solve the problems to avert disaster.

Further reading

Holding, D. H. (1988) *Human Skills,* 2nd edn. Wiley.
Legge, D., and Barber, P. J. (1976) *Information and Skill.* Methuen.
Stammers, R., and Patrick, J. (1975) *The Psychology of Training.* Methuen.

Chapter twenty-six

Studying and examinations

John Radford

'Freud is said to have worked with wealthy middle-aged neurotic women in Vienna at the turn of the century. It is hardly fair but rather apt. It is true he worked with many wealthy people, most were middle-aged women, and he did work in Vienna, but it was he who made them neurotic.' (Examination script)

There is no shortage of advice on how to study for and how to pass examinations. At any time there are usually around a score of books in print on the subject. I offer here a personal view based on specific experience as an examiner in psychology at GCE and degree levels, and on some of the published research. (A good summary of much relevant research is given by Burns and Dobson in their *Introductory Psychology*, MTP Press, 1984. As so often with psychological research, findings are by no means unanimous, but I think they are in general not inconsistent with what follows.) Ever aware of individual differences, I realize that what suits one student may not do much for another. If you look elsewhere, beware only of those who suggest there are short-cuts to success or that you can trick examiners. On the whole, I am sure this is not so. But there are ways to make the maximum use of one's time and talents, whatever they may be. I have also included a selection of 'exam howlers' which I have spread throughout the text. They are included, not to mock their authors but to cheer us all up as well as serving to remind us to think carefully. Incidentally most of the commercial systems offering to develop a 'super-power' memory are based on the ancient but effective method of loci for which, as a student of psychology, you need not pay extra (see Chapter 12).

'Memory traces are difficult to trace.'

Examinations

Let us start with examinations, and begin by saying what they are and are not. Nearly all formal courses of study embody examinations, and at GCE 'A' level and above these are usually based on unseen questions requiring written answers in a set time. There may also be course work or some other form of continuous assessment, practical work, or some variation in the form of answer required. Psychology, despite psychologists' study of assessment methods, has so far been very typical. This I think is due partly to inertia but mainly to the fact that, on the whole, the time limited set paper is less demanding administratively than any other method. Since it is obvious that students differ, an ideal system would sample their knowledge by a range of methods. Nevertheless I think some justification can be given for the present system, which in any case is what we shall probably have to deal with for some time to come. I think a set of questions to be answered in (frequently) forty minutes each can be a reasonably fair and accurate sampling of knowledge and understanding. A good examination question should be saying: 'Here is an important issue; from your reading and thinking, what do you make of it?'

A syllabus is a licence to examine; that is you *may* be asked about anything on it, but not about what is not on it. A question paper should be a fair sampling of the syllabus, and it should be comprehensible to anyone with a basic knowledge of the subject. Each question should be clear and unambiguous; if more than one meaning is possible a candidate must not be penalized for choosing one the examiner didn't intend.

The GCE Boards, in my experience, go to enormous trouble to try to ensure that examinations are fair and objective. A typical pattern is that a Chief Examiner prepares a question paper, which is submitted to a Moderator (a sort of watchdog) and to a subject panel which includes several teachers. The Chief Examiner will also prepare a marking scheme, showing what is to count as a right answer and how many marks each part of an answer is to score. With the essay type of question so common in psychology, different approaches to the question have to be allowed for. When the scripts come in there will be a standardization meeting at which all examiners will mark a sample and agree, under the guidance of the Chief Examiner, on how each answer is to be assessed. There will be further checks throughout the whole process of marking. Finally there is a list of candidates and marks. These have to be turned into grades, which involves further marking of samples to decide where the cut-off points are to fall – in other words what counts as an A grade, a B, and so on. It is sometimes thought that Boards decide this on the basis of how many candidates they want to achieve various grades. All I can say is that in nine years as a Chief Examiner I never saw this. The decisions were based solely on the standards of the answers. It would be foolish to suggest that the system is perfect. Administrative errors can occur, and marking does depend on human judgement. Boards will arrange for re-marking of individual scripts (normally for a fee) where a result is queried. My experience of this is that in nearly every case a candidate had failed to do her or himself justice, perhaps misreading questions or just not bringing out relevant knowledge.

One has to say that on the whole degree examinations are much less systematic than this. Questions are usually approved by an Examinations Board consisting mainly of staff teaching the course plus External Examiners (frequently two). Scripts are usually marked blind by two examiners, and the Externals check all or a sample. Final grades are determined by the Board, based on marks obtained but usually with some leeway for condoning poorer performance in some parts if compensated by better marks elsewhere. Generally a Board goes out of its way to award the best grades it feels can be justified.

To a certain extent, therefore, whatever the system, a candidate is competing in something like a qualitative sport such as gymnastics, rather than in a race in which time provides an indisputable decision. And this gives rather a good analogy, because what I want to suggest is essentially a skills based approach to examinations. An examination is not an attempt by the examiner to outwit the candidate – nor vice versa. And it is not, or at least is not intended to be, a trial by ordeal. Of course, some candidates find examinations stressful, though others enjoy them. One main cause of stress is lack of confidence. One remedy is to become familiar with the examination task under non-stressful conditions. Another is to build up the skills needed to do well. Both imply practice. It also follows that while success is a true indication of ability – you can't, in general, fake it – failure on a particular day may be due to many causes. However, while in sport you can generally keep trying, if you want to, until you find your own level, with examinations you often get only one chance, or perhaps two.

It is characteristic of outstanding sports people – gymnasts, footballers, cricket, snooker or tennis players – that they make it look easy. Actions are smooth and flowing; they always seem to have time to make the shot. It is obvious that such displays don't spring into existence at the moment of the event itself. They are the result of talent plus training. I can't do anything about your talent, though I'm sure you have some or you would not be reading this; I can do something about training. A book, however, is not a good medium for developing skills, just as a map is only a guide to travel, not travel itself. I can only suggest some things you may try, and hope they work for you as they have done for others.

Among the better-established findings of psychology are some things about skills: in particular that they improve with practice and with feedback. Skills can be practised slowly at first, then speeded up. It is also often possible to analyse skills into component parts, which can be learned separately. When a skill is well practised, fewer cues are necessary, and one quickly picks out those that are relevant from those that are not. All this is true, for example, of learning a game, or learning to drive a car; and it is also true of examinations. What then are the component parts of the skill of passing examinations? First let us distinguish two main groups of examination procedures: essays (and 'short notes'); and practicals, including project work. There are many other possible procedures but these form by far the greatest part of 'A' levels and degrees; and there is no need to be afraid of them.

'Phobias may be cured by removing the hypothalamus.'

Essays and notes

At the risk of apparent procrastination, I am going to leave the composition of essays to the section on studying. I shall assume for the moment that you can do it, and deal with the examination itself. I suggest there are three groups of activities: (a) organization; (b) writing; (c) expression.

Organization

I mean first such small but necessary matters as having enough writing implements and any calculators, etc. that may be required; but much more important, is the use of time. There are two main parts to this, concerned with the paper as a whole and with individual questions. The first step is to read, and make sure you understand, the instructions. In nearly every examination some candidate will lose marks through failure to do what is actually required – answering from the wrong section, leaving out a compulsory question, etc. The second step is to read through the whole paper and make at least a preliminary decision as to which questions to answer and in what order. The point of this is that you will be recalling, consciously or not, material for the later questions while answering the earlier ones.

It should already be apparent that these activities, simple as they are, are actually skills that can be practised *before the examination,* until they become second nature. Most students will look up previous papers: when you do so, make a point of reading quickly through the instructions, then checking to make sure you have understood. This may seem trivial, yet it takes only a few seconds and could mean vital marks. Similarly with reading through the questions: which questions, exactly, would you answer? This partly involves quickly reviewing one's knowledge on each topic, to which I will return. At first it can be taken slowly, then practised until you can do the whole thing in five minutes or less.

Now the second aspect of organization. After the initial five minutes (some examinations allow extra time for reading long papers), the remainder must be devoted to the actual answers. Examinations normally indicate the time that should be given to each part or question. A common format is four, three, or two questions with equal marks each. In that case *the time you spend should be equal also.* I have hardly marked an examination in which some candidates have not failed through a weak or non-existent last question. It is so tempting to spend extra time on the topic you know most about, but the tactic is practically always wrong. One reason is that if the last answer is going to be difficult, you will certainly not need less time to try to work something out. The main reason, however, is that in an essay type of examination, it is extremely difficult to score very high marks. No answer can ever be perfect, and examiners are always, consciously or not, reluctant to use the top end of the scale. Conversely, of course, few answers are so bad as to score zero. Thus in a typical format of four questions with 25 per cent of marks each, four at 15 or 16 must do better than say one (very good) 20, a 17, a 12 and a five (or, if not attempted, zero).

Writing

By this I mean the components of writing an answer. There are three: planning, the actual writing, and checking. The first is the most important but also the most neglected. Here, above all, is the case for practising the skill before you have to exhibit it. There are in turn two parts: one is collecting information, and one is putting it in order. The first step is to jot down anything that occurs to you that might be relevant to the answer. The difficult part is to avoid jumping prematurely to a decision as to what to include. Of course some questions are much more specific than others, and what you jot down will be more narrow in range; still it can do no harm to enter an apparently irrelevant word or two, no one will see it but you. In the studying section I will mention some ways to improve this recall process. The next thing is to decide on the plan of an answer: what are you going to include, and in what order? This, more than anything else, is what distinguishes the good candidate from the mediocre. Again I shall return to this under studying; the point here is that it is something that very few people can do well without practice, and this practice must be done before the examination – indeed throughout the period of study. Planning has to be done in five minutes or so, since most of the time is needed for the physical task of writing. The main thing here is to keep an eye on the clock, but one should know from experience how much one can write in the time available. What goes into the answer has already been decided, though it always may happen that something additional occurs to one. A practised writer can often weave it in later. Footnotes or supplementary sections are of course perfectly allowable but are almost certain to give an impression of confusion – another reason for getting the plan right in the first place. Still it is always better to risk this rather than leave out something you are quite sure should be said. Similarly, if despite everything you have more to say and almost no time to say it, brief notes at the end are better than nothing. Examiners are not impressed by messages saying, 'sorry – ran out of time'. Finally it is desirable if you can to leave two or three minutes to read what you have written and correct any glaring mistakes. I myself would seldom subtract marks for mere carelessness, but too much looks like ignorance. The occasional 'howler' may relieve the tedium of marking but cannot be recommended as a deliberate ploy; indeed the real thing would be hard to match. *'Harlow's experiments consisted of two wire suffragette monkeys'*, or *'Skinner was able to form an association with the rat in the box by flashing at it'*.

Expression

This means language and handwriting. The English language, in which your answers will be expressed, is an exceedingly complex and subtle instrument. Consider the enormous gulf between someone who struggles with a short letter, and a master such as Dickens, Orwell, or Wodehouse. Marks are not deducted for poor English (including poor spelling), but why handicap yourself? At worst, if the meaning is not clear, you risk not scoring marks you ought to get. More important, language is the means you have for conveying what you want the examiner to know; for showing what you can do. Because of the time limits it is important to say what you have to say as concisely and effectively as possible. I can't offer here a course in good English, but here are three points. There are numerous excellent books on the subject; in bookshops, sometimes under the heading 'English as a foreign language'. Second, read and compare good authors – not just in psychology. Try to improve on Beatrix Potter; and ask yourself why you can't. Third, as ever, practise. Each time you write, try to be as clear as you can. One specific form of practice now rather neglected, is précis: the exercise of trying to reduce a given passage to half or a third of its length, without losing meaning. Since this is essentially what one does in taking notes, it is doubly useful. (I will also offer a piece of advice from Dr Johnson. He said something like this: 'Read over what you have written, and whenever you come to a passage you think particularly fine, strike it out!')

Most examinations still depend on handwriting, though one wonders how long this can last. Many studies show that although handwriting is not supposed to count, it can lose a significant number of marks. Consider the poor examiner, faced with a seemingly endless pile of scripts, all saying more or less the same thing, yet which must be given accurate marks, and which are needed first thing tomorrow. Why make this task worse by writing which is hard – in some cases impossible – to read? One does not look for perfection, merely legibility. If you cannot write a hand that can be easily read *even when done quickly,* it is well worth trying to improve at once. Again there are many excellent books. With or without one as a guide, it is possible to effect a steady improvement by concentrating on one's worst formed letter. Whatever it is, try to get it right each time; when that is achieved, move on to the next. Layout can also help: writing to the left hand margin, leaving a line between paragraphs, *occasional* underlining done with a ruler.

All that has been said about essays applies to the 'write short notes on' question. But in this case writing must be even more concise: usually one, two, or at most three main points are all that are necessary or possible to score full marks.

Some examinations include a 'long' essay, that is, taking anything from one and a half to three hours to write. The good answer is not just an extended short one. The title is usually a rather general one, and it is necessary to think out, at the planning stage, what issues are raised and what sorts of solutions are possible, as well as what evidence is available. This rather different kind of planning must also be practised before the examination.

Finally in this section, the three worst faults of essays (and notes) are: not answering the question; lack of knowledge; lack of organization; and to all of these we shall return.

'Thoughts give people ideas.'

Practical work and projects

Generally these are done under non-examination conditions, though there are often time limits for handing in. The skills involved are thus largely those that are taught in the practical course, such as experimental design and analysis. Early in the book we deal with a good deal of this. Here I am more concerned with practical management.

Inasmuch as routine practicals are largely prescribed, the main advice (and I fully realize it is easier said than done) is to try to keep up to date with reports. The ideal is to write up the investigation, if you are going to do it at all, immediately after completing it. Even a short delay, and one forgets why things were done. One small help is to keep notes as one goes along, *under the same headings as will be used in the write-up.* Individual teachers have their own versions of these, and other conventions, so I shall not go into further details. The criterion to keep in mind is that a report should be such that someone else, reading it, could go away and repeat what you did. Here, as elsewhere, it is quite easy to check this by asking someone to read what you write.

Practical work as it progresses usually calls for the student to contribute more and more to the ideas and planning, and at degree level if not before this usually leads to an individual project which is nearly all the student's own work. Many students find difficulty here, largely I think because there is too big a jump from set practicals to what is in effect a small piece of research. Thus they lack a clear idea of what is required, and consequently lack confidence. Here are a few hints. As all researchers know, it is much easier to devise a big project than a small one. Thus one should start by thinking of a project as simply an extension of an ordinary practical. At the end of a write-up one usually gives suggestions as to how it might be improved or extended. If this were done it would be a project. Another tactic is to start from a replication of what someone else has done. Look at a few recent published experiments and ask yourself, 'Could I do that – or something like it, perhaps part of it?' It is usually easy to see how a slight variation would make it more original. Originality is the least difficulty; the clever part is to think of something that can be done and completed in the time available. At least two things are necessary here. One is keep in mind the practical considerations, without letting them dominate. What sort of subjects may be needed, and will they be available? How long will data collection take (time for one subject multiplied by likely number of subjects)? Will complex apparatus be required? (it will very likely break down at some point). At the same time it is usually not helpful to jump to a decision as to technique just because it is available, before deciding what one is trying to find out. The other thing is to have a timetable and try to stick to it. It is helpful to write out the various steps such as thinking of an idea, planning, data collection, etc., with expected dates. They will all have to be revised as one goes on but to some extent it guards against merely drifting. And there must be an element of what I usually call bloody-mindedness: moments come when one must settle on the best that can be done even if it is far from perfect, since the alternative will be ending up with nothing. Dr Johnson put it more neatly saying, 'What *must* be done, Sir, will be done'.

Having got what seems like a reasonable idea, a plan or proposal should be written out *using the headings of a practical write-up*. This means that you have to be specific about a hypothesis, a procedure, and an analysis. Many projects come to grief because this has not been done; above all because those undertaking the projects have not specified the analysis to be used, and ensured that the data can be treated in that way. At the planning stage, specify what sort of data will result (e.g. what scale of measurement, see Chapter 4); and draw up the table in which results will be entered.

It is usually, if not always, wise to do one or more pilot investigations. These may be no more than trying out one or two subjects to ensure that apparatus works or that instructions can be understood; or they may be more elaborate, and form part of the final report.

'Once a scheme has been formed inertia often sets in.'

Studying

Research bears out the common-sense view that students who are strongly motivated, either by intrinsic interest or the wish to succeed, tend to do better than those without such a drive. To a large extent any advice on study methods has to take motivation for granted, though there are some techniques for maintaining it. And motivation is not the same as anxiety, which may actually impair performance. The long-established Yerkes–Dodson principle shows that there is an optimum level of arousal for peak performance. Many students, in my experience, become so anxious as examinations approach that they work desperately but not effectively.

It will not be a surprise that I think the answer to this lies largely in study habits, in other words in the skills of studying. Research shows that there is, in general, an association between 'good' study habits and success. Successful students are on the whole those who work regularly and systematically, revise periodically, and practise examination techniques. Theoretically it might be the case that both habits and success are caused by some third variable, such as ability. More likely there is a complex interaction of these and other factors such as personality and environmental conditions. Looked at simply, it makes sense to emulate those who do well. It is, however, the principles rather than the details that are important. Evidence suggests, not so much that a particular pattern of study is right for everyone, as that what matters is to have some system rather than none, and to use methods which there is some reason to think psychologically sound.

'When the infant monkeys had grown into adults, Harlow decided to mate and observe the offspring.'

Organization

My own feeling is that the most basic principle is organization. This applies at several levels. Take, first, physical conditions. Some people can study successfully in the most adverse environments, but on the whole it is better, if at all possible, to have some quiet and reasonably comfortable place without constant distractions. At the same time while much study necessarily has to be done alone, many people find it helpful to work with a partner or a small group at least part of the time. Discussion can often help to clarify ideas; and it is salutary to get someone else to read what one writes, if only as a test of whether it is comprehensible. Of course tutors will usually mark written work, but they already know what ought to be there (at least in many cases); and their comments are often rather short, even unhelpful. It is actually much more difficult to make helpful positive comments than negative ones. Working with others also helps to maintain interest and motivation.

'When two people's eyes touch, they are in love.'

Time

Then there is organization of one's time. It is generally desirable to have a fairly consistent plan for which parts of the year, term, week, and day are to be used for work and for other things. Research does not suggest a very high correlation between sheer amount of time spent studying and success. Rather what matters is how the time is used. On the whole it seems to be better to have a regular pattern of work and leisure, and to keep each activity fairly separate. I confess I still find this hard, and not infrequently find at the end of a morning of 'work' that I have done very little and really might almost as well have taken the day off. One device here is, if one finds creative work such as writing an essay is stalling, to have on hand some routine but useful occupation such as filing or checking notes, or perhaps statistical calculations; something which has to be done but is not too demanding. Another device which many writers use is to end a work session with some task unfinished. This, some people find, makes it easier to start again in the next session. Personally, writing a short piece comparable to an essay, I might often do it over several sessions, not necessarily of equal length, involving collecting material; sorting through material and making a rough plan; making a fuller plan; starting to write; writing the bulk of it; completing and checking through; final revision. This is only an example of something that happens to suit me, yet it has some psychological justification. It allows time for review and for what is often called incubation. And it makes the task less formidable by breaking it into sub-units, each of which can be achieved. This in turn is reinforcing, on good operant conditioning principles, and so helps to maintain motivation. How long one can work effectively at a stretch varies between individuals, but many people find about an hour is right, followed by a short break – provided, of course, it does not turn into a long one. A change of topic can also help to combat fatigue, but this must be balanced against interrupting an effective sequence of work.

Similarly it is helpful to organize work within the time available. Here I think a rolling plan is needed. However well organized one is, the situation changes as some pieces of work are completed, or take longer than anticipated, and new ones come in. A regular, say weekly, review and listing of what has to be done and when does help to keep it in proportion, as well as giving feedback as to whether one is keeping up or falling behind. Usually, too, one has various categories of work which need to be kept going in parallel, when the temptation is to neglect the least enjoyable.

'Thorndike enforced the Law of Effect.'

Knowledge

Let us now turn to the organization of material or knowledge. I think the physical means for this are of some importance. For example, it is better to standardize on one size of paper rather than end up with notes on scraps of various sizes which will only get lost. Generally nowadays A4 is so universally used for examinations, and may be compulsory for practicals, that it is better to use it for everything. Another advantage is that handouts will fit into whatever you keep your own notes in; looseleaf systems are best. Personally I preferred always to write on one side of the paper. Although obviously more expensive, this allows one to add material in the right place on the blank side. Index cards are useful to build up a revision system which can be carried about and used in odd moments.

What goes into the looseleaf system will be mostly handouts, essays, and notes made from lectures and reading. We will come to essays later. Note taking is an individual matter, but very few people have such good memories that they can do without it. Lecturers also vary enormously, some virtually dictating notes and some (I'm told) rambling so as to make notetaking impossible. Usually, however, one wants to try to record the main points of what is said, and my own opinion is that the exercise of trying to grasp and summarize is in itself useful. How much one writes depends on the style of the lecturer and one's own ability to précis and write quickly and legibly. Since these are, in fact, examination skills it is useful to try to improve them. For my part I tried always to write in sentences; I found if I merely jotted down unconnected words they generally meant nothing to me later. Whatever style you adopt, however, I think it is useful, if not essential, to go over the notes afterwards to make sure they do make some sense. Some people advocate 'writing up' the notes in a more complete form, but I think this soon becomes such an impossible task that it is abandoned. My own habit was to spend five minutes reading through the notes, amending if not clear, and jotting down in the margin a subheading for each section or paragraph. This serves as an index and a revision guide.

Making notes from books or papers is usually a bit more leisurely. The first point in my opinion is, *always write down the complete reference in the conventional form as used in publications*. This may seem merely a chore, but if it is neglected the moment will inevitably come when you wish to look up the original and cannot, because all your note tells you s 'Smith, 1980'. It is also in itself a good learning device. And, of course, it is necessary for practicals and projects. How detailed the notes are will depend on their purpose and on how much you already have on the topic. It is *sometimes* useful to write out a short passage verbatim, when you want to make sure you have the author's exact words. Sometimes there will be a phrase or sentence (such as a definition) which it may be worth not only noting but learning so as to quote later.

Students sometimes ask how important is it to remember names and dates? In theory, the purpose of quoting names and dates is to enable the reader to check on what you have written. In practice this rarely happens because the reader is usually too busy. Tutors and examiners, unless they are exceptionally conscientious, seldom look up references except when something strikes them as outlandish (Freud has been said to live from 1832 to 1922; alternatively from 1856 to 1859). On the other hand they will, of course, notice glaring mistakes, and these create a bad impression. (*'Many of Freud's ideas were developed further by his daughter Melanie Kline.'*) So the only real answer is to learn as much as you can reliably remember. As an examiner, I personally would be more impressed by relevant arguments and facts than just a string of names; but names correctly used do strengthen an answer. The importance of names and dates from the student's point of view, I think, is to help to construct some framework of what has been done. When one starts, one is often overwhelmed with names, which seem all of equal importance. With further information, some come to stand out as major figures. Similarly with dates; some are landmarks, and getting them right helps to put events in the proper sequence. Some historical perspective is important because so much of psychology consists of changing ways of viewing behaviour, and the development of ideas out of, or in reaction to, others. (In the Department of which I was once Head, we had two tea ladies, Rose and Gladys, known as Glad. It was said that when stuck for a name in an exam, one would be wise to quote Rosenglad; but I can't really advise this for general use.)

It will be seen that one psychological principle which underlies much of what has been said is that of active rather than passive learning. Another principle is that of conceptual rather than rote learning. This can be seen as yet another example of organization. The material you accumulate, whether in your head or your notebooks, is much more easily remembered if it is arranged in some order. And the exercise of ordering is again in itself a learning device. For this purpose it is necessary to have some framework or index system. The simplest system will be the headings of the examination, or of the course of lectures, or a basic textbook. These, however, very seldom match each other exactly, nor do they necessarily correspond to the conceptual systems of psychology. For example, in this book we have a chapter on 'Thinking'. A GCE or degree course might well have no lectures or examination with that label, because what we call 'Thinking' is subsumed under 'Cognitive' (as it is in the *Psychological Abstracts*). Part might be under 'Developmental' or even 'Social'. An important part of studying psychology, in my view, is trying to see what justification, if any, the various divisions have, and whether and how the different parts fit together. Appendix I gives some examples of this sort of thinking.

'Gestalt however argued that a circle was a circle no matter what size it was.'

Topics

The objects of all this notetaking and other work are, of course, not the accumulation of material but some level of mastery of the subject, and success in examinations – two things which I consider quite compatible. It is not the slightest use having masses of notes if the material is not (a) accurate and (b) reproducible on demand. (a) is the reason for checking through notes and keeping complete references. (b) is the reason for active learning and organization. Both, however, also require selectivity. No one could possibly read, let alone retain, all the psychology there is; there are about 35,000 new publications each year. Many students, especially at degree level, in my opinion make the mistake of trying to learn too much and learning it very badly, so that they cannot reproduce it when the time comes. In GCE work good teachers guide students away from this. The opposite mistake, however, is to try to spot questions, and learn only what is needed for them. When the questions are, inevitably, not quite what was expected, an inappropriate answer results, with consequent low marks. This leads us back by another route to the need for organization. Knowledge for examinations should usually be organized by topics or issues. Questions are too specific; textbook chapters or examination papers too wide. What these topics are to be can only be decided from the actual syllabus. And topics are not necessarily all of the same size or status. But an example might be, say, 'the effects of early experience on later behaviour'. Notice that this crosses many conventional boundaries: it would include imprinting, intelligence, and emotional development, for example. It includes both issues and facts. And while it *might* form an examination answer in itself, it is more likely to provide material, or part of it, for several different questions. A topic, I have sometimes said, is rather like a piece of Lego or Meccano; a unit which can be used with others to make many different structures (answers).

Topics, as has been implied, need to be organized both conceptually and physically. Material can be collected conveniently in looseleaf form – in some cases with duplication where topics overlap. They can be summarized in card form for handy revision.

It would be quite wrong to suggest that passing examinations is the only point of studying. But it is certainly one point; and the means of doing so, in particular writing essays or papers, is also one of the main vehicles of studying. There is no contradiction therefore in concentrating on the skills involved. The advantage of writing regular essays, even when they are not required for continuous assessment, is that this is both good practice and active processing. (A colleague used to say that, quite simply, 100 essays during the course, that is roughly one a week, equalled a first, 75 an upper second, and so on. This is a bit simplistic but he had a point.)

> *'From birth boys are indoctrinated to be tough and masculine and girls, soft and delicate. They are dressed in blue and pink respectably.'*

Essays

Students, especially in examinations, often seem somehow to lose sight of what an essay is. In my view it is an answer to a question. If this appears a pointless remark, consider. It is *an* answer; not *the* answer. Usually in psychology there is no one correct answer. There are findings and arguments, and at any level we have to make the most useful or sensible selection we can of them. It is an *answer*. The examiner does not mean 'tell me all you can remember about this'; if he meant that he would say so. And it is an answer to a *question*. This question ought to be a sensible one, and it is being asked by someone who wants to know the answer. (There is supposed once to have been an Oxbridge examiner who asked, 'Is this a good question?'; and a student who got high marks for writing, 'Yes, if this is a good answer'. Fortunately perhaps few of us will meet such conundrums.) At the same time while an essay is an answer, it is not any answer. In the sciences dealing with human beings, including psychology, many questions are the subject of general conversation, and even of ignorant pronouncement by otherwise educated persons such as politicians and judges, who ought to know better. The student is expected to produce something other than what I sometimes call the 'saloon bar' answer. He is expected to know at least the main psychological approaches to the issue. At a simplistic level, this means knowing what there is about it in books labelled 'psychology'. At a slightly higher level it means appreciating the advantages and difficulties of an objective, empirical (that is, based on evidence), and, in particular, experimental approach.

A question then should be taken at face value, and the first step is to review what one knows that may be relevant. One way to improve this is to free associate to *each word of the question.* 'To what extent is intelligence inherited?' What does one know of intelligence; of inheritance; of the inheritance of intelligence; and of extent (how can it be measured, etc.)? Another way, more useful the more general a question is, is to run through one or more of the classificatory systems you may have. Is there anything relevant in the physiology box, the cognitive box, and so on? But to repeat what has already been said, this recollection of material is not the answer. Time and again students, particularly when panicking in examinations, simply write down the first thing they can remember; then think of something else; and so on until they run out.

A device here is to imagine that someone is actually asking you the question. This someone knows a bit about psychology but not enough to answer the question; she or he wants to find out. What would you say? (Such an imaginary conversation can be practised in odd moments, on the bus, for example.) Taking it seriously, you would first have to collect your thoughts, and then put them in some sort of order. This order need not be complicated, in fact the simpler the better. And a device here is to ask oneself, what is a one sentence answer? Here, it might be, 'To quite a large extent; but of course it does depend on what you mean by intelligence'; or it might be, 'Not at all'. (In that case the answer would involve refuting the 'inheritance' evidence as well as quoting the 'environmental' evidence.) An order of presentation might be: evidence for; evidence against; conclusion. Or it might be: the problem of 'intelligence'; attempts to answer the inheritance question; why they are inconclusive. Many others are possible. What matters is that there is some plan, and that each succeeding part of the essay helps to answer the question. A colleague used to ask, can you draw a line back from each paragraph to the original question?

It is sometimes said that an essay should have a beginning, a middle and an end; and I sometimes have said that in my view it should have a middle. I have in mind an old bit of advice to the young journalist: First set the scene and outline the situation; then tell your story; then draw conclusions. Then take a pair of scissors and cut off the beginning and the end of your piece. This exaggerates a little; but I am very unimpressed by opening paragraphs that are really waffle, of the type, 'many people have investigated this problem for many years ...' Then the second paragraph may well start, 'Smith, 1988, attacked this problem by ...' – and this might make quite an impressive beginning to the essay. This is as much a matter of style as of planning, and the exercise of précis mentioned above trains one to make sure that every sentence and every word serves a useful purpose. (And if you think I myself need to go back to some basic exercises, well, I probably do. But there is a place for redundancy in teaching which does not exist in essay writing.)

Until one is skilled at it – and for many writers even then – it is generally necessary to make one or more drafts before the final version. Try to read the draft as though you wanted to find out the answer; check its structure; trim the redundancy.

Particularly in GCE work one is often asked to 'assess' or to 'compare and contrast'. All too often what appears is simply a description; sometimes with a sentence of assessment or comparison at the end. It is the balance between description and evaluation that makes the good answer. And one does not have to describe before evaluating; rather, description should be brought in to support the evaluation. In order to assess or compare one has to have some criteria. (Compare Freud and Eysenck. In what way? They are both of German origin; Eysenck is a keen tennis player while Freud collected antiques.) Here again a classification system can help. A simple device, however, is to think of the usual headings of a practical report. Can he or they be assessed on background; hypotheses; method; procedure and subjects; data; analysis; conclusions; further work (influence)? Once more, this is not the answer, but a way of finding material for an answer. What was X trying to do? How did he go about it? How far did he succeed? What evidence is there for his ideas? What followed from his work? These are some questions to *ask yourself about the topic* (see also Appendix I). As in all essays, one is trying to organize arguments and evidence to answer a question.

Perhaps this is the place to mention definitions. Essays often start 'Before we can discuss X we must define it'. To begin with this is usually not so. 'What did you have for breakfast?' 'Before I can answer that I must define "breakfast"' would usually be an odd response. But not always; you might want to point out that you had nothing at the normal time, so that your 'breakfast' was actually lunch. Secondly it is exceedingly difficult to devise a good definition (especially in an examination). Thirdly a definition right at the beginning may well not cover what you are going to want to mention later. One dodge is to leave the question of definition, if it is indeed important, to later, even to the end. Another is to use someone else's definition which you have learned for the purpose, and which you can criticize later if necessary. (Dictionaries, either psychological or general, can sometimes be useful.) What I do think is important, is that *you are clear in your own mind what you mean*. If you are muddled the answer will be muddled. Thus it is worthwhile in studying to stop and ask oneself what one understands by words and concepts. (Imagine, or actually try, explaining to someone what 'instinct' or 'conditioning' means.)

'Those children who were inanimate were badly behind their contemporaries.'

Revision

Research suggests that periodic revision throughout a course is more effective than a last minute rush. Indeed, ideally one might say that revision should not be necessary if sound study methods have been followed. In practice few people are so confident. This is where summary cards come in. But there are very few, if any, single facts that are vital in themselves or will make any difference to a result. Of course one must have enough knowledge, but it is much better to use revision to be sure of a number of topics, which can be used to answer different questions, than to try to add yet more detail at the last minute. As with all learning, active practice is best. Alone, or with a partner, one can pose hypothetical (or past) questions and compose, or just plan, answers.

A lot has been said about practice, and less on feedback. Here are a few devices. Normally work is marked by someone, but as has been said, comments are often negative. In that case there is usually no reason why you cannot ask tactfully for something more constructive. As has been suggested several times, friends can read each others' work. If alone, it is useful to look at work – notes or essays – again after a period, and try to read it as if it were new. Does it make sense? Do essays answer the question? As with notes, essays can benefit from subheadings. These not only act as a revision aid, but help to bring out the plan of the essay. Is it what you intended? Could it be improved – for example, could you say the same thing in fewer words?

Studying and examinations are not the most important things in life but they do often open doors. And it seems to me in an old-fashioned way that if one sets out to do something it is usually worth doing it as well as one can. In any case, if you are faced with such tasks, may good fortune attend you – though I expect the more you practise, the less you will need it.

'Hackman and Lawler got 39 female operators with 22 supervisors to see if there would be any kind of satisfaction but this was found not to be so.'

Information

Most degree and GCE students will be enrolled on a course and will get plenty of information, indeed it may seem overwhelming at times. But there are some ways in which, nevertheless, it may be useful to supplement it.

About examinations

Syllabuses for GCE examinations should be available in the institution offering courses; or they can be obtained direct from the relevant Board. Make sure the syllabus is up to date. Past papers are available in the same way. The existence of Chief Examiners' reports is not always widely known. These usually report on how each question in a particular examination was answered, and point out the main deficiencies.

At degree level under the CNAA system (that is, in institutions other than universities) each course is defined by a lengthy course document, usually a large volume or two, including all the syllabuses and details about staff and resources. These may be available in the institution's library, but shortened course documents are usually published for students. Past papers are normally available. External examiners' reports may be regarded as confidential, but in any case do not usually refer to specific questions but only to the overall standards of the course and examining. In universities course documents and syllabuses are often more perfunctory, and past papers, plus course handouts, are usually the best guide.

About study methods

There are numerous books on study methods, and it would be difficult and invidious to review them here. However, one institution, the Open University, has put a great deal of thought into this topic because its students mostly work on their own. Many of the OU publications are available to everyone from bookshops or from the Publications Department, BBC, London W1A 1AA. OU television programmes which include study methods can also be watched by anyone. And many institutions offer short courses in study methods, perhaps especially for those returning to study later in life.

About psychology

Even a quite large book such as this can provide only an introduction to some parts of psychology, though we hope to have provided a fair overview, and specifically to have met the needs of GCE 'A' level and at least first year degree students. Particularly at degree level, institutions will provide far more than can be found in any one book. Here, however, are a few extras.

Some students have suggested that this textbook should include, as many do, a glossary. We decided against this, partly on the grounds of length and hence cost, and partly because we simply thought the job too difficult to do well. There are, besides, a number of dictionaries of psychology, some in paperback form and cheap enough to buy. Other publications are more encyclopaedic and may be found in a university or college library, or even in a general reference library. General dictionaries and encyclopaedias are not to be despised. It can often be useful to consider the 'ordinary' definition of a word, such as intelligence, which psychologists use in a technical way. Large encyclopaedias often contain articles on major psychological issues and important historical figures (see Appendix II).

The soaring price of books, and reductions in educational expenditure, have created problems for both students and libraries. It may be useful to explore the resources of the public library system and perhaps some more specialized collections. Some details of the latter are given in *Teaching Psychology: Information and Resources,* edited by Rose and Radford and published by the British Psychological Society, 1990. (Although intended mainly for teachers this may be of use to students; it also deals with such things as careers and courses, do-it-yourself equipment, and ethical issues.) It may be worthwhile for a small group of students to club together and buy and share books. It may likewise be worthwhile to explore second-hand

and, more especially, remainder bookshops, which generally sell at half the last retail price. As with angling, the catch may be small but the activity is pleasant.

Presentation of psychology in the mass media is variable, and it is nearly always equated with psychiatry. Nevertheless serious treatment of psychological topics is not infrequent. There are the excellent programmes of the Open University (though not always at convenient hours), and there are other good television and radio items which can be looked out for. Popular/specialist magazines such as *New Society, New Scientist* and especially *Scientific American* frequently contain good articles. Even the daily press can be helpful. Surveys of newspapers by students of mine showed the *Sunday Times* and *The Times* to have the greatest frequency of psychological items, though even they are far from immune to misconceptions; for example a piece in the *Sunday Times*, 24 January 1988, starts: 'It must be the supreme irony of sport that Pat Cash is aided and abetted by a psychologist' – presumably because the tennis player is the epitome of normality. Still, making a newspaper collection can be an interesting exercise.

Students of academic psychology are often warned against including personal experiences in what they write. There is force in this, for mere anecdote is no substitute for systematic evidence and experiment. Nevertheless psychology is (mostly) about people, and if an experiment, or more often a theory, seems to contradict common sense it should at least make us question it. At least one formal examination, that for the International Baccalaureate (equivalent to GCE), actually asks candidates to say how they think psychology applies to themselves. One's own observations, experiences, or general reading, used appropriately, are among the sources that can help to make a psychological answer. Similarly, ethical issues are relevant to a number of problems, and may indeed be specifically asked for; a discussion may well include one's own viewpoint, with arguments to back it, but it should not be just an unsupported diatribe – the 'saloon bar' answer. Nor should it be a personal attack on the real or supposed opinions of an individual; it is evidence and reasoning that are needed. There is nothing contradictory in holding strong views and at the same time being able to understand, and state, the arguments on both sides. The popular view of the moment may, or may not, command the best support in the long run, and it is the ability to see things in a wider perspective that characterizes the scientific approach.

Appendix I:

Some classification systems

What follows may seem very formalistic. It must be stressed that the various lists are simply tools: devices to help one investigate the complex material that counts as 'psychology'. Psychology as one studies it some-times seems like a vast jigsaw puzzle with no picture and some of the pieces missing. Nevertheless there are some ways of considering which pieces might go together.

1. One of the earliest modern systematic accounts was given by the philosopher Thomas Hobbes (1588–1679). He saw that to be complete any account of behaviour must deal with three levels, which we might now call physiological, individual, and social. Few psychologists have actually tried to do this. Freud, for example, originally hoped to produce a neurological explanation of behaviour which would ultimately be consistent with the other two levels. His shot at this, dated 1895, was posthumously published as the *Project for a Scientific Psychology*; but the neurology of his day was not adequate for the purpose, and his later theories dealt with the individual and social levels. H. J. Eysenck could reasonably claim to be one of the few to have worked out a system consistent at all three levels. Innate differences in conditionability (physiology) determine the degree of introversion/extraversion (individual personality) which in turn determines social behaviour. Skinner similarly seeks to take account of genetics, an individual's learning history, and the functional importance of social environments. Consistency does not of itself prove that a system is correct. Nevertheless it is useful to ask at what level a theory is supposed to be working, and whether it is consistent or inconsistent with findings from the other levels.

2. R. S. Peters (1953), in condensing to one volume Brett's massive *History of Psychology,* argued that those who have thought about behaviour have generally been concerned with one or more of four basic sorts of question, which he called questions of theory, of technology, of policy, and of philosophy and metaphysics. Questions of theory are 'scientific': questions about what is the case and always will be – the attempt to establish general laws. Questions of technology are concerned with how to bring about a specific effect, whether or not it is understood scientifically. Much of psychology is in practice like this – how to select for a particular job, remedy a learning deficiency, etc. Questions of policy are about what ought to be done – moral and ethical issues. The last category of question is to do both with what sort of enquiry psychology itself is, is it a science, if so of what kind, and so on; and with the general assumptions we make about behaviour and the nature of human beings, the models that are adopted (e.g. man as a closed energy system, as a computer, etc.). These questions often overlap and intermingle. For example, take an issue such as corporal punishment, only recently removed from British schools after fierce debates. What is the evidence that it works? How does that evidence affect its rightness or wrongness? What sort of creatures do we imagine children to be? and so on.

3. A rather obvious way of sorting things out is by content, but usually syllabuses and textbook headings are somewhat arbitrary and influenced by fashion or special interests. I have found it more useful to try to distinguish some main groups of issues: (a) biological bases of behaviour; (b) information processing; (c) interaction; (d) causes of behaviour (emotion and motivation); (e) individual differences; (f) disorders; (g) development. Notice that these overlap in content, even though they are concerned with different questions. For example the study of mother–child language would come in (b), (c), and (g).

4. Behaviour can be looked at from many different theoretical orientations, each with its own assumptions, not always clearly stated, about what is important and how to go about investigations. (In *Thinking in Perspective*, Methuen (1978), Andrew Burton and I tried to show how this applies to one subject area.) Some of the main orientations are: introspective; behavioural; psychometric; dynamic (e.g. psychoanalytic); phenomeno-logical; 'humanistic'; structural. Sometimes a given investigator will not fall neatly into one class, or perhaps will deliberately borrow from more than one. Like all the lists given here, this is not a filing system, just a way of thinking about what is going on. (There are other perspectives, such as those of the various world religions, which are of great importance but which generally, as here, get no more than a passing nod in textbooks of psychology.)

5. Many of those who have studied behaviour have been mainly engaged in one or more of several different sorts of activity, which might be called (a) philosophical/theoretical (analysing issues and speculating); (b) empirical or experimental (collecting facts under particular conditions); (c) psycho-metric (measuring, particularly individual differences); (d) clinical (treat-ing people in some remedial way). Again they overlap, for example (d) often involves (c). On the other hand (b) and (c) would appear to be closely related, yet historically often developed almost in isolation.

6. Many systems of psychology look for the explanation of behaviour in the past; for example, psychoanalysts and behaviourists agree on this if nothing else. But some, such as Piaget and Lewin, emphasize the present (for example, in Piaget's system it is the current state of the mental structures that determines how we think and react); and some even the future. McDougall, an early champion of this approach, is now virtually forgotten; but much social psychology deals with what we expect from others – in other words, the future.

7. Finally for the reader who is still with us, a bow in the direction of one of the first Western psychologists, Aristotle (384–322 BC). His doctrine of the four causes suggests what must be considered to give a complete account of a phenomenon. The material cause is that of which the thing is made; the

805

formal cause is the pattern or 'law of development'; the efficient cause is the agency which makes something move or happen; the final cause is the end towards which something is moving or developing. It is true, as Peters points out, that in practice Aristotle's system tended to equate the last three, making them the same as another of his concepts, the 'essence' or real nature of something, the identification of which was for Aristotle the business of science. Aristotle's science thus tended to be descriptive rather than explanatory as we now consider explanation. Nevertheless, the four causes can be applied to behaviour. Is it a better or worse explanation to say that a man works hard in order to buy a house (final cause) than because he has been conditioned (efficient cause)? Piaget, and perhaps Jung, might be said to deal with formal causes; and so on.

Appendix II:

Some dictionaries and encyclopaedias with relevant information

Of purely general publications, the *Encyclopaedia Britannica* is particularly useful on the history of psychology and major figures in psychology. Two other general works among many are the *McGraw-Hill Encyclopaedia of Science and Technology* (15 vols, 1982); and the *Oxford Companion to Science* (OUP, 1989). There are also dictionaries of psychological terms, some giving translations between English and French, German, and Spanish. Of those listed below, perhaps the most useful to consider buying is that by Reber (note that it cannot be guaranteed that any item will remain in print).

Encyclopedic Dictionary of Psychology (1986). Dushkin Publications.
Bruno, F. J. (1986) *Dictionary of Key Words in Psychology*. Methuen.
Chaplin, J. P. (1985) *Dictionary of Psychology*. Dell.
Corsini, R. J. (1984) *Encyclopaedia of Psychology,* 4 Vols. Wiley.
Corsini, R. J. (1987) *Concise Encyclopaedia of Psychology* (abridgement of 4 Vol. work). Wiley.
Eysenck, H. J. (1979) *Encyclopaedia of Psychology*, 2nd edn. Continuum.
Godwin, D. M. (1989) *Dictionary of Neuropsychology*. Springer.
Goldenson, R. M. (1984) *Longman Dictionary of Psychology and Psychiatry*. Longman.
Gregory, R. L., and Zangwill, O. L. (1987) *The Oxford Companion to the Mind*. OUP.
Harre, R., and Lamb, R. (1983) *The Encyclopaedic Dictionary of Psychology*. Blackwell.
Harre, R., and Lamb, R. (1986) *Dictionary of Developmental and Educational Psychology*. Blackwell.
Harre, R., and Lamb, R. (1986) *Dictionary of Ethology and Animal Learning*. Blackwell.
Harre, R., and Lamb, R. (1986) *Dictionary of Personality and Social Psychology*. Blackwell.
Harre, R., and Lamb, R. (1986) *Dictionary of Physiological and Clinical Psychology*. MIT Press.

Leigh, D., *et al* (1977) *A Concise Encyclopaedia of Psychiatry*. M.T.P.

Matson, K. (1977) *The Psychology Today Omnibook of Personal Development*. William Morrow.

Naaramore, C. M. (1984) *Compact Encyclopaedia of Psychological Problems*. Zondervan.

Reber, A. S. (1986) *Dictionary of Psychology*. Viking; also published by Penguin Books.

Rosenberg, J. M. (1986) *Dictionary of Artificial Intelligence and Robotics*. Wiley.

Rycroft, C. (1972) *A Critical Dictionary of Psychoanalysis*. Penguin.

Shapiro, S. C. (1987) *Encyclopaedia of Artificial Intelligence*, 2 Vols. Wiley.

Skinner, S. W. (1986) *Dictionary of Psychotherapy*. Routledge.

Slater, P. J. B. (1986) *Encyclopaedia of Animal Behaviour*. Collins.

Statt, D. A. (1981) *Dictionary of Human Behaviour*. Harper and Row.

Statt, D. A. (1989) *Concise Dictionary of Psychology*, 2nd edn. Routledge.

Thakurdas, H., and Thakurdas, L. (1979) *Dictionary of Psychiatry*. M.T.P.

Walton, H. (1985) *Dictionary of Psychiatry*. Blackwell.

Wolman, B. B. (1977) *International Encyclopedia of Psychiatry, Psychology, Psychoanalysis and Neurology*, 12 Vols. Van Nostrand Reinhold.

Wolman, B. B. (1979) *Dictionary of Behavioral Science*. Van Nostrand.

The book details were compiled by Pat Triggs, Psychology Librarian at Polytechnic of East London.

Bibliography

Abernethy, E. (1940) 'The effect of changed environmental conditions upon the results of college examinations'. *Journal of Psychology*, 10, 293–301.

Abramovitch, R., Pepler, D., and Corter, C. (1982) 'Patterns of sibling interaction among pre-school children'. In M. E. Lamb and B. Sutton-Smith, eds., *Sibling Relationships: Their nature and significance across the lifespan*. Hillsdale, N.J., Lawrence Erlbaum Associates.

Abramson, L. Y., Seligman. M. E. P., and Teasdale, J. D. (1978) 'Learned helplessness in humans: critique and reformulation'. *Journal of Abnormal Psychology*, 89, 49–74.

Adorno, T. W., Frenkel-Brunswick, E., Levinson, D. J., and Sanford, R. N. (1950) *The Authoritarian Personality*. New York, Harper and Row.

Ader, R., and Cohen, N. (1985) 'CNS-immune system interactions: conditioning phenomena'. *The Behavioral and Brain Sciences*, 8, 3, 379–426.

Ainscow, M., and Tweddle, D. (1979) *Preventing Classroom Failure: An objective approach*. Chichester, Wiley.

Ainsworth, M. D. S. (1967) *Infancy in Uganda: Infant care and the growth of love*. Baltimore, Johns Hopkins University Press.

Ainsworth, M. D. S., Blehar, M. C., Waters, E., and Wall, S. (1978) *Patterns of Attachment*. Hillsdale, N.J., Lawrence Erlbaum Associates.

Aitchison, J. (1982) *The Articulate Mammal*, 2nd edn. London, Hutchinson.

Aitchison, J. (1987) *Words in the Mind: An introduction to the mental lexicon*. Oxford, Blackwell.

Ajzen, I. (1982) 'On behaving in accordance with one's attitudes'. In M. P. Zanna, E. T. Higgins, and C. P. Herman, eds, *Consistency in Social Behaviour*. The Ontario Symposium, Vol. 2. Hillsdale, N.J., Lawrence Erlbaum Associates.

Ajzen, I., and Fishbein, M. (1980) *Understanding Attitudes and Predicting Social Behavior*. Englewood Cliffs, N.J., Prentice-Hall.

Allport, G. W. (1935) 'Attitudes'. In C. Murchison, ed., *A Handbook of Social Psychology*. Worcester, Mass., Clark University Press.

Allport, G. (1954) *The Nature of Prejudice*. Reading, Mass., Addison-Wesley.

Allport, G. W. (1961) *Pattern and Growth in Personality*. New York, Holt, Rinehart and Winston.

American Psychological Association (1954) 'Technical recommendations for tests'. *Psychological Bulletin*, 51, pt 2.

Anand, B. K., and Brobeck, J. R. (1951) 'Hypothalamic control of food intake in rats and cats'. *Yale Journal of Biological Medicine*, 24, 123–40.

Anastasi, A. (1958) *Differential Psychology*. New York, Macmillan.

Annett, J. (1969) *Feedback and Human Behaviour*. Harmondsworth, Penguin.

Antell, S. E. G., and Caron, A. J. (1985) 'Neonatal perception of spatial relationships'. *Infant Behaviour and Development*, 8, 15–23.

Archer, S. L. (1982) 'The lower age boundaries of identity development'. *Child Development*, 53, 1551–6.

Arend, R. A., Grove, F. L., and Sroufe, L. A. (1979) 'Continuity of early adaptation: from attachment in infancy to ego resilience and curiosity at age five'. *Child Development*, 50, 950–9.

Arkin, R. M., and Lake, E. A. (1983) 'Plumbing the depths of the bogus pipeline: a reprise'. *Journal of Research in Personality*, 17, 81–8.

Arlin, K. P. (1975) 'Cognitive development in adulthood. A fifth stage?'. *Developmental Psychology*, 11, 602–6.

Arlin, K. P. (1984) 'Adolescent and adult thought'. In M. L. Commons, *et al*, eds., *Beyond Formal Operations*. New York, Praeger.

Aronson, E. (1969) 'The theory of cognitive dissonance: a current perspective'. In L. Berkowitz, ed., *Advances in Experimental Social Psychology*, Vol. 4. New York, Academic Press.

Asch, S. (1946) 'Forming impressions of personality'. *Journal of Abnormal and Social Psychology*, 41, 258–90.

Asch, S. (1956) 'Studies in independence and submission to group pressures. A minority of one against a unanimous majority'. *Psychological Monographs*, 70 (9) (Whole No. 416).

Association of Educational Psychologists (1986) *Educational Psychologists: Their work and the implications for training – a statement of policy*, 3 Sunderland Road, Durham, DH1 2LH, July.

Atkinson, R., and Shiffrin, R. (1968) 'Human memory: a proposed system and its control processes'. In K. Spence and J. Spence, eds, *The Psychology of Learning and Motivation: Advances in research and theory*, Vol. 2. New York, Academic Press.

Atkinson, R., and Shiffrin, R. (1971) 'The control of short-term memory'. *Scientific American*, 225, 89–90.

Au, T. K. -F. (1983) 'Chinese and English counterfactuals; the Sapir-Whorf hypothesis revisited'. *Cognition*, 15, 155–87.

Ausubel, D., Novak, J., and Hanesian, H. (1978) *Educational Psychology: A cognitive view*, 2nd edn. London, Holt, Rinehart and Winston.

Averill, J. R., O'Brien, L., and Dewitt, G. W. (1977) 'The influence of response effectiveness on the preference for warning and on psychophysiological stress reactions'. *Journal of Personality*, 45, 395–418.

Ax, A. F. (1953) 'Physiological differentiation of emotional states'. *Psychosomatic Medicine*, 15, 433–42.

Axelrod, R. (1984) *The Evolution of Co-operation*. New York, Basic Books.

Baars, B. J. (1980) 'The competing plans hypothesis: a heuristic viewpoint on the problem of speech errors'. In H. W. Dechert and R. M. Raupach, eds., *Temporal Variables in Speech*. The Hague, Mouton.

Baddeley, A. (1978) 'The trouble with levels: a re-examination of Craik and Lockhart's framework for memory research'. *Psychological Review*, 85, 139–52.

Baddeley, A. (1982) 'Amnesia: a minimal model and an interpretation'. In L. S. Cermak, ed., *Human Memory and Amnesia*. Hillsdale, N.J., Lawrence Erlbaum Associates.

Baddeley, A. (1988) 'Cognitive psychology and human memory'. *Trends in Neurosciences*, 11, 176–81.

Baddeley, A., and Hitch, G. (1974) 'Working memory'. In G. Bower, ed., *Recent Advances in Learning and Motivation*, Vol. VIII. New York, Academic Press.

Baddeley, A., and Scott, D. (1971) 'Short-term forgetting in the absence of inhibition'. *Quarterly Journal of Experimental Psychology*, 23, 275–83.

Badia, P., Harsh, J., and Abbot, B. (1979) 'Choosing between predictable and unpredictable shock conditions: data and theory'. *Psychological Bulletin*, 86, 1107–31.

Baltes, P. B., and Nesselroade, J. R. (1972) 'Developmental analysis of individual differences on multiple measures'. In J. R. Nesselroade and Reese, eds., *Life-span Developmental Psychology*. New York, Academic Press.

Baltes, P. B., *et al* (1980) 'Life-span developmental psychology'. *Annual Review of Psychology*, 31, 65–110.

Bandura, A. (1973) *Aggression: A social learning analysis*. Englewood Cliffs, N.J., Prentice-Hall.

Bandura, A. (1977a) 'Self-efficacy: towards a unifying theory of behavioural change'. *Psychological Review*, 84, 191–215.

Bandura, A. (1977b) *Social Learning Theory*. Englewood Cliffs, N.J., Prentice-Hall.

Baratz, S. S., and Baratz, J. C. (1970) 'Early childhood intervention'. *Harvard Educational Review*.

Barnard, W. A., and Benn, M. S. (1988) 'Belief congruence and prejudice reduction in an interracial contact setting'. *Journal of Social Psychology*, 128, 125–34.

Baron, A., Myerson, J., and Hale, S. (1988) 'An integrated analysis of the structure and function of behaviour: aging and the cost of dividing attention'. In G. Davey and C. Cullen, *Human Operant Conditioning and Behaviour Modification*. Chichester, Wiley.

Baron, J. (1978) 'The word superiority effect: perceptual learning from reading'. In W. K. Estes, ed., *Handbook of Learning and Cognitive Processes*, Vol. 6. Hillsdale, N.J., Lawrence Erlbaum, pp. 131–66.

Baron, J. B., and Sternberg, R. J. (1987) *Teaching Thinking Skills: Theory and practice*. Oxford, W. H. Freeman.

Baron, R. S., Moore, D., and Saunders, G. S. (1988) 'Distraction as a source of drive in social facilitation research'. *Journal of Personality and Social Psychology*, 8, 816–24.

Barrett, M. D. (1979) *Semantic Development during the Single Word Stage of Language Development*. Unpublished doctoral thesis, University of Sussex.

Bartlett, F. C. (1932) *Remembering: A study in experimental and social psychology*. Cambridge University Press.

Basseches, M. (1980) 'Dialectical schemata'. *Human Development*, 23, 400–21.

Basso, A., Spinnler, H., Vallar, G., and Zanobio, E. (1982) 'Left hemisphere damage and selective impairment of auditory verbal short-term memory: a case study'. *Neuropsychologia*, 20, 263–74.

Bates, E., Bretherton, I., Beeghly-Smith, M., and McNew, S. (1982) 'Social bases of language development'. In H. W. Reese and L. P. Lipsitt, eds., *Advances in Child Development and Behaviour*, Vol. 16. London, Academic Press.

Baum, W. M. (1975) 'Time allocation in human vigilance'. *Journal of Experimental Analysis of Behaviour*, 22, 321–42.

Baumrind, D. (1973) 'The development of instrumental competence through socialization'. In A. E. Pick, ed., *Minnesota Symposia on Child Psychology*. Minneapolis, University of Minnesota Press.

Beattie, G. (1983) *Talk – An Analysis of Speech and Non-Verbal Behaviour in Conversation*. Milton Keynes, Open University Press.

Beattie, G. W., Cutler, A., and Pearson, M. (1982) 'Why is Mrs Thatcher interrupted so often?'. *Nature*, 300, 744–7.

Beck, A. T. (1967) *Depression: Clinical, experimental and theoretical aspects*. New York, Harper and Row.

Bee, H. L., and Mitchel, S. K. (1980) *The Developing Person: A life-span approach*. New York, Harper and Row.

Belsky, J., Robins, E., and Gamble, W. (1984) 'The determinants of parental competence'. In M. Lewis, ed., *Beyond the Dyad*. New York, Plenum.

Belsky, J., and Rovine, M. (1987) 'Temperament and attachment security in the strange situation: an empirical rapprochement'. *Child Development*, 58, 787–95.

Bem, D. J. (1965) 'An experimental analysis of self-perception'. *Journal of Experimental Social Psychology*, 1, 199–218.

Bem, D. J. (1967) 'Self-perception: an alternative interpretation of cognitive dissonance phenomena'. *Psychological Review*, 74, 183–200.

Bem, D. J. (1972) 'Self-perception theory'. In L. Berkowitz (ed.), *Advances in Experimental Social Psychology 6*. New York, Academic Press.

Bem, S. L. (1975) 'Fluffy women and chesty men'. *Psychology Today*, September.

Benedict, R. (1934) *Patterns of Culture*. New York, New American Library.

Bennett, N. (1976) *Teaching Styles and Pupil Progress*. London, Open Books.

Berger, H. (1929) 'Uber das Elektrenkephalogramm des Menschen'. *Archiv für Psychiatrie und Nervenkrankheiten*, 87, 527–70.

Berkowitz, L. (1969) 'The frustration-aggression hypothesis revisited'. In L. Berkowitz, ed., *Roots of Aggression*. New York, Atherton Press.

Berkowitz, L., and Frodi, A. (1977) 'Stimulus characteristics that can enhance or decrease aggression'. *Aggressive Behaviour*, 3, 1–15.

Bernstein, B. (1970) 'Education cannot compensate for society'. In Colin Stoneman and David Rubinstein, eds., *Directions in Sociolinguistics*. New York, Holt, Rinehart and Winston.

Berry, J. W. (1984) 'Towards a universal psychology of cognitive competence'. *International Journal of Psychology*, 19, 335–61.

Berscheid, E., and Walster, E. (1974) 'Physical attractiveness'. In L. Berkowitz, ed., *Advances in Experimental Social Psychology*, Vol. 7. New York, Academic Press.

Berzonski, M. D. (1978) 'Formal reasoning in adolescence: an alternative view'. *Adolescence*, 13, 279–90.

Bever, T. G. (1970) 'The cognitive basis for linguistic structures'. In J. R. Hayes, ed., *Cognition and the Development of Language*. New York, Wiley.

Biblow, E. (1973) 'Imaginative play and the control of aggressive behaviour'. In J. L. Singer, ed., *The Child's World of Make-Believe*. New York, Academic Press.

Bierwisch, M. (1970) 'Semantics'. In J. Lyons, ed., *New Horizons in Linguistics*, Hammondsworth, Penguin.

Birren, J. E. (1955) 'Age changes in speed of responses'. In J. E. Birren, *In Old Age in the Modern World*. Livingstone.

Blakemore, C. (1973) 'Environmental constraints on developments in the visual system'. In R. A. Hinde and J. Stevenson-Hinde, eds., *Constraints on Learning*. London, Academic Press, Ch. 3, pp. 51–75.

Blinkov, S. M., and Glezer, I. I. (1968) *The Human Brain in Figures and Tables: A quantitative handbook*. New York, Basic Books.

Bloom, A. H. (1981) *The Linguistic Shaping of Thought: A study in the impact of language on thinking in China and the West*. Hillsdale, N.J., Lawrence Erlbaum Associates.

Bloom, B. (1979) *Alterable Variables: The new direction in educational research*. Edinburgh, Scottish Council for Research in Education.

Bloom, L. (1970) *Language Development*. Cambridge, Mass., MIT Press.

Blos, P. (1962) *On Adolescence*. Basingstoke, Collier-Macmillan.

Blum, J. (1978) *Pseudoscience and Mental Ability*. London, Monthly Review Press.

Blurton-Jones, N., and Konner, M. J. (1976) '!Kung knowledge of animal behaviour'. In R. B. Lee and L. Devore, eds., *Kalahari Hunter Gatherers:*

Studies of the !Kung and their neighbours. Cambridge, Mass., Harvard University Press.

Boden, M. A. (1987) *Artificial Intelligence and Natural Man*. London, MIT Press.

Bogardus, C., Lillioja, S., Ravussin, E., Abbott, W., Zawadzki, J. K., Young, A., Knowler, W. C., Jacobowitz, R., and Moll, P. P. (1986) 'Familial dependence of the resting metabolic rate'. *New England Journal of Medicine*, 315, 96–100.

Bolgar, H. (1965) 'The case study method'. In B. B. Wolman, ed., *Handbook of Clinical Psychology*, New York, McGraw-Hill.

Bornstein, M. H. (1984) 'Perceptual development'. In M. H. Bornstein and M. E. Lamb, eds., *Developmental Psychology: An advanced textbook*. Hillsdale, N.J., Lawrence Erlbaum Associates.

Bornstein, M. H., Kessen, W., and Weiskopf, S. (1976) 'Colour vision and hue categorization in young human infants'. *Journal of Experimental Psychology: Human Perception and Performance*, 2, 115–29.

Botwinick, J. (1978) *Ageing and Behaviour*. New York, Springer.

Bouchard, T. J., and McGue, M. (1981) 'Familial studies of intelligence: a review'. *Science*, 212, 1055–8.

Bourne, L. E., Ekstrand, B. R., and Dominowski, R. L. (1971) *The Psychology of Thinking*. Englewood Cliffs, N.J., Prentice-Hall.

Bousfield, W. (1953) 'The occurrence of clustering in the recall of randomly arranged associates'. *Journal of General Psychology*, 49, 229–40.

Bower, G., and Karlin, M. (1974) 'Depth of processing pictures of faces and recognition memory'. *Journal of Experimental Psychology*, 103, 751–7.

Bower, T. G. R., Broughton, J. M., and Moore, M. K. (1971) 'Infant responses to approaching objects: an indicator of response to distal variables'. *Perception and Psychophysics*, 9, 193–6.

Bowlby, J. (1951) *Child Care and the Growth of Love*. Harmondsworth, Penguin.

Bowlby, J. (1969) *Attachment and Loss: Vol. 1. Attachment*. London, Hogarth.

Bowles, B., and Gintis, H. (1972 and 1973) 'IQ in the United States class structure'. *Social Policy*, 3 (4 and 5).

Boxall, M. (1976) *The Nurture Group in the Primary School*. Inner London Education Authority.

Bradshaw, J. L., and Nettleton, N. C. (1981) 'The nature of hemispheric specialization'. *Behavioral and Brain Sciences*, 4, 51–91.

Brady, J. V. (1958) 'Ulcers in "executive make-up"'. *Scientific American*, 199, 4, 95–100.

Braine, M. (1963) 'On learning the grammatical order of words'. *Monographs of the Society for Research in Child Development*, 41.

Bransford, J., and Johnson, M. (1973) 'Considerations of some problems of comprehension'. In W. Chase, ed., *Visual Information Processing*. New York, Academic Press.

Brehm, J. W. (1966) *A Theory of Psychological Reactance*. New York, Academic Press.

Brehm, J. W., and Cohen, A. R., eds. (1962) *Explorations in Cognitive Dissonance*. New York, Wiley.

Brehm, S. S., and Brehm, J. W. (1981) *Psychological Reactance: A theory of freedom and control*. New York, Academic Press.

Brekke, N., and Borgida, E. (1988) 'Expert psychological testimony in rape trials: a social-cognitive analysis'. *Journal of Personality and Social Psychology*, 55, 372–86.

Bremer, F. (1937) 'L'activité cérébrale au course du sommeil et de narcose: contribution à l'étude du mécanisme du sommeil'. *Bulletin de l'Académie Royale de Médecine Belgique*, 4, 68–86.

Bremer, F. (1977) 'Cerebral hypnogenic centers'. *Annals of Neurology*, 2, 1– 6.

Broadbent, D. E. (1958) *Perception and Communication*. Oxford, Pergamon.

Broca, P. (1861) 'Remarques sur le siège de la faculté du langage articulé suivees d'une observation d'aphemie'. *Bulletin de la Société Anatomique* (Paris), 6, 330–57.

Brodmann, K. (1909) *Vergleichende Lokalisationlehre der Grosshirnrinde in ihren Prinzipien dargestellt auf Grund des Zellenbaues*. Leipzig, J. A. Barth.

Bronfenbrenner, U. (1970) *Two Worlds of Childhood: U.S. and USSR*. New York, Basic Books.

Bronfenbrenner, U. (1979) *The Ecology of Human Development*. Harvard University Press.

Bronfenbrenner, U. (1986) 'Ecology of the family as a context for human development: research perspectives'. *Developmental Psychology*, 22, 723–42.

Bronfenbrenner, U., and Gabarino, J. (1976) 'The socialization of moral judgement and behaviour in cross-cultural perspective'. In T. Lockona, ed., *Moral Development and Behaviour*. New York, Holt, Rinehart and Winston.

Brophy, J. (1983) 'Research on self-fulfilling prophesy and teacher expectations'. *Journal of Educational Psychology*, 75, 631–61.

Brophy, J. (1986) 'Teacher influences on student achievement'. *American Psychologist*, 41, 1069–77.

Brophy, J. *et al* (1973) 'Effect of teacher sex and student sex on classroom interaction'. *Journal of Educational Psychology*, 65, 1, 74–87.

Browman, C. P. (1978) *Tip of the Tongue and Slip of the Ear: Implications for language processing*. UCLA Working Papers in Phonetics 42.

Brown, G., and Desforges, C. (1979) *Piaget's Theory: A psychological critique*. London, Routledge and Kegan Paul.

Brown, L. K., and Fritz, G. K. (1988) 'Children's knowledge and attitudes about AIDs'. *Journal of the American Academy of Child and Adolescent Psychiatry*, 27, 504–8.

Brown, R. (1965) *Social Psychology*, New York, Wiley.

Brown, R. (1973) *A First Language*. London, Allen & Unwin.

Brown, R. (1986) *Social Psychology*, 2nd edn, New York, Free Press.

Brown, R., and McNeill, D. (1966) 'The "tip of the tongue" phenomenon', *Journal of Verbal Learning and Verbal Behaviour*, 5, 325–37.

Bruce, V., and Green, P. (1985) *Visual Perception: Physiology, psychology and ecology*. Hillsdale, N.J., Lawrence Erlbaum.

Bruner, J. (1959) 'Inhelder and Piaget's "The growth of logical thinking"'. *British Journal of Psychology*, 50, 363–70.

Bruner, J. (1975) 'From communication to language – a psychological perspective'. *Cognition*, 3, 255–87.

Bruner, J. S. (1978) 'Learning how to do things with words'. In J. S. Bruner and A. Garton, eds., *Human Growth and Development: Wolfson College Lectures. 1976*. Oxford, Oxford University Press.

Bruner, J. S. and Goodman, C. C. (1947) 'Value and need as organizing factors in perception'. *Journal of Abnormal and Social Psychology*, 42, 33–44.

Bruner, J. S., and Minturn, A. L. (1955) 'Perceptual identification and perceptual organization'. *Journal of General Psychology*, 53, 21–8.

Bruner, J. S., and Tagiuri, R. (1954) 'The perception of people'. In G. Lindzey, ed., *Handbook of Social Psychology*, Vol. 2. Reading, MA, Addison-Wesley.

Bruner, J. S., Goodnough, J. J., and Austin, G. A. (1956) *A Study of Thinking*. New York, Wiley.

Bryant, P. (1982) Special Issue: 'Piaget: issues and questions'. *B.L.P.* 73, 2. 151–311.

Bryant, P. E., and Trabasso, T. (1971) 'Transitive inferences and memory in young children'. *Nature*, 232, 456–8.

Bugelski, B. R., and Alampay, D. A. (1961) 'The role of frequency in developing perceptual sets'. *Canadian Journal of Psychology*, 15, 205–11.

Bull, P. E., and Mayer, K. (1988) 'Interruptions in political interviews: a study of Margaret Thatcher and Neil Kinnock'. Paper presented to Annual Conference of the British Psychological Society, 15–18 April, Leeds.

Burns, R. B. and Dobson, C. B. (1984) *Introductory Psychology*. Netherlands, Kluwer Academic Publishers.

Burt, C. (1921) *Mental and Scholastic Tests*. London, King.

Burt, C. (1955) 'The evidence for the concept of intelligence'. *British Journal of Educational Psychology*, 25, 158–77.

Burt, C. (1966) 'The genetic determination of differences in intelligence'. *British Journal of Psychology*, 57, 137–53.

Butcher, H. J. (1968) *Human Intelligence: Its nature and assessment*. London, Methuen.

Butler, N. R., and Golding, J., eds. (1986) *From Birth to Five: A study of the health and behaviour of Britain's five-year-olds*. Oxford, Pergamon.

Butterworth, B. L. (1975) 'Hesitation and semantic planning in speech'. *Journal of Psycholinguistic Research*, 4, 75–87.

Campbell, D. T. (1963) 'Social attitudes and other acquired behavioral dispositions'. In S. Koch, ed., *Psychology: A study of science*, Vol. 6. New York, McGraw-Hill.

Campione, J. C., Brown, A. L., Ferrara, R. A., Jones, R. S., and Steinberg, E. (1985) 'Breakdowns in flexible use of information: intelligence-related differences in transfer following equivalent learning performance'. *Intelligence*, 9, 297–315.

Campos, J. J., Langer, A., and Krowitz, A. (1970) 'Cardiac responses on the visual cliff in prelocomotor human infants'. *Science*, 170, 196–7.

Cannon, W. B. (1929) *Bodily Changes in Pain, Hunger, Fear and Rage*. New York, Appleton.

Carey, S., and Diamond, R. (1977) 'From piecemeal to configurational representation of faces'. *Science*, 195, 312–14.

Caro, P. W. (1973) 'Aircraft simulators and pilot training'. *Human Factors*, 15, 502–9.

Caron, A. J., and Caron, R. F. (1981) 'Processing of relational information as an index of infant risk'. In S. Friedman and M. Sigman, eds., *Preterm Birth and Psychological Development*. New York, Academic Press.

Carraher, T., Carraher, D. W., and Schliemann, A. L. (1985) 'Mathematics in streets and schools'. *British Journal of Developmental Psychology*, 3, 21–30.

Carrigan, P. M. (1960) 'Extraversion–introversion as a dimension of personality: a reappraisal'. *Psychological Bulletin*, 57, 329–60.

Casey, M. B. (1986) 'Individual differences in selective attention among pre-readers: a key to mirror-image confusions'. *Developmental Psychology*, 22, 58–66.

Cattell, R. B. (1963) 'Theory of fluid and crystallized intelligence: a critical experiment'. *Journal of Educational Psychology*, 54, 1–22.

Cattell, R. B. (1965) *The Scientific Analysis of Personality*. Harmondsworth, Penguin.

Cattell, R. B., and Nesselroade, J. R. (1967) 'Likeness and completeness – theories examined by the 16-personality factor measure on stably and unstably married couples'. *Journal of Personality and Social Psychology*, 351–61.

Chaiken, S. (1979) 'Communicator physical attractiveness and persuasion'. *Journal of Personality and Social Psychology*, 37, 1387–97.

Chaiken, S., and Eagly, A. H. (1976) 'Communication modality as a determinant of message persuasiveness and message comprehensibility'. *Journal of Personality and Social Psychology*, 34, 605–14.

Chaiken, S., and Eagly, A. H. (1983) 'Communication modality as a determinant of persuasion: the role of communicator salience'. *Journal of Personality and Social Psychology*, 45, 241–56.

Chapanis, N., and Chapanis, A. (1964) 'Cognitive dissonance: five years later'. *Psychological Bulletin*, 61, 1–22.

Cherry, C. (1953) 'Some experiments on the reception of speech with one and with two ears'. *Journal of the Acoustical Society of America*, 25, 975–9.

Cherry, F., Byrne, D., and Mitchell, H. E. (1976) 'Clogs in the bogus pipeline: demand characteristics and social desirability'. *Journal of Research in Personality*, 10, 69–75.

Chow, L. L., Riesen, A. H., and Newell, F. W. (1957) 'Degeneration of retinal ganglion cells in infant chimpanzees reared in darkness'. *Journal of Comparative Neurology*, 107, 27–42.

Cialdini, R. B., Baumann, D. J., and Kenrick, D. T. (1981) 'Insights from sadness: a three step model of the development of altruism as hedonism'. *Developmental Review*, 1, 207–23.

Cialdini, R. B., Petty, R. E., and Cacioppo, J. T. (1981) 'Attitude and attitude change'. *Annual Review of Psychology*, 32, 357–404.

Ciricelli, V. G. (1982) 'Sibling influence throughout the lifespan'. In M. E. Lamb and B. Sutton-Smith, eds., *Sibling Relationships: Their nature and significance across the lifespan*. Hillsdale, N.J., Lawrence Erlbaum Associates.

Clark, E. (1973) 'What's in a word?: on the child's acquisition of semantics in his first language'. In T. E. Moore, ed., *Cognitive Development and the Acquisition of Language*, New York, Academic Press.

Clark, H. H., and Chase, W. G. (1972) 'On the process of comparing sentences against pictures'. *Cognitive Psychology*, 3, 472–517.

Clark, H. H., and Haviland, S. E. (1977) 'Comprehension and the given-new contract'. In R. O. Freedle, ed., *Discourse Production and Comprehension*. Norwood, N.J., Ablex.

Clark, Margaret M. (1976) *Young Fluent Readers: What can they teach us?* London, Heinemann Educational Books.

Clarke, A. D. B., and Clarke, A. M. (1960) 'Some recent advances in the study of early deprivation'. *Journal of Child Psychology and Psychiatry*, 1, 26–36.

Clarke, A. D. B., and Clarke, A. M. (1986) 'Thirty years of child psychology'. *Journal of Child Psychology and Psychiatry*, 27 (6), 719–59.

Clarke, J. E., and Whitehurst, G. S. (1974) 'Asymmetrical stimulus control and the mirror-image problem'. *Journal of Experimental Psychology*, 17, 147–66.

Clarke-Stewart, K. A. (1978) 'And Daddy makes three: The mother–father–infant interaction'. *Child Development*, 49, 466–78.

Clift, S. M., and Stears, D. F. (1988) 'Belief and attitudes regarding AIDS among British college students: a preliminary study of change between November 1987 and May 1987'. *Health Education Research*, 3, 75–88.

Coates, J. (1986) *Women, Men and Language: A sociolinguistic account of sex differences in language*. London, Longman.

Cohen, B. (1966) 'Some-or-none characteristics of coding behaviour'. *Journal of Verbal Learning and Verbal Behaviour*, 5, 182–7.

Cohen, G. (1979) 'Language comprehension in old age'. *Cognitive Psychology*, 11, 412–29.

Cohen, G. (1981) 'Inferential reasoning in old age'. *Cognition*, 9, 59–72.

Cohen, G. (1983) *The Psychology of Cognition*. London, Academic Press.

Cohen, L. B., and Salapatek, P. (1975) *Infant Perception: From sensation to cognition*, Vols. 1 and 2. New York, Academic Press.

Coladarci, A. P. (1956) 'The relevance of educational psychology'. *Educational Leadership*, 12, 489–92.

Colby, A., and Kohlberg, L., *et al* (1983) *A Longitudinal Study of Moral Judgement*. Harvard, Harvard University Press.

Cole, M., and Bruner, J. S. (1971) 'Cultural differences and inferences about psychological processes'. *American Psychologist*, 26, 867–76.

Cole, M., Gay, J., Glick, J. A., and Sharp, D. W. (1971) *The Cultural Context of Learning and Thinking: An exploration in experimental anthropology*. London, Methuen.

Coleman, J. C. (1980) *The Nature of Adolescence*. London, Methuen.

Coles, M. G., Gale, A., and Kline, P. (1971) 'Personality and habituation of the orienting reaction: tonic and response measures of electrodermal activity'. *Psychophysiology*, 8, 54–63.

Collett, P., and Marsh, P. (1974) 'Patterns of public behaviour: collision avoidance on a pedestrian crossing'. *Semiotica*, 12, 281–99.

Collins, A., and Loftus, E. (1975) 'A spreading-activation theory of semantic processing'. *Psychological Review*, 82, 407–28.

Collins, A., and Quillian, M. R. (1969) 'Retrieval time from semantic memory'. *Journal of Verbal Learning and Verbal Behaviour*, 8, 240–7.

Collins, A., and Quillian, M. R. (1972) 'Experiments on semantic memory and language comprehension'. In L. Gregg, ed., *Cognition in Learning and Memory*. New York, Wiley.

Coltheart, M., Patterson, K., and Marshall, J. C., eds. (1980) *Deep Dyslexia*. London, Routledge and Kegan Paul.

Condry, J., and Condry, S. (1976) 'Sex differences: a study of the eye of the beholder'. *Child Development*, 47, 812–19.

Conger, R., and Killeen, P. (1974) 'Use of concurrent operants in small group research'. *Pacific Sociological Review*, 17, 399–416.

Conrad, R. (1962) 'An association between memory errors and errors due to acoustic maskings of speech'. *Nature*, 193, 1314–15.

Conrad, R. (1964) 'Acoustic confusion in immediate memory'. *British Journal of Psychology*, 55, 75–84.

Cook, M. (1984) *Levels of Personality*. London, Holt, Rinehart and Winston.

Cooke and Lawson (1984) 'Support for carers of disabled children'. *Child: Care, Health and Development*, 10, 67–79.

Coren, S., and Porac, C. (1978) 'Iris pigmentation and visual-geometric illusions'. *Perception*, 7, 473–8.

Corteen, R. S., and Wood, B. (1972) 'Autonomic responses to shock-associated words in an unattended channel'. *Journal of Experimental Psychology*, 94, 308–13.

Corter, C., Abramovitch, R., and Pepler, D. J. (1983) 'The role of the mothers in sibling interactions'. *Child Development*, 54, 1599–1605.

Craik, F. I. M., and Lockhart, R. (1972) 'Levels of processing: a framework for memory research'. *Journal of Verbal Learning and Verbal Behaviour*, 11, 671–84.

Craik, F. I. M., and Watkins, M. (1973) 'The role of rehearsal in short-term memory'. *Journal of Verbal Learning and Verbal Behaviour*, 12, 599–607.

Crispin, L., Hamilton, W., and Trickey, G. (1984) 'The relevance of visual sequential memory to reading'. *British Journal of Educational Psychology*, 54 (I), 24–31.

Cromer, R. F. (1974) 'The development of language and cognition: the cognition hypothesis'. In B. Foss, ed., *New Perspectives in Child Development*, Harmondsworth, Penguin.

Cronbach, L. J. (1960) *Essentials of Psychological Testing*. New York, Harper and Row.

Crossman, E. R. (1957) 'The speed and accuracy of simple hand movements'. In *The Nature and Acquisition of Industrial Skills*. Report to M.R.C. and D.S.I.R. Joint Committee on Individual Efficiency in Industry.

Crouter, A. C., Perry-Jenkins, M., Huston, T. L., and McHale, S. M. (1987) 'Processes underlying fathers' involvement in dual-earner and single-earner families'. *Developmental Psychology*, 23, 431–40.

Cumming, E., and Henry, W. E. (1961) *Growing Old*. New York, Basic Books.

Curran, H. V. (1988) 'Relative universals: perspectives on culture and cognition'. In G. Claxton, ed., *Growth Points in Cognition*. London, Routledge.

Curtiss, S. (1977) *Genie*. New York, Academic Press.

Curtiss, S. (1988) 'The special talent of grammar acquisition'. In L. K. Obler and D. Fein, eds., *The Exceptional Brain*. N.Y., Guilford Press.

Czeisler, C. A., Weitzman, E. D., Moore-Ede, M. C., Zimmerman, J. C., and Knauer, R. S. (1980) 'Human sleep: its duration and organization depend on its circadian phase'. *Science*, 210, 1264–7.

Darley, B. W., and Gross, P. H. (1983) 'A hypothesis-confirming bias in labelling effects'. *Journal of Personality and Social Psychology*, 44, 20–33.

Daston, P. G. (1956) 'Perception of homosexual words in paranoid schizophrenia'. *Perceptual Motor Skills*, 45–55.

Davey, A. (1983) *Learning to be Prejudiced: Growing up in a multi-ethnic Britain*. London, Arnold.

Davey, G., and Cullen, C. (1988) *Human Operant Conditioning and Behaviour Modification*. Chichester, Wiley.

David, O. J. (1984) 'The relationship of lead to learning and behavioural disabilities'. *Advances in Learning and Behavioural Disabilities*, 3, 41–56.

Davison, G. C., and Neale, J. M. (1990) *Abnormal Psychology – An experimental clinical approach*, 4th edn. New York, Wiley.

Davitz, J. R. (1955) 'Social perception and sociometric choice in children'. *Journal of Abnormal Social Psychology*, 50, 173–6.

Dawkins, R. (1976) *The Selfish Gene*. Oxford, Oxford University Press.

Dawkins, R. (1987) *The Blind Watchmaker*. Harmondsworth, Penguin.

Dawson, M. E., and Schell, A. M. (1982) 'Electrodermal responses to attended and nonattended significant stimuli during dichotic listening'. *Journal of Experimental Psychology: Human Perception and Performance*, 8, 82–6.

De Bono, E. (1976) *Teaching Thinking*. Harmondsworth, Penguin.

Deci, E. L., and Ryan, R. M. (1980) 'The empirical exploration of intrinsic motivational processes'. In L. Berkowitz, ed., *Advances in Experimental Social Psychology*, Vol. 13. New York, Academic Press.

DeFleur, M. I., and Westie, F. R. (1963) 'Attitude as a scientific concept'. *Social Forces*, 42, 17–31.

Deregowski, J. B. (1980) *Illusions, Patterns and Pictures*. London, Academic Press.

Deutsch, J. A., and Deutsch, D. (1963) 'Attention: some theoretical considerations'. *Psychological Review*, 70, 80–90.

Diener, E. (1979) 'Deindividuation, self-awareness and disinhibition'. *Journal of Personality and Social Psychology*, 37, 1160–71.

Diener, E., Fraser, S. C., Beaman, A. L., and Kelem, R. T. (1976) 'Effects of deindividuation variables on stealing among Hallowe'en "trick or treaters"'. *Journal of Personality and Social Psychology*, 33, 497–507, 178–83.

Ditchburn, R. W., and Ginsborg, B. L. (1952) 'Vision with a stabilized retinal image'. *Nature*, 170, 36–7.

Dobson, V., and Teller, D. Y. (1978) 'Visual acuity in human infants: a review and comparison of behavioural and electrophysiological studies'. *Vision Research*, 18, 1469–83.

Dobzhansky, T. (1962) *Mankind Evolving: The evolution of the human species*. Newhaven, Conn., Yale University Press.

Dollard, J. Doob, L. W., Miller, N. E., Mowrer, O. H., and Sears, R. R. (1939) *Frustration and Aggression*. Newhaven, Conn., Yale University Press.

Donaldson, M., and McGarrigle, J. (1974) 'Some clues to the nature of semantic development'. *Journal of Child Language*, 1, 185–94.

Doob, L. W. (1947) 'The behaviour of attitudes'. *Psychological Review*, 54, 135–56.

Dore, J. (1977) 'Oh them sheriff: a pragmatic analysis of children's responses to questions'. In S. M. Ervin-Tripp and C. Mitchell-Kernan, eds, *Adult–Child Conversation*. London, Croom Helm.

Douglas, J. W. B., and Ross, J. M. (1964) 'Age of puberty related to educational ability'. *Journal of Child Psychology and Psychiatry*, 5, 185–96.

Dudycha, G. J. (1936) 'An objective study of punctuality in relation to personality and achievement'. *Archives of Psychology*, 204.

Duncan, B. (1976) 'Differential social perception and attribution of intergroup violence: testing the lower limits of stereotyping blacks'. *Journal of Personality and Social Psychology*, 34, 590–8.

Duncan, C. (1949) 'The retroactive effect of electro-shock on learning'. *Journal of Comparative Physiology*, 42, 32–44.

Duncan, S., and Fiske, D. W. (1977) *Face to Face Interaction: Research methods and theory*. Hillsdale, N.J., Lawrence Erlbaum Associates.

Dunn, J. (1977) *Distress and Comfort*. London, Fontana.

Dunn, J. (1984) *Brothers and Sisters*. London, Fontana.

Dunn, J. (1986) 'Growing up in a family world: issues in the study of social development in young children'. In M. Richards and P. Light, eds, *Children of Social Worlds*. Cambridge, Polity Press.

Dunn, J. (1988) *The Beginnings of Social Understanding*. Oxford, Blackwell.

Dunn, J., and Kendrick, C. (1982) *Siblings: Love, envy and understanding*. London, Grant McIntyre.

Duval, S., and Wicklund, R. A. (1972) *A Theory of Objective Self Awareness*, New York, Academic Press.

Eagly, A. H. and Warren, R. (1976) 'Intelligence, comprehension and opinion change'. *Journal of Personality*, 44, 226–42.

Eccles, J. C., Fatt, P., and Koketsu, K. (1954) 'Cholinergic and inhibitory synapses in a pathway from motor-axon collaterals to motor neurones'. *Journal of Physiology*. (London), 216, 524–62.

Edwards, A. (1957) *Techniques of Attitude Scale Construction*. New York, Appleton-Century-Crofts.

Egan, J. P. (1975) *Signal Detection Theory and ROC Analysis*. New York, Academic Press.

Eisenberg, R. (1976) *Auditory Competence in Early Life: The roots of communicative behaviour*. Baltimore, University Park Press.

Eiser, R. J. (1978) 'Co-operation and competition between individuals'. In H. Tajfel and C. Fraser, eds, *Introducing Social Psychology*. Harmondsworth, Penguin.

Ekman, P., Levenson, R. W., and Friesen, W. V. (1983) 'Autonomic nervous system activity distinguishes among emotions'. *Science*, 221, 1208–10.

Ellis, A. (1984) 'Rational-emotive therapy'. In R. J. Corsini, ed., *Current Psychotherapies*, 3rd edn. Itaska, Ill., Peacock Press.

Ellis, A., and Beattie, G. (1986) *The Psychology of Language Communication*. London, Weidenfeld and Nicolson.

Ellis, A. W., Miller, D., and Sin, G. (1983) 'Wernicke's aphasia and normal language processing: a case study in cognitive neuropsychology'. *Cognition*, 15, 111–14.

Ellis, H., and Hunt, R. (1983) *Fundamentals of Human Memory Cognition*. Iowa, W.C. Brown.

Ericsson, K., and Simon, H. (1980) 'Verbal reports as data'. *Psychological Review*, 87, 215–51.

Erikson, E. (1965) *Childhood and Society*. London, Pelican.

Esposito, A. (1979) 'Sex differences in children's conversations'. *Language and Speech*, 22, 213–21.

Estes, W. K. (1975) 'The locus of inferential and perceptual processes in letter identification'. *Journal of Experimental Psychology: General*, 2, 122–45.

Evans, C. (1973) 'Parapsychology – what the questionnaire revealed'. *New Scientist*, 57, 209.

Evans, J. St. B. T. (1984) 'Heuristic and analytic processes in reasoning'. *British Journal of Psychology*, 75, 451–68.

Evans, J. St. B. T., and Lynch, J. S. (1973) 'Matching bias in the selection task'. *British Journal of Psychology*, 64, 391–7.

Evans, P. D., and Moran, P. (1987) 'The Framingham Type A scale, vigilant coping and heart-rate activity'. *Journal of Behavioural Medicine*, 10, 311–21.

Evans, P. D., Phillips, K., and Fearn, J. (1984) 'On choosing to make aversive events predictable or unpredictable: some behavioural and psychophysiological findings'. *British Journal of Psychology*, 75, 377–91.

Evans, P. D., Pitts, M. K., and Smith, K. (1988) 'Minor infection, minor life events and the four-day desirability dip'. *Journal of Psychosomatic Research*, 32, 4/5, 533–9.

Ewart, P. H. (1930) 'A study of the effect of inverted retinal stimulation upon spatially co-ordinated behaviour'. *Genetic Psychology Monographs*, 7, 177–366.

Eysenck, H. J. (1952) *The Scientific Study of Personality*. London, Routledge and Kegan Paul.

Eysenck, H. J. (1955) 'Cortical inhibition, figural after-effects and theory of personality'. *Journal of Abnormal and Social Psychology*, 51, 94–106.

Eysenck, H. J. (1971a) *Race, Intelligence and Education*. London, Temple Smith/ New Society.

Eysenck, H. J. (1971b) *Readings in Extraversion–Introversion*, Vol. 3. London, Staples Press.

Eysenck, H. J. (1972) 'The experimental study of Freudian concepts'. *Bulletin, British Psychological Society*, 25, 261–7.

Eysenck, H. J. (1986) 'Toward a new model of intelligence'. *Personality and Individual Differences*, 7, 731–6.

Eysenck, H. J., and Eysenck, S. B. G. (1969) *The Structure and Measurement of Personality*. London, Routledge and Kegan Paul.

Eysenck, M. (1975) 'I remember you, you're ...'. *New Behaviour*, 2, 222–3.

Eysenck, M. (1978) 'Verbal remembering'. In B. M. Foss, ed., *Psychology Survey No. 1*. London, Allen and Unwin.

Eysenck, M. (1984) *A Handbook of Cognitive Psychology*. London, Lawrence Erlbaum Associates.

Eysenck, M. (1986) 'Working memory'. In G. Cohen, M. Eysenck and M. LeVoi, eds, *Memory: A cognitive approach*. Milton Keynes, Open University Press.

Eysenck, M. W., and Eysenck, H. J. (1980) 'Mischel and the concept of personality'. *British Journal of Psychology*, 71, 71–83.

Fantz, R. L. (1961) 'The origin of form perception'. *Scientific American*, 204(5), 66–72.

Fairweather, H. (1982) 'Sex differences: little reason for females to play midfield'. In J. G. Beaumont, ed., *Divided Visual Field Studies of Cerebral Organization*. London, Academic Press.

Fantino, E., and Logan, C. (1979) *The Experimental Analysis of Behavior: A biological approach*. San Francisco, Freeman.

Faust, M. S. (1960) 'Developmental maturity as a determinant in prestige of adolescent girls'. *Child Development*, 31, 173–84.

Fawl, C. (1963) 'Disturbances experienced by children in their natural habitat'. In R. G. Barker, ed., *The Stream of Behaviour*. New York, Appleton.

Ferster, C. B., and Skinner, B. F. (1957) *Schedules of Reinforcement*. Englewood Cliffs, N.J., Prentice-Hall.

Feshbach, S., and Singer, R. D. (1971) *Television and Aggression: an experimental field study*, San Francisco, Jossey-Bass.

Festinger, L. (1957) *A Theory of Cognitive Dissonance*. Evanston, Ill., Row, Peterson.

Festinger, L., and Maccoby, N. (1964) 'On resistance to persuasive communications'. *Journal of Abnormal and Social Psychology*, 68, 359–66.

Feuerstein, R., Rand Y., Hoffman, M. B., and Miller, R. (1980) *Instrumental Enrichment*. Baltimore, University Park Press.

Fiedler, F. E. (1978) 'The contingency model and the dynamics of the leadership process'. In L. Berkowitz, ed., *Advances in Experimental Social Psychology*, Vol. 11. New York, Academic Press.

Field, T. (1978) 'Interaction patterns of primary versus secondary caretaking fathers'. *Developmental Psychology*, 14, 183–5.

Fine, S. (1987) 'Children in divorce, custody and access situations: an update'. *Journal of Child Psychology and Psychiatry*, 28, 361–4.

Firestone, G., and Brody, N. (1975) 'Longitudinal investigation of teacher–student interactions and their relation to academic performance'. *Journal of Educational Psychology*, 67, 544–50.

Fishbein, M., and Ajzen, I. (1975) *Belief, Attitude, Intention and Behavior: An introduction to theory and research*. Reading, Mass., Addison-Wesley.

Fiske, S. T., and Taylor, S. E. (1984) *Social Cognition*. Reading, Mass., Addison-Wesley.

Flavell, J. H. (1963) *The Developmental Psychology of Jean Piaget*. New York, Van Nostrand Reinhold.

Floyd, H. H. jnr., and South, D. R. (1972) 'Dilemma of youth: the choice of parents or peers as a frame of reference for behaviour'. *Journal of Marriage and the Family*, 34, 627–34.

Fodor, J. (1983) *The Modularity of Mind*. MIT Press.

Fogelman, K. (1976) *Britain's sixteen-year-olds*. National Children's Bureau.

Fong, G., Krantz, D. H., and Nisbett, R. E. (1986) 'The effects of statistical training on thinking about everyday problems'. *Cognitive Psychology*, 18, 253–92.

Fontana, D., ed. (1984) *Behaviourism and Learning Theory in Education*. British Journal of Educational Psychology Monograph Series No. 1, Edinburgh, Scottish Academic Press.

Francis, H., ed. (1985) *Learning to Teach: Psychology in teacher training*. Lewes, Falmer.

Frankenhaeuser, M. (1983) 'The sympathetic-adrenal and pituitary-adrenal response to challenge: comparison between the sexes'. In T. M. Dembroski, T. H. Schmidt and G. Blumchen, eds, *Behavioral Bases of Coronary Heart Disease*. Basel, S. Karger.

Frankenhaeuser, M., Dunne, E., and Lundberg, U. (1976) 'Sex differences in sympathetic-adrenal medullary reactions induced by different stressors'. *Psychopharmacology*, 47, 1–5.

Frankenhaeuser, M., Fauste-Von Wright, M., Collins, A., von Wright, J., Sedvall, G., and Swahn, C. G. (1978) 'Sex differences in psychoneuroendocrine reactions to examination stress'. *Psychosomatic Medicine*, 40, 334–43.

Franks, C. M. (1956) 'Conditioning and personality. A study of normal and neurotic subjects'. *Journal of Abnormal and Social Psychology*, 52, 143.

Frederiksen, N. (1986) 'Toward a broader conception of intelligence'. *American Psychologist*, 41, 445–52.

Freeman, D. (1983) *Margaret Mead and Samoa: the making and unmaking of an anthropological myth*. Harvard University Press.

Freeman, F. S. (1962) *Theory and Practice of Psychological Testing*. New York, Holt.

French, J. R. P., and Raven, B. (1959) 'The bases of social power'. In D. Cartwright, ed., *Studies in Social Power*, Ann Arbor, University of Michigan Press.

Freud, S. (1900) *The Interpretation of Dreams*. London, Allen and Unwin (1938).

Freud, S. (1901) *The Psychopathology of Everyday Life*. Harmondsworth, Penguin (1975).

Friedman, M., and Rosenman, R. H. (1974) *Type A Behaviour and Your Heart*. New York, Knopf.

Friedrich, L. K., and Stein, A. H. (1973) 'Aggressive and pro-social television programmes and the natural behaviour of pre-school children'. *Monographs of the Society for Research in Child Development*, 38, 4.

Fromkin, V. A., ed. (1973) *Speech Errors as Linguistic Evidence*. The Hague, Mouton.

Fromkin, V. A., ed. (1980) *Errors in Linguistic Performance: Slips of the tongue, ear, pen and hand*. New York, Academic Press.

Funkenstein, D. H. (1956) 'Norepinephrine-like and epinephrine-like substances in relation to human behavior'. *Journal of Mental Diseases*, 24, 58–68.

Furstenburg, F. F., and Seltzer, J. A. (1986) 'Divorce and child development'. In P. A. Adler and P. Adler, eds, *Sociological Studies of Child Development*, Vol. 1. London, J.A.I. Press.

Gaes, G. G., Quigley-Fernandez, B., and Tedeschi, J. T. (1978) 'Unclogging the bogus pipeline: a critical reanalysis of the Cherry, Byrne and Mitchell study'. *Journal of Research in Personality*, 12, 189–92.

Gagné, R. M. (1962) 'Military training and principles of learning'. *American Psychologist*, 17, 83–91.

Gagné, R. M. (1985) *The Conditions of Learning*, 4th edn. London, Holt, Rinehart and Winston.

Gardner, H. (1983) *Frames of Mind: The theory of multiple intelligences*. London, Paladin.

Gardner, H. (1986) *The Mind's New Science: A history of the cognitive revolution*. New York, Basic Books.

Gardner, R. A., and Gardner, B. T. (1969) 'Teaching language to a chimpanzee'. *Science*, 165, 664–72.

Garmezy, N. (1984) 'Risk and protective factors in children vulnerable to major mental disorders'. In L. Grinspoon, ed., *Psychiatry 1983*, Vol. 3. Washington, DC, American Psychiatric Press.

Garn, S. M. (1961) *Human Races*. Springfield, Ill., Thomas.

Garvey, C. (1977) *Play*. London, Fontana.

Garvey, C., and Berninger, G. (1981) 'Timing and turn-taking in children's conversations'. *Discourse Processes*, 4, 27–57.

Gellert, E. (1955) 'Systematic observation: a method in child study'. *Harvard Educational Review*, 25, 179–95.

Gellhorn, E., and Loufbourrow, G. N. (1963) *Emotions and Emotional Disorders: A neurophysiological study*. New York, Harper and Row.

Gerbner, G. (1972) 'Violence in TV drama'. In *TV and Social Behaviour*, Vol. 1, Washington, DC, Government Printing Office.

Gibbs, J., Young, R. C., and Smith, G. P. (1972) 'Effect of gut hormones on feeding behaviour in the rat'. *Federation Proceedings*, 31, 397.

Gibson, E. J., and Spelke, E. S. (1983) 'The development of perception'. In J. H. Flavell and E. M. Markman, eds, *Handbook of Child Psychology: Cognitive development*, Vol. 3. New York, Wiley.

Gibson, E. J., and Walk, R. D. (1961) 'A comparative and analytical study of visual depth perception'. *Psychological Monographs*, 75 (15), 2–34.

Gibson, J. J. (1933) 'Adaptation, after-effect and contrast in the perception of curved lines'. *Journal of Experimental Psychology*, 16, 1–31.

Gibson, J. J. (1979) *The Ecological Approach to Visual Perception*. Boston, Houghton Mifflin.

Gick, M. L., and Holyoak, K. J. (1980) 'Analogical problem solving'. *Cognitive Psychology*, 12, 306–55.

Giles, H., and Powesland, P. F. (1975) 'Speech Style and Social Evaluation'. *European Monographs in Social Psychology, 7*. London, Academic Press.

Gillig, P. M., and Greenwald, A. G. (1974) 'Is it time to lay the sleeper effect to rest?' *Journal of Personality and Social Psychology*, 29, 132–9.

Gilligan, C. (1972) *In a Different Voice: Psychological theory and women's development*. Cambridge, Mass., Harvard University Press.

Gleitman, L., Newport, E., and Gleitman, H. (1984) 'The current status of the motherese hypothesis'. *Journal of Child Language*, 11, 43–79.

Gleitman, L. R., and Wanner, E., eds (1982) *Language Acquisition: The state of the art*. Cambridge University Press.

Glucksberg, S. (1988) 'Language and thought'. In R. J. Sternberg and E. E. Smith, eds, *The Psychology of Human Thought*. Cambridge University Press.

Glueck, S., and Glueck, E. (1956) *Physique and Delinquency*. New York, Harper.

Goffman, E. (1968) *Asylums: Essays on the social attitudes of mental patients and other inmates*. Harmondsworth, Penguin.

Goffman, E. (1971) *The Presentation of Self in Everyday Life*. Harmondsworth, Penguin.

Goldberg, S. B. (1981) 'Infant irritability, mother responsiveness, and social support influences on the security of infant–mother attachment'. *Child Development*, 52, 857–65.

Goldman-Eisler, F. (1968) *Psycholinguistics: Experiments in spontaneous speech*. London, Academic Press.

Golinkoff, R. M., and Ames, G. J. (1979) 'A comparison of fathers' and mothers' speech with their young children'. *Child Development*, 50, 28–32.

Goodall, J. (1963) 'My life among wild chimpanzees'. *National Geographic*, 124, 272–308.

Goodenough, F. L. and Leahy, A. M. (1927) 'The effect of certain family relationships upon the development of personality'. *Journal of Genetic Psychology*, 34, 45–71.

Gordon, W. J. J. (1961) *Synectics*. New York, Harper and Row.

Gottesman, I. I. (1963) 'Heritability of personality: a demonstration'. *Psychological Monographs*, 77 (9), 21.

Gottesman, I., and Shields, J. (1972) *Schizophrenia and Genetics: A twin study vantage point*. New York, Academic Press.

Govier, E., and Pitts, K. (1982) 'Contextual disambiguation of a polysemous word in an unattended message'. *British Journal of Psychology*, 73, 537–45.

Gray, J. (1971) *The Psychology of Fear and Stress*. London, Weidenfeld and Nicolson.

Greenfield, P. M., and Smith, J. H. (1976) *The Structure of Communication in Early Language Development*. New York, Academic Press.

Greenwald, A. G. (1975) 'On the inconclusiveness of "crucial" cognitive tests of dissonance versus self-perception theories'. *Journal of Experimental Social Psychology*, 11, 490–9.

Gregor, A. J., and McPherson, D. A. (1965) 'A study of susceptibility to geometric illusions among cultural outgroups of Australian aborigines'. *Psychologica Africana*, 11, 1–13.

Gregory, R. L. (1966) *Eye and Brain*. London, Weidenfeld and Nicolson.

Gregory, R. L., and Wallace, J. (1963) *Recovery from Early Blindness*. Cambridge, Heffer.

Grice, H. P. (1975) 'Logic and conversation'. In P. Cole and J. L. Morgan, eds, *Syntax and Semantics*, Vol. 3. New York, Academic Press.

Grossman, F. K., Pollack, W. S., and Golding, E. (1988) 'Fathers and children: predicting the quality and quantity of fathering'. *Developmental Psychology*, 24, 82–91.

Gruder, C. L., Cook, T. D., Hennigan, K. M., Flay, B. R., Allessis, C., and Halamaj, J. (1978) 'Empirical test of the absolute sleeper effect predicted from the discounting cue hypothesis'. *Journal of Personality and Social Psychology*, 36, 1061–74.

Guilford, J. P. (1967) *The Nature of Human Intelligence*. New York, McGraw-Hill.

Guilford, J. P. (1982) 'Cognitive psychology's ambiguities: some suggested remedies'. *Psychological Review*, 89, 48–59.

Hagen, M. A., and Jones, R. K. (1978) 'Cultural effects on pictorial perception: how many words is one picture really worth?'. In R. D. Walk and H. L. Pick, eds, *Perception and Experience*. New York, Plenum.

Haith, M. M. (1980) *Rule that Babies Look By*. Hillsdale, N.J., Lawrence Erlbaum Associates.

Haith, M. M., Bergman, T., and Moore, M. J. (1977) 'Eye contact and face scanning in early infancy'. *Science*, 198, 853–5.

Halford, G. S. (1972) 'The impact of Piaget in the seventies'. In B. M. Foss, ed., *New Horizons in Psychology*, Harmondsworth, Penguin.

Hall, G. S. (1904) *Adolescence*. Englewood Cliffs, N.J., Prentice-Hall.

Halliday, M. A. K. (1975) *Learning How to Mean*. London, Edward Arnold.

Halsey, A. H. (1972) *Educational Priority*, Vol. 1 *E.P.A. Problems and Policies*. HMSO.

Hammerton, M. (1977) 'Transfer and simulation'. In *Human Operators and Simulation*. London, Institute of Measurement and Control.

Haney, C., Banks, W., and Zimbardo, P. (1973) 'Interpersonal dynamics in a simulated prison'. *International Journal of Criminology*, 1, 69–97.

Hannon, P. (1987) 'A study of the effect of parental involvement in the teaching of reading on children's reading test performance'. *British Journal of Educational Psychology*, 57, 56–73.

Hanson, D. J. (1980) 'Relationship between methods and findings in attitude-behavior research'. *Psychology*, 17, 11–13.

Hardyck, C., and Petrinovich, L. F. (1977) 'Left-handedness'. *Psychological Bulletin*, 84, 385–404.

Hargreaves, D. (1967) *Social Relations in a Secondary School*. London, Routledge and Kegan Paul.

Hargreaves, D., Hestor, S. K., and Mellor, F. J. (1975) *Deviance in Classrooms*. London, Routledge and Kegan Paul.

Harper, J. F., and Collins, J. K. (1972) 'The effects of early or late maturation on the prestige of the adolescent girl'. *Australian and New Zealand Journal of Sociology*, 8, 83–8.

Hartshorne, H., and May, M. (1932) *Studies in the Nature of Character*. New York, Macmillan.

Harre, R., and Secord, P. (1972) *The Explanation of Social Behaviour*. Oxford, Blackwell.

Harris, M., and Coltheart, M. (1986) *Language Processing in Children and Adults*. London, Routledge and Kegan Paul.

Harris, M., Jones, D., Brookes, S., and Grant, J. (1986) 'Relations between the non-verbal context of maternal speech and rate of language development'. *British Journal of Developmental Psychology*, 4.

Harris, M. J., and Rosenthal, R. (1985) 'Mediation of interpersonal expectancy effects: 31 meta analyses'. *Psychological Bulletin*, 97, 363–86.

Hartshorne, H., and May, M. A. (1928) *Studies in the Nature of Character, Vol. 1: Studies in Deceit*. New York, Macmillan.

Hartup, W. W. (1983) 'Peer relations'. In E. M. Hetherington, ed., *Handbook of Child Psychology, Vol. 4: Socialization, Personality and Social Development*, 4th edn. New York, Wiley.

Harvey, P. G. (1984) 'Lead and children's health: recent research and future questions'. *Journal of Child Psychology and Psychiatry and Allied Disciplines*, 25, 517–22.

Hass, R. G. (1981) 'Effects of source characteristics on the cognitive processing of persuasive messages and attitude change'. In R. Petty, T. Ostrom and T. Brock, eds, *Cognitive Responses in Persuasion*. Hillsdale, N.J., Lawrence Erlbaum Associates.

Havighurst, R. J. (1952) *Developmental Tasks and Education*. New York, McKay.

Havighurst, R. J. (1972) *The History of Developmental Psychology*. New York, Academic Press.

Havighurst, R. J., *et al* (1968) 'Disengagement and patterns of ageing'. In B. L. Neugarten, ed., *Middle Age and Ageing*. University of Chicago Press.

Haviland, S. E., and Clark, H. H. (1974) 'What's new? Acquiring new information as a process in comprehension'. *Journal of Verbal Learning and Verbal Behaviour*, 13, 512–21.

Hebb, D. (1949) *The Organization of Behaviour*. New York, Wiley.

Hebb, D., and Foord, E. (1945) 'Errors of visual recognition and the nature of the trace'. *Journal of Experimental Psychology*, 35, 335–48.

Heider, F. (1958) *The Psychology of Interpersonal Relations*. New York, Wiley.

Heinicke, C. M. (1984) 'The impact of prebirth parent personality and marital functioning on family development'. *Developmental Psychology*, 20, 1044–53.

Held, R., and Hein, A. (1963) 'Movement-produced stimulation in the development of visually guided behaviour'. *Journal of Comparative and Physiological Psychology*, 56, 607–13.

Henle, M. (1962) 'On the relation between logic and thinking'. *Psychological Review*, 69, 366–78.

Hensall, C., and McGuire, J. (1986) 'Gender development'. In M. Richards and P. Light, eds, *Children of Social Worlds*. Cambridge, Polity Press.

Herman, R. (1984) 'The genetic relationship between identical twins'. *Early Child Development*, 16, 265–75.

Herrnstein, R. J. (1970) 'On the law of effect'. *Journal of Experimental Analysis of Behavior*, 13, 243–66.

Hess, R. D., and Shipman, V. C. (1965) 'Early experience and socialization of cognitive modes in children'. *Child Development*, 34 (4), 869–86.

Hetherington, A. W., and Ranson, S. W. (1942) 'The relation of various hypothalamic lesions to adiposity in the rat'. *Journal of Comparative Neurology*, 76, 475–99.

Hetherington, E. M., Cox, M., and Cox, R. (1982) 'Effects of divorce on parents and children'. In M. Lamb, ed., *Non-Traditional Families*. Hillsdale, N.J., Lawrence Erlbaum Associates.

Hill, J. P. (1980) *The Early Adolescent and the Family*. University of Chicago Press.

Himmelfarb, S., and Eagly, A. H. (1974) 'Orientations to the study of attitudes and their change'. In S. Himmelfarb and A. H. Eagly, eds, *Readings in Attitude Change*. New York, Wiley.

Hitch, G. (1980) 'Developing the concept of working memory'. In G. Claxton, ed., *Cognitive Psychology: New directions*. London, Routledge and Kegan Paul.

Hoffman, L. W. (1984) 'Work, family and the socialization of the child'. In R. D. Parke, ed., *Review of Child Development Research, Vol. 7: The Family*. Chicago, University of Chicago Press.

Hoffman, M. (1975) 'Developmental synthesis of affect and cognition and its implications for altruistic motivation'. *Developmental Psychology*, 11, 607–22.

Holding, D. H. (1988) *Human Skills*, 2nd edn. Chichester, Wiley.

Holmes, D. S. (1974) 'Investigations of repression: differential recall of material experimentally or naturally associated with ego threat'. *Psychological Bulletin*, 81, 632–53.

Holmes, D. S., and Schallow, J. R. (1969) 'Reduced recall after ego threat: repression or response competition?'. *Journal of Personality and Social Psychology*, 13, 145–52.

Hopkins, W. (1988) 'Needle sharing and street behavior in response to AIDS in New York City'. *National Institute on Drug Abuse: Research Monograph Series*, 80, 18–27.

Horn, J. L. (1970) 'Organization of data on lifespan development of human abilities'. In L. Goule and P. Balters, eds, *Lifespan and Developmental Psychology*. New York, Academic Press.

Horn, J. L. (1982) 'The ageing of human abilities'. In B. B. Wolman, ed., *Handbook of Developmental Psychology*. Englewood Cliffs, N.J., Prentice-Hall.

Horne, J. A. (1978) 'A review of the biological effects of total sleep deprivation in man'. *Biological Psychology*, 7, 55–102.

Horne, J. A. (1979) 'Restitution and human sleep: a critical review'. *Physiological Psychology*, 7, 115–25.

Hovland, C. I., Lumsdaine, A. A., and Sheffield, F. D. (1949) *Experiments on Mass Communication*. Princeton, N.J., Princeton University Press.

Hovland, C. I., and Weiss, W. (1951) 'The influence of source credibility on communication effectiveness'. *Public Opinion Quarterly*, 15, 635–50.

Howe, M. J. A. (1988) 'Intelligence as an explanation'. *British Journal of Psychology*, 79, 349–60.

Howes, D. H., and Solomon, R. L. (1950) 'A note on McGinnies' emotionality and perceptual defense'. *Psychological Review*, 57, 229–34.

Hubel, D. H. (1979) 'The visual cortex of normal and deprived monkeys'. *American Scientist*, 67 (5), 532–43.

Hubel, D. H., and Wiesel, T. N. (1962) 'Receptive fields, binocular interaction and functional architecture in the cat's visual cortex'. *Journal of Physiology* (London), 160, 106–54.

Hubel, D. H., and Wiesel, T. N. (1979) 'Brain mechanisms of vision'. *Scientific American*. 241, 130–44.

Huesmann, L. R., *et al* (1983) 'Measuring patterns of fantasy behaviour'. *Journal of Personality and Social Psychology*, 42, 2, 347–68.

Hunt, E. (1980) 'Intelligence as an information-processing concept'. *British Journal of Psychology*, 71, 449–74.

Hunt, J. McV. (1963) 'Motivational interest in information processing and action'. In O. J. Harvey, *Motivation and Social Interaction*. Ronald Press.

Huntington, G. S., Simeonson, R. J., Bailey, D. B., and Comfort, M. (1987) 'Handicapped child characteristics and maternal involvement'. *Journal of Reproductive and Infant Psychology*, 5, 105–18.

Huston, A. C. (1983) 'Sex typing'. In E. M. Hetherington, ed., *Handbook of Child Psychology, Vol. 4: Socialization, Personality and Social Development*, 4th edn. New York, Wiley.

Hutt, C. (1966) 'Exploration and play in children'. *Symposia of the Zoological Society of London*, 18, 61–81.

Hytner, B., Da' Cocodia, L., Kagan, C., Spencer, L., and Yakes, A. (1981) *Report of the Moss Side Enquiry Panel*. Manchester, Greater Manchester Council.

Ingenkamp, K. (1977) *Educational Assessment Council for Europe*. Slough, NFER.

Inglis, J., Ruckman, M., Lawson, J. S., MacLean, A. W., and Monga, T. N. (1982) 'Sex differences in the cognitive effects of unilateral brain damage'. *Cortex*, 18, 257–76.

Irvine, S. E. (1966) 'Towards a rationale for testing attainments and abilities in Africa'. *British Journal of Educational Psychology*, 36, 24–32.

Irvine, S. E. (1969) 'Factor analysis of African abilities and attainments: constructs across cultures'. *Psychological Bulletin*, 71, 20–32.

Jacoby, J. (1976) 'Consumer psychology: an octenium'. In M. R. Rosenzweig and L. W. Porter, eds, *Annual Review of Psychology*, 27, 331–58.

Jahoda, G. (1966) 'Geometric illusions and environment: a study in Ghana'. *British Journal of Psychology*, 57, 193–9.

Jahoda, G. (1979) 'On the nature of difficulties in spatial-perceptual tests: ethnic and sex differences'. *British Journal of Psychology*, 70, 351–63.

James, W. (1890) *The Principles of Psychology*, Vol. 2. New York, Holt.

Jenkins, J. (1974) 'Can we have a meaningful memory?'. In R. Solso, ed., *Theories in Cognitive Psychology: The Loyola Symposium*. New York, Wiley.

Jensen, A. R. (1969) 'How much can we boost IQ and scholastic achievement?'. *Harvard Educational Review*, 39, 1–123.

Jerison, H. J. (1973) *Evolution of the Brain and Intelligence*. New York, Academic Press.

Johnson, W. G., and Wildman, H. E. (1983) 'Influence of external and covert food stimuli in insulin secretion in obese and normal subjects'. *Behavioral Neuroscience*, 97, 1025–8.

Johnson-Laird, P. N. (1982) Ninth Bartlett Memorial Lecture: 'Thinking as a skill'. *Quarterly Journal of Experimental Psychology*, 34A, 1–29.

Jones, E. E., and Davis, K. E. (1965) 'From acts to dispositions: the attribution process in person perception'. In L. Berkowitz, ed., *Advances in Experimental Social Psychology*, Vol. 2. New York, Academic Press.

Jones, E. E., and de Charms, R. (1957) 'Changes in social perception as a function of the personal relevance of behaviour'. *Sociometry*, 20, 75–85.

Jones, E. E., and Nisbett, R. E. (1972) 'The actor and the observer: divergent perspectives of the causes of behaviour'. In E. E. Jones, D. E. Kanouse, H. Kelley, R. E. Nisbet, S. Valins, and B. Weiner, eds, *Attribution: Perceiving the causes of behaviour*. Morristown, N.J., Genevore Learning Group.

Jones, E. E., and Sigall, H. (1971) 'The bonus pipeline: a new paradigm for measuring affect and attitude'. *Psychological Bulletin*, 76, 349–64.

Jones, T., and Kamil, A. (1973) 'Tool making and tool using in the northern blue jay'. *Science*, 180, 1076–8.

Jorgansen, C., and Kintsch, W. (1973) 'The role of imagery in the evaluation of sentences'. *Cognitive Psychology*, 4, 110–16.

Jorm, A. (1983) 'Specific reading retardation and working memory: a review'. *British Journal of Psychology*, 74, 311–42.

Jouvet, M. (1969) 'Biogenic amines and the states of sleep'. *Science*, 163, 32–40.

Jouvet, M. (1972) 'The role of monoamines and acetylcholine-containing neurons in the regulation of the sleep–waking cycle'. *Ergebnisse der Physiologie*, 64, 166–307.

Kagan, J., Henker, B. A., Hen-Tov, A., Levine, J., and Lewis, M. (1966) 'Infants' differential reactions to familiar and distorted faces'. *Child Development*, 37, 519–32.

Kahle, L. R. (1984) *Attitudes and Social Adaptation*. Oxford, Pergamon.

Kandel, E. R., and Schwartz, J. H., eds (1985) *Principles of Neural Science*, 2nd edn. New York, Elsevier.

Karlins, M., Coffman, T. L., and Walters, G. (1969) 'On the fading of social stereotypes: studies in three generations of college students'. *Journal of Personality and Social Psychology*, 13, 1–16.

Katchadourian, H. A. (1977) *The Biology of Adolescence*. Oxford, W. H. Freeman.

Katz, D. (1960) 'The functional approach to the study of attitudes'. *Public Opinion Quarterly*, 24, 163–204.

Katz, D., and Braly, K. (1933) 'Racial stereotypes of one hundred college students'. *Journal of Abnormal and Social Psychology*, 28, 280–90.

Keenan, E. O., and Schiffelin, B. (1976) 'Topic as a discourse notion: a study of topic in the conversations of children and adults'. In C. Li, ed., *Subject and Topic*, New York, Academic Press.

Kelley, H. H. (1967) 'Attribution theory in social psychology'. In D. Levine, ed., *Nebraska Symposium on Motivation*. Lincoln, University of Nebraska Press.

Kelley, H. H. (1973) 'The processes of causal attribution'. *American Psychologist*, 8, 107–28.

Kelly, G. A. (1955) *The Psychology of Personal Constructs*. New York, Norton.

Kelman, H. C. (1958) 'Compliance, identification, and internalization: three processes of attitude change'. *Journal of Conflict Resolution*, 2, 51–60.

Keppel, G., and Underwood, B. (1962) 'Proactive inhibition in short-term retention of single items'. *Journal of Verbal Learning and Verbal Behaviour*, 1, 153–61.

Kiel, F. C. (1981) 'Constraint on knowledge and cognitive development'. *Psychological Review*, 88, 197–227.

Kiel, F. C. (1986) 'On the structure-dependent nature of cognitive development'. In J. Levin, ed., *Stage and Structure*, New Jersey, Ablex.

Kimura, D. (1967) 'Functional asymmetry of the brain in dichotic listening'. *Cortex*, 3, 163–8.

Kimura, D. (1977) 'Acquisition of a motor skill after left hemisphere damage'. *Brain*, 100, 527–42.

Kinchla, R. A., and Wolf, J. (1979) 'The order of visual processing: "top-down", "bottom-up", or "middle-out"'. *Perception and Psychophysics*, 25, 225–31.

Kintsch, W. (1970) *Learning, Memory and Conceptual Process*. New York, Wiley.

Kline, P. (1972) *Fact and Fantasy in Freudian Theory*. London, Methuen.

Kline, P. (1983) *Personality: Measurement and theory*. London, Batsford.

Klopfer, P. (1963) 'Behavioural aspects of habitat selection. The role of early experience'. *Wilson Bulletin*, 75, 15–22.

Kohlberg, L. (1966) 'A cognitive developmental analysis of children's sex role concepts and attitudes'. In E. E. Maccoby, ed., *The Development of Sex Differences*. Stanford, CA, Stanford University Press.

Kohlberg, L. (1976) 'Moral stages and moralization'. In T. Lickona, ed., *Moral Development and Behaviour*. New York, Holt, Rinehart.

Kohler, I. (1964) 'The formation and transformation of the visual world'. *Psychological Issues*, 3, 28–46 and 116–33.

Konishi, M. (1965) 'The role of auditory feedback in the control of vocalization in the white-crowned sparrow'. *Zeitschrift der Tierpsychologie*, 22, 770–83.

Kramer, D. (1983) 'Post formal operations'. *Human Development*, 26, 91–105.

Krasner, L. (1958) 'Studies of the conditioning of verbal behaviour'. *Psychological Bulletin*, 55, 148–70.

Krebs, J. R., and Davies, N. B. (1987) *An Introduction to Behavioural Ecology*, 2nd edn. Oxford, Blackwell.

Kuffler, S. W. (1953) 'Discharge patterns and functional organization of mammalian retina'. *Journal of Neurophysiology*, 16, 37–68.

Kurdek, L. A. (1981) 'An integrative perspective on children's divorce adjustments'. *American Psychologist*, 36, 856–66.

Kyriacou, C. (1985) 'Conceptualizing research on effective teaching'. *British Journal of Educational Psychology*, 55 (II), 148–56.

Labouvie-Vief, G. (1980) 'Beyond formal operations'. *Human Development*, 23, 141–61.

Labov, W. (1972) *Sociolinguistic Patterns*. Philadelphia, University of Pennsylvania Press.

Laing, R. D. (1965) *The Divided Self*. Harmondsworth, Penguin.

Lalljee, M., Watson, M., and White, P. (1982) 'Explanations, attributions and the social context of unexpected behaviour'. *European Journal of Social Psychology*, 12(1), 17–29.

Lally, M., and Nettelbeck, T. (1977) 'Intelligence, reaction time and inspection time'. *American Journal of Mental Deficiency*, 82, 273–81.

Lamb, M. E. (1982) 'Maternal employment and child development: a review'. In M. E. Lamb, ed., *Non-traditional Families: Parenting and child development*. Hillsdale, N.J., Lawrence Erlbaum Associates.

Lamb, M. E., Frodi, A. M., Hwang, C. P., Frodi, M., and Steinberg, J. (1982) 'Mother- and father–infant interaction involving play and holding in traditional and non-traditional Swedish families'. *Developmental Psychology*, 18, 215–21.

Lamb, M. E., Pleck, J. H., and Levin, J. A. (1985) 'The role of the father in child development: the effects of increased paternal involvement'. In B. B. Lahey and E. Kazdin, eds, *Advances in Clinical Child Psychology*, Vol. 8. New York, Plenum.

Lane, H. (1977) *The Wild Boy of Aveyron*. London, Allen and Unwin.

Langlois, J. H., and Downs, A. C. (1980) 'Mothers, fathers and peers as socialization agents of sex-typed play behaviors in young children'. *Child Development*, 51, 1237–47.

LaPiere, R. T. (1934) 'Attitudes v actions'. *Social Forces*, 13, 230–7.

Latané, B., and Darley, J. M. (1970) *The Unresponsive Bystander: Why doesn't he help?* New York, Appleton-Century-Crofts.

Latané, B., and Nida, S. (1980) 'Social impact theory and group influence: a social engineering perspective'. In P. B. Paulus, ed., *Psychology of Group Influence*. Lawrence Erlbaum, N.J., Hillsdale.

Latané, B., and Rodin, J. (1969) 'A lady in distress: inhibiting effects of friends and strangers on bystander intervention'. *Journal of Experimental Social Psychology*, 15, 189–202.

Laurendeau, M., and Pinard, A. (1962) *Causal Thinking in the Child*. New York, International Universities Press.

Lazarsfeld, P. F., Berelson, B., and Gaudet, H. (1944) *The People's Choice: How the voter makes up his mind in a presidential campaign*. New York, Duell, Sloan & Pearce.

Lazarus, R. S. (1966) *Psychological Stress and the Coping Process*. New York, McGraw-Hill.

Lazarus, R. S. (1981) 'The stress and coping paradigm'. In C. Eisdorfer, *et al*, eds, *Theoretical Basis in Psycho-Pathology*. New York, Spectrum.

Ledoux, J. E., Risse, G. L., Springer, S. P., Wilson, D. H., and Gazzaniga, M. S. (1977) 'Cognition and commissurotomy'. *Brain*, 100, 87–104.

Leeper, R. (1935) 'A study of a neglected portion of the field of learning – the development of sensory organization'. *Journal of Genetic Psychology*, 46, 41–75.

Legge, D., and Barber, P. J. (1976) *Information and Skill*. London, Methuen.

Le Magnen, J. (1972) 'Regulation of food intake'. *Advances in Psychosomatic Medicine*, 7, 73–90.

Lenneberg, E. M. (1962) 'Understanding language without ability to speak: a case report'. *Journal of Abnormal and Social Psychology*, 65, 419–25.

Lenneberg, E. H. (1967) *Biological Foundations of Language*, New York, Wiley.

Leon, G., and Roth, L. (1977) 'Obesity: psychological causes, correlations, and speculations'. *Psychological Bulletin*, 84, 117–39.

Le Shan, L. (1959) 'Psychological states as factors in the development of malignant disease: a critical review'. *Journal of the National Cancer Institute*, 22, 1–18.

Lesser, G. S. *et al* (1965) 'Mental abilities of children from different social-class and cultural groups'. *Monographs of the Society for Research in Child Development*, 30 (serial No. 103), 1–93.

Leventhal, A. G., and Hirsch, H. V. (1975) 'Cortical effects of early exposure to diagonal lines'. *Science*, 190, 902–4.

Leventhal, H. (1970) 'Findings and theory in the study of fear communications'. In L. Berkowitz, ed., *Advances in Experimental Social Psychology*, Vol. 5. New York, Academic Press.

Levy, J., and Reid, M. (1978) 'Variations in cerebral organization as a function of handedness: hand posture in writing, and sex'. *Journal of Experimental Psychology: General*, 107, 119–44.

Lewin, K., Lippitt, R., and White, R. K. (1939) 'Patterns of aggressive behavior in experimentally created "social climates"'. *Journal of Social Psychology*, 10, 271–99.

Lewis, C. (1986) 'Early sex-role socialization'. In D. J. Hargreaves and A. M. Colley, eds, *The Psychology of Sex Roles*. London, Harper and Row.

Lewis, M., and Weintraub, M. (1974) 'Sex of parent versus sex of child: socio-emotional development'. In R. Riehart, R. Friedman and R. Vande Weide, eds, *Sex Difference in Behavior*. New York, Wiley.

Lewis, M., Feiring, C., McGuffog, C., and Jaskin, J. (1984) 'Predicting psychopathology in six-year-olds from early social relations'. *Child Development*, 55, 123–36.

Leyden, S. (1985) *Helping the Child of Exceptional Ability*. London, Croom Helm.

Likert, R. (1932) 'A technique for the measurement of attitudes'. *Archives of Psychology*, 22, 1–55.

Limber, J. (1977) 'Language in child and chimp'. *American Psychologist*, 32, 280–95.

Little, A. W. (1985) 'The child's understanding of the causes of academic success and failure: a case study of British schoolchildren'. *British Journal of Educational Psychology*, 55(I), 11–24.

Loehlin, C. (1980) 'Recent adoption studies of IQ'. *Human Genetics*, 55, 297–302.

Loewi, O., and Navratil, E. (1926) 'Ueber humorale Uebertragbarkeit der Herzennervenwirkung. X. Ueber das Schicksal des Vagusstoffes'. *Pfeugers Archiv Gesamte Physiologie*, 214, 678–88.

Lorenz, D. N., and Goldman, S. A. (1982) 'Vagal mediation of the cholecystokinin satiety effect in rats'. *Physiology and Behavior*, 29, 599–604.

Lotze, H. (1852) *Outlines of Psychology*, tr G. T. Ladd. Boston, Ginn.

Lovibond, S. H., Adams, Mithiran, and Adams, W. G. (1979) 'Effects of three experimental prison environments on the behaviour of non-convict volunteer subjects'. *Australian Psychologist*, 14(3), 273–87.

Lucas, E. A., and Sterman, M. B. (1975) 'The effect of forebrain lesions upon the polycyclic sleep–wake cycle and sleep–wake patterns in the cat'. *Experimental Neurology*, 46, 368–88.

Luria, A. R. (1976) *Cognitive Development: Its cultural and social foundations*. Cambridge, Mass., Harvard University Press.

Lynn, R., and Hampson, S. (1986) 'The rise of national intelligence: evidence from Britain, Japan and the USA'. *Personality and Individual Differences*, 7, 23–32.

Maccoby, E. E., and Jacklin, C. N. (1975) *The Psychology of Sex Differences*. Stanford, California, Stanford University Press.

Maccoby, E. E., and Martin, J. A. (1983) 'Socialization in the context of the family'. In E. M. Hetherington, ed., *Handbook of Child Psychology, Vol. 4: Socialization, Personality and Social Development*, 4th edn. New York, Wiley.

MacDonald, K., and Parke, R. D. (1984) 'Bridging the gap: the relationship between parent–child play and peer inter-active competence'. *Child Development*, 55, 1265–77.

Macintosh, H. G., and Hale, D. E. (1976) *Assessment and the Secondary School Teacher*. London, Routledge and Kegan Paul.

Mackintosh, N. J. (1986) 'The biology of intelligence'. *British Journal of Psychology*, 77, 1–18.

Macnamara, J. (1972) 'Cognitive basis of language learning in infants'. *Psychological Review*, 79, 1–13.

Madsen, K. B. (1988) *A History of Psychology in Metascientific Perspective*. Amsterdam, Elsevier.

Maher, C. A., and Illback, J. R. (1982) 'Organizational school psychology: issues and considerations'. *Journal of School Psychology*, 20(3), 244–53.

Maier, N. R., and Thurber, J. A. (1968) 'Accuracy of judgements of deception when an interview is watched, heard and read'. *Personnel Psychology*, 21, 23–30.

Main, M., and Weston, D. (1981) 'The quality of the toddler's relationship to mother and father: related to conflict behavior and readiness to establish new relationships'. *Child Development*, 52, 932–40.

Mandler, G. (1972) 'Organization and recognition'. In E. Tulving and W. Donaldson, eds, *Organization of Memory*. New York, Academic Press.

Mange, A. P., and Mange, E. J. (1980) *Genetics: Human aspects*. Philadelphia, Saunders College.

Manis, M., Nelson, T. E., and Shedler, J. (1988) 'Stereotypes and social judgement: extremity, assimilation, and contrast'. *Journal of Personality and Social Psychology*, 55, 28–36.

Mann, L. (1981) 'The baiting crowd in episodes of threatened suicide'. *Journal of Personality and Social Psychology*, 41, 703–9.

Manning, A. (1973) *An Introduction to Animal Behaviour*. London, Arnold.

Maranon, G. (1924) 'Contribution à l'étude de l'action émotive de l'adrénaline'. *Revue Française d'Endrocrinologie*, 2, 301–25.

Marcia, J. (1980) 'Identity in adolescence'. In J. Adelson, ed., *Handbook of Adolescent Psychology*, New York, Wiley.

Marcia, J. E. (1966) 'Development and validation of ego-identity status'. *Journal of Personality and Social Psychology*, 3, 551–8.

Marcus, P. E., and Overton, W. F. (1978) 'The development of cognitive gender constancy'. *Child Development*, 49, 2, 434–44.

Markus, H. (1977) 'Self-schemata and the processing of information about the self'. *Journal of Personality and Social Psychology*, 35, 63–78.

Marler, P., and Tamura, M. (1964) 'Culturally transmitted patterns of vocal behaviour in sparrows'. *Science*, N.Y., 146, 1483–6.

Marlowe, M. (1985) 'Low lead exposure and learning disabilities'. *Research Communications in Psychology, Psychiatry and Behaviour*, 10, 155–66.

Marr, D. (1982) *Vision: A computational investigation in the human representation and processing of visual information*. Oxford, W. H. Freeman.

Marsh, P. (1978) *Aggro: The illusion of violence*. London, Dent.

Marshall, G. D., and Zimbardo, P. G. (1979) 'Affective consequences of inadequately explained physiological arousal'. *Journal of Personality and Social Psychology*, 37, 970–88.

Marslen-Wilson, W. D. (1980) 'Speech understanding as a psychological process'. In J. C. Simon, ed., *Spoken Language Generation and Understanding*. Dordrecht, D. Reidel.

Marslen-Wilson, W. D., and Tyler, L. K. (1980) 'The temporal structure of spoken language understanding'. *Cognition*, 8, 1–71.

Martin, E. G., Stambrook, M., Tataryn, D. J., and Beihl, H. (1984) 'Conditioning in the unattended left ear'. *International Journal of Neuroscience*, 23, 95–102.

Martin, I., and Venables, P. H. (1980) *Techniques in Psychophysiology*. Chichester, Wiley.

Maslach, C. (1979) 'Negative emotional biasing of unexplained arousal'. *Journal of Personality and Social Psychology*, 37, 953–69.

Maslow, A. H. (1954) *Motivation and Personality*. New York, Harper and Row.

Maslow, C., Yoselson, K., and London, H. (1971) 'Persuasiveness of confidence expressed via language and body language'. *British Journal of Social and Clinical Psychology*, 10, 234–40.

McClelland, J. L., and Elman, J. E. (1986) 'The TRACE model of speech perception'. *Cognitive Psychology*, 18, 1–86.

McGinnies, E. (1949) 'Emotionality and perceptual defence'. *Psychological Review*, 56, 244–51.

McGlone, J. (1980) 'Sex differences in human brain asymmetry: a critical survey'. *Behavioral and Brain Sciences*, 3, 215–27.

McGuinness, D. (1972) 'Hearing: individual differences in perceiving'. *Perception*, 1, 465–73.

McGuinness, D. (1976) 'Sex differences in the organization of perception and cognition'. In B. Lloyd and U. Archer, eds, *Exploring Sex Differences*, 123–56. New York, Academic Press.

McGuire, J. (1982) 'Gender specific differences in early childhood: the impact of the father'. In N. Beail and J. McGuire, eds, *Fathers: Psychological perspectives*. London, Junction.

McGuire, W. J. (1968) 'Personality and susceptibility to social influence'. In E. F. Borgatta and W. W. Lambert, eds, *Handbook of Personality Theory and Research*. Chicago, Rand McNally.

McGuire, W. J. (1969) 'The nature of attitudes and attitude change'. In G. Lindzey and E. Aronson, eds, *Handbook of Social Psychology*, 2nd edn, Vol. 3. Reading, Mass., Addison-Wesley.

McHale, S. M., and Huston, T. L. (1984) 'Men and women as parents: Sex-role orientation, employment and parental roles with infants'. *Child Development*, 55, 1349–61.

McKay, D. (1973) 'Aspects of the theory of comprehension, memory and attention'. *Quarterly Journal of Experimental Psychology*, 25, 22–40.

McKeever, W. F., and Van Deventer, A. D. (1977) 'Visual and auditory language processing asymmetries: influence of handedness, familial sinistrality, and sex'. *Cortex*, 13, 225–41.

McMahon, A., Bolam, R., Abbott, R., and Holly, P. (1984) *Guidelines for Review: Internal development in schools*. London, Schools Council Publications (now Schools Curriculum Development Council).

McNiell, D. (1970) *The Acquisition of Language: The study of developmental psycholinguistics*. New York, Harper and Row.

McShane, J. (1980) *Learning to Talk*. Cambridge, Cambridge University Press.

Mead, M. (1928) *Coming of Age in Samoa*. New York, Morrow.

Meddis, R. (1979) 'The evolution and function of sleep'. In D. A. Oakley and H. C. Plotkin, eds, *Brain, Behaviour and Evolution*. London, Methuen.

Mednick, S. A., Schulsinger, F., and Griffiths, J. (1981) 'Children of schizophrenic mothers: The Danish High-risk Study'. In F. Schulsinger, S. A. Mednick and J. Knopf, eds, *Longitudinal Research: Methods and uses in behavioral science*. Hingham, Mass., Martinus Nijhoff.

Meehl, P. E. (1950) 'On the circularity of the law of effect'. *Psychological Bulletin*, 47, 52–75.

Meehl, P. E. (1978) 'Theoretical risks and tabular asterisks: Sir Karl, Sir Ronald and the progress of soft psychology'. *Journal of Consulting and Clinical Psychology*, 46, 806–34.

Mehler, J., and Carey, P. W. (1967) 'Role of surface and base structure in the perception of sentences'. *Journal of Verbal Learning and Verbal Behaviour*, 6, 335–8.

Meichenbaum, D., Bowers, K., and Ross, R. (1969) 'A behavioural analysis of teachers' expectancy effect'. *Journal of Personality and Social Psychology*, 13, 306–16.

Melzack, R., and Wall, P. D. (1988) *The Challenge of Pain*. Harmondsworth, Penguin.

Meltzoff, A. N. (1985) 'The roots of social and cognitive development: models of man's original nature'. In T. M. Field and N. A. Fox, eds, *Social Perception in Infants*. Norwood, N.J., Ablex.

Meumann, E. (1913) *Die Entstehung der Ersten Worbedeut Ungen Bein Kinde*. Leipzig, W. Engelmann.

Meyer, A. (1973) 'Remember, remember'. *New Society*, 1 March.

Mezrick, J. J. (1973) 'The word superiority effect in brief visual displays: elimination by vocalization'. *Perception and Psychophysics*, 13, 45–8.

Miles, T. R. (1957) 'Contributions to intelligence testing and the theory of intelligence: I. On defining intelligence'. *British Journal of Educational Psychology*, 27, 153–65.

Milgram, S. (1965) 'Some conditions of obedience and disobedience to authority'. *Human Relations*, 18, 57–76.

Miller, G. (1956) 'The magical number seven, plus or minus two: some limits of our capacity for processing information'. *Psychological Review*, 63, 81–97.

Miller, G. A. (1965) 'Some preliminaries to psycholinguistics'. *American Psychologist*, 20, 15–20.

Miller, N. E. (1941) 'The frustration–aggression hypothesis'. *Psychological Review*, 48, 337–42.

Mills, J., and Harvey, J. (1972) 'Opinion change as a function of when information about the communicator is received and whether he is attractive or expert'. *Journal of Personality and Social Psychology*, 21, 52–5.

Mineka, S. (1979) 'The role of fear in theories of avoidance learning, flooding and extinction'. *Psychological Bulletin*, 86, 985–1010.

Minsky, M. (1975) 'A framework for representing knowledge'. In P. Winston, ed., *The Psychology of Computer Vision*. New York, McGraw–Hill.

Minsky, M. (1978) 'Frame-system theory'. In P. Johnson-Laird and P. Wason, eds, *Thinking: Readings in cognitive science*. Cambridge University Press.

Mischcl, W. (1968) *Personality and Assessment*. New York, Wiley.

Money, J. (1965) 'Psychosexual differentiation'. In J. Money, ed., *Sex Research: New developments*, 3–23. New York, Holt.

Montemayor, R., and Eisen, M. (1977) 'The development of self-conceptions from childhood to adolescence'. *Developmental Psychology*, 13, 314–19.

Moos, R. H. (1969) 'Sources of variance in responses to questionnaires and in behaviour'. *Journal of Abnormal Psychology*, 74, 405–12.

Moray, N. (1969) *Attention*. London, Hutchinson.

Morgan, C. D., and Murray, H. A. (1935) 'A method for inventing fantasies'. *Archives of Neurological Psychiatry*, 34, 289–306.

Morgan, J. J. B., and Morton, J. T. (1944) 'The distortion of syllogistic reasoning produced by personal conviction'. *Journal of Social Psychology*, 20, 39–59.

Morgane, P. J., Stern, W. C., and Bronzino, J. D. (1977) 'Experimental studies of sleep in animals'. In R. D. Myers, ed., *Methods in Psychobiology*, Vol. 3. New York, Academic Press.

Morris, B. (1958) 'Social learning: some aspects of character formation'. *Educational Review*, 10, 141–5.

Morris, D. (1959) 'The comparative ethnology of grassfinches and mannakins'. *Proceedings of the Zoological Society of London*, 131, 389–439.

Mortimer, P., Sammons, P., Stoll, L., Ecob, R., and Lewis, D. (1988) 'The effects of school membership on pupils' educational outcomes'. *Research Papers in Education*, 3, 3–26.

Moruzzi, G., and Magoun, H. W. (1949) 'Brain stem reticular formation and activation of the EEG'. *Electroencephalography and Clinical Neurophysiology*, 1, 455–73.

Motley, M. T. (1980) 'Verification of "Freudian slips" and semantic prearticulatory editing via laboratory spooncrisms'. In V. A. Fromkin, ed., *Errors in Linguistic Performance: Slips of the tongue, ear, pen and hand*. New York, Academic Press.

Movshon, J. A., and Van Sluyters, R. C. (1981) 'Visual neural development'. *Annual Review of Psychology*, 32, 477–522.

Mueller, K., and Hsiao, S. (1979) 'Consistency of cholecystokinin satiety effect across deprivation levels and motivational states'. *Physiology and Behavior*, 22, 809–15.

Mundy-Castle, A. C. (1966) 'Pictorial depth perception in Ghanaian children'. *International Journal of Psychology*, 1, 290–300.

Mundy-Castle, A. C., and Nelson, G. K. (1962) 'A neuro-psychological study of the Knysna forest workers'. *Psychologia Africana*, 9, 240–72.

Munro, G., and Adams, G. R. (1977) 'Ego-identity formation in college students and working youth'. *Developmental Psychology*, 13, 523–4.

Myerson, J., and Hale, S. (1984) 'Practical implications of the matching law'. *Journal of Applied Behavior Analysis*, 17, 367–80.

Nachshon, I. (1988) 'Dichotic listening models of cerebral deficit in schizophrenia'. In K. Hugdahl, ed., *Handbook of Dichotic Listening: theory, methods and research*, New York, Wiley.

Nauta, W. J. H. (1946) 'Hypothalamic regulation of sleep in rats: an experimental study'. *Journal of Neurophysiology*, 9, 285–316.

Navon, D. (1977) 'Forest before trees: the precedence of global features in visual perception'. *Cognitive Psychology*, 9, 353–83.

Neale, M. D. (1966) *The Neale Analysis of Reading Ability*, 2nd edn. London, Macmillan.

Nelson, K. (1973) 'Structure and strategy in learning to talk'. *Monographs of the Society for Research in Child Development*, 38, 1–2.

Nelson, K. (1981) 'Individual differences in language development: implications for development and language'. *Developmental Psychology*, 17(2), 170–87.

Nesselroade, J. R., and Baltes, P. B. (1972) 'Adolescent personality development and historical change'. *Monographs of the Society for Research in Child Development*, 1974, 39.

Nesselroade, J. R., Schaie, K. W., and Baltes, P. B. (1972). In R. Gross, ed., *Psychology, The Science of Mind and Behaviour*, London, Edward Arnold. (1987).

Neugarten, B. L. (1972) 'Personality and the ageing process'. *Gerontologist*, 12(1,1), 9–15.

Neugarten, B. L. (1973) 'Personality change in later life'. In Eisdorfer and Lawton, *The Psychology of Adult Development and Ageing*. APA.

Newell, A., and Simon, H. A. (1972) *Human Problem Solving*. Englewood Cliffs, N.J., Prentice-Hall.

Newson, J., and Newson, E. (1968) *Four Years Old in an Urban Community*. Harmondsworth, Penguin.

Newson, J., and Newson, E. (1976) *Seven Years Old in the Home Environment*. Harmondsworth, Penguin.

Newson, J., and Newson, E. (1986) 'Family and sex roles in middle childhood'. In D. J. Hargreaves and A. M. Colley, eds, *The Psychology of Sex Roles*. London, Harper and Row.

Nisbett, R., and Wilson, T. (1977) 'Telling more than we can know: verbal reports on mental processes'. *Psychological Review*, 84, 231–59.

Norman, D. A. (1981) 'Categorization of action slips'. *Psychological Review*, 88, 1–15.

Norwich, B. (1983) 'The unique contribution of child psychological services'. *Bulletin of the British Psychological Society*, 36, 116–19.

O'Barr, W., and Atkins, B. (1980) 'Women's language or powerless language'. In McConnell-Ginet *et al*, eds, *Women and Language in Literature and Society*. New York, Praeger.

O'Connell, A. N. (1976) 'The relationship between lifestyle and identity synthesis and resynthesis in traditional, neo-traditional and non-traditional women'. *Journal of Personality*, 4, 675–88.

Ohman, A., and Dimberg, V. (1984) 'An evolutionary perspective on human social behaviour'. In W. M. Waid, ed., *Sociophysiology*. New York, Springer-Verlag.

Ojemann, G. A. (1983) 'Brain organization for language from the perspective of electrical stimulation mapping'. *Behavioural and Brain Science*, 6, 189–230.

Olds, J., and Milner, P. (1954) 'Positive reinforcement produced by electrical stimulation of septal area and other regions of rat brain'. *Journal of Comparative Physiology Psychology*, 47, 419–27.

Olds, J., and Olds, M. (1956) 'Drive, rewards and the brain'. In T. M. Newcombe, ed., *New Directions in Psychology II*. New York, Holt, Rinehart and Winston.

Orloff, H., and Weinstock, A. (1975) 'A comparison of parent and adolescent attitude factor structures'. *Adolescence*, 10, 201–5.

Osborn, A. F., and Milbank, J. E. (1987) *The Association of Pre-School Educational Experience with Subsequent Ability, Attainment and Behaviour*. Draft report prepared for the D.E.S.

Osgood, C. E., Suci, G. J., and Tannenbaum, P. H. (1957) *The Measurement of Meaning*. Urbana, Ill., University of Illinois Press.

Oswald, I. (1976) 'The function of sleep'. *Postgraduate Journal*, 52, 15–18.

Oswald, I. (1980) *Sleep*, 4th edn. Harmondsworth, Penguin.

Palmar, S. E. (1975) 'The effects of contextual scenes on the identification of objects'. *Memory and Cognition*, 3, 519–26.

Parke, R. D. (1974) In R. Gross, ed., *Psychology of the Science of Mind and Behaviour*, London, Edward Arnold. (1987).

Parke, R. D., *et al* (1974) 'Child and adult perceptions of the impact of reactions to discipline on adult behaviour'. Unpublished research. Fels Research Institute.

Parten, M. B. (1932) 'Social participation among pre-school children'. *Journal of Abnormal Psychology*, 27, 243–69.

Passingham, R. (1982) *The Human Primate*. Oxford, Freeman.

Pederson, F. A., Cain, R., and Zaslow, M. (1982) 'Variations in infant experience associated with alternative family roles'. In L. Laosa and I. Sigel, eds, *The Family as a Learning Environment*. New York, Plenum.

Peel, E. A. (1956) 'Some contributions of psychology to education'. *International Review of Education*, 2, 67–71.

Perrett, D. I., Rolls, E. T., and Caan, W. (1982) 'Visual neurones responsive to faces in the monkey temporal cortex'. *Experimental Brain Research*, 47, 329–42.

Perry, W. B. (1968) *Forms of Intellectual and Ethical Development in the College Years*. New York, Holt Rinehart.

Peterson, A. C. (1976) 'Physical androgyny and cognitive functioning in adolescence'. *Development Psychology*, 12, 524–33.

Peterson, J., and Peterson, J. K. (1938) 'Does practice with inverting lenses make vision normal?' *Psychological Monographs*, 50, 12–37.

Pettigrew, T. F., Allport, G. W., and Barnett, E. O. (1958) 'Binocular resolution and perception of race in South Africa'. *British Journal of Psychology*, 49, 265–78.

Petty, R. E., and Cacioppo, J. T. (1977) 'Forewarning, cognitive responding, and resistance to persuasion'. *Journal of Personality and Social Psychology*, 35, 645–55.

Petty, R. E., and Cacioppo, J. T. (1981) *Attitudes and Persuasion: Classic and contemporary approaches*. Dubuque, Iowa, Wm. C. Brown.

Phillips, D. (1977) 'Motor vehicle fatalities increase just after publicized suicide stories'. *Science*, 196, 1464–5.

Piaget, J. (1926) *The Language and Thought of the Child*. Routledge and Kegan Paul.

Piaget, J. (1952) *The Child's Conception of Number*. Routledge and Kegan Paul.

Piliavin, J., Vovidio, J. F., Gaertner, S. L., and Clarke, R. D. III (1981) *Emergency Intervention*. New York, Academic Press.

Pinker, S. (1979) 'Formal models of language learning'. *Cognition*, 7, 217–83.

Pi-Sunyer, X., Kissileff, H. R., Thornton, J., and Smith, G. P. (1982) 'C-Terminal octapeptide of cholecystokinin decreases food intake in obese men'. *Physiology and Behavior*, 29, 627–30.

Pollio, H., and Foote, R. (1971) 'Memory as a reconstructive process'. *British Journal of Psychology*, 62, 53–8.

Pollitzer, A. (1958) 'The Negroes of Charleston, S.C.: a study of haemoglobin types, serology and morphology'. *American Journal of Physical Anthropology*, 16, 241–63.

Posner, M. I. (1969) 'Abstraction and the process of recognition'. In G. H. Bower and J. T. Spence, eds, *The Psychology of Learning and Motivation*, Vol. 3. New York, Academic Press.

Posner, M. I., and Keele, S. W. (1968) 'On the genesis of abstract ideas'. *Journal of Experimental Psychology*, 77, 353–63.

Postman, L. (1972) 'A pragmatic view of organization theory'. In E. Tulving and W. Donaldson, eds, *Organization of Memory*. New York, Academic Press.

Postman, L., Bruner, J. S., and McGinnies, E. (1948) 'Personal values as selective factors in perception'. *Journal of Abnormal and Social Psychology*, 43, 142–54.

Power, M. J., Benn, R. T., and Morris, J. N. (1972) 'Neighbourhood, school and juveniles before the courts'. *British Journal of Criminology*, 12, 111–32.

Power, M. J., and Champion, L. A. (1987) 'Cognitive approaches to depression: a theoretical critique'. *British Journal of Clinical Psychology*, 25, 201–13.

Powley, T. L., and Opsahl, C. A. (1974) 'Ventromedial hypothalamic obesity abolished by subdiaphragmatic vagotomy'. *American Journal of Physiology*, 226, 25–33.

Pratkanis, A. R., Greenwald, A. G., Leippe, M. R., and Baumgardner, M. H. (1988) 'In search of reliable persuasion effects: III. The sleeper effect is dead. Long live the sleeper effect'. *Journal of Personality and Social Psychology*, 54, 203–18.

Prelec, D. (1982) 'Matching, maximizing, and the hyperbolic reinforcement feedback function'. *Psychological Review*, 89, 189–230.

Premack, D. (1962) 'Reversibility of the reinforcement relation'. *Science*, 136, 255–7.

Prosser, G. (1985) 'Play: a child's eye view'. In A. Braithwaite and D. Rogers, eds, *Children Growing Up*. Open University Press.

Raaheim, K. (1984) *Why Intelligence is not Enough*. London, Sigma Forlag.

Raber, H. (1948) 'Analyse des Belzverhaltens eines domestizierten Truthahns'. (Meleagries). *Behaviour*, 1, 237–66.

Rachlin, H. (1976) *Behavior and Learning*. Oxford, Freeman.

Radke-Yarrow, M., *et al* (1975) 'Perspective taking and pro-social behaviour'. *Developmental Psychology*, 13, 1, 87–8.

Ramm, P. (1979) 'The locus coeruleus, catecholamines and REM sleep; a critical review'. *Behavioral and Neural Biology*, 25, 415–48.

Randle, C. W. (1956) 'How to identify promotable executives'. *Harvard Business Review*, 34, 122–34.

Rasmussen, J., Duncan, K., and Leplat, J., eds (1987) *New Technology and Human Error*. Chichester, Wiley.

Rasmussen, T., and Milner, B. (1977) 'The role of early left-brain injury in determining lateralization of cerebral speech functions'. *Annals of the New York Academy of Sciences*, 299, 355–69.

Razran, G. (1950) 'Ethnic dislikes and stereotypes: a laboratory study'. *Journal of Abnormal and Social Psychology*, 45, 7–27.

Reason, J. (1987) 'Generic error-modelling system (GEMS)'. In J. Rasmussen, K. Duncan, and J. Leplat, eds, *New Technology and Human Error*. Chichester, Wiley.

Reicher, G. (1969) 'Perceptual recognition as a function of meaningfulness of stimulus material'. *Journal of Experimental Psychology*, 81, 275–80.

Reicher, S. (1984) 'The St. Paul's riot; an explanation of the limits of crowd action in terms of a social identity model'. *European Journal of Social Psychology*, 14, 1–21.

Restle, F. (1974) 'Critique of pure memory'. In R. Solso, ed., *Theories in Cognitive Psychology: the Loyola Symposium*. New York, Wiley.

Reynolds, D. (1987) 'The effective school: do educational psychologists help or hinder?'. *Educational Psychology in Practice*, 3(3) (October), 22–8.

Rezek, M., Kroeger, E. A., Lesiuk, H., Havlicek, V., and Novin, D. (1977) 'Cerebral and hepatic glucoreceptors: assessment of their role in food intake control by the uptake of 3H-2 Deoxy-D-Glucose'. *Physiology and Behavior*, 18, 679–83.

Richards, J. E., and Rader, N. (1983) 'Affective, behavioural, and avoidance responses on the visual cliff: effect of crawling onset age, crawling experience, and testing age'. *Psychophysiology*, 20, 633–42.

Riesen, A. H. (1966) 'Sensory deprivation'. In E. Stellar and J. M. Sprague, eds, *Progress in Physiological Psychology*. New York, Academic Press.

Rim, Y. (1977) 'Personality variables and interruptions in small group discussions'. *European Journal of Social Psychology*, 7, 247–51.

Rivers, W. H. R. (1901) 'Vision'. In A. C. Haddon, ed., *Reports of the Cambridge Anthropological Expedition to the Torres Straits*, Vol. 2(1). Cambridge University Press and *British Journal of Psychology*, I, 321 (1905).

Robberson, M. R., and Rogers, R. W. (1988) 'Beyond fear appeals: negative and positive persuasive appeals to health and self esteem'. *Journal of Applied Social Psychology*, 18, 277–87.

Rogers, C. R. (1961) *On Becoming a Person*. Boston, Houghton Mifflin.

Roland, P. E. (1984) 'Metabolic measurements of the working frontal cortex in man'. *Trends in Neuroscience*, 7, 430–5.

Rolls, B. J., Rowe, E. A., and Rolls, E. T. (1982) 'How sensory properties of foods affect human feeding behavior'. *Physiology and Behavior*, 29, 409–17.

Rosch, E. (1978) 'Principles of categorization'. In E. Rosch, and B. Lloyd, eds, *Cognition and Categorization*, Hillsdale, N.J., Lawrence Erlbaum Associates.

Rosenberg, M. (1965) *Society and the Adolescent Self-Image*. Princeton, N.J., Princeton University Press.

Rosenberg, M. J. (1960) 'Cognitive reorganization in response to the hypnotic reversal of attitudinal affect'. *Journal of Personality*, 28, 39–63.

Rosenberg, S., and Jones, R. A. (1972) 'A method for investigating and representing a person's implicit theory of personality: Theodor Dreiser's view of people'. *Journal of Personality and Social Psychology*.

Rosenhan, D. L. (1973) 'On being sane in an insane place'. *Science*, 179, 250–8.

Rosenthal, R. (1966) *Experimenter Effects in Behavioural Research*. Irvington, Century Psychology Series.

Rosenthal, R., and Jackson, L. (1968) *Pygmalion in the Classroom*. New York, Rinchart-Winston.

Ross, L., Amabile, T., and Steinmetz, J. (1977) 'Social roles, social control and biases in social perception processes'. *Journal of Personality and Social Psychology*, 35, 485–94.

Rotter, J. B. (1966) 'Generalized expectancies for internal versus external control of reinforcement'. *Psychological Monographs*, 80, 1 (Whole No. 709).

Rovee-Collier, C. K., and Lipsitt, L. P. (1982) 'Learning, adaptation and memory in the newborn'. In P. Stratton, ed., *Psychobiology of the Human Newborn*. Chichester, Wiley.

Rowe, M. (1974) 'Wait time and rewards as instructional variables'. *Journal of Research in Science*, 11, 291–308.

Rowntree, D. (1977) *Assessing Students: How shall we know them?* London, Harper and Row.

Rubin, J. Z., Provenzano, F. J. and Luria, Z. (1974) 'The eye of the beholder: parents' view on sex of newborns'. *American Journal of Orthopsychiatry*, 44, 512–19.

Russell, B. (1927) *An Outline of Philosophy*. London, Allen and Unwin.

Rutter, D. R., and Bunce, D. J. (1989) 'The theory of reasoned action of Fishbein and Ajzen: a test of Towriss's amended procedure for measuring beliefs'. *British Journal of Social Psychology*, 28, 39–46.

Rutter, M. (1978) 'The origins of security and competence'. In J. S. Bruner and A. Garton, eds, *Human Growth and Development*. Oxford, Clarendon.

Rutter, M. (1981) *Maternal Deprivation Reassessed*. Harmondsworth, Penguin.

Rutter, M., Maughan, B., Mortimer, P., and Ouston, J. (1979) *Fifteen Thousand Hours*. London, Open Books.

Rutter, M., and Tizard, J. *et al* (1976) 'Research Report. Isle of Wight Studies 1964–1974'. *Psychological Medicine*, 6, 313–32.

Rybash, J. M., Hoyer, W. J., and Roodin, P. A. (1986) *Adult Cognition and Ageing*. Oxford, Pergamon.

Ryle, G. (1949) *The Concept of Mind*. London, Hutchinson.

Sacks, H., Schegloff, E. A., and Jefferson, G. A. (1974) 'A simplest systematics for the organization of turn-taking in conversation'. *Language*, 50, 697–735.

Saffran, E. M., Schwartz, M. J., and Marin, O. S. M. (1980) 'Evidence from aphasia: isolating the components of a production model'. In B. Butterworth, ed., *Language Production*, Vol. 1. London, Academic Press.

Salapatek, P. (1975) 'Pattern perception in early infancy'. In L. B. Cohen and P. Salapatek, eds, *Infant Perception from Sensation to Cognition, Volume 1*. New York, Academic Press.

Salthouse, T. A. (1986) *A Theory of Cognitive Ageing*. Oxford, Pergamon.

Santrock, J. W., Warshak, R. A., and Elliott, G. L. (1982) 'Social development and parent–child interaction in father custody and stepmother families'. In M. E. Lamb, ed., *Non-traditional Families: Parenting and child development*. Hillsdale, N.J., Lawrence Erlbaum Associates.

Sapir, E. (1927) *Language*. N.Y., Harcourt Brace.

Scarman Report (1981) *The Brixton Disorders 10–11 April 1981*. London, HMSO Cmnd 8427.

Schachter, S. (1964) 'The interaction of cognitive and physiological determinants of emotional states'. In L. Berkowitz, ed., *Advances in Experimental Social Psychology*, Vol. 1. New York, Academic Press.

Schachter, S., and Singer, J. E. (1962) 'Cognitive, social and physiological determinants of emotional state'. *Psychological Review*, 69, 379–99.

Schachter, S., and Singer, J. E. (1979) 'Comments on the Maslach and Marshall/Zimbardo experiments'. *Journal of Personality and Social Psychology*, 37, 989–95.

Schaffer, H. R., and Crook, C. K. (1978) 'The role of the mother in early social development'. In H. McGurk, ed., *Issues in Childhood Social Development*. London, Methuen.

Schank, R., and Abelson, R. (1977) *Scripts, Plans, Goals and Understanding*. Hillsdale, N.J., Lawrence Erlbaum Associates.

Schneider, D. J., Hastorf, A. H., and Ellsworth, P. C. (1979) *Person Perception*, 2nd edn. Reading, Mass., Addison-Wesley.

Schofield, N. J., and Ashman, A. F. (1987) 'The cognitive processing of gifted high average and low average ability students'. *British Journal of Educational Psychology*, 57(I), 9–21.

Schonell, F. J. (1942) *Backwardness in the Basic Subjects*. Edinburgh, Oliver and Boyd.

Schultz, R. (1976) 'Effects of control and predictability on the psychological well-being of the institutionalized aged'. *Journal of Personality and Social Psychology*, 33, 563–73.

Schwartz, A. N., Campsos, J. J., and Baisel, E. J. (1973) 'The visual cliff: cardiac and behavioural responses on the deep and shallow sides at five and nine months of age'. *Journal of Experimental Child Psychology*, 15, 86–99.

Schwartz, G. M., Izard, C. E., and Ansul, S. E. (1985) 'The five-month-old's ability to discriminate facial expressions of emotion'. *Infant Behaviour and Development*, 8, 65–77.

Schweinhart, L. J., and Weikhart, D. P. (1980) *Young Children Grow Up*. Ypsilanti, Michigan, The High/Scope Press.

Sclafani, A., and Springer, D. (1976) 'Dietary obesity in adult rats: similarities to hypothalamic and human obesity syndromes'. *Physiology and Behavior*, 17, 461–71.

Scribner, S. (1984) 'Studying working intelligence'. In B. Rogoff and J. Lave, eds, *Everyday Cognition: Its development and social context*. Cambridge, Mass., Harvard University Press.

Searle, J. (1980) 'Minds, brains and programs'. *The Behavioural and Brain Sciences*, 3, 417–57.

Segal, E. (1969) 'Hierarchical structure in free recall'. *Journal of Experimental Psychology*, 80, 59–63.

Segal, S. J., and Fusella, V. (1970) 'Influence of imaged pictures and sounds on detection of visual and auditory signals'. *Journal of Experimental Psychology*, 83, 458–64.

Segall, M. H., Campbell, D. T., and Herskovits, M. J. (1963) *The Influence of Culture on Visual Perception*. New York, Bobbs-Merrill.

Seligman, M. (1972) *Biological Boundaries of Learning*. New York, Appleton-Century-Croft.

Seligman, M. (1975) *Helplessness: On depression development and death*. San Francisco, W. H. Freeman.

Serpell, R. (1971) 'Discrimination of orientation by Zambian children'. *Journal of Comparative Physiology*, 75, 312.

Serpell, R. (1979) 'How specific are perceptual skills? A cross-cultural study of pattern reproduction'. *British Journal of Psychology*, 70, 365–80.

Seyfarth, R. M., and Chesney, D. L. (1984) 'Grooming alliances and reinforced altruism in vervet monkeys'. *Nature*, 308, 541–3.

Shagass, C., and Kerenyi, A. B. (1958) 'Neurophysiological studies of personality'. *Journal of Nervous and Mental Disease*, 126, 141–7.

Shallice, T., and Warrington, E. (1970) 'Independent functioning of verbal memory stores. A neuropsychological study'. *Quarterly Journal of Experimental Psychology*, 22, 261–73.

Sharpe, S. (1978) *Just Like A Girl: How girls learn to be women*. Harmondsworth, Penguin.

Shatz, M. (1983) Section 2, part 4 of E. Warner and L. R. Gleitman, eds, *Language Acquisition*. Cambridge, Cambridge University Press.

Shaw, L., and Sichel, N. S. (1970) *Accident Proneness*. Oxford, Pergamon.

Sherif, M. (1936) *The Psychology of Social Norms*. New York, Harper and Row.

Sherif, M., Harvey, O. J., White, B. J., Hood, W. R., and Sherif, C. W. (1961) *Inter-group conflict and co-operation: the Robbers' Cave experiment*. Norman, Oklahoma, University of Oklahoma Press.

Sherif, M., and Hovland, C. I. (1961) *Social Judgement: Assimilation and contrast effects in communication and attitude change*. New Haven, Conn., Yale University Press.

Shuey, A. M. (1966) *The Testing of Negro Intelligence*. New York, Social Science Press.

Shulman, H. (1970) 'Encoding and retention of semantic and phonetic information in short term memory'. *Journal of Verbal Learning and Verbal Behaviour*, 9, 499–508.

Siddle, D. A., Morish, R. B., White, K. D., and Mangen, G. L. (1969) 'Relation of visual sensitivity to extraversion'. *Journal of Experimental Research in Personality*, 3, 264–7.

Sidman, M., and Kirk, B. (1974) 'Letter reversals in naming, writing, and matching to sample'. *Child Development*, 45, 616–25.

Sidtis, J. J. (1981) 'The complex tone test: implications for the assessment of auditory laterality effects'. *Neuropsychologia*, 19, 103–12.

Sigall, H., and Page, R. (1971) 'Current stereotypes: a little fading, a little faking'. *Journal of Personality and Social Psychology*, 18, 247–55.

Sigel, R. S. (1964) 'Effect of partisanship on the perception of political candidates'. *Public Opinion Quarterly*, 28, 488–96.

Simon, H. A. (1957) *Models of Man*. New York, Wiley.

Simonini, R. C. (1956) 'Phonemic and analogic lapses in radio and television speech'. *American Speech*, 31, 252–63.

Sinclair-de-Zwart, H. (1969) 'Developmental psycholinguistics'. In D. Elkind and J. H. Flavell, eds, *Studies in Cognitive Development*. Oxford University Press.

Skeels, H. M. (1966) 'Adult status of children with contrasting early life experiences'. *Monographs of the Society for Research in Child Development*, 31, 3 (Serial No. 105).

Skinner, B. F. (1957) *Verbal Behaviour*. New York, Appleton-Century-Crofts.

Skoff, E., and Pollack, R. H. (1969) 'Visual acuity in children as a function of hue'. *Perception and Psychophysics*, 6, 244–6.

Slobin, D. I. (1966) 'Grammatical transformations and sentence comprehension in childhood and adulthood'. *Journal of Verbal Learning and Verbal Behaviour*, 5, 219–27.

Smith, Frank (1978) *Reading*. Cambridge, Cambridge University Press.

Smith, M. (1985) 'Recent work on low lead level exposure and its impact on behavior, intelligence, and learning: a review'. *Journal of the American Academy of Child Psychiatry*, 24, 24–32.

Smyth, M. M., Morris, P. E., Levy, P., and Ellis, A. W. (1987) *Cognition in Action*. London, Lawrence Erlbaum Associates.

Snyder, F. W., and Pronko, N. H. (1952) *Vision with Spatial Inversion*. Wichita, Kansas, University of Wichita Press.

Snyder, M. (1974) 'Self-monitoring of expressive behaviour'. *Journal of Personality and Social Psychology*, 36, 526–37.

Snyder, M., Tanke, E., and Berscheid, E. (1977) 'Social perception and interpersonal behaviour: on the self-fulfilling nature of social stereotypes'. *Journal of Personality and Social Psychology*, 35, 656–66.

Snyder, M., and Uranowitz, S. (1978) 'Reconstructing the past: some cognitive consequences of person perception'. *Journal of Personality and Social Psychology*, 36, 941–50.

Solity, J., and Bull, S. (1987) *Special Needs: Bridging the curriculum gap*. Milton Keynes, Open University Press.

Solman, R. T., May, J. G., and Schwartz, B. D. (1981) 'The word superiority effect: a study using parts of letters'. *Journal of Experimental Psychology: Human Perception and Performance*, 7, 552–9.

Solomon, R. L. (1980) 'The opponent process theory of acquired motivation: the costs of pleasure and the benefits of pain'. *American Psychologist*, 35, 691–712.

Spence, J. T., and Helmreich, R. L. (1978) *Masculinity and Femininity*. University of Texas Press.

Sperry, R. W. (1982) 'Some effects of disconnecting the cerebral hemispheres'. *Science*, 217, 1223–6.

Sroufe, R. A. (1983) 'Individual patterns of adaptation from infancy to pre-school'.

In M. Permutter, ed., *Minnesota Symposium on Child Psychology*, Vol. 16. Hillsdale, N.J., Lawrence Erlbaum Associates.

Stammers, R., and Patrick, J. (1975) *The Psychology of Training*. London, Methuen.

Stein, A. H., and Friedrich, L. K. (1975) 'Impact of television on children and youth'. In E. M. Hetherington, ed., *Review of Child Development Research*, Vol. 5. University of Chicago Press.

Stelmack, R. M., Achorn, E., and Michaud, A. (1977) 'Extraversion and individual differences in auditory evoked responses'. *Psychophysiology*, 14, 368–74.

Stern, D. (1977) *The First Relationship: Infant and mother*. London, Fontana.

Stern, E., Parmelee, A. H., and Harris, M. A. (1973) 'Sleep state periodicity in prematures and young infants'. *Developmental Psychobiology*, 6, 357–65.

Sternberg, R. J. (1984) 'Toward a triarchic theory of human intelligence'. *Behavioral and Brain Sciences*, 7, 269–87.

Sternberg, R. J. (1985a) *Beyond IQ: A triarchic theory of human intelligence*. Cambridge University Press.

Sternberg, R. J. (1985b) *Human Abilities: An information processing approach*. Oxford, W. H. Freeman.

Sternberg, R. J., and Berg, C. A. (1986) 'Quantitative integration: definitions of intelligence: a comparison of the 1921 and 1986 symposia'. In R. J. Sternberg and D. K. Detterman, eds, *What is Intelligence? Contemporary viewpoints on its nature and definition*. Norwood, N.J., Ablex.

Sternberg, R. J., and Gardner, H. (1983) 'Unities in inductive reasoning'. *Journal of Experimental Psychology: General*, 112, 80–116.

Stewart, R. B. (1983) 'Sibling attachment relations'. *Developmental Psychology*, 19, 192–9.

Stratton, G. M. (1896) 'Some preliminary experiments on vision'. *Psychological Review*, 3, 611–17.

Stratton, G. M. (1897) 'Vision without inversion of the retinal image'. *Psychological Review*, 4, 341–60 and 463–81.

Stratton, P. (1982) *The Psychobiology of the Human Newborn*. Chichester, Wiley.

Super, C. M. (1983) 'Cultural variation in the meaning and uses of children's "intelligence"'. In J. Deregowski, S. Oziurawec and R. Annis, eds, *Explorations in Cross Cultural-Psychology*. Amsterdam, Swets and Zeitlinger.

Svancara, J. (1984) 'Mutual influences of genetic and environmental factors in life span developmental research'. *Sbornik Praci Filosofike Faculty Brenenske U*, 19, 43–51.

Swann, J., and Read, S. (1981) 'Self-verification processes: how we sustain our self-conceptions'. *Journal of Experimental Social Psychology*, 17, 351–72.

Szasz, T. S. (1970) *The Manufacture of Madness*. New York, Harper and Row.

Tajfel, H. (1978) 'Intergroup behaviour, I and II'. In H. Tajfel and C. Fraser, eds, *Introducing Social Psychology*. Harmondsworth, Penguin.

Tajfel, H., Billig, M. G., Bundy, R. P., and Flament, C. (1971) 'Social categorization and intergroup behaviour'. *European Journal of Social Psychology*, 1, 149–78.

Tanner, J. M. (1972, 1973) *Foetus into Man*. London, Open Books.

Taylor, S. E., and Fiske, S. T. (1978) 'Salience, attention and attribution: top of the head phenomena'. In L. Berkowitz, ed., *Advances in Experimental Social Psychology*, Vol. 11. New York, Academic Press.

Teasdale, T. W., and Owen, D. R. (1984) 'Heredity and familial environment in intelligence and educational level: a sibling study'. *Nature*, 309, 620–2.

Tedford, W. H., Warren, D. E., and Flynn, W. E. (1977) 'Alternation of shock aversion thresholds during menstrual cycle'. *Perception and Psychophysics*, 21, 2, 193–6.

Telch, M. J., Killen, J. D., McAlister, A. L., Perry, C. L., and Maccoby, N. (1982) 'Long-term follow-up of a pilot project on smoking prevention with adolescents'. *Journal of Behavioral Medicine*, 5, 1–8.

Terman, L. (1925–1957) *Genetic Studies of Genius*, Vol. 1: 1925, Vol. 2: 1926, Vol. 3: 1930, Vol. 4: 1957. Stanford, California, Stanford University Press.

Thomas, A., and Chess, S. (1977) *Temperament and Development*. New York, Brunner-Mazel.

Thomas, C. B., and Duszynski, K. R. (1974) 'Closeness to parents and the family constellation in a prospective study of five disease states: suicide, mental illness, malignant tumor, hypertension and coronary heart disease'. *Johns Hopkins Medical Journal*, 134, 251–70.

Thomas, W. I., and Znaniecki, F. (1918) *The Polish Peasant in Europe and America*, Vol. 1. Boston, Badger.

Thompson, S. C. (1981) 'Will it hurt less if I can control it? A complex answer to a simple question'. *Psychological Bulletin*, 90, 89–101.

Thurstone L. L. (1928) 'Attitudes can be measured'. *American Journal of Sociology*, 33, 529–44.

Thurstone, L. L. (1931) 'The measurement of social attitudes'. *Journal of Abnormal and Social Psychology*, 26, 249–69.

Thurstone, L. L. (1938) 'Primary mental abilities'. *Psychometric Monographs*, No. 1.

Tinbergen, N. (1952) 'Derived activities'. *Quarterly Review of Biology*, 27, 1–32.

Tinsley, B. R., and Parke, R. D. (1984) 'Grandparents as support and socialization agents'. In M. Lewis, ed., *Beyond the Dyad*. New York, Plenum.

Tizard, B., and Hughes, M. (1984) *Young Children Learning*. London, Fontana.

Tizard, J., *et al* (1982) 'Collaboration between teachers and parents in assisting children's reading'. *British Journal of Educational Psychology*.

Tolman, E. C. (1932) *Purposive Behaviour in Animals and Man*. New York, Appleton-Century-Crofts.

Tolman, E. C., and Honzig, C. H. (1930) 'Introduction and renewal of reward and maze performance in rats'. *Berkeley University of California Publications in Psychology*, 4, 19, 267.

Topping, K., and Wolfendale, S., eds, (1985) *Parental Involvement in Children's Reading*. London, Croom Helm (New York, Nichols).

Treisman, A. (1960) 'Contextual cues in selective listening'. *Quarterly Journal of Experimental Psychology*, 12, 242–8.

Treisman, A. (1964) 'Verbal cues, language and meaning in attention'. *American Journal of Psychology*, 77, 206–14.

Treisman, A. M., and Gelade, G. (1980) 'A feature-integration theory of attention'. *Cognitive Psychology*, 12, 97–136.

Trevarthen, C. (1974) 'Conversations with a two-month-old'. *New Scientist*, 62, 230–5.

Triplett, N. (1897) 'The dynamogenic factors in pacemaking and competition'. *American Journal of Psychology*, 9, 507–33.

Trudgill, P. (1974) *Sociolinguistics*. Harmondsworth, Penguin.

Tulving, E. (1966) 'Subjective organization and effects of repetition in multi-trial free recall learning'. *Journal of Verbal Learning and Verbal Behaviour*, 5, 193–7.

Tulving, E. (1968) 'Theoretical issues in free recall'. In T. Dixon and D. Horton, eds, *Verbal Behaviour and General Behaviour Theory*. Englewood Cliffs, N.J., Prentice-Hall.

Tulving, E. (1972) 'Episodic and semantic theory'. In E. Tulving and W. Donaldson, eds, *Organization of Memory*. New York, Academic Press.

Tulving, E., and Pearlstone, Z. (1966) 'Availability versus accessibility of information in memory for words'. *Journal of Verbal Learning and Verbal Behaviour*, 5, 381–9.

Tulving, E., and Thomson, D. (1971) 'Retrieval processes in recognition memory: effects of associate context'. *Journal of Experimental Psychology*, 87, 116–24.

Tulving, E., and Thomson, D. (1973) 'Encoding specificity and retrieval processes in episodic memory'. *Psychological Review*, 80, 352–73.

Turner, C. W., Layton, J. F., and Simons, L. S. (1975) 'Naturalistic studies of aggressive behaviour: aggressive stimuli, victim visibility and horn honking'. *Journal of Personality and Social Psychology*, 31, 1098–107.

Turner, J. (1980) *Made for Life: Coping, competence and cognition*. London, Methuen.

Ullman, S. (1980) 'Against direct perception'. *Behavioural and Brain Sciences*, 3, 373–415.

Underwood, J., and Underwood, G. (1987) 'Data organization and retrieval by children'. *British Journal of Educational Psychology*, 57(III), 313–30.

Ungerleider, L. G., and Mishkin, M. (1982) 'Two cortical visual systems'. In D. J. Ingle, M. A. Goodale, and R. J. W. Mansfield, eds, *Analysis of Visual Behavior*. Cambridge, Mass., MIT Press.

United States of America (1972) *Report of Surgeon General's Advisory Committee on Television and Social Behaviour*. Washington, D.C., Government Printing Office.

United States of America (1982) *American National Institute of Mental Health*. Report. Washington, D.C., Department of Health.

Vandell, D. L. (1979) 'A microanalysis of toddlers' social-interaction with mothers and fathers'. *The Journal of Genetic Psychology*, 134, 299–312.

Vandenberg, S. G. (1966) 'Contributions of twin research to psychology'. *Psychological Bulletin*, 66, 327–52.

Vandenberg, S. G. (1984) 'Does a special twin situation contribute to similarities for abilities in MZ and DZ twins?' *Acta Geneticae Medicae et Gemellelogiae: Twin Research*, 33, 219–22.

Van Dijk, T. (1981) 'Review of R. O. Freedle's *New Directions in Discourse Processing*'. *Journal of Linguistics*, 17, 140–8.

van Lawick-Goodall, J. (1968) 'Tool using birds: the Egyptian vulture'. *National Geographic*, 133, 631–41.

Vargas, J. (1977) *Behavioural Psychology for Teachers*. London, Harper and Row.

Vaughn, B., Egeland, B., Sroufe, L. A., and Waters, E. (1979) 'Individual differences in infant–mother attachments at twelve and eighteen months: stability and change in families under stress'. *Child Development*, 50, 971–5.

Vernon, P. E. (1960) 'Development of current ideas about intelligence tests'. *Modern Concepts of Intelligence*, Association of Educational Psychologists.

Vernon, P. E. (1965a) 'Ability factors and environmental influences'. *American Psychologist*, 20, 723–33.

Vernon, P. E. (1965b) 'Environmental handicaps and intellectual development'. *British Journal of Education Psychology*, 35, 117–36.

Vernon, P. E. (1969) *Intelligence and Cultural Environment*. London, Methuen.

Von Senden, M. (1932) *Space and Sight*, tr. P. Heath. Methuen/Free Press, 1960.

Von Wright, J. M., Anderson, K., and Stenman, U. (1975) 'Generalization of conditional GSRs in dichotic listening'. In P. Rabbit and S. Dornic, eds, *Attention and Performance*, Vol. 5. Oxford and Stockholm, Academic Press.

Vygotsky, L. S. (1934) *Thought and Language*. Edited and translated by E. Hanfmann and G. Vakar (1962). Cambridge, Mass., MIT Press.

Wachs, T. D., and Gruen, G. E. (1982) *Early Experience and Human Development*. New York, Plenum.

Walker, S. (1983) *Animal Thought*. London, Routledge and Kegan Paul.

Wallerstein, J. S., and Kelly, J. S. (1980) *Surviving the Breakup: How children and parents cope with divorce*. London, Grant McIntyre.

Walsh, K. W. (1978) *Neuropsychology*, Edinburgh, Churchill Livingstone.

Walster, E., Aronson, E., and Abrahams, D. (1966) 'On increasing the persuasiveness of a low prestige communicator'. *Journal of Experimental Social Psychology*, 2, 325–42.

Wanner, E., and Maratsos, M. (1978) 'An ATN approach to comprehension'. In M. Halle, J. Bresnan and G. A. Miller, eds, *Linguistic Theory and Psychological Reality*. Cambridge, Mass., MIT Press.

The Warnock Report (1978) *Special Educational Needs*. London, HMSO.

Wason, P. C. (1965) 'The context of plausible denial'. *Journal of Verbal Learning and Verbal Behaviour*, 4, 7–11.

Wason, P. C. (1968) 'Reasoning about a rule'. *The Quarterly Journal of Experimental Psychology*, 20, 273–81.

Wason, P. C.. (1969) 'Regression in reasoning'. *British Journal of Psychology*, 60, 471–80.

Wason, P. C., and Johnson-Laird, P. N. (1970) 'A conflict between selecting and evaluating information in an inferential task'. *British Journal of Psychology*, 61, 509–15.

Wason, P. C., and Shapiro, D. (1971) 'Natural and contrived experience in a reasoning problem'. *Quarterly Journal of Experimental Psychology*, 23, 63–71.

Wasz-Hockert, O., Lind, J., Vourenkoski, V., Partanen, T., and Valenne, E. (1968) *A Spectographic and Auditory Analysis*. Suffolk, Lavenham Press.

Waterman, A. S., *et al* (1974) 'A longitudinal study of changes in ego-identity status from the freshman to the senior year at college'. *Developmental Psychology*, 10, 387–92.

Waugh, N., and Norman, D. (1965) 'Primary memory'. *Psychological Review*, 72, 89–104.

Weiner, B. (1974) *Achievement Motivation and Attribution Theory*. Morristown, N.J., General Learning Press.

Weisberg, H., and Bowen, B. (1977) *An Introduction to Survey Research and Data Analysis*. San Francisco, Freeman.

Weiskrantz, L. (1958) 'Sensory deprivation and the cat's optic nervous system'. *Nature*, 181, 1047–50.

Weiss, J., and Brown, P. (1977) *Self-insight Error in the Explanation of Mood*. Unpublished manuscript, Harvard University.

Weiss, J. M. (1977) 'Psychological and behavioural influences on gastrointestinal lesions in animal models'. In J. D. Maser and M. E. P. Seligman, eds, *Psychopathology: Experimental Models*. San Francisco, Freeman.

Weiss, W. (1957) 'Opinion congruence with a negative source on one issue as a factor influencing agreement on another issue'. *Journal of Abnormal and Social Psychology*, 54, 180–6.

Weizenbaum, J. (1987) 'Artificial intelligence', In R. Finnegan, G. Salaman and K. Thompson, eds, *Information Technology: A reader*. London, Hodder and Stoughton.

Welch, J. (1898) 'On the measurement of mental activity through muscular activity and the determination of a constant attention'. *American Journal of Psychology*, 1, 288–306.

Werner, E. E., and Smith, R. S. (1982) *Vulnerable but Invincible: A longitudinal study of resilient children and youth*. New York, McGraw-Hill.

Wernicke, C. (1874) *Der aphasische Symptomenkomplex*. Breslau, Cohn und Weigert.

Wertsch, J. V. (1985a) *Culture, Communication and Cognition: Vygotskian perspectives*. Cambridge University Press.

Wertsch, J. V. (1985b) *Vygotsky and the Social Formation of Mind*. Cambridge, Mass., Harvard University Press.

Wessells, M. G. (1982) *Cognitive Psychology*. New York, Harper and Row.

Westie, F. R. and DeFleur, M. L. (1959) 'Autonomic responses and their relationship to race attitudes'. *Journal of Abnormal and Social Psychology*, 58, 340–7.

Westlin-Lindgren, G. (1982) 'Achievement and mental ability of physically late and early maturing school children related to their social background'. *Journal of Child Psychology and Psychiatry*, 23, 407–20.

Westmacott, E. V. S., and Cameron, R. J. (1981) *Behaviour Can Change*. London, Macmillan Education.

Wexler, B. E. (1988) 'Dichotic presentation as a method for single hemisphere stimulation studies'. In K. Hugdahl, ed., *Handbook of Dichotic Listening: Theory, methods and research*. Chichester, Wiley.

Wheeler, M. P. (1983) 'Context related age change in mothers' speech: joint book reading'. *Journal of Child Language*, 10, 259–63.

Whimbey, A., and Lochhead, J. (1980) *Problem Solving and Comprehension: A short course in analytical reasoning*. Philadelphia, The Franklin Institute Press.

White, D. G., Woollett, E. A., and Lyon, M. L. (1982) 'Fathers' involvement with their infants: the relevance of holding'. In N. Beail and J. McGuire, eds, *Fathers: Psychological perspectives*. London, Junction.

Whiting, B. B., and Whiting, J. W. M. (1975) *Children of Six Cultures*. Harvard University Press.

Whorf, B. L. (1957) *Language, Thought and Reality*. Cambridge, Mass., MIT Press.

Wicker, A. W. (1969) 'Attitudes versus actions: the relationship of verbal and overt behavioral responses to attitude objects'. *Journal of Social Issues*, 25, 41–78.

Wicklund, R. (1975) 'Objective self-awareness'. In L. Berkowitz, ed., *Advances in Experimental Social Psychology*, Vol. 8. New York, Academic Press.

Wilkins, W. (1971) 'Desensitization: social and cognitive factors underlying the effectiveness of Wolpe's procedure'. *Psychology Bulletin*, 76, 311–17.

Wilson, E. O. (1975) *Sociobiology: The new synthesis*. Cambridge, Mass., Harvard University Press.

Wilson, R. S. (1977) 'Twins and siblings: concordance for school-age mental development'. *Child Development*, 38, 211–16.

Wilson, R. S. (1986) 'Continuity and change in cognitive ability profile'. *Behavior Genetics*, 16, 45–60.

Wilson, R. W. (1979) 'Synchronics in mental development: an epigenetic perspective'. *Annual Progress in Psychiatry and Child Development*, 144–67.

Winkler, J., and Taylor, S. E. (1979) 'Preference, expectations and attributional bias: two field studies'. *Journal of Applied Psychology*, 9, 183–97.

Winneke, G. C., and Kraemer, V. (1984) 'Neuropsychological effects of lead in children: interactive effects with social background variables'. *Neuropsychobiology*, 11, 195–202.

Winograd, T. (1972) 'Understanding natural language'. *Cognitive Psychology*, 3, 1–191.

Witkin, H. A. (1949) 'The nature and importance of individual differences in perception'. *Journal of Personality*, 18, 145–70.

Witkin, H. A., and Berry, J. W. (1975) 'Psychological differentiation in cross-cultural perspective'. *Journal of Cross-Cultural Psychology*, 6, 4–87.

Wober, J. M. (1988) 'Informing the British public about AIDS'. *Health Education Research*, 3, 19–24.

Wober, M. (1972) 'Culture and the concept of intelligence'. *Journal of Cross Cultural Psychology*, 3, 327–8.

Wollen, K., Weber, A., and Lowry, D. (1972) 'Bizarreness versus interaction of mental images as determinants of learning'. *Cognitive Psychology*, 2, 518–23.

Wolpe, J. (1958) *Psychotherapy by Reciprocal Inhibition*. Stanford, Calif., Stanford University Press.

Wood, W., and Eagly, W. H. (1981) 'Stages in the analysis of persuasive messages: the role of causal attributions and message comprehension'. *Journal of Personality and Social Psychology*, 40, 246–59.

Woodhead, M. (1985) 'Pre-school education has long term effects: but can they be generalized?' *Oxford Review of Education*, 11, 133–55.

Woodworth, R. S., and Sells, S. B. (1935) 'An atmosphere effect in formal syllogistic reasoning'. *Journal of Experimental Psychology*, 18, 451–60.

Woollett, A. (1986) 'The influence of older siblings on the language environment of young children'. *British Journal of Developmental Psychology*, 4, 235–45.

Woollett, E. A., White, D. G., and Lyon, M. L. (1982) 'Observations of fathers at birth'. In N. Beail and J. McGuire, eds, *Fathers: Psychological perspectives*. London, Junction.

Worthington, A. G. (1969) 'Paired comparison scaling of brightness judgements; a method for the measurement of perceptual defence'. *British Journal of Psychology*, 60(3), 363–8.

Wulf, F. (1922) 'Uber die Veranderung von Verstellunge (Gedachtnis und Gestalt)'. *Psychologisch Forschung*, 1, 333–73.

Yates, F. (1966) *The Art of Memory*. London, Routledge and Kegan Paul.

Yen, W. (1975) 'Sex-linked major gene influence on selected types of spatial performance'. *Behaviour Genetics*, 5, 281–98.

Zahavi (1979) 'Ritualization and the evolution of movement signals'. *Behaviour*, 72, 77–81.

Zajonc, R. (1965) 'Social facilitation'. *Science*, 149, 269–74.

Zarbatany, L., and Lamb, M. E. (1985) 'Social referencing as a function of information source: mothers versus strangers'. *Infant Behaviour and Development*, 8, 25–33.

Zeller, A. (1950) 'An experimental analogue of repression: the effect of individual failure and success on memory measured by relearning'. *Journal of Experimental Psychology*, 40, 411–22.

Zimbardo, P. G. (1970) 'The human choice: individuation, reason, and order versus deindividuation, impulse and chaos'. In W. J. Arnold and D. Levine, eds, *Nebraska Symposium on Motivation*, 17, 237–307.

Zimbardo, P. G. (1973) 'The psychological power and pathology of imprisonment'. In E. Aronson and R. Helmreich, eds, *Social Psychology*. New York, Van Nostrand.

Zimmerman, D. H., and West, C. (1970) 'Sex roles, interruptions and silences in conversation'. In B. Thorne and N. Henley, eds, *Language and Sex, Difference and Dominance*. Rowley, Mass., Newbury House.

Zucker, K. J. (1985) 'The infant's construction of his parents in the first six months of life'. In T. M. Fiels and N. A. Fox, eds, *Social Perception in Infants*. Norwood, N.J., Ablex.

Zuckerman, M. (1979) 'Attribution of success and failure revisited, or, the motivational bias is alive and well in attribution theory'. *Journal of Personality*, 47, 245–87.

Significance tables

Table A.1 One-tailed probabilities (p) for values of the standard normal deviate (z). (Abridged from Table 1 of *The Biometrika Tables for Statisticians*, Vol. I, edited by Pearson, E. S. and Hartley, H. O., with permission of E. S Pearson and the trustees of Biometrika.)

z	p	z	p	z	p	z	p
0.00	.5000	0.35	.3632	0.70	.2420	1.05	.1469
0.01	.4960	0.36	.3594	0.71	.2389	1.06	.1446
0.02	.4920	0.37	.3557	0.72	.2358	1.07	.1423
0.03	.4880	0.38	.3520	0.73	.2327	1.08	.1401
0.04	.4840	0.39	.3483	0.74	.2296	1.09	.1379
0.05	.4801	0.40	.3446	0.75	.2266	1.10	.1357
0.06	.4761	0.41	.3409	0.76	.2236	1.11	.1335
0.07	.4721	0.42	.3372	0.77	.2206	1.12	.1314
0.08	.4681	0.43	.3336	0.78	.2177	1.13	.1292
0.09	.4641	0.44	.3300	0.79	.2148	1.14	.1271
0.10	.4602	0.45	.3264	0.80	.2119	1.15	.1251
0.11	.4562	0.46	.3228	0.81	.2090	1.16	.1230
0.12	.4522	0.47	.3192	0.82	.2061	1.17	.1210
0.13	.4483	0.48	.3156	0.83	.2033	1.18	.1190
0.14	.4443	0.49	.3121	0.84	.2005	1.19	.1170
0.15	.4404	0.50	.3085	0.85	.1977	1.20	.1151
0.16	.4364	0.51	.3050	0.86	.1949	1.21	.1131
0.17	.4325	0.52	.3015	0.87	.1922	1.22	.1112
0.18	.4286	0.53	.2981	0.88	.1894	1.23	.1093
0.19	.4247	0.54	.2946	0.89	.1867	1.24	.1075
0.20	.4207	0.55	.2912	0.90	.1841	1.25	.1056
0.21	.4168	0.56	.2877	0.91	.1814	1.26	.1038
0.22	.4129	0.57	.2843	0.92	.1788	1.27	.1020
0.23	.4090	0.58	.2810	0.93	.1762	1.28	.1003
0.24	.4052	0.59	.2776	0.94	.1736	1.29	.0985
0.25	.4013	0.60	.2743	0.95	.1711	1.30	.0968
0.26	.3974	0.61	.2709	0.96	.1685	1.31	.0951
0.27	.3936	0.62	.2676	0.97	.1660	1.32	.0934
0.28	.3897	0.63	.2643	0.98	.1635	1.33	.0918
0.29	.3859	0.64	.2611	0.99	.1611	1.34	.0901
0.30	.3821	0.65	.2578	1.00	.1587	1.35	.0885
0.31	.3783	0.66	.2546	1.01	.1562	1.36	.0869
0.32	.3745	0.67	.2514	1.02	.1539	1.37	.0853
0.33	.3707	0.68	.2483	1.03	.1515	1.38	.0838
0.34	.3669	0.69	.2451	1.04	.1492	1.39	.0823

z	p	z	p	z	p	z	p
1.40	.0808	1.90	.0287	2.40	.0082	2.90	.0019
1.41	.0793	1.91	.0281	2.41	.0080	2.91	.0018
1.42	.0778	1.92	.0274	2.42	.0078	2.92	.0018
1.43	.0764	1.93	.0268	2.43	.0075	2.93	.0017
1.44	.0749	1.94	.0262	2.44	.0073	2.94	.0016
1.45	.0735	1.95	.0256	2.45	.0071	2.95	.0016
1.46	.0721	1.96	.0250	2.46	.0069	2.96	.0015
1.47	.0708	1.97	.0244	2.47	.0068	2.97	.0015
1.48	.0694	1.98	.0239	2.48	.0066	2.98	.0014
1.49	.0681	1.99	.0233	2.49	.0064	2.99	.0014
1.50	.0668	2.00	.0228	2.50	.0062	3.00	.0013
1.51	.0655	2.01	.0222	2.51	.0060	3.01	.0013
1.52	.0643	2.02	.0217	2.52	.0059	3.02	.0013
1.53	.0630	2.03	.0212	2.53	.0057	3.03	.0012
1.54	.0618	2.04	.0207	2.54	.0055	3.04	.0012
1.55	.0606	2.05	.0202	2.55	.0054	3.05	.0011
1.56	.0594	2.06	.0197	2.56	.0052	3.06	.0011
1.57	.0582	2.07	.0192	2.57	.0051	3.07	.0011
1.58	.0571	2.08	.0188	2.58	.0049	3.08	.0010
1.59	.0559	2.09	.0183	2.59	.0048	3.09	.0010
1.60	.0548	2.10	.0179	2.60	.0047	3.10	.0010
1.61	.0537	2.11	.0174	2.61	.0045	3.11	.0009
1.62	.0526	2.12	.0170	2.62	.0044	3.12	.0009
1.63	.0516	2.13	.0166	2.63	.0043	3.13	.0009
1.64	.0505	2.14	.0162	2.64	.0041	3.14	.0008
1.65	.0495	2.15	.0158	2.65	.0040	3.15	.0008
1.66	.0485	2.16	.0154	2.66	.0039	3.16	.0008
1.67	.0475	2.17	.0150	2.67	.0038	3.17	.0008
1.68	.0465	2.18	.0146	2.68	.0037	3.18	.0007
1.69	.0455	2.19	.0143	2.69	.0036	3.19	.0007
1.70	.0446	2.20	.0139	2.70	.0035	3.20	.0007
1.71	.0436	2.21	.0136	2.71	.0034	3.21	.0007
1.72	.0427	2.22	.0132	2.72	.0033	3.22	.0006
1.73	.0418	2.23	.0129	2.73	.0032	3.23	.0006
1.74	.0409	2.24	.0125	2.74	.0031	3.24	.0006
1.75	.0401	2.25	.0122	2.75	.0030	3.30	.0005
1.76	.0392	2.26	.0119	2.76	.0029	3.40	.0003
1.77	.0384	2.27	.0116	2.77	.0028	3.50	.0002
1.78	.0375	2.28	.0113	2.78	.0027	3.60	.0002
1.79	.0367	2.29	.0110	2.79	.0026	3.70	.0001
1.80	.0359	2.30	.0107	2.80	.0026		
1.81	.0351	2.31	.0104	2.81	.0025		
1.82	.0344	2.32	.0102	2.82	.0024		
1.83	.0336	2.33	.0099	2.83	.0023		
1.84	.0329	2.34	.0096	2.84	.0023		
1.85	.0322	2.35	.0094	2.85	.0022		
1.86	.0314	2.36	.0091	2.86	.0021		
1.87	.0307	2.37	.0089	2.87	.0021		
1.88	.0301	2.38	.0087	2.88	.0020		
1.89	.0294	2.39	.0084	2.89	.0019		

Table A.2 Critical values of chi square. Values of χ^2 that equal or exceed the tabled value are significant at, or beyond, the level indicated. (Abridged from Table IV of Fisher, R. A. and Yates, F.: *Statistical Tables for Biological, Agricultural and Medical Research*. Longman 1963. Previously published by Oliver and Boyd Ltd, Edinburgh. By permission of the authors and publishers.)

	Level of significance	
Degrees of freedom	.05	.01
1	3.84	6.64
2	5.99	9.21
3	7.82	11.34
4	9.49	13.28
5	11.07	15.09
6	12.59	16.81
7	14.07	18.48
8	15.51	20.09
9	16.92	21.67
10	18.31	23.21
11	19.68	24.72
12	21.03	26.22
13	22.36	27.69
14	23.68	29.14
15	25.00	30.58
16	26.30	32.00
17	27.59	33.41
18	28.87	34.80
19	30.14	36.19
20	31.41	37.57
21	32.67	38.93
22	33.92	40.29
23	35.17	41.64
24	36.42	42.98
25	37.65	44.31
26	38.88	45.64
27	40.11	46.96
28	41.34	48.28
29	42.56	49.59
30	43.77	50.89

Table A.3 Critical values of t that equal or exceed the tabled value are significant at, or beyond, the level indicated. (Taken from Table III of Fisher, R. A. and Yates, F.: *Statistical Tables for Biological, Agricultural and Medical Research*. Longman 1963. Previously published by Oliver and Boyd Ltd, Edinburgh. By permission of the authors and publishers.)

	Level of significance for a one-tailed test			
	.05	.025	.01	.005
Degrees	Level of significance for a two-tailed test			
of freedom	.10	.05	.02	.01
1	6.314	12.706	31.821	63.657
2	2.920	4.303	6.965	9.925
3	2.353	3.182	4.541	5.841
4	2.132	2.776	3.747	4.604
5	2.015	2.571	3.365	4.032
6	1.943	2.447	3.143	3.707
7	1.895	2.365	2.998	3.499
8	1.860	2.306	2.896	3.355
9	1.833	2.262	2.821	3.250
10	1.812	2.228	2.764	3.169
11	1.796	2.201	2.718	3.106
12	1.782	2.179	2.681	3.055
13	1.771	2.160	2.650	3.012
14	1.761	2.145	2.624	2.977
15	1.753	2.131	2.602	2.947
16	1.746	2.120	2.583	2.921
17	1.740	2.110	2.567	2.898
18	1.734	2.101	2.552	2.878
19	1.729	2.093	2.539	2.861
20	1.725	2.086	2.528	2.845
21	1.721	2.080	2.518	2.831
22	1.717	2.074	2.508	2.819
23	1.714	2.069	2.500	2.807
24	1.711	2.064	2.492	2.797
25	1.708	2.060	2.485	2.787
26	1.706	2.056	2.479	2.779
27	1.703	2.052	2.473	2.771
28	1.701	2.048	2.467	2.763
29	1.699	2.045	2.462	2.756
30	1.697	2.042	2.457	2.750
40	1.684	2.021	2.423	2.704
60	1.671	2.000	2.390	2.660
120	1.658	1.980	2.358	2.617
∞	1.645	1.960	2.326	2.576

Table A.4 Critical values of F at the 5% level of significance. Values of F that equal or exceed the tabled value are significant at or beyond the 5% level. (Abridged from Table 18 of *The Biometrika Tables for Statisticians*, Vol. I, edited by Pearson, E. S. and Hartley, H. O. with the permission of E. S. Pearson and the trustees of Biometrika.)

Degrees of freedom for the denominator	Degrees of freedom for the numerator																		
	1	2	3	4	5	6	7	8	9	10	12	15	20	24	30	40	60	120	∞
1	161.4	199.5	215.7	224.6	230.2	234.0	236.8	238.9	240.5	241.9	243.9	245.9	248.0	249.1	250.1	251.1	252.2	253.3	254.3
2	18.51	19.00	19.16	19.25	19.30	19.33	19.35	19.37	19.38	19.40	19.41	19.43	19.45	19.45	19.46	19.47	19.48	19.49	19.50
3	10.13	9.55	9.28	9.12	9.01	8.94	8.89	8.85	8.81	8.79	8.74	8.70	8.66	8.64	8.62	8.59	8.57	8.55	8.53
4	7.71	6.94	6.59	6.39	6.26	6.16	6.09	6.04	6.00	5.96	5.91	5.86	5.80	5.77	5.75	5.72	5.69	5.66	5.63
5	6.61	5.79	5.41	5.19	5.05	4.95	4.88	4.82	4.77	4.74	4.68	4.62	4.56	4.53	4.50	4.46	4.43	4.40	4.36
6	5.99	5.14	4.76	4.53	4.39	4.28	4.21	4.15	4.10	4.06	4.00	3.94	3.87	3.84	3.81	3.77	3.74	3.70	3.67
7	5.59	4.74	4.35	4.12	3.97	3.87	3.79	3.73	3.68	3.64	3.57	3.51	3.44	3.41	3.38	3.34	3.30	3.27	3.23
8	5.32	4.46	4.07	3.84	3.69	3.58	3.50	3.44	3.39	3.35	3.28	3.22	3.15	3.12	3.08	3.04	3.01	2.97	2.93
9	5.12	4.26	3.86	3.63	3.48	3.37	3.29	3.23	3.18	3.14	3.07	3.01	2.94	2.90	2.86	2.83	2.79	2.75	2.71
10	4.96	4.10	3.71	3.48	3.33	3.22	3.14	3.07	3.02	2.98	2.91	2.85	2.77	2.74	2.70	2.66	2.62	2.58	2.54
11	4.84	3.98	3.59	3.36	3.20	3.09	3.01	2.95	2.90	2.85	2.79	2.72	2.65	2.61	2.57	2.53	2.49	2.45	2.40
12	4.75	3.89	3.49	3.26	3.11	3.00	2.91	2.85	2.80	2.75	2.69	2.62	2.54	2.51	2.47	2.43	2.38	2.34	2.30
13	4.67	3.81	3.41	3.18	3.03	2.92	2.83	2.77	2.71	2.67	2.60	2.53	2.46	2.42	2.38	2.34	2.30	2.25	2.21
14	4.60	3.74	3.34	3.11	2.96	2.85	2.76	2.70	2.65	2.60	2.53	2.46	2.39	2.35	2.31	2.27	2.22	2.18	2.13
15	4.54	3.68	3.29	3.06	2.90	2.79	2.71	2.64	2.59	2.54	2.48	2.40	2.33	2.29	2.25	2.20	2.16	2.11	2.07
16	4.49	3.63	3.24	3.01	2.85	2.74	2.66	2.59	2.54	2.49	2.42	2.35	2.28	2.24	2.19	2.15	2.11	2.06	2.01
17	4.45	3.59	3.20	2.96	2.81	2.70	2.61	2.55	2.49	2.45	2.38	2.31	2.23	2.19	2.15	2.10	2.06	2.01	1.96
18	4.41	3.55	3.16	2.93	2.77	2.66	2.58	2.51	2.46	2.41	2.34	2.27	2.19	2.15	2.11	2.06	2.02	1.97	1.92
19	4.38	3.52	3.13	2.90	2.74	2.63	2.54	2.48	2.42	2.38	2.31	2.23	2.16	2.11	2.07	2.03	1.98	1.93	1.88
20	4.35	3.49	3.10	2.87	2.71	2.60	2.51	2.45	2.39	2.35	2.28	2.20	2.12	2.08	2.04	1.99	1.95	1.90	1.84
21	4.32	3.47	3.07	2.84	2.68	2.57	2.49	2.42	2.37	2.32	2.25	2.18	2.10	2.05	2.01	1.96	1.92	1.87	1.81
22	4.30	3.44	3.05	2.82	2.66	2.55	2.46	2.40	2.34	2.30	2.23	2.15	2.07	2.03	1.98	1.94	1.89	1.84	1.78
23	4.28	3.42	3.03	2.80	2.64	2.53	2.44	2.37	2.32	2.27	2.20	2.13	2.05	2.01	1.96	1.91	1.86	1.81	1.76
24	4.26	3.40	3.01	2.78	2.62	2.51	2.42	2.36	2.30	2.25	2.18	2.11	2.03	1.98	1.94	1.89	1.84	1.79	1.73
25	4.24	3.39	2.99	2.76	2.60	2.49	2.40	2.34	2.28	2.24	2.16	2.09	2.01	1.96	1.92	1.87	1.82	1.77	1.71
26	4.23	3.37	2.98	2.74	2.59	2.47	2.39	2.32	2.27	2.22	2.15	2.07	1.99	1.95	1.90	1.85	1.80	1.75	1.69
27	4.21	3.35	2.96	2.73	2.57	2.46	2.37	2.31	2.25	2.20	2.13	2.06	1.97	1.93	1.88	1.84	1.79	1.73	1.67
28	4.20	3.34	2.95	2.71	2.56	2.45	2.36	2.29	2.24	2.19	2.12	2.04	1.96	1.91	1.87	1.82	1.77	1.71	1.65
29	4.18	3.33	2.93	2.70	2.55	2.43	2.35	2.28	2.22	2.18	2.10	2.03	1.94	1.90	1.85	1.81	1.75	1.70	1.64
30	4.17	3.32	2.92	2.69	2.53	2.42	2.33	2.27	2.21	2.16	2.09	2.01	1.93	1.89	1.84	1.79	1.74	1.68	1.62
40	4.08	3.23	2.84	2.61	2.45	2.34	2.25	2.18	2.12	2.08	2.00	1.92	1.84	1.79	1.74	1.69	1.64	1.58	1.51
60	4.00	3.15	2.76	2.53	2.37	2.25	2.17	2.10	2.04	1.99	1.92	1.84	1.75	1.70	1.65	1.59	1.53	1.47	1.39
120	3.92	3.07	2.68	2.45	2.29	2.17	2.09	2.02	1.96	1.91	1.83	1.75	1.66	1.61	1.55	1.50	1.43	1.35	1.25
∞	3.84	3.00	2.60	2.37	2.21	2.10	2.01	1.94	1.88	1.83	1.75	1.67	1.57	1.52	1.46	1.39	1.32	1.22	1.00

Degrees of freedom for the denominator

Table A.5 Critical values of F at the 1% level of significance. Values of F that equal or exceed the tabled value are significant at or beyond the 1% level. (Abridged from Table 18 of *The Biometrika Tables for Statisticians*, Vol. I, edited by Pearson, E. S. and Hartley, H. O. with the permission of E. S. Pearson and the trustees of Biometrika.)

						Degrees of freedom for the numerator												
1	2	3	4	5	6	7	8	9	10	12	15	20	24	30	40	60	120	∞
4052	4999.5	5403	5625	5764	5859	5928	5982	6022	6056	6106	6157	6209	6235	6261	6287	6313	6339	6366
98.50	99.00	99.17	99.25	99.30	99.33	99.36	99.37	99.39	99.40	99.42	99.43	99.45	99.46	99.47	99.47	99.48	99.49	99.50
34.12	30.82	29.46	28.71	28.24	27.91	27.67	27.49	27.35	27.23	27.05	26.87	26.69	26.60	26.50	26.41	26.32	26.22	26.13
21.20	18.00	16.69	15.98	15.52	15.21	14.98	14.80	14.66	14.55	14.37	14.20	14.02	13.93	13.84	13.75	13.65	13.56	13.46
16.26	13.27	12.06	11.39	10.97	10.67	10.46	10.29	10.16	10.05	9.89	9.72	9.55	9.47	9.38	9.29	9.20	9.11	9.02
13.75	10.92	9.78	9.15	8.75	8.47	8.26	8.10	7.98	7.87	7.72	7.56	7.40	7.31	7.23	7.14	7.06	6.97	6.88
12.25	9.55	8.45	7.85	7.46	7.19	6.99	6.84	6.72	6.62	6.47	6.31	6.16	6.07	5.99	5.91	5.82	5.74	5.65
11.26	8.65	7.59	7.01	6.63	6.37	6.18	6.03	5.91	5.81	5.67	5.52	5.36	5.28	5.20	5.12	5.03	4.95	4.86
10.56	8.02	6.99	6.42	6.06	5.80	5.61	5.47	5.35	5.26	5.11	4.96	4.81	4.73	4.65	4.57	4.48	4.40	4.31
10.04	7.56	6.55	5.99	5.64	5.39	5.20	5.06	4.94	4.85	4.71	4.56	4.41	4.33	4.25	4.17	4.08	4.00	3.91
9.65	7.21	6.22	5.67	5.32	5.07	4.89	4.74	4.63	4.54	4.40	4.25	4.10	4.02	3.94	3.86	3.78	3.69	3.60
9.33	6.93	5.95	5.41	5.06	4.82	4.64	4.50	4.39	4.30	4.16	4.01	3.86	3.78	3.70	3.62	3.54	3.45	3.36
9.07	6.70	5.74	5.21	4.86	4.62	4.44	4.30	4.19	4.10	3.96	3.82	3.66	3.59	3.51	3.43	3.34	3.25	3.17
8.86	6.51	5.56	5.04	4.69	4.46	4.28	4.14	4.03	3.94	3.80	3.66	3.51	3.43	3.35	3.27	3.18	3.09	3.00
8.68	6.36	5.42	4.89	4.56	4.32	4.14	4.00	3.89	3.80	3.67	3.52	3.37	3.29	3.21	3.13	3.05	2.96	2.87
8.53	6.23	5.29	4.77	4.44	4.20	4.03	3.89	3.78	3.69	3.55	3.41	3.26	3.18	3.10	3.02	2.93	2.84	2.75
8.40	6.11	5.18	4.67	4.34	4.10	3.93	3.79	3.68	3.59	3.46	3.31	3.16	3.08	3.00	2.92	2.83	2.75	2.65
8.29	6.01	5.09	4.58	4.25	4.01	3.84	3.71	3.60	3.51	3.37	3.23	3.08	3.00	2.92	2.84	2.75	2.66	2.57
8.18	5.93	5.01	4.50	4.17	3.94	3.77	3.63	3.52	3.43	3.30	3.15	3.00	2.92	2.84	2.76	2.67	2.58	2.49
8.10	5.85	4.94	4.43	4.10	3.87	3.70	3.56	3.46	3.37	3.23	3.09	2.94	2.86	2.78	2.69	2.61	2.52	2.42
8.02	5.78	4.87	4.37	4.04	3.81	3.64	3.51	3.40	3.31	3.17	3.03	2.88	2.80	2.72	2.64	2.55	2.46	2.36
7.95	5.72	4.82	4.31	3.99	3.76	3.59	3.45	3.35	3.26	3.12	2.98	2.83	2.75	2.67	2.58	2.50	2.40	2.31
7.88	5.66	4.76	4.26	3.94	3.71	3.54	3.41	3.30	3.21	3.07	2.93	2.78	2.70	2.62	2.54	2.45	2.35	2.26
7.82	5.61	4.72	4.22	3.90	3.67	3.50	3.36	3.26	3.17	3.03	2.89	2.74	2.66	2.58	2.49	2.40	2.31	2.21
7.77	5.57	4.68	4.18	3.85	3.63	3.46	3.32	3.22	3.13	2.99	2.85	2.70	2.62	2.54	2.45	2.36	2.27	2.17
7.72	5.53	4.64	4.14	3.82	3.59	3.42	3.29	3.18	3.09	2.96	2.81	2.66	2.58	2.50	2.42	2.33	2.23	2.13
7.68	5.49	4.60	4.11	3.78	3.56	3.39	3.26	3.15	3.06	2.93	2.78	2.63	2.55	2.47	2.38	2.29	2.20	2.10
7.64	5.45	4.57	4.07	3.75	3.53	3.36	3.23	3.12	3.03	2.90	2.75	2.60	2.52	2.44	2.35	2.26	2.17	2.06
7.60	5.42	4.54	4.04	3.73	3.50	3.33	3.20	3.09	3.00	2.87	2.73	2.57	2.49	2.41	2.33	2.23	2.14	2.03
7.56	5.39	4.51	4.02	3.70	3.47	3.30	3.17	3.07	2.98	2.84	2.70	2.55	2.47	2.39	2.30	2.21	2.11	2.01
7.31	5.18	4.31	3.83	3.51	3.29	3.12	2.99	2.89	2.80	2.66	2.52	2.37	2.29	2.20	2.11	2.02	1.92	1.80
7.08	4.98	4.13	3.65	3.34	3.12	2.95	2.82	2.72	2.63	2.50	2.35	2.20	2.12	2.03	1.94	1.84	1.73	1.60
6.85	4.79	3.95	3.48	3.17	2.96	2.79	2.66	2.56	2.47	2.34	2.19	2.03	1.95	1.86	1.76	1.66	1.53	1.33
6.63	4.61	3.78	3.32	3.02	2.80	2.64	2.51	2.41	2.32	2.18	2.04	1.88	1.79	1.70	1.59	1.47	1.32	1.00

Row labels (Degrees of freedom for the denominator): 1, 2, 3, 4, 5, 6, 7, 8, 9, 10, 11, 12, 13, 14, 15, 16, 17, 18, 19, 20, 21, 22, 23, 24, 25, 26, 27, 28, 29, 30, 40, 60, 120, ∞

Degrees of freedom for the denominator

Table A.6 One-tailed probabilities associated with particular values of x in the Sign test

n \ x	0	1	2	3	4	5	6	7	8	9	10	11	12	13	14	15
4	063	313	688	938												
5	031	188	500	812	969											
6	016	109	344	656	891	984										
7	008	062	227	500	773	938	992									
8	004	035	145	363	637	855	965	996								
9	002	020	090	254	500	746	910	980	998							
10	001	011	055	172	377	623	828	945	989	999						
11		006	033	113	274	500	726	887	967	994						
12		003	019	073	194	387	613	806	927	981	997					
13		002	011	046	133	291	500	709	867	954	989	998				
14		001	006	029	090	212	395	605	788	910	971	994	999			
15			004	018	059	151	304	500	696	849	941	982	996			
16			002	011	038	105	227	402	598	773	895	962	989	998		
17			001	006	025	072	166	315	500	685	834	928	975	994	999	
18			001	004	015	048	119	240	407	593	760	881	952	985	996	999
19				002	010	032	084	180	324	500	676	820	916	968	990	998
20				001	006	021	058	132	252	412	588	748	868	942	979	994
21				001	004	013	039	095	192	332	500	668	808	905	961	987
22					002	008	026	067	143	262	416	584	738	857	933	974
23					001	005	017	047	105	202	339	500	661	798	895	953
24					001	003	011	032	076	154	271	419	581	729	846	924
25						002	007	022	054	115	212	345	500	655	788	885

Table A.7 Critical values of T or T^1, whichever is the smaller, in the Wilcoxon Rank-Sum test. Values of T or T^1 that are equal to or less than the tabled value are significant at, or beyond, the level indicated. (Taken from Table L of Tate, M. W. and Clelland, R. C., *Non-Parametric and Shortcut Statistics*. Interstate Printers and Publishers Inc., Danville, Illinois, 1957. With permission of the authors and publishers.)

Number of scores in the smaller sample (n_1)

Number of scores in the larger sample (n_2)	One-tailed	Two-tailed	1	2	3	4	5	6	7	8	9	10	11	12	13	14	15	16	17	18	19	20
3	.10	.20		3	7	(4)																
	.05	.10			6																	
	.025	.05																				
	.005	.01																				
4	.10	.20		3	7	13	(5)															
	.05	.10			6	11																
	.025	.05				10																
	.005	.01																				
5	.10	.20		4	8	14	20	(6)														
	.05	.10		3	7	12	19															
	.025	.05			6	11	17															
	.005	.01					15															
6	.10	.20		4	9	15	22	30	(7)													
	.05	.10		3	8	13	20	28														
	.025	.05			7	12	18	26														
	.005	.01				10	16	23														
7	.10	.20		4	10	16	23	32	41	(8)												
	.05	.10		3	8	14	21	29	39													
	.025	.05			7	13	20	27	36													
	.005	.01				10	16	24	32													
8	.10	.20		5	11	17	25	34	44	55	(9)											
	.05	.10		4	9	15	23	31	41	51												
	.025	.05		3	8	14	21	29	38	49												
	.005	.01				11	17	25	34	43												

Level of significance

Table A.7 cont'd

Number of scores in the larger sample (n_2)	One-tailed	Two-tailed	1	2	3	4	5	6	7	8	9	10	11	12	13	14	15	16	17	18	19	20
9	.10	.20	1	5	11	19	27	36	46	58	70											
	.05	.10		4	9	16	24	33	43	54	66											
	.025	.05		3	8	14	22	31	40	51	62											
	.005	.01			6	11	18	26	35	45	56	(10)										
10	.10	.20	1	6	12	20	28	38	49	60	73	87										
	.05	.10		4	10	17	26	35	45	56	69	82										
	.025	.05		3	9	15	23	32	42	53	65	78										
	.005	.01			6	12	19	27	37	47	58	71	(11)									
11	.10	.20	1	6	13	21	30	40	51	63	76	91	106									
	.05	.10		4	11	18	27	37	47	59	72	86	100									
	.025	.05		3	9	16	24	34	44	55	68	81	96									
	.005	.01			6	12	20	28	38	49	61	73	87	(12)								
12	.10	.20	1	7	14	22	32	42	54	66	80	94	100	127								
	.05	.10		5	11	19	28	38	49	62	75	89	104	120								
	.025	.05		4	10	17	26	35	46	58	71	84	99	115								
	.005	.01			7	13	21	30	40	51	63	76	90	105	(13)							
13	.10	.20	1	7	15	23	33	44	56	69	83	98	114	131	149							
	.05	.10		5	12	20	30	40	52	64	78	92	108	125	142							
	.025	.05		4	10	18	27	37	48	60	73	88	103	119	136							
	.005	.01			7	14	22	31	41	53	65	79	93	109	125	(14)						
14	.10	.20	1	7	16	25	35	46	59	72	86	102	118	136	154	174						
	.05	.10		5	13	21	31	42	54	67	81	96	112	129	147	166						
	.025	.05		4	11	19	28	38	50	62	76	91	106	123	141	160						
	.005	.01			7	14	22	32	43	54	67	81	96	112	129	147	(15)					

Table A.7 cont'd

Number of scores in the smaller sample (n_1)

Number of scores in the larger sample (n_2)	One-tailed	Two-tailed	1	2	3	4	5	6	7	8	9	10	11	12	13	14	15	16	17	18	19	20
15	.10	.20	1	8	16	26	37	48	61	75	90	106	123	141	159	179	200	(16)				
	.05	.10		6	13	22	33	44	56	69	84	99	116	133	152	171	192					
	.025	.05		4	11	20	29	40	52	65	79	94	110	127	145	164	184					
	.005	.01			8	15	23	33	44	56	69	84	99	115	133	151	171					
16	.10	.20	1	8	17	27	38	50	64	78	93	109	127	145	165	185	206	229	(17)			
	.05	.10		6	14	24	34	46	58	72	87	103	120	138	156	176	197	219				
	.025	.05		4	12	21	30	42	54	67	82	97	113	131	150	169	190	211				
	.005	.01			8	15	24	34	46	58	72	86	102	119	136	155	175	196				
17	.10	.20	1	9	18	28	40	52	66	81	97	113	131	150	170	190	212	235	259	(18)		
	.05	.10		6	15	25	35	47	61	75	90	106	123	142	161	182	203	225	249			
	.025	.05		5	12	21	32	43	56	70	84	100	117	135	154	174	195	217	240			
	.005	.01			8	16	25	36	47	60	74	89	105	122	140	159	180	201	223			
18	.10	.20	1	9	19	30	42	55	69	84	100	117	135	155	175	196	218	242	266	291	(19)	
	.05	.10		7	15	26	37	49	63	77	93	110	127	146	166	187	208	231	255	280		
	.025	.05		5	13	22	33	45	58	72	87	103	121	139	158	179	200	222	246	270		
	.005	.01			8	16	26	37	49	62	76	92	108	125	144	163	184	206	228	252		
19	.10	.20	2	10	20	31	43	57	71	87	103	121	139	159	180	202	224	248	273	299	325	(20)
	.05	.10	1	7	16	27	38	51	65	80	96	113	131	150	171	192	214	237	262	287	313	
	.025	.05		5	13	23	34	46	60	74	90	107	124	143	163	182	205	228	252	277	303	
	.005	.01		3	9	17	27	38	50	64	78	94	111	129	147	168	189	210	234	258	283	
20	.10	.20	2	10	21	32	45	59	74	90	107	125	144	164	185	207	230	255	280	306	333	361
	.05	.10	1	7	17	28	40	53	67	83	99	117	135	155	175	197	220	243	268	294	320	348
	.025	.05		5	14	24	35	48	62	77	93	110	128	147	167	188	210	234	258	283	309	337
	.005	.01		3	9	18	28	39	52	66	81	97	114	132	151	172	193	215	239	263	289	315

Level of significance

Number of scores in the larger sample (n_2)

Number of scores in the larger sample (n_2)

Table A.8 Critical values of T for the Wilcoxon Signed-Rank test. Values of T that are equal to or less than the tabled value are significant at, or beyond, the level indicated. (Taken from Table 1 of McCormack, R. L. 'Extended tables of the Wilcoxon matched pair signed rank statistic.' *Journal of the American Statistical Association*, 1965, Vol. 60, pp. 864–871. With permission of the publishers.)

	Level of significance for a two-tailed test			
	.10	.05	.02	.01
	Level of significance for a one-tailed test			
n	.05	.025	.01	.005
5	0			
6	2	0		
7	3	2	0	
8	5	3	1	0
9	8	5	3	1
10	10	8	5	3
11	13	10	7	5
12	17	13	9	7
13	21	17	12	9
14	25	21	15	12
15	30	25	19	15
16	35	29	23	19
17	41	34	27	23
18	47	40	32	27
19	53	46	37	32
20	60	52	43	37
21	67	58	49	42
22	75	65	55	48
23	83	73	62	54
24	91	81	69	61
25	100	89	76	68

Table A.9 Critical values of r_s. Values of r_s that equal or exceed the tabled value are significant at, or beyond, the level indicated. (Taken from Zar, J. H.: 'Significance Testing of the Spearman Rank Correlation Coefficient.' *Journal of the American Statistical Association*, 1972, Vol. 67, pp. 578–580. With permission of the author and publisher.)

		Level of significance for a two-tailed test			
		.10	.05	.02	.01
		Level of significance for a one-tailed test			
		.05	.025	.01	.005
n =	4	1.000			
	5	.900	1.000	1.000	
	6	.829	.886	.943	1.000
	7	.714	.786	.893	.929
	8	.643	.738	.833	.881
	9	.600	.700	.783	.833
	10	.564	.648	.745	.794
	11	.536	.618	.709	.755
	12	.503	.587	.671	.727
	13	.484	.560	.648	.703
	14	.464	.538	.622	.675
	15	.443	.521	.604	.654
	16	.429	.503	.582	.635
	17	.414	.485	.566	.615
	18	.401	.472	.550	.600
	19	.391	.460	.535	.584
	20	.380	.447	.520	.570
	21	.370	.435	.508	.556
	22	.361	.425	.496	.544
	23	.353	.415	.486	.532
	24	.344	.406	.476	.521
	25	.337	.398	.466	.511
	26	.331	.390	.457	.501
	27	.324	.382	.448	.491
	28	.317	.375	.440	.483
	29	.312	.368	.433	.475
	30	.306	.362	.425	.467

For n > 30, the significance of r_s can be tested by using the formula:

$$t = r_s \sqrt{\frac{n-2}{1-r_s^2}} \qquad df = n - 2$$

and referring to Table A.3.

Table A.10 Critical values of Pearson's r.Values of r that equal or exceed the tabled value are significant at, or beyond, the level indicated. (Adapted from Table 13 of *The Biometrika Tables for Statisticans*, Vol. 1, edited by E. S. Pearson and H. O. Hartley, with the permission of E. S. Pearson and the trustees of Biometrika.)

	Level of significance for a one-tailed test		Level of significance for a two-tailed test	
	.05	.01	.05	.01
Degree of freedom				
1	.988	.999	.997	.999
2	.900	.980	.950	.990
3	.805	.934	.878	.959
4	.729	.882	.811	.917
5	.669	.833	.754	.874
6	.622	.789	.707	.834
7	.582	.750	.666	.798
8	.549	.716	.632	.765
9	.521	.685	.602	.735
10	.497	.658	.576	.708
11	.476	.634	.553	.684
12	.458	.612	.532	.661
13	.441	.592	.514	.641
14	.426	.574	.497	.623
15	.412	.558	.482	.606
16	.400	.542	.468	.590
17	.389	.528	.456	.575
18	.378	.516	.444	.561
19	.369	.503	.433	.549
20	.360	.492	.423	.537
21	.352	.482	.413	.526
22	.344	.472	.404	.515
23	.337	.462	.396	.505
24	.330	.453	.388	.496
25	.323	.445	.381	.487
26	.317	.437	.374	.479
27	.311	.430	.367	.471
28	.306	.423	.361	.463
29	.301	.416	.355	.456
30	.296	.409	.349	.449
35	.275	.381	.325	.418
40	.257	.358	.304	.393
45	.243	.338	.288	.372
50	.231	.322	.273	.354
60	.211	.295	.250	.325
70	.195	.274	.232	.303
80	.183	.256	.217	.283
90	.173	.242	.205	.267
100	.164	.230	.195	.254

Table A.11 Critical values of W.Values of W that equal or exceed the tabled value are significant at, or beyond, the level indicated. (Taken from Tate, M. W. and Clelland, R. C. *Non-Parametric and Shortcut Statistics*, Interstate Inc., Illinois, 1957. Values to the left of the line are from Kendall, M. G. *Rank Correlation Methods*, Griffin, 1948. With permission of the authors and publishers.)

n	Level of significance	k 3	4	5	6	7	8	9	10
3	.05	1.00	.82	.71	.65	.62	.60	.58	.56
	.01		.96	.84	.77	.73	.70	.67	.65
4	.05	.81	.65	.54	.51	.48	.46	.45	.44
	.01	1.00	.80	.67	.62	.59	.56	.54	.52
5	.05	.64	.52	.44	.41	.39	.38	.36	.35
	.01	.84	.66	.56	.52	.49	.46	.44	.43
6	.05	.58	.42	.37	.35	.33	.32	.31	.30
	.01	.75	.56	.49	.45	.42	.40	.38	.37
7	.05	.51	.36	.32	.30	.29	.27	.26	.26
	.01	.63	.48	.43	.39	.36	.34	.33	.32
8	.05	.39	.32	.29	.27	.25	.24	.23	.23
	.01	.56	.43	.38	.35	.32	.31	.29	.28
9	.05	.35	.28	.26	.24	.23	.22	.21	.20
	.01	.48	.38	.34	.31	.29	.27	.26	.25
10	.05	.31	.25	.23	.21	.20	.20	.19	.18
	.01	.48	.35	.31	.28	.26	.25	.24	.23
12	.05	.25	.21	.19	.18	.17	.16	.16	.15
	.01	.36	.30	.26	.24	.22	.21	.20	.19
14	.05	.21	.18	.17	.16	.15	.14	.14	.13
	.01	.31	.26	.23	.21	.19	.18	.17	.17
16	.05	.19	.16	.15	.14	.13	.12	.12	.12
	.01	.28	.23	.20	.18	.17	.16	.15	.15
18	.05	.17	.14	.13	.12	.11	.11	.11	.10
	.01	.25	.20	.18	.16	.15	.14	.14	.13
20	.05	.15	.13	.12	.11	.10	.10	.10	.09
	.01	.22	.18	.16	.15	.14	.13	.12	.11
25	.05	.12	.10	.09	.09	.08	.08	.08	.07
	.01	.18	.15	.13	.12	.11	.10	.10	.09
30	.05	.10	.09	.08	.07	.07	.07	.07	.06
	.01	.15	.12	.11	.10	.09	.09	.08	.08

Table A.12 Critical values of H in the Krukal-Wallis test. Values of H that equal or exceed the tabled value are significant at, or beyond, the level indicated. (Abridged from Kruskal, W. H. and Wallis, W. A. 'Use of ranks in one-criterion variance analysis.' *Journal of the American Statistical Association*, 1952, Vol. 47, pp. 584–621. With permission of the publishers.)

Sample sizes			Level of significance	
n_1	n_2	n_3	.05	.01
3	2	2	4.71	
3	3	1	5.14	
3	3	2	5.36	6.25
3	3	3	5.60	6.49
4	2	1		
4	2	2	5.33	
4	3	1	5.21	
4	3	2	5.44	6.30
4	3	3	5.73	6.75
4	4	1	4.97	6.67
4	4	2	5.45	6.87
4	4	3	5.60	7.14
4	4	4	5.69	7.54
5	2	1	5.00	
5	2	2	5.16	6.53
5	3	1	4.96	
5	3	2	5.25	6.82
5	3	3	5.44	6.98
5	4	1	4.99	6.84
5	4	2	5.27	7.12
5	4	3	5.63	7.40
5	4	4	5.62	7.74
5	5	1	5.13	6.84
5	5	2	5.25	7.27
5	5	3	5.63	7.54
5	5	4	5.64	7.79
5	5	5	5.66	7.98

Table A.13 Critical values of P in Jonckheere's Trend test. Values of P that equal or exceed the tabled value are significant at, or beyond, the level indicated. (Taken from Jonckheere, A. R., 'A distribution-free k-sample test against ordered alternatives'. *Biometrika*, Vol. 41, pp. 133–145. With permission of the author and publisher).

		Number of samples (k)						
		3		4		5		6	
Level of significance		.05	.01	.05	.01	.05	.01	.05	.01
Number per sample (n)	2	10	—	14	20	20	26	26	34
	3	17	23	26	34	34	48	44	62
	4	24	32	38	50	51	72	67	94
	5	33	45	51	71	71	99	93	130
	6	42	59	66	92	92	129	121	170
	7	53	74	82	115	115	162	151	213
	8	64	90	100	140	140	197	184	260
	9	76	106	118	167	166	234	219	309
	10	88	124	138	195	194	274	256	361

Table A.14 Critical values of L in Page's Trend test. Values of L that equal or exceed the tabled value are significant at, or beyond, the level indicated. (Taken from Page, E. B. 'Ordered hypotheses for multiple trements: a significance test for linear rank.' *Journal of the American Statistical Association*, Vol. 58, pp. 216–230. With permission of the publishers.)

		Number of samples (k)						
		3		4		5		6	
Level of significance		.05	.01	.05	.01	.05	.01	.05	.01
Number per sample (n)	2	28	—	58	60	103	106	166	173
	3	41	42	84	87	150	155	244	252
	4	54	55	111	114	197	204	321	331
	5	66	68	137	141	244	251	397	409
	6	79	81	163	167	291	299	474	486
	7	91	93	189	193	338	346	550	563
	8	104	106	214	220	384	393	625	640
	9	116	119	240	246	431	441	701	717
	10	128	131	266	272	477	487	777	793

For values of k and n beyond those tabled above, the significance of L can be tested by using the formula:

$$z = \frac{12L - 3nk(k+1)^2}{\sqrt{nk^2(k^2-1)(k+1)}}$$

Index